KU-245-367

# Contents at a Glance

Introduction.................................................................................1

**Part I    Microsoft Exchange Server 2003 Overview**
1    Exchange Server 2003 Technology Primer.......................................7
2    Planning, Prototyping, Migrating, and Deploying
      Exchange Server 2003................................................................35
3    Installing Exchange Server 2003..................................................69

**Part II    Exchange Server 2003**
4    Designing Exchange Server 2003 for a Small to Medium Network...........113
5    Designing an Enterprise Exchange Server 2003 Environment.................135
6    Integrating Exchange Server 2003 in a Non-Windows Environment.......163

**Part III    Networking Services Impact on Exchange**
7    Domain Name System Impact on Exchange Server 2003 .........................185
8    Global Catalog and Domain Controller Placement...............................211
9    Securing Exchange Server 2003 with ISA Server 2004.............................233
10    Configuring Outlook Web Access and Exchange Mobile Services ............287

**Part IV    Securing an Exchange Server 2003 Environment**
11    Client-Level Security.................................................................337
12    Server-Level Security...............................................................361
13    Transport-Level Security...........................................................391

**Part V    Migrating to Exchange Server 2003**
14    Migrating from NT4 to Windows Server 2003.................................421
15    Migrating from Exchange v5.5 to Exchange Server 2003......................451
16    Migrating from Exchange 2000 to Exchange Server 2003.....................483
17    Compatibility Testing..............................................................509

**Part VI    Exchange Server 2003 Administration and Management**
18    Administering Exchange Server 2003.............................................533
19    Exchange Server 2003 Management and Maintenance Practices.............581
20    Documenting an Exchange Server 2003 Environment .........................605
21    Using Terminal Services to Manage Exchange Services.......................625

**Part VII**   **New Mobility Functionality in Exchange Server 2003**

    **22**   Designing Mobility in Exchange Server 2003 ............................................641

    **23**   Implementing Mobile Synchronization in Exchange Server 2003...........657

    **24**   Configuring Client Systems for Mobility ......................................................673

**Part VIII**   **Client Access to Exchange Server 2003**

    **25**   Getting the Most Out of the Microsoft Outlook Client ..........................707

    **26**   Everything You Need to Know About the Outlook Web Access
         (OWA) Client..................................................................................................749

    **27**   Outlook for Non-Windows Systems .............................................................801

**Part IX**   **Client Administration and Management**

    **28**   Deploying the Client for Exchange...............................................................829

    **29**   Group Policy Management for Exchange Clients.......................................853

**Part X**   **Fault Tolerance and Optimization Technologies**

    **30**   System-Level Fault Tolerance (Clustering/Network Load Balancing)........877

    **31**   Backing Up the Exchange Server 2003 Environment ...............................909

    **32**   Recovering from a Disaster ...........................................................................935

    **33**   Capacity Analysis and Performance Optimization ...................................975

**Part XI**   **Cross-Platform Migrations to Exchange 2003**

    **34**   Migrating from Novell GroupWise to Exchange 2003 .............................999

    **35**   Migrating from Lotus Notes to Exchange Server 2003 ...........................1057

         Index

# Microsoft®
# Exchange Server 2003

## UNLEASHED

## Second Edition

Rand H. Morimoto, Ph.D., MCSE
Michael Noel, MCSE+I, CISSP, MCSA
Kenton Gardinier, MCSE, CISSP, MCSA
Joe R. Coca Jr., MCSE, MCSA

 800 East 96th Street, Indianapolis, Indiana 46240

# Microsoft Exchange Server 2003 Unleashed, Second Edition

International Standard Book Number: 0-672-32807-0

Library of Congress Catalog Card Number: 2003111834

Printed in the United States of America

First Printing: September 2005

06   05   04   03          4   3   2   1

## Trademarks

All terms mentioned in this book that are known to be trademarks or service marks have been appropriately capitalized. Sams Publishing cannot attest to the accuracy of this information. Use of a term in this book should not be regarded as affecting the validity of any trademark or service mark.

## Warning and Disclaimer

Every effort has been made to make this book as complete and as accurate as possible, but no warranty or fitness is implied. The information provided is on an "as is" basis. The authors and the publisher shall have neither liability nor responsibility to any person or entity with respect to any loss or damages arising from the information contained in this book.

## Bulk Sales

Sams Publishing offers excellent discounts on this book when ordered in quantity for bulk purchases or special sales. For more information, please contact

> U.S. Corporate and Government Sales
> 1-800-382-3419
> corpsales@pearsontechgroup.com

For sales outside of the U.S., please contact

> International Sales
> international@pearsoned.com

**Publisher**
Paul Boger

**Acquisitions Editor**
Neil Rowe

**Development Editor**
Mark Renfrow

**Managing Editor**
Charlotte Clapp

**Project Editor**
George Nedeff

**Copy Editors**
Nancy Albright
Karen Annett

**Indexer**
Larry Sweazy

**Proofreader**
Jessica McCarty

**Publishing Coordinator**
Cindy Teeters

**Interior Designer**
Gary Adair

**Cover Designer**
Gary Adair

**Page Layout**
Toi Davis

**Contributing Writers (2nd Edition)**
Alex Lewis, MCSE

Chris Amaris, MCSE, CISSP

Peter Handley, MCSE, CNE

Sarah Holden, MCSE

# Table of Contents

**Introduction**     **1**

**Part I**    **Microsoft Exchange Server 2003 Overview**

   **1**    **Exchange Server 2003 Technology Primer**     **7**

Using Exchange Server 2003 As an Email and Calendaring Solution ..........8

Taking Advantage of Active Directory in Exchange ......................................8

Leveraging Exchange Server 2003 As a Web Access Solution ......................9

Expanding into the New Wireless and Mobility Technologies ..................10

Choosing the Right Time to Migrate to
   Exchange Server 2003 ...............................................................................11

     Adding an Exchange Server 2003 Server to an Existing
      Exchange Organization .......................................................................12

     Migrating from Exchange 2000 to Exchange Server 2003 ................12

     Migrating from Exchange 5.5 to Exchange Server 2003 ...................12

     Migrating from Novell GroupWise to Exchange Server 2003 ...........13

     Migrating from Lotus Notes to Exchange Server 2003 ......................13

Understanding the Two Versions of Exchange Server 2003 ......................13

     Getting to Know the Exchange Server 2003 Standard Edition .........14

     Expanding into the Exchange Server 2003 Enterprise Edition .........14

Understanding How Improvements in Windows 2003 Enhance
   Exchange Server 2003 ...............................................................................15

     Drag-and-Drop Capabilities in Administrative Tools ........................15

     Built-in Setup, Configuration, and Management Wizards ................15

     Improvements in Security .................................................................16

     IPSec and Wireless Security Improvements .......................................16

     Microsoft Internet Security and Acceleration Server (ISA) 2004
      Enhancements .....................................................................................16

     Performance and Functionality Improvements ................................17

     Global Catalog Caching on a Domain Controller .............................17

     Remote Installation Service for Servers .............................................17

     Scaling Reliability with 8-Node Clustering .......................................18

     Taking Advantage of the Windows 2003 SP1 Security
      Configuration Wizard .......................................................................19

     Improving Mailbox Recovery Through Volume Shadow
      Copy Services .....................................................................................19

Reliability Enhancements in Exchange Server 2003 ...................................20
  Simplifying Mailbox Recovery Using Integrated Tools .....................20
  Leveraging Recovery Storage Group Functionality ...........................20
Expanding on Manageability and Administration Benefits of
  Exchange Server 2003 ....................................................................21
  Improving the Speed of Mailbox Moves ...........................................21
  Establishing Dynamic Distribution Lists ...........................................21
  Replicating Directories Between Forests ...........................................22
  Simplifying Migrations Using Structured Migration Tools ...............23
  Taking Advantage of Microsoft Operations Manager ......................24
Improvements in Exchange Server 2003 Security ....................................25
  Establishing Security Between Front-End and Back-End Servers ......25
  Creating Cross-Forest Kerberos Authentication ...............................25
  Restricting Distribution Lists to Authenticated Users ......................25
  Using Safe and Blocked Lists ............................................................26
  Filtering of Inbound Recipients Functionality .................................26
  Blocking Attachments in Outlook Web Access (OWA) .....................27
  Supporting S/MIME for OWA Attachments ......................................27
  Supporting SenderID Messaging Framework ....................................27
Leveraging Mobility in Exchange Server 2003 .......................................27
  Improving Outlook Web Access's Functionality ...............................28
  Using Outlook 2003 over HTTPS ......................................................28
  Leveraging ActiveSync for Exchange Replication .............................29
  Connecting Users Through Wireless Technologies ...........................29
Performance Improvements in Exchange Server 2003 .............................29
  Allocating Memory to Improve Performance ...................................30
  Using Caching on Distribution Lists ................................................30
  Controlling Message Notification .....................................................30
Solidifying Core Technologies for Exchange Server 2003 ........................31
  Solidifying DNS for Proper Message Routing ...................................31
  Deploying Global Catalogs for Reliable Directory Lookup ...............32
  Completing a Migration to Windows 2003 ......................................32
Summary ..................................................................................................32
Best Practices ...........................................................................................32

2   Planning, Prototyping, Migrating, and Deploying Exchange
    Server 2003                                                                               35
Initiation, Planning, Prototype, and Pilot: The Four Phases
  to the Upgrade ..........................................................................................36
  Documentation Required During the Phases ....................................36
Initiation Phase: Defining the Scope and Goals ....................................37
  The Scope of the Project ....................................................................37
  Identifying the Goals .........................................................................38

Initiation Phase: Creating the Statement of Work ....................................42
   Summarizing the Scope of Work .......................................................42
   Summarizing the Goals ...................................................................43
   Summarizing the Timeline and Milestones ........................................44
   Summarizing the Resources Required ..............................................44
   Summarizing the Risks and Assumptions ..........................................45
   Summarizing the Initial Budget ......................................................45
   Getting Approval on the Statement of Work ....................................46
Planning Phase: Discovery ....................................................................46
   Understanding the Existing Environment .........................................46
   Understanding the Geographic Distribution of Resources ................47
Planning Phase: Creating the Design Document ......................................48
   Collaboration Sessions: Making the Design Decisions .....................48
   Disaster Recovery Options ..............................................................49
   Design Document Structure ............................................................50
   Agreeing on the Design .................................................................53
Creating the Migration Document .........................................................53
   The Project Schedule ....................................................................54
   Creating the Migration Document ..................................................55
The Prototype Phase ............................................................................60
   What Is Needed for the Lab? .........................................................60
   Disaster Recovery Testing ..............................................................61
   Documentation from the Prototype ................................................62
   Final Validation of the Migration Document ....................................62
The Pilot Phase: Validating the Plan to a Limited Number of Users ..........62
   The First Server in the Pilot ...........................................................63
   Choosing the Pilot Group ..............................................................63
   Gauging the Success of the Pilot Phase ..........................................64
The Production Migration/Upgrade .......................................................64
   Decommissioning the Old Exchange Environment ...........................65
   Supporting the New Exchange Server 2003 Environment ................65
Summary .............................................................................................65
Best Practices ......................................................................................66

3   Installing Exchange Server 2003                                              69
Preparing for Implementation of Exchange 2003 ....................................69
   Implementing Active Directory ......................................................70
   Realizing the Impact of Windows on Exchange ...............................70
   Global Catalog Placement .............................................................70
   Choosing Between Active Directory Mixed and Native Mode in
      Exchange 2003 .........................................................................71
   Selecting a Windows 2000/Windows 2003 Group Model ................71

Extending the Active Directory Schema ...........................................73

Preparing the Windows 2000 or Windows 2003 Domain ................74

Preparing to Install Exchange 2003 ........................................................75

Planning Your Exchange 2003 Installation ....................................75

Choosing to Install Exchange in Either a Test or Production
Environment ...................................................................................75

Prototyping Your Exchange 2003 Installation ..............................76

Conducting Preinstallation Checks on Exchange 2003 ..........................76

Verifying Core Services Installation ..............................................77

Preparing the Forest ........................................................................77

Preparing the Domain ....................................................................77

Reviewing All Log Files ...................................................................78

Performing an Interactive Installation of Exchange Server 2003 ..............78

Performing a Scripted Installation of Exchange Server 2003 ....................80

Creating the unattend Install File .................................................81

Running setup in Unattended Mode .............................................81

Completing the Installation of Exchange 2003 .......................................82

Creating Administrative Group and Routing Group Structure .........82

Creating Storage Groups .................................................................85

Managing Databases ........................................................................87

Creating Additional Mailbox Stores ...............................................87

Creating a Public Folder Store ........................................................89

Performing Postinstallation Configurations ...........................................89

Disabling Services ............................................................................90

Removing Information Stores ..........................................................90

Setting Up Routing Group Connectors .........................................91

Enabling Logging and Message Tracking .......................................93

Dismounting and Deleting Public Folder Stores ...........................94

Using System Policies to Manage Mailbox and Public Stores ..........95

Best Practices for Configuring Storage Groups and Databases .........96

Delegating Administration in Exchange 2003 ...............................97

Configuring Additional Server Services ...................................................98

Installing a Bridgehead Server ........................................................98

Enabling SSL for Services on Front-End Servers ...........................99

Managing Public Folders ...............................................................100

Creating New Public Folder Trees .................................................101

Using Dedicated Public Folder Servers .........................................102

Designing Public Folder Trees .......................................................102

Understanding Public Folder Replication .....................................103

System Folders ...............................................................................103

SMTP Connectors and Virtual Servers .........................................104

Securing SMTP Mail Relays ...........................................................105

Testing the Exchange 2003 Installation ....................................................106

    Creating a Mailbox .............................................................................106

    Testing Mail Flow Using OWA ..........................................................107

    Installing the Exchange System Manager ..........................................107

Summary .............................................................................................108

Best Practices .....................................................................................109

**Part II   Exchange Server 2003**

**4   Designing Exchange Server 2003 for a Small to Medium Network       113**

Formulating a Successful Design Strategy .............................................113

Getting the Most Out of Exchange Server 2003 Functionality ...............113

    Outlining Significant Changes in Exchange Server 2003 ...............114

    Reviewing Exchange and Operating System Requirements ............115

    Scaling Exchange Server 2003 .........................................................117

    Having Exchange Server 2003 Coexist with an

        Existing Network Infrastructure ......................................................117

    Identifying Third-Party Product Functionality ...............................118

Understanding Active Directory Design Concepts for

    Exchange Server 2003 ..........................................................................118

    Understanding the Active Directory Forest ......................................118

    Understanding the Active Directory Domain Structure ..................120

    Reviewing Active Directory Infrastructure Components ...............120

    Understanding Multiple Forests Design Concepts Using

        Microsoft Identity Integration Server 2003 ...................................123

Determining Exchange Server 2003 Placement .....................................123

    Designing Administrative Groups ....................................................123

    Planning Routing Group Topology ..................................................124

    Examining Public Folder Design Concepts .....................................125

    Understanding Environment Sizing Considerations ......................125

    Identifying Client Access Points .....................................................125

Configuring Exchange Server 2003 for Maximum Performance and

    Reliability ...........................................................................................127

    Designing an Optimal Operating System Configuration

        for Exchange ..................................................................................127

    Avoiding Virtual Memory Fragmentation Issues ............................128

    Configuring Disk Options for Performance ....................................128

    Working with Multiple Exchange Databases and Storage

        Groups ............................................................................................129

    Understanding Clustering for Exchange Server 2003 .....................130

    Monitoring Design Concepts with Microsoft

        Operations Manager 2005 .............................................................131

Outlining Backup and Restore Design Concepts and the Volume
Shadow Copy Service ....................................................................131
Uncovering Enhanced Antivirus and Spam Features .....................131
Securing and Maintaining an Exchange Server 2003 Implementation ....131
Patching the Operating System Using Windows Software
Update Services ........................................................................131
Using Front-End Server Functionality ..........................................132
Implementing Maintenance Schedules .........................................132
Using Antivirus and Backup Solutions .........................................132
Summary ............................................................................................133
Best Practices ....................................................................................133

5   **Designing an Enterprise Exchange Server 2003 Environment**     **135**

Designing for Small Organizations—Company123 ..................................135
Designing for Midsize Organizations—OrganizationY ....................136
Designing for Large Organizations—CompanyABC ........................136
Designing Active Directory for Exchange Server 2003 ...........................136
Understanding Forest and Domain Design ....................................137
Outlining AD Site and Replication Topology Layout .....................138
Reviewing Domain Controller and Global Catalog Placement
Concepts .....................................................................................138
Configuring DNS ...........................................................................139
Outlining Active Directory Design Decisions for
Small Organizations ...................................................................139
Outlining Midsize Organization AD Design Decisions ..................140
Outlining Large Organization AD Design Decisions ......................142
Determining Hardware and Software Components ...................................142
Designing Server Number and Placement .....................................142
Providing for Server Redundancy and Optimization .....................143
Reviewing Server Memory and Processor Recommendations .........143
Outlining Server Operating System Considerations .......................144
Designing Clustering and Advanced Redundancy Options ............145
Reviewing Small Organization Hardware and Software
Design Decisions .......................................................................145
Reviewing Midsize Organization Hardware and Software
Design Decisions .......................................................................146
Reviewing Large Organization Hardware and Software
Design Decisions .......................................................................146
Designing Exchange Infrastructure .......................................................147
Determining Exchange Version and Org Name ..............................148
Outlining Administrative Group and Routing Group Structure .....149

Designing Public Folder Structure and Replication ...........................149
Determining Exchange Databases and Storage Groups Layout .......149
Outlining Exchange Recovery Options ............................................150
Considering Exchange Antivirus and Antispam Design ................150
Monitoring Exchange .....................................................................151
Reviewing Small Organization Exchange
  Infrastructure Design Decisions ...................................................151
Reviewing Midsize Organization Exchange
  Infrastructure Design Decisions ...................................................151
Reviewing Large Organization Exchange
  Infrastructure Design Decisions ...................................................153
Integrating Client Access into Exchange Server 2003 Design ...................154
Outlining Client Access Methods ..................................................154
Determining Front-End Server Design ...........................................155
Reviewing Small Organization Client Access Design Decisions ......156
Reviewing Midsize Organization Client Access Design
  Decisions ....................................................................................156
Reviewing Large Organization Client Access Design Decisions ......157
Summarizing Design Examples ............................................................157
Summarizing the Sample Small Organization Design Model .........157
Summarizing the Sample Midsize Organization Design Model ......158
Summarizing the Sample Large Organization Design Model ..........159
Summary .............................................................................................160
Best Practices .....................................................................................160

**6   Integrating Exchange Server 2003 in a Non-Windows Environment     163**
Synchronizing Directory Information with Microsoft Identity
  Integration Server (MIIS) 2003 ......................................................164
Understanding MIIS 2003 ..............................................................164
Understanding MIIS 2003 Concepts ..............................................165
Exploring MIIS 2003 Account Provisioning ...................................166
Outlining the Role of Management Agents (MAs) in MIIS 2003 ....167
Defining MIIS 2003 and Group Management ................................168
Installing MIIS 2003 with SQL 2000 .............................................168
Synchronizing Exchange Server 2003 with Novell eDirectory ...............169
Understanding Novell eDirectory ..................................................169
Deploying MIIS 2003 for Identity Management with eDirectory ...169
Using Microsoft Directory Synchronization Services to
  Integrate Directories ...................................................................170
Installing the Microsoft Directory Synchronization Service ...........172
Synchronizing eDirectory/NDS with Active Directory
  Using Services for NetWare .........................................................172

Implementing MSDSS ..................................................................173

Identifying Limitations on Directory Synchronization with
MSDSS .................................................................................174

Backing Up and Restoring MSDSS Information ..............174

Managing Identity Information Between LDAP Directories and
Exchange Server 2003 ............................................................175

Understanding LDAP from a Historical Perspective ........176

Understanding How LDAP Works .....................................177

Outlining the Differences Between LDAP2 and LDAP3
Implementations ..............................................................177

Using Services for Unix to Integrate Unix Environments with
Exchange Server 2003 ............................................................178

Defining Services for Unix .................................................179

Understanding Services for Unix Prerequisites ...............179

Outlining the Role of Interix As a Component of Services
for Unix .............................................................................180

Understanding Interix Scripting .......................................180

Outlining Interix Tools and Programming Languages ...181

Synchronizing Users with SFU ..........................................181

Detailing User Name Mapping in SFU .............................181

Performing Password Synchronization with SFU ............181

Summary ....................................................................................182

Best Practices .............................................................................182


Part III    Networking Services Impact on Exchange


7    Domain Name System Impact on Exchange Server 2003            185

Defining the Domain Name Service .......................................185

How DNS Is Used ................................................................186

Understanding Who Needs DNS ........................................187

Outlining the Types of DNS Servers .......................................187

Examining Unix BIND DNS ...............................................188

Exploring Third-Party (Checkpoint-Meta IP or Lucent
Vital QIP) DNS .................................................................188

Examining DNS Compatibility Between DNS Platforms ...188

Examining DNS Components ...................................................189

DNS Zones ...........................................................................189

DNS Queries .........................................................................191

DNS Replication or Zone Transfer ....................................192

DNS Resource Records ........................................................192

Using DNS to Route SMTP Mail in Exchange Server 2003 ....197

Using DNS in Exchange 2003 ............................................197

Understanding SMTP Mail Routing ................................................198
Examining Client DNS Use for Exchange ......................................199
Understanding DNS Requirements for Exchange Server 2003 .................199
Exchange 5.5 and E2k3 DNS/WINS Name
Resolutions Requirements ................................................199
DNS and SMTP RFC Standards ...........................................200
Virtual SMTP Servers ......................................................200
Routing Groups ...........................................................200
Mixed Environment Mail Routing ......................................201
SMTP Mail Security, Virus Checking, and Proxies ...................201
SMTP Server Scalability and Load Balancing .......................203
Configuring DNS to Support Exchange Servers .........................204
External DNS Servers for the Internet ...............................205
Internal DNS Servers for Outbound Mail Routing .................205
Internal DNS Servers for Internal Routing of Email
Between Exchange Servers ............................................205
Troubleshooting DNS Problems ........................................205
Using Event Viewer to Troubleshoot ...............................205
Troubleshooting Using the ipconfig Utility .......................206
Monitoring Exchange Using Performance Monitor ...............207
Using nslookup for DNS Exchange Lookup .......................207
Troubleshooting with DNSLINT .....................................208
Using dnscmd for Advanced DNS Troubleshooting .............209
Summary ...................................................................209
Best Practices .............................................................210

**8   Global Catalog and Domain Controller Placement          211**

Understanding Active Directory Structure .............................212
Exploring AD Domains ................................................212
Exploring AD Trees ...................................................212
Exploring AD Forests .................................................212
Understanding AD Replication with Exchange Server 2003 ...........213
Examining the Role of Domain Controllers in AD ...................214
Examining Domain Controller Authentication in
Active Directory ......................................................214
Determining Domain Controller Placement with Exchange
Server 2003 .........................................................215
Defining the Global Catalog .........................................215
Understanding the Relationship Between Exchange
Server 2003 and the AD Global Catalog .......................216
Understanding Global Catalog Structure .........................216
Creating Global Catalog Domain Controllers .................216

Verifying Global Catalog Creation ...............................................218

Using Best Practices for Global Catalog Placement ........................219

Optimizing Global Catalog Promotion ...........................................219

Exploring Global Catalog Demotion ..............................................219

Deploying Domain Controllers Using the Install from
Media Option .............................................................................220

Understanding Universal Group Caching for AD Sites ...................221

Exploring DSAccess, DSProxy, and the Categorizer ............................222

Understanding DSAccess ..............................................................223

Determining the DSAccess Roles ...................................................223

Understanding DSProxy .................................................................224

Outlining the Role of the Categorizer ...........................................224

Understanding AD Functionality Modes and Their Relationship to
Exchange Groups ..........................................................................225

Understanding Windows Group Types ............................................225

Defining Security Groups ..............................................................225

Defining Distribution Groups in Exchange Server 2003 .................225

Outlining Mail-Enabled Security Groups in Exchange
Server 2003 ...............................................................................226

Explaining Group Scope ................................................................226

Functional Levels in Windows Server 2003 Active Directory .........227

Exchange Server 2003 Functional Modes ......................................228

Summary ...........................................................................................230

Best Practices ....................................................................................230

**9   Securing Exchange Server 2003 with ISA Server 2004          233**

Understanding Internet Security and
Acceleration (ISA) Server 2004 ....................................................234

Outlining the Need for ISA Server 2004 in Exchange Environments ......234

Outlining the High Cost of Security Breaches ................................234

Outlining the Critical Role of Firewall Technology in a Modern
Connected Infrastructure ..........................................................235

Understanding the Growing Need for Application-Layer
Filtering ....................................................................................236

Outlining the Inherent Threat in Exchange
OWA/EMS Traffic ........................................................................237

Understanding Web (HTTP) Exploits ..............................................237

Securing Encrypted (Secure Sockets Layer) Web Traffic ................238

Outlining ISA Server 2004's Messaging Security Mechanisms ........238

Securing Exchange Outlook Web Access with ISA Server 2004 .............239

Exporting and Importing the OWA Certificate to the ISA Server ...240

Creating an Outlook Web Access Publishing Rule ..........................243

Redirecting HTTP OWA Traffic to HTTPS Traffic .............................247
Customizing Forms-Based Authentication .......................................252
Securing Exchange Mobile Services (EMS) with ISA ..................................252
Supporting Mobile Services in ISA When Using Forms-Based
Authentication for OWA ...............................................................253
Assigning a New IP Address on the ISA Server for the
Additional Web Listener ...............................................................254
Setting Up an Outlook Mobile Access (OMA) and ActiveSync
Publishing Rule ..........................................................................254
Securing RPC over HTTPS Servers with an ISA Publishing Rule .....258
Securing Exchange MAPI Access ....................................................258
Configuring MAPI RPC Filtering Rules .............................................259
Deploying MAPI Filtering Across Network Segments .......................260
Securing POP and IMAP Exchange Traffic .........................................261
Creating and Configuring a POP Mail Publishing Rule ..................261
Creating and Configuring an IMAP Mail Publishing Rule .............264
Managing and Controlling Simple Mail Transfer Protocol
(SMTP) Traffic ..............................................................................266
Installing and Configuring the SMTP Service on the ISA Server ....268
Installing the ISA SMTP Screener Component ...............................268
Enabling Outbound and Inbound SMTP Filtering with the
SMTP Message Screener ...............................................................269
Configuring Exchange to Forward Outbound Messages to ISA ......275
Customizing the SMTP Filter ........................................................276
Logging ISA Traffic ........................................................................277
Examining ISA Logs ......................................................................277
Customizing Logging Filters .........................................................278
Monitoring ISA from the ISA Console ...............................................279
Customizing the ISA Dashboard ...................................................279
Monitoring and Customizing Alerts ..............................................280
Monitoring Session and Services Activity ......................................283
Creating Connectivity Verifiers ....................................................283
Summary .......................................................................................285
Best Practices ...............................................................................285

10 Configuring Outlook Web Access and Exchange Mobile Services 287

Understanding OWA and the Exchange Virtual Server ..........................288
Designing an OWA Infrastructure ................................................288
Designing an Exchange Front-End/Back-End OWA Architecture ............289
Describing Front-End and Back-End Servers ..................................289
Planning for Front-End OWA Servers ............................................290
Securing Communications on Front-End Servers ...........................291

Configuring a Firewall for Front-End Servers ...................................291

Disabling Unnecessary Services on the Front-End Server ...............293

Reducing Server Configuration .......................................................294

Configuring Network Load Balancing for Front-End Servers ..........294

Configuring Front-End and Back-End Servers ...............................294

Enabling Secure Sockets Layer (SSL) Support for Exchange
Outlook Web Access .......................................................................294

Understanding the Need for Third-Party CAs ..................................296

Installing a Third-Party CA on an OWA Server ...............................297

Using an Internal Certificate Authority for OWA Certificates ........300

Forcing SSL Encryption for OWA Traffic .........................................303

Customizing and Securing an OWA Web
Site from Internal Access ...............................................................304

Redirecting Clients to the Exchange Virtual Directory ...................305

Creating a Custom SSL Error to Redirect HTTP Traffic to SSL .........306

Enabling Forms-Based Authentication on the OWA Server ............309

Summarizing OWA Virtual Server Settings .....................................310

Enabling the Change Password Feature in OWA .............................313

Configuring OMA and ActiveSync Access to Exchange ...........................315

Enabling and Supporting OMA and ActiveSync on the OWA Server ......316

Enabling OMA and ActiveSync in Exchange System Manager .......316

Enabling or Disabling OMA and EAS on a Per-Mailbox Basis .........317

Supporting OMA and ActiveSync on an OWA Server
Configured As a Back-End Mailbox Server ....................................317

Deploying Multiple OWA Virtual Servers .............................................322

Adding IP Addresses to an OWA Server ..........................................323

Creating an Additional OWA Virtual Server ....................................323

Assigning a Second SSL Certificate to the New
OMA-EAS Virtual Server ................................................................325

Configuring Exchange System Manager to Not Override SSL
Settings ..........................................................................................325

Using RPC over HTTP(S) with Exchange Server 2003 ............................326

Installing the RPC over HTTP Proxy ...............................................326

Configuring RPC over HTTPS on an Exchange Back-End Server ....327

Configuring RPC over HTTPS on an Exchange Front-End Server ...328

Modifying the Registry to Support a Single-Server Exchange
RPC over HTTP Topology ...............................................................329

Creating the RPC Virtual Directory on the Proper Virtual Server ...330

Setting Up an Outlook 2003 Profile to Use RPC over HTTP ..........331

Summary ..............................................................................................333

Best Practices .......................................................................................333

**Part IV    Securing an Exchange Server 2003 Environment**

**11    Client-Level Security**                                                                337

Tips and Tricks for Hardening Windows .................................................337

Windows Server 2003 Security Improvements ..................................338

Windows XP Professional Security Improvements ...........................338

Windows Firewall Protection .........................................................339

Standardizing Security with Security Templates ............................340

Keeping Up with Security Patches and Updates .............................342

Client-Based Virus Protection .......................................................343

Windows Lockdown Guidelines and Standards ..............................343

Exchange Server 2003 Client-Level Security Enhancements ..................343

Securing Outlook 2003 .........................................................................344

Securely Accessing Exchange over the Internet
(RPC over HTTPS) ..................................................................344

Encrypting Outlook 2003 and Exchange Server 2003
Communications ....................................................................346

Authenticating Users ....................................................................347

Blocking Attachments ...................................................................348

Protecting Against Spam ......................................................................349

Spam and Antispam Tools .............................................................349

Protecting Against Web Beaconing ...............................................350

Filtering Junk Mail ........................................................................351

Filtering with Safe and Block Lists ...............................................352

Blocking Read Receipts .................................................................353

Information Rights Management in Office 2003 ............................353

Securing Outlook Web Access ...............................................................354

Protecting Against Potentially Harmful Message Content ..............354

Blocking Attachments Through OWA .............................................354

Using Safe and Block Lists ...........................................................355

Using Digital Signatures and Encryption .............................................356

Simplified Fundamentals of Using Digital Signatures and
Encryption ............................................................................356

Configuring Outlook 2003 for Secure Messaging ..........................357

Configuring OWA for Secure Messaging ........................................358

Sending Secure Messages ..............................................................358

Summary ..............................................................................................360

Best Practices .......................................................................................360

**12    Server-Level Security**                                                                361

Microsoft's Trustworthy Computing Initiative .......................................361

Secure by Design ...........................................................................361

Secure by Default ................................................................362
Secure by Deployment ........................................................362
Building Communications and Community ..................................362
Assessing Your Risks ................................................................362
Designing a Secure Messaging Environment ............................364
Establishing a Corporate Email Policy ..............................364
Securing Exchange Server 2003 Through Administrative
    Policies ......................................................................365
Using Email Disclaimers ................................................365
Exchange Server-Side Security Improvements ..........................366
Security Roles in Exchange Server 2003 ..........................368
Tips, Tricks, and Best Practices for Hardening Windows Server 2003 ......370
Layered Approach to Server Security ..............................370
Physical Security Considerations ....................................370
Restricting Logon Access ..............................................370
Auditing Security Events ................................................370
Securing Groups ..........................................................372
Keeping Services to a Minimum ....................................373
Locking Down the File System ......................................373
Using the Microsoft Baseline Security Analyzer ................374
Consulting Standards and Guidelines ..............................374
Using the Security Configuration Wizard ..........................374
Securing Servers with Security Templates ........................376
Keeping Up with Security Patches and Updates ................377
Hardening IIS ..............................................................378
IIS Hardening Checklist ................................................378
Other Hardening Techniques for Windows Server 2003 ................379
Securing by Functional Roles of the Server ..............................380
Standardizing Exchange Server 2003 Servers ............................382
Standardizing Server Builds ..........................................382
Protecting Exchange Server 2003 from Viruses ........................382
The AVAPI 2.5 Specification ..........................................383
Combating Spam ....................................................................384
Using Intelligent Message Filter ......................................384
Using SenderID ............................................................385
Using Blacklists ............................................................386
Reporting Spammers ....................................................386
Using a Third-Party Antispam Product ............................387
Do Not Use Open SMTP Relays ....................................387
Using the Work Email Address for Work Only ..................387
Protecting Distribution Lists ..........................................387
Taking Caution When Sharing Your Email Address ............388

Looking for Privacy Statements and Mailing Options ....................388
Removing or "Unsubscribing" at Your Own Discretion ...............388
Summary ...............................................................................................388
Best Practices ........................................................................................389

**13   Transport-Level Security                                          391**

The Onion Approach .............................................................................391
Using Public Key Infrastructure with Exchange Server 2003 ................392
Certificate Services in Windows Server 2003 ..............................392
PKI Planning Considerations ......................................................394
Installing Certificate Services .....................................................395
Fundamentals of Private and Public Keys ...................................396
Understanding Certificates ..........................................................396
Certificate Templates ...................................................................397
Smartcards in a PKI Infrastructure .............................................399
Certificate Enrollment .................................................................400
Supporting S/MIME ...............................................................................402
Supporting Digital Signatures .....................................................402
Message Encryption .....................................................................403
Comparing PGP and S/MIME .....................................................403
Protecting Communications with IP Security (IPSec) ...........................403
Fundamentals of IPSec .................................................................404
IPSec NAT Transversal (NAT-T) ..................................................404
Configuring IPSec ...................................................................................405
Establishing an IPSec Policy ........................................................406
Transport Layer Security ..............................................................407
Locking Down SMTP .............................................................................407
General SMTP Security Best Practices .........................................407
Configuring Message Delivery Limits .........................................407
Securing SMTP Virtual Servers ....................................................408
Controlling SMTP Relaying .........................................................410
Securing Routing Group Connectors .....................................................412
Using X.400 ..................................................................................412
Securing SMTP Connectors ..........................................................413
Using the Internet Mail Wizard ..................................................413
Securing Other Exchange-Supported Protocols .....................................414
Protecting Client–to–Front-End–Server Communications ......................415
Automatic SSL Redirection ...........................................................415
Locking Down Front-End and Back-End Server Communications ..........416
TCP and UDP Ports ......................................................................416
Summary ...............................................................................................418
Best Practices ........................................................................................418

**Part V    Migrating to Exchange Server 2003**

**14    Migrating from NT4 to Windows Server 2003                         421**

Microsoft Active Directory Configuration ...............................................421
   Defining the Migration Process .......................................................421
   Defining Exchange Server 2003 Objectives ......................................422
   Establishing Migration Project Phases ............................................422
   Examining In-Place Upgrade Versus New Hardware Migration
      Approaches ..................................................................................423
   Choosing a Migration Strategy .......................................................423
   Exploring Migration Options ...........................................................424
Upgrading a Single Member Server ......................................................424
   Verifying Hardware Compatibility ...................................................424
   Verifying Application Readiness ......................................................425
   Backing Up and Creating a Recovery Process .................................425
   Outlining Standalone Server Upgrade Steps ...................................426
Upgrading an NT 4.0 Domain Structure to Active Directory via
   the In-Place Upgrade Process ........................................................427
   Upgrading the Windows NT4 Primary Domain Controller ............427
   Upgrading to Active Directory ........................................................428
   Migrating and Replacing Backup Domain Controllers ...................429
Migrating Existing NT4 Domains to a New Windows
   Server 2003 Forest .........................................................................429
   Installing and Configuring a New Windows Server 2003 Forest
      and Domain .................................................................................430
   Configuring a Domain Trust Between Source Windows NT4
      and Target Windows Server 2003 Domains .................................430
   Migrating Account and Resource NT Domains to Active
      Directory Domains ......................................................................432
   Implication of Migrating Security Principles ..................................432
Understanding and Using the Microsoft Active Directory
   Migration Tool 2.0 (ADMT v2) .......................................................433
   Deploying ADMT in the Lab ...........................................................434
   Installing and Configuring ADMT ..................................................434
   Outlining Domain Migration Prerequisites ....................................435
   Creating Two-Way Trusts Between Source and Target Domains .....435
   Assigning Proper Permissions on Source Domain and Source
      Domain Workstations .................................................................435
   Creating a Target OU Structure ......................................................435
   Modifying Default Domain Policy on Target Domain ...................435
   Exporting Password Key Information ..............................................436

Installing Password Migration DLL on the Source Domain ...........436
Setting Proper Registry Permissions on the Source Domain ..........438
Migrating Accounts Using the Active Directory Migration Tool .............438
Migrating Groups Using ADMT .......................................................438
Migrating User Accounts Using ADMT .............................................442
Migrating Computer Accounts Using ADMT ...................................445
Migrating Service Accounts Using ADMT .......................................448
Migrating Other Domain Functionality .........................................449
Summary ...........................................................................................449
Best Practices ...................................................................................450

**15   Migrating from Exchange v5.5 to Exchange Server 2003        451**

Understanding Exchange 5.5 Migration Options and Strategies .............451
Comparing Exchange 5.5 and Exchange Server 2003 .............................451
Detailing Design Limitations in Exchange 5.5 .................................452
How Exchange Server 2003 Addresses Exchange 5.5
Shortcomings ................................................................................453
Reviewing the Prerequisites for Migrating to Exchange Server 2003 .......454
Checking the Current Environment with the Exchange
Server 2003 Deployment Tools .....................................................454
Preparing the Exchange 5.5 Organization for the Migration ..........454
Structuring the Migration for Best Results .........................................457
Performing Single Site Exchange 5.5 Migrations ............................457
Performing Multisite Exchange 5.5 Migrations ..............................458
Performing Multiorganization Exchange 5.5 Migrations ...............458
Preparing the Active Directory Forest and Domain for
Exchange Server 2003 ........................................................................458
Extending the Active Directory Schema .........................................458
Preparing the Windows Server 2003 Domains to Support
Exchange Server 2003 ...................................................................459
Verifying the Organization Settings with OrgPrepCheck ...............460
Installing and Configuring the Active Directory Connector ...................460
Installing the ADC ..........................................................................460
Creating Connection Agreements ..................................................461
Installing the First Exchange Server 2003 System in an
Exchange 5.5 Site ...............................................................................466
Installing the First Exchange Server 2003 System ..........................466
Understanding What Happens Behind the GUI During the
Installation ....................................................................................468
Understanding the Configuration Connection Agreement ...........469
Examining the Site Replication Service (SRS) ................................469

No Service Account in Exchange Server 2003 ..................................469

Using the Recipient Update Service (RUS) ......................................470

Understanding Exchange Server 2003 Mailbox-Migration Methods .......470

Migrating Using the Move Mailbox Approach ................................470

Leapfrogging Server Migrations to Reduce Costs ...........................472

Using ExMerge to Migrate Mailboxes .........................................473

Migrating Exchange 5.5 Public Folders to Exchange Server 2003 ...........475

Migrating Exchange 5.5 Connectors and Services to Exchange
Server 2003 .............................................................................475

Migrating the Internet Mail Service ............................................476

Migrating Site Connectors ........................................................477

Migrating Foreign Mail Connectors ............................................477

Creating Support for Unsupported Connectors ...........................477

Completing the Migration to Exchange Server 2003 .........................478

Converting to Native Mode ......................................................478

Deleting All Directory Replication Connectors ............................479

Performing Post-Migration Clean-Up .........................................480

Summary .....................................................................................481

Best Practices ..............................................................................481


16    Migrating from Exchange 2000 to Exchange Server 2003          483

Outlining Migration Options from Exchange 2000 to Exchange
Server 2003 .............................................................................484

Understanding Exchange Server 2003 Migration Prerequisites ......484

Identifying Exchange Server 2003 Migration Incompatibilities .....485

Understanding Exchange Server 2003 Deployment
Enhancements ......................................................................485

Migration Techniques Using the In-Place Upgrade Method ..........486

Understanding Migration Techniques Using the Move
Mailbox Method ..................................................................487

Understanding Complex and Combined Approach Migration
Techniques .........................................................................488

Deploying a Prototype Lab for the Exchange Server 2003
Migration Process ..................................................................489

Creating Temporary Prototype Domain Controllers to Simulate
Migration ...........................................................................489

Seizing Operations Master (OM) Roles in the Lab Environment ....490

Restoring the Exchange Environment for Prototype Purposes .......491

Validating and Documenting Design Decisions and Migration
Procedures .........................................................................491

Migrating to Exchange Server 2003 Using the In-Place Upgrade
Approach ..............................................................................491

Making Use of the Exchange Server 2003 Deployment Tools ........492

Upgrading the Active Directory Schema with Exchange
ForestPrep ...................................................................................492

Preparing Each Domain for Exchange Server 2003 with
DomainPrep ...................................................................................494

Running the In-Place Upgrade of an Exchange 2000 System to
Exchange Server 2003 ...............................................................495

Upgrading the Operating System from Windows 2000 to
Windows Server 2003 ................................................................496

Upgrading Additional Exchange 2000 Servers to
Exchange Server 2003 ...............................................................497

Migrating to Exchange Server 2003 Using the Move Mailbox Method ...497

Deploying Exchange 2003 Servers in Advance of the
Move Mailbox Migration ............................................................498

Enabling New Server "Burn-In" and Pilot Testing ..........................500

Moving Mailboxes to the New Exchange Server 2003 Databases ...500

Replicating Public Folders from Exchange 2000 to Exchange
Server 2003 ...............................................................................502

Moving Connectors from Exchange 2000 to Exchange
Server 2003 ...............................................................................503

Changing the Recipient Update Service (RUS) Server from
Exchange 2000 to Exchange Server 2003 ....................................504

Retiring Legacy Exchange 2000 Servers ...........................................505

Summary ..................................................................................................506

Best Practices .........................................................................................506

**17  Compatibility Testing**                                                      **509**

The Importance of Compatibility Testing ..............................................510

Preparing for Compatibility Testing ......................................................511

Determining the Scope for Application Testing ...............................511

Defining the Goals for Compatibility Testing .................................513

Documenting the Compatibility Testing Plan .................................517

Researching Products and Applications ...............................................517

Creating an Inventory of the Messaging Applications ...................518

Prioritizing the Applications on the List .........................................518

Verifying Compatibility with Vendors ...................................................519

Tracking Sheets for Application Compatibility Research ...............520

Six States of Compatibility ...............................................................520

Using an Exchange Server 2003–Compatible Application ..............521

Requiring a Minor Update or Service Patch for Compatibility .......522

Applications That Require a Version Upgrade for Compatibility ...522

Noncompatible Applications That Will Be Used Anyway ...............522

Noncompatible Applications That Will Be Eliminated and
Applications That Are Not Compatible and Will Not Be Used .....523
Noncompatible Applications That Seem to Work ...........................523
Creating an Upgrade Decision Matrix ...........................................524
Assessing the Effects of the Compatibility Results on the
Compatibility Testing Plan ..............................................524
Lab Testing Existing Applications ........................................................525
Allocating and Configuring Hardware ...........................................525
Allocating and Configuring the NOS and Exchange Server 2003 ...525
Loading the Remaining Applications ............................................526
Application Compatibility Testing Tool ..........................................527
Testing the Migration and Upgrade Process ...................................528
Documenting the Results of the Compatibility Testing ...........................528
Determining Whether a Prototype Phase Is Required ..............................529
Summary .............................................................................529
Best Practices ........................................................................530

**Part VI    Exchange Server 2003 Administration and Management**

**18    Administering Exchange Server 2003                                    533**

Exchange Administration and the Delegation Wizard ...........................533
Implementing Role-Based Administration ......................................534
Understanding and Implementing Extended Permissions ..............536
Delegating Administrative Rights ..................................................537
Auditing Administrative Tasks in Exchange Server 2003 ...............539
Managing Mailboxes and Message Settings in Exchange Server 2003 .....540
Managing Exchange Mailboxes .....................................................540
Implementing Message Limits and Storage Limits ..........................541
Understanding and Implementing User Mailbox Options ...........541
Managing New Mailbox Features .......................................................543
Using Wireless Services ................................................................543
Managing User Protocols ..............................................................544
Changing the Status of Exchange Features ....................................545
Managing and Monitoring Mailbox Usage .....................................545
Running the User Monitor tool .....................................................546
Exporting Collection Data to a File ...............................................547
Moving Exchange User Mailboxes ......................................................547
Simple Tasks to Prepare for Moving Mailboxes ..............................547
Moving Mailboxes Between Storage Groups and Servers ...............548
Creating and Managing Exchange Contacts .........................................551
Creating Exchange Contacts .........................................................551

Mail-Forwarding Options with Contacts ........................................... 552

Contact Email Address Types .......................................................... 552

Modifying and Adding Contact Email Addresses .......................... 553

Planning and Creating Distribution Groups .......................................... 553

Determining Distribution Group Scopes ...................................... 554

Creating Distribution Groups ....................................................... 555

Creating Query-Based Distribution Groups .................................. 556

Managing and Maintaining Distribution Groups ......................... 557

Mail-Enabling Groups .................................................................. 558

Creating and Managing Exchange Server 2003 Administrative

Groups ................................................................................................ 558

Mixed Mode ................................................................................ 559

Native Mode ................................................................................ 559

Administrative Groups Models ..................................................... 559

Creating Administrative Groups in Exchange Server 2003 ............ 560

Delegating Control over Administrative Groups .......................... 560

Creating and Managing Routing Groups ............................................. 561

Understanding Exchange Server 2003 Routing Groups ............... 562

Installing Routing Groups ............................................................ 562

Moving Exchange Servers Between Routing Groups ..................... 563

Using Recipient Policies ....................................................................... 563

Implementing Email Address Recipient Policies .......................... 564

Defining Recipient Policy Naming Standards ............................... 565

Defining Recipient Policy Membership Using Search Filters .......... 565

Implementing Mailbox Recipient Policies .................................... 566

Editing and Changing Existing Recipient Policies ....................... 567

Administering Recipient Update Services ............................................. 568

Understanding Recipient Update Services .................................... 568

Deploying Recipient Update Services ........................................... 569

Managing Recipient Update Services ............................................ 570

Using the Mailbox Recovery Center Tool ............................................ 571

Identifying Disconnected Mailboxes ............................................ 571

Resolving Mailbox Conflicts ........................................................ 572

Matching and Recovering Mailboxes ........................................... 573

Using the Mailbox Manager Utility ..................................................... 574

Accessing the Mailbox Manager .................................................. 574

Understanding Mailbox Manager Options .................................... 574

Reporting with Mailbox Manager ................................................ 575

Configuring Mailbox-Cleanup Tasks ............................................ 576

Scheduling Mailbox Manager Tasks ............................................. 577

Summary ............................................................................................. 578

Best Practices ...................................................................................... 579

**19    Exchange Server 2003 Management and Maintenance Practices          581**

Managing Exchange Server 2003 ................................................................581
    Managing by Server Roles and Responsibilities ...............................582
Auditing the Environment .......................................................................583
    Audit Logging ...............................................................................584
    Protocol Logging ...........................................................................585
    Message Tracking ..........................................................................585
Managing Exchange Server 2003 Remotely ...........................................586
Maintenance Tools for Exchange Server 2003 .......................................587
    Managing Exchange with the Exchange System Manager ..............587
    Active Directory Users and Computers ...........................................588
    Windows Server 2003 Backup ........................................................590
    Exchange Maintenance with the ntdsutil Utility ........................590
    Integrity Checking with the isinteg Utility ...................................590
    Database Maintenance with the eseutil Utility ............................591
    Exchange Message Tracking ...........................................................592
    Exchange Queue Viewer ................................................................592
Best Practices for Performing Database Maintenance ............................592
    Online Database Maintenance .......................................................593
    Performing Offline Database Maintenance ....................................594
    Database Maintenance Through Mailbox Moves ...........................597
Prioritizing and Scheduling Maintenance Best Practices .......................597
    Daily Maintenance .......................................................................598
    Weekly Maintenance .....................................................................599
    Monthly Maintenance ...................................................................600
    Quarterly Maintenance .................................................................601
Post-Maintenance Procedures ................................................................602
Reducing Management and Maintenance Efforts ..................................602
    Using Microsoft Operations Manager ............................................602
Summary .................................................................................................603
Best Practices ..........................................................................................603

**20    Documenting an Exchange Server 2003 Environment          605**

Planning Exchange Server 2003 Documentation ...................................606
Benefits of Documentation .....................................................................606
    Knowledge Sharing and Knowledge Management .........................607
    Financial Benefits of Documentation ............................................607
    Baselining Records for Documentation Comparisons ....................607
    Using Documentation for Troubleshooting Purposes ...................608
Design and Planning Documentation .....................................................608
    Documenting the Design ...............................................................608
    Creating the Migration Plan ..........................................................610

Outlining the Project Plan ......................................................610
Developing the Test Plan ........................................................611
Developing the Migration Documentation ............................................612
Server Migration Procedures ....................................................612
Desktop Client Configuration Procedures .....................................613
Mail Migration Procedures ......................................................613
Example of a Mail Migration Checklist .......................................613
Exchange Server 2003 Environment Documentation ...........................614
Server Build Procedures ........................................................614
Configuration (As-Built) Documentation .....................................615
Topology Diagrams ................................................................615
Administration and Maintenance Documentation .................................616
Step-by-Step Procedure Documents ..........................................616
Organizational Policy Documents .............................................617
Documented Checklists ..........................................................617
Disaster Recovery Documentation ................................................617
Disaster Recovery Planning .....................................................618
Backup and Recovery Development ..........................................619
Exchange System Failover Documentation ...................................619
Performance Documentation ........................................................619
Routine Reporting .................................................................620
Management-Level Reporting ...................................................620
Technical Reporting ...............................................................620
Security Documentation ..............................................................621
Change Control .....................................................................621
Procedures ...........................................................................621
Training Documentation ..............................................................622
End-User ...............................................................................622
Technical ...............................................................................622
Summary ..................................................................................622
Best Practices .............................................................................623

**21   Using Terminal Services to Manage Exchange Servers          625**
Terminal Services Modes of Operation ........................................625
Remote Desktop for Administration .........................................625
Planning for Remote Desktop for Administration Mode ................626
Enabling Remote Desktop for Administration ............................626
Remote Administration (HTML) ..............................................627
Remote Desktop Administration Tips and Tricks .........................630
Terminal Services ..................................................................631
Planning Considerations for Using Terminal Services ...................631

Terminal Services Security ................................................631

Terminal Server Licensing ..............................................632

Using Terminal Services on Pocket Devices ................................633

Locking Down PDA Terminal Services ................................633

Using Exchange System Manager to Remotely

Manage Exchange Server 2003 ..........................................635

Benefits of Remote Management Using the ESM ............................636

Managing a Mixed Exchange Environment with ESM ....................636

Summary ..................................................................637

Best Practices ..............................................................637

**Part VII    New Mobility Functionality in Exchange Server 2003**

**22    Designing Mobility in Exchange Server 2003                    641**

Mobilizing Exchange Server 2003 ........................................641

Accessing Outlook Using VPN Connectivity ..........................641

Connecting Outlook over HTTP Proxy ................................642

Using Outlook Web Access As a Remote Client ......................642

Using Exchange ActiveSync for PDA Connectivity ..................643

Using Mobile Web Access for Wireless Phone Access ..............643

Using Non-Windows Systems to Access Exchange ....................644

Automatic Update on Mobile Devices ................................644

Leveraging Exchange ActiveSync for PDA Mobile Communications ......644

Flexibility of Information Synchronization ..........................645

Customizing Synchronization Characteristics ........................645

Improving Mobile Performance ......................................646

Improving Mobile Security ..........................................646

Using Outlook Mobile Access for Browser-Based Devices ..............647

Simplified Browser-Centric Commands ..............................647

Minimizing Downloads Through Enhanced Features ................647

Designing the Appropriate Use of Exchange 2003

Mobility Capabilities ....................................................648

Identifying Mobile Devices in Use ..................................648

Choosing the Right Mobile Solution ................................650

Understanding Exchange ActiveSync and OMA ......................650

Active Prototype and Pilot Testing of Exchange Mobility ..........651

Organizational Scalability of Exchange Mobility ..................652

Using Exchange Mobility for the Mobile Executive ..................653

Technologies Used by Mobile Executives ..........................653

Achieved Benefits by Executives ....................................653

Replacing Laptops with Mobile Pocket Devices ......................653

Technologies Used for Mobile Laptop Users ........................654

Achieved Benefits by Mobile Laptop Users ........................654

Leveraging a Low-Cost PDA Instead of an Expensive Tablet ...................654
    Technologies Used for Pocket PC Mobility .....................................654
    Achieved Benefits of Pocket Device Use .........................................655
Summary .............................................................................................655
Best Practices ....................................................................................655

**23  Implementing Mobile Synchronization in Exchange Server 2003        657**

Preparing for Mobility in an Exchange 2003 Environment ....................657
    Understanding ActiveSync Versus Outlook Mobile Access .............658
    Functionality in Exchange 2003 ....................................................658
    Designing and Planning a Mobile Access Exchange
        Environment ..............................................................................658
    Optimizing the Number of Front-End Servers ...............................659
    Trying Mobility Before Making a True Investment ........................661
Installing an Exchange Server 2003 Server for Mobile Access .................662
    Creating a Separate Front-End Server for Mobile Connections ......662
    Adding Additional Front-End Servers for Scalability .....................664
    Configuring Firewall Ports to Secure Communications ..................664
Migrating from Microsoft Mobile Information Server .............................665
    Installing Mobile Information Server from Scratch ........................665
    Replacing an Existing Mobile Information Server ..........................666
Configuring Mobile Exchange Features ...................................................666
    Viewing Mobile Services ...............................................................666
    Configuring Mobile Services ........................................................667
    Configuring Mobile Services Properties for ActiveSync .................668
    Configuring Mobile Services Properties for OMA ..........................670
Summary .............................................................................................670
Best Practices ....................................................................................671

**24  Configuring Client Systems for Mobility        673**

Identifying Mobile Devices to Be Supported .........................................673
Supporting the Pocket PC 2002 Synchronization with
    Microsoft Exchange 2003 .....................................................................674
    Installing the Pocket PC 2002 Emulator ......................................675
    Configuring a Pocket PC 2002 Device for Network
        Connectivity ..............................................................................679
    Establishing a Connection Between the Pocket PC 2002
        and Exchange 2003 ...................................................................683
    Synchronizing Data Between Pocket PC 2002 and
        Exchange 2003 ...........................................................................683
Supporting Pocket PC 2003 Synchronization with Exchange 2003 .........684
    Installing the Pocket PC 2003 Emulator ......................................685

Configuring a Pocket PC 2003 Device for Network
Connectivity .................................................................688
Establishing a Connection Between the Pocket PC 2003
and Exchange 2003 ......................................................692
Synchronizing Data Between Pocket PC 2003 and
Exchange 2003 .............................................................693
Using the Pocket PC 2002 and Pocket PC 2003 ..................693
Viewing Inbox Information ............................................693
Viewing Calendar and Contacts Information ...................694
Working with Smartphones ..................................................695
Using a Smartphone Wireless Device ..............................695
Using a Smartphone Emulator ......................................696
Synchronizing Data Between the Smartphone and
Exchange 2003 .............................................................698
Establishing a Link from a Mobile Phone to Exchange 2003 ...................699
Establishing Connectivity for a Mobile Phone Device ...................700
Connectivity of a Web-Enabled Wireless Phone ...........700
Connectivity Using a Web-Enabled Phone Emulator .....................700
Using Outlook Mobile Access to Exchange Server 2003 .........................701
Summary ...........................................................................702
Best Practices ...................................................................702

**Part VIII    Client Access to Exchange Server 2003**

**25    Getting the Most Out of the Microsoft Outlook Client         707**
What's Common Across All Versions of Outlook ...................707
Comparing Outlook 97, Outlook 98, Outlook 2000,
Outlook XP/2002, and Outlook 2003 ...........................708
The Basic Outlook Features ............................................708
Security .........................................................................708
Collaboration ................................................................708
Other Enhancements .....................................................709
What's New in Outlook 2003 ...............................................709
Understanding the New Outlook 2003 Interface ............709
Methods for Highlighting Outlook Items .......................710
Proposing a New Meeting Time .....................................711
Using the New Search Functionality ..............................712
Associating Items with Specific Contacts ......................713
Managing Multiple Email Accounts from One Place ......715
Customizing the End-User Experience ..................................715
Using the Custom Installation Wizard ...........................716
Creating a PRF File Using the Custom Installation Wizard .............716

Configuring Registry Keys During Installation ................................718
Using PRF Files .................................................................................718
Applying PRF Files ...........................................................................719
Security Enhancements in Outlook 2003 ...............................................719
Support for Secured Messaging ......................................................719
Attaching Security Labels ...............................................................722
Using Junk Email Filters .................................................................722
Preventing Spam Beaconing ...........................................................725
Understanding RPC over HTTP ..............................................................725
Installing and Configuring RPC over HTTP on the Server End ......725
Installing and Configuring RPC over HTTP on the End-User
    Workstation ..............................................................................727
Using Outlook 2003 Collaboratively ......................................................729
Viewing Shared Calendars in Multiple Panes .................................729
Enabling Calendar Sharing ..............................................................729
Sharing Other Personal Information ...............................................731
Delegating Rights to Send Email "On Behalf Of" ..........................731
Sharing Information with Users Outside the Company .................731
Using iCalendar and vCalendar ......................................................733
Using Public Folders to Share Information ....................................736
Using Group Schedules .................................................................. 736
Using Synchronized Home Page Views ..........................................738
Using Outlook Cached Mode for Remote Connectivity .........................739
The User Experience in Cached Mode .............................................740
Deploying Cached Exchange Mode .................................................740
Using Cached Exchange Mode ........................................................743
Cached Exchange Mode and OSTs and OABs .................................744
Outlook Features That Decrease Cached Mode's Effectiveness .......745
Summary ................................................................................................746
Best Practices ........................................................................................747

26  Everything You Need to Know About the Outlook Web Access
    (OWA) Client                                                                     749
Understanding Microsoft's Direction on OWA ........................................750
Creating a Common Interface .........................................................750
Making a Full-Feature Web Client ..................................................750
Integrating XML in the Client Interface .........................................751
Leveraging the .NET Framework .....................................................751
Using the Basics of OWA 2003 ..............................................................751
Understanding User Modes .............................................................751
What's New in the OWA Client (Since Exchange 2000 Server) ..............753
Logging On ......................................................................................755

Getting to Know the Look and Feel of OWA 2003 ......................................757
    Using Multiple Panes ...........................................................757
    Using Pull-Down Menus ......................................................759
    Moving Through the OWA Features ...................................760
    Moving Through Email Pages ..............................................760
    Changing the Viewing Order and Using the Two-Line View ..........760
    Using the Reading Pane .......................................................761
    Creating New Folders ..........................................................762
    Displaying Public Folders in Their Own Windows ..........763
    Using OWA Help ..................................................................763
    Logging Off OWA 2003 ........................................................764
Using OWA Mail Features ...........................................................764
    Creating an Email ................................................................764
    Addressing an Email ............................................................764
    Removing a User from the To, CC, or BCC Fields in a Message .....765
    Adding Attachments ............................................................765
    Sending an Email .................................................................766
    Reading an Email .................................................................767
    Reading Attachments ..........................................................767
    Replying or Forwarding an Email .....................................768
    Deleting Email .....................................................................769
    Configuring Message Options: Importance,
      Sensitivity, and Tracking Options .................................769
    Changing the Look of the Text in an Email Message ......771
Taking Advantage of Advanced OWA Features ...........................771
    Moving Email Messages to Folders ...................................771
    Using the Address Book .......................................................771
    Marking Messages Read/Unread .......................................773
    Viewing User Property Sheets ...........................................773
    Using the OWA 2003 Spell Checker ..................................774
    Configuring Rules Using the Rules Editor .......................775
    Displaying Context Menus .................................................777
    Enabling Quick Flags for Easier Reminders .....................778
    Performing Searches with Outlook ...................................779
    Using Keyboard Shortcuts to Save Time ..........................780
    Understanding the Deferred View Update .......................781
Customizing OWA Options ..........................................................781
    Configuring the Out of Office Assistant ..........................781
    Configuring Items Per Page ...............................................781
    Setting Default Signatures .................................................782
    Reading Pane Options .........................................................783
    Spelling Options ..................................................................783

Email Security .................................................................783
Privacy and Junk Email Prevention ...............................784
Color Scheme Appearance ..............................................785
Configuring Date and Time Formats ...............................785
Configuring Calendar Options .......................................786
Configuring Reminder Options ......................................786
Configuring Contact Options .........................................786
Recovering Deleted Items ..............................................786
Changing the Active Directory Password ........................787
Using the Calendar in OWA ...............................................788
Using Views ....................................................................788
Creating an Appointment in Calendar ...........................788
Creating a Meeting Request in Calendar ........................789
Gaining Functionality from the Meeting Invitation Functions ..............792
Forwarding and Replying to Meeting Requests ...............792
Setting Preferred Reminder Time Changes .....................792
Launching an Invitation in Its Own Window .................792
Receiving Task and Calendar Reminders ........................793
Using Tasks in OWA ...........................................................793
Creating Tasks ................................................................793
Task Views .....................................................................794
Using Contacts in OWA ......................................................794
Creating Contacts ..........................................................794
Editing Contacts ............................................................795
Mapping Addresses from Contacts ................................795
Changing Contact Views ................................................795
Deleting Contacts ..........................................................796
Finding Names ...............................................................796
Sending Mail from Contacts ..........................................796
Creating New Distribution Lists ....................................796
Understanding OWA Security Features ...............................797
S/MIME: Sending and Receiving Digitally Signed and
   Encrypted Messages ....................................................797
Understanding Spam Beacon Blocking ...........................797
Understanding Attachment Blocking .............................798
Understanding Cookie Authentication Timeout and
   Timed Logoff ..............................................................798
Clearing User Credentials at Logoff ..............................798
Tips for OWA Users with Slow Access ................................798
Summary ............................................................................799
Best Practices .....................................................................800

27    **Outlook for Non-Windows Systems**                                      **801**

Understanding Non-Windows-Based Mail Client Options ....................802
  Supporting Mac Clients with Microsoft Solutions .........................802
  Providing Full Functionality with Virtual PC and
    Remote Desktop for Mac ............................................................803
  Using the Internet for Exchange Connectivity ..............................804
  Comparing Client Functionality and Compatibility ......................804
Outlook for Macintosh .........................................................................805
  Outlook Options for Macintosh ...................................................806
  Configuring Support for Mac Clients ...........................................806
  Configuring Outlook for Macintosh .............................................808
  Supporting Macintosh Clients .....................................................809
Outlook Express ....................................................................................810
  Compatibility with Non-Windows Systems ..................................810
  Installing and Enabling Support for Outlook Express 5 ................811
  Configuring POP Access with Outlook Express 5 for Mac .............812
  Migrating and Backing Up Personal Address Books ......................813
Configuring and Implementing Entourage 2004 for Mac .......................815
  Features and Functionality ...........................................................815
  Deploying Entourage 2004 ...........................................................816
Terminal Services Client for Mac ..........................................................818
  Compatibility, Features, and Functionality ..................................818
  Installing the Terminal Services Client ........................................820
Understanding Other Non-Windows Client Access Methods .................822
  POP3 Access to Exchange ..............................................................822
  IMAP Access to Exchange ..............................................................822
  Pocket PC Access ..........................................................................823
  HTML Access ................................................................................823
  Outlook Web Access .....................................................................823
Summary ...............................................................................................824
Best Practices .......................................................................................824

Part IX    **Client Administration and Management**

28    **Deploying the Client for Exchange**                                    **829**

Understanding Deployment Options .....................................................829
  Available Methods of Deployment ...............................................830
  Outlook Profile Generation ..........................................................830
  Configuring Outlook Client Options ............................................831
  Deploying Non–Windows-Based Options ......................................832
Planning Considerations and Best Practices ........................................832
  Network Topology Bandwidth Consideration ..............................832

Planning Best Practices ................................................................833

Addressing Remote and Mobile Client Systems ..............................833

Managing the Outlook Deployment ..............................................834

Preparing the Deployment ...................................................................834

Outlook Systems Requirements .....................................................834

Planning Predefined Configuration Options ..................................835

Creating Administrative Installation Points ...................................836

Automating Outlook Profile Settings .............................................836

Creating Transforms and Profile Files ...........................................838

Installing the Exchange Client .............................................................842

Using Transforms and PRF Files When Installing Outlook .............842

Installing the Outlook Clients with PRF Files .................................843

Manually Installing Outlook with Transforms ...............................843

Pushing Client Software with Windows 2003 Group Policies ...............844

Deploying Outlook with Group Policy Overview ...........................844

Best Practices for Deploying Outlook Clients ................................846

Pushing Outlook Client ..................................................................846

Testing the Outlook Client Deployment ........................................848

Deploying with Microsoft Systems Management Server ......................848

Planning and Preparing Outlook Deployments with SMS .............848

Deploying with Systems Management Server 2003 ........................849

Configuring the SMS Package for an Unattended Installation .......849

Managing Post-Deployment Tasks .......................................................850

Validating Successful Installations ..................................................850

Summary ...............................................................................................851

Best Practices ........................................................................................851

**29  Group Policy Management for Exchange Clients          853**

Understanding Group Policy Management with Outlook .....................854

Managing Group Policies ................................................................854

Understanding Policies and Preferences .........................................855

Group Policy Templates ..................................................................855

Defining the Order of Application ..................................................856

Group Policy Refresh Intervals .......................................................856

Baseline Administration for Group Policy Deployment .......................857

Delegating GP Management Rights .................................................857

Working with Resultant Set of Policies (RSoP) ..............................858

Managing Group Policy Inheritance ...............................................858

Group Policy Backup, Restore, Copy, and Import ..........................859

Outlook Client Group Policies .............................................................859

Exchange Client Policy Options ......................................................860

Adding the Outlook Administrative Template .................................860

Assigning Group Policy Delegates ....................................................863
Managing Group Policy Configurations .........................................864
Administering Outlook Through Group Policy ......................................864
Defining Baseline Outlook Preferences .........................................865
Managing the Look and Feel of the Exchange Client ...................867
Configuring and Applying Outlook Group Policy Settings ...........867
Updates and Patch Management with Group Policies ...........................870
Deployment Options When Updating Exchange Clients ..............870
Deploying Client Updates ...............................................................871
Pushing Client Updates ...................................................................872
Determining the Success of a Push ...............................................873
Summary .....................................................................................................873
Best Practices ...........................................................................................874

**Part X    Fault Tolerance and Optimization Technologies**

**30    System-Level Fault Tolerance (Clustering/Network Load Balancing)    877**

Clustering and Load Balancing with Exchange Server 2003 ...................878
Clustering Terminology ...................................................................878
Fault Tolerance Options .................................................................879
Cluster Permissions with Exchange Server 2003 Environments .....882
Management Options with Exchange Server 2003 ........................883
Clusters and Load-Balancing Requirements .............................................883
Cluster Node Hardware Requirements .........................................883
Software Requirements ...................................................................884
Networking Requirements ...............................................................885
Shared Storage and Disks Requirements ......................................885
Implementing Fault-Tolerant Exchange Systems .....................................886
Preparing to Install Exchange Server 2003 Clusters ......................887
General Features Overview ...........................................................887
Planning Exchange Server 2003 Clusters ....................................888
Installing Exchange Server 2003 Clusters ...............................................891
Setting Up Windows Server 2003 Clusters ..................................892
Adding Additional Nodes to a Cluster ..........................................893
Installing the Cluster-Aware Version of Exchange Server 2003 ......894
Configuring Exchange Server 2003 in a Cluster ..........................896
Managing Exchange Server 2003 Clusters ...............................................898
Configuration and Management Options .....................................899
Backing Up and Restoring Exchange Server 2003 Clusters .............899
Failover and Failback ......................................................................902
Outlook Web Access Front-End Server and Load-Balancing Clusters ......903
Using Network Load Balancing .....................................................903

NLB Modes and Port Configuration Overview ................................904

NLB Network Card Configurations ................................904

Configuring Network Load Balancing with OWA ........................904

Summary ................................907

Best Practices ................................907

**31  Backing Up the Exchange Server 2003 Environment        909**

Using Backup to Solve Department Challenges ........................910

Understanding What Should Be Ready for Restoral ....................910

Maintaining Documentation on the Exchange Environment ................912

Server Configuration Documentation ............................913

The Server Build Document ................................913

Hardware Inventory ................................913

Network Configurations ................................914

Recovery Documentation ................................914

Updating Documentation ................................914

Developing a Backup Strategy ................................915

Creating a Master Account List ................................915

Assigning Tasks and Designating Team Members ....................915

Creating Regular Backup Procedures ............................916

Creating a Service-Level Agreement for Each Critical Service ........916

Selecting Devices to Back Up ................................917

Backing Up the Windows Server 2003 and Exchange Server 2003 ..........918

Backing Up Boot and System Volumes ............................918

Backing Up Exchange Data Volumes ............................919

Backing Up Windows Server 2003 Services ........................919

Backing Up the System State ................................920

Using the Active Directory Restore Mode Password ....................920

Volume Shadow Copy Services and Exchange Server 2003 ................920

What Role VSS Plays in Backup ................................921

Shadow Copies and Snapshots ................................921

VSS Requirements and Prerequisites ............................921

Using the Windows Backup Utility (Ntbackup.exe) ....................922

Modes of Operation ................................922

Using the Windows Backup Advanced Mode ........................923

Automated System Recovery ................................924

Backing Up Specific Windows Services ............................927

Disk Configuration (Software RAID Sets) ........................927

Certificate Services ................................927

Internet Information Services (IIS) ................................929

Managing Media in a Structured Backup Strategy ....................................930

    Media Pools ..........................................................................................931

Summary ..............................................................................................932

Best Practices ......................................................................................932

**32    Recovering from a Disaster                                                    935**

Identifying the Extent of the Problem ..................................................935

    Mailbox Content Was Deleted, Use the Undelete Function of

    Exchange and Outlook ....................................................................936

    Data Is Lost, Must Restore from Backup ..........................................936

    Data Is Okay, Server Just Doesn't Come Up ....................................937

    Data Is Corrupt—Some Mailboxes Are Accessible, Some

    Are Not ............................................................................................937

    Data Is Corrupt, No Mailboxes Are Accessible ................................937

    Exchange Server Is Okay, Something Else Is Preventing

    Exchange from Working ..................................................................938

What to Do Before Performing Any Server-Recovery Process ................938

    Validating Backup Data and Procedures ..........................................938

Preparing for a More Easily Recoverable Environment ..........................939

    Documenting the Exchange Environment ........................................939

    Documenting the Backup Process ....................................................940

    Documenting the Recovery Process ..................................................940

    Including Test Restores in the Scheduled Maintenance ..................940

Recovering from a Site Failure ..............................................................941

    Creating Redundant and Failover Sites ............................................941

    Creating the Failover Site ..................................................................941

    Failing Over Between Sites ................................................................942

    Failing Back After Site Recovery ......................................................943

    Providing Alternative Methods of Client Connectivity ..................943

Recovering from a Disk Failure ..............................................................944

    Hardware-Based RAID Array Failure ................................................944

    System Volume ..................................................................................944

    Boot Volume ......................................................................................945

    Data Volume ......................................................................................945

Recovering from a Boot Failure ..............................................................945

    The Recovery Console ........................................................................947

Recovering from a Complete Server Failure ..........................................947

    Restoring Versus Rebuilding ............................................................947

    Manually Recovering a Server ..........................................................948

    Restoring a Server Using a System State Restore ............................949

    Restoring a System Using an Automated System Recovery

    Restore ..............................................................................................951

    Restoring the Boot Loader File ..........................................................953

Recovering Exchange Application and Exchange Data ............................953
    Recovering Using Ntbackup.exe ................................................953
    Performing a Restore of Only Exchange Database Files ................954
Recovering from Database Corruption ...............................................956
    Flat File Copying the Exchange Databases ...............................956
    Moving Mailboxes to Another Server in the Site ......................957
    Extracting Mail from a Corrupt Mailbox .................................958
    Running the ISINTEG and ESEUTIL Utilities ................................961
Using the Recovery Storage Group in Exchange Server 2003 ..............963
    Recovering Data with a Recovery Storage Group ....................964
Recovering Internet Information Services ...........................................966
    Recovering IIS Data and Logs .................................................966
Recovering the Cluster Service ........................................................966
Recovering Windows Server 2003 Domain Controllers .......................967
Recovering Active Directory .............................................................967
    The Active Directory Database ...............................................967
Summary .......................................................................................973
Best Practices ................................................................................974

**33   Capacity Analysis and Performance Optimization          975**

Examining Exchange Server 2003 Performance Improvements ..............976
    Communication Improvements ...............................................976
    Client-Side Performance Enhancements .................................977
    Outlook Web Access (OWA) Performance Enhancements ..............978
    Improved Public Folder Store Replication ...............................978
    Performance Scalability Improvements ...................................979
Analyzing Capacity .........................................................................979
    Establishing Baselines .........................................................980
Monitoring Exchange Server 2003 ...................................................981
    Using the Performance Monitor Console ................................981
    Using Network Monitor .......................................................982
    Using Task Manager ............................................................982
    Simulating Stress with Jetstress ...........................................982
Analyzing and Monitoring Core Elements .........................................983
    Memory Subsystem Optimizations.........................................984
    Improving Virtual Memory Usage ..........................................985
    Monitoring Processor Usage..................................................986
    Monitoring the Disk Subsystem ............................................986
    Monitoring the Network Subsystem .......................................987
Properly Sizing Exchange Server 2003 .............................................987
    Optimizing the Disk Subsystem Configuration ........................987
    Database Sizing and Optimization .........................................989

Optimizing Exchange Logs ...............................................990

Sizing Memory Requirements ........................................991

Sizing Based on Server Roles ........................................991

Optimizing Exchange Through Ongoing Maintenance ........................993

Monitoring Exchange with Microsoft Operations Manager ..................994

Summary ...............................................................995

Best Practices ........................................................995

**Part XI    Cross-Platform Migrations to Exchange 2003**

**34    Migrating from Novell GroupWise to Exchange 2003            999**

Similarities and Differences Between GroupWise and

Exchange Server 2003 ...............................................1000

Comparing Messaging and Collaboration Capabilities ...............1000

Comparing Administrative Tools ...................................1001

Exchange Migration and the Impact of Active Directory ................1001

Implementing Exchange in a Native Active Directory

Environment ...................................................1002

Running Exchange in an NDS/eDirectory Environment .............1002

Evaluating the Existing Environment .................................1002

Understanding the Tools Available to Migrate from NDS/

eDirectory to Active Directory .....................................1004

Services for NetWare ............................................1004

Microsoft Directory Synchronization Services ....................1004

File Migration Utility ..........................................1005

Automating the Migration Using Services for NetWare 5.03 .............1006

Setting Up Directory Synchronization ............................1006

Migrating Data with the File Migration Utility (FMU) ............1008

Planning Your Migration from GroupWise .............................1010

Choosing a Phased Migration from GroupWise .....................1011

Choosing the Direct Migration Approach .........................1015

Conducting Preinstallation Checks on Exchange Server 2003 ...........1016

Verifying Core Services Installation ............................1017

Preparing the Forest ...........................................1017

Preparing the Domain ...........................................1017

Reviewing All Log Files ........................................1017

Performing a Core Installation of Exchange Server 2003 ..............1018

Implementing Active Directory ..................................1018

Extending the Active Directory Schema ..........................1018

Preparing the Windows 2003 Domain .............................1019

Step-by-Step Installation of Exchange Server 2003 ..............1020

Detailing the Exchange Server 2003 Installation ....................1022

Creating Administrative Group and Routing Group Structure .....1022
Creating Storage Groups .........................................................1025
Managing Databases .................................................................1027
Creating Additional Mailbox Stores ........................................1028
Creating a Public Folder Store .................................................1029
Performing Postinstallation Configurations .................................1030
Disabling Services ......................................................................1030
Removing Information Stores ....................................................1030
Setting Up Routing Group Connectors .....................................1031
Enabling Logging and Message Tracking ..................................1034
Installing and Configuring a Gateway Between GroupWise
and Exchange .............................................................................1035
Prerequisites for Migrating to Exchange Server 2003 ...................1035
Migration Considerations for All GroupWise Environments ........1036
Installing an Exchange Server 2003 Server with the Connector
for GroupWise .......................................................................1037
Enabling and Customizing Novell GroupWise Proxy
Addresses ...............................................................................1038
Configuring the Connector for Novell GroupWise .......................1039
Starting the Connector for Novell GroupWise ............................1041
Configuring Directory Synchronization .......................................1041
Manually Testing Directory Synchronization ..............................1044
Installing and Configuring Calendar Connector in a GroupWise
Environment ...............................................................................1044
Prerequisites for the Calendar Connector for GroupWise ............1044
Installing the Calendar Connector ................................................1045
Adding a Local Replica for the Schedule+ Free/Busy Public
Folder .....................................................................................1045
Configuring the Calendar Connector ...........................................1046
Starting Calendar Connector Service ...........................................1048
Reviewing the Results of the Lab Environment ..........................1048
Using the Exchange Migration Wizard to Migrate User Data ...............1048
Setting Up a Migration Server for Novell GroupWise and
Exchange Server 2003 ............................................................1048
Preparing the Users' Novell GroupWise Mailboxes .......................1049
Deploying Outlook 2003 Client Software to Pilot User
Workstations ..........................................................................1050
Running the Exchange Migration Wizard Process .......................1050
Confirming Migration Operations ................................................1052
Details on the Effects of the GroupWise
Migration Tools ..........................................................................1053
Migration of Local Archives .........................................................1053
Migration of Personal Address Books ...........................................1054

Migration of Personal Dictionaries ............................................1054

Migration of Client Rules and Proxy Access ...............................1054

Migration of Shared Folders ......................................................1055

Migration of External Entities ...................................................1055

Summary .........................................................................................1055

Best Practices .................................................................................1056

**35    Migrating from Lotus Notes to Exchange Server 2003    1057**

Similarities and Differences Between Lotus Notes and Exchange Server
    2003 Comparing Messaging and Collaboration Capabilities ..............1058

Comparing Administrative Tools ................................................1059

Exchange Migration and the Impact of Active Directory ......................1059

Implementing Exchange in a Native Active Directory
    Environment .........................................................................1059

Migrating to Exchange in an Environment
    That Has No Windows Network ..............................................1060

Evaluating the Existing Environment ..................................................1060

Planning Your Migration from Lotus Notes .........................................1061

Choosing a Phased Migration from Lotus Notes .........................1062

Choosing the Direct Migration Approach ..................................1066

Conducting Preinstallation Checks on Exchange Server 2003 .............1067

Verifying Core Services Installation ...........................................1067

Preparing the Forest ...................................................................1067

Preparing the Domain ...............................................................1067

Reviewing All Log Files ..............................................................1068

Performing a Core Installation of Exchange Server 2003 .....................1068

Implementing Active Directory .................................................1068

Extending the Active Directory Schema ....................................1068

Preparing the Windows 2003 Domain .......................................1069

Step-by-Step Installation of Exchange Server 2003 .....................1070

Detailing the Exchange Server 2003 Installation .................................1072

Creating the Administrative Group and Routing Group
    Structure ...............................................................................1072

Creating Storage Groups ............................................................1075

Managing Databases ...................................................................1077

Creating Additional Mailbox Stores ..........................................1078

Creating a Public Folder Store ...................................................1079

Performing Postinstallation Configurations .......................................1079

Disabling Services ......................................................................1080

Removing Information Stores .....................................................1080

Setting Up Routing Group Connectors ......................................1081

Enabling Logging and Message Tracking ...................................1084

Installing and Configuring a Gateway Between Lotus Notes and
    Exchange ...........................................................................................1085
    Prerequisites for Migrating to Exchange Server 2003 ....................1085
    Migration Considerations for All Lotus Notes Environments .......1085
    Installing an Exchange Server 2003 Server with the Connector
        for Lotus Notes ...........................................................................1086
    Enabling and Customizing Lotus Notes Proxy Addresses ............1087
    Configuring the Connector for Lotus Notes ..................................1088
    Starting the Connector for Lotus Notes ........................................1089
    Configuring Directory Synchronization ........................................1089
    Manually Testing Directory Synchronization ................................1092
Installing and Configuring Calendar Connector in a Lotus Notes
    Environment ....................................................................................1092
    Prerequisites for the Calendar Connector for Lotus Notes ...........1092
    Installing the Calendar Connector ................................................1093
    Adding a Local Replica for the Schedule+ Free/Busy Public
        Folder ..........................................................................................1093
    Configuring the Calendar Connector ............................................1094
    Starting Calendar Connector Service ............................................1095
    Reviewing the Results of the Lab Environment ............................1096
Using the Exchange Migration Wizard to Migrate User Data ................1096
    Prerequisites for the Exchange Migration Wizard ........................1096
    Preparing Your Lotus Domino Environment .................................1097
    Creating a Mail File for the Lotus Notes Account ........................1098
    Preparing Your Microsoft Exchange 2003 Server ..........................1098
    Running the Exchange Migration Wizard Process ........................1099
    Confirming Migration Operations .................................................1101
    Problems and Errors That May Occur During the Migration
        Process .........................................................................................1102
Details on the Effects of the Lotus Notes Migration Tools ....................1105
    Migration of Local Archives .........................................................1105
    Migration of Personal Address Books ...........................................1106
    Migration of Personal Dictionaries ..............................................1106
    Migration of Client Rules and Proxy Access .................................1106
    Migration of Shared Folders .........................................................1107
Summary ...................................................................................................1107
Best Practices ...........................................................................................1108

# About the Authors

**Rand H. Morimoto, Ph.D., MCSE**   Rand Morimoto has been in the computer industry for over 25 years and has authored, co-authored, or been a contributing writer for over a dozen books on Windows 2003, Security, Exchange Server 2003, BizTalk Server, and Remote and Mobile Computing. Rand is the president of Convergent Computing, an IT-consulting firm in the San Francisco Bay area that has been one of the key early adopter program partners with Microsoft, implementing beta versions of Microsoft Exchange Server 2003, SharePoint 2003, and Windows Server 2003 in production environments over 2 years before the initial product releases. Besides speaking at over 50 conferences and conventions around the world in the past year on tips, tricks, and best practices on planning, migrating, and implementing Exchange Server 2003, Rand is also a special advisor to the White House on cyber-security and cyber-terrorism.

**Michael Noel, MCSE+I, CISSP, MCSA**   Michael Noel has been involved in the computer industry for more than a decade, and has significant real-world experience with enterprise Exchange Server environments. In addition to his writings on Exchange, Michael is the author of ISA Server 2004 Unleashed and has co-authored *Microsoft Windows Server 2003 Unleashed* and *Microsoft SharePoint 2003 Unleashed*. Currently a senior consultant at Convergent Computing in the San Francisco Bay area, Michael's writings leverage his real-world experience designing, deploying, and administering Exchange Server environments.

**Kenton Gardinier, MCSE, CISSP, MCSA**   Kenton Gardinier manages the systems engineering team at Peopleclick, Inc., a total workforce acquisition solution provider. His team is responsible for a "software as a service" (SaaS) model that continuously supports clients on a global scale. He has designed and implemented technical- and business-driven solutions for organizations of all sizes around the world for more than 10 years. He has also led early adopter engagements implementing products such as Windows Server 2003, Exchange Server 2003, and SharePoint Portal Server 2003 prior to the products' release for numerous organizations. Kenton is an internationally recognized author and public speaker on a variety of technologies. He has authored, co-authored, and contributed to several books and articles on Windows, Exchange, security, performance tuning, administration, and systems management. He holds many certifications including MCSE, CISSP, and MCSA.

**Joe R. Coca Jr., MCSE**   Joe Coca has been a leading architect of migration and deployment strategies in the computer industry for more than 10 years. Along with his involvement in the Silicon Valley supporting business solutions for industry leading technology companies, Joe has also been a contributing writer and co-author of several books, such as *Microsoft Windows Server 2003 Unleashed, Windows 2000 Design and Migration, Microsoft Windows Server 2003 Insider Solutions*, and most recently the first edition of *Microsoft Exchange Server 2003 Unleashed*. In addition to writing, Joe has also been a guest speaker with the Enterprise Networking Association Conference and the president of a large user group with members ranging from the Silicon Valley area to the San Francisco Bay area. Working with key companies based throughout the greater Bay Area and Silicon Valley, Joe has designed and implemented numerous large Active Directory and Exchange 2000 and 2003 environments, including designing and leading several worldwide migrations from previous platforms to the latest Microsoft Windows and Exchange Server platforms.

# Dedication

*I dedicate this book to Greg Visscher, who got me involved in the very first early adopter program of the Exchange Server product almost a dozen years ago. Your introduction of this product to me has led to a career of wonderful opportunities. Thanks, Greg!!!*

—Rand H. Morimoto, Ph.D., MCSE

*This book is dedicated to the Sefanovs—Regina, Vadim, Zachary, and Joshua. I am eternally grateful for the love and devotion that you show to our family.*

—Michael Noel, MCSE+I, MCSA

*I dedicate this book to Vincent Fajardo and all Fajardo family members; your loving ways heal us all. And to my niece Vanessa, your talent and spirit brings joy and happiness to those that are fortunate to have you in their lives.*

—Joe R. Coca Jr., MCSE

*This book is dedicated to my daughter Hailey. Thank you for brightening every day. You are truly a gift from God.*

—Kenton Gardinier, MCSE, CISSP, MCSA

# Acknowledgments

**Rand H. Morimoto, Ph.D., MCSE**   I want to thank Alex Lewis and Pete Handley for their help with the new Cross-Platform Migration chapters. Your expertise in the areas of Lotus Notes and Novell GroupWise respectively was very helpful in putting together those two new chapters! Additionally, I want to thank all of the consultants and staff at Convergent Computing who work with the Microsoft Exchange product day in and day out, building up our wealth of knowledge and experience on the technology!

I want to acknowledge the contributors to the first edition of the book, whose work and effort laid the initial foundation for this text. Those individuals include Amanda Acheson, Brian Peladeau, Chista Ashti, Chris Amaris, Colin Spence, Ed Roberts, Ilya Eybelman, Jeff Guillet, Kathi Honegger, and Làzlò Somi.

I also want to thank our acquisitions editor, Neil Rowe, who believes in us and continues to provide us opportunities to write for Sams Publishing! To all those on the Sams Publishing team, including Mark Renfrow, George Nedeff, and Karen Annett, who take our work, clean it up, and prepare it to be published!

And thank you to our dozens of early adopter clients who, in many cases, were our guinea pigs as we worked together years before the product release (even now as we implement Exchange E12 beta in production environments), helping build case experience and knowledge of the technology.

Last but not least, to Kelly and Andrew, thank you for being good while daddy wrote in the wee hours of the night. Thank you to my parents, Ed and Vickie, for teaching me good work ethics. And to my brother Bruce and sister Lisa, thank you for all your support over the years!

**Michael Noel, MCSE+I, CISSP, MCSA**   Well, once again I got myself into one of these books and, once again, I couldn't have made it through without the help of some truly gifted, dedicated, and patient people. First off, I would like to thank Rand Morimoto for his valuable insight and technical guidance once again. You have never hesitated to share your knowledge with me and with the people you work with, and I am eternally grateful for this. Thanks as well go to my co-workers at Convergent Computing who work side by side with me, providing me with valuable tips and tricks and some really great ideas. Big thanks also go to Neil Rowe at Sams Publishing for putting up with us once again.

Of course, once again, my family were the ones to suffer the most from the long hours I put into this revision, and I must thank them. Marina, you are an amazing woman, and I couldn't have done it without you! To Julia, my daughter, you are destined for great things. To my in-laws, who put up with me once again, and to my parents, who helped to shape who I am.

**Kenton Gardinier, MCSE, CISSP, MCSA**   I realize that every time I commit myself to writing a book, I'm asking for others to commit as well, especially my family. Amy, you are an incredible person and wife. I'm truly blessed that you are a part of my life.

It is a privilege working with many talented people over the course of writing this book. It has been great co-authoring with Rand on yet another book. Thank you to all those who do the behind-the-scenes work at Sams Publishing, especially Neil Rowe, who always amazes me.

I would also like to thank the many dedicated people at Microsoft and Peopleclick for providing their resources and expertise and who helped us gain practical, real-world experience with Exchange Server 2003. It has been wonderful working closely with each and every one of you. Although there are countless individuals to thank, I'd like to point out Will Anderson, Carol Vercellino, Patrick Reardon, Tim Jenkins, and Doug Drum for their support. You have greatly enhanced the content of this book.

**Joe R. Coca Jr., MCSE**   With many challenges faced during the course of writing this book, I want to first thank Rand Morimoto—your believing in me and encouragement is truly a driving force. Thank you for making this all possible. To Sams Publishing and Neil Rowe, thanks again for believing in the people here at CCO. And to Andrew Abbate and all my peers at CCO, your dedication, teamwork and support are what makes our success!

I would also like to thank a very special family member who was so important during the creation of this book. Vincent Fajardo, your commitment to Michele inspires; God bless you both. And to my family members, Carmen, Raymon, Vinni, Javier, and brother Richard, all the kids, and friends Angel and Johnny, thank you all for the many years of support while I served with the U.S. Marines and over the past 10 years while I have been with CCO.

# We Want to Hear from You!

As the reader of this book, *you* are our most important critic and commentator. We value your opinion and want to know what we're doing right, what we could do better, what areas you'd like to see us publish in, and any other words of wisdom you're willing to pass our way.

As an associate publisher for Sams Publishing, I welcome your comments. You can email or write me directly to let me know what you did or didn't like about this book—as well as what we can do to make our books better.

*Please note that I cannot help you with technical problems related to the topic of this book. We do have a User Services group, however, where I will forward specific technical questions related to the book.*

When you write, please be sure to include this book's title and author as well as your name, email address, and phone number. I will carefully review your comments and share them with the author and editors who worked on the book.

**Email:**     feedback@samspublishing.com

**Mail:**      Paul Boger
              Associate Publisher
              Sams Publishing
              800 East 96th Street
              Indianapolis, IN 46240 USA

For more information about this book or another Sams Publishing title, visit our Web site at www.samspublishing.com. Type the ISBN (excluding hyphens) or the title of a book in the Search field to find the page you're looking for.

# Introduction

When my coauthors and I set out to produce the second edition of the very successful Exchange Server 2003 Unleashed book, we wanted to make sure we not only added content to chapters where things have been added since the original product release, but we also wanted to make sure we went through the entire book start to finish to rewrite sections where tips, tricks, and best practices may have changed since we wrote the first edition of the book. So before we even read the old chapter content to determine what we will fix or edit, we started off by outlining each and every chapter from scratch. We thought about what we would want to make sure was covered in each chapter if we were to write the chapters from a blank sheet. What resulted was our ability to then read the chapter, add content, delete content, and make changes that met the current best practices in the industry.

Do note, this second edition of the book takes into account Exchange Server 2003 Service Pack 2 as well as earlier releases of Exchange Server 2003 (Service Pack 1, and the original Exchange Server 2003 release). This takes in account all versions of Exchange Server 2003 before the next major version of Exchange.

By taking a clean view on the appropriate content for this book, we believe we are providing to you, our reader, a fresh perspective on planning, designing, implementing, and migrating to an Exchange Server 2003 environment. The four of us (Rand, Mike, Kenton, and Joe) started working with Exchange Server 2003 more than 18 months prior to the original product release to the public. We had several clients who were large beta implementers of Exchange Server 2003 that had dozens of servers in production using the Exchange Server 2003 beta. Now, a few years after the original product launch, we have produced this second edition of the book based on our work with organizations having hundreds of thousands of mail users. The text of this book leverages knowledge and best practices on how to successfully migrate to Exchange Server 2003.

This book is organized into 11 parts, each part focusing on core Exchange Server 2003 areas, with several chapters making up each part:

- **Part I: Microsoft Exchange Server 2003 Overview**—This part provides an introduction to Exchange Server 2003, not only from the perspective of a general technology overview, but also to note what is truly new in Exchange Server 2003 that made it compelling enough for organizations to implement the technology in beta in a production environment. We also cover basic planning, prototype testing, and migration techniques, and provide a full chapter on the installation of Exchange Server 2003.

- **Part II: Exchange Server 2003**—This part covers the design of an Exchange Server 2003 messaging environment for small, medium, and large organizations. It also covers the integration of Exchange Server 2003 in a non-Windows environment. We understand that the implementation of Exchange is different for organizations of different sizes. Small organizations typically do not have the need for extensive routing groups and administrative groups, so the design illustrations focus on limited server environments. Exchange for large organizations frequently involves extensive front-end, back-end, and distributed user environments, so specific design recommendations are made for these types of organizations.

- **Part III: Networking Services Impact on Exchange**—This part covers DNS, Global Catalog and domain controller placement, Microsoft routing and remote access configuration, and Outlook Web Access configuration from the perspective of planning, integrating, migrating, and coexistence. Notes, tips, and best practices provide valuable information on features that are new in Exchange Server 2003. You explore what's new and different that you can leverage after a migration to Exchange Server 2003.

- **Part IV: Securing an Exchange Server 2003 Environment**—Security is on everyone's mind these days, and Microsoft knew it and included several major security enhancements to Exchange Server 2003. We dedicate three chapters of the book to security, breaking the information into client-level security, such as remote client access, message encryption, and attachment encryption; server-level security, such as encrypted front-end and back-end server configuration, certificates, and privacy and antispam protection; and transport-level security, such as IPSec, RPC over HTTPS, and system-to-system encrypted communications.

- **Part V: Migrating to Exchange Server 2003**—This part is dedicated to migrations. We provide a chapter specifically on migrating from Windows NT4 to Windows Server 2003 as it applies to planning and preparing Active Directory with Exchange Server 2003 in mind. Other chapters in this part of the book address migrating Exchange 5.5 to Exchange Server 2003, Exchange 2000 to Exchange Server 2003, and compatibility testing of Exchange add-ins and components in a Windows 2003 and Exchange Server 2003 environment. These chapters are loaded with tips, tricks, and cautions on migration steps and best practices.

- **Part VI: Exchange Server 2003 Administration and Management**—In this part, four chapters focus on the administration of an Exchange Server 2003 environment. This is where the importance of a newly written book (as opposed to a modified Exchange 2000 book) is of value to you, the reader. The administration and management of mailboxes, distribution lists, and sites have been greatly enhanced in Exchange Server 2003. Although you can continue to perform tasks the way you did in Exchange 2000, because of significant changes in replication, background transaction processing, secured communications, integrated mobile communications, and changes in Windows 2003 Active Directory, there are better ways to work with Exchange Server 2003. These chapters drill down into specialty areas helpful to administrators of varying levels of responsibility.

- **Part VII: New Mobility Functionality in Exchange Server 2003**—Mobility is a key improvement in Exchange Server 2003, so this part focuses on enhancements made in the mobile phone and PDA replication tools to Exchange. Instead of just providing a remote node connection, Exchange Server 2003 provides true end-to-end secured anytime/anywhere access functionality. The wireless mobility functions provide access to Exchange, using mobile phone, wireless device, and PDA support. The chapters in this part highlight best practices on implementing and leveraging these technologies.

- **Part VIII: Client Access to Exchange Server 2003**—This part of the book focuses on the enhancements to the Outlook Web Access client, various Outlook client capabilities, and Outlook for non-Windows systems. Outlook Web Access is no longer just a simple browser client, but one that can effectively be a full primary user client to Exchange. Different versions of the full Outlook client have varying levels of support in Exchange Server 2003 relative to security, XML-based forms support, data recovery, and information manageability. The chapters in this part of the book focus on providing details on leveraging the client capabilities.

- **Part IX: Client Administration and Management**—As many organizations choose to upgrade the client software on their desktop and mobile users, new capabilities in Windows Group Policies and various deployment techniques simplify the process. The two chapters in this part of the book cover best practices, tips, and techniques to automate the client administration and management process.

- **Part X: Fault Tolerance and Optimization Technologies**—This part of the book addresses fault tolerance, data recovery, and system optimization in Exchange Server 2003. Exchange Server 2003 must be reliable, and Microsoft included several new enhancements in fault-tolerant technologies and data recovery to Exchange 2003. The four chapters in this part address system-level fault tolerance in leveraging clustering and network load balancing technologies, best practices in backup and restore procedures, tested procedures at recovering from a disaster, and capacity analysis and performance optimization of an Exchange 2003 environment. When these new technologies are implemented in an Exchange messaging environment, an organization can truly achieve better enterprise-level reliability and recoverability.

- **Part XI: Cross-Platform Migrations to Exchange 2003**—The last part of the book addresses the migration to Exchange Server 2003 from non-Microsoft messaging environments. This section has chapters on migrating from Novell GroupWise and Lotus Notes to Microsoft Exchange Server 2003. The chapters cover tips, tricks, and best practices using the Microsoft migration tools for migrating mailbox content to Exchange such as email messages and calendar appointments. The section also covers the connectors that interlink Novell GroupWise and Lotus Notes to Exchange for environments where the coexistence of other messaging environments to Exchange is necessary.

The real-world experience we have had in working with Exchange Server 2003 and our commitment to writing this book from scratch enables us to relay to you information that we hope will be valuable in your successful planning, implementation, and migration to an Exchange Server 2003 environment.

# PART I

# Microsoft Exchange Server 2003 Overview

## IN THIS PART

| | | |
|---|---|---|
| CHAPTER 1 | Exchange Server 2003 Technology Primer | 7 |
| CHAPTER 2 | Planning, Prototyping, Migrating, and Deploying Exchange Server 2003 | 35 |
| CHAPTER 3 | Installing Exchange Server 2003 | 69 |

# Exchange Server 2003 Technology Primer

**IN THIS CHAPTER**

- Using Exchange Server 2003 As an Email and Calendaring Solution
- Taking Advantage of Active Directory in Exchange
- Leveraging Exchange Server 2003 As a Web Access Solution
- Expanding into the New Wireless and Mobility Technologies
- Choosing the Right Time to Migrate to Exchange Server 2003
- Understanding the Two Versions of Exchange Server 2003
- Understanding How Improvements in Windows 2003 Enhance Exchange Server 2003
- Reliability Enhancements in Exchange Server 2003
- Expanding on Manageability and Administration Benefits of Exchange Server 2003
- Improvements in Exchange Server 2003 Security
- Leveraging Mobility in Exchange Server 2003
- Performance Improvements in Exchange Server 2003
- Solidifying Core Technologies for Exchange Server 2003

Exchange Server 2003 is the latest release of the electronic messaging–focused application server products from Microsoft. When Exchange Server 2003 first shipped, some called it a major service pack for Exchange Server 2000. However, a couple years after its release, with a couple service pack updates and several feature pack releases later, organizations have found Exchange Server 2003 a strategic evolution of the Exchange messaging product's extension beyond just email and calendaring.

Organizations migrating from earlier releases of Exchange have found the migration process to Exchange Server 2003 a relatively simple and user accepted process. Because a migration from Exchange 5.5 or Exchange 2000 typically does not require a change in the Outlook client used by email users, many users never knew they were upgraded to Exchange Server 2003. However, when you look under the hood, Exchange Server 2003 is a major improvement of the Exchange messaging system, with significant changes that improve mobile user access, server reliability, message and server fault tolerance, and system scalability.

This chapter introduces the significant enhancements and diverse capabilities of the Exchange Server 2003 messaging system and references the chapters through the balance of this book that detail these improvements. The differences that Exchange Server 2003 adds to a messaging environment require a re-education so that design and implementation decisions take full advantage of the enhanced communications capabilities.

# Using Exchange Server 2003 As an Email and Calendaring Solution

Exchange Server 2003 is a versatile messaging system, one that meets the needs of a variety of different business functions. Like earlier versions of Exchange, Exchange Server 2003 can provide all the basic email and calendaring functionality, but now it offers a lot more. An example of the Outlook 2003 client in Exchange Server 2003 is shown in Figure 1.1.

**FIGURE 1.1**    Outlook 2003 client to Exchange Server 2003.

Because Exchange Server 2003 provides a variety of different functions, an organization should choose how to best implement Exchange Server 2003 and the various messaging features to meet the needs of the organization. In small network environments with less than 50 users, an organization may choose to implement all the Exchange Server 2003 features on a single server. However in larger environments, multiple servers may be implemented to improve system performance and provide fault tolerance and redundancy.

# Taking Advantage of Active Directory in Exchange

One of the major additions to the messaging system role introduced with the release of Windows 2000 and Windows 2003 is Active Directory. Active Directory is more than a simple list of users and passwords for authentication into a network. It also is a directory that extends to other business applications. When fully leveraged, an organization can have its human resources (HR) department add an employee to the organization's HR software; then the HR software automatically creates a user in the Active Directory that generates a network logon, an email account, a voicemail account, and remote access capabilities—and links pager and mobile phone information to the employee. Likewise, if an employee is terminated, a single change in the HR software can issue automated commands to disable the individual's network, email, remote logon, and other network functions.

Exchange Server 2003 extends the capabilities of the Active Directory by integrating the email, mobile phone, and remote access functionality into a centralized administration tool. Organizations that purchase add-ins to Exchange—such as voicemail, pager, or faxing tools—expand the list of commonly managed resources.

Through the integration of better management tools, Exchange Server 2003 provides a more robust implementation of Active Directory and enables better scalability and redundancy to improve communication capabilities. Exchange Server 2003 effectively adds more reliability, faster performance, and better management tools to an enterprise, which can be leveraged as a robust text, data, and mobile communications system.

When planning the implementation of Exchange Server 2003, a network architect needs to consider which communication services are needed, and how they will be combined on servers or how they will be made redundant across multiple servers for business continuity failover. For a small organization, the choice to combine several server functions to a single system or to just a few systems is one of economics. The reason to distribute server services to multiple servers, however, also could be a decision for improving performance (see Chapter 33, "Capacity Analysis and Performance Optimization"), Exchange administration (see Chapter 18, "Administering Exchange Server 2003"), creating redundancy (see Chapter 30, "System-Level Fault Tolerance"), and enabling security (covered in three chapters in Part IV, "Securing an Exchange Server 2003 Environment").

## Leveraging Exchange Server 2003 As a Web Access Solution

A significant improvement in the Exchange Server 2003 Outlook Web Access (OWA) interface, shown in Figure 1.2, now provides organizations the ability to use OWA as their primary mail client for users. With previous versions of Exchange, organizations used the full Outlook client as the primary messaging client for their users. Outlook Web Access was limited in features and functions, leaving OWA as a secondary client for use when the primary client was unavailable or harder to access.

OWA 2003 adds spell-checking, forms, rules, pull-down menus, preview mode, and the ability to view other calendars and folders. These additions in OWA 2003 provide organizations the ability to make OWA 2003 the primary message client for their users, eliminating the need for a full desktop configuration, lowering the cost and effort of deploying desktop application software, and improving an organization's ability to provide access to mail from user's homes, from Internet kiosks, or from other remote locations.

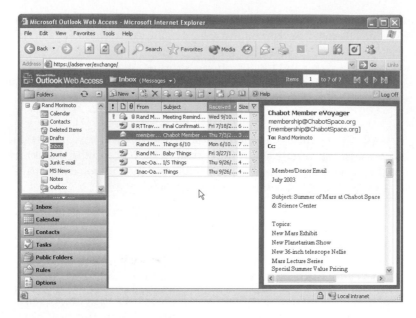

**FIGURE 1.2**   Outlook Web Access 2003.

The OWA 2003 client is covered in Chapter 26, "Everything You Need to Know About the Outlook Web Access (OWA) Client"; back-end server configuration of OWA is explored in Chapter 10, "Configuring Outlook Web Access and Exchange Mobile Services."

# Expanding into the New Wireless and Mobility Technologies

In addition to the Outlook Web Access client, Exchange Server 2003 also added wireless and mobility technologies for the use of wireless phones and pocket PC devices for access to mail and messaging, as shown in Figure 1.3. The new mobility technologies built in to Exchange Server 2003 minimize the need for users to have a separate mobile phone, PDA, and wireless email device lining their beltline. With multifunction mobile phones enabled with pocket PC technologies, a user can have a single device that provides real-time email, calendar, contacts, and Internet access. Exchange Server 2003 provides real-time synchronization of information with mobile devices.

Although mobile device synchronization has existed for several years, the utilities were typically add-ons to messaging systems that required additional costs and had complicated integration requirements. With mobility technologies built directly in to Exchange Server 2003, the licensing is part of the user cost, so a single-user license covers the cost of a full Outlook client, Web access client, and mobile phone, or mobile device access client license. Because the mobility software is built directly in to Exchange Server 2003, there are no special installation or integration requirements. A user's mailbox is mobility-enabled, simplifying the process of providing mobile access to mail, calendars, contacts, and other Exchange system information.

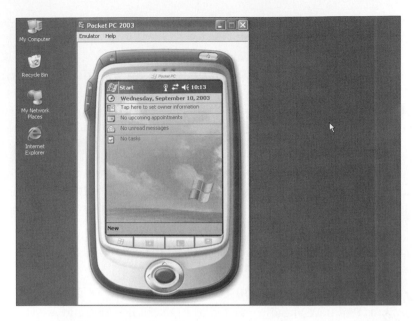

**FIGURE 1.3**    Outlook client on pocket PC.

Mobility is covered in Part VII, "New Mobility Functionality in Exchange Server 2003" in three chapters of the book: Chapter 22, "Designing Mobility in Exchange Server 2003," Chapter 23, "Implementing Mobile Synchronization in Exchange Server 2003," and Chapter 24, "Configuring Client Systems for Mobility."

## Choosing the Right Time to Migrate to Exchange Server 2003

With the popularity of Exchange Server 2003 along with the proven business productivity benefits and communication capabilities of Exchange Server 2003, many organizations not running the latest version of Exchange wonder when is the right time to migrate to the late Microsoft Exchange messaging system. As with any technology, the decision typically starts with identifying the value of migrating versus the cost and effort to migrate.

This chapter introduces the many features and functions in Exchange Server 2003 that have helped other organizations plan a migration. Improvements in security, performance, and manageability provide benefits to organizations looking to minimize administration costs while providing more functionality to users.

The cost and effort to migrate to Exchange Server 2003 varies based on the current state of an organization's messaging environment and the features and functions of Exchange Server 2003 to be implemented. Some of the common states and needed functions are adding Exchange Server 2003 into an existing Exchange 5.5 or Exchange 2000 organization, doing a migration from Exchange 2000 to Exchange Server 2003, and migrating from Exchange 5.5 to Exchange Server 2003. Additional migration to Exchange processes involve the migration from non-Microsoft messaging systems like Novell GroupWise or Lotus Notes to Microsoft Exchange 2003.

## Adding an Exchange Server 2003 Server to an Existing Exchange Organization

Many organizations want to add a specific Exchange Server 2003 function, such as Outlook Web Access 2003, Outlook RPC over HTTP, or mobile phone access. Functions such as these can be added on an Exchange Server 2003 server in an existing Exchange 5.5 or Exchange 2000 organization. This enables an organization to get Exchange Server 2003 application functionality fairly quickly and easily without having to do a full migration to Exchange Server 2003. In many cases, an Exchange Server 2003 server simply can be added to an existing network without impact. This provides extremely low messaging system impact, but provides an organization the ability to prototype and test the new technology, pilot it for a handful of users, and slowly roll out the technology to its client base as part of a regular system replacement or upgrade process.

## Migrating from Exchange 2000 to Exchange Server 2003

For organizations that have already migrated to an Exchange 2000 and Active Directory environment, migrating to Exchange Server 2003 can provide access to several additional capabilities built on top of Windows 2003, such as mailbox recovery.

Fortunately, organizations that have already implemented Exchange 2000 or have already migrated from Windows NT4 to Windows 2000 have completed the hard part of their migration process. Effectively, Exchange Server 2003 uses the same Active Directory organizational structure that was created with Windows 2000, so forests, domain trees, domains, organizational users, sites, groups, and users all transfer directly into an Exchange Server 2003 organizational structure. If the organizational structure in Windows 2000 and Exchange 2000 meets the needs of the organization, the migration to Exchange Server 2003 is predominantly the moving of mailboxes from the old Exchange server to a new Exchange server.

Migrating from Exchange 2000 to Exchange 2003 requires a handful of preparatory steps. More details on the migration process from Exchange 2000 is covered in Chapter 16, "Migrating from Exchange 2000 to Exchange Server 2003."

## Migrating from Exchange 5.5 to Exchange Server 2003

Organizations that still have Exchange 5.5 as their messaging environment just need to plan their migration to Exchange Server 2003. Deciding factors include what features and functions in Exchange Server 2003 the organization wants and the cost and effort to migrate. Organizations do not have to migrate completely to Exchange Server 2003 to get Exchange Server 2003 functionality. An organization can choose to migrate just a couple of servers from Exchange 5.5 to Exchange Server 2003 without having to migrate the whole organization. This can be a first step for an organization to get Exchange Server 2003 functionality into its network.

If an organization has already begun its migration to Exchange 2000, it may choose to just complete their migration process as an Exchange Server 2003 migration. Even if an organization has Exchange 2000 in its environment, it can migrate some of the Exchange 2000 servers to Exchange Server 2003 as an interim process.

The planning, design, prototype, and migration steps to assist an organization in its migration from Exchange 5.5 to an Exchange Server 2003 environment is covered in Chapter 15, "Migrating from Exchange v5.5 to Exchange Server 2003."

### Migrating from Novell GroupWise to Exchange Server 2003

Many organizations that are migrating to Exchange Server 2003 don't even have an earlier version of Microsoft Exchange today, but rather are migrating off of Novell NetWare to Windows Active Directory for the networking environment, and at the same time migrating from Novell GroupWise to Exchange 2003. As with any cross-platform migration, there is a learning curve for users to adopt the new messaging system; however, many organizations find employees use Outlook at home for their personal email, or new employees come from companies that had Microsoft Exchange as their messaging platform, so the migration from GroupWise to Exchange has been well accepted by users.

Chapter 34 of this book, "Migrating from Novell GroupWise to Exchange 2003," covers the free tools provided by Microsoft to assist in organizations in migrating from Novell NDS and eDirectory to Active Directory, as well as from GroupWise to Microsoft Exchange. The chapter covers a single step migration where all users are migrated at once from GroupWise to Exchange, and a longer coexistence migration process where the migration is completed over an extended period of time.

### Migrating from Lotus Notes to Exchange Server 2003

Other organizations using a messaging system different than Exchange today seeking to migrate to Exchange Server 2003 are organizations with Lotus Notes. Because many business applications leverage Microsoft Outlook and the integration tools with Microsoft Office, organizations with Lotus Notes have been migrating to Exchange Server 2003 to take advantage of the tight application integration.

In Chapter 35 of this book, "Migrating from Lotus Notes to Exchange Server 2003," the process of migrating Lotus Notes mailboxes as well as establishing a gateway to maintain a link between a Lotus Notes environment and Exchange Server 2003 environment are presented in detail in step-by-step guidelines and procedures.

## Understanding the Two Versions of Exchange Server 2003

Exchange Server 2003 comes in two versions (as did Exchange 2000): Exchange Server 2003 Standard Edition and Exchange Server 2003 Enterprise Edition. This is similar to the naming designations used for Exchange 5.5 and Exchange 2000. Typically, the Standard Edition is used for either a small organization or as a utility server in a large environment.

The Enterprise Edition has more expandability for larger organizations or those organizations that need to take advantage of some of the advanced capabilities of Exchange.

## Getting to Know the Exchange Server 2003 Standard Edition

The Exchange Server 2003 Standard Edition is the basic message server version of the software. The Standard Edition supports one mailbox database up to 16GB for the original release of Exchange Server 2003 and Exchange Server 2003 Service Pack 1, and up to 75GB for Exchange Server 2003 Service Pack 2. The Standard Edition has full support for Web access, mobile access, and server recovery functionality.

The Standard Edition is a good version of Exchange to support a messaging system for a small organization, as a front-end server for a larger environment, or as a bridgehead server for an Exchange organization. Many small and medium-sized organizations find the capabilities of the Standard Edition sufficient for most messaging server services, and even large organizations use the Standard Edition for message routing servers or as the primary server in a remote office. The Standard Edition meets the needs of effectively any environment wherein a server with a limited database storage capacity is sufficient.

> **NOTE**
>
> Unlike Exchange 2000, which required an Enterprise Edition version of the messaging system for a server to be a front-end server, an Exchange Server 2003 front-end server can run on a Standard Edition version of the messaging system. By enabling an organization to acquire a Standard Edition license of Exchange, the licensing cost can be significantly lowered for organizations that split their back-end mailbox server from their front-end client access server.

## Expanding into the Exchange Server 2003 Enterprise Edition

The Exchange Server 2003 Enterprise Edition is focused at server systems that require more than a single Exchange messaging database. With support for up to 20 databases per server, the Enterprise Edition is the appropriate version of messaging system for organizations that have a lot of mailboxes or a lot of mail storage.

> **NOTE**
>
> Typically, organizations implementing Exchange Server 2003 Standard Edition install the messaging system on top of Windows Server 2003 Standard Edition. Choosing to install the Standard Edition of Exchange 2003 on top of a Standard Edition of Windows limits the organization's ability to migrate the server to the Enterprise Edition of Exchange. Although an organization may choose to upgrade Exchange to the Enterprise Edition, the organization would also want to upgrade Windows to the Enterprise Edition, making it a challenging task to upgrade the version of the Exchange license.

Table 1.1 summarizes the differences between the Standard and Enterprise Editions.

**TABLE 1.1**   Exchange Server 2003 Standard Versus Enterprise Editions

| Exchange Server 2003 Function | Standard Edition | Enterprise Edition |
| --- | --- | --- |
| # of storage groups supported | 1 | 4 |
| # of databases per storage group supported | 2 (1 private, 1 public) | 5 |
| Maximum database size | 16GB-75GB (SP0-SP2) | Unlimited (16TB maximum) |
| Clustering support | None | Up to 8-node |
| X.400 connector support | None | Included |
| OS support | Windows 2000 SP3+ or Windows Server 2003 Standard or Enterprise Windows 2000 SP3+ or Windows Server 2003 Standard or Enterprise | |

# Understanding How Improvements in Windows 2003 Enhance Exchange Server 2003

With the introduction of Windows Server 2003, Microsoft added several new features and functions to the operating system. Some of the features are general system enhancements, and other features directly add benefits and improvements for organizations using Exchange Server 2003. Enhancements in Windows 2003 improve user administration, security, data replication, and system performance.

## Drag-and-Drop Capabilities in Administrative Tools

Many of the new administrative tools with Windows Server 2003, including the Exchange Server 2003 System Manager, provide drag-and-drop capabilities that enable administrators to select objects with a mouse and drag and drop the object to a new location. In Windows 2000, an administrator would have to select the objects, right-click the mouse, select Move, and choose the destination from a menu or graphical tree. Although this might seem trivial, for any administrator reorganizing users between organizational units in the Active Directory Users and Computers utility, the ability to drag and drop objects can greatly simplify the time and effort it takes to organize and manage objects in the Active Directory.

## Built-in Setup, Configuration, and Management Wizards

Other major additions to Windows 2003 that simplify tasks are a series of configuration and management wizards that come built in to the Windows 2003 and Exchange Server 2003 systems. Instead of having to walk through menus of commands to manually create or modify networking roles, the 2003 versions provide wizards that enable an administrator to add, modify, or remove system configurations. No doubt these wizards are a significant benefit to novices of the messaging system, because the questions in the wizards are typically simple to answer. However, even Windows experts find the wizards simplify the configuration process over manual installation tasks, because it is easier and faster to start with the base settings created by the wizard and then manually adjust changes.

## Improvements in Security

Significantly more than just cosmetic updates are the security enhancements added to Windows Server 2003. During the middle of the development of the Windows Server 2003 product, Microsoft launched its Trustworthy Computing Initiative, which stipulated that all products and solutions from Microsoft meet very stringent requirements for security. Although Exchange Server 2003 was already slated to have several new security enhancements, Trustworthy Computing created an environment where the Exchange Server 2003 product added and enhanced security significantly in the system environment.

Additionally, with the release of Windows 2003 Service Pack 1, along with Exchange Server 2003 SP1 and SP2, Microsoft has continued to expand the security capabilities of the core operating system and the Exchange messaging system.

Chapters 11, "Client-Level Security," 12, "Server-Level Security," and 13, "Transport-Level Security," of this book are focused on security in different core areas. Chapter 12 addresses some of the new Exchange Server 2003 defaults and Windows 2003 SP1 updates wherein most services are disabled on installation or configuration and must be enabled for access. Although this also might seem like a trivial change in a messaging system environment, it provides a relatively secured server immediately from initial installation. Previous versions of Exchange could easily take an hour going through all the unneeded features and manually locking down a server system. The server defaults and the functional or operational differences are noted in Chapter 12.

## IPSec and Wireless Security Improvements

Transport-level security in the form of IPSec was included in Windows 2000; however, organizations have been slow to adopt IPSec security, typically because they don't understand how it works. Chapter 13 of this book addresses how IPSec is enabled in organizations, providing a high level of server-to-server, site-to-site, and remote user–to–LAN secured communications. Also covered in Chapter 13 is the new secured wireless LAN (802.1X) technology that is built in to Windows Server 2003. Windows Server 2003 includes dynamic key determination for improvements in wireless security over the more common Wired Equivalency Protocol (WEP) that is used with standard 802.11 wireless communications. By improving the encryption on wireless communications, an organization can increase its confidence that Exchange Server 2003 can provide a truly secured messaging environment.

## Microsoft Internet Security and Acceleration Server (ISA) 2004 Enhancements

A new addition to the Microsoft server product line is the Internet Security and Acceleration Server, or ISA 2004, product. ISA 2004 provides firewall and reverse proxy capabilities that help expand the secured communications and access to Exchange Server 2003. Rather than opening up several ports on a firewall for remote access, ISA 2004 provides an organization the ability to simply open up ports 80 (HTTP) and 443 (HTTPS) for remote access communications. Additionally, by implementing an ISA 2004 server in place of or in addition to a front-end Exchange server, an organization can manage, monitor, and improve secured communications to their Exchange environment. ISA 2004 for an Exchange Server 2003 environment is covered in Chapter 13.

## Performance and Functionality Improvements

A network end-user would likely never notice many new features added to Exchange Server 2003, and in many cases a network administrator would not even be aware that the technologies were updated and improved. These are technologies that help the network operate more efficiently and effectively so that a user might experience faster message transmission. (Although even if the network were able to respond twice as fast, many times a process that used to take three seconds to complete and now takes less than two seconds to complete is not something a user would particularly notice.) The key benefit typically comes in the area of overall network bandwidth demand improvements. For very large organizations, the performance improvements prevent the organizations from having to add additional servers, processors, or site connections; they gain system efficiencies from improvements in the core operating system and Exchange application.

## Global Catalog Caching on a Domain Controller

One of the significant back-end improvements to Windows Server 2003 is the server's capability of caching Global Catalog (GC) information on domain controllers. In a Windows 2000 environment, for users to access the Global Catalog to view mail accounts and distribution lists, an organization typically put out a Global Catalog server to every site in the organization. This distributed Global Catalog server function minimized the ongoing traffic of users querying the catalog over a WAN connection every time they wanted to send an email to someone else in the organization. With Windows Server 2003, an organization has the ability to place a domain controller in a remote location, and the Global Catalog information is cached to the remote domain controller system. This provides the best of both worlds: The directory information is readily available to remote users, but because it is just a cache of the information and not a fully replicated copy, synchronization and distribution of catalog information is done only when initially requested, and not each time a change is made to the directory.

## Remote Installation Service for Servers

New to Windows Server 2003 is a server tool called Remote Installation Service for Servers, or RIS for Servers. RIS for Servers enables an organization to create images of server configurations, which can then be pushed up to a RIS server that can later be used to re-image a new system. RIS was standard with Windows 2000; however, it only supported the re-imaging of desktop systems.

RIS for Servers can be used several ways. One way organizations have leveraged RIS for Servers has been to create a new, clean server image with all of a company's core utilities installed. Every time the organization needs to install a new server, rather than starting from scratch with an installation CD, it can use the template RIS server installation. The image could include service packs, patches, updates, or other standard setup utilities.

RIS for Servers can also be used as a functional disaster recovery tool. After a server has been configured as an Exchange Server 2003 server with the appropriate program files and parameters configured, the organization can then run the RIPrep to back up the Exchange server image to a RIS server. In the event of a system failure, the organization can recover the server image from the state of the system before system failure.

> **NOTE**
>
> Creating RIS images for production servers requires planning and testing before relying on the system function for successful disaster recovery. Certain applications require services to be stopped before RIPrep is run. Chapter 32, "Recovering from a Disaster," addresses steps to conduct system server recovery.

RIS for Servers is a versatile tool that helps organizations quickly build new servers or recover from application server failures. Besides being covered in Chapter 32, RIS for Servers is also covered in detail in Chapter 3, "Installing Exchange Server 2003."

## Scaling Reliability with 8-Node Clustering

Another Windows 2003 enhancement that is supported in Exchange Server 2003 is the support for 8-node clustering. Previous versions of Exchange supported up to 2-node clustering, which enabled an organization to have two systems available to support a series of mailboxes. Windows 2003 supports 8-node clustering, so an organization can now have up to eight servers clustered for a combination of performance load balancing and real-time system failover.

With active clustering, the load of the users accessing mailboxes hosted on the cluster can be distributed across the active servers, thus providing improved performance to users accessing mail. With 2-node clustering, the load was distributed to just two systems, thus limiting realistic access to thousands of simultaneous mail access connections. By expanding to up to 8-nodes, an organization can now have several thousand users simultaneously connecting to the mail store, distributing the load to up to eight systems for much better scalability.

In addition to providing load balancing, clustering provides failover and fault-tolerance capabilities, enabling an organization to have several thousand mailboxes protected by real-time fault failover and recovery. Through the implementation of active and passive clustering, an IT organization can choose the level of system recovery.

Details on how to plan, test, and implement a clustered Exchange Server 2003 environment is covered in Chapter 30. That chapter also covers other tools, technologies, and techniques on methods of improving Exchange system reliability and mailbox recovery in the event of a system failure.

## Taking Advantage of the Windows 2003 SP1 Security Configuration Wizard

One of the enhancements added to Windows 2003 SP1 is the Security Configuration Wizard (SCW). SCW provides the ability for an administrator to set a security role for each server in the environment for the purpose of role-based security. SCW supports the lockdown of servers specific to the function of a front-end server or back-end server, enabling the secured configuration for Web access or mailbox storage specific to the role of the server. SCW disables Windows services such as RPC, IIS Web, and the like if they are not used in the role of the server. Additionally, SCW closes all ports on the server that are not used, further decreasing the attack surface of a server and minimizing the potential for a security breach of the server system. SCW is covered in Chapter 12 of this book.

## Improving Mailbox Recovery Through Volume Shadow Copy Services

A significant addition to Windows Server 2003 is the Volume Shadow Copy Service (VSS) technology. Volume Shadow Copy takes a snapshot of a network volume and places the copy onto a different volume on the network. After a mirrored snapshot has been taken, at any time, files from the read-only shadow can be accessed without complications typical of network volumes in use. Exchange Server 2003 is one of the first application server products that takes advantage of the Volume Shadow Copy Service. VSS is used to improve online backups of Exchange databases, and it provides the basis from which mailbox recovery capabilities are provided in an Exchange Server 2003 environment. There are two primary ways VSS provides better system management support in Exchange Server 2003:

- **Online Backup of Files**—VSS provides the ability to back up open files, such as Exchange EDB data. Backing up open files has always been a challenge for organizations. Old tape backup software skipped files in use because there was no easy way to back up the files being used by applications such as Exchange. Improvements in tape backup software now provide the ability for an organization to add an Exchange backup agent so that Exchange databases can be backed up. However, the process of backing up Exchange data during production usage time significantly slows down the normal access to messages in the Exchange database.

  Windows Server 2003 Volume Shadow Copy provides the ability to create a snapshot to another volume. With the read-only shadow volume available, tape backup software can now launch a backup on the shadowed version of the database without having to contend with database access on the primary disk volume of the network. Furthermore, because the database on the shadowed volume is not in use, the backup system does not have to stop, unlock a file, back up the file, and then relock the file for user access.

- **Simple Mailbox Recovery**—Volume Shadow Copy Service technology is also used in Exchange Server 2003 to provide administrators the ability to recover lost or damaged mailboxes. Rather than having to go back to the last tape backup on a system, a mail administrator can go to a third party utility that supports Exchange

VSS recovery and choose to recover a mailbox. More details on mailbox recovery is covered in Chapter 32.

# Reliability Enhancements in Exchange Server 2003

In addition to the enhancements in Windows Server Server 2003 that improve the functionality of Exchange Server 2003, there are several new enhancements added to Exchange Server 2003 specifically to improve messaging reliability. These enhancements include long-awaited tools for mailbox and database recoverability. The tools provide simple mail message and mailbox folder recovery to complete recovery of deleted or damaged mailboxes.

## Simplifying Mailbox Recovery Using Integrated Tools

One of the major enhancements added to Exchange Server 2003 is the Mailbox Recovery Center, shown in Figure 1.4. This tool provides mail administrators the ability to recover a mailbox of individual users that might have been accidentally deleted or disconnected from a user's network logon account. The mailbox recovery tool is integrated directly in the Exchange System Manager administration tool, making it easy for administrators to provide mailbox recovery assistance when recovery or reconnection is required.

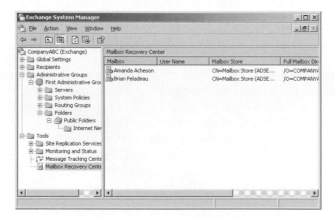

**FIGURE 1.4**   Mailbox Recovery Center in Exchange Server 2003.

The mailbox recovery tool and other disaster recovery tips and techniques are covered in Chapter 32.

## Leveraging Recovery Storage Group Functionality

Any disaster recovery and system reliability plan includes techniques to plan, prepare, and implement system and data recovery. Exchange Server 2003 introduces the concept of a recovery storage group that is used as a spare data location where information can be recovered. The recovery storage group prepares the Exchange system for the capability of restoring and recovering mailboxes. With the release of Exchange Server 2003 Service

Pack 1, any database from any server can be restored to the recovery storage group of another server in the same Administrative Group for the purpose of message, mailbox, or entire database recovery. Additionally, SP1 simplifies the movement of mailbox data from the recovery storage group to an online mailbox store by simply right-clicking the recovery storage group and choosing Exchange Tasks to launch a recovery wizard. Chapter 32 presents more details on the implementation of a recovery storage group.

## Expanding on Manageability and Administration Benefits of Exchange Server 2003

Exchange Server 2003 introduced a series of functions that help Exchange administrators better manage and administer the Exchange environment. Some of those tools include improvements in the ExMerge utility for mailbox moves, the ability to create dynamic distribution lists, a simplified method of replication address lists between forests, step-by-step migration tools to upgrade from previous versions of Exchange, and better integration with Microsoft Operations Manager.

### Improving the Speed of Mailbox Moves

For most Exchange administrators, the ExMerge utility is a familiar tool. When ExMerge first became available years ago, it was an Exchange Resource Kit of tools that enabled an administrator to export and import mailboxes. Over the years, Exchange administrators have found many occasions to export and import mailboxes—whether to back up a mailbox for future recovery, transfer the mailbox from one server or Exchange organization to another, or clean up a corrupt mailbox by exporting good messages and leaving bad messages behind.

Microsoft has continued to revise the ExMerge utility posting the latest version of the tool on the downloads section of the Exchange page of their Web site (`http://www.microsoft.com/exchange/downloads/2003/default.mspx`). The latest ExMerge utility provides the ability to schedule ExMerge tasks, specify a date range for the extraction and importation of message data, skips bad or corrupt messages, and is now multithreaded. As a multithreaded tool, the utility can migrate multiple mailboxes at the same time, as shown in Figure 1.5, using more bandwidth and the capabilities of a server.

ExMerge is covered in more detail in Chapter 5, "Designing an Enterprise Exchange Server 2003 Environment."

### Establishing Dynamic Distribution Lists

New to Exchange Server 2003 is the ability to dynamically create a mail distribution list. Prior to this feature, distribution lists were static groups in which members were added or deleted from a list. With dynamic group creation, a distribution list can be created by specifying LDAP query information. A group can be created that looks for all members who live in a particular city, or a query created that looks for all individuals who live in California (CA), as shown in Figure 1.6, or a dynamic query created that looks for all individuals with manager, director, or VP in their title.

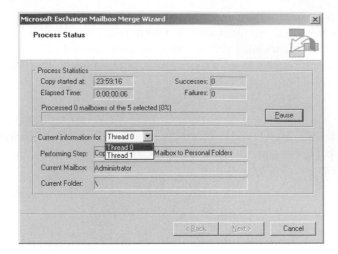

**FIGURE 1.5**    Multithreaded mailbox moves with the new ExMerge.

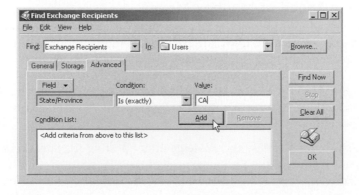

**FIGURE 1.6**    Setting a query-based distribution rule.

The dynamic lookup function requires that data fields serving as queries have consistent information or that the query takes into account matching for similarities—for example, matching for the words manager, mgr, or mngr if there is a lack of consistency in naming. However, the query-based group lookup is done through LDAP queries and can look in default or custom attribute fields to build a distribution list for users.

Query-based distribution lists are covered in Chapter 18.

## Replicating Directories Between Forests

Although not new to Windows, Exchange Server 2003 formally introduces the Identity and Integration Feature Pack (IIFP) that synchronizes address book information between

Exchange organizations. Before Exchange Server 2003, organizations were able to acquire a copy of Microsoft Metadirectory Service (MMS) under special license arrangements with Microsoft and with limited support. Because of the success of MMS in synchronizing directories between Active Directory forests, Identity and Integration Feature Pack (formerly known as MMS 3.0) is now freely downloadable from Microsoft.

With the inclusion of a synchronization wizard, Identity and Integration Feature Pack has the capability of synchronizing the address books between multiple Exchange forests, thus enabling an organization with multiple Active Directory forests to share directories. For more robust directory synchronization needs, Microsoft provides the Microsoft Identity and Integration Server (MIIS) that supports synchronization with non–Active Directory directories, such as LDAP, Novell NDS/e-Directory, and Exchange 5.5 Directory.

Chapter 18 explores more on the Identity and Integration Pack as well as directory replication.

## Simplifying Migrations Using Structured Migration Tools

To help simplify the process of migrating from Exchange 5.5 and Exchange 2000 to Exchange Server 2003, Microsoft is providing an interactive step-by-step migration guide and migration tools. The interactive guide, shown in Figure 1.7, not only walks an administrator through the steps, but it also links each step to tools with applicable wizards and parameters needed for each migration step.

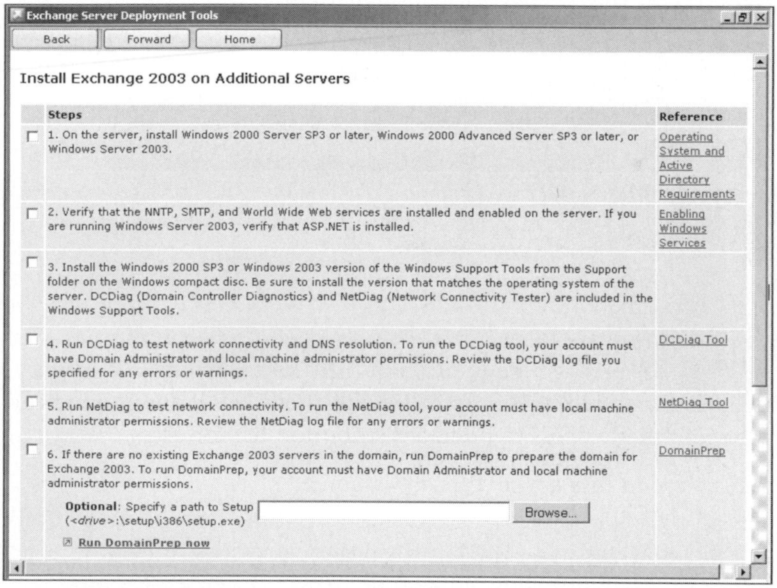

FIGURE 1.7    Step-by-step migration guide in Exchange Server 2003.

The tools can be launched manually to follow custom configuration steps; however, for organizations needing common tested procedures, the migration guide provides a simplified process.

The migration process from Exchange 5.5 is covered in Chapter 15; the migration process from Exchange 2000 is covered in Chapter 16.

## Taking Advantage of Microsoft Operations Manager

Another management and administration tool that has been available from Microsoft to help Exchange administrators is the Microsoft Operations Manager, or MOM. Because manageability is so important to Exchange administrators to validate message routing, connect to the Internet, and monitor email traffic and spam, Microsoft includes the Exchange components for MOM with Exchange 2003. The Exchange 2003 agent for MOM, shown in Figure 1.8, includes over 1700 of the box rules and a copy of the Microsoft knowledgebase.

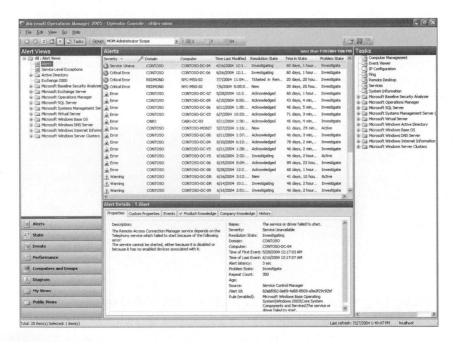

**FIGURE 1.8**    Microsoft Operations Manager for Exchange Server 2003.

The 1700 rules monitor and produce reports on everything from message traffic, server uptime, and replication statistics. The knowledgebase provides integrated access to debugging information for event errors or problem reports.

All this information helps an Exchange administrator gain better control for managing and administering the Exchange environment in an organization. Exchange Server 2003 management and maintenance practices are covered in Chapter 19, "Exchange Server 2003 Management and Maintenance Practices."

# Improvements in Exchange Server 2003 Security

Security has been on the minds of most organizations, and very much so for the employees at Microsoft, which went through several secured computing initiative steps to improve security of all of its products. After designing Exchange Server 2003, Microsoft tested it repeatedly for security in the application code; Microsoft also integrated several security technologies either already present in Windows 2000 or new to Windows 2003 and Exchange Server 2003.

## Establishing Security Between Front-End and Back-End Servers

All future products from Microsoft will include IP Security (IPSec) as an intra-domain/intra-forest secured communication standard. Rather than leaving the security between Exchange front-end and back-end servers to simple server-to-server communications, Microsoft now provides IPSec encryption between front-end and back-end servers.

By integrating IPSec's 168-bit encryption between servers, the security and integrity of information between servers in an Exchange forest is ensured. Security used to look at just external breaches, such as a hacker taking control of servers connected to the Internet. However with privacy of information—and legislation requiring security of personal information, healthcare patient information, or financial services data—organizations are leveraging the industry standard IPSec for server-to-server security even inside the firewall.

Chapter 13 covers IPSec security, along with securing internal and external Exchange servers.

## Creating Cross-Forest Kerberos Authentication

Besides replicating directory information between forests, Windows 2003 provides the capability of creating cross-forest trusts and establishing cross-forest Kerberos authentication. Cross-forest Kerberos authentication provides the ability for an organization to share messages and attachments with trust-level security, which enhances secured communications.

You'll find more information on cross-forest Kerberos authentication in Chapter 5.

## Restricting Distribution Lists to Authenticated Users

A minor function—but something that is a major enhancement for improved secured messaging interaction—is the ability to restrict distribution lists to authenticated users. With previous versions of Exchange, anyone could send an email to a distribution list if they knew the SMTP address name for the list. Although there were ways of blocking the ability for external access to distribution list message distribution, it was an all-or-nothing action.

With Exchange Server 2003, the Exchange administrator now has the ability to restrict distribution lists to authenticated users. An authenticated user in Exchange Server 2003 is someone who successfully logs on to an authorized domain or forest. With the implementation of authenticated user access to distribution lists, security is improved. Chapter 18 explores distribution lists.

## Using Safe and Blocked Lists

Unwanted emails, or spam, account for over 50% of all emails transmitted over the Internet, and for some organizations, spam has extended beyond being a nuisance for users to delete. With inappropriate or undesired spam messages flashing pictures and displaying obscenities on screens of employees, spam has become a human resource issue. Exchange Server 2003 includes the ability to create lists for safe and blocked addresses, as shown in Figure 1.9, enabling Exchange administrators to control message flow. With Exchange Server 2003 SP1, Microsoft added a Spam Confidence Level (SCL) that provides an administrator the ability to actively filter messages on a rating of 1 through 9, choosing to delete, manage, or allow users to manage SPAM or potentially unwanted messages.

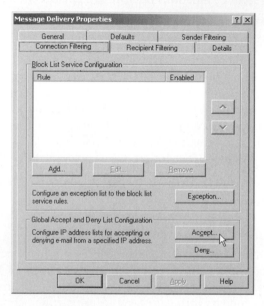

**FIGURE 1.9**    Safe and blocked lists in Exchange Server 2003.

Chapter 12 presents details on the SPAM protection and the safe and blocked list functionality in Exchange Server 2003.

## Filtering of Inbound Recipients Functionality

Filtering inbound recipients is a new feature built in to Exchange Server 2003. By being able to filter for inbound recipients, an organization can extend the restriction of desired or undesired message communications. Additionally, Microsoft has been active in supporting Sender ID standards for the active registration and identification of legitimate electronic messages. Sender ID can be enabled in an Exchange Server 2003 environment to support the standards for message identification. Sender ID and the inbound recipient filter is covered in Chapter 12.

### Blocking Attachments in Outlook Web Access (OWA)

Attachments in Outlook Web Access pose a threat for the distribution of viruses and message beaconing, which is a method spammers use to identify qualified email addresses. Outlook Web Access in Exchange Server 2003 provides the ability for the Exchange administrator to block attachments, thus minimizing the risk of the spread of viruses and awareness by spammers of valid email addresses. Chapter 12 covers attachment blocking in detail.

### Supporting S/MIME for OWA Attachments

Included as part of the security functions built in to Exchange Server 2003 is the ability for organizations to send and receive attachments using S/MIME encryption. With previous versions of Exchange, in order to support certificates that enabled attachment encryption, the organization had to use the full Outlook client. With Exchange Server 2003, however, the Outlook Web Access client now supports S/MIME attachments, thus providing the capability of securely communicating between email users. Chapter 13 explores S/MIME attachments in OWA.

### Supporting SenderID Messaging Framework

With Exchange Server 2003 Service Pack 2, Microsoft has included support for the SenderID messaging framework. SenderID is an authentication prototocol, the domain name from which emails are sent. SenderID is intended to decrease the potential for email spoofing and phishing. SenderID validates the domains of the source of email messages by verifying IP addresses of the sender against a list of valid IP addresses registered by each organization. SenderID is addressed in Chapter 12.

## Leveraging Mobility in Exchange Server 2003

As noted in an earlier section, "Expanding into the New Wireless and Mobility Technologies," Microsoft has included mobile communication capabilities for wireless phones and PDAs into Exchange Server 2003. This provides an organization the ability to enable users to access their email, calendars, and contacts from a wireless phone or pocket PC device. Because the technology is built in to Exchange Server 2003, there is no need to add special software, servers, or integration with Exchange to provide this functionality. Mobility is now an integrated part of Exchange, providing access to users anytime and anywhere.

Additionally, mobility in Exchange Server 2003 includes a new and improved version of the Outlook Web Access Web client so that users can view, create, and manage their email, calendar, contacts, and public folder information from a Web browser.

Remote access to messaging information has been greatly enhanced with the added improvements of wireless and Web access communications.

## Improving Outlook Web Access's Functionality

The first improvement in Exchange Server 2003 for remote and mobile access is a significant improvement to the Outlook Web Access client. Instead of organizations having to use the full Outlook client and full Windows desktop for users to check their email, the OWA in Exchange Server 2003 provides pull-down menus, spell-check, rules, filters, global address list access, and other functions that users want in their mail client.

With a more robust Web client for Exchange, organizations can choose to have OWA as the primary client for users, thus minimizing the need for setting up virtual private networks (VPNs), having laptops for all mobile users, or creating Citrix or Terminal Services farms for remote users. Outlook Web Access 2003 is covered in detail in Chapter 26.

## Using Outlook 2003 over HTTPS

For organizations that still need the full Outlook client—possibly for integration with a client relationship management software—or power users with sophisticated access needs, Outlook 2003 combined with Exchange Server 2003 provides the ability to have a client-to-server connection over secured HTTP, as shown in Figure 1.10. This feature enables organizations to securely connect a full Outlook client to Exchange without having to set up a VPN, and without having to open up special ports for client/server access.

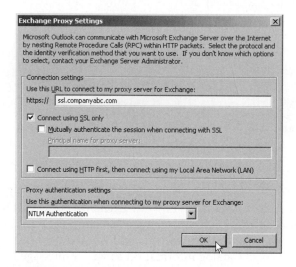

**FIGURE 1.10**    Outlook 2003 client configuration for secured HTTP access.

Setting up a remote full Outlook client can now take only a minute or two on a system running Outlook 2003, thus improving remote and mobile access while simplifying the security configuration process. Outlook 2003 over HTTPS improves an organization's ability to extend client access in a secured manner without the normal complexity of creating sophisticated client connections.

Chapter 11 explains secured client communication.

### Leveraging ActiveSync for Exchange Replication

ActiveSync in Exchange Server 2003 is a utility that provides the synchronization of Exchange information to pocket PC devices. Instead of having a cradle on each computer with a pocket PC computer—or setting up ActiveSync for pocket PC users to update their calendars, contacts, and other information—Exchange Server 2003 now includes ActiveSync as part of the core messaging system.

Pocket PC users with Ethernet, 802.11b wireless, or wireless phone connectivity can now synchronize security from their pocket PC to Exchange Server 2003. Because ActiveSync is built in to Exchange Server 2003, there are no special server integration tools, dedicated sync gateway servers, or other devices necessary. All an organization needs is physical connectivity from either a wired or wireless pocket PC device, and then the mobile devices can communicate with the Exchange environment.

Chapter 23 describes pocket PC–ActiveSync integration.

### Connecting Users Through Wireless Technologies

Besides synchronizing pocket PC devices to Exchange Server 2003, the Exchange Server 2003 product also provides mobile phone connectivity to Exchange for devices supporting General Packet Radio Service (GPRS) or Single Carrier Radio Transmission Technology (1×RTT). In addition to GPRS and 1×RTT support, Exchange Server 2003 can also communicate with standard cellular phone or packet radio devices. Wireless phone connectivity in Exchange Server 2003 means that users with simple character-based phones can send and receive email messages and query calendars and contact lists from their mobile phones. Exchange Server 2003 also supports xHTML (WAP 2.x), cHTML, and HTML standards for mobile phone connectivity.

With Outlook Web Access 2003, Outlook over HTTPS, ActiveSync for pocket PC devices, and mobile phone access, Exchange Server 2003 provides access to virtually any client device for access to information from anywhere. Chapter 23 explores mobile connectivity built in to Exchange Server 2003.

## Performance Improvements in Exchange Server 2003

There are several additions to Exchange 2003 that help organizations better improve the performance of their Exchange servers. Exchange Server 2003 includes improvements such as better memory allocation and management through technologies that cache distribution lists and Global Catalog information as well as message notification suppression.

Performance improvements not only decrease the overhead of a server, enabling an organization to grow its organization, but performance improvements also enable an organization to minimize the number of servers needed in its environment. If an organization with five Exchange servers can decrease performance demands by 20%, the organization can eliminate an entire server from its network environment with no performance degradation seen by users.

## Allocating Memory to Improve Performance

One of the improvements in Exchange Server 2003 is the ability to optimize the memory for servers greater than 1GB. This is actually a function of Windows 2003 memory management, which enables memory to be tuned between kernel and application memory. Rather than allocating memory equally between kernel and application memory, an organization can specifically allocate memory about 1GB to optimize kernel memory.

Chapter 33 covers tuning an optimization of memory and other recommendations based on best practices for optimizing a server configuration.

## Using Caching on Distribution Lists

Exchange Server 2003 takes advantage of caching of information in several ways to improve system and message environment performance. One way caching improves Exchange is in its capability of caching Global Catalog information on domain controllers. Rather than requiring a Global Catalog server to query the directory for each lookup to the Global Catalog, Exchange Server 2003 takes advantage of Windows 2003 Global Catalog caching. When an Exchange client queries the Global Catalog, the response can now come from a cache off a domain controller, thus minimizing the need to query across a WAN connection to a remote Global Catalog server or to put a domain controller in each location.

Additionally, Exchange Server 2003 provides caching of distribution lists for email message distribution. By using the cache for distribution list information, fewer queries need to be made directly to the Global Catalog database, resulting in faster message transmission.

Chapter 33 explains caching distribution lists and Global Catalog information.

## Controlling Message Notification

Exchange Server 2003 adds a new feature that enables the Exchange administrator to specify which message notifications get sent from an Exchange server. Normally when a message comes in to an Exchange server, if the Exchange server cannot find the recipient, a non-delivery receipt (NDR) is sent to the sender. However, with spam messages accounting for over 50% of incoming messages for many organizations, the number of NDRs could be significant.

By controlling message notification, as shown in Figure 1.11, an Exchange administrator can designate what to do with message notification and can control the amount of responses generated from messages that might otherwise be undesired.

Controller message notification is a tuning and optimization function and is covered in Chapter 33.

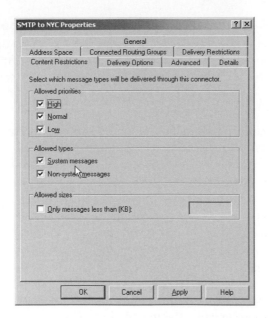

**FIGURE 1.11**    Controlling message notification in Exchange Server 2003.

# Solidifying Core Technologies for Exchange Server 2003

Although this chapter has covered a variety of new features, functions, and capabilities built in to Exchange Server 2003, there are also a number of core technologies that Microsoft improved as well. Some of these core technology improvements come in the area of DNS improvements, reliable Global Catalog lookup improvements, tools, and strategies for successfully planning and migrating from Exchange 5.5 and Exchange 2000, and core technologies at leveraging Windows 2000 and Windows 2003 capabilities.

## Solidifying DNS for Proper Message Routing

Domain Name System, or DNS, has been the core name resolution technology for Active Directory from which Exchange 2000 and Exchange Server 2003 extend the directory lookup scheme. Having a solid DNS infrastructure is critical to the success of proper email message routing. Organizations that do not clearly understand how to implement DNS, or integrate Active Directory DNS with existing Unix-based enterprise DNS systems, can impact efficient and effective message routing.

Chapter 7, "Domain Name System Impact on Exchange Server 2003," covers the basics as well as best practices and lessons learned at implementing DNS, which improves name resolution for an organization. Chapter 7 also addresses a core infrastructure need for reliable message routing and communications.

## Deploying Global Catalogs for Reliable Directory Lookup

Global Catalogs are the directories used within an Active Directory or Exchange messaging environment for looking up other internal email users and distribution lists. Microsoft made changes in Windows 2003 on how Global Catalogs can be positioned in the Active Directory. The improvements in Global Catalog caching, replication of site information, and distribution list information have changed the way many organizations operate.

Chapter 8, "Global Catalog and Domain Controller Placement," covers new tips, tricks, and techniques on GC and DC placement, and provides a method in which the number of servers can be reduced, or at least optimize systems for better directory lookup and replication.

## Completing a Migration to Windows 2003

Some organizations might still be running Windows NT4 or Exchange 5.5 and will take this opportunity to make a major upgrade to Windows 2003 and Exchange Server 2003. There are many reasons highlighted in this introduction chapter on why to upgrade to the latest Windows and Exchange systems, but Chapter 14, "Migrating from NT4 to Windows Server 2003," and Chapter 15 focus on specific areas for planning, prototype testing, and successfully completing the migration process.

Upgrading is not just getting the latest operating system and messaging system from Microsoft; the upgrade also provides the Exchange administrator with a more reliable messaging system with tools that help keep the system more secure, run more efficiently, and provide access from virtually anywhere and from any device in use in an organization.

# Summary

This chapter highlighted the new features, functions, migration tools, and management utilities in Exchange Server 2003 that will help administrators take advantage of the capabilities of the new messaging system. An upgrade to Exchange Server 2003 is more than just a simple upgrade from one messaging system to another, because email hasn't changed much from version to version. This upgrade is an opportunity to benefit from the messaging system enhancements and the capabilities of the Windows Server 2003 and Exchange Server 2003. With these new tools, an organization can change the way users access the system remotely, improve security both in the background and at the client, and have the tools available to maintain, manage, and recover from a disaster.

The steps to proper planning and successful implementation are highlighted throughout this book, with tips, tricks, and best practices noted throughout the chapters.

# Best Practices

This chapter highlighted the new features, functions, and core technologies built in to Exchange Server 2003. The following are best practices from this chapter:

- Use the step-by-step migration tools highlighted in Chapter 15 (for migrations from Exchange 5.5) and Chapter 16 (for migrations from Exchange 2000) to work through the upgrade process.

- Consider using the new Outlook Web Access 2003—not only as a Web browser client, but possibly as the primary mail client for many users, thus eliminating the need to support full desktop OSs and client software for users.

- Leverage the Outlook-over-HTTPS functionality covered in Chapter 11 to enable remote full client Outlook users connectivity to Exchange Server 2003 without the need to implement VPNs or other secured connection systems.

- Review Chapter 8 to determine whether you can decrease the number of domain controllers or Global Catalog servers on your network with an upgrade to Windows Server 2003, where GC and DC caching simplifies the requirement for domain controller placement.

- Test the mailbox recovery process highlighted in Chapter 32 to ensure that if you need to recover from mailbox deletion or corruption, you have successfully tested the functionality.

- Review your use of IPSec and whether you want to begin implementing server-to-server encryption to create a more secure networking environment. See Chapter 13 for more details on server-level security.

- Evaluate the use of RIS for Servers as a possible disaster recovery process to recover a failed Exchange server, or for adding additional Exchange servers to a network.

- Consider changing distribution lists to query-based distribution lists so that lookups can be dynamic instead of requiring manual addition and changes of users.

- If your organization needs to replicate directories with other Exchange organizations or with other directories, review Chapter 18 on IIFP and MIIS 2003.

- For better Exchange server management, administration, and reporting, review Chapter 19, "Exchange Server 2003 Management and Maintenance Practices," on tips and techniques on leveraging the Microsoft Operations Manager add-in that comes with Exchange Server 2003.

- To minimize spam and unwanted messaging, leverage the capabilities of the Spam Confidence Level as well as safe and blocked lists, inbound recipient filtering, Sender ID, and attachment blocking, which are covered in more detail in Chapter 12 of this book.

- Consider using Exchange Server 2003's built-in remote and mobile capabilities for wireless phone and PDA device communications for messaging, calendaring, and contact communications.

- Look for updates from Microsoft (`http://www.microsoft.com/exchange/ downloads/2003/default.mspx`) that might provide better administration, management, or migration to Exchange Server 2003.

- Review exiting enterprise configurations for network settings that may be modified or reconfigured with an upgrade to Windows 2003 and Exchange Server 2003.

# CHAPTER 2

# Planning, Prototyping, Migrating, and Deploying Exchange Server 2003

**IN THIS CHAPTER**

- Initiation, Planning, Prototype, and Pilot: The Four Phases to the Upgrade

- Initiation Phase: Defining the Scope and Goals

- Initiation Phase: Creating the Statement of Work

- Planning Phase: Discovery

- Planning Phase: Creating the Design Document

- Creating the Migration Document

- The Prototype Phase

- The Pilot Phase: Validating the Plan to a Limited Number of Users

- The Production Migration/Upgrade

Messaging has evolved from an alternative to "snail mail" to an intricate communications and information storage environment. Exchange and Outlook users rely on it for formal and informal communications, keeping track of appointments, storing addresses and phone numbers, and (it's been said) receiving stock quotes, health tips, and urban myths. These tools are also available remotely in most environments, making them even more important at keeping the mobile professional productive and connected to his or her world.

It has become such a critical tool that the upgrade process should not be taken lightly. Although an upgrade from Exchange 5.5 or Exchange 2000 might at first appear to be a simple process, its success relies on your understanding of current issues with the messaging environment, defining both the objectives of the upgrade, and its potential effects on the user community. Adding more features and complexity to the messaging "ecosystem" might not result in ecstatic users, but reducing spam and the resulting impact on in-boxes might more than justify the cost of the upgrade. Reducing the number of milliseconds it takes to send an email probably won't get noticed, but being able to guarantee access to email anywhere and anytime should. An enthusiastic user community tends to generate support and momentum for projects, which extend the functionality of the messaging system.

Important decisions include whether the entire network operating system (NOS) needs to be upgraded (if Active Directory is not yet in place) or only a subset of it, and what other infrastructure components need to be changed or replaced.

The examples used in this chapter assume that the environments being migrated are primarily based on Exchange v5.5 or Exchange 2000, and except where noted that Active Directory is already in place. The same process can be applied to other messaging migration projects, such as GroupWise or Notes. The migration process is covered in detail in Chapters 14, "Migrating from NT4 to Windows Server 2003"; 15, "Migrating from Exchange v5.5 to Exchange Server 2003"; and 16, "Migrating from Exchange 2000 to Exchange Server 2003."

# Initiation, Planning, Prototype, and Pilot: The Four Phases to the Upgrade

This chapter presents a structured process for upgrading to Exchange Server 2003 and highlights some best practice recommendations to enhance the success of the project. The standard project management phases of *initiation*, *planning*, *testing*, and *implementation* can be used for organizations of any size. Between each phase is a "go/no go" step, in which the results of the phase are reviewed, and the decision-makers determine whether the project should move forward. Any problems that were encountered are assessed to determine whether they require attention before moving forward. This ensures that issues identified are addressed, rather than being overlooked, to inevitably crop up at the worst possible moment.

## Documentation Required During the Phases

A number of documents are produced during each phase to ensure that it is well defined and ultimately successful. In the initiation phase the goals of the project can be identified and documented in a *Statement of Work* document. In the planning phase, more time and energy can be applied to detailing the end-state of the migration in a *Design* document. Although this document paints the picture of what the end-state looks like, the roadmap of how to get there is detailed in the *Project Schedule and Migration* documents. These documents are only drafts during this phase, because they need to be validated in the testing phase before they can be labeled "final."

The testing phase validates that the new technologies will effectively meet the organization's needs, and determines whether modifications to the project are needed. Any additional documents that would help with the implementation process, such as *Server Build* documents, *Business Continuity* or *Disaster Recovery* documents, and checklists for workstation configurations are also created during the testing phase. Finally, the appropriate *Maintenance* documents are created during the implementation phase. These phases and the documents to be created are discussed in more detail later in this chapter.

The following list summarizes the standard phases of an Exchange Server 2003 upgrade and the standard documents created in each phase:

- **Initiation Phase**—Statement of Work document

- **Planning Phase**—Design Document Draft, Migration Document Draft, and Migration Schedule Draft (Gantt Chart)

- **Testing Phase**—Design Document Final, Migration Document Final, Migration Schedule Final (Gantt Chart), Server Build Documents, Migration Checklists, and Training Documents for End-Users

- **Implementation Phase**—Maintenance Documents

For smaller projects, not all of these items are required, but it's important to have each document created *before* it is needed, to avoid show-stoppers during the migration process. For example, having a Statement of Work document that is well constructed and agreed upon in the initiation phase will smooth the way for the creation of the Design document and Migration document. A detailed Migration Schedule Gantt chart facilitates scheduling of resources for the actual work and clarifies the roles and responsibilities.

# Initiation Phase: Defining the Scope and Goals

Upgrading to Exchange Server 2003 can be a simple process for basic messaging environments, or as challenging as a complete network operating system upgrade for more complex organizations. In most environments Exchange is implemented on multiple servers, and an upgrade will affect a number of other software applications. In fact, changes to the Exchange environment may affect the daily lives of the employees to a much greater extent than moving from NT to Windows Server 2003 (or even more than an upgrade from a non-Microsoft environment), because they will most likely receive a new Outlook client and change the way they access email remotely. With an operating system upgrade, the end-users often don't even know that anything has changed.

The upgrade process is also a great opportunity to help the business achieve its business objectives by leveraging the messaging components of the technology infrastructure and to help justify the never-ending IT expenses. Messaging, in essence, enables the sharing of information and access to data and other resources within the company to help the company deliver its products or services. With this critical purpose in mind, it makes sense to engage in a structured and organized process to determine the goals of the project, control the variables and risks involved, and make sure that a clear definition of the end-state has been crafted. The Statement of Work is the key deliverable from this phase that paints the overall picture of the upgrade project and gains support from the key decision-makers (and allocates an initial budget).

## The Scope of the Project

Before the entire Statement of Work can be written, time should be allocated to define the scope of the project. The scope of the project simply defines what is included in the project and what is not. For a simpler environment this may be very easy to define— for example, an environment in which there is only one Exchange server used for email and scheduling, with a dedicated backup device and virus protection software. If this organization has not migrated to Active Directory yet, the scope might expand to include the upgrade of additional servers or simply upgrade the single server. A desktop upgrade might be included in the scope of the project if the features and benefits of Outlook 2003 are desired. In any case, it's important to clarify this level of detail at the beginning of the planning process. "Scope creep" is a lot more manageable if it can be predicted in advance!

> **NOTE**
>
> An example of a scope of work for a small organization is
>
> - Upgrade the Exchange 5.5 NT 4 Server to Exchange Server 2003 with Windows Server 2003.
> - Upgrade the Tape Back-up and Virus Protection software to Exchange Server 2003–compatible versions.
> - Upgrade the Outlook client to Outlook 2003 on all workstations.
> - Provide OWA access to all remote users.

In a larger company, "what's in" and "what's out" can be correspondingly more complicated. A company with multiple servers dedicated to Exchange functions—such as front-end and back-end servers, bridgehead servers, or servers dedicated to faxing or conferencing—requires the scope definition to get that much more detailed. Multiple sites and even different messaging systems complicate the scope, especially if the company has grown via mergers over the last few years.

> **NOTE**
>
> An example of a scope of work for a larger organization is
>
> - Upgrade the four Exchange 5.5 NT 4 Servers to two Exchange Server 2003 cluster pairs on Windows Server 2003, and upgrade the six NT file and print servers to two Windows Server 2003 cluster pairs.
> - Upgrade the Enterprise Tape Back-up and Virus Protection software on all servers to the latest versions that are Windows Server 2003–compatible and Exchange Server 2003–compatible.
> - Upgrade the outlook client to Outlook 2003. Provide OWA access to all remote users.

The scope of work might change as the initiation phase continues and in the more detailed planning phase as the Design and Migration documents are created and reviewed. This is especially true for more complex migration projects after the detailed planning phase is completed and the all-important budget is created. At this point, the scope might need to be reduced, so that the budget requested can be reduced.

## Identifying the Goals

As a next step in the initiation phase, it helps to spend time clearly identifying the goals of the project before getting too caught up in the technical details. All too often everyone runs up the whiteboard and starts scribbling and debating technology before agreeing on the goals. Although this conversation is healthy and necessary, it should be part of the planning phase, after the high-level goals for the project and initial scope have been defined. Even if there is a very short timeline for the project, the goals—from high-level business objectives, to departmental goals, to the specific technology goals—should be specified.

### High-Level Business Goals

The vision statement of an organization is an excellent place to start because it tells the world where the company excels and what differentiates that company from its competitors. There will typically be several key objectives behind this vision, which are not so publicly stated, that can be related to the Exchange Server 2003 upgrade. These should be uncovered and clarified, or it will be difficult, if not impossible, to judge whether the project succeeds or fails from a business standpoint.

> **NOTE**
>
> High-level business goals that pertain to an Exchange Server 2003 upgrade can include better leveraging of company knowledge and resources through efficient communications and collaboration, controlling IT costs to lower overhead and enable products to be more competitively priced, or improving security to meet governmental requirements.

Although this process sounds basic, it might be more difficult if the company hasn't documented or updated its business objectives in some time (or *ever*). Different divisions of larger companies might even have conflicting business goals, which can make matters more complicated. High-level business goals of a company can also change rapidly, whether in response to changing economic conditions or as affected by a new key stakeholder or leader in the company. So even if a company has a standard vision statement in place, it is worth taking time to review and ensure that it still accurately reflects the opinions of the key stakeholders.

This process helps clarify how the messaging upgrade fits into the overall company strategy and should help ensure that support will be there to approve the project and keep its momentum going. In this time of economic uncertainty, a project must be strategic and directly influence the delivery of the company's services and products; otherwise, the danger exists of a key stakeholder "pulling the plug" at the first sign of trouble or shifting attention to a more urgent project.

For example, a consulting organization might have a stated vision of providing the latest and greatest processes and information to its clients, and the internal goal could be to make its internal assets (data) available to all employees at all times to best leverage the knowledge gained in other engagements. The Exchange environment plays a key role in meeting this goal, because employees have become so dependent on Outlook for communicating and organizing information and many of the employees rely on portable devices and pocket PCs.

A different company, one which specializes in providing low-cost products to the market-place, might have an internal goal of cost control, which can be met by Exchange Server 2003 through reduction in the total server count and more cost-effective management to help reduce downtime. For this company, user productivity is measured carefully, and the enhancements in the Outlook 2003 client would contribute positively.

## High-Level Messaging Goals

At this point the business goals that will guide and justify the Exchange upgrade should be clearly defined, and the manner in which Exchange Server 2003's enhanced features will be valuable to the company are starting to become clear. The discussion can now turn to learning from key stakeholders what goals they have that are specific to the messaging environment that will be put in place.

The high-level goals tend to come up immediately, and be fairly vague in nature; but they can be clarified to determine the specific requirements. A CEO of the company might simply state, "I need access to my email and calendar from anywhere." The CTO of the same company might demand "zero downtime of the Exchange servers and easy adminis-tration." The CFO may want to "reduce the costs of the email system." If the managers in different departments are involved in the conversation, a second level of goals might well be expressed. The IT manager might want 4-node clustering, the ability to restore a single user's mailbox, and reduced user complaints about spam and performance. The marketing manager might want better tools to organize the ever-increasing amount of "stuff" in his employees' in-boxes and mail folders.

Time spent gathering this information helps ensure that the project is successful and the technology goals match up with the business goals. It also matters who is spearheading the process and asking the questions, because the answers might be very different if asked by the president of the company rather than an outside consultant who has no direct influence over the career of the interviewee.

> **NOTE**
>
> An example of some high-level messaging goals include a desire to have no downtime of the Exchange servers, access to email and calendars from anywhere, better functionality of the OWA client, and increased virus and spam protection.

A specific trend or theme to look for in the expression of these goals is whether they are focused on fixing and stabilizing or on adding new functionality. When a company is fixated on simply "making things work properly," it might make sense to hold off on implementing a variety of new functionality (such as video conferencing or providing Windows-powered mobile devices such as pocket PCs) at the same time.

## Business Unit or Departmental Messaging Goals

After these higher-level goals have been identified, the conversations can be expanded to include departmental managers and team leads. The results will start to reveal the complexity of the project and the details needed to complete the statement of work for the migration project. For an Exchange upgrade project to be completely successful, these individuals, as well as the end-users, need to benefit in measurable ways.

Based on the business and technology goals identified thus far, the relative importance of different departments will start to become clear. Some organizations are IT-driven, especially if they are dependent on the network infrastructure to deliver the company's products and services. Others can survive quite well if technology isn't available for a day or even longer.

> **NOTE**
>
> An example of some departmental goals include a desire to ensure encrypted transmission of human resource and personnel emails, an OWA client that has the same functionality as the Outlook client, and support for SmartPhone and Pocket PC devices. The IT department might also like better mailbox recovery tools and Exchange-specific management tools that can be used from MOM.

All departments use email, but the sales department might also receive voicemails through the Outlook client and updates on product pricing, and thus need the best possible reliability and performance. This includes ensuring that viruses don't make it into employee in-boxes and that spam be reduced as much as possible.

Certain key executives are rarely in the office and aren't happy with the existing Outlook Web Access client. They also carry BlackBerry wireless devices and need to make sure that they remain fully functional during and after the upgrade.

The marketing department uses the email system for sharing graphics files via public folders, which have grown to an almost unmanageable size, but this enables them to share the data with strategic partners outside of the company. This practice won't change, and the amount of data to be managed will continue to grow over time.

The finance and human resources departments are very concerned about security and want to make sure that all email information and attached files are as safe as possible when traveling within the organization, or being sent to clients over the Internet.

The IT department has a very aggressive service level agreement (SLA) to meet and is interested in clustering, reducing the number of servers that need to be managed, and improving the management tools in place. In addition, Exchange Server 2003's integration with Active Directory will facilitate the management of users and groups and additions and changes to existing user information.

In the process of clarifying these goals, the features of the Exchange messaging system that are most important to the different departments and executives should become apparent.

A user focus group might also be helpful, which can be comprised of employee volunteers and select managers, to engage in detailed discussions and brainstorming sessions. In this way the end-users can participate in the initial planning process and help influence the decisions that will affect their day-to-day work experience. New features offered by the

Outlook 2003 client include the Exchange Cached Mode, optimized network traffic with data compression, and an improved Outlook 2003 client and OWA capabilities.

Other outcomes of these discussions should include an understanding of which stakeholders will be involved in the project and the goals that are primary for each person and each department. A sense of excitement should start to build over the possibilities presented by the new technologies that will be introduced to make managers' lives easier and workers' days more productive.

# Initiation Phase: Creating the Statement of Work

Executives generally require a documented Statement of Work that reflects strategic thinking, an understanding of the goals and objectives of the organization, and a sense of confidence that the project will be successful and beneficial to the company. The document needs to be clear and specific and keep its audience in mind, which generally means not going into too much technical detail. This document also needs to give an estimate of the duration of the project, the costs involved, and the resources required.

The initial scope of work might have changed and evolved as discussions with the executives, managers, and stakeholders reveal problems that weren't obvious and requirements that hadn't been foreseen. Although the scope started out as a "simple Exchange upgrade" it might have expanded to include an upgrade to Active Directory, the addition of new features for remote access to the messaging environment, or management and business continuity features.

The following is a standard outline for the Statement of Work document:

1. Scope of Work

2. Goals

3. Timeline and Milestones

4. Resources

5. Risks and Assumptions

6. Initial Budget

The following sections cover the different components of the Statement of Work. This document is arguably the most important in the entire process because it can convince the executives who hold the purse strings to move forward with the project—or, of course, stop the project in its tracks.

## Summarizing the Scope of Work

At this point in the initiation phase, a number of conversations have occurred that have clarified the basic scope of the project, the high-level business goals as they pertain to the messaging upgrade, and the more specific goals for each department and of key stakeholders. Armed with this wealth of information, the lead consultant on the project should now organize the data to include in the Statement of Work and get sign-off to complete the phase and move to the more detailed planning phase.

The Scope section of the Statement of Work document should answer these essential questions:

- How many Exchange and Windows servers need to be upgraded?

- Where do these servers reside?

- What additional applications need to be upgraded (especially backup, virus protection, disaster recovery [DR], and remote access) as part of the project?

- What additional hardware needs to be upgraded or modified to support the new servers and applications (especially tape backup devices, storage area networks, and routers)?

- Will the desktop configurations be changed?

The answers to these questions may still be unclear at this point, and require additional attention during the planning phase.

## Summarizing the Goals

As discussed earlier, a number of conversations have been held previously on the topic of goals, so there may be a fairly long list of objectives at this point. A structure to organize these goals is suggested in the following list:

- Business continuity/disaster recovery (Clustering, Storage, Backup and Restore)

- Performance (Memory Allocation Improvements, Public Folders, Email)

- Security (Server, Email)

- Mobility (Outlook Web Access, Pocket PC and SmartPhone Support)

- Collaboration (Real-time Collaboration—replacement for Exchange Instant Messaging—SharePoint Portal)

- Serviceability (Administration, Management, Deployment)

- Development (Collaboration Data Objects, Managed API)

By using a framework such as this, any "holes" in the goals and objectives of the project will be more obvious. Some of the less glamorous objectives, such as a stable network, data recovery abilities, or protection from the hostile outside world, might not have been identified in the discussions. This is the time to bring up topics that might have been missed, before moving into the more detailed planning phase.

It might also be valuable to indicate what will be corrected by the upgrade ("pain points") and what new capabilities will be added.

## Summarizing the Timeline and Milestones

A bulleted list of tasks is typically all that is needed to help define the time frame for the upgrade (more complex projects might benefit from a high-level Gantt chart of no more than 10–20 lines). The time frame should be broken down by phase to clarify how much time is to be allocated for the planning phase and testing phases. The actual implementation of the upgrade also should be estimated.

Depending on the complexity of the project, a time frame of 1–2 months could be considered a "short" time frame, with 2–4 months offering a more comfortable window for projects involving more servers, users, and messaging-related applications. Additional time should be included if an outside consulting firm will assist with part or all of the project.

Because every project is different, it's impossible to provide rules for how much time to allocate to which phase. Experience has shown that allocating additional time for the planning and testing phase helps the upgrade go more smoothly, resulting in a happier user base. If little or no planning is done, the testing phase will most likely miss key requirements for the success of the project. Remember also to allocate time during the process for training of the administrative staff and end-users.

The key to successfully meeting a short timeline is to understand the added risks involved and define the scope of the project so that the risks are controlled. This might include putting off some of the functionality that is not essential, or contracting outside assistance to speed up the process and leverage the experience of a firm that has performed similar upgrades many times. Hardware and software procurement can also pose delays, so for shorter time frames, they should be procured as soon as possible after the ideal configuration has been defined.

Some upgrades can actually take place over a single weekend; then on Monday morning users show up for training and are up and running on the new messaging platform.

## Summarizing the Resources Required

Typical roles that need to be filled for an Exchange Server 2003 upgrade project include

- Project Sponsor
- Exchange Server 2003 Design Consultant
- Exchange Server 2003 Technical Lead
- Exchange Server 2003 Consulting Engineer
- Project Manager
- Systems Engineer(s)
- Technical Writer
- Administrative Trainer
- End-user Trainer

2

The organization should objectively consider the experience and skills as well as available time of internal resources before deciding whether outside help is needed. For the most part, few companies completely outsource the whole project, choosing instead to leverage internal resources for the tasks that make sense and hiring external experts for the planning phase and testing phases. Often internal resources simply can't devote 100% of their energy to planning and testing the messaging technologies, because their daily duties will get in the way. Contracted resources, on the other hand, are able to focus just on the messaging project.

The resulting messaging environment needs to be supported after the dust settles, so it makes sense for the administrative staff to receive training in the early phases of the upgrade (such as planning and testing) rather than after the implementation. Many consultants provide hands-on training during the testing and implementation phases.

For larger projects, a team may be created for the planning phase, a separate team allocated for the testing phase, and a third team for the implementation. Ideally the individuals who perform the testing participate in the implementation for reasons of continuity. Implementation teams can benefit from less-experienced resources for basic server builds and workstation upgrades.

## Summarizing the Risks and Assumptions

More time is spent discussing the details of the risks that could affect the successful outcome of the project during the planning phase, but if there are immediately obvious risks they should be included in the statement of work.

Basic risks could include

- Existing Exchange problems, such as corrupt database, lack of maintenance

- Lack of in-house expertise and bandwidth for the project

- Using existing hardware that might not have enough RAM, storage capacity, or processor speed

- WAN or LAN connectivity issues, making downtime a possibility

- A production environment that cannot experience any downtime or financial losses will occur

- Customized applications that interface with Exchange Server and that need to be tested and possibly rewritten for Exchange Server 2003

- Short timeline that will require cutting corners in the testing process

## Summarizing the Initial Budget

The decision-makers will want to start getting a sense for the cost of the project, at least for the planning phase of the project. Some information might already be quite clear, such as how many servers need to be purchased. If the existing servers are more than a few years old, chances are they need to be replaced, and price quotes can easily be gathered for new machines. Software upgrades and licenses can also easily be gathered, and costs for peripheral devices such as tape drives or SANs should be included.

If external help is needed for the planning, testing, and implementation, some educated guesses should be made about the order of magnitude of these costs. Some organizations set aside a percentage of the overall budget for the planning phase, assuming outside assistance, and then determine whether they can do the testing and implementation on their own.

As mentioned previously, training should also not be forgotten—for both the administrative staff and the end-users.

### Getting Approval on the Statement of Work

After the initial information has been presented in the Statement of Work format, formally present and discuss it with the stakeholders. If the process has gone smoothly this far, the Statement of Work should be approved or, if not, items that are still unclear can be clarified. After this document has been agreed on, a great foundation is in place to move forward with the planning phase.

## Planning Phase: Discovery

The planning phase enables the Exchange Server 2003 design consultant time to paint the detailed picture of what the end-state of the upgrade will look like, and also to detail exactly how the network will evolve to this new state. The goals of the project are clear, what's in and what's out are documented, the resources required are defined, the timeline for the planning phase and an initial sketch of the risks are anticipated, and the budget is estimated.

### Understanding the Existing Environment

If the organization has multiple Exchange servers in place, third-party add-on applications, multiple sites, complex remote access, or security requirements, a network audit makes sense. If an outside company is spearheading the planning phase, this is its first real look at the configuration of the existing hardware and network, and it is essential to help create an appropriate end-state and migration process. Standard questionnaires are helpful to collect data on the different servers that will be affected by the upgrade.

The discovery process typically starts with onsite interviews with the IT resources responsible for the different areas of the network and proceeds with a hands-on review of the network configuration. Focus groups or whiteboarding sessions can also help dredge up concerns or issues that might not have been shared previously. External consultants often generate better results because they have extensive experience with network reviews and analysis and with predicting the problems that can emerge midway through a project.

Network performance can be assessed at the same time to predict the level of performance the end-users will see and whether they are accessing email, public folders, or calendars from within the company, from home, or from an Internet kiosk in an airport.

Existing network security policies might be affected by the upgrade, and should be reviewed. If AD is being implemented, group policies—which define user and computer configurations and provide the ability to centralize logon scripts and printer access—can be leveraged.

Anyone using Exchange is familiar with the challenges of effectively managing the data that builds up, and in grooming and maintaining these databases. The existing database structure should be reviewed at least briefly so the Exchange Server 2003 design consultant understands where the databases reside, how many there are and their respective sizes, and whether regular maintenance has been performed. Serious issues with the database(s) crashing in the past should be covered. Methods of backing up this data should also be reviewed.

Desktop configurations should be reviewed if the upgrade involves an upgrade to the Outlook client. If there are a variety of different desktop configurations, operating systems, and models, the testing phase might need to expand to include these.

Disaster recovery plans or service level agreements (SLAs) can be vital to the IT department's ability to meet the needs of the user community, and should be available for review at this time.

What remote and mobile connections to the messaging system are currently in use? OWA is used by most organizations, as well as Terminal Services, or VPNs. The features in Exchange Server 2003 may enable the organization to simplify this process; VPNs might no longer be needed because Outlook can be accessed via HTTP.

Although the amount of time required for this discovery process varies greatly, the goals are to fully understand the messaging infrastructure in place as the foundation on which the upgrade will be built. New information might come to light in this process that will require modifications to the Statement of Work document.

## Understanding the Geographic Distribution of Resources

If network diagrams exist, they should be reviewed to make sure they are up to date and contain enough information (such as server names, roles, applications managed, switches, routers, firewalls, IP address info, gateways, and so forth) to fully define the location and function of each device that plays a role in the upgrade. These diagrams can then be modified to show the end-state of the project.

Existing utility servers—such as bridgehead servers, front-end servers, DNS naming servers, and DHCP or WINS servers—should be taken into account.

Has connectivity failure been planned for a partial or fully meshed environment? Connections to the outside world and other organizations need to be reviewed and fully understood at the same level, especially with an eye toward the existing security features.

Companies with multiple sites bring added challenges to the table. As much as possible, the same level of information should be gathered on all the sites that will be involved in and affected by the messaging upgrade. Also, a *centralized* IT environment has different requirements from a *distributed* management model.

If time permits, the number of support personnel in each location should be taken into account, as well as their ability to support the new environment. Some smaller sites might not have dedicated support staff and network monitoring, and management tools, such as MOM or SMS, might be required.

How is directory information replicated between sites, and what domain design is in place? If the company already has Active Directory in place, is a single domain with a simple organizational unit (OU) structure in place, or are there multiple domains with a complex OU structure? Global Catalog placement should also be clarified.

The answers to these questions directly shape the design of the solution, the testing phase, and the implementation process.

# Planning Phase: Creating the Design Document

When the initial discovery work is complete, attention can be turned to the Design document itself, which paints a detailed picture of the end-state of the network upgrade. In essence, this document expands on the Statement of Work document and summarizes the process that was followed and the decisions that were made along the way.

The second key deliverable in the planning phase is the Migration document, which tells the story of how the end-state will be reached. Typically, these documents are separate, because the Design document gives the "what" and "why" information, and the Migration document gives the "how" and "when" information.

## Collaboration Sessions: Making the Design Decisions

The planning phase kicked off with discovery efforts and review of the networking environment, and additional meetings with the stakeholders and the Project Team should be scheduled for collaborative discussions. This process covers the new features that Exchange Server 2003 offers and how these could be beneficial to the organization as a whole and to specific departments or key users. Typically, several half-day sessions are required to discuss the new features and whether implementing them makes sense.

Ideally, quite a bit of thought has already gone into what the end-state will look like, as reflected in the Statement of Work document, so everyone attending these sessions will be on the same page in terms of goals and expectations for the project. If they aren't, this is the time to resolve differing opinions, because the Design document is the blueprint for the results of the messaging upgrade.

The collaborative sessions should be led by a consultant with hands-on experience in designing and implementing Exchange Server 2003 solutions. Agendas should be provided in advance to keep the sessions on track (see Figure 2.1 for a sample agenda) and enable attendees to prepare specific questions. A technical writer should be invited to take notes and start to become familiar with the project as a whole, because that individual will most likely be active in creating the Design document and additional documents required.

**Agenda – Exchange 2003 Design**

1. Goals and Objectives
   a.  Overall Project Goals
   b.  Department Goals
   c.  Requirement for Scalability
   d.  Need for Fault Tolerance / Redundancy

2. AD Topolgy
   a.  Forests/Domains/Sites/GCs
   b.  OUs/Groups/Users
   c.  DNS/DDNS

3. Exchange 2003 Architecture
   a.  Mailbox Server Placement
   b.  Public Folder Servers
   c.  Connector Servers
   d.  OWA
   e.  Global Catalog Placement
   f.  Administrative Groups
   g.  Routing  Groups
   h.  Mixed Mode vs. Native Mode
   i.  Server Loading
   j.  Server Sizing
   k.  Client Performance over WAN
   l.  High Availability

4. Exchange 2003 Database
   a.  Storage Group Design
   b.  Databases
   c.  Log Files
   d.  Database Sizing
   e.  Users per server
   f.  Mailbox Sizing
   g.  Mailbox Cleanup
   h.  Backup – Storage Group

   i.  Restore – Database
   j.  Service Level Agreements

5. Connectors
   a.  Recipient Synch
   b.  Bulletins/Public Folders Synch
   c.  Configuration Synch
   d.  One-way or Two-way

6. Security Model
   a.  Groups
   b.  Administrators
   c.  Enterprise Administrators
   d.  OWA/FE Servers

7. Administrative Model
   a.  Server Administration
   b.  View-Only Administrator
   c.  Administrator
   d.  Full Administrator
   e.  User Administration
   f.  Delegation
   g.  System Policy
   h.  Recipient Policy

8. Application Integration
   a.  BlackBerry

9. Exchange Clients
   a.  Outlook 2003/Outlook 2000 / XP
   b.  OWA/HTTP-DAV/HTTPS
   c.  POP3/SMTP
   d.  IMAP4

**FIGURE 2.1**   Sample Exchange Server 2003 design agenda.

The specifics of the upgrade should be discussed in depth, especially the role that each server will play in the upgrade. A diagram is typically created during this process (or an existing Visio diagram updated) that defines the locations and roles of all Exchange 2003 servers and any legacy Exchange servers that need to be kept in place.

The migration process should be discussed as well, although often organizations prefer to discuss the minutiae of the migration *after* the Design document has been completed. Why spend hours discussing how to get to end-state A when the budget ends up being too high, and design B needs to be crafted?

## Disaster Recovery Options

A full disaster recovery assessment is most likely out of the scope of the messaging upgrade project, but the topic should be covered at this phase in the project.

Most people would agree that the average organization would be severely affected if the messaging environment were to go offline for an extended period of time.

Communications between employees would have to be in person or over the phone, document sharing would be more complex, communication with clients would be affected, and productivity of the remote work force would suffer. Employees in the field rarely carry pagers any more, and some have even discarded their cell phones, so many employees would be hard to reach. This dependence on messaging makes it critical to adequately cover the topic of disaster recovery as it pertains to the Exchange messaging environment.

Existing service level agreements (SLAs) should be reviewed and input gathered on the "real" level of disaster recovery planning and testing that has been completed. Few companies have spent the necessary time and energy to create plans of action for the different failures that could take place, such as power failures in one or more locations, Exchange database corruptions, or server failures. A complete disaster recovery plan should include offsite data and application access as well.

## Design Document Structure

The Design document expands on the content created for the Statement of Work document defined previously, but goes into greater detail and provides historical information on the decisions that were made. This is helpful if questions come up later in the testing or implementation process, such as "Whose idea was that?" or "Why did we make that decision?"

The following is a sample table of contents for the Exchange Server 2003 Design document:

1. Executive Summary

2. Goals and Objectives

    - Business Objectives

    - Departmental Goals

3. Background

    - Overview of Process

    - Summary of Discovery Process

4. Exchange Design

    - Exchange 2000 Design Diagram

    - Exchange Mailbox Server Placement (where do they go)

    - Organization (definition of and number of Exchange Organizations)

    - Administrative Groups (definition of and number of)

    - Routing Groups (definition of and number of)

    - Storage Groups (definition of and number of)

- Mixed Mode Versus Native Mode (choice and decision)

- Global Catalog Placement (definition and placement)

- Recipient Policies (definition and usage)

- Front-end and Bridgehead Servers (definition and usage, includes remote access)

- Server Specifications (recommendations and decisions, role for each server defined, redundancy, disaster recovery options discussed)

- Virus Protection (selected product with configuration)

- Administrative Model (options defined, and decisions made for level of administration permitted by administrative group)

- System Policies (definition and decisions on which policies will be used)

- Exchange Monitoring (product selection and features described)

- Exchange Backup/Recovery (product selection and features described)

5. Budget Estimate

    - Hardware and Software Estimate

## Executive Summary

The Executive Summary should summarize the high-level solution for the reader in under one page by expanding upon the scope created previously. The importance of the testing phase can be explained and the budget summarized.

## Design Goals and Objectives

Goals and objectives have been discussed earlier in this chapter and should be distilled down to the most important and universal goals. They can be broken down by department if needed. The goals and objectives listed can be used as a checklist of sign-off criteria for the project. The project is complete and successful when the goals are all met.

## Background

In the background section, the material gathered in the discovery portion of the planning phase should be included in summary form (details can always be attached as appendixes); also helpful is a brief narrative of the process the project team followed to assemble this document and make the decisions summarized in the design portion of the document.

## Design

The design section defines how the Exchange Server 2003 environment will be configured. Exchange Server 2003 was designed to be extremely flexible in how it can be added to the network. In Figure 2.2, the possibilities are listed for Exchange 5.5, Exchange 2000, Exchange Server 2003, Windows NT, Windows 2000, and Windows Server 2003. This flexibility can be very important if there are third-party applications used to extend the functionality of the current version of Exchange that are not available for Exchange Server 2003 or that have been written specifically for a previous version of Exchange or to control the costs of the overall upgrade. For instance, a unified messaging solution currently in place on Exchange 2000 could simply be left as is while the rest of the messaging environment is upgraded to Exchange Server 2003.

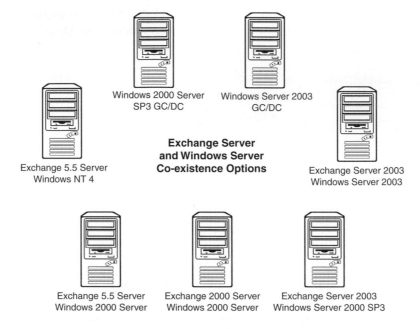

**FIGURE 2.2**    Exchange and Windows server coexistence.

> **NOTE**
>
> Note also that Exchange 5.5 and 2000 cannot run directly on servers running Windows 2003 Server; they can, however, operate in a Windows Server 2003 Active Directory environment.

Additional information on the options for coexistence of different Windows Server Operating Systems and Exchange Server versions is covered in Part II, "Exchange Server 2003."

**Technical Advantages of Exchange Server 2003 Running on Windows Server 2003**
Exchange Server 2003 can run on Windows 2000 and Windows Server 2003, but the latter provides a number of technical advantages. Note that Exchange Server 2003 cannot be run on Windows Server 2003 Web Edition.

Using Exchange Server 2003 with Windows Server 2003 provides memory tuning, database snapshot through Volume Shadow Copy Services (VSS), secured HTTP support for Outlook 2003, OWA compression support, IPSec support between front-end and back-end clusters, object quotas, and SID filtering. If Windows Server 2003 Enterprise is the platform, there is support for up to 8-way PIII or P4 processors, and up to 8-node clustering.

If the Enterprise version of Exchange Server 2003 is used, the 16GB database limit is removed; instead of 1 mailbox store, there can be up to 20 databases per server.

Future chapters cover these topics in greater detail, especially in Parts III, "Networking Services Impact on Exchange"; IV, "Securing an Exchange Server 2003 Environment"; VI, "Exchange Server 2003 Administration and Management"; VII, "New Mobility Functionality in Exchange Server 2003"; and X, "Fault Tolerance and Optimization Technologies."

### Agreeing on the Design

When the document is complete, it should be presented to the project stakeholders and reviewed to make sure that it fully meets their requirements, and to see whether any additional concerns come up. If there were significant changes since the initiation phase's Statement of Work document, they should be highlighted and reviewed at this point. Again, it is valuable in terms of time and effort to identify any issues at this stage in the project, especially when the Migration document still needs to be created.

Some organizations choose to use the Design document to get competitive proposals from service providers, and having this information levels the playing field and results in proposals that promise the same end results.

## Creating the Migration Document

With the Design document completed and agreed to by the decision-makers, the Migration document can now be created. There are always different ways to reach the desired Exchange Server 2003 configuration, and the Migration document presents the method best suited to the needs of the organization—in terms of timeline, division of labor, and cost—based on the goals and objectives defined in the initiation and planning processes. The Migration document makes the project real; it presents specific information on "who does what" in the actual testing and migration process, assigns costs to the resources as applicable, and creates a specific timeline with milestones and due dates.

The Migration document should present enough detail about the testing and upgrade process that the resources performing the work have guidance and understand the purpose and goals of each step. The Migration document is not a step-by-step handbook of how to configure the servers, implement the security features, and move mailboxes. The Migration document is still fairly high level, and the resources performing the work need real-world experience and troubleshooting skills.

Additional collaborative meetings might be needed at this point to brainstorm and decide both on the exact steps that will be followed and when the testing and upgrade will be (see Figure 2.3).

**Agenda – Exchange 2003 Migration Planning**

1. Goals and Objectives

2. Project Management
   a. Benefits of Phased Approach
   b. Phase 1 - Design/Planning
   c. Phase 2 - Prototype
   d. Phase 3 - Pilot
   e. Phase 4 - Implement
   f. Phase 5 - Support
   g. Timeline, Milestones
   h. Resource Requirements
   i. Risk Management
   j. Checkpoints

3. Migration Planning
   a. ForestPrep/DomainPrep
   b. Site Replication Service (SRS)
   c. Existing Mail PO Infrastructure/Routing
   d. PO Consolidation
   e. PO Pre-migration Maintenance
   f. Client Personal Folders Renaming
   g. One-to-one Mailbox Mapping
   h. Exchange Security Groups
   i. Universal Groups, DL, and Native Mode
   j. Move Mailboxes
   k. Migrating Mobile Users
   l. Direct/Gradual/Rolling Upgrade
   m. NTDSNoMatch Option
   n. Switching to Native Mode

4. Deployment Tools
   a. Scripting
   b. Built-in Exchange Migration Wizard
   c. Third-party

5. Building
   a. Normalize Environment

   b. Datacenter First
   c. Branch Offices Second
   d. Deployment Strategies
   e. Staged vs. Scripted vs. Manual

6. Documentation
   a. Design/Plan
   b. As-builts
   c. Build Guides
   d. Migration Guides
   e. Administration Guides
   f. Maintenance Guides
   g. Disaster Recovery Guides
   h. User Guides/Informational Updates

7. Training
   a. Users
   b. Administrators
   c. Migration Team
   d. Technical Experts

8. Communications
   a. Migration Team
   b. Executives and Management
   c. Administrators
   d. Users
   e. Methods
   f. Frequency
   g. Detail Level

9. Administration and Maintenance
   a. Administration
   b. Maintenance
   c. Disaster Recovery
   d. Guides
   e. Periodic Schedules
   f. Daily / Weekly / Monthly
   g. Planned Downtime
   h. Checklists
   i. Testing

**FIGURE 2.3**    Migration session agenda.

Part V, "Migrating to Exchange Server 2003," provides additional information about the various strategies and processes for moving from previous versions of Exchange to Exchange Server 2003.

## The Project Schedule

A *project schedule* or *Gantt Chart* is a standard component of the Migration document, and it presents tasks organized by the order in which they need to be completed, in essence creating a detailed roadmap of how the organization will get from the current state, test the solution, and then implement it.

Other important information is included in the project schedule: resources assigned to each task, start dates and durations, key checkpoints, and milestones. Milestones by definition have no duration and represent events such as the arrival of hardware items, sign-off approval on a series of tasks, and similar events. Some additional time should be allocated (contingency time) if possible during the testing phase or between phases, in case stumbling blocks are encountered.

A good rule of thumb is to have each task line represent at least four hours of activities; otherwise, the schedule can become too long and cumbersome. Another good rule is that a task should not be less than 1% of the total project, thus limiting the project to 100 lines. The project schedule is not intended to provide detailed information to the individuals performing the tasks, but to help schedule, budget, and manage the project.

To create a project schedule, a product such as Microsoft Project is recommended, which facilitates the process of starting with the high-level steps and then filling in the individual tasks. The high-level tasks, such as those shown in Figure 2.4, should be established first and can include testing the server configurations and desktop designs, performing one or more pilot implementations, the upgrade or migration process, and the support phase.

Dependencies can also be created between tasks to clarify that Task 40 needs to be completed before Task 50 can start. A variety of additional tools and reports are built in to see whether resources are overburdened (for example, being expected to work 20 hours in one day), which can be used for *resource leveling*. A *baseline* can also be set, which represents the initial schedule, and then the *actuals* can be tracked and compared to the baseline to see whether the project is ahead or behind schedule.

Microsoft Project is also extremely useful in creating budgetary information and creating what-if scenarios to see how best to allocate the organization's budget for outside assistance, support, or training.

If the timeline is very short, the Gantt Chart can be used to see if multiple tasks take place simultaneously or if this will cause conflicts.

## Creating the Migration Document

With the project schedule completed, the Migration document will come together quite easily, because it essentially fills out the "story" told by the Gantt Chart. Typically the Migration document is similar to the structure of the Design document (another reason why many organizations want to combine the two), but the Design document relates the design decisions made and details the end-state of the upgrade, and the Migration document details the process and steps to be taken.

The following is a sample table of contents for the Migration document:

1. Executive Summary

2. Goals and Objectives of the Migration Process

3. Background

4. Summary of Migration-Specific Decisions

5. Risks and Assumptions

6. Roles and Responsibilities

7. Timeline and Milestones

8. Training Plan

9. Migration Process

- Hardware and Software Procurement Process

- Prototype Proof of Concept Process

- Server Configuration and Testing

- Desktop Configuration and Testing

- Documentation Required from Prototype

- Pilot Phase(s) Detailed

- Migration/Upgrade Detailed

- Support Phase Detailed

- Support Documentation Detailed

10. Budget Estimate

- Labor Costs for Prototype Phase

- Labor Costs for Pilot Phase

- Labor Costs for Migration/Upgrade Phase

- Labor Costs for Support Phase

- Costs for Training

11. Project Schedule (Gantt Chart)

The following sections delve into the information that should be covered in each section. Part V of this book provides in-depth information on the steps involved in migrating to Exchange Server 2003 from Exchange 5.5 or Exchange 2000, and Part IX, "Client Administration and Management," provides details on the client configuration options and processes.

### Executive Summary
As with the Design document, the executive summary section summarizes what the Migration document covers, the scope of the project, and the budget requested.

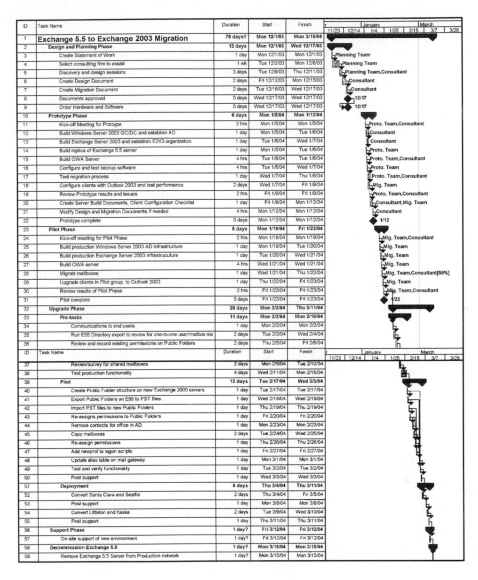

| ID | Task Name | Duration | Start | Finish |
|----|-----------|----------|-------|--------|
| 1 | **Exchange 5.5 to Exchange 2003 Migration** | 76 days? | Mon 12/1/03 | Mon 3/15/04 |
| 2 | Design and Planning Phase | 13 days | Mon 12/1/03 | Wed 12/17/03 |
| 3 | Create Statement of Work | 1 day | Mon 12/1/03 | Mon 12/1/03 |
| 4 | Select consulting firm to assist | 1 wk | Tue 12/2/03 | Mon 12/8/03 |
| 5 | Discovery and design sessions | 3 days | Tue 12/9/03 | Thu 12/11/03 |
| 6 | Create Design Document | 2 days | Fri 12/12/03 | Mon 12/15/03 |
| 7 | Create Migration Document | 2 days | Tue 12/16/03 | Wed 12/17/03 |
| 8 | Documents approved | 0 days | Wed 12/17/03 | Wed 12/17/03 |
| 9 | Order Hardware and Software | 0 days | Wed 12/17/03 | Wed 12/17/03 |
| 10 | Prototype Phase | 6 days | Mon 1/5/04 | Mon 1/12/04 |
| 11 | Kick-off Meeting for Prototype | 2 hrs | Mon 1/5/04 | Mon 1/5/04 |
| 12 | Build Windows Server 2003 GC/DC and establish AD | 1 day | Mon 1/5/04 | Tue 1/6/04 |
| 13 | Build Exchange Server 2003 and establish E2K3 organization | 1 day | Tue 1/6/04 | Wed 1/7/04 |
| 14 | Build replica of Exchange 5.5 server | 1 day | Mon 1/5/04 | Tue 1/6/04 |
| 15 | Build OWA Server | 4 hrs | Tue 1/6/04 | Tue 1/6/04 |
| 16 | Configure and test backup software | 4 hrs | Tue 1/6/04 | Wed 1/7/04 |
| 17 | Test migration process | 1 day | Wed 1/7/04 | Thu 1/8/04 |
| 18 | Configure clients with Outlook 2003 and test performance | 2 days | Wed 1/7/04 | Fri 1/9/04 |
| 19 | Review Prototype results and issues | 2 hrs | Fri 1/9/04 | Fri 1/9/04 |
| 20 | Create Server Build Documents, Client Configuration Checklist | 1 day | Fri 1/9/04 | Mon 1/12/04 |
| 21 | Modify Design and Migration Documents if needed | 4 hrs | Mon 1/12/04 | Mon 1/12/04 |
| 22 | Prototype complete | 0 days | Mon 1/12/04 | Mon 1/12/04 |
| 23 | Pilot Phase | 5 days | Mon 1/19/04 | Fri 1/23/04 |
| 24 | Kick-off meeting for Pilot Phase | 2 hrs | Mon 1/19/04 | Mon 1/19/04 |
| 25 | Build production Windows Server 2003 AD infrastructure | 1 day | Mon 1/19/04 | Tue 1/20/04 |
| 26 | Build production Exchange Server 2003 infrastrucuture | 1 day | Tue 1/20/04 | Wed 1/21/04 |
| 27 | Build OWA server | 4 hrs | Wed 1/21/04 | Wed 1/21/04 |
| 28 | Migrate mailboxes | 1 day | Wed 1/21/04 | Thu 1/22/04 |
| 29 | Upgrade clients in Pilot group to Outlook 2003 | 1 day | Thu 1/22/04 | Fri 1/23/04 |
| 30 | Review results of Pilot Phase | 2 hrs | Fri 1/23/04 | Fri 1/23/04 |
| 31 | Pilot complete | 0 days | Fri 1/23/04 | Fri 1/23/04 |
| 32 | Upgrade Phase | 29 days | Mon 2/2/04 | Thu 3/11/04 |
| 33 | Pre-tasks | 11 days | Mon 2/2/04 | Mon 2/16/04 |
| 34 | Communications to end users | 1 day | Mon 2/2/04 | Mon 2/2/04 |
| 35 | Run E55 Directory export to review for one-to-one user/mailbox ma | 2 days | Tue 2/3/04 | Wed 2/4/04 |
| 36 | Review and record existing permissions on Public Folders | 2 days | Thu 2/5/04 | Fri 2/6/04 |

| ID | Task Name | Duration | Start | Finish |
|----|-----------|----------|-------|--------|
| 37 | Review/survey for shared mailboxes | 2 days | Mon 2/9/04 | Tue 2/10/04 |
| 38 | Test production functionality | 4 days | Wed 2/11/04 | Mon 2/16/04 |
| 39 | Pilot | 12 days | Tue 2/17/04 | Wed 3/3/04 |
| 40 | Create Public Folder structure on new Exchange 2000 servers | 1 day | Tue 2/17/04 | Tue 2/17/04 |
| 41 | Export Public Folders on E55 to PST files | 1 day | Wed 2/18/04 | Wed 2/18/04 |
| 42 | Import PST files to new Public Folders | 1 day | Thu 2/19/04 | Thu 2/19/04 |
| 43 | Re-assigns permissions to Public Folders | 1 day | Fri 2/20/04 | Fri 2/20/04 |
| 44 | Remove contacts for office in AD | 1 day | Mon 2/23/04 | Mon 2/23/04 |
| 45 | Copy mailboxes | 2 days | Tue 2/24/04 | Wed 2/25/04 |
| 46 | Re-assign permissions | 1 day | Thu 2/26/04 | Thu 2/26/04 |
| 47 | Add newprof to logon scripts | 1 day | Fri 2/27/04 | Fri 2/27/04 |
| 48 | Update alias table on mail gateway | 1 day | Mon 3/1/04 | Mon 3/1/04 |
| 49 | Test and verify functionality | 1 day | Tue 3/2/04 | Tue 3/2/04 |
| 50 | Post support | 1 day | Wed 3/3/04 | Wed 3/3/04 |
| 51 | Deployment | 6 days | Thu 3/4/04 | Thu 3/11/04 |
| 52 | Convert Santa Clara and Seattle | 2 days | Thu 3/4/04 | Fri 3/5/04 |
| 53 | Post support | 1 day | Mon 3/8/04 | Mon 3/8/04 |
| 54 | Convert Littleton and Itaska | 2 days | Tue 3/9/04 | Wed 3/10/04 |
| 55 | Post support | 1 day | Thu 3/11/04 | Thu 3/11/04 |
| 56 | Support Phase | 1 day? | Fri 3/12/04 | Fri 3/12/04 |
| 57 | On-site support of new environment | 1 day? | Fri 3/12/04 | Fri 3/12/04 |
| 58 | Decommission Exchange 5.5 | 1 day? | Mon 3/15/04 | Mon 3/15/04 |
| 59 | Remove Exchange 5.5 Server from Production network | 1 day? | Mon 3/15/04 | Mon 3/15/04 |

**FIGURE 2.4**    Sample project schedule.

### Goals and Objectives of the Migration Process

The goals and objectives of the migration overlap with those of the overall project, but should focus also on what the goals are for use and development of internal resources, and the experience of the user community. A goal of the overall project could be "no interruption of messaging services," and this would certainly be a goal to include in the Migration document.

Subphases of the Migration document have their own specific goals that might not have been included in the Design document. For example, a primary goal of the prototype phase, which takes place in a lab environment so it won't interfere with the production network, is to validate the design and to test compatibility with messaging-related applications. Other goals of the prototype phase can include hands-on training for the migration team, creating documents for configuration of the production servers, and creating and validating the functionality of the desktop configurations.

### Background

A summary of the migration-specific decisions should be provided to answer questions such as "Why are we doing it that way?" Because there is always a variety of ways to implement new messaging technologies—such as in-place upgrades instead of buying new hardware—and a number of conversations will have taken place during the planning phase, it is worth summarizing them early in the document.

### Risks and Assumptions

Risks pertaining to the phases of the migration should be detailed, and typically are more specific than in the Design document. For example, a risk of the prototype phase might be that the hardware available won't perform adequately and needs to be upgraded. Faxing, virus protection, or backup software might not meet the requirements of the Design document and thus need upgrading. Custom-designed messaging applications, or Exchange add-ons might turn out not to be Exchange Server 2003–compatible.

### Roles and Responsibilities

The Design document focuses on the high-level "who does what"; the Migration document should be much more specific, because the budget for labor services is part of this deliverable. Rather than just defining the roles (such as project sponsor, Exchange Server 2003 design consultant, Exchange Server 2003 technical lead, and project manager) the Migration document specifically indicates the level of involvement of each resource throughout the prototype, pilot, and migration phases. The project sponsor should stay involved throughout the process, and regular project status meetings keep the team on the same page.

The project manager is expected to keep the project on time, on budget, and within scope, but generally needs support from the project sponsor and key stakeholders involved in the project. Depending on how the project manager role is defined, this individual may be either a full-time resource, overseeing the activities on a daily basis, or a part-time resource, measuring the progress, ensuring effective communications, and raising flags when needed. A cautionary note: Expecting the project manager to be a technical resource—such as the Exchange Server 2003 technical lead—can lead to a conflict of interest and generally does not yield the best results. Projects tend to be more successful if even 10% of an experienced project manager's time can be allocated to assist.

### Timeline and Milestones

Specific target dates can be listed, and should be available directly from the project schedule already created. This summary can be very helpful to executives and managers, whereas the Gantt Chart contains too much information. Constraints that were identified in the discovery process need to be kept in mind here, because there might be important dates (such as the end of the fiscal year), seasonal demands on the company that black out certain date ranges, and key company events or holidays.

### Training Plan

Will training happen during the prototype testing process in a hands-on fashion for the project team, or will classroom-style training be required? Will the end-users be trained while their desktops are being upgraded, or be left with a training document, or be directed to a training video on the network? If management tools are being added to the environment, who will train the appropriate resources on how to effectively use them and not be overwhelmed by false alarms?

### Migration Process

The project schedule Gantt Chart line items should be included and expanded upon so that it is clear to the resources doing the work what is expected of them. The information does not need to be on the level of step-by-step instructions, but it should clarify the process and results expected from each task. For example, the Gantt Chart might indicate that an Exchange server needs to be configured, and in the Migration document, information would be added about which Service Pack is to be used for the NOS and for Exchange, how the hard drives are to be configured, and which additional applications (virus protection, tape backup, faxing, and network management) need to be installed.

If the Gantt Chart lists a task of, for example, "Configure and test Outlook 2003 on sales workstation," the Migration document gives a similar level of detail: Which image should be used to configure the base workstation configuration, which additional applications and version of Office should be loaded, how is the workstation to be locked down, and what testing process should be followed (is it scripted or will an end-user from the department do the testing)?

Documentation also should be described in more detail. The Gantt Chart might simply list "Create as-built documents," with *as-built* defined as "a document containing key server configuration information and screenshots so that a knowledgeable resource can rebuild the system from scratch."

Sign-off conditions for the prototype phase are important and should be included. Who needs to sign off on the results of the prototype phase to indicate that the goals were all met and that the design agreed upon is ready to be created in the production environment?

Similar levels of information are included for the pilot phase and the all-important migration itself. Typically during the pilot phase, all the upgraded functionality needs to be tested, including remote access to email, voicemail access, BlackBerry and personal information managers, and public folders.

After the Exchange Server 2003 infrastructure is fully in place, what level of support will be provided? If an outside firm has assisted, will it leave staff onsite for a period of time to hold users' hands and troubleshoot any issues that crop up?

If documentation is specified as part of the support phase, such as Exchange maintenance documents, disaster recovery plans, or procedural guides, expectations for these documents should be included to help the technical writers make sure the documents are satisfactory.

### Budget Estimate

At this point in the process the budgetary numbers should be within 10%–20% of the final costs, bearing in mind any risks already identified that could affect the budget. Breaking the budget into prototype, pilot, migration, support, and training sections helps the decision-makers understand how the budget will be allocated and make adjustments if needed. No matter how much thought has gone into estimating the resources required and risks that could affect the budget, the later phases of the project may change based on the outcome of the prototype phase or the pilot phase.

# The Prototype Phase

Exchange Server 2003 offers a wealth of new features when compared to Exchange Server 2000 or Exchange 5.5, including database backup through Volume Shadow Copy Service (VSS), public folder store replication improvements, Outlook 2003 Cached Exchange Mode, cross-forest Kerberos authentication, front-end and back-end Kerberos authentication, secured HTTP access from Outlook 2003, public folder search capabilities, and Exchange-specific events for use with MOM. Other features are upgrades from Exchange Server 2000 capabilities—such as Outlook Mobile Access (OMA), which is a rewrite of Mobile Information Server—and some of the previous functionality—such as Exchange Conferencing Server—are not supported on the Windows Server 2003 platform.

Depending on the design that was decided on by the organization, the prototype phase varies greatly in complexity and duration. It is still critical to perform a prototype, even for the simplest environments, to validate the design, test the mailbox migration process, and ensure that there won't be any surprises during the actual upgrade. The prototype lab should be isolated from the production network via a VLAN or physical separation to avoid interfering with the live users.

The prototype phase also gives the project team a chance to get acquainted with the new features of Exchange Server 2003 and any new add-on applications that will be used, and to configure the hardware in a pressure-free environment. If an external company is assisting in this phase, informal or formal knowledge transfer should take place. Ideally, the prototype lab exactly mirrors the final messaging configuration so that training in this environment will be fully applicable to the administration and support skills needed after the upgrade.

## What Is Needed for the Lab?

At a bare minimum, the lab should include a new Exchange Server 2003 server, one each of the standard desktop and laptop configurations, the tape drive that will be used to back up the public and private information stores, and application software as defined in the Design document. Connectivity to the Internet should be available for testing OWA and mobile access.

Additional information on testing applications and devices for compatibility with Exchange Server 2003 is provided in Chapter 17, "Compatibility Testing."

Existing data stores should be checked for integrity and then imported to Exchange Server 2003 to ensure that the process goes smoothly. Exchange Server 2003 comes with improved mailbox migration tools, which are more resistant to failure when corrupt mailboxes are encountered and are multithreaded for better performance.

> **NOTE**
>
> The recommended route for customers with Exchange 5.5 servers to get to Exchange 2003 is to install Exchange Server 2003 into the site and move mailboxes. If Exchange 2000 is already in place, an in-place upgrade process can be used (SP3 needed for both the Exchange and the NOS), but Exchange should actually be upgraded to Exchange Server 2003, and then Windows 2000 should be upgraded to Windows Server 2003. Note that in this case, Mobile Information Server, Instant Messenger, and/or Chat should be uninstalled.

If site consolidation or server consolidation are goals of the project, the prototype lab can be used for these purposes. Multiforest connectivity can now be tested, but this requires an MMS server in one or more of the forests to enable directory synchronization.

Exchange Server 2003 also comes with a number of new tools to aid in the testing and migration process, which are covered in detail in Chapter 17. These include a prescriptive guide that walks through the deployment process, preparation tools that scan the topology and provide recommendations, and validation tools.

For more complex environments and larger companies, the lab should be kept in place even after the upgrade is completed. Although this requires the purchase of at least one additional Exchange server and related software, it provides a handy environment for testing patches and upgrades to the production environment, performing offline database maintenance, and in worst-case scenarios, a server to scavenge from in times of dire need.

After the lab is configured to match the end-state documented in the Design document, representative users from different departments with different levels of experience and feature requirements should be brought in and given a chance to play with the desktop configurations and test new features and remote access. Input should be solicited to see whether any changes need to be made to the client configurations or features offered, and to help get a sense for the training and support requirements.

## Disaster Recovery Testing

Another important testing process that can be performed prior to implementation of the new solution on the live network is business continuity or disaster recovery testing. Ideally this was covered in the design process and DR requirements were included in the design itself.

## Documentation from the Prototype

During the prototype phase, a number of useful documents can be created that will be useful to the deployment team during the pilot and production upgrade phases, and to the administrators when the upgrade is complete.

As-built documents capture the key configuration information on the Exchange Server 2003 systems so that they can easily be replicated during the upgrade or rebuilt from scratch in case of catastrophic failure. Generally the as-built documents include actual screenshots of key configuration screens to facilitate data entry.

Assuming that DR requirements for the project were defined as suggested previously, this is a perfect time to summarize the testing that was performed in the lab and record the steps a knowledgeable administrator should take in the failure scenarios tested.

## Final Validation of the Migration Document

When the testing is complete, the migration plan should be reviewed a final time to make sure that the testing process didn't reveal any show-stoppers that will require a change in the way the upgrade will take place or in the components of the final messaging solution.

The end-users who have had a chance to get their feet wet and play with the new Outlook 2003 client and learn about the new capabilities and enhanced performance of Exchange Server 2003 should be spreading the word by now, and the whole company should be excited for the upgrade!

# The Pilot Phase: Validating the Plan to a Limited Number of Users

With the testing completed, the Exchange Server 2003 upgrade team has all the tools needed for a successful upgrade, if the steps outlined so far in this chapter have been followed. The Design document is updated based on the prototype testing results so that the end-state that the executives and decision-makers are expecting has been conceptually proven. Unpleasant surprises or frantic midnight emails requesting more budget are nonexistent. The roadmap of how to get to the end-state is created in detail, with the project schedule outlining the sequential steps to be taken and the Migration document providing the details of each step. Documentation on the exact server configurations and desktop configuration are created to assist the systems engineers who will be building and configuring the production hardware.

The project team has gained valuable experience in the safe lab environment, so it is brimming with confidence and excited to forge ahead. End-users representing the different departments, who tested and approved the proposed desktop configurations, are excited about the new features that will soon be available.

To be on the safe side, a rollback strategy should be clarified, in case unforeseen difficulties are encountered when the new servers are introduced to the network. Disaster recovery testing can also be done as part of the first pilot, so that the processes are tested with a small amount of data and a limited number of users.

## The First Server in the Pilot

The pilot phase officially starts when the first Exchange Server 2003 is implemented in the production environment. The same testing and sign-off criteria that were used in the lab environment can be used to verify that the server is functioning properly and coexisting with the present Exchange servers. Surprises might be waiting that will require some troubleshooting, because the production environment will add variables that weren't present in the lab, such as large quantities of data consuming bandwidth, non-Windows servers, network management applications, and applications that have nothing to do with messaging but may interfere with Exchange Server 2003.

The migration of the first group of mailboxes is the next test of the thoroughness of the preparation process. Depending on the complexity of the complete design, it might make sense to limit the functionality offered by the first pilot phase to basic Exchange Server 2003 functionality, and make sure that the foundation is stable before adding on the higher-end features, such as voicemail integration, mobile messaging, and faxing. The first server should have virus protection software and tape backup software installed. Remote access via OWA is an important item to test as soon as possible, because there can be complexities involved with DMZ configurations and firewalls.

## Choosing the Pilot Group

The first group of users—preferably more than 10—represents a sampling of different types of users. If all members in the first pilot group are in the same department, the feedback won't be as thorough and revealing as if different users from different departments with varied needs and expectations are chosen. It's also generally a good idea to avoid managers and executives in the first round, no matter how eager they are, because they will be more likely to be the most demanding, be the least tolerant of interruptions to network functionality, and have the most complex needs.

Although a great deal of testing has taken place already, these guinea pigs should understand that there will most likely be some fine-tuning that needs to take place after their workstations are upgraded; they should allocate time from their workdays to test the upgrades carefully with the systems engineer performing the upgrade.

After the initial pilot group is successfully upgraded and functional, the number of users can be increased, because the upgrade team will be more efficient and the processes finetuned to where they are 99% error free.

For a multisite messaging environment, the pilot process should be carefully constructed to include the additional offices. It might make sense to fully implement Exchange Server 2003 and the related messaging applications in the headquarters before any of the other locations, but issues related to WAN connectivity might crop up later, and then the impact is greater than if a small pilot group is rolled out at HQ and several of the other offices. It is important to plan where the project team and help desk resources will be, and they ideally should travel to the other offices during those pilots, especially if no one from the other office participated in the lab testing phase.

The help desk should be ready to support standard user issues, and the impact can be judged for the first few subphases of the pilot. Issues encountered can be collected and tracked in a knowledge base, and the most common issues or questions can be posted on the company intranet or in public folders, or used to create general training for the user community.

## Gauging the Success of the Pilot Phase

When the pilot phase is complete, a sampling of the participants should be asked for input on the process and the results. Few companies do this on a formal basis, but the results can be very surprising and educational. Most employees should be informed of when the upgrade will take place, that no data will be lost, and that someone will be there to answer questions immediately after the upgrade. Little changes to the workstation environment—such as the loss of favorites or shortcuts, or a change in the network resources they have access to—can be very distressing and result in disgruntled pilot testers.

A project team meeting should be organized to share learning points and review the final outcome of the project. The company executives must now make the go/no go decision for the full migration, so they must be updated on the results of the pilot process.

# The Production Migration/Upgrade

When the pilot phase is officially completed and any lingering problems have been resolved with the upgrade process, there will typically be 10%–20% of the total user community upgraded. The project team will have all the tools it needs to complete the remainder of the upgrade without serious issues. Small problems with individual workstations or laptops will probably still occur but the help desk is probably familiar with how to handle these issues at this point.

A key event at this point is the migration of large amounts of Exchange data. The public and private information stores should be analyzed with eseutil and isinteg, and complete backup copies should be made in case of serious problems. The project team should make sure that the entire user community is prepared for the migration and that training has been completed by the time a user's workstation is upgraded.

It is helpful to have a checklist for the tasks that need to be completed on the different types of workstations and laptops so that the same steps are taken for each unit, and any issues encountered can be recorded for follow-up if they aren't critical. Laptops will most likely be the most problematic because of the variation in models, features, and user requirements, and because the mobile employees often have unique needs when compared to workers who remain in the office. If home computers need to be upgraded with the Outlook 2003 client and if, for instance, the company VPN is being retired, these visits need to be coordinated.

As with the pilot phase,  the satisfaction of the user community should be verified. New public folders or SharePoint discussions can be started, and supplemental training can be offered for users who might need some extra or repeat training.

### Decommissioning the Old Exchange Environment

As mentioned previously, some upgrades require legacy Exchange servers to be kept online, if they are running applications that aren't ready or can't be upgraded right away to Exchange Server 2003. Even in environments where the Exchange 5.5 or 2000 servers should be completely removed, this should not necessarily be done right away.

### Supporting the New Exchange Server 2003 Environment

After the dust has settled and any lingering issues with users or functionality have been resolved, the project team can be officially disbanded, and possibly receive some extra monetary reward for the extra hours and a job well done. If they haven't been created already, Exchange Server Maintenance documents should be created to detail the daily, weekly, monthly, and quarterly steps to ensure that the environment is performing normally and the databases are healthy.

If the prototype lab is still in place, this is an ideal testing ground for these processes and for testing patches and new applications.

## Summary

Exchange used to mean email and scheduling to the average user, but it has grown to become a critical business communications and collaboration tool. Email must be available at any hour of the day, and must be protected from viruses and spam. Calendars must be accessible to co-workers for scheduling meetings, or for company resources—such as conference rooms—to be allocated. Public folders enable company information to be shared on an as-needed basis and are replacing intranets in many organizations. The new productivity tools in Outlook 2003 make it an even more valuable tool for the average user.

The Outlook client has become an invaluable filing cabinet for the average user and a way of listening to voicemails, reading faxes, and keeping up on industry news. More "road warriors" can be fully functional because of their ability to access the network remotely, but email and scheduling access are major requirements. Any change to the Exchange messaging environment has an impact on every user on the network, and many organizations worry more about an Exchange upgrade than an NOS.

With these added features comes complexity in how the Exchange environment is configured and how it integrates with the network as a whole. An organization can have multiple Exchange Mail servers, front-end servers to provide OWA access, bridgehead servers to connect sites, and conferencing and mobile information servers.

Exchange Server 2003 was designed to be very flexible in how it can be integrated with the existing messaging environment. Exchange 5.5, 2000, and 2003 can coexist, and Exchange Server 2003 can be installed on Windows 2000 Server (with some limitations) or Windows Server 2003. This flexibility requires a phased implementation that starts with creating a scope for the project (what's in, what's out), understanding the goals from a business standpoint and a technology standpoint, and creating a more detailed Statement of Work document. As the process moves forward, time should be spent on discovery of the existing environment and collaborative design sessions to agree on what the end result of the migration will be. After the design is documented and agreed on by the company executives and project stakeholders, a roadmap needs to be created to detail how to get from point A to point Z. A project schedule in the form of a Gantt Chart paints the high-level picture, and a Migration document tells the details of the resources required, the specifics of the tasks to be performed, and the risks involved.

After all this documentation, lab testing is essential to prove the conceptual design and train the project team on the new technologies and prepare any documents needed for the migration. Assuming no show-stoppers are encountered in the testing process, Exchange Server 2003 can be introduced to the production network on a pilot basis, with a handful of users with different needs. When this process is complete and any snags are resolved, the full migration can be performed, with a high level of confidence that no major problems will be encountered. Upon completion of the migration, maintenance procedures should be created to ensure that the new messaging ecosystem is optimized and tuned.

The process can be summarized by saying that a thorough understanding of the needs of the organization, an assessment of the current environment, and a structure design and testing process yield more successful results.

## Best Practices

This chapter focuses on the planning, prototype testing, migration, and deployment overview for a Microsoft Exchange 2003 implementation. The following are best practices from this chapter:

- An upgrade to Exchange 2003 should follow a process that keeps the project on schedule. Set up such a process with a four-phase approach, including initiation, planning, testing, and implementation.

- Documentation is important to keep track of plans, procedures, and schedules. Create some of the documentation that could be expected for an upgrade project, including a Statement of Work document, a Design document, a project schedule, and a Migration document.

- Key to the initiation phase is the definition of the scope of work. Create such a defi-nition, identifying the key goals of the project.

- Make sure that the goals of the project are not just IT goals, but also include goals and objectives of the organization and business units of the organization. This ensures that business needs are tied to the migration initiative, which can later be quantified to determine cost savings or tangible business process improvements.

- Set milestones in a project that can ensure that key steps are being achieved and the project is progressing at an acceptable rate. Review any drastic variation in attaining milestone tasks and timelines to determine whether the project should be modified or changed, or the plans reviewed.

- Allocate skilled or qualified resources that can help the organization to better achieve technical success and keep it on schedule. Failure to include qualified personnel can have a drastic impact on the overall success of the project.

- Identify risks and assumptions in a project to provide the project manager the ability to assess situations and proactive work and avoid actions that might cause project failures.

- Plan the design around what is best for the organization, and then create the migration process to take into account the existing configuration of the systems within the organization. Although understanding the existing environment is important to the success of the project, an implementation or migration project should not predetermine the actions of the organization based on the existing enterprise configuration.

- Ensure that key stakeholders are involved in the ultimate design of the Exchange 2003 implementation. Without stakeholder agreement on the design, the project might not be completed and approved.

- Document decisions made in the collaborative design sessions as well as in the migration planning process to ensure that key decisions are agreed upon and accepted by the participants of the process. Anyone with questions on the decisions can ask for clarification before the project begins rather than stopping the project midstream.

- Test assumptions and validate procedures in the prototype phase. Rather than learning for the first time in a production environment that a migration will fail because an Exchange database is corrupt or has inconsistencies, the entire process can be tested in a lab environment without impacting users.

- Test the process in a live production environment with a limited number of users in the prototype phase. Although key executives (such as the CIO, or IT Director) want to be part of the initial pilot phase, it is usually not recommended to take such high-visibility users in the first phase. The pilot phase should be with users that will accept an incident of lost email or inability to send or receive messages for a couple days while problems are worked out. In many cases, a pre-pilot phase could include the more tolerant users, with a formal pilot phase including insistent executives of the organization.

- Migrate, implement, or upgrade after all testing has been validated. The production process should be exactly that, a process that methodically follows procedures to implement or migrate mailboxes into the Exchange 2003 environment.

# CHAPTER 3

# Installing Exchange Server 2003

**IN THIS CHAPTER**

- Preparing for Implementation of Exchange 2003

- Preparing to Install Exchange 2003

- Conducting Preinstallation Checks on Exchange 2003

- Performing an Interactive Installation of Exchange Server 2003

- Performing a Scripted Installation of Exchange Server 2003

- Completing the Installation of Exchange 2003

- Performing Postinstallation Configurations

- Configuring Additional Server Services

- Testing the Exchange 2003 Installation

This chapter explains the basic installation of a new Exchange 2003 server. In this latest version of Exchange, Microsoft has taken a big step in improving the installation process to make it a lot more intuitive than previous versions of Exchange. The tools included on the installation CD walk you through the preinstallation tasks to verify the environment prior to installing the server.

When you execute `setup.exe`, you are not launched immediately into the installation program. You are taken through a step-by-step checklist of tasks prior to launching the setup executable.

This chapter does not present upgrading or migrating from previous versions of Exchange and other messaging platforms. You read about migrations in Chapters 14, "Migrating from NT4 to Windows Server 2003"; 15, "Migrating from Exchange 5.5 to Exchange Server 2003"; 16, "Migrating from Exchange 2000 to Exchange Server 2003; 34, "Migrating from Novell GroupWise to Exchange 2003"; and 35, "Migrating from Lotus Notes to Exchange 2003."

## Preparing for Implementation of Exchange 2003

Several tasks should be done prior to installing Exchange 2003. The choice of running Exchange 2003 on Windows 2000 or Windows 2003 affects the preinstallation steps that need to take place and the functionality of Exchange. Some tasks are optional, such as forest prep and domain prep (automatically done when setup is run), but most tasks are requirements that would stop the install process, such as having a Global Catalog available on the network or not having the NNTP service installed on the server where you are installing Exchange.

## Implementing Active Directory

Before you install Exchange Server 2003 on your network you need to make sure that Active Directory is properly deployed. The Active Directory infrastructure and DNS need to be healthy and without replication errors prior to installing your first Exchange 2003 server. It is so important to perform health checks and verification steps in your environment prior to installation that the Exchange development team has designed the installation program to include these steps. Exdeploy walks you through all the preinstallation health checks before running the setup program for Exchange 2003.

## Realizing the Impact of Windows on Exchange

Because Windows is the base infrastructure for Exchange 2003, take into account key factors prior to implementing Exchange:

- Global Catalog placement

- Windows Mixed versus Native Mode

- Group type used

- Extension of the forest schema

- Preparation of the Active Directory domain

## Global Catalog Placement

One item to review is the placement of Global Catalogs within the Active Directory site configuration. The importance of the Global Catalog server cannot be overstated. The Global Catalog is used for the address list that users see when they are addressing a message. If the Global Catalog server is not available, the recipient's address will not resolve when users address a message, and the message will immediately be returned to the sender.

One well-equipped Global Catalog server can support several Exchange 2003 servers on the same LAN segment. There should be at least one Global Catalog server in every Active Directory site that contains an Exchange 2003 server. For large sites, two Global Catalogs are much better and provide redundancy in the event the first Global Catalog server is unavailable.

For optimization, plan on having a Global Catalog server close to the clients to provide efficient address list access. Making all domain controller servers Global Catalog servers is recommended for an organization that has a single Active Directory domain model and a single site, and it's also not a bad idea for Active Directory designs that use a placeholder domain as the forest root with one or two first-level domains. A good Active Directory site design helps make efficient use of bandwidth in this design. This design helps reduce some of the overhead with multiple Global Catalogs in every Active Directory site.

The Active Directory Replication Monitor (ReplMon) can be used to help determine the number of Global Catalogs in the Active Directory forest. To start the Active Directory Replication Monitor, click Start, All Programs, Windows Support Tools, Command Prompt, and then run replmon.exe. Use the Edit menu to add a monitored server. When the server is displayed, right-click the server and select Show Global Catalog Servers in Enterprise.

> **TIP**
>
> To access the Windows 2003 support tools, install them from the Windows 2003 CD. Go to the original CD, select Support, Tools, and run the Suptools.msi installer, which installs the Windows 2003 support utilities into the \Program Files\Support Tools\ directory.

## Choosing Between Active Directory Mixed and Native Mode in Exchange 2003

If the domain that will host Exchange 2003 is or was in mixed mode, a message may be displayed during domain prep saying that the domain might possibly be insecure because of the Pre-Windows 2000 Compatible Access group. This is just a warning, and the installation of Exchange can proceed with just the understanding that Exchange may be insecure due to the current configuration of the domain.

Members of the Pre-Windows 2000 Compatible Access group will be able to see the members of groups that have their membership marked as hidden. In order to secure group membership, users and groups must be removed from this group before installing Exchange 2003. It is not necessary to resolve this security issue prior to installing Exchange 2003, because the removal of objects from this group can be done soon after Exchange 2003 has completed installation.

> **NOTE**
>
> Frequently, confusion occurs when Exchange implementers hear that Windows Active Directory must be in Native Mode for the organization to be able to implement Exchange 2003. That's not true. As covered in Chapter 15, during a migration from Exchange v5.5, if the destination domain is not in Native Mode, certain public folder group attributes are not migrated properly. Workarounds during a migration are covered in Chapter 15. However, for a clean installation of Exchange 2003, Exchange *can* be implemented in a Mixed Mode domain structure if that fits the needs of the organization.

## Selecting a Windows 2000/Windows 2003 Group Model

Groups can be a big issue in Exchange 2003, especially in multidomain Windows 2000 or Windows 2003 Active Directory environments. Exchange 2003 uses Windows 2000 groups in place of the distribution lists that were used in Exchange 5.5. Distribution lists in Exchange 5.5 have been replaced by distribution groups in Active Directory. A Windows 2000 or Windows 2003 distribution group is the same as an Exchange 5.5

distribution list except it cannot be assigned permissions on an access control list. This means the strategy to secure calendars, public folders, and resources in Exchange 5.5 has to be redesigned for Exchange 2003. There are two major issues with groups that architects and administrators need to be concerned about:

- Visibility

- Permissions

### Viewing Group Membership with Visibility

Visibility enables users to view the membership of the group. This is obviously an important requirement when sending an email to a group of users, because the users would like to see the list of recipients to whom they are sending the message.

Here is the way the group types affect visibility:

- **Domain Local**—Domain membership is not in the Global Catalog. Users in a domain can see the membership of domain local groups only from their own domain. They can see the group entry for domain local groups from other domains in the Global Address List (GAL), but they cannot see the members.

- **Global**—Domain membership is not in the Global Catalog. Users in a domain can see the membership of global groups only from their own domain. They can see the group entry for global groups from other domains in the Global Address List but they cannot see the members.

- **Universal**—Domain membership is in the Global Catalog. Users can see the membership of the group no matter where the group resides.

In a single domain model or a domain model that uses a placeholder for the forest root and just one first-level domain, this issue is fairly simple to solve. Any group model will work in this design as long as all mailbox-enabled users reside in the same domain. If the plan is to add more domains later, universal groups should be used because of their flexibility. Another option would be to use domain local groups and then convert them to universal groups after the additional domains are installed.

### Permissions

Security groups are required for assigning permissions to calendars, public folders, and resources. A security group type of domain local, global, or universal must be selected to control permissions on objects. Because controlling access to collaboration objects is essential, it's best to avoid distribution groups to reduce confusion for end-users and administrators. If the organization is supporting multiple mail platforms, it might be forced to support the distribution group as a representation of the foreign mail system's mailing list, but try to avoid using them for collections of Exchange 2003 users.

For full functionality, the best solution is to use universal security groups. This provides the ability to see group membership across all domains and to assign permissions to calendars, file shares, public folders, and other resources—all with the same group. In larger environments, there are some obvious challenges with using universal groups that are mostly political because of the segmentation of which group controls email, directory, and file resources.

The second challenge with universal security groups is that the Active Directory domain must be in native mode to support universal security groups. This means all DCs in the domain must be running Windows 2000 or Windows 2003 Active Directory and not Windows NT 4.0.

The last challenge with using universal security groups is that they incur a replication penalty. If the group membership changes for one user, the entire group is replicated to all DCs in the local domain and to all Global Catalogs in the forest. This usually does not make or break a design decision to use universal security groups, but architects need to keep it in mind if they have remote Global Catalogs across bandwidth-choked links. The way Active Directory handles group membership changes might change in future revisions of the product.

> **NOTE**
>
> The way Active Directory handles group membership changes could be a problem for organizations that use in-house applications or third-party applications that automatically rebuild Universal Security Group membership daily, depending on list size, rebuild frequency, and the number of lists.
>
> Although Active Directory in Windows 2000 had a practical limit of 5,000 users for a single group membership, Active Directory in Windows 2003 has extended that far beyond 5,000 users. If very large lists are required, you can choose to use nested lists and keep each individual list to a functionally limited basis.

## Extending the Active Directory Schema

The first step to the actual implementation of Exchange 2003 is to extend the Active Directory schema. The *schema* comprises the rules that apply to the directory and controls what type of information can be stored in the directory. It also describes how that information is stored in the directory—such as string, string length, integer, and so on. Exchange 2003 almost doubles the amount of attributes in the Active Directory schema.

Extending the schema is the easiest part of the installation, but it is also the place where many organizations make mistakes. To extend the Active Directory schema, use the /forestprep switch on setup.exe for Exchange 2003 or follow the steps outlined in the deployment tool. A few tips to note before extending the Active Directory schema:

- The schema must be extended on the server that holds the Schema Master FSMO role. By default, the first server installed in the forest contains the Schema Master; however, this role could have been moved to another server. To locate which server contains the Schema Master FSMO role, use the Active Directory Schema MMC snap-in, right-click the Active Directory Schema icon under the console root, and select Operations Master.

To use the Active Directory Schema MMC snap-in, the `adminpak.msi` file must be installed on the server. Use the `run` command and execute `adminpak.msi` to install the adminpak. After the adminpak is installed, open the MMC from the run prompt by executing MMC; then use the Add/Remove snap-in option from the Console menu to add the Active Directory Schema MMC snap-in.

- The account used to extend the schema must be a member of the schema admins group and domain admins or enterprise admins groups. The schema admins and enterprise admins groups are available only in the first domain in the forest. If the messaging group does not control the forest root domain, this process must be delegated to the group that does.

- A schema change forces a full replication of domain databases and Global catalog information in Active Directory. Many administrators are scared of full replications and have heard stories of bandwidth-saturated WAN links due to schema extensions. However, when a full replication occurs, the directory information is compressed before it is sent across the network. The actual amount of data sent across the wire will be approximately 15%–20% of the actual Active Directory database size.

For Windows NT 4.0 organizations still in the Active Directory planning stages, to get an approximate size of the Active Directory database size multiply the Windows NT 4.0 SAM database by a factor of 3. This is a good ballpark estimate to use for the database size that will be seen immediately after migration. To calculate the size after implementing Exchange 2003 and other new directory information, use the AdSizer tool from Microsoft, available at `http://www.microsoft.com/windowsserver2003/downloads/`.

## Preparing the Windows 2000 or Windows 2003 Domain

The second step in preparing to install Exchange 2003 is to prepare the Windows 2000 or Windows 2003 domain that will host the Exchange servers or mailbox-enabled users. To prepare the Windows 2000 or Windows 2003 domains, use the `/domainprep` switch on `setup.exe` for Exchange 2003 or follow the steps outlined in the deployment tool.

The account used to prepare the Windows 2000 or Windows 2003 domains must be a member of the domain admins group in the domain where the `/domainprep` command is being run. Running `domainprep` performs the following operations on the domain:

- Creates the global security group Exchange Domain Servers

- Creates the domain local security group Enterprise Exchange Servers

- Adds the Exchange Domain Servers group to Enterprise Exchange Servers group

- Grants appropriate rights to the domain controller used for the Recipient Update Service

For domains that will host mailbox-enabled users and not host Exchange servers, administrators have the choice of running domainprep or manually creating a Recipient Update Service for the domain in Exchange System Manager. If the domain will never host Exchange servers, the Recipient Update Service should be manually created. If the domain will eventually host Exchange servers, domainprep should be used.

# Preparing to Install Exchange 2003

After a solid Windows 2000/Windows 2003 infrastructure has been put in place, Exchange 2003 can be planned for implementation. The installation preparation process follows standard project methodology, which includes planning, prototype testing, implementing, and ongoing support.

## Planning Your Exchange 2003 Installation

Chapter 1, "Exchange Server 2003 Technology Primer," covers the differences between the Exchange 2003 Standard Edition and the Enterprise Edition, and why an organization would choose one version over the other for a server. Chapters 4, " Designing Exchange Server 2003 for a Small to Medium Network," and 5, " Designing an Enterprise Exchange Server 2003 Environment," of this book address the planning and design of an Exchange 2003 implementation for a small/medium versus a medium/large organization, respectively.

## Choosing to Install Exchange in Either a Test or Production Environment

When installing Exchange 2003 for the first time, the organization should make the decision whether the implementation will be exclusively a test environment implementation, or whether the test will be simply a preinstallation of a future production environment. It is typically suggested to have the first implementation of Exchange 2003 be one of building a completely isolated test environment.

Having a test environment isolates test functional errors so that if there are any problems in the testing phase, they will not be injected into the existing networking environment. Any decision to move forward or hold back the implementation of Exchange will not change the impact the decisions have for the organization.

Many times when an organization begins to install Exchange as if it is a test environment, it loads an evaluation copy of the Windows or Exchange license on a low-end hardware system. Then because it has so much success from the initial tests, the organization puts the system into a production environment. This creates a problem because the system is built on expiring licenses and substandard hardware. When committed to being solely a test environment, the results should be to rebuild from scratch, and not put the test environment into position as a full production configuration.

### Prototyping Your Exchange 2003 Installation

When the decision is made to build in a test or production environment, build Exchange 2003 in the expected environment. If the system will be solely a test configuration, the implementation of Exchange 2003 should be in an isolated lab. If the system will be used in production, the implementation of Exchange 2003 should be focused on building the appropriate best-practice server configuration, which will give the organization a better likelihood of a full production implementation success.

Some of the steps an organization should go through when considering to build a test Exchange environment include

- Building Exchange 2003 in a lab

- Testing email features and functions

- Verifying design configuration

- Testing failover and recovery

Much of the validation and testing should occur during the test process. It's a lot easier testing a disaster recovery rebuild of Exchange in an exclusively test environment than to test the recovery of an Exchange server for the first time during a very tense server rebuild and recovery process after a system crash. Additionally, this is a good time to test application compatibility, as covered in Chapter 17, "Compatibility Testing," before migrating to a full messaging environment and then testing to see whether a third-party fax, voicemail, or paging software will work with Exchange 2003.

Another item to test during the prototype testing phase is directory replication in a large multisite environment to ensure that the Global Catalog is being updated fast enough between sites. And of course, security is of concern for many organizations these days, and the appropriate level of security for the organization should be tested and validated. Many times the plan for securing mailbox or public folder access sounds great on paper, but when implemented, is too limiting for the average user to get functionality from the service. Slight adjustments in security levels help minimize user impact while strengthening existing security in the organization.

## Conducting Preinstallation Checks on Exchange 2003

When it comes to the actual installation of Exchange 2003, you can run setup manually or you can create an unattend file so that the install can be automated for a branch office with no technical staff at the site. There are also different configurations of Exchange, such as Mailbox Server, Public Folder Server, Front-end Server, Back-end Server, and Bridgehead Server. This section covers the preinstallation tasks prior to installing the first Exchange server in the environment.

There are some changes in the Exchange 2003 setup program when compared to Exchange 2000. These changes include identical schema files in the Active Directory connector and Exchange 2003 setup, meaning that the schema gets updated only once when using the ADC. Exchange 2003 also does not require full permissions at the organizational level when installing your second Exchange server. After the first Exchange server is installed, all subsequent servers can be installed with administrative group–level permissions instead of organizationwide permissions. The setup program will no longer contact the Schema FSMO Role holder, as it did with Exchange 2000 setup.

## Verifying Core Services Installation

When installing Exchange 2003 on a Windows 2000 SP3 server, you must make sure that IIS, NNTP, and SMTP are installed and running. This can be done by checking the services applet within administrative tools from the Start menu. The setup program looks for IIS, NNTP, and SMTP services before it begins the install and fails if they are not present. If you are installing on a Windows 2000 SP3 server, the Exchange 2003 setup program will automatically install and enable ASP.NET and .NET framework for you.

If you are installing Exchange Server 2003 on a Windows Server 2003 server, none of these services are enabled by default. You have to enable these services manually prior to running the Exchange 2003 setup program.

> **TIP**
>
> In a new server installation, only the required services are enabled by default. If you are upgrading a server to Exchange 2003, it will retain the services status of the server. We recommend checking services postinstallation and disabling those that you are not using (for example, POP3, IMAP, NNTP).

## Preparing the Forest

The forest prep process extends the Active Directory schema to include the Exchange 2003 classes and attributes required for the application to run. In order to run the forest prep process, you must have the following permissions by belonging to these groups: enterprise admins, schema admins, domain admins, and local administrator on the Exchange server. During the forest prep process, you assign an account that has full Exchange administrator rights to the organization object in Exchange 2003.

> **NOTE**
>
> Notice that you no longer have to enter an organization name for Exchange during the forest prep process. This is now entered only at the point of installation.

## Preparing the Domain

The domain prep process creates groups and permission within the Active Directory forest so that Exchange 2003 can modify user attributes. To run the domainprep setup parameter you must be a member of the domain admins and local administrator groups.

The groups that are created during this process are Exchange domain servers and Exchange enterprise servers. The Exchange domain servers group is a domain global security group and the Exchange enterprise servers group is a domain local security group.

### Reviewing All Log Files

Each of the utilities that you execute has some output in its respective log files. Review the log file after running each utility to ensure no errors are encountered.

## Performing an Interactive Installation of Exchange Server 2003

When installing Exchange Server 2003 for the first time in an environment, the easiest way to conduct the installation is to insert the Exchange 2003 CD and follow the step-by-step installation instructions. This section of the chapter focuses on the step-by-step installation of a basic Exchange Server 2003 server.

> **NOTE**
>
> For those who have installed previous versions of Exchange, the setup program now has a new switch that can be used during installation. Running setup with a /ChooseDC {dcname}, followed by the name of a domain controller, tells the setup program to look for a specific DC to write schema changes to or check for permissions and groups.

To install the first Exchange server in an organization using the interactive installation process of Exchange Server 2003, use the following steps:

1. Insert the Exchange 2003 CD (Standard or Enterprise).

2. Autorun should launch a splash screen with options for Resources and Deployment Tools. (If autorun does not work, select Start, Run. Then type **CDDrive:\setup.exe** and click OK.)

3. Click on Exchange Deployment Tools.

4. At the Deployment Tools welcome screen, click on Deploy the first Exchange 2003 Server.

5. Click on New Exchange 2003 installation.

6. Verify that your server has met all the operating system and Active Directory requirements. (Click on the reference link in the right column.)

7. Check that your server is running NNTP, SMTP, and World Wide Web Services. If you're running Windows 2003, you also need ASP.NET. (Check the reference link to the right of the window for details.)

8. Install the Windows 2003 Support Tools to use the preinstallation utilities (located on the Windows 2003 CD under \support\tools\).

9. Run `DCDiag` and view the log file output. Click on the reference link to the right for details. The syntax is

```
DCDiag /f: log file /s:domain controller
```

10. Run `NetDiag` and view the log file output in `netdiag.log`.

11. Click Run Forestprep Now.

12. Click Next.

13. Read the license agreement, and then click I Agree if you agree with the licensing. Click Next.

14. Click Next to accept the default administrator account.

15. Click Finish when the forest prep is done.

The next step is to run the domain prep on the domain that will hold the Exchange servers and user accounts. To prepare the domain, use the following steps:

1. Click Run Domainprep Now.

2. Click Next.

3. After reading the license agreement, click I Agree, and then click Next.

4. Click Next again.

5. Click Finish.

After the domain has been prepared, it's time to install the Exchange messaging system:

1. Run Setup Now.

2. Click Next.

3. Select I Agree after agreeing with the licensing requirements, and then click Next.

   In the Component Selection window, the default will be Typical for Microsoft Exchange, Install for Microsoft Exchange Messaging and Collaboration Services, and Install for Microsoft Exchange System Management Tools. The configuration screen should look something like Figure 3.1.

4. Click Next.

5. Select Create New Exchange Organization and click Next.

6. Type the Exchange organization name and click Next.

7. Select I Agree That I Have Read and Will Be Bound by the License Agreements for This Product.

8. Click Next.

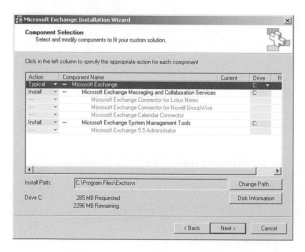

**FIGURE 3.1**   Component Selection screen for installation.

9. If you already created the admin group and routing group structure, you will be prompted to select where to install this server. Choose an administrative group and click Next. Then choose a routing group and click Next.

10. Review the Installation Summary and click Next.

11. If you are installing in a Mixed Mode domain, you will get a security warning. Click OK to the security group warning.

12. Click on Finish.

13. Click on OK if prompted to reboot.

> **NOTE**
>
> Before proceeding with the installation of other Exchange services, connect the server to the Internet and download and install the latest updates and service packs for Exchange 2003. Many features have been updated with Exchange 2003 Service Pack 1 and Service Pack 2 that require the installation of the service packs to be properly configured. Access updates and service packs at http://www.microsoft.com/exchange/downloads/2003/default.mspx.

# Performing a Scripted Installation of Exchange Server 2003

If you want to install Exchange with automation instead of manually choosing options, you can create an unattend file to run along with the setup program. This method is frequently used to script a standard series of configuration steps so that a script can be sent to branch offices, allowing local system administrators the option of installing the server onsite with minimal intervention.

## Creating the unattend Install File

To create an unattend installation file, use the following steps:

1. Insert the Exchange CD.

2. Close the autorun splash screen.

3. Click on Start and choose Run.

4. Type

   `cddrive:\setup.exe /createunattend drive:\filename.ini`

   supplying your drive and filename—for example:

   `F:\setup.exe /createunattend d:\e2kunattend.ini`

5. Click Next.

6. Select I Agree and click Next.

7. Select the Exchange components you want to install, change or keep the installation path, and click Next to continue.

8. Keep the default installation, type `create a new Exchange organization`, and click Next.

9. Type an organization name and click Next.

10. Choose I Agree on the license agreement page and click Next.

11. Review the installation summary and click Next to accept and continue.

12. You should get a window that says the unattend file was successfully created. Click Finish.

13. Review the unattend file that you created; it is an .ini file and is around 14KB.

## Running setup in Unattended Mode

After the script file has been created, execute the script file:

1. Insert the Exchange CD.

2. Close the autorun splash screen.

3. Click on Start and choose Run.

4. Type

   `cddrive:\setup.exe /unattendfile filename.ini`

   The setup program will run automatically with no input required. You will see the progress window as it runs through the installation process. When the install is complete, the installation wizard will close.

5. Verify that the installation was successful by looking in the Start menu programs and checking for Exchange services.

# Completing the Installation of Exchange 2003

After the first Exchange 2003 server has been installed, the Exchange environment will likely need to be customized to meet the needs and requirements of the organization. The custom options include

- Creating administrative groups

- Creating routing groups

- Creating storage groups

- Creating additional mailbox databases

- Creating a public folder store

## Creating Administrative Group and Routing Group Structure

By default, the Exchange installation program will create an administrative group and routing group called first administrative group and first routing group. If your company wants to create an administrative group structure prior to installing Exchange, it can do so by installing the Exchange System Manager and creating the group structure.

### Setting Administrative Views

To begin managing and administering the administrative groups and routing groups in Exchange 2003, Administrative Views needs to be configured. To enable Administrative Views, follow these steps:

1. Start the Exchange System Manager.

2. Right-click and select Properties on the Exchange organization.

3. On the properties page, select Display Routing Groups and Display Administrative Groups, as shown in Figure 3.2.

4. Click OK.

### Creating Administrative Groups

For a clean installation of Exchange, the organization is set up in a single administrative group. The Exchange administrator can create additional administrative groups to delegate the administration of the organization to other administrators. To create an additional administrative group, follow these steps:

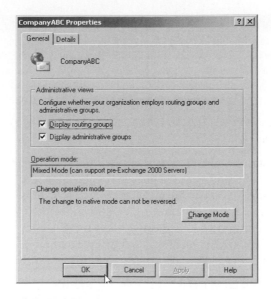

**FIGURE 3.2**    Enabling administrative views.

1. Start Exchange System Manager.

2. Right-click Administrative Groups and select New Administrative Group, as shown in Figure 3.3.

3. Type the name of the group and click OK.

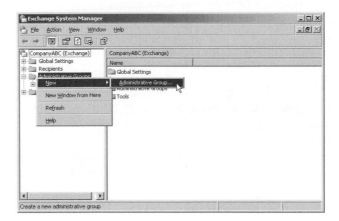

**FIGURE 3.3**    Adding an administrative group.

### Creating Routing Groups

The default installation of administrative groups is to create a single administrative boundary; routing groups also create a single boundary for mail delivery. Routing groups are created to control message flow. A routing group connector then connects routing groups. A new routing group is usually created when there is a transition in bandwidth, such as from a LAN to a WAN. Servers separated by a WAN link or highly saturated or unstable LAN link are usually contained in separate routing groups.

In every routing group one server is identified as the routing group master (RGM). This server is responsible for propagating link state information to other servers in the routing group. The RGM is responsible for tracking which servers are up or down in their own routing group and propagating that information to the RGM servers in other routing groups on the network. Only two states are tracked for the message link, which are up or down.

Routing groups also affect a client's connection to a public folder. When a client attempts to access a public folder, the client uses the copy of the folder on its home server if it exists. If the folder cannot be located on the home server, the client uses a copy in its home server's routing group. If a copy is not available in the local routing group, clients attempt to locate the folder in a remote routing group. The arbitrary cost assigned to the routing group connector by the administrator determines which routing group is selected first.

If the organization has only a single location, a complicated routing structure is unnecessary. However, routing groups can enable the Exchange administrator(s) to throttle the routing of messages between servers and sites. This may be done if an organization has a very low bandwidth between sites and wants to prevent large attachments from saturating the limited bandwidth between locations. Standard messages could be sent throughout the day; however, messages with large attachments can be delayed until the evening when bandwidth is more readily available.

To create an additional routing group, follow these steps:

1. Start Exchange System Manager.

2. Expand the administrative groups/administrative group name.

3. Right-click on Routing Groups, and then select New Routing Group, as shown in Figure 3.4.

4. Type the routing group name and click OK.

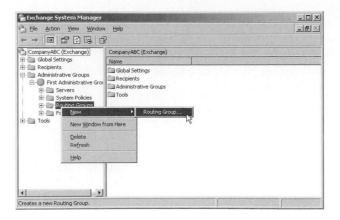

**FIGURE 3.4**   Adding a routing group.

---

**NOTE**

You can also rename any new administrative group you create and any of the routing group names after the first server is installed in your organization. To do so, right-click, select Properties, and choose Rename.

---

## Creating Storage Groups

Storage groups are collections of Exchange databases that the Exchange server manages with a separate process. Each storage group shares a set of transaction logs. Log files are not purged until the entire storage group has been backed up. All databases in the storage group are also subject to the Circular Logging setting on the storage group. Exchange 2003 Standard Edition supports a single storage group on a server, and a total of four storage groups are supported on each Exchange 2003 Enterprise Edition server.

---

**NOTE**

Circular logging is a process that can be enabled to save disk space by overwriting transaction logs. Enabling circular logging is dangerous because, in the event the database fails and has to be restored from tape, a replay of the information in the logs might not contain all the messages since the last backup. For data integrity and recovery reasons, Exchange administrators should never enable circular logging on the storage group. Instead, they should allocate sufficient disk space for the transaction logs and verify that a successful backup of the storage group is being performed each night. Running a *full* backup and then flagging the tape backup software to purge the log files is the best practice of ensuring that the database has been properly backed up and logs have been cleared.

---

As an administrator, you should create additional storage groups when

- **You can use separate physical transaction log drives to increase performance**—Putting an additional storage group on the same physical transaction log drive might actually reduce performance because of transaction log management and should be considered only if the first storage group is full.

- **You need to back up multiple databases simultaneously**—Databases are backed up at the storage group level. Using multiple storage groups allows simultaneous backups of each storage group.

- **The first storage group already has the maximum number of databases supported**—When another database is required on a server where the first storage group has the maximum number of supported databases, an additional storage group has to be created.

To create a new storage group, right-click the Exchange server in Exchange System Manager and select New, Storage Group. A set of options, as shown in Figure 3.5, is shown:

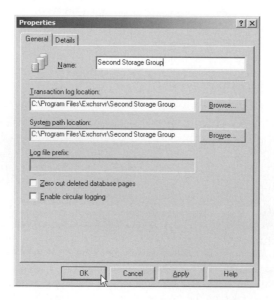

**FIGURE 3.5**    Options for creating a new storage group.

- **Name**—The name of the storage group appears in Exchange System Manager and Active Directory Users and Computers when managing users.

- **Transaction log location**—Put transaction logs on a different drive than the databases that will be part of this storage group; if the hard drive that the database is on crashes and you have to restore the database from tape, the logs are not affected by the database drive hardware failure. This method can improve data integrity and recoverability.

- **System path location**—The system path is the location of temporary files, such as the checkpoint file and reserve logs.

- **Log file prefix**—The log file prefix is assigned to each log file and is automatically assigned by the server.

- **Zero out deleted database pages**—This option clears deleted data from the drive, and although that process creates additional overhead, it also increases security.

- **Enable circular logging**—Never enable this setting. Make sure the backup jobs are completing successfully to prevent filling the transaction log drive.

## Managing Databases

Exchange 2003 Enterprise allows five databases per storage group. The number of databases can be any combination of public and private stores. Exchange 2003 stores data in two types of databases:

- **EDB**—Stores rich text messages and Internet Message headers.

- **STM**—Stores all MIME content. Stores audio, voice, and video as a stream of MIME data without conversion. This reduces the amount of space for storage and reduces the overhead on the server by not converting the data. Message bodies from the Internet messages are also stored in the STM database; the message header is converted to rich text format and stored in the EDB database.

A feature in Exchange 2003 mailbox and public store databases is full-text indexing. In earlier versions of Exchange, every folder and message was searched when users initiated a search. In Exchange 2003, the administrator can configure an index that is updated and rebuilt periodically. This enables fast searches for Outlook 2003, Outlook XP, and Outlook 2000 users. The following attachment types are also included in the index: doc, xls, ppt, html, htm, asp, txt, and eml (embedded MIME messages). Binary attachments are not included in the index. To initiate a full-text index, right-click the Mail or Public store and select Create Full Text Index.

## Creating Additional Mailbox Stores

New mailbox stores should be created when the size of the existing mailbox store is growing too large to manage. To create a new mailbox store, right-click the storage group and select New, Mailbox Store. When creating a new mailbox store, the options to configure appear as tabs, as shown in Figure 3.6:

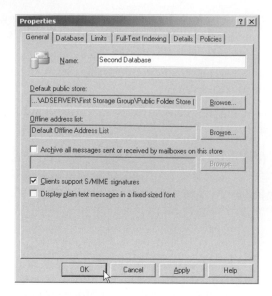

**FIGURE 3.6**    Options for creating a new database.

- **General**—Defines the database name, the offline address book to use, message archiving, whether digitally signed messages are allowed, and plain text display.

- **Database**—Sets the location for the EDB and STM databases. These should be stored on a hardware RAID 5 or 0+1 drive. Also controls the online database maintenance schedule.

- **Limits**—Configures the message storage limit at which users are warned that sending and receiving are prohibited. Also sets the deleted items and mailbox policy.

- **Full-Text Indexing**—Configures how often the full-text index is updated and rebuilt.

- **Details**—Notes any information about the configuration that is manually keyed in to this page by an administrator or Exchange Server manager.

- **Policies**—Defines the system mailbox store policies that apply to the mailbox store.

Three entries are listed below the mailbox store that can provide the administrator information regarding the status of the store:

- **Logons**—Last logon time, last access time, client type used to log on, and the Windows 2000 or Windows 2003 account that was used.

- **Mailboxes**—Number of items in the mailbox, mailbox size, and last logon and logoff time.

- **Full-Text Indexing**—Index information, such as location, size, state, number of documents, and the last build time.

### Creating a Public Folder Store

Unlike the mailbox store, new public stores should be created only when there is a need for a new public folder tree, because each public folder store needs to be associated with a public folder tree. Public folder trees can be created under the folders container in each storage group. Only one public store from each Exchange server can be associated with a public folder tree. To create a new public store, right-click the storage group and select New, Public Store. The majority of the tabs are identical to those of the mailbox store. The following are tabs that contain unique public folder store settings:

- **Replication**—Sets the replication schedule, interval, and size limit for public folder replication messages.

- **Limits**—Includes an age limit setting for the number of days for folder content to be valid.

The entries listed below the public folder store provide the administrator information regarding the status of the store:

- **Logons**—Last logon time, last access time, client type used to log on, and the Windows 2000 or Windows 2003 account that was used.

- **Public Folder Instances**—Information about folders that are being replicated to other servers.

- **Public Folders**—Folder size, number of items, creation date, and last access time.

- **Replication Status**—Replication status of each folder in the public folder store—for example, In Sync indicates that the folder is up to date.

- **Full-Text Indexing**—Index information, such as location, size, state, number of documents, and the last build time.

## Performing Postinstallation Configurations

After Exchange 2003 has been installed and customized, there are a few cleanup and implementation steps you should take:

- Disable unnecessary services.

- Remove information stores that won't be used.

- Set up routing group connections.

- Enable logging and message tracking.

- Delete mailbox and public folder stores.

## Disabling Services

Although Exchange 2003 does a much better job by not automatically installing dozens of different utilities and services the way previous versions of Exchange did, it still installs some default services that might not be used by the organization. For security and administration purposes, if a service is not used, it should be disabled. To disable services that are commonly unused—such as IMAP, POP3, NNTP, or SMTP—do the following:

1. Select Start, All Programs, Administrative Tools, Services.

2. Scroll down to the IMAP4 Service.

3. Double-click on the service.

4. Under the Startup Type section, choose Disabled.

5. Under the Service Status section, click Stop.

6. Repeat steps 1–5 for POP3, NNTP, and SMTP, as applicable.

> **NOTE**
>
> If IMAP, POP3, and NNTP are used on a server, such as a front-end system hosting remote mail users, those services should not be disabled. It's common on back-end servers where IMAP or POP3 is not used that the service could be disabled; it's also common for organizations that use Exchange just for email and do not need NNTP on any of their servers. For servers or systems that are not routing mail, such as those set up solely as Exchange System Manager administration servers, the SMTP service should be disabled.

## Removing Information Stores

By default, an information store that holds Exchange databases is created on each Exchange server installed in the organization. However, dedicated front-end servers that are just the Web front-end systems do not require information stores or databases. In those cases, the information stores should be deleted. To delete the information stores that are unneeded on front-end servers, follow these steps:

1. Select Start, All Programs, Microsoft Exchange, System Manager.

2. Navigate to Administrative Groups, Administrative Group Name, Servers, Server Name, Storage Groups.

3. Right-click on the mailbox store and choose Delete.

4. Click Yes.

5. Click OK and delete the database files manually.

> **CAUTION**
>
> Before deleting any database or information store, unless you are positive the database or information store is completely empty and unused, you might want to do a full backup of the database, store, and system—in case a user's mailbox was inadvertently hosted on the system. Sometimes during an early implementation of Exchange, an organization might start with just one or two servers in a pilot test environment. If a mailbox was stored on one of the test servers, it might eventually become the front-end server for the organization. Backing up a system is safer than making assumptions and regretting the decision later. Using the NTBackup utility covered in Chapter 31, "Backing Up the Exchange Server 2003 Environment," is a quick way to back up a system.

## Setting Up Routing Group Connectors

Routing group connectors should be used in situations where there is greater than 64KB of available bandwidth between the routing groups. If there is not sufficient bandwidth, SMTP or X.400 connectors should be used to connect the routing groups. Routing group and routing group connector designs should follow the organization's physical connectivity links. Four basic routing group connector strategies can be implemented based on the organization's physical network links:

- **Full Mesh**—In a full mesh all routing groups connect to all other routing groups. Unless there are only a few routing groups the administrative overhead for implementation becomes unbearable. This design can also be a waste of administrative resources if there isn't the WAN link redundancy to support the design.

- **Partial Mesh**—A partial mesh tries to create the benefits of a full mesh without the added administrative overhead. If the WAN design is a partial mesh, build the routing groups to follow the partial mesh.

- **Hub and Spoke**—In a hub-and-spoke design one routing group becomes the center of the universe and all other routing groups connect to it. In larger networks there can be multiple hubs in the enterprise, and the hubs are joined together in a full or partial mesh. This design is simple to implement and maintain but creates a single point of failure at the hub. This design is an option for locations that do not have any WAN link redundancy.

- **Linear**—In a linear design routing groups connect to only one other routing group in a straight line. Linear designs are not recommended.

To create a new routing group, follow these steps:

1. Navigate to Administrative Groups, Admin Group, Routing Groups, HO, as shown in Figure 3.7.

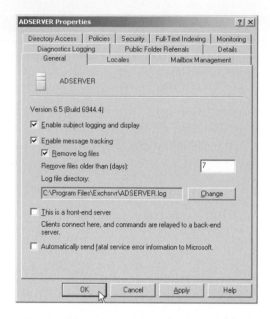

**FIGURE 3.7**    Traversing the Exchange System Manager for routing groups.

2. Right-click Connectors and choose New Routing Group Connector.

3. Type a name for the connector, as shown in Figure 3.8.

**FIGURE 3.8**    Routing group configuration screen.

4. Click These Servers Can Send Mail over the Connector, and click Add to choose a server or check Any Local Server Can Send Mail over the Connector.

   The General tab of the routing group connector defines a few significant items that administrators should understand when configuring the connector:

   • **Connect this routing group with**—Specifies the destination routing group for the RGC.

- **Cost**—Arbitrary cost assigned by the administrator, which can be used to control which connector is used first if multiple connectors exist.

- **Server**—Allows any server, or specifies specific servers allowed, to transfer mail to the destination routing group. By specifying specific servers, a bridgehead server is nominated. By specifying multiple servers, backup bridgehead servers are identified. The order of the servers in the list specifies which server is used first.

- **Do not allow public folder referrals**—Disables the user's ability to access public folder content that is homed in the routing group connected to that server.

5. Click on the Remote Bridgehead tab and click Add to choose a server. After entering the bridgehead server selection, you will see a screen similar to Figure 3.9.

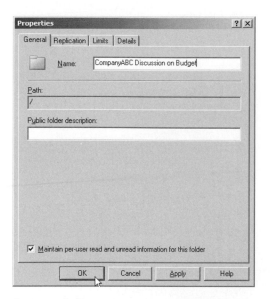

**FIGURE 3.9**    Bridgehead server configuration.

6. Click OK.

7. Select Yes to create a routing group connector in the remote routing group.

## Enabling Logging and Message Tracking

Logging and message tracking are common functions enabled by Exchange administrators early on in an Exchange implementation to help the administrator validate that messages are flowing through the environment. By enabling the logging and message tracking function, the administrator can then run a report to find out which route a message took to get from one server to another, and how long it took for the message to be transmitted.

Many administrators never use the logging and message tracking function and simply assume that messages are getting from point A to point B successfully. In many environments, although messages reach their destination, they are routed from one site to another and once around the globe before being received by a mail user in the same site facility. Misconfigured routing group connectors, DNS errors, or other networking problems are often the cause. So it's usually helpful to monitor messages to ensure that they are being routed and processed as expected.

To enable logging and message tracking, follow these steps:

1. Open Exchange System Manager.

2. Navigate to Administrative Groups, Admin Group, Servers, Server Name.

3. Right-click on the server object and choose Properties.

4. Select Enable Subject Logging and Display and Enable Message Tracking.

5. Type a number indicating days to keep the message-tracking log files, as shown in Figure 3.10.

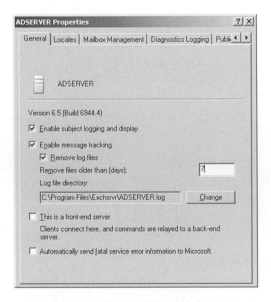

**FIGURE 3.10**    Configuring logging for message tracking.

## Dismounting and Deleting Public Folder Stores

Unused public folder stores should be removed for security and administration purposes. Frequently, organizations that separate mailbox servers from front-end servers from public folder servers do not need public folder databases on the front-end or mailbox servers.

To dismount and delete public folder stores, follow these steps:

1. Expand the servers and storage group.

2. Right-click the public folder store and choose Dismount.

3. Click Yes to dismount the store.

4. Right-click the public folder store and choose Delete.

5. Click Yes twice.

6. Click Yes to delete the store.

7. Select OK to the message that says you have to select another public folder store for the system folders and that public folder store will have to be dismounted and remounted for the changes to take effect.

8. Choose a new public folder store for this server's system folders.

9. Click OK. You have to manually delete the database files for the store by going to the mdbdata directory and deleting pub1.edb and pub1.stm.

10. Right-click the mailbox store and choose Dismount.

11. Click Yes to dismount the store.

12. Right-click the mailbox store and choose Delete.

13. Click Yes.

14. Click OK. You have to manually delete the database files again as previously stated.

---

**CAUTION**

Unless you are positive that the database or information store is empty, you should do a full backup of the database, store, and system, in case the public folder store hosted the authoritative copy of the public folder information.

---

## Using System Policies to Manage Mailbox and Public Stores

Many of the settings that can be manually set on each mail and public store can be set through a system policy to simplify the settings configuration. Standardizing Exchange Server settings in a large deployment was always tough for Exchange Server 5.5 because each setting had to be manually set on every server. With a system policy, the mail and public store settings for limits, deleted item retention, and so on can be set through the policy, and the policy can be applied to the stores. Each administrative group has its own set of policies for the stores. When a policy is applied, the setting that the policy overrides displays as grayed out on the mailbox or public store. Administrators have the choice of choosing which property pages for the mail or public store they want to configure policies.

To configure and apply a policy, follow these steps:

1. In the Exchange System Manager, in the Administrative Groups container, right-click on the administrative group you want to manage and select New, System Policies Container.

2. Right-click on the System Policies container and select New. Then select either Mailbox Policy, Public Store Policy, or Server Policy.

3. When a properties pages appears, enter a name you want to identify with this policy.

> **NOTE**
>
> Because the icon for the Mailbox or Public policies are the same, name the policy something descriptive to indicate it's a Mailbox or Public store policy.

4. Right-click the new policy and select Add Mailbox Store, Add Public Store, or Add Server, and then select the appropriate store or server. Click on OK to complete this task.

5. To force the policy to be applied immediately to all stores, right-click the policy and select Apply Now.

After the policy is created, it can be modified by right-clicking the policy and selecting Properties.

## Best Practices for Configuring Storage Groups and Databases

After configuring hundreds—if not thousands—of storage groups and databases in beta and production environments, the following best practices have been determined:

- Keep databases small to keep restore and maintenance intervals short. The database size is organization-specific and depends on the speed that maintenance and restores run on the server hardware and the organization's Service Level Agreements for messaging services.

- Choose to create additional databases before creating additional storage groups to avoid overhead on the server for log file management.

- Use no more than four databases per storage group. This will leave one database position open in each storage group for offline database maintenance.

- Do not use circular logging.

- Verify that a successful backup is performed every day and the logs have been purged.

- Use full backups every day if possible.

- Periodically verify the backup using an isolated lab.

- Leave online system maintenance on and stagger the database maintenance times so that all databases and storage groups aren't trying to run maintenance at the same time.

- Do not use the prohibit-send option when configuring storage limits as a courtesy to end-users.

- Keep deleted items for at least 7 days and deleted mailboxes for 30 days. Use the option to not remove the items permanently until the store is backed up.

## Delegating Administration in Exchange 2003

The delegation of permissions can occur at the organizational or administrative levels. There are three levels of permissions that exist in Exchange 2003:

- **Exchange Full Administrator**—This level enables the administrator to add, delete, modify, and rename objects, with the ability to change security permissions. These rights are granted to global messaging administrators and at the administrative group where boundary of control changes.

- **Exchange Administrator**—This administrator level offers the add, delete, modify, and rename objects permissions. However, this level cannot change security permissions. This level is usually the standard level granted to individuals who need to manage or administer Exchange on a regular basis.

- **Exchange View Only Administrator**—With this level, you can view the configuration settings in Exchange System Manager. This level is usually granted to administrators who provide operational support (reviewing logs, creating reports, validating connectivity, and message routing) and do not necessarily need to change settings or configurations directly.

It's easier to delegate administration to a group than to a user. To delegate administration, right-click the administrative group or organization and select Delegate Control to launch the Delegation Wizard. Select the group or user from the Active Directory Object Picker dialog box and set the Exchange administration role, as shown in Figure 3.11. Then click Next and Finish to apply the permissions throughout the Exchange organization.

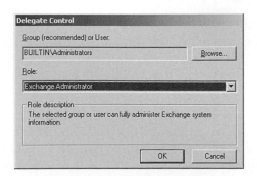

**FIGURE 3.11**    Delegating administration to an AD group.

# Configuring Additional Server Services

In addition to basic Exchange servers that host mailboxes for user email accounts, there are other Exchange Server 2003 services that can be configured:

- Bridgehead servers

- Front-end servers

- Public folder servers

- SMTP mail routing servers

## Installing a Bridgehead Server

A *bridgehead server* is a routing server that accepts mail from another server and then distributes the mail to the next server in the route. Similar to the hub-and-spoke system used by airlines to prevent having to fly nonstop flights to and from every single city around the world, the bridgehead server minimizes the site-to-site direct-traffic flow by focusing mail between bridgehead servers.

Many times administrators with high-speed WAN bandwidth question why they wouldn't just have all Exchange servers route mail directly to all other Exchange servers. An example gives the best explanation: If a manager in the United States sends a message with a 20MB attachment to managers in 10 different European offices, 200MB of mail is routed between continents. However, if the organization had a bridgehead server in the U.K., only one 20MB message, with attachment, would go between the U.S. and the U.K. Then the message would be distributed from the U.K. to the rest of the European sites. Even between local sites with a T1 line, the belief is that there is plenty of bandwidth between the sites and users can send any size email because it's a local office. So unless attachment restrictions are placed on servers, a user could send a 40MB attachment to dozens of offices, taking up hundreds of megabytes of bandwidth. A bridgehead server can consolidate bandwidth between an East Coast and West Coast connection, minimizing traffic across the country.

To configure a bridgehead server, from the Remote Bridgehead tab on the routing group connector Properties page, a target server can be specified that will receive messages in the destination routing group. Multiple servers can be specified, and connections to the server are attempted in the order of the servers listed in the remote bridgehead list.

The Delivery Restrictions, Content Restrictions, and Delivery Options tabs are used to control which users can send messages and of what type across the connection. The Delivery Options tab includes the option of scheduling large messages across a specific message route during a specific period of time. For example, large attachments from one site to another site that has a slow connection can schedule all attachments of a certain size to be transported later in the day or evening. Using this option for messages greater than a few megabytes on busy or slow links can keep mail flowing without clogging the link.

When the connector is configured, the administrator is then prompted to create a corresponding connector in the remote routing group. The administrator should keep this in mind when naming the connector, because automatically configured connectors in the remote routing group will use the same name as the connector configured in the local routing group.

Routing group connectors are not the only option for administrators to link routing groups. The SMTP and X.400 connectors also can be used for linking. Both connectors have a Connected Routing Groups tab that can be used to connect routing groups when bandwidth is limited or other services, such as encryption, are required.

## Enabling SSL for Services on Front-End Servers

You can enable most of the protocols on the front-end server from within the Exchange System Manager. To enable SSL for POP3, IMAP4, SMTP, and NNTP, use the following steps:

1. Open Exchange System Manager.

2. Navigate to Administrative Groups, Servers, Protocols.

3. Select a protocol and expand it.

4. Right-click on the protocol and choose Properties.

5. Click on the Access tab.

6. Under Secure Communications, click on Certificate.

7. Select Next.

8. Select Create a New Certificate and click Next.

9. If you have an internal Certificate Authority (CA), you can choose Send the Request Immediately to a CA; otherwise, choose Prepare Now and Send Later, and then click Next.

10. Type a name for the certificate, choose the bit length, and click Next.

11. Type the organization name and unit and then click Next.

12. Type a common name for the Web site or fully qualified DNS name.

13. Type the country, state, and city, and then click Next. (Do not use abbreviations.)

14. Type a path and filename for the CSR file and click Next.

15. Review the summary and click Next.

16. Click Finish.

If your organization uses a third-party certificate authority such as Verisign, Tharte, or others, send the CSR file created in the previous steps to the third-party certificate authority to have a valid certificate file created. After a certified file is issued by the third-party CA, do the following:

1. Open Exchange System Manager.

2. Navigate to Administrative Groups, Servers, Protocols.

3. Select a protocol and expand it.

4. Right-click on the protocol and choose Properties.

5. Click on the Access tab.

6. Under Secure Communications, click on Certificate, and then click Next.

7. Choose Process the Pending Request and Install the Certificate, and then click Next.

8. Click and browse to select the certificate file you received from the third-party CA, and click Next.

9. Review the summary of the certificate to verify that it is correct and click Next.

10. Click Next on the confirmation screen.

## Managing Public Folders

Public folders are collaboration objects in Microsoft Exchange that can be used to share information with a group of individuals in the organization, and are the basis of work-flow applications.

Public folders can be created either through the Outlook 2003, Outlook XP, or Outlook 2000 client or through Exchange System Manager. To create folders through the Exchange System Manager, locate the folders container in the administrative group. Right-click the default public folder tree and select New, Public Folder. The tabs, shown in Figure 3.12, are for the following:

- **General**—Contains the option of configuring an address list display name to be different from the folder name and whether folder content read and unread information is tracked for each user.

- **Replication**—Controls which public folder stores receive a copy of the folder and at what frequency the information is replicated.

- **Limits**—Configures the storage, deletion, and age limit settings. These settings can be inherited from the public store database settings or from a public store system policy.

- **Details**—Allows for the entry of administrative notes.

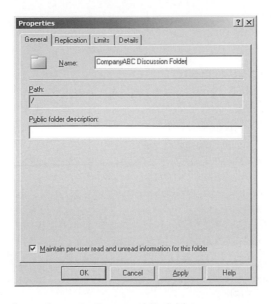

**FIGURE 3.12**   Tab options when creating a public folder.

To mail-enable the folder, right-click the folder in Exchange System Manager and select Mail Enable. After the folder is mail-enabled, right-click the folder and select Properties to view the following tabs:

- **Exchange General**—Displays the folder's alias and the public folder tree that contains the folder. Options also exist for Delivery Restrictions and Delivery Options, which are inherited from the Exchange organization.

- **Email Addresses**—Lists email addresses for the object, which are defined in the Recipient Policies from Exchange System Manager. This includes the SMTP, X.400 address, and addresses for other mail platforms.

- **Exchange Advanced**—Includes settings that control address list visibility and the custom attributes.

Folders can also be created in Outlook 2003, Outlook XP, or Outlook 2000 by accessing the Public Folders, All Public Folders container.

## Creating New Public Folder Trees

MAPI clients can use only the default public folder tree, so this process does not apply to organizations that use only the Outlook 2003, Outlook XP, or Outlook 2000 client. Only

Web-based clients can use other public folder trees. Organizations might want to consider creating a new public folder tree to support customized Web-based applications that use the Web store capabilities of the public store. Creating new public folder trees is a four-step process:

1. Create the tree.

2. Create a public store associated with the tree.

3. Link the tree with the public store by using the Associated Public Store dialog box when creating the store.

4. Mount the public store.

To create new public folder trees, use Exchange System Manager to locate the folders container in the administrative group. Right-click the folders container and select New, Public Folder Tree; enter the name of the folder tree. The second step is to create a public folder store by right-clicking a storage group and selecting New, Public Store. The third step is to use the Browse button to select the new public folder tree as the associated public folder tree when creating the public store. The final step is to mount the store. To mount the store, choose Yes when prompted to mount the store.

> **NOTE**
>
> To mount stores created on remote servers, Active Directory must complete replication of the store configuration information.

## Using Dedicated Public Folder Servers

Many Exchange 5.5 organizations used dedicated public folder servers to support their folder installations and keep the load of collaboration applications and repositories off their mail servers. This is still an acceptable practice; however, do not remove the private store from the dedicated public folder server if the organization plans to administer the public folder tree on the server from Exchange System Manager. To configure dedicated public folder servers, leave the mailbox store unpopulated or permanently dismount the mailbox store by marking the store with the Do Not Mount This Store at Start-up option on the Database tab of the mailbox store.

## Designing Public Folder Trees

The first level of the public folder tree is called top-level public folders. In most organizations, the top few levels of the public folder structure are designed with some hierarchy in mind. This is done to organize the information and also to control the replication of information across the network. It might not be efficient to replicate the entire public folder tree to every server in the organization if the information is needed in only certain areas of the company. Generally, the first few levels are designed with a department or geographic organization. Most Exchange administrators usually lock down the top-level folders to prevent the hierarchy from being corrupted by users. To lock down the top-level folders, set the following permissions:

1. Right-click the Public Folder tree under the folders container in the administrative group and select properties.

2. Click the Security tab.

3. Select the Everyone group.

4. Select the Deny option for the Create Top Level Public Folder permissions.

## Understanding Public Folder Replication

Public folder replication enables information that's created in one folder to be replicated to all other public stores configured on its Replication tab. Public folders operate in a multimaster replication hierarchy where every public store has a read and write copy of the folder. By default, a public folder inherits the replication schedule from the public store Replication tab or the public store system policy that is applied to the server.

Plan on spending some time developing the replication scheme for the public folder hierarchy. Not all information in the tree needs to replicate immediately. Exchange administrators should make sure that top-level folder administrators understand which folders replicate more quickly than others and should be used for time-sensitive information.

## System Folders

The Exchange system folders control many of the underlying components of the Exchange organization, such as storing the Offline Address Book and the public free and busy time information that users see when they create meeting requests. The Exchange system folders include EForms Registry, Events Root, Nntp Control Folder, Offline Address Book, Schedule+ Free Busy, StoreEvents, and System Configuration. Administrators might need to view information about the system folders when troubleshooting problems on the server. By default, the system folders are not displayed in Exchange System Manager. To view system folders, follow these steps:

1. Open Exchange System Manager.

2. In Exchange System Manager, expand the Folders container.

> **TIP**
>
> For Native Mode Exchange environments, use the Folders container under Administrative Group.

3. Right-click Public Folders.

4. Select View System Folders.

## SMTP Connectors and Virtual Servers

SMTP is the primary message routing protocol used in Exchange 2003 and is the backbone of many other services, such as OWA, POP3, and IMAP. Exchange 2003 uses the base SMTP service configuration provided by IIS and extends its functionality to link state routing, advanced queuing engine, and enhanced message categorization. Many of the features that are added to the base SMTP service are Exchange-specific commands.

Two basic components need to be configured for SMTP on the Exchange 2003 server: the SMTP Virtual Server and the SMTP Connector. The SMTP Virtual Server is used to define settings—such as the domain and authentication—for connections. Multiple SMTP virtual servers can be used on a physical server to support the needs of different groups in the organization. The purpose of the SMTP connector is to use SMTP to route external mail. The SMTP Connector is the replacement for the Internet Mail Service in Exchange 5.5. The connector defines how that mail is delivered and any restrictions on messages or connectivity that apply to the delivery.

### Creating SMTP Connectors

The following process assumes the connector is being installed to send messages to the Internet.

To install the SMTP connector, right-click the routing group's connectors container and select New, SMTP Connector. To configure the connector, use the following steps:

1. On the General tab enter a descriptive name for the connector, such as
   `SMTP(Internet)`.

2. Select the method to deliver the SMTP messages, either DNS or smart host. If you're using a smart host, it's better to use a hostname rather than an IP address; an IP address change in the organization will not cause mail routing to fail as long as DNS properly resolves the name to another IP address. If you're using IP addresses, they must be enclosed in brackets ([]). Multiple smart hosts can be entered but must be separated by semicolons (;) or commas (,).

3. Add a server in the local routing group as the local bridgehead. This will be the server responsible for delivering SMTP messages in this routing group.

4. Add an address space entry. If this connector will route all mail to the Internet, create an SMTP address entry and leave the default setting to send all addresses. If there are multiple connectors with the same address space entry, the cost can be modified to set one of the connectors to a higher or lower priority. The higher the cost, the lower the priority.

5. Set Connector Scope for Entire Organization or the routing group. If using Entire Organization, all servers in the organization can send messages through this connector.

6. Set the advanced settings for security if necessary. For sending mail to servers on the Internet, set the option for HELO instead of EHLO for ensured interoperability.

The General tab of the SMTP connector is configured to deliver SMTP mail to the Internet. The other tabs on the SMTP connector can be configured as needed, but most organizations leave the settings as the default when configuring connectors to send SMTP mail to the Internet.

### Creating SMTP Virtual Servers

In most Exchange organizations, it's not necessary to create additional SMTP virtual servers. Unless the organization is supporting multiple domain names that require different settings or POP3 and IMAP users that require secured SMTP relays, creating additional SMTP virtual servers is not necessary.

To create a new SMTP Virtual Server, right-click the SMTP protocol container and select New, SMTP Virtual Server. The wizard then prompts for the name of the virtual server and the IP address. It's best to use a descriptive name for the virtual server, such as the domain name (in this example, smtp.companyabc.com). Only IP addresses that have been configured on the server's LAN adapters appear in the IP address selection box.

The following tabs are available for the SMTP Virtual Server:

- **General**—The General tab can be used to limit the number of connections and the connection timeout and contains the IP address and port number combinations configured for the virtual server. When you're adding additional IP addresses, the Enable Filter option can be used to apply message filters that have been configured in the Message Delivery options under the Global container for the organization. Logging for the SMTP connection can also be enabled here.

- **Access**—The Access tab controls the Authentication mechanism in place and can be used to enable secure communication under the Certificate and Communication buttons. Connections and SMTP message relaying can also be controlled.

- **Messages**—The Messages tab controls the number of messages that can be transferred and the handling of nondelivery reports. A setting that's really helpful during mail migrations is the Forward All Mail with Unresolved Recipients to Host option, which enables mail for the same domain name to be delivered to another mail platform that may have been previously responsible for the SMTP domain name for the Exchange organization.

- **Delivery**—The Delivery tab configures outbound message retry intervals, authentication, DNS, and smart host configuration information.

## Securing SMTP Mail Relays

The Relay button on the Access tab of the SMTP Virtual Server is responsible for controlling the capability for remote hosts of relaying SMTP messages off the Exchange SMTP server. Open SMTP mail relays are a target for spammers, who use the open relay to send unsolicited email messages anonymously.

By default, SMTP message relaying is not enabled. Only the hosts specifically entered in the relay configuration can relay SMTP messages. By selecting the option All Except the

List Below, you open the relay to any server on the Internet. The check box Allow All Computers Which Successfully Authenticate to Relay is an override for the lists of hosts listed above the check box that are either allowed or not allowed to relay. This check box is selected by default and will allow POP3 and IMAP clients to relay SMTP messages off the server as long as they can authenticate.

To configure Outlook Express for authentication, use the Servers tab of the mail account and mark the check box under the Outgoing Mail Server for My Server Requires Authentication. The Settings button enables the user to enter a different account or use the same account as the Incoming Mail Server.

If the organization needs to support POP3 and IMAP users, the next step in configuring the SMTP relay is to select the authentication method under the Authentication button on the Access tab. If this SMTP virtual server will be used for all SMTP connections, the Anonymous Access selection should remain on. If only POP3 and IMAP users will use this virtual server, Anonymous Access should be disabled.

The most secure method to access the SMTP server over the Internet is to remove the Integrated Windows Authentication method and enable the check box for Requires TLS Encryption. In order to select Requires TLS Encryption, you must install a certificate on the server, which can be obtained through the Certificate button on the Access tab for the SMTP virtual server. After the certificate is installed, encryption can be required under the Communication button on the Access tab of the SMTP virtual server.

Select the Require Secure Channel check box under the Communication button if this server will be used to relay messages exclusively for POP3 and IMAP clients. If this server is receiving SMTP mail for the organization, connections will be rejected if they cannot support SSL.

In order to use TLS security for sending messages, the POP3 and IMAP clients need to support TLS or SSL. To configure Outlook Express for SSL, use the Advanced tab of the POP3 or IMAP mail account and select This Server Requires a Secure Connection (SSL).

# Testing the Exchange 2003 Installation

After Exchange 2003 has been installed and appears to be working, or at least nothing has reported an error that would indicate a problem with the installation, there are a few things that can be tested to validate the installation. Some of these steps involve actually setting up a test user, testing the sending and receiving of email from a test user, checking the flow of mail between servers, and checking to make sure the Outlook Web Access function is working properly.

## Creating a Mailbox

The easiest way to confirm whether Exchange is working properly is to create a mailbox and test sending and receiving email. To create a mailbox, use the following steps:

1. Click on Start, All Programs, Microsoft Exchange, Active Directory Users and Computers.

2. Right-click on the user account you want to create a mailbox for, select All Tasks, and then select Exchange Tasks.

3. At the Welcome to Exchange Tasks screen, click Next to bypass the welcome page. You can disable the welcome page by clicking on the box next to Do Not Show This Welcome Page Again.

4. Verify that Create Mailbox is highlighted and click Next.

5. Accept the default or type an alias name for the user, server name, and mailbox store name.

6. Click Next to continue.

7. Click Finish. (You can click on the box next to View detailed report when this wizard closes if you want to see the full report of the mailbox creation.)

## Testing Mail Flow Using OWA

Another test can involve whether the user can log on to Outlook Web Access. Successful OWA access validates that the Web services are working properly, that the front-end and back-end servers are communicating properly, and that the organization's firewall supports the passing of OWA traffic. To test mail flow using Outlook Web Access, follow these steps:

1. Open Internet Explorer and go to http://{*servername*}/exchange.

2. Log in as an Exchange user and send messages to another Exchange user.

3. Open a second Internet Explorer window and log in as the other Exchange user.

4. Verify that mail has been received by the second user.

5. Send a reply to the first user and confirm that the messages were successfully sent and received.

> **NOTE**
>
> More specific details on using Outlook Web Access is covered in Chapter 26, "Everything You Need to Know About Outlook Web Access (OWA) Client."

## Installing the Exchange System Manager

If you have an administrative machine and you want to install the Exchange System Manager on it to perform administrative tasks for Exchange, you can install the Exchange System Manager program locally.

> **NOTE**
>
> When installing the Exchange System Manager only, you still are required to have the IIS SMTP and NNTP service installed on your PC. However, for a standalone administration system, the IIS, SMTP, and NNTP services are not required after installation and should be disabled after the installation is complete.

To install the Exchange System Manager program, follow these steps:

1. Insert the Exchange 2003 CD (Standard or Enterprise).

2. Autorun should launch a splash screen with options for Resources and Deployment Tools. (If autorun does not work, select Start, Run. Then type **CDDrive:\setup.exe** and click OK.)

3. Click on Exchange Deployment Tools.

4. At the Deployment Tools welcome screen, click on Install Exchange System Management Tools only.

5. Review the prerequisite options, and when you comply with the initial configuration, click on Run Setup now.

6. Click Next.

7. Review the license agreement, and when in agreement, select I Agree, and then click Next.

8. In the component selection window, confirm that the Microsoft Exchange System Management tools option has been selected.

9. Click Next to begin the installation of the tools.

10. Click Finish when done.

# Summary

Microsoft has simplified the process for installing the Exchange Server product, and Exchange Server 2003 is the easiest-to-install Exchange version to date. As with any simplified installation process, however, it's important to understand the steps leading to a successful installation so that any appropriate planning or preparation is done prior to the live installation. Additionally, because Exchange Server 2003 includes many new functions that extend beyond basic email messaging and calendaring, getting the first Exchange 2003 server installed properly sets the foundation for a successful enterprise rollout of the Exchange messaging system.

# Best Practices

The following are best practices from this chapter:

- Review Chapter 1 to understand the common reasons organizations plan and deploy the Exchange 2003 messaging system.

- Leverage the planning and design details in Chapters 4 and 5 of this book to prepare the business for an appropriate messaging system design and configuration.

- The easiest way to install the first Exchange 2003 server in a new environment is to follow the interactive installation process initiated by an autorun automatic load from the Exchange Server 2003 CD.

- For an organization that will be installing many Exchange servers and wants to ensure an identical build between servers, creating an unattended installation script can ensure that a common installation process is followed.

- After installing Exchange 2003, consider locking down services that may not be needed—such as POP3, IMAP, and the like—which can improve security on the Exchange server.

- Create additional Exchange databases when the database file size begins to reach 15–20GB, to keep data backup, maintenance, and recovery to a more manageable level.

- Use system policies to minimize the effort it takes to manage servers individually when a single change in a group policy can automatically make changes on all servers simultaneously.

- Use a bridgehead server to minimize the traffic between site boundaries that can be better served by managed message transmission and routing.

- SMTP relaying should be enabled only when absolutely necessary, and when enabled should be properly locked down. This prevents spammers from gaining unauthorized access to relay spam messages.

# PART II

# Exchange Server 2003

## IN THIS CHAPTER

CHAPTER 4    Designing Exchange Server 2003 for
             a Small to Medium Network          113

CHAPTER 5    Designing an Enterprise Exchange
             Server 2003 Environment            135

CHAPTER 6    Integrating Exchange Server 2003
             in a Non-Windows Environment       163

# Designing Exchange Server 2003 for a Small to Medium Network

**IN THIS CHAPTER**

- Formulating a Successful Design Strategy

- Getting the Most Out of Exchange Server 2003 Functionality

- Understanding Active Directory Design Concepts for Exchange Server 2003

- Determining Exchange Server 2003 Placement

- Configuring Exchange Server 2003 for Maximum Performance and Reliability

- Securing and Maintaining an Exchange Server 2003 Implementation

## Formulating a Successful Design Strategy

The fundamental capabilities of Exchange Server 2003 are impressive. Improvements to security, reliability, and scalability enhance an already road-tested and stable Exchange platform. Along with these impressive credentials comes an equally impressive design task. Proper design of an Exchange Server 2003 platform will do more than practically anything to reduce headaches and support calls in the future. Many complexities of Exchange may seem daunting, but with a proper understanding of the fundamental components and improvements, the task of designing the Exchange Server 2003 environment becomes manageable.

This chapter focuses specifically on the Exchange Server 2003 components required for design. Key decision-making factors influencing design are presented and tied into overall strategy. All critical pieces of information required to design Exchange Server 2003 implementations are outlined and explained.

## Getting the Most Out of Exchange Server 2003 Functionality

Designing Exchange Server used to be a fairly simple task. When an organization needed email and the decision was made to go with Exchange Server, the only real decision to make was how many Exchange servers were needed. Primarily, organizations really needed only email and eschewed any "bells and whistles."

Exchange Server 2003, on the other hand, takes messaging to a whole new level. No longer do organizations require only an email system, but other messaging functionality as well. After the productivity capabilities of an enterprise email platform have been demonstrated, the need for more productivity improvements arises. Consequently, it is wise to understand the integral design components of Exchange before beginning a design project.

## Outlining Significant Changes in Exchange Server 2003

There have been two major areas of improvement in Exchange Server 2003. The first is in the realm of user access and connectivity. The needs of many organizations have changed and they are no longer content with slow remote access to email and limited functionality when on the road. Consequently, many of the improvements in Exchange focus on various approaches to email access and connectivity. The improvements in this group focus on the following areas:

- **Outlook Web Access (OWA)**—The Outlook Web Access (OWA) client is now almost completely different from the one that debuted in Exchange 5.5. Improvements over the Exchange 2000 OWA client are also impressive, with support for nearly all functionality that exists in the standard Outlook client. In fact, from first glance, there are few distinguishable differences between the two clients.

- **Outlook Mobile Access (OMA)**—Outlook Mobile Access (OMA) was developed to fill the vast, growing niche of mobile phone, pager, and PDA Internet access to email. Because the screen sizes on these clients are much smaller and the connection requirements so different, a mail client more suited for these conditions was created. OMA simplifies and streamlines Exchange mail access from these clients and adds an additional access option to Exchange.

- **Outlook 2003 Offline Improvements**—One major improvement in client access for Exchange 2000 comes in the form of improvements to the "heavy" Outlook client. In addition to improved MAPI compression, Outlook 2003 dramatically improves offline and slow-link connections to make it more feasible to access Exchange from remote locations. In addition, the concept of "RPC over HTTP" enables Outlook 2003 access to Exchange data across the HTTP or HTTPS ports, reducing the need for cumbersome VPN connections.

The second major area of improvement in Exchange Server 2003 has been in the area of back-end improvements. End-users are not aware of these improvements, but they make the Exchange Administrator's job much easier. These improvements include the following:

- **New Deployment Tools**—One of the major problems that Microsoft had with Exchange 2000 was the steep learning curve associated with its deployment. In general, Microsoft products had always been easy to set up, with wizards showing the way. With Exchange 2000, however, the complexity of deployment required command-line `forestprep` and `domainprep` commands; manual Active Directory Connector ADC setup; and confusing concepts, such as Config_CAs, the Site Replication Service, and schema extensions. With Exchange Server 2003, all of these requirements are still present, but the means with which they are accomplished have been streamlined. A step-by-step process known as the Exchange Deployment Wizard leads an administrator through the installation process, reducing the potential for error or major directory issues.

- **Administrative Tool Improvements**—The development team for Exchange Server 2003 listened to Exchange administrator feedback and drastically improved the functionality and capabilities of the Exchange System Manager administrative toolset. Enhanced queue viewing capabilities, move mailbox tool enhancements, dynamic distribution list functionality, and the ability to run Exchange System Manager on Windows XP have greatly simplified the job of the Exchange Administrator.

- **Database Backup and Restore Capabilities**—The overall backup and restore functionality of Exchange has been improved in Exchange Server 2003. New Enhancements, such as the Volume Shadow Copy Service, the Mailbox Recovery Center, and the Recovery Storage Group concept, help position Exchange Server 2003 for simplified and enhanced backup and restore capabilities.

It is important to incorporate the concepts of these improvements into any Exchange design project, because their principles often drive the design process.

## Reviewing Exchange and Operating System Requirements

Exchange Server 2003 has some specific requirements, both hardware and software, that must be taken into account when designing. These requirements fall into several categories:

- Hardware requirements
- Operating system
- Active Directory
- Exchange version

Each requirement must be addressed before Exchange Server 2003 can be deployed.

### Reviewing Hardware Requirements

It is important to design Exchange hardware to scale out to the user load, which is expected for up to three years from the date of implementation. This helps retain the value of the investment put into Exchange. Specific hardware configuration advice is offered in later sections of this chapter.

### Reviewing Operating System Requirements

Exchange Server 2003 is optimized for installation on Windows Server 2003. The increases in security and the fundamental changes to Internet Information Services (IIS) in Windows Server 2003 provide the basis for many of the improvements in Exchange Server 2003. That said, Exchange Server 2003 also can be installed on Windows 2000. The specific compatibility matrix, which indicates compatibility between Exchange versions and operating systems, is illustrated in Table 4.1.

**TABLE 4.1**    Exchange Version Compatibility

| Version | Windows NT 4.0 | Windows 2000 | Windows 2003 |
|---|---|---|---|
| Exchange 5.5 | Yes | Yes | No |
| Exchange 2000 | No | Yes | No |
| Exchange 2003 | No | Yes | Yes |

### Understanding Active Directory Requirements

Exchange originally maintained its own directory. With the advent of Exchange 2000, however, the directory for Exchange was moved to the Microsoft Active Directory, the enterprise directory system for Windows. This gave greater flexibility and consolidated directories, but at the same time increased the complexity and dependencies for Exchange. Exchange Server 2003 uses the same model, with either Windows 2000 or Windows Server 2003 Active Directory as its directory component.

> **NOTE**
>
> Active Directory is loosely modeled on the original Exchange 5.5 Directory. Administrators familiar with the Exchange 5.5 Directory will notice similarities between the environments, particularly in the replication engines.

### Outlining Exchange Version Requirements

As with previous versions of Exchange, there are separate Enterprise and Standard versions of the Exchange Server 2003 product. The Standard version supports all Exchange Server 2003 functionality with the exception of the following key components:

- **Greater than 75GB Mailbox Store**—The Service Pack 2 standard version of Exchange Server 2003 can support only a single database of up to 75GB in size. Pre-SP2 Standard Exchange only supported up to 16GB databases. Organizations with small numbers of users or strict storage limits can use this version of Exchange without problems.

> **NOTE**
>
> There is no direct upgrade path from the Exchange Standard version to the Enterprise version. Only a mailbox migration procedure that can transfer mailboxes from a Standard version server to an Enterprise version server will be able to accomplish an upgrade. Consequently, it is

important to make an accurate determination of whether the Enterprise version of the software is needed.

---

- **Multiple Mailbox Database Stores**—One of the key features of Exchange Server 2003 is the capability of the server to support multiple databases and storage groups with the Enterprise version of the software. This capability is not supported with the Standard version of the product.

- **Clustering Support**—Exchange Server 2003 clustering is available only when using the Enterprise version of the software. Support for up to an 8-way active-active or active-passive cluster on Windows Server 2003 is available. Microsoft recommends at least one passive node per cluster.

- **X.400 Connectors**—Although becoming increasingly less common, the ability to install and configure X.400 Connectors for remote site connectivity is available only in the Enterprise version of the software.

## Scaling Exchange Server 2003

The days of the Exchange server "rabbit farm" are gone. No longer is it necessary to set up multiple Exchange server implementations across an organization. Exchange 2000 originally provided the basis for servers that could easily scale out to thousands of users in a single site, if necessary. Exchange Server 2003 enables even more users to be placed on fewer servers through the concept of site consolidation.

Site consolidation enables organizations that might have previously deployed Exchange servers in remote locations to have those clients access their mailboxes across WAN links or dial-up connections by using the enhanced Outlook 2003 or Outlook Web Access clients. This solves the problem that previously existed of having to deploy Exchange servers and Global Catalog (GC) servers in remote locations, with only a handful of users, and greatly reduces the infrastructure costs of setting up Exchange.

## Having Exchange Server 2003 Coexist with an Existing Network Infrastructure

Exchange is built upon a standards-based model, which incorporates many industry-wide compatible protocols and services. Internet standards—such as DNS, IMAP, SMTP, LDAP, and POP3—are built in to the product to provide coexistence with existing network infrastructure.

In a design scenario, it is necessary to identify any systems that require access to email data or services. For example, it might be necessary to enable a third-party monitoring application to relay mail-off of the SMTP engine of Exchange so that alerts can be sent. Identifying these needs during the design portion of a project is subsequently important.

### Identifying Third-Party Product Functionality

Microsoft built specific hooks into Exchange Server 2003 to enable third-party applications to improve upon the built-in functionality provided by the system. For example, built-in support for antivirus scanning, backups, and spam filtering exist right out of the box, although functionality is limited without the addition of third-party software. The most common additions to Exchange implementation are

- Antivirus

- Backup

- Spam filtering

- Fax software

# Understanding Active Directory Design Concepts for Exchange Server 2003

After all objectives, dependencies, and requirements have been mapped out, the process of designing the Exchange Server 2003 environment can begin. There are several key areas where decisions should be made:

- Active Directory design

- Exchange Server placement

- Global Catalog placement

- Client access methods

### Understanding the Active Directory Forest

Because Exchange Server 2003 relies on the Windows Server 2003 Active Directory for its directory, it is subsequently important to include Active Directory in the design plans. In many situations, an Active Directory implementation, whether based on Windows 2000 or Windows Server 2003, already exists in the organization. In these cases, it is necessary only to plan for the inclusion of Exchange Server into the forest.

If an Active Directory structure is not already in place, a new AD forest must be established. Designing the Active Directory forest infrastructure can be complex, and can require nearly as much thought into design as the actual Exchange Server configuration itself. Subsequently, it is important to understand fully the concepts behind Active Directory before beginning an Exchange 2003 design.

In short, a single "instance" of Active Directory consists of a single Active Directory forest. A forest is composed of Active Directory trees, which are contiguous domain namespaces in the forest. Each tree is composed of one or more domains, as illustrated in Figure 4.1.

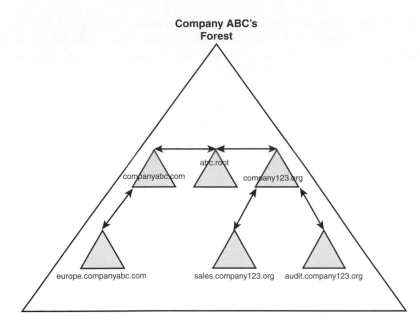

**FIGURE 4.1**    Multi-tree forest design.

Certain cases exist for using more than one Active Directory forest in an organization:

- **Political Limitations**—Some organizations have specific political reasons that force the creation of multiple Active Directory forests. For example, if a merged corporate entity required separate divisions to maintain completely separate IT infrastructures, more than one forest would be necessary.

- **Security Concerns**—Although the Active Directory domain serves as a de facto security boundary, the "ultimate" security boundary is effectively the forest. In other words, it is possible for user accounts in a domain in a forest to hack into domains within the same forest. Although these types of vulnerabilities are not common and are difficult to do, highly security-conscious organizations should implement separate AD forests.

- **Application Functionality**—A single Active Directory forest shares a common directory schema, which is the underlying structure of the directory and must be unique across the entire forest. In some cases, separate branches of an organization require that certain applications, which need extensions to the schema, be installed. This might not be possible or might conflict with the schema requirements of other branches. These cases might require the creation of a separate forest.

- **Exchange-Specific Functionality**—In certain circumstances, it might be necessary to install Exchange Server 2003 into a separate forest, to enable Exchange to reside in a separate schema and forest instance. An example of this type of setup would be an organization with two existing Active Directory forests that creates a third forest specifically for Exchange and uses cross-forest trusts to assign mailbox permissions.

The simplest designs often work the best. The same principle applies to Active Directory design. The designer should start with the assumption that a simple forest and domain structure will work for the environment. However, when factors such as those previously described create constraints, multiple forests can be established to satisfy the requirements of the constraints.

## Understanding the Active Directory Domain Structure

After the Active Directory forest structure has been laid out, the domain structure can be contemplated. As with the forest structure, it is often wise to consider a single domain model for the Exchange Server 2003 directory. In fact, if deploying Exchange is the only consideration, this is often the best choice.

There is one major exception to the single domain model: the placeholder domain model. The placeholder domain model has an isolated domain serving as the root domain in the forest. The user domain, which contains all production user accounts, would be located in a separate domain in the forest, as illustrated in Figure 4.2.

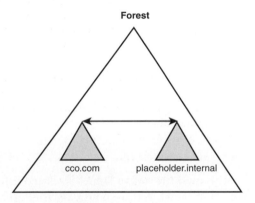

**FIGURE 4.2**    The placeholder domain model.

The placeholder domain structure increases security in the forest by segregating high-level schema-access accounts into a completely separate domain from the regular user domain. Access to the placeholder domain can be audited and restricted to maintain tighter control on the critical schema. The downside to this model, however, is the fact that the additional domain requires a separate set of domain controllers, which increases the infrastructure costs of the environment. In general, this makes this domain model less desirable for smaller organizations, because the tradeoff between increased cost and less security is too great. Larger organizations can consider the increased security provided by this model, however.

## Reviewing Active Directory Infrastructure Components

There are several key components of Active Directory that must be installed within an organization to ensure proper Exchange Server 2003 and Active Directory functionality. In smaller environments, many of these components can be installed on a single machine, but all need to be located within an environment to ensure server functionality.

### Outlining the Domain Name Service (DNS) Impact on Exchange Server 2003 Design

In addition to being tightly integrated with Active Directory, Exchange Server 2003 is joined with the Domain Name Server (DNS). DNS serves as the lookup agent for Exchange Server 2003, Active Directory, and most new Microsoft applications and services. DNS translates common names into computer-recognizable IP addresses. For example, the name www.cco.com translates into the IP address of 12.155.166.151. Active Directory and Exchange Server 2003 require that at least one DNS server be made available so that name resolution properly occurs.

Given the dependency that both Exchange Server 2003 and Active Directory have on DNS, it is an extremely important design element. For an in-depth look at DNS and its role in Exchange Server 2003, see Chapter 7, "Domain Name System Impact on Exchange Server 2003."

### Reviewing DNS Namespace Considerations for Exchange

Given Exchange Server 2003's dependency on DNS, a common DNS namespace must be chosen for the Active Directory structure to reside in. In multiple tree domain models, this could be composed of several DNS trees, but in small organization setups, this normally means choosing a single DNS namespace for the AD domain.

There is a great deal of confusion between the DNS namespace in which Active Directory resides, and the email DNS namespace in which mail is delivered. Although they are often the same, in many cases there are differences between the two namespaces. For example, CompanyABC's Active Directory structure is composed of a single domain named companyabc.internal, and the email domain to which mail is delivered is companyabc.com. The separate namespace, in this case, was created to reduce the security vulnerability of maintaining the same DNS namespace both internally and externally (published to the Internet).

For simplicity, CompanyABC could have chosen companyabc.com as its Active Directory namespace. This choice increases the simplicity of the environment by making the Active Directory login User Principal Name (UPN) and the email address the same. For example, the user Pete Handley is pete@companyabc.com for login, and pete@companyabc.com for email. This option is the choice for many organizations, because the need for user simplicity often trumps the higher security.

### Outlining Global Catalog Caching and GC/DC Placement

Because all Exchange directory lookups use Active Directory, it is vital that the essential Active Directory Global Catalog information is made available to each Exchange server in the organization. For many small offices with a single site, this simply means that it is important to have a full Global Catalog server available in the main site.

Recall that the Global Catalog is an index of the Active Directory database that contains a partial copy of its contents. All objects within the AD tree are referenced within the Global Catalog, which enables users to search for objects located in other domains. Every attribute of each object is not replicated to the Global Catalogs, only those attributes that are commonly used in search operations, such as first name and last name. Exchange Server 2003 uses the Global Catalog for the email-based lookups of names, email addresses, and other mail-related attributes.

Windows Server 2003 domain controllers and sites enable the concept of Universal Group Membership Caching, which enables a standard (non–Global Catalog) domain controller to cache the membership of commonly referenced universal groups in the organization. Because this is one of the most common types of objects that are looked up using the Global Catalog, the addition of this functionality enables the placement of domain controllers in remote sites without a local Global Catalog, as illustrated in Figure 4.3.

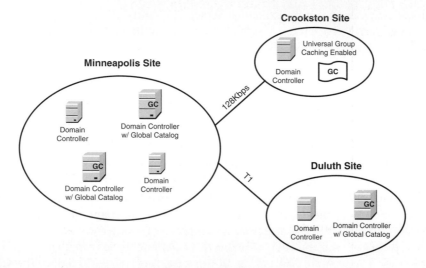

**FIGURE 4.3**    Global Catalog and domain controller placement.

Because full Global Catalog replication can consume more bandwidth than standard domain controller replication, it is important to design a site structure to reflect the available WAN link capacity. If a sufficient amount of capacity is available, a full Global Catalog server can be deployed. If, however, capacity is limited, universal group membership caching can be enabled to reduce the bandwidth load.

---
**NOTE**

It is critical to note that Universal Group Caching can be useful to reduce replication latency and speed logins, but that Exchange Server still requires the use of a full Global Catalog server to be locally available to the clients. For this reason, Universal Group Caching does not provide many benefits from an Exchange design perspective.

---

## Understanding Multiple Forests Design Concepts Using Microsoft Identity Integration Server 2003

Microsoft Identity Integration Server 2003 enables out-of-the-box replication of objects between two separate Active Directory forests. This concept becomes important for organizations with multiple Exchange implementations that want a common Global Address List for the company. Previous iterations of MIIS required an in-depth knowledge of scripting to be able to synchronize objects between two forests. MIIS 2003, on the other hand, includes built-in scripts that can establish replication between two Exchange Server 2003 AD forests, making integration between forests easier.

> **NOTE**
>
> The built-in scripts in MIIS 2003 enable synchronization only between two forests that have a full Exchange Server 2003 schema. In other words, if synchronization between an Exchange 2000 forest or an Exchange 5.5 directory is required, customized scripts must be developed.

# Determining Exchange Server 2003 Placement

Previous versions of Exchange essentially forced many organizations into deploying servers in sites with greater than a dozen or so users. With the concept of site consolidation in Exchange Server 2003, however, smaller numbers of Exchange servers can service clients in multiple locations, even if they are separated by slow WAN links. For small and medium-sized organizations, this essentially means that one or two servers should suffice for the needs of the organization, with few exceptions. Larger organizations require a larger number of Exchange servers, depending on the number of sites and users. Designing Exchange Server 2003 placement must take into account both administrative group and routing group structure.

## Designing Administrative Groups

An Exchange Server 2003 administrative group is a logical assortment of Exchange Servers that are administered by the same IT team. A single administrative group can encompass multiple physical locations, depending on the administrative requirements of the organization. For example, in Figure 4.4, CompanyABC has two administrative groups, one for the IT team in North America, and one for the team in Europe.

Administrative groups enable the simple delegation of granular administrative rights to specific groups. In CompanyABC's case, this means that specific rights can be granted to the IT team in Europe to administer only European servers, and not North American servers—and vice versa.

> **TIP**
>
> It is often beneficial to maintain fewer administrative groups in an organization as the flexibility provided between servers within the same admin group is greater. For example, it is more straightforward and seamless to move mailboxes between servers within the same admin group. In addition, Recovery Storage Groups can only be used to restore data from other servers within

the same admin group. Because of this, Exchange designers should start with a design of a single admin group, and only add additional admin groups if there is a specific need to do so.

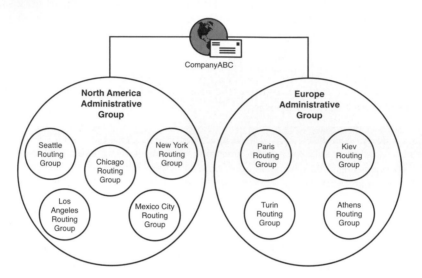

**FIGURE 4.4**    Multiple administrative groups in Exchange Server 2003.

## Planning Routing Group Topology

The concept of the routing group in Exchange enables a distinction to be made between administration of servers and the actual physical sites in which servers are located.

> **NOTE**
>
> Administrative groups and routing groups in Exchange 5.5 were not separate concepts, but both existed in the form of the Exchange 5.5 site. Consequently, administrative groups and routing groups in Exchange Server 2003 cannot be separated from each other unless the Exchange organization is running in Exchange 2003 native mode.

Figure 4.4 shows that CompanyABC used multiple routing groups within the two administrative groups that have been created. Subsequently, designing administrative group and routing group structure for an organization simply requires outlining the administrative needs and the physical routing restrictions in place in the organization. In many cases, a single administrative group is all that is required, because single IT teams often manage organizations of this size. On the same thread of reasoning, it is often the case that a single routing group can encompass all the servers in a small organization, especially when taking into account the site consolidation strategies mentioned in the previous sections of this chapter.

## Examining Public Folder Design Concepts

The public folder structure in Exchange Server 2003 is the main storehouse of publicly accessed information in the messaging infrastructure. For example, departmental calendars or contact lists can be stored in Exchange public folders.

The Exchange Server 2003 public folder store is a separate database, which is used to store public folder information. In a small or medium-sized organization, a single public folder store can be created and used. In larger organizations, multiple servers can contain multiple public folder stores, each configured to contain a read/write replica of public folder information for redundancy purposes.

## Understanding Environment Sizing Considerations

In some cases with small organizations, the number of users is small enough to warrant the installation of all Active Directory and Exchange Server 2003 components on a single server. This scenario is possible, as long as all necessary components—DNS, a Global Catalog domain controller, and Exchange Server 2003—are installed on the same hardware.

## Identifying Client Access Points

At its core, Exchange Server 2003 essentially acts as a storehouse for mailbox data. Access to the mail within the mailboxes can take place through multiple means, some of which may be required by specific services or applications in the environment. A good understanding of what these services are and if and how your design should support them is warranted.

### Outlining MAPI Client Access with Outlook 2003

The "full" client of Outlook, Outlook 2003, has gone through a significant number of changes, both to the look and feel of the application, and to the back-end mail functionality. The look and feel has been streamlined based on Microsoft research and customer feedback. Although it might take some getting used to, the layout and configuration is much more efficient, making checking email, scheduling, and other messaging features easier to accomplish.

On the back end, Outlook 2003 improves the MAPI compression that takes place between an Exchange Server 2003 system and the Outlook 2003 client. The increased compression helps reduce network traffic and improve the overall speed of communications between client and server.

In addition to MAPI compression, Outlook 2003 introduces the ability to run in cached mode, which automatically detects slow connections between client and server and adjusts Outlook functionality to match the speed of the link. When a slow link is detected, Outlook can be configured to download only email header information. When emails are opened, the entire email is downloaded, including attachments if necessary. This drastically reduces the amount of bits across the wire that are sent, because only those emails that are required are sent across the connection.

The Outlook 2003 client is the most effective and full-functioning client for users who are physically located close to an Exchange Server. With the enhancements in cached mode functionality, however, Outlook 2003 can also be effectively used in remote locations. The decision about which client to deploy as part of a design should keep these concepts in mind.

### Accessing Exchange with Outlook Web Access (OWA)

The Outlook Web Access (OWA) client in Exchange Server 2003 has been revamped and optimized for performance and useability. There is now very little difference between the full function client and OWA. With this in mind, OWA is now an even more efficient client for remote access to the Exchange Server. The one major piece of functionality that OWA does not have, but the full Outlook 2003 client does, is offline mail access support. If this is required, the full client should be deployed. Aside from this, however, the improvements in OWA make this a difficult choice.

### Using Outlook Mobile Access (OMA)

Microsoft anticipates that the wireless messaging market will expand by leaps and bounds in the coming years. The company subsequently has invested heavily in gearing its technologies toward wireless access methods. Exchange Server 2003 is one) of those technologies, and the instruction of Outlook Mobile Access (OMA) gives an indication of Microsoft's push into this arena.

OMA enables wireless devices, such as handheld organizers, wireless phones, and other small-screen appliances to have an access method to Exchange mailbox data that is customized to the uniquely small reading areas of these devices. The OMA client enables an optimized mail experience, and is ideal for those types of clients that use wireless devices.

### Reviewing Exchange ActiveSync (EAS)

Exchange ActiveSync (EAS) support in Exchange Server 2003 allows a mobile client, such as a Pocket PC device, to synchronize with the Exchange Server, allowing for access to email from a handheld device. EAS also supports the Always Up to Date feature, which allows for instantaneous email delivery to handheld devices via the SMS Protocol.

### Using the POP3 Protocol

Exchange Server 2003 enables access to email via the older, but industry-standard POP3 Protocol. POP3 is often used with clients such as Outlook Express and Eudora, and is limited in its functionality beyond basic mail retrieval. If a specific need exists to maintain POP3 functionality, this protocol can be designed into the environment. If there is no distinct need to use it, it should be disabled to minimize potential security risks.

### Accessing Exchange with the IMAP Protocol

Similar to POP3, the IMAP protocol is an older industry standard that relates to mail sending and retrieval. Many Unix mail clients, such as PINE, use IMAP for mail. As with the POP3 protocol, unless a specific need exists to support IMAP clients, the IMAP protocol should be disabled.

### Understanding the Simple Mail Transport Protocol (SMTP)

The Simple Mail Transfer Protocol (SMTP) is an industry-standard protocol that is widely used across the Internet for mail delivery. The SMTP protocol is built in to Exchange servers and is used by Exchange systems for relaying mail messages from one system to another, which is similar to the way that mail is relayed across SMTP servers on the Internet. Exchange is dependent on SMTP for mail delivery and uses it for internal and external mail access.

> **NOTE**
>
> Previously, Exchange 5.5 (and earlier) used the X.400 protocol to relay messages internally from one Exchange Server to another. This feature changed in Exchange 2000 and later in Exchange Server 2003, where X.400 is used only for backward compatibility with Exchange 5.5 systems.

By default, Exchange Server 2003 uses DNS to route messages destined for the Internet out of the Exchange topology. If, however, a user wants to forward messages to a smarthost before he or she is transmitted to the Internet, an SMTP connector can be manually set up to enable mail relay out of the Exchange system. SMTP connectors also reduce the risk and load on an Exchange Server by offloading the DNS lookup tasks to the SMTP smarthost. SMTP connectors can be specifically designed in an environment for this type of functionality.

### Using RPC over HTTP(S) (Outlook over HTTPS)

The new access mechanism added to Exchange Server 2003 is RPC over HTTP(S) (also known as Outlook over HTTPS), which enables standard Outlook 2003 access across firewalls. The Outlook 2003 client encapsulates RPC packets into HTTP or HTTPS packets and sends them across standard Web ports (80 and 443), where they are then extracted by the Exchange Server 2003 system. This technology enables Outlook to communicate using its standard RPC protocol, but across firewalls and routers that normally do not allow RPC traffic. The potential uses of this protocol are significant, because many situations do not require the use of cumbersome VPN clients.

## Configuring Exchange Server 2003 for Maximum Performance and Reliability

After decisions have been made about Active Directory design, Exchange Server placement, and client access, optimization of the Exchange Server itself helps ensure efficiency, reliability, and security for the messaging platform.

### Designing an Optimal Operating System Configuration for Exchange

As previously mentioned, Exchange Server 2003 operates best when run on Windows Server 2003. The enhancements to the operating system, especially in regard to security, make Windows Server 2003 the optimal choice for Exchange. Unless clustering or network load balancing is required, which is rare for smaller organizations, the Standard version of Windows Server 2003 can be installed as the OS.

> **NOTE**
>
> Contrary to popular misconception, the Enterprise version of Exchange can be installed on the Standard version of the operating system, and vice versa.
>
> Although there has been a lot of confusion on this concept, both versions of Exchange were designed to interoperate with either version of Windows.

## Avoiding Virtual Memory Fragmentation Issues

Windows Server's previous iterations have suffered from a problem with virtual memory (VM) fragmentation. The problem would manifest itself on systems with greater than 1GB of RAM, which run memory-intensive applications such as SQL Server or Exchange. The Advanced Server Edition of Windows 2000 enabled a workaround for this problem, in the form of a memory allocation switch that allocated additional memory for the user kernel.

Windows Server 2003 includes the capability of using this memory optimization technique in both the Standard and the Enterprise versions of the software, so that the switch can now be used on any Windows Server 2003 system with more than 1GB of physical RAM. The switch is added to the end of the boot.ini file, as illustrated in Figure 4.5.

**FIGURE 4.5**   *boot.ini* parameter switch setting.

The /3GB switch tells Windows to allocate 3GB of memory for the user kernel, and the /USERVA=3030 switch optimizes the memory configuration, based on tests performed by Microsoft that determined the perfect number of megabytes to allocate for optimal performance and the least likely instance of VM fragmentation.

## Configuring Disk Options for Performance

The single most important design element, which improves the efficiency and speed of Exchange, is the separation of the Exchange database and the Exchange logs onto a separate hard drive volume. Because of the inherent differences in the type of hard drive operations performed (logs perform primarily write operations, databases primarily read), separating these elements onto separate volumes dramatically increases server performance. Keep these components separate in even the smallest Exchange server implementations. Figure 4.6 illustrates some examples of how the database and log volumes can be configured.

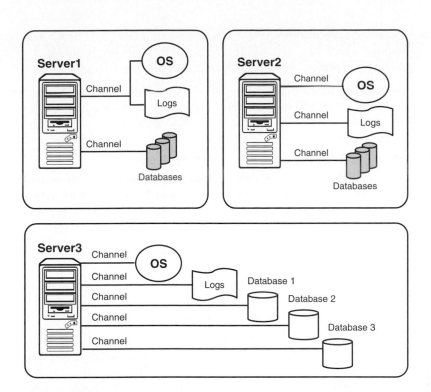

**FIGURE 4.6**   Database and log volume configuration.

On Server1, the OS and logs are located on the same mirrored C:\ volume and the database is located on a separate RAID5 drive set. With Server2, the configuration is taken up a notch, with the OS only on C:\, the logs on D:\, and the database on the RAID5 E:\ volume. Finally, Server3 is configured in the optimal configuration, with separate volumes for each database and set of logs. The more advanced a configuration, the more detailed and complex the drive configuration can get. However, the most important factor that must be remembered is to separate the Exchange database from the logs wherever possible.

## Working with Multiple Exchange Databases and Storage Groups

The Enterprise version of Exchange Server 2003 not only enables databases of larger than 75GB (16GB for pre-Exchange SP2), it also enables the creation of multiple separate databases on a single server. This concept gives great flexibility in design while enabling reduced downtime and increased performance.

A storage group is a logical grouping of databases that share a single set of logs. Each Exchange Server 2003 Enterprise system can handle a maximum of 4 storage groups per server, and each storage group can contain a maximum of 5 databases. This means that each server could theoretically hold up to 20 databases.

In practice, however, each instance of a storage group that is created uses a significant amount of resources, so it is wise to create additional storage groups only if absolutely necessary. Multiple databases, on the other hand, can solve several problems:

- **Reduce Database Restore Time**—Smaller databases take less time to restore from tape. This concept can be helpful if there is a group of users who require quicker recovery time (such as management). All mailboxes for this group could then be placed in a separate database to provide quicker recovery time in the event of a server or database failure.

- **Provide for Separate Mailbox Limit Policies**—Each database can be configured with different mailbox storage limits. For example, the standard user database could have a 200MB limit on mailboxes, and the management database could have a 500MB limit.

- **Mitigate Risk by Distributing User Load**—By distributing user load across multiple databases, the risk of losing all user mail connectivity is reduced. For example, if a single database failed that contained all users, no one would be able to mail. If those users were divided across three databases, however, only one-third of those users would be unable to mail in the event of a database failure.

- **Provide for a Recovery Storage Group**—Exchange Server 2003 provides a concept called a recovery storage group, which enables the creation of a special storage group to which entire databases can be restored. This can be run on a production mail server and can greatly simplify the task of restoring mailbox data to production accounts.

> **NOTE**
>
> One disadvantage to multiple databases is that the concept of single-instance storage is lost across databases. Single-instance storage occurs when only one copy of an email message sent to multiple people is stored on the server, dramatically reducing the space needed to store mass mailings. Each separate database must keep a copy of mass mailings, however, which increases the aggregate total size of the databases.

## Understanding Clustering for Exchange Server 2003

Exchange Server 2003 is configured to use Windows Server 2003 clustering for enhanced redundancy and increased uptime. Clustering is a relatively expensive option, but one that will increase reliability of the Exchange Server 2003 implementation.

> **NOTE**
>
> Microsoft no longer recommends a full active-active clustering configuration. Consequently, at least 1 cluster node should be configured as passive. With 8-way clustering, this means that 7 nodes can be active, and 1 node passive.

## Monitoring Design Concepts with Microsoft Operations Manager 2005

The enhancements to Exchange Server 2003 do not stop with the improvements to the product itself. New functionality has been added to the Exchange Management Pack for Microsoft Operations Manager (MOM) 2000/2005 that enables MOM to monitor Exchange servers for critical events and performance data. The MOM Management Pack is preconfigured to monitor for Exchange-specific information, and enable administrators to proactively monitor Exchange servers.

## Outlining Backup and Restore Design Concepts and the Volume Shadow Copy Service

The backup and restore functionality for Exchange Server 2003 has been enhanced via integration with the Volume Shadow Copy Service (VSS) of Windows Server 2003. VSS enables an Exchange database to be backed up via snapshots of the database, which create full data images that can be used for restores. This functionality can also be leveraged by software companies that create backup software for Exchange to further improve the capabilities for Exchange Server 2003 backup and restore.

## Uncovering Enhanced Antivirus and Spam Features

Exchange Server 2003 provides an improved Anti-Virus API (AVAPI), which enables preemptive identification of potential viruses in email attachments. The improved AVAPI can be integrated with antivirus software for Exchange written by third-party software companies and helps secure an Exchange environment.

# Securing and Maintaining an Exchange Server 2003 Implementation

One of the greatest advantages of Exchange Server 2003 is its emphasis on security. Along with Windows Server 2003, Exchange Server 2003 was developed during and after Microsoft's Trustworthy Computing initiative, which effectively put a greater emphasis on security over new features in the products. In Exchange Server 2003, this means that the OS and the application were designed with services "Secure by Default."

With Secure by Default, all nonessential functionality in Exchange must be turned on if needed. This is a complete change from the previous Microsoft model, which had all services, add-ons, and options turned on and running at all times, presenting much larger security vulnerabilities than was necessary. Designing security effectively becomes much easier in Exchange Server 2003, because it now becomes necessary only to identify components to turn on, as opposed to identifying everything that needs to be turned off.

## Patching the Operating System Using Windows Software Update Services

Although Windows Server 2003 presents a much smaller target for hackers, viruses, and exploits by virtue of the Secure by Default concept, it is still important to keep the OS up to date against critical security patches and updates. Currently, two approaches can be used to automate the installation of server patches. The first method involves configuring the Windows Server 2003 Automatic Updates client to download patches from Microsoft and install them on a schedule. The second option is to set up an internal server to coordinate patch distribution and management. The solution that Microsoft supplies for this functionality is known as Windows Software Update Services (WSUS).

WSUS enables a centralized server to hold copies of OS patches for distribution to clients on a preset schedule. SUS can be used to automate the distribution of patches to Exchange Server 2003 servers, so that the OS components will remain secure between service packs. Windows Software Update Services may not be necessary in smaller environments, but can be considered in medium-sized to large organizations that want greater control over their patch management strategy.

## Using Front-End Server Functionality

The OWA component of Exchange Server 2003 can be further optimized through the use of a dedicated Exchange Server 2003 front-end server. A front-end server is an Exchange server that acts as a proxy for mail access. No working databases are kept on a front-end server; the front-end server relays requests from clients to the back-end Exchange mailbox server. For more information on front-end/back-end design, see Chapter 10, "Configuring Outlook Web Access and Exchange Mobile Services."

## Implementing Maintenance Schedules

Exchange uses the Microsoft JET Database structure, which is effectively the same database engine that has been used with Exchange from the beginning. This type of database is useful for storing the type of unstructured data that email normally carries, and has proven to be a good fit for Exchange Server. Along with this type of database, however, comes the responsibility to run regular, scheduled maintenance on the Exchange databases on a regular basis.

Although online maintenance is performed every night, it is recommended that Exchange databases be brought offline on a quarterly or, at most, semiannual basis for offline maintenance. Exchange database maintenance utilities, `eseutil` and `isinteg`, should be used to compact and defragment the databases, which can then be mounted again in the environment.

Exchange databases that do not have this type of maintenance performed run the risk of becoming corrupt in the long term, and will also never be able to be reduced in size. Consequently, it is important to include database maintenance into a design plan to ensure data integrity.

## Using Antivirus and Backup Solutions

It has become a must for organizations to employ antivirus and backup solutions for Enterprise email applications. As previously mentioned, one of the major advantages of Exchange is that the OS and the application itself support advanced backup and antivirus technologies that can be tied into by third-party software resellers. This third-party support is broad, and should be part of any Exchange design.

## Summary

Exchange Server 2003 offers a broad range of functionality and improvements to messaging and is well suited for organizations of any size. With proper thought for the major design topics, a robust and reliable Exchange email solution can be put into place that will perfectly complement the needs of any organization.

When Exchange design concepts have been fully understood, the task of designing the Exchange Server 2003 infrastructure can take place.

## Best Practices

The following are best practices from this chapter:

- Use site consolidation strategies to reduce the number of Exchange servers to deploy.

- Separate the Exchange log and database files onto separate physical volumes whenever possible.

- Install Exchange Server 2003 on Windows Server 2003 with Service Pack 1.

- Use the \3GB and \USERVA=3030 switches in the boot.ini file of any Exchange Server 2003 server with greater than 1GB of physical RAM.

- Integrate an antivirus and backup strategy into Exchange Server design.

- Keep a local copy of the Global Catalog close to any Exchange servers.

- Implement quarterly or semiannual maintenance procedures against Exchange databases by using the ISINTEG and ESEUTIL utilities.

- Keep the OS and Exchange up to date through service packs and software patches, either manually or via Windows Software Update Services.

- Keep the Active Directory design simple, with a single forest and single domain, unless a specific need exists to create more complexity.

- Identify the client access methods that will be supported and match them with the appropriate Exchange Server 2003 technology.

- Implement DNS in the environment on the AD domain controllers.

# CHAPTER 5

**IN THIS CHAPTER**

- Designing for Small Organizations—Company123
- Designing Active Directory for Exchange Server 2003
- Determining Hardware and Software Components
- Designing Exchange Infrastructure
- Integrating Client Access into Exchange Server 2003 Design
- Summarizing Design Examples

# Designing an Enterprise Exchange Server 2003 Environment

Exchange Server 2003 was designed to accommodate the needs of multiple organizations, from the small businesses to large multinational corporations. In addition to the scalability features present in previous versions of Exchange, Exchange Server 2003 offers more opportunities to scale the back-end server environment to the specific needs of any group.

This chapter addresses specific design guidelines for organizations of various sizes. Throughout the chapter, specific examples of small, medium, and large organizations are presented and general recommendations are made. This chapter assumes a base knowledge of design components that can be obtained by reading Chapter 4, "Designing Exchange Server 2003 for a Small to Medium Network."

In this chapter, sample companies have been chosen to illustrate how Exchange Server 2003's design principles can be applied to organizations of varying sizes. Each major section of the chapter details the best practice design decisions taken by each of these organizations, to more effectively illustrate the common approaches to Exchange Server 2003 design. The end of the chapter summarizes the design decisions taken by each organization.

## Designing for Small Organizations— Company123

Small businesses account for a large portion of the install base for Exchange. Consequently, a great deal of work went into creating a more cost-effective Exchange model that works for smaller organizations. In addition to the advanced feature set of Exchange 2000, Exchange Server 2003 offers more opportunities to scale the implementation to fit the size of the organization deploying it.

The example of a small organization, for the purposes of this chapter, is Company123. Company123 is the manufacturer of a line of boutique microfiber towels and distributes its product through various resellers. Company123 has 13 employees in its San Francisco headquarters and another 3 in an office in London. As part of a messaging deployment for Company123, the decision was made to deploy Exchange Server 2003. The specific design decisions reached by Company123 are detailed in later sections.

## Designing for Midsize Organizations—OrganizationY

The heart of the target market for Exchange is the realm of the midsize organization. Exchange has always been a good choice for organizations of this size, and recent improvements in design components make it an even better match.

The example of a midsize organization is OrganizationY. OrganizationY is a software company headquartered in Manchester, Missouri. OrganizationY is composed of approximately 1,200 users: 500 in Manchester, 300 in Los Angeles, 100 in Saint Petersburg, Russia, and an additional 300 scattered in various smaller locations worldwide. OrganizationY determined that Exchange was best suited for its messaging needs and designed an Exchange Server 2003 infrastructure using the design criteria outlined in later sections.

## Designing for Large Organizations—CompanyABC

One of the last, heavily fought realms for "frontiers" in the messaging world is that of the large, enterprise organizations. Microsoft has invested considerable resources into expanding the install base of Exchange Server into this arena, and has fixed many of the problems with Exchange that previously kept it geared toward small and midsize organizations.

The example of a large organization for the purposes of this chapter is CompanyABC. CompanyABC is a large, multinational medical services company headquartered in Minneapolis. A total of 50,000 users worldwide work for CompanyABC, with major centers in San Francisco, Dallas, New York, Paris, Moscow, Tokyo, and Singapore. Multiple smaller offices are spread around the globe. CompanyABC recently acquired a competitor, effectively doubling its size, but requiring thought into integration of the new environment. The decision to deploy Exchange Server 2003 was based on the improvements made to Exchange in areas of site consolidation, clients, and total cost of ownership. Specific design decisions reached by CompanyABC are outlined in later sections.

# Designing Active Directory for Exchange Server 2003

Active Directory is a necessary and fundamental component of any Exchange Server 2003 implementation. That said, organizations of any size do not necessarily need to panic about setting up Active Directory in addition to Exchange, as long as a few straightforward design steps are followed. The following areas of Active Directory must be addressed to properly design and deploy Exchange Server 2003:

- Forest and Domain Design
- AD Site and Replication Topology Layout
- Domain Controller and Global Catalog Placement
- DNS Configuration

## Understanding Forest and Domain Design

Because Exchange Server 2003 uses Active Directory for its underlying directory structure, it is necessary to link Exchange with a unique Active Directory forest.

In many cases, an existing Active Directory forest and domain structure is already in place in organizations considering Exchange Server 2003 deployment. In these cases, Exchange can be installed on top of the existing AD environment, and no additional AD design decisions need to be made. It is important to note that Exchange Server 2003 can be installed on either a Windows 2000 or Windows Server 2003 Active Directory implementation.

In some cases, there may not be an existing AD infrastructure in place, and one needs to be deployed to support Exchange. In these scenarios, design decisions need to be made for the AD structure in which Exchange will be installed. In some specific cases, Exchange may be deployed as part of a separate forest by itself, as illustrated in Figure 5.1. This is often the case in an organization with multiple existing AD forests.

In any case, AD should be designed with simplicity in mind. A single-forest, single-domain model, for example, will solve the needs of many organizations. If Exchange itself is all that is required of AD, this type of deployment is the best practice to consider.

> **NOTE**
>
> The addition of Exchange Server 2003 into an Active Directory forest requires an extension of the AD forest's Active Directory schema.
>
> Considerations for this factor must be taken into account when deploying Exchange onto an existing AD forest.

Microsoft has gotten serious recently about support for Exchange Server across multiple forests. This was previously an onerous task to set up, but the ability to synchronize between separate Exchange organizations has been simplified through the use of Microsoft Identity Integration Server (MIIS) 2003. MIIS now comes with a series of preconfigured scripts to replicate between Exchange forests, enabling organizations which, for one reason or another, cannot use a common forest to unite the email structure through object replication.

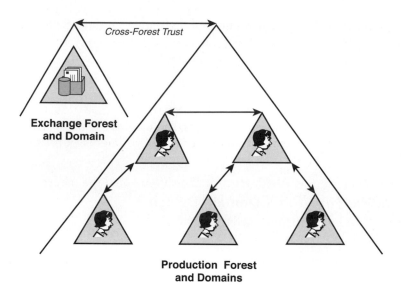

**FIGURE 5.1**    Multi-forest Exchange configuration.

## Outlining AD Site and Replication Topology Layout

Active Directory sites should mirror existing network topology. Where there are pools of highly connected AD domain controllers, for example, Exchange sites should be created to optimize replication. Smaller organizations have the luxury of a simplified AD site design. In general, the number of sites is small—or, in most cases, composed of a single physical location. Small organizations should subsequently configure their Active Directory implementation with a single AD Site. Midsize and larger organizations may require the creation of multiple Active Directory sites to mirror the WAN connectivity of the organization.

## Reviewing Domain Controller and Global Catalog Placement Concepts

In small or midsize organizations, there are effectively two options regarding domain controller placement. The first option involves using the same physical server for domain controller and Exchange Server duties. This option is feasible for smaller organizations because its impact on the server is minimal.

The second option is to separate the Active Directory domain controller duties onto a separate physical server from Exchange Server 2003. This option is more expensive, but has the advantages associated with distributed computing. As the anticipated load on the server increases with the number of users using the system, this option becomes necessary.

## Configuring DNS

Because AD and Exchange are completely dependent on DNS for lookups and overall functionality, configuring DNS is an important factor to consider. In the majority of cases, DNS is installed on the domain controller(s), which enables the creation of Active Directory–Integrated DNS Zones. AD-Integrated Zones enable DNS data to be stored in AD with multiple read/write copies of the zone available for redundancy purposes. Although using other non-Microsoft DNS for AD is supported, it is not recommended. See Chapter 7, "Domain Name System Impact on Exchange Server," for more information on third-party DNS scenarios.

The main decision regarding DNS layout is the decision about the namespace to be used within the organization. The DNS namespace is the same as the AD domain information, and it is difficult to change later. The two options in this case are to configure DNS to use either a published, external namespace that is easy to understand, such as cco.com, or an internal, secure namespace that is difficult to hack into, such as cconet.internal. In general, the more security-conscious an organization, the more often the internal namespace will be chosen.

## Outlining Active Directory Design Decisions for Small Organizations

Company123 did not have an existing Active Directory infrastructure in place, so design decisions regarding AD were necessary. Because its needs were not complex, however, the AD design decisions were not complex. Small organizations rarely need to spend a great deal of time worrying about Active Directory forests, trees, and domains. In reality, the vast majority of these small organizations use a single-forest, single-domain model for their Active Directory.

In Company123's case, the size of the company dictated a simple Active Directory design. Because it had no specific need for a complex forest design, it settled for a single-forest, single-domain AD design, as illustrated in Figure 5.2.

**Company123 Forest**

company123.org

**FIGURE 5.2**    Single-forest, single-domain Active Directory design.

In Company123's case, 12 of the 15 employees are physically located in the San Francisco headquarters. An additional 3 employees are located in a London office, but it was determined that the number of employees in this location was too small to warrant the creation of a second AD site. A single San Francisco site was created for AD.

When the decision about domain controller placement arose, Company123 chose the simple structure of having a single domain controller for the entire forest. This meant that there were no decisions to be made regarding Global Catalog placement either, because the first domain controller is, by default, a Global Catalog server. In addition, most small organizations opt to have their domain controller on the same hardware as their Exchange Server, which is the configuration chosen by Company123.

Company123 installed and configured DNS on the single server chosen as the domain controller and Exchange server for the organization. A single forward lookup zone for the AD domain was created (`company123.org`) and a reverse lookup zone was created for the subnet (`10.0.0.0/24`), as illustrated in Figure 5.3.

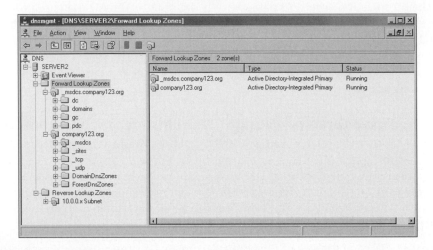

**FIGURE 5.3**    Forward lookup and reverse lookup zone configuration.

The DNS namespace chosen for the Active Directory domain was the same as the external DNS namespace registered to Company123 on the Internet: `company123.org`. This option was less secure, but because the security needs of Company123 were not great, the decision was made to assume the same namespace for convenience purposes and therefore not confuse the end-users.

## Outlining Midsize Organization AD Design Decisions

OrganizationY already had an Active Directory domain infrastructure in place and wanted to integrate Exchange Server 2003 into the forest. The AD domain structure used a placeholder root structure, which isolated the schema master role, as illustrated in Figure 5.4.

OrganizationY had three major locations, so separate Active Directory sites had been configured for each location to optimize replication traffic. In advance of the Exchange Server 2003 project, the three sites each were given full Global Catalog domain controllers so that Exchange traffic would be optimized.

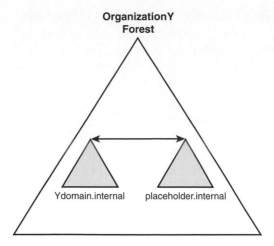

**FIGURE 5.4**   Placeholder root Active Directory design structure.

The primary user domain used an internally published DNS namespace named Ydomain.internal. DNS zones were configured for both the placeholder root domain (placeholder.internal) and the user resource domain (ydomain.internal). The local copy of the zone was configured as AD-Integrated, and the other domain zone was configured as a stub zone, as illustrated in Figure 5.5. This enabled the highest level of security along with the most efficient levels of replication.

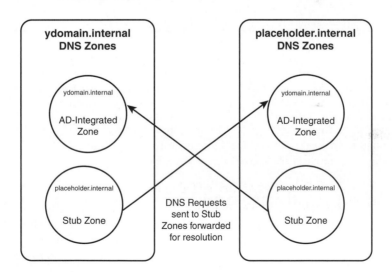

**FIGURE 5.5**   AD-integrated and stub zone configuration.

## Outlining Large Organization AD Design Decisions

CompanyABC was faced with a complex Active Directory problem. Separate AD forests had already been deployed in two locations within the company, and it was determined to be too complex an undertaking to consolidate the AD forests into a single forest for Exchange.

CompanyABC was left with the decision to either deploy Exchange Server 2003 in two locations and synchronize the address lists between them using Microsoft Identity Integration Server (MIIS) 2003, or deploy a dedicated forest for Exchange. The second option was chosen, and CompanyABC designed a completely separate AD forest for Exchange, but with cross-forest transitive trusts established between the forests, as illustrated in Figure 5.6.

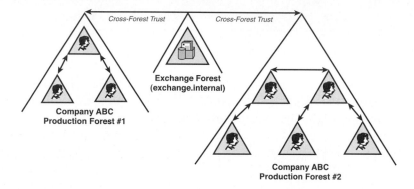

**FIGURE 5.6**    Multiple Active Directory forest with cross-forest trusts.

The AD Site structure was set up to follow existing WAN topology, with Active Directory sites for Minneapolis, San Francisco, Dallas, New York, Paris, Moscow, Tokyo, and Singapore. Each site contained Global Catalog domain controllers for fast Exchange access.

As evident in Figure 5.6, CompanyABC chose a single domain model with a DNS namespace of `exchange.internal` for the Exchange forest. All external forest accounts would be granted permissions to their mailboxes across the cross-forest trusts.

# Determining Hardware and Software Components

Justifying hardware and software purchases is often a difficult task for organizations of any size. It is therefore important to balance the need for performance and redundancy with the funds available in the budget, and thus deploy the optimal Exchange server hardware and software configuration.

## Designing Server Number and Placement

Exchange scales very well to a large number of mailboxes on a single machine, depending on the hardware chosen for the Exchange server. Exchange Server 2003 also does not require dedicated systems for connectors, as did some previous versions. Subsequently, Exchange Server 2003 is optimal for organizations that want to limit the amount of servers that are deployed and supported in an environment.

Exchange 2000 previously had one major exception to this concept, however. If multiple sites required high-speed access to an Exchange server, multiple servers were necessary for deployment. Exchange Server 2003, on the other hand, introduces the concept of site consolidation, which enables smaller sites to use the Exchange servers in the larger sites through the more efficient bandwidth usage present in Outlook 2003 and the OWA and OMA technologies.

## Providing for Server Redundancy and Optimization

The ability of the Exchange server to recover from hardware failures is more than just a "nice-to-have" feature. Many server models come with an array of redundancy features, such as multiple fans and power supplies, and mirrored disk capabilities. These features incur additional costs, however, so it is wise for smaller organizations to perform a cost-benefit analysis to determine what redundancy features are required. Midsize and larger organizations should seriously consider robust redundancy options, however, because the increased reliability and uptime is often well worth the up-front costs.

One of the most critical but overlooked performance strategies for Exchange is the concept of separating the Exchange logs and database onto separate physical drive sets. Because Exchange logs are very write-intensive, and the database is read-intensive, having these components on the same disk set would degrade performance. Separating these components onto different disk sets, however, is the best way to get the most out of Exchange.

In addition to separating the Exchange database onto a striped RAID5 set, the SMTP component used by Exchange can be optimized by moving it to the same partition as the database. By default, the SMTP component is installed on the system (OS) partition, but can be easily moved after an Exchange server has been set up. You can easily move the SMTP folder by accessing the Messages tab under the default SMTP Virtual Server in Exchange System Manager, as illustrated in Figure 5.7.

## Reviewing Server Memory and Processor Recommendations

Exchange Server is a resource-hungry application that, left to its own devices, will consume a good portion of any amount of processor or memory that is given to it. Although it operates best with multiple processors and more RAM, small organizations may not need the enhanced performance that this investment brings. The amount of processors and RAM required should reflect the budgetary needs of the organization. In general, 1GB of RAM and dual processors is a good rule of thumb for smaller organizations, but a single processor and as low as 500MB of RAM could also work.

Midsize and larger organizations should consider multiprocessor servers and greater amounts of RAM—2GB or 4GB. This will help increase the amount of mailboxes that can be homed to any particular server.

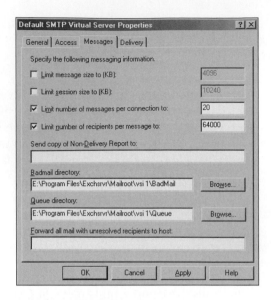

**FIGURE 5.7**   Moving the SMTP folder in ESM.

> **NOTE**
>
> Any Exchange Server 2003 system with greater than 1GB of physical RAM should include the
> /3GB  /USERVA=3030 switches, which optimize the memory allocation for these systems.

## Outlining Server Operating System Considerations

Exchange Server 2003 is optimized for use with Windows Server 2003, and it is therefore
logical to place Exchange on a server with the new OS installed. Exchange Server 2003
takes advantage of the increased security and feature set of Windows Server 2003, and is
therefore the recommended approach for small organizations deploying Exchange.

> **NOTE**
>
> Although it is preferable to install Exchange Server 2003 on Windows Server 2003, this does not
> mean that the entire network needs to be Windows Server 2003–only. All other servers, includ-
> ing Exchange 2000 and Windows 2000 Active Directory, can coexist in the environment at the
> same time.

The base OS for Exchange, Windows Server 2003, comes in two versions, Enterprise and
Standard. Some midsize and larger organizations could deploy the Enterprise version of
the Windows Server 2003 product, namely for clustering support and/or greater than 4GB
RAM or more than 4 processors. If this functionality is not required, the Standard version
of the OS is sufficient.

Small organizations, on the other hand, will almost exclusively require only the Standard version, rather than the Enterprise version, of the Windows Server 2003 product. The Enterprise version is seldom required for small server deployments, as the advanced functionality described above is rarely needed for organizations of this size.

## Designing Clustering and Advanced Redundancy Options

In larger organizations, the need to ensure a very high level of reliability is paramount. These organizations often require a level of uptime for their email that equates to "5 nines" of uptime, or 99.999% uptime a year. For this level of redundancy, a higher level of Exchange redundancy is required than the standard models. For these organizations, the clustering features built in to Windows Server 2003 Enterprise Edition and used by Exchange are ideal.

> **NOTE**
>
> It is now Microsoft's recommendation, however, that at least 1 node in a cluster be set up in passive mode for the most effective failover strategy. For more information on using clustering with Exchange Server 2003, see Chapter 30, "System-Level Fault Tolerance (Clustering/Network Load Balancing)."

## Reviewing Small Organization Hardware and Software Design Decisions

Because 12 of the 15 employees were located in San Francisco, Company123 deployed a single Exchange Server 2003 system, running on the same hardware as the Active Directory and DNS components. It was designed to enable the three London users to access Exchange using the slow-link and offline capabilities of Outlook 2003.

Company123 decided to deploy server hardware with RAID redundant disks and dual power supplies and fans. Because messaging was a critical aspect for the company, the additional cost was determined to be warranted for the small organization. In addition, the Exchange database, SMTP engine, and Exchange logs were separated onto different physical drive sets, as illustrated in Figure 5.8. This helped Company123 to get the most out of its hardware investment.

Company123 purchased enterprise-level server hardware with dual processors and 1GB of RAM. Because it was deploying all Active Directory and Exchange components on a single machine, it decided to invest in hardware so that its Exchange implementation would be relevant for several years to come.

The decision was made to deploy its Exchange Server using Windows Server 2003 Standard Edition, because the company wanted the optimal OS configuration for Exchange and didn't have any need for server clustering or large RAM support.

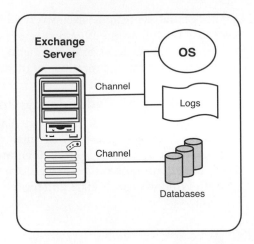

**FIGURE 5.8**    Separating Exchange components on separate drive sets.

## Reviewing Midsize Organization Hardware and Software Design Decisions

OrganizationY determined that Exchange mailbox servers would run in two sites, Manchester and Los Angeles, and that the St. Petersburg location and all other smaller sites would connect to these Exchange servers using the improved slow-link functionality in Outlook 2003. This significantly reduced hardware and support expenditures because the number of servers that would have been required was reduced to two for the entire organization, as illustrated in Figure 5.9.

Each server was optimized for the Exchange role with 4GB of RAM, quad processors, redundant fans and power supplies, and RAID controllers providing redundant disks. Each server had a separate RAID set for the OS, a separate one for the logs, and a RAID5 set for the database and SMTP folder, as illustrated in Figure 5.9.

The servers were installed with Windows Server 2003 Standard Edition. Because clustering was determined to be unnecessary, the Standard Edition of Windows sufficed.

## Reviewing Large Organization Hardware and Software Design Decisions

CompanyABC deployed Exchange mailbox servers in the largest sites: Minneapolis, San Francisco, Dallas, New York, Paris, Moscow, Tokyo, and Singapore. All other users within the organization were configured to use the mailbox servers in these locations for email access.

The largest site, Minneapolis, clustered its Exchange mailbox servers into a 4-node cluster, with 3 active nodes and 1 passive node. The server hardware for these cluster nodes was composed of enterprise grade servers with redundant fans and power supplies, 4GB of RAM, quad processor, and RAID redundant disks. The disk arrays were configured with separate RAID sets for the OS, Logs, and Databases/SMTP Folder, as illustrated in Figure 5.10.

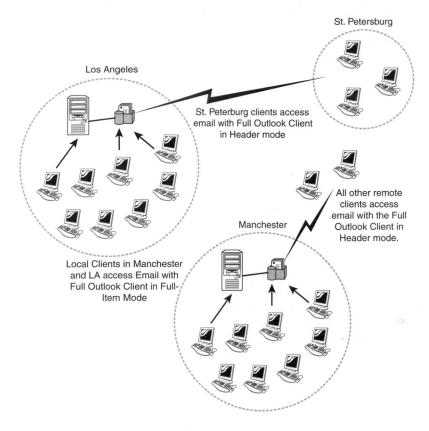

St. Petersburg

Los Angeles

St. Peterburg clients access email with Full Outlook Client in Header mode

All other remote clients access email with the Full Outlook Client in Header mode.

Manchester

Local Clients in Manchester and LA access Email with Full Outlook Client in Full-Item Mode

**FIGURE 5.9**   Exchange organization with a reduction of servers.

The servers in the other large sites were configured with the same hardware, but without clustering capabilities. Windows Server 2003 Standard Edition was installed on all servers with the exception of the clustered servers, which were installed with the Enterprise version of the software.

# Designing Exchange Infrastructure

After Active Directory and the physical OS has been chosen and deployed, the Exchange infrastructure can be set up and optimized for the specific needs of the organization. With these needs in mind, there are several things that can be done to optimize an Exchange Server 2003 setup, as detailed in the following sections.

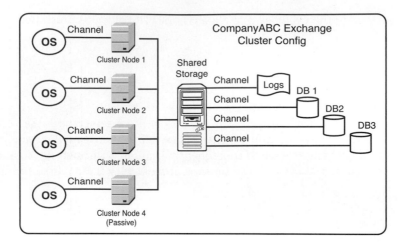

**FIGURE 5.10**    Separate drive sets for an Exchange 2003 configuration.

## Determining Exchange Version and Org Name

When installing Exchange, the choice of Exchange version needs to be made. As with Windows Server 2003, there are two versions of Exchange, Standard and Enterprise. The Standard version enables all Exchange Server 2003 functionality except the following:

- Multiple databases

- Databases larger than 75GB (16GB for pre SP2)

- Clustering support

- X.400 Connectors

In smaller organizations, nearly all implementations of Exchange require only the Standard version; the advanced feature set of the Enterprise Edition is geared toward larger deployments. The critical factor that pushes the midsize-to-large organizations to the Enterprise version, however, is the 75GB database limit. Some organizations require large mailbox sizes and could potentially require multiple databases larger than 75GB. Because this functionality is available only with the Enterprise version of the software, it must be installed.

> **CAUTION**
>
> Because the standard version of Exchange does not support databases larger than 75GB, and the pre-SP2 version only supports up to 16GB, keep track of the size of the private database store, ensuring that it stays well below the designated limit. The database will shut down if it reaches this limit.

When installing the first Exchange Server 2003 system, the setup program prompts for the creation of the Exchange Organization. The information entered in the Exchange

Organization is fairly trivial, because end-users do not access this information. However, the Exchange Organization is unique across the forest and should reflect the name of the organization that will use the Exchange Server 2003 implementation.

## Outlining Administrative Group and Routing Group Structure

Exchange Server 2003 continues with the Exchange 2000 concept of separating the administration of servers with the physical location of those servers. In other words, Exchange servers could exist in multiple sites but be administered by the same group. The administration of Exchange servers is subsequently facilitated through the creation of administrative groups, and the physical server routing facility is facilitated through routing groups.

In a nutshell, administrative groups in Exchange Server 2003 should be established to designate administrative boundaries for Exchange components. In other words, if the entire organization is centrally administered, there should be only a single admin group for the entire organization. If there is a separate admin group—for servers in Europe, for example—multiple admin groups can be created to provide eased delegation of administration.

Routing groups, on the other hand, are used to optimize replication between "islands" of high connectivity, similar to the concept of Active Directory and Exchange 5.5 sites. Servers within the same routing group communicate with each other faster and more often, and Exchange systems in remote routing groups can be configured to replicate information on a scheduled basis.

## Designing Public Folder Structure and Replication

Public folders in Exchange have a somewhat mixed relationship with administrators and users. Many organizations widely use the group calendaring and posting features of public folders, but others maintain a public folder database with little or no data in it.

Public folder architecture for small organizations is usually quite simple; because there is normally only one Exchange server, only one public folder instance is possible. If there is more than one server and fast access to public folder information is required, it may be necessary to create a second public folder instance.

Midsize-to-large organizations, on the other hand, can take advantage of the ability to have multiple read/write copies of public folder trees by deploying public folder instances in various servers across the organization. This ensures fast public folder access for users.

## Determining Exchange Databases and Storage Groups Layout

As previously mentioned, the Enterprise version of Exchange enables the concept of multiple databases, up to a maximum of 20. This enables a greater amount of design freedom and gives administrators more flexibility. A maximum of four production storage groups can be created, and each storage group can contain up to five databases.

> **NOTE**
>
> Exchange Server 2003 introduces a concept called a recovery storage group, which enables the restoration of mailbox data to a completely separate storage group from the regular mail data. An Exchange Recovery storage group can be installed as a fifth storage group on the Enterprise version of Exchange, but it also can be used on the Standard version.

## Outlining Exchange Recovery Options

Deploying Exchange requires considerable thought about backup and recovery solutions. Because Exchange is a live, active database, special considerations need to be taken into account when designing the backup strategy for email.

Microsoft designed Exchange Server 2003 to use the new backup APIs from Windows Server 2003. These APIs support the Volume Shadow Copy service, which enables Exchange databases to be backed up through creation of a "shadow copy" of the entire disk at the beginning of the backup. The shadow copy is then used for the backup, so that the production disk is not affected.

> **NOTE**
>
> The Windows Server 2003 backup utility can be used to back up Exchange using the traditional online backup approach. Volume Shadow Copy requires a third-party solution that has been written to support the new Windows Server 2003 backup and restore APIs.

Exchange Server 2003 also includes support for the concept of a recovery storage group, which is an additional storage group (available with either Standard or Enterprise Exchange) and which can be used on a running server to restore databases and mailboxes "on the fly." This streamlines the mailbox recovery process, because restore servers are no longer a necessity. For more information on backup and recovery options, see Chapter 31, "Backing Up the Exchange Server 2003 Environment."

## Considering Exchange Antivirus and Antispam Design

Viruses are a major problem for all organizations today. Email is especially vulnerable, because it is typically unauthenticated and insecure. Consequently, design of an Exchange implementation should include consideration for antivirus options.

Exchange Server 2003 improves upon the Virus Scanning Application Programming Interface (VSAPI) that was introduced in Exchange 2000. The enhanced VSAPI 2.5 engine enables quarantine of email messages, as opposed to simply attachments, and enables virus scanning on gateway servers. Third-party virus products can be written to tie directly into the new VSAPI and use its functionality.

Spam, unsolicited email, has become another major headache for most organizations. In response to this, Exchange Server 2003 has some built-in antispam functionality that enables email messages to contain a spam rating. This helps determine which emails are legitimate, and can be used by third-party antispam products as well.

## Monitoring Exchange

Email services are required in many organizations. The expectations of uptime and reliability are increasing, and end-users are beginning to expect email to be as available as phone service. Subsequently, the ability to monitor Exchange events, alerts, and performance data is optimal.

Exchange Server 2003 is a complex organism with multiple components, each busy processing tasks, writing to event logs, and running optimization routines. There are several methods of monitoring Exchange, the most optimal being Microsoft Operations Manager (MOM) 2005. MOM is essentially a monitoring, alerting, and reporting product that gathers event information and performance data, and generates reports about Microsoft servers. An Exchange-specific management pack for MOM contains hundreds of pre-packaged counters and events for Exchange Server 2003. Use of the management pack is ideal in midsize and larger environments to proactively monitor Exchange.

Although close monitoring of multiple Exchange servers is best supported through the use of MOM, this may not be the most ideal approach for smaller organizations because MOM is geared toward medium and large organizations. Exchange monitoring for small organizations can be accomplished through old-fashioned approaches, such as manual reviews of event log information, performance counters using perfmon, and simple SNMP utilities to monitor uptime, which is the approach taken by Company123.

## Reviewing Small Organization Exchange Infrastructure Design Decisions

In small organizations such as CompanyABC, it is typical for a single group (or single individual) to administer the entire organization, so a single administrative group should suffice. In addition, there may be only one site (or a small number of sites) and Exchange Server 2003 can be configured with a single routing group for each site. Because of its size, Company123 used a single routing group and a single administration group, as illustrated in Figure 5.11.

The Exchange infrastructure was deployed at Company123 with Exchange Standard Edition on its single server. The Exchange organization was named Company123 for simplicity.

Because Company123 was using the Standard version of Exchange Server 2003, it did not require additional thought into database or storage group design. Following this logic, it deployed a single private information store, a single public information store, and a single storage group.

## Reviewing Midsize Organization Exchange Infrastructure Design Decisions

Administration within OrganizationY is centralized, and required the creation of a single admin group for the Exchange organization. The Exchange organization was named OrganizationY and the routing group structure was divided into separate routing groups for Manchester and Los Angeles, as illustrated in Figure 5.12.

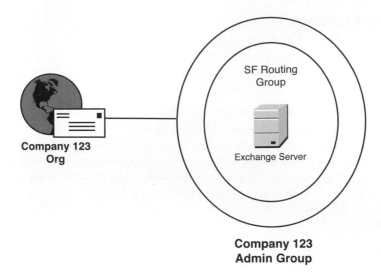

**FIGURE 5.11**    Routing group and admin group design for a small organization.

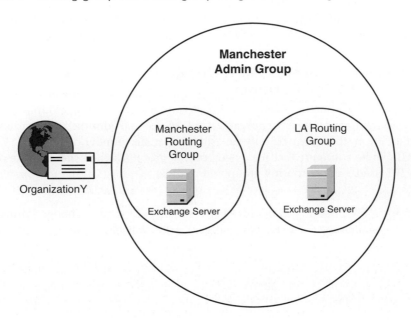

**FIGURE 5.12**    Routing group and admin group design for a mid-size organization.

Each Exchange Server in the organization used the Enterprise version of Exchange, because support for large and multiple databases was required. A third-party backup and antivirus solution were chosen to protect the mail data. The Exchange servers were each configured with three private store databases for mailboxes, and one public folder store, as illustrated in Figure 5.12. Users were distributed across the databases by practice group—with management in one database and marketing in another, for example. This helped OrganizationY shorten recovery time for certain groups while also enabling separate mailbox limits and database options.

Microsoft Operations Manager (MOM) 2005 was deployed in the Manchester location to monitor all AD and Exchange servers and provide for proactive systems management.

## Reviewing Large Organization Exchange Infrastructure Design Decisions

CompanyABC was divided into two separate IT Teams. One IT team managed the parent company, which included the Minneapolis, San Francisco, Moscow, and Tokyo offices. The second IT team managed the company that had been acquired, which included the Dallas, New York, Paris, and Singapore offices. Consequently, two administrative groups were created and a total of eight routing groups were created, as illustrated in Figure 5.13. The Exchange organization was named CompanyABC.

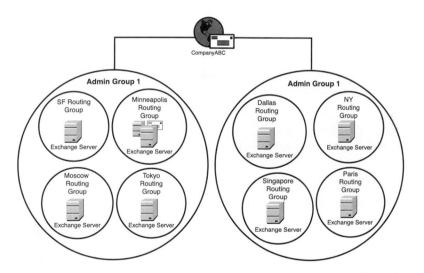

**FIGURE 5.13**    Routing group and admin group design for a large organization.

All servers across the entire organization were installed with the Enterprise version of Exchange to enable large databases, as illustrated in Figure 5.13. The user base was distributed across the databases alphabetically to ease the administration of the mailboxes. Each site contained a local copy of the public folder tree to ensure quick response time. Finally, third-party antispam, antivirus, and backup solutions were put in place to protect Exchange.

Microsoft Operations Manager 2005 was deployed with the Exchange Server 2003 Management Pack and configured to monitor all components of Active Directory and Exchange Server 2003.

# Integrating Client Access into Exchange Server 2003 Design

Although the Exchange Server is a powerful systems component, it is only half the equation for an email platform. The client systems compose the other half, and are a necessary ingredient that should be carefully determined in advance.

## Outlining Client Access Methods

Great effort has been put into optimizing and streamlining the client access approaches available in Exchange Server 2003. Not only have traditional approaches such as the Outlook client been enhanced, but support for nontraditional access with POP3 and IMAP clients is also available. The following options exist for client access with Exchange Server 2003:

- **Outlook 2003**—The full Outlook 2003 client has been streamlined and enhanced. MAPI communications with Exchange 2003 systems have been compressed, and the addition of slow-link detection enables speedy mail retrieval for remote users.

- **Outlook Web Access (OWA)**—The Outlook Web Access (OWA) client is now nearly indistinguishable from the full Outlook 2003 client. The one major component missing is offline capability, but nearly every other Outlook 2003 functionality is part of OWA.

- **Exchange ActiveSync (EAS)**—EAS provides for synchronized access to email from a handheld device, such as a PocketPC. It allows for real-time send and receive functionality to and from the handheld, through the use of the Always Up to Date feature of EAS.

- **RPC over HTTPS**—RPC over HTTPS is a method by which a full Outlook 2003 client can dynamically send and receive messages directly from an Exchange server over an HTTP or HTTPS web connection. This allows for VPN-free access to Exchange data, over a secured HTTPS connection.

- **Outlook Mobile Access (OMA)**—Outlook Mobile Access (OMA) is a version of Outlook Web Access, which has been optimized for use on handheld devices, such as cellular phones, PDAs, and other small-screen units.

> **TIP**
>
> OMA functionality can be tested from an Internet Explorer 6.0 client by accessing the following:
>
> `http://servername/oma`
>
> where *servername* is the name of the Exchange Server where OMA is running. This is a useful trick if a real OMA client is not available for testing purposes.

- **Post Office Protocol (POP3)**—The Post Office Protocol (POP3) is a legacy protocol that is supported in Exchange 2003. POP3 enables simple retrieval of mail data via applications that use the POP3 protocol. Mail messages, however, cannot be sent with POP3 and must use the SMTP engine in Exchange. By default, POP3 is not turned on and must be explicitly activated.

- **Interactive Mail Access Protocol (IMAP)**—Legacy Interactive Mail Access Protocol (IMAP) access to Exchange is also available, which can enable an Exchange Server to be accessed via IMAP applications, such as some Unix mail clients. As with the POP3 protocol, IMAP support must be explicitly turned on.

> **NOTE**
>
> Exchange Server 2003 supports the option of disallowing MAPI access or allowing only specific Outlook clients MAPI access. This can be configured if an organization desires only OWA access to an Exchange server. It can also, for security reasons, stipulate that only Outlook 2003 can access the Exchange server. The registry key required for this functionality is the following:
>
> ```
> Location:HKLM\System\CurrentControlSet\Services\MSExchangeIS\ParametersSystem
> Value Name: Disable MAPI Clients
> Data Type: REG_SZ
> String: Version # (i.e. v4, v5, etc)
> ```
>
> See Microsoft Technet Article 288894 for more information:
>
> ```
> http://support.microsoft.com/default.aspx?scid=KB;EN-US;288894
> ```

Each organization will have individual needs that determine which client or set of clients will be supported. In general, the full Outlook 2003 client offers the richest messaging experience with Exchange Server 2003, but many of the other access mechanisms, such as Outlook Web Access, are also valid. The important design consideration is identifying what will be supported, and then enabling support for that client or protocol. Any methods that will not be supported should be disabled or left turned off for security reasons.

## Determining Front-End Server Design

As noted, Exchange Server 2003 enables an Exchange Server to act as a proxy agent for mail, which is also known as a front-end server. Front-end servers relay client requests back to the back-end mailbox store. Front-end servers offload processor-intensive activities, such as decryption of SSL client traffic, and provide for a single entry point to multiple back-end mailbox servers.

By default, all Exchange Server 2003 systems have front-end capabilities built in, which effectively means that organizations can use a single Exchange server without the need to deploy a dedicated front-end system, if not required. In most cases for small businesses, this would be the preferred option to spending more on a second Exchange server. Larger and midsize organizations may want to deploy front-end technology as part of a design to increase security and scalability.

## Reviewing Small Organization Client Access Design Decisions

Company123 deployed the full Outlook 2003 client for all of its users, to take advantage of the full-featured set offered by the application. The users in the London office use Outlook in the auto-detected slow-link header mode, which enables them to more efficiently use their slower access.

Since it was a small organization and did not require the security and scalability of a dedicated front-end server, Company123 opted to use a single Exchange server with front-end support.

## Reviewing Midsize Organization Client Access Design Decisions

OrganizationY used a mixed approach to client access. The majority of users in the main Manchester and Los Angeles sites were given full Outlook 2003 clients for access to the Exchange servers. Users in St. Petersburg, however, accessed mail through Outlook Web Access for most individuals, and the full Outlook 2003 client for traveling users who required offline access. Users in smaller sites across the organization used a combination of the two technologies, with some individuals using Outlook Mobile Access from cell phones and other handheld devices, as illustrated in Figure 5.14.

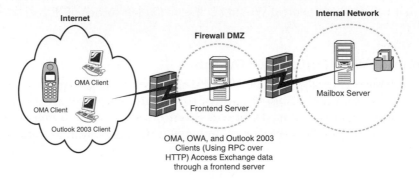

**FIGURE 5.14**    Outlook Mobile Access from handheld devices.

A dedicated front-end server was set up in the DMZ of the firewall in Manchester to enable Internet access to corporate email. This enabled remote users to access their corporate email from any location on the Internet by using RPC over HTTP capabilities in the Outlook 2003 client. The traffic was encrypted through SSL to protect the data. This design model gave great flexibility and accessibility to users across the organization.

### Reviewing Large Organization Client Access Design Decisions

CompanyABC was configured to enable access to email from several different client access mechanisms. The preferred client was established as Outlook 2003, but MAPI access from downlevel Outlook clients (XP/2000/97) was also provided. POP3 and IMAP access were also given to specific offices that had special needs. In addition, access to Outlook Web Access was provided for all mailboxes through a series of load-balanced front-end servers, as illustrated in Figure 5.15.

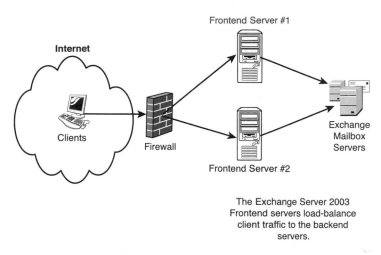

**FIGURE 5.15**   Load balancing Outlook Web Access.

The slow-link cache mode and improved OWA client greatly increased CompanyABC's capabilities to consolidate email services to its largest sites and subsequently helped decrease the total cost of ownership for the entire organization.

## Summarizing Design Examples

Every organization is unique, but there are certain similarities that organizations of varying sizes possess. In general, the following company examples can be used as a starting point to match its needs to the needs of any similar organization. The following sections summarize the design decisions presented by the sample organizations in this chapter.

### Summarizing the Sample Small Organization Design Model

As illustrated throughout this chapter, Company123 followed a best practice model from small organizations for its Exchange Server 2003 design strategy. Each organization is unique, and there might be other factors that would change some of these design decisions, but they are presented to give a better understanding of how the needs of a sample small organization fit into Exchange Server 2003 design.

In summary, the following key design elements were implemented as part of Company123's small organization Exchange Server 2003 design:

- **Forest and Domain Design**—Single forest/Single domain—`company123.org`

- **AD Site and Replication Topology Placement**—Single site

- **AD Domain Controller and Global Catalog Placement**—Single domain controller/Global Catalog server

- **DNS Layout**—AD-integrated `company123.org` zone

- **Server Number and Placement**—Single Exchange Server 2003 system, on same hardware as AD domain controller

- **Server Redundancy and Optimization**—RAID1 drive set for OS and logs; RAID5 drive set for database and SMTP folder

- **Server Memory and Processor**—1GB RAM, single processor

- **Server Operating System**—Windows Server 2003 Standard Edition

- **Exchange Version and Org Name**—Exchange Server 2003 Standard Edition/org name: Company123

- **Administrative Group and Routing Group Structure**—Single admin group/single routing group

- **Public Folder Structure and Replication**—Single public folder store

- **Exchange Database and Storage Group Structure**—Single private folder store/single public folder store

- **Exchange Monitoring Solution**—Manual monitoring via event log parsing and using perfmon counters

- **Client Access Methods**—Outlook 2003 client for all users; Outlook 2003 in slow-link header mode for remote users

- **Front-end Server Design**—Single Exchange Server with front-end capabilities

## Summarizing the Sample Midsize Organization Design Model

OrganizationY is fairly typical of the run-of-the-mill, midsize organization in today's environment. The following design decisions can be useful in designing Exchange Server 2003 for these types of organizations:

- **Forest and Domain Design**—Used existing placeholder root domain AD structure with placeholder domain (`placeholder.internal`) and user resource domain (`ydomain.internal`)

- **AD Site and Replication Topology Placement**—Separate AD sites for three main locations

- **AD Domain Controller and Global Catalog Placement**—Full Global Catalogs in all sites

- **DNS Layout**—AD-integrated zones for local DNS trees; stub zone for separate tree in the forest

- **Server Number and Placement**—Exchange Servers in Manchester and Los Angeles; all other sites to access Exchange using auto-detected slow-link capabilities of Outlook 2003 or OWA

- **Server Redundancy and Optimization**—Redundant fans and power supplies; RAID sets for OS, logs, and database

- **Server Memory and Processor**—4GB RAM, quad processors

- **Server Operating System**—Windows Server 2003 Standard Edition

- **Exchange Version and Org Name**—Exchange Server 2003 Enterprise Edition

- **Administrative Group and Routing Group Structure**—Single admin group; two routing groups (Manchester, Los Angeles)

- **Public Folder Structure and Replication**—Two public folder instances, one for each routing group

- **Exchange Database and Storage Group Structure**—Three private store databases for each Exchange Server, divided by practice group; single production storage group

- **Exchange Monitoring Solution**—MOM deployed

- **Client Access Methods**—Outlook 2003 client for most users, OWA for Internet users

- **Front-end Server Design**—Single front-end server deployed for RPC over HTTP access to Exchange from the Internet

## Summarizing the Sample Large Organization Design Model

The complexities of larger organizations were not lost on the Exchange design team. Exchange Server 2003 was built upon the lessons learned by large organizations with Exchange 2000 and is consequently a better product. The sample large organization shown in this chapter is not unique, and some of the following design strategies can be used for similar designs:

- **Forest and Domain Design**—Separate, dedicated AD forest (`exchange.internal`) for Exchange with cross-forest transitive trusts to the two existing AD production forests

- **AD Site and Replication Topology Placement**—AD sites for each large location

- **AD Domain Controller and Global Catalog Placement**—Full Global Catalog servers in each AD site

- **DNS Layout**—Single AD-integrated DNS zone (`exchange.internal`)

- **Server Number and Placement**—Exchange Mailbox Servers in each major location; 4-node Exchange cluster with one passive node in Minneapolis

- **Server Redundancy and Optimization**—Redundant fans and power supplies; RAID drive sets; cluster in Minneapolis

- **Server Memory and Processor**—4GB RAM, quad processors

- **Server Operating System**—Windows Server 2003 Standard for non–cluster systems; Windows Server 2003 Enterprise for cluster nodes

- **Exchange Version and Org Name**—Exchange Server 2003 Enterprise Edition

- **Administrative Group and Routing Group Structure**—Two admin groups, eight routing groups

- **Public Folder Structure and Replication**—Public folder instance in each routing group

- **Exchange Database and Storage Group Structure**—Three private stores on each mailbox server, divided alphabetically; single storage group for each server

- **Exchange Monitoring Solution**—Microsoft Operations Manager deployed for all AD and Exchange System monitoring needs

- **Client Access Methods**—Preferred client Outlook 2003; support for older MAPI clients, OWA, OMA, IMAP, and POP3

- **Front-end Server Design**—Dual load-balanced front-end servers to provide for remote RPC over HTTP Internet access to Exchange data

## Summary

Exchange Server 2003 offers a broad range of functionality and improvements to messaging and is well suited for organizations of any size. With proper thought into the major design topics, a robust and reliable Exchange email solution can be put into place that will perfectly complement the needs of organizations of any size.

In short, Exchange easily scales up to support thousands of users on multiple servers, and it also scales down very well. Single Exchange server implementations can easily support hundreds of users, even those that are scattered in various locations. This flexibility helps establish Exchange as the premier messaging solution for organizations of any size.

## Best Practices

- Try to create an Active Directory design that is as simple as possible. Expand the directory tree with multiple subdomains and forests at a later date if needed.

- Even if the organization has high bandwidth between sites, create a site to better control replication and traffic between sites.

- When possible, DNS in an organization should be Microsoft DNS; however, Windows 2003 (and Windows 2000) also can be integrated with non-Microsoft DNS.

- Minimize the number of servers needed by consolidating services into as few systems as possible; however, after systems have been consolidated, take the left-over spare systems and create redundancy between systems.

- Use the /3GB /USERVA=3030 switch in boot.ini to optimize system memory in an Exchange Server with more than 1GB of physical RAM.

5

# CHAPTER 6

# Integrating Exchange Server 2003 in a Non-Windows Environment

**IN THIS CHAPTER**

- Synchronizing Directory Information with Microsoft Identity Integration Server (MIIS) 2003

- Synchronizing Exchange Server 2003 with Novell eDirectory

- Managing Identity Information Between LDAP Directories and Exchange Server 2003

- Using Services for Unix to Integrate Unix Environments with Exchange Server 2003

By using Active Directory for its own directory system, Exchange Server 2003 reduces the amount of administration required in an Exchange environment by eliminating the need for a redundant directory. But beyond the boundaries of Active Directory, organizations have needed the capabilities of further extending their directories, ideally reducing the maintenance required to a single administrative point. When a new employee starts, for example, a single entry would then ideally create a mailbox, enter the new employee into an HR database, create a Unix account, create a Novell Directory Services (NDS) account, and the like.

These types of capabilities and integration in non-Windows environments have become more streamlined and capable with the release of several new tools that possess these types of metadirectory capabilities. The use of these tools in an Exchange Server 2003 environment can greatly reduce the administrative overhead associated with having multiple directories, and subsequently make it less costly to operate.

This chapter focuses on the integration of Exchange Server 2003's directory system, Active Directory, with non-Windows environments, such as Unix, Novell, and Lightweight Directory Access Protocol (LDAP) directories. Various tools, such as Microsoft Identity Integration Server (MIIS) 2003 that can be used to accomplish this are presented, and the pros and cons of each are analyzed.

# Synchronizing Directory Information with Microsoft Identity Integration Server (MIIS) 2003

In most enterprises today, each individual application or system has its own user database or directory to track who is permitted to use that resource. Identity and access control data reside in different directories as well as applications such as specialized network resource directories, mail servers, human resource, voice mail, payroll, and many other applications.

Each has its own definition of the user's "identity" (name, title, ID numbers, roles, membership in groups). Many have their own password and process for authenticating users. Each has its own tool for managing user accounts, and sometimes its own dedicated administrator responsible for this task. Further, most enterprises have multiple processes for requesting resources and for granting and changing access rights. Some of these are automated, but many are paper-based. Many differ from business unit to business unit, even when performing the same function.

Administration of these multiple repositories often leads to time-consuming and redundant efforts in administration and provisioning. It also causes frustration for users, requiring them to remember multiple IDs and passwords for different applications and systems. The larger the organization, the greater is the potential variety of these repositories and the effort required to keep them updated.

In response to this problem, Microsoft developed Microsoft Metadirectory Services (MMS) to provide for identity synchronization between different directories. As the product improved, it was re-released under the new name Microsoft Identity Integration Server (MIIS) 2003.

## Understanding MIIS 2003

MIIS is a system that manages and coordinates identity information from multiple data sources in an organization, enabling you to combine that information into a single logical view that represents all of the identity information for a given user or resource.

MIIS enables a company to synchronize identity information across a wide variety of heterogeneous directory and non-directory identity stores. This enables customers to automate the process of updating identity information across heterogeneous platforms while maintaining the integrity and ownership of that data across the enterprise.

Password management capabilities enable end-users or helpdesk staff to easily reset passwords across multiple systems from one easy-to-use Web interface. End-users and helpdesk staff no longer have to use multiple tools to change their passwords across multiple systems.

> **NOTE**
>
> There are actually two versions of MIIS. The first version, known as the Identity Integration Feature Pack for Microsoft Windows Server is free to anyone licensed for Windows Server 2003 Enterprise Edition. It provides functionality to integrate identity information between multiple Active Directory forests or between Active Directory and Active Directory Application Mode (ADAM).
>
> The second version requires a separate licensing scheme and also requires SQL Server 2000 for the back-end database. This version is known as the Microsoft Identity Integration Server 2003—Enterprise Edition. It provides classic metadirectory functionality that enables administrators to synchronize and provision identity information across a wide variety of stores and systems.

## Understanding MIIS 2003 Concepts

It is important to understand some key terms used with MIIS 2003 before comprehending how it can be used to integrate various directories. Keep in mind that the following terms are used to describe MIIS 2003 concepts but might also help give you a broader understanding of how metadirectories function in general:

- **Management Agent (MA)**—An MIIS 2003 management agent is a tool used to communicate with a specific type of directory. For example, an Active Directory management agent enables MIIS 2003 to import or export data and perform tasks within Active Directory.

- **Connected Directory (CD)**—A connected directory is a directory that MIIS 2003 communicates with using a configured MA. An example of a connected directory is a Microsoft Exchange 5.5 directory database.

- **Connector Namespace (CS)**—The connector namespace is the replicated information and container hierarchy extracted from or destined to the respective connected directory.

- **Metaverse Namespace (MV)**—The metaverse namespace is the authoritative directory data created from the information gathered from each of the respective connector namespaces.

- **Metadirectory**—Within MIIS 2003, the metadirectory is made up of all the connector namespaces plus the authoritative metaverse namespace.

- **Attributes**—Attributes are the fields of information that are exported from or imported to directory entries. Common directory entry attributes are name, alias, email address, phone number, employee ID, or other information.

MIIS 2003 can be used for many tasks but is most commonly used for managing directory entry identity information. The intention here is to manage user accounts by synchronizing attributes, such as login ID, first name, last name, telephone number, title, and department. For example, if a user named Jane Doe is promoted and her title is changed from manager to vice president, the title change could first be entered in the HR or Payroll databases; then through MIIS 2003 management agents, the change could be replicated to other directories within the organization. This ensures that when someone looks up the title attribute for Jane Doe, it is the same in all the directories synchronized with MIIS 2003. This is a common and basic use of MIIS 2003 referred to as *identity management*. Other common uses of MIIS 2003 include account provisioning and group management.

> **NOTE**
>
> MIIS 2003 is a versatile and powerful directory synchronization tool that can be used to simplify and automate some directory management tasks. Because of the nature of MIIS 2003, it can also be a very dangerous tool as management agents can have full access to the connected directories. Misconfiguration of MIIS 2003 management agents could result in data loss, so careful planning and extensive lab testing should be performed before MIIS 2003 is released to the production directories of any organization. In many cases, it might be prudent to contact Microsoft consulting services and certified Microsoft solution provider/partners to help an organization decide whether MIIS 2003 is right for its environment, or even to design and facilitate the implementation.

## Exploring MIIS 2003 Account Provisioning

MIIS enables administrators to easily provision and de-provision users' accounts and identity information, such as distribution, email and security groups across systems, and platforms. Administrators will be able to quickly create new accounts for employees based on events or changes in authoritative stores such as the human resources system. Additionally, as employees leave a company they can be immediately de-provisioned from those same systems.

Account provisioning in MIIS 2003 enables advanced configurations of directory management agents, along with special provisioning agents, to be used to automate account creation and deletion in several directories. For example, if a new user account is created in Active Directory, the Active Directory MA could tag this account. Then, when the respective MAs are run for other connected directories, a new user account could be automatically generated.

One enhancement of MIIS 2003 over MMS is that password synchronization is now supported for specific directories that manage passwords within the directory. MIIS 2003 provides an application programming interface (API) accessed through the Windows Management Interface (WMI). For connected directories that manage passwords in the directory's store, password management is activated when the management agent is configured in Management Agent Designer. In addition to enabling password management for each management agent, Management Agent Designer returns a system name attribute using the WMI interface for each connector space object.

## Outlining the Role of Management Agents (MAs) in MIIS 2003

A management agent links a specific connected data source to the metadirectory. The management agent is responsible for moving data from the connected data source and the metadirectory. When data in the metadirectory is modified, the management agent can also export the data to the connected data source to keep the connected data source synchronized with the metadirectory. Generally, there is at least one management agent for each connected directory. MIIS 2003, Enterprise Edition, includes management agents for the following identity repositories:

- Active Directory

- Active Directory Application Mode (ADAM)

- Attribute-value pair text files

- Comma-separated value files

- Delimited text files

- Directory Services Markup Language (DSML) 2.0

- Exchange 5.5

- Exchange 2000 and Exchange Server 2003 Global Address List (GAL) synchronization

- Fixed-width text files

- LDAP Directory Interchange Format (LDIF)

- Lotus Notes/Domino 4.6/5.0

- Novell NDS, eDirectory, DirXML

- Sun/iPlanet/Netscape directory 4.x/5.x (with "changelog" support)

- Microsoft SQL Server 2000, SQL Server 7.0

- Microsoft Windows NT4 Domains

- Oracle 8i/9i

- Informix, dBase, ODBC and OLE DB support via SQL Server Data Transformation Services

> **NOTE**
>
> Service Pack 2 for MIIS introduced integrated support for synchronization with additional directories such as SAP. In addition, it also introduced the ability for end users to reset their own passwords via a web management interface.

Management agents contain rules that govern how an object's attributes are mapped, how connected directory objects are found in the metaverse, and when connected directory objects should be created or deleted.

These agents are used to configure how MIIS 2003 will communicate and interact with the connected directories when the agent is run. When a management agent is first created, all the configuration of that agent can be performed during that instance. The elements that can be configured include which type of directory objects will be replicated to the connector namespace, which attributes will be replicated, directory entry join and projection rules, attribute flow rules between the connector namespace and the metaverse namespace, plus more. If a necessary configuration is unknown during the MA creation, it can be revisited and modified later.

## Defining MIIS 2003 and Group Management

Just as MIIS 2003 can perform identity management for user accounts, it also can perform management tasks for groups. When a group is projected into the metaverse namespace, the group membership attribute can be replicated to other connected directories through their management agents. This enables a group membership change to occur in one directory and be replicated to other directories automatically.

## Installing MIIS 2003 with SQL 2000

Both versions of MIIS 2003 require a licensed version of SQL Server 2000 with SP3 or greater to run, and an install of the product will prompt for the location of a SQL 2000 Server, as illustrated in Figure 6.1.

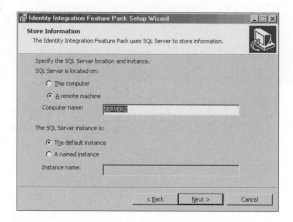

**FIGURE 6.1**    SQL install options with MIIS 2003.

It is not necessarily required to install a new instance of SQL, because an existing SQL 2000 SP3 or greater system can be used as well. If an existing SQL 2000 server is not available, SQL 2000 can be installed on the same system as MIIS 2003. This particular system must be running Windows Server 2003 as MIIS requires this version of the OS.

# Synchronizing Exchange Server 2003 with Novell eDirectory

Novell eDirectory and NDS environments are relatively commonplace in business environments, and there is often a need to integrate them into deployed Exchange infrastructures. Several tools exist that can make this a reality, including the MIIS 2003 tools discussed. In addition, tools in the Microsoft-supplied Services for NetWare can be used to synchronize directory information between the two directory systems.

## Understanding Novell eDirectory

Novell eDirectory is a distributed, hierarchical database of network information that is used to create a relationship between users and resources. It simplifies network management because network administrators can administer global networks from one location (or many) and manage all network resources as part of the eDirectory tree.

User administration is simplified because the users dynamically inherit access to network resources from their placement in the eDirectory tree. For example, eDirectory enables a user to dynamically inherit access to departmental resources, such as applications and printers, when that user is placed in the department's eDirectory container.

eDirectory information is typically stored on several servers, which are often at different locations. This enables information to be stored near the users who need it and provides efficient operation even if the users are geographically dispersed. Names are organized in a top-down hierarchy or tree structure. This helps users find resources in a structured manner. It also enables an administrator to administer a large network by delegating portions of the tree to local administrators.

The entries in an eDirectory database represent network resources available on the network and are referred to as objects. An object contains information that identifies, characterizes, and locates information pertaining to the resource it represents. eDirectory uses a single naming system that encompasses all servers, services, and users in an internetwork. In the past, names were administered separately on each server. Now, eDirectory enables information entered once to be accessible everywhere and lets a user log in once to access diverse, geographically separated resources.

An eDirectory database can be divided into logical partitions according to business needs, network use, geographical location, access time, and other factors. These partitions can be distributed to any server represented in the directory. When an eDirectory database is distributed to multiple servers, eDirectory maintains the equality of the distributed logical partitions by distributing object information changes to the appropriate servers.

## Deploying MIIS 2003 for Identity Management with eDirectory

MIIS 2003 can be an effective tool for managing identities between Novell eDirectory environments and Active Directory. Identity information could include names, email and physical addresses, titles, department affiliations, and much more. Generally speaking, identity information is the type of data commonly found in corporate phone books or intranets. To use MIIS 2003 for identity management between Active Directory and Novell eDirectory, follow these high-level steps:

1. Install MIIS 2003 and the latest service packs and patches.

2. Create a management agent for each of the directories, including an Active Directory management agent and a Novell eDirectory management agent.

3. Configure the management agents to import directory object types into their respective connector namespaces.

4. Configure one of the management agents—for example, the Active Directory MA—to project the connector space directory objects and directory hierarchy into the metaverse namespace.

5. Within each of the management agents, a function can be configured called attribute flow, which defines which directory object attributes from each directory will be projected into the respective metaverse directory objects. Configure the attribute flow rules for each management agent.

6. Configure the account-joining properties for directory objects. This is the most crucial step because it determines how the objects in each directory are related to one another within the metaverse namespace. To configure the account join, certain criteria can be used, such as employee ID or first name and last name combination. The key is to find the most unique combination to avoid problems when two objects with similar names are located—for example, if two users named Tom Jones exist in Active Directory.

7. After completely configuring the MAs and account joins, configure management agent runs profiles to tell the management agent what to perform with the connected directory and connector namespace. For example, perform a full import or export of data. The first time the MA is run, the connected directory information is imported to create the initial connector namespace.

8. After running the MAs once, you can run them a second time to propagate the authoritative metaverse data to the respective connector namespaces and out to the connected directories.

These steps outline the most common use of MIIS 2003; these steps can be used to simplify account maintenance tasks when several directories need to be managed simultaneously. When more sophisticated functionality using MIIS 2003 is needed, such as the automatic creation and deletion of directory entries, extensive scripting and customization of MIIS 2003 can be done to create a more complete enterprise account provisioning system.

## Using Microsoft Directory Synchronization Services to Integrate Directories

Microsoft Directory Synchronization Services (MSDSS), part of the Services for NetWare Toolkit, is a tool used for synchronization of directory information stored in the Active

Directory and NDS. MSDSS synchronizes directory information stored in Active Directory with all versions of NetWare; MSDSS supports a two-way synchronization with NDS and a one-way synchronization with Novell 3.x bindery services.

Because Active Directory does not support a container comparable to an NDS root organization and because Active Directory security differs from Novell, MSDSS, in migration mode only, creates a corresponding domain local security group in Active Directory for each NDS organizational unit (OU) and organization. MSDSS then maps each Novell OU or organization to the corresponding Active Directory domain local security group.

MSDSS provides a single point of administration; with one-way synchronization, changes made to Active Directory will be propagated over to NDS during synchronization. Synchronization from Active Directory to NDS allows changes to object attributes, such as a user's middle name or address, to be propagated. In two-way synchronization mode, changes from NDS to Active Directory require a full synchronization of the object (all attributes of the user object).

One of the key benefits to MSDSS is password synchronization. Passwords can be administered in Active Directory and the changes propagated over to NDS during synchronization. Password synchronization allows users access to Windows Server 2003 and Novell NDS resources with the same logon credentials.

The MSDSS architecture is made up of the following three components. These components manage, map, read, and write changes that occur in Active Directory, NDS, and NetWare bindery services:

- The configuration of the synchronization parameters is handled by the session manager.

- An object mapper relates the objects to each other (class and attributes), namespace, rights, and permissions between the source and target directories.

- Changes to each directory are handled by a DirSync (read/write) provider. LDAP is used for Active Directory calls and NetWare NCP calls for NDS and NetWare binderies.

In addition to the core components of MSDSS, the session configuration settings (session database) are securely stored in Active Directory. Specific scenarios for MSDSS include the following:

- A company is migrating directly from Novell to a Windows Server 2003 network. All network services—such as DNS, DHCP, and IIS services—are running on a single server. MSDSS can be used to migrate all users and files over to Windows Server 2003 after all services have been migrated.

- A company is gradually migrating from Novell to a Windows Server 2003 network. The network services—such as DNS, DHCP, and IIS—are installed on multiple servers and sites. MSDSS can be used to migrate and synchronize AD and NDS directories during the migration.

## Installing the Microsoft Directory Synchronization Service

MSDSS needs to be installed on a Windows domain controller to properly synchronize directory information between the two different network environments. To install MSDSS on a Windows Server 2003 domain controller, follow these steps:

1. On the domain controller computer on which the MSDSS will be installed, insert the CD into the CD-ROM drive.

2. Go into the MSDSS directory on the CD-ROM (such as d:\msdss) and run the msdss.msi script package. This launches the installation wizard.

3. Choose to install the Microsoft Directory Synchronization Service.

> **NOTE**
>
> Installing MSDSS initiates an extension of the schema of the Active Directory forest. As with any schema update, the Active Directory should be backed up (see Chapter 31, "Backing Up the Exchange Server 2003 Environment," for details on doing a full backup of the Active Directory). Also with a schema update, because the update will replicate directory changes to all global catalogs throughout the organization, the replication should be done at a time when a Global Catalog synchronization can take place without impact on the normal production environment.

## Synchronizing eDirectory/NDS with Active Directory Using Services for NetWare

For organizations that have both a Windows Active Directory and a Novell eDirectory (or NDS) environment, there are two primary methods of performing directory synchronization between the two directories. One method is using the Novell DirXML product, and the other method is using the MSDSS utility. To set up directory synchronization with MSDSS, do the following:

1. Launch the MSDSS utility by selecting Start, Programs, Administrative Tools, Directory Synchronization.

2. Right-click on the MSDSS tool option and select New Session.

3. Click Next at the New Session Welcome screen.

4. At the Synchronization and Migration Tasks screen, choose either NDS or Bindery for the type of service.

> **NOTE**
>
> Use the NDS option if Novell NetWare 4.x or higher running NDS or eDirectory is used. Use the Bindery option if Novell NetWare 3.2 or lower Bindery mode is running on the Novell network.

5. Dependent on the synchronization option, choose either a one-way (from Active Directory to NDS/Bindery), a two-way (AD to NDS/Bindery and back), or a migration from NDS/Bindery to Active Directory. Click Next.

6. For the Active Directory container and domain controller, choose the AD container to which objects will be synchronized, as well as the name of the domain controller that'll be used to extract and synchronize information, similar to the settings shown in Figure 6.2. Click Next.

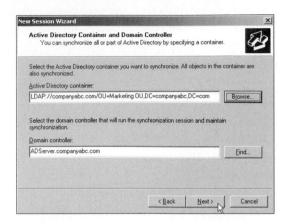

**FIGURE 6.2**   Setting server synchronization information settings.

7. For the NDS Container and Password, select the NDS container to and/or from which AD information will be synchronized. Enter a logon name and password for a supervisor account on Novell to access the Novell directory. Click Next.

8. On the initial reverse synchronization screen, select the password option to define passwords to be either blank, same as the username, set to a random value (that can be viewed in the log file), or set to an organizational default. Click OK after making the password option, and then click Next to continue.

9. Click Finish to begin the synchronization/migration process.

## Implementing MSDSS

MSDSS runs on a Windows 2000 or Windows 2003 domain controller and replicates user account and password information between the Active Directory environment and a Novell eDirectory or NDS environment. MSDSS is a Windows service that synchronizes user account information between Active Directory and NetWare. The following are best practices determined in the implementation of MSDSS in an enterprise environment:

- Ensure that the Microsoft MSDSS server that is running on a Windows Active Directory domain controller and the Novell directory server are on the same network segment or have limited hops between each other.

- Because directory synchronization reads and writes information directly to the network directory, test the replication process between mirrored domain and directory services in a test lab environment before implementing MSDSS for the first time in a production environment.

- Monitor directory and password synchronization processing times to confirm the transactions are occurring fast enough for users to access network resources. If users get an authentication error, consider upgrading the MSDSS server to a faster system.

- Password characteristic policies (requiring upper- and  lowercase letters, numbers, or extended characters in the password, and password change times) should be similar on both the Microsoft and Novell environments to minimize inconsistencies in authorization and update processes.

## Identifying Limitations on Directory Synchronization with MSDSS

Although directory synchronization can provide common logon names and passwords, MSDSS does not provide dual client support or any application-level linkage between multiple platform configurations. This means that if a Novell server is running IPX as a communication protocol and Windows is running TCP/IP, MSDSS does not do protocol conversion. Likewise, if an application is running on a Novell server requiring the Service Advertising Protocol (SAP), because Windows servers commonly use NetBIOS for device advertising, a dual client protocol stack must be enabled to provide common communications.

MSDSS merely links the logon names and passwords between multiple environments. The following are areas that need to be considered separate from the logon and password synchronization process:

- Protocols, such as TCP/IP and IPX/SPX, should be supported by servers and clients.

- Applications that require communication standards for logon authentication may require a client component to be installed on the workstations or servers in the mixed environment.

- Applications that were written for Novell servers (such as Network Loadable Modules [NLMs] or BTrieve databases) should be converted to support Windows.

- Login scripts, drive mappings, or other access systems compatible with one networking environment may not work across multiple environments, so those components should be tested for full compatibility.

- Backup utilities, antivirus applications, network management components, or system monitoring tools that work on one system should be purchased or relicensed to support another network operating configuration.

## Backing Up and Restoring MSDSS Information

MSDSS configuration, tables, and system configurations are critical to the operations of the MSDSS synchronization tool. Microsoft provides a backup and restore utility that enables the storage and recovery of MSDSS information. To back up MSDSS, do the following:

1. Select Start, Programs, Administrative Tools, MSDSS Backup & Restore Utility. A screen similar to the one shown in Figure 6.3 should appear.

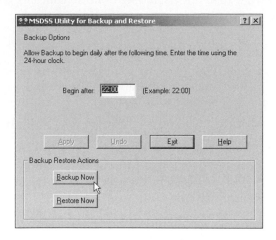

**FIGURE 6.3**   Backing up MSDSS information.

2. Either click on Backup Now to back up the MSDSS session directory, or change the default time when the MSDSS information should be backed up.

3. If it is required to back up the session directory information, the process will notify that the MSDSS service will need to be stopped. Choose Yes to continue.

4. Upon completion of the backup, there will be a prompt that the MSDSS service will need to be restarted. Choose Yes to restart the MSDSS service.

At any time, if the MSDSS session directory information gets corrupt or behaves erratically, the MSDSS information can be restored. To restore MSDSS, do the following:

1. Select Start, Programs, Administrative Tools, MSDSS Backup & Restore Utility.

2. Click on Restore Now to restore the MSDSS session directory.

3. When notified that the MSDSS service will need to be stopped, choose Yes to continue.

4. Upon completion of the restore, a final prompt will appear to signify that the MSDSS service will need to be restarted. Choose Yes to restart the MSDSS service.

## Managing Identity Information Between LDAP Directories and Exchange Server 2003

LDAP Directories are commonplace today and can be found in many business environments. Unix applications in particular make wide use of the LDAP standard for directories. Along with this proliferation of LDAP directory structures comes a need to synchronize the information contained within them to an Exchange Server 2003 environment. The Enterprise version of MIIS 2003 contains MAs that support synchronization to LDAP directories. Consequently, a good understanding of LDAP concepts is required before synching between the environments.

## Understanding LDAP from a Historical Perspective

To understand LDAP better, it is useful to consider the X.500 and Directory Access Protocol (DAP) from which it is derived. In X.500, the Directory System Agent (DSA) is the database in which directory information is stored. This database is hierarchical in form, designed to provide fast and efficient search and retrieval. The Directory User Agent (DUA) provides functionality that can be implemented in all sorts of user interfaces through dedicated DUA clients, Web server gateways, or email applications. The DAP is a protocol used in X.500 directory services for controlling communications between the DUA and DSA agents. The agents represent the user or program and the directory, respectively.

The X.500 directory services are application-layer processes. Directory services can be used to provide global, unified naming services for all elements in a network, translate between network names and addresses, provide descriptions of objects in a directory, and provide unique names for all objects in the Directory. These X.500 objects are hierarchical with different levels for each category of information, such as country, state, city, and organization. These objects may be files (as in a file system directory listing), network entities (as in a network naming service such as NDS), or other types of entities.

Lightweight protocols combine routing and transport services in a more streamlined fashion than do traditional network and transport-layer protocols. This makes it possible to transmit more efficiently over high-speed networks—such as ATM or FDDI—and media—such as fiber-optic cable.

Lightweight protocols also use various measures and refinements to streamline and speed up transmissions, such as using a fixed header and trailer size to save the overhead of transmitting a destination address with each packet.

LDAP is a subset of the X.500 protocol. LDAP clients are, therefore, smaller, faster, and easier to implement than X.500 clients. LDAP is vendor-independent and works with, but does not require, X.500. Contrary to X.500, LDAP supports TCP/IP, which is necessary for any type of Internet access. LDAP is an open protocol, and applications are independent of the server platform hosting the directory.

Active Directory is not a pure X.500 directory. Instead, it uses LDAP as the access protocol and supports the X.500 information model without requiring systems to host the entire X.500 overhead. The result is the high level of interoperability required for administering real-world, heterogeneous networks.

Active Directory supports access via the LDAP protocol from any LDAP-enabled client. LDAP names are less intuitive than Internet names, but the complexity of LDAP naming is usually hidden within an application. LDAP names use the X.500 naming convention called Attributed Naming.

An LDAP URL names the server holding Active Directory services and the Attributed Name of the object—for example:

```
LDAP:// Server1.fastportfolio.com/CN=LSomi, ,OU=Users,O=fastportfolio,C=US
```

By combining the best of the DNS and X.500 naming standards, LDAP, other key protocols, and a rich set of APIs, the Active Directory enables a single point of administration for all resources, including files, peripheral devices, host connections, databases, Web access, users, arbitrary other objects, services, and network resources.

## Understanding How LDAP Works

LDAP directory service is based on a client-server model. One or more LDAP servers contain the data making up the LDAP directory tree. An LDAP client connects to an LDAP server and asks it a question. The server responds with the answer or with a pointer to where the client can get more information (typically, another LDAP server). No matter which LDAP server a client connects to, it sees the same view of the directory; a name presented to one LDAP server references the same entry it would at another LDAP server. This is an important feature of a global directory service such as LDAP.

## Outlining the Differences Between LDAP2 and LDAP3 Implementations

LDAP 3 defines a number of improvements that enable a more efficient implementation of the Internet directory user agent access model. These changes include

- Use of UTF-8 for all text string attributes to support extended character sets

- Operational attributes that the directory maintains for its own use—for example, to log the date and time when another attribute has been modified

- Referrals enabling a server to direct a client to another server that might have the data that the client requested

- Schema publishing with the directory, enabling a client to discover the object classes and attributes that a server supports

- Extended searching operations to enable paging and sorting of results, and client-defined searching and sorting controls

- Stronger security through an SASL-based authentication mechanism

- Extended operations, providing additional features without changing the protocol version

LDAP 3 is compatible with LDAP 2. An LDAP 2 client can connect to an LDAP 3 server (this is a requirement of an LDAP 3 server). However, an LDAP 3 server can choose not to talk to an LDAP 2 client if LDAP 3 features are critical to its application.

> **NOTE**
>
> LDAP was built on Internet-defined standards and is composed of the following RFCs:
>
> - **RFC 2251**—Lightweight Directory Access Protocol (v3)
> - **RFC 2255**—The LDAP URL Format
> - **RFC 2256**—A Summary of the X.500(96) User Schema for use with LDAPv3
> - **RFC 2253**—Lightweight Directory Access Protocol (v3): UTF-8 String Representation of Distinguished Names
> - **RFC 2254**—The String Representation of LDAP Search Filters

# Using Services for Unix to Integrate Unix Environments with Exchange Server 2003

In addition to the MIIS 2003 directory synchronization tools available for synching to Unix-based directory systems, a series of tools is available from Microsoft to supply this functionality as well. The tools are known as Services for Unix (SFU), as illustrated in Figure 6.4, and include advanced functionality that can be used to integrate Unix systems into an Exchange Server 2003 environment.

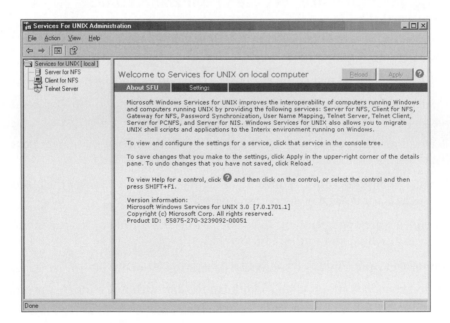

**FIGURE 6.4** Understanding Services for Unix.

## Defining Services for Unix

For many years, Unix and Windows systems were viewed as separate, incompatible environments that were physically, technically, and ideologically different. Over the years, however, organizations found that supporting two completely separate topologies within their environments was inefficient and expensive; much redundant work was also required to maintain multiple sets of user accounts, passwords, environments, and so on.

Slowly, the means to interoperate between these environments was developed. At first, most of the interoperability tools were written to join Unix with Windows, as evident with Samba, a method for Linux/Unix platforms to be able to access Windows NT file shares. Other interoperability tools were developed as well, but Microsoft was accused of pretending that Unix did not exist, and subsequently its Unix interoperability tools were not well developed.

The development of SFU for Windows Server 2003 signaled a change to this strategy. Microsoft developers spent a great deal of time developing tools for Unix that not only focused on migration, but also on interoperability. Long-awaited functionality—such as password synchronization, Unix scripts on Windows, joint security credentials, and the like—were presented as viable options and can be considered as part of a migration to, or interoperability scenario with, Windows Server 2003.

SFU is composed of several key components, each of which provides a specific integration task with different Unix environments. Any or all of these components can be used as part of SFU because the installation of the suite can be customized, depending on an organization's needs. The major components of SFU are as follows:

- Interix
- Gateway for NFS
- NFS Client
- NFS Server
- User Name Mapping
- Password Synchronization
- NIS Domains

Each component can be installed separately, or multiple components can be installed on a single server, as required. Each component is described in more detail in the following sections.

## Understanding Services for Unix Prerequisites

SFU interoperates with various "flavors" of Unix but was tested and specifically written for use with the following Unix iterations:

- Sun Solaris 2.7

- Red Hat Linux 7.0

- Hewlett-Packard HP-UX 11

- IBM AIX 4.3.3

---

**NOTE**

SFU is not limited to Sun Solaris, Red Hat Linux, HP-UX, or IBM AIX. It actually performs quite well in various other similar Unix implementations, but has not been tested to the same degree as with the most common Unix versions.

---

SFU has some other important prerequisites and limitations that must be taken into account before considering it for use in an environment:

- The Server for NIS must be installed on an Active Directory domain controller.

- The NFS Client and Gateway for NFS components cannot be installed on the same server.

- Password synchronization requires installation on domain controllers in each environment.

- The Server for NIS Authentication component must be installed on all domain controllers in the domain in which security credentials will be used.

## Outlining the Role of Interix As a Component of Services for Unix

There is one major change to the new version of SFU. Interix, a previously standalone product from SFU 2.0, has been integrated into the Services for Unix package. Interix is an extension to the Windows POSIX subsystem that enables the native execution of Unix scripts and applications in a Windows environment. Interix is not an emulation product, and all applications and scripts run natively in the built-in POSIX subsystem of Windows Server 2003.

Interix fills the gap between development on Unix platforms and development in Windows. It was written to enable programmers familiar with Unix to continue to use the most familiar programming tools and scripts, such as `grep`, `tar`, `cut`, `awk`, and many others. In addition, with limited reprogramming efforts, applications that run on Unix-based systems can be ported over to the Wintel platform, building on the low cost of ownership of Windows while retaining software investments from Unix.

## Understanding Interix Scripting

The Korn and C Shells are both available in the Interix environment, and both behave exactly as they would in Unix. SFU also supports the single-rooted file system through these shells, which negates the need to convert scripts to support drive letters.

## Outlining Interix Tools and Programming Languages

Interix supports all common Unix tools and utilities, with all the familiar commands such as grep, man, pr, nice, ps, kill, and many others. Each tool was built to respond exactly the way it is expected to behave, and Interix users can build or import their own customizable tools using the same procedures that they would in a Unix environment.

SFU streamlines the sharing of information between Unix and Windows Server 2003, allowing users from both environments to seamlessly access data from each separate environment, without the need for specialized client software. Using the Gateway for NFS, Server for NFS, and NFS Client enables this level of functionality and provides a more integrated environment.

## Synchronizing Users with SFU

The goal of single sign-on, in which users on a network log in once and then have access to multiple resources and environments, is still a long way off. It is common for a regular user to maintain and use three or more separate usernames and associated sets of passwords. SFU goes a long way toward making Single Sign-on a reality, however, with the User Name Mapping and Password Synchronization capabilities.

## Detailing User Name Mapping in SFU

User Name Mapping enables specific user accounts in Windows Server 2003 Active Directory to be associated with corresponding Unix user accounts. Because Exchange Server 2003 uses AD, it becomes easier to integrate Unix user accounts with their corresponding mailboxes in Exchange. In addition to mapping identically named user accounts, User Name Mapping enables the association of user accounts with different names in each organization. This factor is particularly useful considering the fact that Unix user accounts are case-sensitive, whereas Windows accounts are not. User Name Mapping, along with many components of Services for Unix, can be installed on a stand-alone server. In addition, User Name Mapping supports the ability to map multiple Windows user accounts to a single user account in Unix. This capability enables, for example, multiple administrators to map Windows Server 2003 Active Directory accounts with the Unix root administrator account.

## Performing Password Synchronization with SFU

Going hand in hand with the User Name Mapping service, password synchronization enables those user accounts that have been mapped to automatically update their passwords between the two environments. This functionality allows users on either side to change their passwords and have the changes reflected on the mapped user accounts in the opposite platform.

As previously mentioned, password synchronization must be installed on all domain controllers on the Active Directory side because all the DCs must be able to understand the Unix password requests forwarded to them. In addition, password synchronization is supported "out of the box" in only the following Unix platforms:

- Solaris 7 and 8

- Red Hat Linux 6.2 and 7.0

- HP-UX 11

All other flavors of Unix require a recompile of the platform, which is made easier by the inclusion of make files and SFU source code.

## Summary

Exchange Server 2003 running on Active Directory already goes far toward the goal of maintaining a single directory system for managing enterprise user accounts. The addition of advanced tools such as MIIS 2003, Services for NetWare, and Services for Unix further extends the capabilities of an organization to achieve this goal by providing for single metadirectory functionality. Proper use of these tools can significantly reduce the overhead associated with maintaining separate Exchange, Unix, NetWare, LDAP, and other directory implementations.

## Best Practices

- Use the Identity Integration Feature Pack (IIFP) version of MIIS 2003 for synchronizing information between various versions of Active Directory.

- Use the Enterprise version of MIIS 2003 for synchronization between non-AD directories, such as Novell eDirectory, LDAP, and Unix directories.

- Consider Services for NetWare when synching directories or integrating a Novell NetWare environment with Exchange Server 2003.

- Deploy Services for Unix to integrate Unix directories and functionality into an Exchange Server 2003 environment.

- Use Account Provisioning in MIIS 2003 to reduce the overhead associated with creating and deleting user accounts.

# PART III

# Networking Services
# Impact on Exchange

## IN THIS PART

| CHAPTER 7 | Domain Name System Impact on Exchange Server 2003 | 185 |
| CHAPTER 8 | Global Catalog and Domain Controller Placement | 211 |
| CHAPTER 9 | Securing Exchange Server 2003 with ISA Server 2004 | 233 |
| CHAPTER 10 | Configuring Outlook Web Access and Exchange Mobile Services | 287 |

# Domain Name System Impact on Exchange Server 2003

**IN THIS CHAPTER**

- Defining the Domain Name Service

- Outlining the Types of DNS Servers

- Examining DNS Components

- Using DNS to Route SMTP Mail in Exchange Server 2003

- Understanding DNS Requirements for Exchange Server 2003

- Configuring DNS to Support Exchange Servers

- Troubleshooting DNS Problems

The capability of any one resource to locate other resources is the centerpiece of a functional network. Consequently, the name-resolution strategy chosen for a particular NOS must be robust and reliable and should conform to industry standards.

Name resolution plays a major part in any electronic mail environment. As mail travels from the sender to the recipient, servers that handle the mail need to be able to resolve the name of the destination. This concept is similar to the way that post offices handle mail that is routed from one destination to the next. Just as the post office relies on ZIP Codes to route the mail between regions, electronic mail systems such as Exchange Server 2003 use the Domain Name System (DNS) to resolve where the mail server responsible for handling mail for a particular destination is located. It is subsequently a critical component of an Exchange messaging environment.

This chapter gives an overview of the main components of the Domain Name System (DNS) and how it works. Particular focus is given to the interaction between DNS and Exchange Server 2003 environments. In addition, troubleshooting advice and best practices are outlined and defined.

## Defining the Domain Name Service

Network naming services were developed to overcome the obstacle of humans having to remember complex computerized addresses. The DNS is a distributed database indexed by domain names. Recall that each domain name exists as a path in a large inverted tree, the domain namespace. The structure of this tree is hierarchical.

All DNS implementations adhere to a specific set of criteria:

- Each node in the tree has a text label that can be up to 63 characters long.

- The root of the tree is labeled with a zero-length name.

- The full name of any node in the tree is the path from the node to the root, using the text labels separated by a dot. When the root node's label is printed, it appears as the name of the node, ending with a dot.

- An absolute domain name is also referred to as a *fully qualified domain name (FQDN)*.

- DNS specification requires that nodes under the same parent have different labels. This restriction guarantees that a single node is uniquely defined within the tree, regardless of its location in the structure.

## How DNS Is Used

DNS is composed of two main components, clients and servers. The servers store information about specific components of the DNS structure and service requests, and the clients issue requests.

Each server contains a partial subset of the entire DNS namespace. These subsets are known as *zones*. DNS servers can contain copies of either forward or reverse lookup zones. *Forward lookup zones* are used to resolve DNS names to IP addresses. For example, the forward lookup zone for `microsoft.com` resolves `www.microsoft.com` to its numerical IP address. *Reverse lookup zones* are responsible for resolving IP addresses to DNS names, or the reverse of the forward lookup zones.

The key to understanding how a DNS client resolves DNS queries is to understand the order in which name resolution occurs. The DNS client follows through these steps when resolving DNS names. If a match is found, the results are returned and no further steps are taken. If all steps have been exhausted, the client receives an error. Initially, the DNS client will attempt to resolve the request using local resources:

- The local cache, which is obtained from previous queries, is searched. The items in this cache remain until the Time-to-Live (TTL) period, which is set on each item, expires. Every time the DNS client is shut down or the ipconfig /flushdns command is run, the cache is cleared.

- The local hosts file, which is stored in the `%systemroot%\system32\drivers\etc` directory is queried. The hosts file contains hostname-to-address mappings to enable manual hard-coding of DNS-to-IP addresses. These entries remain static and remain on the system even if it is rebooted. In addition, the hosts file is always queried before DNS servers are.

When the client has exhausted all its locally available options, it sends a query to the DNS server for the record that it is seeking. The DNS server attempts to resolve the client's query the following way:

- If the query result is found in any of the zones for which the DNS server is authoritative, the server responds to the host with an authoritative answer.

- If the result is in the zone entries of the DNS server, the server checks its own local cache for the information.

If the local resources fail to provide an answer to the client's query it attempts to resolve the query by sending the request to other DNS servers in the form of a recursive query. This query is sent to either the server that is listed as a Forwarder, or to the set of servers set up in the DNS server's Root Hints file.

The DNS query is then sent around the Internet until it comes into contact with the DNS servers that are listed as being authoritative for the zone listed in the query. That DNS server then sends back the reply as either affirmative (with the IP address requested) or negative.

## Understanding Who Needs DNS

Not all situations require the use of the DNS. There are other name resolution mechanisms that exist beside DNS, some of which come standard with the operating system that companies deploy. Managing name servers in a domain sometimes is too much overhead. DNS makes life easier, but not all scenarios have the requirement of a complex name resolution structure.

In the past, an organization with a standalone, non-interconnected network could get away with using only host files or Microsoft's Windows Internet Naming Service (WINS) to provide NetBIOS-to-IP address name translation. Some very small environments could also use broadcast protocols such as NetBEUI to provide name resolution. In modern networks, however, DNS becomes a necessity, especially in Active Directory environments.

In addition to local name translation, connecting to the Internet makes DNS connectivity a must. The World Wide Web, mail services, file transfer, and remote access services all use DNS services. Simply gaining access to the Internet does not, however, mean that every company or individual connecting to the Internet has to set up its own DNS server. Internet Service Providers (ISPs) can take care of managing DNS services on behalf of the user. A small organization might have a few hosts that access the Internet and might rely on its ISP to host those records. When a company wants to have more control over the domain and the name servers for that domain, it sets up its own DNS servers.

# Outlining the Types of DNS Servers

DNS is an integral and necessary part of any Windows Active Directory implementation. In addition, it has evolved to be the primary naming service for the Unix OS and the Internet. Because of Microsoft's decision to make Windows Server 2000 (and Windows

Server 2003) Internet-compatible, DNS has replaced WINS as the default name resolution technology. Microsoft followed IETF standards and made its DNS server compatible with other DNS implementations.

## Examining Unix BIND DNS

Many organizations have significant investment in Unix DNS implementations. Microsoft Exchange heavily relies on Active Directory, and Active Directory heavily relies on DNS. Microsoft Active Directory can coexist and use third-party DNS implementations as long as they support active updates and SRV records. In some cases, organizations choose not to migrate away from the already implemented Unix DNS environment; instead, they coexist with Microsoft DNS. Companies using Unix DNS for Microsoft AD clients should consider the following:

- The Unix DNS installation should be at least 8.1.2.

- For incremental zone transfers, the Unix DNS implementation should be at least 8.2.1.

## Exploring Third-Party (Checkpoint-Meta IP or Lucent VitalQIP) DNS

Third-party DNS implementations can provide significant enhancements in enterprise-class IP management. They either provide integrated management of Unix, Linux, and Microsoft DNS and DHCP servers from a central location or can be used in place of the previously mentioned implementations. Latest versions fully support dynamic DNS updates, SRV records, and Incremental Zone Transfer, which should be considered a necessity if Active Directory uses the third-party DNS servers.

## Examining DNS Compatibility Between DNS Platforms

DNS clients should, in theory, be able to query any DNS server regardless of who wrote that implementation. Active Directory, in particular, has some unique requirements from all DNS servers, however. Clients that authenticate to Active Directory look specifically for server resources, which means that the DNS server has to support SRV records. In Active Directory, DNS clients can dynamically update the DNS server with their IP address using Dynamic DNS. It is important to note that Dynamic DNS is not supported by all DNS implementations.

> **NOTE**
>
> In a mixed DNS environment, Microsoft specifically recommends using Microsoft DNS server as the primary DNS server for clients, with other DNS servers set up as forwarders or secondary zone servers. This is because Microsoft clients natively support dynamic registration and lookups against Microsoft DNS.

# Examining DNS Components

As previously mentioned, name servers, or DNS servers, are systems that store information about the domain namespace. Name servers can have either the entire domain namespace or just a portion of the namespace. When a name server only has a part of the domain namespace, the portion of the namespace is called a zone.

## DNS Zones

There is a subtle difference between zones and domains. All top-level domains, and many domains at the second and lower level, are broken into zones—smaller, more manageable units by delegation. A zone is the primary delegation mechanism in DNS over which a particular server can resolve requests. Any server that hosts a zone is said to be authoritative for that zone, with the exception of stub zones, defined later in the chapter.

A name server can have authority over more than one zone. Different portions of the DNS namespace can be divided into zones, each of which can be hosted on a DNS server or group of servers.

### Forward Lookup Zones

A forward lookup zone is created to do forward lookups on the DNS database, resolving names to IP addresses and resource information.

### Reverse Lookup Zones

A reverse lookup zone performs the opposite operation as the forward lookup zone. IP addresses are matched up with a common name in a reverse lookup zone. This is similar to knowing the phone number but not knowing the name associated with it. Reverse lookup zones must be manually created, and do not exist in every implementation. Reverse lookup zones are primarily populated with PTR records, which serve to point the reverse lookup query to the appropriate name.

> **TIP**
>
> It is good practice for the SMTP mail server to have a record in the reverse lookup zone. Spam control sites check for the existence of this record. It is possible to be placed on a spammer list if the site does not have a PTR record for the MX entry in the DNS reverse lookup zone.

### Active Directory–Integrated Zones

A Windows 2003 DNS server can store zone information in two distinct formats: Active Directory–integrated, or standard text file. An Active Directory–integrated zone is an available option when the DNS server is installed on an Active Directory domain controller. When a DNS zone is installed as an Active Directory zone, the DNS information is automatically updated on other server AD domain controllers with DNS by using Active Directory's multimaster update techniques. Zone information stored in the Active Directory allows DNS zone transfers to be part of the Active Directory replication process secured by Kerberos authentication.

### Primary Zones

In traditional (non–Active Directory–integrated) DNS, a single server serves as the master DNS server for a zone, and all changes made to that particular zone are done on that particular server. A single DNS server can host multiple zones, and can be primary for one and secondary for another. If a zone is primary, however, all requested changes for that particular zone must be done on the server that holds the master copy of the zone. As illustrated in Figure 7.1, `fastportfolio.com` is set up on `SERVER1` as the primary zone. On `SERVER2`, `development.fastportfolio.com` zone is located, and the server is the primary for that zone as well as for the `hq.fastportfolio.com` primary zone. `SERVER1` also holds a secondary zone copy of `development` and `hq` zone, and `SERVER2` holds a secondary zone for `fastportfolio.com`.

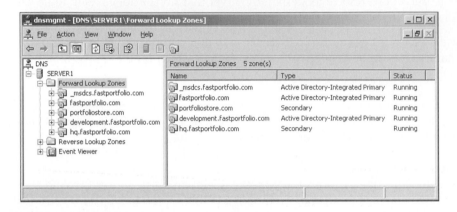

**FIGURE 7.1**    DNS primary and secondary zones.

Creating a new primary zone manually is a fairly straightforward process. Follow these steps to create a standard DNS zone:

1. Open the DNS MMC snap-in (Start, Administrative Tools, DNS).

2. Navigate to DNS\<Servername>\Forward Lookup Zones.

3. Right-click Forward Lookup Zones and choose New Zone.

4. Click Next on the Welcome screen.

5. Select Primary Zone from the list of zone types available and click Next to continue.

6. Type the name of the primary zone to be created and click Next.

7. Because a new zone file will be created, as opposed to importing an existing zone file, select Create a New File with This File Name and click Next.

8. Determine whether dynamic updates will be allowed in this zone. If not, select Do Not Allow Dynamic Updates and click Next to continue.

9. Click Finish on the Summary page to create the zone.

### Secondary Zones

A secondary zone is established to provide redundancy and load balancing for the primary zone. Secondary zones are not necessary if the zone has been set up as the Active Directory, because the zone will be replicated to all domain controllers in the domain. With secondary zones, each copy of the DNS zone database is read-only, however, because all recordkeeping is done on the primary zone copy. A single DNS server can contain several zones that are primary and several that are secondary. The zone creation process is similar to the one outlined in the preceding section on primary zones, but with the difference being that the zone is transferred from an existing primary server.

### Stub Zones (Delegated Zones)

A *stub zone* is a zone that contains no information about the members in a domain but simply serves to forward queries to a list of designated name servers for different domains. A stub zone subsequently contains only NS, SOA, and glue records. *Glue records* are A records that work in conjunction with a particular NS record to resolve the IP address of a particular name server. A server that hosts a stub zone for a namespace is not authoritative for that zone.

As illustrated in Figure 7.2, the stub zone effectively serves as a placeholder for a zone that is authoritative on another server. It allows a server to forward queries that are made to a specific zone to the list of name servers in that zone.

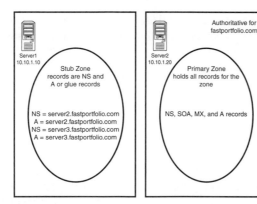

**FIGURE 7.2**    Understanding stub zones.

## DNS Queries

The primary function of DNS is to provide name resolution for requesting clients, so the query mechanism is one of the most important elements in the system. Two types of queries are commonly made to a DNS database: recursive and iterative.

### Recursive Queries

Recursive queries are most often performed by resolvers, or clients that need to have a specific name resolved by a DNS server. Recursive queries are also accomplished by a DNS server if forwarders are configured to be used on a particular name server. A *recursive query* asks whether a particular record can be resolved by a particular name server. The response to a recursive query is either negative or positive.

### Iterative Queries

*Iterative queries* ask a DNS server to either resolve the query or make best-guess referrals to a DNS server that might contain more accurate information about where the query can be resolved. Another iterative query is then performed to the referred server and so on until a result, positive or negative, is obtained.

## DNS Replication or Zone Transfer

Copying the DNS database from one server to another is accomplished through a process known as a *zone transfer*. Zone transfers are required for any zone that has more than one name server responsible for the contents of that zone. The mechanism for zone transfer varies, however, depending on the version of DNS and whether the zone is Active Directory–integrated.

### Primary-Secondary (Master-Slave) (RW-RO)

The primary name server holds the authoritative copy of the zone. For redundancy and load sharing, a secondary or slave name server should be set up. The DNS name resolution does not care that it is dealing with a primary or secondary server.

The main difference between the primary and secondary server is where the data comes from. The primary server reads it from a text file, and the secondary server loads it from another name server over the network via the zone transfer process. A slave name server is not limited to loading its data from a primary master name server; a slave server can load a zone from another slave server.

A big advantage of using a secondary name server is that only one set of DNS databases needs to be maintained, since all secondaries are read-only (RO) databases. All updates to the zone file have to be done at the server holding the primary zone file.

### AD-Integrated Replication

One of the most significant changes from Windows Server 2000 to Windows Server 2003 is the location where the zone file is stored in Active Directory. Windows Server 2003 Active Directory–integrated zones are stored in the application partition, whereas in Windows Server 2000 the zones were part of the Global Catalog (GC). This change in the location of the zone file reduces cross-forest replication traffic, because the application partition is unique to each domain.

## DNS Resource Records

In the DNS hierarchy, objects are identified through the use of *resource records (RR)*. These records are used for basic lookups of users and resources within the specified domain and are unique for the domain in which they are located. Because DNS is not a flat namespace, multiple identical RRs can exist at different levels in a DNS hierarchy.

### Start of Authority Record

The *Start of Authority (SOA) record* indicates that this name server is the best source for information within the zone. An SOA record is required for each zone. The server referenced by the SOA record maintains and updates the zone file.

The SOA record also contains other useful information, such as the latest serial number for the zone file, the email address of the responsible person for the zone, and Time to Live (TTL).

### Host Records

A *host (A) record* is the most common form of DNS records; its data is an Internet address in a dotted decimal form (for example, `10.32.1.132`). There should be only one A record for each address of a host.

### Name Server Records

*Name Server (NS) records* indicate which servers are available for name resolution for that zone. All DNS servers are listed as NS records within a particular zone. When slave servers are configured for the zone, they will have an NS record as well.

### Mail Exchange Record

A *mail exchanger (MX) record* specifies a mail forwarder or delivery server for Simple Mail Transfer Protocol (SMTP) servers. MX records are the cornerstone of a successful Internet mail routing strategy.

One of the advantages of a DNS over HOSTS files is its support for advanced mail routing. LMHOST files allowed only attempts to deliver mail to the host's IP address. If that failed, they could either defer the delivery of the message and try again later or bounce the message back to the sender. DNS offers a solution to this problem, by allowing the setup of backup mail server records.

Backup mail server records are also MX records, but with a higher priority number as the primary MX record for the domain. In Figure 7.3, `whitehouse.gov` has two mail servers, one with priority `100` and one with priority `200`.

The preference values of MX determine the order in which a mailer uses a record. The preference value of an MX record is important only in relation to the other servers for the same domain. Mail servers will attempt to use the MX record with the lower number first; if that server is not available, they will try to contact the server with a higher number, and so on.

MX record preference can also be used for load sharing. When several mail hosts have the same preference number associated with them, a sender can choose which mail server to contact first.

Mail routing based on preference numbers sounds simple enough, but there are major caveats that mail administrators have to understand. When troubleshooting mail routing problems, administrators use the following concepts to pinpoint the problem.

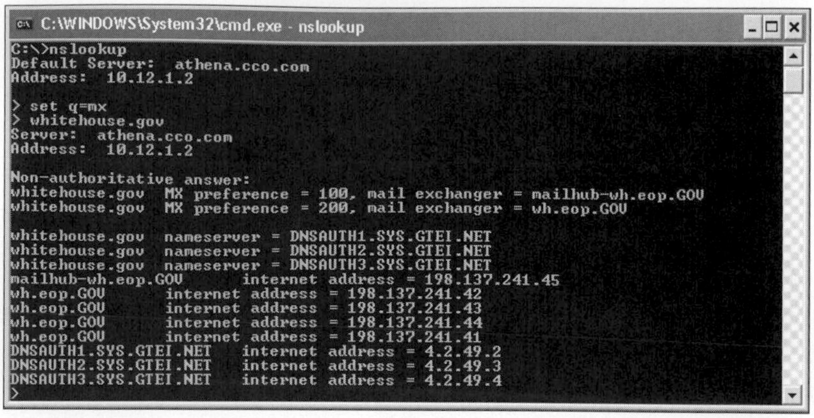

**FIGURE 7.3**    `whitehouse.gov` mail server entries.

Mail routing algorithms based on preference numbers can create routing loops in some situations. The logic in mail servers helps circumvent this problem:

```
Companyabc.com  IN     MX     10     m1.companyabc.com
Companyabc.com  IN     MX     20     m2.companyabc.com
Companyabc.com  IN     MX     30     m3.companyabc.com
```

Using this example, if a message is sent from a client to Bob@companyabc.com from an email address outside of companyabc.com, the mail server looks up the available mail server for companyabc.com based on the MX records set up for that domain. If the first mail server with the lowest priority is down (m1.companyabc.com), the mail server attempts to contact the second server (m2.companyabc.com). m2 will try to forward the message to m1.companyabc.com because that server is on the top of the list based on preferences. When m2 notices that m1 is down, it will try to contact the second server on the list (itself), creating a routing loop. If m2 would try to send the message to m3, m3 would try to contact m1, then m2, and then itself, creating a routing loop. To prevent these loops from happening, mail servers discard certain addresses from the list before they decide where to send a message. A mailer sorts the available mail host based on preference number first, and then checks the canonical name of the domain name on which it's running. If the local host appears as a mail exchange, the mailer discards that MX record and all MX records with the same or higher preference value. In this example, m2 will not try to send mail to m1 and m3 for final delivery.

The second common mistake administrators have to look out for with an MX record is the alias name. Most mailers do not check for alias names; they check for canonical names. Unless an administrator uses canonical names for MX records, there is no guarantee that the mailer will find itself and create a mail loop.

Hosts listed as mail exchangers must have A records listed in the zone so that mailers can find address records for each MX record and attempt mail delivery.

Another common mistake when configuring mail hosts is the configuration of the hosted domain local to the server. ISPs and organizations commonly host mail for several domains on the same mail server. As mergers and acquisitions happen, this situation becomes more common. The following MX record illustrates that the mail server for companyabc.com is really the server mail.companyisp.com:

```
companyabc.com IN MX 10 mail.companyisp.com
```

Unless mail.companyisp.com is set up to recognize companyabc.com as a local domain, it will try to relay the message to itself, creating a routing loop and resulting in the following error message:

```
554 MX list for companyabc.com points back to mail.companyisp.com
```

In this situation, if mail.companyisp.com was configured not to relay messages to unknown domains, it would refuse delivery of the mail.

### Service (SRV) Record

*Service (SRV) records* are RRs that indicate which resources perform a particular service. Domain controllers in Active Directory are referenced by SRV records that define specific services, such as the Global Catalog, LDAP, and Kerberos. SRV records are relatively new additions to DNS and did not exist in the original implementation of the standard. Each SRV record contains information about a particular functionality that a resource provides. For example, an LDAP server can add an SRV record indicating that it can handle LDAP requests for a particular zone. SRV records can be very useful for Active Directory because domain controllers can advertise that they can handle GC requests.

> **NOTE**
>
> Because SRV records are a relatively new addition to DNS, they are not supported by several downlevel DNS implementations, such as Unix BIND 4.1 and NT 4.0 DNS. It is therefore critical that the DNS environment that is used for Windows Server 2003's Active Directory has the capability of creating SRV records. For Unix BIND servers, version 8.1.2 or higher is required.

### Canonical Name Record

A *canonical name (CNAME)* represents a server alias or allows any one of the member servers to be referred to by multiple names in DNS. The record redirects queries made to the A record for the particular host. CNAME records are useful when migrating servers, and for situations in which friendly names, such as mail.companyabc.com, are required to point to more complex, server-naming conventions, such as sfoexch01.companyabc.com.

> **CAUTION**
>
> Though DNS entries for MX records can be pointed to canonical (CNAME) host records, doing so is not advised, and is not a Microsoft recommended best practice. Increased administrative overhead and the possibility of misrouted messages can result. Microsoft recommends that

mail/DNS administrators always link MX records to fully qualified principal names or domain literals. For further details, see Microsoft support article #153001.

## Other Records

Other, less common forms of records that may exist in DNS have specific purposes, and there might be cause to create them. The following is a sample list, but it is by no means exhaustive:

- **AAAA**—Maps a standard IP address into a 128-bit IPv6 address. This type of record becomes more prevalent as IPv6 is adopted.

- **ISDN**—Maps a specific DNS name to an ISDN telephone number.

- **KEY**—Stores a public key used for encryption for a particular domain.

- **RP**—Specifies the Responsible Person for a domain.

- **WKS**—Designates a particular Well Known Service.

- **MB**—Indicates which host contains a specific mailbox.

## Multihomed DNS Servers

For multihomed DNS servers, an administrator can configure the DNS service to selectively enable and bind only to IP addresses that are specified using the DNS console. By default, however, the DNS service binds to all IP interfaces configured for the computer.

This can include

- Any additional IP addresses configured for a single network connection.

- Individual IP addresses configured for each separate connection where more than one network connection is installed on the server computer.

- For multihomed DNS servers, an administrator can restrict DNS service for selected IP addresses. When this feature is used, the DNS service listens for and answers only DNS requests that are sent to the IP addresses specified on the Interface tab in the Server properties.

By default, the DNS service listens on all IP addresses and accepts all client requests sent to its default service port (UDP 53 or TCP 53 for zone transfer requests). Some DNS resolvers require that the source address of a DNS response be the same as the destination address that was used in the query. If these addresses differ, clients could reject the response. To accommodate these resolvers, you can specify the list of allowed interfaces for the DNS server. When a list is set, the DNS service binds sockets only to allowed IP addresses used on the computer.

In addition to providing support for clients that require explicit bindings to be used, specifying interfaces can be useful for other reasons:

- If an administrator does not want to use some of the IP addresses or interfaces on a multihomed server computer

- If the server computer is configured to use a large number of IP addresses and the administrator does not want the added expense of binding to all of them

When configuring additional IP addresses and enabling them for use with the Windows 2003 DNS server, consider the following additional system resources that are consumed at the server computer:

- DNS server performance overhead increases slightly, which can affect DNS query reception for the server.

- Although Windows 2003 provides the means to configure multiple IP addresses for use with any of the installed network adapters, there is no performance benefit for doing so.

- Even if the DNS server is handling multiple zones registered for Internet use, it is not necessary or required by the Internet registration process to have different IP addresses registered for each zone.

- Each additional address might only slightly increase server performance. In instances when a large overall number of IP addresses are enabled for use, server performance can be degraded noticeably.

- In general, when adding network adapter hardware to the server computer, assign only a single primary IP address for each network connection.

- Whenever possible, remove nonessential IP addresses from existing server TCP/IP configurations.

# Using DNS to Route SMTP Mail in Exchange Server 2003

Simple Mail Transfer Protocol (SMTP) has become the standard Internet protocol for electronic mail. Commonly used on Unix and Linux environments, and more recently in Windows, SMTP is used not only for mail delivery across the Internet, but also used within Active Directory as an alternative transport mechanism for site traffic.

Domains that want to participate in electronic mail exchange need to set up MX record(s) for their published zone. This advertises the system that will handle mail for the particular domain, so that SMTP mail will find the way to its destination.

## Using DNS in Exchange 2003

For name resolution, Microsoft Exchange Server 2003 primarily uses DNS. In addition to talking to a DNS server for local name lookup, it also uses DNS to communicate over the Internet via SMTP mail services.

Each user has to authenticate to the Active Directory in order to access an Exchange mailbox. Exchange Server 2003 itself has information about authenticating other servers in the domain. This information can be found in Exchange System Manager under the Server Properties, Directory Access tab. The Exchange server obtains this information from the DNS server.

## Understanding SMTP Mail Routing

Email is probably the most widely used TCP/IP and Internet application today, with the possible exception of the World Wide Web. SMTP defines a set of rules for addressing, sending and receiving mail between systems, based on the model of communication shown in Figure 7.4. As a result of a user mail request, the SMTP sender establishes a two-way connection with the SMTP receiver. The SMTP receiver can be either the ultimate destination or an intermediate (mail gateway). The SMTP sender generates commands that are replied to by the receiver. All this communication takes place over TCP port 25. When the connection is established, a series of commands and replies are exchanged between the client and server. This connection is similar to a phone conversation, and the commands and responses are equivalent to verbal communication.

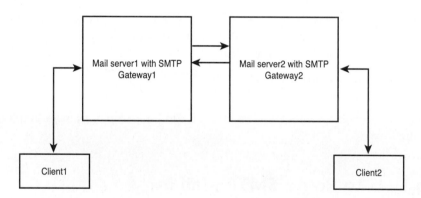

**FIGURE 7.4**    SMTP communications.

> **NOTE**
>
> In various implementations, there is a possibility of exchanging mail between the TCP/IP SMTP mailing system and the locally used mailing systems. These applications are called *mail gateways* or *mail bridges*. Sending mail through a mail gateway may alter the end-to-end delivery specification, because SMTP guarantees delivery only to the mail gateway host, not to the real destination host, which is located beyond the TCP/IP network. When a mail gateway is used, the SMTP end-to-end transmission is host-to-gateway, gateway-to-host, or gateway-to-gateway; the behavior beyond the gateway is not defined by SMTP.

## Examining Client DNS Use for Exchange

Before users can access their mailboxes on an Exchange server, they must be authenticated. Authentication requires a DNS lookup in order to locate a domain controller on which the users' accounts can be authenticated.

Clients normally cannot deliver messages directly to destination mail hosts. They typically use a mail server to relay messages to destinations. Using SMTP, clients connect to a mail server, which first verifies that the client is allowed to relay through this server, and then accepts the message destined for other domains.

A client uses DNS to resolve the name of a mail server. For example, when configuring an Outlook mail client to connect to an Exchange server, only the short name and not the FQDN is used to connect to the server. The short name is resolved by DNS to the FQDN of the Exchange server to which the client is connected.

# Understanding DNS Requirements for Exchange Server 2003

In Active Directory, all client logons and lookups are directed to local domain controllers and GC servers through references to the SRV records in DNS. Each configuration has its DNS and resource requirements. In a member server configuration, Exchange relies on other servers for client authentication and uses DNS to find those servers. In an Active Directory domain controller configuration, on the other hand, the Exchange server also participates in the authentication process for Active Directory.

### Exchange 5.5 and E2k3 DNS/WINS Name Resolutions Requirements

Exchange 5.5 and NT4 use different name resolution orders when trying to resolve a name. NT4 relies on the local hostname, HOST, DNS NetBIOS name cache, WINS, B-Cast NetBIOS broadcasts, and the LMHOSTS file for name resolution. Windows 2000 and higher clients, on the other hand, use a significantly different approach for name resolution. Windows 2000 uses hostname resolution first, rather than NetBIOS name resolution techniques. In addition, a local cache is used to reduce network traffic.

Windows NT servers and Exchange 5.5 servers find Exchange 2003 servers via DNS, but name resolution might be slightly slower because of the order previously outlined. Windows 2003 and Exchange rely on DNS, so these servers must be part of a DNS name resolution schema. When older clients and servers are used that do not have DNS as the primary name resolution, it is best to add Windows 2003 servers and Exchange Server to the WINS database statically—directly to the WINS database—or dynamically—adding the WINS server IP address under the TCP/IP configuration section.

> **TIP**
>
> When migrating from Windows NT4, one of the first tasks is to update the DNS server to a version that supports dynamic updates and, most importantly, SRV records.

## DNS and SMTP RFC Standards

In 1984, the first DNS architecture was designed. The result was released as RPC 882 and 883. These were superseded by RFC 1034 (Domain Names—concepts and facilities) and 1035 (Domain Names—implementation and specification), the current specifications of the DNS. RFCs 1034 and 1035 have been improved by many other RFCs, which describe fixes for potential DNS security problems, implementation problems, best practices, and performance improvements to the current standard.

RFC 2821 defines the SMTP, which replaced the earlier versions of RFC 821 and 822.

## Virtual SMTP Servers

The SMTP protocol is an essential part of Exchange 2003 and Active Directory. Although Exchange 4.x and 5.x messaging is primarily based on X.400 mail transfer standards, Exchange 2000 and 2003 are native SMTP messaging systems. However, when an Exchange 2000/2003 server has to communicate to an Exchange 5.5 server, it still uses the MTA and x.400 for communication.

A single virtual SMTP server runs by default on all Exchange 2003 servers. In most cases, this is the SMTP server needed for external and internal communications. An administrator might want to install an additional SMTP virtual server for the following reasons:

- To maintain multiple domain namespaces on the same server

- To establish different authentication methods for different users or groups

- To configure different SMTP options to different users

## Routing Groups

A *routing group* is a collection of servers that enjoy a persistent high-bandwidth connection and it's used to organize server communication based on bandwidth constraints. All servers within a routing group communicate with each other directly when transferring mail. This is also known as *mesh topology*. Reasons for setting up routing groups include the following:

- Low speed or unreliable connection between Exchange servers

- Administrators wanting more control over the message flow within the organization

- Fault tolerance or high availability between routing groups

Exchange messages can be routed from sender to recipient the following ways:

- With sender and recipient located on the same server

- With sender and recipient located in the same routing group

- Between routing groups

- To a server outside the Exchange organization

The preferred method for connecting routing groups in Exchange is via the routing group connector. Routing groups themselves do not use a particular protocol, but will use SMTP for all traffic to and from Exchange 2000/2003 servers and Remote Procedure Calls (RPCs) for Exchange 5.5 servers. Email routing between routing groups is funneled through the bridgehead server or servers, which is fully configurable on a per–routing group basis.

## Mixed Environment Mail Routing

Companies with multiple email systems usually use SMTP mail transport between these dissimilar systems. Microsoft Exchange Server 2003 can connect to any other RFC-compliant SMTP gateway. It also supports authenticated and secure transfer between SMTP gateways.

## SMTP Mail Security, Virus Checking, and Proxies

Spamming and security issues are daily concerns for email administrators. As the Internet grows, so too does the amount of spam that mail servers have to confront. Unwanted messages not only can take up a lot of space on mail servers, but can also carry dangerous payloads or viruses. Administrators have to maintain a multilayered defense against spam and viruses.

There are several security areas that have to be addressed:

- Gateway security to control access to the mail server delivering messages to/from the Internet

- Mail database security where messages are stored

- Client mail security where messages are opened and processed

Gateway security is a primary concern for administrators because a misconfigured gateway can become a gateway used by spammers to relay messages. Unauthenticated message relay is the mechanism spammers rely on to deliver their messages. When a server is used for unauthenticated message relay, it not only puts a huge load on server resources, but also might get the server placed on a spam list. Companies relying on spam lists to control their incoming mail traffic refuse mail delivered from servers listed in the database; therefore, controlling who can relay messages through the mail relay gateway is a major concern.

Application-level firewalls such as Microsoft's Internet Security and Acceleration (ISA) Server 2004 allow mail proxying on behalf of the internal mail server. Essentially, mail hosts trying to connect to the local mail server have to talk to the proxy gateway, which is responsible for relaying those messages to the internal server. Going one step further, these proxy gateways can also perform additional functions to check the message they are relaying to the internal host or to control the payload passed along to the internal server.

This configuration is also helpful in stopping dangerous viruses from being spread through email. For example, dangerous scripts could potentially be attached to email, which could execute as soon as the user opens the mail. A safe configuration allows only permitted attachment types to pass through. Even those attachments have to pass virus checking before they are passed to an internal mail server. Figure 7.5 illustrates the schematics of how an application gateway works.

The following process describes how one server contacts another server to send email messages that include virus checking:

1. The sender contacts its SMTP gateway for message delivery.

2. The SMTP gateway looks up the MX record for the recipient domain and establishes communication with it. The application proxy acting as the SMTP server for the recipient's domain receives the message. Before the recipient gateway establishes communication with the sender gateway, it can check whether the sender SMTP gateway is listed on any known spam lists. If the server is not located on any spam lists, communication can resume and the message can be accepted by the proxy server.

3. The application proxy forwards the message for virus checking.

4. After virus checking, the mail is routed back to the application proxy.

5. Mail is delivered to the internal SMTP gateway.

6. The recipient picks up the mail message.

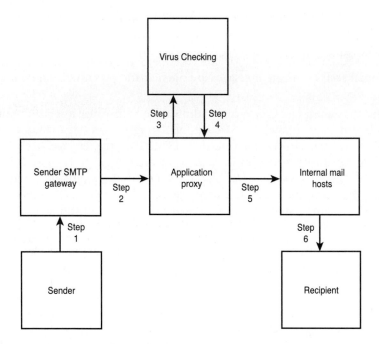

**FIGURE 7.5**    Examining an Application gateway.

> **NOTE**
>
> Application proxy and virus or spam checking might be done within the same host. In that case, steps 2–5 are done in a single system without having to transfer a message to a separate host.

Third-party products can be used for virus checking not only at the gateway level, but also directly on an Exchange email database. Database level scans can be scheduled to run at night when the load is lower on the server; real-time scans can perform virus checking in real time before any message is written to the database.

The final checkpoint for any multilayered virus protection is on the workstation. The file system and the email system can be protected by the same antivirus product. Messages can be scanned before a user is able to open the message or before a message is sent.

Protecting email communications and message integrity puts a large load on administrators. Threats are best dealt with using a multilayered approach from the client to the server to the gateway. When each step along the way is protected against malicious attacks, the global result is a secure, well-balanced email system.

## SMTP Server Scalability and Load Balancing

In a larger environment, administrators might set up more than one SMTP server for inbound and/or outbound mail processing. Windows Server 2003 and Exchange Server 2003 provide a very flexible platform to scale and balance the load of SMTP mail services. DNS and Network Load Balancing (NLB) are key components for these tasks.

Administrators should not forget about hardware failover and scalability. Multi-network interface cards are highly recommended. Two network cards can be teamed together for higher throughput, can be used in failover configuration, or can be load balanced by using one network card for front-end communication and another for back-end services, such as backup.

Network design can also incorporate fault tolerance by creating redundant network routes and by using technologies that can group devices together for the purpose of load balancing and delivery failover. Load balancing is the process where requests can be spread across multiple devices to keep individual service load at an acceptable level.

Using NLB, Exchange Server SMTP processes can be handed off to a group of servers for processing, or incoming traffic can be handled by a group of servers before it gets routed to an Exchange server. The following example outlines a possible configuration for using NLB in conjunction with Exchange. Figure 7.6 illustrates the layout of the message flow.

DNS, in this example, has been set up to point to the name of the NLB cluster IP address. Externally, the DNS MX record points to 196.8.10.15 as the mail relay gateway for companyabc.com. Exchange server uses smarthost configuration to send all SMTP messages to the NLB cluster. The NLB cluster is configured in balanced mode where the servers share equal load. Only port 25 traffic is allowed on the cluster servers. This configuration would offload SMTP mail processing from the Exchange servers because all they have to do is to pass the message along to the cluster for delivery. They do not need to contact any outside SMTP gateway to transfer the message. This configuration allows scalability because when the load increases, administrators can add more SMTP gateways to the cluster. This setup also addresses load balancing, because the NLB cluster is smart enough to notice whether one of the cluster nodes has failed or is down for maintenance. An additional ramification of this configuration is that message tracking will not work beyond the Exchange servers.

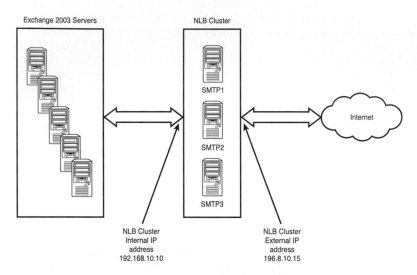

**FIGURE 7.6**    Message flow with NLB and Exchange Server 2003.

> **NOTE**
>
> Administrators should not forget about the ramifications of antivirus and spam-checking software with NLB. These packages in gateway mode can also be used as the SMTP gateway for an organization. In an NLB clustered mode, an organization would need to purchase three sets of licenses to cover each NLB node.

A less used but possible configuration for SMTP mail load balancing uses DNS to distribute the load between multiple SMTP servers. This configuration, known as DNS round robin, does not provide as robust a message routing environment as the NLB solution.

## Configuring DNS to Support Exchange Servers

Because DNS is already required and integrated with Active Directory before Exchange Server is installed, most companies already have a robust DNS environment in place. Exchange by itself accesses DNS servers to find resources on the local network, such as Global Catalog servers and domain controllers. It also uses DNS to search for MX records of other domains.

## External DNS Servers for the Internet

The external DNS server for Exchange (or any other mail system) is responsible for giving out the correct MX and A records for the domain for which it is authoritative. Administrators should take security precautions regarding who can change these records—and how. Intentionally or accidentally changing these records can result in undelivered mail.

Most companies let their ISP host the external DNS entries for their domain. ISPs provide internal administrators with methods of managing DNS entries for their domain. In some cases it has to be done over the phone, but normally a secure Web interface is provided for management. Although this setup is convenient and ISPs usually take care of load balancing and redundancy, some companies opt to host their own zone records for the Internet. In this case companies have to host their own DNS server in-house with the ISP responsible only for forwarding all requests to their DNS server. When hosting an external DNS server, in-house administrators have to think about security issues and DNS configuration issues.

## Internal DNS Servers for Outbound Mail Routing

Exchange SMTP gateways are responsible for delivering mail to external hosts. As with any name process involving resolving names to IP addresses, DNS plays a major part in successful mail delivery.

Exchange can route mail to outbound destinations two ways. One is by using smarthosts to offload all processing of messages destined to other domains. As seen in the previous section, an NLB cluster can be used to route Internet mail to its final destination.

The second way is the default, with Exchange Server 2003 taking care of delivering messages to other domains. In this scenario, Exchange queries DNS servers for other domains' MX records and A records for address resolution.

## Internal DNS Servers for Internal Routing of Email Between Exchange Servers

Exchange 2003 depends entirely on SMTP for mail routing, both internally and externally. Internally, Exchange servers have to be able to resolve either the short name (for example, server1) or the FQDN (for example, server1.companyabc.com).

# Troubleshooting DNS Problems

Troubleshooting is part of everyday life for administrators. DNS is no exception to this rule. Subsequently, understanding how to use the following tools to troubleshoot DNS will not only help avoid mistakes when configuring DNS-related services, but will also provide administrators with a useful toolbox to resolve issues.

## Using Event Viewer to Troubleshoot

The first place to look for help when something is not working, or it appears that it is not working, is the system logs. With Windows Server 2003, the DNS logs are conveniently located directly in the DNS MMC console. Parsing this set of logs can help the administrator troubleshoot DNS replication issues, query problems, and other issues.

For more advanced Event Log diagnosis, administrators can turn on Debug Logging on a per-server basis. Debugging should be turned on only for troubleshooting, because log files can fill up fast. To enable Debug Logging, follow these steps:

1. Open the DNS MMC snap-in (Start, Administrative Tools, DNS).

2. Right-click on the server name and choose Properties.

3. Select the Debug Logging tab.

4. Check the Log Packets for Debugging box.

5. Configure any additional settings as required and click OK.

Turn off these settings after the troubleshooting is complete.

## Troubleshooting Using the `ipconfig` Utility

The `ipconfig` utility is used not only for basic TCP/IP troubleshooting, but can also be used to directly resolve DNS issues. These functions can be invoked from the command prompt with the correct flag, detailed as follows:

- **`ipconfig /displaydns`**—This command displays all locally cached DNS entries. This is also known as the DNS resolver cache.

- **`ipconfig /flushdns`**—This switch can be used to save administrators from a lot of headaches when troubleshooting DNS problems. This command flushes the local DNS cache. The default cache time for positive replies is 1 day; for negative replies, it is 15 minutes.

- **`ipconfig /registerdns`**—This flag informs the client to automatically re-register itself in DNS, if the particular zone supports dynamic zone updates.

---

**NOTE**

Client-side DNS caching is configurable in the registry via the following key:

`\\HKLM\System\CurrentControlSet\Services\DNSCach\Parameters`

Set `MaxCacheEnrtyTtlLimit = 1` (default = 86400)

Set `NegativeCacheTim = 0` (default = 300)

The first entry overwrites the TTL number in the cached address to 1 second, essentially disabling the local cache. The second entry changes the negative cache from 15 minutes to 0, essentially disabling the negative cache facility.

---

## Monitoring Exchange Using Performance Monitor

Performance monitor is a built-in, often overlooked utility that enables a great deal of insight into issues in a network. Many critical DNS counters can be monitored relating to queries, zone transfers, memory use, and other important factors.

## Using `nslookup` for DNS Exchange Lookup

In both Windows and Unix environments, `nslookup` is a command-line administrative tool for testing and troubleshooting DNS servers. Simple query structure can provide powerful results for troubleshooting. A simple query contacts the default DNS server for the system and looks up the inputted name.

To test a lookup for www.companyabc.com, type

```
nslookup www.companyabc.com
```

at the command prompt. `nslookup` can also be used to look up other DNS resource types—for example, an MX or SOA record for a company. To look up an MX record for a company type, use the following steps, as illustrated in Figure 7.7:

1. Open a command prompt instance.

2. Type **nslookup** and press Enter.

3. Type **set query=mx** (or simply **set q=mx**) and press Enter.

4. Type **microsoft.com** and press Enter.

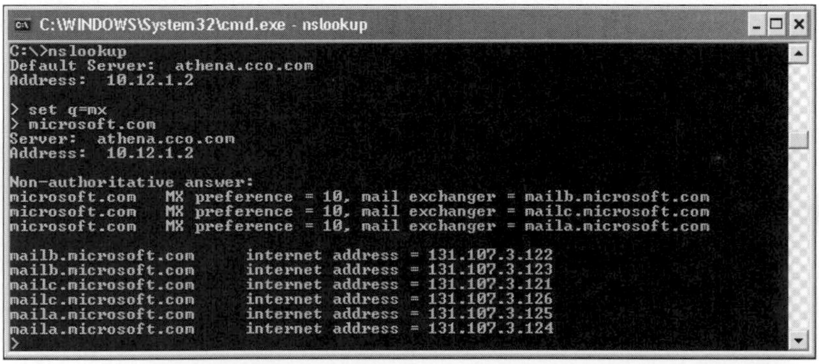

FIGURE 7.7    `nslookup` MX query.

An MX record output not only shows all the MX records that are used for that domain, their preference number, and the IP address they are associated with, the name server for the domain is also displayed.

By default, `nslookup` queries the local DNS server the system is set up to query. Another powerful feature of `nslookup` is that it can switch between servers to query. This feature enables administrators to verify that all servers answer with the same record as expected.

For example, if an organization is moving from one ISP to another, it might use this technique, because the IP addresses for its servers might change during the move. The DNS change takes an administrator only a few minutes to do, but replication of the changes through the Internet might take 24–72 hours. During this time, some servers might still use the old IP address for the mail server. To verify that the DNS records are replicated to other DNS servers, an administrator can query several DNS servers for the answer through the following technique:

1. Open a command prompt instance.

2. Type **nslookup** and press Enter.

3. Type **server <server IP address>** for the DNS server you want to query.

4. Type **set query=mx** (or simply **set q=mx**) and press Enter.

5. Type **microsoft.com** and press Enter.

Repeat from step 3 for other DNS servers.

nslookup can also help find out the version of BIND used on a remote Unix DNS server. An administrator may find it useful to determine which version of BIND each server is running for troubleshooting purposes. To determine this, the following steps must be performed:

1. From the command line, type **nslookup**, and then press Enter.

2. Type **server <server IP address>** for the IP address of the DNS server queried.

3. Type **set class=chaos** and then press Enter.

4. Type **set type=txt** and then press Enter.

5. Type **version.bind** and then press Enter.

If the administrator of the BIND DNS server has configured the server to accept this query, the BIND version that the server is running is returned. As previously mentioned, the BIND version must be 8.1.2 or later to support SRV records.

## Troubleshooting with DNSLINT

DNSLINT is a Microsoft Windows utility that helps administrators diagnose common DNS name resolution issues. The utility is not installed by default on Windows servers and has to be downloaded from Microsoft. Microsoft Knowledge Base Article 321046 contains the link to download this utility.

When this command-line utility runs, it generates an HTML file in the directory it runs from. It can help administrators with Active Directory troubleshooting and also with mail-related name resolution and verification. Running DNSLINT /d <domain_name> /c tests DNS information as known on authoritative DNS servers for the domain being tested; it also checks SMTP, POP3, and IMAP connectivity on the server. For the complete options for this utility, run DNSLINT /?.

## Using dnscmd for Advanced DNS Troubleshooting

The dnscmd utility is essentially a command-line version of the MMC DNS console. Installed as part of the Windows Server 2003 Support tools, this utility enables administrators to create zones, modify zone records, and perform other vital administrative functions. To install the support tools, run the support tools setup from the Windows Server 2003 CD (located in the \support\tools directory). You can view the full functionality of this utility by typing **DNSCMD** **/?** at the command line, as illustrated in Figure 7.8.

**FIGURE 7.8**  dnscmd functionality.

# Summary

DNS is the cornerstone of name resolution on the Internet and within Windows Server 2003 and Active Directory. Subsequently, it is also an integral part of any modern email solution such as Exchange Server 2003. It is impossible to fully understand Exchange without a solid understanding of DNS and the tie-ins DNS has with the messaging platform. A good understanding of DNS, on the other hand, helps keep both Exchange and Active Directory stable and reliable.

# Best Practices

The following are best practices from this chapter:

- Use Windows 2000/2003 DNS for client AD name resolution whenever possible. If not possible, ensure that the Unix BIND version is 8.1.2 or higher to support SRV records.

- Administrators should set up redundant name resolution servers in the event that one server fails.

- Use caching-only DNS servers to help leverage load and minimize zone transfer traffic across WAN links.

- Make any DNS implementations compliant with the standard DNS character set so that zone transfers are supported to and from non–Unicode-compliant DNS implementations, such as Unix BIND servers. This includes a–z, A–Z, 0–9, and the hyphen (-) character.

- Set up multiple MX records for all mail servers for redundancy. ISPs usually function as a secondary mail relay gateway for the hosted domain.

- It is wise to segregate inbound and outbound SMTP traffic from direct exposure to the Internet by deploying an SMTP smarthost in the DMZ of the firewall.

# CHAPTER 8

# Global Catalog and Domain Controller Placement

**IN THIS CHAPTER**

- Understanding Active Directory Structure

- Examining the Role of Domain Controllers in AD

- Defining the Global Catalog

- Exploring DSAccess, DSProxy, and the Categorizer

- Understanding AD Functionality Modes and Their Relationship to Exchange Groups

There is simply no way around it; Active Directory is a critical and necessary component of any Exchange Server 2003 deployment. With the release of Exchange 2000, Exchange's personal directory was replaced by Active Directory. This initially was the cause of much grumbling as the learning curve associated with Active Directory was steep. The advent of Windows Server 2003 and Exchange Server 2003 brought the optimization and simplification of the Active Directory environment. Lessons learned from Active Directory 1.0 have been integrated into the newest version of Active Directory, available with Windows Server 2003.

Notwithstanding the improvements, there is still a great deal of misunderstanding about Active Directory and its core components. The Global Catalog, for example, is a critical component of Exchange and requires a solid grasp of its concepts.

This chapter explains the relationship between Exchange Server 2003 and Active Directory and how the placement of domain controllers and Global Catalog servers affects it. Components of Exchange Server 2003 that access Active Directory are explained, and troubleshooting techniques for directory access problems are detailed. In addition, this chapter offers best practice recommendations for domain controller and Global Catalog placement and presents detailed fine-tuning information.

# Understanding Active Directory Structure

Active Directory (AD) is a robust, standards-based Light Directory Access Protocol (LDAP) directory developed by Microsoft. In addition to serving as the central directory for Windows Server 2003, AD is also used to store the Exchange Server 2003 directory information. All Exchange attributes, such as email address, mailbox location, home server, and a whole range of other information used by Exchange is directly stored in Active Directory.

## Exploring AD Domains

An Active Directory domain is the main logical boundary of Active Directory. In a stand-alone sense, an AD domain looks very much like a Windows NT domain. Users and computers are all stored and managed from within the boundaries of the domain. However, several major changes have been made to the structure of the domain and how it relates to other domains within the Active Directory structure.

Domains in Active Directory serve as a security boundary for objects and contain their own security policies. For example, different domains can contain different password policies for users. Keep in mind that domains are a logical organization of objects and can easily span multiple physical locations. Consequently, it is no longer necessary to set up multiple domains for different remote offices or sites, because replication concerns can be addressed with the proper use of Active Directory sites, which are described in greater detail later in this chapter.

## Exploring AD Trees

An Active Directory tree is composed of multiple domains connected by two-way transitive trusts. Each domain in an Active Directory tree shares a common schema and Global Catalog. The transitive trust relationship between domains is automatic, which is a change from the domain structure of NT 4.0, wherein all trusts had to be manually set up. The transitive trust relationship means that because the asia domain trusts the root companyabc domain, and the europe domain trusts the companyabc domain, the asia domain also trusts the europe domain. The trusts flow through the domain structure.

## Exploring AD Forests

Forests are a group of interconnected domain trees. Implicit trusts connect the roots of each tree into a common forest.

The overlying characteristics that tie together all domains and domain trees into a common forest are the existence of a common schema and a common Global Catalog. However, domains and domain trees in a forest do not need to share a common namespace. For example, the domains microsoft.com and msnbc.com could theoretically be part of the same forest, but maintain their own separate namespaces (for obvious reasons).

> **NOTE**
>
> Each separate instance of Exchange Server 2003 requires a completely separate AD Forest. In other words, AD cannot support more than one Exchange organization in a single forest. This is an important factor to bear in mind when examining AD integration concepts.

## Understanding AD Replication with Exchange Server 2003

An understanding of the relationship between Exchange and Active Directory is not complete without an understanding of the replication engine within AD itself. This is especially true because any changes made to the structure of Exchange must be replicated across the AD infrastructure.

Active Directory replaced the concept of Primary Domain Controllers (PDCs) and Backup Domain Controllers (BDCs) with the concept of multiple domain controllers that each contain a master read/write copy of domain information. Changes that are made on any domain controller within the environment are replicated to all other domain controllers in what is known as *multimaster replication.*

Active Directory differs from most directory service implementations in that the replication of directory information is accomplished independently from the actual logical directory design. The concept of Active Directory sites is completely independent from the logical structure of Active Directory forests, trees, and domains. In fact, a single site in Active Directory can actually host domain controllers from different domains or different trees within the same forest. This enables the creation of a replication topology based on your WAN structure, and your directory topology can mirror your organizational structure.

From an Exchange point of view, the most important concept to keep in mind is the delay that replication causes between when a change is made in Exchange and when that change is replicated throughout the entire AD structure. The reason for these types of discrepancies lies in the fact that not all AD changes are replicated immediately. This concept is known as replication latency. Because the overhead required in immediately replicating change information to all domain controllers is large, the default schedule for replication is not as often as you might want. To immediately replicate changes made to Exchange or any AD changes, use the following procedure:

1. Open Active Directory Sites and Services.

2. Drill down to Sites, *sitename*, Servers, *servername*, NTDS Settings. The server name chosen should be the server you are connected to, and from which the desired change should be replicated.

3. Right-click each connection object and choose Replicate Now, as illustrated in Figure 8.1.

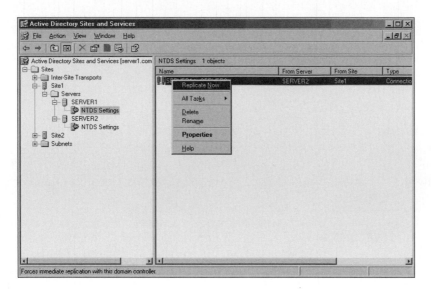

**FIGURE 8.1**    Forcing AD replication.

# Examining the Role of Domain Controllers in AD

Exchange has always relied on domain controllers for authentication of user accounts. Mailboxes in Exchange 5.5 were controlled through the application of security from Windows NT 4.0 and, later, Active Directory domain accounts. It should come as no surprise, consequently, that Exchange Server 2003 also relies on Active Directory domain controllers for authentication purposes. Proper placement of DCs is also important.

## Examining Domain Controller Authentication in Active Directory

To understand how Exchange manages security, an analysis of Active Directory authentication is required. This information aids in troubleshooting the environment, as well as in gaining a better understanding of Exchange Server 2003 as a whole.

Each object in Exchange, including all mailboxes, can have security directly applied for the purposes of limiting and controlling access to those resources. For example, a particular administrator may be granted access to control a certain set of Exchange Servers, and users can be granted access to mailboxes. What makes Exchange particularly useful is that security rights can be assigned not only at the object level but at the attribute level too. This enables granular administration, by allowing such tasks as a Telecom group being able to modify only the phone number field of a user, for example.

When a user logs in to a domain, the domain controller performs a lookup to ensure a match between the username and password. If a match is made, the client is then authenticated and given the rights to gain access to resources, including Exchange Server 2003 mailboxes.

Because the domain controllers provide users with the keys to access the resources, it is important to provide local access to domain controllers for all Exchange servers. If a local domain controller became unavailable, for example, users would be unable to authenticate to their mailboxes in Exchange, effectively locking them out.

### Determining Domain Controller Placement with Exchange Server 2003

As previously identified, Exchange relies heavily on the security authentication performed by Active Directory domain controllers. This concept is important for Exchange Server 2003 design, because placement of domain controllers becomes an important concept. In general, at least one Active Directory domain controller must be within close proximity to any Exchange Server to enable quick authentication for local users and mailboxes. While it may be tempting to place the domain controller role on an Exchange server, it is important to note, however, that the separation of the domain controller function from Exchange is more ideal, and gives the greatest performance boost.

Other sites may deploy more than one Active Directory domain controller for user authentication. This enables the distribution of domain controller tasks, but also builds redundancy into the design. Because each DC is multimaster, if one goes down the other will be able to take over domain controller responsibilities.

> **NOTE**
>
> Although Active Directory domain controllers are multimaster, downlevel clients (Windows NT 4.0 and lower) still require access to a Windows NT Primary Domain Controller (PDC) equivalent. A single Windows 2000/2003 DC acts as the PDC Emulator for each domain, and is not multimaster for that role. If the AD DC with this role goes down, the downlevel clients are disrupted as if their NT PDC went down. Windows 2000/XP-and-higher clients do not have this problem, however, because they are able to take advantage of the multimaster DC approach.

# Defining the Global Catalog

The Global Catalog is an index of the Active Directory database that contains a partial copy of all objects in all domains in the forest. All objects within the AD tree are referenced within the Global Catalog, which enables users to search for objects located in other domains. Every attribute of each object is not replicated to the Global Catalogs— only those attributes that are commonly used in search operations, such as first name, last name, and so on.

Global Catalog servers, commonly referred to as GCs or GC/DCs, are Active Directory domain controllers that contain a copy of the Global Catalog. Locating a minimum of one Global Catalog server in each physical location is a wise move, because the Global Catalog must be referenced often by clients, and the traffic across slower WAN links would limit this traffic. In addition, technologies such as Exchange Server 2003 need fast access to Global Catalog servers for all user transactions, making it very important to have a Global Catalog server nearby.

## Understanding the Relationship Between Exchange Server 2003 and the AD Global Catalog

In the past, an Exchange server could continue to operate by itself with few dependencies on other system components. Because all components of the mail system were locally confined to the same server, downtime was an all-or-nothing prospect. The segregation of the directory into Active Directory has changed the playing field somewhat. In many cases, downlevel clients no longer operate independently in the event of a Global Catalog server failure. Keep this in mind, especially when designing and deploying a domain controller and Global Catalog infrastructure.

> **NOTE**
>
> Because Outlook clients and Exchange can behave erratically if the Global Catalog they have been using goes down, it is important to scrutinize which systems receive a copy of the Global Catalog. In other words, it is not wise to set up a GC/DC on a workstation or substandard hardware, simply to offload some work from the production domain controllers. If that server fails, the effect on the clients is the same as if their Exchange server failed.

## Understanding Global Catalog Structure

The Global Catalog is an oft-misunderstood concept with Active Directory. In addition, design mistakes with Global Catalog placement can potentially cripple a network, so a full understanding of what the Global Catalog is and how it works is warranted.

As mentioned earlier, Active Directory was developed as a standards-based LDAP implementation, and the AD structure acts as an X.500 tree. Queries against the Active Directory must therefore have some method of traversing the directory tree to find objects. This means that queries that are sent to a domain controller in a subdomain need to be referred to other domain controllers in other domains in the forest. In large forests, this can significantly increase the time it takes to perform queries.

In Active Directory, the Global Catalog serves as a mechanism for improving query response time. The Global Catalog contains a partial set of all objects (users, computers, and other AD objects) in the entire AD forest. The most commonly searched attributes are stored and replicated in the Global Catalog (that is, first name, username, email address). By storing a read-only copy of objects from other domains locally, full tree searches across the entire forest are accomplished significantly faster. So, in a large forest, a server that holds a copy of the Global Catalog contains information replicated from all domains in the forest, as illustrated in Figure 8.2.

## Creating Global Catalog Domain Controllers

With the exception of the first domain controller in a domain, all domain controllers in Active Directory are not Global Catalog servers by default; they must first be established as such through the following procedure:

1.  Open Active Directory Sites and Services.

**2.** Navigate to Sites, *sitename*, Servers, *servername*.

**3.** Right-click NTDS Settings and then select Properties.

**4.** Check the box labeled Global Catalog, as indicated in Figure 8.3.

**5.** Click OK.

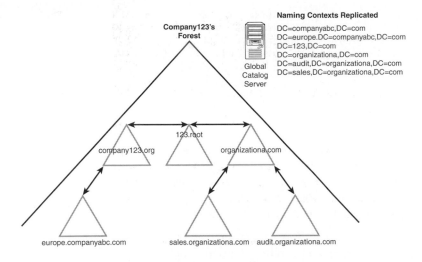

FIGURE 8.2    Global catalog replication.

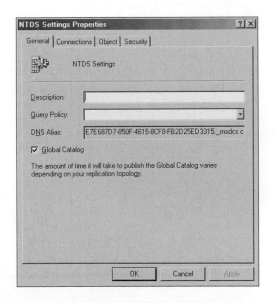

FIGURE 8.3    Making a domain controller a Global Catalog server.

Once this setting is applied, the server must be rebooted before it will assume full GC responsibilities. After being made into Global Catalog servers, domain controllers then receive their read-only copy of the partial domain naming context from each domain in the forest. To remove a domain controller from Global Catalog duties, uncheck the box; the DC will then no longer hold a copy of the GC information.

> **NOTE**
>
> In large forests, replicating a full set of Global Catalog information can be a time- and band-width-consuming activity. Schedule the creation of Global Catalog servers during periods of low network activity, such as over an evening or weekend.

## Verifying Global Catalog Creation

When a domain controller receives the orders to become a Global Catalog server, there is a period of time when the GC information will replicate to that domain controller. Depending on the size of the Global Catalog, this could take a significant period of time. To determine when a domain controller has received the full subset of information, use the replmon (replication monitor) utility from the Windows Server 2003 support tools. The replmon utility indicates which portions of the AD database are replicated to different domain controllers in a forest, and how recently they have been updated.

Replmon enables an administrator to determine the replication status of each domain naming context in the forest. Because a Global Catalog server should have a copy of each domain naming context in the forest, determine the replication status of the new GC with replmon. For example, the fully replicated Global Catalog server in Figure 8.4 contains the default naming contexts, such as Schema, Configuration, and DnsZones, in addition to domain naming contexts for all domains. In this example, both the companyabc.com domain and the europe.companyabc.com domain are replicated to the ELG-DC1 domain controller.

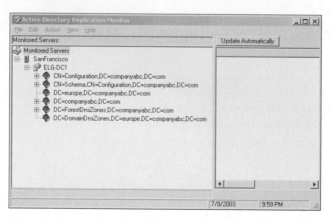

**FIGURE 8.4**    ReplMon GC creation verification.

## Using Best Practices for Global Catalog Placement

The general rule of thumb with GC placement is to place at least one GC in close network proximity to any major service that requires use of the Global Catalog (3268) port. Exchange Server 2003 makes extensive use of this port, and it is therefore wise to include a local GC in any site that contains an Exchange server.

These requirements do not mean that an unnecessary number of Global Catalog servers needs to be deployed, however. In reality, the total number of GCs that need to be deployed can be reduced in many situations through the concept of site consolidation in Exchange Server 2003. This concept enables multiple physical sites to use a central Exchange Server or set of servers, as opposed to having Exchange Servers (and their corresponding GCs) deployed to each site. Site consolidation works by having remote clients use the improved client remote access capabilities of Outlook 2003, OWA, and OMA. For more information on site consolidation strategies, see Chapter 4, "Designing Exchange Server 2003 for a Small to Medium Network."

## Optimizing Global Catalog Promotion

As previously mentioned, domain controllers can easily be promoted or demoted into Global Catalog servers with a single check box. The ease of this operation should not be taken lightly, however, because there can be a significant impact on network operations during this procedure.

When promoting a domain controller to Global Catalog status, the server immediately writes SRV records into DNS indicating its status as a Global Catalog server. In the past, this would cause problems, because Exchange 2000 servers would immediately begin using the incomplete Global Catalog on a newly created GC server, which would yield improper results. Since the release of Service Pack 2 for Exchange 2000 and subsequently Exchange Server 2003, a mechanism for detecting the readiness of a Global Catalog server was built into Exchange, specifically into the DSAccess service. This prevented Exchange from using those GCs until it received a full copy of the Global Catalog.

> **NOTE**
>
> After a domain controller has been promoted to Global Catalog status, the server will require a reboot at some point. Although an administrator who sets up a GC server will never be prompted to reboot, the Name Service Provider Interface (NSPI) service, which is used by Outlook for address book lookups, will not function properly until the newly promoted GC server has been rebooted. In general, Exchange should be able to proxy this service for the clients, but it is still a good idea to plan for a reboot of a GC shortly after its creation.

## Exploring Global Catalog Demotion

Removing a Global Catalog server from production can also have a detrimental effect in certain cases. Outlook 2000-and-older clients, for example, experience lockup issues if the Global Catalog server they have been using is shut down or removed from GC service. The loss of a GC server is the equivalent of the loss of an Exchange server, and should therefore not be taken lightly. Outlook 2002-and-greater clients, however, automatically detect the failure of their Global Catalog server and reroute themselves within 30 seconds. Scheduling Global Catalog or domain controller demotions for the off-hours, therefore, is important.

> **NOTE**
>
> If a production Global Catalog server goes down, downlevel (pre-2002) versions of Outlook can regain connectivity via a restart of the Outlook client. In some cases, this means forcing the closure of OUTLOOK.EXE and MAPISP32.EXE from the Task Manager or rebooting the system.

## Deploying Domain Controllers Using the Install from Media Option

When deploying a remote site infrastructure to support Exchange Server 2003, take care to examine best-practice deployment techniques for domain controllers in order to optimize the procedure. In the past, deploying domain controller and/or Global Catalog servers to remote sites was a rather strenuous affair. Because each new domain controller would need to replicate a local copy of the Active Directory for itself, careful consideration into replication bandwidth was taken into account. In many cases, this required one of these options:

- The domain controller was set up remotely at the start of a weekend or other period of low bandwidth.

- The domain controller hardware was physically set up in the home office of an organization and then shipped to the remote location.

This procedure was unwieldy and time-consuming with Windows 2000 Active Directory. Fortunately, Windows Server 2003 addressed this issue through use of the Install from Media option for Active Directory domain controllers.

The concept behind the media-based GC/DC replication is straightforward. A current, running domain controller backs up the directory through a normal backup process. The backup files are then copied to a backup media, such as a CD or tape, and shipped to the remote GC destination. Upon arrival, the dcpromo command can be run with the /adv switch (dcpromo /adv), which activates the option to install from media, as illustrated in Figure 8.5.

After the dcpromo command restores the directory information from the backup, an incremental update of the changes made since the media was created is performed. Because of this, you still need network connectivity throughout the DCPROMO process, although the amount of replication required is significantly less. Because some dcpromo operations have been known to take days and even weeks, this concept can dramatically help deploy remote domain controllers.

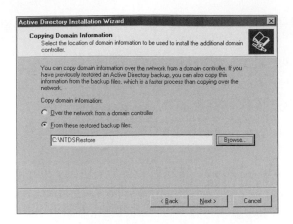

**FIGURE 8.5**    Install from Media option.

---

**NOTE**

If the copy of the Global Catalog that has been backed up is older than the tombstone date for objects in the Active Directory (which by default is 60 days), this type of dcpromo will fail. This built-in safety mechanism prevents the introduction of lingering objects and also assures that the information is relatively up to date and no significant incremental replication is required.

---

## Understanding Universal Group Caching for AD Sites

Windows Server 2003 Active Directory enables the creation of AD Sites that cache universal group membership. Any time a user uses a universal group, the membership of that group is cached on the local domain controller and is used when the next request comes for that group's membership. This also lessens the replication traffic that would occur if a Global Catalog was placed in remote sites.

One of the main sources of replication traffic is group membership queries. In Windows 2000 Active Directory, every time clients logged in, their universal group membership was queried, requiring a Global Catalog to be contacted. This significantly increased login and query time for clients who did not have local Global Catalog servers. Consequently, many organizations had stipulated that every site, no matter the size, have a local Global Catalog server to ensure quick authentication and directory lookups. The downside of this was that replication across the directory was increased, because every site would receive a copy of every item in the entire AD, even though only a small portion of those items would be referenced by an average site.

Universal Group Caching solved this problem because only those groups that are commonly referenced by a site are stored locally, and requests for group replication are limited to the items in the cache. This helps limit replication and keeps domain logins speedy.

Universal Group Caching capability is established on a per-site basis, through the following technique:

1. Open Active Directory Sites and Services.

2. Navigate to Sites, *sitename*.

3. Right-click NTDS Site Settings and choose Properties.

4. Check the Box labeled Enable Universal Group Membership Caching, as illustrated in Figure 8.6.

5. Click OK to save the changes.

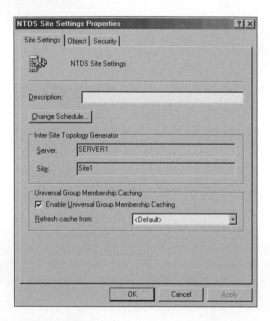

**FIGURE 8.6**    Universal group caching.

---

**NOTE**

Universal group (UG) caching is useful for minimizing remote-site replication traffic and optimizing user logins. Universal group caching does not replace the need for local Global Catalog servers in sites with Exchange 2000/2003 servers, however, because it does not replace the use of the GC Port (3268), which is required by Exchange. UG caching can still be used in remote sites without Exchange servers that use the site consolidation strategies of Exchange Server 2003 previously mentioned.

---

## Exploring DSAccess, DSProxy, and the Categorizer

The relationship that Exchange Server 2003 has with Active Directory is complex and often misunderstood. Because the directory is no longer local, special services were written for Exchange to access and process information in AD. Understanding how these systems work is critical for understanding how Exchange interacts with AD.

## Understanding DSAccess

DSAccess is one of the most critical services for Exchange Server 2003. DSAccess, via the `dsacccess.dll` file, is used to discover current Active Directory topology and direct Exchange to various AD components. DSAccess dynamically produces a list of published AD domain controllers and Global Catalog servers and directs Exchange resources to the appropriate AD resources.

In addition to simple referrals from Exchange to AD, DSAccess intelligently detects Global Catalog and domain controller failures, and directs Exchange to fail over systems dynamically, reducing the potential for downtime caused by a failed Global Catalog server. DSAccess also caches LDAP queries made from Exchange to AD, speeding up query response time in the process.

DSAccess polls the Active Directory every 15 minutes to identify changes to site structure, DC placement, or other structural changes to Active Directory. By making effective use of LDAP searches and Global Catalog port queries, domain controller and Global Catalog server suitability is determined. Through this mechanism, a single point of contact for the Active Directory is chosen, which is known as the Configuration Domain Controller.

## Determining the DSAccess Roles

DSAccess identifies AD servers as belonging to one of four groups:

- **Domain Controllers**—Up to 10 domain controllers, which have been identified by DSAccess to be fully operational, are sorted into this group.

- **Global Catalog Servers**—Up to 10 identified Global Catalog domain controllers are placed in this group.

- **Configuration Domain Controller**—A single AD domain controller is chosen as the configuration domain controller to reduce the problems associated with replication latency among AD domain controllers. In other words, if multiple domain controllers were chosen to act as the configuration DC, changes Exchange makes to the directory could conflict with each other. The configuration domain controller role is transferred to other local DCs in a site every eight hours.

- **All Domain Controllers**—This group includes all identified domain controllers, Global Catalog servers, and the configuration domain controller. It often contains multiple listings for the same server if that server appears in more than one group.

The roles that have been identified by DSAccess can be viewed in the Directory Access tab of Exchange Server properties in Exchange System Manager, as illustrated in Figure 8.7. In addition, manual overrides can be performed in this dialog box as necessary.

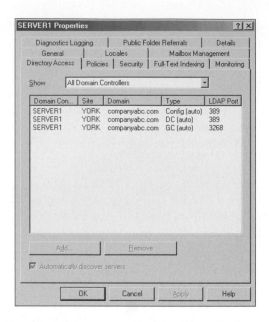

**FIGURE 8.7**    Viewing DSAcess roles.

## Understanding DSProxy

DSProxy is a component of Exchange that parses Active Directory and creates an address book for downlevel Outlook (pre–Outlook 2000 SR2) clients. These clients assume that Exchange uses its own directory, as opposed to directly using the Active Directory by itself, as Outlook 2000 SR2-and-greater clients do. The DSProxy service provides these higher-level clients with a referral to an Active Directory Global Catalog server, which they then use without accessing the Exchange servers directly. The newer Outlook clients do not refresh this information unless a server failure has occurred or the client is restarted.

> **NOTE**
>
> DSProxy uses NSPI instead of LDAP for address list lookups, because NSPI is a more efficient interface for that type of lookup. Only Global Catalog servers support NSPI, so they are necessary for all client address list lookups.

## Outlining the Role of the Categorizer

The SMTP Categorizer is a component of Exchange that is used to submit mail messages to their proper destination. When a mail message is sent, the Categorizer queries the DSAccess component to locate an Active Directory server list, which is then directly queried for information that can be used to deliver the message.

Although the Categorizer in Exchange gets a list of all Global Catalog servers from DSAccess, it normally opens only a single LDAP connection to a GC server to send mail, unless a large number of messages are queued for delivery.

> **TIP**
>
> Problems with the Categorizer are often the cause of DNS or AD lookup issues. When troubleshooting mail-flow problems, use message tracking in Exchange Server 2003 to follow the course of a message. If the message stops at the Categorizer, it is often wise to start troubleshooting the issue from a directory access perspective.

## Understanding AD Functionality Modes and Their Relationship to Exchange Groups

Exchange Server 2003 and Active Directory functionality was designed to break through the constraints that limited Exchange 5.5 implementations. In order to accomplish this, however, levels of compatibility with downlevel NT domains and Exchange 5.5 organizations were required. These requirements stipulated the creation of several functional modes for AD and Exchange that limit the application of new functionality. Several of the limitations of the AD functional modes in particular impact Exchange Server 2003 itself, specifically Active Directory group functionality. Consequently, a firm grasp of these concepts is warranted.

### Understanding Windows Group Types

Groups in Windows Server 2003 come in two flavors: security and distribution. In addition, groups can be organized into different scopes: machine local, domain local, global, and universal. It might seem complex, but the concept, once defined, is simple.

### Defining Security Groups

The type of group that administrators are most familiar with is the security group. This type of group is used to apply permissions to resources en masse, so that large groups of users can be administered more easily. Security groups could be established for each department in an organization. For example, users in the marketing department could be given membership in a marketing security group. This group would then have permissions on specific directories in the environment. This concept should be familiar to anyone who has administered downlevel Windows networks, such as NT or Windows 2000.

### Defining Distribution Groups in Exchange Server 2003

The concept of distribution groups in Windows Server 2003 was introduced in Windows 2000 with its implementation of Active Directory. Essentially, a distribution group is a group whose members are able to receive SMTP mail messages that are sent to the group. Any application that has the capability of using Active Directory for address book lookups can use this functionality in Windows Server 2003.

Distribution groups are often confused with mail-enabled security groups, a concept in environments with Exchange 2000/2003. In addition, in most cases distribution groups are not used in environments without Exchange 2000/2003, because their functionality is limited to infrastructure that can support them.

> **NOTE**
>
> In environments with Exchange 2000/2003, distribution groups can be used to create email distribution lists that cannot be used to apply security. However, if separation of security and email functionality is not required, you can make security groups mail-enabled instead of using distribution groups.

## Outlining Mail-Enabled Security Groups in Exchange Server 2003

With the introduction of Exchange 2000/2003 into an Active Directory environment comes a new concept: mail-enabled groups. These groups are essentially security groups that are referenced by an email address, and can be used to send SMTP messages to the members of the group. This type of functionality becomes possible only with the inclusion of Exchange 2000 or greater. Exchange 2000 actually extends the forest schema to enable Exchange-related information, such as SMTP addresses, to be associated with each group.

Most organizations will find that the concept of mail-enabled security groups satisfies most of the needs, both security and email, in an organization. For example, a single group called Marketing, which contains all users in that department, could also be mail-enabled to allow users in Exchange to send emails to everyone in the department.

## Explaining Group Scope

Groups in Active Directory work the way that previous group structures, particularly in Windows NT, have worked, but with a few modifications to their design. As mentioned earlier, group scope in Active Directory is divided into several groups:

- **Machine Local Groups**—Machine local groups, also known as local groups, previously existed in Windows NT 4.0 and can theoretically contain members from any trusted location. Users and groups in the local domain, as well as in other trusted domains and forests, can be included in this type of group. However, local groups allow resources only on the machine they are located on to be accessed, which greatly reduces their useability.

- **Domain Local Groups**—Domain local groups are essentially the same as local groups in Windows NT, and are used to administer resources located only on their own domain. They can contain users and groups from any other trusted domain and are typically used to grant access to resources for groups in different domains.

- **Global Groups**—Global groups are on the opposite side of domain local groups. They can contain only users in the domain in which they exist, but are used to grant access to resources in other trusted domains. These types of groups are best used to supply security membership to user accounts who share a similar function, such as the sales global group.

- **Universal Groups**—Universal groups can contain users and groups from any domain in the forest, and can grant access to any resource in the forest. With this added power comes a few caveats: First, universal groups are available only in Windows 2000 or 2003 AD Native Mode domains. Second, all members of each universal group are stored in the Global Catalog, increasing the replication load. Universal group membership replication has been noticeably streamlined and optimized in Windows Server 2003, however, because the membership of each group is incrementally replicated.

Universal groups are particularly important for Exchange Server 2003. When migrating from Exchange 5.5 to Exchange 2003, for example, Exchange 5.5 distribution lists are converted into universal groups for the proper application of public folder and calendaring permissions. An AD domain that contains accounts that have security access to Exchange 5.5 mailboxes must be in AD Native Mode before performing the migration. This is because the Universal Groups are made as Universal Security Groups, which are only available in AD Native Mode. For more information on this concept, see Chapter 15, "Migrating from Exchange v5.5 to Exchange Server 2003."

## Functional Levels in Windows Server 2003 Active Directory

Active Directory was designed to be backward-compatible. This helps to maintain backward compatibility with Windows NT domain controllers. Four separate functional levels exist at the domain level in Windows Server 2003, and three separate functional levels exist at the forest level:

- **Windows Server 2003 Mixed**—When Windows Server 2003 is installed in a Windows 2000 Active Directory forest that is running in Mixed Mode, Windows Server 2003 domain controllers will be able to communicate with Windows NT and Windows 2000 domain controllers throughout the forest. This is the most limiting of the functional levels, however, because certain functionality—such as universal groups, group nesting, and enhanced security—is absent from the domain. This is typically a temporary level to run in, because it is seen more as a path toward eventual upgrade.

- **Windows Server 2003 Native**—Installed into a Windows 2000 Active Directory that is running in Windows 2000 Native Mode, Windows Server 2003 runs itself at a Windows 2000/2003 functional level. Only Windows 2000 and Windows Server 2003 domain controllers can exist in this environment.

- **Windows Server 2003 Interim**—Windows Server 2003 interim mode gives Active Directory the capability of interoperating with a domain composed of Windows NT 4.0 domain controllers only. Although a confusing concept at first, the Windows Server 2003 interim functional level does serve a purpose. In environments that seek to upgrade directly from NT 4.0 to Windows Server 2003 Active Directory, interim mode enables Windows Server 2003 to manage large groups more efficiently than if an existing Windows 2000 Active Directory exists. After all NT domain controllers have been removed or upgraded, the functional levels can be raised.

• **Windows Server 2003**—The most functional of all the various levels, Windows Server 2003 functionality is the eventual goal of all Windows Server 2003 Active Directory implementations. Functionality on this level opens the environment to features such as schema deactivation, domain rename, domain controller rename, and cross-forest trusts. To get to this level, first all domain controllers must be updated to Windows Server 2003. Only after this can the domains, and then the forest, be updated to Windows Server 2003 functionality.

---

**NOTE**

Beginning with Exchange Server 2003 Service Pack 1, Microsoft extended the ability to perform domain rename on an Active Directory forest that was previously extended for Exchange. Before SP1, it was not possible to rename an AD domain within a forest that contained Exchange.

---

As previously mentioned, it is preferable to convert AD domains into Windows Server 2003 Native Mode, or Windows Server 2003 Functional Mode before migrating Exchange 5.5 Servers that use those domains. The universal group capabilities that these modes provide for make this necessary.

To change domain or forest functional levels in Active Directory to the highest level for Windows Server 2003, follow these steps:

1. Open Active Directory Domains and Trusts from Administrative Tools.

2. In the left scope pane, right-click Active Directory Domains and Trusts and then click Raise Domain Functional Level.

3. In the box labeled Select an Available Domain Functional Level, select Windows Server 2003 and then choose Raise.

4. Click OK, and then OK again to complete the task.

5. Repeat the steps for all domains in the forest.

6. Perform the same steps on the forest root, except this time click Raise Forest Functional Level and follow the prompts.

After the domains and the forest have been upgraded, the Functional Mode will indicate Windows Server 2003, as shown in Figure 8.8.

## Exchange Server 2003 Functional Modes

Not to be confused with Windows Server 2003 functional modes, Exchange can be run under two operations modes:

- **Mixed Mode**—An Exchange Server 2003 Organization running in Mixed Mode can support Exchange 5.5 Servers as part of the organization. Exchange routing groups and administrative groups cannot be separated when running in this mode, however.

- **Native Mode**—Native Mode in Exchange Server 2003 supports both Exchange 2000 and Exchange 2003 servers. In addition, Native Mode Exchange organizations support multiple routing groups within the same administrative group.

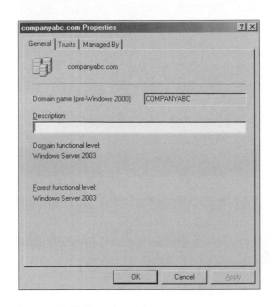

**FIGURE 8.8**    Windows Server 2003 functional forest.

> **NOTE**
>
> There is no difference in functionality between Exchange Server 2003 and Exchange 2000 from a functional mode perspective. Subsequently, there is no option to upgrade to an Exchange Server 2003–only mode.

To make the change from Exchange Mixed Mode to Native Mode, click the Change Mode button in the properties of the organization, as illustrated in Figure 8.9.

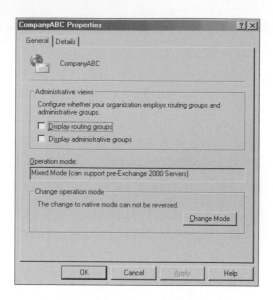

**FIGURE 8.9**    Switching to Exchange Server 2003 Native Mode.

# Summary

Exchange Server 2003 is a powerful but complicated piece of technology. With the scalability and performance enhancements comes an increased degree of interdependence with other system components, most notably the Global Catalog. Access to the Global Catalog and AD domain controllers is critical and cannot be overlooked. A good Exchange deployment plan takes these factors into account.

# Best Practices

- Deploy at least one domain controller in each physical location with more than 10 users.

- Use the Install from Media option to deploy remote Global Catalog servers when bandwidth is constrained.

- Promote or demote Global Catalog servers and domain controllers during off-hours.

- Use Exchange Server 2003 site consolidation concepts to reduce the total number of deployed Exchange Servers and Global Catalog servers.

- Understand the role of DSAccess, DSProxy, and the Categorizer and how Global Catalog or domain controller failures can affect them.

- Place at least one GC in close network proximity to any major service (such as Exchange Server 2003) that requires use of the Global Catalog (3268) port.

- Ensure that the AD domain is in Windows Server 2003 functional mode before migrating to Exchange Server 2003.

- Do not use substandard or workstation hardware for Global Catalog servers, as failures can affect Outlook clients.

- Use Outlook 2003 clients when possible to reduce the threat of client lockup in the event of GC failure.

- Consider the use of universal group caching for domain controllers in sites without local Exchange servers.

# CHAPTER 9

# Securing Exchange Server 2003 with ISA Server 2004

**IN THIS CHAPTER**

- Understanding Internet Security and Acceleration (ISA) Server 2004

- Outlining the Need for ISA Server 2004 in Exchange Environments

- Outlining the Inherent Threat in Exchange OWA/EMS Traffic

- Securing Exchange Outlook Web Access with ISA Server 2004

- Securing Exchange Mobile Services (EMS) with ISA

- Securing Exchange MAPI Access

- Securing POP and IMAP Exchange Traffic

- Managing and Controlling Simple Mail Transfer Protocol (SMTP) Traffic

- Logging ISA Traffic

- Monitoring ISA from the ISA Console

In today's risk-fraught computing environment, any exposed service is subject to frequent attack from the Internet. This is particularly true for Web services, including those offered by Exchange's Outlook Web Access (OWA), Exchange Mobile Services (EMS) of Outlook Mobile Access (OMA), Exchange ActiveSync (EAS), and RPC over HTTP. Exploits using the Hypertext Transfer Protocol (HTTP) that these services use are becoming very commonplace, and it is no longer acceptable to make an Exchange OWA (front-end) server directly accessible via the Internet.

Fortunately, the productivity gains of OWA/EMS can still be utilized and made more accessible by securing them behind a reverse-proxy server such as Microsoft Internet Security and Acceleration (ISA) Server 2004. ISA Server 2004 allows for advanced Application-layer filtering of network traffic, greatly securing the overall SharePoint environment. In addition, ISA Server supports deployment models in the demilitarized zone (DMZ) of existing firewalls, giving organizations the ability to deploy advanced Application-layer filtering for OWA without reconfiguring existing security infrastructure.

This chapter details the ways that Exchange services can be secured using the ISA Server 2004 product. Deployment scenarios for securing OWA, OMA, EAS, RPC-HTPPS, MAPI, POP, IMAP, and SMTP using ISA are outlined, and specific step-by-step guides are illustrated.

# Understanding Internet Security and Acceleration (ISA) Server 2004

The rise in the prevalence of computer viruses, threats, and exploits on the Internet has made it necessary for organizations of all shapes and sizes to re-evaluate their protection strategies for edge services such as SharePoint Portal Server. No longer is it possible to ignore or minimize these threats as the damage they can cause can cripple a company's business functions. A solution to the increased sophistication and pervasiveness of these viruses and exploits is becoming increasingly necessary.

Corresponding with the growth of these threats has been the development and maturation of the ISA Server product from Microsoft. The latest release of the product, ISA Server 2004, is fast becoming a business-critical component of many organizations, which are finding that many of the traditional packet-filtering firewalls and technologies don't necessarily stand up to the modern threats of today. The ISA Server 2004 product provides for that higher level of application security required, particularly for common tools such as Exchange OWA and related services.

# Outlining the Need for ISA Server 2004 in Exchange Environments

A great deal of confusion exists about the role that ISA Server can play in an Exchange environment. Much of that confusion stems from the misconception that ISA Server is only a proxy server. ISA Server 2004 is, on the contrary, a fully functional firewall, VPN, Web-caching proxy, and application reverse-proxy solution. In addition, ISA Server 2004 addresses specific business needs to provide a secured infrastructure and improve productivity through the proper application of its built-in functionality. Determining how these features can help to improve the security and productivity of an Exchange environment is subsequently of key importance.

In addition to the built-in functionality available within ISA Server 2004, a whole host of third-party integration solutions provide additional levels of security and functionality. Enhanced intrusion detection support, content filtering, Web-surfing restriction tools, and customized application filters all extend the capabilities of ISA Server and position it as a solution to a wide variety of security needs within organizations of many sizes.

## Outlining the High Cost of Security Breaches

It is rare when a week goes by without a high-profile security breach, denial of service (DoS) attack, exploit, virus, or worm appearing in the news. The risks inherent in modern computing have been increasing exponentially, and effective countermeasures are required in any organization that expects to do business across the Internet.

It has become impossible to turn a blind eye toward these security threats. On the contrary, even organizations that would normally not be obvious candidates for attack from the Internet must secure their services as the vast majority of modern attacks do not focus on any one particular target, but sweep the Internet for any destination host,

looking for vulnerabilities to exploit. Infection or exploitation of critical business infrastructure can be extremely costly for an organization. Many of the productivity gains in
business recently have been attributed to advances in information technology functionality, including Exchange-related gains, and the loss of this functionality can severely
impact the bottom line.

In addition to productivity losses, the legal environment for businesses has changed
significantly in recent years. Regulations such as Sarbanes Oxley (SOX), HIPAA, and
Gramm Leach Bliley have changed the playing field by requiring a certain level of security
and validation of private customer data. Organizations can now be sued or fined for
substantial sums if proper security precautions are not taken to protect client data. The
atmosphere surrounding these concerns provides the backdrop for the evolution and
acceptance of the ISA Server 2004 product.

## Outlining the Critical Role of Firewall Technology in a Modern Connected Infrastructure

It is widely understood today that valuable corporate assets such as Exchange OWA
cannot be exposed to direct access to the world's users on the Internet. In the beginning,
however, the Internet was built on the concept that all connected networks could be
trusted. It was not originally designed to provide robust security between networks, so
security concepts needed to be developed to secure access between entities on the
Internet. Special devices known as firewalls were created to block access to internal
network resources for specific companies.

Originally, many organizations were not directly connected to the Internet. Often, even
when a connection was created, there was no type of firewall put in place as the percep-
tion was that only government or high-security organizations required protection.

With the explosion of viruses, hacking attempts, and worms that began to proliferate,
organizations soon began to understand that some type of firewall solution was required
to block access to specific "dangerous" TCP or UDP ports that were used by the Internet's
TCP/IP protocol. This type of firewall technology would inspect each arriving packet and
accept or reject it based on the TCP or UDP port specified in the packet of information
received.

Some of these firewalls were ASIC-based firewalls, which employed the use of solid-state
microchips, with built-in packet-filtering technology. These firewalls, many of which are
still used and deployed today, provided organizations with a quick-and-dirty way to filter
Internet traffic, but did not allow for a high degree of customization because of their
static nature.

The development of software-based firewalls coincided with the need for simpler management interfaces and the capability to make software changes to firewalls quickly and
easily. The most popular firewall in organizations today, CheckPoint, falls into this category, as do other popular firewalls such as SonicWall and Cisco PIX. ISA Server 2004 was
built and developed as a software-based firewall, and provides the same degree of packet-
filtering technology that has become a virtual necessity on the Internet today.

More recently, holes in the capabilities of simple packet-based filtering technology has made a more sophisticated approach to filtering traffic for malicious or spurious content a necessity. ISA Server 2004 responds to these needs with the capabilities to perform Application-layer filtering on Internet traffic.

## Understanding the Growing Need for Application-Layer Filtering

Nearly all organizations with a presence on the Internet have put some type of packet-filtering firewall technology in place to protect the internal network resources from attack. These types of packet-filtering firewall technologies are useful in blocking specific types of network traffic, such as vulnerabilities that utilize the RPC protocol, by simply blocking TCP and UDP ports that the RPC protocol would use. Other ports, on the other hand, are often left wide open to support certain functionality, such as the TCP port 80, utilized for HTTP Web browsing and for access to OWA/EMS. As previously mentioned, a packet-filtering firewall is only able to inspect the header of a packet, simply understanding which port the data is meant to utilize, but unable to actually read the content. A good analogy to this is if a border guard was instructed to only allow citizens with specific passports to enter the country, but had no way of inspecting their luggage for contraband or illegal substances.

The problems that are becoming more evident, however, is that the viruses, exploits, and attacks have adjusted to conform to this new landscape, and have started to realize that they can conceal the true malicious nature of their payload within the identity of an allowed port. For example, they can "piggyback" their destructive payload over a known "good" port that is open on a packet-filtering firewall. Many modern exploits, viruses, and "scumware," such as illegal file-sharing applications, piggyback off of the TCP 80 HTTP port, for example. Using the border guard analogy to illustrate, the smugglers realized that if they put their contraband in the luggage of a citizen from a country on the allowed list, they could smuggle it into the country without worrying that the guard would inspect the package. These types of exploits and attacks are not uncommon, and the list of known Application-level attacks continues to grow.

In the past, when an organization realized that they had been compromised through their traditional packet-filtering firewall, the common, knee-jerk reaction was to lock down access from the Internet in response to threats. For example, an exploit that would arrive over HTTP port 80 might prompt an organization to completely close access to that port on a temporary or semipermanent basis. This approach can greatly impact productivity as OWA access would be affected. This is especially true in a modern connected infrastructure that relies heavily on communications and collaboration with outside vendors and customers. Traditional security techniques would involve a trade-off between security and productivity. The tighter a firewall was locked down, for example, the less functional and productive an end-user could be.

In direct response to the need to maintain and increase levels of productivity without compromising security, Application-layer "stateful inspection" capabilities were built in to ISA Server that could intelligently determine if particular Web traffic is legitimate. To illustrate, ISA Server inspects a packet using TCP port 80 to determine if it is a properly formatted HTTP request. Looking back to the previous analogy, ISA Server is like a border guard who not only checks the passports, but is also given an X-ray machine to check the luggage of each person crossing the border.

The more sophisticated Application-layer attacks become, the greater the need becomes for a security solution that can allow for a greater degree of productivity while reducing the type of risks that can exist in an environment that relies on simple packet-based filtering techniques.

## Outlining the Inherent Threat in Exchange OWA/EMS Traffic

The Internet provides somewhat of a catch-22 when it comes to its goal and purpose. On one hand, the Internet is designed to allow anywhere, anytime access to information, linking systems around the world together and providing for that information to be freely exchanged. On the other hand, this type of transparency comes with a great deal of risk, as it effectively means that any one system can be exposed to every connected computer, either friendly or malicious, in the world.

Often, this inherent risk of compromising systems or information through their exposure to the Internet has led to locking down access to that information with firewalls. Of course, this limits the capabilities and usefulness of a free-information exchange system such as what Web traffic provides. Many of the Web servers need to be made available to anonymous access by the general public, which causes the dilemma, as organizations need to place that information online without putting the servers it is placed on at undue risk.

Fortunately, ISA Server 2004 provides for robust and capable tools to secure Web traffic, making it available for remote access but also securing it against attack and exploit. To understand how it does this, it is first necessary to examine how Web traffic can be exploited.

### Understanding Web (HTTP) Exploits

It is an understatement to say that the computing world was not adequately prepared for the release of the Code Red virus. The Microsoft Internet Information Services (IIS) exploit that Code Red took advantage of was already known, and a patch was made available from Microsoft for several weeks before the release of the virus. In those days, however, less emphasis was placed on patching and updating systems on a regular basis, as it was generally believed that it was best to wait for the bugs to get worked out of the patches first.

So, what happened is that a large number of Web sites were completely unprepared for the huge onslaught of exploits that occurred with the Code Red virus, which sent specially formatted HTTP requests to a Web server to attempt to take control of a system. The following URL is an example of an exploit that executes an embedded command that the user might not want run on his or her system:

6

```
http://webmail.companyabc.com/scripts/..%5c../winnt/system32/
cmd.exe?/c+dir+c:\
```

This one in particular attempts to launch the command prompt on a Web or OWA server. Through proper manipulation, viruses such as Code Red found the method for taking over Web servers and using them as drones to attack other Web servers.

These types of HTTP attacks were a wakeup call to the broader security community as it became apparent that firewalls that operate at the packet-layer that can only open and close ports were worthless against the threat of an exploit that packages its traffic over a legitimately allowed port such as HTTP.

HTTP filtering and securing, fortunately, is something that ISA Server does extremely well, and ISA Server offers a large number of customization options that allow administrators to have control over the traffic and security of the Web server.

## Securing Encrypted (Secure Sockets Layer) Web Traffic

As the World Wide Web was maturing, organizations realized that if they encrypted the HTTP packets that were transmitted between a Web site and a client, it would make it virtually unreadable to anyone who would potentially intercept those packets. This led to the adoption of Secure Sockets Layer (SSL) encryption for HTTP traffic.

Of course, encrypted packets also create somewhat of a dilemma from an intrusion detection and analysis perspective, as it is impossible to read the content of the packet to determine what it is trying to do. Indeed, many HTTP exploits in the wild today can be transmitted over secure SSL-encrypted channels. This poses a dangerous situation for organizations that must secure the traffic against interception, but must also proactively monitor and secure their Web servers against attack.

ISA Server 2004 is uniquely positioned to solve this problem, fortunately, as it includes the ability to perform end-to-end SSL bridging. By installing the SSL certificate from the OWA server on the ISA server itself, along with a copy of the private key, ISA is able to decrypt the traffic, scan it for exploits, and then re-encrypt it before sending it to the Exchange server. Very few products on the marketplace can do this type of end-to-end encryption of the packets, and, fortunately, ISA allows for this level of security.

## Outlining ISA Server 2004's Messaging Security Mechanisms

As a backdrop to these developments, ISA Server 2004 was designed with messaging security in mind. A great degree of functionality was developed to address email access and communications, with particularly tight integration with Exchange Server built in. To illustrate, ISA Server 2004 supports securing the following messaging protocols and access methods:

- Simple Mail Transfer Protocol (SMTP)
- Messaging Application Programming Interface (MAPI)
- Post Office Protocol version 3 (POP3)

- Internet Message Access Protocol version 4 (IMAP4)

- Exchange Outlook Web Access (OWA), with or without forms-based authentication (FBA)

- Exchange Outlook Mobile Access (OMA)

- Exchange ActiveSync (EAS)

- Remote Procedure Call over Hypertext Transfer Protocol (RPC over HTTP/HTTPS), also called Outlook over HTTP

Securing each of these types of messaging access methods and protocols is detailed in subsequent sections of this chapter. For an understanding of how to initially set up Web-related mail access with OWA/OMA, ActiveSync, and RPC over HTTPS, you should review Chapter 10, "Configuring Outlook Web Access and Exchange Mobile Services," as this chapter only deals with securing existing OWA/EMS deployments.

## Securing Exchange Outlook Web Access with ISA Server 2004

As previously mentioned, OWA is one of the most commonly secured services that ISA servers protect. This stems from the critical need to provide remote email services while at the same time securing that access. The success of ISA deployments in this fashion give tribute to the tight integration Microsoft built between its ISA and Exchange products.

An ISA server used to secure an OWA implementation can be deployed in multiple scenarios, such as an edge firewall, an inline firewall, or a dedicated reverse-proxy server. In all these scenarios, ISA secures OWA traffic by "pretending" to be the OWA server itself, scanning the traffic that is destined for OWA for exploits, and then repackaging that traffic and sending it on, as illustrated in Figure 9.1.

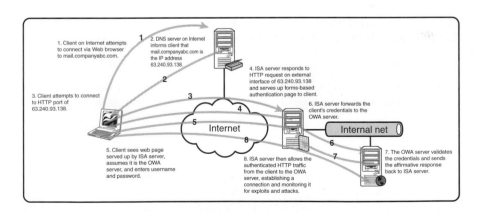

**FIGURE 9.1**   Explaining OWA publishing with ISA Server 2004.

ISA performs this type of OWA securing through a mail publishing rule, which automatically sets up and configures a Listener on the ISA server. A Listener is an ISA component that listens to a specific IP address and port combination for traffic, and processes that traffic for the requesting client as if it were the actual server itself. For example, an OWA Listener on an ISA server would respond to OWA requests made to it by scanning them for exploits and then repackaging them and forwarding them on to the OWA server itself. Using Listeners, the client cannot tell the difference between the ISA server and the OWA server itself.

ISA Server is also one of the few products that has the capability to secure Web traffic with SSL encryption from end to end. It does this by using the OWA server's own certificate to re-encrypt the traffic before sending it on its way. This also allows for the "black box" of SSL traffic to be examined for exploits and viruses at the Application layer and then to be re-encrypted to reduce the chance of unauthorized viewing of OWA traffic. Without the capability to scan this SSL traffic, exploits bound for an OWA server could simply hide themselves in the encrypted traffic and pass right through traditional firewalls.

## Exporting and Importing the OWA Certificate to the ISA Server

For ISA to be able to decrypt the SSL traffic bound for the Exchange OWA server, ISA needs to have a copy of the SSL certificate used on the OWA server. This certificate is used by ISA to decode the SSL packets, inspect them, and then re-encrypt them and send them on to the OWA server itself. For this certificate to be installed on the ISA server, it must first be exported from the OWA server as follows:

> **NOTE**
>
> The steps in Chapter 10 for setting up an OWA site and securing it with an SSL certificate must be run before performing these steps.

1. From the OWA server (not the ISA server), open IIS Manager (Start, All Programs, Administrative Tools, Internet Information Services (IIS) Manager).

2. Navigate to Internet Information Services, SERVERNAME (local computer), Web Sites.

3. Right-click on the OWA virtual server (typically named Default Web Site), and then click Properties.

4. Choose the Directory Security tab.

5. Click View Certificate.

6. Click the Details tab.

7. Click Copy to File.

8. At the wizard, click Next to begin the export process.

9. Select Yes, Export the Private Key, as shown in Figure 9.2, and click Next to continue.

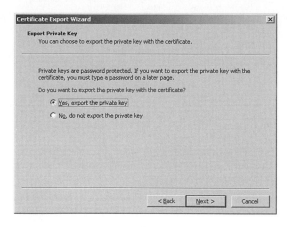

**FIGURE 9.2**   Exporting the SSL private key.

10. Select Include All Certificates in the Certification Path and also select to Enable Strong Protection, and click Next to continue.

11. Type and confirm a password, and click Next to continue.

12. Enter a file location and name for the file, and click Next.

13. Click Finish.

After the `.pfx` file has been exported from the OWA server, it can then be imported to the ISA server via the following procedure:

> **CAUTION**
>
> It is important to securely transmit this `.pfx` file to the ISA server and to maintain high security over its location. The certificate's security could be compromised if it were to fall into the wrong hands.

1. From the ISA server, open the MMC console (Start, Run, `mmc.exe`, OK).

2. Click File, Add/Remove Snap-in.

3. Click the Add button.

4. From the list shown in Figure 9.3, choose the Certificates snap-in and click Add.

**FIGURE 9.3**    Customizing an MMC Certificates snap-in console for import of the OWA certificate.

5. Choose Computer Account from the list when asked what certificates the snap-in will manage, and click Next to continue.

6. From the subsequent list in the Select Computer dialog box, choose Local Computer: (The Computer This Console Is Running On), and click Finish.

7. Click Close and then click OK.

After the custom MMC console has been created, the certificate that was exported from the OWA server can be imported directly from the console via the following procedure:

1. From the MMC console root, navigate to Certificates (Local Computer), Personal.

2. Right-click the Personal folder, and choose All Tasks, Import.

3. At the wizard welcome screen, click Next to continue.

4. Browse for and locate the .pfx file that was exported from the OWA server. The location can also be typed into the File Name field. Click Next when located.

5. Enter the password that was created when the certificate was exported, as illustrated in Figure 9.4. Do not check to mark the key as exportable. Click Next to continue.

6. Choose Automatically Select the Certificate Store Based on the Type of Certificate, and click Next to continue.

7. Click Finish to complete the import.

After it is in the certificate store of the ISA server, the OWA SSL certificate can be used as part of the publishing rules.

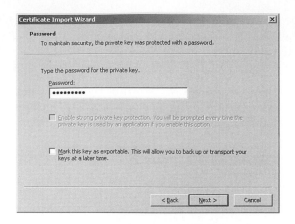

**FIGURE 9.4**    Installing the OWA certificate on the ISA server.

> **NOTE**
>
> If a rule that makes use of a specific SSL certificate is exported from an ISA server, either for backup purposes or to transfer it to another ISA server, the certificate must also be saved and imported to the destination server, or that particular rule will be broken.

## Creating an Outlook Web Access Publishing Rule

After the OWA SSL has been installed on the ISA server, the actual ISA mail publishing rule can be generated to secure OWA via the following procedure:

> **NOTE**
>
> The procedure outlined here illustrates an ISA OWA publishing rule that uses FBA for the site, which allows for a landing page to be generated on the ISA server to preauthenticate user connections to Exchange. This forms-based authentication page can only be set on ISA, and must be turned off on the Exchange server itself to work properly. Therefore, this particular rule does not configure the ancillary services of OMA, ActiveSync, and RPC over HTTP. If FBA is not used, these services can be installed as part of the same rule. See later sections of this chapter for information on how to do this.

1. From the ISA Management console, click once on the Firewall Policy node from the console tree.

2. From the Tasks tab in the task pane, click the Publish a Mail Server link.

3. Enter a name for the rule, and click Next to continue.

4. From the Access Type dialog box, select Web Client Access (OWA), Outlook Mobile Access, Exchange Server ActiveSync, and click Next to continue.

5. From the Select Services dialog box, ensure that the boxes for Outlook Web Access and Enable High Bit Characters Used by Non-English Character Sets are checked (OMA and ActiveSync should not be checked because they need to be secured with a different rule if forms-based authentication is used), and click Next to continue.

6. From the Bridging Mode dialog box, shown in Figure 9.5, click the Secure Connection to Clients and Mail Server check box. This ensures that the communications are encrypted from end to end. Click Next to continue.

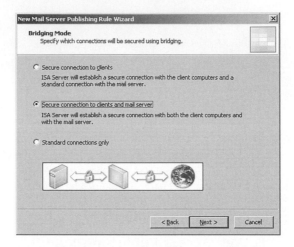

**FIGURE 9.5**     Selecting the OWA publishing rule bridging mode.

7. Enter the fully qualified domain name (FQDN) of the OWA server. This should match the external name referenced by the client (for example, mail.companyabc.com). Click Next to continue.

---

**CAUTION**

For an SSL-based OWA rule to work, the FQDN entered in this dialog box must exactly match what the clients will be entering into their Web browsers. If it does not match, the host header for the SSL traffic from the ISA server to the Exchange OWA server changes, which causes an upstream chaining error when the site is accessed. It is also very important that the ISA server is able to resolve the FQDN to the internal OWA server, and not to an outside interface. This might involve creating a hosts file to redirect the ISA server to the proper address. This type of scenario is often the case when the ISA server is configured in the DMZ of an existing firewall.

---

8. In the Public Name Details dialog box, select the Accept Request for This Domain Name (Type Below) option, and enter the FQDN of the server into the Public Name field (for example, mail.companyabc.com). Click Next to continue.

9. In the Web Listener dialog box, click the New button, which invokes the New Web Listener Wizard.

10. In the Welcome dialog box, enter a descriptive name for the Web Listener (for example, OWA SSL Listener with FBA), and click Next.

11. In the IP Addresses dialog box, check the External check box to allow it to listen from the external network, and click Next to continue.

12. In the Port Specification dialog box, uncheck Enable HTTP; then check Enable SSL.

13. Click the Select button to locate the certificate installed in the previous steps, select it from the list displayed, and click OK to save the settings.

14. Click Next to continue.

15. Click Finish to complete the Listener Wizard.

16. While still in the Select Web Listener dialog box, with the new Listener selected, click the Edit button.

17. Select the Preferences tab.

18. On the Preferences tab, select the Authentication button, as shown in Figure 9.6.

**FIGURE 9.6**  Configuring the OWA SSL Listener.

19. Uncheck Integrated from the list of allowed authentication methods.

20. Click OK to acknowledge the warning about requests being denied with no methods of authentication in place.

21. Check the box for OWA forms-based authentication.

22. Click the Configure button to configure FBA.

23. Enter OWA FBA settings in the dialog box shown in Figure 9.7. The settings chosen should reflect the particular security requirements of the organization. Click OK when you are finished.

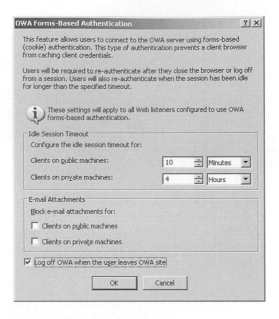

**FIGURE 9.7**     Configuring forms-based authentication.

24. Click OK and OK again to save the changes to the Listener, and then click Next to continue.

25. In the User Sets dialog box, accept the default of All Users, and click Next to continue.

26. Click Finish to complete the wizard.

27. Click the Apply button at the top of the details pane.

28. Click OK to acknowledge that the changes are complete.

At this point, the ISA server is set up to reverse proxy the OWA traffic and scan it for Application-layer exploits. This rule applies only to HTTPS traffic, however, so additional rules need to be created if HTTP traffic should be automatically redirected to HTTPS traffic.

One final configuration step for many environments is to force the SSL traffic to use 128-bit encryption, as opposed to as low as 40-bit (the default). Making this change also makes it possible to take a good look at the options and features of the rule itself. Double-click on the newly created rule in the details pane, and look through the tabs to see the options created in the rule. The particular option for forcing 128-bit SSL is located on the Traffic tab, as shown in Figure 9.8.

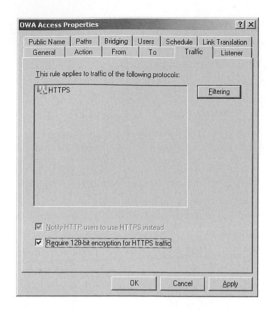

**FIGURE 9.8**    Forcing 128-bit encryption.

Checking the Require 128-bit Encryption for HTTPS Traffic check box, clicking OK, and then saving changes to ISA forces all connections to use the highly secured 128-bit SSL traffic.

> **CAUTION**
>
> It is important not to be confused by some of the options listed on the tabs of the individual publishing rule itself. Some of the options might seem to be necessary, but end up breaking the rule itself. If testing a different scenario, be sure to export it out to an XML file for backup purposes before making changes. ISA publishing rules need to be set up "just so," and minor changes to the rules can break the rules, so it is useful to save the specific rule so that it can be restored in the event of a problem.

## Redirecting HTTP OWA Traffic to HTTPS Traffic

Securing SSL traffic through OWA is a good start, but many organizations require some HTTP traffic to be handled, mainly to provide external clients with ease of use by automatically redirecting their requests for an http:// URL to one that starts with https://. For example, a user on the Internet typically types in the URL of the OWA Web page simply as mail.companyabc.com. The problem with this is that the browser assumes that it is regular, unencrypted HTTP traffic and attaches an http:// prefix, forcing the traffic to run as HTTP traffic.

When configured with the rule described in the previous section on configuring the OWA rule in ISA, ISA refuses this HTTP traffic because it has a very strict rule that specifies that only HTTPS traffic should be used. This is the case even if the ASP file that redirects traffic described in the previous section is used. This creates somewhat of a dilemma: The need to provide for ease of use clashes with the need to secure the environment.

Many organizations have found it useful to perform the automatic redirection on the OWA server itself, primarily through a custom 403.4 error ASP message, as previously described. This technique is a useful mechanism for performing a simple type of redirect on the virtual server of OWA itself.

The only downside to this type of redirect is that it requires unauthenticated HTTP traffic to hit the OWA server. This occurs either by adding HTTP functionality to the Listener or creating a new Listener and associated rule to allow the traffic through. This is not too large of a concern because ISA scans the traffic for exploits and the OWA server automatically rejects the HTTP traffic and forces the redirection. However, many security administrators have looked for ways to further secure this scenario, particularly if ISA is deployed in the DMZ of an existing firewall, and the preference is to keep all unauthenticated traffic to the DMZ itself.

Fortunately, there is a relatively straightforward way to accomplish both creating a secure OWA environment and providing for automatic redirection of the HTTP traffic, without requiring any unauthenticated traffic to pass through into the internal network. In this scenario, a special rule is configured on the ISA server to redirect any HTTP traffic sent to the OWA server to a single HTML file on a Web server in an isolated network, such as a DMZ network, as illustrated in Figure 9.9.

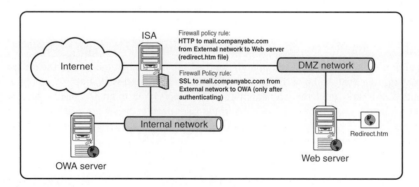

**FIGURE 9.9**    Automatically redirecting HTTP OWA traffic to HTTPS.

An existing Web server, be it Windows IIS, Linux Apache, or any other standard HTML 1.2–compliant Web server, can be used for this, and the only requirement is that a virtual directory should be created to house the simple, three-line HTML file that performs the redirection.

> **NOTE**
>
> Although it might seem as if ISA is a likely candidate to do the redirection itself, there is no built-in mechanism to perform this. The Web component of IIS should never be installed on an ISA server itself. This procedure requires that some Web server be made available.

The process to implement this solution requires two steps. First, the HTML redirect page is created on the Web server in the DMZ. Second, the ISA rule is created to redirect the traffic.

### Setting Up the HTTP Redirect File on the Web Server

For the first step, a separate server with Web services enabled must be identified and the HTML Web file must be placed into a virtual directory on that server.

The text of the HTML Web file should be as follows:

```
<html>
<meta HTTP-EQUIV="REFRESH" content="0; url=https://mail.companyabc.com/exchange"
<html/>
```

Note that the mail.companyabc.com portion of the file should be replaced with the publicly accessible name of the OWA Web site. The procedure for placing this file on the Web server in question varies based on the type and version of Web server being used, but it essentially involves saving the lines of HTML code into a file named redirect.htm (or any other descriptive name) and placing it into a virtual directory such as /isa on the Web server. For example, the following URL represents one particular Web structure for accessing the file:

```
http://www.companyabc.com/isa/redirect.htm
```

The procedure for installing this file varies depending on the version of Web services software installed. For Internet Information Services v6, the steps would be as follows:

1. From the Web server in the DMZ, create a directory named isa anywhere on the server (for example, C:\isa).

2. Create the redirect.htm file in Notepad, using the example given, and save that file in the isa folder, making sure that it is saved as an .htm file and not a .txt file.

3. Open IIS Manager (Start, All Programs, Administrative Tools, Internet Information Services (IIS) Manager) and navigate to SERVERNAME, Web Sites.

4. Right-click on the virtual server to which the virtual directory will be added (for example, the WWW site for the organization), point to New, and then click Virtual Directory.

5. Click Next at the welcome screen.

6. Under Alias, enter **isa** and click Next.

7. In the Web Site Content Directory dialog box, enter the path of the directory created earlier (for example, **C:\isa**).

8. In the Virtual Directory Access Permissions dialog box, select to allow only Read (uncheck Run scripts and leave the others blank), and then click Next to continue.

6

> **NOTE**
>
> The `redirect.htm` file does not need to be directly accessible from the Internet; it needs to be accessible only from the ISA server itself. In this scenario, ISA is configured to reverse proxy the site.

### Creating the ISA Server HTTP Redirect Rule

The second step in the redirection process is to create the ISA rule that redirects traffic sent to `http://mail.companyabc.com` to `http://www.companyabc.com/isa/redirect.htm`, which, in turn, repoints the user to `https://mail.companyabc.com/exchange`.

> **NOTE**
>
> The procedure outlined here also applies to a unihomed ISA configuration, where the ISA server is deployed into the DMZ of an existing firewall.

To create the ISA redirect rule, perform the following steps:

1. From the ISA console, select the Firewall Policy node from the console tree.

2. On the Tasks tab of the tasks pane, click the Publish a Web Server link.

3. For the Web Publishing Rule Name, enter a descriptive name, such as OWA HTTP Redirect, and click Next to continue.

4. Under Rule Action, select Allow, and click Next.

5. In the Define Website to Publish dialog box, shown in Figure 9.10, enter the name or IP address of the server to which the redirect file was saved, keeping in mind that the IP or name entered must be accessible from the ISA server itself, not necessarily to users from the Internet. Enter **isa/redirect.htm** as the path, and click Next to continue.

6. In the Public Name Details dialog box, select to accept requests from the domain name of the OWA server, and change the path to blank, as shown in Figure 9.11. Click Next to continue.

7. In the Select Web Listener dialog box, click New.

8. Enter a descriptive name for the Web Listener, such as HTTP Redirect Listener, and click Next.

9. Select to listen for requests from the external Web site by checking the External check box, and click Next to continue.

10. In the Port Specification dialog box, accept the default of HTTP Traffic Only, and click Next.

11. Click Finish to create the Listener.

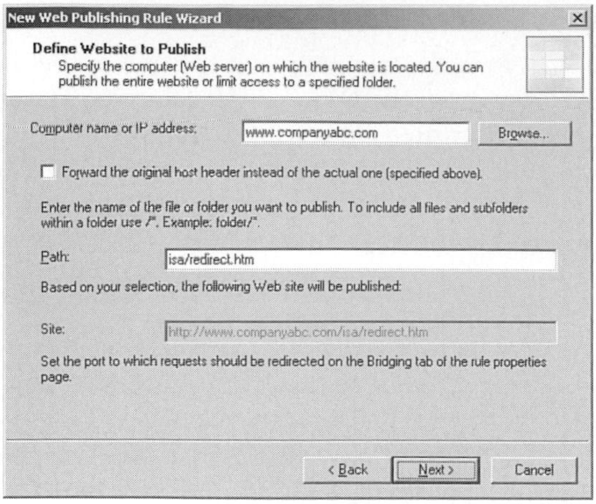

**FIGURE 9.10**    Defining the location of the HTTP redirect file.

12. Click Next to continue.

13. Accept the default of All Users under User Sets, and click Next.

14. Click Finish to finalize the settings.

15. Click Apply at the top of the details pane.

16. Click OK to acknowledge that the changes were saved to ISA.

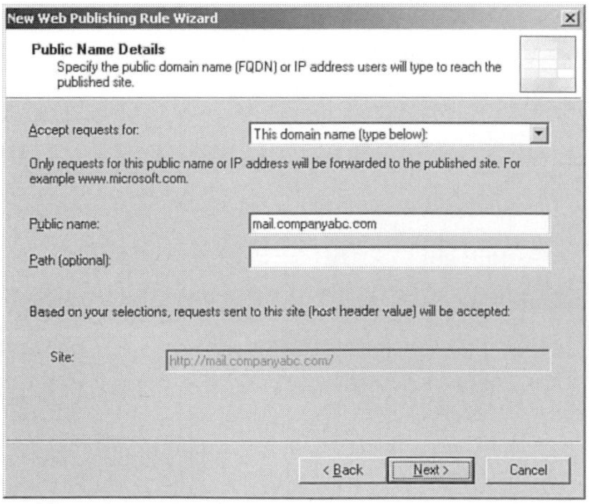

**FIGURE 9.11**    Configuring the HTTP redirect rule.

When used in combination with the HTTPS OWA mail publishing rule, the HTTP redirect rule can be a useful way to provide ease of use while maintaining a high level of security.

## Customizing Forms-Based Authentication

The FBA mechanism allows for a flexible approach to OWA authentication and keeps unauthenticated packets away from the OWA server. Many organizations require that custom OWA landing pages be created, however, so that they can incorporate special wording, or simply to rename the "domain\username" field in the form to simply "user-name." Fortunately, ISA Server 2004 makes customization of key wording in the OWA FBA page straightforward and uncomplicated.

The text in the FBA page is pulled from a single text file, located in the following location on the ISA server:

```
\Program Files\Microsoft ISA Server\CookieAuthTemplates\strings.txt
```

This file, shown in Figure 9.12, is a simple text file that can be modified to match an organization's needs. After it is modified, the firewall service needs to be restarted to view the changes.

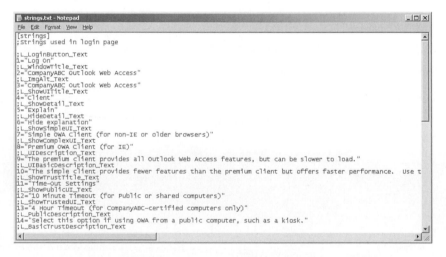

**FIGURE 9.12** Editing the `strings.txt` file to customize FBA.

> **CAUTION**
>
> If the ISA server being modified is placed in production, be certain to warn users or schedule the downtime that will be associated with a firewall service reset. Resetting the service effectively kills all connections traveling through the firewall, including Web servers, terminal service sessions, and VPN connections.

# Securing Exchange Mobile Services (EMS) with ISA

If the need exists to secure the EMS of Exchange, such as OMA, EAS, and RPC over HTTPS, it might be as simple as allowing the specific path statements as part of the same ISA publishing rule (for example, `/oma`, `/Microsoft-Server-ActiveSync`, or `/rpc`). In certain cases, however, when FBA is used with OWA, special procedures need to be followed to secure these services through ISA.

## Supporting Mobile Services in ISA When Using Forms-Based Authentication for OWA

For environments that have OWA configured to use forms-based authentication through ISA, there is somewhat of a catch-22 in regard to enabling OMA, ActiveSync, and RPC-HTTP (commonly referred to as the *Exchange Mobile Services, or EMS*). The problem arises from the fact that the Listener that the FBA-enabled OWA site uses must be the only Listener that can be bound to the IP address and port where it is assigned, and that the mobile services cannot support FBA authentication tied to the Listener that they use.

To illustrate with a hypothetical situation, suppose that CompanyABC hosts an OWA presence on the Internet that corresponds to mail.companyabc.com. In this scenario, DNS lookups to this address correspond to 63.240.93.138. CompanyABC's ISA server, which owns the 63.240.93.138 IP address, is configured with an HTTPS Listener that corresponds to that IP address and answers to all HTTPS requests sent to it.

The problem arises when OMA, RPC-HTTP, and/or ActiveSync traffic need to be sent through the same connection. It fails as the traffic sent to the virtual directory for these mobile services cannot understand FBA authentication. Fortunately, however, there is a workaround for this, but it involves installing and configuring an additional IP address on the external interface of the ISA server. This IP address is then used by ISA to create an additional Listener that uses Basic Authentication (encrypted via SSL), which is supported by OMA and ActiveSync.

---

**Avoiding Dual-Authentication Approaches**

If FBA is not utilized directly on the ISA server, this problem does not exist, and the OMA and ActiveSync publishing rules can be configured as part of the same OWA publishing rule itself, or a new rule can be configured to use the same Listener. In this scenario, the additional IP address, DNS A record, and additional certificate are no longer necessary; standard SSL-encrypted Basic Authentication can be used. The downside is that the increased security and functionality of FBA is lost and the user is prompted with the standard Username/Password dialog box.

---

The only additional requirement is that this traffic be directed to an additional DNS namespace, such as `http://mail2.companyabc.com`, so that it can be configured to point the external A record for mail2 to the different external IP address. Of course, this requires installing a separate certificate for the additional presence, which might add additional cost to the environment, depending on whether third-party CAs are used. To finish the example, in this case, CompanyABC would install and configure a certificate for mail2.companyabc.com and associate all non-FBA traffic with that particular FQDN.

This solution provides a less-than-elegant, but fully supported solution to the problem of enabling OMA, ActiveSync, and OWA with FBA at the same time.

> **TIP**
>
> If it is not feasible to obtain an additional external IP, DNS name, and certificate, the fallback solution to the problem is to simply use standard Basic Authentication with OWA. This allows all services, including OWA, OMA, ActiveSync, and RPC over HTTPS, to be enabled on the same virtual server and with the same ISA rule.

## Assigning a New IP Address on the ISA Server for the Additional Web Listener

The first step to enabling support for OMA and ActiveSync on an ISA server that supports OWA with FBA is to add an additional IP address to the ISA server for the additional Listener to attach itself to. To do this, perform the following steps on the ISA server:

> **NOTE**
>
> If the ISA server is directly connected to the Internet, an additional public IP address needs to be obtained directly from the Internet service provider (ISP) to support this process. In addition, the additional DNS A record must be registered for the new namespace.

1. From the ISA server, click Start, Control Panel, Network Connection; locate the external NIC from the list; right-click it; and click Properties.

2. On the General tab, double-click Internet Protocol (TCP/IP).

3. Click the Advanced button.

4. Under IP Settings, click Add.

5. Enter the additional IP address (see the preceding note about obtaining an additional public IP address) and its corresponding mask, and click Add.

6. Click OK three times to save the settings.

## Setting Up an Outlook Mobile Access (OMA) and ActiveSync Publishing Rule

After the necessary IP prerequisites and Listener requirements have been satisfied, the OMA and ActiveSync publishing rule can be created.

As an initial cleanup step, the original OWA rule needs to be modified to use only the first IP address, and not all IP addresses on the server (the default). To set this up, do the following:

1. In the details pane of the ISA console, double-click the OWA rule previously created.

2. Select the Listener tab.

3. Click Properties.

4. Select the Networks tab.

5. Double-click on the external network.

6. Select to listen for requests on specified IP addresses, select the primary IP address of the ISA server, and click Add, similar to what is shown in Figure 9.13.

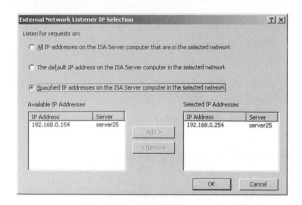

**FIGURE 9.13**   Modifiying the OWA rule to use only the primary IP address on the server.

7. Click OK, OK, OK, Apply, and OK to save the changes.

After setting the primary OWA rule to use only the IP associated with the FBA traffic, the following process can be used to set up the OMA-EAS rule in ISA:

1. Open the ISA Management console and select the Firewall Policy node from the console tree.

2. On the Tasks tab of the tasks pane, click the Publish a Mail Server link.

3. Enter a descriptive name for the rule, such as OMA-EAS Access, and click Next.

4. Keep the default at Web Client Access, and click Next to continue.

5. Uncheck Outlook Web Access and check Outlook Mobile Access and Exchange ActiveSync instead, as shown in Figure 9.14.

6. Select to maintain a secure connection to both clients and server, and click Next.

7. Enter the mail server name (for example, mail2.companyabc.com). Make sure the hostname is addressable from the ISA server and that it points to the secondary IP address of the OWA server. Click Next to continue.

8. Enter the FQDN again (for example, mail2.companyabc.com) on the Public Name Details tab, as shown in Figure 9.15, and click Next to continue.

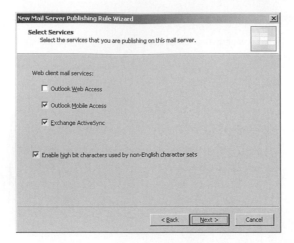

FIGURE 9.14    Setting up an OMA-EAS ISA publishing rule.

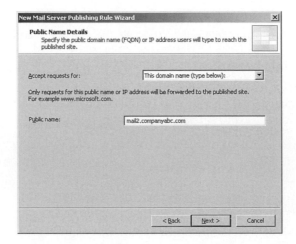

FIGURE 9.15    Setting up the public name details of the OMA-EAS ISA publishing rule.

9.  Under Web Listener, click New.

10. Enter a descriptive name for the Web Listener into the Name field, and click Next.

11. Check to listen for requests from the external network, and click the Address button.

12. Select Specified IP Addresses on the ISA Server Computer in the Selected Network, and choose the secondary IP address configured in the previous steps. Click Add when selected and click OK.

13. Click Next to continue.

14. Uncheck Enable HTTP and check Enable SSL. Click the Select button to select the new certificate and click OK. Click Next to continue.

15. Click Finish to create the new Listener.

16. Click Edit to edit the settings of the newly created Listener.

17. Select the Preferences tab.

18. Under Configure Allowed Authentication Methods, click the Authentication button.

19. Uncheck Integrated and click OK to acknowledge the warning.

20. Select Basic by checking the box next to it, as shown in Figure 9.16.

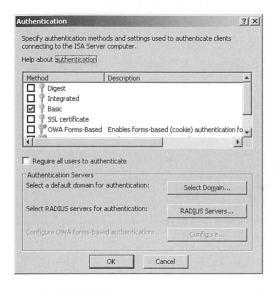

**FIGURE 9.16**    Configuring the OMA-EAS Listener.

21. Click the Select Domain button.

22. Enter the default domain name into the field (for example, companyabc.com), if one will be needed. This enables users to simply enter a username instead of domain/username. Click OK three times to save the settings.

23. Click Next to continue.

24. Keep the default at All Users, and click Next.

25. At the completion screen, click Finish.

26. Click Apply and then OK to save the changes to ISA.

> **NOTE**
>
> The concept described in this section could easily be extended to create multiple presences for an organization, depending on the type of service being set up—for example, owa.companyabc.com, oma.companyabc.com, eas.companyabc.com, rpc.companyabc.com, pop.companyabc.com, imap.companyabc.com, and so forth. The only limitation is the number of IP addresses and certificates that can be created.

## Securing RPC over HTTPS Servers with an ISA Publishing Rule

Securing an RPC over HTTPS proxy server involves publishing the RPC virtual directory as part of a publishing rule. This is typically done on the rule where OMA and ActiveSync have been set up, unless forms-based authentication is used, and then it is typically enabled on the standard OWA rule.

> **CAUTION**
>
> Once again, it is important to note that RPC over HTTP cannot utilize a Listener on a rule that uses forms-based authentication. Instead, it must utilize a Basic Authentication–enabled Listener. Consult the previous sections for more information on this.

To modify an existing ISA mail publishing rule to include RPC over HTTPS support, perform the following steps:

1. From the ISA Server console, select the Firewall Policy node.

2. Double-click on the rule that will be modified (typically the OMA-EAS rule previously set up, or the OWA rule if FBA is not used).

3. Select the Paths tab and click the Add button.

4. Enter **/rpc/\*** and click OK.

5. Click OK, Apply, and OK to save the changes.

> **NOTE**
>
> For access to an internal RPC over HTTP topology over the Internet, the server's hostname must be published via external DNS so that it can be propagated across the Internet and made available for lookups.

# Securing Exchange MAPI Access

The Messaging Application Programming Interface (MAPI) has traditionally been used for communications between the client and an Exchange server. This type of traffic is highly functional, but can pose a security threat to an Exchange server because it requires the use of the dangerous Remote Procedure Call (RPC) protocol, which has become notorious through recent exploits that take advantage of the open nature of the RPC protocol to take over services on poorly coded services.

In the past, organizations have been handcuffed by the fact that blocking RPC requires blocking a huge range of ports (all dynamic ports from 1024 to 65,536, plus others) because of the dynamic nature in which RPC works. Blocking RPC access to an Exchange server was not feasible either. This type of block also blocked client access through MAPI, effectively crippling email access to an Exchange server.

ISA Server 2004 greatly simplifies and secures this process through its capability to filter RPC traffic for specific services, dynamically opening only those ports that are negotiated for use with MAPI access itself. This greatly limits the types of exploits that can take advantage of an Exchange server that is protected with MAPI filtering techniques.

## Configuring MAPI RPC Filtering Rules

To configure an ISA server to filter and allow only MAPI access across particular network segments, use the following technique:

1. From the ISA console, navigate to the Firewall Policy node in the console tree.

2. On the Tasks tab, click the Publish a Mail Server link.

3. Enter a name for the rule, such as MAPI Access from Clients Network, and click Next.

4. Select Client Access from the list of access types, and click Next.

5. Check the box for Outlook (RPC), as shown in Figure 9.17, and click Next to continue.

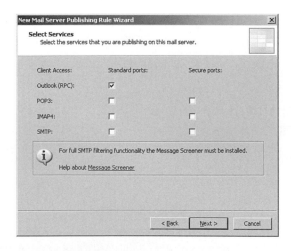

**FIGURE 9.17**  Enabling a MAPI filtering rule.

6. Enter the IP address of the Exchange server that is to be published, and click Next.

7. Select from which networks the rule will listen to requests, and click Next to continue.

8. Click Finish, Apply, and OK.

To set up more advanced MAPI filtering, examine the Traffic tab of the rule that was created and click on either the Filtering, Configure Exchange RPC, and/or the Properties buttons. Advanced settings can be found under the Interfaces tab, such as which Universal Unique IDs (UUIDs) to allow, as shown in Figure 9.18.

**FIGURE 9.18**   Examining advanced MAPI filtering.

## Deploying MAPI Filtering Across Network Segments

Where MAPI filtering really shines is in scenarios in which the ISA server is used to protect a server's network from the client's network in an organization, similar to that shown in Figure 9.19.

In these scenarios, the ISA server acts as an Exchange firewall, providing secured mail, OWA, POP, and any other necessary services to the ISA server through a secured, Application-layer filtered environment. This type of deployment scenario is very useful for organizations that want to reduce the exposure to security threats faced from unruly or exploited clients. It allows for a great degree of control over what type of access to an Exchange environment can be set up.

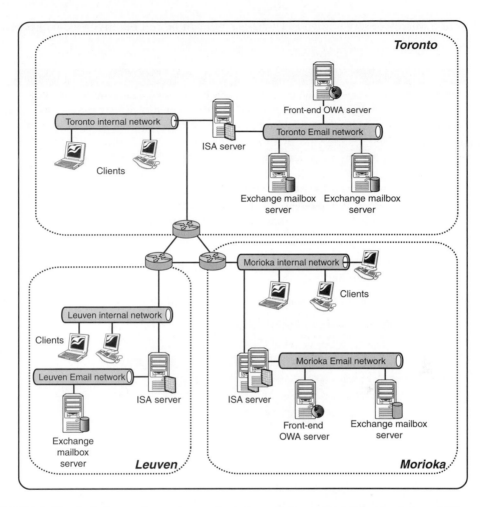

**FIGURE 9.19**   Isolating and securing an Exchange environment behind an internal ISA firewall.

# Securing POP and IMAP Exchange Traffic

The ancillary mail services of the Post Office Protocol version 3 (POP3) and Internet Message Access Protocol version 4 (IMAP4) can be secured through an ISA server. This is particularly important for organizations that require support of these legacy protocols; they are less secure than the newer forms of mail access available.

### Creating and Configuring a POP Mail Publishing Rule

POP3 servers are secured in ISA through the creation of a special rule that enables ISA to examine all traffic sent to the POP3 server and perform intrusion detection heuristics on it with an advanced POP intrusion detection filter. The POP server does not necessarily need to be a Microsoft server, such as Exchange, but can be run on any POP3-compliant messaging system.

> **CAUTION**
>
> Enable POP support in a messaging environment only if there is no other viable option. POP3 support is less secure than other access methods, and can cause mail delivery and security issues. For example, many POP clients are configured to pull all the mail off the POP server, making it difficult to do disaster recovery of mail data.

### Enabling POP3 Access on an Exchange Server

If no existing POP3 server is available, but support for the protocol needs to be enabled, the service can be enabled on an internal Exchange Server 2003 system via the following procedure:

1. On the Exchange server, open the Services MMC console (Start, All Programs, Administrative Tools, Services).

2. Right-click the Microsoft Exchange POP3 service, and choose Properties.

3. Change the Startup Type to Automatic, as shown in Figure 9.20.

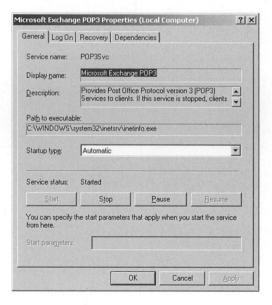

**FIGURE 9.20**    Enabling POP support on the Exchange server.

4. Click Start to start the service, and click OK.

### Enabling SSL Support on the POP Virtual Server

Realistically, all POP traffic across an untrusted network such as the Internet should be encrypted as well, using Secure Sockets Layer. This involves installing a certificate on the POP virtual server.

> **NOTE**
>
> An existing certificate can be used for POP-SSL traffic as well as HTTPS traffic. ISA is intelligent enough to decipher whether the traffic hitting its interface is HTTPS or POP-SSL traffic, and it forwards the requests to the appropriate rule. That said, some organizations do decide to create an additional name (such as pop.companyabc.com) for POP traffic to create a logical separation. Although this is convenient, this is not necessary with ISA.

To configure the POP virtual server for SSL by using an existing certificate (for example, mail.companyabc.com), do the following:

1. On the Exchange server (or front-end Exchange server), open Exchange System Manager (Start, All Programs, Microsoft Exchange, System Manager).

2. Navigate to ORGANIZATIONNAME, Administrative Groups, ADMINGROUPNAME, Servers, SERVERNAME, Protocols, POP3.

3. Right-click the POP virtual server, and select Properties.

4. Select the Access tab.

5. Under Secure Communication, click the Certificate tab.

6. Click Next at the Welcome dialog box.

7. Select Assign an Existing Certificate, and click Next.

8. Select the certificate desired (for example, mail.companyabc.com) from the list, and click Next to continue.

9. Click Next at the summary page.

10. Click Finish.

The final step is to force SSL on the POP virtual server. To do this in the same dialog box, perform the following steps:

1. Click the Communication button.

2. Check Require Secure Channel and Require 128-Bit Encryption, and click OK.

3. Click the Authentication button.

4. Clear the button for Simple Authentication and leave Basic Authentication checked. Check the box for Requires SSL/TLS Encryption, as shown in Figure 9.21, and click OK.

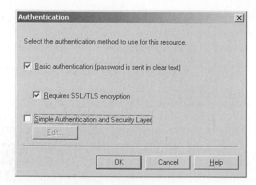

**FIGURE 9.21**    Forcing SSL on the POP virtual server.

   5. Click OK.


### Configuring an ISA POP Filtering Rule

After a POP server has been enabled or established on the internal network, it can be secured via modification of an existing rule or creation of a new rule to secure POP traffic as follows:

   1. From the ISA console, select the Firewall Policy node from the console tree.

   2. In the Tasks pane, click the Publish a Mail Server link.

   3. Enter a descriptive name for the rule (for example, POP-SSL Access), and click Next.

   4. Select the Client Access: RPC, IMAP, OP3, SMTP option button, and click Next.

   5. In the Select Services dialog box, select Secure Ports for POP3, and click Next.

   6. Enter the internal IP address of the POP server, and click Next.

   7. Select to which networks the ISA server will listen by checking the boxes next to them, and click Next.

   8. Click Finish, Apply, and OK.


## Creating and Configuring an IMAP Mail Publishing Rule

The Internet Message Access Protocol (IMAP) is often used as a mail access method for Unix systems and even for clients such as Outlook Express. It also can be secured through an ISA server, using the same rule as a POP rule, or through the configuration of a unique IMAP publishing rule.

### Enabling IMAP4 Access on an Exchange Server

If IMAP protocol support is required, but an internal IMAP server is not currently available, Exchange Server 2003 can be configured to provide for IMAP functionality through the following procedure:

1. On the Exchange server, open the Services MMC console (Start, All Programs, Administrative Tools, Services).

2. Right-click the Exchange IMAP4 service, and choose Properties.

3. Change the Startup Type to Automatic.

4. Click Start to start the service, and click OK.

### Configuring SSL on the IMAP Virtual Server

As with POP traffic, it is preferable to force SSL encryption for IMAP traffic. The procedure to configure this is very similar to POP SSL configuration, and can be done with the following steps:

1. On the Exchange server (or front-end Exchange server), open Exchange System Manager (Start, All Programs, Microsoft Exchange, System Manager).

2. Navigate to ORGANIZATIONNAME, Administrative Groups, ADMINGROUPNAME, Servers, SERVERNAME, Protocols, IMAP4.

3. Right-click the IMAP virtual server, and select Properties.

4. Select the Access tab.

5. Under Secure Communication, click the Certificate tab.

6. Click Next at the Welcome dialog box.

7. Select Assign an Existing Certificate, and click Next.

8. Select the certificate desired (for example, mail.companyabc.com) from the list, and click Next to continue.

9. Click Next at the summary page.

10. Click Finish.

The final step is to force SSL on the IMAP virtual server. To do this, perform the following steps in the same dialog box:

1. Click the Communication button.

2. Check Require Secure Channel and Require 128-Bit Encryption, and click OK.

3. Click the Authentication button.

4. Clear the button for Simple Authentication and leave Basic Authentication checked. Check the box for Requires SSL/TLS Encryption, and click OK.

5. Click OK.

### Configuring an ISA IMAP Filtering Rule

After the internal IMAP presence has been established, an ISA rule can be created to allow IMAP traffic to the IMAP server. The following procedure outlines this process:

1. From the ISA console, select the Firewall Policy node from the console tree.

2. In the Tasks pane, click the Publish a Mail Server link.

3. Enter a descriptive name for the rule (for example, IMAP-SSL Access), and click Next.

4. Select the Client Access: RPC, IMAP, POP3, SMTP option button, as shown in Figure 9.22, and click Next.

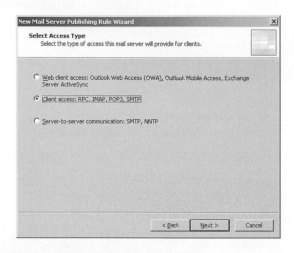

**FIGURE 9.22**    Setting up an ISA IMAP publishing rule.

5. In the Select Services dialog box, select Secure Ports for IMAP4, and click Next.

6. Enter the internal IP address of the POP server, and click Next.

7. Select to which networks the ISA server will listen by checking the boxes next to them, and click Next.

8. Click Finish.

# Managing and Controlling Simple Mail Transfer Protocol (SMTP) Traffic

The Simple Mail Transfer Protocol (SMTP) is the second most commonly used protocol on the Internet, after the Web HTTP protocol. It is ubiquitously used as an email transport mechanism on the Internet, and has become a critical tool for online collaboration.

Unfortunately, SMTP is also one of the most abused protocols on the Internet. Unsolicited email (spam), phishing attacks, and email-borne viruses all take advantage of the open, unauthenticated nature of SMTP, and it has become a necessity for organizations to control and monitor SMTP traffic entering and leaving the network.

ISA Server 2004's Application-layer inspection capabilities allow for a high degree of SMTP filtering and attack detection. By default, ISA supports the protocol as part of standard rules and policies. In addition, ISA also includes the SMTP Screener component, which enables the ISA server itself to become an SMTP smart host, and to filter and scan the SMTP traffic, as well as proxy the SMTP traffic for internal clients.

What this means is that ISA enables an environment to be further secured. The SMTP Screener off-loads the need to have an outside MX record point to an internal server, and instead points directly to it instead, as shown in Figure 9.23. This keeps potential SMTP exploits at bay because external intruders do not have direct access to the SMTP port of internal servers. In addition, it can also provide for outbound SMTP filtering to protect an organization from the liability associated with its own clients sending viruses and exploits out unwittingly or deliberately.

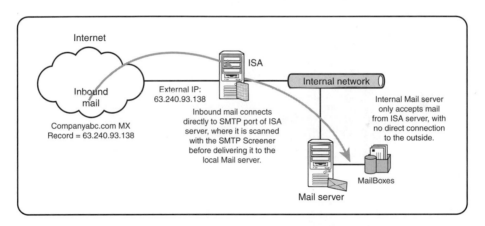

**FIGURE 9.23**   Examining SMTP screening with ISA Server 2004.

The one caveat with the SMTP Screener service is that, by itself, it really provides for only a base level of SMTP filtering. It does not have built-in intelligence to filter out email-borne viruses. It can, however, be extended with a third-party virus filter product that is designed for use with ISA Server 2004. The list of these products keeps growing over time, but it can be found at the following URL:

`http://www.microsoft.com/isaserver/partners/contentsecurity.asp`

With the addition of one of these third-party extensions to the SMTP filter, the capabilities of ISA Server can be further extended to include enterprise SMTP virus scanning and content filtering.

## Installing and Configuring the SMTP Service on the ISA Server

The first step to installing the SMTP Screener component of ISA is to install the SMTP Service on the ISA server. To install this service in Windows Server 2003, do the following:

1. Click Start, Control Panel, Add or Remove Programs.

2. Click Add/Remove Windows Components.

3. Select Application Server (by clicking on the name, not the check box), and click the Details button.

4. Select Internet Information Services (IIS) by clicking on the name (not the check box), and click Details.

5. Scroll down and select the SMTP Service, as shown in Figure 9.24. This has the effect of selecting other necessary components that go along with the SMTP Service.

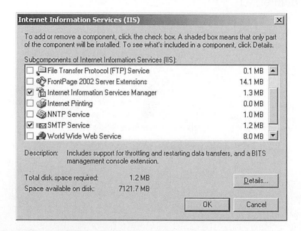

**FIGURE 9.24**    Installing the SMTP Service.

6. Click OK, OK, and Next.

7. Insert the Windows Server 2003 media (if prompted) or point to the i386 files on a local drive or network location, and click OK.

8. Click Finish.

After installing the SMTP Service, it is a good idea to check with Windows Update for any patches that apply to the server in its new configuration.

## Installing the ISA SMTP Screener Component

After the SMTP Service is installed, the ISA SMTP Screener component can be installed on the ISA server. If ISA is installed from scratch, the key to installing the SMTP Screener is to choose a custom installation and add the SMTP Screener to the installation options. If ISA is already installed, the following steps can ensure that the service is added:

1. Click Start, Control Panel, Add or Remove Programs.

2. Select Microsoft ISA Server 2004 from the list of installed programs, and click the Change/Remove button.

3. Click Next at the Welcome screen.

4. Select the Modify option button.

5. From the Custom Setup Screen, shown in Figure 9.25, select the SMTP Screener component, and choose This Feature Will Be Installed on Local Hard Drive.

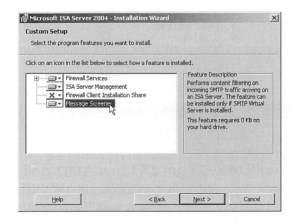

**FIGURE 9.25**    Installing the SMTP Screener component.

6. Click Next and then click Install.

7. Insert the media if prompted.

8. Click Finish and then reboot the server.

## Enabling Outbound and Inbound SMTP Filtering with the SMTP Message Screener

As with most things with ISA Server, simply installing the service does not automatically enable the functionality. Because ISA is a firewall, rules must be created to allow SMTP traffic to the ISA server. Several different varieties of SMTP rules can be set up with an SMTP Screener, depending on the type of traffic that will be allowed, such as

- **Inbound SMTP Filtering**—Inbound SMTP filtering is the most common type of SMTP filtering deployed. The primary security need for organizations with SMTP mail is to secure the anonymous email traffic coming into their networks from the untrusted Internet. At a minimum, inbound SMTP filtering should be enabled.

- **Outbound SMTP Filtering**—Outbound SMTP filtering is becoming more important. Organizations are finding that they are being held liable for internal employees launching attacks and sending spam (often without their knowledge) to external employees. Filtering and scanning the outbound traffic from a network can help to mitigate these risks.

- **Inbound and Outbound SMTP Filtering**—The best and most secure approach is to deploy an SMTP filtering strategy that makes use of both inbound and outbound SMTP filtering for an environment. This also has the advantage of enforcing SMTP communications through the ISA server itself, rather than opening up any direct communications from internal clients or servers.

### Creating an Outbound SMTP Filtering Rule

The different types of rules are set up in similar ways, using the standard ISA rule methodology discussed throughout this book. To set up a rule to allow inbound SMTP filtering (to ISA from the Internet), do the following:

> **TIP**
>
> For inbound SMTP filtering to work properly, the MX record on the Internet needs to resolve to the external IP address of the ISA server, either through the public IP address on ISA or through the single IP address, when ISA is configured as a unihomed server in the DMZ of an existing firewall. In these configurations, the extra firewall needs to establish a Network Address Translation (NAT) relationship between the IP address that the public MX record references, and the ISA Server IP address.

1. From the ISA console, click the Firewall Policy node.

2. In the Tasks pane, select the Publish a Mail Server link.

3. Enter a descriptive name for the publishing rule, such as "Outbound SMTP to ISA," and click Next to continue.

4. Select the Server-to-Server Communication option button, and click Next to continue.

5. Select SMTP from the check boxes in the Select Services dialog box, as shown in Figure 9.26, and click Next to continue.

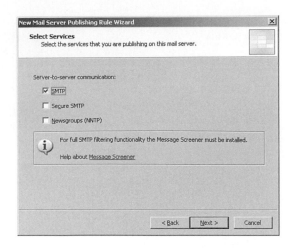

**FIGURE 9.26**   Setting up an outbound SMTP rule.

6. Enter the IP address of the internal ISA interface (the rule needs to specify that the internal email server can send directly to ISA), and click Next to continue.

7. Select Listen to Requests from the Internal Network, and click Next.

8. Click Finish, Apply, and OK to save the changes.

### Configuring an Inbound SMTP Filter Rule

To configure the Inbound SMTP Filtering rule, perform the following steps:

1. From the ISA console, click the Firewall Policy node.

2. In the Tasks pane, select the Publish a Mail Server link.

3. Enter a descriptive name for the publishing rule, such as "Inbound SMTP to ISA," and click Next to continue.

4. Select the Server-to-Server Communication option button, as shown in Figure 9.27, and click Next to continue.

5. Select SMTP from the check boxes under Select Services, and click Next to continue.

6. Enter the IP address of the external ISA interface (the rule needs to specify that external email servers can send directly to ISA), and click Next to continue.

7. Select to listen to requests from the external network, and click Next.

8. Click Finish, Apply, and OK to save the changes.

9

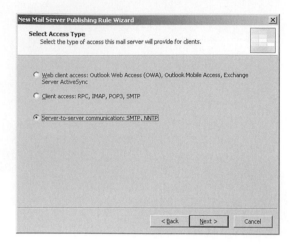

**FIGURE 9.27** Setting up an inbound SMTP filter rule.

### Configuring ISA SMTP Service Security Settings

To make sure that ISA allows mail sent to the proper domain name to be accepted internally, and to also secure the server and allow Exchange to relay outbound messages, the SMTP virtual server on the ISA server itself needs to be configured. To do this, follow these steps:

1. On the ISA server, open IIS Manager (Start, All Programs, Administrative Tools, Internet Information Services [IIS] Manager).

2. Expand to SERVERNAME, Default SMTP Virtual Server.

3. Right-click the SMTP virtual server, and choose Properties.

4. Select the Access tab.

5. Click the Relay button.

6. Leave the Only the List Below setting enabled, and click Add to add the IP address of the internal Exchange server. Also, uncheck the box for Allow All Computers Which Successfully Authenticate to Relay, Regardless of the List Above, similar to what is shown in Figure 9.28. Click OK.

7. Expand the virtual server, and select Domains.

8. Right-click Domains, point to New, and then click Domain.

9. For the Domain Type, select Remote.

10. Enter the address space for the domain, such as companyabc.com. This allows inbound mail sent to internal domains to be forwarded to Exchange. Click Finish.

11. Right-click the newly created domain, and choose Properties.

**FIGURE 9.28**    Restricting relaying on the ISA SMTP Service.

12. Under Route Domain, choose to forward all mail to the smart host (the internal Exchange server). Note that an IP address must be surrounded by brackets, as shown in Figure 9.29. Click OK when finished.

**FIGURE 9.29**    Setting inbound domain smart host settings.

13. Restart IIS by right-clicking the server name and choosing All Tasks, Restart IIS and then clicking OK to confirm.

**Configuring an Access Rule for ISA to Forward Outbound Messages**

The final step toward configuring ISA to send outbound messages is to allow the actual SMTP traffic from the ISA server to all external mail servers on the Internet. This can be configured with a simple access rule, set up as follows:

1. On the ISA server, open the ISA console and choose the Firewall Policy node from the console tree.

2. On the Tasks pane, click the Create New Access Rule link.

3. Enter a descriptive name, such as Allow SMTP Outbound from ISA, and click Next.

4. Select Allow from the Rule Action List, and click Next.

5. Under This Rule Applies To, select Specified Protocols.

6. Click Add under Protocols, then drill down and choose Common Protocols, SMTP, as shown in Figure 9.30. Click Add.

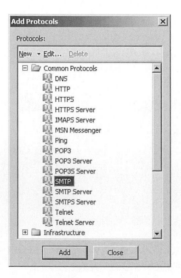

**FIGURE 9.30**   Adding an SMTP access rule for ISA outbound SMTP traffic.

7. Click Close and Next.

8. Under Access Rule Sources, click Add.

9. Drill down to Networks, select Local Host, and click Add, then Close.

10. Under Access Rule Destinations, click Add.

11. Under Networks, select External, and then click Add and Close.

12. Click Next, Next, Finish.

13. Click the Apply button at the top of the details pane and the OK button to confirm.

## Configuring Exchange to Forward Outbound Messages to ISA

As a final step in this process, the Exchange organization needs to be configured to forward all outbound mail to the ISA server, to off-load this functionality from the internal servers. To do this in an Exchange Server 2003 organization, perform the following steps:

1. On an Exchange server in the organization, open Exchange System Manager (Start, All Programs, Microsoft Exchange, System Manager).

2. Right-click on the organization name (at the top of the console hierarchy), and choose Properties.

3. Make sure that the box for Display Routing Groups is checked, and then click OK.

4. Drill down to ORGNAME (Exchange), Administrative Groups, ADMINGROUPNAME, Routing Groups, ROUTINGGROUPNAME, Connectors.

5. Right-click Connectors, point to New, and then click SMTP Connector.

6. Enter a descriptive name in the Name field, and check the Forward All Mail Through the Following Smart Host check box, as shown in Figure 9.31. Note that the ISA server's internal IP must be placed in brackets.

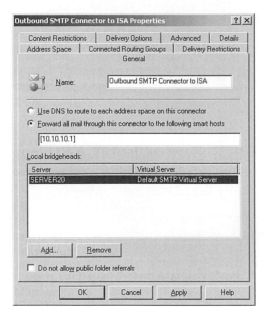

**FIGURE 9.31**  Creating an Exchange outbound SMTP connector to forward mail to the ISA Message Screener.

7. Click the Add button, select a local Exchange bridgehead from the list, and click OK.

8. Select the Address Space tab.

9. Click Add.

10. Select SMTP from the address type, and click OK.

11. For email domain, leave it at * and a cost of 1, and click OK.

12. Click OK to save the changes.

## Customizing the SMTP Filter

After SMTP rules have been set up to allow the traffic to flow through the SMTP screener, the ISA SMTP filter can be customized to block specific types of SMTP commands and content. To access the SMTP filter settings on the ISA server, do the following:

1. From the ISA console, click the Add-ins node in the console tree.

2. Under Application Filters in the details pane, double-click on SMTP Filter.

3. Examine and configure the settings in the SMTP Filter Properties dialog box, some of which are shown in Figure 9.32.

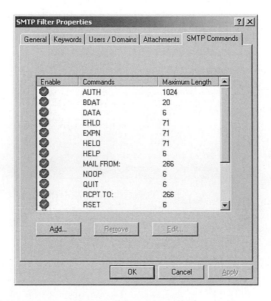

**FIGURE 9.32**    Configuring SMTP filter settings.

The SMTP Screener filter allows for the following default filtering functionality:

- Keyword filtering

- Email address/domain name filtering

- Attachment filtering

- SMTP command filtering

To take full advantage of the SMTP Screener and its Application-layer filtering technology, a third-party SMTP filtering product from an antivirus vendor is recommended. It will tie the ISA SMTP Screener engine to the built-in intelligence that these products use to look for viruses and to perform content filtering. Be sure to validate that the specific product is verified for ISA Server 2004.

# Logging ISA Traffic

One of the most powerful troubleshooting tools at the disposal of SharePoint and ISA administrators is the Logging mechanism, which gives live or archived views of the logs on an ISA server, and allows for quick and easy searching and indexing of ISA Server log information, including every packet of data that hits the ISA server.

Many of the advanced features of ISA logging are only available when using MSDE or SQL databases for the storage of the logs.

## Examining ISA Logs

The ISA logs are accessible via the Logging tab in the details pane of the Monitoring node, as shown in Figure 9.33. They offer administrators the ability to watch, in real time, what is happening to the ISA server, whether it is denying connections, and what rule is being applied for each Allow or Deny statement.

The logs include pertinent information on each packet of data, including the following key characteristics:

- **Log Time**—The exact time the packet was processed.
- **Destination IP**—The destination IP address of the packet.
- **Destination Port**—The destination TCP/IP port, such as port 80 for HTTP traffic.
- **Protocol**—The specific protocol that the packet utilized, such as HTTP, LDAP, RPC, or others.
- **Action**—The type of action the ISA server took on the traffic, such as initiating the connection or denying it.
- **Rule**—The particular firewall policy rule that applied to the traffic.
- **Client IP**—The IP address of the client that sent the packet.
- **Client Username**—The username of the requesting client. Note that this is only populated if using the Firewall Client.
- **Source Network**—The source network that the packet came from.

9

- **Destination Network**—The network where the destination of the packet is located.

- **HTTP Method**—If HTTP traffic, this column displays the type of HTTP method utilized, such as GET or POST.

- **URL**—If HTTP is used, this column displays the exact URL that was requested.

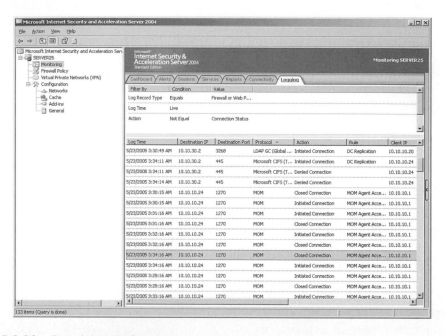

**FIGURE 9.33**    Examining ISA logging.

By searching through the logs for specific criteria in these columns, such as all packets sent by a specific IP address or all URLs that match `http://sharepoint.companyabc.com`, advanced troubleshooting and monitoring is simplified.

## Customizing Logging Filters

What is displayed in the details pane of the Logging tab is a reflection of only those logs that match certain criteria in the log filter. It is highly useful to use the filter to weed out the extraneous log entries that just distract from the specific monitoring task. For example, on many networks, an abundance of NetBIOS broadcast traffic makes it difficult to read the logs. For this reason, a specific filter can be created to only show traffic that is not NetBIOS traffic. To set up this particular type of rule, do the following:

1. From the ISA Admin console, click the Monitoring node from the console tree and select the Logging tab in the details pane.

2. From the Tasks tab in the tasks pane, click the Edit Filter link.

3. Under the Edit Filter dialog box, change the Filter By, Condition, and Value fields to display Protocol – Not Equal – NetBios Datagram, and click Add to List.

4. Repeat for the NetBios Name Service and the NetBios Session values, so that the dialog box looks like the one displayed in Figure 9.34.

5. Click Start Query.

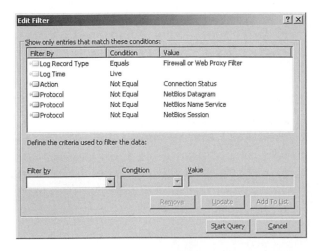

**FIGURE 9.34**    Creating a custom logging filter.

> **NOTE**
>
> It cannot be stressed enough that this logging mechanism is quite literally the best tool for troubleshooting ISA access. For example, it can be used to tell if traffic from clients is even hitting the ISA server, and if it is, what is happening to it (denied, accepted, and so on).

# Monitoring ISA from the ISA Console

In addition to the robust logging mechanism, the ISA Monitoring node also contains various tabs that link to other extended troubleshooting and monitoring tools. Each of these tools performs unique functions, such as generating reports, alerting administrators, or verifying connectivity to critical services. It is subsequently important to understand how each of these tools works.

## Customizing the ISA Dashboard

The ISA Dashboard, shown in Figure 9.35, provides for quick and comprehensive monitoring of a multitude of ISA components from a single screen. The view is customizable, and individual components can be collapsed and/or expanded by clicking on the Arrow buttons in the upper-right corner of each of the components. All of the individual ISA monitoring elements are summarized here.

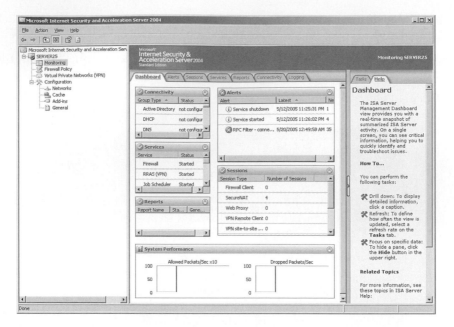

**FIGURE 9.35**    Viewing the ISA Dashboard.

> **TIP**
>
> The ISA Dashboard is the logical "parking" page for ISA administrators, who can leave the screen set at the Dashboard to allow for quick views of ISA health.

## Monitoring and Customizing Alerts

The Alerts tab, shown in Figure 9.36, lists all of the status alerts that ISA has generated while it is in operation. It is beneficial to look through these alerts on a regular basis, and acknowledging them when no longer needing to display them on the Dashboard. If alerts need to be permanently removed, they can be reset instead. Resetting or acknowledging alerts is as simple as right-clicking on them and choosing Reset or Acknowledge.

Alerts that show up in this list are listed because their default alert definition specified an action to display them in the console. This type of alert behavior is completely customizable, and alerts can be made to do the following actions:

- Send email
- Run a program
- Report to Windows event log
- Stop selected services
- Start selected services

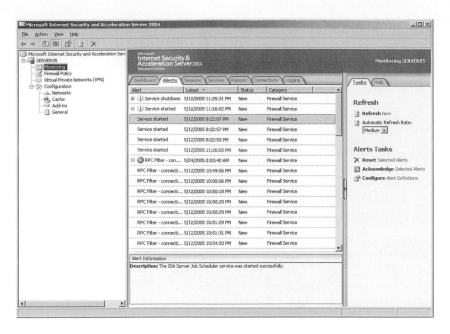

**FIGURE 9.36**    Viewing the ISA Alerts tab.

For example, it might be necessary to force a stop of the firewall service if a specific type of attack is detected. Configuring alert definitions is relatively straightforward. For example, the following process illustrates how to create an alert that sends an email to an administrator when a SYN attack is detected:

1. From the Alerts tab of the ISA Monitoring node, select the Tasks tab in the tasks pane.

2. Click the Configure Alert Definitions link.

3. In the Alert Definitions dialog box, shown in Figure 9.37, choose SYN Attack and click Edit.

4. Choose the Actions tab from the SYN Attack Properties dialog box.

5. Check the Send E-mail check box.

6. Enter the appropriate information in the SMTP Server, From, To, and CC fields, similar to what is shown in Figure 9.38.

7. Click the Test button to try the settings, and then click OK to acknowledge a successful test.

8. Click OK, OK, Apply, and OK to save the settings.

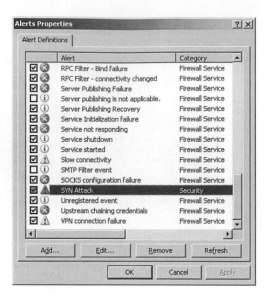

**FIGURE 9.37**    Creating a custom alert definition.

As is evident from the list, a vast number of existing alert definitions can be configured, and a large number of thresholds can be set. In addition, more potential custom alerts can be configured by clicking the Add button on the Alerts Properties dialog box and following the wizard.  This allows for an even greater degree of customization.

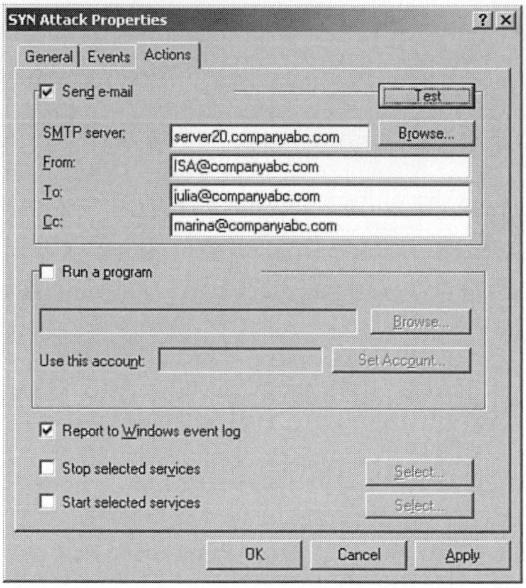

**FIGURE 9.38**    Entering the SMTP server info into a custom alert definition.

## Monitoring Session and Services Activity

The Services tab, shown in Figure 9.39, allows you to view the ISA Services, if they are running, and determine how long they have been up since last being restarted. The services can also be stopped and started from this tab.

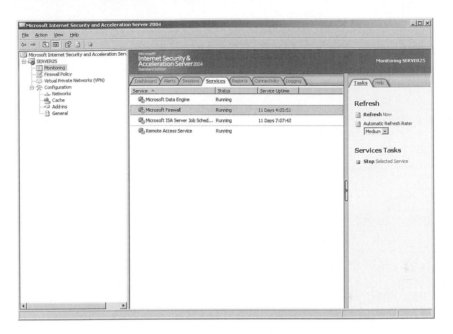

**FIGURE 9.39**   Monitoring ISA Services.

The Sessions tab allows for more interaction, as individual unique sessions to the ISA server can be viewed and disconnected as necessary. For example, it might be necessary to disconnect any users who are on a VPN connection, if a change to the VPN policy has just been issued. This is because VPN clients that have already established a session with the ISA server are only subject to the rules of the VPN policy in effect when the user logged on. To disconnect a session, right-click on the session and choose Disconnect Session, as shown in Figure 9.40.

## Creating Connectivity Verifiers

Connectivity verifiers can be a useful way of extending ISA's capabilities to include monitoring of critical services within an environment, such as DNS, DHCP, HTTP, or other custom services. Connectivity verifiers are essentially a "quick-and-dirty" approach to monitoring an environment with very little cost, as they take advantage of ISA's alerting capabilities and the Dashboard to display the verifiers.

For example, the following step-by-step process illustrates setting up a connectivity verifier that checks the status of an internal SharePoint server.

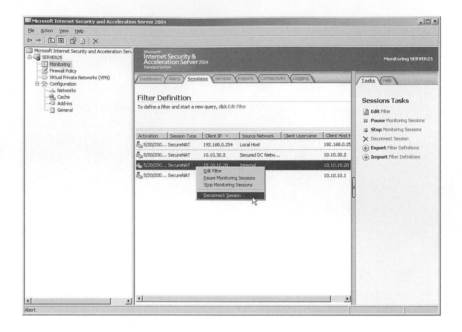

**FIGURE 9.40**    Disconnecting a session.

1. On the Monitoring tab of the ISA console, click the Connectivity tab of the details pane.

2. On the Tasks tab of the tasks pane, click the Create New Connectivity Verifier link.

3. Enter a name for the connectivity verifier, such as Web Server Verifier, and click Next.

4. In the Connectivity Verification Details dialog box, enter the server FQDN, the Group Type (which simply determines how it is grouped on the Dashboard), and what type of verification method to use, in this case an HTTP GET request, as shown in Figure 9.41.

5. Click Finish.

6. Click Yes when prompted to turn on the rule that allows ISA Server to connect via HTTP to selected servers.

7. Click Apply and then click OK.

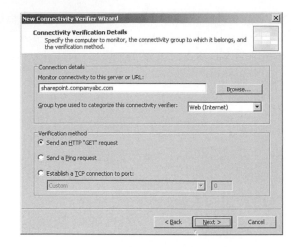

**FIGURE 9.41**    Configuring a SharePoint HTTP connectivity verifier.

After being created, connectivity verifiers that fit into the major group types are reflected on the Dashboard. Creating multiple connectivity verifiers in each of the common group types can make the Dashboard a more effective monitoring tool.

## Summary

ISA Server 2004 has often been called the Exchange Server Firewall, and for good reason. The capabilities of ISA Server 2004 to secure and protect Exchange services, whether through reverse proxying HTTP traffic, filtering MAPI traffic, or screening SMTP messages gives it capabilities not present in other firewall solutions. In addition, ISA's capability to be easily deployed in the DMZ of existing firewalls as a dedicated security appliance further extends its capabilities and allows it to be deployed in environments of all shapes and sizes.

## Best Practices

The following are best practices from this chapter:

- Filter MAPI traffic destined for Exchange servers using ISA Server 2004's RPC filtering technology.

- Use SSL-encryption on any edge-facing service, such as OWA, POP, or IMAP.

- Monitor ISA Server using the MSDE or SQL logging approaches to allow for the greatest level of monitoring functionality.

- If using forms-based authentication with OWA and Exchange Mobile Services on the same ISA server, deploy an additional IP address on the ISA server to allow for Basic Authentication for EMS.

- Secure any edge-facing service, such as OWA and EMS, with a reverse-proxy system such as ISA Server 2004.

- Deploy ISA reverse-proxy capability in the existing DMZ of a firewall if it is not feasible to replace existing firewall technologies.

CHAPTER **10**

# Configuring Outlook Web Access and Exchange Mobile Services

**IN THIS CHAPTER**

- Understanding OWA and the Exchange Virtual Server

- Designing an Exchange Front-End/Back-End OWA Architecture

- Enabling Secure Sockets Layer (SSL) Support for Exchange Outlook Web Access

- Customizing and Securing an OWA Web Site from Internal Access

- Configuring OMA and ActiveSync Access to Exchange

- Enabling and Supporting OMA and ActiveSync on the OWA Server

- Deploying Multiple OWA Virtual Servers

- Using RPC over HTTP(S) with Exchange Server 2003

Beginning with Exchange Server 5.5, the Outlook Web Access (OWA) tool has offered users the ability to view email information from a Web browser. Early versions of the OWA client were cumbersome, lacked functionality, and didn't scale very well beyond a few hundred connections. With Exchange 2000 Server, the OWA client was rewritten and improved, but still lacked many of the functional characteristics of the full Outlook client. The Outlook Web Access Client in Exchange Server 2003, however, is vastly improved and closer than ever to full Outlook client functionality.

In addition to the improvements made to the OWA client, Exchange Server 2003 integrated mobile access functionality that was previously part of a separate product into the system. This includes the services of Outlook Mobile Access (OMA), Exchange ActiveSync (EAS), and RPC over HTTPS. These various email access mechanisms allow for new methods of accessing email via WAP-enabled phones, handheld devices, and Outlook clients across restricted firewalls.

This chapter focuses on configuring Exchange Server 2003 to support OWA functionality. It focuses on best practices of front-end/back-end server configuration, including Network Load Balancing (NLB) and front-end server upgrade considerations. In addition, it covers the OWA-related services such as OMA, RPC over HTTPS, and EAS.

# Understanding OWA and the Exchange Virtual Server

Unlike Exchange Server 5.5, every deployed Exchange 2000 and Exchange 2003 server has OWA functionality built in via the HTTP virtual server component of IIS. The HTTP virtual server acts as a proxy to the Information Store, relaying requests made through OWA to the mailboxes. The IIS installation on each Exchange server also handles POP3, IMAP4, NNTP, and SMTP access in a similar fashion, through virtual servers for each component, as illustrated in Figure 10.1.

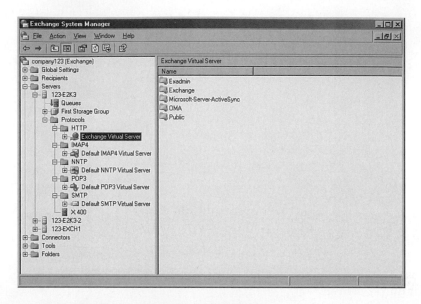

**FIGURE 10.1**   Virtual servers in Exchange Server 2003.

---

**NOTE**

For security reasons, the POP3, IMAP4, and NNTP Services are disabled in Exchange Server 2003. To enable these virtual servers, the services must first be started and set to run automatically. After this has been done, the virtual servers can be started to provide access via these protocols.

---

The virtual server concept is important because it provides the basis for more advanced and secure OWA designs.

## Designing an OWA Infrastructure

All deployed Exchange Server 2003 systems will be running OWA, and it is general best practice not to expose mailbox servers directly to HTTP access, especially from unsecured networks such as the Internet. In organizations with fewer security requirements, allowing port 80 (or preferably encrypted SSL traffic over port 443) through a firewall to the Exchange 2003 server will suffice. Larger or more security-conscious organizations might require an additional buffer of security, in the form of a front-end/back-end topology and some form of reverse proxy, such as that provided by Microsoft Internet Security and Acceleration (ISA) Server. More information on configuring ISA Server to secure Exchange OWA can be found in Chapter 9, "Securing Exchange Server 2003 with ISA Server 2004."

# Designing an Exchange Front-End/ Back-End OWA Architecture

The ability to configure front-end servers is a new concept introduced in Exchange 2000 Server and improved upon in Exchange Server 2003. Exchange Server 5.5 allowed an ASP-based front-end server for OWA by enabling a dedicated IIS server to handle OWA client traffic, but Exchange 2000/2003 enables an increased degree of flexibility by off-loading all protocols and enabling load balancing of those servers.

Front-end servers contain no mailboxes, and proxy HTTP, POP3, and IMAP traffic to a back-end server. They cannot, however, handle MAPI requests in the same way because MAPI clients must communicate directly with the server containing the client's mailbox. The term *back-end server* refers to any Exchange 2000/2003 server that contains the mailbox store and is configured to communicate with a front-end server for IMAP, HTTP, or POP3. Back-end servers could handle all the tasks that the front-end servers handle, but separating front-end/back-end responsibilities provides the following benefits:

- **Off-loads processing overhead for encryption/decryption processes**—SSL-based encryption and decryption processes, which are used to secure HTTP, POP3, and IMAP, add 15% to 40% processor overhead to the Exchange server and can be delegated to the front-end server.

- **Enables multiple servers to have the same alias in DNS**—Front-end servers allow multiple mailbox servers to be addressed by a single DNS namespace, by acting as a gateway to the OWA traffic.

- **Enables automatic referrals to public folder content for IMAP clients**—Many IMAP clients do not handle referrals to other servers. When an IMAP client needs folder content that might be available on another server, a front-end server handles the referral and provides the public folder content for the IMAP client.

## Describing Front-End and Back-End Servers

When a client connects to a front-end server for HTTP access, the front-end server queries Active Directory to find the correct back-end server that contains the user's mailbox. The front-end server then sends the request to the back-end server, with the HTTP host header unmodified.

For the back-end server to respond to the front-end server's request, an HTTP virtual server must exist on the back-end server that is configured to communicate with the front-end server. Both the front-end server and back-end server must have identical HTTP virtual servers for this communication to take place. This is an important consideration because it effectively means that the back-end HTTP virtual server or servers must be enabled for front-end OWA to function properly. The back-end server treats the front-end server the same as it would a client who connected directly to the back-end server. When the back-end server responds to the client request, the communication travels through the front-end server unchanged.

> **NOTE**
>
> Each Exchange Server 2003 system can contain multiple HTTP virtual servers. This is useful in situations in which an OWA server needs to respond to requests from OWA clients from multiple domains. For example, if a single OWA server will respond to owa.companyabc.com, owa.company123.org, and owa.organizationy.com, virtual servers need to be set up for each domain on both the front-end and back-end server, because the host header information does not change when proxying requests.

The following are a few facts to note regarding the communication between the front-end and back-end server:

- **Front-end and back-end servers communicate OWA requests with each other only over port 80**—Trying to use any other port on the virtual server, such as 8080, does not work.

- **SSL cannot be used between front-end and back-end servers to secure communication**—Use IPSec to secure traffic between front-end/back-end servers when it must traverse unsecured networks.

- **Front-end servers support only HTTP 1.1 basic authentication**—If users will be connecting to the server over the Internet, SSL should be enabled on the front-end server to secure the session and the user's credentials.

- **When authenticating to the front-end server, users need to enter the domain name**—User credentials need to be entered in the format domain/username. This can be overridden with a default domain, if necessary.

## Planning for Front-End OWA Servers

The general recommendation from Microsoft is to plan for one front-end server for no more than four back-end servers. Front-end servers require fast processors to handle tasks such as encryption through SSL or IPSec, and they should also be configured with sufficient memory. Large disks are not required in the front-end servers because they have unpopulated mail store databases or no databases at all. The level of fault tolerance in the front-end server is really up to the organization. If features such as NLB are enabled, it might not be worth spending the extra dollars for RAID controllers, redundant fans, and network adapters. If NLB is not used, organizations should consider at least hardware RAID 1 disk configuration.

## Securing Communications on Front-End Servers

If the front-end server will be used for Internet clients, the communication between the client and the server should be secured using SSL.

> **NOTE**
>
> For steps on configuring a front-end server for SSL, see the section later in this chapter, "Enabling Secure Sockets Layer (SSL) Support for Exchange Outlook Web Access."

If secure communication is needed between the front-end and back-end servers, IPSec can be implemented. The back-end server should be configured for Client (respond only) so that IPSec is not required for MAPI client access. On the front-end server, only HTTP traffic initiated by the front-end server on port 80 should be configured for IPSec. Any firewalls between the servers will have to be opened for IP identifiers 50 and 51.

## Configuring a Firewall for Front-End Servers

To use a front-end/back-end server configuration in which there is a firewall between the front-end and back-end servers, certain ports must be opened between the servers for proper communication to take place.

> **NOTE**
>
> Although previous security designs for OWA often focused on placing an Exchange front-end server in the demilitarized zone (DMZ) of a packet-filter firewall, this is not recommended best practice as it requires such a large number of ports to be open that it effectively negates most of the security advantages of placing the server in the DMZ. Current best practice is to utilize a reverse proxy system such as Microsoft ISA Server 2004 that only requires port 443 or 80 to be open to and from the DMZ. For more information on configuring ISA to secure Exchange, see Chapter 9.

For client access to the front-end server, the following ports must be open from the clients to the front-end server or servers. If one or more of these protocols will not be supported, they can be disabled:

- **443/TCP HTTPS**—HTTP secured with SSL.

- **993/TCP IMAPS**—IMAP secured with SSL.

- **995/TCP POP3S**—POP3 secured with SSL.

- **25/TCP SMTP**—Required for relaying from POP3 and IMAP clients or receiving Internet mail from the outside. This is not required if SMTP mail is relayed from another location or not allowed.

10

> **NOTE**
>
> Although it is not normally recommended to allow nonencrypted traffic over the "normal" ports for HTTP, IMAP4, and POP3 (80, 143, and 110), it can be allowed, depending on the security requirements of the organization. In addition, if port 80 is open, clients need to be educated to access the server over an `https://` connection. If this is not feasible, port 80 has to be opened, and a special web page can be placed that automatically redirects clients to use the SSL port.

For the front-end server to communicate with the back-end server, the following ports must be open between the front-end server(s) and the internal network:

- 80/TCP HTTP

- 143/TCP IMAP (if utilized)

- 110/TCP POP3 (if utilized)

- 25/TCP SMTP (not required if the server is not forwarding SMTP messages)

- 389/TCP LDAP Access to Active Directory

- 3268/TCP Access to the global catalog

- 88/TCP/UDP Kerberos authentication

It's also recommended to open port 53 for TCP and UDP to enable the front-end server to query DNS for the global catalog and domain controller records. If the DNS ports are not open, a host file can be used on the server. The host file should list all global catalog and domain controller servers that the front-end server needs to contact.

Exchange Server 2003 front-end servers have reduced their reliance on requiring RPC between the front-end servers and the AD domain controllers, but unfortunately have not completely divorced themselves from this role. Specifically, front-end servers require RPC for client authentication and to do queries to locate AD domain controllers and global catalog servers.

To support client authentication on the front-end server, the following additional ports should be opened:

- 135/TCP RPC Port Endpoint Mapper

- 1024+/TCP RPC Service Ports

- 445/TCP Netlogon

If it is not possible to open dynamic RPC ports between front-end servers and the AD domain controllers, it might be possible to force AD to communicate over specific ports through a Registry change on all domain controllers. Because this requires production domain controller changes that differ from general best practice, it is not normally recommended. In addition, as the preceding note describes, it is often better practice to use a reverse proxy system in the DMZ than an Exchange front-end server.

## Disabling Unnecessary Services on the Front-End Server

Front-end servers require only a few services to operate. Listed are the services that are required by each protocol on the front-end server:

- **HTTP**—World Wide Web Publishing Service and Exchange System Attendant

- **POP3**—Exchange POP3, Exchange System Attendant, and Exchange Information Store

- **IMAP**—Exchange IMAP, Exchange System Attendant, and Exchange Information Store

> **NOTE**
>
> All Exchange services other than the HTTP, POP3, and IMAP services should be left disabled in the Services snap-in on the front-end servers. This ensures that the front-end server processes only the tasks necessary to be dedicated to service.

By default, in POP3 and IMAP configurations, the front-end server requires a storage group on the server even though it might not contain any databases. The storage group can be removed if the dependencies on the Exchange Information Store are removed in the Registry. To remove the POP3 and IMAP front-end servers' dependency on the Exchange Information Store, remove the `MSExchangeIS` entry from the `DependOnService` Registry entries in the following Registry keys:

`HKEY_LOCAL_MACHINE\System\CurrentControlSet\Services\IMAP4SVC`

`HKEY_LOCAL_MACHINE\System\CurrentControlSet\Services\POP3SVC`

When a firewall separates the front-end and back-end servers and the RPC ports are not open, the POP3 and IMAP dependency on the Exchange Information Store must be removed.

For HTTP, POP3, and IMAP configurations, all public folder store databases should be deleted from the server. Mail store databases can be left on the server as long as they do not contain any mailboxes. Leaving the mail store databases on the server enables the Internet Service Manager to be run against the server, so items such as the SSL configuration can be modified.

Front-end servers that receive mail from the Internet need to retain at least one private Information Store so nondelivery receipts (NDRs) can be sent to Internet users. If one store is not mounted, the message conversion cannot take place and the NDR messages become stuck in the local delivery queue. An Information Store database is also required if there are Exchange 5.5 servers in the same routing group to enable the MTA to transfer mail over RPC.

## Reducing Server Configuration

As the number of front-end servers grows, the overhead of configuring each back-end server to communicate with the front-end servers grows too. Remember that each back-end server must have a corresponding HTTP virtual server for each front-end server. Using a single HTTP virtual server on the back-end server configured for all front-end servers is possible and can help reduce the HTTP virtual server configuration overhead with a large number of front-end servers. This technique can be used as long as the front-end server configurations are identical.

## Configuring Network Load Balancing for Front-End Servers

A DNS-based round-robin can be used to load balance between front-end servers by creating multiple A records for each front-end server with the same hostname—for instance, mail.companyabc.com. This solution provides primitive load balancing and works well while all servers are online. The disadvantage to this solution is that the DNS still returns the IP address of a failed server in the round-robin.

A better solution for load balancing is to use the NLB feature of Windows Server 2003. NLB uses a virtual IP address for all connections to the front-end servers. NLB does not attempt to connect with an offline server. SSL can also be used on front-end servers in the NLB cluster to secure client communication. When using SSL and NLB, use the default Client Affinity setting of Single to preserve the client session state between a client and a specific node in the NLB cluster.

## Configuring Front-End and Back-End Servers

Exchange 2000 Server previously required that all front-end servers run the Enterprise version of Exchange to be able to run as a front-end server. This is no longer the case in Exchange Server 2003, and the Standard version of the software can run as a front-end server. To configure a front-end server, use Exchange System Manager to access the properties of the front-end server and click the check box This Is a Front-End Server, as shown in Figure 10.2.

# Enabling Secure Sockets Layer (SSL) Support for Exchange Outlook Web Access

Traffic to and from an OWA server uses the Web-based Hypertext Transfer Protocol (HTTP) to communicate with both client and server. The upside to using this protocol is that the OWA server can be accessed from any client on the Internet that supports HTTP. This enables employees to access mail services from airport kiosks, libraries, home computers, or other systems with ease.

The downside to OWA access with HTTP is that the traffic is sent in clear text, easily readable to any third party that intercepts the traffic sent across untrusted networks.

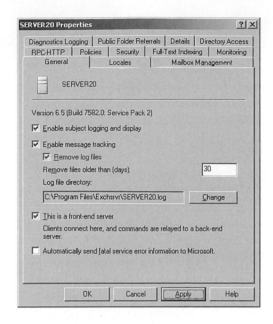

**FIGURE 10.2**   Creating a front-end server.

After the server has been made into a front-end server, the Exchange POP3, Exchange IMAP, and World Wide Web Publishing Service services must be restarted.

Fortunately, HTTP can be encrypted with a technology known as Secure Sockets Layer (SSL), which scrambles the packets sent between client and server by using a set of keys tied to an SSL certificate installed on the OWA server, such as is illustrated in Figure 10.3. This certificate ensures the identify of the server itself, and allows the traffic to be virtually uncrackable, particularly if strong 128-bit encryption is used.

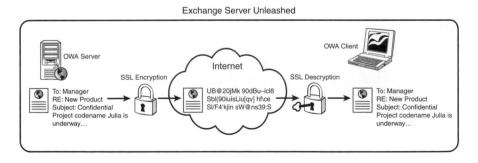

**FIGURE 10.3**   Examining SSL encryption for OWA traffic.

The upshot of this discussion is that it is vital, and almost always necessary, to secure OWA-based traffic using digital SSL certificates. It is less and less common to run into OWA implementations that are not secured with SSL, and this chapter focuses on deploying and securing OWA sites that use SSL to encrypt the traffic.

Installing a digital certificate on the Exchange OWA server involves a two-step process. In the first step, the certificate request must be generated from the OWA server and sent to a certificate authority. Second, the certificate authority must then verify the identity of the site and send a certificate back to the organization to be installed on the OWA server. The key to this process is to either use a third-party certificate authority such as VeriSign or Thawte to provide the certificates, or to install and configure an internal enterprise certificate authority. Each of these processes is described in more detail in the subsequent section of this chapter.

## Understanding the Need for Third-Party CAs

By and large, the most common approach to securing an OWA server with SSL is to buy a certificate from a third-party certificate authority such as VeriSign, Thawte, or one of many other enterprise certificate authorities. These companies exist as a trusted third-party vendor of digital identity. Their job is to validate that their customers are really who they say they are, and to generate the digital certificates that validate this for digital communications that require encryption, such as SSL.

For example, if CompanyABC wants to create a certificate to install on its OWA server, it sends the certificate request to the third-party certificate authority (CA), who then follows up by researching the company, calling the CompanyABC employees, and conducting interviews to determine the validity of the organization. Based on the information obtained from this process, the third-party CA then encrypts the certificate and sends it back to CompanyABC, which then installs it on its server.

Because the third-party CA is registered on nearly all the Web browsers (the most common ones always are), the client automatically trusts the CA and, subsequently, trusts the certificate generated by CompanyABC. It is because of this seamless integration with the majority of the world's browsers that third-party enterprise CAs are commonly utilized.

Internal certificate authorities, built and maintained by the internal IT branch of an organization, are more cost effective. Expensive third-party certificates (which can run up to $1,000 per year in some cases) can be eschewed in favor of internally generated certificates. This also gives an organization more flexibility in the creation and modification of certificates. Windows Server 2003 includes the option of installing an enterprise certificate authority on an internal server or set of servers, giving administrators more options for SSL communications. The biggest downside to an internal CA is that, by default, not all browsers have the required certificate patch that includes the internal CA as part of the default installation and, therefore, receive the error illustrated in Figure 10.4 when accessing a site secured by this certificate.

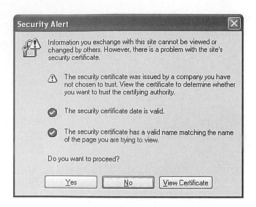

**FIGURE 10.4**   Viewing a common SSL certificate error.

The only way to avoid this type of error message from appearing is to add the internal CA to the client's list of trusted root authorities, which can be a difficult prospect if OWA access is to be made available to browsers around the world. An enterprise certificate authority is automatically trusted by domain members, which can make this easier for an organization to deploy, but can still limit the deployment of a seamless solution. It is this limitation that sometimes stops organizations from installing their own CAs.

Either third-party CA certificate generation or internal CA generation is required for SSL support on OWA. These deployment options are illustrated in the subsequent sections of this chapter.

## Installing a Third-Party CA on an OWA Server

If a third-party certificate authority will be used to enable SSL on an OWA server, a certificate request must first be generated directly from the OWA server. After this request has been generated, it can be sent off to the third-party CA, who then verifies the identify of the organization and sends it back, where it can be installed on the server.

If an internal CA will be utilized, this section and its procedures can be skipped, and readers can proceed directly to the subsequent section, "Using an Internal Certificate Authority for OWA Certificates."

To generate an SSL certificate request for use with a third-party CA, perform the following steps:

1. From the OWA server, open IIS Manager (Start, All Programs, Administrative Tools, Internet Information Services (IIS) Manager).

2. Under the console tree, expand SERVERNAME (local computer), Web Sites and right-click the OWA virtual server (typically named Default Web Site), and then click Properties.

3. Select the Directory Security tab.

4. Under Secure Communications, click the Server Certificate button.

5. At the Welcome page, click Next to continue.

6. From the list of options displayed, select Create a New Certificate, and click Next to continue.

7. From the Delayed or Immediate Request dialog box, select Prepare the Request Now, But Send It Later, and then click Next.

8. Type a descriptive name for the certificate, such as what is shown in Figure 10.5, leave the Bit Length at 1024, and click Next to continue.

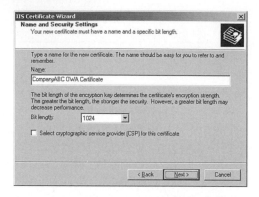

**FIGURE 10.5**    Generating an SSL certificate request for an OWA virtual server.

9. Enter the name of the organization and what organizational unit will be associated with the certificate. These fields will be viewable by external users, and should accurately reflect the organizational structure of the requestor.

10. Enter a common name for the OWA Web site in the form of the fully qualified domain name (FQDN). An example of this is mail.companyabc.com. Click Next to continue.

> **NOTE**
>
> If the OWA site will be made accessible from the Internet, the common name of the site needs to be made accessible from the Internet via a DNS A record.

11. Enter the appropriate information into the Geographical Information dialog box, such as State, City, and Country. Abbreviations are not allowed. Click Next to continue.

12. Enter a filename for the certificate request, such as `C:\owacert.txt`, and click Next to continue.

13. On the Request File Summary dialog box, review the summary page for accuracy, and click Next to continue.

14. Click Finish to end the Web Server Certificate Wizard.

After the certificate request has been generated, the text file, which will look similar to the one shown in Figure 10.6, can then be emailed or otherwise transmitted to the certificate authority via its own individual process. Each CA has a different procedure, and the exact steps need to follow the individual CA's process. After an organization's identity has been proven by the CA, it sends back the server certificate, typically in the form of a file, or as part of the body of an email message.

**FIGURE 10.6**   Viewing a certificate request file.

The certificate then needs to be installed on the server itself. If it was sent in the form of a .cer file, it can be imported via the process described in the following steps. If it was included in the body of an email, the certificate itself needs to be cut and pasted into a text editor such as Notepad and saved as a .cer file. After the .cer file has been obtained, it can be installed on the OWA server through the following process:

1. From the OWA server, open IIS Manager (Start, All Programs, Administrative Tools, Internet Information Services (IIS) Manager).

2. Under the console tree, expand SERVERNAME (local computer), Web Sites, and right-click the OWA virtual server (typically named Default Web Site), and then click Properties.

3. Select the Directory Security tab.

4. Under Secure Communications, click the Server Certificate button.

5. At the Welcome page, click Next to continue.

6. From the Pending Certificate Request dialog box, select Process the Pending Request and Install the Certificate, and click Next to continue.

7. Enter the pathname and filename where the .cer file was saved (the Browse button can be used to locate the file), and click Next to continue.

8. Click Finish to finalize the certificate installation.

At this point in the process, SSL communication to the OWA server can be allowed, but forcing SSL encryption requires more configuration, which is outlined in the later section titled "Forcing SSL Encryption for OWA Traffic."

## Using an Internal Certificate Authority for OWA Certificates

If a third-party certificate authority is not utilized, an internal CA can be set up instead. There are several different CA options, including several third-party products, and it may be advantageous to take advantage of an existing internal CA. If none is available, however, one can be installed on an internal Windows Server 2003 system in an organization.

### Installing an Internal Certificate Authority

On a domain member server or, more commonly, on a domain controller, the Certificate Authority component of Windows Server 2003 can be installed using the following procedure:

> **NOTE**
>
> This procedure outlines the process on a Windows Server 2003 system. It is possible to install and configure a CA on a Windows 2000 system, through a slightly different procedure.

1. Click Start, Control Panel, Add or Remove Programs.

2. Click Add/Remove Windows Components.

3. Check the box labeled Certificate Services.

4. At the warning box, shown in Figure 10.7, click Yes to acknowledge that the server name cannot be changed.

**FIGURE 10.7**    Installing a local certificate authority.

5. Click Next to continue.

From the subsequent dialog box, shown in Figure 10.8, select what type of certificate authority is to be set up. Each choice of CA type has different ramifications, and each one is useful in different situations. The following is a list of the types of CAs available for installation:

• **Enterprise root CA**—An enterprise root CA is the highest-level certificate authority for an organization. By default, all members of the forest where it is installed trust it, which can make it a convenient mechanism for securing OWA or other services within a domain environment. Unless an existing enterprise root CA is in place, this is the typical choice for a homegrown CA solution in an organization.

- **Enterprise subordinate CA**—An enterprise subordinate CA is subordinate to an existing enterprise root CA, and must receive a certificate from that root CA to work properly. In certain large organizations, it might be useful to have a hierarchy of CAs, or the desire might exist to isolate the CA structure for OWA to a subordinate enterprise CA structure.

- **Standalone root CA**—A standalone root CA is similar to an enterprise CA, in that it provides for its own unique identity and can be uniquely configured. It differs from an enterprise CA in that it is not automatically trusted by any forest clients in an organization.

- **Standalone subordinate CA**—A standalone subordinate CA is similar to an enterprise subordinate CA, except that it is not directly tied or trusted by the forest structure, and must take its own certificate from a standalone root CA.

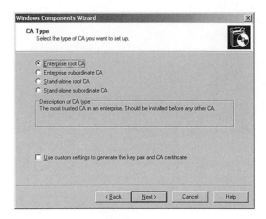

**FIGURE 10.8**   Selecting a CA type to install.

After choosing the type of CA required, continue the CA installation process by performing the following steps:

1. In this example, an enterprise certificate authority is chosen. Click Next to continue.

2. Enter a common name for the certificate authority, such as what is shown in Figure 10.9. Click Next to continue.

3. Enter locations for the certificate database and the database log (the defaults can normally be chosen), and click Next to continue.

4. Click Yes when warned that the IIS Services will be restarted.

5. Click Finish after the installation is complete.

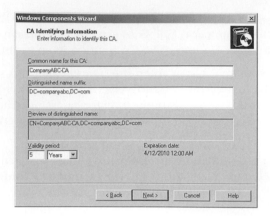

**FIGURE 10.9** Entering a common name for the certificate authority.

## Installing an Internal Certificate on the OWA Server

After the internal CA is in place, the OWA server can automatically use it for generation of certificates. To use an internal CA to generate and install a certificate on an OWA server, use the following technique:

1. From the OWA server, open IIS Manager (Start, All Programs, Administrative Tools, Internet Information Services (IIS) Manager).

2. Under the console tree, expand SERVERNAME (local computer), Web Sites, and right-click the OWA virtual server (typically named Default Web Site), and then click Properties.

3. Select the Directory Security tab.

4. Under Secure Communications, click the Server Certificate button.

5. At the Welcome page, click Next to continue.

6. Select Create a New Certificate, and click Next to continue.

7. From the Delayed or Immediate Request dialog box, select Send the Request Immediately to an Online Certification Authority, and click Next to continue.

8. Enter a name for the certificate, such as CompanyABC OWA Certificate, leave the bit length at 1024, and click Next to continue.

9. Enter the organization and organizational unit name, keeping in mind that they should accurately reflect the real name of the requestor. Click Next to continue.

10. Enter the FQDN of the OWA server, such as mail.companyabc.com.

11. In the Geographical Information dialog box, enter an unabbreviated State, City, and Country, and click Next to continue.

12. Specify the SSL port (443 is the default) that the server is to use, and click Next to continue.

13. In the Choose a Certification Authority dialog box, shown in Figure 10.10, select the CA that was set up in the previous steps, and click Next to continue.

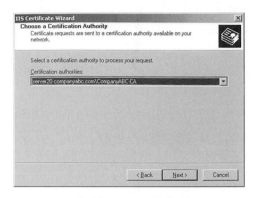

**FIGURE 10.10**    Installing a local CA certificate on an OWA server.

14. Review the request in the Certificate Request Submission dialog box, and click Next to continue.

15. Click Finish when complete.

After installation, the certificate can be viewed by clicking on the View Certificate button of the Directory Services tab under the Virtual Server properties.

After SSL is placed on a server, SSL encryption is made available on the OWA server. If the enterprise certificate authority was installed in an Active Directory domain, all the domain members include the internal CA as a trusted root authority and connect to OWA via SSL with no errors. External or nondomain members, however, need to install the enterprise CA into their local trusted root authorities to avoid the error message described in the previous section.

## Forcing SSL Encryption for OWA Traffic

After either a third-party or a local internal certificate has been installed on an OWA server, it is typical to then set up the OWA server to force SSL traffic, rather than allow that traffic to use the unencrypted HTTP protocol. This is especially necessary given the fact that most users simply connect to the OWA server from their browser by typing in the name of the server, such as mail.companyabc.com, which defaults to the unencrypted http:// prefix, rather than the encrypted https:// prefix. To solve this problem, SSL encryption must be forced from the OWA server via the following procedure:

1. On the OWA server, open IIS Manager (Start, All Programs, Administrative Tools, Internet Information Services (IIS) Manager).

2. Navigate to Internet Information Services, Web Sites, OWA Web Site (usually named Default Web Site).

10

3. Right-click on the Exchange virtual directory (under the OWA virtual server), and choose Properties.

4. Choose the Directory Services tab.

5. Under Secure Communications, click the Edit button.

6. From the Secure Communications dialog box, shown in Figure 10.11, check the boxes for Require Secure Channel (SSL) and Require 128-bit Encryption.

**FIGURE 10.11**   Forcing SSL encryption on the Exchange virtual directory.

7. Click OK, OK.

8. Repeat the process for the Public virtual directory.

> **NOTE**
>
> Although it might seem like it is better to force SSL on the entire site, it is not actually required, and can also interfere with some of the functionality that might be needed, such as automatic redirection of users, covered in the next section of this chapter. The Exchange and Public virtual directories are the only default directories that should have their information encrypted.

## Customizing and Securing an OWA Web Site from Internal Access

The OWA Web site should be secured and optimized to allow internal clients to access the server safely. This helps to mitigate the risk of internal attack against the OWA server. The following section deals with best practice methods to optimize and secure the OWA site with standard Windows and Exchange methods.

## Redirecting Clients to the Exchange Virtual Directory

By default, any clients that access an OWA implementation by simply typing in the name of the server, such as mail.companyabc.com, do not gain access to OWA, as the full path to the Exchange virtual directory (for example, `http://mail.companyabc.com/exchange`) must be entered. A simple trick automates this procedure. To set up the automatic redirection to the Exchange virtual directory, perform the following steps on the OWA server:

1. On the OWA server, open IIS Manager (Start, All Programs, Administrative Tools, Internet Information Services (IIS) Manager).

2. Navigate to SERVERNAME, Web Sites.

3. Right-click on the OWA virtual server (usually Default Web Site), and choose Properties.

4. Select the Home Directory tab.

5. Change the setting under the heading The Content for This Resource Should Come From to A Redirection to a URL, and enter **/exchange** into the Redirect To field, as shown in Figure 10.12.

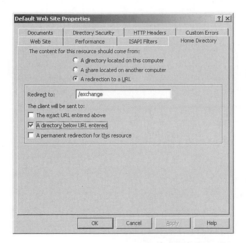

**FIGURE 10.12**    Setting the OWA virtual server to automatically use the Exchange virtual directory.

6. Check the check box labeled A Directory Below URL Entered.

7. Click OK.

8. When prompted about inheritance overrides, click OK.

9. Restart the IIS Services by right-clicking on the name of the server in IIS Manager and choose All Tasks, Restart IIS.

10. Click OK to complete the restart of IIS.

10

With the automatic redirect in place, the OWA server is configured to automatically add the /exchange to the URL that the user enters.

## Creating a Custom SSL Error to Redirect HTTP Traffic to SSL

One of the downsides to forcing SSL encryption on the OWA server is that the users receive a 403.4 error message similar to the one shown in Figure 10.13 when they try to connect to the OWA server using the standard HTTP protocol.

**FIGURE 10.13**    Examining the 403.4 error message.

Although a handful of users would be able to recover from this error message and put the https:// as the prefix to the URL, a large number of them would probably not, which could make the OWA logon process less than transparent and frustrating to many. A simple fix to this problem is to generate a custom error message to replace the 403.4 message with one that automatically redirects the users to the https:// OWA namespace.

The 403.4 error message must be replaced by a custom ASP Web page that redirects the requestor to the SSL Web site and the Exchange virtual directory on the server. The code of the ASP file can be input in Notepad and should be exactly as follows (do not replace any of the variables with real server names):

```
<%
    If Request.ServerVariables("SERVER_PORT")=80 Then
        Dim strSecureURL
        strSecureURL = "https://"
        strSecureURL = strSecureURL & Request.ServerVariables("SERVER_NAME")
        strSecureURL = strSecureURL & "/exchange"
        Response.Redirect strSecureURL
    End If
%>
```

The high-level process to create this message is as follows:

1. Create a directory in C:\Inetpub\wwwroot called owaasp (where C:\ is the OS drive).

2. In Notepad, create a file named owahttps.asp, with the code listed in the preceding passages, and place it in the C:\Inetpub\wwwroot\owaasp directory.

3. Open IIS Manager (Start, All Programs, Administrative Tools, Internet Information Services (IIS) Manager).

4. Expand SERVERNAME, Web Sites.

5. Right-click the OWA virtual server (usually called Default Web Site), point to New, and then click Virtual Directory.

6. Click Next at the wizard welcome dialog box.

7. Under the Virtual Directory Alias dialog box, enter **OWA_Redirect** as the Alias name, as shown in Figure 10.14.

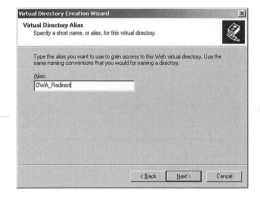

**FIGURE 10.14**   Creating a virtual directory for OWA HTTP Redirection to SSL.

8. Enter **C:\Inetpub\wwwroot\owaasp** as the directory path, and click Next to continue.

9. In the Virtual Directory Access Permissions dialog box, choose only Read and Run Scripts from the permissions displayed (the defaults), and click Next to continue.

10. Click Finish.

After the file is created, the virtual directory must be changed to allow anonymous connections and to use the proper application pool. If this is not done, users will not be properly redirected. Perform the following steps to set this up:

1. From IIS Manager, expand the OWA Web Site, right-click on the newly created OWA_Redirect virtual directory, and choose Properties.

10

2. Under the Virtual Directory tab, in the Application Settings section, choose ExchangeApplicationPool from the drop-down list under Application_pool, as shown in Figure 10.15.

**FIGURE 10.15**    Setting virtual directory settings in OWA.

3. Select the Directory Security tab.

4. Under Authentication and Access Control, click the Edit button.

5. Keep the default check box checked for Enable Anonymous Access and accept the default anonymous account. Uncheck (do not enable) any other type of access.

6. Click OK and OK to save the changes.

The last step is to actually change the 403.4 error message to use the custom ASP page. To do this, follow these steps:

1. Under the same OWA virtual server in IIS Manager, right-click the Exchange virtual directory and choose Properties.

2. Choose the Custom Errors tab.

3. Select the HTTP Error of 403.4 and click the Edit button.

4. Change the message type to URL, enter **/owa_redirect/owahttps.asp**, and click OK.

5. The Custom Errors dialog box should now look like the one shown in Figure 10.16. Click OK to save the changes.

6. Right-click the server name and choose All Tasks, Restart IIS.

7. Click OK to confirm the restart.

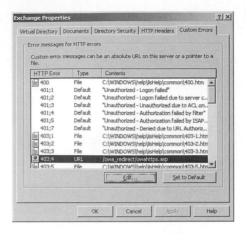

**FIGURE 10.16**    Customizing the 403.4 error to redirect OWA users to HTTPS.

At this point, the Exchange Outlook Web Access server is now configured to automatically redirect all users to SSL encrypted traffic, the first step to securing the OWA server for access from the Internet. In addition, the server is positioned to have a reverse proxy solution such as ISA Server 2004 secure the server through the use of an ISA Mail Publishing Rule. For more information on using ISA to secure OWA, see Chapter 9.

> **NOTE**
>
> For more information on using this technique to redirect to SSL connections, reference the Knowledge Base article #555126 at the following URL:
>
> http://support.microsoft.com/kb/555126

## Enabling Forms-Based Authentication on the OWA Server

Exchange Server 2003 allows for the use of forms-based authentication (FBA) for OWA, which provides end-users with a custom form similar to the one shown in Figure 10.17 that can be used to log on to the OWA site.

The advantage to using forms-based authentication with OWA is that it is cookie-based, which means that clients can be automatically timed out of the connection after a specific period of time. In addition, it allows for users to choose from options such as Simple OWA versus Advanced, so as to support the version of browser that they are using.

> **CAUTION**
>
> There are two important things to keep in mind when enabling FBA on the OWA server itself. First, if FBA is used in conjunction with an ISA Server 2004 reverse proxy, it must be enabled only in ISA, and not in OWA, or it will break. Second, enabling FBA on a virtual server effectively disables Basic Authentication on that virtual server, which will break OMA, EAS, and RPC-HTTPS access. To fix this, a second virtual server must be created. For information on how to do this, see the later section of this chapter titled "Deploying Multiple OWA Virtual Servers."

10

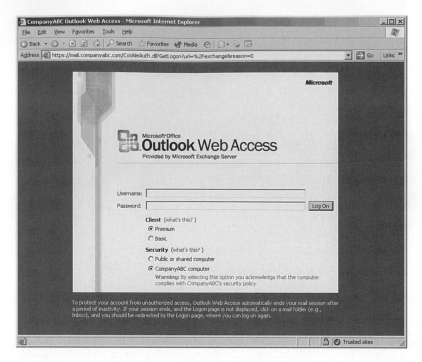

**FIGURE 10.17**    Using forms-based authentication with OWA.

To enable FBA on an OWA virtual server, perform the following steps:

1. From Exchange System Manager, navigate to OrganizationName, Administrative Groups, AdminGroupName, Servers, ServerName, Protocols, HTTP.

2. Right-click on the OWA virtual server and choose Properties.

3. Click the Settings tab.

4. Check the box labeled Enabled Forms Based Authentication, as shown in Figure 10.18.

5. Leave the compressions settings at the default and click OK and OK again to save the settings.

## Summarizing OWA Virtual Server Settings

It is sometimes difficult to keep track of the particular SSL and authentication settings that constitute best practice OWA design. Consequently, Table 10.1 is provided to give administrators a quick glance at best practice OWA virtual server and virtual directory settings. This table is meant to be used as a general guideline for organizations seeking a laundry list of standard settings.

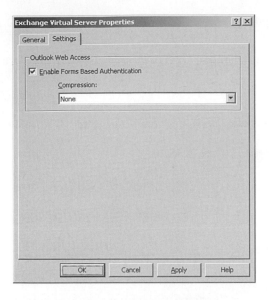

**FIGURE 10.18**    Enabling Forms-Based Authentication for OWA.

**TABLE 10.1**    OWA Virtual Server Settings

| Virtual Directory | SSL | Authentication | Notes |
|---|---|---|---|
| Root (at the virtual server level) | Not enabled | Anonymous only | Change home directory to redirect to URL /exchange. Check the check box for A Directory Below this One under the Home Directory tab. |
| Exadmin | Not enabled | Integrated Windows Authentication | Not used for remote access; only needed to allow for public folders to be displayed when the local Exchange System Manager tool is accessed from the server. |
| Exchange | Required | Basic Authentication only | Create a custom 403.4 error to point to URL of /owa_redirect/ owahttps.asp. |

10

**TABLE 10.1**    Continued

| Virtual Directory | SSL | Authentication | Notes |
|---|---|---|---|
| ExchWeb | Required | Anonymous only | Note that enabling anonymous connections on this directory does not decrease security because the files themselves are secured. |
| Iisadmpwd | Required | Basic Authentication only | Used to enable the Change Password feature in OWA, disabled by default in Exchange Server 2003. See the step-by-step examples in the section titled "Enabling the Change Password Feature in OWA." |
| Microsoft-Server-ActiveSync | Required | Basic Authentication only | Special considerations exist for OWA servers that are not dedicated front-end servers. See the subsequent section of this chapter on ActiveSync. |
| OMA | Required | Basic Authentication only | Special considerations exist for OWA servers that are not dedicated front-end servers. |
| ExchDAV | Not enabled | Integrated Windows Authentication Basic Authentication | Used only when OWA server is also a back-end database server and SSL is enabled on the Exchange virtual server. This is for supporting OMA and EAS in this configuration, referenced in later sections of this chapter. Configure it to deny all connections except the local OWA server's IP address (for security reasons). |
| OWA_Redirect | Required | Anonymous only | Create this virtual directory and point to the owahttps.asp redirect file. |
| Public | Required | Basic Authentication only | Used for public folder access. |
| Rpc | Required | Basic Authentication only | Used for RPC over HTTPS communications. See the later section of this chapter on how to do this. |

> **CAUTION**
>
> Service packs and hotfixes can have the effect of erasing custom changes made in IIS Manager, including SSL and Authentication settings on virtual directories. One of the first things that should be done after applying patches or service packs should be to double-check these settings and validate functionality.

## Enabling the Change Password Feature in OWA

By default, Exchange Server 2003 does not display the Change Password button in OWA. This option was previously made available by default in Exchange 2000 OWA, so many administrators may be looking to provide for this same functionality.

The Change Password button was removed to provide for a higher degree of default security in Exchange Server 2003, particularly because the Exchange 2000 Change Password feature was highly insecure in its original implementations. Fortunately, however, the Exchange Server 2003 Change Password option in OWA was recoded to operate at a much lower security context, and is subsequently much safer. Despite this fact, however, this functionality must still be enabled on the Exchange server.

Enabling the Change Password feature on the Exchange OWA server involves a three-step process: creating a virtual directory for the password reset, configuring the virtual directory, and modifying the Exchange Server Registry to support the change. To start the process and create the virtual directory, do the following:

1. From the OWA server, open IIS Manager (Start, All Programs, Administrative Tools, Internet Information Services (IIS) Manager).

2. Right-click the OWA virtual server (typically named Default Web Site), point to New, and then click Virtual Directory.

3. At the Welcome dialog box, click Next.

4. Under Alias, enter **iisadmpwd** and click Next.

5. Enter **C:\windows\system32\inetsrv\iisadmpwd** into the Path field, as shown in Figure 10.19 (where C:\ is the system drive), and click Next to continue.

6. Check the boxes for Read and Run Scripts permissions and click Next.

7. Click Finish.

After it is created, the IISADMPWD virtual directory needs to be configured to use the Exchange application pool, and also be forced to use Basic Authentication with SSL (highly recommended for security reasons). To do so, perform the following steps:

1. In IIS Manager, under the OWA virtual server, right-click the newly created iisadmpwd virtual directory and choose Properties.

2. Under the Virtual Directory tab, in the Application Settings field, choose ExchangeApplicationPool from the drop-down list labeled Application Pool, as shown in Figure 10.20.

10

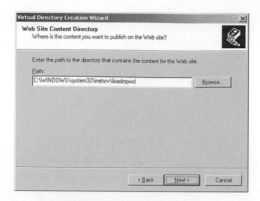

**FIGURE 10.19**     Creating the IISADMPWD virtual directory.

**FIGURE 10.20**     Modifying the IISADMPWD virtual directory.

3. Choose the Directory Security tab, and click the Edit button under Authentication and Access Control.

4. Deselect Enable Anonymous Access, and check Basic Authentication.

5. Click Yes to acknowledge the warning (SSL will be used, so this warning is moot).

6. Click OK to save the authentication methods changes.

7. Under Secure Communications, click the Edit button.

8. Check the boxes for Require Secure Channel (SSL) and Require 128-bit Encryption, and click OK twice to save the changes.

After the virtual directory has been created, a Registry change must be made to allow password resets to take place. To do this, perform the following tasks:

1. Click Start, Run, type in **regedit.exe**, and click OK.

2. Navigate to My Computer\HKEY_LOCAL_MACHINE\SYSTEM\CurrentControlSet\
   Services\MSExchangeWEB\OWA.

3. Look for the DWORD value labeled DisablePassword, as shown in Figure 10.21, double-click on it, enter **0** in the Value Data field, and click OK. Entering 0 forces changes to be made in SSL, which is highly recommended.

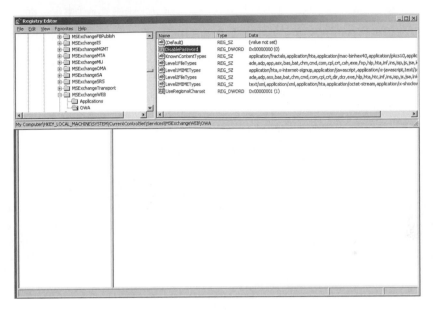

**FIGURE 10.21**   Changing the Registry to support password resets.

4. Back in IIS Manager, restart IIS by right-clicking on the server name in IIS Manager and choosing All Tasks, Restart IIS, and then clicking OK.

## Configuring OMA and ActiveSync Access to Exchange

The OMA, EAS, and RPC over HTTP services are similar to OWA in that they all use Web protocols to provide access to mail resources. Each of these services provides for unique methods of access to an Exchange server, as follows:

- **Outlook Mobile Access (OMA)**—OMA allows Web-enabled phones and other mobile devices to have access to mailbox resources via a simple, streamlined interface that displays only simple text.

- **Exchange ActiveSync (EAS)**—Exchange ActiveSync allows ActiveSync-enabled phones, such as those running Mobile 2003 or PocketPC 2002, to synchronize content remotely with the Exchange server wirelessly or while docked to a workstation. This combined with the "always up-to-date" functionality of Exchange Server

10

2003 allows ActiveSync-enabled devices to have full real-time send and receive capabilities, similar to that offered by products such as RIM BlackBerry devices.

- **RPC over HTTP(S)**—RPC over HTTP(S) is an extremely useful method of accessing Exchange servers from Outlook 2003 clients anywhere in the world. It uses secure SSL-encrypted Web communications between the client and the server. RPC over HTTP(S) can be used in conjunction with Cached Mode on Outlook 2003 to offer instant available access to up-to-date email, calendar information, and other mail data whenever a roaming laptop is connected to a network that has SSL access back to the Exchange server, which typically covers most networks on the Internet.

OMA and ActiveSync can be enabled in an Exchange organization relatively easily: All that's required is that a box be checked. RPC over HTTP access is more complex, however, and is described in the upcoming section of this chapter, titled "Using RPC over HTTP(S) with Exchange Server 2003."

# Enabling and Supporting OMA and ActiveSync on the OWA Server

Enabling OMA and ActiveSync is a relatively straightforward process, but one that requires that certain special steps be taken in particular circumstances. Particular attention needs to be taken when SSL is used and when Exchange front-end servers are not. First and foremost, the Exchange Mobile Services must be enabled in an Exchange organization.

## Enabling OMA and ActiveSync in Exchange System Manager

OMA and EAS can be enabled in an Exchange organization by an Exchange administrator via the following procedure:

1. On any Exchange server in the organization, open Exchange System Manager (Start, All Programs, Microsoft Exchange, System Manager).

2. Navigate to Global Settings, Mobile Services.

3. Right-click on Mobile Services and choose Properties.

4. Check the appropriate boxes for ActiveSync and OMA, as shown in Figure 10.22. Enable partial or full access to the services by checking some or all of these check boxes and configuring options with the Device Security button. Click the Help (question mark) for more information on the options.

> **NOTE**
>
> Depending on the Exchange service pack in use, the settings here might differ. Exchange Server 2003 Service Pack 2 added additional functionality to these options, allowing for Direct Push over HTTP and Device Security options.

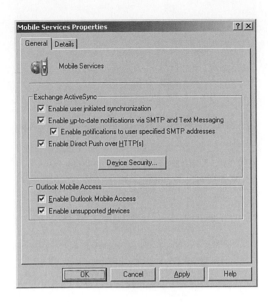

**FIGURE 10.22**    Enabling OMA and EAS in an Exchange 2003 organization.

5. Click OK to save the changes.

6. Click OK when warned about enabling up-to-date notifications. This dialog box is only displayed when using Service Pack 2 for Exchange.

## Enabling or Disabling OMA and EAS on a Per-Mailbox Basis

By default, all mailbox-enabled users in an Exchange organization have OMA and EAS individually enabled. If OMA and EAS access needs to be disabled for an individual user, or to verify that it is indeed enabled for that user, the individual setting can be found on the Exchange Features tab of an individual user account in Active Directory, as shown in Figure 10.23.

## Supporting OMA and ActiveSync on an OWA Server Configured As a Back-End Mailbox Server

One of the most misunderstood and confusing topics with OMA and EAS has to do with how to enable mobile services on an Exchange OWA server that operates both as an Exchange SSL-enabled OWA server and an Exchange mailbox server. In these cases, mobile services fail to work properly, with error messages such as Synchronization Failed Due to an Error on the Server... or Currently Your Mailbox Is Stored on an Older Version of Exchange Server.... To understand why these error messages occur, and how to fix them, it is important to understand how EAS and OMA access mail resources, and how specific SSL or forms-based authentication settings can break this.

10

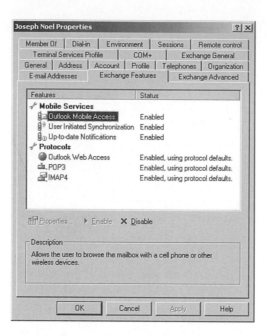

**FIGURE 10.23**    Validating OMA and EAS per-mailbox settings.

A standard IIS virtual server for Web-based mail access uses specific virtual directories to make calls into the Exchange database. For example, the /exchange virtual directory is used to display individual mailboxes; the /public virtual directory is used for public folders; and the /exchweb virtual directory is used for mailbox maintenance tasks, such as rule configuration and out-of-office settings. When SSL encryption is forced on an OWA server, however, the /exchange and /public directories are modified to force all connections made to them to use SSL only.

Now, this is all fine when OWA is the only Web-based access mechanism used. OWA users negotiate SSL encryption, and open a secured tunnel directly to the secured virtual directories. Figure 10.24 illustrates this concept.

OMA and EAS, however, work in a different way. They have their own virtual directories (/oma and /Microsoft-Server-ActiveSync). As a throwback to the origins of OMA and EAS (which were previously part of a separate product called Mobile Information Server), the server decrypts the OMA and EAS traffic, then opens up a DAV logon from the Exchange server itself to the /exchange virtual directory on the server where the mailboxes for that user are located. The problem arises when the /exchange directory on the server with the mailbox is encrypted via SSL. The DAV logon cannot establish an encrypted session with the virtual directory, and communications fails.

For environments with front-end servers, this is not a problem because the DAV calls are made to the back-end server with the user's mailbox on it. Because front-ends can only communicate to back-end servers over HTTP, an Exchange back-end mailbox server would not be configured with SSL anywhere on the virtual server, and OMA and EAS would not have a problem accessing the mailboxes.

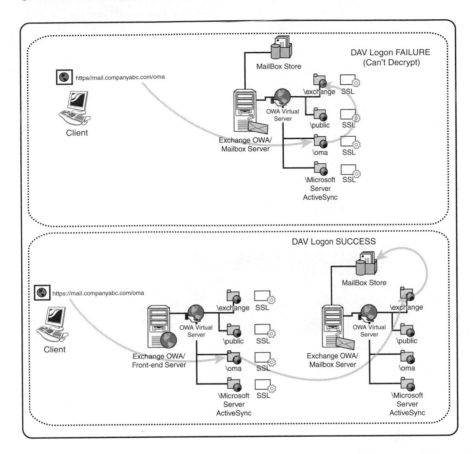

**FIGURE 10.24**   Understanding how OMA and EAS work.

For many organizations, however, a single Exchange server is the only system in place, and it performs the duties of both an Exchange front-end and back-end server. These organizations may require the use of SSL or forms-based authentication, and subsequently encrypt the /exchange virtual directory, breaking OMA and EAS traffic.

The solution to this problem is to configure a separate virtual directory for mobile services that has the same functionality as the /exchange virtual directory, but without SSL enabled on it. If the Registry is modified, the Exchange server makes the DAV call to this additional virtual server instead. To avoid having users bypass SSL encryption on the server, this virtual directory must be configured to allow only the local OWA server to access it and to deny connections from other IP addresses. To start the process, the configuration of the /exchange virtual directory must first be saved to an XML file, so it can be used to make a copy of itself. To do this, perform the following steps:

10

> **CAUTION**
>
> Remember, the entire ExchDAV procedure is necessary only if the environment is configured with a single Exchange server. If front-ends are used, this procedure is not necessary and can interfere with the default front-end/back-end topology.

1. On the Exchange server, start IIS Manager (Start, All Programs, Administrative Tools, Internet Information Services (IIS) Manager).

2. Expand SERVERNAME (local computer), Web Sites, and choose the OWA Web Site (usually Default Web Site).

3. Right-click on the /exchange virtual directory and choose All Tasks, Save Configuration to a File.

4. Enter a filename and a path to which the XML file should be saved, as shown in Figure 10.25. As an optional security precaution, a password can be entered to encrypt the XML file. Click OK.

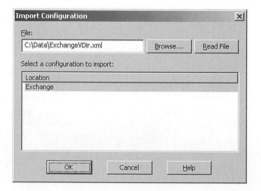

FIGURE 10.25   Exporting the Exchange virtual directory to an XML file.

After the XML file has been created, it can be imported as part of a new virtual directory via the following process:

1. Right-click the OWA virtual server (Default Web Site), point to New, and then click Virtual Directory (from file).

2. Type the path of the XML file created in the previous steps and click Read File.

3. Select the Exchange configuration and click OK.

4. When prompted that the virtual directory still exists, select Create a New Virtual Directory, enter **ExchDAV** as the alias, and click OK.

5. Enter the password entered when exporting the file (if prompted).

Now the virtual directory is in place, and the authentication and IP restriction parameters can be inputted. To do this, proceed as follows:

1. Right-click the ExchDAV virtual directory, and choose Properties.

2. Select the Directory Security tab, and click the Edit button in the Authentication and Access Control section.

3. Check only Integrated Windows Authentication and Basic Authentication; leave everything else unchecked and click OK.

4. Under Secure Communications, click the Edit button.

5. Make sure that SSL is not enabled (uncheck the boxes for Require Secure Channel if they are checked), and click OK.

6. Under IP Address and Domain Name Restrictions, click the Edit button.

7. Configure all connections to be denied by changing the setting to Denied Access. Enter an exception for the local Exchange server by clicking Add and entering the IP address of the local server, as shown in Figure 10.26.

**FIGURE 10.26**   Locking down the ExchDAV folder so that only the local server can initiate DAV logon calls for OMA and EAS.

8. Click OK and OK to save the changes.

The final step to set this up on the Exchange server is to edit the Registry to point mobile services DAV logons to the ExchDAV virtual directory. To do this, follow this procedure:

1. Open regedit (Start, Run, regedit.exe, OK).

2. Navigate to HKEY_LOCAL_MACHINE\SYSTEM\CurrentControlSet\Services\MasSync\ Parameters.

3. Right-click the Parameters folder, point to New, and then click String Value.

4. Enter **ExchangeVDir** as the name of the value.

5. Double-click on ExchangeVDir and enter /**ExchDAV** as the value data; click OK to save the changes. The setting should look like what is shown in Figure 10.27.

10

**FIGURE 10.27**    Configuring the Registry settings for the ExchDAV changes.

6. Close the Registry Editor, and restart IIS from the IIS Manager (right-click the Servername and choose All Tasks, Restart IIS, OK).

> **NOTE**
>
> For more information on this particular solution, reference Microsoft Knowledge Base article #817379 at the following URL:
>
> `http://support.microsoft.com/kb/817379/EN-US/`

## Deploying Multiple OWA Virtual Servers

To make things more complex, an OWA server that uses SSL to access OMA requires an Exchange server to have a different Web "identity," so that it can use the new certificate name (for example, mail2.companyabc.com). In addition, if the OWA site uses forms-based authentication, a different identity for OMA/RPC-HTTPS/EAS must be configured as well. There are a few ways to do this, but the most straightforward way is to configure an additional virtual server on the Exchange OWA server. This configuration can also be used in other scenarios, such as the following:

- A need exists to have an SSL-secured OWA (for external clients) in addition to a standard HTTP OWA (for internal clients).

- Different SSL OWA Web presences need to be implemented (such as mail.companyabc.com, mail2.companyabc.com, mail.companyxyz.com) with unique certificates.

- OWA with forms-based authentication and OWA without FBA need to be allowed.

- OWA with FBA through ISA Server, and OWA with FBA directly to Exchange, need to be set up.

Fortunately, these scenarios can be accommodated on the OWA server through the creation of additional OWA virtual servers that are associated with a different IP address on the OWA server.

Once again, as previously mentioned, this step can be avoided if basic authentication (without FBA) is used for OMA and EAS.

## Adding IP Addresses to an OWA Server

To start the process of configuring the OWA server to support the second certificate for OMA-EAS, a second IP address needs to be added to the OWA server. Follow the procedure outlined here:

1. From the OWA server, click Start, Control Panel, Network Connection; then locate the OWA NIC from the list, right-click it, and choose Properties.

2. On the General tab, double-click Internet Protocol (TCP/IP).

3. Click the Advanced button.

4. Under IP Settings, click Add.

5. Enter the additional IP address and its corresponding mask and click Add.

6. Add any additional IP addresses to the dialog box.

7. Click OK three times to save the settings.

Before a new virtual server can be created, the original OWA virtual server must be configured to use the first IP address, rather than all the IP addresses on the server (the default setting). To change this, do the following:

1. Open IIS Manager.

2. Right-click the original OWA virtual server (often called Default Web Site), and choose Properties.

3. Under IP Address, change the drop-down list to display only the first IP address on the server, and click OK.

## Creating an Additional OWA Virtual Server

After additional IP addresses have been added, they can be used to create the additional OWA presence. After it is created, the additional OWA presence can be individually configured from the original virtual server, enabling an administrator to have two or more instances of OWA running on the same server. This procedure should be performed in Exchange System Manager, not in IIS Manager. To set up an additional virtual server on the OWA server, do the following:

1. On the OWA server, open Exchange System Manager (Start, All Programs, Microsoft Exchange, System Manager).

2. Expand ORGNAME (Exchange), Administrative Groups, ADMINGROUPNAME, Servers, SERVERNAME, Protocols, HTTP.

3. Right-click the HTTP folder, point to New, and then click HTTP Virtual Server.

4. Enter a descriptive name in the Name field, and change the IP address to match the additional IP address added to the server in the previous steps.

10

5. Select the Access tab and click the Authentication button.

6. Change the authentication settings to allow only Basic Authentication and clear Integrated Windows Authentication. Click OK twice when finished making changes.

After the virtual server is created, the virtual directories for Exchange need to be created. To do this, perform the following steps:

1. Right-click the newly created virtual server, point to New, and then click Virtual Directory.

2. Enter **Exchange** for the name, and leave the default path as Mailboxes for SMTP Domain, as shown in Figure 10.28.

**FIGURE 10.28**    Creating a second instance of the Exchange virtual directory.

3. Change the authentication settings under the Authentication button to support Basic Authentication and click OK, OK.

4. Right-click the virtual server again, point to New, and then click Virtual Directory.

5. Enter a name of **Public** in the Name field, and choose Public Folder under Exchange Path, set the Access Authentication to Basic Only (no Integrated for the rest of the virtual folders), and then click OK, OK.

6. Right-click the virtual server again, point to New, and then click Virtual Directory.

7. Enter a name of **oma** in the Name field and choose Outlook Mobile Access under Exchange Path. This time, authentication does not need to be changed because it is inherited from the root. Click OK.

8. Right-click the virtual server again, point to New, and then click Virtual Directory.

9. Enter a name of `Exchange-Server-ActiveSync`, and choose Exchange ActiveSync under the Exchange Path field. No need to change authentication, so click OK.

10. Restart IIS by right-clicking the server name and choosing All Tasks, Restart IIS and clicking OK.

The capability to create multiple virtual servers for an OWA server gives a great deal of flexibility in supporting a heterogeneous environment that requires different types of authentication mechanisms, access methods, and certificate identities.

## Assigning a Second SSL Certificate to the New OMA-EAS Virtual Server

Before SSL can be enabled for the new virtual server, a SSL certificate must be installed and enabled on the site. In addition, the virtual directories must be configured to require SSL. Follow the steps in the previous section titled "Enabling Secure Sockets Layer (SSL) Support for Exchange Outlook Web Access" to create the new certificate (for example, mail2.companyabc.com). The only addition to the steps in this section are to ensure that the OMA and EAS virtual directories are configured to force SSL, and the Exchange virtual directory is configured *not* to force SSL, per the reasoning described in the section of this chapter titled "Supporting OMA and ActiveSync on an OWA Server Configured as a Back-End Mailbox Server."

## Configuring Exchange System Manager to Not Override SSL Settings

One of the more frustrating aspects of Exchange in regard to IIS virtual servers is that settings in Exchange System Manager (ESM) overwrite manual settings made in IIS Manager. This can cause havoc for OWA and Exchange Mobile Services access as eventually SSL-encrypted virtual servers that were manually created will suddenly stop accepting SSL connections. This occurs as ESM overwrites the SSL port setting in IIS Manager. To prevent this from occurring, the SSL port must be manually entered on the virtual server in ESM via the following process:

1. Open Exchange System Manager.

2. Navigate to OrganizationName, Administrative Groups, AdminGroupName, Servers, ServerName, Protocols, HTTP.

3. Right-click on the new virtual server that was previously created and choose Properties.

4. To the right of the IP Address button, click the Advanced button.

5. Click Add.

6. Under IP address, select the IP address that is associated with that virtual server.

7. Clear the '80' entry from the TCP Port field (until this is done, the SSL port will be grayed out).

10

8. Under the SSL Port field, enter **443**, as shown in Figure 10.29.

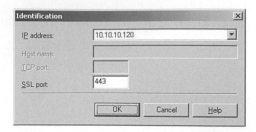

**FIGURE 10.29**    Preventing ESM from overwriting SSL port settings.

9. Click OK, Yes, OK, and OK to save the settings.

# Using RPC over HTTP(S) with Exchange Server 2003

Quite often, mobile and roaming users rely on the functionality of the full Outlook client, as it provides for offline use and enhanced functionality. The problem they faced was that the default access mechanism between Outlook and Exchange was using MAPI, which relies on RPC ports to be open between client and server, a rare and dangerous setup on the Internet. This dilemma forced many organizations to require connection via a VPN client before Outlook access could be obtained.

With Exchange Server 2003, however, functionality has been added that allows an Outlook 2003 client to connect to an Exchange 2003 server over the HTTP/HTTPS protocols, using a protocol known as RPC over HTTP, or Outlook over HTTP. The big advantage to using this protocol is that it is VPN-less, and email access can be obtained from anywhere on the Internet that has the HTTP/HTTPS ports open, which includes most networks. Using RPC-HTTPS with Outlook 2003 gives organizations better mobile access capabilities, and is becoming widespread in implementation.

> **NOTE**
>
> Client support of RPC over HTTP requires Outlook 2003 to be running on Windows XP SP2 (or Windows XP SP1 with the Knowledge Base article #331320 patch installed) or higher. The Knowledge Base article can be found at the following URL:
>
> `http://support.microsoft.com/kb/331320`

## Installing the RPC over HTTP Proxy

The RPC over HTTP service requires the use of an RPC-HTTP proxy that assists in the management of RPC-HTTP requests to the Exchange mailbox server. This proxy is normally installed on an Exchange front-end server, but can also be installed on a single all-in-one Exchange server that acts as both the back-end and front-end server, if special Registry changes are made to that server, as described in the following sections.

To install the RPC over HTTP service on the front-end or all-in-one back-end server, perform the following steps:

1. From the Exchange front-end or all-in-one back-end server, go to Start, All Programs, Add or Remove Programs.

2. Click the Add/Remove Windows Components button.

3. Scroll down and select Networking Services by clicking once on the name (not the check box) and then clicking the Details button.

4. Check the box next to RPC over HTTP Proxy, as shown in Figure 10.30. Click OK.

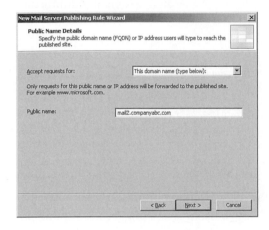

**FIGURE 10.30**   Installing the RPC over HTTP Proxy service.

5. Click Next to continue.

6. Click Finish when complete.

## Configuring RPC over HTTPS on an Exchange Back-End Server

After the networking service for RPC over HTTP has been installed, the Exchange server must be configured to act as an RPC over HTTP back-end server. In the case of the all-in-one Exchange server, where there is no unique front-end server and a single Exchange server acts as the primary mailbox and OWA server for the enterprise, this configuration is performed on the Exchange server where the RPC over HTTP Networking Service was installed, and must be followed by the Registry change outlined in the following sections.

In deployment scenarios in which there are separate front-end and back-end servers, the back-end server must first be configured as an RPC over HTTP back-end, followed by configuration of the front-end server as an RPC-HTTP front-end. To configure the back-end server for RPC over HTTP, do the following:

10

> **NOTE**
>
> The scenarios outlined in this book assume that Exchange Server 2003 Service Pack 1 is installed. SP1 adds a lot of configuration enhancements, including a much more simplified RPC over HTTP configuration. It is not recommended to use RPC over HTTP on pre-SP1 Exchange Server 2003 implementations, and the scenarios presented in this book will not be accurate without SP1 installed.

1. From the Exchange back-end mailbox server, open ESM by clicking on Start, All Programs, Microsoft Exchange, System Manager.

2. Navigate to ORGANIZATIONNAME (Exchange), Administrative Groups, ADMINGROUPNAME, Servers.

3. Right-click on the back-end server and click Properties.

4. Select the RPC-HTTP tab (if it doesn't appear, it probably means that Exchange Server 2003 Service Pack 1 is not installed).

5. Select RPC-HTTP back-end server from the list.

6. Click OK if warned that there are no RPC-HTTP front-end servers in the organization.

7. Click OK to save the changes.

8. When prompted with the warning message shown in Figure 10.31, select OK to change the ports automatically.

**FIGURE 10.31**    Examining the RPC over HTTP port changes warning.

9. Click OK to acknowledge that the role change will not be effective until reboot.

10. Reboot the server (when feasible to do so).

## Configuring RPC over HTTPS on an Exchange Front-End Server

As previously mentioned, deployment scenarios involving separate hardware for Exchange front-end servers and Exchange back-end servers require the front-end server or servers to be configured as RPC over HTTP front-ends. In single all-in-one server deployments, this step can be skipped and the Registry change outlined in the next section of this chapter should instead be run.

That said, the following procedure allows an Exchange Server 2003 SP1 front-end server to act as a proxy for RPC-HTTPS traffic:

1. From the Exchange back-end mailbox server, open ESM by clicking on Start, All Programs, Microsoft Exchange, System Manager.

2. Navigate to ORGANIZATIONNAME (Exchange), Administrative Groups, ADMINGROUPNAME, Servers.

3. Right-click on the front-end server and click Properties.

4. Select the RPC-HTTP tab.

5. Select RPC-HTTP front-end server from the list and click OK.

6. Reboot the server to complete the changes.

## Modifying the Registry to Support a Single-Server Exchange RPC over HTTP Topology

As previously mentioned, if there is not a dedicated front-end server in the RPC-HTTP topology, a special Registry change needs to be performed on the all-in-one Exchange server. To make this change, do the following:

---

**CAUTION**

Be sure that the Registry change is made to only back-end servers that do not have any front-end RPC-HTTP servers in the environment. This procedure is meant only for Exchange servers that serve dual roles as both front-end and back-end servers.

---

1. On the all-in-one Exchange front-end/back-end server, open the Registry Editor (Start, Run, cmd.exe, regedit.exe).

2. Navigate through the console tree to HKEY_LOCAL_MACHINE\Software\Microsoft\Rpc\RpcProxy.

3. Right-click the ValidPorts entry, and then click Modify.

4. In the Edit String field, under Value Data, type in the following and click OK, as shown in Figure 10.32:

    ```
    SERVERNAME:6001-6002;server.companyabc.com:6001-6002;
    SERVERNAME:6004;server.companyabc.com:6004;
    ```

    (where SERVERNAME is the NetBIOS name of the server and server.companyabc.com is the FQDN of the server as it will appear for RPC services).

---

**CAUTION**

It is critical to match the FQDN entered into this Registry with the FQDN that will be used from the Internet for RPC over HTTP traffic. This might or might not be different from the FQDN used

---

10

for OWA, depending on whether a different namespace is used so as to allow forms-based authentication.

**FIGURE 10.32**    Entering the Registry change for RPC-HTTP support on an all-in-one Exchange front-end/back-end server.

5. Close the Registry Editor.

## Creating the RPC Virtual Directory on the Proper Virtual Server

In certain scenarios, such as when a separate virtual server has been created for non-forms-based authentication traffic, the RPC virtual directory needs to be exported from the default OWA virtual server to the secondary virtual server, such as in the scenarios described in this chapter. To export and import this setting, do the following:

> **NOTE**
>
> This procedure needs to be followed only if multiple OWA virtual servers have been created, and the RPC traffic will be directed at the one that doesn't currently have the \rpc virtual directory.

1. From the OWA server, open IIS Manager (Start, All Programs, Administrative Tools, Internet Information Services (IIS) Manager.

2. Navigate to SERVERNAME, Web Sites, Default Web Site (or the name of the primary OWA virtual server).

3. Right-click the RPC virtual directory listed under the OWA Web site and select All Tasks, Save Configuration to a File.

4. Enter **rpc** as the filename and a local path, and click OK.

5. Right-click the Secondary Virtual Server, point to New, and then click Virtual Directory (from file).

6. Enter the path and name of the XML file that was exported, and click the Read File button. Select RPC from the list, as shown in Figure 10.33, and click OK.

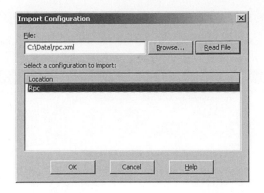

**FIGURE 10.33**   Importing the RPC virtual directory to a secondary virtual server.

7. Right-click the servername and choose All Tasks, Restart IIS, and then click OK to confirm.

## Setting Up an Outlook 2003 Profile to Use RPC over HTTP

The final step involved with enabling RPC over HTTP support for clients is to configure the client Outlook 2003 mail profiles to use it as a service. First, ensure that Windows XP Service Pack 2 (or the hotfix for RPC over HTTP previously mentioned) is installed, along with the Outlook 2003 client. After it is verified, a mail profile can be created via the following procedure:

> **NOTE**
>
> Unfortunately, the profile cannot be set up remotely, or at least not without RPC access to the Exchange server to create the initial connection. The initial creation of the profile itself should be performed on the internal network, or somewhere with standard RPC access (essentially full network access) to the Exchange server. After it has been set up for the first time and all mail has been synchronized, it can then be sent out into the field indefinitely. The upside to this is that the initial synchronization of the offline folder settings, which can be quite extensive, can be done on a fast local network segment.

1. From the Outlook 2003 client (connected to the internal network, with full access to the Exchange server), click Start, Control Panel.

2. Double-click on the Mail item (switching to Classic View might be required to see it).

3. Click Show Profiles.

4. At the General tab, select either Always Use This Profile (if this is the only mail server that will be set up as part of a profile), or prompt for a profile to be used. Click Add.

5. Enter a name for the profile, such as Exchange-RPC-HTTP.

6. Select Add a New E-mail Account, and click Next.

7. Select Microsoft Exchange Server from the list shown in Figure 10.34 and click Next.

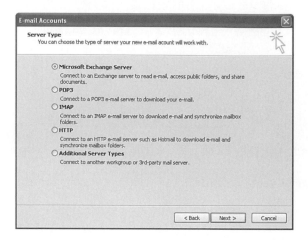

**FIGURE 10.34**    Configuring an RPC over HTTP–enabled Outlook profile.

8. Enter the local name of the back-end mailbox server, such as server20, and make sure that Use Cached Exchange Mode is checked.

9. Enter the name of the mailbox that will be set up (for example, the user's username or full name), and click More Settings.

10. Select the Security tab and check the box for Always Prompt for User Name and Password.

11. Select the Connection tab and check the box for Connect to My Exchange Mailbox Using HTTP, then click the Exchange Proxy Settings button.

12. Using the Exchange Proxy Settings dialog box, enter the FQDN of the external name of the RPC-HTTP topology, such as mail2.companyabc.com. Check the box to Mutually Authenticate the Session, and enter **msstd:*serverfqdn*** (for example, msstd:mail2.companyabc.com). Change the Proxy Authentication Settings to Basic Authentication, as shown in Figure 10.35.

13. To force RPC over HTTP for all connections, select the box labeled On Fast Networks, Connect Using HTTP First, Then Connect Using TCP/IP. If this is not checked, MAPI is attempted first when the connection to the server is fast. Click OK twice.

14. The username and Exchange server should be underlined at this point; click Next to continue.

15. Click Finish and then click OK.

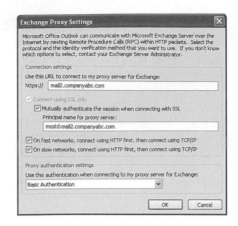

**FIGURE 10.35**    Reviewing Exchange proxy settings for the RPC-HTTPS Outlook profile.

Outlook needs to be opened and the mailbox synchronized with the client at this point. After the full mailbox data has been copied locally, the system is free to roam around on the Internet, wherever HTTPS access back to the Exchange server is granted.

## Summary

The improvements to the Outlook Web Access client and Exchange Mobile Services are profound, and provide great incentive for organizations to upgrade to Exchange Server 2003. Indeed, the variety of ways in which email can be accessed with Exchange Server 2003 has proliferated, and Exchange can be easily configured to provide for multiple access methods such as OWA, OMA, EAS, and RPC-HTTPS. Along with this functionality, however, comes the need to properly design an Exchange environment to provide for secure and robust access to these services, through deploying front-end servers and/or reverse proxy systems to protect the Exchange environment from untrusted networks. With the proper precautions in place, however, the functionality of an Exchange Server environment can be greatly enhanced using these technologies.

## Best Practices

- Use a reverse proxy server such as ISA Server 2004 in the DMZ of a firewall  for secure OWA client access from the Internet.

- Use SSL encryption wherever possible for client access from the Internet.

- Upgrade or replace all Exchange 2000 Server front-end servers before upgrading any back-end mailbox servers to Exchange Server 2003.

- Disable any unnecessary services or protocols on a front-end server.

- Use NLB to load balance multiple front-end servers.

- Deploy multiple virtual servers on Exchange front-end servers to provide for Exchange Mobile Services and forms-based authentication in the same environment.

10

- Consider enabling RPC-HTTPS to provide for robust VPN-less Outlook client access from anywhere on the Internet.

- Replace, rather than upgrade, existing Exchange 2000 Server front-end servers to recover expensive Exchange Enterprise licenses.

# PART IV

# Securing an Exchange Server 2003 Environment

## IN THIS PART

| CHAPTER 11 | Client-Level Security | 337 |
| CHAPTER 12 | Server-Level Security | 361 |
| CHAPTER 13 | Transport-Level Security | 391 |

CHAPTER **11**

# Client-Level Security

**IN THIS CHAPTER**

- Tips and Tricks for Hardening Windows

- Exchange Server 2003 Client-Level Security Enhancements

- Securing Outlook 2003

- Protecting Against Spam

- Securing Outlook Web Access

- Using Digital Signatures and Encryption

Security in general is often regarded as a significant and sometimes complex part of the network environment. Although some environments take security more seriously than others, it is a topic that must be properly addressed and implemented. Microsoft is continually tackling security head-on, ensuring that not only are known vulnerabilities not an issue but also that future threats can be avoided.

Microsoft's approach to security spans across its entire business product line, and Exchange Server 2003 is no exception. In fact, Microsoft has gone to great lengths to provide a rich array of security features at the client, server, and transport layers in Exchange Server 2003 to protect the messaging environment investment. This approach helps ensure that every link in the messaging chain is as secure as the other links.

## Tips and Tricks for Hardening Windows

Exchange Server 2003 and its client counterparts are only as secure as the underlying operating system that supports them. The good news is that by default both Windows Server 2003 and Windows XP Professional are more secure than any other Windows operating system. Despite this fact, default installations are not going to magically secure any environment, so security customizations are almost always going to be recommended.

Securing Windows Server 2003 or Windows XP Professional can be broken down into smaller, more manageable components, including—but not limited to—authentication, access control, patch management, and communications. Organizations of all sizes should at least take these focal areas into consideration, especially when implementing new services or technologies.

## Windows Server 2003 Security Improvements

Out of the box, Windows Server 2003 reduces its attack surface, making it more difficult from the start to gain unauthorized access. This reduction in the attack surface area stems from many improvements, including—but not limited to—the following:

- The number of services running by default is significantly reduced.

- Internet Information Services (IIS) has been completely overhauled and is no longer installed by default. In addition, group policies can be implemented that prevent rogue IIS installations.

- Access Control Lists (ACLs) have been redefined and are stronger by default.

- Security can be defined by server and user roles.

- Public Key Infrastructure (PKI) Certificate Services has been greatly improved and includes advanced support for automatic smart card enrollment, Certificate Revocation List (CRL) deltas, and more.

- Wireless security features, such as IEEE 802.1X, are supported.

- The Security Configuration Wizard, included in Windows Server 2003 Service Pack (SP) 1, can further lock down security based on server role and function.

## Windows XP Professional Security Improvements

Windows XP Professional complements Windows Server 2003 from the client-computer perspective and supports the security features that are built in to Windows Server 2003. Among the notable security improvements built into Windows XP Professional are

- Core system files and kernel data structures are protected against corruption and deletion.

- Software policies can be used to identify and restrict which applications can run.

- Wireless security features, such as IEEE 802.1X, are supported.

11

- Sensitive or confidential files can be encrypted using the Encrypting File System (EFS).

- Communications can be encrypted using IP Security (IPSec).

- Kerberos-based authentication is supported.

- Enhanced support for security devices, such as smart cards, are available.

Additional improvements such as those included in Windows XP SP2 (for example, Windows Firewall and pop-up blocker) offer enhanced and modifiable security mechanisms.

## Windows Firewall Protection

Exchange Server 2003 for many environments is intended to provide access to messaging anytime and virtually anywhere. Many users must securely access their mail from not only corporate office locations but also from hotels, client sites, and other locations. As a result, users are often more susceptible to viruses and intrusions. To minimize security risks, client computers should have the Windows Firewall enabled (as shown in Figure 11.1), especially when they are directly connected to the Internet.

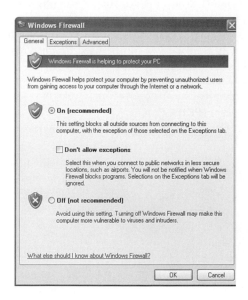

**FIGURE 11.1**    Enabling Windows Firewall to protect Windows XP.

As the name implies, the Windows Firewall serves as a firewall for a Windows XP client computer. The Windows Firewall uses stateful packet inspection to monitor all communications to and from the computer and records which traffic originates from the computer it is protecting (that is, outbound traffic). The Windows Firewall can also be customized to allow exceptions based on an application or port as well as to log security events.

## Standardizing Security with Security Templates

Security templates are a practical and effective means to standardize an environment on security policies and configurations. These security templates can be customized to adhere to security requirements of the organization, and these security templates can be applied to client computers as well as to servers using the Security Configuration and Analysis Microsoft Management Console (MMC) snap-in.

> **TIP**
>
> Microsoft provides several security templates based on functional roles within the network environment that can easily be applied to client computers and the server. However, as a best practice, always customize the security template to ensure that application and operating system functionality is not broken or negatively affected.

This not only ensures that computers are identically configured with the same security configurations, but it also is an easy way to configure appropriate security measures for those computers that are not managed using Group Policy Objects (GPOs).

### Using the Security Configuration and Analysis Tool

The Security Configuration and Analysis tool, shown in Figure 11.2, is a utility that can apply security templates to computers. It compares a computer's security configurations with a security template. When the computer's security configuration does not conform to the settings in the security template, it can be used to apply the modifications and standardize the computer's security configuration.

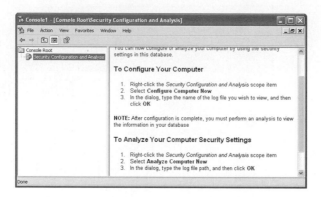

**FIGURE 11.2**    Using the Security Configuration and Analysis tool.

This utility has two modes of operation: analysis and configuration. It is always a good idea to analyze the computer prior to making any modifications, because it enables administrators to manually compare the differences and select which settings to change. To analyze a computer, do the following:

1. Start the MMC by typing **MMC** in the Start, Run menu.

2. From the File menu, select Add/Remove Snap-in and then click the Add button.

3. Choose the Security Configuration and Analysis snap-in and then click the Add button again.

4. Click the Close button to close and then the OK button to return to the MMC.

5. In the MMC, right-click the Security Configuration and Analysis snap-in and select Open Database.

6. Type a database name, select a location to store the database, and then click Open.

7. Choose a security template and then click Open.

8. Right-click the Security Configuration and Analysis snap-in and choose Analyze Computer Now. Click OK when done.

The tool displays which security settings are and are not in compliance with the security template settings. When the analysis is reviewed, you can choose to configure the system with the template setting by right-clicking the snap-in and choosing Configure Computer Now.

### Customizing Security Templates

One of the primary purposes of customizing security templates is to ensure that the organization's specific security requirements are met. It is also a way to ensure that business requirements and goals that are supported through the use of applications and systems' functional roles are not compromised. Typically, the larger the organization, the more systems it has and thus there might be a need for more customized security templates. For instance, if there are different security and business requirements for the various Exchange Server 2003 functional roles, administrators can customize a security template for each of those roles.

> **TIP**
>
> Use security templates provided by Microsoft, the National Security Agency (NSA), or the National Institute of Standards and Technology (NIST) as baselines for customizing the organization's security templates.

Windows Server 2003 and Windows XP Professional are equipped with the Security Templates MMC snap-in that enables administrators to quickly and easily customize security templates to fit the requirements for specific systems. To begin using this tool, add the Security Templates MMC snap-in by following the steps outlined in the previous section "Using the Security Configuration and Analysis Tool."

When the Security Templates snap-in is expanded, it displays the default search path to where the built-in security templates are stored, which is the `%SystemRoot%\security\templates` directory. Other paths can be opened to display other security templates that may reside on the system. Either select New Template after right-clicking on the path, or as a best practice use the Save As selection after right-clicking an existing or baseline security template to create a new, customized template. After creating and naming the new security template, expand it to display all the security settings that can be modified, as shown in Figure 11.3. When the security template has been customized, save it to a network share and use the Security Configuration and Analysis tool to apply the template to the appropriate systems.

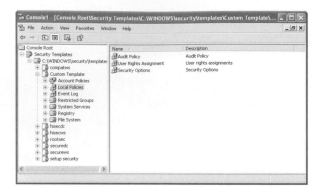

**FIGURE 11.3**    Using the Security Template MMC snap-in to customize a security template.

## Keeping Up with Security Patches and Updates

Service packs and hotfixes for both the operating system and applications are vital parts to maintaining availability, reliability, performance, and security. Microsoft packages these updates into SPs or as individual updates (hotfixes).

There are several ways an administrator can update a system with the latest SP or individual update: CD-ROM, manually entered commands, Windows Update, Microsoft Windows Software Update Services (WSUS), Microsoft System Management Server (SMS), or third-party patch management software.

> **NOTE**
>
> Thoroughly test and evaluate SPs and hotfixes in a lab environment before installing them on production servers and client machines. Also, install the appropriate SPs and hotfixes on each production server and client machine to keep all systems consistent.

### Windows Update

Windows Update is a Web site that scans a local system and determines whether there are updates to apply to that system. Windows Update is a great way to update individual systems, but this method is sufficient for only a small number of systems. If administrators choose this method to update an entire organization, there is an unnecessary amount of administration.

### Windows Server Update Services (WSUS)

Realizing the increased administration and management efforts administrators must face when using Windows Update to keep up with security updates for anything other than small environments, Microsoft has created Windows Server Update Services (WSUS) to

11

minimize administration, management, and maintenance of mid- to large-sized organizations. WSUS communicates directly and securely with Microsoft to gather the latest security updates. Unlike Software Update Services (WSUS's predecessor), WSUS updates a variety of Microsoft products as well as provides reporting and target capabilities.

The security updates downloaded onto WSUS can then be distributed to either a lab server for testing (recommended) or to a production server for distribution. After these updates are tested, WSUS can automatically update systems inside the network.

> **NOTE**
>
> You can find more information on WSUS and download the product from
> `http://www.microsoft.com/windowsserversystem/updateservices/default.mspx`.

### Client-Based Virus Protection

Viruses might be one of the most dangerous threats faced by computer systems. Many viruses are written to exploit specific vulnerabilities that might be present in clients and servers. Due to the large percentage of companies that use Microsoft products, many such viruses are specifically written to attack the Windows operating system. Consequently, it is extremely important to consider using an enterprise antivirus solution on all clients and servers. All the major antivirus manufacturers include robust scanners that detect, quarantine, or remove viruses.

An aggressive plan should be in place to keep antivirus signature files and engines up to date. Because virus outbreaks can wreak havoc worldwide in a matter of hours, rather than days, it is wise to have the antivirus solution check for updates daily.

### Windows Lockdown Guidelines and Standards

Microsoft has gone to great lengths to provide secure and reliable products. Moreover, it has worked closely with companies, government agencies, security consultants, and others to address security issues in the computer industry. Through this concerted effort and teamwork, secure standards and guidelines have been developed for not just Microsoft products but also other leading vendors as well.

In addition to Microsoft security standards and guidelines, it is advisable that organizations use recommended best practices compiled by the National Institute of Standards and Technologies (NIST) and the National Security Agency (NSA). Both NIST and NSA provide security lockdown configuration standards and guidelines that can be downloaded from their Web site (`http://www.nist.gov` and `http://www.nsa.gov`, respectively).

## Exchange Server 2003 Client-Level Security Enhancements

As mentioned earlier, Exchange Server 2003 has many new and improved security features at the client level. At a glance, these features include—but are not limited to—the following:

- Support for MAPI (RPC) over HTTP or HTTPS and can be configured to use either Secure Sockets Layer (SSL) or NTLM-based authentication

- Support for authentication methods, such as Kerberos and NTLM

- Antispam features, such as safe and block lists, as well as advanced filtering mechanisms to control the amount of unwanted emails

- Protection against Web beaconing, which is used by advertisers and spammers to verify email addresses and determine whether emails have been read

- Attachment-blocking by Exchange Server 2003 before it reaches the intended recipient

- Rights management support, which prevents unauthorized users from intercepting emails

# Securing Outlook 2003

Exchange Server 2003 and Microsoft Office 2003 are very well integrated, and the teaming provides a formidable security front. Both new and improved features help provide a safe and reliable messaging environment and are described in the following sections.

## Securely Accessing Exchange over the Internet (RPC over HTTPS)

In previous versions of Exchange (and Outlook), Outlook users that needed to connect to Exchange over the Internet needed to establish a VPN connection prior to using Outlook. The only alternative solution was to open all sorts of RPC ports to the Internet or make a few Registry modifications to statically map RPC ports. Either way presents more of a security risk for the Exchange messaging environments than most are willing to afford.

Now, with Exchange Server 2003 and Outlook 2003, Outlook 2003 users can connect securely over the Internet via an HTTPS proxy connection. This feature reduces the need for VPN solutions and keeps the messaging environment as secure as possible. VPN solutions are still viable and can be used to provide a host of other services for mobile users.

> **NOTE**
>
> For more information on configuring the server side of RPC over HTTPS, refer to Chapter 26, "Everything You Need to Know About the Outlook Web Access (OWA) Client."

To enable this type of secure connectivity, do the following:

1. Within Outlook 2003, select E-mail Accounts from the Tools menu.

2. Select View or change existing email accounts and then click Next to continue.

3. Click Change and, on the next screen, click the More Settings button.

4. Under the Connection tab, check Connect to My Exchange Mailbox Using HTTP and then click the Exchange Proxy Settings button.

5. Type the URL. This can be the same URL as the OWA or Outlook Mobile Access (OMA) URL, as shown in Figure 11.4.

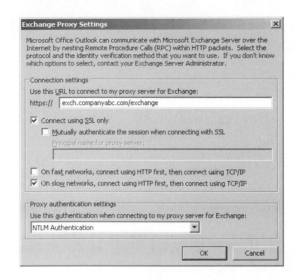

**FIGURE 11.4**    Configuring a secure Outlook 2003 connection to Exchange Server 2003 over the Internet.

6. Verify that Connect Using SSL Only is checked. If SSL is not used, the connection will use HTTP and will not be secure.

7. Optionally, select whether this SSL connection requires mutual authentication. Mutual authentication ensures that both parties (the server and the client) are who they say they are.

8. Choose whether to use NTLM or Basic proxy authentication (NTLM is the strongest of the two and is used by default). The best practice is to use only NTLM to keep security at its highest.

9. Click OK when done.

> **NOTE**
>
> This feature requires several components before functioning. It requires that the client is running Windows XP Professional with Service Pack 1 or higher and that the server infrastructure is running Windows Server 2003 and Exchange Server 2003 (that is, mailbox, front-end, Global Catalog, and public folder servers).

*RPC over HTTPS* is commonly used by mobile laptop users who connect to the Internet over various wireless hotspots, or network connections; however, many organizations have started to use this technology to connect home office users to their corporate email network. This technology provides a reliable and secure connection, without the need to set up complicated VPNs, or specialized, secured access systems.

> **TIP**
>
> Outlook 2003 users who will be using RPC over HTTPS as described in this section should be using Cached Exchange mode. Cached Exchange mode optimizes the communications between Exchange Server 2003 and Outlook 2003.

## Encrypting Outlook 2003 and Exchange Server 2003 Communications

As a MAPI client, Outlook 2003 uses Remote Procedure Calls (RPCs) to communicate with Exchange Server 2003. RPCs are interprocess communications (IPC) mechanisms that, during the transfer of information, can either use or not use encryption. By default, Outlook 2003 does not use encrypted RPC communication. It is important to note that using this form of encryption is different from using RPC over HTTPS as described earlier in the section "Securely Accessing Exchange over the Internet (RPC over HTTPS)." RPC over HTTPS is still required if the Outlook 2003 client needs to securely communicate over a public network such as the Internet.

In Figure 11.5, a user or administrator can enable encrypted RPC communication between Outlook 2003 and Exchange Server 2003 by simply checking the box within the Encryption section. To modify this setting, do the following:

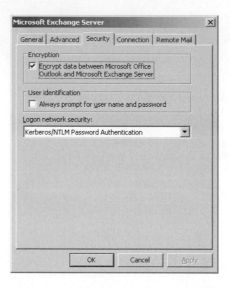

**FIGURE 11.5**   Enabling encrypted RPC communications in a LAN environment.

1. In Outlook 2003, click on E-mail Accounts from the Tools menu.

2. Select View or Change Existing Email Accounts and then click Next.

3. Click the Change button and, on the next window, click the More Settings button.

4. Select the Security tab and then check Encrypt Data Between Microsoft Office Outlook and Microsoft Exchange Server.

5. Click OK to close the window.

6. Click Next and then Finish when done.

Because encryption requires additional processing overhead, it is important to thoroughly test this feature prior to deploying it in a production environment.

## Authenticating Users

By default, Outlook 2003 uses the credentials of the user who is logged on to the local computer to access the Outlook 2003 profile and mailbox. It first tries to use Kerberos for the authentication process and then NT LAN Manager (NTLM). Administrators can also set Outlook 2003 to use Kerberos Password Authentication or NTLM solely, as illustrated in Figure 11.6.

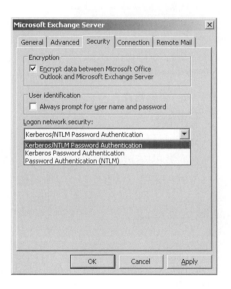

**FIGURE 11.6**    Configuring authentication options for Outlook 2003.

> **TIP**
>
> For stronger security, use Kerberos-only authentication. Use the Kerberos/NTLM or the NTLM options only for backward compatibility with older systems. Kerberos provides encryption of a user's credentials when communicating with Active Directory for authentication.

Although the default setting is a secure method of authenticating users, some users might still be prone to leave their computers unattended and therefore leave open the opportunity for someone to gain unauthorized access to the user's email. For instance, a user leaves to run an errand and forgets to lock the computer or log off. Someone in the office can then simply open Outlook 2003 and have full access to the user's mailbox.

Many organizations do not necessarily think that this is either a high security risk or the organization's responsibility but Outlook 2003 can be configured nonetheless to mitigate the chances of this occurring. Outlook 2003 can be configured to always prompt for the user's username and password before accessing the mailbox on Exchange Server 2003. To increase this level of security, do the following:

1. Within Outlook 2003, select E-mail Accounts from the Tools menu and then select View or Change Existing Email Accounts. Click Next to continue.

2. Click the Change button and, in the next window, click More Settings.

3. Go to the Security tab and then in the User Identification section, check Always Prompt for Username and Password.

## Blocking Attachments

A common and often effective way for viruses and malicious scripts to spread is through email. When a user receives a message with an attachment, all the user needs to do is to try opening the attachment for the virus to infect the computer.

As a result of this threat, Microsoft has incorporated attachment blocking in Outlook, and Outlook Web Access (OWA), to help prevent such infections. By default, Outlook does not block attachments with common Microsoft Office file formats—such as .doc, .xls, and .ppt—but it does block executables—such as .exe, .bat, and .vbs files. It is important to note that the common Microsoft Office file attachments that are not blocked by default can contain viruses. However, using an antivirus on the client computer can significantly reduce the chances of these types of attachments causing any harm.

Outlook does not provide any way for the end-user to unblock these attachments. If files with these file formats need to be shared, users must rename the file, zip the files in question, or place the files on a network share.

> **NOTE**
>
> If an Outlook 2003 user tries sending an attachment that is blocked by default, a warning message is displayed informing the user that the attachment may be unsafe and recipients using Outlook 2003 may not be able to open the attachment. It then asks the user if the attachment should be sent anyway.

# Protecting Against Spam

If you have ever had an email account, odds are you have also been a victim of at least one spam message. If you have only had a few spam messages, you are one of the lucky ones. Unfortunately, having an email account somewhere is going to put you at risk of receiving unsolicited and often pornographic email messages.

> **NOTE**
>
> It has been estimated by many organizations that billions upon billions of spam messages will be sent in less than a year's time. In fact, some estimates predict that out of all of the Internet email messages, roughly 70% or more will be spam. Whatever the numbers turn out to be, it is definitely too high.

Spam does not just affect your patience and productivity. It affects companies, Internet service providers, and anyone else who is hosting messaging services. The battle against spam is just beginning, and legal battles are well underway against both known spammers and companies that host the messaging services. In some cases, employees are suing employers on grounds that the employer is not implementing strong enough measures to keep spam from entering someone's mailbox. In any scenario, spam and its effects cost the computer industry billions of dollars, which ultimately affects everyone relying on messaging.

## Spam and Antispam Tools

Spam is not new to the Internet community. It has been around for many years and probably for many more to come. It has become more prevalent over the last several years because of the increasing number of people using the Internet—many of whom are using it for the first time. With more people and larger target audiences for spammers, spam has proven to be a corrupt but effective way of making profits.

> **NOTE**
>
> Spammers are becoming increasingly more creative and cunning. For instance, spammers frequently change email addresses, domain names, content, and more to get past a company's protective measures and into someone's mailbox. Some message content (for example, a word or phrase) that is not legitimate in one message may be legitimate in another.

Microsoft has provided at least some basic form of antispam technologies in Exchange since version 5.5 and Outlook 98. For example, junk mail filters were provided to help identify messages that had either offensive material or other keywords indicating the message was spam. This form of spam prevention placed most, if not all, of the responsibility on the end-user to block unwanted email messages.

> **NOTE**
>
> Microsoft's Internet Message Filter (IMF) for Exchange Server 2003 is a free tool that evaluates whether or not incoming messages are spam. IMF can be managed at the client level and used

to determine what action is to be taken if a potential spam message is received. For more information on IMF, refer to Chapter 12, "Server-Level Security."

---

Other methods of antispam technology relied on reverse DNS lookups and IP blocking features that helped verify who the sender was and determined whether the spam was coming from a legitimate source. These techniques are still employed with Exchange Server 2003, but they are also complemented by a host of other techniques to provide the most comprehensive coverage against spam as possible.

## Protecting Against Web Beaconing

A common and very popular format for email messages is HTML. This is primarily because of the rich content that can be presented, including graphics, images, font formatting, and more. A less-known fact, however, is that HTML-based messages can also present security problems and annoyances because of the various code and hidden images that the message can contain.

*Web beaconing* is a term used to describe the method of retrieving valid email addresses and information on whether a recipient has opened a message. Advertisers, spammers, and the like thrive on Web beaconing to help them become more profitable and improve audience targeting. For instance, when an unsuspecting user opens an email message that contains a Web beacon, the user's email address and possibly other information is sent to the solicitor. The user is oblivious that personal information has been given.

Outlook 2003 can be used to block Web beacons and consequently prevent the user's email address from ending up in the wrong hands. By default, if Outlook 2003 suspects that the content of a message could be used as a Web beacon, it presents a pop-up window warning users that to help protect their privacy, links to images, multimedia, or other external content have been blocked. The text content of the email message is viewable by the user, and the user is then presented with an option to unblock the content. This enables the user to make a conscious decision of whether to display all the contents of the message.

Although the default setting is recommended because it is an excellent way to protect end-users from a barrage of unwanted emails and it helps minimize unsolicited emails, it is possible to disable this option. To change the default settings, do the following:

1. In Outlook 2003, select Options from the Tools menu.

2. Click on the Security tab and then click Change Automatic Download Settings.

3. In the Automatic Picture Download Settings window, choose whether to download pictures or other content automatically. Outlook 2003 can also be customized to automatically download content from safe lists or from Web sites listed in the trusted IE security zones, as illustrated in Figure 11.7.

## Filtering Junk Mail

As mentioned earlier, junk mail filtering has been available in earlier versions of Exchange and Outlook. This feature has been improved from earlier versions and minimizes the responsibility of end-users to configure junk mail filtering options. In fact, junk mail filtering is primarily controlled by Exchange Server 2003 administrators, but options can be set by the users. Most junk mail or spam is filtered before it reaches the user's mailbox.

**FIGURE 11.7**    Configuring Automatic Picture Download Settings.

---

**TIP**

Despite the fact that Exchange Server 2003 and Outlook 2003 have sound, practical spam-fighting techniques and features built in, organizations should evaluate third-party antispam tools. Third-party tools provide advanced features and customizations that offer stronger protection against spam.

---

Outlook 2003, by default, presents four levels of junk mail protection:

- **No Protection**—The only filtering that occurs is when email originates from the manually configured blocked senders list. This is fairly ineffective, considering that spammers change source email addresses constantly.

- **Low**—Safe and block lists are consulted with this level of protection, but Outlook 2003 also searches for key words and phrases in the message's subject and body.

- **High**—This uses the features of the low setting plus it is more aggressive with filtering. Users should not permanently delete suspected spam and should check the junk email folder more frequently to find possible false positives.

- **Safe Lists Only**—This setting is the most restrictive because it allows only messages from preapproved senders to be delivered to the inbox. Although this is a good option to have, it probably will not be one that is chosen very often. You might get a legitimate message from someone you do not know, or in many cases there might be a spam message from a trusted domain.

> **TIP**
>
> With any filtering level that you use, send mail to the Junk E-mail folder, at least initially, rather than deleting it. Use the high level to ensure that most, if not all, spam is filtered. Most of the false positives are likely to come from mailing lists and newsletters. If this is the case, it is easier to use this setting and unblock those mailing lists that are legitimate. Testing has shown that the high-level setting cuts as much as 90% of spam out of a user's mailbox.

As illustrated in Figure 11.8, Outlook 2003 by default is set to Low to keep only the most obvious spam out. Any filtered messages are placed in the Junk E-mail folder unless the Delete All Junk E-mail option is checked.

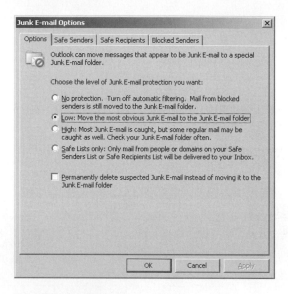

**FIGURE 11.8**    Outlook 2003 Junk E-mail filtering options.

## Filtering with Safe and Block Lists

Outlook 2003 enables users to create and manage their own safe and block lists. A safe list is a list of email addresses or domains that are trustworthy; a block list contains those email addresses or domains that are always considered spam or junk mail.

There are actually two safe lists that Outlook 2003 users can create and manage: Safe Senders and Safe Recipients. The Safe Senders list is intended to store email addresses or domains of individual users, and the Safe Recipients list covers members of email lists or groups. An example of when the latter should be used is when you are a member of a discussion group where many members pass emails back and forth through the mailing list.

As the name implies, block lists can contain known spamming email addresses or domains. Depending on how your organization is taking a stance on spam, there might be only a few entries in this list.

Outlook 2003 also gives users the ability to import whitelists and blacklists, which are similar to safe lists and block lists, respectively. These lists may be quite large, though, and have been known to cause performance problems, because each message had to be checked and verified against the potentially large list that was imported.

> **NOTE**
>
> Outlook 2003 trusts the user's contacts by default. This keeps messages from those contacts away from the Junk E-mail folder.

## Blocking Read Receipts

Most email applications, such as Outlook, enable users to request read receipts for the messages that they send. Read receipts tell the sender that the intended recipient has at least opened the email.

Outlook 2003 prompts a user by default on whether the user wants to send a read receipt if a message requests one. To ensure that users do not accidentally send read receipts, it is recommended to turn off sending read receipts and consequently turn off the prompting. To do so, use the following steps:

1. In Outlook 2003, select Options from the Tools menu.

2. Click the E-mail Options button to display the E-mail Options window.

3. Click the Tracking Options button to display the Tracking Options window and then select Never Send a Response.

4. Click OK three times to close all the options windows.

## Information Rights Management in Office 2003

Information Rights Management (IRM), also known as Rights Management (RM), is an unprecedented new feature that enables users to create and control information. More specifically, it gives the creator of the specific information control over the following:

- What can be done with the information

- Who can perform actions or tasks with the information (for example, who can forward a specific message, print a document, or copy a file)

- The lifetime of the information (that is, the message expiration on a specific date)

IRM granularizes security for Microsoft Office 2003 Professional applications such as Word, Excel, PowerPoint, Outlook, and any other IRM-aware application. IRM is intended to complement other security technologies, such as S/MIME and PGP. It secures the contents of information (for example, documents and messages), but it does not provide authentication to the information. In addition, it is important to keep the appropriate access controls on the information as an added layer of security.

There is an IRM server component that resides on Windows Server 2003, and support is built in to Office 2003 Professional. When implemented, Outlook 2003 users can use a toolbar icon to manage and secure their outgoing messages. For instance, user1 can send a message intended only for user2. Depending on the IRM settings for that message, user2 might be able to only read the message and not be able to forward it, copy it, or print it. This keeps the message's contents from falling into the wrong hands and is particularly useful for sensitive or confidential information.

## Securing Outlook Web Access

OWA provides the interface for users to access their mail through Internet Explorer (IE). When compared to previous versions, OWA is far superior, not just in functionality but also in terms of security. At a quick glance, OWA provides the following security features and enhancements:

- Built-in S/MIME support
- Stripping of Web beacons, referrals, and other potentially harmful content from messages
- Attachment blocking
- OWA form-based (cookie) authentication
- Session inactivity timeout
- OWA infrastructure using IPSec and Kerberos
- Safe and block lists

### Protecting Against Potentially Harmful Message Content

Outlook 2003 gives the option to read messages in HTML (default), rich text, and plain text formats. If these users are employing plain text format to read their messages, they are not at risk of Web beacons giving away their information. The messaging experience is not as rich, but security vulnerabilities are minimized. OWA users, on the other hand, are particularly susceptible to Web beacons because all messages are read using the HTML format.

This risk is easily thwarted, however, by keeping the default OWA setting of blocking external content in HTML messages. On the OWA Options page, there is a single check box under the Privacy and Junk E-mail Prevention section that helps prevent such a risk.

### Blocking Attachments Through OWA

The concept and functionality of blocking attachments is similar to that of Outlook 2003. The implementation, however, is different; an administrator enables attachment blocking by modifying the Registry. To enable attachment blocking for OWA, do the following:

1. Start the Registry Editor by typing **regedit** in the Start, Run dialog box on the OWA server.

2. Locate the following Registry key:

   HKEY_LOCAL_MACHINE\SYSTEM\CurrentControlSet\Services\MSExchangeWeb\OWA

3. Create a new DWORD value by selecting New, DWORD Value from the Edit menu.

4. In the right window pane, type **DisableAttachments** for the name of the DWORD value.

5. Right-click Disable Attachments and select Modify.

6. Select Decimal and then type one of the following values for the configuration that is required:
   **0** to allow all attachments
   **1** to block all attachments
   **2** to allow only attachments from the back-end servers

7. Click OK when done.

## Using Safe and Block Lists

Like the Outlook 2003 features, many of the OWA counterparts match the functionality. This holds true when using safe and block lists. These lists are managed in the Options page within OWA. On the OWA Options page, locate the Privacy and Junk E-mail Prevention section and click on the Manage Junk E-mail Lists button to modify the Safe Senders, Safe Recipients, or Blocked Senders list, as illustrated in Figure 11.9.

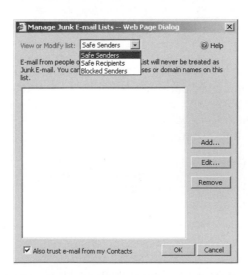

**FIGURE 11.9**    Managing safe and block lists in OWA.

# Using Digital Signatures and Encryption

Secure/Multipurpose Internet Mail Extensions (S/MIME) is used to digitally sign and encrypt messages. Digital signatures provide authentication, nonrepudiation, and data integrity; encryption keeps message contents confidential.

> **NOTE**
>
> S/MIME for Outlook 2003 and OWA can work with an organization's (for example, Windows Server 2003 Certificate Services) or outsourced Public Key Infrastructure (PKI) solution. The following sections on S/MIME assume that a PKI is in place. For information on implementing PKI for Exchange Server 2003, refer to Chapter 12.

## Simplified Fundamentals of Using Digital Signatures and Encryption

Digital signatures and encryption are fundamental components to S/MIME. S/MIME is in turn a small subset of PKI, which has a large reach into many different security facets. For instance, PKI supports smart cards, SSL, user certificates, and much more. For the purposes of this chapter it is important to have an understanding of S/MIME and how it can be used to secure the messaging environment.

X.509 is a digital certificate standard that defines the format of the actual certificate used by S/MIME. The certificate identifies information about the certificate's owner and includes the owner's public key information. X.509 is the most widely used digital certificate and therefore has become the industry standard digital certificate. PKI products, such as Microsoft's Certificate Services included in Windows Server 2003, are products that generate X.509 digital certificates to be used with S/MIME-capable clients.

### The Signing Process

When a user chooses to sign a message, a random checksum is generated from and added to the message. The random checksum is the digital signature (also known as a digital ID). This signature is then encrypted using the user's private signing key. The user then sends the message to the recipient that includes three items: the message in plain text, the sender's X.509 digital certificate, and the digital certificate.

The recipient then checks its Certificate Revocation List (CRL) to see whether the sender's certificate is on the list. If the certificate is not on the list, the digital signature is decrypted with the sender's public signing key. If it is on the CRL, the recipient is warned that the sender's certificate has been revoked. Remember that the digital certificate included the sender's public signing key. The recipient's client then generates a checksum from the plain text message and compares it to the digital signature. If the checksums match, the recipient knows the sender is the one who sent the message. If they do not match, the recipient is warned that the message has been tampered with.

### The Encryption Process

When a user chooses to encrypt a message, the client generates a random bulk encryption key that is used to encrypt the contents of the message. The sender then uses the recipient's public key to encrypt the bulk encryption key. This is referred to as a *lockbox*. If there are multiple recipients for the message, individual lockboxes are created for each recipient, using his or her own public encryption key. The contents of the lockbox (the bulk signing key) are the same, however. This saves the client the overhead of encrypting the message multiple times and still ensures that the message contents stay secure.

For this process to work, the sender must have a copy of the recipient's digital certificate. The certificate can be retrieved from either the Global Address List (GAL) or the sender's Contact list. The digital certificate contains the recipient's public encryption key, which is used to create the lockbox for the bulk encryption key.

When the recipient receives the message, he or she will use a private encryption key to decrypt the lockbox that contains the bulk encryption key used to encrypt the message contents. The bulk encryption key is then used to decrypt the message.

## Configuring Outlook 2003 for Secure Messaging

To configure Outlook 2003 clients for secure messaging, do the following:

1. In Outlook 2003, click Tools, Options and select the Security tab.

2. Obtain a secure email certificate if one does not already exist by either choosing the Get a Digital ID option (to obtain the certificate from a third party) or by using the Certificate snap-in (`certmgr.msc`) to request one from the organization's PKI.

3. Select Options from the Tools menu and then click on the Security tab.

4. On the Security tab, click Settings to display the default security settings, as shown in Figure 11.10. Ensure that the Security Setting Preferences reflect the S/MIME settings.

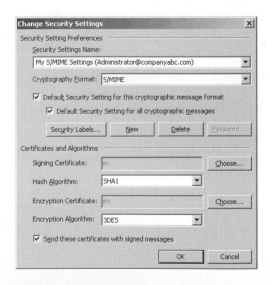

**FIGURE 11.10**    Verifying Outlook 2003 S/MIME settings.

5. Click OK.

6. Check Encrypt Contents and Attachments for Outgoing Messages and Add Digital Signature to Outgoing Messages.

7. Click OK when done.

## Configuring OWA for Secure Messaging

Earlier versions of Outlook supported digital signatures and encryption, but OWA did not. The Exchange Server 2003 OWA version now supports these S/MIME features, using an S/MIME ActiveX control.

Users can download the S/MIME ActiveX control from Exchange Server 2003 by clicking on the Download button under the E-mail Security section on the OWA Options page. Two windows prompt the user to accept or decline the installation and execution of the S/MIME ActiveX control, as illustrated in Figure 11.11. Simply selecting Yes to both of these prompts allows the user to enable S/MIME.

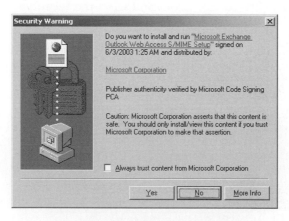

**FIGURE 11.11**    Accepting S/MIME certificates.

To configure default S/MIME settings for OWA, do the following:

1. Scroll down to the E-mail Security section on the OWA Options page.

2. Check Encrypt Contents and Attachments for Outgoing Messages and Add a Digital Signature to Outgoing Messages.

If these options are left unchecked, the OWA user can still use S/MIME on a per message basis.

## Sending Secure Messages

To configure S/MIME on a per message basis in Outlook 2003, do the following:

1. Create a new message and then click the Options button within the message window.

2. Click the Security Settings button to display the Security Properties window.

3. Check either email security setting (Encrypt Message Contents and Attachments or Add a Digital Signature to This Message).

4. In the Security Settings section, select the appropriate S/MIME configuration and then click OK.

5. Click Close when done.

To configure S/MIME on a per message basis in OWA, do the following:

1. Create a new message and then click the Options button within the message window.

2. Check either email security setting (Encrypt Message Contents and Attachments or Add a Digital Signature to This Message), as shown in Figure 11.12.

**FIGURE 11.12**   Using S/MIME for an individual message.

3. Click Close when done.

---

**TIP**

The easiest way to enable secure messaging with users outside of the Exchange 2000 organization is to send the user a digitally signed message. Outlook 2000 and later sends a copy of the sender's certificate with any signed message by default. The recipient of the signed message can then add the sender and certificate to the Contacts folder. When both users have a copy of each other's certificates, they can send and receive encrypted messages. When users receive an encrypted message they need to enter their security password to decrypt the message. In Outlook XP/Outlook 2000, encrypted messages display with a padlock in the lower-right corner of the message header.

# Summary

Keeping messaging clients secure is a critical facet to any Exchange environment and it involves careful planning, design, and testing in order to meet the requirements of the organization. Properly securing messaging clients and access to the messaging infrastructure requires security configurations of the operating system (both Windows Server 2003 and Windows XP Professional), Exchange Server 2003, and Microsoft Office 2003. This provides a robust, well-rounded, and secure solution.

# Best Practices

The following are best practices from this chapter:

- Customize security templates to ensure that application and operating system functionality are not broken or negatively affected.

- Use security templates provided by Microsoft, the National Security Agency (NSA) or the National Institute of Standards and Technology (NIST) as baselines for customizing the organization's security templates.

- Keep servers and client computers up-to-date with the latest service pack and security updates.

- Consult Microsoft, NIST, and NSA security guidelines for securing the operating system.

- Use third-party antivirus software.

- Authenticate clients to the Exchange Server 2003 messaging infrastructure, using Kerberos whenever possible.

- Outlook 2003 users should use Cached Exchange mode if they will be using RPC over HTTPS connections over the Internet.

- Combine Exchange Server 2003, Outlook 2003, and third-party features to combat spam.

- Block all read receipts.

- Implement IRM.

- Use S/MIME to encrypt sensitive or confidential messages.

# CHAPTER 12

# Server-Level Security

**IN THIS CHAPTER**

- Microsoft's Trustworthy Computing Initiative

- Assessing Your Risks

- Designing a Secure Messaging Environment

- Exchange Server-Side Security Improvements

- Tips, Tricks, and Best Practices for Hardening Windows Server 2003

- Securing by Functional Roles of the Server

- Standardizing Exchange Server 2003 Servers

- Protecting Exchange Server 2003 from Viruses

- Combating Spam

Exchange Server 2003 server-level security involves a combination of policy, configuration, and practices. With any type of system, these aspects require thorough planning, designing, and testing. This includes, but is not limited to, the development of messaging-related security policies, standardization of Windows Server 2003 and Exchange Server 2003 security mechanisms, and implementing industry-standard best practices.

Server-level security for the messaging environment is one of the most important considerations for a secure messaging environment because Exchange Server 2003 not only stores messaging data, it is also a mission-critical form of communication. As a result, it is important to establish a server-level security plan and to gain a full understanding of the security capabilities of both the operating system that it is dependent on and Exchange.

## Microsoft's Trustworthy Computing Initiative

Microsoft has undergone a vast transformation in regard to security. Microsoft seeks to provide server products, like Exchange Server 2003, that are "secure by design, secure by default, and secure by development." Every security aspect in virtually all of its server products is scrutinized. Specific features, vulnerabilities, and code have been analyzed to ensure that Exchange Server 2003 is as secure as possible.

### Secure by Design

Microsoft's Trustworthy Computing Initiative is the cornerstone of Exchange Server 2003 development. The initiative began by providing security-focused training to the entire

Exchange Server 2003 team and specially created cross-component, security-focused teams. These teams shared developer best practices to increase code quality and minimize the attack surface. Microsoft then performed code reviews to ensure that changes made to one feature set did not impose or create a security risk in others. This entire process is performed constantly.

In addition to constant code reviews, teams of security experts, called Red Teams, performed product testing and threat reviews. These teams essentially acted as hackers, attempting to compromise systems and exploit vulnerabilities based on function or feature.

### Secure by Default

Another integral part of the security initiative was to minimize the attack surface areas possible with Exchange Server 2003. This translates to keeping default installations more secure. By minimizing the number of services and functions that are enabled by default, organizations are less likely to have features unknowingly enabled that might present a security risk. For instance, frequently used protocols are no longer enabled by default. These protocols include Post Office Protocol 3 (POP3), Internet Message Access Protocol 4 (IMAP4), Network News Transfer Protocol (NNTP), and Outlook Mobile Access (OMA). Other features, such as new user restrictions and messaging limitations, have also been enabled to reduce the likelihood that default installations are unsecure.

### Secure by Deployment

Microsoft equips IT personnel with the necessary tools and documentation to securely and successfully deploy Exchange Server 2003. The deployment tools and documentation ensure that the network environment is healthy, properly configured, and ready to accept Exchange Server 2003.

Coupling these tools and documentation with the appropriate training helps prepare Exchange Server 2003 administrators. It gives them the necessary resources and knowledge to adequately secure the messaging environment based on the security requirements of the specific organization.

### Building Communications and Community

Another focal point to the security initiative is building communications and community around all server products. This framework for encouraging the sharing of information is analogous to user groups in which groups of IT professionals shared experiences, insights, and other pertinent knowledge. Communications and community can be fostered through a number of different mediums, such as newsgroups, discussion lists, user groups, and security Web sites.

## Assessing Your Risks

A key consideration for security is risk and the costs associated with securing information. This is not just about determining the monetary value of the information but equally important is assessing the different types of risks and the value of the information. Ask yourself how much would it cost the organization if the information was destroyed, altered, or stolen.

This is not an easy task; in fact, it is often a daunting one. Although monetary values can easily be associated with some types of information, other information might be nearly impossible to assess. The important thing to remember is that it's essential to secure your resources and a balance must be struck between the cost of securing the information with the information's value.

After the assessment process is initiated, it is important to begin analyzing possible security vulnerabilities for the service or functionality that the organization is offering. The following are some of the security risks to investigate and protect against for Exchange Server 2003:

- **Denial of service**—A denial of service, or DoS, occurs when a user either maliciously or surreptitiously performs some action that causes a service interruption. The interruption might affect targeted users or the entire server. An example might be the "ping of death" or a specially crafted email header that consumes the entire Exchange server processing time.

- **Viruses or Trojan Horse messages**—Viruses, email worms, and Trojan Horse messages are the bane of the messaging world. They can cause many hours of lost productivity, and keeping on top of this issue can be a full-time job. Thankfully, Exchange Server 2003 has numerous features that help administrators and antivirus vendors combat this problem.

- **Spam**—Unfortunately, unsolicited email (spam) is destined to be a part of the messaging community's life for a very long time—if not forever. It forces unwanted and frequently objectionable material into users' inboxes, costing Internet users billions of dollars annually. The reason is simple: Spam is a cheap way for mass-marketers to get their message out to a wide segment of people.

- **Intentional attacks**—These attacks are usually targeted at a specific entity or messaging system. Attacks might occur to disrupt normal business operations or compromise a known vulnerability in the company's messaging system. The administrator should bear in mind that some intentional attacks are used to focus attention away from the "real" attack.

- **Message spoofing**—Message spoofing is a tactic used by many email worms, such as KLEZ and BugBear, as well as some intentional attacks by malicious users. Message spoofing alters Simple Mail Transfer Protocol (SMTP) headers so that mail appears as though it came from a different address or messaging server. These messages are sometimes difficult and time-consuming to troubleshoot.

# Designing a Secure Messaging Environment

The messaging environment is composed of much more than just the Exchange servers and client machines. Firewalls, network perimeters, accessibility options for users, security policies, and more are integral components that must be thoroughly designed as well.

## Establishing a Corporate Email Policy

Corporate or organizational email policies are used to govern and enforce appropriate business use of the messaging environment. They are also used to provide grounds for investigations of inappropriate use of corporate email. It is recommended to establish these policies and get the business to approve them as soon as possible.

> **NOTE**
>
> Corporate email policies not only define how the system can and should be used, but they also limit liability.

The following are possible considerations and guidelines to include in the corporate email policy:

- The policy should expressly state that the email system is not to be used for the creation or distribution of any offensive or disruptive messages, including messages containing offensive comments about race, gender, age, sexual orientation, pornography, religious or political beliefs, national origin, or disability. State that employees who receive any emails with this content should report the matter to their supervisor immediately.

- Employees should not use email to discuss competitors, potential acquisitions, or mergers, or to give their opinion about another firm. Unlawful messages, such as copyright infringing emails, should also be prohibited. Include examples and be clear about measures taken when these rules are breached.

- Include a list of "email risks" to make users aware of the potential harmful effects of their actions. Advise users that sending an email is like sending a postcard or letter; if they do not want it posted on the bulletin board, they should not send it.

- If the organization monitors the content of its employees' emails, it must mention this in the email policy. It is important to note that most states and countries are allowed to monitor employees' emails if the employees are cognizant that the messages are being monitored. Organizations should warn users that there is no expectation of privacy in anything they create, store, send, or receive on the company's computer system. In addition, organizations should warn employees that messages can be viewed without prior notice.

- Establish clear email retention policies.

- Include a point of contact for questions arising from the email policy.

The corporate email policy should be made available in a variety of different places on a variety of different mediums. For instance, include the corporate email policy on the intranet, in employee handbooks, and periodically in the company newsletter. The policy can also be included as users log on to the messaging system using forms-based authentication.

## Securing Exchange Server 2003 Through Administrative Policies

Similar to the corporate email policy for users, it is recommended to establish administrative policies that govern the operation and usage of the Exchange Server 2003 messaging system. Considerations for the organization's administrative policies include the following:

- Administrative and operator accounts should not have mailboxes.

- Grant permissions to groups rather than to users.

- SMTP addresses should not match the User Principle Name (UPN).

- Require complex (strong) passwords for all users.

- Require users to close the browser when finishing an Outlook Web Access (OWA) session.

- Require Secure Sockets Layer (SSL) for HTTP, POP3, IMAP4, NNTP, and LDAP clients.

- Set policies globally and customize other user policies.

- Set storage limits and reply-to policies.

## Using Email Disclaimers

Email disclaimers inform recipients of corporate legal information and policies. For all practical purposes, email disclaimers are used to reduce liability and caution recipients about misusing the information contained within the message. Email disclaimers can be tacked onto the bottom of all outgoing messages automatically when sent through a particular server.

The following is a sample email disclaimer:

> The information contained in this message is intended solely for the individual to whom it is specifically and originally addressed. This message and its contents may contain confidential or privileged information. If you are not the intended recipient, you are hereby notified that any disclosure or distribution, or taking any action in reliance on the contents of this information, is strictly prohibited.

**TIP**

The organization's legal department or representative should approve the contents of the email disclaimer. If there were ever a situation in which the information could potentially be used in a court of law, the email disclaimer will hold more relevance under scrutiny.

Exchange Server 2003 SMTP event sinks are used to add email disclaimers to all outgoing mail or outgoing mail from a specific server. Third-party products are available as well but also come with a cost. To create an email disclaimer, follow these high-level steps:

1. Install the Exchange Software Development Kit (SDK).

2. Create an event sink using Visual Basic Script and save it as `EventSinkScript.vbs`.

3. Open the command prompt by typing **cmd** at the Start, Run dialog box and browse to the `...\Exchange SDK\SDK\Support\CDO\Scripts` directory.

4. Register the event sink using the `smtpreg.vbs` script provided in the Exchange SDK. For example, at the command prompt, type

   ```
   cscript smtpreg.vbs /
   add 1 onarrival SMTPScriptingHost CDO.SS_SMTPOnArrivalSink "mail

   from=*@your-domain-here.com"
   ```

   Press Enter when you are finished.

5. Type

   ```
   cscript smtpreg.vbs /setprop 1 onarrival SMTPScriptingHost Sink ScriptName

   "C:\EventSinkScript.vbs"
   ```

6. Test the SMTP event sink and email disclaimer.

For more information on creating an SMTP event sink for an email disclaimer, refer to Knowledge Base article 317680.

# Exchange Server-Side Security Improvements

Exchange Server 2003 has numerous product enhancements and new features, including those that are security related. The following are some of the most notable server-level security features:

- **Distribution Lists Restricted to Authenticated Users**—You can allow sending only from authenticated users or specify which users can or cannot send mail to specified distribution lists.

- **Support of Real-Time Safe and Block Lists**—Reduce the amount of unsolicited mail delivered to your organization with connection filtering.

- **Inbound Recipient Filtering**—Reduce unsolicited email messages by filtering inbound messages based on the recipient. Messages that are addressed to users who are not found, or to whom the sender does not have the permissions to send, are rejected. This applies only to messages sent by anonymously authenticated users.

- **Kerberos Authentication Between a Front-End and Back-End Server**—To help ensure that credentials are securely passed from front-end to back-end servers, Exchange Server 2003 uses Kerberos delegation when sending user credentials.

- **Virus Scanning API 2.5**—Third-party antivirus products can run on servers running Exchange Server 2003 that do not have resident Exchange mailboxes. These products can be configured to send messages to the sender and to delete messages.

- **Antispam Integration with Outlook 2003 and Outlook Web Access**—You can upload the Safe and Block Senders List to Exchange Server 2003 for filtering.

- **Clustering Security**—Exchange Server 2003 clustering supports Kerberos authentication against an Exchange virtual server. Exchange Server 2003 also supports Internet Protocol Security (IPSec) between front-end servers and clustered back-end servers running Exchange.

- **Public Folder Permissions for Unknown Users**—Public folders, with distinguished names in access control lists (ACLs) that cannot be resolved to security identifiers, drop the unresolvable distinguished names.

- **Domain Users Denied Local Logon to Exchange Server 2003 Servers by Default**—When Exchange Server 2003 is installed on a member server, the domain users group is denied local logon rights in the local security configuration. This prevents nonadministrators from logging on to the server even if they should gain physical or Remote Desktop access to the Exchange server.

- **Removal of Top-Level Public Folder Creation Permissions for Everyone and Anonymous Logon**—Exchange Server 2003 secures rampant public folder creation by removing the ability of these groups to create top-level public folders.

- **Maximum Message Size Limitations**—By default, Exchange Server 2003 limits public folder message sizes to 10MB. In addition, inbound and outbound messages have the same cap on message size.

- **Selected Services Disabled by Default**—With the exception of in-place upgrades, services such as POP3, IMAP4, and Outlook Mobile Access (OMA) are installed but disabled by default. Administrators must manually enable these services.

- **Sender ID**—With Exchange Server 2003 Service Pack 2 (SP2), Sender ID provides an additional layer of protection against spoofing and phishing.

- **Updated Intelligent Message Filter (IMF)**—Spam is significantly reduced with Version 2 of the IMF provided in SP2. Among the most notable improvements with IMF is the updated SmartScreen Technology.

- **Mobile Services Properties**—With SP2, administrators can better control and secure mobile devices. Some important security features provided with SP2 include the ability to enforce password policies, remotely delete data from lost or stolen devices, periodically refresh device settings, employ certification-based authentication, and utilize Secure/Multipurpose Internet Mail Extensions (S/MIME).

## Security Roles in Exchange Server 2003

Exchange Server 2003 administration is determined through permissions and Exchange roles. Roles determine the level to which IT personnel can administrate Exchange objects within the Exchange organization.

The Exchange Server 2003 roles work in conjunction with standard Windows Server 2003 groups and permissions structures. However, they are different and can be a bit confusing at first. For instance, the Exchange Full Administrator role is not found in Active Directory Users and Computers like a standard user or group would be. Rather, the Exchange Server 2003 roles should be viewed as templates that can define how administrators manage and maintain Exchange.

In previous versions, permissions were set through applying rights to Active Directory users' and groups' Exchange objects property pages. Now, role-based administration is assigned using the Exchange Server 2003 Delegation Wizard.

> **NOTE**
>
> For more information on Exchange Server 2003 administration, refer to Chapter 18, "Administering Exchange Server 2003."

Depending on where and which roles are assigned, different levels of permissions can be applied to different Exchange Server objects. Leveraging each of the three Exchange Server administrative roles are

- **Exchange Full Administrator**—The Exchange Full Administrator role is the least restrictive of all three Exchange Server 2003 roles. Similar to Full Control, using this role allows administrators to manage Exchange objects (that is, add, delete, and change permissions and objects). Assign this role only to Exchange administrators who require complete access to the Exchange Server 2003 organization. The Exchange administrator with this role must also manually be added to the Exchange Server 2003 server's local administrators group.

- **Exchange Administrator**—This role is ideal for performing daily Exchange administration by allowing Exchange Server 2003 administrators the ability to add, change, or modify objects. This role cannot modify permissions of other Exchange administrative roles and it is recommended to place the administrator with this role into the server's local administrators group.

- **Exchange View Only Administrator**—The Exchange View Only Administrator role is the most restrictive of all Exchange roles because it allows administrators to view Exchange objects only. Use this role to restrict administrative permissions between Exchange administrative groups.

### Required Roles to Install Additional Exchange Server 2003 Servers

In previous versions of Exchange, the Exchange Full Administrator role was required to install additional Exchange servers in the organization. This is no longer required in

Exchange Server 2003. Exchange Full Administrator rights at the administrative group level can now be delegated to allow other Exchange administrators to add new Exchange Server 2003 servers within their location. This reduces the amount of administrative overhead.

To delegate control to other Exchange administrators to install additional Exchange Server 2003 servers, do the following:

1. Open the Exchange System Manager (ESM) from the Start, All Programs, Microsoft Exchange menu by selecting System Manager.

2. Expand Administrative Groups and then right-click on the administrative group that requires delegated control and select Delegate Control.

3. In the Exchange Administration Delegation Wizard, click Next.

4. In the next window, shown in Figure 12.1, click Add to add the user or group who will add an Exchange Server 2003 server in the site.

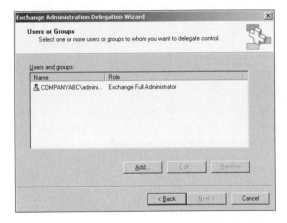

**FIGURE 12.1**    Using the Exchange Administration Delegation Wizard.

5. Select the role of Exchange Full Administrator and click OK.

6. Click Next and then click Finish.

> **TIP**
>
> The user or group should also be a member of the local administrators group on the server. Run the Exchange Administration Delegation Wizard again on either the organization or administrative group to view who has been delegated Exchange roles.

# Tips, Tricks, and Best Practices for Hardening Windows Server 2003

Exchange Server 2003 is only as secure as Windows Server 2003. Therefore, it is imperative to secure Windows Server 2003 to ensure it conforms to the security standards for the organization.

## Layered Approach to Server Security

Security works best when it is applied in layers. It is much more difficult to rob a house, for example, if a thief not only has to break through the front door, but also has to fend off an attack dog and disable a home security system. The same concept applies to server security: Multiple layers of security should be applied so that the difficulty in hacking into a system becomes that much greater.

Windows Server 2003 seamlessly handles many of the security layers that are required, using Kerberos authentication, NTFS file security, and built-in security tools to provide for a great deal of security out of the box. After Windows Server 2003 is secured according to the organization's requirements, Exchange Server 2003 security can be integrated to conform to the security requirements of the organization.

## Physical Security Considerations

An Exchange Server 2003 server can be very restrictive in what resources are accessible but if the server is not physically secured, an unauthorized user or hacker can more easily gain unauthorized access. For example, simply unplugging the server can have serious repercussions even if the unauthorized user was not able to access messaging data.

Physical security should be a requirement for any organization because it is the most common cause of security breaches. Despite this fact, many organizations have loose levels, or no levels, of physical security for their mission-critical servers.

Servers should be physically secured behind locked doors, preferably in an environmentally controlled room. Other methods of physically securing servers include hardware-locking devices, video surveillance, and more.

## Restricting Logon Access

All servers should be configured to allow only administrators to physically log on to the console. By default, Exchange Server 2003 does not allow any members of the domain users group local logon privileges. This prevents nonadministrators from logging on to the server even if they can gain physical access to the server.

## Auditing Security Events

Auditing is a way to gather and keep track of activity on the network, devices, and entire systems. By default, Windows Server 2003 enables some auditing, whereas many other auditing functions must be manually turned on. This allows for easy customization of the features the system should have monitored.

Auditing is typically used for identifying security breaches or suspicious activity. However, auditing is also important to gain insight into how the servers are accessed. Windows Server 2003's auditing policies must first be enabled before activity can be monitored.

### Auditing Policies

Audit policies are the basis for auditing events on a Windows Server 2003 system. Depending on the policies set, auditing may require a substantial amount of server resources in addition to those resources supporting the server's functionality. Otherwise, it could potentially slow server performance. Also, collecting lots of information is only as good as the evaluation of the audit logs. In other words, if a lot of information is captured and a significant amount of effort is required to evaluate those audit logs, the whole purpose of auditing is not as effective. As a result, it's important to take the time to properly plan how the system will be audited. This enables the administrator to determine what needs to be audited and why without creating an abundance of overhead.

Audit policies can track successful or unsuccessful event activity in a Windows Server 2003 environment. These policies can audit the success and failure of events. The types of events that can be monitored include the following:

- **Account Logon Events**—Each time a user attempts to log on, the successful or unsuccessful event can be recorded. Failed logon attempts can include logon failures for unknown user accounts, time restriction violations, expired user accounts, insufficient rights for the user to log on locally, expired account passwords, and locked-out accounts.

- **Account Management**—When an account is changed, an event can be logged and later examined. Although this pertains more to Windows Server 2003 than to Exchange Server 2003, it is still very relevant because the Exchange directory is stored in Active Directory.

- **Directory Service Access**—Any time a user attempts to access an Active Directory object that has its own system access control list (SACL), the event is logged.

- **Logon Events**—Logons over the network or by services are logged.

- **Object Access**—The object access policy logs an event when a user attempts to access a resource (for example, a printer or shared folder).

- **Policy Change**—Each time an attempt to change a policy (user rights, account audit policies, trust policies) is made, the event is recorded.

- **Privilege Use**—Privileged use is a security setting and can include a user employing a user right, changing the system time, and more. Successful or unsuccessful attempts can be logged.

- **Process Tracking**—An event can be logged for each program or process that a user launches while accessing a system. This information can be very detailed and can take a significant amount of resources.

- **System Events**—The system events policy logs specific system events, such as a computer restart or shutdown.

The audit policies can be enabled or disabled through either the local system policy or Group Policy objects. Audit policies are located within the `Computer Configuration\Windows Settings\Security Settings\Local Policies\Audit Policy` folder, as shown in Figure 12.2.

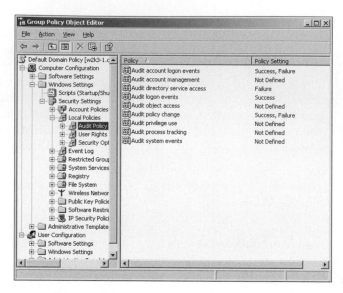

**FIGURE 12.2**    Windows Server 2003 audit policies.

## Securing Groups

An important way to secure your messaging environment is by securing distribution and mail-enabled security groups. For instance, CompanyABC is a medium-sized company with 1,000 users. To facilitate companywide notifications, the HR department created a distribution group called "All Employees." All employees are members of the "All Employees" group. By default, there are no message restrictions for new groups, meaning that anyone can send to this list. If CompanyABC has an Internet Mail SMTP Connector, this group will also have an SMTP address.

Consider what would happen if a new user sent an email to "All Employees" advertising a car for sale. Now imagine that the user sent it with a read receipt and delivery notification requested. This can have disastrous results if the server is unable to process this many requests at once.

In a similar scenario, intentions are not as innocent as the new user trying to sell a car. In fact, it can be an attempted denial of service (DOS) attack. An attacker sends an SMTP message to the "All Employees" group with a delivery notification receipt requested and spoofs the Return to Address field as the same SMTP address as the distribution group. The effect is (1 + 1000 + 1000 * 1000) 1,001,001 messages! Because a delivery notification receipt was requested, this single email results in over 1 million messages processed by the system.

Exchange Server 2003 now offers an easy solution for this problem by configuring message restrictions for the distribution group. To secure distribution groups so that only authenticated users can use it, do the following:

1. Open Active Directory Users and Computers from the Start, All Programs, Microsoft Exchange menu.

2. Right-click the distribution group and select Properties.

3. Select the Exchange General tab and under the Message Restrictions section, check the check box to Accept Messages: From Authenticated Users Only.

4. Click OK.

An administrator could further restrict the usage of this group by allowing only a specific security group to use it. To restrict access to the distribution group to a specific user or group, do the following:

1. In the Active Directory Users and Computers snap-in, right-click the distribution group and select Properties.

2. Select the Exchange General tab and under the Message Restrictions section, select the Only From radio button.

3. Click Add and enter the security group that has permissions to send to the distribution group.

4. Click OK.

## Keeping Services to a Minimum

Depending on the role that an Exchange Server 2003 server will fulfill, not all services that are installed by default are necessary for the server to function. It is considered good practice to limit the number of entry points (services) into a server. Any services that are not required for the system to function should be disabled. Note that this can be performed using a customized security template.

## Locking Down the File System

Files secured on Windows Server 2003 are only as secure as the permissions that are set on them. Subsequently, it is good to know that Windows Server 2003, for the first time in a Microsoft operating system, does not grant the Everyone group full control over share-level and NTFS-level permissions. In addition, critical operating system files and directories are secured, to disallow their unauthorized use.

Despite the overall improvements made, a complete understanding of file-level security is recommended to ensure that the file-level security of a server is not neglected.

> **NOTE**
>
> The Exchange Server 2003 installation process requires that partitions on the server are formatted as NTFS.

## Using the Microsoft Baseline Security Analyzer

The Microsoft Baseline Security Analyzer (MBSA) is a tool that identifies common security misconfigurations and missing hotfixes via local or remote scans of Windows systems. MBSA provides users with the ability to scan a single Windows system and obtain a security assessment as well as a list of recommended corrective actions. Furthermore, administrators may use the MBSA tool to scan multiple functional roles of a Windows-based server on the network for vulnerabilities to help ensure systems are up to date with the latest security-related patches.

To run MBSA, do the following:

1. Download the latest security XML file to use with MBSA. This file contains a list of current service packs and hotfixes that should be applied to a system.

2. Keep the default settings and scan the server(s).

## Consulting Standards and Guidelines

As mentioned in Chapter 11, "Client-Level Security," Microsoft has gone to great lengths to provide secure and reliable products. Moreover, it has worked closely with companies, government agencies, security consultants, and others to address security issues in the computer industry.

In addition to Microsoft security standards and guidelines, it is advisable that organizations use recommended best practices compiled by the National Institute of Standards and Technologies (NIST) and the National Security Agency (NSA). Both NIST and NSA provide security lockdown configuration standards and guidelines that can be downloaded from their Web sites (http://www.nist.gov and http://www.nsa.gov, respectively).

## Using the Security Configuration Wizard

The Security Configuration Wizard (SCW) is a tool provided in Windows Server 2003 Service Pack 1 that can significantly improve a computer's or a group of computers' security. As the name implies, SCW is wizard-based, designed to determine the specific functionality required by the server. All other functionality that is not intended or required by the server can then be disabled. This reduces the computer's attack surface by limiting functionality to only that which is required and necessary.

SCW reviews the computer's configuration, which includes but is not limited to the following:

- **Services**—SCW limits the number of services in use.

- **Packet filtering**—SCW can configure certain ports and protocols.

- **Auditing**—Auditing can be configured based on the computer's role and the organization's security requirements.

- **IIS**—SCW can secure IIS, including Web extensions and legacy virtual directories.

- **Server roles and tasks**—The role (file, database, messaging, Web server, and so on), specific tasks (backup, content indexing, and so on), and placement in an environment that a computer may have is a critical component in any lockdown process or procedure. Some of the roles and tasks that are evaluated are illustrated in Figure 12.3. Application services are also evaluated from products such as Exchange Server 2003, SQL Server 2000, ISA Server, SharePoint Portal Server 2003, and Operations Manager.

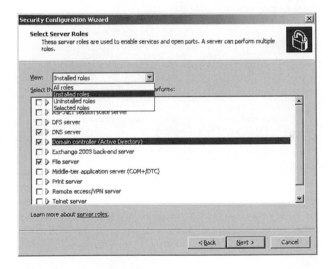

**FIGURE 12.3**  Analyzing computer roles.

- **IPSec**—SCW can be used to properly configure IPSec.

- **Registry settings**—After careful analysis, SCW can modify the LanMan Compatibility level, SMB security signatures, NoLMHash, and LDAP Server Integrity parameters based on down-level computer compatibility requirements.

---

**CAUTION**

SCW is a very flexible and powerful security analysis and configuration tool. As a result, it is important to keep control over when and how the tool is used. Equally important is testing possible configurations in a segmented lab environment prior to implementation. Without proper testing, environment functionality can be stricken or completely locked.

---

SCW is used to assist in building specific security-related policies and to analyze computers against those policies to ensure compliance. In many ways, SCW can be considered a replacement for other Microsoft security-related tools that are also mentioned in this chapter. For instance, SCW can take existing security templates created from the Security Configuration and Analysis tool and expand upon the restrictions to meet an organization's security policy requirements. In addition, SCW can analyze computers for any security updates that are needed, integrate with Group Policy, and provide a knowledge base repository, as shown in Figure 12.4.

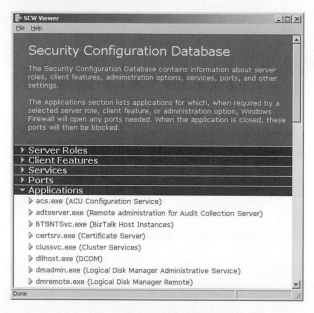

**FIGURE 12.4**    Viewing SCW's knowledge base.

## Securing Servers with Security Templates

Security templates are a practical and effective means to apply security policies and configurations to Exchange Server 2003 servers. Although security templates are provided with Windows Server 2003, it is recommended to customize them prior to applying them using the Security Configuration and Analysis Microsoft Management Console (MMC) snap-in.

This not only ensures that computers are identically configured with the same security configurations, but it also is an easy way to configure appropriate security measures for those computers that are not managed using GPOs.

> **TIP**
>
> E2k3SecOps11.exe contains security templates specific for Exchange Server 2003. It is still important, however, to customize these scripts to properly address your environment's security policy.

> **NOTE**
>
> For more information on customizing and using security templates, refer to Chapter 11.

## Keeping Up with Security Patches and Updates

Service packs (SPs) and hotfixes for both the operating system and applications, such as Exchange Server 2003, are vital parts to maintaining availability, reliability, performance, and security. An administrator can update a system with the latest SP in several ways: CD-ROM, manually entered commands, Windows Update, or Microsoft Software Update Server (SUS).

> **NOTE**
>
> Thoroughly test and evaluate SPs and hotfixes in a lab environment before installing them on production servers. Also, install the appropriate SPs and hotfixes on each production server to keep all systems consistent.

### Windows Update

Windows Update is a Web site that scans a local system and determines whether there are updates to apply to that system. Windows Update is a great way to update individual systems, but this method is sufficient for only a small number of systems. If administrators choose this method to update an entire organization, there would be an unnecessary amount of administration.

### Windows Server Update Services

Windows Server Update Services (WSUS), an upgrade from its predecessor Software Update Services (SUS), minimizes administration, management, and maintenance of small- to midsized organizations communicating directly and securely with Microsoft to gather the latest security updates and SPs (for Windows Server 2003, Windows 2000 (SP4 or later), Windows XP (SP1 or later), Exchange Server 2003, SQL Server 2000, and Office XP or higher). Some of the most notable changes from the previous version include the following:

- Support for a greater number of products, including service pack updates

- The capability to target computers using Group Policy or scripts

- Reports on update installation status

- The capability to perform basic hardware inventory

The updates downloaded onto WSUS can then be distributed to either a lab server for testing (recommended) or to targeted production servers. After these updates are tested, WSUS can automatically distribute them inside the network.

> **NOTE**
>
> You can find more information on WSUS and download the product from
> `http://www.microsoft.com/windowsserversystem/updateservices/default.mspx`.

## Hardening IIS

IIS is an integral part of Windows Server 2003 and it has come a long way from its predecessors especially in terms of security. Several key enhancements, such as a reduced attack surface and enhanced application isolation, deliver a robust and secure Web platform.

IIS installs only the features needed to fill its defined role or function. It works by turning off unnecessary features, much like the IISLockdown utility performed, thus reducing the attack surface available to attackers. For previous versions of Windows, the IISLockdown tool was available as a separate download. It is now, however, built in to IIS. IIS maintains a `UrlScan.ini` file with a specific section for DenyUrlSequences and can limit the length of specific fields and requests. This functionality replaces some of the features of URLScan, a complementary component of using IISLockdown.

## IIS Hardening Checklist

Although IIS does a good job at installing and enabling only what is needed, it is important to review IIS security configurations on the organization's Exchange Server 2003 servers. Table 12.1 summarizes key hardening aspects of IIS as well as presents other key recommendations for securing the Web components on the messaging server.

**TABLE 12.1**    IIS Hardening Checklist

| Recommendation | Description |
| --- | --- |
| Enable logging using W3C. Use the extended properties sheet to add more information to the logs. | IIS logging can identify many different parameters and record them for later analysis. Add client IP address, username, method, URI Stem, HTTP status, Win32 status, User Agent, server IP address, and server port. |
| Set log file ACLs (admin—Full Control, system—Full Control, everyone— write, create). | This prevents someone from covering his tracks. Any log file that IIS generates will be stored in the `%SystemRoot%\system32\LogFiles` folder on the system partition. If the access control settings for these files are not secured, an attacker might cover up his actions on the server by deleting associated log entries. |
| Remove unused script mappings. | Unused script mappings—such as `.htr`, `.ida`, `.htw`, `.idc`, `.printer`, `.shtm`, `.stm`, and `.shtml` could be used to gain access to the system. If any script mappings within IIS are not being used, they should be removed. |
| Set appropriate directory permissions. | Set appropriate ACLs on virtual directories. |

> **NOTE**
>
> `URLScan.exe` can be used to only allow HTTP requests that follow a specific ruleset, such as length or character set, to an IIS server.

## Other Hardening Techniques for Windows Server 2003

Although not all inclusive, Table 12.2 provides a quick checklist of recommended security precautions to take on an Exchange Server 2003 server.

**TABLE 12.2** Windows Server 2003 Hardening Checklist

| Recommendation | Description |
| --- | --- |
| Secure default Windows Repair Directory (`\%SystemRoot%\Repair`). | Set an appropriate level of access to this directory to prevent unauthorized access to system files. |
| Protect against data remnants. | The Recycle Bin saves a copy of a file when it is deleted through Windows Explorer. On critical servers, this could pose a security risk. A sensitive file might be deleted, yet a copy of that file would remain in the Recycle Bin. To configure the Recycle Bin to prevent deleted files from being saved, use the following procedure: |
| | 1. Right-click the Recycle Bin icon on the desktop, and select Properties. |
| | 2. Check the box labeled Do Not Move Files to the Recycle Bin. Remove Files Immediately on Delete. |
| | 3. Click OK. |
| | 4. Empty the Recycle Bin of any preexisting files. |
| Automatically clear the pagefile before the system shuts down. | Virtual Memory support in Windows Server 2003 uses a system pagefile to swap pages from memory when they are not being actively used. On a running system, this pagefile is opened exclusively by the operating system and, hence, is well protected. However, to implement a secure Windows Server 2003 environment, the system pagefile should be wiped clean when the system shuts down. To do so, change the data value of the `ClearPageFileAtShutdown` value in the following Registry key to a value of 1: `HKEY_LOCAL_MACHINE\SYSTEM\CurrentControlSet\Control\Session Manager\Memory Management`. If the value does not exist, add the following value: |
| | Value Name: **`ClearPageFileAtShutdown`** |
| | Value Type: **`REG_DWORD`** |
| | Value: **1** |

**TABLE 12.2**   Continued

| Recommendation | Description |
|---|---|
| Rename the administrator account. | Renaming the administrator account helps prevent unauthorized access by using the default administrator account. In addition, consider establishing a decoy account named "Administrator" with no privileges. Scan the event log regularly to identify attempts to use this account. |
| Remove all unnecessary file shares. | Scrutinize all shares to determine whether they should be removed or shares should be locked down. |

## Securing by Functional Roles of the Server

Exchange Server 2003 servers can participate in various responsibilities in a given messaging environment. Some of these responsibilities may be intertwined due to budget constraints, business requirements, or technical justifications. No matter how the roles and responsibilities play out in the environment, it's important to secure them appropriately based on the roles of the server.

Some examples of the functional roles that Exchange Server 2003 servers can have within the messaging environment include, but are not limited to, the following:

- **Front-end servers**—Front-end servers relay client requests to back-end servers and should not host Information Stores.

- **Connector and relay servers**—Connector or relay servers act as a bridge between different Exchange sites or organizations, as well as to foreign servers on different networks.

- **Back-end servers**—Back-end servers refer to Exchange servers that are located on the internal network and do not directly face the Internet. These servers generally host Information Stores containing mailboxes or public folders.For instance, administrators must take a different approach to securing an OWA, front-end server compared to a back-end mailbox server. The following is a list of role-specific lock-down procedures that are recommended for an OWA server:

- Stop and disable unnecessary services (for example, Alerter, Help and Support, Microsoft Exchange Information Store, Microsoft Exchange MTA Stacks, and Microsoft Exchange Routing Engine).

- Remove databases and storage groups to prevent data being stored on the front-end server.

- Use SSL and enable forms-based authentication to improve authentication and session control.

- Change the look and feel as well as possible error messages of the OWA site and remove references to Microsoft or their products.

Now, compare the list of lockdown procedures for OWA with one for a mailbox server. Although the two might have some similarities especially with regard to operating system lockdown, there can be significant differences.

- Stop and disable unnecessary services.

- Review and set appropriate store permissions for mailboxes and public folders.

- Scan stores for viruses in addition to mail scanning at the gateway.

- Review and configure appropriate send, receive, and recipient limits.

### Exchange Server 2003 Running on Domain Controllers

Some smaller messaging environments might consider implementing Exchange Server 2003 on a global catalog/domain controller (GC/DC) to save on costs and administration. On the contrary, this configuration can actually increase costs by increasing administration and maintenance, and potentially cause more downtime (both scheduled and unscheduled). An equally important reason for avoiding this configuration is to minimize security risks and other implications, such as the following:

- Clustering is not available.
- Performance is affected.
- DSAccess, DSProxy, and global catalog services will not be load-balanced or have failover capabilities.
- All services run under LocalSystem might pose a greater chance of compromise.
- Exchange administrators require physical access to the DC.
- The server takes much longer to shut down.

### Special Security Considerations for Exchange and Operating System Upgrades

If Exchange Server 2003 runs on top of Windows 2000 SP3, the administrator has the option of doing an in-place upgrade of the NOS to Windows 2003 Server. Because of the new security and functionality of Windows 2003, Exchange Server 2003 must make some adjustments to IIS 6.0 after the upgrade.

As the server starts up, it looks for a /lm.ds2mb/61491 key in the IIS metabase. If the key does not exist, Exchange performs the following steps:

1. IIS switches from Compatibility mode to Worker Process Isolation mode.
2. Exchange ISAPI extensions are enabled and an application pool is created.
3. IIS creates the /lm.ds2mb/61491 key in the metabase.
4. IIS automatically restarts the W3SVC service for the changes to take effect.

Each of these changes are logged in the application event log.

# Standardizing Exchange Server 2003 Servers

Organizations are challenged by varying IT infrastructure standards because all too often systems vary in the type of components used, how they are built, how they are configured, and more. The variations require significantly more administration and maintenance especially in mid- to large-sized environments. The result of this increases the number of IT personnel needed to support such a solution and the associated IT expenditures.

Standardizing the messaging environment is in the organization's best interest not only to save on administration, maintenance, and troubleshooting, but also to help promote a more secure environment. Standardization ensures that each server has been properly secured based on the role or function that it serves.

## Standardizing Server Builds

When organizations build servers from scratch, typically the build parameters, including security configurations, are inconsistent. From an administration, maintenance, troubleshooting, and security point of view, this can be a nightmare. Each server must be treated individually and administrators must try to keep track of separate, incongruent configurations.

> **NOTE**
>
> Use ExchDump to report on how the Exchange server is configured. Also periodically scan each Exchange server using the Exchange Best Practices Analyzer (ExBPA) to review configurations and identify potential issues. For more information on using ExBPA, refer to Chapter 33, "Capacity Analysis and Performance Optimization."

# Protecting Exchange Server 2003 from Viruses

Exchange Server 2003 does not provide what is typically thought of as antivirus software (that is, an application that gets installed and enabled to scan for viruses), but it does provide various tools and an Antivirus Application Program Interface (AVAPI) that help to protect the messaging infrastructure from viruses and worms. Third-party vendors, such as the ones listed in Table 12.3, can hook their antivirus applications into the AVAPI to gain access to messages as they are handled by Exchange.

**TABLE 12.3**    Third-Party Antivirus Products for Exchange Server 2003

| Vendor/Product | Web Site |
| --- | --- |
| Sybari's Antigen for Exchange | http://www.sybari.com |
| Aladdin's eSafe Mail | http://www.aladdin.com/ |
| GFI MailSecurity for Exchange | http://www.gfi.com/mailsecurity |
| Panda Antivirus for Exchange Server | http://www.pandasecurity.com |
| Trend's ScanMail for Microsoft Exchange | http://www.trend.com |

**TABLE 12.3**  Continued

| Vendor/Product | Web Site |
| --- | --- |
| Symantec's AntiVirus/Filtering for Microsoft Exchange | http://enterprisesecurity.symantec.com |
| Sophos PureMessage for Windows/Exchange | http://www.sophos.com |

Many mechanisms can be used to protect the messaging environment from viruses and other malicious code. Most third-party virus-scanning products scan for known virus signatures as well as provide some form of heuristics to scan for unknown viruses. Other antivirus products block suspicious or specific types of message attachments at the point of entry before a possible virus reaches the Information Store.

As alluded to, there are two fundamental ways for antivirus products to keep viruses from affecting the Information Store:

- **Gateway scanning**—Gateway scanning works by scanning all messages as they go through the SMTP gateway (typically to the Internet). If the message contains a virus or is suspected of carrying a virus, the antivirus product can clean, quarantine, or delete it before Exchange has to do any further processing. More specifically, a transport event sink takes the message and places it into a queue to be scanned.

- **Mailbox scanning**—Mailbox scanning is useful to remove viruses that have entered the Information Store. For example, a new virus might make it into the Exchange Information Store before a signature file that can detect it is applied, so the virus is not detected by the gateway scanner. The Information Store can be rescanned after the new pattern file is installed, cleaning the viruses that made it in. If a user opens a virus-laden message, the mailbox scanner cleans it. A mailbox scanner also scans messages created from the internal network so that if a user brings a floppy disk from home with an infected file that is then emailed to a colleague, the message does not go through the SMTP gateway but the mailbox scanner detects and cleans it upon submission to the mail store.

## The AVAPI 2.5 Specification

Antivirus vendors use the Exchange Server 2003 AVAPI 2.5 specification to provide a robust solution against viruses, worms, and spam.

The more notable features of AVAPI version 2.5 in Exchange Server 2003 include the following:

- Gateway scanning occurs before mail even gets to the mailbox.

- The ability to clean, quarantine, or delete messages is available.

- Additional message properties are now exposed.

- More detailed status codes are available to Outlook from vendor software.

- Guaranteed outbound scanning is offered.

# Combating Spam

Spam is a global problem that affects everyone with an Internet-accessible email address. It is not just a frustration anymore; it affects many things, including an organization's ability to be productive among other things. In Chapter 11 and Chapter 13, "Transport-Level Security," many methods and features such as blocking attachments, filtering, and preventing Web beaconing were examined to help prevent spam in the organization. To continue with that examination, the following sections describe common best practices to minimize or alleviate spam.

## Using Intelligent Message Filter

The Exchange 2003 Intelligent Message Filter (IMF) uses SmartScreen Technology, which uses a probability-based algorithm to learn and then characterize what is and what is not spam (that is, distinguishing between legitimate and unsolicited commercial email [UCE]). As a result, there are no pattern files or keywords to download; however, as you would expect, Microsoft provides occasional updates to IMF. Exchange SP2 improves IMF's learning capability to reduce false positives and includes the ability to identify and ward off phishing scams.

> **NOTE**
>
> IMF best serves the organization when installed on the gateway server so that it can scan and filter all incoming messages. If you are using a third-party gateway product, Microsoft recommends that you install it on a bridgehead server. Smaller organizations with single server environments may use IMF on the mailbox server if implementing a gateway is not an option.

As IMF scans an incoming message, it assigns a number rating (ranging from 1 to 9 from least to most probable) on how probable the message is UCE and then stores the spam confidence level (SCL) within the SMTP header.

The high-level tasks for implementing IMF are as follows. For more detailed information, refer to Microsoft's Exchange Server 2003 Intelligent Message Filter deployment guide.

1. Create an account on the Exchange server that accepts all incoming connections (for example, gateway or bridgehead server) and give the Send As permissions.

2. Create a connector in the connecting forest that requires authentication using the account you just created.

3. Download `ExchangeIMF.msi` from Microsoft's download Web page (go to `http://www.microsoft.com/downloads/` and search for Intelligent Message Filter). You should also note if updates are available for IMF and download those as well.

4. Within the Exchange System Manager, expand Global Settings, right-click Message Delivery, and then select Properties.

5. On the Intelligent Message Filtering tab, assign an SCL threshold and instruct IMF to take a certain action when a message is blocked like the one depicted in Figure 12.5.

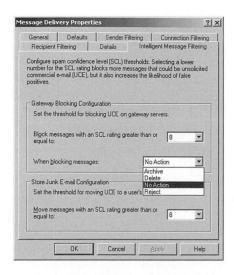

**FIGURE 12.5**   Configuring IMF to take an action when a message is blocked.

> **TIP**
>
> Allow IMF to scan incoming messages for a period of time without taking action. This allows you to fine-tune the configuration and ensure that false positives are minimized. If you are using MOM, also consider using the IMF management pack to help monitor and optimize the installation.

6. Within the servers's SMTP protocol settings, enable IMF on the server's SMTP Virtual server, as shown in Figure 12.6.

## Using SenderID

Although spammers can use several tools to successfully send unwanted emails, two very popular methods are spoofing and phishing. Spoofing is deceptive in that it masks a sender's email address with a fake one that either looks like it originated from your domain or from a trusted one. Phishing, on the other hand, uses spam to draw attention to official-looking but fraudulent Web sites such as a bank. For instance, a person receiving the spam is convinced that the spam is originating from an online vendor, clicks on a link to a fraudulent (but official-looking) site, and then proceeds to enter in personal or financial information just as they would for the legitimate site.

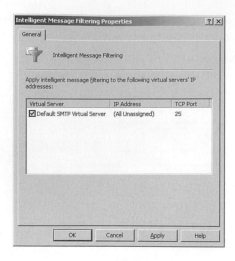

**FIGURE 12.6**   Enabling IMF on SMTP virtual servers.

Exchange SP2 adds support for another spam fighter called Sender ID. Sender ID uses an authentication protocol and Sender Policy Framework (SPF) DNS record to verify that the email sender is who she really says she is. It verifies the IP address of the email sender against a list of registered servers that are authorized to send email for the domain in question. Sender ID can then send the information to IMF.

## Using Blacklists

Many companies are unknowingly serving as open relays, which aid spammers by essentially permitting them to use the company's messaging system for unsolicited email. When a company or domain is reported as an open relay, the domain can be placed on a blacklist. This blacklist, in turn, can be used by other companies to prevent incoming mail from a known open relay source. Blacklists are useful because they can help prevent spam.

You can find some organizations that maintain blacklists at the following addresses:

- http://www.dsbl.org
- http://www.mail-abuse.com
- http://www.spamcop.net
- http://ordb.org

## Reporting Spammers

Organizations and laws are getting tougher on spammers, but spam prevention requires users and organizations to report the abuse. Although this often is a difficult task because many times the source is undecipherable, it is nonetheless important to take a proactive stance and report abuses.

Users should contact the system administrator or help desk if they receive or continue to receive spam, virus hoaxes, and other such fraudulent offers. System administrators should report spammers and contact mail abuse organizations, such as the ones listed earlier in the section "Using Blacklists." System administrators must also use discretion based on the offense, the frequency, and the possible ramifications of various ways of dealing with the spam. For instance, if a few spam messages appear to originate from yahoo.com, it might serve the company better to filter messages based on a message's language contents rather than blocking the entire domain.

## Using a Third-Party Antispam Product

Microsoft has equipped users, system administrators, and third-party organizations with the tools necessary to combat spam. Using third-party products strengthens the company's defense and complements the tools that Microsoft provides in Exchange Server 2003. Third-party products also provide a multitude of features that help with reporting, customizations, and filtering mechanisms to keep only the unwanted mail away from the messaging environment and users.

## Do Not Use Open SMTP Relays

By default, Exchange Server 2003 is not configured to allow open relays. If an SMTP relay is necessary in the messaging environment, take the necessary precautions to ensure that only authorized users or systems have access to these SMTP relays.

> **NOTE**
>
> Use ExBPA or other tools such as Sam Spade (http://www.samspade.org/) to check for SMTP open relays.

## Using the Work Email Address for Work Only

Although this is self-explanatory, it is important to note that this policy and practice not only helps minimize spam in the workplace, but it also helps prevent the messaging environment from being used for unauthorized purposes. It is recommended for everyone, including system administrators, to use a personal email address for subscribing to or signing up for non-business-related services.

## Protecting Distribution Lists

An easy way for spammers to increase their target audience is by finding and using distribution lists. There are several ways to prevent unauthorized use of distribution lists in the organization, including, but not limited to, hiding group membership, using a gateway and DNS to prevent external emails from being sent to the list, and allowing only authenticated users to send messages. To prevent anyone other than an authenticated user from sending to the list, open the property page of the distribution list within Active Directory Users and Computers. Next click the Exchange General tab and check From Authenticated Users Only, as shown in Figure 12.7.

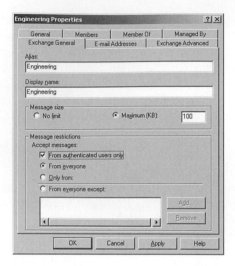

**FIGURE 12.7**    Restricting access to distribution lists.

### Taking Caution When Sharing Your Email Address

Whether you use your email address for business or nonbusiness purposes, think twice before giving away your email address. Some people have gone so far as to not list their email address on business cards. Others use a secondary email address for those higher-risk situations. Take the time to determine the appropriateness of giving out your email address and be aware of the possible consequences.

### Looking for Privacy Statements and Mailing Options

When submitting information through an online form, look for a privacy statement and mailing options. Make sure the statement includes protection of all your information, including your email address, and make sure that you are not opting to be put on a mailing list.

### Removing or "Unsubscribing" at Your Own Discretion

A general rule of thumb to follow is that if it looks like spam, it probably is. Removing your name or "unsubscribing" only validates your account and can result in more spam.

## Summary

Securing Exchange Server 2003 from a server-level perspective is multifaceted. It involves proper planning and design, hardening Windows Server 2003, developing policies, implementing or enabling Exchange Server 2003 features, and much more. This chapter focused on the server-level aspects that promote a secure messaging environment.

# Best Practices

The following are best practices from this chapter:

- Assess the messaging environment's risks.

- Establish a corporate email policy.

- Establish administrative policies.

- Use email disclaimers and have them approved by a legal representative.

- Plan and design Exchange Server 2003 security roles.

- Use a layered approach when hardening Windows Server 2003.

- Perform periodic security assessments.

- Keep updated with the latest service packs and hotfixes.

- Assess the functional role of the server and secure it accordingly.

- Do not install Exchange Server 2003 on a domain controller.

- Standardize Exchange Server 2003 security.

- Implement a mailbox and gateway antivirus scanner.

# CHAPTER 13

# Transport-Level Security

**IN THIS CHAPTER**

- The Onion Approach
- Using Public Key Infrastructure with Exchange Server 2003
- Supporting S/MIME
- Protecting Communications with IP Security (IPSec)
- Configuring IPSec
- Locking Down SMTP
- Securing Routing Group Connectors
- Securing Other Exchange-Supported Protocols
- Protecting Client–to–Front-End–Server Communications
- Locking Down Front-end and Back-end Server Communications

Organizations of all sizes use Exchange Server 2003, not as simply an email system, but also for internal and external communications. This communication is vital to any organization and it must be efficient and secure. The level of security depends on the business, security policies, type and content of information being communicated, and which parties are communicating.

Securing external communication is vital—especially information that is transmitted over public networks such as the Internet. External communication is an important facet to address when considering transport-level security, but it is not the only important aspect to secure. Internal communication, whether it is internal employees sending messages or server-to-server interactions, are equally important. This chapter focuses on the mechanisms that exist to protect and encrypt information sent between computers on a network.

## The Onion Approach

Security is a relative term, because even the most secure infrastructures are subject to vulnerabilities, and an environment is only as secure as its weakest link. One of the best defenses, however, is deploying multiple layers of security on critical network data. Using multiple layers of security is often referred to as the *onion approach*, where different stages or layers of security are used to protect the information. Generally speaking, as the information becomes more sensitive or confidential, the number of onion layers increases to thwart unauthorized access.

The premise behind the onion approach is that if a single layer of security is compromised, the intruder will have to bypass the second, third, fourth, and so on layers of security to gain access to the information. For example, relying on a complex 128-bit "unbreakable" encryption scheme is worthless if an intruder uses simple social engineering to acquire the password or PIN from a validated user. Putting in a second or third layer of security makes it that much more difficult for intruders to break through all layers.

On the other hand, adding security layers also affects usability and sometimes even functionality. As the security layers are applied, the complexity increases for authorized users trying to gain access to the information. The key to providing multiple layers of security is that the information is worthwhile to protect and the mechanisms that are put into place are as transparent as possible to authorized users.

When working with Windows Server 2003 and Exchange Server 2003, there are many security facets to consider implementing. Transport-level security is just one of those facets, but it is an important one to consider for organizations of all sizes. Transport-level security also uses an onion approach, wherein multiple levels of authentication, encryption, and authorization can be implemented for an enhanced degree of security on a network.

# Using Public Key Infrastructure with Exchange Server 2003

Public Key Infrastructure (PKI), in a nutshell, is an extensible infrastructure used to provide certificate-based services. It is a conglomeration of digital certificates, registration authorities, and Certificate Authorities that can be used to provide authentication, authorization, non-repudiation, confidentiality, and verification. A Certificate Authority (CA) is a digital signature of the certificate issuer.

PKI implementations are widespread and are becoming more of a critical component of modern networks. Windows Server 2003 fully supports the deployment of various PKI configurations. PKI deployments can range from simple to complex, as illustrated in Figures 13.1 and 13.2, with some PKI implementations using internal and external PKIs to supply a wide range of services and trust relationships with other entities. Although entire books are dedicated to PKI, this chapter focuses on how PKI can be used to secure Exchange Server 2003 implementations.

## Certificate Services in Windows Server 2003

Windows Server 2003 includes a built-in Certificate Authority (CA) known as Certificate Services. Certificate Services can be used to create certificates and subsequently manage them; it is responsible for ensuring their validity. Certificate Services can also be used to trust outside PKIs, such as a third-party PKI, to expand services and secure communication with other organizations.

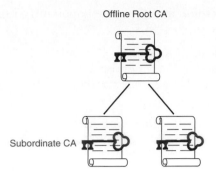

**FIGURE 13.1**  A simple PKI.

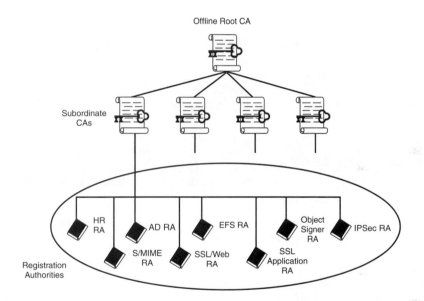

**FIGURE 13.2**  A complex PKI.

The type of CA that you install and configure depends on the purpose or purposes of the Windows Server 2003 PKI. Certificate Services for Windows Server 2003 can be installed as one of the following CA types:

- **Enterprise Root Certification Authority**—The enterprise root CA is the most trusted CA in an organization and, if required in an organization, should be installed before any other CA. All other CAs are subordinate to an enterprise root CA. Enterprise root CAs store certificates in Active Directory (AD) by default.

- **Enterprise Subordinate Certification Authority**—An enterprise subordinate CA must get a CA certificate from an enterprise root CA but can then issue certificates to all users and computers in the enterprise. These types of CAs are often used for load balancing of an enterprise root CA; more importantly, using subordinates provides stronger security for the PKI.

- **Standalone Root Certification Authority**—A standalone root CA is the root of a hierarchy that is not related to the enterprise domain information, and therefore certificates are not stored in AD. Multiple standalone CAs can be established for particular purposes.

- **Standalone Subordinate Certification Authority**   A standalone subordinate CA receives its certificate from a standalone root CA and can then be used to distribute certificates to users and computers associated with that standalone CA.

Windows Server 2003 PKI can also be either online or offline. The key difference is the level of security that is required in the organization.

> **TIP**
>
> An enterprise root CA is the most versatile CA in Windows Server 2003 because it integrates tightly with AD and offers more certificate services. If you're unsure as to what CA to use, choose an enterprise root or subordinate CA for use with messaging. Most importantly, however, is that with any PKI there must be careful planning and design.

## PKI Planning Considerations

Any PKI implementation requires thorough planning and design, as noted earlier. Possible planning and design considerations include the following:

- Multinational legal considerations, including creation and standardization of a formal Certificate Practice Statement (CPS)

- Policies and procedures for issuing, revoking, and suspending certificates

- PKI hardware identification and standardization, including employee badge integration

- Determination of CA hierarchy administration model

- Creation of a redundant CA infrastructure based on geographical location

- Policies and procedures for creation of CAs as subordinates and policy enforcers within a greater hierarchy including qualified subordination and cross-certification

- Policies and procedures for creation of Registration Authorities (RAs) and their placement within the CA hierarchy

- CA trust strategies

- Policies and procedures for maintaining the CA as a 7×24×365 operation

- Policies and procedures for key and certificate management, including—but not limited to—key length, cryptographic algorithms, certificate lifetime, certificate renewal, storage requirements, and more

- Policies and procedures for securing the PKI

- Published plans for providing high availability and recoverability

- Policies and procedures for integrating the CA with LDAP and/or Active Directory

- Policies and procedures for integrating with existing applications

- Policies and procedures for security-related incidents (for example, bulk revocation of certificates)

- Policies and procedures for delegation of administrative tasks

- Standards for PKI auditing and reporting

- Policies and procedures for change control

- Standards for key length and expiration of certificates

- Policies and procedures for handling lost certificates (that is, smartcard)

- Policies and procedures for safe distribution of the CA public key to end-users

- Policies and procedures for enrollment (for example, auto-enrollment, stations, and so forth)

- Policies and procedures for incorporating external users and companies

- Procedures for using certificate templates

As you can see from this list, implementing PKI is not to be taken lightly. Even if the organization is implementing PKI just for enhanced Exchange Server 2003 messaging functionality, the considerations should be planned and designed.

## Installing Certificate Services

To install Certificate Services on Windows Server 2003, follow these steps:

1. Choose Start, Control Panel, Add or Remove Programs.

2. Click Add/Remove Windows Components.

3. Check the Certificate Services box.

4. A warning dialog box will be displayed indicating that the computer name or domain name cannot be changed after you install Certificate Services. Click Yes to proceed with the installation.

5. Click Next to continue.

6. The next screen enables you to create the type of CA required. Refer to the preceding list for more information about the different types of CAs that you can install. In this example, choose Enterprise Root CA and click Next to continue.

7. Enter a common name for the CA—for example, `TestCA`.

8. Enter the validity period for the Certificate Authority and click Next to continue. The cryptographic key will then be created.

9. Enter a location for the certificate database and then database logs. The location you choose should be secured to prevent unauthorized tampering with the CA. Click Next to continue. Setup will then install the CA components.

10. If IIS is not installed, a prompt will be displayed indicating that Web Enrollment will be disabled until you install IIS. If this box is displayed, click OK to continue.

11. Click Finish after installation to complete the process.

## Fundamentals of Private and Public Keys

Encryption techniques can primarily be classified as either symmetrical or asymmetrical. *Symmetrical encryption* requires that each party in an encryption scheme hold a copy of a *private key*, which is used to encrypt and decrypt information sent between the two parties. The problem with private key encryption is that the private key must somehow be transmitted to the other party without it being intercepted and used to decrypt the information.

*Asymmetrical encryption* uses a combination of two keys, which are mathematically related to each other. The first key, the private key, is kept closely guarded and is used to encrypt the information. The second key, the *public key*, can be used to decrypt the information. The integrity of the public key is ensured through certificates. The asymmetric approach to encryption ensures that the private key does not fall into the wrong hands and only the intended recipient is able to decrypt the data.

## Understanding Certificates

A *certificate* is essentially a digital document issued by a trusted central authority that is used by the authority to validate a user's identity. Central, trusted authorities such as VeriSign are widely used on the Internet to ensure that software from Microsoft, for example, is really from Microsoft, and not a virus in disguise.

Certificates are used for multiple functions, including, but not limited to, the following:

- Secure email
- Web-based authentication
- IP Security (IPSec)
- Secure Web-based communications

- Code signing

- Certification hierarchies

Certificates are signed using information from the subject's public key; identifier information such as name, email address, and so on; and the CA.

## Certificate Templates

As mentioned earlier, there are multiple functions for certificates, and hence there are multiple types of certificates. In other words, one certificate may be used to sign code and another certificate used to provide support for secure email. This is a one-to-one relationship wherein a certificate is used for a single purpose. Certificates can also have a one-to-many relationship wherein one certificate is used for multiple purposes.

> **TIP**
>
> One of the best examples of a certificate that uses a one-to-many relationship is the user certificate. A User certificate by default provides support for user authentication, secure email, and the Encrypting File System (EFS), as shown in Figure 13.3.

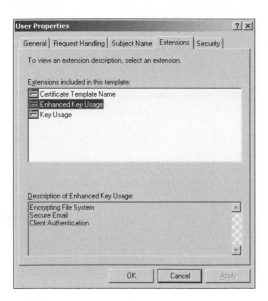

**FIGURE 13.3**    Default properties for the User certificate.

Windows Server 2003 contains a large number of certificates, and each has an assigned set of settings and purposes. In essence, certificates can be categorized into six different functional areas:

- **Server Authentication**—These certificates can be used to authenticate servers to clients as well as provide authentication between servers.

- **Client Authentication**—These certificates are used to provide client authentication to servers or server-side services.

- **Secure Email**—Users can digitally sign and encrypt email.

- **Encrypting File System**—These certificates are used to encrypt and decrypt files using EFS.

- **File Recovery**—These certificates are used for recovering encrypted EFS files.

- **Code Signing**—These certificates can sign content and applications. Code signing certificates help users and services trust code.

### Customizing Certificate Templates

To customize a certificate template to be used in the network environment, use the Certificate Templates snap-in, as shown in Figure 13.4. To use this snap-in, do the following:

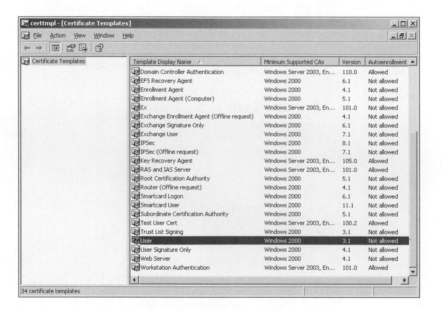

**FIGURE 13.4**    The Certificate Templates snap-in.

1. Open the Run dialog box from the Start menu and type **MMC**.

2. In the MMC console window, select Add/Remove Snap-in from the File menu.

3. Click the Add button and select the Certificate Templates snap-in.

4. Click Add and then click Close.

5. Click OK when done.

6. In the left pane, select Certificate Templates. This will display in the right pane all the available certificate templates.

7. Right-click the template to modify and select Duplicate Template. For this example, select the User certificate template.

8. Type the certificate template display name from within the General tab, as shown in Figure 13.5.

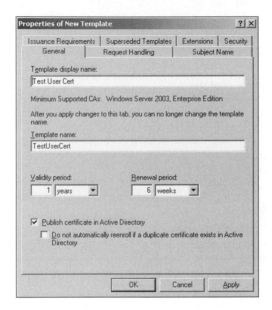

**FIGURE 13.5**    Customizing a certificate template.

9. Within the Request Handling tab, verify that the purpose of the certificate is to provide signature and encryption capabilities.

10. On the Issuance Requirements tab, select whether the certificate requires manager approval and the number of authorized signatures that are required. These options control how and when users can get the certificate.

11. On the Security tab, check which users will have enroll or auto-enroll rights. By default, the Domain Users group has enroll permissions.

12. Click OK when done.

## Smartcards in a PKI Infrastructure

A robust solution for PKI can be found in the introduction of smartcard authentication for users. Smartcards are small devices that have a microchip embedded in them; this chip enables them to store unique information in each card. User login information, as well as certificates installed from a CA server, can be placed on a smartcard. When a user needs to log in to a system, the user places the smartcard in a smartcard reader or simply swipes it across the reader itself. The certificate is read, and the user is prompted only for a PIN, which is uniquely assigned to each user. After the PIN and the certificate are verified, the user can log in to the domain.

> **NOTE**
>
> Smartcards can also be used to complement the use of passwords. For instance, strong passwords can be used in addition to a PIN number if the organization's security policy dictates very strong authentication requirements.

Smartcards have obvious advantages over standard forms of authentication. It is no longer possible to simply steal or guess someone's username and password, because the username can be entered only via the unique smartcard. If stolen or lost, the smartcard can be immediately deactivated and the certificate revoked. Even if a functioning smartcard were to fall into the wrong hands, the PIN would still need to be used to properly access the system. Smartcards are fast becoming a more accepted way to integrate the security of certificates and PKI into organizations.

## Certificate Enrollment

Users must first be issued certificates before they are able to sign or encrypt messages. How users obtain the certificates depends on the organization's security policy and procedures and the infrastructure that is in place to support certificate services. If the organization is using Windows Server 2003 Certificate Services, users can obtain certificates in the following manner:

- Auto-enrollment
- Using smartcards
- Using the Web enrollment form
- Using the MMC

> **NOTE**
>
> When using Windows Server 2003 Certificate Services (PKI), public keys are stored in the AD, which enables users in the AD to encrypt messages for others in the AD. Private keys, on the other hand, are typically stored on the user's computer or on a smartcard.

Use the following steps to request a certificate using the MMC:

1. Type `certmgr.msc` from the Start, Run command window.

2. In the Certificate Manager window, expand Certificates—Current User.

3. Right-click on Personal and select All Tasks, Request New Certificate.

4. Click Next in the Certificate Request Wizard and then select the User certificate. It is important to note that these certificates must be made available to the users. Refer to the section "Customizing Certificate Templates," earlier in this chapter, for more information on how to provide certificates to users.

5. Click Next and then type the friendly name for the certificate.

6. Click Next and then Finish when done.

In the Certificate Manager window, click on the Personal, Certificates folder to display the certificates that have been issued to the current user, as shown in Figure 13.6.

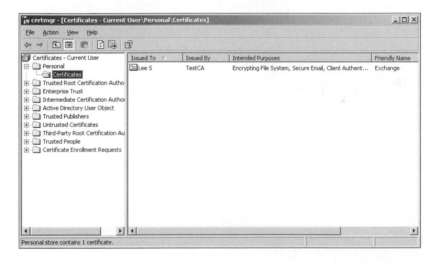

**FIGURE 13.6**   Displaying issued certificates of a user, using the Certificate Manager.

---

**TIP**

The Active Directory Users and Computers snap-in can be used to display which certificates have been issued to a user. Select Advanced Features from the View menu and then double-click the user. The certificates can be viewed on the Published Certificates tab, as illustrated in Figure 13.7.

---

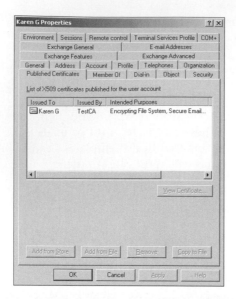

**FIGURE 13.7** Displaying issued certificates of a user, using Active Directory Users and Computers.

# Supporting S/MIME

Secure/Multipurpose Internet Mail Extensions (S/MIME) is used to digitally sign and encrypt messages. Digital signatures provide authentication, non-repudiation, and data integrity, and encryption keeps message contents confidential.

To support S/MIME, X.509 digital certificates are used. The certificate identifies information about the certificate's owner and includes the owner's public key information. X.509 is the industry standard for digital certificates. The Windows Server 2003 certificate templates that support S/MIME are Exchange User, Exchange Signature Only (for only digital signatures), Smartcard User, and User.

## Supporting Digital Signatures

Signing a message generates a random checksum that is added to the message. The random checksum is the message's fingerprint or digital signature, which is then encrypted using the user's private signing key. The user then sends the message to the recipient that includes three items: the message in plain text, the sender's X.509 digital certificate, and the digital certificate.

The recipient checks the Certificate Revocation List (CRL) to see whether the sender's certificate is on the list. If the certificate is not on the list, the digital signature is decrypted with the sender's public signing key. If it is on the CRL, the recipient is warned that the sender's certificate has been revoked. The recipient's client then generates a checksum from the plain text message and compares it to the digital signature. If the checksums match, the recipient knows the sender is the one who sent the message. If they do not match, the recipient is warned that the message has been tampered with.

## Message Encryption

The process of encrypting a message generates a random *bulk encryption key* that is used to encrypt the contents of the message. The sender uses the recipient's public key to encrypt the bulk encryption key. For this process to work, the sender must have a copy of the recipient's digital certificate. The certificate can be retrieved from either the Global Address List (GAL) or the sender's Contact list. The digital certificate contains the recipient's public encryption key, which is used to create the lockbox for the bulk encryption key.

When the recipient receives the message, he or she will use a private encryption key to decrypt and gain access to the bulk encryption key. The bulk encryption key is then used to decrypt the message. The Exchange User, Smartcard User, and User certificate templates have encryption and decryption capabilities.

> **NOTE**
>
> With Exchange SP1 and higher, antivirus software using the Virus Scanning API (VSAPI) 2.5 can scan digitally signed or encrypted messages.

## Comparing PGP and S/MIME

Pretty Good Privacy (PGP) is similar to S/MIME because it can sign and encrypt messages. It is an alternative to using S/MIME.

Use PGP in the following situations:

- For single users or small workgroups
- If there are many different types of mail clients

Use S/MIME for the following situations:

- For larger environments
- For standardization
- If Outlook is the primary (or only) mail client
- If you want to make secure email transparent to the end-user

# Protecting Communications with IP Security (IPSec)

IPSec is a mechanism or policy for establishing end-to-end encryption of all data packets sent between computers. IPSec operates at Layer 3 of the OSI model and subsequently uses packets for all traffic between computers participating in the IPSec policy.

13

IPSec is often considered to be one of the best ways to secure the traffic generated in an environment, and is useful for securing servers and workstations, both in high-risk Internet access scenarios and also in private network configurations as an enhanced layer of security.

## Fundamentals of IPSec

As mentioned earlier, all traffic between participating computers (whether initiated by an application, the operating system, services, and so on) is encrypted. IPSec places its own header on each encrypted packet and sends the packets to the destination server to be decrypted. The primary advantage to this is that it helps prevent eavesdropping and discourages unauthorized access.

As you can imagine, IPSec requires additional processing overhead in order to efficiently encrypt and decrypt data as it moves among the participating computers. There are network interface cards (NICs) that have built-in support for IPSec and which offload much of the processing overhead. These NICs are highly recommended in a production environment.

### Key IPSec Functionality

IPSec in Windows Server 2003 provides the following key functionality:

- **Data Privacy**—All information sent from one IPSec machine to another is thoroughly encrypted by such algorithms as 3DES, which effectively prevent the unauthorized viewing of sensitive data.

- **Data Integrity**—The integrity of IPSec packets is enforced through ESP headers, which verify that the information contained within an IPSec packet has not been tampered with.

- **Anti-Replay Capability**—IPSec prevents streams of captured packets from being re-sent, known as a "replay" attack.

- **Per Packet Authenticity**—IPSec uses certificates or Kerberos authentication to ensure that the sender of an IPSec packet is actually an authorized user.

- **NAT Transversal**—Windows Server 2003's implementation of IPSec now enables IPSec to be routed through current NAT implementations, a concept that will be defined more thoroughly in the following sections.

- **Diffie-Hellman 2048-Bit Key Support**—Virtually unbreakable Diffie-Hellman 2048-bit key lengths are supported in Windows Server 2003's IPSec implementation, assuring that the IPSec key cannot easily be broken.

## IPSec NAT Transversal (NAT-T)

IPSec in Windows Server 2003 supports the concept of Network Address Translation Transversal (NAT-T). Understanding how NAT-T works requires a full understanding of the need for NAT itself.

Network Address Translation (NAT) was developed because not enough IP addresses were available for all the clients on the Internet. Because of this, private IP ranges were established (10.x.x.x, 192.168.x.x, and so on) to enable all clients in an organization to have a unique IP address in their own private space. These IP addresses were designed to not route through the public IP address space, and a mechanism was needed to translate them into a valid, unique public IP address.

NAT was developed to fill this role. It normally resides on firewall servers or routers to provide NAT capabilities between private and public networks. RRAS for Windows Server 2003 also provides NAT capabilities.

Because the construction of the IPSec packet does not enable NAT addresses, IPSec traffic has, in the past, been dropped at NAT servers, because there was no way to physically route the information to the proper destination. This posed major barriers to the widespread implementation of IPSec because many of the clients on the Internet today are addressed via NAT.

NAT Transversal, which is a new feature in Windows Server 2003's IPSec implementation, was jointly developed as an Internet standard by Microsoft and Cisco Systems. NAT-T works by sensing that a NAT network needs to be transversed and subsequently encapsulating the entire IPSec packet into a UDP packet with a normal UDP header. NAT handles UDP packets flawlessly, and they are subsequently routed to the proper address on the other side of the NAT.

NAT Transversal works well but requires that both ends of the IPSec transaction understand the protocol so as to properly pull the IPSec packet out of the UDP encapsulation. With the latest IPSec client and server, NAT-T becomes a reality and is positioned to make IPSec into a much bigger success than it is today.

## Configuring IPSec

IPSec is built into Windows Server 2003 and is also available for clients. In fact, basic IPSec functionality can easily be set up in an environment that is running Windows Server 2003's Active Directory, because IPSec can use the Kerberos authentication functionality in lieu of certificates. While the process of installing IPSec is a fairly straightforward process, configuring it properly so that traffic is filtered as desired is not. Adequate time should be spent thoroughly testing the IPSec implementation. The prototype should include building filter lists to help define what should be filtered such as the example provided in Table 13.1, working with IPSec templates, and analyzing server to server as well as client to server communication in a lab environment.

**TABLE 13.1**  Sample IPSec filter list

| Service | Protocol | Src. Port | Dest. Port | Src. Addr. | Dest. Addr. | Action | Mirror |
|---------|----------|-----------|------------|------------|-------------|--------|--------|
| ICMP | ICMP | ANY | ANY | ME | ANY | ALLOW | YES |
| DNS | TCP | ANY | 53 | ANY | ME | ALLOW | YES |
| All IP Traffic | ANY | ANY | ANY | ANY | ME | NEGOTIATE | YES |

## Establishing an IPSec Policy

Although other policies can be customized to fit the organization's security requirements, three predefined IPSec policies are built into Windows Server 2003:

- **Server (Request Security)**—This policy option requests but does not require IPSec communications. Choosing this option enables the server to communicate with other non-IPSec clients, and is recommended for organizations with fewer security needs or those in the midst of, but not finished with, an implementation of IPSec.

- **Client (Respond Only)**—This option enables the configured client computer to respond to requests for IPSec communications.

- **Secure Server (Require Security)**   The most secure policy option is the Require Security option, which stipulates that all network traffic to and from the server must be encrypted with IPSec.

To establish a simple IPSec policy on a server, do the following:

1. Choose Local Security Policy from the Start, Administrative Tools menu.

2. Navigate to Security Settings\IP Security Policies on Local Computer.

3. In the right pane, right-click Server (Request Security) and select Assign.

To establish a simple IPSec policy on a Windows XP client, do the following:

1. Choose Local Security Policy from the Start, Administrative Tools menu. The Administrative Tools must be enabled in the Task Manager view settings.

2. Navigate to Security Settings\IP Security Policies on Local Computer.

3. In the right pane, right-click Client (Respond Only) and select Assign.

To configure more complex IPSec policies, it is recommended to use the `netsh` command. You can determine the arguments to `netsh` by simply typing it on the command line. The arguments that you use with the command can be used to create and manage IPSec filters and rules as well. Two simple samples of the command-line options follow. Microsoft's "Windows Server 2003 Security Guide" that can be downloaded at http://www.microsoft.com/downloads/ provides a full sample IPSec script that you can tailor and test.

```
netsh ipsec static add filter filterlist="ICMP" srcaddr=any dstaddr=me
description="ICMP traffic" protocol=ICMP srcport=0 dstport=0

netsh ipsec static add rule name="ICMP Rule" policy="Packet Filters - DC"
filterlist="ICMP" kerberos=yes filteraction=SecPermit
```

## Transport Layer Security

Transport Layer Security (TLS) is another, lesser-known method of encrypting traffic. It is essentially a newer version of SSL and is used primarily to encrypt SMTP-specific traffic, particularly SMTP connector–related traffic. TLS encryption can also be used with Basic or Integrated Windows Authentication to protect credentials as they are being transmitted.

# Locking Down SMTP

SMTP is the de facto messaging standard—not only for Exchange Server 2003 but also for the industry. This service is not built into Exchange Server 2003 but rather is a service provided by Windows Server 2003. Nonetheless, SMTP security and other parameters can be easily configured through the Exchange System Manager (ESM).

## General SMTP Security Best Practices

Some general security best practices for SMTP include, but are not limited to, the following:

- **Limit Message Size**—Limiting the size of incoming and outgoing emails not only helps save disk space on the Exchange Server 2003 server, it also minimizes Denial of Service (DoS) vulnerabilities.

- **Disable Auto-replies**—The classic out-of-office or on-vacation message that users may configure are essentially messages informing a hacker that "I'm not at home." Users are notorious for also giving information, such as contact information, in these auto-reply receipts that should not necessarily be shared with anyone that sends them an email.

- **Restrict User Access**—Allowing only authenticated users to send email prevents unauthorized users from using the system for spam or other nonapproved messaging.

- **Control SMTP Connections**—Controlling which IP addresses or domains that can send emails will greatly reduce spam, spam-relaying, and DoS attacks.

- **Hide the SMTP Greeting**   Hide the SMTP greeting so that hackers must work even harder to discover which messaging system they are trying to attack.

## Configuring Message Delivery Limits

Message delivery limits prevent users from sending large messages through Exchange. Large messages tie up Exchange resources (processing time, queue availability, disk storage, and more) and if misused can be just as bad as experiencing a DoS attack. It also molds users into using better, alternative delivery methods, such as file shares, compression of attachments, and even document management portals. Exchange Server 2003 uses a 10,240KB (10MB) message size limit by default, and this can be easily set to smaller sizes.

Another important message delivery limit that can be used to secure Exchange Server 2003 involves the number of recipients that a message can be sent to at any one time. Limiting the maximum number of recipients limits internal users' ability to essentially spam the enterprise with large numbers of emails. Exchange Server 2003 limits the number of recipients per message to 5,000 recipients. Using public folders in addition to a limitation on the maximum number of recipients can also mold users into working more efficiently with Exchange Server 2003.

To configure Exchange Server 2003 message delivery limits, do the following:

1. Open the ESM by choosing System Manager from the Start, All Programs, Microsoft Exchange menu.

2. Expand Global Settings and then right-click Message Delivery and select Properties.

3. On the Defaults tab, adjust the limits for Sending message size or Receiving message size.

4. To control the number of recipients per message, adjust the Recipients limits setting.

> **TIP**
>
> Distribution Groups are expanded when evaluating the maximum recipients limit. It might be necessary to override some users (for example, the Human Resources [HR] department) with No Limit in Active Directory Users and Computers to allow them to use an All Employees distribution group.

## Securing SMTP Virtual Servers

Security configuration parameters can be found within the SMTP virtual server's Property pages. To view the Property pages for a server's SMTP virtual server, do the following:

1. Open the ESM by choosing System Manager from the Start, All Programs, Microsoft Exchange menu.

2. Expand the Exchange Organization, the Administrative Group where the server resides, the Exchange Server 2003 server, the Protocols folder, and finally the SMTP folder.

3. Right-click the Default SMTP Virtual Server and select Properties.

### Using Authentication Controls

All three of the supported authentication methods supported by the SMTP virtual server (that is, anonymous, Basic, and Integrated Windows Authentication) are enabled as illustrated in Figure 13.8. Although this configuration might appear to be completely insecure, it depends on the organization's security policy and whether the SMTP virtual server is accessible by a host on the Internet. Many SMTP hosts do not require usernames and passwords and instead rely on other methods to secure access. If the organization has only a small number of SMTP hosts accessing the SMTP virtual server, use either Basic with TLS or Integrated Windows Authentication.

**FIGURE 13.8**   Authentication methods supported by SMTP virtual servers.

> **CAUTION**
>
> Checking the option to resolve anonymous email might leave the messaging environment susceptible to spoofing. Spoofing is essentially the ability for an unauthorized user to masquerade as a valid or authorized user. It can give users and hackers the ability to forge messages as if they were being sent from a legitimate user.

These options are accessible by clicking the Authentication button on the Access tab within the SMTP virtual server's Property pages.

### Securing Communications

Communications with the SMTP virtual server can be secured using digital certificates and encryption. More specifically, using encryption can be made a requirement through the use of TLS. To secure communications using TLS, do the following:

1. Within the SMTP virtual server's Property pages, select the Access tab.

2. Click on the Certificate button within the Secure communications section to start the Web Server Certificate Wizard. Click Next to bypass the welcome screen.

3. As illustrated in Figure 13.9, there are several options for obtaining a digital certificate, including creating a new one, assigning an existing certificate, importing, or copying a certificate from another site.

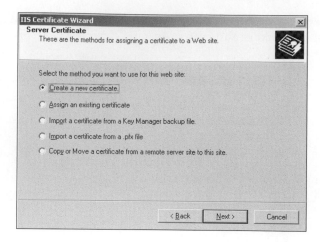

**FIGURE 13.9**    Requesting a digital certificate for the SMTP virtual server.

4. Click Next and then select the certificate to use. The options vary depending on the option chosen in the previous step.

5. Click Next and then review the certificate summary window.

6. Click Next and then Finish when done.

At this point, the certificate is installed but the secure communications is not enabled. To require encrypted communications, do the following:

1. Click on the now visible Communications button.

2. In the Security window check the check box to require encrypted communications.

3. Optionally, check the check box to require 128-bit encryption. This option is recommended when using TLS.

### Restricting Access to the SMTP Virtual Server

Access to the SMTP virtual server can be restricted based on the IP address, subnet, or domain. These options are found by clicking the Connection button on the Access tab.

## Controlling SMTP Relaying

SMTP relay servers deliver messages without regarding the recipient or sender. This functionality is very useful to many organizations, but if the relay is wide open, spammers can and will prey on it whenever possible so that thousands upon thousands of messages can be easily broadcast without ever disclosing their true point of origin. For instance, an organization might need to relay alerts and notifications from internal systems to users. A monitoring solution, such as Microsoft Operations Manager (MOM), can be configured to send email alerts to the administrator via a relay server if the Exchange server goes down. Another example would be to enable Unix servers to relay backup reports and logs to administrators.

> **NOTE**
>
> Relaying can also be enabled on an SMTP connector if the Allow Messages to Be Relayed to These Domains option is checked on the Address Space tab of the SMTP connector's Property pages.

The good news is that Exchange Server 2003 must be manually configured to enable any SMTP relaying. However, more often than not many organizations still are unknowingly SMTP relays because of misconfigurations or carelessness.

As spam enters an organization, administrators can view the SMTP header to reveal the SMTP relay server from which the message originated. The spammed organization can then either complain to the organization that was used as a relay—or worse, add the SMTP relay server to a relay blacklist. These blacklists, which Exchange Server 2003 supports, help reduce spam but can wreak havoc for organizations that are unknowingly relaying because messages can be blocked so that spam is not further propagated using your SMTP relay.

> **NOTE**
>
> Use the Exchange Best Practices Analyzer (ExBPA) tool to check whether or not the server is configuring to relay. For more information on ExBPA, refer to Chapter 12, "Server-Level Security."

If your organization must use relaying, there are security measures that can be taken to prevent SMTP relay abuse. Connection control methods, similar to what was described in the earlier section "Restricting Access to the SMTP Virtual Server," can restrict access to the SMTP relay based on IP addresses, subnets, and domains. Domain restrictions require reverse lookups, however, which can severely affect server performance. In addition to connection control, relaying can be controlled through the use of authentication methods.

### Using Authentication to Secure a Relay Server

In Exchange 2003, the administrator can grant or deny relay permissions to specific users and groups. Relay permissions give the user the right to use the SMTP virtual server to send mail to a destination outside the organization. More specifically, relaying can be restricted using Discretionary Access Control Lists (DACLs), which enables more granularities with restrictions. Restricting relaying on SMTP virtual servers is useful to allow a group of users to relay mail to the Internet, but deny relay privileges for others.

For outbound connections, authentication can be configured to control connections from the SMTP relay server to other messaging servers. These options can be located by doing the following:

13

1. Click the Delivery tab within the SMTP virtual server's Property pages.

2. Click Outbound Security to view the authentication options.

The authentication options for outbound security allow you to choose only one type of authentication to use, which is not the case for the inbound security settings. When either Basic or Integrated Windows Authentication is used, additional information must be supplied and the other servers must support authentication. If Basic is chosen, a username and password must be supplied by the SMTP relay server. On the other hand, if Integrated Windows Authentication is to be used, a valid account and password must be supplied. In either case, TLS can be used and is recommended.

# Securing Routing Group Connectors

A collection of messaging servers connected via high-speed bandwidth (512KB or higher) in Exchange Server 2003 is defined as a *routing group*. By default, one routing group is created. Anytime a server is added to a routing group the connections between the servers are automatically configured.

Another purpose for the routing group is communicating with other routing groups through specialized connectors. When routing groups communicate with other routing groups, they do so through designated servers most commonly known as *bridgehead servers*. Exchange Server 2003 provides many such connectors that can connect to other Exchange servers as well as foreign messaging environments, such as Lotus Notes. The most common connector in Exchange Server 2003 is the SMTP connector. As the name implies, the SMTP connector uses the SMTP protocol, but other connectors use SMTP by default as well. Other commonly used routing groups include the X.400 and the routing group connectors.

> **NOTE**
>
> Routing group connector security is strong by default and there is minimal configuration. However, this connector does not support encryption unless the servers participate in an IPSec policy where all traffic is encrypted. If connector communications traffic flows through public networks, use the SMTP connector instead to support encrypted communications.

## Using X.400

X.400 is a long-standing messaging standard that Exchange Server 2003 uses for compatibility with older or foreign messaging systems. It can be configured using either X.25 or TCP/IP.

From a security perspective, X.400 has been superceded by SMTP. One of the key reasons is because SMTP supports strong authentication whereas X.400's authentication is much weaker. For instance, X.400 supports the use of passwords, but the passwords are transmitted in plain text. Use the SMTP connector instead of the X.400 connector whenever possible.

## Securing SMTP Connectors

Exchange Server 2003's SMTP connector can be used to connect to the Internet, to other Exchange servers, to other Exchange organizations, or to other messaging systems. With regard to security there are several key considerations to take in account, including content restrictions, authentication, encryption, and relaying.

### Outbound Security Controls

Outbound security controls can be set on the SMTP connector and are very similar to those mentioned earlier in the section "Using Authentication Controls." These controls provide authentication (anonymous, Basic, and Integrated Windows Authentication) and encryption (using TLS) options. The basic difference between these options and those for the SMTP virtual server is that only one authentication method can be selected.

To configure outbound security controls for the SMTP connector, do the following:

1. In the ESM, expand the administrative and routing groups.

2. Under the defined routing group for the messaging environment, expand the Connectors folder to reveal the SMTP connector.

3. Right-click the SMTP connector and select Properties.

4. Click the Outbound Security button on the Advanced tab.

5. Select the authentication method and whether or not the connector will use TLS. By default, the SMTP connector uses anonymous access.

Integrated Windows Authentication with TLS offers the strongest and securest form of authentication for outbound security and is therefore recommended.

## Using the Internet Mail Wizard

The Internet Mail Wizard is designed to create a secure, reliable, nonrelaying Internet mail SMTP connector. This wizard is not only for inexperienced Exchange Server 2003 administrators, but it is also very useful for even the most experienced. It walks the administrator through the creation of an Internet mail SMTP connector.

To use the Internet Mail Wizard, do the following:

1. Open the ESM by choosing System Manager from the Start, All Programs, Microsoft Exchange menu.

2. Right-click the Exchange organization name and select Internet Mail Wizard.

3. Click Next twice to bypass the Welcome and Prerequisites for Internet Mail windows.

4. Select the Exchange Server 2003 server to create the SMTP connector. The wizard then checks whether the server meets the prerequisites. Click Next when it has completed and passed.

5. Choose whether this connector will send or receive Internet email, as shown in Figure 13.10 and then click Next.

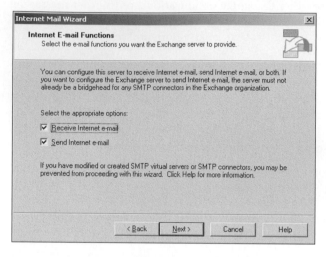

**FIGURE 13.10**    Using the Internet Mail Wizard.

6. Review the domains that will receive email for this Exchange organization and then click Next. Domains can be added or removed at this point if necessary.

7. Select the SMTP virtual server that will be the bridgehead for outbound Internet email and then click Next.

8. Specify whether to use DNS or a smarthost to send Internet email. If DNS will be used and the Exchange Server 2003 will not resolve DNS addresses, enter the external DNS servers. If a smarthost is used, enter the hostname or IP address enclosed in brackets (for example, `[192.168.1.20]`). Click Next to continue.

9. Specify whether to allow delivery to all domains or to specific domains and then click Next.

10. Review the configuration and then click Next.

11. Click Finish when done. Optionally, check the check box to view a detailed configuration report.

# Securing Other Exchange-Supported Protocols

Examining Exchange Server 2003 transport-level security would not be complete without discussing protocols other than SMTP. In addition to SMTP, Exchange Server 2003 supports the following:

- Network News Transfer Protocol (NNTP)

- Post Office Protocol version 3 (POP3)

- Internet Message Access Protocol (IMAP4)

Some notable security features Exchange Server 2003 provides regarding these protocols includes, but is not limited to, the following:

- These protocols are not enabled by default unless the system was upgraded from a previous version of Exchange that also had these services running.

- Each protocol runs as a service and the service is disabled by default.

- IMAP4 and POP3 support Basic authentication over SSL or TLS as well as NTLM-based authentication.

- NNTP supports anonymous (disabled by default), Basic authentication, Integrated Windows Authentication, and SSL client authentication.

- Each protocol supports secure, certificate-based communications.

- Each protocol can use connection controls (IP address or domain names) to grant or deny access.

## Protecting Client–to–Front-End–Server Communications

When clients connect to an Outlook Web Access (OWA) server, the information must be protected to ensure that usernames, passwords, and messaging data are not susceptible to compromise. This protection can be accomplished through the use of SSL on the Internet Information Services (IIS) virtual server. SSL requires a digital certificate that can be supplied either by the organization's PKI or through a third-party, such as VeriSign.

> **NOTE**
>
> Forms-based authentication can be used to help secure OWA by requiring the use of SSL and also improving control over sessions. For instance, user credentials are stored in cookies and when the session times out or the user logs off the cookie is cleared. For information on implementing forms-based authentication, refer to Chapter 10, "Configuring Outlook Web Access and Exchange Mobile Services."

### Automatic SSL Redirection

If SSL is used on the OWA server (and it should be), clients connect to the OWA server by typing `https://<FQDN>/exchange` to log on and use Exchange Server 2003 over the SSL connection. One of the biggest hassles for clients, however, is remembering to use https rather than just http. Using http means using the nonsecure URL. Another hassle is remembering to use `/exchange` to get to OWA.

Administrators can configure automatic redirection for users to more easily connect to and use Exchange Server 2003. This prevents users from mistakingly trying to use the non-secure URL—not to mention keeps the number of helpdesk calls to a minimum if users are not able to gain access to email.

To configure automatic SSL redirection when forms-based authentication is not in use, create a new HTM file called `HTTPSRedirect.htm` with the following contents:

```
<!DOCTYPE HTML PUBLIC "-//W3C//DTD HTML 4.01//EN"
"http://www.w3.org/TR/html4/strict.dtd">
<HTML><HEAD>
<meta http-equiv="refresh" content="0; url=https://webmail.companyabc.com">
</HEAD></HTML>
```

> **NOTE**
>
> For information on how to use forms-based authentication and SSL redirection for OWA, refer to Chapter 10.

## Locking Down Front-End and Back-End Server Communications

The very nature and capabilities of a front-end (FE) and back-end (BE) Exchange Server 2003 configuration lends itself to a more secure environment. An FE server hosts only the Internet Information Services (IIS) virtual server that provides the interface to users and communicates with the BE virtual server. It should not, by definition, host Exchange information stores containing messaging data. Only the back-end servers contain information stores so that messaging data is not easily accessible from outside the organization.

### TCP and UDP Ports

Many organizations place FE servers in the perimeter network (also known as the DMZ) to segment the internal network from those servers requiring some degree of exposure to the Internet. As a result, ports must be opened on the firewall to enable the FE and BE servers to communicate. Other ports might also be necessary depending on the services being offered and the configuration of the messaging environment.

Table 13.2 lists the common inbound ports to open to the OWA FE servers.

**TABLE 13.2**   Inbound Ports to the OWA FE

| Protocol | TCP/UDP | Port Number |
| --- | --- | --- |
| HTTP | TCP | 80 |
| HTTPS | TCP | 443 |
| SMTP | TCP | 25 |
| POP3 | TCP | 110 |
| IMAP | TCP | 143 |

Table 13.3 lists the commonly required ports between FE and BE Exchange Server 2003 servers. Some of these ports are optional, and the specific ports that the organization might require will vary depending on the messaging environment.

> **NOTE**
>
> SSL cannot be used between an FE and BE server. If the organization's security policy dictates that communication between the FE and BE servers is encrypted, implement IPSec. For more information on IPSec, refer to "Protecting Communications with IP Security (IPSec)" earlier in this chapter.

**TABLE 13.3**  Commonly Used Ports Between FE and BE Exchange Servers

| Protocol | TCP/UDP | Port Number |
|---|---|---|
| HTTP | TCP | 80 |
| DNS Lookup | TCP/UDP | 53 |
| Kerberos | TCP/UDP | 88 |
| Network Time Protocol (NTP)— optional | TCP | 123 |
| RPC End Point Mapper | TCP | 135 |
| LDAP | TCP/UDP | 389 |
| Server Message Block (SMB) | TCP | 445 |
| Link State Algorithm | TCP | 691 |
| Global Catalog | TCP | 3268 |

The ports listed in Table 13.4 are optional.

**TABLE 13.4**  Optional Ports Between FE and BE Exchange Servers

| Protocol | TCP/UDP/ID | Port/ID Number |
|---|---|---|
| POP3 | TCP | 110 |
| IMAP | TCP | 143 |
| SMTP | TCP | 25 |
| RPC | TCP | 1024+ |
| IPSec | IP Protocol ID | 50, 51 |
| IPSec | UDP | 500 |

> **TIP**
>
> To avoid having to leave a large number of RPC ports open, statically map them to a standardized port number. To statically map the port, create a registry key value called `TCP/IP Port` of type `REG_DWORD` in `HKEY_LOCAL_MACHINE\SYSTEM\CurrentControlSet\Services\NTDS\Parameters`.

# Summary

Transport-level security is a major security consideration for any organization and can significantly impact server and client-level security methods. Securing the communications between users and servers on a network is vital, and in some cases required by law. This chapter examined the various transport-level security methods supported by Windows Server 2003 and Exchange Server 2003 and provided best practices for securely configuring and effectively locking down an organization's transmission of data.

# Best Practices

The following are best practices from this chapter:

- Thoroughly plan and design the organization's PKI.

- Use a User certificate when users require access to multiple certificate services.

- Customize certificate templates.

- Use smartcards.

- Use S/MIME to sign and encrypt messages.

- Use IPSec to encrypt communications between front-end and back-end servers.

- Thoroughly plan and test IPSec in a lab environment prior to production implementation.

- Limit SMTP message size.

- Use TLS to secure SMTP.

- Disable auto-replies.

- Control the distribution group maximum recipients limit.

- Use the strongest authentication methods possible.

- Avoid allowing anonymous access.

- Secure mail relay servers.

- Configure automatic SSL redirection.

- Open only ports that are absolutely necessary for communication.

# PART V

## Migrating to Exchange Server 2003

## IN THIS PART

| | | |
|---|---|---|
| **CHAPTER 14** | Migrating from NT4 to Windows Server 2003 | 421 |
| **CHAPTER 15** | Migrating from Exchange v5.5 to Exchange Server 2003 | 451 |
| **CHAPTER 16** | Migrating from Exchange 2000 to Exchange Server 2003 | 483 |
| **CHAPTER 17** | Compatibility Testing | 509 |

# Migrating from NT4 to Windows Server 2003

**IN THIS CHAPTER**

- Microsoft Active Directory Configuration

- Upgrading a Single Member Server

- Upgrading an NT 4.0 Domain Structure to Active Directory via the In-Place Upgrade Process

- Migrating Existing NT4 Domains to a New Windows Server 2003 Forest

- Understanding and Using the Microsoft Active Directory Migration Tool 2.0 (ADMT v2)

- Migrating Accounts Using the Active Directory Migration Tool

## Microsoft Active Directory Configuration

Before the many benefits of Exchange Server 2003 can be realized, the directory for Exchange, Microsoft's Active Directory, must be created and configured. In some cases where no existing infrastructure is in place, this involves designing and implementing an Active Directory infrastructure from scratch. Most environments, however, use an existing Windows 2000 or Windows NT domain infrastructure. Organizations wherein Windows 2000 Active Directory is deployed can upgrade to Windows Server 2003 Active Directory, or simply not upgrade before deploying Exchange. Because Exchange Server 2003 can be installed on either directory platform, the decision is not critical.

With Windows NT 4.0 domains, however, you must upgrade to Active Directory to be able to support the directory requirements of Exchange Server 2003. For this reason, this chapter details the options available for migrations from NT to Windows Server 2003 and explores the various pros and cons of each approach. In addition, step-by-step example best-practice migration strategies are presented and detailed.

### Defining the Migration Process

Any migration procedure requires a defined procedure that details the reasons for migration, steps involved, fallback precautions, and other important factors that can influence the migration process. When these items have been finalized, the steps toward performing the migration implementation can be accomplished and the performance increases can be realized.

## Defining Exchange Server 2003 Objectives

As part of any migration project, establishing project objectives are a critical but often overlooked aspect of a project. Without objectives, it becomes difficult to define whether a project has been successful. Although there are significant improvements between Windows NT 4.0 domains and Windows Server 2003 AD, the ultimate decision to upgrade might be to support Exchange Server 2003. As previously mentioned, Exchange Server 2003 requires a functional Windows 2000/2003 Active Directory implementation for its directory, and this might force an organization to upgrade.

> **NOTE**
>
> Although it is necessary for Exchange 2000/2003 to use an Active Directory forest for directory and authentication purposes, there is one scenario in which an existing NT 4.0 domain can be preserved, if desired or required. Exchange Server 2003 can be installed in a new, separate AD forest, with a manual trust established to the production NT domain. The NT domain accounts can then be granted full mailbox privileges to the Mailbox-enabled user accounts that can be created in the AD domain. This type of design is referred to as the "Resource forest" Exchange model.

## Establishing Migration Project Phases

After the decision has been made to upgrade, a detailed plan of the resources, timeline, scope, and objectives of the project should be outlined. Establishing a project plan, whether ad hoc or professionally drawn up, should be part of any migration plan, to assist in accomplishing the planned objectives in a timely manner with the correct application of resources.

A condensed form of the standard phases for a migration project is detailed as follows:

- **Discovery**—The first portion of a design project should be a discovery, or fact-finding portion. This section focuses on the analysis of the current environment and documentation of the results of the analysis. Current network diagrams, server locations, WAN throughputs, server application dependencies, and all other relevant sections should be detailed as part of the Discovery phase.

- **Design**—The Design portion of a project is a straightforward concept. All key components of the actual migration plan should be documented and key data from the Discovery phase should be used to draw up Design and Migration documents. The project plan itself would normally be drafted during this phase. This is especially true with Windows NT 4.0 because there are significant differences in structure between NT and Windows Server 2003.

- **Prototype**—The Prototype phase of a project involves the essential lab work to test the design assumptions that were made during the Design phase. The ideal prototype would involve a mock production environment that is migrated from Windows NT 4.0 to Windows Server 2003. Step-by-step procedures for migration can also be outlined and produced as deliverables for this phase.

- **Pilot**—The Pilot phase, or Proof-of-Concept phase, involves a production "test" of the migration steps, on a limited scale. For example, a single domain controller could be upgraded to Windows Server 2003 in advance of the migration of all other domain controllers.

- **Implementation**—The Implementation portion of the project is the full-blown migration of network functionality or upgrades to the operating system. This process can be done quickly or slowly over time, depending on the needs of an organization. Make the timeline decisions in the Design phase and incorporate them into the project plan.

- **Training and Support**—Learning the ins and outs of the new functionality that Windows Server 2003 can bring to an environment is essential towards the realization of the increased productivity and reduced administration that the OS can bring to an environment. Consequently, it is important to include a training portion in a migration project, so that the design objectives can be fully realized.

For more detailed information on the project plan phases of a migration, reference Chapter 2, "Planning, Prototyping, Migrating, and Deploying Exchange Server 2003."

## Examining In-Place Upgrade Versus New Hardware Migration Approaches

Because the underlying operating system kernel is similar between Windows NT 4.0 and Windows Server 2003, the possibility exists to simply upgrade an existing Windows NT Server in place. Depending on the type of hardware currently in use in a Windows NT 4.0 network, this type of migration strategy becomes an option. That said, it is highly recommended and definitely safer to simply introduce newer systems into an existing environment and retire the current servers from production. This type of technique normally has less impact on current environments and can also support fallback more easily.

Which migration strategy to choose depends on one major factor: the condition of the current hardware environment. If Windows NT 4.0 is taxing the limitations of the hardware in use, it might be preferable to introduce new servers into an environment and retire the old Windows NT 4.0 servers. If, however, the hardware in use for Windows NT 4.0 is newer and more robust, and could conceivably last for another 2–3 years, it might be easier to perform in-place upgrades of the systems in an environment.

In most cases, a dual approach to migration is taken. Older hardware is replaced by new hardware running Windows Server 2003. Newer Windows NT 4.0 systems are upgraded in place to Windows Server 2003. Consequently, performing an audit of all systems to be migrated and determining which ones will be upgraded and which ones will be retired is an important step in the migration process.

## Choosing a Migration Strategy

As with many technology implementations, there are two approaches that can be taken regarding deployment: a quick, "Big-Bang" approach, or a phased, slower approach. The

Big-Bang option involves quickly replacing the entire Windows NT 4.0 infrastructure (often over the course of a weekend) with the new Windows Server 2003 environment. The phased approach involves a slow, server-by-server replacement of Windows NT 4.0. Each approach has its advantages and disadvantages, and there are key factors of Windows Server 2003 to take into account before a decision is made.

Because there are fundamental structural changes between the NT domain structure and Active Directory, the argument of not maintaining two conflicting and redundant environments for long periods of time supports the Big-Bang approach. That said, there are situations in which the phased approach might be more appealing. Larger organizations with a heavy investment in Windows NT 4.0 might determine that a phased approach will help divide the upgrade into manageable components. Other risk-averse organizations might decide to minimize risk through the use of this strategy. Windows Server 2003 easily accommodates both migration options.

## Exploring Migration Options

Migration to Windows Server 2003 can be precipitated by one of many factors. In the case of Exchange Server 2003, the necessity of an Active Directory infrastructure in place requires that the infrastructure be upgraded to support it. Other reasons also might justify the upgrade, such as improvements in reliability, scalability, and a lower Total Cost of Ownership (TCO). In any case, an upgrade from NT 4.0 to Windows Server 2003 can be done in several ways.

# Upgrading a Single Member Server

The direct upgrade approach from Windows NT 4.0 to Windows Server 2003 is the most straightforward approach to migration. The upgrade takes all settings on a single server and upgrades them to Windows Server 2003. If a Windows NT 4.0 server handles WINS, DNS, and DHCP, the process upgrades all WINS, DNS, and DHCP components, as well as the base operating system. This type of migration is very tempting, and it can be extremely effective, as long as all prerequisites (mentioned later) are satisfied.

Often, upgrading a single server can be a project. The standalone member servers in an environment are often the workhorses of the network, loaded with a myriad of different applications and critical tools. Performing an upgrade on these servers would be simple if they were used only for file or print duties and if their hardware systems were all up-to-date. Because this is not always the case, it is important to detail the specifics of each server that is marked for migration.

## Verifying Hardware Compatibility

Testing the hardware compatibility of any server that will be directly upgraded to Windows Server 2003 is critical. During the installation process is not the most ideal time to be notified of problems with compatibility between older system components and the drivers required for Windows Server 2003. Verify the hardware in a server for Windows

Server 2003 on the manufacturer's Web site, or on Microsoft's Hardware Compatibility List (HCL).

Microsoft offers minimum hardware levels that Windows Server 2003 will run on, but it is *highly* recommended to install the OS on systems of a much higher caliber, as these recommendations do not take into account any application loads, domain controller duties, and so forth. The following is a list of Microsoft's recommended hardware levels for Windows Server 2003:

- 550MHz CPU

- 256MB RAM

- 1.5GB free disk space

It cannot be stressed enough that it is almost always recommended to exceed these levels to provide a robust computing environment.

14

> **NOTE**
>
> One of the most important features that mission-critical servers can have is redundancy. Putting the operating system on a mirrored array of disks, for example, is a simple yet effective way of increasing redundancy in an environment.

## Verifying Application Readiness

Nothing ruins a migration process like a mission-critical application that will not work in the new environment. List all applications on a server that will be required in the new environment. Applications that will not be used or whose functionality is replaced in Windows Server 2003 can be retired and removed from consideration. Applications that have been verified for Windows Server 2003 can be designated as "safe" for upgrade. Delegate any other applications that might not be compatible but are necessary to another server, or force the upgrade to wait on that specific server.

In addition to the applications, the version of the operating system that will be upgraded is an important consideration in the process. A Windows NT 4.0 Server install can be upgraded to either Windows Server 2003 Standard Server or Windows Server 2003 Enterprise. A Windows NT 4.0 Enterprise Edition install can be upgraded *only* to Windows Server 2003 Enterprise, however.

## Backing Up and Creating a Recovery Process

It is critical that a migration does not cause more harm to an environment than good. A good backup system put in place is essential for quick recovery in the event of upgrade failure. Often, especially with the in-place upgrade scenario, a full system backup is the only way to recover, and you should detail fallback steps in the event of problems.

## Outlining Standalone Server Upgrade Steps

After all considerations regarding applications and hardware compatibility have been thoroughly validated, the process of upgrading a standalone server can be accomplished. The following steps detail the process involved with this type of upgrade process:

1. Insert the Windows Server 2003 CD into the CD drive of the server to be upgraded.

2. The welcome page should appear automatically. If not, select Start, Run, and type *X:\Setup* (where *X:* is the CD drive).

3. Click on Install Windows Server 2003.

4. Select Upgrade from the drop-down box, as illustrated in Figure 14.1, and click Next to continue.

**FIGURE 14.1**    Upgrading to Windows Server 2003.

5. Click I Accept This Agreement at the License screen and click Next to continue.

6. The next dialog box prompts you to enter the 25-character product key. This number can be found on the CD case or in the license documentation from Microsoft. Enter it and click Next to continue.

7. The next prompt is crucial. It indicates which system components are not compatible with Windows Server 2003. It will indicate important factors such as the fact that IIS will be disabled as part of the install. IIS can be reenabled in the new OS, but is turned off for security reasons. Click Next after reviewing these factors.

8. The system then copies files and reboots, continuing the upgrade process. After all files have been copied, the system is then upgraded to a fully functional install of Windows Server 2003.

> **NOTE**
>
> Many previously enabled components, such as IIS, are turned off by default in Windows Server 2003. Ensure that one of the post-upgrade tasks performed is an audit of all services, so that those disabled can be reenabled.
>
> Additionally, before proceeding with the installation of other Exchange services, connect the server to the Internet and download and install the latest updates and service packs for Exchange 2003. Many features have been updated with Exchange 2003 Service Pack 1 and Service Pack 2 that require the installation of the service packs to be properly configured. Access updates and service packs at `http://www.microsoft.com/exchange/downloads/2003/default.mspx`.

## Upgrading an NT 4.0 Domain Structure to Active Directory via the In-Place Upgrade Process

Upgrading an NT 4.0 domain environment to Windows Server 2003 Active Directory can be accomplished through two methods. As previously mentioned, the first method involves upgrading the domain structure in place. This method is more straightforward and easy to accomplish, but involves a greater degree of risk and does not immediately give the advantages of domain consolidation that can be achieved through the second option, which is migrating the domain accounts into a new AD structure.

This section details the steps required if the first option is chosen. The sample scenarios outlined assume a fairly simple environment, but the overall strategy can easily be ported into a more complex domain structure.

### Upgrading the Windows NT4 Primary Domain Controller

Performing an in-place upgrade of a Windows NT 4.0 domain to Active Directory requires that the machine running the Primary Domain Controller (PDC) role be upgraded to Windows Server 2003. This can either be an existing domain controller, or a new one created solely for the purposes of the upgrade. To perform an in-place upgrade, insert the Windows Server 2003 installation CD-ROM into the CD-ROM drive of the PDC. Then, follow these steps:

1. If the server has autorun enabled, the Windows Server 2003 Setup Wizard screen appears. If it is not enabled, launch the Windows Server 2003 Setup Wizard by running the `Setup.exe` program from the Windows Server 2003 CD-ROM.

2. On the Welcome to Windows Server 2003 Family page, select Install Windows Server 2003 to begin upgrading the PDC to Windows Server 2003 and Active Directory. This step launches the Windows Setup Wizard.

3. On the Welcome to Windows Setup page, select the installation type of Upgrade (Recommended). This begins the upgrade of the Windows NT4 server operating system to Windows Server 2003 and Active Directory. Select Next to continue.

4. On the Licensing Agreement page, use the scroll button to read the Microsoft licensing agreement. After reading the license page, select I Accept This Agreement, and select Next to continue.

5. The copy of Windows Server 2003 should have a license key that came with the Windows Server 2003 CD-ROM software. Enter the 25-character product code and select Next.

The Setup Wizard begins the installation of Windows Server 2003 by copying necessary files to the PDC's hard drive. The upgrade progress can be monitored from the progress bar in the lower-left corner of the installation screen. When the Setup Wizard has completed copying files, the server automatically restarts.

## Upgrading to Active Directory

When the Server Setup Wizard has completed upgrading the operating system to Windows Server 2003, the system restarts automatically and begins running the Active Directory Installation Wizard. To install Microsoft's Active Directory, follow these steps:

1. At the Welcome to the Active Directory Installation Wizard screen, select Next. This upgrades the existing Windows NT4 domain and domain security principles to Active Directory.

> **NOTE**
>
> Choosing this option maintains the existing NT4 Domain and upgrades all domain security principles directly to Active Directory. All NT4 user accounts, domain groups, and computer accounts will automatically be upgraded into the new Active Directory domain. In addition, by using this approach the migration appears transparent to the end-users.

When the installation of Active Directory has completed, the next step is to review the Active Directory Users and Computers management console to ensure that all security principles have been upgraded properly.

2. Because this is an in-place upgrade, at the Create New Domain page, select the option to create a new Domain in a New Forest, and select Next.

3. As mentioned earlier, Active Directory requires Domain Name System (DNS) to be installed before the Active Directory installation can continue. If the network has a DNS Server compatible with Windows Server 2003 and Active Directory, select Yes, I Will Configure the DNS Client.

4. If there is no DNS server on the network and this server is intended to be the first DNS server within the new Active Directory domain, select No, Just Install and Configure DNS on This Computer, and select Next to continue.

5. On the New Domain page, type the DNS name of the domain—for example, **companyabc.com**. Select Next to continue. Before completing the installation, use the

scrollbar to review the server configuration summary page. Ensure that the configuration information is correct. If changes are required, use the Back button to modify the server configuration. If the installation summary is correct, click Next to continue.

6. Before choosing Finish to complete the in-place upgrade, review the Installation Wizard information. This information can identify whether any errors were experienced during setup.

> **NOTE**
>
> It is a good practice to review the server event and system logs upon completing any upgrade. Review each log and identify errors and warnings that can potentially affect the stability of the server that is being upgraded and cause problems with domain authentication.
>
> Also review the Active Directory Users and Computers snap-in to ensure that all security principles have been migrated successfully to Windows Server 2003 and Active Directory.

### Migrating and Replacing Backup Domain Controllers

When the PDC upgrade has been completed, the next step is to either upgrade or replace the remaining network Backup Domain Controllers (BDCs). The preferred method of replacing BDC functionality is by promoting new servers to be Windows Server 2003 domain controllers via the DCPROMO process. However, there may be some instances where existing hardware should be preserved through direct upgrades of the BDCs. In these instances, a direct upgrade can take place.

When performing an upgrade of Windows NT4 BDCs, the Active Directory Installation Wizard offers the opportunity to change a server's domain membership type or server roles. For example, an exiting NT BDC can be migrated to Windows Server 2003 and Active Directory as a member server or a domain controller.

As a rule, upgrading BDCs hosting network services such as DHCP and WINS should be considered first. By migrating vital network services, network downtime and interruption of server-to-server communications are minimized.

## Migrating Existing NT4 Domains to a New Windows Server 2003 Forest

In many instances, it might be more ideal to simply abandon a  badly designed or inefficient NT domain structure and migrate the accounts into a new Active Directory forest. This process can be streamlined through the use of a tool included on the Windows Server 2003 CD: Microsoft Active Directory Migration Tool (ADMT) 2.0 (ADMT v2).

By installing and configuring a new Windows Server 2003 Active Directory domain with pre–Windows 2000 permissions and creating a domain trust between source and target domains, the ADMT can then be used to migrate any Windows NT4 security principle to

Active Directory Domains and Organizational Units. By using this tool, organizations can then migrate security principles incrementally and still maintain shared resources located on each domain.

When using the ADMT to restructure domains, all NT4 security principles are copied or cloned from the Windows NT4 domain and placed into Active Directory in the form of what is called *SIDHistory*. By cloning NT4 security principles, the source domain is left completely in place and uninterrupted, enabling administrators to easily roll back to the previous domain if required.

## Installing and Configuring a New Windows Server 2003 Forest and Domain

Installing a new domain requires the installation of a new AD structure. One of the biggest advantages to this approach is that best-practice AD design can be used, and efficient, effective, and secure AD forests can be constructed. For more information on the best ways to design AD, specifically regarding deployment of Exchange Server 2003, refer to Chapters 4, "Designing Exchange Server 2003 for a Small to Medium Network," and 5, "Designing an Enterprise Exchange Server 2003 Environment."

## Configuring a Domain Trust Between Source Windows NT4 and Target Windows Server 2003 Domains

When migrating existing NT4 domains to a new Active Directory forest root or child domain, the trust relationships must be created between the existing Windows NT4 domains. The existing Windows NT4 domains are referred to as the *source domains*, and the newly created Windows Server 2003 Active Directory domains are the *target domains*. Follow these steps:

1. Begin by first configuring a trust on the target domain. On the Windows Server 2003 domain controller, open the administrator tools and launch Active Directory Domains and Trust Manager. From the Action menu option, open the Properties page for the Active Directory domain and select the Trust tab. This opens the Domain Trust configuration page.

2. Windows Server 2003 and Active Directory trusts are created using the New Trust Wizard. Select New Trust to start the wizard and be guided through the creation of a domain trust. Select Next at the Welcome to the New Trust page. On the Trust Name page, type the name of the Windows NT4 source domain. This enables Active Directory to establish connectivity with the source Windows NT4 domain. Select Next to continue.

---

NOTE

When configuring a domain trust, each domain must have the capability of resolving the domain name to a domain controller's TCP/IP Address. Install the Windows Internet Naming Service (WINS) on the target domain controller and configure the TCP/IP properties on the target and source domain controllers to use the newly installed WINS.

---

3. Select the type of trust to be established. On the Direction of Trust page, select Two-Way, Allowing Connectivity and Access to Resources in Both the Target and Source Domains When Migrating; select Next to continue.

4. To configure outgoing trust properties, select Allow Authentication for All Resources in the Local Domain. This option allows Windows NT4 security principles access to all resources within the Active Directory target domain. Windows Server 2003 will automatically authenticate existing NT4 security principles within the target domain; this allows required administrator accounts access to each domain and domain group memberships. Select Next to continue.

5. The *trust password* is a password other than the domain administrator password. The trust password is unique to the trust being created and will be used by both the source and target domains to authenticate the trust. The same trust password must be used on both the Windows NT4 target domain and Windows Server 2003 source domain trust configurations. Enter a password for this trust to use and select Next to continue.

6. At this point, review the trust configuration; select Back to modify any setting that needs to be changed or select Next to complete creating the trust and view the configuration changes created by the Trust Wizard. Click the Next button to continue.

7. A dialog box will appear asking for confirmation of the ongoing trust. Before continuing, create and establish a trust relationship on the Windows NT4 source domain's Primary Domain Controller. At the Confirm Outgoing Trust page, select No, Do Not Confirm the Outgoing Trust and click Next to continue.

8. Choose No, Do Not Confirm the Incoming Trust option from the Confirm Incoming Trust page. Choose Next to complete the trust configuration. Review the trust configuration and select Finish to close the Trust Wizard.

9. To successfully establish a trust on the Windows NT source domain, the trusted domain must first be configured. To add the target domain to the Windows NT4 trusted domains, open the User Manager for Domains on the Windows NT4 Primary Domain Controller. Click Policies from the menu options and select Trust Relationships. This opens the Windows NT4 Trust Relationship page.

10. Begin by selecting the Add button under Trusted Domains. Enter the name of the target domain and a password that will be used by both domains to authenticate the trust. As mentioned earlier, this password is unique to the trust configuration and should be different from the domain administrator account password. This password will be used only to authenticate the domain trust between the source and target domains.

11. After the trusted domain has been established successfully, select Add under the Trusting Domain section of the page. Enter the name of the target domain and the password used to establish the trust. This adds the target domain to the Windows NT4 trusting domains and completes the configuration of the Windows NT4 trust. Click Close to close the Trust Relationships Dialog screen.

14

**12.** When the trust is created successfully, the New Trust Wizard can now confirm the trust settings. If choosing to validate the trust, use the administrator account name and password of the source domain to test access for both incoming and outgoing connectivity of the domain trust. Click OK to close the open dialog box.

## Migrating Account and Resource NT Domains to Active Directory Domains

Using this option enables administrators to restructure existing Windows NT4 accounts and resources into newly created Windows Server 2003 Active Directory domains and organizational units (OUs).

Migrating account domains and resource domains to Active Directory organizational units allows enhanced security and ease of delegation within the Active Directory domain tree. When the Active Directory domain organizational unit (OU) structure is configured, the domain resources and security principles can be migrated by using the ADMT shown in Figure 14.2.

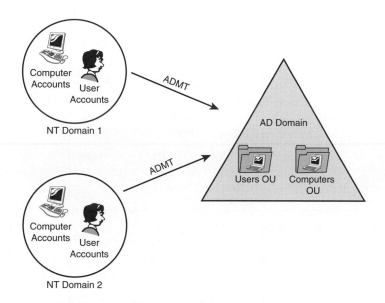

**FIGURE 14.2**    Consolidating NT domains into AD.

## Implication of Migrating Security Principles

When security principles are created in a Windows NT4 domain, each individual object is assigned a unique security identifier or (SID). SIDHistory is a record of each security principle's previous Windows NT4 group and domain membership, and each SID is unique.

When these types of security principles are migrated to Windows Server 2003 and Active Directory, each security principle is assigned a new SID with information about its new domain and group membership. Because the new SID does not contain information about the security principle's previous domain membership, when a user or group accesses domain resources on the old Windows NT4 domain, such as files, users might find that they no longer have permission to specific resources.

To avoid these issues during and after the migration, use the Microsoft ADMT to migrate a security principle's SIDHistory. The ADMT can migrate the security principles SIDHistory for each object, maintaining previous information and avoiding permissions issues later in the migration.

## Understanding and Using the Microsoft Active Directory Migration Tool 2.0 (ADMT v2)

The Active Directory Migration Tool (ADMT) is an effective way to migrate users, groups, and computers from one domain to another. It is robust enough to migrate security permissions and Exchange mailbox domain settings, and it supports a rollback procedure in the event of migration problems. ADMT is composed of several components and functions:

- **ADMT Migration Wizards**—ADMT includes a series of wizards, each specifically designed to migrate specific components. Different wizards exist for migrating Users, Groups, Computers, Service Accounts, and Trusts.

- **Low Client Impact**—ADMT automatically installs a service on source clients, which negates the need to manually install client software for the migration. In addition, after the migration is complete, these services are automatically uninstalled.

- **SIDHistory and Security Migrated**—Users will continue to maintain network access to file shares, applications, and other secured network services through migration of the SIDHistory attributes to the new domain. This preserves the extensive security structure of the source domain.

- **Test Migrations and Rollback Functionality**—An extremely useful feature in ADMT v2 is the ability to run a mock migration scenario with each Migration Wizard. This helps identify any issues that might exist prior to the actual migration work. In addition to this functionality, the most recently performed user, computer, or group migration can be "undone," providing rollback in the event of migration problems.

ADMT v2 installs very easily, but requires knowledge of the various wizards to properly use. In addition, a best-practice process should be used when migrating from one domain to another.

The migration example illustrated in the following sections describes the most common use of the ADMT, an inter-forest migration of domain users, groups, and computers into another domain. This procedure is by no means exclusive, and many other migration techniques can be used to achieve proper results. Matching the capabilities of ADMT with the migration needs of an organization are important.

## Deploying ADMT in the Lab

ADMT v2 comes with unprecedented rollback capabilities. Not only can each wizard be tested first, the last wizard transaction can also be rolled back in the event of problems. In addition to this, however, the environment should be reproduced in a lab setting and test a migration in advance, to mitigate potential problems that might arise.

The most effective lab can be created by creating new domain controllers in the source and target domains, and then physically segregating them into a lab network, where they cannot contact the production domain environment. The Operations Master (OM or FSMO) roles for each domain can then be seized for each domain using the ntdsutil utility, which creates exact replicas of all user, group, and computer accounts that can be tested with the ADMT.

## Installing and Configuring ADMT

The installation of the ADMT component should be accomplished on a domain controller in the target domain to which the accounts will be migrated. To install, follow these steps:

1. Insert the Windows Server 2003 CD into the CD drive of a domain controller in the TARGET domain.

2. Select Start, Run, type **X:\i386\admt\admigration.msi** (where **X:** is the CD drive), and press Enter.

3. At the welcome screen, click Next to continue, as illustrated in Figure 14.3.

**FIGURE 14.3**    Installing ADMT v2.

4. Accept the EULA and click Next to continue.

5. Accept the default installation path and click Next to continue.

6. When ready to begin the installation, click Next at the next screen.

7. After installation, click Finish to end the wizard.

## Outlining Domain Migration Prerequisites

As previously mentioned, the most important prerequisite for migration with ADMT is lab verification. Testing as many aspects of a migration as possible helps establish the procedures required and identify potential problems before the procedures are done in the production environment.

There are several functional prerequisites that must be accomplished before the ADMT can function properly. Many of these requirements revolve around the migration of passwords and security objects, and are critical for this functionality.

## Creating Two-Way Trusts Between Source and Target Domains

The source domain and the target domains must be able to communicate with each other and share security credentials. Consequently, it is important to establish trusts between the two domains before the ADMT can be run.

## Assigning Proper Permissions on Source Domain and Source Domain Workstations

The account that will run the ADMT in the target domain must be added into the Builtin\Administrators group in the source domain. In addition, each workstation must include this user as a member of the local administrators group for the computer migration services to be able to function properly. Domain group changes can be easily accomplished, but a large workstation group change must be scripted, or manually accomplished, prior to migration.

## Creating a Target OU Structure

The destination for user accounts from the source domain must be designated at several points during the ADMT migration process. Establishing an OU for the source domain accounts can help simplify and logically organize the new objects. These objects can be moved to other OUs after the migration and this OU can be collapsed, if desired.

## Modifying Default Domain Policy on Target Domain

Unlike previous versions of Windows Operating Systems, Windows Server 2003 does not support anonymous users authenticating as the Everyone group. This functionality was designed to increase security. However, for ADMT to be able to migrate the accounts, this functionality must be disabled. After the process is complete, the policies can be reset to the default levels. To change the policies, follow this procedure:

1. Open the Domain Security Policy (Start, All Programs, Administrative Tools, Domain Security Policy).

2. Navigate to Console Root, Default Domain Policy, Windows Settings, Security Settings, Local Policies, Security Options.

3. Double-click on Network Access: Let Everyone Permissions Apply to Anonymous Users.

4. Check Define This Policy Setting and choose Enabled, as indicated in Figure 14.4. Click OK to finish.

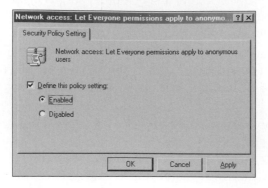

**FIGURE 14.4**    Allowing Anonymous Access for ADMT.

5. Repeat the procedure for the Domain Controller Security Policy Snap-In.

## Exporting Password Key Information

If current passwords will be migrated, a 128-bit encrypted password key from the target domain should be installed on a server in the source domain. This key allows the migration of password and SIDHistory information from one domain to the next.

To create this key, perform the following procedure from the command prompt of a domain controller in the target domain where ADMT was installed:

1. Insert a floppy disk into the drive to store the key (the key can be directed to the network but, for security reasons, is better off directed to a floppy).

2. Change to the ADMT directory by typing `cd program files\active directory migration tool` and pressing Enter.

3. Type `admt key` *SOURCEDOMAINNAME* `a:` *password* and press Enter (where *SOURCEDOMAINNAME* is the NetBIOS name of the source domain, `a:` is the destination drive for the key, and *password* is a password that is used to secure the key). Refer to Figure 14.5 for an example.

4. Upon successful creation of the key, remove the floppy disk and keep it in a safe place.

## Installing Password Migration DLL on the Source Domain

A special Password Migration DLL should be installed on a domain controller in the source domain. This machine will become the Password Export Server for the source domain. The following procedure outlines this installation:

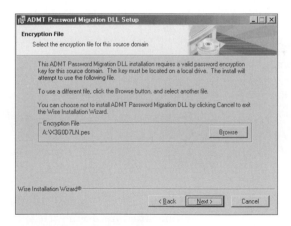

```
C:\WINDOWS\system32\cmd.exe

C:\>cd program files\active directory migration tool

C:\Program Files\Active Directory Migration Tool>admt key companyxyz a: password
The password export server encryption key for domain 'companyxyz' was successfully created
and saved to 'A:\EBP6XN8P.pes'.

C:\Program Files\Active Directory Migration Tool>
```

FIGURE 14.5    Creating a password export key.

1. Insert the floppy disk with the exported key from the target domain into the disk drive of the server.

2. Insert the Windows Server 2003 CD into the CD drive of the domain controller in the source domain where the Registry change was enacted.

3. Start the Password Migration Utility by selecting Start, Run, and typing **X:\i386\ADMT\Pwdmig\Pwdmig.exe** (where **X:** is the drive letter for the CD).

4. At the welcome screen, click Next.

5. Enter the location of the key that was created on the target domain; normally this will be the A: drive, as indicated in Figure 14.6. Click Next to continue.

ADMT Password Migration DLL Setup

**Encryption File**
Select the encryption file for this source domain

This ADMT Password Migration DLL installation requires a valid password encryption key for this source domain. The key must be located on a local drive. The install will attempt to use the following file.

To use a different file, click the Browse button, and select another file.

You can choose not to install ADMT Password Migration DLL by clicking Cancel to exit the Wise Installation Wizard.

Encryption File
A:\X3G0D7LN.pes                                                    Browse

Wise Installation Wizard®
< Back    Next >    Cancel

FIGURE 14.6    Accessing the password export key.

6. Enter the password twice that was set on the target domain and click Next.

7. At the Verification page, click Next to continue.

8. Click Finish after the installation is complete.

9. The system must be restarted; click Yes when prompted to automatically restart. Upon restart, the proper settings will be in place to make this server a Password Export Server.

### Setting Proper Registry Permissions on the Source Domain

The installation of the proper components creates special Registry keys, but leaves them disabled by default, for security reasons. A specific Registry key should be enabled to allow passwords to be exported from the Password Export server. To export the passwords, do the following:

1. On a domain controller in the source domain, open Registry Editor (Start, Run, Regedit).

2. Navigate to

   HKEY_LOCAL_MACHINE\SYSTEM\CurrentControlSet\Control\Lsa

3. Double-click on the AllowPasswordExport DWORD value.

4. Change the properties from 0 to 1 - Hexadecimal.

5. Click OK and close Registry Editor.

6. Reboot the machine for the Registry changes to be enacted.

At this point in the ADMT process, all prerequisites have been satisfied and both source and target domains are prepared for the migration.

## Migrating Accounts Using the Active Directory Migration Tool

When the target domain structure has been finalized, built, and "burnt in" as part of a pilot, and ADMT has been installed, the process of migrating the user, computer, and other accounts can begin. As previously mentioned, the built-in wizards in ADMT streamline the process and give a great deal of flexibility regarding migration options.

### Migrating Groups Using ADMT

In most cases, the first objects to be migrated into a new domain should be groups. The reason for this suggestion is the fact that if users are migrated first, their group membership does not transfer. However, if the groups exist before the users are migrated, they automatically find their place in the group structure. To migrate groups using ADMT v2, use the Group Account Migration Wizard:

1. Open the ADMT MMC snap-in (Start, All Programs, Administrative Tools, Active Directory Migration Tool).

2. Right-click on Active Directory Migration Tool in the left pane and choose Group Account Migration Wizard.

3. Click Next to continue.

4. On the next screen, illustrated in Figure 14.7, the option to test the migration is available. As previously mentioned, the migration process should be thoroughly tested before actually being done in production. In this example, however, the migration will be done. Choose Migrate Now? and click Next to continue.

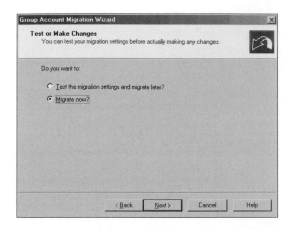

FIGURE 14.7    ADMT test run options.

5. Select the source and destination domains and click Next to continue.

6. The subsequent screen allows for the group accounts from the source domain to be selected. Select all required by using the Add button and selecting the objects manually. After the groups have been selected, click Next to continue.

7. Enter the destination OU for the accounts from the source domain by clicking Browse and selecting the OU created in the prerequisite steps outlined previously. Click Next to continue.

8. On the following screen, several options appear that will determine the nature of the migrated groups. Clicking the Help button details the nature of each setting. In the sample migration, the settings detailed in Figure 14.8 are chosen. After choosing the appropriate settings, click Next to continue.

9. If auditing has not been enabled on the source domain, the prompt illustrated in Figure 14.9 will appear, which gives the option to enable auditing. This is required for migration of the SIDHistory. Click Yes to continue.

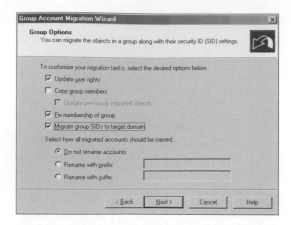

FIGURE 14.8    Examining Group options in ADMT.

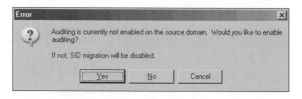

FIGURE 14.9    The Enable Auditing dialog box.

10. Another prompt might appear if auditing is not enabled on the target domain. Enabling auditing is required for migration of SIDHistory and can be disabled after the migration. Click Yes to enable and continue.

11. A local group named SOURCEDOMAIN$$$ is required on the source domain for migration of SIDHistory. A prompt asking to create this group will be displayed at this point, as illustrated in Figure 14.10, if it has not been created beforehand. Click Yes to continue.

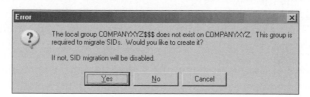

FIGURE 14.10    Local group creation for ADMT.

12. Another dialog box may appear asking to create a Registry key named TcpipClientSupport in the source domain. This is also required for SIDHistory migration. Click Yes to continue.

13. If the Registry key was created, an additional prompt is displayed asking whether the PDC in the source domain will require a reboot. In most cases, it will, so click Yes to continue.

14. The next prompt, illustrated in Figure 14.11, exists solely to stall the process while the reboot of the source PDC takes place. Wait until the PDC is back online and then click OK to continue.

**FIGURE 14.11**    Waiting for the source domain PDC to reboot.

15. The subsequent screen allows for the exclusion of specific directory-level attributes from migration. If the need arises to exclude any attributes, they can be set here. In this example, no exclusions are set. Click Next to continue.

16. A user account with proper administrative rights on the source domain should now be entered in the screen shown in Figure 14.12. After it's entered, click Next to continue.

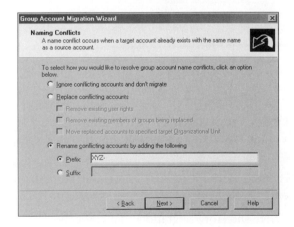

**FIGURE 14.12**    Resolving naming conflicts.

17. Naming conflicts often arise during domain migrations. In addition, different naming conventions may apply in the new environment. The screen illustrated in Figure 14.12 allows for these contingencies. In the example illustrated, any conflicting names have the XYZ- prefix attached to the account names. After the settings have been defined, click Next to continue.

18. The verification screen is the last wizard screen before any changes have been made. Ensure that the procedure has been tested before running it, because ADMT will henceforth write changes to the target Windows Server 2003 Active Directory environment. Click Finish when ready to begin group migration.

19. The Group migration process will then commence. Changing the refresh rate, as illustrated in Figure 14.13, allows a quicker analysis of the current process. When the procedure is complete, the log can be viewed by clicking on View Log. After you complete these steps, click the Close button to end the procedure.

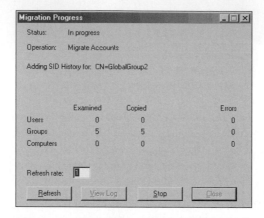

**FIGURE 14.13**    The group account migration process.

## Migrating User Accounts Using ADMT

User accounts are the bread and butter of domain objects, and are one of the most important components in the domain. The biggest shortcoming of ADMT v1 was its inability to migrate passwords of user objects, which effectively limited its use. However, ADMT v2 does an excellent job of migrating users, their passwords, and the security associated with them. To migrate users, follow this procedure:

1. Open the ADMT MMC Console (Start, All Programs, Administrative Tools, Active Directory Migration Tool).

2. Right-click on Active Directory Migration Tool and choose User Account Migration Wizard, as indicated in Figure 14.14.

3. Click Next at the welcome screen.

4. The next dialog box offers the option to test the migration before actually performing it. As previously mentioned, this is a recommended process; in this example, the full migration will be performed. Select Migrate Now and then click Next.

5. Select the source and target domains in the subsequent screen and click Next to continue.

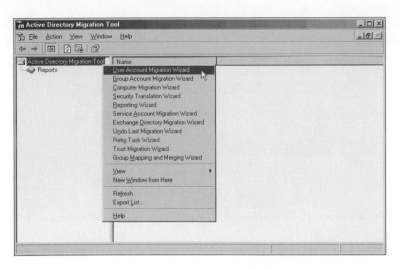

**FIGURE 14.14**    Starting the user account migration process.

6. The following screen enables you to choose user accounts for migration; click the Add button and select the user accounts to be migrated. After all user accounts have been selected, click Next to continue.

7. The next screen enables you to choose a target OU for all created users. Choose the OU by clicking the Browse button. After the OU has been selected, similar to what is shown in Figure 14.15, click Next to continue.

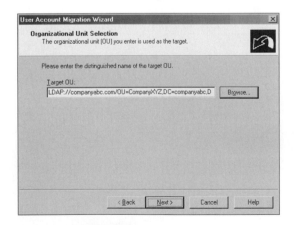

**FIGURE 14.15**    Selecting the organization unit in the Migration Wizard.

8. The new password migration functionality of ADMT v2 is enacted through the following screen. Select Migrate Passwords and select the server in the source domain that had the Password Migration DLL installed in previous steps. Click Next to continue.

9. The subsequent screen deals with security settings in relation to the migrated users. Click Help for an overview of each option. In this example, the settings illustrated in Figure 14.16 are chosen. Click Next to continue.

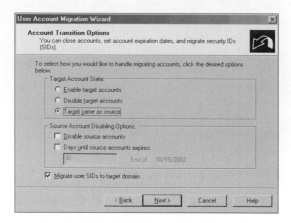

**FIGURE 14.16**    Outlining account transition options.

10. Enter the username, password, and domain of an account that has Domain Admin rights in the source domain. Click Next to continue.

11. Several migration options are presented as part of the next screen. As before, press Help to learn more about some of these features. In this example, the options illustrated in Figure 14.17 are selected. Click Next to continue.

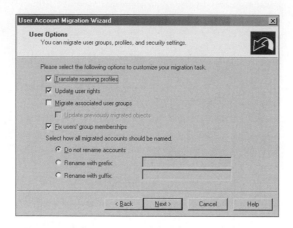

**FIGURE 14.17**    User options in ADMT.

12. The next screen is for setting exclusions. Any property of the user object that should not be migrated should be specified here. In this example, no exclusions are set. Click Next to continue.

13. Naming conflicts for user accounts are common. A procedure for dealing with duplicate accounts should be addressed in advance and can be designated in the next wizard screen, as illustrated in Figure 14.18. Select the appropriate options for duplicate accounts and click Next to continue.

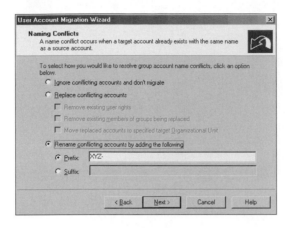

**FIGURE 14.18**    Examining naming conflict settings.

14. The following verification screen presents a summary of the procedure that will take place. This is the last screen before changes are written to the target domain. Verify the settings and click Next to continue.

15. The Migration Progress status box displays the migration process as it occurs, indicating the number of successful and unsuccessful accounts created. When the process is complete, review the log by clicking View Log and verify the integrity of the procedure. A sample log file from a user migration is illustrated in Figure 14.19. Click Close when finished.

## Migrating Computer Accounts Using ADMT

Another important set of objects that must be migrated is also one of the trickier ones. Computer objects must not only be migrated in AD, they must also be updated at the workstations themselves so that users can log in effectively from their consoles. ADMT seamlessly installs agents on all migrated computer accounts and reboots them, forcing them into their new domain structures. This process is outlined in the following steps:

1. Open the ADMT MMC Console (Start, All Programs, Administrative Tools, Active Directory Migration Tool).

2. Right-click on Active Directory Migration Tool and choose Computer Migration Wizard.

3. Click Next at the welcome screen.

**FIGURE 14.19**    Viewing a sample user migration log.

4. As in the previous wizards, the option for testing the migration is given at this point. It is highly recommended to test the process before migrating computer accounts. In this case, a full migration will take place and Migrate Now is chosen. Click Next to continue.

5. Type the names of the source and destination domains in the drop-down boxes of the next screen and click Next to continue.

6. In the following dialog box, select the computer accounts that will be migrated by clicking the Add button and picking the appropriate accounts. Click Next to continue.

7. Select the OU to which the computer accounts will be migrated and click Next to continue.

8. The next screen enables for the specification of which settings on the local computers will be migrated. Click the Help button for a detailed description of each item. In the example, all items are checked, as illustrated in Figure 14.20. Click Next to continue.

9. The subsequent screen prompts you to choose whether existing security will be replaced, removed, or added on to. In this example, the security will be replaced. Click Next to continue.

10. A prompt is displayed informing you that the user rights translation will be performed in Add mode only. Click OK to continue.

11. The next screen is important. It enables an administrator to specify how many minutes a computer will wait before restarting itself. In addition, the naming convention for the computers can be defined, as illustrated in Figure 14.21. After choosing options, click Next to continue.

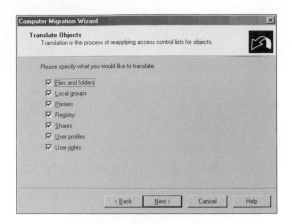

**FIGURE 14.20**    Specifying settings to be migrated.

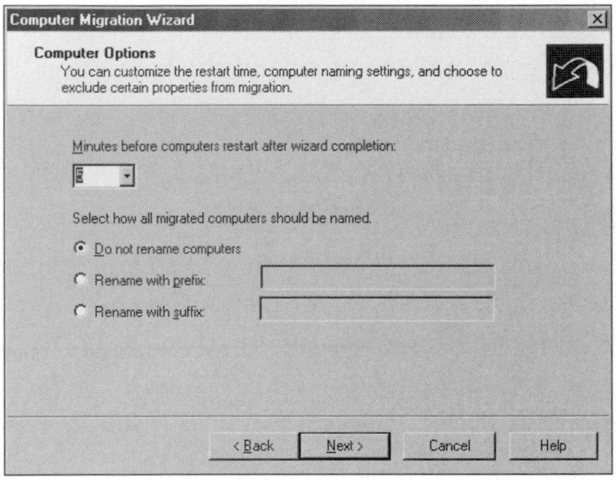

**FIGURE 14.21**    Exploring computer timing options.

12. As in the previous wizards, exclusions for specific attributes may be set in the following wizard. Select any exclusions desired and click Next to continue.

13. Naming conflicts are addressed in the subsequent screen. If any specific naming conventions or conflict resolution settings are desired, enter them here. Click Next to continue.

14. The completion screen lists a summary of the changes that will be made. Review the list and click Finish when ready. All clients that will be upgraded will subsequently be rebooted.

15. After the migration process has completed, the migration log will be available for viewing by clicking the View Log button. After all settings have been verified, click Close.

16. The client agents will be distributed to all clients that have been migrated. Each agent is installed automatically, and counts down until the designated time limit that was set during the configuration of the migration wizard. The dialog box illustrated in Figure 14.22 appears on each workstation.

**FIGURE 14.22**    Viewing the automatic workstation restart.

17. Click Close on the Migration Console to end the wizard.

## Migrating Service Accounts Using ADMT

With the combination of performing an in-place upgrade and the need to support applications that require service accounts—such as Microsoft Exchange and other third-party products—the ADMT Service Account Migration Wizard can assist in moving this account information to Active Directory. To migrate these service accounts, perform the following steps:

1. From the ADMT management console, launch the Service Account Migration Wizard by selecting Action.

2. Select the source domain from which the service accounts reside and the target domain where the service accounts will be migrated. Select the Next button when ready to continue.

3. The Update Service Account Information page gathers service account information for the selected sources domain. If this is the first time you are using the Service Account Migration Wizard, select Yes, Update the Information.

4. The No, Use Previously Collected Information option is not available if the wizard has not been run previously. This option enables the migration of service accounts without collecting service account information each time the wizard is run.

5. On the Service Account Selection page, enter the computer that will host the service accounts that are being migrated. Click the Add button to enter and check the computer account names that host the service accounts being migrated. Click OK to continue.

6. The Active Directory Migration Tool Monitor will appear. Review the status as the ADMT installs the agent on the computers selected.

7. On the Service Account Information page, review the service account being migrated. Use the Skip/Include button to select or deselect accounts for this migration. The Update CSM Now option updates the service control entry. After the proper accounts have been selected, choose Next to continue.

The Service Account Migration Wizard summary verifies the tasks and results of the migration. Use the scrollbar to review the tasks of the service account migration. Click Finish to close the Service Account Wizard.

The Active Directory Migration Tool can be used to migrate additional Windows NT4 Domain resources to Active Directory. Always review the results of each migration and test permissions and functionality before continuing with any of the migrations.

## Migrating Other Domain Functionality

In addition to the Group, User, and Computer Migration Wizards, several other wizards exist that can migrate specific domain-critical components. These wizards operate using the same principles that the wizards previously presented use, and are as straightforward in their operation. The following is a list of the additional wizards included in ADMT v2:

- Security Translation Wizard

- Reporting Wizard

- Exchange Directory Migration Wizard

- Retry Task Wizard

- Trust Migration Wizard

- Group Mapping and Merging Wizard

Virtually all necessary functionality that needs to be replaced when migrating from one domain to another can be transferred by using ADMT v2. It has proven to be a valuable tool that gives administrators an additional option to consider when migrating and restructuring Active Directory environments.

## Summary

Many organizations have been waiting for that "killer app" to justify an upgrade from an NT 4.0 domain structure to Active Directory. Exchange Server 2003 often qualifies as such an application. Before deploying Exchange Server 2003, Active Directory must be in place, which normally means that a migration from NT 4.0 to Windows Server 2003 AD must take place. The upgrade path to Windows Server 2003 can be accomplished via an in-place upgrade of each NT domain into AD, or via a migration from the old NT domain structure into a brand new AD forest via the Active Directory Migration Tool. Each option has its pros and cons, and it is important to determine which option is the most ideal for each organization, as the benefits of Exchange Server 2003 cannot be achieved without this very important step.

## Best Practices

- Choose the in-place Upgrade method when looking for a speedier and more straightforward upgrade process.

- Choose the Migration with ADMT method when it is preferable to create a new domain structure and consolidate existing domains.

- Test the hardware compatibility of any server that will be directly upgraded to Windows Server 2003 against the published Hardware Compatibility List from Microsoft.

- Migrate groups before users when using the Active Directory Migration Tool. This preserves the user's group membership.

- Use the Microsoft Compatibility Check Tool on the Windows Server 2003 CD to test application compatibility.

- Review the server event and system logs upon completing any upgrade.

- When possible, replace NT Backup Domain Controllers with new Windows Server 2003 Domain Controllers, as opposed to upgrading them.

- Test the ADMT migration process before performing the actual migration.

# CHAPTER 15

# Migrating from Exchange v5.5 to Exchange Server 2003

**IN THIS CHAPTER**

• Understanding Exchange 5.5 Migration Options and Strategies

• Comparing Exchange 5.5 and Exchange Server 2003

• Reviewing the Prerequisites for Migrating to Exchange Server 2003

• Structuring the Migration for Best Results

• Preparing the Active Directory Forest and Domain for Exchange Server 2003

• Installing and Configuring the Active Directory Connector

• Installing the First Exchange Server 2003 System in an Exchange 5.5 Site

• Understanding Exchange Server 2003 Mailbox-Migration Methods

• Migrating Exchange 5.5 Public Folders to Exchange Server 2003

• Migrating Exchange 5.5 Connectors and Services to Exchange Server 2003

• Completing the Migration to Exchange Server 2003

## Understanding Exchange 5.5 Migration Options and Strategies

In the past, Microsoft has taken a great deal of heat over the complexity of its migration path from Exchange 5.5 to Exchange 2000. Because of these difficulties, special consideration was given to making the process of migration from Exchange 5.5 to Exchange Server 2003 a much more structured, risk-averse approach. Consequently, a set of very well-designed tools known as the Exchange Deployment Tools was created to assist administrators with the task of migrating off Exchange 5.5. In addition to these tools, specific knowledge of the architecture of both Exchange 5.5 and Exchange Server 2003, and how they interact in a migration process, is recommended.

This chapter focuses on best-practice migration from Exchange 5.5 to Exchange Server 2003. It discusses the differences between Exchange 5.5 and Exchange Server 2003, and it then details specific steps required to migrate an environment. Close attention is given to new migration techniques made available with the Exchange Deployment Tools, in addition to the more "manual" approaches to migration.

## Comparing Exchange 5.5 and Exchange Server 2003

Exchange 5.5 was a fantastic product in small and medium-size companies and for collaboration at the department level, but often had shortcomings in more enterprise environments. This section examines some of the ways that Exchange 5.5 was typically deployed and how its shortcomings are resolved in Exchange Server 2003. The idea behind this section is to give Exchange 5.5 architects and administrators some ideas of how they can leverage the capabilities of Exchange Server 2003. In most environments, upgrading all the Exchange 5.5 servers to Exchange Server 2003 will not be the best solution to leverage Exchange Server 2003. Some places in the environment could or should be consolidated or eliminated.

## Detailing Design Limitations in Exchange 5.5

Exchange 5.5 environments generally followed a distributed deployment model in which Exchange servers were placed in each remote location that had more than 20–30 users. This was especially true for organizations that were deployed in early Exchange deployments and was due to several factors in how the product was architected and the inability of clients to reliably connect across remote network links. In addition to this limitation, Exchange 5.5 also had other architectural shortcomings that were addressed in Exchange Server 2003.

### Combined Administration and Routing

Exchange 5.5 tied the hands of messaging architects by limiting Exchange designs around the site boundary. The Site in Exchange 5.5 was the boundary for administration as well as message routing. Exchange 5.5 directory replication occurs every 15 minutes within an Exchange site, and every server in a site communicates with every other server in that site. Messages also route within a site directly from the source to the destination server. Unless bandwidth was unlimited in the organization, architects had to draw site boundaries to control message routing and directory replication. Many organizations that chose a single-site design paid the price with frequent RPC message timeouts and eventually switched to a multisite design. Because message routing and administration are linked, a distributed administration model was automatically created that was an additional headache. Windows NT 4.0 didn't do a good job of providing granular administration. Anyone with administrative rights in the domain could add himself to the global group that was assigned rights in the Exchange Administrator program. This really meant that distributed message routing and centralized administration just was not possible if someone in the remote office needed to manage the Exchange server.

### Lack of Scalability

In Exchange 5.5 environments, scalability was usually a cap that was set based on the size of the mail and public folder server database size or the number of users supported per server. When the cap was reached, users were moved from one server to another. Mailbox limits could vary widely between organizations, from a conservative 500 users to a less conservative number of about 2,500. Many organizations capped the database size or number of users per server due to the 16GB mail and public folder store limitation of the standard edition of the Exchange Server software. Even after the limitation was removed in the enterprise edition, organizations were limited in the size of the database by the amount of time offline maintenance, backup, and restore operations took on the server.

The cap was then set based on the organization's comfort level with the risk of losing the server and the amount of recovery time to get a failed server operational. Many organizations found that when they began to exceed about 30GB, the store became unmanageable.

### Small Degree of Redundancy

In most Exchange 5.5 deployments, mail servers were distributed to locations that had more than 20–30 users, an arbitrary number of users that was selected on the size and availability of WAN bandwidth, whether backup links existed, and the organization's comfort with the level of risk. This was due to the desire to provide a decent level of performance with the capability to keep mail services running in the remote location online in case of WAN failure. Redundancy was also provided through the use of multiple connector servers for foreign mail, SMTP, and OWA. Having multiple connector servers allowed one connector server to fail or have a fault; another connector server would be available to service messaging routing needs.

### Questionable Stability

In corporate locations, stability was achieved by keeping databases small and by separating public folders and message-routing services from mail-message services. Distributed services came in the form of dedicated public folder servers and connector servers such as cc:Mail connector servers, Outlook Web Access servers, and SMTP bridgehead servers for Internet Mail.

## How Exchange Server 2003 Addresses Exchange 5.5 Shortcomings

Exchange Server 2003 provides the features necessary to build a more robust messaging environment. It removes many of the boundaries that tied the hands of architects and administrators in Exchange 5.5. As Exchange Server 2003 matures, the messaging designs continue to centralize, with only a portion of the services still being distributed. Exchange Server 2003 improves upon the shortcomings of Exchange 5.5 in the following ways:

- **Separate administration and routing**—In Exchange Server 2003, separate routing and administration can be achieved through the creation of Routing and Administrative Groups. To fully use these new containers, the organization must be converted to Native Mode Exchange Server 2003. This requires all Exchange 5.5 servers to be converted to Exchange Server 2003 or be uninstalled from the organization. The combination of Administrative and Routing Groups with the granular permission of Active Directory helps messaging administrators better control access to the messaging services in the organization.

- **Increased degree of scalability**—Scalability is provided in multiple mail and public folder databases that can be used to keep the database performance high while keeping backup and restore times low. This means that the number of users supported per server can be increased, reducing the number of servers on the network. Each database can be mounted and dismounted individually, allowing the server to continue to function even when some databases are offline.

15

- **Improved redundancy**—Redundancy in Exchange Server 2003 is provided through full support of the Microsoft Cluster Service (MCS). Connectors in Exchange Server 2003 can also be redundant. By using SMTP for message delivery and a link-state routing algorithm, message-routing designs can be built to route messages efficiently and to take advantage of redundant links on the WAN.

- **Enhanced stability**—Stability is provided within the Windows Server 2003 operating system and at the core of Exchange Server 2003 in the Extensible Storage Environment (ESE) database. Small efficient databases, redundant connector designs, and clustering technology all increase the stability of Exchange Server 2003, improving the end-user experience and letting information technology groups create service level agreements that they can stand by.

# Reviewing the Prerequisites for Migrating to Exchange Server 2003

Before moving the Exchange 5.5 organization to Exchange Server 2003, several items need to be addressed from a technical implementation and design standpoint. Refer to Chapter 4, "Designing Exchange Server 2003 for a Small to Medium Network," and Chapter 5, "Designing an Enterprise Exchange Server 2003 Environment," for information on Exchange Server 2003 design concerns.

## Checking the Current Environment with the Exchange Server 2003 Deployment Tools

The Exchange Deployment Tools are an invaluable asset to any deployment team. They are straightforward and robust, and they cover a multitude of migration scenarios. Even die-hard Exchange upgrade enthusiasts with years of Exchange 2000 migration experience under their belt can benefit from the tactical advice and safeguards built into the tools.

The Exchange Deployment Tools guide administrators through the Exchange Server 2003 migration process in a step-by-step fashion. The tools themselves can be invoked by simply inserting the Exchange Server 2003 CD (or clicking Setup.exe if autorun is disabled) and then clicking on the Exchange Deployment Tools link. The tools, illustrated in Figure 15.1, initially lead the migration team through a series of prerequisite steps.

These prerequisite steps should be followed exactly as described in the tool. In fact, the entire migration process outlined in this chapter can be followed via the Exchange Deployment Tools. In addition to running through the prerequisite steps listed in the tools, several key factors must be taken into account before deploying Exchange Server 2003.

## Preparing the Exchange 5.5 Organization for the Migration

When moving to Exchange Server 2003, one of the biggest items that organizations should be concerned about is that Exchange Server 2003 is a one-to-one Exchange Organization to Active Directory forest environment. This means that there can only be one Exchange Server 2003 organization per Active Directory forest. Some organizations have one or more Exchange organizations in their environment. This type of installation can result from mergers and acquisitions that were never fully meshed or breakaway lines of business that established their own organization, or it could be done by design to create an SMTP relay routing hub. In any case, only one organization can remain in Exchange Server 2003, and this organization must be chosen before the start of the migration.

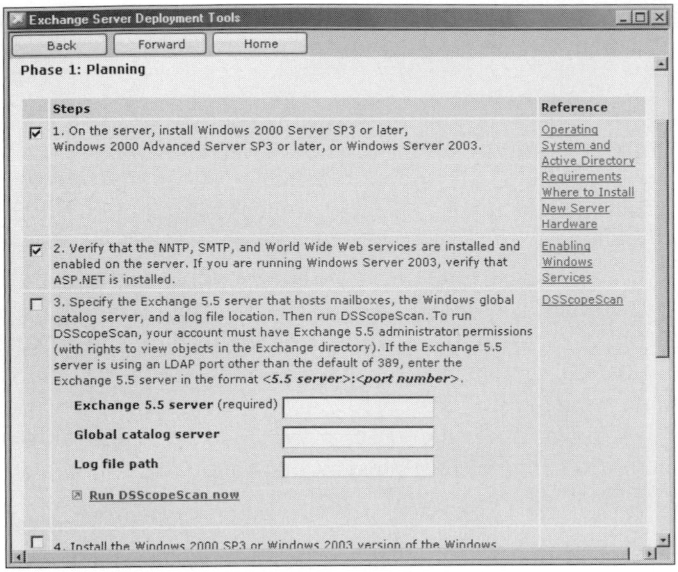

**FIGURE 15.1**   Using the Exchange Deployment Tools.

---

**TIP**

For organizations designed to support SMTP relay functions, continue to use them through the migration process and then replace them with Routing Groups. If the Exchange 5.5 relay servers are under the control of another group in the organization, place the Routing Group with the relay server in its own Administrative Group.

---

The second piece of the one-to-one environment that must be one-to-one is the number of mailboxes per Active Directory account. In Exchange 5.5, a Windows NT account could have an unlimited number of mailboxes associated with it. In Active Directory, the messaging components of the user account are just additional attributes of the user, so the mailbox is really part of the user account. It was quite common for Exchange 5.5 administrators to use a single account for multiple mailboxes, especially for administrative functions such as backup and virus-scanning products, and also for resources such as conference rooms. Linking the Active Directory accounts to the Exchange 5.5 mailboxes can be done either manually for a few mailboxes or for a large number of mailboxes by using the NTDSNoMatch utility, or by using the Resource Mailbox Wizard in the ADC Tools, described in more detail later in this chapter.

> **TIP**
>
> To view the Windows NT Accounts with multiple mailboxes, use the Exchange 5.5 Administrator program and run a directory export to a CSV file. In the Exchange Administrator program, select Tools, Directory Export and export all mailboxes from the Global Address List container. Open the export file in Excel and sort the spreadsheet by the Primary Windows NT account column. Scrolling through the Excel sheet or running a duplicate query in Microsoft Access reveals all of the Windows NT 4.0 accounts that were used on more than one mailbox.

## Compacting the Exchange 5.5 Organization

The more items that exist in Exchange 5.5, the more items must be migrated to Exchange Server 2003. It's a given that mail database and public folder servers need to be migrated, but all the connector servers might not be necessary in the Exchange Server 2003 environment. Now is the time to rethink the Exchange design. By consolidating servers and using features such as clustering, it is now possible to locate all the Exchange installations at a few central hubs on the WAN where the administrators with the best Exchange skills reside. In addition, the enhanced remote client access capabilities introduced in Exchange Server 2003 allow for site consolidation, further reducing the number of servers that must be supported. Of course, the migrated Exchange Server 2003 environment can mirror the exact same configuration as Exchange v5.5. It's just an option (and opportunity) to rethink the best configuration for the organization.

Later revisions of Exchange 5.5 introduced a utility called the Move Server Wizard that allows for the consolidation of Exchange 5.5 organizations and sites. This tool allowed an organization to consolidate servers into a single site. Service Pack 1 for Exchange Server 2003 introduced the ability to move mailboxes between Administrative Groups while in mixed mode, which greatly improved the migration options available.

## Connecting with Foreign Mail Systems

One of the changes which may affect organizations moving from Exchange 5.5 to Exchange Server 2003 regarding foreign mail connectivity is that there is no Exchange Server 2003 version of the PROFS/SNADS connector. The easiest solution to this problem is to leave a single Exchange 5.5 site behind to handle the PROFS/SNADS connectivity. The downside to this solution is that it delays the organization's move to Exchange Server 2003 Native Mode until another solution is put into place. For a long-term solution, investigate using SMTP to connect the systems, or migrate the PROFS user to Exchange Server 2003.

A second issue regarding foreign mail connectivity is that organizations might have put so much effort into getting their connectors stable and configured properly that they might not want to move their foreign mail connectors to Exchange Server 2003. As long as the organization can remain in Mixed Mode, it's okay to leave the connectors in Exchange 5.5. As with the PROFS/SNADS connector, it's better to leave all Exchange 5.5

connectors in a single Exchange 5.5 site than multiple sites. If this means moving the connector anyway to consolidate to a single Exchange 5.5 site, or if a single Exchange site doesn't make sense because of geography or WAN issues, consider moving the connectors sooner rather than later to Exchange Server 2003.

### Upgrading Service Pack Levels

To migrate from Exchange 5.5 to Exchange Server 2003, some or all of the Exchange 5.5 servers must be running at least Service Pack 3, and preferably Service Pack 4. Most organizations are already at that level, but those that are not should plan to perform the Service Pack 3 upgrade before starting the Exchange migration. Although it is wise to upgrade all, only one Exchange 5.5 server in the organization technically must run SP3—the one in each Site that the ADC replicates to.

If the organization is planning to consolidate services before migrating to Exchange Server 2003, it makes sense to postpone the Service Pack 3 upgrade until the consolidation through the Move Server Wizard is completed.

## Structuring the Migration for Best Results

When structuring the migration, the end goal is to move to the new platform without disrupting current services or losing functionality. The only way to be sure that service and functionality will not be lost during the migration is to perform lab testing. Having a fallback plan and solid disaster-recovery processes are also essential when planning the Exchange Server 2003 deployment. By breaking the migration into sections, the organization can move cautiously through the migration without making too many changes at one time. The following best practices deploy Exchange Server 2003 by migrating each service type at a time. For many smaller remote locations, this might not be feasible and all services might have to be migrated at the same time. Migrating by service type is usually the best solution for corporate sites and large remote offices.

## Performing Single Site Exchange 5.5 Migrations

Within the same Exchange 5.5 site, administrators have the flexibility of moving users between servers. Single-site Exchange 5.5 installations become a single Administrative Group with a single Routing Group when converted to Exchange Server 2003. If granular message routing is needed, additional Routing Groups can be added and servers within the Administrative Group can be moved to new Routing Groups after the conversion to Native Mode.

Because servers cannot be moved between Administrative Groups even after the conversion to Native Mode, administrators need to examine whether a single Administrative Group will fulfill the organization's administrative needs. Additional Administrative Groups can be added to the organization, but only by installing new Exchange Server 2003 systems. Users can be moved between Administrative Groups by moving the mailbox from Admin group to group, either before the switch to Native Mode by using the cross-site migration tool introduced in Service Pack 1 or normally when in Native Mode.

## Performing Multisite Exchange 5.5 Migrations

Multisite migrations are a bit more complex than single-site migrations. After the first Exchange server is installed, administrators can use the *Move Mailbox method* to migrate users to Exchange Server 2003.

Understanding why the multiple sites were established might help in deciding how to handle the multiple sites. If the decision to have multiple sites was to originally delegate control of administration, the multiple Administrative Groups might still be needed. If multiple sites were implemented to control message flow and directory replication, consolidating many of the Administrative Groups might be desired.

## Performing Multiorganization Exchange 5.5 Migrations

Multiorganization environments must consolidate to a single Exchange Server 2003 organization to migrate to Exchange Server 2003 unless the organization plans to support multiple Active Directory forests. Multiple organization environments have the following choices when moving to Exchange Server 2003:

- **Select one organization to be migrated to Exchange Server 2003**—Use the most heavily populated organization if it fits the company's standards. Create new Exchange Server 2003 mailboxes for users in the other organization. Use ExMerge or the Exchange Migration Wizard to move user data from the abandoned organization to Exchange Server 2003.

- **Start with a clean Exchange Server 2003 organization and do not migrate either organization**—Both organizations feel equal pain that might be politically acceptable. Look at the ExMerge utility or the Exchange Migration Wizard to migrate user data, or run both Exchange 5.5 organizations for a short period of time and allow users to forward mail to their Exchange Server 2003 mailbox.

# Preparing the Active Directory Forest and Domain for Exchange Server 2003

After the prerequisite steps have been satisfied, the Exchange Deployment Tools prompt the administrator to run the Forestprep and Domainprep processes. These processes can be invoked manually via setup.exe switches (/forestprep and /domainprep), or they can simply be launched via the Exchange Deployment Tools, as illustrated in Figure 15.2.

A greater understanding of what tasks these two utilities perform is crucial to understanding the Exchange deployment process as a whole.

## Extending the Active Directory Schema

To extend the Active Directory schema, Exchange Setup relies on the capabilities of the /forestprep switch, which can be invoked via the Exchange Deployment Tools. Running the ForestPrep procedure requires that the account invoking the command have Schema Admin privileges in the schema root domain because the command extends the Active Directory schema to support the attributes that Exchange Server 2003 requires. The schema extension is quite extensive, and the changes are replicated to all domain controllers in the Active Directory forest. This might require special consideration into replication issues if the AD forest is large and spread out across slow replication links.

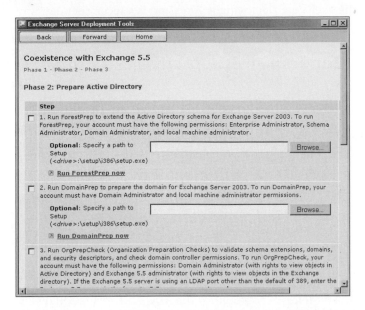

**FIGURE 15.2**   Launching ForestPrep and DomainPrep from the Exchange Deployment Tools.

> **NOTE**
>
> The ForestPrep performed by the Exchange Deployment tools is different than the ForestPrep procedure that is performed during a Windows Server 2003 schema extension. Indeed, Exchange Server 2003 does not require the schema extensions for Windows Server 2003 to function, as the Windows 2000 schema is sufficient.

## Preparing the Windows Server 2003 Domains to Support Exchange Server 2003

The Active Directory domains that will host Exchange servers or mailbox-enabled users must be prepared before installing the first Exchange Server 2003 system. Prepare the Windows Server 2003 domains using the /domainprep switch, also invoked via the Exchange Deployment Tools. The /domainprep process configures the Recipient Update Service parameters, which are responsible for keeping Exchange address lists up-to-date and for creating proxy addresses for users based on recipient policy addressing configuration. In addition, it creates the Exchange Server 2003–specific groups that allow Exchange services to run without a service account.

### Verifying the Organization Settings with OrgPrepCheck

Exchange Server 2003 introduces a new utility named OrgPrepCheck to validate that the ForestPrep and DomainPrep utilities were functionally successful. The OrgPrepCheck utility is invoked via the Exchange Deployment Tools and is a recommended way of determining whether it is safe to proceed with the migration process.

## Installing and Configuring the Active Directory Connector

Unlike in Exchange 2000, the Active Directory Connector (ADC) does not need to be installed until after the /forestprep command has run. This was designed so that only a single schema extension is required for upgrading to Exchange Server 2003, as opposed to the dual-extension that was performed with Exchange 2000.

After the Exchange Deployment Tools have run through the ForestPrep and DomainPrep processes, the ADC can be installed. The connection agreements in ADC are necessary to synchronize directory entries between the Exchange 5.5 and Exchange Server 2003 systems. Unlike in Exchange 2000, the Exchange Server 2003 ADC can be installed on a member server and is often installed on the first Exchange Server 2003 system in a site.

Organizations can choose to implement one or more Active Directory Connectors in the organization. Implementing additional ADC connectors and connection agreements should not be seen as a fault-tolerant solution for the ADC. The ADC should be seen as a temporary coexistence solution, with migration being the intended end goal.

ADC installations are better off being left as simple as possible. A single ADC installed with one connection agreement to each Exchange 5.5 site is much easier to manage than multiple ADCs, all with their own connection agreements. This might or might not be possible based on the Exchange 5.5 site design and WAN layout. The ADC and its connection agreements should communicate with servers on the same network segment that will require multiple ADC installations.

### Installing the ADC

Both the Active Directory domain controller and the Exchange 5.5 server that will be joined through the Active Directory Connector should be on the same physical network segment. Schema Admin and Enterprise Administrator rights are required to install the ADC.

Plan a few days to install and configure the ADC and the connection agreements. The initial installation and configuration take only a few hours, but it generally takes a few days to work out the kinks and resolve the errors in the Application Event Log. Problems in the ADC will show up later and complicate the migration, so don't rush the ADC installation. Microsoft recommends allocating 2 hours for replicating about 5,000 objects in a single direction, but the length of time for replication really varies on the number of connection agreements, recipient containers, and populated attributes on the actual directory objects.

The ADC has the capability to delete objects in both directories, so check whether the backup media and procedures have been recently verified before configuring the ADC. The organization should be familiar with how to perform an authoritative restore through NTDSUTIL for the Active Directory database.

The first step in installing the ADC is to create or choose a user account that will be used to run the ADC service and manage the connection agreements. This account does not have to be the same account that is used in each of the connection agreements configured later in the chapter. This account needs to be added to the Administrators group in the domain if the ADC is installed on a domain controller or to the local Administrators group if the ADC is installed on a member server.

To manually start the ADC installation, insert the Exchange Server 2003 CD and select ADC Setup from the autorun menu, or simply invoke the setup from the Exchange Deployment Tools. The ADC prompts for the component selection and allows just the MMC administration snap-in to be installed or the ADC service. Select both components when installing the ADC on the server. If the ADC will need to be remotely managed, the administration component can be installed later on the administrator's workstation.

Next, the installation prompts for the path to install the ADC and the ADC service account credentials. When the installation is complete, the next step is to configure the connection agreements to begin synchronizing the Active Directory and Exchange 5.5 directories.

## Creating Connection Agreements

Configuring connection agreements (CAs) has been the bane of many an Exchange 2000 administrator. Improperly configured connection agreements can seriously corrupt an Active Directory or Exchange 5.5 database, so it is extremely important to properly configure CAs for the migration process. Luckily, Exchange Server 2003 includes a series of ADC Tools that streamline the process of creating CAs for migration, as illustrated in Figure 15.3. After installation, it is highly recommended that you use these wizards to install and configure the CAs.

Two tools in particular are extremely helpful in the migration process. The first tool, the Resource Mailbox Wizard, illustrated in Figure 15.4, can help to identify users with multiple mailboxes and fix them in advance of the migration. This tool streamlines the process that the NTDSUTIL utility previously utilized.

The second tool, the Connection Agreement Wizard, walks an administrator through the tricky process of creating the connection agreements required to migrate from Exchange 5.5. The wizard helps to identify "gotchas" such as the AD domain being in Mixed Mode (it should be changed to Native Mode in advance of the migration) and other important factors. As illustrated in Figure 15.5, it automatically creates a recipient CA and a public folder CA, which can then be manually tweaked as necessary.

**FIGURE 15.3**    Using the ADC Tools.

**FIGURE 15.4**    Viewing the Resource Mailbox Wizard.

After initial setup, several properties can be configured on the ADC to give the administrator more information and control over the ADC and its connection agreements. Attribute replication, account-matching rules, and diagnostic logging properties should all be configured before building the connection agreements and replicating directory entries. Even when using the default settings on the ADC, it is a best practice to prototype the ADC replication processes in a lab before attempting the synchronization on production systems.

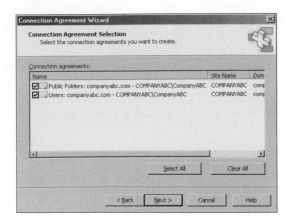

**FIGURE 15.5**   Connection Agreement Wizard.

Connection agreements are configured by an administrator who controls the type of objects that are replicated between Active Directory and Exchange 5.5. They also contain the credentials and connection information needed to connect to both systems and other attributes, such as handling deletion and what to do when there is no matching account for the mailbox in the destination directory. Connection agreements operate using two different approaches:

- **One way**—Information is synchronized only one way. The connection agreement can be from Windows or from Exchange, but not from both. After the direction is selected, the opposite system's tabs and controls are grayed out.

- **Two way**—Information is synchronized in both directions. This is generally the preferred method and keeps the configuration simple.

Connection agreements also need to be designated as primary or not. A primary connection agreement has the capability to create objects in the directory. A connection agreement that is not marked as primary cannot create new objects and can only update the attributes of existing objects. To ensure that objects are created, the ADC marks all connection agreements as primary by default.

**Understanding Configuration Connection Agreements**

Configuration connection agreements are used for coexistence between the Exchange 5.5 and Exchange 2003 servers, and they transfer information such as site addressing and routing information between the Exchange platforms. The configuration connection agreement cannot be created manually and is created by the Exchange Server 2003 setup program when the first Exchange Server 2003 system is installed. After the replication of the configuration information, Exchange 5.5 sites are visible in the Exchange System Manager program and are represented as Administrative Groups. Exchange Server 2003 systems are also visible in the Exchange 5.5 Administrator program.

### Defining Recipient Connection Agreements

Recipient connection agreements are responsible for replicating mailbox, distribution list, and custom recipient information from the Exchange 5.5 directory to Active Directory. They are also used to send users, groups, and contacts from Active Directory to Exchange 5.5. Recipient Connection Agreements can be configured as one-way or two-way connection agreements. Most often a two-way connection agreement is used. Each connection agreement has its own schedule, so using one-way connection agreements might be preferred if the organization has specific requirements on when each side should be updated.

### Using Public Folder Connection Agreements

Public folder connection agreements are responsible for replicating mail-enabled public folder information from and to Exchange 5.5 and Active Directory. Public folder connection agreements can be configured only as two-way connection agreements. It is a best practice to create one public folder connection agreement per Exchange 5.5 site. This is true even if the organization does not mail-enable public folders. Administrators might not be aware of some folders that are mail-enabled, and it is best to create the connection agreement for each Exchange 5.5 site, to reduce the likelihood of problems with the folders during the migration.

### Configuring Connection Agreements

As previously mentioned, it is wise to allow the ADC Tools to create the necessary CAs for the migration process. If a manual CA will need to be configured, however, it can be done in the following fashion. Open the ADC MMC snap-in on the domain controller running the ADC by selecting Start, All Programs, Microsoft Exchange, Active Directory Connector. Right-click the Active Directory Connector service icon for the server and select New, Recipient Connection Agreement.

The following tabs must be populated:

- **General**—Select the direction and the ADC server responsible for the connection agreement. It's usually best to select a two-way connection agreement for the primary connection agreement.

- **Connections**—Enter the username and password combination that will be used to read and write to Active Directory. Next enter the server name and LDAP port number for the Exchange 5.5 server, and the username and password that will be used to read and write to the Exchange 5.5 directory. When entering the user credentials, use the format domain\user—such as companyabc.com\administrator.

---

**TIP**

To locate the LDAP port number on the Exchange 5.5 server, open Exchange Administrator and access the LDAP protocol properties under the Protocols container beneath the server object.

- **Schedule**—The directory synchronization process takes place between midnight and 6:00 a.m. daily under the default schedule. Use the grid to modify the schedule, or select Always, which replicates every five minutes.

- **From Exchange**—Select all the recipient containers in the Exchange 5.5 site to synchronize with Active Directory. Remember to select any containers that might be used as import containers for foreign mail connectors. Next select the destination container in Active Directory where the ADC will search for matching accounts and create new accounts. Select the object types to replicate, such as mailboxes, distribution lists, and custom recipients.

- **From Windows**—Select the Organizational Units in Active Directory to take updates from and the Exchange 5.5 container to place the updates in. The object types to replicate are selectable for users, groups, and contacts. The check boxes for Replicate Secured Active Directory Objects to the Exchange Directory and Create Objects in Location Specified by Exchange 5.5 DN are best left blank in most instances. Click Help while in the From Windows tab for more information on these options.

- **Deletion**—The Deletion option controls whether deletions are processed or stored in a CSV or LDF file, depending on the platform. If this is a short-term connection for migration, it's usually best to mark these options to not process the deletions and store the change in a file. The CSV and LDF files get created in the path that the ADC was installed into. Each connection agreement has its own subdirectory, and the output CSV and LDF files get created there.

- **Advanced**—The Advanced tab is set correctly for the first primary connection agreement and does not need to be modified. The settings on this tab should be modified when multiple connection agreements exist or when configuring the ADC to replicate between Exchange organizations. Leaving the Primary Connection Agreement check box selected on multiple connection agreements for the same containers creates duplicate directory entries. Never have the ADC create contacts unless the ADC is being used to link two Exchange organizations for collaboration purposes.

To configure a public folder connection agreement, right-click the Active Directory Connector service icon for the server and select New, Public Folder Connection Agreement.

- **General**—Select the ADC server responsible for the connection agreement. The direction can be only two-way on public folder connection agreements.

- **Connections**—Enter the username and password combination that will be used to read and write to Active Directory. Next enter the server name and LDAP port number for the Exchange 5.5 server, and the username and password that will be used to read and write to the Exchange 5.5 directory. When entering the user credentials, use the format domain\user—in this case, companyabc\administrator.

15

- **Schedule**—The directory-synchronization process will take place between midnight and 6:00 a.m. daily under the default schedule. Use the grid to modify the schedule. Select the check box for Replicate the Entire Directory the Next Time the Agreement Is Run to perform a full synchronization on the first run.

- **From Windows**—The only option available here is the check box for Replicate Secured Active Directory Objects to the Exchange Directory. This replicates objects that contain an explicit deny in the Access Control List to Exchange 5.5. Exchange 5.5 does not support explicit deny entries, so the objects are not replicated by default.

The final step is to force the connection agreement to replicate immediately. To force the replication, right-click the connection agreement and select Replicate Now. Be sure to check the Application Event Log in Event Viewer for errors during the replication process.

# Installing the First Exchange Server 2003 System in an Exchange 5.5 Site

Because there are many prerequisite tasks and processes to run, getting to the point of the actual Exchange Server setup is a watershed event. The following section double-checks that the prerequisites have been fulfilled. When installing the first Exchange Server 2003 system, it is recommended that you use a server that has been wiped clean and has a fresh installation of Windows Server 2003. This is because the first server in Exchange holds many critical Exchange organizational management and routing master tables, and having a new, clean server ensures that the masters are created and stored on a solidly configured system.

## Installing the First Exchange Server 2003 System

The actual Exchange Server 2003 installation of the first server is quite easy after the prerequisite conditions are met. The installation takes about 30 minutes on average.

> **TIP**
>
> The first Exchange 2003 server in a Site runs the Site Replication Service, which is used to synchronize Site topology information between Exchange 5.5 and Exchange Server 2003. Because of this special role, larger organizations may want to install this role onto a dedicated server, rather than a production mailbox server. This is also highly recommended if the mailbox servers are to be set up as cluster nodes.

One final step before running the Exchange Server 2003 setup is to run a tool called SetupPrep, shown in Figure 15.6. This tool validates that all necessary prerequisites are in place for the installation of the first Exchange Server 2003 in the Site.

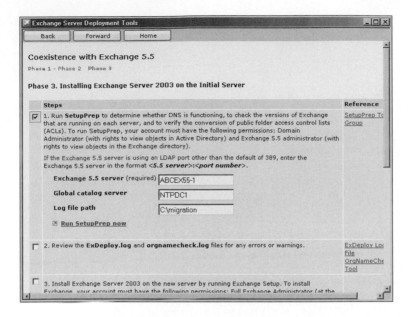

**FIGURE 15.6**   Running SetupPrep.

After SetupPrep has been run, the actual setup of the server can be invoked via the tools or simply by running the Setup.exe in the \setup\i386 folder. The following steps properly install Exchange Server 2003 on the system on which they are run:

1. Click Next at the Welcome Wizard.

2. Agree to the end-user licensing agreement and click Next.

3. Choose the installation path and ensure that Typical Installation is chosen. Click Next.

4. Select Join or Upgrade an Existing Exchange 5.5 Organization, as illustrated in Figure 15.7, and click Next.

> **NOTE**
>
> It is imperative that Join or Upgrade an Existing Exchange 5.5 Organization is chosen at this point. If Create a New Exchange Organization is chosen, connectivity will be lost to the Exchange 5.5 organization, and the organization will have to be removed completely by using the setup /removeorg option.

5. Enter the name of an Exchange 5.5 server in a site the Exchange Server 2003 system will join.

6. Click OK at the prompt to test prerequisite conditions.

7. Select I Agree to agree to the license agreement.

15

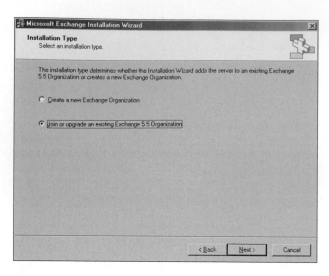

**FIGURE 15.7**    Joining an Exchange 5.5 organization.

8. Enter the password of the Exchange 5.5 service account.

9. Verify the installation options, and click Next to start the installation.

10. When the installation is complete, click Finish.

To install additional Exchange Server 2003 systems, the installation process is almost identical, and the same procedure can be followed.

## Understanding What Happens Behind the GUI During the Installation

Quite a few items are installed and configured during the installation. The following items describe some of the major components that are installed and configured during setup. The new terms and features are discussed more in depth in the next few sections.

- **Exchange Server 2003 binaries and services installed**—All the basic services for Exchange Server 2003 are installed and started. The SMTP and NNTP services from IIS are modified for Exchange Server 2003.

- **Changes to Active Directory Configuration container**—Information about the Exchange installation, such as Administrative and Routing Group configurations, are in the Services container.

- **Exchange Server added to Exchange Domain Servers security group**—The machine account for the server is added to the Exchange Domain Servers security group to let Exchange Server 2003 run under the local system account.

- **Configuration connection agreement created**—A new connection agreement is added to the ADC to replicate configuration and routing information between Exchange 5.5 and Exchange Server 2003.

- **Recipient Update Service created**—The RUS is created to update address lists and recipient policies in Active Directory.

- **Site Replication Service (SRS) installed**—The SRS is installed and synchronizes the directory with the Exchange 5.5 server in the site.

## Understanding the Configuration Connection Agreement

During the installation, a new connection agreement called the ConfigCA is added to the Active Directory Connector. The ConfigCA is responsible for replicating the configuration information between the Exchange platforms. The ConfigCA replicates items such as the Site Addressing Policies and the routing information in the Gateway Address Routing Table (GWART).

## Examining the Site Replication Service (SRS)

The Site Replication Service (SRS) provides directory interoperability between the Exchange 5.5 and Exchange 2003 servers. The SRS runs as a service and is needed only during the migration period. SRS uses LDAP to communicate between directories, and to Exchange 5.5 servers it looks just like another Exchange 5.5 server. The SRS works in conjunction with the Active Directory Connector for directory synchronization.

Only one SRS is allowed per Exchange Server 2003 system. Additional SRSs can be added, as long as there are additional Exchange Server 2003 systems available to run the service. The SRS has no configuration parameters in the Exchange Server 2003 System Manager. Synchronization can be forced through the SRS by accessing the SRS from the Exchange 5.5 Administrator program.

SRSs are created on all servers that house Exchange 5.5 Directory Replication Connectors. The Directory Replication Connector is replaced by the SRS to perform intersite replication with the remote Exchange 5.5 site; if an Exchange Server 2003 is configured to communicate with an Exchange 5.5 server, the Site Replication Service automatically is installed and configured at the time of Exchange Server 2003 installation.

> **TIP**
>
> To view the Directory Replication Connector endpoints in the SRS, open Exchange System Manger and expand the Tools icon. Next click the Site Replication Services icon and then select Directory Replication Connector View from the View menu. Each Exchange 5.5 site's Directory Replication Connector is now displayed under the Site Replication Service.

## No Service Account in Exchange Server 2003

Exchange Server 2003 runs under the Local System account. This is a major change from Exchange 5.5, where the Exchange Service account was used on all servers. The benefit of the new architecture is that the service account was a single point of failure in case of a password change or if the account was deleted. When Exchange Server 2003 systems communicate between servers, they are authenticated by the server's machine account in Active Directory.

When the /domainprep option is run, it creates two groups called Exchange Domain Servers and Exchange Enterprise Servers. During Exchange setup, the Exchange server's machine account is added to a Global Security group called Exchange Domain Servers. The Exchange Domain Servers group is granted permissions on all Exchange objects to allow the Exchange Server 2003 services to access and update Active Directory. The Exchange Enterprise Servers group contains the Exchange Domain Servers groups from all domains in the forest and provides cross-domain access between all Exchange Server 2003 systems.

### Using the Recipient Update Service (RUS)

The Recipient Update Service (RUS) is responsible for updating address lists and email addresses in Active Directory. Two objects are contained in the Recipient Update Services container by default. The Recipient Update Service (with "Enterprise Configuration" in brackets) is responsible for updating the Enterprise Configuration information in Active Directory, such as Administrative and Routing Group information. The domain specified is responsible for updating the address lists and email addresses configured on objects in the Active Directory domain that the Exchange server resides in. The address list and email addresses are configured under the Recipient Policies and Address List icon, discussed previously in this section.

# Understanding Exchange Server 2003 Mailbox-Migration Methods

Two methods exist for moving mailboxes to Exchange Server 2003, and each differs in hardware requirements and the amount of risk and interoperability during and after the migration. The following migration methods for mailboxes are covered in this section:

- Move Mailboxes
- ExMerge

### Migrating Using the Move Mailbox Approach

Moving user mailboxes between servers is the safest migration method because the servers' databases are not in jeopardy if the migration fails. Moving the users also provides the opportunity to use new hardware with little or no downtime. In addition, moving users allows the organization to migrate users in sizeable chunks over time. Outlook profiles automatically are updated on the desktop, and users are redirected to the new Exchange Server 2003 systems when they log on. The limitation of moving users to a new server is that they can be moved only to an Exchange Server 2003 system in the same Administrative Group. Moving users can also slow the speed of the migration, which can be seen as a positive or negative, depending on the organization's goals.

The Exchange Server 2003 database is much more efficient than Exchange 5.5 was at storing messages. Even with full copies of all messages created by moving the users, administrators might actually see the database size shrink when comparing the size of the Exchange 5.5 and Exchange Server 2003 databases before and after migration. Quite a bit of empty space in the Exchange 5.5 database might also account for a portion of the reduced database size.

To move user mailboxes, open the Active Directory Users and Computers administrative tool and right-click the user to move; then select Exchange Tasks, as illustrated in Figure 15.8.

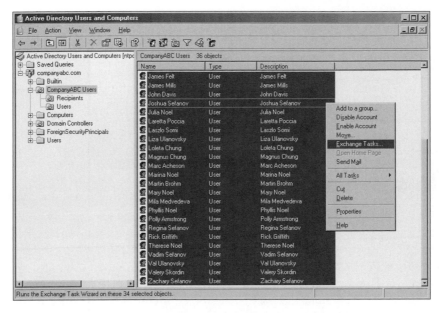

**FIGURE 15.8**    Selecting mailbox-enabled users to move.

1. Click Next at the welcome screen.

2. Choose the option for Move Mailbox and click Next.

3. When prompted for the type of move, select Same Administrative Group Move and click Next.

4. Select the destination server and mailbox store, and click Next.

5. At the next screen, choose either to create a failure report if corruption is detected or to skip corrupted items and continue the mailbox move. Click Next to continue.

6. At the next prompt, you can specify what time the Move Mailbox command should start and finish by. This is very useful when scheduling mailbox moves for off-hour periods. Click Next to continue.

Connections are then made to the source and destination server, and the mailbox contents are moved four at a time, as illustrated in Figure 15.9. If the move is unsuccessful, the user's mailbox still is available on the source Exchange 5.5 server.

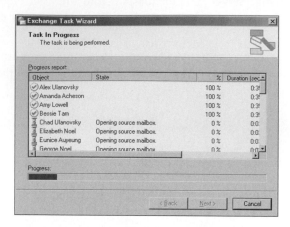

**FIGURE 15.9**   Moving mailboxes to Exchange Server 2003.

## Leapfrogging Server Migrations to Reduce Costs

If server hardware or budget is a limiting factor in the project, the organization might want to consider using a leapfrog method (also called the swing upgrade method) to migrate the users to Exchange Server 2003. Using the leapfrog method, fewer servers need to be purchased to perform the migration through the move users method.

One server still needs to be installed into the Exchange 5.5 site to house the SRS. Users can then be moved to that server or a second Exchange Server 2003 system installed into the site. After all users, connectors, and public folders are moved off the Exchange 5.5 server, that server can be formatted and reinstalled as an Exchange Server 2003 system, allowing the next Exchange 5.5 server's users to be migrated to Exchange Server 2003.

This greatly reduces the speed of the migration process and also requires a Native Mode Windows Server 2003 domain to support the public folders if they are scattered across the Exchange 5.5 servers. Another option for public folders in this scenario is to consolidate the public folders by replicating all the folders to a single Exchange 5.5 server in the site if a Native Mode Windows Server 2003 domain is not available. Connectors could also pose a problem with this method and require a solution before starting the leapfrog process.

One problem with this leapfrog method to be aware of is to not remove the first Exchange 5.5 server in a site until it's the last remaining 5.5 system in that site. The first Exchange server in the site hosts folders and other functions that are required by the Exchange 5.5 organization.

## Using ExMerge to Migrate Mailboxes

Exmerge.exe is a Microsoft utility that can extract the contents of a user's mailbox to a personal store (PST) file. The PST file created by ExMerge can be added to a user's Outlook profile so the user can access the contents of his old mailbox. ExMerge can also import the PST file to a destination mailbox to another server, site, or organization. On the destination server, ExMerge can merge the imported PST file or overwrite data in the target mailbox.

ExMerge can be used in disaster recovery and in migration scenarios to move user data from point A to point B by selecting the source and destination Exchange servers. ExMerge can be used when an organization wants to start with a clean Exchange Server 2003 environment and wants to be able to move mailbox contents to the new Exchange Server 2003 mailbox or archive the contents of the Exchange 5.5 mailbox in case a user needs access to his old information. ExMerge can also be used to move mailbox contents in organization-naming hierarchies that are the same or different. This is beneficial to organizations that want to build a new naming context when converting to Active Directory and Exchange Server 2003.

A few issues should be considered when using ExMerge to move mailbox contents to a new organization. The biggest one is that the capability to reply to all recipients on old messages could be lost. At a minimum, end-users need to force the names on old messages to be resolved against the new directory by using Alt+K or the Check Name button on the toolbar. End-users might be confused and frustrated if the new system cannot locate all of the users. This can occur if all users have not been migrated from the old organization or if mail connectivity to foreign mail systems has not been re-established in the new Exchange organization.

The second-biggest issue is that appointments on the user's calendar that contain other attendees are severed. The original appointments were resolved to the attendee's old addresses when they were created. This means that if the user deletes the appointment or makes a change to the time or location of the meeting, the other attendees will not be notified.

Even with these issues, ExMerge can be just the thing organizations are looking for, especially when they have survived multiple mergers and acquisitions and are looking to start over with Exchange Server 2003. If the organization plans to use ExMerge for the entire migration process, spend extensive time prototyping the merge process to catch other issues the organization might encounter.

ExMerge merges the following information:

- User folders
- User messages
- Outlook calendars
- Contacts
- Journal

15

- Notes

- Tasks

- Folder rules that were created in Exchange 5.0 or later

ExMerge does not support the following:

- Forms

- Views

- Schedule+ data

- Folder rules that were created in Exchange 4.0

ExMerge also supports advanced options such as extracting folder permissions. It can filter the messages for extraction from the source store by attachment name or subject that are accessible under the Options button on the source server selection screen.

ExMerge can be configured in either a one- or a two-step merge process. One-step merge processes copy the data from the source mailbox to a PST and then merge the data into the same mailbox on the destination server. The distinguished name of the mailbox and container path of the source and destination servers must be identical to perform a one-step merge.

When using ExMerge to move mailbox data from different organizations and sites, administrators need to be aware that ExMerge cannot create a mailbox on a destination server or set alternative recipient and forwarding rules on the source server. Another item that administrators should be aware of is that ExMerge runs only on Windows Server 2003. ExMerge needs to be able to access several Exchange Server 2003 DLL files. To run ExMerge, copy the `Exmerge.exe` and `Exmerge.ini` files to the Exchange `\bin` directory, or update the system path to include the Exchange `\bin` directory if ExMerge will run from another file location.

To run ExMerge using Exchange 5.5 as the source and Exchange Server 2003 as the destination, the credentials used for ExMerge must have Service Account Administrator privileges in Exchange 5.5 at the Organization, Site, and Configuration container levels. The credentials must also have at least Receive As permission on the destination Exchange 2003 mailbox.

> **NOTE**
>
> For inter-org migrations, ExMerge can be useful, but administrators should also look into using the built-in Exchange Migration Wizard, as it will preserve legacy directory information on mail items and can be a useful tool in the migration process.

# Migrating Exchange 5.5 Public Folders to Exchange Server 2003

Exchange mailboxes on the new Exchange Server 2003 systems must be able to access system and public folders, and subsequently require copies of the information that existed in those folders. Previously, in Exchange 2000, this required a fairly manual process of marking top-level public folders for replication and then propagating those changes down to subfolders. With Exchange Server 2003, however, a utility called `pfmigrate` automates this functionality. The options for `pfmigrate` are illustrated in Figure 15.10.

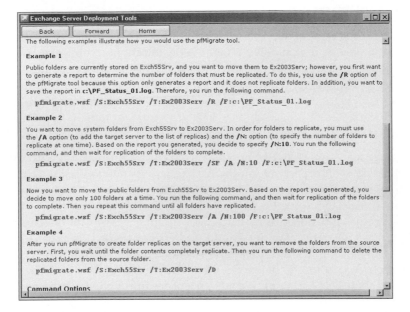

**FIGURE 15.10**    pfMigrate options.

The `pfmigrate` utility can be used in advance of a migration to make copies of public folders on the new servers; it then can be used later to remove the public folder copies from the old Exchange 5.5 servers.

# Migrating Exchange 5.5 Connectors and Services to Exchange Server 2003

With connectors in general, the best migration path is to build parallel connectors on Exchange Server 2003 systems. This way, the Exchange 5.5 connectors can remain intact and continue to route mail and perform directory synchronization with the foreign mail system.

The benefits of running connectors on both systems are as follows:

- Involves less risk when migrating the connectors

- Enables administrators to view Exchange 5.5 connector configuration when configuring and administering the Exchange Server 2003 connector

- Allows for controlled mail flow testing

- Provides a fallback plan if software defects or configuration issues are encountered with the Exchange Server 2003 connector

While testing the Exchange Server 2003 connectors, configure the Exchange Server 2003 connector with a higher cost and limited address space. This enables administrators to perform controlled tests of mail flow. When the organization is comfortable with the test results, the address space can be configured to match that of the Exchange 5.5 connectors. Also, the cost parameter on the connector can be dropped below that of the Exchange 5.5 connector, and the Exchange Server 2003 connector can begin routing all mail to the foreign system. The Exchange 5.5 connectors can remain in place until the organization is comfortable shutting them down.

Many Exchange 5.5 connectors also provide directory synchronization with foreign mail systems. Directory synchronization on the Exchange Server 2003 version of the connector should not be enabled until the mail flow through the connector works properly and the organization is ready to use the Exchange Server 2003 connector full-time. Most connectors such as GroupWise and Lotus Notes provide filtering options for directory synchronization. Marking the option Do Not Import Address Entries of This Type and using an asterisk (*) as a wildcard means that no entries will be imported and directory synchronization will remain on the Exchange 5.5 Server. Also do not export address entries to the foreign mail system, to avoid duplicate address entries in the foreign mail system's address list.

> **TIP**
>
> Take screenshots of all connector configuration property pages before attempting to migrate any connector. A lost setting such as an address space entry that is not transferred to the Exchange Server 2003 connector can cause a major routing or directory synchronization disaster on both mail platforms.

## Migrating the Internet Mail Service

The Internet Mail Service has been replaced by several components in Exchange Server 2003:

- SMTP Connector

- Internet Message Format

- Message Delivery Properties

The Internet Mail Service needs to be replaced by an equivalent SMTP Connector in Exchange Server 2003. After the migration, the new connector must be reconfigured to match the settings of the old IMS.

## Migrating Site Connectors

Site Connectors in Exchange v5.5 are replaced by Routing Group Connectors in Exchange Server 2003. Routing Group Connectors that communicate with Exchange 5.5 Server communicate over RPC. When Routing Group Connectors communicate between Exchange Server 2003 systems, they communicate over SMTP.

To build parallel connectors to Exchange 5.5 sites, create a Routing Group Connector to the remote Exchange 5.5 site and configure the local bridgehead server as the new Exchange Server 2003 connector server.

## Migrating Foreign Mail Connectors

Exchange Server 2003 includes support for the following foreign mail connectors:

- GroupWise Connector

- Lotus Notes Connector

- X.400 Connector

The best strategy to migrating these connectors is to use a parallel connector strategy. The following configuration settings must be reconfigured after an upgrade is in place on the foreign mail connectors:

- Directory synchronization schedule

- Address spaces

- Import container and export container configurations

- Delivery restriction options, such as message size

Always prototype the configuration, mail transfer, and directory synchronization for foreign mail connectors in a lab environment before implementing them in production. Mistakes in foreign mail connector configuration are usually quite costly and require extensive clean-up on both sides of the connection.

## Creating Support for Unsupported Connectors

To support unsupported connectors such as the PROFS/SNADS, cc:Mail, and MSMAIL connectors, remain in Mixed Mode Exchange Server 2003 and leave an Exchange 5.5 site to handle the unsupported connector. For a long-term solution, consider an SMTP solution for mail transfer and LDAP for directory synchronization. Another solution is to locate a third-party replacement connector.

# Completing the Migration to Exchange Server 2003

When all Exchange 5.5 servers are no longer required, the organization can convert to Native Mode Exchange Server 2003. This section covers the steps that need to be accomplished before the conversion to Native Mode can be executed. This section also covers some of the post-migration clean-up processes that need to be run in the Exchange Server 2003 organization. Not all of the clean-up processes need to be run in all environments; this depends on the method the organization used to populate Active Directory.

## Converting to Native Mode

Converting to Native Mode provides the organization with the following benefits and flexibility:

- Multiple Routing Groups are supported.

- Routing Groups can contain servers from different Administrative Groups.

- Servers can move between Routing Groups.

- Mailboxes can be moved between Administrative Groups.

- SMTP becomes the default routing protocol.

There are very few reasons to keep an Exchange organization in Mixed Mode after all Exchange 5.5 servers have been removed. You should change your Exchange organization to Native Mode in the following scenarios:

- No more Exchange 5.5 servers exist in the organization.

- No plans exist to add Exchange Server 5.5 servers to the organization in the future—the likelihood for a merger or acquisition is low.

- No need exists for connectors or gateways that run only on Exchange 5.5.

To convert to Native Mode Exchange Server 2003, the following steps must be accomplished in the following order:

1. Delete all Directory Replication Connectors.

2. Delete all Exchange 5.5 servers from each remaining site.

3. Delete the recipient connection agreements and all other connection agreements for each Exchange 5.5 site.

4. Delete the Site Replication Service (SRS) from all Exchange Server 2003 systems.

5. Switch to Native Mode using the Change Mode button on the organization's properties.

## Deleting All Directory Replication Connectors

For any remaining Exchange 5.5 site that will not be migrated to Exchange Server 2003, the Directory Replication Connectors must be deleted.

Use the Exchange System Manager to delete all Directory Replication Connectors. To delete the Directory Replication Connectors, click Tools to view Site Replication Service. Click the View menu and select Directory Replication Connector View. Click each Directory Replication Connector and press Delete.

Next force replication to propagate the deletion of the Directory Replication Connectors in the Active Directory Connector Manager by using the Replicate Now option on the connection agreements for the site. Verify the deletion of the Directory Replication Connectors by opening the Exchange System Manager on another Exchange Server 2003 system and viewing the Site Replication Service with the Directory Replication Connector view. When the Directory Replication Connector no longer appears, the deletion has been replicated.

### Removing All Exchange 5.5 Servers from the Organization

When all the Exchange 5.5 servers are no longer needed, they should be uninstalled through the Exchange 5.5 setup program. The last server to be uninstalled should be the server that was the first server in the site or that contains the first server in the site components.

After all the servers have been uninstalled, the last server must be deleted manually from the Exchange hierarchy. To delete the server from the hierarchy, use the Exchange 5.5 Administrator program to connect to the Exchange Server 2003 system running the Site Replication Service and locate the list of servers in the site. Click the server to be removed and then click Edit, Delete. A warning appears if the server still contains mailboxes or connectors. Click Yes to continue the deletion. Another warning appears if there are still public folder replicas on the server. Click Yes to continue the deletion.

The next step is to force replication through the ADC for all connection agreements for the site by using the Replicate Now option. Verify that the server has been removed from Active Directory through the ADC before deleting the connection agreements and uninstalling the ADC. The server should no longer appear in the Exchange System Manager.

### Removing the ADC

Open the Active Directory Connector Manager and delete all connection agreements. If the connection agreements are not deleted, the membership of distribution groups could be lost.

If the Active Directory Connector is no longer needed and all connection agreements have been removed, uninstall the Active Directory Connector through Control Panel, Add/Remove Programs. Also remember to disable or delete the service account used for the ADC if it's not used for any other services.

### Deleting the SRS

The Site Replication Services are the last services to be deleted before the conversion to Native Mode can take place. To delete the Site Replication Service, open the Exchange System Manager and expand the Tools icon. Next expand the Site Replication Services icon, and then right-click each Site Replication Service and click Delete.

### Throwing the Native Mode Switch

After the conversion to Native Mode, there is no way to return to mixed mode. The organization should be completely confident about the transition. When all the prerequisite steps have been accomplished, the Change Mode button on the organization properties in the Exchange System Manager should be available. Use the following steps to convert to Native Mode Exchange Server 2003:

1. Open the Exchange System Manager.

2. Right-click the organization and click Properties.

3. Click the General tab, and then click Change Mode under Change Operations Mode. Click Yes to permanently switch the organization's mode to Native Mode.

After the conversion to Exchange Server 2003 Native Mode, Administrative Groups are always displayed in the organization. Administrators have the choice of disabling the display of Routing Groups.

## Performing Post-Migration Clean-Up

Depending on the method that was used to populate the Active Directory, the organization might have to use a utility called ADClean that merges duplicate Active Directory accounts created during the migration process to Exchange Server 2003. If the Active Directory Connector was used to populate the Active Directory from the Exchange 5.5 directory before the Windows NT 4.0 domain accounts were migrated to Active Directory, two entries will exist for each user. The two user account entries should be merged through ADClean to complete the migration and clean up Active Directory.

The most efficient method of migrating to Exchange Server 2003 is to migrate the Windows NT 4.0 user accounts to Active Directory before beginning the Exchange Server 2003 migration, either through an in-place upgrade of the Windows NT 4.0 Primary Domain Controller or by using a migration tool such as the Active Directory Migration Tool (ADMT) v2.0 or other third-party tool. This eliminates the need to run the ADClean utility because the ADC will automatically match the Active Directory account to the mailbox, as long as it's specified as the primary Windows NT account for the mailbox. The ADC will then add the attributes for the mailbox to the existing Active Directory user account.

Duplicate accounts in Active Directory can also occur if two ADC recipient connection agreements were created and marked as primary on a particular container. One account displays as disabled with a red x in the user icon and with a –1 appended to the display name. The other account displays normally. ADClean can also be used to merge these accounts. To merge accounts created due to duplicate connection agreements, run ADClean and select the container to search. On the next screen, verify the accounts to merge and then choose the option to begin the merge or export the merge to a file for import through ADClean later.

> **TIP**
>
> The Search Based on Exchange Mailboxes Only option allows ADClean to search for only duplicate accounts created by the ADC.

The ADClean utility is installed during setup in the \exchsrvr\bin directory. ADClean gives administrators the capability to manually select accounts to be merged or run the wizard to search for and suggest accounts to be merged. The merge can be executed immediately or exported to a .csv file to be reviewed by the administrator and then executed later through ADClean.

## Summary

Migration from Exchange 5.5 to Exchange 2000 was a wild ride and required a great deal of planning and insight into the migration process to ensure success. Exchange Server 2003 greatly improves upon the migration capabilities, however, with the addition of the Exchange Deployment Tools. Using these tools, in addition to understanding best practices of the underlying procedures taking place, can do much to increase the reliability and success rate of an Exchange migration and more easily lead an Exchange 5.5 environment to the advanced feature set of Exchange Server 2003.

## Best Practices

- Utilize the Exchange Deployment Tools for the entire migration process to streamline the deployment and reduce risk.

- Migrate using the Move Mailbox process whenever possible, and resort to the ExMerge process only if migrating between Exchange Organizations.

- Install the Active Directory Connector on the first Exchange Server in the Site. Consider making this server a dedicated ADC/SRS server rather than a mailbox server.

- Switch the AD domain to Native Mode in advance of the ADC setup and Exchange migration, to ensure proper replication of security groups.

- Use the site and server consolidation strategies in Exchange Server 2003 to significantly reduce the number of servers that will need to be supported.

- Rely on the ADC Tools to configure the connection agreements, and modify them only if there is a specific reason to do so.

- Leave an Exchange 5.5 server in place only if it is needed to support connectors that are unsupported in Exchange Server 2003.

15

# Migrating from Exchange 2000 to Exchange Server 2003

**IN THIS CHAPTER**

- Outlining Migration Options from Exchange 2000 to Exchange Server 2003

- Deploying a Prototype Lab for the Exchange Server 2003 Migration Process

- Migrating to Exchange Server 2003 Using the In-Place Upgrade Approach

- Migrating to Exchange Server 2003 Using the Move Mailbox Method

The differences between Exchange 2000 and Exchange Server 2003 are not monumental. In many ways, Exchange Server 2003 is more akin to a major service pack to Exchange 2000 than anything. Keeping this in mind, upgrading an existing Exchange 2000 implementation to Exchange Server 2003 might not be high on many organizations' wish lists. However, the lack of major architectural differences between the two builds of Exchange can actually work to make an upgrade a more tempting prospect. The ease of upgrading from Exchange 2000 can bring the enhanced capabilities of Exchange Server 2003, particularly in the areas of remote connectivity and productivity, closer.

Ease of upgrade aside, due diligence should still be used when planning the deployment. A well-constructed prototype environment can help facilitate a smooth deployment of Exchange Server 2003, test design assumptions, and reduce the risk associated with any migration project. In addition, a migration to Exchange Server 2003 can also serve as a good opportunity to restructure an inefficient or ill-designed Exchange 2000 implementation.

This chapter focuses on best practice approaches to migrating from an existing Exchange 2000 implementation to Exchange Server 2003. Pros and cons of various migration approaches are presented, and sample step-by-step guides are detailed. In addition, special scenarios, such as cross-forest migrations, are discussed and illustrated.

# Outlining Migration Options from Exchange 2000 to Exchange Server 2003

The upgrade process from Exchange 2000 to Exchange Server 2003 was sold by Microsoft to be something that even a manager could perform. The idea was that an upgrade could involve simply throwing in an Exchange Server 2003 CD and clicking a few buttons. In many situations, the upgrade process can truly be this simple. Other more complex migrations involve additional thought into the migration process, however, because there are some fundamental security differences between the two products that can affect a migration process.

Among the upgrade scenarios available for Exchange 2000 to 2003 migrations, the field can essentially be narrowed to two major options: migrations using the move mailbox approach, and migrations using the in-place upgrade method. Other migration scenarios typically use a combination of these approaches or involve a significant degree of complexity.

## Understanding Exchange Server 2003 Migration Prerequisites

Because Exchange 2000 and Exchange Server 2003 are similar in many ways, there are fewer incompatibilities between them than one might think. A few of the lesser-used features in Exchange 2000 are not available in Exchange Server 2003, however, and should be called out in advance of a migration. In addition, several prerequisites exist that need to be satisfied before the upgrade takes place.

The following is a list of prerequisites that an Exchange 2000 environment should accomplish before upgrading to Exchange Server 2003:

- **OS and Exchange Level**—Exchange Server 2003 must be installed on either Windows 2000 SP3 or greater, or Windows Server 2003. Exchange 2000 also must be running at Exchange SP3 or greater.

- **Hardware Level**—The minimum requirements for running Exchange Server 2003 are a 133MHz processor, 256MB of RAM, and 500MB of available disk space. That said, a production Exchange Server will run much more efficiently with faster equipment.

- **Applicable Services Installed on Exchange System**—An Exchange Server 2003 System requires that the SMTP, NNTP, and WWW Services be enabled. If running Windows Server 2003, ASP.NET must also be enabled. These services, with the exception of SMTP, can be disabled if OWA and/or NNTP will not be used in Exchange.

- **Exchange Front-End Servers Upgraded First**—If front-end server architecture is deployed on Exchange 2000 servers, then all front-end servers in each Admin Group must be upgraded to Exchange Server 2003 first.

- **DNS and WINS**—DNS and WINS must be properly configured within the environment.

- **AD Requirements**—At least one, and preferably all, domain controllers in each AD site must be running with Windows 2000 SP3 or greater (or Windows Server 2003) to upgrade to deploy Exchange Server 2003 in the forest. In addition, a Global Catalog server must be located at no more than one AD Site away, although preferably in the same site.

## Identifying Exchange Server 2003 Migration Incompatibilities

The following services, which run on Exchange 2000, are incompatible and must either be removed or left on a running Exchange 2000 system:

- Exchange Conferencing Server

- Chat and Instant Messenger

- Key Management Server

- Mobile Information Server (MIS) (replaced with built-in Exchange Mobile Services functionality)

- cc:Mail and MS Mail connector

Any Exchange 2000 server that is running these services and is marked for upgrade must remove these services before proceeding. If their functionality is required, a legacy Exchange 2000 server can be left after the upgrade to run the components required. Mailboxes on Exchange Server 2003 systems will still be able to access their functionality in this scenario.

## Understanding Exchange Server 2003 Deployment Enhancements

Many of the changes between Exchange 2000 and Exchange Server 2003 are in the realm of server deployment. The process of deploying Exchange servers has been streamlined and optimized over the process used in Exchange 2000. Unlike most Microsoft applications, the process to deploy Exchange 2000 was not straightforward, and involved a series of command-line setup options and counter-intuitive procedures. Although Exchange Server 2003 greatly improves upon this model, it also can make changes that affect current server functionality. It is important to note the major changes to the Exchange setup process, to more accurately scope an upgrade scenario. The following list is a breakdown of the changes made to the setup process:

- **Deployment Tools**—The CD for Exchange Server 2003 includes a powerful set of deployment tools, which walk an administrator through the process of deploying Exchange Server 2003 under multiple scenarios. The step-by-step technique employed by this utility helps eliminate common mistakes and reduces the risk associated with deploying Exchange.

- **Granular Permissions Improvements**—Exchange Server 2003 handles installation permissions more intelligently, by allowing Exchange Full Administrators at the

16

Admin Group level to install Exchange, and by not overwriting custom permissions each time a new server is set up. In addition, security improvements remove the ability of regular domain users to physically log in to Exchange Servers.

- **Intelligent Setup**—Exchange Server 2003 improves the intelligence of the setup process by monitoring for such common errors as the Exchange Groups having been moved or renamed, and combines the schema extensions necessary for both the ADC and Setup components into a single extension process. In addition, it is no longer required for the setup of an Exchange server to contact the schema master Operations Master (OM) Role.

- **Default Public Folder and Message Size Limits**—Exchange Server 2003 defaults all public folders to a 10MB limit, in addition to defaulting maximum message size to 10MB. Unless a custom setting is already applied in Exchange 2000, upgrading to Exchange Server 2003 will default to these values regardless of whether they are wanted.

- **IIS Secured and Configured**—When upgrading an Exchange 2000/Windows 2000 system to Exchange Server 2003/Windows Server 2003, the functionality of IIS is upgraded and secured. Through this process, however, functionality for other IIS applications might break. Examine IIS functionality in advance of the migration to ensure that the securing process will not affect current functionality.

- **ActiveSync and OMA Components Installed**—Exchange Server 2003 automatically installs the components required to support Outlook Mobile Access (OMA) and Exchange ActiveSync.

## Migration Techniques Using the In-Place Upgrade Method

The in-place upgrade method is one of the simplest approaches to migration and can be an important tool if used effectively. In short, the in-place upgrade is composed of two steps: upgrading the Exchange 2000 component to Exchange Server 2003, and then upgrading the operating system from Windows 2000 to Windows Server 2003.

> **NOTE**
>
> Although the operating system upgrade is not technically required, it is desirable to run Exchange Server 2003 on IIS 6.0, which is available only with Windows Server 2003. IIS 6.0 provides a series of security and uptime enhancements for Exchange, and is subsequently highly recommended.

The in-place upgrade method has several advantages to its execution:

- **Design Simplicity**—When the design of the Exchange 2000 environment is already proven to be sound and reliable, the in-place upgrade approach enables a continuation of the elements of that design. The same servers contain the same mailboxes, and the overall design structure remains intact. The need for a long, drawn-out design process is reduced, and the focus shifts to simply scheduling the downtime for the server upgrade.

- **Hardware Reuse**—Existing hardware can be easily reused through the simple upgrade process. Organizations with an investment in current hardware can easily reallocate that hardware to the new environment through the upgrade process and eliminate the need to purchase new hardware.

- **Database Conversion Streamlined**—The in-place upgrade approach simply upgrades the Exchange 2000 databases in place, which is a faster procedure than the move mailbox method.

- **Eliminated Client-Reconfiguration**—By keeping the same servers and server names, non-Outlook clients, such as POP3 and IMAP clients, do not need to be reconfigured to point to a new set of servers. Although Outlook clients automatically reconfigure themselves if mailbox locations change, non-Outlook clients that may access Exchange normally have to be reconfigured to point to the new location. The in-place upgrade process eliminates this.

In general, this approach is useful for organizations with a solid existing Exchange 2000 design, who are simply interested in deploying Exchange Server 2003 for the increased productivity and security improvements. It is extremely useful for "quick and dirty" upgrades and can be successfully used for many organizations.

## Understanding Migration Techniques Using the Move Mailbox Method

One of the most flexible, safe, and effective approaches to upgrading is the move mailbox method. This method involves the introduction of new Exchange Server 2003 systems into an existing environment, testing them out and "burning" them in, and then migrating the mailboxes from Exchange 2000 to Exchange Server 2003. After the mailboxes are migrated, the Exchange 2000 servers can be retired.

The flexibility of this approach stems from the following distinct advantages:

- **Simplified Rollback**—By not reformatting or removing the old servers, the rollback procedure is optimized. A simple restore of premigration databases to the old servers can have users back up and running in the event of a problem with the migration.

- **Hardware Replacement**—This approach is useful if the servers that host Exchange 2000 are on older or overused hardware, because the present mailboxes can be easily moved to newer or more robust servers.

- **System Burn-in Time**—By allowing the new servers to be deployed in advance of the migration, they can be preconfigured with all security settings, antivirus configuration, software updates, and other settings. In addition, the hardware itself, such as disk drives and power supplies, can be stress-tested in advance of the production move to the new servers. This helps eliminate the risk associated with moving to new hardware and software.

16

- **New OS Builds**—By building the Windows Server 2003 and Exchange Server 2003 systems from scratch, legacy issues with software on old systems can be avoided. Although the in-place upgrade procedures have been improving in recent years, it is still good practice to build a system from scratch rather than perform an upgrade.

- **New Database Structure**—Migrations using the move mailbox method create new Exchange databases for the migrated users. This can resolve some lingering database corruption issues and also serves to defragment existing Exchange 2000 databases.

- **Architecture Changes Facilitated**—Organizations that are not happy with their current Exchange 2000 database or server structure can use this technique to restructure their environment. For example, organizations that originally deployed Exchange 2000 Standard Edition and were limited to a single database can use the move mailbox approach to move their mailboxes to multiple databases on servers running the Enterprise Edition of Exchange Server 2003.

- **Pilot Availability**—By deploying the new servers in advance of the migration, a small subset of users can be migrated in advance to test the functionality of the new system. These users can be members of a pilot group, which enables any bugs to be worked out of the system in advance of the migration.

The move mailbox method also enables a certain degree of flexibility in the execution of the approach. If the old hardware is still robust and is required to be recycled into Exchange Server 2003 servers, a leapfrog approach to the move mailbox process can be used by moving mailboxes from one server to the next, rebuilding the old server with new software, and then moving those mailboxes back. Combinations of this approach can also be used, which increases the flexibility of this option.

## Understanding Complex and Combined Approach Migration Techniques

The larger the organization, the more potential for complexity in the existing Exchange 2000 design. Some Exchange deployments make use of multiple separate Exchange organizations running in separate Exchange forests. These types of environments can make use of advanced tools—such as Microsoft Identity Integration Server 2003 (MIIS 2003), InterOrg/PF, and dedicated Exchange forests—to achieve their migration goals.

Organizations may choose to migrate to Exchange Server 2003 using a combined approach, wherein some of the systems that are migrated are upgraded in place and other systems use the move mailbox approach. The strength in each of the two strategies is that they enable the flexibility to be used in conjunction with each other.

In the case of multiple Exchange 2000 organizations, the decision can be made to collapse those organizations and their corresponding AD forests into a single forest, or to synchronize the information between the organizations using MIIS 2003. A third option enables the creation of a dedicated Windows Server 2003 forest and Exchange Server 2003 organization that is used by the various existing forests in the environment. Domain trusts between the domains and the Exchange forest are used to grant rights for users' accounts to access Exchange data, as illustrated in Figure 16.1. This model is referred to as the Exchange Resource Forest model.

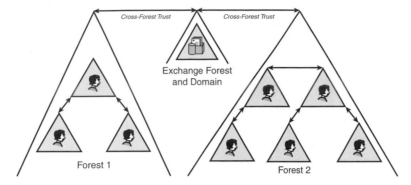

**FIGURE 16.1**  Viewing an Exchange organization configured in a Resource forest model.

## Deploying a Prototype Lab for the Exchange Server 2003 Migration Process

Regardless of the method that is chosen to migrate Exchange, care should be taken to test design assumptions as part of a comprehensive prototype lab. A prototype environment can help simulate the conditions that will be experienced as part of the migration process. Establishing a functional prototype environment also can help reduce the risk associated with migrations. In addition to traditional approaches for creating a prototype lab, which involves restoring from backups, several techniques exist to replicate the current production environment to simulate migration.

### Creating Temporary Prototype Domain Controllers to Simulate Migration

Construction of a prototype lab to simulate existing Exchange 2000 infrastructure is not particularly complicated, but requires thought in its implementation. Because an exact copy of the Active Directory is required, the most straightforward way of accomplishing this is by building a new domain controller in the production domain and then isolating that domain controller in the lab to create a mirror copy of the existing domain data. DNS and global catalog information should be transferred to the server when in production, to enable continuation of these services in the testing environment.

> **NOTE**
>
> There are several considerations to keep in mind if planning this type of duplication of the production environment. First, when the temporary domain controller is made into a Global Catalog server, the potential exists for Exchange 2000 to identify it as a working Global Catalog server and refer clients to it for directory lookups. When the server is brought offline, the clients would experience connectivity issues. For these reasons, it is good practice to create a temporary domain controller during off-hours.

A major caveat to this approach is that the system must be completely separate, with no way to communicate with the production environment. This is especially the case because the domain controllers in the prototype lab respond to requests made to the production domain, authenticating user and computer accounts and replicating information. Prototype domain controllers should never be added back into a production environment.

## Seizing Operations Master (OM) Roles in the Lab Environment

1. Because Active Directory is a multimaster directory, any one of the domain controllers can authenticate and replicate information. This factor is what makes it possible to segregate the domain controllers into a prototype environment easily. There are several different procedures that can be used to seize the OM (also referred to as FSMO) roles. One approach uses the `ntdsutil` utility: Open a Command Prompt by selecting Start, Run and typing **cmd**. Press Enter.

> **CAUTION**
>
> Remember, this procedure should only be performed in a lab environment or in disaster recovery situations. Never perform against a running production Domain Controller unless the intent is to forcibly move OM roles.

2. Type **ntdsutil** and press Enter.

3. Type **roles** and press Enter.

4. Type **connections** and press Enter.

5. Type **connect to server** *SERVERNAME* (where *SERVERNAME* is the name of the target Windows Server 2003 domain controller that will hold the OM Roles) and press Enter.

6. Type **quit** and press Enter.

7. Type **seize schema master** and press Enter.

8. Click Yes at the prompt asking to confirm the OM change.

9. Type **seize domain naming master** and press Enter.

10. Click Yes at the prompt asking to confirm the OM change.

11. Type **seize pdc** and press Enter.

12. Click OK at the prompt asking to confirm the OM change.

13. Type **seize rid master** and press Enter.

14. Click OK at the prompt asking to confirm the OM change.

15. Type **seize infrastructure master** and press Enter.

**16.** Click OK at the prompt asking to confirm the OM change.

**17.** Exit the Command Prompt window.

After these procedures have been run, the domain controllers in the prototype lab environment will control the OM roles for the forest and domain, which is necessary for additional migration testing.

> **NOTE**
>
> Although the temporary domain controller procedure just described can be very useful toward producing a copy of the AD environment for a prototype lab, it is not the only method that can accomplish this. The AD domain controllers can also be restored via the backup software's restore procedure. A third option—which is often easier to accomplish but is somewhat riskier—is to break the mirror on a production domain controller, take that hard drive into the prototype lab, and install it in an identical server. This procedure requires the production server to lose redundancy for a period of time while the mirror is rebuilt, but is a "quick and dirty" way to make a copy of the production environment.

### Restoring the Exchange Environment for Prototype Purposes

After all forest and domain roles have been seized in the lab, the Exchange server or servers must be duplicated in the lab environment. Typically, this involves running a restore of the Exchange server on an equivalent piece of hardware. All of the major backup software implementations contain specific procedures for restoring an Exchange 2000 environment. Using these procedures is the most ideal way of duplicating the environment for the migration testing.

### Validating and Documenting Design Decisions and Migration Procedures

The actual migration process in a prototype lab should follow, as closely as possible, any design decisions made regarding an Exchange Server 2003 implementation. It is ideal to document the steps involved in the process so that they can be used during the actual implementation to validate the process. The prototype lab is not only an extremely useful tool for validating the upgrade process, it can also be useful for testing new software and procedures for production servers.

The migration strategy chosen—whether it be an in-place upgrade, a move mailbox method, or another approach—can be effectively tested in the prototype lab at this point. Follow all migration steps as if they were happening in production.

## Migrating to Exchange Server 2003 Using the In-Place Upgrade Approach

As previously mentioned, the in-place upgrade method is the most straightforward approach toward migration. Existing server architecture and database structure is maintained. In many ways, this type of upgrade simply involves throwing in the Exchange Server 2003 CD and performing the upgrade.

An upgrade to Exchange Server 2003 is a two-step process. The first step involves upgrading the Exchange application component to Exchange Server 2003. The second step involves upgrading the operating system from Windows 2000 to Windows Server 2003. Exchange Server 2003 supports upgrading only Exchange first, because Exchange 2000 cannot function on a Windows Server 2003 operating system. The OS does not technically *require* upgrading, but it is recommended to do so to take advantage of all the new Exchange Server 2003 features that tie into the new OS.

## Making Use of the Exchange Server 2003 Deployment Tools

Microsoft has streamlined its Exchange deployment process by creating a set of deployment tools to assist with the Exchange installation process. With Exchange 2000, Microsoft found that the complexity of the upgrade process created confusion among the uninitiated, and led to some rather serious support calls. The Exchange deployment tools provide step-by-step checklists to ensure that the upgrade process is uneventful.

Using the Exchange Deployment Tools is a straightforward process and is the first step toward upgrading an existing Exchange 2000 server in place. To initiate the upgrade process, perform the following steps:

1. Insert the Exchange Server 2003 CD into the CD drive.

2. Select Start, Run, and type **X:\setup.exe** (where **X** is the CD drive).

3. At the welcome screen, click the Exchange Deployment Tools link.

4. Select Deploy the First Exchange 2003 Server.

5. Select Upgrade from Exchange 2000 Native Mode.

6. Review and perform the tasks listed under the prerequisites list in Deployment Tools, as illustrated in Figure 16.2.

The prerequisite tasks listed should be performed in any situation, and can help ensure that everything is in place before beginning intrusive tasks, such as upgrading the AD schema. Microsoft included these tasks in the deployment tools to proactively identify potential issues with the Exchange Server setup before they become major production incidents.

## Upgrading the Active Directory Schema with Exchange ForestPrep

Exchange Server 2003 requires that the Active Directory schema be modified to support the new enhancements in the product. The schema of Active Directory contains a list of all attributes and objects that can exist in the directory, and is the core framework around which Active Directory operates. It is a critical piece of an enterprise directory, and great care should be taken when examining changes to its structure, such as those enacted during Exchange Server setup. After the initial steps have been followed with the Exchange deployment tools, Exchange ForestPrep can be run on a domain controller in the schema root domain. It can be run manually or from the command line, or it can be invoked from the Exchange deployment tools, as follows:

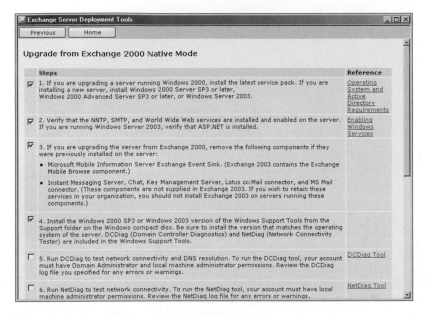

**FIGURE 16.2**   Viewing Exchange setup prerequisites.

1. While in Exchange Deployment Tools, ensure that all prerequisite steps have been completed.

2. Click the Run ForestPrep Now link.

3. After waiting for Setup to initialize, click Next at the welcome screen.

4. Select I Agree and click Next.

5. Review and ensure that ForestPrep is selected for the Action, as illustrated in Figure 16.3, and click Next.

6. Enter the name of the account that will be used for subsequent installations of Exchange. This account will be granted Exchange Full Administrator rights at the Organization level. Click Next to continue.

7. Click Finish at the final screen for the ForestPrep procedure.

> **NOTE**
>
> The changes made to the AD schema can be viewed via low-level LDAP tools, such as ADSI Edit. This particular tool can be installed as part of the Windows Server 2003 Support Tools pack, which is located on the Windows Server 2003 CD in the \Support\Tools directory.

16

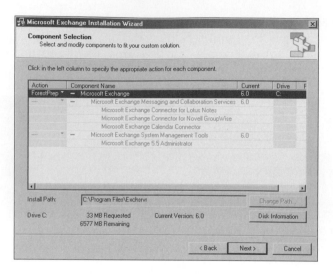

FIGURE 16.3    Exchange ForestPrep.

## Preparing Each Domain for Exchange Server 2003 with DomainPrep

After the AD schema has been upgraded and the changes have propagated throughout the AD forest, each domain in the forest must be prepared for Exchange Server 2003 via the DomainPrep procedure. Although DomainPrep can be run via the command prompt (setup /domainprep), it can also be launched via the deployment tools as follows:

1. On a domain controller in the root domain, restart Deployment Tools and continue from the end of the ForestPrep procedure.

2. Click Run DomainPrep now to start the DomainPrep procedure.

3. Click Next at the welcome screen.

4. Select I Agree and click Next.

5. Ensure that DomainPrep is selected under Action and click Next.

6. Click OK to any messages that appear about insecure groups that might exist in the domain. DomainPrep will run, as illustrated in Figure 16.4.

7. Click Finish when complete.

8. Repeat on a DC in each domain in the AD forest.

---

**NOTE**

DomainPrep must be run on each domain in a forest where Exchange servers or mailboxes will reside, even though it might have been run during the setup of Exchange 2000, as Exchange Server 2003 DomainPrep performs additional required tasks beyond those performed with the Exchange 2000 domainprep utility.

---

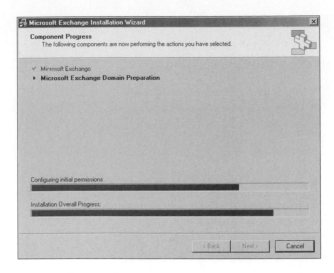

**FIGURE 16.4**   Running Exchange DomainPrep.

The DomainPrep procedure creates groups necessary for Exchange and sets appropriate permissions for the accounts required. The groups that it creates (Exchange Domain Servers and Exchange Enterprise Servers) must be kept in the default Users container in AD and must not be renamed to ensure functionality.

## Running the In-Place Upgrade of an Exchange 2000 System to Exchange Server 2003

After all the prerequisites have been satisfied, ForestPrep has been run and replicated, and DomainPrep has created the appropriate groups and permissions in each domain, the actual upgrade procedure for Exchange Server 2003 can commence. The upgrade process should be run from the server that is to be upgraded, and can be manually initiated or invoked via the Deployment Tools, as follows:

1. Run Exchange Deployment Tools on the Exchange 2000 Server to be upgraded and verify that all tasks up to the DomainPrep have been completed.

2. Click Run Setup Now.

3. Click Next at the welcome screen.

4. Select I Agree and click Next.

5. Ensure that Upgrade is listed under Action, as illustrated in Figure 16.5, and click Next.

6. Review the final settings and click Next; Exchange will update.

7. When the installation is complete, click Finish.

16

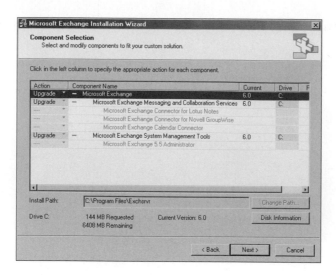

**FIGURE 16.5**    Upgrading an Exchange server.

At this point, Exchange is updated from Exchange 2000 to Exchange Server 2003. The new Exchange System Manager tool is installed, and the bulk of Exchange Server 2003 functionality is present for all mailboxes on the server. In addition to installing the base Exchange Server 2003 files, it is highly recommended to apply Exchange Server 2003 Service Pack 2 to the server as well.

## Upgrading the Operating System from Windows 2000 to Windows Server 2003

The final piece of the puzzle, which makes an Exchange 2003 system complete, is the upgrade of the base operating system to Windows Server 2003. Certain functionality, especially regarding security, cannot be achieved until the base OS for Exchange Server 2003 is running the new OS. Fortunately, the upgrade from Windows 2000 to Windows Server 2003 is straightforward, and can be accomplished via the following steps:

1. Insert the Windows Server 2003 CD.

2. Run the appropriate Setup.exe (Enterprise or Standard Edition).

3. Select Install Windows Server 2003 (Enterprise Edition).

4. Verify the Installation Type to be Upgrade, as illustrated in Figure 16.6, and click Next.

5. Select I Accept This Agreement and click Next.

6. Enter the appropriate License Key and click Next.

7. Select No, Skip This Step and Continue Installing Windows, when prompted to download update files.

8. Review any incompatibilities on the next screen and click Next. Setup will start copying files, reboot, and complete the installation.

**FIGURE 16.6**  Upgrading to Windows Server 2003.

Upon the successful completion of the steps outlined in this section, an Exchange 2000 system will be upgraded to Exchange Server 2003, using the in-place upgrade method. At this point, any additional servers that have been marked for upgrade can use this procedure.

### Upgrading Additional Exchange 2000 Servers to Exchange Server 2003

Each additional server that is running Exchange 2000 can be upgraded using the same technique described in the previous sections. The prerequisite steps, ForestPrep and DomainPrep, do not need to be repeated for each additional server, however. Unlike with Exchange 5.5, there is no functional difference between an all–Exchange 2003 or mixed Exchange 2000/2003 environment, so there is no such thing as an Exchange Server 2003 Native Mode. Most of the differences will be noticeable at the client level, however, in the form of improvements to the client experience, such as OMA, ActiveSync, RPC over HTTP, and improved security.

## Migrating to Exchange Server 2003 Using the Move Mailbox Method

As previously mentioned, the move mailbox method of migration can be ideal for organizations that require a new set of hardware for their Exchange servers or that desire to reconstruct some portions of their Exchange infrastructure. The move mailbox method is also an effective way of minimizing the risk associated with a migration to Exchange Server 2003.

## Deploying Exchange 2003 Servers in Advance of the Move Mailbox Migration

The greatest advantage to the move mailbox approach lies in the ability to deploy a new system to function as an Exchange 2003 Server. The server can be set up and configured with all applicable settings and third-party utilities before a single mailbox is moved to it.

Just as the in-place upgrade process (described earlier) required AD to be upgraded, the move mailbox approach has the same requirements. This process involves running the ForestPrep and DomainPrep options before the first server is deployed. After these prerequisites are satisfied, the setup of the server can begin:

1. Insert the Exchange Server 2003 CD into the CD drive.

2. Select Start, Run, and type **D:\setup.exe** (where **D** is the CD drive).

3. At the welcome screen, click the Exchange Deployment Tools link.

4. Select Deploy the First Exchange 2003 Server, as illustrated in Figure 16.7.

**FIGURE 16.7**    Using the Exchange Server Deployment Tools.

5. Select Upgrade from Exchange 2000 Native Mode.

6. Review and check off the prerequisites list in the Deployment Tools.

7. Click the Run ForestPrep Now link.

8. After waiting for Setup to initialize, click Next at the welcome screen.

9. Select I Agree and click Next.

10. Review and ensure that ForestPrep is selected for the Action and click Next.

11. Enter the name of the account that will be used for subsequent installations of Exchange, as illustrated in Figure 16.8, and click Next.

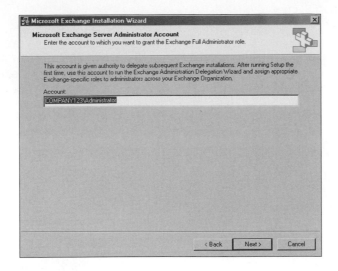

**FIGURE 16.8**    Selecting the Exchange Administrator during ForestPrep.

12. Click Finish at the final screen for the ForestPrep procedure.

13. Click Run DomainPrep now to start the DomainPrep procedure.

14. Click Next at the welcome screen.

15. Select I Agree and click Next.

16. Ensure that DomainPrep is selected under Action and click Next.

17. Click OK to any messages that appear about insecure groups that might exist in the domain.

18. Click Finish when complete.

19. Click Run Setup Now from the Deployment Tools.

20. Click Next at the welcome screen.

21. Select I Agree and click Next.

22. Ensure that Typical is listed under Action and click Next.

23. Review the final settings and click Next; Exchange will update.

24. When the installation is complete, click Finish.

All these steps are necessary to install the first Exchange Server 2003 system into an existing Exchange 2000 environment. Subsequent Exchange 2003 systems can also be set up at this point, via the post–DomainPrep procedures outlined earlier.

16

## Enabling New Server "Burn-In" and Pilot Testing

One of the main advantages to the move mailbox approach is that the new systems can now be "burnt in" and tested without affecting production users. A small subset of mailboxes can also be migrated to the new system to test functionality and ensure compatibility with an organization's systems. After the pilot is complete, a full mailbox migration can then take place with less overall risk.

## Moving Mailboxes to the New Exchange Server 2003 Databases

After all Exchange Server 2003 systems have been deployed and their configurations finalized, the actual migration process of moving mailboxes from Exchange 2000 to Exchange Server 2003 can begin. The move mailbox procedure in Exchange Server 2003 has been vastly improved over the one that was present in Exchange 2000. Features such as error detection, multiple migration streams, and scheduling enable a much-improved experience.

The move mailbox procedure should be scheduled to run during off-hours, because it effectively takes a user's mailbox out of service during the move operation. The mailbox is out of service for only the duration of the move, and is available again after the process is complete for that mailbox. Migration time varies, depending on network connectivity and hardware speed, but at least 2GB/hr can be expected during the move operation.

To move mailboxes from an Exchange 2000 server to one of the new Exchange 2003 systems previously set up, perform the following tasks:

1. From the new Exchange 2003 server, select Start, All Programs, Microsoft Exchange, Active Directory Users and Computers.

2. Select the Mailbox-Enabled Users who are to be migrated. Right-click on them and choose Exchange Tasks.

3. At the welcome page, click Next.

4. Select Move Mailbox and click Next.

5. Select the Server and Information Store to move the mailboxes to and click Next.

6. Select Skip Corrupted Items and Create a Failure Report, as illustrated in Figure 16.9, and click Next.

7. Choose the time to begin migrating and the time to stop migrating and click Next. The wizard will begin moving mailboxes, four at a time, as illustrated in Figure 16.10.

8. Upon completion of the migration process, the migration dialog box will indicate the success or failure of each mailbox migrated, which can be reviewed.

After a mailbox is migrated, a user can then access it via Outlook or other clients. The Outlook client automatically detects the change in Exchange Home Server and updates itself, connecting to the new mailbox automatically. Other functionality—such as OWA for Exchange Server 2003 and ActiveSync with pocket PC devices—also becomes available after the move, once they are enabled in Exchange System Manager.

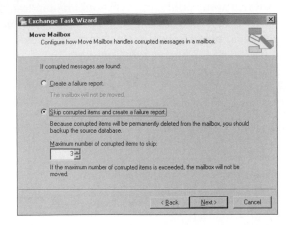

**FIGURE 16.9**    Move Mailbox corrupt item options.

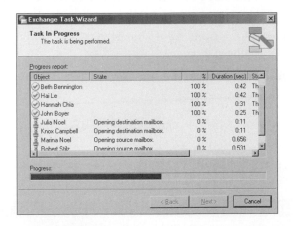

**FIGURE 16.10**    Moving mailboxes.

> **NOTE**
>
> Although the Outlook client will automatically update itself with the new server settings, any manually configured clients, such as POP3 and IMAP clients, should be manually reconfigured with the name of the new server. This factor also commonly affects third-party Exchange synchronization tools, such as Palm devices.

## Replicating Public Folders from Exchange 2000 to Exchange Server 2003

Just as the mailboxes are migrated from one set of Exchange 2000 servers to another set of Exchange Server 2003 systems, the public folders should be replicated before retiring the old Exchange 2000 servers. Previously, this procedure involved a manual replication of folder hierarchy, which could prove to be a tedious process. Microsoft addressed this drawback with a new utility called PFMigrate, which is accessible via the Exchange Deployment Tools. PFMigrate can create public and system folder replicas on new systems, and remove them from old servers. The following procedure outlines how to use PFMigrate to migrate from an Exchange 2000 Server to an Exchange Server 2003 system:

1. Open a Command Prompt (select Start, Run; type **cmd**; and press Enter).

2. Type **cd D:\support\Exdeploy** and press Enter.

3. To create a report of current public folder replication, type the following:

   **pfmigrate.wsf /S:*OLDSERVERNAME* /T:*NEWSERVERNAME* /R /F:c:\LOGNAME.log**

   This generates a report named LOGNAME.log on the C: drive. *OLDSERVERNAME* should be the name of the Exchange 2000 system, and *NEWSERVERNAME* should be the new Exchange Server 2003 system.

4. To replicate System Folders from the Exchange 2000 server to the Exchange 2003 server, type the following:

   **pfmigrate.wsf /S:*OLDSERVERNAME* /T:*NEWSERVERNAME* /SF /A /N:10000**
   **/F:c:\LOGNAME.log**

5. To replicate Public Folders from Exchange 2000 to Exchange Server 2003, type the following:

   **pfmigrate.wsf /S:*OLDSERVERNAME* /T:*NEWSERVERNAME* /A /N:10000 /F:c:\LOGNAME.log**

> **NOTE**
>
> The /N:#### field determines how many public folders should be addressed by the tool. If a larger number of public folder than 10,000 exists, the parameter should be increased to match.

6. After all public folders have replicated, the old replicas can be removed from the Exchange 2000 servers by typing the following, as illustrated in Figure 16.11:

   **pfmigrate.wsf /S:*OLDSERVERNAME* /T:*NEWSERVERNAME* /D**

7. The LOGNAME.log file can be reviewed to ensure that replication has occurred successfully and that a copy of each public folder exists on the new server. A sample log from this procedure is illustrated in Figure 16.12.

**FIGURE 16.11** Command-line PFMigrate functionality.

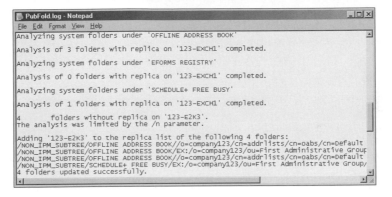

**FIGURE 16.12** Viewing a sample PFMigrate log file.

> **TIP**
>
> Become familiar with the command-line options that are available with the PFMigrate tool, because they can be useful for managing the replication of public folders across a newly deployed Exchange Server 2003 environment.

## Moving Connectors from Exchange 2000 to Exchange Server 2003

If the eventual goal of the migration process involves retiring the Exchange 2000 infrastructure, it will be necessary to move all connectors from the Exchange 2000 servers to the new Exchange 2003 systems. The most important consideration when moving connectors is to ensure that no messages that use or flow through the connectors are lost.

In some cases, Exchange 2000 might have been deployed with specific SMTP connectors to provide outgoing mail flow through specific servers. These types of connectors should

16

be rerouted to pass through Exchange 2003 systems and ensure the proper flow of outgoing mail. This can be done by modifying the cost of the connectors.

As previously mentioned, there are some Exchange 2000 components that are not supported in Exchange Server 2003. This includes two connectors: the MS Mail connector and the cc:Mail connector. If these connectors are in use, an Exchange 2000 server must be left in the organization to support them, because they cannot be migrated over to Exchange 2003 servers.

## Changing the Recipient Update Service (RUS) Server from Exchange 2000 to Exchange Server 2003

Before Exchange 2000 can be retired, an Exchange Server 2003 system must be designated as the Recipient Update Service (RUS) Exchange Server for the organization and for each domain. To do this, perform the following:

1. On the Exchange Server 2003 System, open Exchange System Manager (select Start, All Programs, Microsoft Exchange, System Manager).

2. Navigate to Recipients, Recipient Update Service.

3. Right-click Recipient Update Service (Enterprise Configuration) and choose Properties.

4. Under Exchange Server, click Browse.

5. Type the name of the Exchange 2003 server that will become the RUS system and click OK.

6. Click OK when the new server is listed, as illustrated in Figure 16.13.

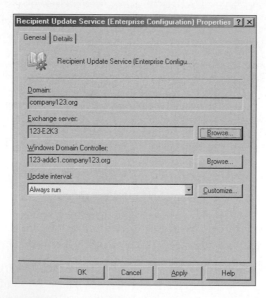

**FIGURE 16.13**    Changing RUS server settings.

7. Repeat for all domain Recipient Update Service settings.

## Retiring Legacy Exchange 2000 Servers

After all mailboxes, public folder replicas, and connectors have been moved off the old Exchange 2000 infrastructure, the old Exchange servers can be retired and removed from service. The easiest and most straightforward approach to this is to uninstall the Exchange 2000 component via the Add-Remove Programs applet in Windows. To perform this operation, do the following:

1. On the Exchange 2000 server, select Start, Settings, Control Panel.

2. Double-click Add/Remove Programs.

3. Select Microsoft Exchange 2000 and click Change/Remove.

4. Click Next at the welcome screen.

5. Under Action, select Remove from the drop-down box, as illustrated in Figure 16.14, and click Next to continue.

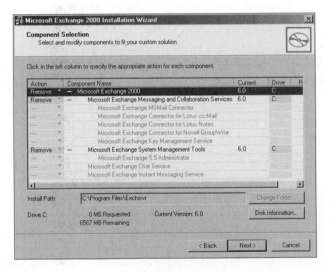

**FIGURE 16.14**    Removing an Exchange 2000 server.

6. At the summary screen, click Next to continue. Exchange 2000 will then be uninstalled.

7. Repeat the process for any additional Exchange 2000 servers.

Upon removal of the last Exchange 2000 system, the environment will then be completely upgraded to Exchange Server 2003, with all mailboxes, public folders, and connectors moved to the new environment.

> **NOTE**
>
> It might be wise to keep old Exchange 2000 servers around for a few weeks after a move mailbox migration, because the old servers will be required to direct clients to their new mailbox locations. After all Outlook clients have connected to their new mailboxes, the old servers can then be safely retired.
>
> If it is not possible to keep an old server around, a "trick" to allow for client redirection to the new server is to create a CNAME record in DNS that points to another Exchange server (not the one where the mailboxes were moved to). This other server will redirect the client to the appropriate server.

## Summary

A migration from Exchange 2000 to Exchange Server 2003 is more of an upgrade than an actual migration. The similarities between the two systems make it not as critical or desirable to migrate in many situations. On the other hand, these same similarities also make it very straightforward to migrate and take advantage of advanced Exchange Server 2003 functionality. With proper diligence, the techniques described in this chapter can be used to migrate an existing Exchange 2000 infrastructure to Exchange Server 2003 using a best practice approach.

## Best Practices

- Use the in-place upgrade procedure for "quick and dirty" upgrades or when server equipment is newer.

- Use the move mailbox procedure when deploying new server hardware or changing basic server architecture, or for risk-averse migrations.

- Create a prototype lab to test the migration process and validate design assumptions.

- Keep an Exchange 2000 server in place only if needing to support legacy tools—such as Conferencing Server, KMS, Chat, and Instant Messenger Server—and other non-supported functionality if it is required in the migrated environment.

- Leave legacy Exchange 2000 servers in place for a few weeks following a move mailbox migration to ensure that all clients are redirected to their new mailbox locations. If it is not possible, use a CNAME record in DNS to point the old server name to a different server than the one that the mailbox was moved to.

- Consider the use of advanced tools—such as MIIS 2003, InterOrg/PF, and dedicated Exchange forests—for complex situations involving multiple Exchange organizations.

- When using the move mailbox approach, allow time between the deployment of the new servers and the migration to enable the new servers to "burn in." This is also an ideal time to migrate a pilot set of users.

- Use the Exchange Deployment Tools to help minimize any issues associated with the migration process.

16

# CHAPTER 17

# Compatibility Testing

IN THIS CHAPTER

- The Importance of Compatibility Testing

- Preparing for Compatibility Testing

- Researching Products and Applications

- Verifying Compatibility with Vendors

- Lab-Testing Existing Applications

- Documenting the Results of the Compatibility Testing

- Determining Whether a Prototype Phase Is Required

At this point in the book, the new features of Exchange Server 2003 have been presented and discussed in depth, as have the essential design considerations and migration processes. The goal of this chapter is to examine the process of testing the actual applications that rely on the Exchange Server infrastructure.

This chapter provides insight into the steps to take in gathering the information needed before the testing process, how to actually test the applications and document the results, and how to determine whether a more extensive prototype testing process is needed. It is vital to go through this process, rather than simply winging it to ensure the success of the project and avoid a displeased user community. The application testing process is intended as a quick way to validate the compatibility and functionality of the proposed end-state for the upgrade.

Currently, many companies are seeking to "right-size" their network environment, and might be using the upgrade as a chance to actually reduce the number of servers that handle Exchange processes on the network. At the end of the process, fewer servers will handle the same tasks as before, and new functionality might have been added, making the configurations of the individual servers that much more complex, and making it even more important to thoroughly test the mission-critical messaging applications on the server. For example, with the improved ability of Exchange Server 2003 to manage and support larger databases with Service Pack 2 and support more RAM, combined with Windows Server 2003's enhanced fault-tolerance features, one Exchange Server 2003 server might replace a handful of Exchange 5.5 or Exchange 2000 servers. Thus, it's even more important that this configuration be tested to ensure that the performance meets user expectations and that the features that are used every day by the employees to share knowledge and collaborate are in place.

The results of the application compatibility testing process will validate the goals of the project or reveal goals that need to be modified due to application incompatibility or instability. If one key application simply won't work reliably on Exchange Server 2003, an Exchange 5.5 server might need to be kept as part of the messaging environment, which changes the overall design. As discussed in Part II of this book, "Exchange Server 2003," a variety of different combinations of Exchange Server software can be combined in the end configuration, so the chances are good that there will be a way to keep the troublesome applications working in the new environment.

# The Importance of Compatibility Testing

The process presented in this chapter is an essential step to take in validating the design for the end-state of the migration or upgrade. The size of the organization and the breadth and scope of the upgrade are important factors to consider in determining the level of testing needed, and whether a full prototype should be conducted.

The differences between a prototype phase and an application testing phase can be dramatic or negligible based on the nature of the upgrade. A prototype phase replicates the end-state as completely as possible, often using the same hardware in the test lab that will be used in the production rollout.

> **CAUTION**
>
> Application testing can be performed on different hardware with different configurations than the end-state, but be aware that the more differences there are between the testing environment and the actual upgraded environment, the more risk for unexpected results there will be. Essentially, you can do an application testing phase without a complete prototype phase, but you shouldn't do a prototype phase without a thorough application testing process.

Most network users don't know or care which server or how many servers perform which task or house which application, but they will be unhappy if the application that allows them to synchronize their pocket PC, BlackBerry, or Palm device no longer works. If the ability to fax from the desktop suddenly disappears, instant messaging vanishes, or they can't access email from an Internet café, the Exchange administrator can expect emails with a lot of capital letters in them. Many companies have integrated voicemail with Exchange so that users simply click on a voicemail to listen to it, and changes to this functionality can harm the business processes of the company. New antispam software can inadvertently block messages from key customers, if they contain a word such as `sale` or `act now`.

If the organization already has Active Directory in place and is on Exchange 2000 Server, the risk of application incompatibility is likely to be less than if the organization is moving from an older operating system, such as NT 4.0 Server, or a competing operating system, such as Novell NetWare. The upgrade from Exchange 2000 Server might well use the existing server hardware and perform in-place upgrades, or in the case of an upgrade from Exchange Server 5.5, it might involve implementing entirely new server hardware and new server fault-tolerance features, which further change the operating environment. If this is the case, a full prototype phase might not be needed, but applications testing should still take place.

# Preparing for Compatibility Testing

Although the amount of preparation needed will vary based on a number of factors, certain steps should be followed in any organization: The scope of the testing should be identified (what's in and what's out), the goals of the testing process should be clarified, and the process should be mapped out.

A significant advantage of following a phased design methodology, as presented in Chapter 2, "Planning, Prototyping, Migrating, and Deploying Exchange Server 2003" is in the planning discussions that take place and in the resulting Statement of Work and Design and Migration documents that are created as deliverables. Often, companies contract messaging experts, who help companies avoid classic mistakes, to assist in the process. By the end of this planning process, it will be very clear why the project is happening, which departments need which features and capabilities, and what budget is available to perform the work. The timeline and key milestones also will be defined.

If a phased discovery and design process hasn't been followed, this information needs to be gathered to ensure that the testing process addresses the goals of the project stakeholders and that the right applications are, in fact, tested and verified by the appropriate people.

## Determining the Scope for Application Testing

At this point in the process, a list should be put together that clarifies which Exchange Server 2003 version is to be used, which version of server software will be used, which add-in features are required, and which third-party applications are needed. As discussed previously, Exchange Server 2003 can be installed on either Windows 2000 Server or Windows Server 2003, and on the Standard or Enterprise versions of the NOS. Smaller companies might choose to use the Standard versions of Windows Server 2003 and Exchange Server 2003, whereas larger organizations might require the Enterprise versions of each.

A key issue to discuss at this point is whether it is acceptable to have multiple versions of the Windows Server operating system and of Exchange Server in the final solution. Some organizations want to control costs of both software and support services and require a single NOS and single version of Exchange Server. These organizations would rather choose a different messaging application than keep an older application in place that isn't compatible with the newest NOS and version of Exchange.

Besides the core Exchange Server 2003 software, additional components can be installed that extend the functionality of the software, such as Outlook Mobile Access (OMA), Mobile Information Server (MIS), or Real Time Collaborations (RTC).

17

NOTE

Although the Standard Edition of Exchange Server 2003 is significantly cheaper than the Enterprise Edition of the license, cost should not be the primary reason for choosing one version over another. It is not as simple to upgrade from the Standard to Enterprise Edition as just changing a software license key. It typically requires setting up a brand-new server with the Exchange Server 2003 Enterprise Edition (on top of Windows Server 2003 Enterprise Edition) and migrating mailboxes from server to server. An organization should seriously consider whether it needs the functionality of the Enterprise Edition before choosing to buy and install the Standard Edition to upgrade easily later.

Third-party applications should be identified as well. The applications most often used include tape backup software modules or agents, antivirus software, fax software, and voicemail integration products. Additional third-party add-on products may include

- Administration

- Antispam

- Backup and storage

- Collaboration

- Customer relationship management (CRM)

- Content checking

- Disclaimers

- Email antivirus

- Fax connectors

- List server software

- Log monitoring

- Migration

- POP3 downloaders

- Reporting

- Security and encryption

- SMS and paging

The hardware to be used should be listed as well, to ensure that it is available when needed. Ideally, the exact hardware to be used in the upgrade will be ordered for the application testing process, but if that is not possible, hardware with specifications similar to that of the servers that will eventually be used should be allocated. Although processor speed and amount of RAM will most likely not make a difference to whether the application functions properly on the server platform, certain hardware devices should be as similar as possible. Tape drives, for example, should have the same features as the ones to be used in the production environment because this is one of the most critical components. If an autoloader will be used in the production environment, one should be made available for the application testing process. If faxing from the Outlook Inbox is required, the same faxing hardware should be allocated as well.

Some applications require clients to be present for the testing process, so at least one workstation class system should be available for this purpose. Connectivity to the Internet might also be needed for testing the functionality of remote access products and antivirus software.

Table 17.1 shows a sample checklist of requirements for summarizing the scope of the application testing phase.

**TABLE 17.1**    Checklist for Application Testing

| Server #1 | Details (Include Version #s) |
| --- | --- |
| Server specs required: | |
| Processor | |
| RAM | |
| Hard drive configuration | |
| Other | |
| Network OS and service packs: | |
| Exchange version and service packs: | |
| Tape backup software version and agents: | |
| Antivirus software and related modules: | |
| Additional third-party apps required: | |
| Additional hardware required: | |
| SAN device | |
| Tape drive | |
| UPS | |
| Switch/hub | |
| Other | |
| Internet access required? | Yes / No |

This process should not take a great deal of time if previous planning has taken place. If the planning phase was skipped, some brainstorming will be required to ensure that the scope includes all of the key ingredients required for the application testing. The goals for the application testing process will also affect the scope, which is covered in the following section.

## Defining the Goals for Compatibility Testing

As with the previous step of defining the scope of the testing process, defining the goals might be a very quick process, or might require some discussions with the stakeholders involved in the project.

One useful way of looking at the goals for the project is to treat them as the checklist for successful completion of the testing. What conditions need to be met for the organization to confidently move forward with the next step in the Exchange upgrade? The next step might be a more complete prototype testing phase, or it might be a pilot rollout, in which the new messaging environment is offered to a select group of savvy users.

These goals are separate from the business goals the company may have, such as "more reliable messaging infrastructure," or "improved feature set of email client." A more complete prototype phase could seek to address these goals, while the application testing process stays focused on the performance of the specific combinations of operating system, Exchange Server 2003, and embedded and connected applications.

A convenient way to differentiate the goals of the project is to split them into key areas, as described in the following sections.

### Time Frame for Testing

This goal can be defined with the statement "The testing must be completed in $X$ days/weeks."

If there is very little time available to perform the testing, this limits how much time can be spent on each application and how many end-users can put each through its paces. It also necessitates a lesser degree of documentation. Remember to include time for researching the application's compatibility with the vendors as part of the timeline. A quick project plan might be useful in this process as a way to verify the assumptions and sell the timeline to the decision-makers.

---

**Estimating the Duration of the Application Testing Process**

A good rule of thumb is to allow four hours per application for basic testing, and eight hours for a more thorough testing process. This allows time for the initial research with the vendors, configuration of the NOS and Exchange Server 2003 software, and testing of the applications. Of course, the total time required will vary based on the types of applications to be tested.

For example, a Windows Server 2003 system with Exchange Server 2003, tape backup software, antivirus software, fax software, and voicemail connectivity (six total applications) would take an estimated three days to test for basic compatibility and functionality and six days for more rigorous testing.

If another system configuration is to be tested in the same lab—which has Windows 2000 Server SP3, tape backup software, antivirus software, fax software, and voicemail connectivity—allocate the same amount of time even though only one component is different: three to six days. Note that if more than one resource is available to perform the testing, these configurations can be tested in parallel, shortening the *duration* of the process, but not the *work effort*.

It's always better to have some extra time during the testing phase. This time can be used for more extensive user testing, training, or documentation.

---

Contingency time should ideally be built in to this goal. Resources assigned to the testing can get sick, or applications might require additional testing when problems are encountered. Vendors might not provide trial versions of the software as quickly as desired, or new versions of software or even the hardware itself can be delayed. With many companies seeking to consolidate the number of servers in use, it is not uncommon to see labs evolve through the testing process. Different versions of the Windows operating system are used, as are different versions of the Exchange Server 2003 software.

### Budget for the Testing

This goal can be defined with the statement "The testing must be completed within a budget of $X."

Of course, there might be no budget allocated for testing, but it's better to know this as soon as possible. A lack of budget means that no new hardware can be ordered, that evaluation copies of the software (both Microsoft and the third-party applications) need to be used, and that no external resources will be brought in. If budget is available or can be accessed in advance of the production upgrade, a subset of the production hardware should be ordered for this phase. Testing on the exact hardware that will be used in the actual upgrade, rather than a cast-off server, will yield more valuable results.

### Resources to Be Used

This goal can be defined with the statement "The testing will be completed by in-house resources and/or external consultants."

Often, the internal Exchange Admin staff is too busy with daily tasks or tackling emergencies that spring up (which might be the reason for the upgrade in the first place), and staff personnel should not be expected to dedicate 100% of their time to the testing process.

If an outside consulting firm with expertise in Exchange Server 2003 is going to be used in the testing process, it can be a good leverage point to have already created and decided upon an internal budget for the testing process. This cuts down on the time it takes to debate the approaches from competing firms.

### Extent of the Testing

The extent of compatibility testing can be defined with the statement "Each application will be tested for basic, mid-level, or complete compatibility and feature sets."

This goal might be different for different types of applications—for example, mission-critical applications need extensive testing, whereas less critical applications might have more basic testing performed. A short time frame with a tightly limited budget won't allow extensive testing, so basic compatibility will most likely be the goal.

**Defining the Different Levels of Compatibility Testing**

Basic compatibility testing, as used in this chapter, essentially means that the mission-critical applications are tested to verify that they load without errors and perform their primary functions properly with Exchange Server 2003. Often, the goal with basic testing is to simply see if the application works, without spending a lot of time or money on hardware and resources, and with a minimum amount of documentation and training. Note that this level of testing reduces but does not eliminate the risks involved in the production rollout.

Mid-level testing is defined as a process whereby Exchange Server 2003 is configured with *all* of the applications that will be present in the eventual implementation, so that the test configuration matches the production configuration as closely as possible to reduce the chance of surprise behavior during the rollout. This level of testing requires more preparation to understand the configuration and more involvement from testing resources, and should include end-users. Some training should take place during the process, and documentation is created to record the server configurations and details of the testing process. Although this level of testing greatly reduces the risks of problems during the production migration or upgrade, the migration process of moving data between servers and training the resources on this process hasn't been covered, so some uncertainty still exists.

*Complete testing* adds additional resource training and possibly end-user training during the process, and should include testing of the actual migration process. Complete training requires more documentation to record the processes required to build or image servers and perform the migration steps. Complete testing is what is typically defined as a prototype phase.

### Training Requirements During Testing

This goal can be defined with the statement "Company IT resources will/will not receive training during the application testing process."

Although the IT resources performing the testing will learn a great deal by going through the testing process, the organization might want to provide additional training to these individuals, especially if new functionality and applications are being tested. If external consultants are brought in, it is important that the organization's own resources are still involved in the testing process, for training and validation purposes. The application testing phase might be an excellent time to have help desk personnel or departmental managers in the user community learn more about new features that will soon be offered so they can help support the user community and generate excitement for the project.

### Documentation Required

This goal can be defined with the statement "Documentation will/will not be generated to summarize the process and results."

Again, the budget and timeline for the testing will affect the answer to this question. Many organizations require a paper trail for all testing procedures, especially when the Exchange infrastructure will have an impact on the viability of the business itself. For other organizations, the messaging environment is not as critical, and less or no documentation may be required.

The application testing phase is a great opportunity to document the steps required for application installations or upgrades if time permits, and this level of instruction can greatly facilitate the production rollout of the upgraded messaging components.

For more information on documenting the Exchange Server 2003 project components, refer to Chapter 20, "Documenting an Exchange Server 2003 Environment."

### Extent of User Community Involvement

This goal can be defined with the statement "End-users will be included/not included in the testing process."

If there are applications such as customer relationship management (CRM), document routing, voicemail or paging add-ons, or connectivity to PDAs and mobile devices, a higher level of user testing (at least from the power users and executives) should be considered.

### Fate of the Testing Lab

This goal can be defined with the statement "The application testing lab will/will not remain in place after the testing is complete."

Organizations decide to keep labs in place after their primary purpose has been served for a number of reasons. Whenever a patch or upgrade to Exchange Server 2003 or to a third-party application integrates with Windows Server 2003, it is advisable to test it in a nonproduction environment. Even seemingly innocent patches to antivirus products can crash a production Exchange server. Other updates might require user testing to see whether they should be rolled out to the production servers. Databases can also be taken offline and copied to the lab for grooming and maintenance. So although this might seem like a trivial question, it is important to clarify at this stage.

## Documenting the Compatibility Testing Plan

The information discussed and gathered through the previous exercises needs to be gathered and distributed to the stakeholders to ensure that the members of the team are working toward the same goals. These components are the scope and the goals of the application testing process, and should include timeline, budget, extent of the testing (basic, mid-level, complete), training requirements, documentation requirements, and fate of the testing lab. This step is even more important if a formal discovery and design phase was not completed.

By taking the time to document these constraints, the testing process will be more structured and less likely to miss a key step or get bogged down on one application. The individuals performing the testing will essentially have a checklist of the exact testing process so are less likely to spend an inordinate amount of time on one application, or "get creative" and try products that are not within the scope of work. After the testing is complete, the stakeholders will also have made it clear what is expected in terms of documentation, so the results of the testing can be presented and reviewed efficiently.

This summary document should be presented to the stakeholders of the project for review and approval; then, the organization will be ready to proceed with the research and testing process for Exchange Server 2003 compatibility.

## Researching Products and Applications

Armed with a detailed list of the applications that will be tested, the application testing team can begin contacting the vendors of the products and validate whether the vendor certifies its product(s) to be compatible.

An inventory of the Exchange-related applications should be created, and this spreadsheet can then be expanded as compatibility information is gathered; if designed properly, it can be used throughout the testing process.

17

## Creating an Inventory of the Messaging Applications

It is usually fairly obvious which applications are installed on the Exchange server or connect to it and are considered to be part of the messaging infrastructure. If an application uses Exchange Server resources or is installed on an Exchange server, it should be tested in the application testing phase. If a different messaging system is in place, it is more likely that the exact applications in use will require more significant upgrades or equivalent products will need to be identified.

As illustrated in Table 17.2, a spreadsheet can easily be created that lists the messaging servers currently in place and the software applications installed on each.

**TABLE 17.2**   Server Inventory List

| Server Name | Server OS, SP#, Role | Messaging OS (with SPs) | Software Installed (with version #) |
| --- | --- | --- | --- |
| CAEX1 | Windows 2000 Server, SP3 | Exchange 2000 Enterprise, SP3 | Veritas BackUp Exec v.x |
| | | | Veritas Exchange Agent v.x |
| | | | Trend AntiVirus v.x |
| | | | RIM BlackBerry v.x |
| CAEX2 | Windows 2000 Server, SP3 | Exchange 2000 Conferencing Server, SP3 | Veritas BackUp Exec v.x |

The key items that should be recorded are the names of the server, the versions of the operating system and messaging server software installed, the role of the device, and the names, manufacturers, and versions of add-on software products.

Care should be taken to identify *all* applications running on each messaging server, including tape software, antivirus software, and network monitoring and management utilities, which are in addition to the more obvious database, email messaging, document routing, or other business applications.

If Microsoft Systems Management Server (SMS) or a similar management product capable of generating an inventory list of installed applications (along with hardware capabilities) is in use, it saves time by automatically detecting the software applications installed.

## Prioritizing the Applications on the List

When the list is completed, it's a good idea to assign priorities to the applications. Departmental managers should be consulted for their opinions on which applications are essential and enable their users to perform their work on a day-to-day basis. Often, applications are in place that are rarely used, and can be removed from the new environment.

Prioritization can occur based on the criticality of the application. Three basic levels, which are self-explanatory, are critical, near-critical, and nice to have. After this first level of categorization has taken place, a rough order of installation can be assigned. This order might change based on the results of the application testing.

This additional set of information is helpful during the testing process because applications that are listed as nice-to-haves and are at the bottom of the list can be passed over if time and budget constraints are too tight, or if the application or utility proves problematic. Certain utilities should be considered critical, such as tape backup software and Exchange agents, antivirus software, and—in zero downtime environments—the network management tools required to monitor the performance of the servers.

Paging connectivity software was essential for many organizations, but in many cases has been replaced by newer technologies, such as the Pocket PC or RIM BlackBerry. Faxing software was very popular several years ago but may not be needed any more, so it can be put at the bottom of the list.

## Verifying Compatibility with Vendors

Armed with the full list of applications that need to be tested for compatibility, the application testing team can now start hitting the phones and delving into the vendors' Web sites for compatibility information. Past experience has shown that simply using the Search feature on the vendor's site can be a frustrating process, so having an actual contact to call who has a vested interest in providing the latest and greatest information (such as the company's sales representative) can be a great time-saver.

> **NOTE**
>
> Experience has shown that the applications written by Microsoft that are to be upgraded to the new Exchange Server 2003 environment are not always compatible without updates or patches. Exchange add-ons—such as Instant Messenger, SharePoint Portal, or Conferencing Server—may have changed radically or not be yet upgraded to be compatible with Exchange Server 2003, so compatibility should not be assumed. Information is usually readily available on any such changes on the home pages for the specific products on the Microsoft Web site.

Each vendor tends to use its own terminology when discussing Exchange Server 2003 compatibility (especially when it isn't 100% tested); a functional way to define the level of compatibility is with the following four areas:

- Compatible

- Compatible with patches or updates

- Not compatible (requires version upgrade)

- Not compatible and no compatible version available (requires new product)

When possible, it is also a good practice to gather information about the specifics of the testing environment, such as the version and SP level of the Windows operating system the application was tested with, along with the hardware devices (if applicable, such as tape drives, specific PDAs, and so forth) tested.

## Tracking Sheets for Application Compatibility Research

For organizational purposes, a tracking sheet should be created for each application to record the information discovered from the vendors. A sample product inventory sheet includes the following categories:

- Vendor name

- Product name and version number

- Vendor contact name and contact information

- Level of criticality: critical, near critical, nice to have

- Compatible with Exchange Server 2003: yes/no/did not say

- Vendor-stated requirements to upgrade or make application compatible

- Recommended action: None, patch/fix/update, version upgrade, replace with new product, stop using product, continue using product without vendor support

- Operating system compatibility: Windows Server 2003, Windows 2000 Server, Windows NT Server, Other

- Notes (conversation notes, URLs used, copies of printed compatibility statements, or hard copy provided by vendor)

It is a matter of judgment as to the extent of the notes from discussions with the vendors and materials printed from Web sites that are retained and included with the inventory sheet and kept on file. Remember that URLs change frequently, so it makes sense to print the information when it is located.

In cases in which product upgrades are required, information can be recorded on the part numbers, cost, and other pertinent information.

## Six States of Compatibility

Essentially, six possible states of compatibility can be defined, based on the input from the vendors, and need to be verified during the testing process. These levels of compatibility roughly equate to levels of risk of unanticipated behavior and issues during the upgrade process:

- The application version currently in use is Exchange Server 2003–compatible.

- The application version currently in use is compatible with Exchange Server 2003, with a minor update or service patch.

- The application currently in use is compatible with Exchange Server 2003, with a version upgrade of the application.

- The application currently in use is not Exchange Server 2003–compatible and no upgrade is available, but it will be kept running as is on an older version of Exchange Server (or other messaging platform) in the upgraded Exchange Server 2003 messaging environment.

- The application currently in use is not Exchange Server 2003–compatible, and will be phased out and not used after the upgrade is complete.

- The application currently in use is not Exchange Server 2003–compatible per the vendor, or no information on compatibility was available, but it apparently runs on Exchange Server 2003 and will be run only on the new operating system.

Each of these states is discussed in more detail in the following sections.

## Using an Exchange Server 2003–Compatible Application

Although most applications require some sort of upgrade, the vendor might simply state that the version currently in use will work properly with Exchange Server 2003 and provide supporting documentation or specify a URL with more information on the topic. This is more likely to be the case with applications that don't integrate with the Exchange Server components but interface with certain components and might even be installed on separate servers.

It is up to the organization to determine whether testing is needed to verify the vendor's compatibility statement. If the application in question is critical to the integrity or security of the Exchange data stores, or provides the users with features and capabilities that enhance their business activities and transactions, testing is definitely recommended. For upgrades that have short time frames and limited budgets available for testing (basic testing as defined earlier in the chapter), these applications may be demoted to the bottom of the list of priorities and would be tested only after the applications requiring updates or upgrades had been tested.

A clear benefit of the applications that the vendor verifies as being Exchange Server 2003–compatible is that the administrative staff will already know how to install and support the product and how it interfaces with Exchange and the help desk. End-users won't need to be trained or endure the learning curves required by new versions of the products.

17

> **NOTE**
>
> As mentioned previously, make sure to clarify what NOS and which specific version of Exchange Server 2003 was used in the testing process because seemingly insignificant changes, such as security patches to the OS, can influence the product's performance in your upgraded environment. Tape backup software is notorious for being very sensitive to minor changes in the NOS or version of Exchange, and tape backups can appear to be working but might not be. If devices such as text pagers or PDAs are involved in the process, the specific operating systems tested and the details of the hardware models should be verified if possible to make sure that the vendor testing included the models in use by the organization.
>
> If a number of applications are being installed on one Exchange Server 2003 system, there can be conflicts that would not be predictable. So for mission-critical Exchange Server 2003 applications, testing is still recommended, even for applications the vendor asserts are fully compatible with Exchange Server 2003.

## Requiring a Minor Update or Service Patch for Compatibility

When upgrading from Exchange 2000 Server, many applications simply need a relatively minor service update or patch for compatibility with Exchange Server 2003. This is less likely to be the case when upgrading from Exchange Server 5.5 or a competing messaging product, such as Lotus Notes or Novell GroupWise.

During the testing process, the service updates and patches are typically quick and easy to install, are available over the Internet, and are often free of charge. It is important to read any notes or readme files that come with the update because specific settings in the Exchange Server 2003 configuration might need to be modified for them to work. These updates and patches tend to change and be updated themselves after they are released, so it is worth checking periodically to see whether new revisions have become available.

These types of updates generally do not affect the core features or functionality of the products in most cases, although some new features may be introduced; so, they have little training and support ramifications because the help desk and support staff will already be experienced in supporting the products.

## Applications That Require a Version Upgrade for Compatibility

In other cases, especially when migrating from Exchange Server 5.5 or a competing messaging system, a product version upgrade is required, and this tends to be a more complex process than downloading a patch or installing a minor update to the product. The process will vary by product, with some allowing an in-place upgrade, where the software is not on the Exchange Server 2003 server itself, and others simply installing from scratch.

The amount of time required to install and test these upgrades is greater and the learning curve steeper, and the danger of technical complexities and issues increases. Thus, additional time should be allowed for testing the installation process of the new products, configuring them for optimal Exchange connectivity, and fine-tuning for performance factors. Training for the IT resources and help desk staff will be important because of the probability of significant differences between the new and old versions.

Compatibility with all hardware devices should not be taken for granted, whether it is the server itself, tape backup devices, or storage area network (SAN) hardware.

If a new version of the product is required, it can be difficult to avoid paying for the upgrade, so budget can become a factor. Some vendors can be persuaded to provide evaluation copies that expire after 30–120 days.

## Noncompatible Applications That Will Be Used Anyway

As discussed earlier in this chapter, Exchange Server 2003 can coexist with previous versions of Exchange and of the Windows operating system, so an Exchange Server 2003 migration does not require that every messaging server be upgraded. In larger organizations, for example, smaller offices might choose to remain on Exchange 2000 Server for a period of time, if there are legitimate business reasons or cost concerns with upgrading expensive applications. If custom scripts or applications have been written that integrate and add functionality to Exchange Server 5.5 or Exchange 2000 Server, it might make more sense to simply keep those servers intact on the network.

An example of this scenario could be a paging application that runs on Exchange Server 5.5 but is used by a few users and is being phased out, so it doesn't make financial sense to pay for an upgrade. Another example could be a faxing server for which a number of proprietary fax boards were purchased and it continues to meet the needs of the company.

Although it might sound like an opportunity to skip any testing because the server configurations aren't changing, connectivity to the new Exchange Server 2003 configurations still needs to be tested, to ensure that the functionality between the servers is stable.

Again, in this scenario, the application itself is not upgraded, modified, or changed, so there won't be a requirement for administrative or end-user training.

### Noncompatible Applications That Will Be Eliminated and Applications That Are Not Compatible and Will Not Be Used

An organization might find that an application is not compatible with Exchange Server 2003, no upgrade is available, or the cost is prohibitive, so it decides to simply retire the application. Exchange Server 2003 includes a variety of new features, as discussed throughout the book, that might make certain utilities and management tools unnecessary. For example, a disaster recovery module for a tape backup product might no longer be needed after clustering is implemented. A VPN solution might be retired because OWA provides enhanced performance and provides the look and feel of the full Outlook client.

Care should be taken during the testing process to note the differences that the administrative, help desk, and end-users will notice in the day-to-day interactions with the messaging system. If features are disappearing, a survey to assess the impact can be very helpful. Many users will raise a fuss if a feature suddenly goes away, even if it was rarely used; whereas if they are informed in advance, the complaints can be avoided.

### Noncompatible Applications That Seem to Work

The final category applies to situations in which no information can be found about compatibility. Some vendors choose to provide no information and make no stance on compatibility with Exchange Server 2003. This puts the organization in a tricky situation, and it has to rely on internal testing results to make a decision. Even if the application seems to work properly, the decision might be made to phase out or retire the product if its failure could harm the business process. If the application performs a valuable function, it is probably time to look for, or create, a replacement, or at least to allocate time for this process at a later time.

If the organization chooses to keep the application, it might be kept in place on an older version of Exchange or moved to the new Exchange Server 2003 environment. In either case, the administrative staff, help desk, and end-users should be warned that the application is not officially supported or officially compatible and might behave erratically.

17

## Creating an Upgrade Decision Matrix

Although each application will have its own inventory sheet, it is helpful to put together a brief summary document outlining the final results of the vendor research process and the ramifications to the messaging upgrade project.

Table 17.3 provides a sample format for the upgrade decision matrix.

**TABLE 17.3**    Upgrade Decision Matrix

| Item # | Vendor | Product Name | Version | Exchange 2003 Compatibility Level | Decision |
|---|---|---|---|---|---|
| 1) Compatible as is | | | | | |
| 2) Needs patches | | | | | |
| 3) Needs upgrade | | | | | |
| 4) Not compatible | | | | | |
| (N) No change | | | | | |
| (P) Patch/fix | | | | | |
| (U) Upgrade | | | | | |
| (R) Replace | | | | | |
| 1 | Veritas | BackUp Exec | v.x | 2 | U |
| 2 | Veritas | Exchange Agent | v.x | 3 | U |
| 3 | Trend | ScanMail | v.x | 3 | U |
| 4 | RIM | BlackBerry | v.x | 1 | N |

As with all documents that affect the scope and end-state of the messaging infrastructure, this document should be reviewed and approved by the project stakeholders.

This document can be expanded to summarize which applications will be installed on which messaging server if there are going to be multiple Exchange Server 2003 servers in the final configuration. In this way, the document can serve as a checklist to follow during the actual testing process.

## Assessing the Effects of the Compatibility Results on the Compatibility Testing Plan

After all the data has been collected on the compatibility, lack of compatibility, or lack of information, the compatibility testing plan should be revisited to see whether changes need to be made. As discussed earlier in the chapter, the components of the compatibility testing plan are the scope of the application testing process, and the goals of the process (timeline, budget, extent of the testing, training requirements, documentation requirements, and fate of the testing lab).

Some of the goals might now be more difficult to meet, and might require additional budget, time, and resources. If essential messaging applications need to be replaced with version upgrades or a solution from a different vendor, additional time for testing and training might be required. Certain key end-users might also need to roll up their sleeves and perform hands-on testing to make sure that the new products perform to their expectations.

This might be the point in the application testing process that a decision is made that a more complete prototype testing phase is needed, and the lab would be expanded to more closely, or exactly, resemble the end-state of the migration.

# Lab Testing Existing Applications

With the preparation and research completed, and the compatibility testing plan verified as needed, the actual testing can begin. The testing process should be fairly anticlimactic at this point because the process has been discussed at length, and it will be clear what the testing goals are and which applications will be tested. Due diligence in terms of vendor research should be completed and now it is just a matter of building the test server or servers and documenting the results.

The testing process can yield results that are unforeseen because the exact combination of hardware and software may affect the performance of a key application; but far better to have this occur in a nonproduction environment in which failures won't affect the organization's ability to deliver its services.

During the testing process, valuable experience with the installation and upgrade process will be gained and will contribute to the success of the production migration. The migration team will be familiar with—or possibly experts at—the installation and application migration processes when it counts, and are more likely to avoid configuration mistakes and resolve technical issues.

## Allocating and Configuring Hardware

Ideally, budget is available to purchase the same server hardware and related peripherals (such as tape drives, UPS, PDAs, and text pagers) that will be used in the production migration. This is preferable to using a server machine that has been sitting in a closet for an undetermined period of time, which might respond differently than the eventual hardware that will be used. Using old hardware can actually generate more work in the long run and adds more variables to an already complex process.

If the testing process is to exactly mirror the production environment, this would be considered to be a prototype phase, which is generally broader in scope than compatibility testing, and requires additional hardware, software, and time to complete. A prototype phase is recommended for more complex networks in which the upgrade process is riskier and more involved and the budget, time, and resources are available.

Don't forget to allocate a representative workstation for each desktop operating system that is supported by the organization and a sample remote access system, such as a typical laptop or PDA that is used by the sales force or traveling executive.

## Allocating and Configuring the NOS and Exchange Server 2003

By this point, the software has been ordered, allocated, downloaded, and set aside for easy access, along with any notes taken or installation procedures downloaded in the research phase. If some time has elapsed since the compatibility research with the vendors, it is worth checking to see whether any new patches have been released. The upgrade decision matrix discussed earlier in the chapter is an excellent checklist to have on hand during this process to make sure that nothing is missed that could cause delays during the testing process.

When configuring the servers with the appropriate operating systems, the company standards for configurations should be adhered to, if they have been documented. Standards can include the level of hard drive redundancy, separation of the application files and data files, naming conventions, roles of the servers, approved and tested service packs, and security configurations.

Next, Exchange Server 2003 should be configured to also meet company standards and then for the essential utilities that will protect the integrity of the data and the operating system, which typically include the backup software, antivirus software, and management utilities and applications. After this base configuration is completed, it can be worth performing a complete backup of the system or using an application such as Ghost to take a snapshot of the server configuration in case the subsequent testing is problematic and a rollback is needed.

## Loading the Remaining Applications

With the Exchange Server 2003 configured with the NOS, Exchange, and essential utilities, the value-added applications can be tested. Value-added applications enhance the functionality of Exchange and enable the users to perform their jobs more efficiently and drive the business more effectively. It's helpful to provide a calendar or schedule to the end-users who will be assisting in the testing process at this point so they know when their services will be needed.

There are so many different combinations of applications that might be installed and tested at this point that the different permutations can't all be covered in this chapter. As a basic guideline, first test the most essential applications and the applications that were not identified previously as being compatible. By tackling the applications that are more likely to be problematic early on in the process, the testing resources will be fresh and any flags can be raised to the stakeholders while there is still time left in the testing process for remediation.

Thorough testing by the end-users is recommended, as is inclusion of the help desk staff in the process. Notes taken during the testing process will be valuable in creating any configuration guides or migration processes for the production implementation.

> **NOTE**
>
> Beyond basic functionality, data entry, and access to application-specific data, some additional tests that indicate an application has been successfully installed in the test environment include printing to different standard printers, running standard reports, exporting and importing data, and exchanging information with other systems or devices. Testing should be done by end-users of the application and administrative IT staff who support, maintain, and manage the application. Notes should be taken on the process and the results because they can be very useful during the production migration.

## Application Compatibility Testing Tool

Microsoft offers a tool called the Windows Application Compatibility Toolkit (ACT), which is a collection of documents and tools that can help identify compatibility problems on applications that are installed on a Windows 2000 or 2003 server. This tool isn't designed specifically for Exchange Server 2003 applications, but it can be very helpful in determining whether the application in question—especially an application for which no information is provided by the vendor or a custom application—has obvious problems or potential security holes. This level of testing falls under the medium level or complete levels of testing, mentioned previously in this chapter, which is valuable to organizations with more complex Exchange messaging environments that need to be as stable as possible.

There are three components to this tool: the Application Compatibility Analyzer, the Internet Explorer Compatibility Evaluator, and the Compatibility Administrator.

The Application Compatibility Analyzer, shown in Figure 17.1, gathers an inventory of all the applications running on the server and then cross-references the results online with a database maintained by Microsoft to produce an assessment report.

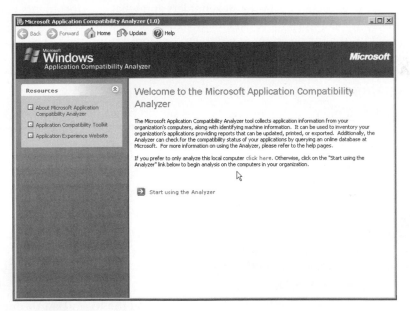

**FIGURE 17.1**   Windows Application Compatibility Analyzer.

For application development, Internet Explorer Compatibility Evaluator then tests for potential compatibility errors caused by common programming mistakes, checks the application for memory-related issues, determines an application's compliance with requirements of the "Certified for Windows Server 2003" Logo Programs, and looks for potential security issues in an application.

At the time of this writing, this application is available for download from `http://www.microsoft.com/downloads` by performing a search for `application compatibility toolkit`.

### Testing the Migration and Upgrade Process

This section touches on the next logical step in the testing process. After it has been verified that the final configuration agreed upon in the planning process is stable and decided which applications and utilities will be installed on which server, the actual upgrade process can be tested. As discussed in Chapters 15, "Migrating from Exchange v5.5 to Exchange Server 2003," 16, "Migrating from Exchange 2000 to Exchange Server 2003," 34, "Migrating from Novell GroupWise to Exchange 2003," and 35, "Migrating from Lotus Notes to Exchange Server 2003," Exchange Server 2003 comes with a number of built-in migration testing and facilitating utilities and tools.

# Documenting the Results of the Compatibility Testing

A number of documents can be produced during the compatibility testing process. Understanding the expectations of the stakeholders and what the documents will be used for is important. For example, more detailed budgetary information might need to be compiled based on the information, or go/no go decisions might need to be reached. Thus, a summary of the improvements offered by Exchange Server 2003 in the areas of reliability, performance visible to the user community, and features improved and added might need to be presented in a convincing fashion.

At a minimum, a summary of the testing process should be created, and a final recommendation for the applications to be included in the production upgrade or migration should be provided to the stakeholders. This can be as simple as the upgrade decision matrix discussed earlier in the chapter, or it can be more thorough, including detailed notes of the exact testing procedures followed. Notes can be made available summarizing the results of end-users testing, validating the applications, and describing results—both positive and negative.

If the testing hardware is the same as the hardware that will be used in the production upgrade, server configuration documents that list the details of the hardware and software configurations can be created; they will ensure that the servers built in the production environment will have the same fundamental configuration as was tested in the lab.

A more detailed build document can be created that walks the technician through the exact steps required to build the Exchange Server 2003 system, in cases in which many messaging servers need to be created in a short period of time.

The level of effort or the amount of time to actually perform the upgrade or the migration of a sample mailbox can be recorded as part of the documentation, and this information can be very helpful in planning the total amount of time that will be required to perform the upgrade or migration.

# Determining Whether a Prototype Phase Is Required

The issue of whether a more complete prototype phase is needed or if a more limited application compatibility testing phase is sufficient has come up several times in this chapter. The essential difference between the two is that the prototype phase duplicates as exactly as possible the actual end-state of the upgrade, from server hardware to peripherals and software, so that the entire upgrade process can be tested to reduce the chance of surprises during the production upgrade. The application testing phase can be less extensive, involve a single server, and be designed to verify that the applications required will work reliably on the Exchange Server 2003 configuration. Compatibility testing can take as little time as a week—from goal definition, to research, to actual testing. A prototype phase takes considerably longer because of the additional steps required.

Following is a checklist that will help your organization make the decision:

- Is sufficient budget available for a subset of the actual hardware that will be used in the upgrade?

- Is sufficient time available for the configuration of the prototype lab and testing of the software?

- Are the internal resources available for a period of time long enough to finish the prototype testing? Or, is budget available to pay for external consulting resources to complete the work?

- Is the Exchange messaging environment mission-critical to the business' ability to go about its daily activities and generate revenues, and will interruption of Exchange services cost the company an unacceptable amount of money?

- Does the actual migration process need to be tested and documented to ensure the success of the upgrade?

- Do resources need to be trained on the upgrade process (building the servers, and configuring the NOS, Exchange Server 2003 software, and related applications)?

If you find that the answers to more than half of these questions are yes, it's likely that a prototype phase will be required.

# Summary

Exchange Server 2003 compatibility testing should be performed before any upgrade or migration. The process can be completed very quickly for smaller networks (basic testing) or for larger networks with fairly simple messaging environments.

The first steps include identifying the scope and goals of the project to make sure that the stakeholders are involved in determining the success factors for the project. Then, research needs to be performed, internal to the company, on which applications are in place that are messaging-related. This includes not only Exchange Server, but tape backup software, antivirus software, network management and monitoring tools, add-ons (such as faxing, text messaging, paging, synchronization utilities for PDAs and remote users, and document routing software), and inventory sheets created summarizing this information. Decisions as to which applications are critical, near critical, or just nice to have should also be made. Research should then be performed with the vendors of the products, tracking sheets should be created to record this information, and the application should be categorized in one of six states of compatibility. Next, the testing begins, with the configuration of the lab environment that is isolated from the production network, and the applications are loaded and tested by both administrative and end-user or help desk staff. The results are then documented, and the final decisions of whether to proceed are made.

With this process, the production upgrade or migration is smoother, and the likelihood of technical problems that can harm the business' ability to transact or provide its services is greatly reduced. The problems are identified beforehand and resolved, and the resources who will perform the work gain familiarity with all the products and processes involved.

## Best Practices

The following are best practices from this chapter:

- Take the time to understand the goals of the project (What will the organization gain by doing the upgrade?) as well as the scope of the project (What is included and what is excluded from the project?).

- Understand all the applications that connect with Exchange Server 2003 and whether they are critical, near critical, or simply nice to have.

- Document the research process for each application because this will prove to be very valuable if problems are encountered during the testing process.

- Create a lab environment that is as close to the final end-state of the upgrade as possible. This reduces the variables that can cause problems at the least opportune time.

- Test applications for compatibility with both typical end-users of the application and application administrators who support, maintain, and manage the application.

# PART VI

# Exchange Server 2003 Administration and Management

## IN THIS PART

| CHAPTER 18 | Administering Exchange Server 2003 | 533 |
| CHAPTER 19 | Exchange Server 2003 Management and Maintenance Practices | 581 |
| CHAPTER 20 | Documenting an Exchange Server 2003 Environment | 605 |
| CHAPTER 21 | Using Terminal Services to Manage Exchange Services | 625 |

# Administering Exchange Server 2003

W ith Exchange Server 2003 and the latest Service Packs, there are new ways of accomplishing familiar administrative tasks along with new features not previously available in earlier releases of Exchange Server and Exchange Server 2003. This chapter guides Exchange administrators through the standard practices of managing basic Exchange Server 2003 Administrative Groups, User Mailbox administration, and the different types of mail-enabled Security and Distribution Groups. Along with basis management, Exchange administrators will find additional newly released tools and tips for performing administrative tasks.

Using the information in this chapter, Exchange administrators can review new features of Exchange Server 2003 with the latest Service Pack available from Microsoft. In this chapter, common scenarios for implementing and managing Exchange Server 2003 mailboxes, permissions, and features will be reviewed to assist in the day-to-day administrative tasks of Exchange.

## Exchange Administration and the Delegation Wizard

As with previous versions of Exchange, the ability to perform administration is determined by permissions. With Exchange Server 2003, administrative rights and permissions are based on the new Exchange roles already built in to the core Exchange Server 2003 platform. These roles determine the level of permissions and administrative rights assigned to an account allowing an administrator access to Exchange objects within the Exchange 2003 organization.

## IN THIS CHAPTER

- Exchange Administration and the Delegation Wizard

- Managing Mailboxes and Message Settings in Exchange Server 2003

- Managing New Mailbox Features

- Moving Exchange User Mailboxes

- Creating and Managing Exchange Contacts

- Planning and Creating Distribution Groups

- Creating and Managing Exchange Server 2003 Administrative Groups

- Creating and Managing Routing Groups

- Using Recipient Policies

- Administering Recipient Update Services

- Using the Mailbox Recovery Center Tool

- Using the Mailbox Manager Utility

In this section, we review each of these new Exchange administrative roles, how to assign and use role-based administration within an Exchange Server 2003 organization, and the rights granted, which are granted to each role when they are assigned.

Also as part of managing and administering Exchange permissions, we look at working with and assigning extended permissions. In this section, we will define what extended permissions are, what they are used for, and how to implement them using Exchange Server 2003 features like the Exchange Server 2003 Delegation Wizard.

## Implementing Role-Based Administration

Administration in Exchange Server 2003 has been simplified from the standard practice of applying permissions by using wizards. As previously required, permissions were set by applying rights to Active Directory users and groups within the permission pages of Exchange objects. In Exchange Server 2003 organizations and administrative groups, assigning permissions has been simplified by implementing role-based administration within the Exchange hierarchy, and Active Directory accounts can be assigned rights by using the Exchange Server 2003 Delegation Wizard. By assigning roles to these objects, delegation of rights and permissions to administer Exchange throughout the organization can easily be assigned to accounts and security groups at the organization and Administrative Group levels.

Depending on where in the Exchange organization tree roles are assigned, different levels of permissions can be applied to different Exchange server objects. Delegating permission in the Exchange organization, administrators can leverage each of these three Exchange server administrative roles to assign permissions at the Exchange Organization and Administrative Group levels:

- Exchange Full Administrator
- Exchange Administrator
- Exchange View Only Administrator

These roles-based permissions can be assigned allowing for different administrative rights at the organizational level and at the Administrative Group level with the Exchange Server 2003 system manager. In larger Exchange designs, these roles can be a powerful tool allowing for decentralized administration. Organizations can leverage this functionality to assign different administrators on separate Administrative Groups within the same Exchange Server 2003 organization. This can be very effective for larger organizations with administrators in multiple locations that are responsible administering objects with their own administrative group.

### Assigning Roles to Groups

When planning and assigning Exchange roles, it is simpler to manage and understand administrative permissions when roles are assigned to groups rather than individual user accounts. Create new Administrative Security Groups and use these groups to assign roles at the desired Exchange server levels.

When assigning Exchange roles using security groups, the accounts that will be used to administer or view Exchange objects must be a member of the security group that has been granted an Exchange role.

### Exchange Full Administrator

The Exchange Full Administrator role is the least restrictive of all three Exchange Server 2003 roles. Similar to Full Control in previous versions of Exchange, using this role allows Exchange administrators to fully administer Exchange objects at the level assigned by giving them the capability to add, delete, and change Exchange permissions and Active Directory objects. Assign the Exchange Full Administrator role to Exchange administrators who require complete access to Exchange for configuring and managing the entire Exchange organization.

> **Exchange Full and Administrator Requirements**
>
> To enable the Exchange Full Administrator or Administrator roles, the security group or users object being assigned these roles must also maintain local administrator group membership to the Exchange server system. This is required on any Exchange server on which these roles are being assigned.

> **Important!**
>
> Adding these permissions to the local administrators group of the Exchange Server 2003 must be completed manually by an account already maintaining local administrative rights. Not having these local administrative rights set correctly will restrict roles from being assigned. This step must be completed for the Exchange Administrator role to be effective.

### Exchange Administrator

The Administrator role is ideal for assigning administrative privileges to users objects and security groups that require the ability to perform the daily administration tasks to objects within Exchange. The Administrator role allows administrators the ability to add, change, or modify objects only.

### Exchange View Only Administrator

The Exchange View Only role is the most restrictive of all Exchange Server 2003 roles. The Exchange View Only role provides permissions to view Exchange objects within the System Manager only. There are no add and modify rights associated with this role, and it is most effectively implemented for security groups and accounts objects that require the capability to view objects in other Exchange organizations and Administrative Groups.

> **NOTE**
>
> The Exchange View Only role can be used to restrict administrative permissions between Exchange Administrative Groups. Assign the Exchange View Only role to allow administrators from separate Administrative Groups to view objects in other Administrative Groups while still restricting the ability to add and modify objects.

18

## Understanding and Implementing Extended Permissions

Another method by which Exchange Server 2003 administrators can manage and control administrative access to Exchange objects is to implement extended permissions. These extended permissions are Exchange-specific and allow for more granular security by giving Full Administrators the capability to set permissions in addition to and beyond the standard Active Directory and role-based permissions. Extended permissions can be applied when roles and rights require a more granular configuration and can be applied to individual objects with the Exchange administrator rather than at organizational or Administrative Group levels.

Exchange Server 2003 extended permissions can be applied to servers within the organization, individual mail store and public folder databases, address lists, and mail protocols.

To implement extended permissions, open the Security tab of an Exchange object. Each Security tab contains both Active Directory–integrated domain-based permissions and Exchange extended permissions, as shown in Figure 18.1.

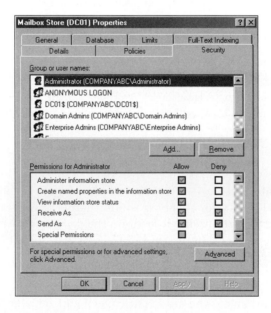

**FIGURE 18.1**    Public folder security and permissions.

---

**NOTE**

When viewing Exchange Server 2003 extended permissions, Windows domain permissions are always viewed first in the Permissions tab and are located at the top of the permissions list. Extended permissions are always viewed after the Windows domain permissions and can be viewed by scrolling down to the bottom of the Permissions list page.

---

## Delegating Administrative Rights

With an understanding of which roles and permissions are available to administer in Exchange Server 2003, the task is now to determine which roles and permissions to apply. To grant permissions effectively, determine which permissions are required for the specific administrative need within each area of Exchange and how to apply them at the different levels of the organization.

For example, as the Exchange Server 2003 organization begins to expand, the Exchange environment might require additional Administrative Groups to be configured and Exchange Server administrators to be granted rights to manage servers. This configuration might also be ideal for decentralizing administrative duties required to maintain each Administrative Group and Exchange object belonging to them.

With multiple Administrative Groups, permission can be applied to individual security Groups, granting them the capability to perform the day-to-day tasks required to manage users, Exchange Server computers, and objects in each Administrative Group. Also, individuals or security groups can be granted extended permissions to provide an even more granular set of rights on objects such as a mailbox store or a public folder tree within a specific Administrative Group.

To apply roles and permission, administrators must perform each addition separately and at different levels. Unlike applying extended permissions, applying Exchange roles can be accomplished by using the Delegation Wizard included in the Exchange System Manager.

The Delegation Wizard is a simple tool built in to the Exchange Server 2003 System Manager that allows a simple method to assign Exchange roles to active Directory objects at the organization and Administrative Group levels within the organization.

The application of extended permission must be performed by opening the property pages of any object in the organization where the permission will be applied. In the properties page of the Exchange object, access to the extended permissions tab can be completed by selecting the Security tab.

### Understanding the Scope of Roles Being Applied

When assigning Exchange roles with the Delegation Wizard, the role-based permissions being assigned is dependent on the level in the Exchange organization tree where the permissions are being assigned.

For example, if an administrative security group called Admins is assigned Full Administrator rights on the Exchange organization, this group and members will be granted full administrative rights to the entire Exchange organization including any Administrative Group within the organizational tree.

Using this strategy, imagine that an object is granted the Full Administrator role on an Administrative Group called Administrative Group 1. This same object is also granted the View Only role to a Send Administrative Group called Administrative Group 2. This object now can fully add, modify, and delete objects in Administrative Group 1 but can only traverse to Administrative Group 2 to view objects only. This account cannot add to or modify anything in Administrative Group 2.

### Using the Delegation Wizard

To implement Exchange roles using the Delegation Wizard, begin by opening the Exchange System Manager and complete these steps:

1. On an Exchange Server or Domain Controller with the Exchange System Manager installed, select Start, Programs, Microsoft Exchange, System Manager.

2. Select the Administrative Group to which the administrative role will be applied.

3. From the Action menu, select Action, Delegate Control. This launches the Welcome to the Exchange Administration Delegation Wizard, shown in Figure 18.2. Select Next to begin.

**FIGURE 18.2**    Welcome to the Exchange Administration Delegation Wizard.

4. On the Users and Groups page, click the Add button to select the group or account and the role that will be applied to the Administrative Group.

5. Select Browse and select the group or account to be used. Select OK when finished.

6. From the Role Selection tab, use the arrow to choose the role Full Administrator, and click OK.

7. Select Next to complete the Delegation Wizard. Review the configuration window to ensure that the selection is correct and that the proper role is being applied. Choose Finish to apply the role to the first Administrative Group.

---

**NOTE**

This procedure can be repeated to add accounts or security groups to any role at the organization and Administrative Group levels within the Exchange System Manager.

---

## Auditing Administrative Tasks in Exchange Server 2003

To help manage changes to the Exchange organization as roles and permissions are assigned to different security groups and accounts, the Windows Server 2003 auditing function can be enabled to help track successful changes and failures as changes are applied by security groups or user objects that have been granted permissions. Auditing can track changes when administrators perform tasks on Exchange containers; however, auditing can only log changes when applied to objects within the Administrative Group of the Exchange organization.

Auditing allows for the tracking of changes, reads, and deletes; the creation of child objects; and send as, receive as, and other helpful tracking information. This is an effective method to assist the administrator in monitoring changes and permissions as they are applied. Auditing can also be configured to be inherited on child objects and subcontainers, as well as applied to a single container with an Administrative Group.

As an example of how to enable auditing on an Exchange container or object, perform the following steps to enable auditing on an object within the first Administrative Group in the Exchange organization.

1. Open the Exchange System Manager and select the first server in the first Administrative Group.

2. Select the properties of the server and select the Security tab.

3. Click the Advanced button in the lower-left corner to open the Advanced Security page for the server.

4. Click the Auditing tab to open the Auditing Configuration page.

5. Click the Add button and select the group or user account on which auditing will be enabled. Click OK when finished.

6. Select the Apply Onto option and select This Object, subcontainers, and children objects. This applies the audit setting to all server containers and objects.

7. Choose the auditing feature that will be applied by placing a check in the box under Access Options. For this scenario, select Create Children and then select Successful.

> **NOTE**
>
> This setting creates an entry in the event logs of the Exchange Server when a child object is created.
>
> Other settings, such as the Read option, automatically enable additional auditing features. This is by design and allows Exchange Server 2003 to enable the proper permission and apply the auditing function correctly.

18

# Managing Mailboxes and Message Settings in Exchange Server 2003

The key function of Exchange Server 2003 is to provide mailbox functionality to end-user objects within Active Directory. This section assists Exchange Server 2003 administrators in enabling and managing end-user mailboxes, mailbox options, and the information stores where they reside.

Also included are the step-by-step tasks to help administrators configure user mailbox options in the Exchange System Manager along with tips for managing new Exchange Server 2003 features, such as wireless browsing, user-initiated synchronization, and always-up-to-date notifications. We also cover methods and tools to use when administering and maintaining mailboxes within mail stores.

## Managing Exchange Mailboxes

Administrators can manage Exchange user mailboxes using two methods. The first and most common is using the Active Directory Users and Computers (ADUC) snap-in. Using Active Directory Users and Computers, administrators can mail-enable and manage mailboxes from an individual object or group of objects perspective as they reside within their perspective Organizational Unit.

The second option is using the Exchange System Manager to manage mailbox attributes and settings. Some user Exchange tasks can also be performed through the Exchange System Manager, but this method is most commonly used to set mailbox options such as message limits and storage limits on a global or storage container level for all mailboxes.

### Mail-Enabling Active Directory Objects

When an account is mail-enabled, Exchange creates a mailbox for the Active Directory object and enables Exchange functionality based on the recipient policies and settings on the Exchange store where the mailbox is created.

Windows Active Directory objects can be mail-enabled using two methods: doing so when the account object is originally created in Active Directory, and using the Exchange Tasks Wizard under the actions tab in the Active Directory Users and Computers snap-in.

Creating a mailbox for any object is known as mail enabling. When mail enabling a new Active Directory account when it is created, select the Create an Exchange Mailbox option during the creation of the account.

When this option is selected, administrators must also select an alias name for the Exchange user and the Exchange Server and mailbox store where the mailbox will reside. This option will create a mail-enabled Active Directory user account.

When active directory objects exist such as a user or group object that were not mail enabled during their creation, objects can be mail enabled individually or in bulk at any time using the Exchange Tasks Wizard in the Active Directory Users and Computers snap-in. To mail enable Active Directory objects, complete these steps:

1. Open the Active Directory Users and Computers snap-in and select the account or account objects to be mail enabled.

2. To open the Exchange Task Wizard, click the Action menu and select the Exchange Task option.

3. At the Welcome to Exchange Task Wizard, select Next.

4. On the Available Task screen, select the Create Mailbox option and click Next.

5. Choose the mail store and server where the mailbox will reside, and select Next.

6. Review the summary and select the Finished button when the mailbox has been created.

> **NOTE**
>
> After a mailbox has been created, the Back button cannot be used to change the Exchange options once the account has been mail enabled.

## Implementing Message Limits and Storage Limits

Implementing message and storage limits is often considered when planning and designing the installation of an Exchange Server 2003 server. Capacity planning and the total number of users planned per server can directly affect the decisions regarding the implementation of information storage limits.

Each can have considerable effects on an Exchange Server 2003 server as well as the server performance that Exchange Server 2003 has installed.

Using storage limits can be beneficial to help manage the total amount of data being stored within a storage group or mail store. Given the total amount of users planned per storage group and the storage limits being implemented, administrators can determine the maximum storage size that any storage container can grow. This can effectively assist Exchange administrators in managing and maintaining information stores to a size that can easily be backed up and restored in a timely manner. Managing the database sizes through storage limits can also assist in shortening the total amount of time needed to perform maintenance on a single Exchange database.

Limits can be implemented with Exchange Server 2003 in two ways. Limits can be configured globally using the Exchange System Manager applying these limits to a mail store or on an individual basis from the Properties tab of a mail-enabled object.

## Understanding and Implementing User Mailbox Options

With each mail-enabled Active Directory object, administrators can configure multiple Exchange options to customize the Exchange mailbox. Each mail-enabled account in Active Directory contains Exchange pages with options specific to the individual account.

18

**Viewing Exchange Options**

To view the Exchange options on a mail-enabled Active Directory object, the Exchange System Manager tools must be installed on the same computer running the Active Directory User and Computer snap-in. Install the administrative tools by running the Exchange Server 2003 installation CD and only selecting the Exchange management tools.

The Exchange options pages in the user's properties can be used and configured to override the storage group container settings applied using the Exchange System Manager. These options are often used when a member of a storage container requires message limits, delivery restrictions, and alternative email addresses that differ from the default setting placed on the container.

To set these options on a specific user object, refer to the following settings to determine which best fits the needs being implemented.

### General Exchange

The General Exchange tab can be used to set mailbox location, message restrictions, and limits for a specific user mailbox. These options and their definitions are listed here:

- **Mailbox Store**—The Mailbox Store tab cannot be modified from the User Option page. It is used to identify the mailbox store of which the account is a member.

- **Alias**—The alias name for a mailbox is used as an alternative logon name for the user account. The option is set when the object is mail enabled and can be changed at any time from this tab.

- **Delivery Restrictions**—Select this option to configure the maximum size limits for outgoing and inbound mail. This option can also be used to specify specific email accounts that the mail-enabled object can and cannot send and receive messages from.

- **Delivery Options**—The most common use for the delivery tab is to configure accounts and enable the Send on Behalf Privileges options for the accounts, as well as limit the total number of addresses the object can send messages to.

- **Storage Limits**—Enabling storage limits sets the total size that a mail-enabled user can allow the mailbox to grow. As a defined mailbox limit is reached, the account is warned that it is reaching the limit set, requiring the user to remove mail objects from within the mailbox. This option also allows an administrator to configure deleted item retention. This determines how long deleted objects will remain hidden within a mailbox for recovery purposes before objects are permanently deleted.

### Email Addresses

The Email options page allows administrators to configure additional addresses for a specific user's account. This option contains preconfigured addresses based on the setting in the Exchange Server 2003 organizations recipient policy configured through the

Exchange System Manager. Most commonly used to add additional SMTP addresses, this tab can also be used to add additional MS mail addresses and X.400 type addresses. Select the New button to add any of the available Microsoft-compatible type addresses.

# Managing New Mailbox Features

With Exchange Server 2003 and the latest service pack, there are new mailbox features that were not available with previous versions of Exchange. With new versions of Exchange, user wireless and mobile device support is included in Exchange operating systems to greatly enhance the ability for end-users to connect to Exchange with built-in compatibility for wireless devices such as cell phones and pocket PCs.

Using Wireless support features, Microsoft Windows Pocket PC clients can now use Microsoft Active Sync and Pocket Outlook to access Exchange Server data and synchronize Outlook information regardless of where they may be.

Using the Properties tab of a mail-enabled object or the Exchange Tasks Wizard, administrators can select the features to enable and disable a user's functionality.

## Using Wireless Services

Exchange Server 2003 now supports advanced wireless cellular and 802.1X connectivity. This was not previously available in early versions of the Exchange Server family. The advanced wireless features enable end-user remote access support and wireless synchronization to Exchange mail using built-in Exchange technology such as Outlook Web Access.

Located on the Exchange Features tab of a mail-enabled user's properties page, the Wireless Services option allows mail-enabled objects access to individual Exchange mailbox data using supported wireless 802.1X devices, Pocket PCs, and Internet-ready cellular phones.

### Wireless Functionality
When Active Directory objects are mail enabled, these features are in an enabled state by default. Each feature is managed and changed through the end-user properties pages by easily disabling and enabling the desired method of wireless access.

Review the wireless features (see Figure 18.3) and their descriptions to better understand Exchange Server 2003 wireless functionality and the options provided with each feature.

- **Outlook Wireless Access**—With Outlook Wireless Access enabled, the user can browse mailbox information from wireless devices and cellular Internet-enabled phones.

- **User Initiated Synchronization**—When enabled, this option allows individual users to synchronize mail information with wireless devices. This option is not associated with active-sync desktop synchronization and is enabled by default.

18

- **Always Up-to-Date Notification**—Enabled and used with user-initiated synchronization, this option notifies wireless users when changes have occurred requiring synchronization.

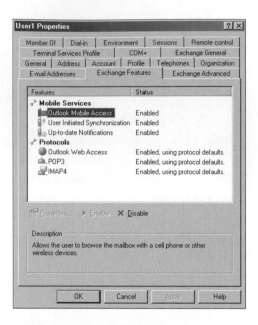

**FIGURE 18.3**    User properties and Exchange features page.

## Managing User Protocols

Protocols allow individual mail enabled users to access Exchange mail using different methods and functionality. Access control to Exchange Mail can be controlled from an individual mail account based on the type of access granted.

By default, Exchange Server 2003 features enable all users to access Exchange using the POP3, Outlook Web Access, and IMAP4 protocols. In most situations, all three of these features are not required for every mail-enabled user in the Exchange organization.

Each feature is fully configurable on an individual account basis and can also be modified by disabling the protocol from the Exchange System Manager. Protocols such as POP3 access cannot be enabled fully unless the Exchange Server 2003 server has been configured to support this protocol.

## Changing the Status of Exchange Features

Any time an Active Directory object is mail enabled, each of the Exchange features are also enabled by default. To control or modify the status of any Exchange feature, use the individual user's Properties tab to change the status of the feature from Enabled to Disabled.

> **NOTE**
>
> Using the Exchange Features tab enables and disables only the functionality for the individual mail-enabled user. When enabling these features, additional configuration is required, such as the implementation of an Outlook Web Access front-end server or the configuration of a server and client to enable POP access to Exchange mail data.
>
> Some additional firewall configuration may also be required for access to Outlook Web Access over the Internet from remote locations.

To change the status of one or more Exchange features for multiple mail-enabled objects in Active Directory and Exchange, use the Exchange Task Wizard.

For example, an organization can disable wireless features for multiple users in Active Directory by following these steps:

1. Open the Active Directory Users and Computers snap-in and select the accounts to be modified.

2. Or, from the Exchange System Manager menu, select Action, Exchange Tasks, and Next at the welcome screen.

3. Select the Configure Exchange Features option and click Next to continue.

4. From the Configure Exchange Features selection, choose the feature to be modified. Select the Disable or Enable tab to change the feature for all users. Modify all options before continuing, and select Next to apply the changes.

5. Review the configured changes and the results of these changes on the Task Summary screen. Select the Back button to adjust any required changes. Select Next to complete the modification and fully apply the settings.

## Managing and Monitoring Mailbox Usage

An Exchange administrator's responsibility goes beyond configuring user mailboxes and settings. An important part of the planning and maintenance of Exchange is to monitor usage and understand what impact users have on a mailbox server when accessing information. Knowing what type of user performance and response times Exchange mailbox

18

servers can provide assist the admin in proactive planning for hardware upgrades and expansion as performance demands grow.

Using the Exchange monitor tool Exmon.exe, administrators can track and review information related to mailbox users accessing in the the following areas:

- Server CPU usage

- TCP/IP addresses and user assignments

- Outlook client versions

- Outlook cached mode information

- Server and network resource usage

---

**Exmon.exe**

The Exmon.exe tool offers extensive information in regard to client access and Exchange Server performance. For additional information on the use of the Exmon.exe tool, review the Using_Exmon.Doc files located in the default installation folder.

To download the Exmon.exe tool, go to Microsoft's web page at `http://www.microsoft.com/exchange/downloads/2003/default.mspx`.

Exmon.exe can also be used in Exchange 2003's mixed mode environments. To use this tool on Exchange 2000, service pack 2 must be installed.

---

## Running the User Monitor Tool

The User Monitor tool can be used when Exchange performance is in question and can be run using several methods. For this exercise, Exmon.exe will be used to gather information about the user, showing CPU usage, operating system, average seek time, and more. Use this tool to gain a clearer insight into the user's impact on your Exchange server, especially during heavy usage times.

To launch the tool and gather information, complete the following steps:

1. Download and install the tool. The default location for installing the tool is c:\Program Files\EXMON.

2. Double click the Exmon.exe file, located in the default installation folder.

3. Select the By User option from the Exchange User Monitor GUI and click the start icon.

4. Information will be collected in one-minute intervals. When desired, select the stop icon to finish the collection of data.

### Exporting Collection Data to a File

With the collection of data complete, administrators must now interpret the information gathered. Because viewing this information can be difficult through the GUI, administrators can export this data to a file by using the following example command:

```
exmon.exe -SU C:\EXMON\Userdata
```

# Moving Exchange User Mailboxes

When moving mailboxes in previous versions of Exchange, moves were completed through the Active Directory Users and Computers snap-in using the Mailbox Move Wizard. These tasks could become difficult when moving multiple mailboxes because administrators were required to locate each mail-enabled account in the Active Directory tree, regardless of where they resided. In addition to this limitation, mailbox moves were also restricted to a single administrative group and could not be moved between different Administrative Groups.

These limitations of Exchange 2000 Server move tools have been eliminated in Exchange Server 2003 installed with the latest service pack. By including the Move Mailbox functionality in the Exchange System Manager, administrators can select and move objects with much greater flexibility. Using the Exchange System Manager to move mailboxes now provides the ability to move multiple mailboxes easily and effectively, including between different Administrative Groups.

Using the Mailbox Move tool through the Exchange System Manager, entire Exchange Server mailbox stores or mailboxes within a store can be selected and moved from one location to another easily.

### Simple Tasks to Prepare for Moving Mailboxes

Before moving a mailbox or multiple mailboxes, tasks can be completed in advance to avoid the loss of mail data and streamline the move process.

By preparing for a mailbox move simply by backing up Exchange information stores and eliminating unwanted mail data using the Mailbox Manager and mailbox recipient policies, administrators can perform moves in less time while eliminating unwanted data in the mailboxes being moved. This allows the newly moved mailboxes in the destination store to be populated only with information needed and in clean fashion.

#### Backing Up Exchange Mailboxes

Before moving and removing mail data from mailboxes, it is always a good practice to back up the Exchange server from where mailboxes are being moved. Also, backing up the individual mailboxes before cleaning and moving allows for the recovery of any messages if mailbox owners identify missing messages after the move that need to be recovered.

To back up a mailbox or a group of mailboxes, administrators can effectively use any of the following methods if the recovery of mail information is required:

- **Full and brick-level backup**—Use a third-party backup product to back up and validate the backup of the Exchange information store or individual Exchange mailboxes.

- **Export mail data to PST files**—Use Exchange utilities such as the Microsoft Exchange Server 2003 Exchange Merge Wizard (Exmerge.exe) to export all user mail data to individual PST files. To obtain the Exchange Merge Wizard, download the tool from Microsoft by going to http://www.microsoft.com/downloads/details.aspx?FamilyId=429163EC-DCDF-47DC-96DA-1C12D67327D5&displaylang=en.

- **Offline copy**—By dismounting the mail store where the mailbox or mailboxes reside, a copy of the stored .MDB and .STM files can be created in a different location allowing for a simple recovery.

### Cleaning Unneeded Mailbox Data

Using the Mailbox Cleanup Wizard to remove unnecessary mailbox information such as deleted items and outdated calendar information shortens the total amount of time required to move mailboxes. Cleaning mailboxes before moving also ensures that the mailbox data being moved is only what is required and clean.

Use the Mailbox Cleanup Wizard to remove unwanted mailbox information before moving mailboxes. To open and schedule mailbox cleanup, see the section "Implementing Mailbox Recipient Policies," later in this chapter.

## Moving Mailboxes Between Storage Groups and Servers

Limitations for moving mailboxes have been greatly reduced in Exchange Server 2003. When leveraging the Mailbox Move tool through the Exchange System Manager, administrators can move mailboxes or groups of mailboxes and can run multiple instances of moves at the same time with very little limitations.

In addition to new features such as moves between Administrative groups, options can now be configured to address corrupted mail items during moves and scheduling that previously interrupted the move process or caused it to fail.

Through the options available with the Mailbox Move tool in Exchange Server 2003, corrupted mailboxes and mailbox items can now be skipped and not moved at all instead of causing corruption in the new mail store or causing the entire move to fail. In addition, these corruptions are now written to a log file and can be retrieved to address issues with specific corrupted mailboxes.

View the Mailbox Move logs to troubleshoot failed item moves and resolve any issues with the move. Move logs can be retrieved by going to C:\Documents and Settings, Profile, My Documents, Exchange Task Wizard Logs folder (where the drive letter is the drive of the Documents and Settings folder and profile represents the account being used).

Options can also be configured to determine the total number of corrupted items to be skipped. Using the Maximum Number of Corrupted Items to Be Skipped option, values can be configured manually between 3 and 100.

> **CAUTION**
>
> When using the Mailbox Move tool options, the default setting for skipping corrupted items is set to three.
>
> When corrupted items are skipped, items are deleted and not retained in the information store. Be sure to back up the Information Store or export mail data to a .PST file to avoid the loss of any mail items not intended to be deleted.

Scheduling and Move Cut Off times are also now available and configurable for mailbox moves. For example, administrators can schedule moves of mailboxes to be run outside business hours. If the move has not completed by the specified cutoff time, the mailbox being moved and the remaining mailboxes are left in the original location.

### Multiple Mailbox Move Tool

The Exchange Server 2003 version of the Move Mailbox tool allows administrators to run several instances of mailbox moves at the same time. Depending on the level of hardware resources, such as available memory and processor speed, multiple instances of the Mailbox Move tool can be run in parallel with adequate performance.

> **TIP**
>
> Test a handful of mailbox moves using the Mailbox Move tool to ensure that the server performance is not affected when running multiple instances of the move function.

### Moving Mailboxes Between Storage Groups

To move mailboxes between administrative storage groups, open the Exchange System Manager and select the Storage Group where the mailboxes to be moved reside. Complete the following steps to move Exchange mailboxes between storage groups:

1. Highlight the mailboxes to be moved.

2. From the Action menu, select the Exchange Tasks option and click the Next button on the welcome screen.

3. At the Available Tasks page, select Move Mailbox and click the Next button to continue.

4. Select the destination mailbox store where the mailboxes will be moved. Click the Mailbox Store option and choose the destination store where the mailboxes will be moved. Select Next when complete.

5. Configure the options for addressing corruption, and set the desired limits for this move. Select the Next button to begin the mailbox move.

6. To continue moving the mailbox, on the Schedule page, select Next to continue.

7. On the Summary page, review the results of the mailbox move, and select Finish.

18

## Moving Mailboxes Between Administrative Groups

New to the latest service pack for Exchange Server 2003 is the ability to move mailboxes between Administrative Groups. Administrators can move user objects and their mailboxes between Administrative Groups as long as the account being used to move mailboxes has permissions to create objects in the destination Administrative Group. To move a mailbox between Administrative Groups, complete the following steps:

1. Highlight the mailbox or mailboxes to be moved.

2. From the Action menu, select the Exchange Tasks option and click the Next button on the welcome screen.

3. On the Available Tasks page, select Move Mailbox and click the Next button to continue.

4. Next, select the new destination Administrative Group and mailbox store where the mailboxes will be moved. Select Next when complete.

5. As with other types of moves, configure the options for addressing corrupted items, and set the desired limits for this move. Select the Next button to begin the mailbox move.

6. To move the mailbox immediately, on the Schedule page, select Next to continue.

7. On the Summary page, review the results of the mailbox move, and select Finish.

## Moving Mailboxes to a Different Exchange Server

Moving mailboxes from one Exchange Server to another is often done to assist administrators in load-balancing multiple Exchange Server environments and even when replacing outdated hardware.

This task is accomplished in the same manner as moving mailboxes between storage groups. Using the Mailbox Move tool, mailboxes can be moved between servers with same options available when moving mailboxes on the same server. This can help administrators ensure that corrupted information is not moved to the new mailbox store, causing failures at a later time.

To move mailboxes between servers, follow these steps:

1. Select the mailbox store where the mailboxes reside. Select and highlight the mailboxes to be moved.

2. From the Action menu, select the Exchange Tasks option and click the Next button on the welcome screen.

3. At the Available Tasks page, select Move Mailbox and click the Next button.

4. Select the destination mailbox store where the mailboxes will be moved. Click the Server option and choose the destination server where the mailboxes will be moved to. Select Next when complete.

5. Configure the options for addressing corruption and set the desired limits for this move. Select the Next button to begin the mailbox move.

6. To continue moving the mailbox, on the Schedule page, select Next.

7. On the Summary page, review the results of the mailbox move and select Finish to complete the move.

> **NOTE**
>
> Mailboxes can be moved between servers only when the servers are part of the same site. When servers are in different sites, the mailboxes cannot be moved using the Move Mailbox function. Moving mailboxes between servers in different sites requires the export of mail data, covered in the section "Backing Up Exchange Mailboxes."

# Creating and Managing Exchange Contacts

In many situations, organizations are required to communicate with non-native Microsoft mail systems, non-Exchange mail recipients, and business contacts with external SMTP addresses. These situations are ideal for an Exchange Server 2003 recipient called contacts.

Known as custom recipients in previous Exchange versions, contacts are created in Active Directory and viewed in the Global Catalog in the same manner as a mail-enabled user object. Each contact can be assigned an SMTP address in the domain where the contact resides allowing internal users easy access to mail communications with external recipients. Using Contacts can also allow a contact to receive external mail using the same email domain as mail-enabled users that is then forwarded to the external account address.

## Creating Exchange Contacts

To create a contact in Exchange Server 2003, begin by opening the Active Directory Users and Computers management console. Select the Organizational Unit where the contact will be created and follow these steps for creating a contacts list:

1. From the Action menu, select New and Contact.

2. Enter the information to identify the contact in Active Directory.

   For example:

   First name = John

   Middle initial = M

   Last name = Doe

   Display name = John Doe

18

3. Select Next to continue.

4. On the Email page, enter the alias name for the contact being created.

5. To create an email address for the contact, ensure that the Create an Exchange Email Address check box is selected.

6. Click the Modify button to begin creating an email address for the contact.

7. Select the SMTP Address option to create a contact address that will forward messages to an external Internet email account.

   Enter the fully qualified Internet email address to be used for the contact; for example: JohnDoe@CompanyABC.com.

   Use the Advanced tab to configure and override the default Internet mail message formats.

8. Click OK when done, validate the email address, and then select Next, Finish. This completes the process of creating a new contact.

## Mail-Forwarding Options with Contacts

The primary function of contacts is to forward internal Exchange messages to external mail recipients that are involved with your business organization. This function allows contacts to accept messages using the same domain name as all mail-enabled objects in Active Directory and to send these messages to a mail system outside the Exchange organization.

To create a contact to forward mail to an external SMTP email address, follow these steps:

1. Open the Active Directory Users and Computers management console, and select the Organizational Unit where the contact will be created.

2. From the Action menu, select New, Contact.

3. Enter the name of the contact and display name that will be used when viewing the contact in the Active Directory Global Catalog. Click the Next button to continue.

4. On the New Object page, ensure that Create an Exchange Email Address is selected. Click the Modify button to create the external SMTP email address where messages will be forwarded. Click Next when complete.

5. Review the information in the Summary page and click Finish when done.

## Contact Email Address Types

Exchange contacts can be configured to communicate with multiple types of mail systems. Using the built-in address types of Exchange Server 2003 contacts, contacts and mail addresses can be configured to provide coexistence between mail systems or to communicate with other mail systems. Built in to Exchange Server 2003, multiple email types are readily available as contact email options. In addition to the built-in mail address types shown in Table 18.1, other mail address types can be configured. Types can also be configured using the Custom Address option.

**TABLE 18.1**   Contact Address Types

| | |
|---|---|
| X.400 Address | Microsoft Mail Address |
| SMTP Address | cc:Mail Address |
| Lotus Notes Address | Novell GroupWise Address |

### Additional Contact Address Types

In addition to these types of addresses, additional contact address types can be configured in the same manner as regular users creating additional custom addresses. This option allows contacts to be enabled with address types not listed in the New Email Address Type options tab.

Using Custom Email options can allow contacts to communicate with other types of mail systems when configuring other types of addresses for use with contacts; the administrator must configure the email address and mail system type. Additional configuration might be required when using this option, to allow Exchange Server 2003 to communicate with nonstandard mail system types.

### Modifying and Adding Contact Email Addresses

When managing users and contacts, administrators are often required to modify addresses and address types. To accomplish this, administrators can simply modify the contact address by opening the Active Directory Users and Computers management console.

Select the contact that will be modified by expanding the domain tree and selecting the Organizational Unit where the contact resides.

**Finding Contacts and Recipients**

An additional method of finding contacts and other Active Directory objects is to use the Find Users, Contacts, and Groups tool built into the Active Directory Users and Computers management console. Properties of Active Directory objects can then be accessed by highlighting and right-clicking the Active Directory object.

Contact attributes can be modified by opening the properties page of the contact and modifying the desired attribute or email address.

## Planning and Creating Distribution Groups

Distribution Groups are created when a collection of Active Directory objects requires membership to a mail-enabled list in Exchange Server 2003. This allows the Distribution Group to receive messages to a single address in Exchange, which can then be distributed to all members of the group.

Also known as distribution lists in Microsoft Exchange 5.5, Distribution Groups can now be created to span domains. However, Distribution Groups posses no capability to be listed in the Active Directory Discretionary Access Control List (DACL) for purposes of assign permissions.

When working with Distribution Groups, functionality and replication depend on several domain and forest factors. Depending on the type of group—Universal, Global, or Local—and the Exchange server and domain functional levels where the group is created, each type of group can be configured to nest other groups or replicate across domains. In this section, we review the different Distribution Group scopes, the functionality of each scope, and how Distribution Groups are created.

> **NOTE**
>
> With Exchange Server 2003 and Active Directory, the scope of the Distribution Groups can easily be converted when the domain functional level is in Native Mode. Using the properties of the Distribution Group, administrators can select the scope and type that the Distribution Group can become.

## Determining Distribution Group Scopes

Before creating Distribution Groups in Exchange Server 2003, it is important to understand what capabilities each scope enables. Distribution Groups can be created in one of the three following scopes: as a Universal Distribution Group, Domain Distribution Group, and Domain Local Distribution Group.

Each scope provides different functionality within the Active Directory domain and forest in which it resides. Depending on the scope of the Distribution Group, other Distribution Groups, user accounts, and even contacts can be members of a single Distribution Group.

Review each type of group to assist in planning and creating the most appropriate Distribution Group for your organization.

- **Domain Local**—Best utilized in a single domain scenario, the Domain Local scope allows the following member types: account objects (user accounts, contacts), additional groups with the Domain Local scope, groups with the Global scope, and groups with the Universal scope. Each Domain Local group exists only within the domain it is created, and group membership is not present when viewing the Global Catalog.

- **Global**—Global Distribution Groups are configured when access to view the group is required in the Global Catalog. Although the Global Distribution Groups can be seen in the Global Catalog, membership of the group is not visible. Each Global group is present only within the domain it is created, and changes are not replicated outside to other domains.

- **Universal**—Universal groups allow administrators to nest nonreplication Global and Domain Local groups for ease of management. Use the Universal scope to consolidate Distribution Groups from multiple domains. All changes to universal groups are replicated to all Global Catalog servers in the forest. Nesting groups requires less replication traffic when changes occur to a member of the nested group.

## Creating Distribution Groups

To create a Distribution Group, administrators must first determine the scope for the groups and the address name that the group will receive messages as. In this scenario, you will create a Distribution Group with the Global scope. This group will be mail enabled to receive and distribute messages to all its members in the local domain.

To begin creating the Distribution Group, open the Active Directory Users and Computers management console and select the Organizational Unit where the Distribution Group will reside. Complete the following steps to add a Distribution Group to Active Directory:

1. From the Action menu tab, select New and then Group.

2. On the New Object Group tab, enter the name of the Distribution Group.

3. Make the scope for the distribution Global, and select the type of group as Distribution.

4. The Create In tab allows you to create the email address for the Distribution Group. Click the check box Create an Exchange Email address. This option mail-enables the Distribution Group.

5. If required, modify the alias name for the Distribution Group and select the Administrative Group that your group will be associated with. Click Next, Finish to finish creating the group.

> **NOTE**
>
> The Associated Administrative Group option is used to determine which default recipient policy and email address will be assigned to the Distribution Group.

### Adding Distribution Group Membership

After the Distribution Group has been created, the administrator can add members to the group. To add members to the group, select the Distribution Group and open the properties of the group by selecting Action, Properties. Then complete the following steps:

1. From the Properties tab of the Distribution Group, select the Members tab.

2. Click the Add button to select the Active Directory accounts to be added to the group.

3. To show all the accounts in the domain, select the Advanced tab. Select the domain where the account resides and click Find Now. This searches Active Directory and displays all accounts and groups in the domain selected.

> **NOTE**
>
> To search for contacts, enable the Contacts search function by selecting the Object Type tab and placing a check in the selection next to Contacts.

4. Select the account objects to be added as members to the Distribution Group. Select OK twice to return to the Members tab.

5. Repeat these steps until all members and objects have been added to the Distribution Group.

## Creating Query-Based Distribution Groups

Query-based Distribution Groups are identical in functionality to a normal Distribution Group. The one benefit to the new Exchange Server 2003 feature is that query-based Distribution Groups assign group membership based on LDAP queries.

Available only in Exchange Server 2003 Native Mode, query-based Distribution Groups allow administrators to dynamically assign members to the group without having to perform the manual task of adding and removing account objects after the group is created.

For example, using the Filter option, if a query-based Distribution Group is created, membership can be defined by selecting all mail-enabled users within the Active Directory domain. This option adds all mail-enabled account objects to the Distribution Group membership; any new accounts also are added as they are mail-enabled in Active Directory.

Filter options for created query-based groups include the following:

- Users with Exchange Mailboxes
- Users with External Mail Addresses
- Mail-Enabled Groups
- Contacts with External Email Addresses
- Mail-Enabled Public Folders
- Customer Filters

To create a query-based Distribution Group, open the Active Directory Users and Computers management console, and select the Advanced Features option from the View menu.

1. Select the Organizational Unit where the query-based Distribution Group will be created. From the Action menu, select New, and Query-Based Distribution Group.

2. On the New Object tab, enter the name for the new query-based Distribution Group and select Next to continue.

3. For this exercise, click the Change button and select Domain.com, Users Organizational Unit. This option applies this filter to all users in the Users Organizational Unit. Next, select the Users with Exchange Mailbox option. This applies the option to all accounts in the User container with a mailbox.

4. Select Next to continue and Finish to finish creating the new query-based Distribution Group.

## Managing and Maintaining Distribution Groups

As organizations grow and the Exchange Server 2003 tree becomes more complicated, administrators can find themselves faced with the task of managing and maintaining large numbers of Distribution Groups, as well as dealing with the effects of these groups when replicating across the network.

To simplify the day-to-day administrative tasks associated with adding and removing group memberships, administrators can now assign an Active Directory user account permissions to manage a Distribution Group. This account can be added to the Managed By tab of the Distribution Group properties, allowing the account to manage and update the membership list of the Distribution Group it is assigned.

### Creating a Distribution Group Manager

To add an account to manage a Distribution Group, select the Distribution Group and open the properties pages of the Distribution Group by selecting File, Properties from the Active Directory Users and Computers management console. To add the account, complete the following steps:

1. Select the Managed By tab and click the Change button to add an account to manage the Distribution Group.

2. Click the Advanced tab and search Active Directory for the account to be added. Select the account and click the OK button when complete.

3. Select the Manager Can Update Membership List check box to enable permission for the account added, and click OK when complete.

The account added can now change and update the membership to the distribution list.

### Managing Distribution Group Replication

Another area related to managing Distribution Groups is maintaining effective and seamless replication. In larger environments, changes to universal group memberships are replicated to all Global Catalog servers in the Active Directory forest and, in some cases, affect bandwidth availability over WAN links.

To avoid replication issues related to Distribution Groups, administrators can nest global groups and local groups with a single Universal group. By nesting groups, account changes and membership changes are completed at the domain level. Because these changes occur within the Global group and not the Universal group level, replication of changes to the Global Catalog server is not required.

18

## Mail-Enabling Groups

With Exchange Server 2003, both distribution and security groups can be mail enabled to receive messages for all members. Unlike a security group, a distribution group is strictly created for the association in Exchange to receive and distribute messages. When groups are converted from one type to another, they are not always automatically mail enabled.

To mail enable a group in Exchange Server 2003, first select the group in Active Directory Users and Computers and complete these steps:

1. From the Action menu, select Exchange Task.

2. On the Welcome to Exchange Task screen, select Next.

3. On the Available Task screen, select Establish Email Address on Groups and click Next.

4. Confirm the mail alias for the group and select Next.

5. Select Finish to finish adding an email address to the group.

It is always a good practice to open the properties page for the group and review the email addresses to ensure that they were added correctly.

# Creating and Managing Exchange Server 2003 Administrative Groups

Exchange Server 2003 Administrative Groups are created to group and maintain Exchange objects for reasons of permissions management and administrative distribution. For example, if an organization is based in three locations worldwide with three groups of Exchange administrators in each location, three separate Administrative Groups can be created and managed by each location to maintain servers and policies in the separate Administrative Groups.

Exchange Server 2003 Administrative Groups are used to manage and maintain Routing Group containers, chat networks, public folder containers, and system policies. Each of these containers can house multiple objects and each can be managed individually.

Also, administrative Group functionality differs depending on the functional level of the Exchange Server 2003 organization, as well as the type of Administrative Group that is created.

---

**Administrative Groups**

By default, Administrative Groups are disabled in the Exchange Server 2003 System Manager. This is, by design, to allow ease of viewing and management in the Exchange System Manager for smaller organizations. To enable Administrative Group functionality, select the properties page for the Exchange Server 2003 organization and select Display Administrative Groups.

---

## Mixed Mode

When a new Exchange Server 2003 organization is installed, the Exchange organization is in Mixed Mode, by default. Mixed Mode facilitates interoperability between Exchange Server 2003 and Exchange 5.X servers. This also means that certain Administrative Group functionality is not available in a Mixed Mode environment.

When Exchange Server 2003 is in a Mixed Mode environment, the following is true:

- Exchange mailboxes cannot be moved between Administrative Groups.

- Routing Groups consist of only the server installed in the Administrative Group.

- Exchange 5.5 sites are mapped to Administrative Groups.

## Native Mode

After an Exchange organization function level is raised to Native Mode, Exchange Administrative Group functionality is enhanced and limitations of a Mixed Mode environment are no longer a consideration. Administrative Group functionality in Native Mode includes the following:

- Exchange Mailboxes can be moved between Administrative Groups.

- Servers can be moved between Routing Groups.

- Routing Groups can contain servers from multiple Administrative Groups.

- Simple Mail Transport Protocol is enabled as the default routing protocol.

## Administrative Groups Models

As we begin to grasp Administrative Groups and the purpose in both Native and Mixed Mode environments, the main design consideration is what model best fits your organizational needs.

In this section, we review two very simple concepts of Exchange Server 2003 Administrative Group management. The first is a centralized management model, and the second is a decentralized one. Because Exchange Administrative Groups are basically collections of objects grouped together for purposes of management, the structure and administrative topology of your organization could dictate the best administrative model for your organization.

### Centralized

A centralized administrative model best fits an organization with fewer locations and a smaller centralized administrative staff. Because there is no need to distribute administrative permission, a centralized model is ideal for smaller organizations.

This model can also be effective in larger organizations. When a larger organization requires individual Exchange functionality to be managed by different groups or user accounts, a centralized model can still be implemented.

18

For example, CompanyABC is a larger organization with multiple Exchange servers and locations. However, the administrative model requires permissions to be configured for one group to manage the Routing Groups within the Administrative Group and another group of administrators to manage recipient policies.

### Decentralized

A decentralized administrative model is very effective when larger organizations have multiple offices and require administration based on each location.

For example, CompanyABC has 40 Exchange servers with administrative staff in 10 separate locations. In this scenario, 10 Administrative Groups can be configured, and Exchange servers and recipient policies can be assigned to the appropriate Administrative Group for management.

## Creating Administrative Groups in Exchange Server 2003

To create an Administrative Group in Exchange Server 2003, administrators must first enable the option to view Administrative Groups in the Exchange Systems Manager.

To enable viewing Administrative Groups, open the properties page of the Exchange organization and complete the following steps:

1. If the Administrative Groups are not visible in the Exchange System Manager, select the organization from the top of the Exchange tree. Select Action and Properties from the Exchange System Manager menu.

2. Check the Display Administrative Groups check box and click OK. This adds the Administrative Groups to the Exchange Systems Manager.

To add additional Administrative Groups in Exchange Server 2003, select the Administrative Groups container in the Exchange Systems Manager. Begin by following these steps:

1. From the Action menu, select New, Administrative Group.

2. On the Properties page, enter the name of the Administrative Group to be added. Click OK to continue.

3. After the Administrative Group is created, administrators can add system policy containers, Routing Group containers, and public folder containers.

## Delegating Control over Administrative Groups

To manage and assign permission to Exchange Server 2003 Administrative Groups, administrators can leverage the Exchange Delegation Wizard.

Using the Delegation Wizard at the Administrative Group level assigns one of three roles to the account or group being assigned permissions over the Administrative Group. These three levels of permission are as follows:

- **Exchange View Only Administrator**—Allows administrators permissions to view objects of the Administrative Group but not change any properties of the Exchange object.

- **Exchange Full Administrator**—This role allows assign permissions to fully administer Exchange system objects and permissions.

- **Exchange Administrator**—The administrator role can fully administer Exchange system information only.

To assign roles and permissions over an Administrative Group using the Delegation Wizard, perform the following steps:

1. Select the Administrative Group where the delegation of roles will be assigned using the Delegation Wizard.

2. From the Action menu, select the Delegate Control options. On the Welcome to the Exchange Administration Delegation Wizard screen, select Next.

3. Click the Add button and select the Active Directory account or group being delegated control over the Administrative Group.

4. When the account or group has been selected, select the Exchange role to be assigned. Select OK to continue.

5. Select Next and Finish to finish delegating control over the Administrative Group.

# Creating and Managing Routing Groups

In all but small single or multiple Exchange server organizations, there is a need for more complex configurations to connect multiple Exchange servers. In these scenarios, locations and Exchange servers are connected using Routing Groups and Routing Group connectors.

As organizations become larger, multiple Routing Groups are created to support the addition of Exchange 2003 servers. Each of these Routing Groups can be connected by creating an Exchange Routing Group connector using multiple connection types:

- Routing Group Connector

- SMTP Connector

- X.400 Connector

Routing Groups are located in the Exchange System Manager and are located in each Administrative Group. A single Routing Group is self-sufficient and possesses certain limitations when in an Exchange Server 2003 Mixed Mode environment.

18

## Understanding Exchange Server 2003 Routing Groups

A Routing Group is a collection of Exchange servers that communicate with each other directly over the same internal network or reliable connection.

When multiple Routing Groups must be created, each individual group must be connected using one of three available Exchange connection types:

- **Routing Group Connector**—This connector is the default connector type. It can be used to connect a single or multiple Exchange bridgehead server for load balancing of message traffic.

- **SMTP Connector**—The SMTP connector uses the Simple Mail Transport Protocol to connect and communicate with remote Routing Groups, non-Exchange mail systems, and the Internet mail host.

- **X.400 Mail Connector**—Limited to a single local and remote host, the X.400 connector is primarily designed for communications between Exchange Server 2003 and X.400 mail systems.

### Mixed Mode

When Exchange Server 2003 is in a mixed environment, Routing Groups can consist of only servers that had been installed directly into the Administrative Group where the Routing Group resides. Additional servers from other Administrative Groups cannot be added to the Routing Group.

### Native Mode

After the functional level has been raised to Native Mode, Exchange servers can be managed and moved between Routing Groups.

Also, Routing Groups in a single Administrative Group can contain servers from other Administrative Groups.

## Installing Routing Groups

Depending on whether you are installing additional Routing Groups into the existing Administrative Group, different tasks must be performed to create new Routing Groups.

To create and establish Routing Groups within a new Exchange Administrative Group, the first step is to create the Routing Group container. The Routing Group container is similar to a folder in Windows Explorer and is used to house and organize one or more Routing Groups.

> **NOTE**
>
> The default first Administrative Group contains the default Routing Group container. Only one Routing Group container is allowed in each Administrative Group. When creating multiple Administrative Groups, multiple Routing Groups can then be added to each Routing Group container.

When creating and configuring a new Routing Group into a new Administrative Group, the first step is to create the routing container. To install the Routing Group container, begin by selecting the new Administrative Group in the Exchange System Manager where the container will be located.

1. Select the Action menu from the Exchange System Manager and select New, Routing Group Container. This creates a container called Routing Groups.

2. To begin installing individual Routing Groups, from the Exchange System Manager, select the Routing Group container where the Routing Groups will reside.

3. From the Action menu, select New, Routing Group.

4. Enter the name of the new Routing Group, and enter any details or administrative descriptions in the Detail tab. Select OK when finished.

## Moving Exchange Servers Between Routing Groups

After Administrative Groups have been populated with Exchange Servers and Routing Groups, one task often completed is moving servers between Routing Groups. This task is usually performed as administrators begin to create a more complex Exchange organization and routing infrastructure.

With Exchange Server 2003, administrators can move Exchange servers between Routing Groups. However, one limitation is that Exchange servers cannot be moved between Administrative Groups.

To move an Exchange server to a different Routing Group, begin by opening the Exchange System Manager. Expand the Routing Group folder where the Exchange server resided, and expand the Routing Group folder where the Exchange server will be placed. Simply drag and drop the Exchange server object from the source Routing Group to the destination Routing Group.

> **CAUTION**
>
> When using and configuring Routing Groups, ensure that new Exchange servers are installed in the proper Administrative Group where their Routing Group resides. Exchange Server 2003 systems cannot be moved between Administrative Groups in Exchange Server 2003.

18

# Using Recipient Policies

Exchange Server 2003 contains two types of recipient policies. The first type of recipient policy deals with mail-enabled objects and how email addresses are created based on naming conventions defined in the policy. The second addresses management of end-user mailboxes and the limitation that can be applied to user mailboxes based on policy membership.

Recipient policies can be created to define how naming conventions will be applied to mail-enabled objects in Exchange. By creating a recipient policy, administrators can define how usernames of specific email address types will be viewed in Exchange when an object is mail enabled.

Different from email-based policies, mailbox recipient policies deal with setting mailbox restrictions such as size limits and age limits; they are configured in the same location as email-based policies. Defining mailbox recipient policies can allow administrators to control and manage the total amount of data retained in the Exchange information store.

> **NOTE**
>
> For more information on mailbox recipient policies, see the section "Using the Mailbox Manager Utility," later in this chapter.

When a policy is created, each type of recipient policy can be assigned to specific users and mail-enabled objects within Active Directory by defining policy membership during the creation of the policy.

For example, an SMTP mail recipient policy can be created to ensure that all users who belong to the Users Organizational Unit will be enabled with an SMTP email address using the following naming convention:

Username = John Doe

SMTP address = CompanyABC.com

SMTP email address = JohnDoe@CompanyABC.com

## Implementing Email Address Recipient Policies

When Exchange Server 2003 is installed, a default recipient policy is created to assign an SMTP address and X.400 address to be used for all mail-enabled Active Directory objects. This recipient policy defines how all mail-enabled Active Directory objects will be assigned email addresses in Exchange. It is based on the Active Directory domain name where the Exchange server is installed.

When creating additional email-based recipient policies, administrators can define several attributes for each policy created. Beginning with policy membership, administrators can assign a recipient policy to a specified group of users only. Additional address types also can be assigned to specific groups of users.

Along with the default email address, other email types are preconfigured and available to be added as recipient policy email addresses. Additional email types are most often defined when creating coexistence between Exchange Server 2003 and other messaging systems. Exchange Server 2003 supports X.400, SMTP, Lotus Notes, Microsoft Mail, cc:Mail, and Novell GroupWise addressing, by default. Custom addresses can be defined for a message type that is not built into Exchange Server 2003.

## Defining Recipient Policy Naming Standards

By default, email-based recipients use the default UserName@domainname.com naming standard. Administrators can define string values to change the default rules that determine how user naming conventions will be implemented. These are naming attributes or values that determine the way a user's name will be defined and displayed—for example, first name.last name or the first initial and then last name. Using the value strings listed here, administrators can modify the default recipient policy or create a new policy to customize the name convention based on specific organizational needs.

Use the following values to modify recipient email addresses and naming conventions:

%g = Given name (first name).

%s = Surname (last name).

%i = Middle name.

%d = Display name.

%m = Exchange alias name.

%r = Replace character x with the character y in the username—for example, in %rxy, if the character x = y, the character will be deleted in the user's name.

Naming conventions can also be defined by the total number of characters in the name, as well as additional characters such as periods between names.

For example, by placing a number in front of the naming value, administrators can define how many characters will be displayed for that name type. Notice the period between the naming values; this adds a period between the first initial and the last name.

Example:

%1g.%s@ComanyABC.com = J.Doe@ComanyABC.com

## Defining Recipient Policy Membership Using Search Filters

Each recipient policy can be applied to Exchange mail-enabled objects by using filters to define policy memberships. As with defining other memberships, policy memberships are defined using the same Active Directory Search tool. The Active Directory Search tool allows membership to be defined in the following areas:

- Users with Exchange Mailboxes
- Users with External Mail Addresses
- Mail-Enabled Groups
- Contacts with External Email Addresses
- Mail Enabled Public Folders
- Query-Based Distribution Groups

18

## Implementing Mailbox Recipient Policies

To create a recipient policy, you need to define the criteria based on the previous informa-tion used in this example:

1. Policy will be applied to users with Exchange mailboxes.

2. Domain name CompanyABC.com will be added as a primary SMTP address.

3. String values will be added to create a first initial and last name standard.

To begin creating the new recipient policy, open the Exchange Server System Manager and follow these steps:

1. Select the recipient container and then Recipient Policies.

2. Select the Action menu and choose New, Recipient Policy.

3. In the New Policy dialog box, check the Email Address options and click OK to continue.

4. On the Properties tab of the new recipient policy, enter the name for the new policy.

5. To define policy membership, select the Modify button under Filter Rules.

6. Ensure that the Users with Exchange Mailboxes is the only option selected and click OK.

7. When you select OK, the message shown in Figure 18.4 appears.

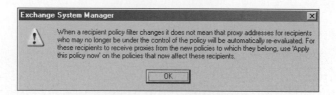

**FIGURE 18.4** Exchange System Manager Proxy Address dialog box.

This dialog box reminds administrators that changes must be applied before they become effective. Click OK to continue.

8. Now that the membership has been defined, select the Email Addresses (Policy) tab to define the email address and naming convention.

9. The default domain name and X.400 address appear in the Address Types dialog box. In this scenario, an additional SMTP address will be defined and added to the policy. Select New to begin adding the CompanyABC.com SMTP address.

10. Select the SMTP Address option, and click OK to continue.

11. On the SMTP Address Properties page, enter **n** the naming values and SMTP domain name defined earlier in the section (see Figure 18.5). Select Apply, OK to continue.

12. On the Email Address Properties page, the new address appears. To set the new address as the primary SMTP address, check the box next to the new address and select Set As Primary. The option sets the new address in bold and creates the address as the primary SMTP address for all policy members.

13. Select OK to continue. You are prompted to update all corresponding email addresses for the members of the new policy. Select Yes to apply the changes.

**FIGURE 18.5**    SMTP Address Properties page.

## Editing and Changing Existing Recipient Policies

Each recipient policy can be modified simply by changing the listed values that already have been defined. When a policy is created in Exchange Server 2003, all attributes and addresses can be modified as long as the account has permissions to manage and change Exchange Server 2003 objects.

To modify existing policies or event default policy, the administrator can simply perform the following steps:

1. Open the policy to be modified for the recipient policy container by selecting the policy. Click the Action menu and select Properties.

2. Modify the desired values and properties of the policy.

3. Select OK from the Policy properties page. A dialog box is displayed. Click OK to apply the changes to all policy members.

> **WARNING**
>
> Clicking OK to apply the changes causes all receipt members to receive the policy change. Review the changes to ensure that no undesired modifications will be applied. Incorrect settings can disable email functionality for all users and may cause changes that do not need to be applied.

# Administering Recipient Update Services

Recipient Update Services, also known as RUS, are used to apply SMTP domains to recipients residing in domains where Exchange Server 2003 is not installed. The RUS is also responsible for managing and maintaining address list membership and updating address changes to ensure that accurate information is available at all times.

When installing Exchange Server 2003, each Exchange organization is installed with a default RUS. When installed, the default service contains two individual services. One is responsible for managing mail addresses and lists at the enterprise level, and the other is responsible for doing so at the domain level.

When working with multidomain environments, it is not always cost-effective or feasible to install multiple Exchange Server 2003 systems to support small amounts of users in each domain. RUS can assist in providing email functionality to accounts that belong to other domains in the Active Directory forest.

## Understanding Recipient Update Services

The Recipient Update Services in Exchange Server 2003 are responsible for providing SMTP domain email functionality within and beyond the default domain where the Exchange server is installed. This means that administrators can now prepare and mail-enable accounts in additional domains without actually installing Exchange Server 2003 directly into the domain.

> **Managing Recipient Update Services**
>
> To create, modify, and delete a RUS, the administrator must possess the Exchange Full Administrator role in the Exchange organization where the service is being managed.
>
> In addition, any Exchange Server services in additional domains will be granted permission to modify Exchange properties in the domain being serviced by the RUS.

Another key function of RUS is to provide and replicate accurate and detailed address list information to other domains in the Active Directory forest.

Each RUS can also be configured to replicate information on a predefined schedule to provide optimal network performance and avoid bandwidth saturation when replicating changes across WAN links.

## Deploying Recipient Update Services

Additional Recipient Update Services can be created to provide support in domains both with and without Exchange Server 2003. Most important, understanding the requirements for creating a RUS can avoid any problems when mail enabling recipients in another domain.

To create a RUS to provide support in a domain where Exchange is not installed, the domain must first be prepped to provide Exchange Server 2003 support:

1. From a domain controller in the domain without Exchange, insert the Exchange Server 2003 CD-ROM into the CD drive.

2. Click Start, Run from the Start menu on the Windows domain controller.

3. The domain where email functionality will be enabled must be Domainprep before the RUS can be created. Using a domain administrator account, enter **D:\I386\Setup.exe /domainprep** in the Run command dialog box (D: represents the drive letter of the CD-ROM drive on the domain controller).

> **NOTE**
>
> For more information on the Domainprep task, see Chapter 3, "Installing Exchange Server 2003."

After the domain has been prepared for Exchange Server 2003, a RUS installation is the same for domains adding additional services and domains without Exchange Server 2003. To establish a RUS to provide email support to the domain members, create the service for the domain by following these steps:

1. Open the Exchange System Manager and select the RUS container.

2. On the Exchange System Manager menu, select the Action option and click New, Recipient Update Service.

3. On the New Object Recipient Update Service dialog box, click Browse. Select the domain where the recipient update service will function. Click OK when complete.

4. On the second New Object Recipient Update Service screen, select the Exchange server responsible for servicing the domain. Click the Browse button to open the Active Directory Search tool, and select the Exchange server providing the service. Click the OK button to return to the New Object screen, and select Next to continue.

5. Review the information provided to ensure that the configuration is correct, and select Finish.

## Managing Recipient Update Services

RUS can be managed in multiple ways to help with server performance and network bandwidth. As an organization becomes larger and server performance, availability, and even replacement become a factor, services and communication can be modified on the RUS to use other domain controllers and Exchange servers in the forest and domain.

Service can also be scheduled to replicate at nonpeak network traffic hours, to avoid bandwidth issues and network performance issues. In addition to scheduled replication, changes and updates to the address list can be pushed manually by administrators to force update changes.

### Performing a Manual Update with Recipient Update Services

Also, when applying changes to the address list, administrators can push changes and update directory information directly from the Exchange System Manager, ensuring that updates are processed immediately. To force a recipient update manually, complete the following steps:

1. From the Exchange System Manager, select the RUS responsible for providing the update needed.

2. On the Exchange System Manager menu, select Action, Update Now. This manually forces the system's update to other Global Catalogs and domains in the forest.

### Setting and Configuring an Update Schedule

When a RUS is created, it must replicate changes with other domains to ensure that the address list and email addresses are applied and viewed correctly and that the information is accurate and always up-to-date. To accomplish this, each RUS is configured with an update schedule that is also created when the service is created.

By default, the replication schedule is set to run every hour. However, the replication schedule is fully configurable and can be changed to meet network and organizational needs.

Administrators might modify the default schedules for several reasons. For example, changes to the address list need to be replicated sooner than every hour in some cases.

---

**Things to Know About Scheduling**

When custom schedules are configured, each update is run at the beginning of the schedule block configured. Allow enough time for the address list to update before the next replication occurs.

Important: When the Never Run schedule option is selected, no changes or modifications to address lists and email addresses are applied. This is true even in the domain that the recipient update service is servicing.

Using the Update Interval Selections drop-down box, preconfigured Exchange replication schedules can be selected and configured to provide accurate replication.

---

To modify the default schedule, open the Exchange System Manager and select the RUS where the schedule will be modified. To change the replication schedule, complete the following steps:

1. Scheduling options are located on the properties page of the RUS. To open the RUS properties, select the Action option from the Exchange System Manager menu and select Properties.

2. To configure a new update schedule, select a preconfigured schedule from the Update Interval drop-down menu or click Customize to create a custom schedule.

3. After the schedule has been configured, select Apply to save the changes and close the properties of the RUS.

# Using the Mailbox Recovery Center Tool

One of the most exciting new features of Exchange Server 2003 is the Mailbox Recovery Center tool. Integrated into the Exchange System Manager, this tool allows administrators to automatically reconnect disassociated mailboxes back to Active Directory accounts. In addition, recovering individual mailboxes and multiple mailboxes can be completed simultaneously using the Exchange System Manager.

Mailbox conflicts between Active Directory accounts can now be identified and resolved using the Mailbox Recovery Center, and mailboxes can be merged as well.

## Identifying Disconnected Mailboxes

When a mailbox is disassociated from the Active Directory object it was originally created for, it becomes a disconnected mailbox in Exchange. This can occur if an Active Directory account is deleted and the mailbox was not marked for deletion at the same time, or if the account has somehow become corrupted and is no longer available.

To identify these disconnected mailboxes, they are displayed in the Exchange Systems Manager by placing a large red X next to the mailbox name, indicating that the mailbox is in a disconnected state. In some instances, these mailboxes are not marked as disconnected and need to be identified as disconnected. When this occurs, the Mailbox Recovery Center tool can be used to identify these mailboxes when their state is not visible as disconnected in a mailbox store.

To identify disconnected mailboxes using the Mailbox Recovery Center tool, begin by adding the mailbox store to the Mailbox Recovery Center in the Exchange Systems Manager. To do so, complete the following steps:

1. Open the Exchange System Manager and open the Tools container. From the Tools container, highlight the Mailbox Recovery Center.

2. From the Exchange System Manager menu, select Action, Add Mailbox Store. Enter the name of the mailbox store to be added, or select the Advanced function to

18

perform a search for the mailbox store. When the appropriate mailbox store has been selected, choose OK to continue.

3. Now that the mailbox store has been added to the Recovery Center, any disconnected mailboxes residing in the mail store will appear in the right pane, as shown in Figure 18.6.

---

**TIP**

When tasks are completed using the Mailbox Recovery Center tool, it is a best practice to remove the mail store from the tool.

---

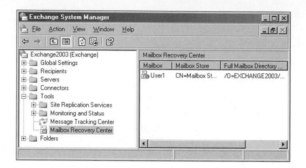

**FIGURE 18.6**   Recovery Center disconnected accounts.

## Resolving Mailbox Conflicts

When mailboxes become disconnected or conflict with multiple Active Directory objects, the Mailbox Recovery Center tool provides a seamless method to resolve these conflicts and prepare the Exchange mailbox for reconnection.

To resolve a conflicting mailbox in Exchange Server 2003, open the Exchange System Manager. Begin by completing these steps:

1. From the Tools container, highlight the Mailbox Recovery Center tool.

2. From the Exchange System Manager menu, select Action, Add Mailbox Store. Enter the name of the mailbox store to be added, or select the Advanced function to perform a search. When the appropriate mailbox store has been selected, choose OK to continue.

3. In the Mailbox Recovery Center tool's right pane, select the mailbox or mailboxes to be resolved by highlighting each mailbox.

4. From the Exchange System Manager menu, select the Action menu and choose Resolve Conflicts.

5. On the Welcome to Exchange Mailbox Conflicts Resolution Wizard screen, select Next.

6. Using the User Matching screen, select the Active Directory account or account to be resolved. If the account is not present, click the Browse button to search Active Directory for the account that the mailbox was associated with.

7. When the account has been selected, choose Next to continue. On the final screen, you should see the message "Wizard has enough information to correct the problem and prepare the account for reconnection." Select Finish to complete the tasks.

## Matching and Recovering Mailboxes

An advantage to using the Mailbox Recovery Center tool is that you can match mailboxes to non–mail-enabled accounts in Active Directory. For example, if an Active Directory account is deleted, administrators can create a new account with the same name and use the Mailbox Recovery Center tool to associate the orphaned mailbox to a new non–mail-enabled account. This option can be used even when the mailbox is marked for deletion.

To re-create an account and reconnect a mailbox, begin by doing the following:

1. Create the account or accounts in Active Directory Users and Computers using the same name or names as the mailboxes being recovered.

2. Open the Exchange System Manager and select the Tools container. Highlight the Mailbox Recovery Center tool.

3. On the Exchange System Manager menu, select Action, Add Mailbox Store. Enter the name of the mailbox store where the mailboxes being recovered reside, or select the Advanced function to search for the mailbox store. When the appropriate mailbox store has been selected, choose OK to continue.

4. In the Mailbox Recovery Center tool's right pane, select the mailbox or mailboxes to be recovered by highlighting each mailbox.

5. From the Exchange System Manager menu, select the Action menu and choose Find Match. This begins the Mailbox Recovery Center tool's search for the correct Active Directory accounts.

6. At the Welcome to Microsoft Exchange Mailbox Matching Wizard, select Next, review the result of the match, and choose Finish to complete matching the mailbox to the Active Directory user account.

> **NOTE**
>
> If no match is found by the Match Wizard, perform the steps in the Resolving Mailbox Conflicts section to search for the mailbox and associate it to a user account. Then repeat the step to match the mailbox to the Active Directory account.

When the Match Wizard has completed, run the Reconnect tool to reconnect the mailboxes to the Active Directory account by performing the following steps:

1. In the Mailbox Recovery Center tool's right pane, select the mailbox or mailboxes to be reconnected by highlighting each mailbox.

2. From the Exchange System Manager menu, select the Action menu and choose Reconnect.

3. At the Welcome to the Exchange Mailbox Reconnect Wizard, select Next.

4. Review the information provided in the Ready to Proceed dialog box and select Next to continue.

5. Review the results of the reconnect, and click Finish when done.

# Using the Mailbox Manager Utility

A familiar tool to Exchange 2000 administrators is the Mailbox Manager utility. This utility is now built in to Exchange Server 2003 and is installed by default when the Exchange server is installed and configured.

In Exchange Server 2003, Mailbox Manager tasks are configured differently in the latest release of Exchange and can be completed using the mailbox recipient policies. Mailbox recipient policies are used to manage and enforce email-retention policies and cleanup tasks in the same manner that these tasks were previously configured. The one benefit to using the policies in Exchange Server 2003 is that they are now replicated to all Exchange servers in the organization by the Recipient Update Service, eliminating the need to configure mailbox management on every server when performing mailbox-cleanup tasks.

These policies can be created and configured to move or delete mailbox items based on size and age limits, specific folders, and times when the Mailbox Manager should be run by the policy.

## Accessing the Mailbox Manager

Mailbox recipient policies are created using the recipient policies container. Using the Exchange System Manager, administrators can add mailbox recipient policies via the same method used to add standard recipient policies.

By selecting the recipient policy container in the Exchange System Manager and choosing the Action menu, new recipient policies can be created to perform the mailbox-cleanup task.

When a policy is configured and created, the recipient policies container can be used on any Exchange server in the organization to view and modify the mailbox recipient policy.

## Understanding Mailbox Manager Options

When creating a policy for the Mailbox Manager to run, administrators need to understand the different tasks' options and the implications of using each option when it is added to a recipient policy.

When configuring options using the mailbox recipient policy, policies can easily be created by selecting the preconfigured tasks available. To understand the different options available, review the following descriptions of the preconfigured tasks.

### Move to Deleted Items

Working with the limits configured in the policy, this option moves all items meeting the configured limits to the Deleted Items folder in the Exchange mailbox.

### Move to System Cleanup

An effective way to move and keep items in case recovery is needed is to use the System Cleanup option. This creates a partial replica of the mailbox folders. Each item exceeding the policy limits is then moved to corresponding system folders and stored.

---

**Using the System Folders**

When the Move Messages to the System Folders option is configured using the Mailbox Manager, a replica of the user mailbox hierarchy is created and placed in a folder called System Cleanup. Deleted messages are then moved to the same folder where they resided in the user's mailbox, creating a partial replica of the user mailbox.

This option is often used as an alternative to placing aged messages in the Deleted Items folder. When the Deleted Items folder option is selected, if a user has selected to enable the option to empty deleted items when logging off, messages are deleted permanently, requiring a restore if a message needs to be recovered.

The system folders can easily restore messages to the original location and archive information based on the recovery period configured through the Mailbox Manager.

---

### Delete Immediately

The Delete Immediately option is the most aggressive of all cleanup task options. This option immediately deletes all items exceeding the configured policy limits.

### Generate Report Only

When using this option, no messages are affected; this option is often best implemented to determine the total effect of actually running a policy that will delete or move items. The result can then be reviewed and evaluated by administrators before performing the actual tasks.

## Reporting with Mailbox Manager

As a best practice, it is often a good idea to create a recipient policy in Generate Report Only mode to identify message totals and sizes that will be deleted when the actual tasks are performed. When this option is selected, a report can be generated in two methods:

- **Send Summary Report to Administrator**—This option provides administrators with the total size of all messages deleted or moved to other folders during the mailbox-cleanup process.

18

- **Send Detailed Report to Administrator**—This option provides administrators with a complete report, listing the policies, folders, and messages that the Mailbox Manager processed during cleanup.

To create a new report-only task, begin by opening the Exchange System Manager and selecting the recipient policies container. Begin configuring the new mailbox recipient policy in Report Only mode by completing the following steps:

1. Select Action from the Exchange System Manager menu, and select New, Recipient Policy.

2. Select the Mailbox Manager Settings option on the New Policy dialog box screen, and click OK to continue.

3. On the Properties page for the mailbox recipient policy, enter the name `Report Policy` in the Name field.

4. Select the Modify tab to assign policy membership for the mailbox policy. For this exercise, select Users with Exchange Mailboxes only and click OK to continue.

5. In the Recipient Policy Change dialog box, click OK.

6. Select the Mailbox Manager Setting (Policy) tab. From the Processing a Mailbox drop-down menu, select Generate Report Only.

7. For this exercise, leave all the default options in place and click the OK button to continue.

## Configuring Mailbox-Cleanup Tasks

To configure an actual mailbox-cleanup task, administrators need to determine the message size limits and age limits before configuring the mailbox recipient policy. When a new policy is created, Exchange Server 2003 defaults the message limits to the following values:

Message size limits = 1024KB.

Message age limits = 30 days.

All folders in the Exchange mailbox are selected.

In this scenario, the default values will be used when creating the new mailbox recipient policy. To create the recipient policy, begin by opening the Exchange System Manager and complete these steps:

1. Click the Recipients container and select the recipients policies container.

2. On the Exchange System Manager menu, select Action, New, Recipient policy.

3. Select the Mailbox Manager Settings option on the New Policy dialog box, and click the OK button to continue.

4. On the Properties page for the mailbox recipient policy, enter the name for the cleanup policy in the Name field.

5. Select the Modify tab to assign policy membership for the mailbox policy. For this exercise, select the Users with Exchange Mailboxes tab and click OK to continue.

6. On the Recipient Policy Change dialog box, click OK.

7. Select the Mailbox Manager Setting (Policy) tab to configure the cleanup tasks for this policy.

8. At the Mailbox Manager Setting page, select the options for the mailbox-cleanup tasks being configured. Review the selection, as shown in Figure 18.7, and select the folder for which the Mailbox Manager will perform the cleanup tasks.

**FIGURE 18.7**   Mailbox Manager settings.

## Scheduling Mailbox Manager Tasks

After the mailbox recipient policy has been created, the next step is to plan and configure the schedule to run the Mailbox Manager task. If no corresponding schedule is created for the mailbox recipient policy, the policy configuration will not be implemented and the tasks will not run.

When planning and configuring a schedule, one important consideration is determining when it is best to run the scheduled task. Because mailbox-cleanup tasks can be demanding on Exchange Server resources and the information store, as a best practice, Exchange administrators should plan and schedule cleanup tasks to occur during off-hours, when the Exchange system is in less demand.

18

To begin configuring the schedule, follow these steps:

1. Open the Exchange System Manager and select the Exchange server where the tasks will run.

2. With the Exchange server highlighted, select the Action option for the Exchange System Manager and select Properties.

3. Click the Mailbox Management tab on the Exchange server to configure the schedule for the policy to run.

   - **Start Mailbox Management Process**—This option allows administrators to select a predefined schedule for the policy to use. Administrators also can select Custom to create a custom schedule by selecting the Customize tab.

   - **Reporting**—With this option, a detailed or summary report is sent to the administrator account defined in the Administrator tab.

   - **Administrator**—Use the Browse tab to select an administrator account that will receive the report when the task is run.

> **NOTE**
>
> Although each mailbox recipient policy is replicated to all Exchange servers, the administrator must configure the schedule for the policy to run on each server in the organization.

## Summary

As validated by the length of this chapter, a lot of things can be done to administer an Exchange environment. Administration can be broken down into delegating administration in Exchange; administering mailboxes, contacts, and Distribution Groups; and managing Administrative Groups and Routing Groups.

The delegation of administration in Exchange Server 2003 gives the organization the capability to distribute administration across multiple Exchange administrators equally or with varying levels of delegated authority. The delegation task sets up the framework from which the task of managing and administering objects in Exchange can be conducted.

After delegation has been assigned, the various levels of administrators can manage mailboxes for creating mailboxes, setting default address settings, moving mail between servers, and even recovering mailboxes that were accidentally deleted. The mail and mailbox administrative tools included in Exchange Server 2003 give administrators a variety of rights and privileges to make administrative changes as necessary.

Beyond just dealing with users with mailboxes, Exchange Server 2003 provides administrative controls over Distribution Groups for mailing lists of users, as well as contacts that are associated with email addresses without mailboxes assigned. Managing these objects provides the administrator naming resources that simplify the addressing of mail users in the organization.

Finally, managing Administrative Groups and Routing Groups separates administrative boundaries as well as message-routing boundaries, to partition administration and management as appropriate for an organization.

All of these administrative functions might be complicated when viewed as a whole, but when trying to make an Exchange environment work in a fashion that suits the needs of an organization, the various tools and functions greatly help administrators with their tasks. After more than five generations in development, Exchange Server 2003 provides a variety of flexible administrative methods for managing the Exchange administrative environment.

## Best Practices

- Most administrators of the Exchange environment should be set as Exchange Administrators, leaving the Exchange Full Administrator role only to one individual, who will have the authority to grant the Exchange Administrator right to others.

- Exchange View Only Administrators should be used for operations staff, network infrastructure staff, or other administrators who need to view the status of Exchange functions but who should not need to directly modify or make changes to the functions.

- Auditing should be enabled to track all administrative changes in Exchange. This ensures a trail for viewing modifications or changes to key Exchange settings.

- Message and storage limits give administrators the capability to control the size of messages sent or received, or the amount of message space a user may store for messages. An organization can set up different groups with different message and storage limits, thus setting an organization standard configuration while allowing certain users to exceed the standard.

- With wireless mobility built into Exchange Server 2003, an administrator can allow users to synchronize their Pocket PC–enabled device or view messages using their HTML-enabled mobile phones.

- The ExMerge utility not only provides administrators the capability to back up mailboxes for a migration, but it also allows for the ease of moving mailboxes from one server to another in case a user needs to move between Exchange sites.

- Moving mailboxes between Administrative Groups, databases, or servers within an Exchange organization can be done by simply using the Mailbox Move tool built in to the Exchange System Manager.

- Contacts are used in the Exchange System Manager to enable an address where mail messages can be forwarded to another address. This is commonly used to reroute or forward messages out of the Exchange environment into another messaging system, possibly during a migration or in a mixed-mail environment.

- Distribution Groups can be used to create internal mailing lists that might be different from security groups created within Windows. When possible, try to create a

Windows security group and mail-enable the group rather than creating separate security groups and Distribution Groups that include the same list of users.

- Query-based Distribution Groups should be used when group membership might change. The use of query-based Distribution Groups can dynamically create a distribution list based on an Active Directory user's Object Properties information.

- Routing Groups should be created any time messages should be throttled between locations. This might be to manage communication between locations over a slow or unreliable communications line, or to provide redundancy between sites.

- Administrative Groups should be created to set up administrative boundaries in an organization. However, if all administrators will share administrative responsibilities (that is, every administrator is a member of each Administrative Group), the organization should seriously consider a single Administrative Group and simplify the process.

- The Mailbox Recovery Center tool can recover disconnected mailboxes or resolve mailbox conflicts. However, it does not fix corrupted mailboxes. An organization should leverage mailbox-recovery functions covered in Chapter 32, "Recovering from a Disaster," for mailbox recovery due to data corruption.

- The Mailbox Manager utility should be used to clean up an Exchange messaging system of unused objects, report on the status of Exchange mail transactions, and perform automated cleanup tasks on mailboxes.

CHAPTER **19**

# Exchange Server 2003 Management and Maintenance Practices

**IN THIS CHAPTER**

- Managing Exchange Server 2003

- Auditing the Environment

- Managing Exchange Server 2003 Remotely

- Maintenance Tools for Exchange Server 2003

- Best Practices for Performing Database Maintenance

- Prioritizing and Scheduling Maintenance Best Practices

- Post-Maintenance Procedures

- Reducing Management and Maintenance Efforts

The messaging system in most environments has come to be considered a mission-critical application. People are reliant on messaging as a primary form of communication. As a direct result, messaging dependability is no longer just a good thing to have—it is a requirement.

An integral part of ensuring that any system is dependable or reliable is care and feeding. Take the classic car example, for instance. You should change the oil every 3,000–6,000 miles, replace air filters, change fuel filters, and more. In fact, even when you buy a new car, the car dealership recommends a maintenance schedule to keep your car healthy.

The same principles apply when you are trying to keep Exchange Server 2003 running as smoothly as possible. Proper management and maintenance minimizes down-time and other problems and keeps the system well tuned. The more Exchange Server 2003 management and mainte-nance processes and procedures are neglected, the higher your chances of the system slowing to a crawl, becoming corrupted, or even being unavailable for any extended period of time. This chapter focuses on the details and best practices necessary for a knowledgeable administrator or engineer to manage and maintain the Exchange Server 2003 messaging environment to keep it stable and reliable.

## Managing Exchange Server 2003

Managing Exchange Server 2003 in this context is not about how to perform necessarily common tasks such as using the interface to add a database. Instead, managing Exchange Server 2003 includes identifying and working with the server's functional roles in the network environment, auditing network activity and usage, and monitoring the environment.

Similarly with Windows Server 2003, Microsoft has come a long way with how servers can be managed. Exchange Server 2003 management can be done locally or remotely. Although local and remote management could be done in previous Exchange versions, Exchange Server 2003 supersedes that functionality with new and improved processes and tools that assist administrators in their management.

## Managing by Server Roles and Responsibilities

Exchange Server 2003 systems can participate in various responsibilities in the messaging environment. Some of these responsibilities may be intertwined due to budget constraints, business requirements, or technical justifications. No matter how the roles and responsibilities play out in the environment, it's important to manage them appropriately based on the roles of the server. The management aspects for some of the roles that Exchange Server 2003 can undertake are listed in the following sections.

### Mailbox Store Server

An Exchange Server 2003 mailbox store server, also known as a back-end server, is primarily responsible for safely storing a mail-enabled user's messages, attachments, files, folders, and other files. Messages sent to a user are stored in the user's mailbox, which is contained within a mailbox store.

For this reason, the mailbox store databases require attention using the Exchange System Manager (ESM) and frequent maintenance routines. Refer to "Best Practices for Performing Database Maintenance" for more information. Equally important, however, is managing user accounts.

### Public Folder Server

Similar to the mailbox store server role, the public folder server role stores message postings and other messages in a hierarchical fashion. Although there isn't a user object specifically associated with a public folder, an entire public folder database is dedicated to a single public folder hierarchy. When the system has multiple public folders, there will be multiple databases to manage and maintain.

### Front-End Server

Front-end (FE) servers are Exchange Server 2003 servers that do not contain mailbox or public folder stores. In fact, FE servers typically serve as proxy servers to back-end (mailbox or public folder) servers. FE servers are possible because Internet Information Server (IIS) manages messaging-related protocols, such as Internet Message Access Protocol version 4 (IMAP4), Post Office Protocol version 3 (POP3), Network News Transfer Protocol (NNTP), and Messaging Application Programming Interface (MAPI). One of the most common roles of an FE server is to provide Web access to back-end mailbox or public folder stores using Outlook Web Access (OWA).

Although there aren't any databases to manage or maintain on an FE server, keep the following important considerations in mind:

- **Connections**—Users connect to FE servers using HTTP. They may also connect via Secure Sockets Layer (SSL) for encrypted communications if the server is configured for increased protection. These connections are important to monitor, especially when the FE server is on the perimeter network (also known as the DMZ) or otherwise facing the Internet. Another management and maintenance aspect to keep in mind is authentication and access controls. Periodically review the event logs to review security issues.

- **IIS Metabase**—Because IIS is one of the driving forces behind an FE server, it is critical to manage the IIS metabase to maximize the server's health. This can involve keeping the metabase backed up, reviewing IIS logs, and reviewing security.

### Bridgehead Server

An Exchange Server 2003 bridgehead server is a connection point among other Exchange servers either inside or outside the organization. It connects other servers that use the same communications protocols. The most notable examples are bridgehead servers connecting routing groups and connecting dissimilar mail systems. These systems require special attention to their specific functionality and often require an administrator to keep closer watch on the server for a given period of time. For instance, a bridgehead server hosting connectors to foreign messaging systems requires an administrator to monitor connections to the server, the specific connectors, and other messaging systems with which it interacts.

### SMTP Relay Server

SMTP relay servers are similar to bridgehead servers in that they both can route messages from one system to another. They serve as mail gateways that relay mail. Mail systems facing the Internet can route mail to internal mail systems or to other external systems. It is not recommended however to allow your SMTP relay server to route messages between two external hosts on the Internet, because your system can then be used for spamming. When managing SMTP relay servers, keep track of how the system is being used and periodically check whether it is routing between external hosts on the Internet.

# Auditing the Environment

Auditing gathers and keeps track of activity on the network, devices, and entire systems. By default, Windows Server 2003 enables some auditing, although many other auditing functions must be manually turned on. Windows Server 2003 should be used with Exchange Server 2003 auditing to customize your auditing requirements and provide comprehensive amounts of information that can be analyzed.

Auditing is typically used for identifying security breaches or suspicious activity. However, auditing is also important to gain insight into how the Exchange Server 2003 systems are performing and how they are accessed. Exchange Server 2003 offers three types of auditing: audit logging, protocol logging, and message tracking.

## Audit Logging

Exchange Server 2003 uses Windows Server 2003 audit policies to audit how users access and use Exchange servers, as shown in Figure 19.1. Audit policies are the basis for auditing events on a Windows Server 2003 system. Depending on the policies set, auditing might require a substantial amount of server resources in addition to those resources supporting the server's functionality. Otherwise, it could potentially slow server performance. Also, collecting lots of information is only as good as the evaluation of the audit logs. In other words, if a lot of information is captured and it takes a significant amount of effort to evaluate those audit logs, the whole purpose of auditing is not as effective. As a result, it's important to take the time to properly plan how the system will be audited. This enables you to determine what needs to be audited, and why, without creating an abundance of overhead.

> **NOTE**
>
> To audit Exchange Server 2003 uses, enable object access auditing. You can audit both successful and unsuccessful events.

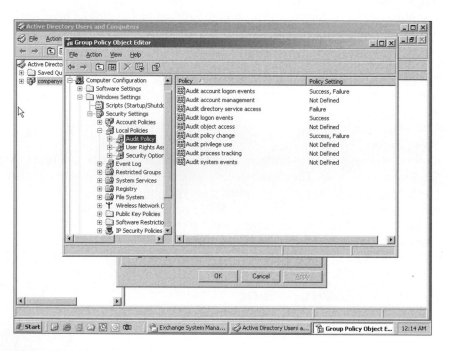

**FIGURE 19.1**    Windows Server 2003 audit policies.

## Protocol Logging

Protocol logging is great for troubleshooting issues with the mail system protocols SMTP, NNTP, or HTTP. It can give you information regarding messaging commands that a user sends to the Exchange Server 2003 server. This includes, but isn't limited to, IP address, bytes sent, data, time, protocol, and domain name.

With the exception of auditing HTTP, which is performed using the IIS snap-in, SMTP and NNTP auditing is enabled through the ESM. To enable protocol logging, follow these steps:

1. Start the ESM by selecting Start, All Programs, Microsoft Exchange, System Manager.

2. In the left pane, expand Servers, Server Name, Protocols and find the protocol to enable logging.

3. In the right pane, right-click on the protocol's virtual server and select Properties.

4. On the General tab, select the Enable Logging check box.

5. From the drop-down list that appears, select the logging format for auditing the protocol. You can choose from Microsoft IIS Log File Format, NCSA Common Log File Format, ODBC Logging, and W3C Extended Log File Format.

## Message Tracking

Out of the three auditing techniques that you can use specifically with Exchange Server 2003, message tracking is by far the least resource-intensive. For this reason, it's more than just a troubleshooting tool. You can use message tracking also for statistical analysis, reporting, and deducing where a message is located in the system.

Message tracking is enabled within the ESM. Simply expand servers and then select properties of the Exchange Server 2003 server for which you want to enable message tracking. Select Enable Message Tracking within the General tab, as shown in Figure 19.2. Click OK when the information window displays. Optionally, you can select Enable Subject Logging and Display.

The information captured by message tracking is kept in the Exchsrvr\<servername>.log file—for example, %SystemDrive%\Program Files\Exchsrvr\server2.log. You can configure Exchange to remove the log file after it is so many days old to conserve disk space. As you can see in Figure 19.3, at first glance the log file might appear somewhat cryptic. It is full of useful information, however, that can be used to track down messages.

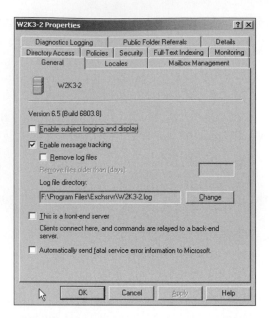

**FIGURE 19.2**    Enabling message tracking.

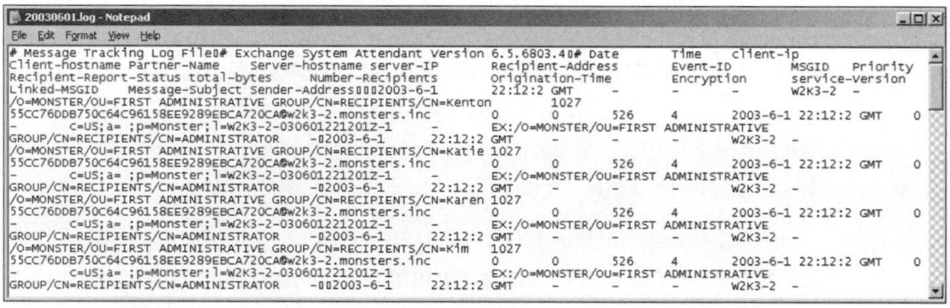

**FIGURE 19.3**    Viewing the message tracking log.

# Managing Exchange Server 2003 Remotely

Windows Server 2003's built-in feature set enables it to be easily managed remotely. This same feature set can be used to manage Exchange Server 2003, which can significantly reduce administration time, expenses, and effort by enabling administrators to manage systems from remote locations rather than having to be physically at the system.

The most common tools available to remotely manage a system are

- **Microsoft Management Console (MMC)**—The MMC not only provides a unified interface for most, if not all, graphical interface utilities, it also can be used to connect and manage remote systems. For example, administrators can use the ESM or Active Directory Users and Computers to manage the local computer and a remote system.

- **Remote Desktop for Administration**—This empowers administrators to log on to a remote system as if they were logging on to the system locally. The desktop and all functions are at the administrators' disposal.

- **Scripting with Windows Script Host (WSH)**—Scripting on Windows Server 2003 can permit administrators to automate tasks locally or remotely. These scripts can be written using common scripting languages. There are many scripts that come bundled with Exchange Server 2003 that can perform myriad tasks, such as configuring recipient policies, newsgroups, virtual servers, and much more.

- **Command-line Utilities**—Many command-line utilities are capable of managing systems remotely.

- **Telnet**—Telnet is a gateway type of service through which an administrator or client can connect and log on to a server running the Telnet Server service. It is not exactly the most flexible or best tool to use for either Windows Server 2003 or Exchange Server 2003 but it can be easily used to test SMTP functionality. By entering

```
telnet <servername or server IP address> 25
```

you can test whether Exchange Server 2003 is responding to SMTP requests.

---

**CAUTION**

By default, Telnet sends usernames and passwords across the network in plain text.

---

# Maintenance Tools for Exchange Server 2003

To effectively and appropriately administer Exchange Server 2003, you must use several tools. These tools include MMC snap-ins that get installed with Exchange Server 2003, tools native to the Windows Server 2003 operating system, and tools you must install separately from the Exchange Server 2003 CD-ROM.

## Managing Exchange with the Exchange System Manager

The ESM shown in Figure 19.4 is one of the primary tools provided with Exchange Server 2003 that you will use to manage the Exchange messaging environment. The ESM is an MMC snap-in that is installed, along with the correct DLL files and Registry entries, from the Exchange Server 2003 CD-ROM. The installation of the ESM is the default and is under Microsoft Exchange System Management Tools.

You can manage the entire Exchange Server 2003 organization from within ESM, assuming that you have the proper access privileges. All the Exchange configurations will be made within this snap-in.

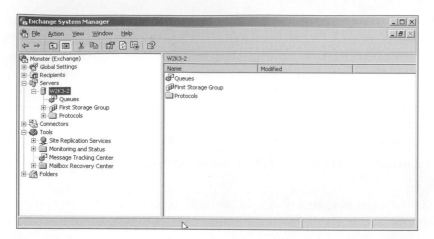

**FIGURE 19.4**    Exchange Server 2003 ESM.

---

**NOTE**

Because Exchange Server 2003 uses Windows Server 2003's Active Directory, mail-enabled Active Directory objects are primarily managed by Active Directory users and computers. The ESM in Exchange Server 2003, however, can be used to move or delete mailboxes.

---

The ESM can also be installed on a client computer or another server and manage the Exchange Server 2003 servers remotely. This provides flexibility for administrators in networks of all sizes.

---

**TIP**

The client computer or server on which the ESM is installed should also be running the same version of the Exchange Server 2003 service pack (SP) as the Exchange Server 2003 servers. Doing so ensures that administrators have full functionality at that location and minimizes even the slightest possibility that compatibility problems or corruption might occur.

---

## Active Directory Users and Computers

Active Directory Users and Computers is an MMC snap-in that is used to manage users, groups, computers, contacts, organizational units, and group policy. It is installed on all domain controllers, but can also be used by installing the Windows Server 2003 Admin Pak (adminpak.msi) located in the i386 directory on the Windows 2003 Server CD-ROM. It is also installed automatically when you install the Exchange System Management Tools from the Exchange Server 2003 CD-ROM.

Active Directory Users and Computers is used instead of the ESM snap-in for managing Active Directory mail-enabled objects, because Exchange Server 2003 uses and stores information in AD rather than its own directory. This tool is the only graphical user interface (GUI) where an administrator can make email-related configuration changes to users, groups, and contacts. The exception to this is moving or deleting mailboxes, which can be done using the ESM.

Common mail-enabled object attributes are readily available in Active Directory Users and Computers, such as delivery restrictions, storage limits, wireless services, protocols, and much more. However, there are several other mail-related fields that can be configured when you select the Advanced Features view mode in the Active Directory Users and Computers snap-in. To enable this mode, simply choose the Advance Features from the view menu from within this snap-in.

The following options are visible with Advanced Features:

- **Exchange Advanced tab**—The Exchange Advanced tab, shown in Figure 19.5, presents options to choose a simple display name, hide the recipient from Exchange address lists, view and modify Exchange custom attributes, configure server and account information for the Internet locator service, and modify mailbox rights.

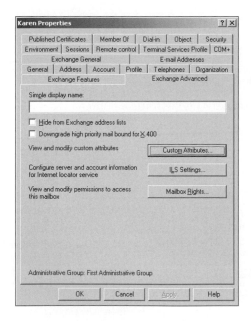

**FIGURE 19.5**   Exchange Advanced tab options.

- **Microsoft Exchange System Objects Container**—This visible container displays Exchange system objects, such as the offline address book, schema-root, SystemMailbox, and more.

## Windows Server 2003 Backup

The Windows Server 2003 backup utility (`ntbackup.exe`) is installed by default on any Windows Server 2003 system and is located under the Start, All Programs, Accessories, System Tools menu. Out of the box, this utility can back up and restore the entire system, including the system state and data.

In order to properly back up and restore Exchange Server 2003 databases and log files using `ntbackup.exe`, the Exchange administrator should either run the backup locally or from another Exchange Server 2003 server. Local and remote Exchange storage groups and databases can be backed up and restored from any Exchange 2000 server, but not from any other server.

Third-party software vendors, such as EMC Legato and Veritas, produce Exchange Server 2003 backup and restore agents for the purpose of remote Exchange database backup.

For more information on Exchange Server 2003 backup and recovery, refer to Chapter 31, "Backing Up the Exchange Server 2003 Environment" and Chapter 32, "Recovering from a Disaster."

## Exchange Maintenance with the `ntdsutil` Utility

Exchange Server 2003 uses Windows Server 2003 AD to store all its directory information. As a result, it is important to keep AD as healthy as possible in order to ensure that Exchange Server 2003 remains reliable and stable.

Windows Server 2003 automatically performs maintenance on AD by cleaning up the AD database on a nightly basis. The process occurs on domain controllers approximately every 12 hours. An example of the data that is removed would be tombstones. *Tombstones* represent the markers for previously deleted objects. The process deletes unnecessary log files and reclaims free space.

The automatic cleanup process does not perform all the maintenance required. The maintenance processes that the automatic cleanup does not perform are compression and defragmentation of the Active Directory database file. To perform this function, use the `ntdsutil` command-line utility to defragment and compress the database.

> **CAUTION**
>
> To avoid possible adverse affects with the AD database, run `ntdsutil` in Directory Service Repair Mode. Reboot the server, press the F8 key, and then select this mode of operation.

## Integrity Checking with the `isinteg` Utility

`isinteg.exe` is an Exchange database integrity checker utility used for maintaining, testing, and repairing database table integrity. The utility is bundled with Exchange Server 2003 and is located in the `Exchsrvr\bin` directory.

> **CAUTION**
>
> Using this utility for anything other than test mode will result in irreversible changes to the database. This utility is not usually used in anything other than test mode, unless there is a specific problem reported.
>
> Therefore, if there is a specific problem to be addressed and corrected, perform the maintenance on a restored copy of the database(s) in a lab environment before attempting to use this utility on a production system.

Dismount the Exchange databases that you plan to perform maintenance on and stop the Microsoft Exchange Information Store prior to running this utility. Keep in mind that this makes the databases unavailable to users before maintenance or problems are corrected.

Database table integrity problems are caused by corruption, which can occur if the server is shut down improperly, if the drive or controller fails, and so forth. To determine whether there are integrity problems with the database, you can do the following:

1. Run isinteg in test mode.

2. View recorded errors in the Event Viewer.

3. Run eseutil /g.

The following is an example of isinteg:

```
isinteg -s ServerName [-fix] [-verbose] [-l logfilename] -test testname[[,
testname]...]
    -s              ServerName
    -fix            check and fix (default - check only)
    -verbose        report verbosely
    -l filename     log file name (default - .\isinteg.pri/pub)
    -t refdblocation (default - the location of the store)
    -test testname,...
       folder message aclitem mailbox(pri only) delfld acllist
       rcvfld(pri only) timedev rowcounts attach morefld ooflist(pri only)
       global searchq dlvrto
       peruser artidx(pub only) search newsfeed(pub only) dumpsterprops
       Ref count tests: msgref msgsoftref attachref acllistref aclitemref
       newsfeedref(pub only) fldrcv(pri only) fldsub dumpsterref
       Groups tests: allfoldertests allacltests
  isinteg -dump [-l logfilename] (verbose dump of store data)
```

## Database Maintenance with the eseutil Utility

Although isinteg, an Exchange-specific utility, is used for maintaining, testing, and repairing database table integrity, eseutil is a database-level utility that is not application-specific. For instance, it can be used to maintain, test, and repair AD and Exchange databases. More specifically, eseutil is used to maintain database-level integrity, perform defragmentation and compaction, and repair even the most severely corrupt databases. It is also the utility to use when maintaining Exchange Server 2003 transaction log files to see which transaction logs you need to replay or which log file the Edb.chk file points to.

---

**CAUTION**

Have either a tape backup or other media backup copy of the databases and an offline copy of the database files prior to using the eseutil utility. This utility can produce irreversible changes within the database and should be used with extreme caution.

---

**NOTE**

While isinteg identifies and fixes database table integrity, ESEUTIL investigates the data that resides in the table for any corruption or errors. This is why it is called a database-level utility. The eseutil options are shown in Table 19.1.

---

**TABLE 19.1**    eseutil Syntax

| Mode of Operation | Syntax |
| --- | --- |
| Defragmentation | eseutil /d <database name> [options] |
| File dump | eseutil /m[mode-modifier] <filename> |
| Recovery | eseutil /r <logfile base name> [options] |
| Integrity | eseutil /g <database name> [options] |
| Repair | eseutil /p <database name> [options] |
| Restore | eseutil /c [mode-modifier] <path name> [options] |

## Exchange Message Tracking

As mentioned earlier, Exchange Server 2003 has a feature called message tracking that gives an administrator the ability to track a message from when it arrives in the Exchange organization until message delivery is complete. Message tracking can also inform the administrator of where a message was delayed or got stuck on the way out of the Exchange organization. This tool is primarily used for finding out where lost messages ended up and to verify which route a message takes for delivery.

## Exchange Queue Viewer

Exchange Queue Viewer is used to view the contents of the queues for each particular protocol on a server. Although this tool is more of a troubleshooting tool, it is important to periodically check protocol queues (for example, SMTP or X.400 queues) to ensure that there are no delivery problems.

# Best Practices for Performing Database Maintenance

Database maintenance is an easy task to put off because it is one of the most involved maintenance practices you will perform with any version of Exchange. It is also, however, one of the most important maintenance tasks to perform, and it is recommended that administrators run database maintenance routinely. Doing so keeps the Exchange Server 2003 system healthy, prevents downtime, helps maintain service levels, minimizes corruption, and reduces chances for data loss.

If your organization requires a reliable and stable messaging environment—and most organizations do—periodic database maintenance can be used to achieve these goals. The primary reason why Exchange systems at some point become less reliable or less stable is that any database that is not maintained suffers from at least a certain level of corruption. There are also other reasons why databases get corrupted:

- Improper shutting down of the system

- Poorly managed systems

- A poorly maintained disk subsystem

- Hardware failures

- Databases exceeding a manageable size

- Failure to use or review systems or operational management tools

- Manual modification of Exchange databases

- Deletion of Exchange transaction logs

- Assumption that Exchange Server 2003 performs all the database maintenance that is required

- Neglect

Database maintenance consists of both online and offline maintenance processes and procedures. Online maintenance is performed automatically by default, and offline maintenance is more involved. It requires dismounting the specific database within a given storage group and running the appropriate utilities against it. It is the offline maintenance that is most often overlooked. As a result, it is recommended to schedule routine offline maintenance procedures. Routinely performing offline maintenance will also assist administrators in disaster recovery situations.

> **CAUTION**
>
> Exchange Server 2003 databases and transaction log files should never be manually modified. Use only the utilities meant to be used for Exchange Server 2003.

## Online Database Maintenance

Similar to AD's automatic maintenance schedule, Exchange Server 2003 out of the box provides general database cleanup maintenance on each of the databases. During the automatic Exchange Server 2003 database cleanup, the following five tasks are performed:

- **Tombstone Maintenance**—Deleted messages are compacted for both user mailboxes and public folders. This process looks for deleted messages and makes sure they have been deleted from the databases, and any references to the deleted messages (including the data space the message actually took up) are cleared from the database.

- **Index Aging**—Index aging cleans up user-defined views that are created within the Outlook client and that have not been accessed or used within the predefined timeframe set in the Aging Keep Time Registry entry.

- **Age Folder Tombstones**—This task applies only to the public folder storage area of the messaging system. All folder tombstone entries that are older than the default 180 days are permanently removed from the list. This event helps control the size of the folder tombstone list.

- **Update Server Versions**—The Exchange public store uses the server's version information to establish and maintain the functionality between different versions of Exchange that might be in use throughout an enterprise.

- **Message Expiration**—Messages in the public folders that have exceeded the predefined time value for remaining on the server are deleted from the system.

Automatic online database maintenance performs approximately 60% of the regular functions needed to maintain integrity of the Exchange databases. These maintenance tasks are all performed while the entire system is online. Another 10%–20% of maintenance can be accomplished by refreshing the Exchange-related services within the Services MMC snap-in.

> **NOTE**
>
> Online database maintenance also reclaims unused whitespace in the database, but it does not compact or defragment it.

Unfortunately, even performing up to 70% or 80% of maintenance is not enough to ensure maximum use of the Exchange Server 2003 production environment. In fact, the remaining percentage of Exchange Server 2003 maintenance is vital to the overall health and integrity of the Exchange databases. Offline maintenance picks up where online maintenance left off.

## Performing Offline Database Maintenance

As mentioned earlier, and as the name implies, offline database maintenance prevents users from accessing the particular database that you are servicing. For this very reason, it is important to perform offline database maintenance during non-business hours. Equally important, it is a good idea to schedule this downtime to minimize its effects on end-users.

Offline database maintenance is useful for repairing, recovering, and defragmenting Exchange Server 2003 databases. The `eseutil` and `isinteg` utilities are used to perform the maintenance. The most common maintenance procedure is defragmenting the databases, and you do not want to repair or recover databases more than you absolutely have to. These maintenance functions are built into `eseutil`. To minimize having to repair or recover a database, include offline database defragmentation maintenance routines in the company's maintenance schedule. A best practice for defragmenting the database is on a quarterly basis. However, this depends on the size of the database, the issues that are being experienced, and scheduling considerations.

> **NOTE**
>
> The following steps to perform offline database maintenance assume that the database has been copied offline to another volume.

To perform offline database maintenance, follow these steps:

1. Log on using an account that has Exchange Full Administrator privileges to the Exchange server that houses the databases that will be maintained.

2. Open the ESM by selecting Start, All Programs, Microsoft Exchange.

3. Expand the Administrative Groups, First Administrative Group, Servers, <ServerName>, <StorageGroupName> in the left pane.

4. Right-click the database that will be maintained and select Dismount Store.

5. Select Yes to continue to dismount the store.

6. Open a Command Prompt by typing **cmd** from the Start, Run dialog box and clicking OK.

7. Change the drives and directory to where `isinteg` resides (the default is

   `%SystemDrive%\Program Files\Exchsrvr\Bin\`)

8. Type **isinteg.exe -s <ServerName> -test allfoldertests** and then press Enter. At this point you will see a list of the databases on the server, indicating which ones are online or offline, as shown in Figure 19.6.

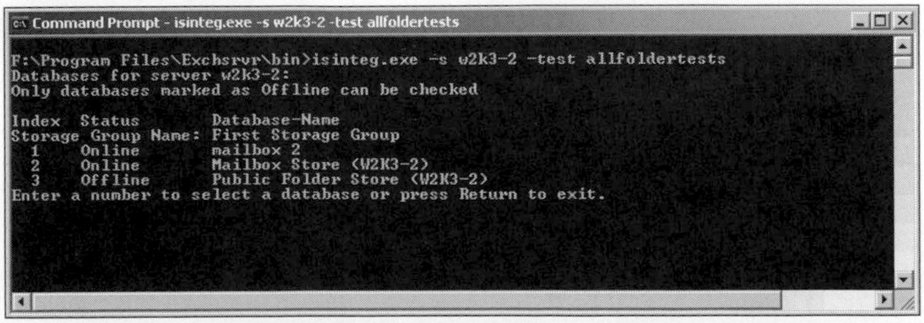

**FIGURE 19.6**    Performing maintenance using `isinteg`.

19

9. Choose to run maintenance on the offline database by typing the appropriate number. Press Enter, then choose Y, and finally press Enter again to confirm.

    If `isinteg` finds errors, run the appropriate fix as recommended and displayed within the command prompt. The same error and recommended fix is recorded in the Application Event log. If necessary, repeat the `isinteg` integrity check until no errors are reported. When no errors are reported continue to the next step.

---

**Preparing to Use** `Eseutil`

The `eseutil` utility requires the administrator to enter the full path and name of the EDB database file. It assumes that the streaming database file (STM) is located in the same directory as its corresponding database and it has the same prefix for the database filename. For example, the database `mailbox store 2` has the following 2 files:

`D:\Program Files\Exchsrvr\MDBDATA\mailboxstore2.edb`

`D:\Program Files\Exchsrvr\MDBDATA\mailboxstore2.stm`

If the filenames or paths are different for the two database files, refer to the online help for `eseutil` to add the switch to specify the path to the STM file.

---

10. At the command prompt, type the following command to perform a database-level integrity check **Eseutil.exe /g "D:\Program Files\Exchsrvr\MDBDATA\ mailboxstore2.edb** and press Enter. The double quotes are necessary for paths with spaces in the names. If errors are reported, refer to Chapter 32.

11. At the command prompt, type the following command to defragment the database **Eseutil.exe /d "D:\Program Files\Exchsrvr\MDBDATA\mailboxstore2.edb"** and press Enter. Again, the double quotes are necessary for paths with spaces in the names.

---

**TIP**

Although it is always a good practice to perform offline database maintenance, including defragmentation, on a quarterly basis, it is necessary only when the amount of free space in the database is greater than 15% of the total database size.

To calculate the percentage of free space, take the total free space recorded in the Application Log (Event ID 1221) and divide that by the total database size (the size of the EDB file plus the size of the STM file).

---

12. When the database compaction completes, mount the database using the ESM.

13. Using Windows Backup or a third-party product, perform a backup of the database.

### Database Maintenance Through Mailbox Moves

When you consider what it means to do database maintenance, it is easy to think about the online and offline maintenance routines mentioned previously. Online and offline database maintenance each have their purposes with offline maintenance routines capable of performing the most thorough maintenance. Offline maintenance, though, requires some downtime and the exact downtime duration depends not only on the size of the database but also on the condition that it is in. For example, offline maintenance of a 40GB database can possibly take well over a day or more to perform defragmentation or corrections on the database.

Another less intrusive method to periodically performing database maintenance that also does not require nearly as much downtime is moving mailboxes to another mailbox store. An Exchange administrator can create a new mailbox store either on the same Exchange Server 2003 server or on a separate server altogether. Once the new mailbox store is created, the administrator can move mailboxes over to the new mailbox store. By moving the mailboxes over to the new mailbox store, the database is in optimal condition.

> **NOTE**
>
> As with any maintenance processes or procedures, it is important to perform backups of Exchange prior to performing the maintenance tasks. Also, moving mailboxes for maintenance reasons should be performed during non-business hours to avoid interrupting users.

In some cases where the 40GB database is experiencing many corruptions, not all mailboxes will be able to be moved without generating errors. For instance, there may be roughly 5%–10% of the mailboxes still on the original mailbox store that generated errors and did not move over to the new mailbox store. If this occurs, the administrator can perform offline maintenance routines mentioned in the "Performing Offline Database Maintenance" section. The benefit is that instead of performing long and arduous offline maintenance routines on a 40GB database, the routines will be run on a much smaller database and consequently will not require a significant amount of downtime. Instead of taking possibly over a day to perform offline maintenance, the routines only require a few hours.

# Prioritizing and Scheduling Maintenance Best Practices

Exchange Server 2003, even without its scheduled maintenance routines, is a very efficient messaging system. However, as mailboxes and public folders are used, there is still logical corruption. Natural wear and tear occurs, as it does in any other system. For this reason, it is important to implement a maintenance plan and schedule to minimize the impact that corruption to these databases has on the overall messaging system.

Scheduled tasks need to be performed daily, monthly, and quarterly. These recommended best practices also are intended to keep administrators informed of the status of the Exchange Server 2003 messaging environment. They can save an abundant amount of time in the long run by minimizing or even avoiding issues that can grow into bigger problems.

TIP

Document the Exchange Server 2003 messaging environment configuration and create a change log to document changes and maintenance procedures.

## Daily Maintenance

Daily maintenance routines require the most frequent attention of an Exchange administrator. However, these tasks should not take a significant amount of time to perform.

### Verify the Online Backup

Daily, online backups should verify that the previous night's backup was successful. The actual verification process depends on the backup solution that is being used. In general, review the backup program's log file to determine whether the backup has successfully completed. If there are errors reported or the backup job set does not complete successfully, identify the cause of the error and take the appropriate steps to resolve the problem.

In addition, it is also a best practice to do the following to back up an Exchange Server 2003 server:

- Include System State data to protect against system failure.

- Keep note of how long the backup process is taking to complete. This time should match any service level agreements that may be in place.

- Verify that transaction logs are deleted if circular logging is disabled. If not, perform a full backup.

### Check Free Disk Space

All volumes that Exchange Server 2003 resides on (Exchange system files, databases, transaction logs, and so forth) should be checked on a daily basis to ensure that ample free space is available. If the volume or partition runs out of disk space, no more information can be written to the disk. Without disk space to write to, the Exchange services stop running. As a best practice, use Microsoft Operations Manager (MOM) or a third-party product to alert administrators if free space dips below 25%.

### Review Message Queues

Message queues should be checked daily to ensure that there are no messages stuck in the queue. Use Queue Viewer to view and manage SMTP, MTA, and connector messaging queues to keep messages flowing.

### Check Event Viewer Logs

On Exchange Server 2003 servers, check the Application Log within the Event Viewer for Warning and Stop error messages. These error messages might directly lead you to an issue on the server, or some error messages may be symptomatic of other issues. Filtering for or alerting on these event types can save a lot of time evaluating whether one of these events has occurred within the last 24 hours. If you are using a systems or operational management solution, this process and more can be automated. In addition, these solutions can also provide enhanced reporting functionality.

## Weekly Maintenance

Tasks that do not require daily maintenance, but still require frequent attention, are categorized in the weekly maintenance routines. These routines are described in the following sections.

### Document Database File Sizes

Unless you set mailbox storage limitations, the size of the mailbox databases can quickly become overwhelmingly large. If the volume housing the databases is not large enough to accommodate the database growth beyond a certain capacity, services can stop, databases can get corrupted, performance can get sluggish, or the system can halt. This holds true even with Exchange Server 2003 SP2 allowing Standard Edition databases growing beyond 16GB. Even when you do set mailbox size limitations, you should know the size of the databases and the growth rate. By documenting the database size(s), you can better understand system usage and capacity requirements.

### Verify Public Folders Replication

Many environments rely on public folders to share information, and the public folder configurations (for example, multiple hierarchies, multiple replicas, and more) vary widely from environment to environment. With environments that replicate public folder information among different Exchange Server 2003 servers, keep abreast of whether the information contained within those folders is kept up to date.

There are several ways to perform quick tests to see whether information is replicating correctly, including manually testing replication, using the Exchange Server 2003 Resource Kit's Public Folder Administration tool (`PFAdmin.exe`), and reviewing the `Ex00yymmdd.log` and `Ex01yymmdd.log` files. If problems exist, you can use the logs just mentioned to troubleshoot.

### Verify Online Maintenance Tasks

Exchange Server 2003 records information in the Application Log about online maintenance that occurs automatically. Check this event log to verify that all the online maintenance tasks and other scheduled tasks are being performed and that no problems are occurring. Using the common event IDs given in the following list, you can easily search by the ID number to review online maintenance and other scheduled tasks. In the right pane of the Event Viewer, click on the Event column to sort events by their ID number:

- **Event ID 1221**—This event reveals how much free space there is in a database. This information is also useful in determining when offline database defragmentation may be necessary.

- **Event ID 1206 and 1207**—Both IDs inform about deleted item retention processing.

- **Event ID 700 and 701**—These IDs indicate the start and stop times of the online database defragmentation process. Check to make sure that the process does not conflict with Exchange database backups, and make sure the process completes without interruptions.

- **Event IDs 9531–9535**—All these IDs are about deleted mailbox retention processing.

### Analyze Resource Utilization

With any system—and Exchange Server 2003 is no different—it is important to know how well the overall system is performing. At a minimum, you should monitor system resources at least once a week. Concentrate on monitoring the four common contributors to bottlenecks: memory, processor, disk subsystem, and network subsystem. The most optimum situation is having a monitoring utility such as MOM keep watch over the system at specified intervals.

### Check Offline Address Book Generation

An Offline Address Book (OAB), also known as an Offline Address List (OAL), is routinely generated for remote users to download and view address lists while offline. By default, the OAL is generated daily if there are changes. Use the ESM to determine the last time it was generated to make sure that remote users can obtain an updated copy. This is performed by viewing the Property pages of the OAL located under the Recipients, Offline Address List container.

> **NOTE**
>
> If you are experiencing problems with OAL generation, enable diagnostic logging and review the Application Log for any OAL Generator category events.

## Monthly Maintenance

Recommended monthly maintenance practices for Exchange Server 2003 do not require the frequency of daily or weekly tasks, but they are nonetheless important to maintaining the overall health of the system. Some general monthly maintenance tasks can be quickly summarized; others are explained in more detail in the following sections.

General tasks include

- Refresh the Exchange Server 2003 services to free up memory resources and kick-start online maintenance routines.

- Install approved and tested service packs and updates.

- Schedule and perform, as necessary, any major server configuration changes, including hardware upgrades.

### Test Uninterruptible Power Supply

Uninterruptible Power Supply (UPS) equipment is commonly used to protect the server from sudden loss of power. Most UPS solutions include supporting management software to assure that the server is gracefully shut down in the event of power failure, thus preserving the integrity of the system. Each manufacturer has a specific recommendation for testing, and its procedure should be followed. However, it should occur no less than once a month, and it is advantageous to schedule the test for the same time as the server reboot.

### Analyze Database Free Space

As mentioned earlier in "Performing Offline Database Maintenance," an approximation of a database's fragmentation can be made using the database size and the amount of free space. The amount of free space that can be recovered from a defragmentation and compaction is provided within Event ID 1221 entries.

## Quarterly Maintenance

Although quarterly maintenance tasks are infrequent, some might require downtime and are more likely to cause serious problems with Exchange Server 2003 if not properly planned or maintained. Therefore proceed cautiously with these tasks.

General quarterly maintenance tasks include the following:

- Check mailbox and public folder stores' Property pages to verify configuration parameters, review usage statistics, determine mailbox sizes, and more.

- Check storage limits to ensure that data storage requirements will not exceed capacity, given the current rate of growth (stemming from the information taken from the weekly maintenance task).

### Perform Offline Maintenance

As mentioned earlier, offline maintenance is one of the most important maintenance tasks to perform, but it can be time consuming and hazardous. Remember to properly plan, schedule during off-hours, and perform both an online and offline backup of the information stores prior to beginning the tasks. A little extra care up front can save you lots of time troubleshooting. For more information on this process, refer to "Performing Offline Database Maintenance," earlier in this chapter.

### Validate Information Store Backups

At first glance, you might consider the process of validating database backups as simply checking the backup logs to see whether they were successful. On the contrary, validating the backups involves performing a full restore onto a test server in a lab environment. This not only ensures that Exchange Server 2003 can be easily recovered in times of disaster but it also irons out any issues in the restore process and keeps administrators in practice for recovering the system; when disaster strikes, they are adequately prepared.

> **TIP**
>
> Document the process of restoring Exchange Server 2003 databases. If documentation already exists, verify that the existing process has not changed. If it has changed, update the documentation.

# Post-Maintenance Procedures

Post-maintenance procedures are designed to quickly and efficiently restore Exchange operations to the environment following maintenance procedures that have required downtime. Devising a checklist for these procedures ensures that there is not unnecessary messaging disruption. The following is a sample checklist for maintenance procedures:

1. Start all the remaining Exchange services.

2. Test email connectivity from Outlook and Outlook Web Access.

3. Perform a full backup of the Exchange Server 2003 server(s).

4. Closely review backup and server event logs over the next few days to ensure that no errors are reported on the server.

# Reducing Management and Maintenance Efforts

As you have seen throughout the chapter, there are numerous utilities available with Exchange Server 2003 for managing, maintaining, and monitoring the messaging system. These utilities can save enormous amounts of time and energy if properly used.

On the other hand, as messaging systems grow in size and complexity, so do the responsibilities of the administrators who work with them on a daily basis.

In any messaging environment, an administrator must consider opportunities for reducing maintenance efforts to maximize effectiveness and efficiency (that is, doing the right jobs or tasks correctly). Besides, management and maintenance that are streamlined or automated can be tied directly to significant cost savings for the company. Equally important, it keeps you one step ahead of the system so that you are proactively managing and maintaining rather than reacting to the problems.

## Using Microsoft Operations Manager

Microsoft Operations Manager (MOM) is one tool that can be used to streamline and automate many of an administrator's messaging responsibilities. More specifically, the MOM Application Management Pack provides the key features required to manage, maintain, and monitor the Exchange Server 2003 environment.

Key features to consider evaluating include, but are not limited to, the following:

- Alerting when various thresholds are met, such as resource utilization statistics or capacity

- Performance baselining and continuous monitoring of system resources and protocols (for example, SMTP, POP3, and IMAP4)

- Trend analysis of usage and performance

- A full knowledgebase of Exchange-specific solutions tied directly to over 1,700 events

- Reporting on usage, problems, security-related events, and much more

## Summary

Messaging is considered a mission-critical application, and it should be well managed and maintained. With proper care and feeding, Exchange Server 2003 can stay healthy and optimized to handle your environment's business and technical requirements.

## Best Practices

The following are best practices from this chapter:

- Manage Exchange Server 2003 based on server roles and responsibilities.

- Audit the messaging environment, using Windows Server 2003 auditing.

- Use Exchange Server 2003's protocol logging and diagnostic logging for troubleshooting purposes.

- Install the ESM on a client computer to remotely administer Exchange Server 2003. Use the same version of Exchange Server 2003 and service pack level of the servers being managed.

- Keep AD well tuned using `ntdsutil`, because Exchange Server 2003 directly relies on it.

- Avoid possible adverse affects with the AD database by running `ntdsutil` in Directory Service Repair mode.

- Perform an online and offline copy of the information stores prior to running offline maintenance tasks.

- Use `isinteg` in test mode unless there is a specific problem reported.

- Never manually modify Exchange Server 2003 databases and transaction log files.

- Document the Exchange Server 2003 messaging environment configuration and create a change log to document changes and maintenance procedures.

- If you are experiencing problems with OAL generation, enable diagnostic logging and review the Application Log for any OAL Generator category events.

- Document the process of restoring Exchange Server 2003 databases. If documentation already exists, verify that the existing process has not changed. If it has changed, update the documentation.

- Create post-maintenance procedures to minimize time needed for restoration.

- Include the System State data in daily backup routines.

- Reduce management and maintenance efforts, using the MOM Application Management Pack.

19

# CHAPTER 20

# Documenting an Exchange Server 2003 Environment

IN THIS CHAPTER

- Planning Exchange Server 2003 Documentation
- Benefits of Documentation
- Design and Planning Documentation
- Developing the Migration Documentation
- Exchange Server 2003 Environment Documentation
- Administration and Maintenance Documentation
- Disaster Recovery Documentation
- Performance Documentation
- Security Documentation
- Training Documentation

Documentation is not only an integral part of the installation or design of an Exchange Server 2003 environment, it is also important for the maintenance, support, and recovery of new or existing environments.

Documentation serves several purposes throughout the life cycle of Exchange Server 2003 and is especially critical on a per-project basis. In the initial stages of a project, it serves to provide a historical record of the options and decisions made during the design process. During the testing and implementation phases, documents such as step-by-step procedures and checklists guide project team members and help ensure that all steps are completed. When the implementation portion of the project is complete, support documentation can play a key role in maintaining the health of the new environment. Support documents include administration and maintenance procedures, checklists, detailed configuration settings, and monitoring procedures.

This chapter is dedicated to providing the breadth and scope of documentation for an Exchange Server 2003 environment. Equally important, it provides considerations and best practices for keeping your messaging environment well documented, maintained, and manageable.

# Planning Exchange Server 2003 Documentation

When planning Exchange Server 2003 documentation (whether for general purposes, specific aspects such as disaster recovery, or a particular project), several factors should be considered:

- The business requirements of the organization

- The technical requirements of the organization

- The audience that will be using the documents

- How and when the documents will be produced and maintained

The extent of the documentation depends on the business and technical requirements of the organization. Some organizations require that each step be documented, and other organizations require that only the configuration be recorded. Careful consideration should be given to any regulatory requirements or existing internal organization policies.

After the specific documentation requirements have been determined, it is important to consider who the audience for each document will be. Who will use each document, in what setting, and for what purpose? It would be impractical to develop a 300-page user guide when all the user wants to do is log on to the messaging system. In that case, all that would be required is a quick reference guide. Properly analyzing the purpose and goals of each document aids in the development of clear and useful documentation.

Planning the schedule for document production often requires a separate project timeline or plan. The plan should include checkpoints, sponsorship or management review, and a clear schedule. Tools such as Microsoft Project facilitate the creation of a documentation project plan (see "Design and Planning Documentation," later in this chapter). The project plan can also provide an initial estimate of the number of hours required and the associated costs. For instance, based on previous documentation projects, there is an estimate that 1-2 pages per hour will be produced.

# Benefits of Documentation

Although many of the benefits of Exchange Server 2003 documentation are obvious and tangible, others can be harder to identify. A key benefit to documentation is that the process of putting the information down on paper encourages a higher level of analysis and review of the topic at hand. The process also encourages teamwork and collaboration within an organization and interdepartmental exchange of ideas.

Documentation that is developed with specific goals, and goes through a review or approval process, is typically well organized and complete, and contributes to the overall professionalism of the organization and its knowledge base. The following sections examine some of the other benefits of professional documentation in the Exchange Server 2003 environment.

## Knowledge Sharing and Knowledge Management

The right documentation enables an organization to organize and manage its data and intellectual property. Company policies and procedures are typically located throughout multiple locations that include individual files for various departments. Consolidating this information into logical groupings can be beneficial.

> **TIP**
>
> Place documentation in at least two different locations where it is easily accessible for authorized users, such as on the intranet, in a public folder, or in hard-copy format. Also consider using a document management system such as SharePoint Portal Server 2003.

A complete design document consolidates and summarizes key discussions and decisions, budgetary concerns, and timing issues. This consolidation provides a single source of information for questions that might emerge at a later date. In addition, a document that describes the specific configuration details of the Exchange server might prove very valuable to a manager in another company office when making a purchasing decision.

All of the documents should be readily available at all times. This is especially critical regarding disaster recovery documents. Centralizing the documentation and communicating the location helps reduce the use of out-of-date documentation and reduce confusion during a disaster recovery. It is also recommended that they be available in a number of formats, such as hard copy, the appropriate place on the network, and even via an intranet.

## Financial Benefits of Documentation

Proper Exchange Server 2003 documentation can be time consuming and adds to the cost of the environment and project. In lean economic times for a company or organization, it is often difficult to justify the expense of project documentation. However, when looking at documents, such as in maintenance or disaster recovery scenarios, it is easy to determine that creating this documentation makes financial sense. For example, in an organization where downtime can cost thousands of dollars per minute, the return on investment (ROI) in disaster recovery and maintenance documentation is easy to calculate. In a company that is growing rapidly and adding staff and new servers on a regular basis, tested documentation on server builds and administration training can also have immediate and visible benefits.

Financial benefits are not limited to maintenance and disaster recovery documentation. Well-developed and professional design and planning documentation helps the organization avoid costly mistakes in the implementation or migration process, such as buying too many server licenses or purchasing too many servers.

## Baselining Records for Documentation Comparisons

Baselining is a process of recording the state of an Exchange Server 2003 system so that any changes in its performance can be identified at a later date. Complete baselining also

20

pertains to the overall network performance, including WAN links, but in those cases it might require special software and tools (such as sniffers) to record the information.

An Exchange Server 2003 system baseline document records the state of the server after it is implemented in a production environment and can include statistics such as memory use, paging, disk subsystem throughput, and more. This information then allows the administrator or appropriate IT resource to determine at a later date how the system is performing in comparison to initial operation.

## Using Documentation for Troubleshooting Purposes

Troubleshooting documentation is a record of identified system issues and the associated resolution. This documentation is helpful both in terms of the processes that the company recommends for resolving technical issues and a documented record of the results of actual troubleshooting challenges. Researching and troubleshooting an issue is time consuming. Documenting the process followed and the results provides a valuable resource for other company administrators that might experience the same issue.

# Design and Planning Documentation

Parts I, "Microsoft Exchange Server 2003 Overview," and II, "Exchange Server 2003," of this book focus on many planning and designing aspects for Exchange Server 2003. Whether you're planning a migration, an entirely new environment, or a specific project, design and planning documentation is critical. All projects, regardless of size, are more successful if they have a well-developed design and migration plan.

## Documenting the Design

As outlined in Chapters 4, "Designing Exchange Server 2003 for a Small to Medium Network," and 5, "Designing an Enterprise Exchange Server 2003 Environment," the first step in the implementation of an Exchange Server 2003 environment is the development and approval of a design. Documenting this design contributes to the success of the project. The design document records the decisions made during the design process and provides a reference for testing, implementation, and support. Typically, a design document includes the following components:

- The goals and objectives of the project
- A summary of the existing environment and the background that led to the project
- The details of the new Exchange Server 2003 environment
- The details of the migration process

Documenting the goals and objectives of the project helps ensure that the project team and stakeholder interests are in alignment. The goals and objectives of the project should be as specific as possible, because after the goals are defined, they help shape design decisions.

Summarizing the existing environment creates a snapshot of the preimplementation environment, which provides a reference point for development of the new design and a historical record should a rollback be required. Including the background behind the decision to implement Exchange Server 2003 further defines the historical record and supports the goals and objectives.

The following is an example of a table of contents for a design document:

```
Exchange Server 2003 Design Document
Project Overview
Design and Planning Process
Existing Environment
        Network Infrastructure
        Active Directory Infrastructure
        Exchange Topology
        Backup and Restore
        Administrative Model
        Client Systems
Exchange Server 2003 Architecture
        Goals and Objectives
        Exchange Server 2003 Mailbox Server Placement
        Public Folder Servers
        Connector Servers
        Front-end Servers/Outlook Web Access
        Global Catalog Placement
        Administrative Groups
        Server Sizing and Loading
        Active Directory Connector
        Administrative Model
        Application Considerations and Integration
        Exchange Server 2003 Clients
Appendix A: Existing Environment Diagrams
```

### Exchange Server 2003 Design

The Exchange Server 2003 design details the decisions made with regard to the end-state of the Exchange Server 2003 environment. These decisions include server configuration information, database design, messaging policies, and more.

The level of detail included in the document, high-level or more specific configurations of each server, depends on the document's audience. However, the design document should not include step-by-step procedures or other details of how the process will be accomplished. This level of detail is better handled, in most cases, in dedicated configuration or training documents.

20

## Creating the Migration Plan

After the end-state or design is developed and documented, the plan on how this state will be implemented can be developed. A migration plan outlines the high-level tasks required to test and implement the design. The development of a well-constructed migration plan helps avoid mistakes and keeps the project on track.

> **NOTE**
>
> The results of testing the design in a prototype or pilot might alter the actual migration steps and procedures. In this case, the migration plan document should be modified to take these changes into account.

The following is a table of contents for an Exchange Server 2003 migration plan:

```
Exchange Server 2003 Migration Plan
Goals and Objectives
Approach
Roles
Process
        Phase I - Design and Planning
        Phase II - Prototype
        Phase III - Pilot
        Phase IV - Implementation
        Phase V - Support
Migration Process
        Active Directory Preparation
        Exchange Server 2003
Summary of Migration Resources
Project Scheduling
Exchange Server 2003 Training
Administration and Maintenance
```

## Outlining the Project Plan

A project plan is essential for more complex migrations and can be useful for managing smaller projects, even single server migrations. Developed from the high-level tasks and outlined in the migration plan, detailed tasks and subtasks are identified in the order in which they occur. The duration of these tasks will vary but it is recommended that they be no less than a half-day duration, because a project plan that tries to track a project hour by hour can be hard to keep up to date. Of course, the size of the project also dictates the project plan's level of detail.

Tools such as Microsoft Project facilitate the creation of project plans (see Figure 20.1). Using Microsoft Project enables the assignment of one or more resources per task and the assignment of duration and links to key predecessor tasks. The project plan can also provide an initial estimate of the number of hours required from each resource and the associated costs if outside resources are to be used. What-if scenarios are easy to create by simply adding resources or cutting out optional steps to determine the effect on the budget and resources.

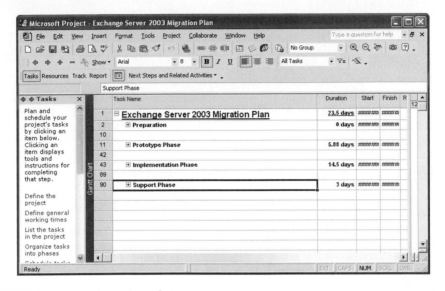

**FIGURE 20.1**  A sample project plan.

## Developing the Test Plan

Thorough testing is critical in the success of any implementation project. A test plan details the resources required for testing (hardware, software, and lab personnel), the tests or procedures to perform, and the purpose of the test or procedure.

It is important to include representatives of every aspect of the network in the development of the test plan. This ensures that all aspects of the Exchange Server 2003 environment or project and its impact will be included in the test plan.

Test plans, although they will vary within each environment, should consider using a framework such as this:

Summary
The purpose of this document is to outline the testing strategy for the migration to Exchange Server 2003. Before Exchange Server 2003 is deployed, the design must be tested in an environment that simulates and protects the production environment. Devising and conducting tests that reflect conditions in the target environment verify the design.

Exchange Server 2003 Testing Methodology
        Testing Phases
        Documentation

20

```
Resources
        Hardware and Software
        Personnel
        Testing Lab Layout
Tests
        Build AD Environment
        Test Schema Modifications
        Build Exchange Server 2003 Servers
        Migrate Data
        Client Software Installation and Customization
Appendix A - Messaging Test Form
Appendix B - Test Questionnaires
```

# Developing the Migration Documentation

Migration documentation is typically created during the testing or prototype phase of the project. Migration documentation, comprised of a combination of procedures and checklists, provides a roadmap of the Exchange Server 2003 migration. The documents might need updating after the initial or pilot implementation to more accurately reflect the migration process.

## Server Migration Procedures

Server migration tasks should be decided on during a design and planning process. Detailed procedures associated with those tasks are then developed and confirmed during a prototype/testing phase. It is also important to validate the documents each time a server is rebuilt to ensure that critical steps are not left out. When complete, this information can save a great deal of time during the implementation.

---

**TIP**

Server migration procedures should be written in such a way so that even less-experienced resources are able to use the procedures for the actual migrations.

---

The procedures covered can include, but are not limited to, the following:

- Server hardware configuration details

- Service pack (SP) and hotfixes to install on each server

- Services (such as DNS and DHCP) to enable or disable (including any appropriate settings)

- Applications (for example, antivirus) to install and appropriate settings

- Security settings

- Steps required to migrate mail to the new server(s)

- Steps required to test the new configuration to ensure full functionality

- Steps required to remove old servers from production

## Desktop Client Configuration Procedures

Desktop configurations might change during the migration to, the implementation of, or the configuration change of Exchange Server 2003. If the Outlook client is already in use, server configuration changes might affect only the Outlook profile. All changes and the change procedure should be documented to ensure that there is a uniform user experience after the implementation.

> **NOTE**
>
> The desktop configuration change process should be discussed in the design and planning phase.

## Mail Migration Procedures

One of the most frequently identified messaging systems implementation goals is to migrate all the existing mail, contacts, mailing lists, calendar items, and more without losing any data. Developing complete and accurate messaging migration procedures during the testing phase helps migrate existing production messaging data and prevents data loss.

## Example of a Mail Migration Checklist

The migration process, based on the amount of data that must be migrated, can often be a long process. It is very helpful to develop both high-level and detailed checklists to guide the migration process. High-level checklists determine the status of the migration at any given point in the process. Detailed checklists ensure that all steps are performed in a consistent manner. This is extremely important if the process is being repeated for multiple sites.

The following is an example of an Exchange Server 2003 server build checklist:

| Task | Initials | Notes |
| --- | --- | --- |
| Verify BIOS and Firmware Revs | | |
| Verify RAID Configuration | | |
| Install Windows Server 2003 Enterprise Edition | | |
| Configure Windows Server 2003 Enterprise Edition | | |
| Install Security Patches | | |
| Install Support Tools | | |
| Install System Recovery Console | | |
| Add Server to Domain | | |
| Install Antivirus | | |
| Install Exchange Server 2003 Enterprise | | |

```
Configure Exchange
Install and Configure Backup Agent on Exchange
Apply Rights for XX-Sysadmins
Set up and Configure Smart UPS
```

Sign off:                                                    Date:

# Exchange Server 2003 Environment Documentation

As the business and network infrastructure changes, it's not uncommon for the messaging infrastructure to change as well. Keep track of these changes as they progress through baselines (how the Exchange Server 2003 environment was built) and other forms of documentation, such as the configuration settings and connectivity diagrams of the environment.

## Server Build Procedures

The server build procedure is a detailed set of instructions for building the Exchange Server 2003 system. This document can be used for troubleshooting and adding new servers, and is a critical resource in the event of a disaster.

The following is an example of a table of contents from a server build procedure document:

```
Windows Server 2003 Build Procedures
        System Configuration Parameters
        Configure the Server Hardware
                Install Vendor Drivers
                Configure RAID
        Install and Configure Windows Server 2003
                Using Images
                Scripted Installations
        Applying Windows Server 2003 Security
                Using a Security Template
                Using GPOs
                Configuring Antivirus
                Installing Service Packs and Critical Updates
        Backup Client Configuration
Exchange Server 2003 Build Procedures
        System Configuration Parameters
        Configuring Exchange as a Mailbox Server
                Creating Storage Groups
                Creating Databases
        Configuring Exchange as a Public Folder Server
                Creating a Public Folder Database
        Configuring Front-end Functionality
                Configuring SSL
```

## Configuration (As-Built) Documentation

The configuration document, often referred to as an as-built, details a snapshot configuration of the Exchange Server 2003 system as it is built. This document contains essential information required to rebuild a server.

The following is an Exchange Server 2003 server as-built document template:

```
Introduction
The purpose of this Exchange Server 2003 as-built document is to assist an
experienced network administrator or engineer in restoring the server in the event
of a hardware failure. This document contains screen shots and configuration set-
tings for the server at the time it was built. If settings are not implicitly
defined in this document, they are assumed to be set to defaults. It is not
intended to be a comprehensive disaster recovery with step-by-step procedures for
rebuilding the server. In order for this document to remain useful as a recovery
aid, it must be updated as configuration settings change.


System Configuration
        Hardware Summary
        Disk Configuration
                Logical Disk Configuration
        System Summary
        Device Manager
        RAID Configuration
        Windows Server 2003 TCP/IP Configuration
        Network Adapter Local Area Connections
Security Configuration
        Services
        Lockdown Procedures (Checklist)
        Antivirus Configuration
Share List
Applications and Configurations
```

## Topology Diagrams

Network configuration diagrams, such as the one shown in Figure 20.2, and related documentation generally include local area network (LAN) connectivity, wide area network (WAN) infrastructure connectivity, IP subnet information, critical servers, network devices, and more. Having accurate diagrams of the new environment can be invaluable when troubleshooting connectivity issues. For topology diagrams that can be used for troubleshooting connectivity issues, consider documenting the following:

- Internet service provider contact names, including technical support contact information

- Connection type (such as frame relay, ISDN, OC-12)

- Link speed

20

- Committed Information Rate (CIR)

- Endpoint configurations, including routers used

- Message flow and routing

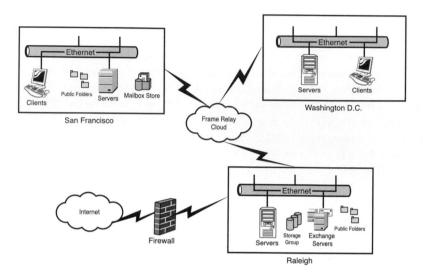

**FIGURE 20.2**    A sample network diagram.

# Administration and Maintenance Documentation

Planning and implementing an Exchange Server 2003 environment is just the beginning of documentation possibilities. Proper documentation can also be critical in maintaining a reliable network. Administration and maintenance documentation helps an administrator organize and keep track of the different steps required to ensure the health of the Exchange environment like the management and maintenance best practices described in Chapter 19, "Exchange Server 2003 Management and Maintenance Practices." This documentation can also facilitate the training of new resources and reduce the variables and risks involved in these transitions.

One key component to administration or maintenance documentation is a timeline detailing when certain procedures should be followed. To properly maintain an Exchange environment, certain daily, weekly, monthly, and quarterly procedures should be followed. These procedures, such as database maintenance and mailbox deletion, should be documented to make sure that the procedures are clearly defined and the frequency in which they should be performed is outlined.

## Step-by-Step Procedure Documents

Administration and maintenance documentation contains a significant amount of procedural documentation. These documents can be very helpful for complex processes or for processes that are not performed on a regular basis. Procedures range from technical processes that outline each step to administrative processes that help clarify roles and responsibilities.

## Organizational Policy Documents

When it comes to messaging, there are a number of system, recipient, and management policies that can and should be established (for example, message size limits, message retention policies, and naming conventions). Establishing clear policies helps establish user expectation and limit database size. In addition, with maintenance and administration policies it helps to have a well-developed, complete, and approved policy document that makes it clear who is responsible for what in specific situations.

## Documented Checklists

Administration and maintenance documentation can be extensive, and checklists can be quick reminders for those processes and procedures. Develop comprehensive checklists that will help administrators perform their scheduled and unscheduled tasks. A timeline checklist highlighting the daily, weekly, monthly, and quarterly tasks helps keep the Exchange environment healthy. In addition, these checklists function as excellent auditing tools.

# Disaster Recovery Documentation

Disaster recovery documentation should be a requirement for every project. Regardless of size, an organization should go through the process of contemplating various disaster scenarios and determining what its needs would be in the event of a disaster. A disaster can range from a hard disk failure to a fire that destroys the entire site. Each type of disaster can pose a different threat to the day-to-day functioning of an organization. Therefore, it's important to determine every possible scenario and begin planning ways to minimize the impact of those disasters.

Planning for a disaster can be time consuming and expensive. However, generally speaking this does not outweigh the benefits of creating such documentation. Even a quick analysis showing how downtime resulting from a disaster might affect the company with regard to reputation, time, productivity, expenses, and loss in profit or revenue versus how much time it takes to create documentation can show the advantages of documenting and being prepared. The true purpose for the evaluation, though, is to assist an organization in determining how much should be invested in remedies to avoid or minimize the impact of a disaster.

A number of different components comprise disaster recovery documentation. Without this documentation, full recovery is difficult at best. The following is a table of contents for the areas to consider when documenting disaster recovery procedures:

```
Executive Summary or Introduction
Disaster Recovery Scenarios
Disaster Recovery Best Practices
        Planning and Designing for Disaster
```

20

```
Business Continuity and Response
        Business Hours Response to Emergencies
        Recovery Team Members
        Recovery Team Responsibilities
        Damage Assessment
        Off-Hours Response to an Emergency
        Recovery Team Responsibilities
        Recovery Strategy
        Coordinate Equipment Needs
Disaster Recovery Decision Tree
Software Recovery
Hardware Recovery
Server Disaster Recovery
Preparation
        Documentation
        Software Management
        Knowledge Management
Server Backup with a Third-party Application
        Client Software Configuration
Restoring the Server
        Build the Server Hardware
        Post Restore
Exchange Disaster Recovery
        Disaster Recovery Service Level Agreements
        Exchange Disaster Recovery Plan
        Exchange Message / Mailbox Restore Scenario
        Complete RAID 5 Failure
        Complete RAID 1 Failure
        NOS Partition Failure
        Complete System Failure
        NIC, RAID Controller Failures
Training Personnel and Practicing Disaster Recovery
```

## Disaster Recovery Planning

The first step of the disaster recovery process is to develop a formal disaster recovery plan. This plan, while time consuming to develop, serves as a guide for the entire organization in the event of an emergency. Disaster scenarios, such as power outages, hard drive failures, and even earthquakes, should be addressed. Although it is impossible to develop a scenario for every potential disaster, it is still helpful to develop a plan to recover from different levels of disaster. It is recommended that organizations encourage open discussions of possible scenarios and the steps required to recover from each one. Include representatives from each department, because each department will have its own priorities in the event of a disaster. The disaster recovery plan should encompass the organization as a whole and focus on determining what it will take to resume normal business function after a disaster.

## Backup and Recovery Development

Another important component of a disaster recovery development process is the evaluation of the organization's current backup policies and procedures. Without sound backup policies and procedures, a disaster recovery plan is useless. It is not possible to recover a system if the backup is not valid.

A backup plan does not just encompass backing up data to tape or other medium. It is an overarching plan that outlines other tasks, including advanced system recovery, offsite storage, testing procedures, and retention policies. These tasks should be carefully documented to accurately represent each backup methodology and how it's carried out. Full documentation of the backup process includes step-by-step procedures, guidelines, policies, and checklists.

Periodically, the backup systems should be reviewed and tested, especially after any configuration changes. Any changes to the system should be reflected in the documentation. Otherwise, backup documents can become stale and can add to the problems during recovery attempts.

Recovery documentation complements backup documentation. The primary purpose of the documented backup process is to provide the ability to recover that backup in the event of an emergency. Recovery documentation should outline where the backup data resides and how to recover from various types of failures, such as hard drive failure, system failure, and natural disasters. Just like backup documentation, recovery documentation takes the form of step-by-step procedures, guidelines, policies, and checklists.

## Exchange System Failover Documentation

Many organizations use clustering in their Exchange environment to provide failover and redundancy capabilities for their messaging systems. When a system fails over, having fully tested and documented procedures helps get the system back up and running quickly. Because these procedures are not used often, they must be thoroughly tested and reviewed in a lab setting so that they accurately reflect the steps required to recover each system.

# Performance Documentation

Performance documentation helps monitor the health and status of the Exchange environment. It is a continuous process that begins by aligning the goals, existing policies, and service level agreements of the organization. When these areas are clearly defined and detailed, baseline performance values can be established, using tools such as the System Monitor, Microsoft Operations Manager (MOM), or third-party tools (such as PerfMon or BMC Patrol). These tools capture baseline performance-related metrics that can include indicators such as how much memory is being used, average processor use, and more. They also can illustrate how the Exchange Server 2003 environment is performing under various workloads.

After the baseline performance values are documented, performance-related information gathered by the monitoring solution should be analyzed periodically. Pattern and trend

20

analysis reports need to be examined at least on a weekly basis. This analysis can uncover current and potential bottlenecks and proactively ensure that the system operates as efficiently and effectively as possible. These reports can range from routine reports generated by the monitoring solution to complex technical reports that provide detail to engineering staff.

## Routine Reporting

Although built-in system monitoring tools log performance data that can be used in reports in conjunction with products such as Microsoft Excel, it is recommended that administrators use products such as MOM for monitoring and reporting functionality. MOM can manage and monitor the Exchange systems and provide preconfigured graphical reports with customizable levels of detail. MOM also provides the framework to generate customized reports that meet the needs of the organization.

## Management-Level Reporting

Routine reporting typically provides a significant amount of technical information. Although helpful for the administrator, it can be too much information for management. Management-level performance reporting should be concise and direct. Stakeholders do not require the specifics of performance data, but it's important to take those specifics and show trends, patterns, and any potential problem areas. This extremely useful and factual information provides insight to management so that decisions can be made to determine proactive solutions for keeping systems operating in top-notch condition.

For instance, during routine reporting, administrators identify and report to management that Exchange Server processor use is on the rise. What does this mean? This information by itself does not give management any specifics on what the problem is. However, if the administrator presents graphical reports that indicate that if the current trends on Exchange Server processor use continue at the rate of a 5% increase per month, an additional processor will be required in 10 months or less. Management can then take this report, follow the issue more closely over the next few months, and determine whether to allocate funds to purchase additional processors. If the decision is made to buy more processors, management has more time to negotiate quantity, processing power, and cost instead of having to pay higher costs for the processors on short notice.

## Technical Reporting

Technical performance information reporting is much more detailed than management-level reporting. It goes beyond the routine reporting to provide specific details on many different components and facets of the system. For example, specific counter values might be given to determine disk subsystem use. This type of information is useful in monitoring the health of the entire Exchange environment. Trend and pattern analysis should also be included in the technical reporting process to not only reflect the current status, but to allow comparison to historical information and determine how to plan for future requirements.

# Security Documentation

Just as with any other aspect of the Exchange environment, security documentation also includes policies, configurations and settings, and procedures. Administrators can easily feel that although documenting security settings and other configurations are important, it might lessen security mechanisms established in the Exchange Server 2003 environment. However, documenting security mechanisms and corresponding configurations are vital to administration, maintenance, and any potential security compromise. Security documentation, along with other forms of documentation—including network diagrams and configurations—should be well guarded to minimize any  potential security risk.

A network environment might have many security mechanisms in place, but if the information—such as logs and events obtained from them—isn't reviewed, security is more relaxed. Monitoring and management solutions, described in the performance documentation section, can help consolidate this information into reports that can be generated on a periodic basis. These reports are essential to the process of continuously evaluating the network's security.

In addition, management should be informed of any unauthorized access or attempts to compromise security. Business policy can then be made to strengthen the environment's security.

## Change Control

Although the documentation of policies and procedures to protect the system from external security risks is of utmost importance, internal procedures and documents should also be established. Developing, documenting, and enforcing a change control process helps protect the system from well-intentioned internal changes.

In environments where there are multiple administrators, it is very common to have the interests of one administrator affect those of another. For instance, an administrator might make a configuration change to limit mailbox size for a specific department. If this change is not documented, a second administrator might spend a significant amount of time trying to troubleshoot a user complaint from that department. Establishing a change control process that documents these types of changes eliminates confusion and wasted resources. The change control process should include an extensive testing process to reduce the risk of production problems.

## Procedures

Although security policies and guidelines comprise the majority of security documentation, procedures are equally as important. Procedures include not only the initial configuration steps, but also maintenance procedures and more important procedures that are to be followed in the event of a security breach.

Additional areas regarding security that can be documented include, but are not limited to, the following:

20

- Auditing policies including review

- Service packs (SPs) and hotfixes

- Certificates and certificates of authority

- Antivirus configurations

- Encrypting File System (EFS)

- Password policies (such as length, strength, age)

- GPO security-related policies

- Registry security

- Lockdown procedures

# Training Documentation

Training documentation for a project can be extensive and ranges from user training to technical training. The most important aspect of training documentation is to make sure that it meets the needs of the individual being trained. The two key documents created and used in organizations are focused for the benefit of end-users, and technical documents are focused toward administrators.

## End-User

Proper end-user training is critical to the acceptance of any new application. Developing clear and concise documentation that addresses the user's needs is key in providing proper training. As discussed earlier, developing specific documentation goals and conducting an audience analysis are especially important to the development of useful training materials.

## Technical

Administrators and engineers are responsible for the upkeep and management of the Exchange environment. As a result, they must be technically prepared to address a variety of issues, such as maintenance and troubleshooting. Training documentation should address why the technologies are being taught and how the technologies pertain to the Exchange environment. In addition, the training documentation should be easy to use and function as a reference resource in the future.

# Summary

The development of documentation for the Exchange Server 2003 environment is important not only to establishing the environment, but to the health, maintenance, and ongoing support of the system. After this documentation is developed, it must be thoroughly tested—preferably by a disinterested party—and maintained. Every change that is made to the environment should be changed in the documentation.

# Best Practices

The following are best practices from this chapter:

- Determine the business needs for documentation.

- Determine the goals of each document.

- Determine the audience and the need for each document.

- Validate and test the documentation.

- Develop audience-level specific training materials.

- Establish a documentation update process.

# CHAPTER 21

# Using Terminal Services to Manage Exchange Servers

**IN THIS CHAPTER**

- Terminal Service Modes of Operation
- Using Terminal Services on Pocket Devices
- Using Exchange System Manger to Remotely Manage Exchange Server 2003

To keep maintenance and administration costs down and promote efficiency in any Exchange Server 2003 messaging environment, you must have a secure and reliable means of managing the servers remotely. Windows Server 2003 and Exchange Server 2003 have these capabilities built in so that you do not have to rely on third-party solutions.

You can manage Exchange Server 2003 systems remotely in different ways, and it is important to understand not only what these options are but also which one is best for your particular environment. This chapter complements Chapter 19, "Exchange Server 2003 Management and Maintenance Practices," and expands on the different remote management capabilities and when to use them.

## Terminal Services Modes of Operation

There are two Terminal Services functions within Windows Server 2003: Remote Desktop for Administration and Terminal Services (formerly known as Terminal Services Application Mode). Remote Desktop for Administration mode is installed (but not enabled) by default; Terminal Services must be manually installed and configured.

### Remote Desktop for Administration

As mentioned earlier, Remote Desktop for Administration is included and installed with the Windows Server 2003 operating system and needs only to be enabled. This eases automated and unattended server deployment by enabling an administrator to deploy servers that can be managed remotely after the operating systems have completed installation. This mode can also be used to manage a headless server, which can reduce the amount of space needed in any server rack. More space can be dedicated to servers instead of switch boxes, monitors, keyboards, and mouse devices.

Remote Desktop for Administration limits the number of terminal sessions to two, with only one Remote Desktop Protocol (RDP) or Secure Sockets Layer (SSL) for remote administration connection per network interface. Only administrators can connect to these sessions. No additional licenses are needed to run a server in this Terminal Services mode, which enables an administrator to perform almost all the server management duties remotely.

Even though Remote Desktop for Administration is installed by default, this mode does not have to be enabled. Some organizations might see Remote Desktop for Administration as an unneeded security risk and choose to keep it disabled. This function can easily be disabled throughout the entire Active Directory (AD) forest by using a Group Policy setting to disable administrators from connecting through Remote Desktop for Administration.

## Planning for Remote Desktop for Administration Mode

Unless Remote Desktop for Administration is viewed as a security risk, you should enable it on all internal servers to allow remote administration. For servers that are on the Internet or for DMZ networks, Remote Desktop for Administration may be used, but access should be even more restricted. For example, consider limiting access to a predefined IP address or set of IP addresses, using firewall ACLs to eliminate unauthorized attempts to log on to the server. Another option is to limit connections to the server based on protocol.

> **NOTE**
>
> The level of encryption for remote sessions by default is 128-bit (bidirectional). It is also important to note that some older Terminal Services clients might not support that level of encryption.

## Enabling Remote Desktop for Administration

Remote Desktop for Administration mode is installed on all Windows Server 2003 servers by default and needs only to be enabled. To manually enable this feature, follow these steps:

1. Log on to the desired server with Administrator privileges.

2. Click Start, right-click the My Computer shortcut, and then click Properties.

3. Select the Remote tab, and under the Remote Desktop section, check the Allow Users to Connect Remotely to Your Computer box, as shown in Figure 21.1.

4. Click OK in the Systems Properties page to complete this process.

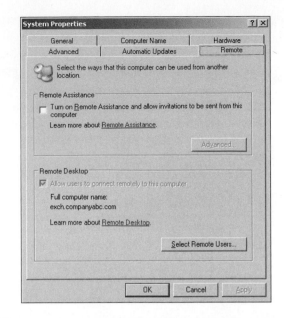

**FIGURE 21.1**     Enabling users to connect to the system remotely.

## Remote Administration (HTML)

Formerly known as the Terminal Services Advanced Client (TSAC) in Windows 2000, the Remote Administration (HTML) tool can also be used to manage Exchange Server 2003. The primary intention of this tool is to provide basic remote administration capabilities for Internet Information Services 6.0 Web servers, as shown in Figure 21.2. However, there are capabilities built in that enable administrators to not only check server status, logs, and IIS functionality, but also to manage server network configurations and email alerts, and use the Exchange System Manager (ESM) through Remote Desktop, as shown in Figure 21.3.

### Installing and Enabling Remote Administration (HTML)

As hinted at in the last section, Remote Administration (HTML) is a Windows Server 2003 IIS component, and it cannot be used to manage earlier versions of IIS. It is also not enabled by default. This does not mean that using this tool creates unnecessary security risks. Instead it keeps Windows Server 2003 security in a more consistent, locked-down state, and you need to manually install and configure its settings to meet the security requirements of your company.

To install Remote Administration (HTML), do the following:

1. Select Add or Remove Programs from the Start, Control Panel menu.

2. Choose Add/Remove Windows Components and then highlight Application Server in the Windows Components Wizard window.

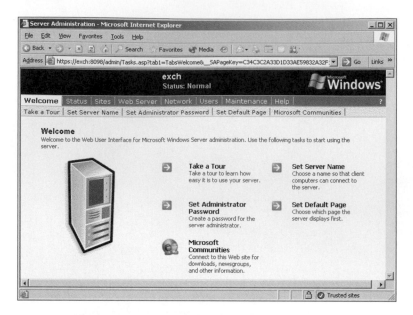

**FIGURE 21.2**    Remote Administration (HTML) tool options.

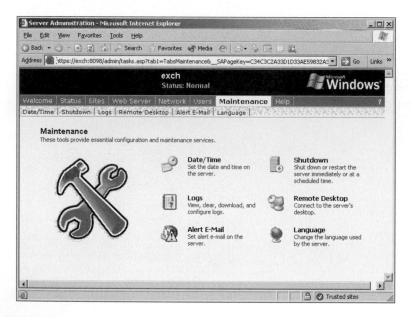

**FIGURE 21.3**    Remote Desktop access from the Remote Administration tool.

3. Click Details and then highlight Internet Information Services (IIS) in the Application Server window.

4. Click Details again and highlight World Wide Web Services. Click Details one more time in order to view the Remote Administration (HTML) option, as shown in Figure 21.4.

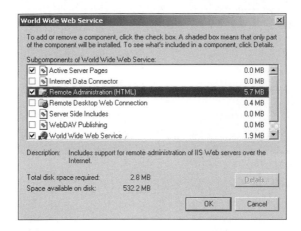

**World Wide Web Service**                                                     ⊠

To add or remove a component, click the check box. A shaded box means that only part of the component will be installed. To see what's included in a component, click Details.

Subcomponents of World Wide Web Service:

| | |
|---|---|
| ☑ 🖹 Active Server Pages | 0.0 MB |
| ☐ 🖹 Internet Data Connector | 0.0 MB |
| ☑ 🖳 Remote Administration (HTML) | 5.7 MB |
| ☐ 🖳 Remote Desktop Web Connection | 0.4 MB |
| ☐ 🖹 Server Side Includes | 0.0 MB |
| ☐ 🖹 WebDAV Publishing | 0.0 MB |
| ☑ 🖳 World Wide Web Service | 1.9 MB |

Description:   Includes support for remote administration of IIS Web servers over the Internet.

Total disk space required:      2.8 MB
Space available on disk:       532.2 MB

[ Details... ]

[ OK ]    [ Cancel ]

**FIGURE 21.4**   Installing the Remote Administration (HTML) tool.

5. Click OK three times to return to the Windows Components Wizard window and then click Next.

6. When installation completes, click Finish.

To enable Remote Administration (HTML), perform the following steps:

1. Select the Internet Information Services Manager from the Start, Administrative Tools menu.

2. Expand the server and also the Web Site folder to display a list of Web sites hosted on the Exchange Server 2003 server.

3. Right-click the Administration Web site and then select Properties.

4. Within the Web site identification section, record the port numbers that are displayed for the TCP and SSL ports. The defaults are 8099 and 8098.

5. Select the Directory Security tab and then click the Edit button under IP address and domain name restrictions section. You can select restrictions either by IP address, a group of IP addresses, or by domain name.

**CAUTION**

Although you can grant access to all computers, all computers in an IP address subnet, or all computers in a domain, you should limit the number of computers that may have access using Remote Administration (HTML) to Exchange Server 2003. Otherwise, unnecessary security vulnerabilities can be introduced on the Exchange Server 2003 server.

6. In the IP Address and Domain Name Restrictions window select Denied Access, and then click the Add button. Note that you can optionally click DNS Lookup to verify the name of the server to which you are granting access.

7. In the Grant Access window, click Single computer and then enter in the IP address of the computer to which you want to grant access.

8. Click OK twice and then close the IIS Manager.

To remotely administer the Exchange Server 2003 Server from the computer that has been granted access, open Internet Explorer and type **https://*servername*:8098** where ***servername*** is the name of the server. You will be prompted to provide username and password credentials in order to log on to the server.

> **NOTE**
>
> As mentioned earlier, Remote Administration (HTML) provides the necessary tools for managing essential IIS components and basic Windows Server 2003 features, but it also provides a link for the Remote Desktop. The Remote Desktop is the Web-based equivalent of Remote Desktop for Administration. This link must be used if you are to manage an Exchange Server 2003 server. Therefore, the Remote Administration (HTML) tool is useful on older or non-Windows computers that need access for remote Exchange Server 2003 management purposes. Otherwise, if the computer accessing Exchange Server 2003 remotely via the Remote Administration (HTML) tool also has the Remote Desktop Connection tool (for the client side), it begs the question of why the Remote Desktop for Administration tool is not being used in the first place. Unless a security policy dictates that the RDP port should not be open on the firewall, the Remote Desktop for Administration tool is recommended.

## Remote Desktop Administration Tips and Tricks

There are several key points to consider before using either Remote Desktop for Administration or Remote Administration (HTML), including, but not limited to, the following:

- **Make sure resources are available**—What IT personnel resources, if any, are available at the remote location or at the Exchange Server 2003 server's location? If a problem arises with the connection to the remote Exchange Server 2003 server or the server itself (for example, a disconnection) there should be contingency plans available to recover and continue to remotely manage the system. Generally speaking it is a good idea to have someone in the vicinity that can assist the administrator in some form or fashion.

- **Use care when modifying network configurations**—With any remote administration tool, you are dependent upon the connectivity between the client computer and the Exchange Server 2003 server that is being remotely managed. If network configuration settings must be modified remotely, consider having alternative methods of access. For instance, dial-up or a separate network connection might minimize downtime or other issues stemming from loss of connectivity.

- **Use disconnect and reset timeout values**—Anytime a connection is accidentally broken or an administrator disconnects, the remote session is placed into a disconnected state that can later be reconnected and used to manage a server remotely. Disconnect and reset timeouts are not configured by default for remote desktop administration tools. These values can be used to ensure that administrators are not unintentionally locked out (for example, when there are two remote sessions that are active but in a disconnected state). Generally speaking, using 10–20-minute timeout values allows enough time for administrators to reconnect if they were accidentally disconnected. Moreover, it helps minimize the number of sessions that are disconnected and not being used.

- **Coordinate remote administration efforts**—The number of remote administration connections is limited to a precious two. Therefore, plan and coordinate efforts to reduce the number of attempts to access Exchange Server 2003 servers remotely. This also helps ensure that remote administration activities do not conflict with other administrators and sessions—or, in the worst of cases, corrupt information or data on the server.

## Terminal Services

Terminal Services mode is available in all editions of Windows Server 2003 (that is, Standard, Enterprise, and Datacenter) except the Web edition. It enables any authorized user to connect to the server and run a single application or a complete desktop session from the client workstation. Because the applications are loaded and running on the Terminal Services server, client desktop resources are barely used; all the application processing is performed by the Terminal Services server. This enables companies to extend the life of old, less-powerful workstations by running applications only from a Terminal Services server session.

Terminal Services is generally not considered a viable technology to manage Exchange Server 2003 remotely. Although it is possible to use Terminal Services to manage Exchange Server 2003, there are several planning considerations that must be addressed to determine whether Terminal Services is suitable in your environment.

## Planning Considerations for Using Terminal Services

Terminal Services can require a lot of planning, especially when you're considering whether to use it to manage Exchange Server 2003 remotely. Because Terminal Services is intended to make applications available to end-users rather than serve as a remote management service, security, server performance, and licensing are key components to consider before using it in a production environment.

## Terminal Services Security

Terminal Services servers should be secured following standard security guidelines defined in company security policies and as recommended by hardware and software vendors. Some basic security configurations include removing all unnecessary services from the

Terminal Services nodes and applying security patches for known vulnerabilities on services or applications that are running on the Terminal server.

An administrator can use Group Policy to limit client functionality as needed to enhance server security, and if increased network security is a requirement, can consider requiring clients to run sessions in 128-bit high-encryption mode.

Windows Server 2003 Terminal Services can be run in either Full Security or Relaxed Security Permission compatibility mode to meet an organization's security policy and application requirements. Permission compatibility mode was created to help lock down the Terminal server environment to reduce the risk of users mistakenly installing software or inadvertently disabling the Terminal Services server by moving directories or deleting Registry keys. This mode can be used for most certified Terminal server applications. Relaxed Security mode was created to support legacy applications that require extended access into the server system directory and System Registry.

In addition to all the more common security precautions that are recommended for Terminal Services, you must also consider how running Terminal Services on an Exchange Server 2003 server affects security. Using a server with both Terminal Services and Exchange Server 2003 roles and responsibilities can be a dangerous combination and should be considered only in the smallest of environments with very relaxed security requirements. In any circumstance, the combination is not recommended.

Combining the two services and configuring Terminal Services to remotely manage Exchange Server 2003 can result in many security-related hazards, including the following:

- A single misconfiguration or setting can enable users to change specific Exchange Server 2003 settings or parameters.

- Users authorized to shut down or restart the system might inadvertently do so, causing messaging downtime.

- Application-specific security might conflict or in some cases unintentionally allow or restrict access to messaging components on the server.

## Terminal Server Licensing

Terminal Services requires the purchase of client access licenses (CALs) for each client device or session. A Terminal Services License Server also must be available on the network to allocate and manage these CALs. When a Terminal Services server is establishing a session with a client, it checks with the Terminal Services License Server to verify whether this client has a license. A license is allocated if the client does not already have one.

> **NOTE**
>
> Using Terminal Services to connect to and remotely manage an Exchange Server 2003 server does not exempt you from needing a Terminal Services CAL. This adds to the overall cost of supporting Exchange Server 2003.

To install licenses on the TS License server, the Terminal Services License server must first be installed and then activated online. The TS License server requires Internet access or dial-up modem access to activate the client access licenses added to the server.

When a Terminal Services server cannot locate a Terminal Services License Server on the network, it still allows unlicensed clients to connect. This can go on for 120 days without contacting a license server, and then the server stops serving Terminal Services sessions. It is imperative to get a license server installed on the network as soon as possible—before Terminal Services servers are deployed to production.

# Using Terminal Services on Pocket Devices

Many mobile devices, such as Pocket PCs, have Terminal Services Client components built in to the device's operating system, as shown in Figure 21.5. The Terminal Services Client connects to the server as a client computer would connect, using Remote Desktop for Administration. After it's connected, as shown in Figure 21.6, administrators can manage the Exchange Server 2003 server from the mobile device the same way they would if they were logged in locally. The obvious downside to using a mobile device is the screen size. Although some mobile devices can resize the screen to accommodate the entire desktop on it, the screen size and resolution is limited.

## Locking Down PDA Terminal Services

Securing mobile devices, such as the Pocket PC illustrated in the figure, is often more challenging than securing a client computer or another server. Because the device is designed for mobility, it opens up the possibility of losing the device or having it stolen. Then an unauthorized person could use it to gain access to the network environment.

An obvious deterrent is securing access to the mobile device's useability. For instance, a person has to use a password in order to use the mobile device. If the mobile device were stolen or found, the person with the device would have to figure out the password before gaining access to the mobile device. Pocket PC 2002 and higher support four-digit PIN numbers (similar to a bank ATM card) and strong, alphanumeric passwords. In addition, each time the wrong password is entered, a timed delay increases before the person can attempt to re-enter a PIN or password. The time delay increases exponentially after each unsuccessful logon attempt. Other mobile devices complement password or PIN support with biometrics such as fingerprint readers.

Another important aspect to secure is mobile device communications with the rest of the world. The type of security that can be used depends on how the mobile device is configured to communicate. Most devices, however, support using SSL or Wired Equivalent Protocol (WEP).

**FIGURE 21.5**    The Terminal Services Client component on a Pocket PC device.

**FIGURE 21.6**    Managing an Exchange Server 2003 server from a Pocket PC device.

> **NOTE**
>
> Although viruses for mobile devices are rare, it is important to implement virus protection software. Antivirus software can also help prevent tracing or monitoring applications from being installed that could record everything that is entered into the mobile device, including passwords.

## Using Exchange System Manager to Remotely Manage Exchange Server 2003

Throughout this book there have been references to using the ESM to perform Exchange-related tasks, such as setting Exchange Server 2003 configuration parameters, monitoring queues, and managing mailboxes. Almost every Exchange-related task that can be done is performed through the ESM. The exceptions include, but are not limited to, those tasks related to AD and offline maintenance of the Exchange databases.

This primary tool for Exchange, shown in Figure 21.7, is a Microsoft Management Console (MMC) snap-in (Exchange System Manager.msc) and it gets installed by default on all Exchange Server 2003 servers. The ESM can also be installed on a client computer so that you can manage Exchange from any location from which you have connectivity to the servers.

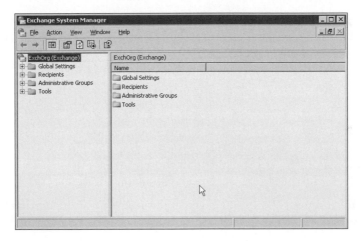

**FIGURE 21.7**    The Exchange System Manager interface.

> **TIP**
>
> Figure 21.7 shows a more advanced view of the ESM, which displays routing and administrative groups. This view can be selected by right-clicking on the Exchange organization within the ESM and selecting Properties. In the Properties window within the General tab, check the routing and administrative group views that you want displayed.

The ESM can be used to manage a single server or groups of servers. As a result, you can manage any of the Exchange servers in your environment, no matter where they are physically located. If you use Remote Desktop for Administration for Exchange management and troubleshooting, it will more than likely still require you to use the ESM. Many tasks for managing Exchange Server 2003 servers, such as monitoring Event Viewer logs and analyzing performance statistics, are related more directly to the operating system and can be managed and maintained through Terminal Services or Remote Desktop for Administration. Other tasks, such as enabling message tracking or configuring front-end server functionality, should be managed through the ESM.

> **CAUTION**
>
> The ESM communicates with servers using Remote Procedure Calls (RPCs). This method of communication is not considered secure by default when traversing over public networks such as the Internet. Therefore, consider either RPC over HTTPS or Remote Desktop for Administration with high encryption when managing Exchange Server 2003 servers remotely over public networks.

## Benefits of Remote Management Using the ESM

There are many inherent benefits of using the ESM to manage and maintain Exchange Server 2003 remotely, including the following four primary advantages:

- **Extensibility**—The ESM snap-in provides the foundation or framework for the Exchange Server 2003–related tasks that can be performed locally and remotely.

- **Convenience**—Given the proper access rights, Exchange administrators can manage multiple Exchange Server 2003 servers, routing groups, and administrative groups from a single, unified interface.

- **Consistency**—As the previous bullet implies, the ESM provides a consistent interface for everyone administering or maintaining the messaging infrastructure. The same snap-in is used, regardless of whether administration has been delegated or different functions—such as public folder administration, connectors, or messaging policies—are being maintained by specific individuals or groups.

- **Mixed Environments**—Most management aspects of Exchange management even in a mixed Exchange environment can be performed using the ESM.

## Managing a Mixed Exchange Environment with ESM

Some network environments, especially large, enterprise networks, might have a period of time where coexistence with previous Exchange versions is necessary or unavoidable. For instance, Exchange 2000 might be kept in the environment for extended periods of time because it is providing functionality, such as Instant Messaging.

In these circumstances it is important to minimize versions of the ESM that are being used to manage the messaging infrastructure; otherwise, compatibility issues might arise.

Microsoft does not recommend or support managing Exchange Server 2003 features using the Exchange 5.5 or Exchange 2000 version of the ESM. There are only a few exceptions to this advisory:

- Use the Exchange 2000 ESM to manage specific Exchange 2000 features that are no longer included with Exchange Server 2003 (for example, Key Management Service or Instant Messaging). Otherwise, use the Exchange Server 2003 ESM.

- Exchange 5.5 servers should be managed using the Exchange 5.5 ESM, except when moving or migrating mailboxes to an Exchange Server 2003 server.

- When you manage connection agreements (for example, during an upgrade to Exchange Server 2003), manage the connection agreements on a per-server basis. In other words, manage connection agreements on an Exchange 2000 server using the Exchange 2000 ESM.

## Summary

Many messaging environments today require an easy and effective way of remotely managing and maintaining systems. Both Windows Server 2003 and Exchange Server 2003 have tools built in that administrators can use to securely manage and maintain Exchange Server 2003 from any location. This chapter examined the most common remote management tools and highlighted which ones are more appropriate in various real-world circumstances.

## Best Practices

The following are best practices from this chapter:

- Carefully plan which Exchange Server 2003 servers should use Remote Desktop for Administration or Remote Administration (HTML) for remote management.

- Restrict Remote Desktop for Administration or Remote Administration (HTML) access on Exchange Server 2003 servers that are facing the Internet (for example, limiting access to a predefined IP address or set of IP addresses).

- Have a person in the vicinity of the server that is being managed remotely assist the administrator in case network connectivity is lost.

- Use care when modifying network configurations over a Remote Desktop for Administration connection.

- Use disconnect and reset timeout values for Remote Desktop for Administration connections.

- Plan and coordinate remote administration efforts to reduce the number of attempts to access Exchange Server 2003 servers remotely.

- Do not implement Terminal Services on an Exchange server solely to manage Exchange Server 2003 remotely.

- Use the advanced view of the ESM when using multiple routing and administrative groups.

- Use RPC over HTTPS or Remote Desktop for Administration with high encryption when managing Exchange Server 2003 servers remotely over public networks using ESM.

# PART VII

# New Mobility Functionality in Exchange Server 2003

## IN THIS PART

**CHAPTER 22**   Designing Mobility in Exchange
Server 2003                                    641

**CHAPTER 23**   Implementing Mobile Synchronization
in Exchange Server 2003                        657

**CHAPTER 24**   Configuring Client Systems
for Mobility                                   673

# Designing Mobility in Exchange Server 2003

**IN THIS CHAPTER**

- Mobilizing Exchange Server 2003

- Leveraging Exchange ActiveSynce for PDA Mobile Communications

- Using Outlook Mobile Access for Browser-Based Devices

- Designing the Appropriate Use of Exchange 2003 Mobility Capabilities

- Using Exchange Mobility for the Mobile Executive

- Replacing Laptops with Mobile Pocket Devices

- Leveraging a Low-Cost PDA Instead of an Expensive Tablet

With previous versions of Microsoft's Exchange product, mobility either meant setting up a dial-up or VPN connection to a full Outlook client on a laptop or ending up being drastically limited in features with a partially featured Outlook Web client, or purchasing a third-party product and integrating it into Exchange. With Exchange 2003, however, mobility now includes several options that provide full access to mail, calendars, and contacts, plus varying built-in methods to access information using mobile phones or PDA devices.

## Mobilizing Exchange Server 2003

Microsoft's strategy on mobility is to provide the ability to have access to email, calendar, contacts, and other important information virtually anywhere. The various mobile access methods to Exchange include

- Full Outlook client access over VPN

- Full Outlook client access using HTTP Proxy

- Outlook Web Access from a browser

- Pocket PC access updated by Exchange ActiveSync

- Mobile phone access using mobile Web

- Accessing Exchange by non-Windows systems

### Accessing Outlook Using VPN Connectivity

One of the long-supported methods of mobile connectivity to Exchange has been to set up a VPN client on the remote system and synchronize content between client and server.

Exchange 2003 continues to support this method, and improvements in the Outlook 2003 client provide improvements in synchronization.

Outlook VPN synchronization enables users, typically with laptop computers, to access the same Outlook information whether they are connected to the LAN or working remotely from the network. When connected remotely, the user works offline and synchronizes his or her client content to the Exchange server.

VPN connectivity for Outlook is covered in depth in Chapter 25, "Getting the Most Out of the Microsoft Outlook Client," which provides best practices on how organizations implement remote access connectivity to Outlook and procedures for installing and configuring the client for synchronization.

## Connecting Outlook over HTTP Proxy

New to Outlook 2003 and Exchange 2003 is the capability of synchronizing between the Exchange server and Outlook client without setting up a VPN connection. This new functionality is commonly referred to as MAPI over HTTP, RPC over HTTP, or HTTP Proxy. Effectively, this functionality, which is new to Windows 2003, enables a user to establish a secured connection over HTTP for data synchronization. Rather than simply allowing secured browser access using SSL, HTTP Proxy provides an Outlook client to connect to an Exchange server for full Outlook synchronization.

Using HTTP Proxy eliminates the challenge of establishing a VPN connection that might otherwise have traditional VPN ports blocked by firewalls. HTTP Proxy is covered in depth in Chapter 25.

## Using Outlook Web Access As a Remote Client

For mobile access to Exchange without the need of transporting mail with a laptop computer, Microsoft Exchange 2003 continues its support of a browser-based client with Outlook Web Access (OWA, pronounced "oh-wah"). Microsoft has drastically improved the OWA client with significant feature enhancements in the Web client, such as spell checker, rules, and preview mode. Many organizations have chosen to implement Outlook Web Access in Exchange Server 2003 as the primary client for users to Exchange because of the full features of the new OWA client.

OWA is good for home access because an IT organization does not have to arrange to install and support the full Outlook client on home systems, and OWA is a good solution for kiosk or Internet café usage. Because OWA uses a standard browser over http port 80 or https port 443, there are few restrictions or limitations on client access to Exchange using OWA.

Implementing OWA in a server environment is covered in Chapter 10, "Configuring Outlook Web Access and Exchange Mobile Services," and the client piece of OWA is covered in Chapter 26, "Everything You Need to Know About the Outlook Web Access (OWA) Client."

## Using Exchange ActiveSync for PDA Connectivity

New to Exchange is the capability of extending mobility from the user property page in Active Directory Users and Computers to enable more than just laptop synchronization and browser access and to include mobile synchronization with devices such as Pocket PCs (see Figure 22.1). In previous versions of Exchange, an organization that wanted to synchronize a Pocket PC device would either have users install ActiveSync software on their desktop and synchronize their Pocket PC devices individually, or purchase a third-party or add-on gateway product, such as Microsoft Mobile Information Server.

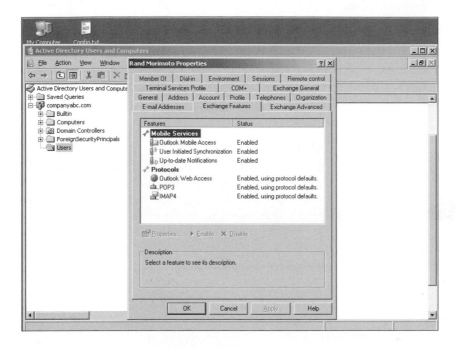

**FIGURE 22.1**    User property page for mobile configuration.

Exchange ActiveSync is built in to Exchange 2003 and supports the synchronization of Pocket PC PDAs, Pocket PC–enabled mobile phones, and SmartPhone devices. Pocket devices that have network connectivity—whether Ethernet, wireless LAN, or mobile public network—can securely synchronize to Exchange 2003. The synchronization connects mail, calendar, contacts, notes, and files linked between Exchange 2003 and the mobile device.

Exchange ActiveSync functionality is covered in more detail in the section "Leveraging Exchange ActiveSync for PDA Mobile Communications," later in this chapter.

## Using Mobile Web Access for Wireless Phone Access

For mobile devices that are not operating under the Windows CE operating system for Pocket PC Exchange ActiveSync synchronization—such as mobile phones—Exchange 2003 supports mobile Web access by these devices. Mobile Web support in Exchange 2003 includes xHTML used in WAP 2.x devices, cHTML, and HTML browser–based device support. With the capability for HTML-type devices to access Exchange client information—such as mail, calendar, contact, and other folder information—users who rely on their mobile phone device can send and receive information directly with Exchange.

Chapter 24, "Configuring Client Systems for Mobility," covers the setup of mobile devices to access mobile Web information in Exchange. The basics of mobile Web access is covered in more detail in the section "Using Outlook Mobile Access for Browser-Based Devices," later in this chapter.

## Using Non-Windows Systems to Access Exchange

When mobile access to Exchange is required that does not fit any of the categories covered so far in this section, see Chapter 27, "Outlook for Non-Windows Systems," which provides alternatives. Mobile system access by non-Windows devices includes Apple Macintosh systems or Unix-based system access to Exchange.

## Automatic Update on Mobile Devices

Key to Microsoft's strategy and offerings for mobile access is the ability for remote users to have access to all of their mail, calendar, contact, and Exchange information, regardless of where they are and what type of device they have available. Part of the strategy is to make sure that Exchange information is always up to date.

Rather than synchronizing information once a day and then working off a cached version for several hours, with the high likelihood that information will be grossly out of date by the next synchronization period, Exchange 2003 provides the ability to keep devices automatically updated throughout the day. In addition to enabling the user to pull down or request a synchronization of information at any time, technology has been built in to Exchange 2003 that pushes updated information to devices, even "waking up" the device—using the Short Message Service (SMS)—to accept updates that can keep important information readily available to the mobile user.

# Leveraging Exchange ActiveSync for PDA Mobile Communications

Pocket PC devices have become more popular over the past couple of years, not only because more devices now include mobile Windows, but also because the ability to fully synchronize calendar, contacts, and other Outlook information makes the functionality more useable. Instead of having to convert contacts, appointments, or messages between disparate applications or learning new tools, a Pocket PC device uses a similar interface to natively synchronize content.

Additionally, because the interface and content remain in native formats, not only do users have the ability to access their email, calendar, and contact information, but they also have full access to other Outlook folder content, such as subfolders and attachments. So if users have managed their Outlook folders with custom containers—

organizing information by client, project, chronological date, or other methods—those folders also can be accessed and synchronized.

Additional improvements in the Exchange ActiveSync with Exchange 2003 include the ability to prevent users from pushing everything, but customizing information synchronization by preventing the sync of nonessential messages, attachments, or content. This offers the ability to create filters and define characteristics on message downloads, decreasing the traffic between the mobile device and the server. Although information can be filtered to prevent the automatic synchronization of this content, Exchange 2003 does provide the ability for the user to manually request the attachment or other filtered information to be transmitted. So the user has the ability to focus bandwidth and information access as effectively as possible.

## Flexibility of Information Synchronization

When synchronizing information between Exchange 2003 and a Pocket PC–enabled device, the device can be connected by a variety of different connectivity methods. The device can be connected through a traditional cradle using the network connectivity of the host system to synchronize with Exchange. A Pocket PC–enabled device can be directly connected to a network using an Ethernet adapter in the device. Through the Ethernet adapter, the device can communicate with the Exchange 2003 server.

A Pocket PC–enabled device can also communicate over wireless methods, and can have a wireless LAN adapter using 802.11a/b, 802.11g, 802.1x, Bluetooth, or infrared. A wireless LAN connection truly disconnects the user from a cradle or physical connection to the network. This provides mobility for the user to access Exchange content anywhere within an office or campus facility. With wireless mobility, the user can keep calendar appointments, email messages, and other up-to-date information accurate and accessible.

When the device is not within the range of a local area network wireless connection, more mobile public network connectivity can extend real-time synchronization regionally, nationally, or globally. Using cellular phone, PCS, GPRS, 1xRTT, GSM, and other public network systems, a properly equipped Pocket PC device can enable users to synchronize their mail, calendar, contact, and other information anytime and anywhere.

## Customizing Synchronization Characteristics

Pocket PC–enabled devices can synchronize folders and subfolders with Exchange and have the capability of filtering and truncating information that is sent and received by the device. Customization of sync characteristics also includes the ability to delete messages or information on the device and have those changes synchronized up to the Exchange server to be deleted on the server copy of the information. The same applies to information that might be deleted using Outlook Web Access, using the full Outlook client software, or by other Exchange client applications that replicate the changes back down to the Pocket PC device. Having full control over the synchronization characteristics, along with the ability to delete in one place what is replicated to all user devices, drastically improves the ability of users to control information regardless of what device they use to access their Exchange information.

## Improving Mobile Performance

As a user accesses Exchange using a variety of different mobile devices, there are times that the bandwidth availability between the Exchange server and the device is grossly limited. Because local area network connections have commonly relied on 100MB speeds, the opening and accessing of large 2MB attachments or 10MB files go unnoticed. However, when a mobile user tries to synchronize a 2MB file over a 9600-baud mobile connection, the file could take 20–30 minutes to transfer, preventing the user from getting urgent emails or other messages during the transfer. Also, many wireless service providers charge based on packets transferred, so the automatic sending and receiving of large attachments could be very expensive. Exchange ActiveSync, included with Exchange 2003, enables the user to choose whether to synchronize attachments.

With Exchange ActiveSync, there is also a smart reply and smart forward function that prevents the need to have an attachment received or sent to the mobile device in order for the user to reply or forward the attachment. For example, a user might receive a large Word document to review. Rather than receiving the document, reviewing it, and then forwarding it to someone where the large attachment would be received and then sent by the mobile device, Exchange ActiveSync enables the user to reply and forward the attachment without the attachment ever being received by the mobile device. The user simply forwards the message to another user. Exchange ActiveSync knows to grab the attachment off the Exchange server and forward it to the user, and not require the mobile device to retransmit the same attachment across the network.

Additional performance-improving features of Exchange ActiveSync are the ability for a user to define peak and nonpeak times to synchronize information and the ability to change those synchronization scheduling options when roaming. By specifying peak time for sending and receiving information, a user can specify higher priority and more frequent transmission of messages. During nonpeak times, the user can specify to have large attachments sent, because message receipt and sending might not be as critical.

Another performance-improving function in Exchange 2003 is the ability for a user to mix the function of ActiveSync with Outlook Mobile Access; this is covered in more detail in the next section, "Using Outlook Mobile Access for Browser-Based Devices." Rather than sending or receiving a large attachment, an HTML Web view of the attachment can be done, enabling the user to view the attachment over a Web browser.

## Improving Mobile Security

Although Exchange 2003 supports sophisticated methods for sending and receiving messages and attachments, organizations must ensure the security and integrity of the information. Exchange ActiveSync supports S/MIME encrypted attachments and 128-bit encryption on transmissions between server and client devices. With support for encryption and encrypted attachments, security of information can be improved.

# 22

# Using Outlook Mobile Access for Browser-Based Devices

As mentioned at the start of this chapter, for devices that are not Pocket PC–enabled, Microsoft Exchange 2003 supports HTML Web browser view of content. This functionality is built in to the Outlook Mobile Access function of Exchange and supports xHTML devices, such as WAP 2.x markup devices, cHTML devices, and standard HTML Web devices. These devices include mobile phones and Web-enabled Palm OS type devices in addition to other mobile wireless devices.

## Simplified Browser-Centric Commands

Outlook Mobile Access, or OMA, provides simple browser-based commands that enable users to manage their email, calendars, contacts, and tasks. Because many of these HTML-based mobile devices do not have large screens or large memories, it is important to minimize the type of information transmitted or sent between the mobile device and Exchange. Because users who send mail to an Exchange 2003 recipient do not know that the recipient is using a mobile phone device for receipt of mail or other information, it is important for the Exchange Outlook Mobile Access tool to do appropriate conversion and modification of content sent to the mobile device.

Some of the browser-centric commands that are part of Outlook Mobile Access include

- **Managing Email**—OMA enables users to have inbox messages, calendar appointment information, and contact data displayed in single-line text that can be more easily read by limited-lined mobile devices. Additionally, OMA enables users to compose, reply, and forward messages using a single button command of a mobile device. Users also can access other folders within Exchange, search the Global Address List, and search contacts.

- **Managing Calendars**—Outlook Mobile Access enables a user to view and create appointments in Exchange, to accept and decline appointments, and to accept appointments as tentative. Through simplified single button commands, a user can reply to a meeting request.

- **Managing Contacts**—The Outlook Mobile Access client enables users to create, delete, and modify contacts in Exchange. In addition to being able to dynamically query the contacts and the Global Address List, users can also add addresses to their personal contacts in the Exchange Global Address List. Contacts can also be used to begin an email message or to initiate a phone call to the contact.

- **Managing Tasks**—Outlook Mobile Access also enables a user to update tasks, mark tasks as complete, and create notes that can be read, reviewed, and accessed not only by the OMA client but also by other Outlook client systems.

## Minimizing Downloads Through Enhanced Features

As mentioned earlier in this section, because the transmission bandwidth to an HTML Web model device typically is done with limited bandwidth, any ability of the messaging client to decrease information transmission drastically improves the user experience. OMA provides the ability for a user to simply and quickly delete a message without having the contents of the message transmitted to the device, and users can mark a message as unread so that they would be reminded to look at the message at a later date.

Additional OMA functions provide the ability to flag a message for follow-up at a later date, similar to a reminder on a message that may require more attention. And OMA provides the ability for users to have only a portion of information sent to their device, with the option to download more if necessary. Many times, after reading the first few words of a document, a user determines that the content of the message is not urgent and then marks the message for view and access at a later time.

# Designing the Appropriate Use of Exchange 2003 Mobility Capabilities

When implementing Exchange 2003 with the expectation of using the Exchange ActiveSync and Outlook Mobile Access functionality, an Exchange design architect needs to determine the best way to take advantage of the technology. Fortunately, the ActiveSync and Outlook Mobile Access functions are relatively low in bandwidth and processing demands on the Exchange environment, so a single server can typically scale to the initial needs of most organizations. Design and scalability of Exchange 2003 mobility do not necessarily require a lot of performance planning, but you do need the right technology for the expected use.

## Identifying Mobile Devices in Use

In defining the organization's use of mobile devices, such as PDAs and mobile phones, it's helpful to start with understanding what type of devices are currently used in the organization. Because there's been neither industry standardization nor support for common gateway or integration products, most organizations have one of every type of mobile device available in their organization. When trying to support one of every device, the organization is challenged with trying to meet the integration and education needs of several different types of devices, and in many cases trying to support devices that do not necessarily meet the needs of the user(s) in the first place.

So rather than trying to support every type of device in the organization, the initial inventory should be intended at understanding the devices in use. To determine the type of devices used and the basic connectivity, ask users to fill out a questionnaire similar to the one in Table 22.1.

**TABLE 22.1**    Identifying Mobile Devices in Use

| Type of Device in Use | Wireless or WAN Connection? | Cradle or Standalone Connection? |
| --- | --- | --- |
| Pocket PC PDA device | | |
| Pocket PC-enabled mobile phone | | |
| Palm pilot device | | |
| Palm OS-enabled device | | |

**TABLE 22.1    Continued**

| Type of Device in Use | Wireless or WAN Connection? | Cradle or Standalone Connection? |
|---|---|---|
| Palm OS-enabled mobile phone xHTML, cHTML, or other browser-supported mobile phone | | |

Users who are determined to have mobile devices should be asked questions to determine their current use of email, calendaring, or other synchronization of information. Ask users questions similar to the ones shown in Table 22.2.

**TABLE 22.2    Identifying Mobile Device Features**

| Feature | Yes | No |
|---|---|---|
| Do you use your mobile device to check email? | | |
| Do you use your mobile device to send email? | | |
| Do you use your mobile device to view and enter contacts? | | |
| Do you use the calendaring function on your mobile device? | | |
| Do you use notes or to-do lists on your mobile device? | | |

Other questions, such as those in Table 22.3, help determine whether the mobile device should be prioritized for integration to Exchange 2003.

**TABLE 22.3    Identifying Exchange 2003 Integration Potential**

| Task | Description |
|---|---|
| How often do you synchronize your mobile device with your desktop system (once a day, once a week, every hour, continuously)? | |
| If you had the ability to synchronize your device more often, would you? | |
| If you do not synchronize your device regularly, is there an impact on information accuracy or business-critical issues? | |
| Does your mobile device meet your mobile information access needs, or do you need access to information (contacts, tasks, calendar appointments) that you do not have access to today? | |

Frequently determined from the answers to these various questionnaires is that most users have minimal mobile information access needs and use their current mobile device for a limited set of features. So rather than trying to integrate every mobile device in the organization to Exchange 2003 initially, identify the users who have the most need and the most functional use of their mobile device now, and add those users to the first round of Exchange 2003–integrated devices. Then add additional users in waves, based on need and anticipated value received from the integration.

Quite commonly, users aren't happy with the device they are using, and connecting their device to Exchange 2003 will still not improve the device or how they use it. So rather than integrating devices that do not meet the need of the users, wait until other users get functional use out of Exchange 2003, and consider recommending a standardization of future mobile devices throughout the organization, based on the successful use by the first few waves of users.

## Choosing the Right Mobile Solution

After interviewing users in the organization about their use of mobile devices, you might find that certain devices meet user needs and other devices do not. There are frequently two types of users: those that are heavy email users and those that are heavy phone users. Trying to make a phone user into a mobile email user, or vice versa, usually does not result in improved user satisfaction.

A mobile phone with 3–4 8-character lines and a numeric phone keyboard is not a device that best suits someone that needs extensive email capabilities. A Pocket PC device that has full Outlook capabilities but does not have public mobile wireless access also lacks appropriate functionality.

Exchange 2003 has the tools and the functionality to meet the needs of organizations, so it's up to the organization to match users with appropriate devices that can then connect to the fully equipped Exchange 2003 environment.

## Understanding Exchange ActiveSync and OMA

An easy way to understand how Exchange 2003 works for mobile users is to leverage the mobile device emulators and software developer's kits for Pocket PC and HTML-based mobile phone units. It's a lot easier and a lot cheaper to download the emulation tools than to buy hardware, set up mobile services, and do initial feature and function testing on real devices.

For Pocket PC functionality testing, Microsoft has a Pocket PC developer's kit that comes with a full functioning Pocket PC emulator. You can download the emulator from Microsoft's home page at http://www.microsoft.com/windowsmobile/developers/ default.mspx.

The software developer's kit, also known as the Windows Mobile 2003 SDK, comes with an emulation program, similar to the one shown in Figure 22.2, that enables you to connect to a network, establish an Exchange ActiveSync connection to Exchange 2003, and synchronize email, calendar, contacts, and other information between Exchange 2003 and this Pocket PC–emulated device.

The Pocket PC emulator requires the installation of eMbedded Visual C++ 4 along with eMbedded Visual C++ Service Pack 4 or higher to run. The emulator can be installed on any workstation connected to the network that the Exchange 2003 server is connected to, or the emulator can be set to VPN from another segment into an RRAS server on the network where the Exchange 2003 server resides.

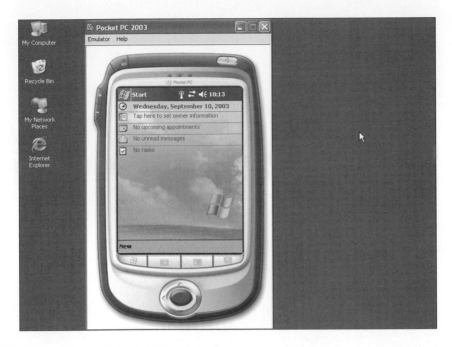

**FIGURE 22.2**    Microsoft Pocket PC emulator.

Similar functionality can be emulated for a mobile phone. Openwave makes a mobile phone simulator, shown in Figure 22.3, that can be downloaded free from its Web site:

```
http://developer.openwave.com/dvl/tools_and_sdk/openwave_mobile_sdk/
phone_simulator/index.htm
```

This emulator enables the testing of mobile phone access to Exchange 2003. An organization can get familiar with how a mobile phone works with Exchange 2003—relative to screens, menu commands, message reply, attachment handling, and other functionality—which might take several weeks with a physical mobile phone.

With an emulator on a workstation, basic connectivity, wireless phone connectivity, and other infrastructure testing is eliminated, thus enabling the Exchange administrator to focus on features and functionality. After the basic features and functions of HTML-based Exchange access are understood, the organization can then make the decision to rent, purchase, and evaluate mobile phone connectivity to Exchange.

## Active Prototype and Pilot Testing of Exchange Mobility

The active prototype and pilot testing phase of Exchange mobility involves actual testing of mobile devices to an Exchange 2003 server. Because basic features and functionality were tested with the emulators, the knowledge learned from software emulation enables the evaluator to better translate the basic functionality knowledge into the specific phone or PDA device. This minimizes the fumbling around of device features and enables the individual to better test the true functionality of the device.

**FIGURE 22.3**    Openwave mobile phone simulator.

The challenge introduced at this phase is physical connectivity of the device to the local area network or to the public network. Whereas the emulators were typically tested right on the network backbone, from a system such as a desktop or laptop already successfully communicating on the network, a real-world test of a device is usually over some wireless network connection. A number of challenges can prevent a user from successfully testing the system: IP address allocation, proper routing of information between device to server, and routing from server to device. Even firewalls and other security devices can prevent a newly connected mobile device from successfully sending and receiving information over the network. In time, the administrator will isolate the problem; fortunately with some testing of the emulators, the tester will at least know the basics of what to try and what to test after the physical connections are established.

## Organizational Scalability of Exchange Mobility

The testing of an emulator—or even a couple of devices—does not necessarily test the full functionality or scalability of the Exchange 2003 network environment. As noted earlier in this chapter, the use of these mobile devices generates very low network and server performance bandwidth demands, and it is actually not too difficult to leverage dozens, if not hundreds, of mobile users off a single Exchange 2003 server, which usually far exceeds the initial prototype testing and pilot phase of most organizations.

For most organizations, the initial phase involves just a handful of users. Even when 5–10 users are involved in a pilot phase, their usage and traffic demands on the Exchange environment is negligible. The level that an organization must start considering performance and bandwidth demands is when the organization exceeds 200–300 simultaneous mobile connections. When the potential server access demand exceeds around 200 simultaneous mobile connections, an additional server should be considered. An additional server may be needed when there is fewer than 200–300 simultaneous mobile connections when the server is also acting as a Global Catalog look-up server, voicemail integration server, private and public folder access server, or an Outlook Web Access server. When additional server services are added to a system, an organization might need to consider moving the Outlook mobile functionality to another server system.

# Using Exchange Mobility for the Mobile Executive

When looking at various scenarios for mobile user access, the mobile executive frequently comes to mind as an individual that can benefit from real-time access to calendar, contacts, and office communications. Prior to Exchange 2003, many executives carried around a mobile phone or a PDA; however, the devices were rarely synchronized on a regular basis, causing calendars on the PDA to be drastically different from the executive's real calendar.

By having Exchange 2003 provide real-time synchronization of information, executives can always look at the most current version of their calendar, and the assistant back at the office has to spend less time adjusting appointments after conflicts are determined.

## Technologies Used by Mobile Executives

Frequently a mobile executive uses a mobile phone to keep in contact with the office or to communicate with other managers or clients. The executive also needs access to up-to-date calendar information and contact information. Some executives add to basic email, calendar, contact, and office communications with real-time email access, using devices such as Research in Motion's Blackberry device, or with a pager and accessible mobile phone. All this functionality leads the executive to have to carry around 2–3 different devices, none of which have the most current information.

## Achieved Benefits by Executives

The benefit of leveraging the mobile capabilities of Exchange is the ability for executives to have the most up-to-date information on their Pocket PC devices without the need to contact their assistant or make last-minute changes to avoid conflicts. Exchange 2003 mobility simplifies the process organizations must go through to connect users to the office network. These benefits improve time to implement and cross-training turnaround, which ensures a more reasonable expectation for accessing the information.

# Replacing Laptops with Mobile Pocket Devices

Many users in organizations have a laptop computer for the sole purpose of checking emails, contacts, and calendars; however, they find it time-consuming to turn on the computer, wait for it to boot up, and then launch Outlook to finally check their calendar. Although a laptop is relatively easy to set up and provides full mobile access to information, laptops are rarely connected on a full-time basis. Users still need to plug in to a phone line to dial up and synchronize their system, or find a high-speed Ethernet or wireless LAN connection to link to their network.

## Technologies Used for Mobile Laptop Users

Pocket PC devices with mobile LAN or WAN connections can provide these types of users with access to their email, calendar, contacts, and other business-critical information with a much smaller device to carry around and at a fraction of the cost. With the instant-on capabilities of the Pocket PC devices and the ability to connect to a public wireless network similar to those used by mobile phones, a Pocket PC device can provide even better access and connectivity to information.

Of course, every organization still has its power users who want or need a full laptop computer with their files and other information. With the ability to read emails, use Word documents, easily make minor edits to documents, view or play PowerPoint presentations, watch or display videos, listen to MP3 files, and other tasks on a Pocket PC device, however, the small instant-on wireless connected devices might be a perfect replacement for many laptop users.

## Achieved Benefits by Mobile Laptop Users

Users who find the functionality of the Pocket PC device meets their needs can frequently eliminate their need for a laptop computer, pager, PDA, cell phone, and wireless email device—such as a BlackBerry—and consolidate all the tasks into a simple Pocket PC–enabled mobile phone.

# Leveraging a Low-Cost PDA Instead of an Expensive Tablet

With the release of the tablet PC in the past several years, many organizations have been reconsidering the use of pen-based technology for business applications. Although pen technologies have been used for years in hospitals, warehouses, and freighting companies, the devices have been focused at very specific tasks in a limited number of industries. However with tablet PCs, an organization can build forms in Microsoft Word or Access and can easily have users fill them in using a pen input device without complicated programming and application development.

Unfortunately, tablet PCs are typically more expensive than normal laptop computers, increasing the cost of input device computing. So the lowering of application cost is transferred to a higher cost per unit of the devices placed in the field.

## Technologies Used for Pocket PC Mobility

Because the Pocket PC device includes Pocket Word, Pocket Access, and Pocket Excel, and has other full application functionality, the pen input function of the Pocket PC can be leveraged for many functions for which dedicated pen-based systems or expensive tablet PC systems have been considered. A form created in Microsoft Word can be transferred to a Pocket PC device, and a user can use the pen to fill in the form and write in comments.

Through integrated wireless LAN and WAN connections on the Pocket PC, a user can transmit information from the Pocket PC over simple Exchange 2003 messaging to a central depository of information.

### Achieved Benefits of Pocket Device Use

Using a Pocket PC device instead of a more expensive laptop, tablet PC, or proprietary pen system, an organization can get a low-cost input system, wireless mobility, easy access to information, and simple mobile data entry. Faster application-creation time and lower-cost input translates to a faster return on investment and an easier way for the organization to leverage the technology into meeting its business needs.

## Summary

Microsoft's strategy on mobility has drastically improved with the release of Exchange 2003, because organizations can now provide several different ways for users to access Exchange information rather than a single Outlook client method, as has been the case in the past. However, because users can access Exchange using a variety of different methods and protocols is not a good reason for all the methods to be activated and used.

Exchange ActiveSync, built in to Exchange 2003, provides an organization the ability to eliminate having their desktop computer systems on all the time. By centralizing synchronization to a server-based component, an organization can now eliminate the need for individual systems with cradles attached to an environment where users can connect to Exchange ActiveSync through Ethernet connections, wireless LAN connections, wireless public access network connections, or even over VPN from another network location.

Exchange 2003 also integrates full support for HTML-Web–based access to Exchange content, thus enabling users with mobile phones to access their Exchange information. Although a mobile phone is not the best device for large extensive emails, by connecting the mobile phone to Exchange mobile access, an organization can simplify its support for email access if users want access only to their contacts, calendar, or other basic information.

In many cases, there is no additional hardware needed to begin using the mobility functions of Exchange 2003, and as the organization needs to scale its use of Exchange mobility, it can add another server to the environment.

## Best Practices

The following are best practices from this chapter:

- Choose the right mobile solution for the right user. No one solution fits all.

- Organizations where users might need extensive email and attachment viewing might consider using a Pocket PC–enabled device.

- Emulators, such as the Pocket PC or the Openwave mobile phone, are easy to set up and can test the functionality of Exchange 2003 mobility without the addition of specialized hardware devices.

- When choosing a mobile access method, a user who frequently uses a mobile phone for communications and wants to limit the number of devices carried around should consider the HTML-Web–based access to Exchange 2003 information.

- Organizations might find that users who currently carry around three to four devices, such as a mobile phone, pager, PDA, and wireless email system, can consolidate to a single Pocket PC mobile phone device that satisfies several needs.

- An organization should not open the pilot testing use of Exchange 2003 mobility devices to all employees, but rather test the functionality with a handful of employees who can then build on best practices of the organization and implement the mobile solution immediately throughout the organization.

- Use Pocket PC devices to replace more expensive tablet PC devices or proprietary pen-based systems that require custom programming. Pocket PC devices can leverage standard Microsoft Word forms and Microsoft Access data entry systems.

- Users who have a mobile phone, PDA, pager, and wireless email device, such as BlackBerry, might find that a Pocket PC device can provide at least as much functionality.

# CHAPTER 23

# Implementing Mobile Synchronization in Exchange Server 2003

**IN THIS CHAPTER**

• Preparing for Mobility in an Exchange 2003 Environment

• Installing an Exchange Server 2003 Server for Mobile Access

• Migrating from Microsoft Mobile Information Server

• Configuring Mobile Exchange Features

With email being critical to business communications, organizations not only want access to their messages, calendar appointments, and contacts at their office computers and home systems, but also from their mobile devices like cell phones and PDA devices. Microsoft Exchange 2003 includes the synchronization of mobile devices. In fact, Exchange 2003 Service Pack 2 includes the ability of maintaining a persistent IP address so a mobile device can continuously synchronize with Exchange instead of requiring a manual or semiautomated request for synchronization. This chapter addresses the options and procedures for enabling and configuring mobile synchronization to Exchange.

## Preparing for Mobility in an Exchange 2003 Environment

The ability to synchronize Pocket PC devices and access Exchange information from a mobile phone no longer needs to be a planned and budgeted decision. It can be just the decision to enable mobile access for mobile devices. Exchange 2003, both the Standard Edition and Enterprise Edition of the server software, fully support the connectivity and synchronization of Pocket PC–enabled devices and access by mobile phone devices. As with any technology that comes free and built in, the key is not how to install the software, but rather how to configure it properly and optimize the configuration to meet the needs of the organization.

## Understanding ActiveSync Versus Outlook Mobile Access

Exchange 2003 mobility includes two separate components, Exchange ActiveSync and Outlook Mobile Access. Exchange ActiveSync is used to synchronize Pocket PC–enabled devices with Exchange data such as email messages, calendar appointments, and contacts. Normally when users with a Pocket PC device want to synchronize their information, they have to place their device in a cradle connected to their desktop computer. Not only does the cradle minimize the user's ability to truly be mobile, it usually means that the calendar and information on the device is not in sync with the information being managed and accessed by others in the organization. Many users of Palm PDAs and early Pocket PC devices complained that they received dozens of appointment conflicts and missed critical information because their mobile device was not updated to the server at the office. For many mobile users, the ability to have an up-to-date calendar or to receive email messages wirelessly required the purchase and use of yet another mobile device, such as a Research in Motion (RIM) Blackberry. However, with full mobile synchronization capabilities of using Exchange 2003 ActiveSync, a mobile Pocket PC user can have real-time synchronization to Exchange data.

The Outlook Mobile Access component built in to Exchange 2003 provides the capability of a mobile phone to access Exchange information using real-time access. With a wireless phone that supports the Wireless Application Protocol (WAP) 2.x or a device that supports XHTML browser access, a mobile phone user can request access to an Exchange 2003 server to view email messages, calendar appointments, and contacts. With Outlook Mobile Access supporting full HTML browsers and i-Mode devices built in to mobile phones and personal digital assistants (PDA), users have flexibility in choosing the type of device they use to access their Exchange information.

> **NOTE**
>
> Users in Japan using Compact HTML (CHTML) can also access Exchange 2003 Outlook Mobile Access to view emails, calendar appointments, and contacts.

## Functionality in Exchange 2003

The mobile functionality for support for Pocket PC synchronization and mobile phone access used to require an organization to purchase the Microsoft Mobile Information Server (MMIS) product as an add-in to Exchange 2000. However, all of the mobile functionality of MMIS is now built directly into Exchange 2003, and the functions have been enhanced.

Simply by installing Exchange 2003, Pocket PC users can immediately configure their Pocket PC device to specify the Exchange 2003 Server as the host server, and the Pocket PC will begin synchronizing mail, calendar, and contacts.

## Designing and Planning a Mobile Access Exchange Environment

The designing and planning process for mobility in Exchange Server 2003 is dependent on the number of servers, location of servers, and security desired in the configuration. In its simplest configuration, a single Exchange 2003 server can act as the mailboxes server, also known as the *back-end server functions*, and as the interface to client systems, known as the *front-end server functions*.

For a small organization with fewer than 50 users all located in a single site, the organization can easily have a single Exchange 2003 server act as the front-end and back-end server. The server can host the mailboxes and be the connection point where users log on and access their mail.

When an organization has multiple locations that span across a wide distance, which could cause degrading, the organization may choose to have one or more Exchange servers in each location. This enables users in one site to access the server closest to their site, and users in another site to access the server closest to them. The two servers can be connected to flow mail between the two locations; however, the users effectively connect to the server closest to them. In this particular case, the organization could have one server in one site acting as the front-end and back-end server, and another server in another site acting as the front-end and back-end server for that site.

An organization may choose to split the front-end services from the back-end services, thus having two separate servers for a single site. The decision to have a dedicated front-end server from a back-end server is a choice of security and scalability. From a security perspective, the organization would expose the front-end server to the Internet for remote mobile access. The organization would secure and protect the back-end server because it has the mailboxes that hold data that might be confidential or require access restrictions. This splitting of the front-end and back-end servers creates a barrier between the two servers that can enable better management of information.

The other reason for having a separate front-end server is to enable scalability for front-end connectivity. If an organization has hundreds of users with very small mailboxes, the organization might *need* only a single back-end mailbox server, but might *choose* to have two to three front-end servers to host the client-to-server connectivity. An organization can load-balance the front-end servers so that the messaging administrators can manage the incoming access to the server in a way that optimizes the connection between users and servers.

In the end, an organization can have one server acting as both the front-end and back-end server, or the organization might choose to have multiple front-end/back-end combination servers for users, which might span several sites in the organization. An organization that wants to optimize the performance of front-end communications might choose to split the front-end from the back-end server, and then have several front-end servers available to load-balance incoming user connectivity.

## Optimizing the Number of Front-End Servers

The correct number of front-end and back-end servers varies based on the size, number of locations, and access demands of each organization. If the decision on the number of locations and placement of servers based on the number of sites has already been made, the decision about how to scale front-end servers for mobility becomes the resulting decision. Exchange 2003 mobility connections to Pocket PC and mobile Web devices is a function of concurrent access. Even though an organization has 500 users—all with mobile devices—the likelihood that all 500 devices are simultaneously accessing the server is minimal. Even if all 500 devices happen to be connected at the same time, the amount of data transacted by the front-end server is limited.

By using the counters in the MMC performance monitoring tool, an administrator can calculate the load being placed on a server. For monitoring Outlook Mobile Access statistics, Exchange 2003 has the following counters:

- Average Response Time
- Browse Count
- Browse Rate
- Calendar Request Rate
- Contact Request Rate
- Cumulative Time for All Requests
- Cumulative Simultaneous Browses
- HTTP status 100 count
- HTTP status 200 count
- HTTP status 300 count
- HTTP status 400 count
- HTTP status 500 count
- Inbox Request Rate
- Last Response Time
- Maximum Simultaneous Browses
- Task Request Rate
- Total Calendar Requests
- Total Contact Requests
- Total Inbox Requests
- Total Number of Task Requests

Of these counters, the ones to monitor include Average Response Time, Cumulative Simultaneous Browses, Maximum Simultaneous Browses, and Late Response Time.

The Average Response Time and Last Response Time indicates how quickly a request is being served by the Exchange 2003 server, and whether any of the requests are being delayed—typically due to congestion on the server. The Cumulative Simultaneous Browses and Maximum Simultaneous Browses provide comparative information about the number of users accessing the system, both on an ongoing basis and at any given time. With the four counters enabled, the performance tool looks similar to Figure 23.1. By understanding the traffic demands, late requests, and the number of users accessing the system simultaneously, an administrator can provide a basic level of assessment about whether the current server is adequate for the organization or whether an additional server is needed.

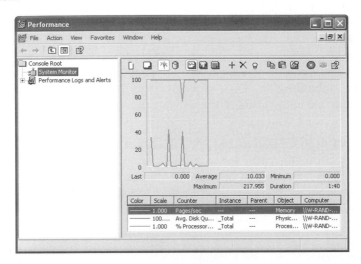

**FIGURE 23.1**   Equivalent site costs on multiple site links.

## Trying Mobility Before Making a True Investment

One of the challenges organizations face in trying to test and evaluate new technologies is the cost of purchasing the devices needed to test the configuration. There are relatively easy ways for an organization to set up and test Pocket PC functionality and mobile phone functionality without having to purchase physical mobile devices.

Microsoft has available a Pocket PC emulator. The emulator provides a fully working Pocket PC 2003 device that can be configured for mobile connections to an Exchange 2003 server. The Pocket PC emulator can be downloaded from Microsoft at http://www.microsoft.com, using keyword pocket pc emulator.

For mobile phone testing, the same requirement applies; most organizations need to have a mobile phone purchased to test the functionality of the technology. Unlike the purchase of many devices, mobile phone services typically require the contracting of at least one year of services. Even if an organization tests the mobility function and does not like how it works, it is obligated to pay for a full year of service or pay an early cancellation penalty. The best way around this is to download mobile phone emulator software, such as the one from OpenWave (http://www.openwave.com), using keyword search phone simulator. OpenWave provides an emulation tool that enables users to establish a connection to Windows 2003.

# Installing an Exchange Server 2003 Server for Mobile Access

The installation of an Exchange 2003 server for mobile connectivity does not require the installation of any special server, software, update, or gateway product. Exchange 2003 has mobility built in to the Exchange 2003 software. By simply installing Exchange 2003 on a server as part of an upgrade from Exchange 5.5 or Exchange 2000, or as part of a completely clean installation, the mobility functions are automatically included. See Chapter 3, "Installing Exchange Server 2003," for the installation of Exchange Server 2003, or Chapters 15, "Migrating from Exchange v5.5 to Exchange Server 2003," and 16, "Migrating from Exchange 2000 to Exchange Server 2003," on the migration from Exchange 5.5 or Exchange 2000. These chapters cover the process of installing or migrating the basic Exchange 2003 server software.

## Creating a Separate Front-End Server for Mobile Connections

As noted in the section "Preparing for Mobility in an Exchange 2003 Environment," earlier in this chapter, an organization may choose to split the front-end client access server from the back-end database server functions. To separate the front-end and back-end server functions follow these steps:

1. Install a new Exchange Server 2003 into an existing Exchange site.

2. Set the properties of the new Exchange server to be a front-end server only.

3. Clean up nonessential components on the new front-end server to prepare it to be just a front-end server.

### Setting an Exchange Server to Be a Front-End Server Only

To be configured as a front-end server to an existing Exchange 2003 site, the server should be configured to be a front-end server only. By default, an Exchange server is activated to be both a front-end and a back-end server. To make a server into a dedicated front-end server, do the following:

1. On an Exchange 2003 server that has already been joined to the site, open the Exchange System Manager.

2. Traverse through the Exchange System Manager through Administrative Groups, Administrative Group Name, Servers.

3. Right-click on the server and select Properties.

4. Click on This Is a Front-End Server, as shown in Figure 23.2.

5. Select OK.

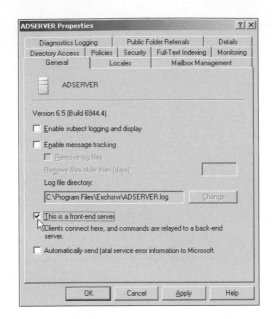

**FIGURE 23.2**    Selecting a server as a front-end server.

### Removing Information Stores

After a server is set to be a front-end server, certain unneeded functions can be deleted from the server. This not only makes the server run more efficiently, but it also makes the server more secure. One of the tasks of cleaning up an Exchange front-end server is to remove the information store and databases.

To delete the information stores on a front-end server, do the following:

1. Click on Start, Programs, Microsoft Exchange, System Manager.

2. Navigate to Administrative Groups, Administrative Group Name, Servers, Server Name, Storage Groups.

3. Right-click on Mailbox Store and Choose Delete.

4. Click Yes.

5. Click OK.

6. Using Windows Explorer, navigate to the directory where the databases are stored and manually delete the database files.

> **CAUTION**
>
> Before deleting any database or information store, unless you are positive the database or information store is completely empty and unused, you might want to do a full backup of the database, store, and system, in case a user's mailbox was inadvertently hosted on the system.

23

Sometimes during an early implementation of Exchange, an organization might start with one or two servers in a pilot test environment. A mailbox stored on one of the test servers might have eventually become the front-end server for the organization. It's always safer to back up a system than to make assumptions and regret the decision later. Using the NTBackup utility covered in Chapter 31, "Backing Up the Exchange Server 2003 Environment," is a quick way to back up a system.

## Adding Additional Front-End Servers for Scalability

After the first dedicated Exchange 2003 front-end server has been added to the site, additional servers can be added by following the same procedure as noted in the section "Installing an Exchange Server 2003 Server for Mobile Access," earlier in this chapter. The addition of front-end servers provides better scalability for client systems to connect to their Exchange mailboxes. The front-end server by default can host any Exchange client, not just Pocket PC and Outlook Mobile Access clients. The front-end servers are also full hosts for Outlook Web Access clients, full Outlook clients, and POP3 and IMAP clients. This provides the organization with the ability to add and remove front-end servers as the client demand increases or decreases in the organization. Because front-end servers do not host mailbox or information routing functions, they are much easier to add and remove than full Exchange servers participating in a site.

## Configuring Firewall Ports to Secure Communications

There are several ways a mobile client can connect to a dedicated Exchange front-end server or Exchange server acting as both the front-end and back-end server. The client system can connect to the Exchange server in the following ways:

- Securely over Port 443, using Secure Sockets Layer (SSL)

- Unsecured over Port 80

- Connected through a VPN client

Of these three methods, the preferred method is to use a secured SSL connection over Port 443. The SSL connection provides both security and the fastest performance. An unsecured connection minimizes the configuration task of installing a certificate on the Exchange server for SSL communications and is simpler to configure; however, without encrypted communications, traffic between the mobile device and the Exchange server is being transmitted in a format that can be intercepted and deciphered by any individual with a radio frequency packet analyzer.

A VPN connection from a mobile device to an Exchange server can leverage existing VPN technologies implemented in an organization; however, the overhead of the VPN client can reduce performance by 5%–15%. Because many of the public wireless services transmit at rates less than 30–50Kbps, the 5%–15% degradation in performance caused by a VPN client can impact the user experience.

By enabling SSL and using SSL encryption between the mobile device and Exchange 2003, an organization can optimize performance while maintaining a secured connection.

If SSL is used, Port 443 should be enabled through the firewall to the Exchange front-end server. If no encryption will be enabled, only standard Port 80 is enabled. If a VPN connection is created, that establishes a connection from the client to the Microsoft Routing and Remote Access (RRAS) server that will then enable the VPN client to route to the Exchange 2003 server for client access.

# Migrating from Microsoft Mobile Information Server

If an organization already has the Microsoft Mobile Information Server (MMIS) installed as part of an Exchange 2000 mobile-enabled environment, the migration path to Exchange 2003 is pretty clear: There is no migration path. The organization has two options to replace Microsoft Mobile Information Server with Exchange 2003. One option is to install Exchange 2003 on a new server and migrate mailboxes from the old MMIS-enabled Exchange 2000 server to the new Exchange 2003 server. Or the organization can uninstall MMIS from the Exchange 2000 server and then do an in-place upgrade to Exchange 2003 on that server.

## Installing Mobile Information Server from Scratch

The more dependable and preferred method of migrating off Microsoft Mobile Information Server to Exchange 2003 is to just start from scratch with a new server, the non-upgrade approach. In this scenario, the existing Exchange 2000 server with MMIS installed remains in the Exchange site. A new Exchange 2003 is installed and joined to the existing Exchange site. Mailboxes are then moved, using the Mailbox Move function in the Exchange Services Manager tool to move mailboxes off the old Exchange 2000 server with MMIS to the new Exchange 2003 server.

This non-upgrade approach of moving mailboxes from an Exchange 2000 server with MMIS to Exchange 2003 enables the administrators of an organization to simply move users' mailboxes off an old server to the new server. There are no conversions of mail, and the mailboxes are migrated in real time with little or no interruption of service to users because mailboxes can be migrated in the middle of a production day.

> **NOTE**
>
> Although mailboxes can be migrated in the middle of a production day, the Mailbox Move process will not move a mailbox in use. Move mailboxes when users are not logged in to the system. This can be done at a time when a user is out to lunch or otherwise not expecting to use Outlook for a period of time. If you attempt to move a mailbox while the mailbox is in use, the Exchange server will wait until the user exits his or her mail client (such as Outlook) and then automatically begin the mailbox move process from the old server to the new server.
>
> Any time a server is added to an Exchange site, or mailboxes are moved from server to server, the Exchange environment should be properly backed up and information validated to ensure that a clean backup has been secured.

After a user's mailbox has been migrated from the old Exchange 2000 server running MMIS to the new Exchange 2003 server, the user now has full mobile access through the Exchange 2003 mobility functions rather than the older MMIS mobility functions. All sequences and processes for the client remain the same; however, because of improvements in compression and algorithms that prioritize the replication of information more effectively in Exchange 2003, the user will experience much better performance. More details on performing a server-to-server migration using the move-mailbox method of migration is covered in Chapter 16.

## Replacing an Existing Mobile Information Server

The other method of replacing the Microsoft Mobile Information Server on an Exchange 2000 server with Exchange 2003 is to do an in-place upgrade from Exchange 2000 to Exchange 2003. This process requires the MMIS software to be uninstalled from the Exchange 2000 server before proceeding with the Exchange 2003 in-place upgrade. To uninstall MMIS, after conducting a full backup for normal best-practice safety purposes, select Start, Settings, Control Panel, Add/Remove Program. Select the Microsoft Mobile Information Server application and click on Remove. This removes the MMIS from the server.

After the MMIS is uninstalled, a server can then be upgraded in place to Exchange 2003. The step-by-step procedure for performing an in-place upgrade from Exchange 2000 to Exchange 2003 is covered in Chapter 16.

> **NOTE**
>
> When a server is being upgraded in place, a full backup should be conducted on the server. This ensures that a safe backup copy is available in the event of a catastrophic failure during the migration process. Because the in-place upgrade provides no easy rollback in the event of a failed upgrade attempt, the Move Mailbox method is the preferred method for improving the integrity of the migration process.

# Configuring Mobile Exchange Features

After an Exchange 2003 server has been installed on the network, the services needed to support mobility are also already installed. By going into the Active Directory Users and Computer utility, an administrator can view the mobility options automatically enabled for a user.

## Viewing Mobile Services

The mobile services are controlled on a user-by-user basis so that an organization can choose to enable or disable mobility on a selected basis. By default, mobility services are enabled for all users. To view the mobile services options available for a user, do the following:

1. Open the Active Directory Users and Computers management tool.

2. Traverse the directory to the user you want and right-click Properties on the user.

3. Click on the Exchange Features tab and a screen similar to the one shown in Figure 23.3 appears.

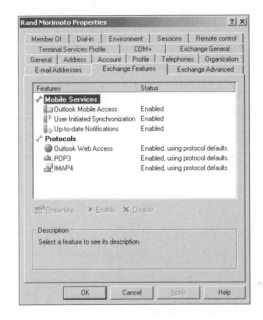

**FIGURE 23.3**    Exchange Features tab in Active Directory Users and Computers.

Notice that on the Exchange Features tab Outlook Mobile Access, User Initiated Synchronization, and Up-to-Date Notifications are automatically enabled. These functions enable users to have access to their mail immediately from a mobile device.

## Configuring Mobile Services

To change the configuration of the mobile services for users, an Exchange administrator can disable the services functions. There are two ways the services can be disabled.

The first way of disabling mobile services is to select the mobile service to be disabled and click on the disable button below the Mobile Services and Protocols window. This method requires the administrator to select each user, select properties, and make the setting changes one setting at a time.

The other way of disabling mobile services that can work for a single user—but also can be used to select multiple users to do a mass disabling of the mobile services—is to use the Exchange Tasks Wizard. To initiate the Exchange Tasks Wizard, do the following:

1. Select the user or users from the Active Directory Users and Computers management tool by holding down the Ctrl key and clicking on the names for which certain mobility functions should be disabled.

2. Right-click and select Exchange Tasks.

3. Click Next on the initial Welcome to the Exchange Task Wizard screen.

4. Select the Configure Exchange Features task and select Next.

5. Select the Exchange features and choose to either enable or disable based on the requirements you want (see Figure 23.4). Select Next to execute the task modifications.

6. Click Finish when done.

This process modifies the Exchange Tasks for the selected users.

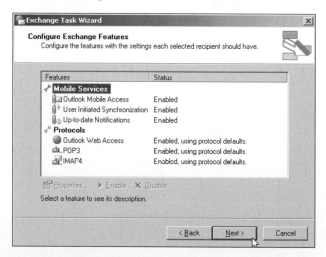

**FIGURE 23.4**    Selecting Exchange task items to modify the settings.

## Configuring Mobile Services Properties for ActiveSync

Besides configuring the mobile services features for each user, the Exchange ActiveSync function can be globally enabled or disabled as a function on the entire Exchange environment. This is done in the Exchange System Manager utility.

The options can be viewed by doing the following:

1. Launch the Exchange System Manager tool.

2. Expand the Global Settings container.

3. Right-click and select Properties on the Mobile Services option. A Mobile Services Properties page is displayed, as shown in Figure 23.5.

4. Select the option for Exchange ActiveSync to enable or disable the function, and then click OK.

**FIGURE 23.5**    Viewing the Exchange Mobile Services Properties page.

The three Mobile Services Properties options are

- **Enable User-Initiated Synchronization**—This option, when enabled, allows a Pocket PC device to synchronize with mailboxes on Exchange. If this option is deselected, users with Pocket PC devices will not be able to synchronize with their mailboxes.

- **Enable Up-to-Date Notifications**—This option uses the new feature in Exchange 2003 that enables an Exchange 2003 server to wake up a Pocket PC device and have the device autoinitiate a synchronization. Because ActiveSync synchronization is a client-initiated task, technically the only way to synchronize with Exchange would be to have a user manually synchronize his or her device, or to create a set schedule where the device autosynchronizes. However, when users are charged for connection time by their service provider, they do not necessarily want to—or should not—synchronize their device unless there is something to synchronize. The up-to-date notifications process initiates the synchronization from a server function when a message or other information needs to be updated with the mobile device.

- **Enable Notifications to User-Specified SMTP Addresses**—By enabling this function, users can use their existing wireless service provider for notifications of changes or updates, rather than having the user autoinitiate synchronization tasks.

> **NOTE**
>
> Exchange 2003 Service Pack 2 has a feature that provides a persistent IP address to mobile devices to maintain continuous synchronization of remote devices. Instead of requiring manual synchronization or semiautomated synchronization, Exchange 2003 SP2 can keep a mobile device up to date.

These mobility property changes can effectively enable the Exchange administrator(s) to disable mobility functions for all users.

### Configuring Mobile Services Properties for OMA

Outlook Mobile Access can also be enabled to allow the Exchange administrator(s) to enable support for the access by OMA devices to Exchange 2003. The two options to enable or disable for Outlook Mobile Access are

- **Enable Outlook Mobile Access**—This option, when enabled, provides access by OMA-supported devices to view their email, calendar, and contact information.

- **Enable Unsupported Devices**—When a device is not directly supported by Exchange 2003 OMA, this option provides best-effort support for nonsupported devices.

By selecting to enable or disable the mobile services properties for OMA, the Outlook Mobile Access functionality can be allowed or disallowed for the entire organization.

## Summary

With mobility built in to Exchange Server 2003, an organization no longer needs to decide whether it wants to add mobility. There are no special servers that need to be added to the network and no special add-ins to load on the servers. Exchange administrators choose whether they want to enable the Pocket PC and the Outlook Mobile Access capabilities for the organization, or to disable the functionality organizationwide for a future date.

The other key decision when rolling out mobility functions across an organization is the infrastructure to support the users connecting to the mobile servers. Front-end servers can be set up and dedicated to enable better scalability and isolation of security to a limited-scope server. For a smaller organization, combining front-end and back-end functions into a single server is frequently more economical and makes a simpler messaging environment. Fortunately with Exchange 2003, an organization can start with a combination front-end/back-end server configuration, and then split off the front-end to a separate server at a later date if the organization wants separate server functions.

The task of providing mobility to users is a relatively simple process, with much of the setup and configuration focused on the mobile devices, covered in Chapter 24, "Configuring Client Systems for Mobility."

# Best Practices

The following are best practices from this chapter:

- If mobility functions are not used in the organization, the Exchange administrator should disable the Pocket PC and the Outlook Mobile Access mobility services from the Exchange Service Manager utility.

- To create a secured mobile connection from mobile devices to the Exchange 2003 server, SSL should be enabled and used rather than the simple Port 80 unsecured access.

- Although a VPN connection can be used to create a secured connection from a mobile device to an Exchange 2003 server, the overhead of the VPN on a relatively low mobile wireless connection could greatly degrade performance. Using SSL for the mobile connection can provide security without all the overhead.

- Organizations with only a few users, or a large organization with a small remote site, may choose to set up Exchange mobility on a single server that hosts both the Exchange mailboxes and acts as the front-end server where users with mobile devices connect for mobile mail, calendar, and contact access.

- Organizations that have a lot of users connecting to their Exchange server(s) should consider splitting off the front-end server functions to a dedicated server. This enables better scalability for user connections to Exchange, and also provides an additional layer of security between user-connected servers and the back-end database housing information.

- Using the Pocket PC 2003 Emulator that is available to be downloaded from Microsoft can help an organization evaluate the functions of Pocket PC mobility and creates a simple way for the organization to test whether mobility and mailbox synchronization is working properly, thus isolating any phone carrier or public wireless network problems that might be preventing successful operations.

- The Pocket PC Emulator can also help an organization train its workforce on how to use mobility functions of the Pocket PC device. The full functions of the mobile device can be run on a workstation or server and displayed on a projection system, or screenshots can be taken for documentation.

- Mobile phone emulators that can be downloaded off the Internet from companies such as OpenWave.com can also simplify the testing process of mobile access. Running OMA functions from an emulator can also simplify the testing, training, and documentation process of validating mobility.

- The simplest way to migrate from Microsoft Mobile Information Server on Exchange 2000 to Exchange 2003 mobility is to add an Exchange 2003 server to an existing Exchange 2000 site and move mailboxes over to the new server. This minimizes the risk of failure of uninstalling MMIS from a server and conducting an in-place upgrade on a production server.

23

# CHAPTER 24

# Configuring Client Systems for Mobility

**IN THIS CHAPTER**

- Identifying Mobile Devices to Be Supported

- Supporting the Pocket PC 2002 Synchronization with Microsoft Exchange 2003

- Supporting Pocket PC 2003 Synchronization with Exchange 2003

- Using the Pocket PC 2002 and Pocket PC 2003

- Working with Smartphones

- Establishing a Link from a Mobile Phone to Exchange 2003

- Using Outlook Mobile Access to Exchange Server 2003

Chapter 22, "Designing Mobility in Exchange Server 2003," provided an overview of the mobility options for Exchange 2003, and Chapter 23, "Implementing Mobile Synchronization in Exchange Server 2003," focused on the server setup for mobile devices. This chapter keys in on the client components for mobility, namely the configuration and operation of Pocket PC–enabled devices using Exchange 2003 ActiveSync and mobile phone devices using Outlook Mobile Access.

## Identifying Mobile Devices to Be Supported

With the release of Exchange 2003, organizations no longer have to purchase add-on products to support access of emails, calendars, contacts, and other Exchange information from Pocket PC or mobile phone devices. As long as a mobile device is supported by Exchange 2003, it just needs to be configured properly and the device will connect to Exchange.

Over the past few years, however, there have been many different versions of the Windows CE and Pocket PC operating system and dozens of different mobile phone/mobile Web access standards. Those supported by Exchange 2003 and highlighted in this chapter include

- Pocket PC 2002 (using ActiveSync)

- Pocket PC 2003 (using ActiveSync)

- Smartphone 2003 (using ActiveSync)

- xHTML used in WAP 2.x devices (using Outlook Mobile Access)

- cHTML (using Outlook Mobile Access)
- HTML browser-based (using Outlook Mobile Access or Outlook Web Access)

Windows CE 2.0 or CE 3.0 devices supported Outlook synchronization, but the operating system supported only cradle-based synchronization. An option that was added in the Pocket PC 2002 and Pocket PC 2003 operating system was a tab that enabled the user to enter the IP address or DNS name of an Exchange server to access. Windows CE 2.0 and 3.0 devices associated with only a PC connection. A user who has an Internet-connected Windows CE device or a CE device that has network or wireless connectivity, however, *can* access Exchange 2003 using the HTML browser-based access. The user with those devices performs a real-time lookup and view of email messages, calendar appointments, contacts, and other Exchange information. The difference is in the ability to synchronize the information for offline access that is built in to the Pocket PC 2002 and 2003 versions of the operating system.

Other organizations might have devices running on the Palm operating system, such as Palm PDAs, Sony Clie, or Handspring devices. The Palm OS devices do not directly synchronize with Exchange 2003, although third-party gateway products have existed since Exchange 5.5 and Exchange 2000; these gateway products connect to an Exchange 2003 environment for synchronization of the Palm OS devices. Just like the support for the Windows CE 2.0 and 3.0 devices, Palm OS devices can access Exchange 2003 email, calendar, and contacts using the Outlook Mobile Access or Outlook Web Access functionality. Using the Web access–based methods to communicate, a Palm OS device can have real-time access to Outlook information; however, the information is not synchronized for offline access.

## Supporting the Pocket PC 2002 Synchronization with Microsoft Exchange 2003

The Pocket PC 2002 operating system was one of the first Windows CE family of products that supported mobile communications. The hardware devices, such as the Compaq iPaq, had either PCMCIA wireless adapters or built-in 802.11 and Bluetooth wireless communications to the devices. Later versions of the Pocket PC 2002 devices came with mobile phone connections for a combination of mobile phone and wireless LAN connectivity.

A three-step process enabled a Pocket PC 2002 device to synchronize information between the device and Exchange 2003:

1. Configure the Pocket PC 2002 network connection.

2. Configure the Pocket PC 2002 ActiveSync parameters.

3. Choose to synchronize the Pocket PC 2002 device to Exchange.

For network or Exchange administrators who want to test out the functionality of Pocket PC 2002 mobility to Exchange, there is a Pocket PC 2002 emulator that is freely downloadable from Microsoft and that has all the functions of the standard Pocket PC 2002 device. The emulator helps an administrator get familiar with setup and configuration without having to actually buy a device or work through unique driver download configurations for mobile connections or wireless adapters.

## Installing the Pocket PC 2002 Emulator

For administrators who want to test the functionality of Pocket PC 2002 emulation, this section focuses on the download and installation of the emulator on a standard Windows workstation. After it's installed on a Windows workstation, the emulator can then be configured and tested against the Exchange 2003 environment.

### Requirements to Run the Pocket PC 2002 Emulator

To install the eMbedded Visual Tools 3.0, Microsoft states that its requirement is a system running Windows 98 Second Edition or higher, 150MHz or faster, 32MB or more of available memory, 720MB of available disk space, network adapter, VGA video, and a mouse. The emulator is a pretty basic tool and does not require a high processing system; however, it does load a fair amount of code into memory, so typically a P3 or faster Windows 2000 or XP workstation with 192MB RAM is recommended. The host workstation also needs a network adapter connected to a network connection that will access the Exchange 2003 server.

It is typically recommended to first test the Pocket PC emulation on an internal backbone segment to make sure the connection to the Exchange server is not blocked by external firewalls, routers, or other external perimeter devices. The host workstation needs network connectivity, and although it's not a requirement to run the Pocket PC 2002 emulator, the system should be able to connect to the Exchange server using Outlook Web Access or from an Outlook client. This ensures that the host workstation has the appropriate network connectivity for the emulator to connect to the server.

> **NOTE**
>
> The Pocket PC 2002 emulator does not require its own IP address on the network, and there is no network connectivity configuration required on the emulator. The emulator simply passes through the existing LAN connection of the host workstation. If the workstation has connectivity to Exchange for Outlook or Outlook Web Access, that same connection is used by the emulator.

### Downloading the Pocket PC 2002 Emulator

The Pocket PC 2002 emulator, also known as the Pocket PC 2002 Software Development Kit (SDK), is a free download from Microsoft. It is included in the eMbedded Visual Tools 3.0—2002 Edition. When the eMbedded Tools 3.0 is installed, the SDK emulator for both Pocket PC 2002 and Smartphone 2002 are also installed, with the core driver and libraries needed to run the software development kit. You will find the eMbedded Tools 3.0 on http://www.microsoft.com (search on `embedded tools 3.0`); the `evt2002web_min.exe` file is 210MB.

**NOTE**

If you already have the eMbedded Visual Tools 3.0 on your host workstation, you can just down-load and install the Pocket PC 2002 emulator. Go to http://www.microsoft.com, search on the words Pocket 2002 SDK, and download the ppc2002_sdk.exe file (66MB).

### Installing eMbedded Visual Tools 3.0 and the Pocket PC 2002 Emulator

After downloading the eMbedded Visual Tools 3.0, install the Embedded Visual Tools application. Use the following steps:

1. Launch the evt2002web_min.exe executable for the eMbedded Visual Tools 3.0 to install it on the host workstation. This extracts the files to a temporary directory and launches the installation wizard.

2. The installation wizard displays a welcome screen; click Next to continue.

3. After reading the end-user license agreement and agreeing to the information, click I Accept the Agreement and then click Next.

4. When prompted for the product license number and user ID, enter the evaluation ID that is noted on the main Web page where you downloaded the eMbedded Visual Tools. The product ID noted is TRT7H-KD36T-FRH8D-6QH8P-VFJHQ. Enter your name and company name so the screen looks similar to Figure 24.1, and then click Next.

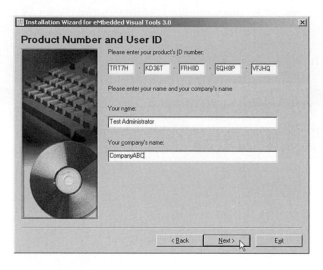

**FIGURE 24.1**    Entering the product ID and username.

5. When prompted, select to install all of the eMbedded tools and then click Next.

> **NOTE**
>
> When installing the eMbedded Visual Tools 3.0, the Pocket PC 2002 and the Smartphone 2002 SDKs are installed by default. This minimizes the need to download and install the emulators separately.

6. Choose a folder you want to install the software in (the default is `c:\Windows CE Tools`) and then click Next.

7. Click OK to pass by the eMbedded tools setup product ID information.

8. Click on Continue when prompted to confirm the installation of the Tools Setup, which includes the eMbedded Visual Basic 3.0, eMbedded Visual C++ 3.0, and Common Components.

9. After the installation of the eMbedded tools, the Pocket PC SDK begins to extract and install. Click on Next at the InstallShield welcome page.

10. Read and accept the license agreement and then click on Next.

11. Enter your name and company name and then click on Next.

12. Select to have a Complete Install and click on Next.

13. Choose to install in the default destination folder and click on Next.

14. Click on Install to complete the installation of the Pocket PC 2002 SDK.

15. When the Pocket PC 2002 SDK has completed its installation, click on Finish, and then the Smartphone 2002 SDK installation begins to extract and install.

16. Click on Next at the InstallShield for the Smartphone 2002 SDK screen.

17. Read and accept the license agreement and then click on Next.

18. Enter your name and company name and then click on Next.

19. Select to have a Complete Install and click on Next.

20. Choose to install in the default destination folder and click on Next.

21. Click on Install to complete the installation of the Smartphone 2002 SDK.

22. When the Smartphone 2002 SDK has completed its installation, click on Finish.

**Launching the Pocket PC 2002 Emulator**

After the installation is complete, the Pocket PC 2002 emulator can be launched. Because this is a Software Development Kit, the launch of the Pocket PC 2002 emulator is done from within the eMbedded Visual Basic 3.0 program. Before the emulator can be launched, the binary emulation image for the proper SDK needs to be selected. To select the binary emulator, perform the following steps:

1. Select Start, Programs, Microsoft Windows SDK for Smartphone 2002, Emulator Binary Switch.

24

2. In the Select SDK window, choose Pocket PC 2002, and then click on OK.

3. When prompted to choose the emulation image, go to

    ```
    c:\Windows CE Tools\wce300\Pocket PC 2002\emulation\English-No Radio
    ```

    Select the `wwenoril.bin` file and click on OK.

After the binary emulation has been selected, the Pocket PC 2002 emulator can be loaded by launching the eMbedded Visual Basic 3.0 program. To launch the emulator, use the following steps:

1. Select Start, Programs, Microsoft eMbedded Visual Tools, eMbedded Visual Basic 3.0.

2. When eMbedded Visual Basic 3.0 loads, from the New Project screen, choose the Windows CE for Pocket PC 2002 icon, as shown in Figure 24.2; then click on Open.

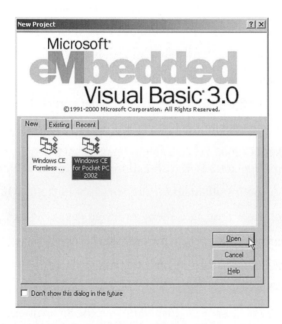

**FIGURE 24.2**    Selecting to open the Pocket PC 2002 emulator.

3. When the Pocket PC 2002 emulator is opened within eMbedded Visual Basic 3.0, select Run, Execute. This launches the emulator, and a screen similar to the one shown in Figure 24.3 appears.

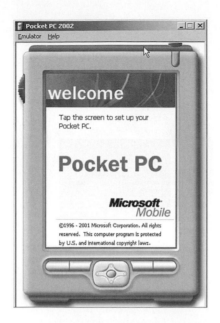

**FIGURE 24.3**    The initial Pocket PC 2002 emulator screen.

The Pocket PC 2002 emulator is now ready to be configured.

## Configuring a Pocket PC 2002 Device for Network Connectivity

After the Pocket PC 2002 emulator has been installed, or for administrators that have a Pocket PC device in front of them, the first thing to do is configure the device for network connectivity. Network connectivity comes in a variety of forms, including the following:

- Pocket PC with an Ethernet adapter or wireless adapter

- Pocket PC with a mobile phone connection to the Internet

- Pocket PC emulator connected to a host workstation

Each configuration is slightly different and is individually highlighted in the next section.

### Configuring a Pocket PC 2002 Device with an Internal Network Adapter

To configure a Pocket PC 2002 device with an internal Ethernet or wireless network adapter, follow these steps:

1. On the Pocket PC device, select Start, Settings, Connections, and then click on the Network Adapters option.

2. Choose the network adapter you want to configure. Figure 24.4 shows the selection of an NE2000 Compatible Ethernet driver.

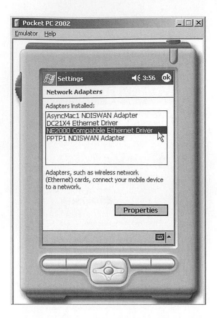

**FIGURE 24.4**    Choosing a network adapter to configure.

3. Click on properties to configure the adapter.

4. Select Use Server-Assigned IP Address If DHCP Is Available on the Network That This Device Will Be Connecting To, or choose Use Specific IP Address and enter a static IP address for the device.

5. If the device is DHCP-configured, skip to step 6; otherwise, click on the Name Servers tab and enter the address for the DNS (and optionally the WINS) servers on the network.

6. Click on OK in the upper-right corner; a notice appears informing you that the adapter will be used. Remove and reinsert the adapter to activate it with the new settings. Click OK to continue.

7. Click OK, and then click on the X in the upper-right corner to complete the network adapter setting.

After the hardware settings on the network adapter have been selected, select the adapter as the default outbound connection. To choose the adapter as the default, use the following steps:

1. Select Start, Settings, Connections, and click on the Connections icon.

2. Make sure that the first option, When Needed, Automatically Connect to the Internet Using These Settings, is set to Work Settings. On the same screen, make sure that the option When Needed, Automatically Connect to Work Using These

Settings and the option My Network Card Connects Are Set to Work, as shown in Figure 24.5.

**FIGURE 24.5**   Choosing the work settings for network connectivity.

3. If a proxy server is used, click on the Modify button to open the Work Settings page.

4. Click on the Proxy Settings tab and click on the This Network Uses a Proxy Server to Connect to the Internet check box. Then enter the name of the proxy server.

5. Click on OK and then on OK again. Click on X in the upper-right corner.

The Pocket PC 2002 device is now configured for network connectivity.

To test whether the Pocket PC 2002 device is working properly, launch Pocket Internet Explorer and confirm whether network connectivity to the Internet is available. To test Internet Explorer, use the following steps:

1. Select Start, Internet Explorer.

2. On the main Internet Explorer home screen, click on the PocketPC.com graphic and then click on the Go to PocketPC.com link toward the bottom of the page.

3. Internet Explorer should traverse the network and provide a Windows Mobile page, assuming the host computer has connectivity to the Internet. If the network segment that the Pocket PC device is on does not have connectivity to the Internet, the Pocket PC device will not have Internet connectivity. Possibly choose an Internet Intranet Web server or other system to check whether the device is communicating properly on the network segment to which it is connected.

### Configuring a Pocket PC 2002 Device with a Mobile Phone Connection

If the Pocket PC 2002 device is a Pocket PC–enabled mobile phone, the service provider of the phone will typically have a GSM or GPRS Internet connection service included with the phone. Follow the instructions provided with the phone to connect the phone to the Internet so that you can effectively surf the Internet with the mobile phone.

Usually the process requires following these steps:

1. Select Start, Settings, Connections, and then click on the Connections icon.

2. For the setting When Needed, Automatically Connect to the Internet Using These Settings, there usually is a pull-down option that says ISP Connection or Internet Provider or GPRS Provider. This varies between mobile phone providers; however, it will likely note that the connection is to the Internet using the mobile phone Internet service connection.

3. Click on OK and then click on the X in the upper-right corner to set the device for Internet connectivity.

To test whether the Pocket PC 2002–enabled mobile phone is working properly, launch Pocket Internet Explorer and confirm whether network connectivity to the Internet is available. To test Internet Explorer, use the following steps:

1. Select Start, Internet Explorer.

2. On the main Internet Explorer home screen, click on the PocketPC.com graphic and then click on the Go to PocketPC.com link toward the bottom of the page.

3. Internet Explorer should traverse the network and provide a Windows Mobile page, assuming the host computer has connectivity to the Internet. If the Pocket PC–enabled mobile phone does not have connectivity to the Internet, check the manual or contact the technical support for the mobile phone to get assistance on connecting the mobile phone to the Internet.

### Configuring a Pocket PC 2002 Emulator

Because the Pocket PC 2002 emulator uses the IP settings built in to the host computer, as long as the host computer has network connectivity, the emulator will have network connectivity. To validate the configuration, use the following steps:

1. Select Start, Settings, Connections, and click on the Connections icon.

2. Make sure that the first option, When Needed, Automatically Connect to the Internet Using These Settings, is set to Work Settings. Additionally, make sure the option When Needed, Automatically Connect to Work Using These Settings and the option My Network Card Connects are set to Work.

---

**NOTE**

No proxy settings should be set on the Pocket PC 2002 emulator, because any proxy settings, DNS settings, or other hardware device settings are taken directly from the host workstation.

---

3. Click on OK and then on OK again. Click on X in the upper-right corner.

The Pocket PC 2002 emulator is now configured for network connectivity.

To test whether the Pocket PC 2002 emulator is working properly, launch Pocket Internet Explorer and confirm whether network connectivity to the Internet is available. To test Internet Explorer, use the following steps:

1. Select Start, Internet Explorer.

2. On the main Internet Explorer home screen, click on the PocketPC.com graphic and then click on the Go to PocketPC.com link toward the bottom of the page.

3. Internet Explorer should traverse the network and provide a Windows Mobile page, assuming the host computer has connectivity to the Internet. If the host computer does not have network connectivity to the Internet, the Pocket PC emulator will not have Internet connectivity either. Possibly choose an Internet Intranet Web server or other system to check whether the device is communicating properly on the network segment to which it is connected.

### Establishing a Connection Between the Pocket PC 2002 and Exchange 2003

After the Pocket PC device has network connectivity, a connection between the device and the Microsoft Exchange server needs to be established. To create the connection, use the following steps:

1. Select Start, ActiveSync to launch the Pocket PC ActiveSync program.

2. Click on Tools at the bottom of the screen, and then click on Options.

3. Click on the Server tab, and for server, enter the DNS name or the IP address of the Exchange server.

4. Click on the Advanced button and enter the logon name, password, and domain of the Outlook/Exchange user account that the Pocket PC device will use to synchronize information. Click to select the Save Password box as the information the password needs to be enabled.

5. Click on OK to go back to the Server screen and choose the options you want to synchronize—such as the Inbox, Calendar, or Contacts—by clicking on the box.

6. Click on OK, and then click on the X in the upper-right corner to save the Exchange server settings.

### Synchronizing Data Between Pocket PC 2002 and Exchange 2003

To synchronize information between the Pocket PC 2002 device and the Exchange 2003 server, use the following steps:

24

1. Select Start, ActiveSync to launch the ActiveSync program.

2. Click on the Sync button to begin synchronization, as shown in Figure 24.6.

**FIGURE 24.6**    Synchronizing the Pocket PC 2002 device with Exchange 2003.

## Supporting Pocket PC 2003 Synchronization with Exchange 2003

When Exchange 2003 started to ship, the Pocket PC 2003 operating system also just started to become available on the market. If an organization has the choice of the Pocket PC 2002 or the Pocket PC 2003 operating system, it should select the Pocket PC 2003 operating system and gain the following advantages:

• Exchange 2003 initiates a sync of information when information becomes available on the Exchange server, such as a new email message or calendar appointment request.

> **NOTE**
>
> The Pocket PC 2002 operation does not support the Exchange 2003 SMS initiation of a synchronization, so Pocket PC 2002 users need to either initiate the sync themselves each time they want to update their information, or schedule the update to occur on a regular basis. Dependent on the frequency of the sync and the service plan with the mobile Internet provider, this continuous synchronization of information can either wear down the battery of the unit or incur connection charges with the Internet provider.

- The Pocket PC 2003 operating system supports the ability to synchronize information without SSL for organizations that might choose to run synchronization unencrypted. The default on the Pocket PC 2002 is always SSL-encrypted.

- The Pocket PC 2003 operating system provides better support for instant messenger, Microsoft Passports, and other network and security functions that are frequently leveraged in mobile communication environments.

The installation and configuration of the Pocket PC 2003–enabled device is similar to that of the Pocket PC 2002 device. Some of the configuration options are slightly different, however, so the following sections cover the installation, configuration, and synchronization specific to Pocket PC 2003 devices.

For network or Exchange administrators who want to test the functionality of Pocket PC 2003 mobility to Exchange, a Pocket PC 2003 emulator is freely downloadable from Microsoft that has all of the functions of the standard Pocket PC 2003 device. The emulator helps an administrator get familiar with setup and configuration without having to actually buy a device or work through unique driver download configurations for mobile connections or wireless adapters.

> **NOTE**
>
> The eMbedded Visual C++ 4.0 for the Pocket PC 2003 emulator and the eMbedded Visual Tools 3.0 used for the Pocket PC 2002 emulator conflict with each other. Effectively, the 4.0 tool over-writes key components of the 3.0 tool that run the Pocket PC 2002 emulator, and the Pocket PC 2002 emulator will not run with the 4.0 tools installed. If you plan to test both Pocket PC 2002 and Pocket PC 2003 emulation, install the eMbedded tools and emulators on separate systems.

## Installing the Pocket PC 2003 Emulator

For administrators who want to test the functionality of Pocket PC 2003 emulation, this section focuses on the download and installation of the emulator on a standard Windows workstation. When installed on a Windows workstation, the emulator can then be configured and tested against the Exchange 2003 environment.

### Downloading the Pocket PC 2003 Emulator

The Pocket PC 2003 emulator is a free download from Microsoft. Go to http://www.microsoft.com, search on the words Pocket 2003 SDK, and download the Microsoft Pocket PC 2003 SDK.msi file (86MB).

In addition to downloading the Pocket PC 2003 emulator, you also need to download a copy of the eMbedded Visual C++ 4.0 and the eMbedded Visual C++ 4.0 Service Pack 4 or higher. The eMbedded Visual C++ 4.0 and Service Pack need to be installed before the SDK emulator to provide the core driver and libraries needed to run the SDK. The eMbedded Visual C++ 4.0 and Service Pack can be found at http://msdn.microsoft.com/mobility/windowsmobile/downloads/default.aspx.

The file eVC4.exe is 235MB, and evc4sp4.exe (Service Pack 4) is 69MB.

## Requirements to Run the Pocket PC 2003 Emulator

To install eMbedded Visual C++ 4.0, Microsoft states its requirement is a system running Windows 2000 or Windows XP, a 450MHz or faster Pentium-II class system, 128–192MB or more of available memory, 200MB of available disk space, network adapter, VGA video, and a mouse. The host workstation needs a network adapter connected to a network connection that will access the Exchange 2003 server.

It is typically recommended to first test the Pocket PC emulation on an internal backbone segment to make sure the connection to the Exchange server is not blocked by external firewalls, routers, or other external perimeter devices. The host workstation needs network connectivity, and although it's not a requirement to run the Pocket PC 2003 emulator, the system should be able to connect to the Exchange server using Outlook Web Access or from an Outlook client. This ensures that the host workstation has the appropriate network connectivity for the emulator to connect to the server.

> **NOTE**
>
> The Pocket PC 2003 emulator does not require its own IP address on the network and there is no network connectivity configuration required on the emulator. The emulator simply passes through the existing LAN connection of the host workstation. If the workstation has connectivity to Exchange for Outlook or Outlook Web Access, that same connection is used by the emulator.

## Installing eMbedded Visual C++ 4.0

After downloading the eMbedded Visual C++ 4.0 and Pocket PC 2003 SDK, the two applications should be installed. To do so, use the following steps:

1. Launch the `eVC4.exe` executable for the eMbedded Visual C++ 4.0 to install it on the host workstation. This extracts the files to a temporary directory (for example, `c:\evc4\`) and launches the installation wizard.

2. Go into the temporary directory and run `setup.exe`. The installation wizard displays a welcome screen; click Next to continue.

3. After reading the end-user license agreement and agreeing to the information, click I Accept the Agreement and then click Next.

4. When prompted for the product license number and user ID, enter the evaluation ID that is noted on the main Web page where you downloaded the eMbedded Visual Tools. The product ID noted is TRT7H-KD36T-FRH8D-6QH8P-VFJHQ.

5. When prompted, select to install all the eMbedded tools and then click Next.

> **NOTE**
>
> Unlike with the eMbedded Visual Tools 3.0 that also installed the Pocket PC 2002 and the Smartphone 2002 SDKs, the eMbedded Visual C++ 4.0 installs only the eMbedded Visual C++ 4.0 tools. Install the Pocket PC 2003 emulator and the Smartphone 2003 emulators separately.

6. Choose a folder you want to install the software in (the default is c:\Windows CE Tools) and then click Next. The Windows CE Platform Manager 4.0 will begin to install.

7. Click OK at the eMbedded tools setup product ID information screen.

8. Click on Continue when prompted to confirm the installation of the eMbedded Visual C++ 4.0 Setup that includes the eMbedded Visual C++ 4.0 and Common Components.

9. After the installation of the eMbedded Visual C++ 4.0 tools, click OK when the setup notes it was completed successfully.

10. The installation wizard for the Standard SDK for Windows CE .NET setup begins to extract and install. Click on Next at the welcome page, and then read and accept the license agreement. Click on Next.

11. Enter your name and company name and then click on Next.

12. Select to have a Complete Install and click on Next.

13. Choose to install in the default destination folder and click on Next.

14. Click on Install to complete the installation of the Standard SDK for Windows CE .NET.

15. When the installation of the Standard SDK for Windows CE .NET has completed its installation, click on Finish.

After the base eMbedded Visual C++ 4.0 has been installed, install eMbedded Visual C++ 4.0 Service Pack 4 or higher. Use the following steps:

1. Run evc4sp4.exe. Choose a directory where you want to expand the files (for example, c:\evcsp4\).

2. Go to the directory you selected, open the DISK1 directory, and run the setup.exe program.

3. At the eMbedded Visual C++ 4.0 SP4 setup welcome screen, click Next.

4. Read and accept the end-user license agreement and click on Next.

5. Click on Install to begin the installation of the Service Pack.

6. When the Service Pack has completed installation, click on Finish.

### Installing the Pocket PC 2003 Emulator

After the eMbedded Visual C++ 4.0 and Service Pack have been installed, install the Pocket PC 2003 SDK. Use the following steps:

1. Launch the Microsoft Pocket PC 2003 SDK.MSI script that you downloaded, which will begin the installation process on your host workstation.

2. At the welcome screen, click on Next.

3. Read the license agreement, select I Accept the Terms in the License Agreement, and click on Next.

4. Confirm your customer information (name and organization name) and then click Next.

5. Select a Complete Installation and then click Next.

6. Click on Next to choose the default destination folders.

7. Click on Install to begin the installation of the Pocket PC 2003 SDK.

8. Click on Finish when completed.

### Launching the Pocket PC 2003 Emulator

After the installation has been completed, the Pocket PC 2003 emulator can now be launched. To launch the Pocket PC 2003 emulator, select Start, Programs, Microsoft Pocket PC 2003 SDK, Pocket PC 2003 Emulator.

> **NOTE**
>
> When you select Start, Programs, Microsoft Pocket PC 2003 SDK, and you do not see a Pocket PC 2003 Emulator icon, as shown in Figure 24.7, confirm that you installed the eMbedded Visual C++ 4.0 Service Pack before installing the Pocket PC 2003 SDK. Missing that step is a common problem with all of the downloads that need to be installed. If the icon does not exist, uninstall the Pocket PC 2003 SDK (from the Start, Settings, Control Panel, Add/Remove Programs tool), reinstall the eMbedded Visual C++ 4.0 Service Pack 4 or higher, and then reinstall the Pocket PC 2003 SDK.

Wait a few seconds and the Pocket PC 2003 emulator will automatically start. The Pocket PC 2003 emulator is now ready to be configured.

## Configuring a Pocket PC 2003 Device for Network Connectivity

After the Pocket PC 2003 emulator has been installed, or for administrators that have a Pocket PC device in front of them, the first thing to do is configure the device for network connectivity. Network connectivity comes in a variety of forms, including:

- Pocket PC with an Ethernet adapter or wireless adapter

- Pocket PC with a mobile phone connection to the Internet

- Pocket PC emulator connected to a host workstation

Each configuration is slightly different and is individually highlighted in the next section.

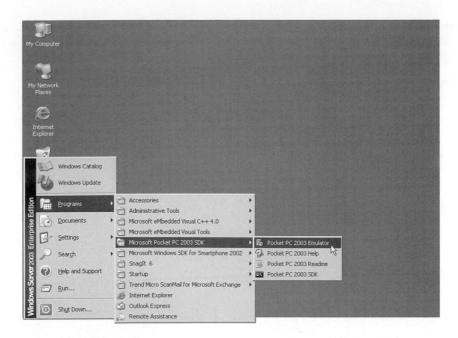

**FIGURE 24.7**   Choosing the Pocket PC.

**Configuring a Pocket PC 2003 Device with an Internal Network Adapter**

To configure a Pocket PC 2003 device with an internal Ethernet or wireless network adapter, follow these steps:

1. On the Pocket PC device, select Start, Settings, Connections. Click on the Connections Icon and then on the Advanced tab.

2. Click on the Network Card button and choose the network adapter you want to configure.

3. Select Use Server-Assigned IP Address If DHCP Is Available on the Network That This Device Will Be Connecting To, or choose Use Specific IP Address and enter a static IP address for the device.

4. If the device is DHCP-configured, skip to step 5; otherwise, click on the Name Servers tab and enter the address for the DNS (and optionally the WINS) servers on the network.

5. Click on OK in the upper-right corner and a notice appears notifying you that the adapter will be used. Remove and reinsert the adapter to activate it with the new settings. Click OK after reading the notice.

6. Click OK and then click on the X in the upper-right corner to complete the network adapter setting.

After the hardware settings on the network adapter have been selected, select the adapter as the default outbound connection. To choose the adapter as the default, use the following steps:

1. Select Start, Settings, Connections. Click on the Connections icon, on Advanced, and on the Select Networks button.

2. Make sure that the first option, Programs That Automatically Connect to the Internet Should Connect Using, is set to My Work Network. Additionally, make sure the option Programs That Automatically Connect to a Private Network Should Connect Using is set to My Work Network.

3. If a proxy server is used, click on the Edit button under the first My Work Network option to open the My Work Network page.

4. Click on the Proxy Settings tab and then on the This Network Uses a Proxy Server to Connect to the Internet check box. Then enter the name of the proxy server.

5. Click on OK three times, and then on X in the upper-right corner.

The Pocket PC 2003 device is now configured for network connectivity.

To test whether the Pocket PC 2003 device is working properly, launch Pocket Internet Explorer and confirm whether network connectivity to the Internet is available. To test Internet Explorer, use the following steps:

1. Select Start, Internet Explorer.

2. On the main Internet Explorer home screen, click on the PocketPC.com graphic.

3. Internet Explorer should traverse the network and provide a Windows Mobile page, assuming the host computer had connectivity to the Internet. If the network segment that the Pocket PC device is on does not have connectivity to the Internet, the Pocket PC device will also not have Internet connectivity. Possibly choose an Internet Intranet Web server or other system to check whether the device is communicating properly on the network segment to which it is connected.

### Configuring a Pocket PC 2003 Device with a Mobile Phone Connection

If the Pocket PC 2003 device is a Pocket PC–enabled mobile phone, the service provider of the phone will typically have a GSM or GPRS Internet connection service included with the phone. Follow the instructions provided with the phone to connect the phone to the Internet so that you can effectively surf the Internet with the mobile phone.

Usually the process is as follows:

1. Select Start, Settings, Connections. Click on the Connections icon, on the Advanced tab, and on the Select Networks button.

2. The first option, Programs That Automatically Connect to the Internet Should Connect Using, usually has a pull-down box that says ISP Connection, Internet Provider, or GPRS Provider. This varies between mobile phone providers; however, it

likely notes that the connection is to the Internet. The option commonly refers to using the mobile phone Internet service connection.

3.  Click on OK, and then on OK again. Click on X and again on X in the upper-right corner.

The Pocket PC 2003 device is now configured for network connectivity.

To test whether the Pocket PC 2003–enabled mobile phone is working properly, launch Pocket Internet Explorer and confirm whether network connectivity to the Internet is available. To test Internet Explorer, use the following steps:

1.  Select Start, Internet Explorer.

2.  On the main Internet Explorer home screen, click on the PocketPC.com graphic.

3.  Internet Explorer should traverse the network and provide a Windows Mobile page, assuming the host computer had connectivity to the Internet. If the Pocket PC–enabled mobile phone does not have connectivity to the Internet, check the manual or contact the technical support for the mobile phone to get assistance on connecting the mobile phone to the Internet.

### Configuring a Pocket PC 2003 Emulator

To configure the Pocket PC 2003 emulator for network connectivity, because the device uses the IP settings built in to the host computer, as long as the host computer has network connectivity, the emulator will have network connectivity. To validate the configuration, use the following steps:

1.  Select Start, Settings, Connections. Click on the Connections icon, on the Advanced tab, and then on the Select Networks button.

2.  Make sure that the first option, Programs That Automatically Connect to the Internet Should Connect Using, is set to My Work Network. Additionally, make sure the option Programs That Automatically Connect to a Private Network Should Connect Using is set to My Work Network, as shown in Figure 24.8.

> **NOTE**
>
> No proxy settings should be set on the Pocket PC 2003 emulator, because any proxy settings, DNS settings, or other hardware device settings are taken directly from the host workstation.

3.  Click on OK, again on OK, and then on the X in the upper-right corner.

The Pocket PC 2003 emulator is now configured for network connectivity.

To test whether the Pocket PC 2003 emulator is working properly, launch Pocket Internet Explorer and confirm whether network connectivity to the Internet is available. To test Internet Explorer, use the following steps:

1. Select Start, Internet Explorer.

2. On the main Internet Explorer home screen, click on the PocketPC.com graphic.

3. Internet Explorer should traverse the network and provide a Windows Mobile page assuming the host computer had connectivity to the Internet. If the host computer does not have network connectivity to the Internet, the Pocket PC emulator will not have Internet connectivity either. Possibly choose an Internet Intranet Web server or other system to check whether the device is communicating properly on the network segment to which it is connected.

**FIGURE 24.8**    Configuring the network settings for connectivity.

## Establishing a Connection Between the Pocket PC 2003 and Exchange 2003

After the Pocket PC device has network connectivity, establish a connection between the device and the Microsoft Exchange server. To create the connection, use the following steps:

1. Select Start, ActiveSync to launch the Pocket PC ActiveSync program.

2. Click on Tools at the bottom of the screen and then click on Options.

3. Click on the Server tab and for server, enter the DNS name or the IP address of the Exchange server.

4. Click on the Options button and enter the logon name, password, and domain of the Outlook/Exchange user account that the Pocket PC device will use to

synchronize information. Click to select the Save Password box as the information the password needs to be enabled.

5. Click on OK to go back to the Server screen and choose the options you want to synchronize—such as Inbox, Calendar, or Contacts—by clicking on the box.

6. Click on OK, and then click on the X in the upper-right corner to save the Exchange server settings.

### Synchronizing Data Between Pocket PC 2003 and Exchange 2003

To synchronize information between the Pocket PC 2003 device and the Exchange 2003 server, use the following steps:

1. Select Start, ActiveSync to launch the ActiveSync program.

2. Click on the Sync button to begin synchronization.

# Using the Pocket PC 2002 and Pocket PC 2003

After connectivity has been established on the Pocket PC device and information has been synchronized, the Pocket PC has Outlook inbox, calendar, and contact information stored in the nonvolatile memory of the device. Users can look at their information; queue up messages to be sent; create and accept calendar appointments; and view, add, and edit contact information. Because the Pocket PC 2002 and Pocket PC 2003 interfaces are similar, the function of using the Pocket PC device is consolidated into a common section.

> **NOTE**
>
> Although the Pocket PC device stores email, calendar, and contact information in nonvolatile memory, the devices are known to lose all memory and configuration settings if the battery is drained and the device is left uncharged for a few days. It's important that users keep their Pocket PC device charged or at least see that the device is not left uncharged for an extended period of time.

### Viewing Inbox Information

Users can access their Inbox, select other folders to synchronize, queue up messages to be sent, and manage their mailbox Outlook information. To access the Outlook email information, select Start, Inbox.

While in the Inbox, a user can open an email message by clicking twice on a mail message. The message can be read. If the user wants to view an attachment, by default, attachments are not sent to the Pocket PC. By clicking on an attachment, the arrow for the attachment turns from gray to green noting that the attachment is flagged for download. The next time the device is synchronized, the attachment will be downloaded.

To create a new mail message, click on New at the bottom of the Inbox screen and a blank email message will appear. Enter the email address and subject, and write the message. Click on Send to have the message queued up to be sent.

To download more than just the Inbox information, select Tools, Manage Folders and then select the folders, as shown in Figure 24.9, that are to be synchronized and managed. Click on OK and then go to ActiveSync and sync the device. Information from the folders will automatically be downloaded.

**FIGURE 24.9**    Choosing other folders to synchronize.

After the managed folders information has been downloaded, within the Inbox, click on the Inbox option in the upper left of the Inbox program to show the Outlook folders. Select a different folder and view the messages that are now managed along with the Inbox.

## Viewing Calendar and Contacts Information

Calendar and contacts information is also common for mobile users to access information remotely. To access the Outlook Calendar or Contacts information, select Start, Calendar or Start, Contacts, respectively.

When viewing calendar appointments, a user can select a day, a week, or a month view. Depending on the option selected, the user sees more detail (such as in a daily view), as shown in Figure 24.10, or less detail (such as in a monthly view).

**FIGURE 24.10**    Viewing a detailed day view.

To add a new appointment, selecting New brings up a page that enables the user to enter details of the appointment. Appointments that are created on the Pocket PC device can note date, time, reminder, and categories; invite other attendees; show status information and sensitivity information; and contain notes about the appointment.

For contacts, a person in the address book can be viewed and edited, or an email or phone call can be initiated from the Pocket PC device from within the contacts. Contacts can be added, deleted, or even beamed from one Pocket PC device to another Pocket PC device.

# Working with Smartphones

Another type of mobile device is a hybrid Windows CE device and mobile phone. Unlike a Pocket PC device that has a touch screen display and looks more like a PDA than a telephone, the Smartphone is a mobile phone that has a Windows interface for viewing inbox messages, calendar appointments, contacts, and other Outlook information.

As with Pocket PC devices, an organization can purchase a Smartphone and test the functionality, or it can download a Smartphone emulator and test the functionality of the Smartphone device to Exchange 2003.

## Using a Smartphone Wireless Device

There are several vendors that have adopted the Smartphone technology into their mobile phone device. The benefit to Exchange administrators is that a Smartphone by definition comes with mobile connectivity, so the device is Internet-ready from the time the device is powered on. Besides being able to use the phone as a mobile phone, a user can also access the Internet using the built-in Internet Explorer browser.

If users have problems with Internet connectivity with a Smartphone, they contact the wireless phone carrier for support. The carrier typically has technical support that helps users connect the Smartphone to the Internet for general browsing. When they can browse the Internet, the Smartphone can be configured to access Exchange 2003 for synchronization of email, contacts, calendar appointments, and other Outlook information.

## Using a Smartphone Emulator

The Smartphone 2003 emulator (the SDK) is a free download from Microsoft. Go to `http://www.microsoft.com`, search on the words `Smartphone 2003 SDK`, and download the `Microsoft Smartphone 2003 SDK.msi` file (55MB).

In addition to downloading the Smartphone 2003 emulator, you also need to download a copy of the eMbedded Visual C++ 4.0 and the eMbedded Visual C++ 4.0 Service Pack 4 or higher—unless you installed the eMbedded Visual C++ 4.0 and Service Pack when you installed the Pocket PC 2003 SDK. The eMbedded Visual C++ 4.0 and Service Pack should be installed before the SDK emulator to provide the core driver and libraries needed to run the software development kit. The eMbedded Visual C++ 4.0 and Service Pack can be found at `http://msdn.microsoft.com/mobility/windowsmobile/downloads/default.aspx`.

The `eVC4.exe` is 235MB and the `evc4sp4.exe` (Service Pack 4) is 69MB.

### Requirements to Run the Smartphone 2003 Emulator

To install eMbedded Visual C++ 4.0, Microsoft states its requirement is a system running Windows 2000 or Windows XP, 450MHz or faster Pentium-II class system, 128–192MB or more of available memory, 200MB of available disk space, network adapter, VGA video, and a mouse. The host workstation also needs a network adapter connected to a network connection that will access the Exchange 2003 server.

It is typically recommended to first test the Smartphone emulation on an internal backbone segment to make sure the connection to the Exchange server is not blocked by external firewalls, routers, or other external perimeter devices. The host workstation needs network connectivity, and although it's not a requirement to run the Smartphone emulator, the system should be able to connect to the Exchange server using Outlook Web Access or from an Outlook client. This ensures that the host workstation has the appropriate network connectivity for the emulator to connect to the server.

---

**NOTE**

The Smartphone 2003 emulator does not require its own IP address on the network, and there is no network connectivity configuration required on the emulator. The emulator simply passes through the existing LAN connection of the host workstation. If the workstation has connectivity to Exchange for Outlook or Outlook Web Access, that same connection is used by the emulator.

---

### Installing eMbedded Visual C++ 4.0

After downloading the eMbedded Visual C++ 4.0 and Smartphone 2003 SDK, install the two applications using the following steps:

1. Launch the eVC4.exe executable for the eMbedded Visual C++ 4.0 to install it on the host workstation. This extracts the files to a temporary directory (for example, c:\evc4\) and launches the installation wizard.

2. Go into the temporary directory and run setup.exe. The installation wizard displays a welcome screen; click Next to continue.

3. After reading the end-user license agreement and agreeing to the information, click I Accept the Agreement and then click Next.

4. When prompted for the product license number and user ID, enter the evaluation ID that is noted on the main Web page where you downloaded the eMbedded Visual Tools. The product ID noted is TRT7H-KD36T-FRH8D-6QH8P-VFJHQ.

5. When prompted, select to install all the eMbedded tools and then click Next.

> **NOTE**
>
> Unlike with the eMbedded Visual Tools 3.0 that also installed the Pocket PC 2002 and the Smartphone 2002 SDKs, the eMbedded Visual C++ 4.0 installs only the eMbedded Visual C++ 4.0 tools. Install the Pocket PC 2003 emulator and the Smartphone 2003 emulators separately.

6. Choose a folder you want to install the software in (the default is c:\Windows CE Tools) and then click Next. The Windows CE Platform Manager 4.0 will begin to install.

7. Click OK past the eMbedded tools setup product ID information.

8. Click on Continue when prompted to confirm the installation of the eMbedded Visual C++ 4.0 Setup, which includes the eMbedded Visual C++ 4.0 and Common Components.

9. After the installation of the eMbedded Visual C++ 4.0 tools, click OK when the setup notes it was completed successfully.

10. The installation wizard for the Standard SDK for Windows CE .NET setup begins to extract and install. Click on Next past the welcome page, read and accept the license agreement, and then click on Next.

11. Enter your name and company name and click on Next.

12. Select to have a Complete Install and click on Next.

13. Choose to install in the default destination folder and click on Next.

14. Click on Install to complete the installation of the Standard SDK for Windows CE .NET.

15. When the installation of the Standard SDK for Windows CE .NET has completed its installation, click on Finish.

After the base eMbedded Visual C++ 4.0 has been installed, install eMbedded Visual C++ 4.0 Service Pack 4 or higher using the following steps:

1. Run `evc4sp4.exe`. Choose a directory where you want to expand the files (for example, `c:\evcsp4\`).

2. Go to the directory you selected, go into the DISK1 directory, and run the `setup.exe` program.

3. At the eMbedded Visual C++ 4.0 SP4 setup welcome screen, click Next.

4. Read and accept the end-user license agreement and click on Next.

5. Click on Install to begin the installation of the Service Pack.

6. When the Service Pack has completed installation, click on Finish.

### Installing the Smartphone 2003 Emulator
After the eMbedded Visual C++ 4.0 and Service Pack have been installed, install the Smartphone 2003 SDK using the following steps:

1. Launch the Microsoft Smartphone 2003 SDK.msi package.

2. At the welcome screen, click on Next.

3. Read the end-user license agreement, select I Accept the Terms in the License Agreement, and click on Next.

4. Enter your name and organization and click on Next.

5. Click on Complete for the type of installation.

6. Click on Next to select the default destination folder information.

7. Click on Install to initiate the installation.

8. When the installation has completed, click on Finish.

### Launching the Smartphone 2003 Emulator
After the Smartphone 2003 SDK has been installed, launch the emulator by selecting Start, Programs, Microsoft Smartphone 2003 SDK, and the Smartphone 2003 Emulator. By default, the Smartphone emulator establishes a link to the Internet as long as the host workstation that the emulator is installed on has Internet connectivity.

## Synchronizing Data Between the Smartphone and Exchange 2003
A user's Outlook information can be synchronized between Exchange 2003 and a Smartphone device. The user can choose to synchronize email, calendar, and contact

information. To synchronize information between the Pocket PC 2003 device and the Exchange 2003 server, use the following steps:

1. Configure ActiveSync by selecting Options in the ActiveSync window.

2. Select Server Settings, Connection, and enter the username, password, and domain. Enable the Save password setting and server name, and then select Done.

3. Select Inbox and enable the check box to synchronize the Inbox with the server.

4. Select Calendar and enable the check box to synchronize the Calendar with the server.

5. Select Contacts and enable the check box to synchronize the Contacts with the server.

6. Select the Sync option to begin synchronization, as shown in Figure 24.11.

**FIGURE 24.11**   Synchronizing Smartphone with Exchange 2003.

## Establishing a Link from a Mobile Phone to Exchange 2003

Exchange 2003 also supports the access of information from mobile phones that are not Pocket PC–enabled devices. Web-enabled phones offer you the ability to view email messages, calendar appointments, contact information, and other Outlook/Exchange information. Unlike the Pocket PC device that downloads and synchronizes information, the Web-enabled device offers a real-time view and information lookup.

The Web-enabled device uses the Outlook Mobile Access capability of Exchange 2003. Outlook Web Access assumes users access their Outlook information from a full-screen desktop computer, but Outlook Mobile Access (OMA) assumes users access their Outlook information from a much smaller screen. In some cases, the OMA screen may be only 8–10 characters wide and 4–5 lines deep, and the device might communicate at speeds equivalent to less than 9600 baud. With limited bandwidth and limited screen view size, the transfer of OMA information must be extremely efficient.

## Establishing Connectivity for a Mobile Phone Device

To connect a mobile phone to Exchange 2003, you first establish network connectivity for the device. Two types of mobile phone devices are addressed in this section. One device is a physical wireless Web-enabled phone, and the other device is a Web-enabled emulator.

## Connectivity of a Web-Enabled Wireless Phone

Fortunately, the nature of a mobile phone is that it has connectivity to some service, typically a mobile phone carrier. The mobile phones that are Web-enabled have HTML, WAP, cHTML, or other wireless Web access and typically are configured from the factory to provide Internet Web access capabilities. To establish Internet connectivity, the best thing to do is read the instructions for the device. The technical support for the phone or carrier vendor will provide assistance on Internet connection.

After the mobile phone has the capability of accessing Web pages on the Internet, the device is ready to be configured for connection to Outlook Mobile Access (covered in the section "Using Outlook Mobile Access to Exchange Server 2003," later in this chapter).

## Connectivity Using a Web-Enabled Phone Emulator

For administrators who want to test Web-enabled Outlook Mobile Access but are not ready to commit to purchasing a mobile phone, a Web-enabled phone emulator is a great way to set up and test the OMA functionality. Openwave Systems, Inc. (`http://www.openwave.com`) provides a mobile phone emulator that can be used with Exchange 2003. The emulator can be set up on a network-connected Windows workstation that can host the emulator. As with the Pocket PC 2002, Pocket PC 2003, and the Smartphone emulators, the system should have connectivity to the Exchange 2003 server that will be tested.

### Downloading the Web-Enabled Emulator
To download the Openwave Mobile SDK, go to `http://www.openwave.com/us/products/developer_products/index.htm`.

From that page, select to download the Openwave Phone Simulator (6.6MB).

### Installing the Web-Enabled Emulator
After the Openwave Phone Simulator has been successfully downloaded, install the Web-enabled mobile phone emulator by running the EXE program downloaded. This installs the emulator on the host workstation.

# Using Outlook Mobile Access to Exchange Server 2003

With either a Web-enabled mobile phone or the Openwave Mobile SDK emulator in front of you, you can now begin to navigate the OMA interface to Exchange 2003. As noted earlier, because OMA is a real-time Web-access tool and not a synchronization tool, the only prerequisite to running the OMA is to have a mobile phone or emulator that has Internet connectivity.

With Internet connectivity, a user enters the Web URL **http://{servername}/OMA**. When OMA is accessed on the Exchange server, the user sees a screen similar to the one shown in Figure 24.12. The user can move around the menu and select to view a message in the Inbox, Calendar, Contacts, or Tasks; search the directory; compose a new message; or change preferences.

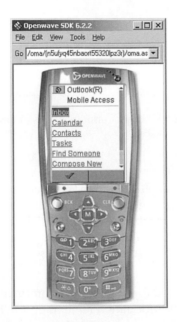

**FIGURE 24.12**  The Outlook Mobile Access screen.

When a user selects the Inbox, the mobile phone establishes a connection with the Exchange 2003 server and displays a list of inbox mail headers. The user can select a message and choose to open it. The mobile phone establishes a connection to the Exchange 2003 server and downloads the message.

Users can also choose to open the calendar and select a day they wish to view calendar appointments. When a day is selected, the phone makes a call to the Internet, and OMA retrieves the calendar appointments for the given day and displays it on the screen, as shown in Figure 24.13.

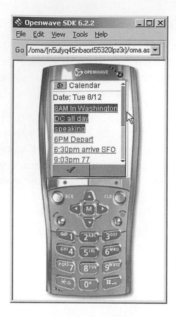

**FIGURE 24.13**   Viewing a calendar day of appointments in OMA.

# Summary

Mobility in Exchange 2003 through the use of Pocket PC devices, Smartphones, and Web-enabled mobile phones provides organizations the ability to extend Exchange to users that might not otherwise have regular connectivity to their messages, calendar appointments, contacts, and other information. With mobile access built in to Exchange 2003, an organization sets up the mobile device and enables users to connect to the Internet and then access their information.

Through the implementation of SSL encryption on information transfers, the data sent and received is secured, and all information remains on the Exchange Server should users lose their mobile device. Mobility has been greatly extended with Exchange 2003 to provide more ways for users to access Outlook and Exchange information.

# Best Practices

The following are best practices from this chapter:

- When evaluating the functions of mobile connectivity, download the emulators for Pocket PC, Smartphone, and Web-enabled mobile phone instead of buying physical devices.

- When testing mobile connectivity, test connectivity internally to a network before testing it externally to minimize any firewall, router, or external communication challenges that might prevent successful communication with an Exchange 2003 server.

- Always use SSL encryption when establishing connectivity between mobile devices and Exchange 2003.

- If you have a choice, get the Pocket PC 2003 version of a device instead of the Pocket PC 2002 version to provide Exchange Server–initiated updates and communications with remote devices as opposed to relying on device-initiated downloads and synchronization.

- Although Pocket PC devices store information in nonvolatile memory, sometimes when a Pocket PC device's battery is completely drained and the device is left uncharged for a period of time, it loses information. Therefore, keep the device charged—or at least make sure to synchronize the device to keep an active copy of all information up on Exchange.

24

# PART VIII

# Client Access to Exchange Server 2003

## IN THIS PART

CHAPTER 25   Getting the Most Out of the
             Microsoft Outlook Client              707

CHAPTER 26   Everything You Need to Know About
             the Outlook Web Access (OWA) Client   749

CHAPTER 27   Outlook for Non-Windows Systems       801

# Getting the Most Out of the Microsoft Outlook Client

**IN THIS CHAPTER**

- What's Common Across All Versions of Outlook

- What's New in Outlook 2003

- Customizing the End-User Experience

- Security Enhancements in Outlook 2003

- Understanding RPC over HTTP

- Using Outlook 2003 Collaboratively

- Using Outlook Cached Mode for Remote Connectivity

## What's Common Across All Versions of Outlook

The Outlook client has "come a long way" since Outlook 97. When Outlook 97 was originally released, the Outlook team developed and created the client without much open communication with the Microsoft Exchange team, which was developing the server platform to run the Outlook application! As a result, the collaborative tools available today didn't exist in previous versions of Outlook. Sarting with Outlook 98, the integration of the two teams began to be improved. This open collaboration culminates in the release of Outlook 2003, which, not by chance, was released at the same time as the first release of Exchange Server 2003, sending a clear message that the two teams now work very closely with each other. To improve on this strategy, during the design process, the Outlook development team also received user input on desired features and functions. Implementing what it could, the team also communicated with the Exchange team to incorporate functionality that the Outlook team couldn't, and to produce better integration on the server side. The results are evident in Outlook 2003 as Exchange and Outlook now have greater integration, enhanced functionality for the end-user, and improved collaborative tools. As a result, it is a better business communication client.

## Comparing Outlook 97, Outlook 98, Outlook 2000, Outlook XP/2002, and Outlook 2003

Many features available in the Outlook 2003 version have been around for many generations of Outlook. However, with each generation, a concerted effort has consistently been made to make Outlook functionality better, faster, a better business tool, and more integrated with Exchange. In the beginning with Outlook 97, the focus of Outlook was almost strictly messaging and calendaring. In subsequent generations of Outlook, the focus turned more toward automated functions such as forms and rules, as well as application integration with Instant Messenger and Internet Explorer.

To meet today's needs, the last few versions have focused more on security, starting with Outlook XP and now Outlook 2003. In addition to these areas, the views, the user interface, and the organization of mail items (it is much easier for the end-user to flag messages) have also become a key focus in Outlook 2003. However, regardless of the Outlook version, the focus has always been to streamline the new version, add new functionality, and make Outlook a more comprehensive business tool. To meet these goals in Outlook 2003, a major focus is on collaborative tools. Leveraging the use and integration of other applications such as Microsoft's Sharepoint Portal in tandem with Exchange Server 2003, the collaborative functionality of Outlook is far superior than that of Outlook 2003 as a standalone client.

### The Basic Outlook Features

As mentioned earlier, the basic Outlook features (such as the Calendar, messaging, and tasks) have been around since the initial release of Outlook 97. However, throughout each version, changes have been made to enhance their ease of use and navigation, and to include new application integration with products like Instant Messenger and Netmeeting.

Although, with regard to messaging, each new version strives to make enhancements when sending and receiving email, such as addressing email, address book changes, and other sending/receiving functionality improvements. Additionally, enhancements to areas like the user dictionaries and the ability to view message sizes, and organize and view messages, generally improves the overall end-user experience.

### Security

Security enhancements have also been included in each Outlook iteration. For example, as spam has become more of an issue, the newer versions of Outlook have included client-configurable antispam options along with updates to Span Sender List along with improved support for S/MIME.

### Collaboration

Collaboration is a major reason companies leverage the Outlook client as their end-user messaging application. With each new version, the collaborative power of Outlook has increased. Although many tools are available for an Outlook 2003 user with just Exchange on the back-end, integration with Microsoft Office and Microsoft's Sharepoint Portal product increases the possibilities for collaboration with Outlook 2003 and Exchange Server 2003. The section on collaboration later in this chapter focuses only on the collaborative tools available to users who aren't using Sharepoint.

## Other Enhancements

Over time, each new release of the Outlook client has introduced added features to enhance functionality and the end-user experience. Whether making it faster, sleeker, or more user-friendly, each new iteration of Outlook has been better than the previous version and integrates better with Exchange as well as other applications. Outlook 2003 is no exception to this rule. In this chapter, we will cover many of the most useful new features available with Outlook 2003 along with leveraging some of the existing features when using the client with Exchange Server 2003.

# What's New in Outlook 2003

As stated previously, new versions of Outlook continue to produce new features and functionality, in addition to enhancements of already existing features. In this section, administrators can find some of the new features that organizations might find beneficial along with new tools for the end-user.

## Understanding the New Outlook 2003 Interface

The new Outlook interface incorporates many changes that have been requested by users and administrators over time.

To meet some of these requests, the new four-pane view is much more user-friendly, and the Preview pane now allows for a greater area of space for previewing email. Also, the new buttons in the Shortcut pane below the Folder pane provide a quick new way to access the different features of Outlook. These new features provide an enhanced way to quickly view and organize email.

### Similarities with OWA

The new Outlook 2003 GUI is extremely similar to the GUI that Outlook Web Access users using Exchange Server 2003 experience. Outlook 2003 provides many more features than OWA does, but the similarities between the two provide the end-user with a much greater comfort level and familiar interface; this also lessens the need for end-user training when implementing OWA usage with Exchange 2003. The similarities between the two products are the result of close work between the two development teams. As a result, administrative overhead when implementing each functionality is greatly improved.

> **NOTE**
>
> To learn more, Outlook Web Access is covered in great detail in Chapter 26, "Everything You Need to Know About the Outlook Web Access (OWA) Client."

## Methods for Highlighting Outlook Items

With each iteration of Outlook, the methods for organizing and finding messages have been enhanced. This is because mail has become more of a way of sharing information, and the pure volume of mail that end-users receive in today's business environment has increased. Now, with Outlook 2003, users are provided an even more enhanced method for highlighting, flagging, alerting, and organizing mail when working with Outlook and Exchange.

### Using Quick Flags

Using Quick flags in Outlook 2003, end-users can right-click on a message and assign a colored flag to that message, making it stand out from other messages and allowing for easier grouping by arranging messages by flag color. And because these flag colors have no predetermined meaning, the end-user can further organize and arrange by assigning importance or categorization to each flag color.

To assign a quick flag in the Outlook 2003 client, complete the following:

1. Right-click on the gray flag icon on the far-right side of the email message in the Inbox to access the flag options.

2. Right-click once on the flag color desired, choose Flag Complete to mark the flag completed and change the colored flag to a check mark.

Another option when working with flags is to configure a reminder on a specific flag. The options for using reminders with flags will allow users to configure a information and a due date associated with each flag. To configure a reminder, complete these steps:

1. Flag the message.

2. Right-click on the flag and choose Add Reminder.

3. Choose the reason to flag the message and then a due date (see Figure 25.1).

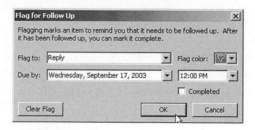

FIGURE 25.1    Adding a reminder to a flag.

Click OK when completed.

> **NOTE**
>
> When using flags, the end-user receives a standard Outlook reminder pop-up when the precon-
> figured reminder comes due.

Once a message is flagged, the messages can then be arranged by clicking on the arrow on the top of the flag column in the Inbox to arrange messages by flagging.

### Making Key Appointments Stand Out with Color

Using the Outlook 2003 Calendar, this new feature allows for the customization and organization of appointments using colors, allowing end-user appointments to stand out when viewing the calendar.

To choose a color and label an appointment, follow these steps:

1. Open the appointment in the Calendar.

2. Click on the drop-down box next to Label, to the right of the Location box.

3. Choose the color and label that best apply to the message.

4. Click Save, Close.

> **TIP**
>
> Organizing the calendar using colors can also be completed while in the Calendar area. Users
> can add colors by clicking on the Calendar Colors button in the toolbar, or by right-clicking on
> the Calendar object before opening it and choosing Label.

### Viewing Information About Email Quickly

Outlook 2003 includes a quick pop-up box that provides information about a specific email. Information in the feature includes sender name, the size of the file, and the date/time the message was received. To view the quick summary, users can simply hold the mouse curser over the desired message; the pop-up box that provides this information will then appear automatically.

## Proposing a New Meeting Time

Another new feature in the Calendar allows meeting invitees, not just the meeting organizer, to be able to propose new meeting times when they receive a meeting invitation. Use this exercise to propose a new time for a meeting as a meeting invitee. Begin by sending an invite to a user as an invitee and complete the following:

1. Open the meeting invitation.

2. Click on the Propose New Time button to the right of the Accept/Tentative/Decline boxes.

3. Choose the new time using any of the standard ways of choosing a meeting time, as shown in Figure 25.2.

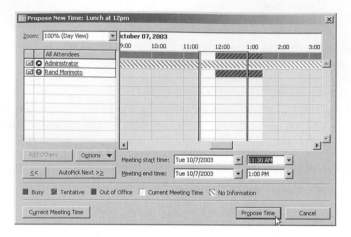

**FIGURE 25.2**    Proposing a new time for a meeting.

4. Click the Propose Time button when done.

5. Click Send when completed.

## Using the New Search Functionality

A power-enhanced feature in Outlook 2003 is the ability to search within the Outlook client and Exchange user mailbox. Users can now save searches: For example, if a user frequently completes the same search, he can save steps and time by saving the search for future use. Additionally, using the Search In functionality from the Outlook toolbar makes accessing the search capability even faster.

### Using the Search In Functionality

The Search In functionality is easily accessible from the top of the toolbar above the main panes. To perform a search, do the following:

1. Enter the word(s) to search for in the Look For box, or click on the Find button in the toolbar.

2. Click the drop-down arrow next to Search In to choose the part of Outlook in which to search.

3. Click Find Now to begin the search. The results are shown in the window below the search.

### Saving Searches

To save a search, the search must be started from within the Folder list under Search Folders. The following steps should be followed:

1. Right-click on Search Folders and choose New Search Folder.

2. Within the New Search Folder pop-up Window, shown in Figure 25.3, choose the search folder and criteria for your search. Depending on what selection is made, the user may be presented with more options to complete before commencing the search. Choose also what part of Outlook to search.

**FIGURE 25.3**   Creating new search folder criteria.

3. Click OK when completed.

4. The search completes and the results are displayed in the center pane. Additionally, the search is saved under the Search Folders area in the Folder list.

5. To delete the saved search, click on it and choose Delete.

> **TIP**
>
> Saved searches are also available when using Outlook Web Access. For saved searches to be accessed via Outlook Web Access (OWA), a user must create the saved search in Outlook 2003 first.

## Associating Items with Specific Contacts

When working with contacts in Outlook 2003, any Microsoft Office document, as well as mail messages, Calendar items, or tasks, can be linked to a contact and linked to the Activities tab of any contact with Outlook 2003. This is useful to keep track of all correspondence and information regarding the contact.

To link an item to the contact, do the following:

1. Open the contact.

2. Go to Actions, Link, Items to link an item within Exchange, as shown in Figure 25.4.

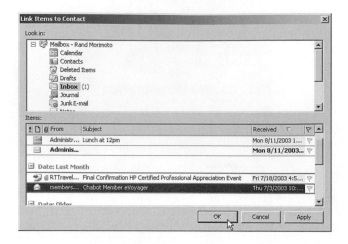

**FIGURE 25.4**    Linking an item to an Outlook contact.

3. Or, go to Actions, Link, File to browse the network or the local hard drive to link a file.

4. Click on Item to choose an Outlook item to link, including items from public folders.

Outlook maintains links in the Activities tab until they are removed manually by the end-user.

To remove a link associated with a contact, there are different methods that can be used for an Outlook component and for a document. To remove a link for an Outlook component, do the following:

- Double-click on the message for which the link should be removed.

- When it's open, go to View, Options.

- To the right of the Contacts button, delete the contact listed there.

- Close the object.

To remove a link for a document, do the following:

- Double-click on the document for which the link should be removed.

- Delete the message that was created with the document included in it.

### Managing Multiple Email Accounts from One Place

Outlook 2003 allows the end-user to access multiple email accounts from the same Outlook client, including IMAP, POP3, and HTTP mail accounts. This allows for multiple mail account configurations for the same user.

To configure Outlook to access multiple mailboxes, do the following:

1. Go to Tools, Email Accounts.

2. Choose Add a New Email Account.

3. Click Next.

4. Select the correct email server for the account, depending on the type of email account (POP3, HTTP, Exchange, IMAP).

5. Click Next.

6. Enter the appropriate information for the email account so that it can be properly connected.

> **TIP**
>
> When configuring an Outlook profile for access to an Exchange Server account, click the Check Name option when configuring access to an Exchange Server 2003 mailbox. Verify that the Exchange server successfully verified the name of the account and server entered; to ensure a successful configuration was competed, the name of the user account will become underlined when this feature is used.
>
> For an MSN Hotmail subscriber, enter the hotmail email address and password only.
>
> For a POP3 server, verify that it is properly configured by clicking Test Account Settings.

7. Click Next.

8. Select Finish to complete the account setup.

> **TIP**
>
> Additional mailboxes associated with user profiles can be enabled automatically by using the Custom Installation Wizard, which is discussed in the next section, "Customizing the End-User Experience."

## Customizing the End-User Experience

The Custom Installation Wizard can be used to modify the user interface and options during the installation or initial rollout of Outlook. However, Group Policy can also be used after the installation is complete to change the user experience. In this section, we will address working with these options using the Custom Installation Wizard.

25

> **NOTE**
>
> For more information regarding customizing Outlook with Windows 2003 Server Group Policy, see Chapter 29, "Group Policy Management for Exchange Clients."

## Using the Custom Installation Wizard

The Custom Installation Wizard (CIW) is available with the Office 2003 Resource Kit (ORK) and can be found in the core set of tools that is installed by default when the kit is installed.

> **TIP**
>
> The Resource Kit can be downloaded from www.microsoft.com/downloads. The CIW is an extremely handy tool to customize the installation choices in Microsoft Office products.

Using the CIW allows administrators to specify what previous Office versions and components will be upgraded or removed, as well as configure features such as Search Folder settings, integration with Instant Messenger, how the messages appear in the Outlook notification area, and the order in which items appear in the navigation pane, among others. Almost anything that is an option or behavior in Outlook can be controlled by the CIW.

## Creating a PRF File Using the Custom Installation Wizard

In this section, administrators can walk through the options available when using the CIW to configure settings and create PRF files. Though detailed directions on how to use the CIW are not covered, administrators can review and configure the choices available for Outlook customization using PRF files.

To use the Custom Installation Wizard, follow these steps:

1. Download and install the Office 2003 Resource Kit.

2. Launch the Custom Installation Wizard. You'll see an initial screen like Figure 25.5.

3. Go through the first few screens until you reach the Set Feature Installation screen that determines what Office product to customize.

4. Make sure that Outlook is selected for installation. Use the drop-down boxes to choose what installation features to install for Outlook. Click Next when done.

5. Continue clicking Next until you reach the Change Office User Settings screen. At this screen, configure the Outlook features to behave as the enterprise requires by enabling or disabling the choices available for Outlook. (The interface is very similar to that of Group Policy.)

6. Continue through the pages by clicking Next until the Outlook: Customize Default Profile page is reached. Here, choose one of the following.

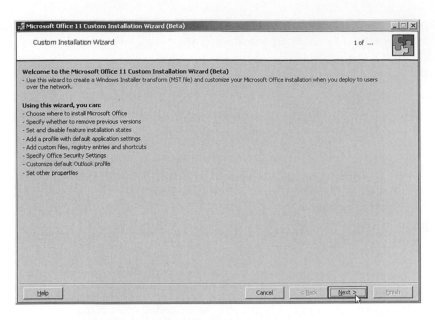

**FIGURE 25.5**   Custom Installation Wizard initial screen.

- **Use Existing Profile**—Outlook will use the existing user Outlook profile. If none exists, it will use the new one.

- **Modify Profile**—Change the existing profile. If none exists, it will use the new one.

- **New Profile**—Use this new profile for all users, whether or not one already exists.

- **Apply PRF**—Apply the profile changes that are configured in the PRF file. Specify the PRF to apply to the users.

7. Click Next when completed.

8. The next screen, Outlook: Specify Exchange Settings, allows for customization of the Exchange settings. Determine the Exchange server, the username, and whether to use the Cached Mode (Configure an Exchange Local Mailbox). Click Next when completed.

9. The next screen, Outlook: Add Accounts, allows for the addition of POP3, IMAP, Internet accounts, PST files, OAB, PABs, and other mailbox options to be included in the Outlook profile automatically.

10. The next screen, Outlook: Remove Accounts and Export Settings, allows the administrator to determine whether other email accounts (MS Mail or Lotus cc:Mail) should be removed, as well as whether to export the PRF for manual text editing. Click Next when done.

11. The next screen, Outlook: Customize Default Settings, allows for the customization of converting the Personal Address Book (PAB) to an Outlook Address Book (OAB) and handles the configuration of the default email editor (such as Wordmail) and default email format (such as HTML). Click Next when done.

12. Continue clicking Next until you reach the final screen, which states "You have completed the Custom Installation Wizard" and tells the name and location of the Custom Installer Transform file.

13. Click Exit.

The PRF file is now created and available for deployment in the enterprise.

## Configuring Registry Keys During Installation

The CIW also allows for the configuration of Registry entries to be included with the installation of Outlook 2003. Registry keys can be created and added, as well as removed, via the CIW, greatly increasing Exchange administrators' ability to customize Outlook 2003. Completing changes to the Registry with the CIW are done using the Add/Remove Registry Entries page (about page 12) in the Custom Installation Wizard.

To do this, the administrator must know the following information and enter it on the Add/Remove Registry Entries page:

1. The root Registry key (such as HKEY_LOCAL_MACHINE or HKEY_CURRENT_USER)

2. The data type value (such as DWORD)

3. The actual Registry key (without the root Registry key at the beginning of it) (such as Software/Microsoft/Office/10.0/etc)

4. The Value name (the name of the key value in the Registry to which the Registry value gets assigned)

5. The value data (such as 1 or 0—whatever is correct for the value name and the configuration desired)

This data must be inputted correctly into the CIW and saved while in the CIW. Then it will become part of the custom installation of Outlook for the enterprise.

## Using PRF Files

Customized Outlook Profile Files (PRF files) are not new to Outlook 2003. In fact, the Outlook 2003 PRF format is the same as it was in Outlook 2000. However, the methods formerly used to create the PRF files (Newprof.exe and Modprof.exe) are no longer used in Outlook 2003. Using the Custom Installation Wizard, an administrator can make the required Outlook interface changes that are desired and then save those changes to a PRF file. The PRF file can then be pushed to the desktop client using several different ways, updating or creating an Outlook profile that is different from the default Outlook profile setting when a basic Outlook installation is completed.

Another option available when working with the CIW addresses previous versions of PRF files. Now older Outlook 98 and Outlook 2000 PRF files can be updated and reused with the newer Outlook 2003 client. Though this option is available, updating older PRF files should be used when settings include corporate or workgroup options only. To perform an update, import the file into the Custom Installation Wizard, complete changes as necessary, and save it through the Custom Installation Wizard to use with newer clients.

> **TIP**
>
> As a best practice when dealing with older PRF files that require major changes or are related to other configurations, such as only Internet mail settings, a new PRF file should be created using the Custom Installation Wizard.
>
> Administrators can also modify or add further customization to a PRF beyond what is available in the CIW by manually editing the file using Notepad.

## Applying PRF files

Additionally, when a new PRF file is used to configure the client, Outlook checks to make sure that no services are duplicated and that all accounts have unique Active Directory names. Many different methods can be used to push the PRF files to the users:

- PRF files are executables, so they can be easily updated by the users by double-clicking on them.

- You can import the PRF file into the Custom Installation Wizard or Custom Maintenance Wizard as a transform. Then use the transform when Outlook is updated or deployed.

- You can configure a Registry key to run the PRF file when Outlook starts up. This key can be included in a transform.

- To specify the PRF as a command-line option for Outlook.exe to import automatically, use the following command:

```
Outlook.exe /importprf \\servername\sharename\outlook.prf
```

# Security Enhancements in Outlook 2003

Microsoft announced its Secure Computing initiative in 2002. For Outlook 2003, this means a great increase in the number of security and antispam features available when using the Outlook 2003 client and Exchange Server 2003.

## Support for Secured Messaging

As a result of Microsoft's security initiatives, as well as the standard increases in security functionality in Outlook that occur with every Outlook iteration, Outlook 2003 expanded its support for secured messaging, including S/MIME V3, digital signing, message encryption, and smart card support.

### S/Mime Support, Digital Signatures, and Email Encryption

Though S/MIME support has been available in previous versions of Outlook, Outlook 2003 provides support for S/MIME V3. Using S/MIME V3, email messages are encrypted by the sender's public key and can be accessed, opened, and decrypted only with the recipient's private key. This private/public key exchange is critical for secure email correspondence.

Use of S/MIME support requires that the Outlook client have a certificate for cryptography on the client computer (and is stored locally either in the Microsoft Windows Certificate Store or on a smart card), and can be pushed through Registry settings or via Group Policy to easily implement S/MIME throughout an organization.

S/MIME V3 support also includes digital signing. Digital signing allows for security labels and signed secure message receipts. Using Outlook 2003 enterprise-wide security labels is enforced, such as "For internal use only" or labeling messages to restrict the forwarding or printing of messages. Additionally, users can now request S/MIME affirmation of receipt of a message. By requesting a receipt, the sender confirms that the recipient recognized and verified the digital signature because no receipt is received unless the recipient, who should have received the message, actually does receive the message. Only then does the sender receive the digitally signed read receipt.

Outlook 2003 also provides support for the X.509v3 standard, which requires third-party encryption keys, such as ones created and sold by digital security companies such as Verisign. By using S/MIME, the sender ensures that the email is encrypted and is read only by the intended recipient.

> **TIP**
>
> The security features mentioned in this entire Security section can also be configured by the administrator via Group Policy, using the `outlk11.adm` Group Policy template. Open the Group Policy that will have the template applied.
>
> For additional tips on using the outlook.adm and Group Policy, see Chapter 29.

### Setting Email Security on a Specific Message

Security such as cryptography can be set for an individual email using the options available with an open email message. Clicking on the Options button opens the Message Options dialog box. There, the end-user clicks on Security Properties to set the security settings for the message. The user can choose to encrypt the message and/or add a digital signature, request S/MIME receipt, and configure the security settings.

To do this, follow these steps:

1. Open a new message.

2. Click on Options.

3. Click the Security Settings button.

4. Add security settings as desired, similar to the ones shown in Figure 25.6.

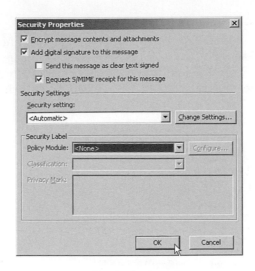

**FIGURE 25.6**   Setting security settings for Outlook mail.

5. Click OK when completed.

### Setting Email Security on the Entire Mailbox

Security settings can also be configured for the whole user mailbox so that they apply at all times.

To do this, follow these steps:

1. Go to Tools, Options.

2. Click on the Security tab.

3. Enable the choices desired for security for the entire mailbox:

   A. Encrypt Contents and Attachments for Outgoing Message

   B. Add Digital Signature to Outgoing Messages

   C. Send Clear Text Signed Messages When Sending Signed Messages (picked by default). (This allows users who don't have S/MIME security to read the message.)

   D. Request S/MIME Receipt for All S/MIME Signed Messages

4. For all choices (except choice C) to work properly, the user must get a digital certificate provided by the administrator. This can be imported by clicking on the Import/Export button at the bottom of the window beneath Digital IDs (Certificates) or by clicking on Get a Digital ID.

5. After you import the digital certificate, the security functionality is complete.

6. Click OK when completed.

## Attaching Security Labels

Also a feature in Outlook 2003, security labels are configured by the administrator and used by the end-user to add security messages to the heading of any email messages. Security labels require digital certificates and denote the sensitivity and security of an email. Security labels include information in the email header such as "Do not forward outside of the company" or "Confidential." They can be configured on a message-by-message basis or for the entire mailbox.

To configure a security label for a single message, follow these steps:

1. Open a new message.

2. Click Options.

3. Click Security settings.

4. Click the check box marked Add Digital Signature to This Message.

5. Choose the security label, classification, and privacy mark that apply to the message.

6. Click OK when completed.


To configure a security label for all messages in the mailbox, follow these steps:

1. Go to Tools, Options.

2. Click the Security tab.

3. Click Settings.

4. Click Security Labels.

5. Choose the policy module, classification, and privacy mark that will apply to all messages.

6. Click OK when completed.


## Using Junk Email Filters

Improved antispam has now been integrated into both Outlook 2003 and Exchange Server 2003. With this feature, the end-user can configure the level of antispam filtering desired and control the level of restriction in which messages will be checked.

With the Junk Email filter, messages are reviewed by determining whether the message should be treated as junk or legitimate email. Before a message is imported to the now spammer list, the filter analyzes each message to determine whether it's a junk email message based on the end-user's class or criteria. When Outlook is installed, the default setting is set to Low, which catches only the most obvious junk email. However, this level of security is configurable by the end-user and can be throttled, increasing the level of sensitivity on the junk email feature to catch more unwanted email. Messages caught by the filter and determined to be junk mail are then moved to a Junk Email folder with

Outlook 2003, where the end-user can then review emails and check for false positives that were accidentally specified as junk. However, the end-user can also configure options to permanently delete junk email messages as they arrive and not save them to the folder at all.

To configure junk email filtering, follow these steps:

1. In Outlook 2003, go to Tools, Options, Preferences tab.

2. Under Email, click on the Junk Email button.

3. On the Options tab, choose the level of blockage desired, as shown in Figure 25.7. Outlook 2003 is configured for Low blockage by default.

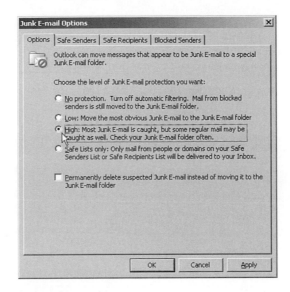

**FIGURE 25.7**   Setting junk mail protection level.

4. Click OK when completed, unless the sender lists will be utilized. The additional tabs are the Safe Senders, Safe Recipients, and Blocked Senders tabs.

### The Safe Senders List

If the filter determines that a wanted message is junk, the end-user can add the sender's email address to a Safe Senders list, thereby preventing the filter from identifying any following emails from that sender to be classified as junk mail. With the Safe Senders list, both the senders email addresses and even entire domains can be added to the Safe Sender list, better tuning the ability to avoid false-positive emails within the filter. By default, all entries in the end-user's contacts list are automatically included in the Safe Senders list, as are any names listed in the Exchange 2003 Global Address List. Finally, for the most aggressive antispam throttling, the end-user can configure mail to receive messages only from the Safe Senders list. However, this is obviously a very aggressive policy and could result in nonreceipt of many wanted emails.

### The Safe Recipients List

The Safe Recipients list basically performs the same functions as the Safe Senders list. The Safe Recipients list is used to configure email lists or mail-enabled groups that the end-user is a member of. When used, any messages sent from these groups are automatically considered "safe."

### The Blocked Senders List

The opposite of the Safe Senders list is the Blocked Senders list. Again, by using configured domains and specific email addresses entered into this list, end-users can completely block and never receive email from those specific configured senders. These messages are then handled and treated as other junk email (either deleted immediately or shunted to a junk email folder).

To add users to the Safe Senders, Safe Recipients, and Blocked Senders lists, do the following:

1. Select Tools, Options and go to the Preference List tab. Select the Junk Email button.

2. Choose one of the tabs (Safe Senders, Safe Recipients, or Blocked Senders), and then click on Add to insert the user into the appropriate list, as shown in Figure 25.8.

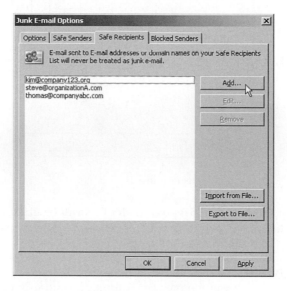

**FIGURE 25.8**    Adding names to one of the Safe Recipients lists.

3. Type in the SMTP email address of the user, group, or domain (such as jdoe@companyabc.com or companyabc.com).

4. Click OK when finished.

> **TIP**
>
> Some third-party companies provide lists of junk senders for import. If your organization wants to provide end-users with a list of trusted or junk senders, end-users can easily import the list by clicking on the Import from File button.

### Preventing Spam Beaconing

One danger with junk mail is HTML messages that include inline references to external content, such as pictures, redirections, or sounds. When the end-user opens the message or views it in the preview pane, his computer retrieves this external content, thus verifying the end-user as a "live" active address to the sender. This technique is known as a Web beacon. If left unblocked, it can make Exchange email recipients and their SMTP addresses vulnerable to and a target for junk mail lists.

To enable spam beacon filtering, from Outlook 2003, do the following:

1. Click Tools, Options and select the Security tab.

2. Under Download Pictures, click the Change Automatic Download Settings button.

3. Configure the necessary security settings. The default is to disallow any pictures or other HTML content.

4. Click OK when finished.

# Understanding RPC over HTTP

RPC over HTTP allows remote users to connect to Exchange Server 2003 using the Outlook 2003 MAPI client over an Internet connection, but without the need for a VPN or other tunneling software, smart cards, or security tokens. This gives remote access users secure communication access to Outlook features found only in the MAPI client.

## Installing and Configuring RPC over HTTP on the Server End

RPC over HTTP requires additional configuration on the Exchange Server to support HTTP Proxy. Two items must be configured on the Exchange Server 2003 front-end server for the remote connection:

- Install RPC over HTTP Windows component
- Configure IIS to support RPC over HTTP secured communications

### Installing the RPC over HTTP Windows Component

To be able to run RPC over HTTP, the RPC over HTTP Windows component needs to be installed. To install the component, do the following:

1. From the Windows 2003 front-end server that will host the RPC over HTTP client connections, run Start, Settings, Control Panel, Add or Remove Programs.

2. Select Add/Remove Windows Components.

3. Highlight the Network Services component and then click Details.

4. Select the RPC over HTTP Proxy option, as shown in Figure 25.9. Then click OK.

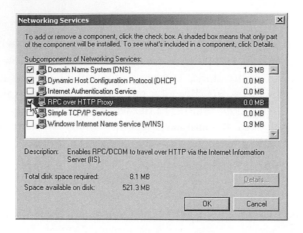

**FIGURE 25.9**    Selecting the RPC over HTTP Proxy Windows component.

5. Click Next to begin installation, and then click Finished when done.

### Configuring IIS to Support RPC over HTTP
After the RPC over HTTP Proxy Windows component has been installed, IIS needs to be configured to support RPC secured communications. To do so, do the following:

1. Select Start, Programs, Administrative Tools, Internet Information Services (IIS) Manager.

2. Traverse the IIS tree past the server, Web sites, RPC. Right-click on the RPC container and select Properties.

3. Select the Directory Services tab and click on Edit.

4. Deselect the Enable Anonymous Access option.

5. Select the Basic Authentication option (the Integrated Windows Authentication option should also be selected by default). Click OK.

6. Click on Edit and select both Require Secure Channel (SSL) and Require 128-Bit Encryption. Click OK.

## Installing and Configuring RPC over HTTP on the End-User Workstation

After HTTP over RPC is configured on the server side, the end-user's workstation system needs to be configured for secure end-to-end communications over the Internet.

Before configuring the Outlook client for RPC over HTTP access, administrators must be installed with the proper operating system. To support this feature, the client operating system must be running Windows XP with SP1 or higher, and Outlook 2003. In addition, the client desktop must be installed with the following hotfix to enable RPC over HTTP.

---

**TIP**

Before configuring HTTP over RPC on any client desktop, install the required hotfix available from Microsoft at `http://support.microsoft.com/default.aspx?scid=KB;EN-US;331320`.

As a best practice, install all security updates and required patches to ensure proper functionality when accessing Exchange over the Internet.

---

To install the required patch and configure the Outlook client for RPC over HTTP access, complete the following:

1. Install the patch.

2. Reboot the PC.

After the hotfix is installed, launch Outlook 2003:

1. Go to Tools, Email Accounts.

2. Choose View or Change Existing Email Accounts.

3. Click Next.

4. Select the Microsoft Exchange Server account and click Change.

5. Click the More Settings button on the Exchange Server Settings page.

6. Click the Connection tab.

7. Click the Connect to My Exchange Mailbox Using HTTP check box, as shown in Figure 25.10.

8. Click on the Exchange Proxy Settings button.

On the Exchange Proxy Settings screen, configure the following:

1. For Connection Settings, enter the URL of the Exchange server that has been configured as the RPC proxy server.

2. Click Connect Using SSL Only.

3. Click Mutually Authenticate the Session When Connecting with SSL.

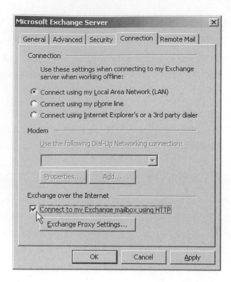

**FIGURE 25.10**    Selecting the connection to Exchange using HTTP.

4. Enter the URL for the proxy server.

5. If the user is located on a fast network, leave the default of connecting via TCP/IP first and then HTTP. If the user is on a slow network, connect using HTTP first and then TCP/IP.

6. For Proxy Authentication settings, choose the method that works best for the enterprise:

    The default method is Password Authentication (NTLM).

    Basic Authentication will prompt a user for a username and password each time the user connects to the Exchange server. If SSL is not being used, the password will be sent in clear text.

7. Click OK twice.

8. Click Next.

9. Click Finish.

The most secure method of connecting uses the following settings, which are also the default settings when RPC over HTTP is first configured:

- Connect with SSL Only

- Mutually Authenticate the Session When Connecting with SSL

- Password Authentication Is NTLM

# Using Outlook 2003 Collaboratively

Outlook 2003 expands on the collaborative tools of previous versions, including providing support for some new features as well. In this section, we will cover working with these collaborative tools and new features available in the Outlook 2003 client.

## Viewing Shared Calendars in Multiple Panes

To enhance collaboration in a business environment, Outlook 2003 now allows a user to view an additional Exchange Calendar in a shared pane. In previous versions, if an additional Calendar was opened, it was opened in a new window. Now, in Outlook 2003, as long as a user is configured with permissions to view a Calendar, multiple Calendars can be viewed at the same time, lined up side by side to view or compare them.

To open more Calendars, do the following:

1. Choose File, Open, Other User's Folder.

2. Choose the name of the user and select Folder Type: Calendar. The Calendar opens in the main window and automatically removes the mailbox owner's Calendar.

3. To view both the end-user Calendar and the additional Calendar, go to the Folder pane. There is an area under the monthly Calendar that provides check boxes for what Calendars the end-user wants to view. Click on the My Calendar box to view both the end-user Calendar and the additional Calendar.

> **TIP**
>
> When viewing multiple Calendars, keep in mind that each additional Calendar is shown in a different color. Also note that the corresponding check box on the left is seen in the same color.

4. Continue to add the Calendars desired and click on the check boxes to remove or add Calendars to view.

5. When completed, click on the My Calendar check box and deselect all the additional Calendars.

> **TIP**
>
> When opening shared Calendars, additional Calendars can also be accessed from the Calendar area by clicking on the Open a Shared Calendar hyperlink in the Folder List pane. Enter the name of the Calendar to open and click OK. This automatically shows both the mailbox owner's Calendar and the new Calendar(s).

## Enabling Calendar Sharing

For security reasons, Calendars are not shared by default. The end-user must specify users with whom to share a Calendar.

To enable the mailbox owner's Calendar to be shared, follow these steps:

1. Click on the hyperlink Share My Calendar in the Folder List area in Calendars.

2. The Calendar Properties box appears.

3. Click on Add.

4. Browse or enter the name or group to get access to the Calendar (see Figure 25.11).

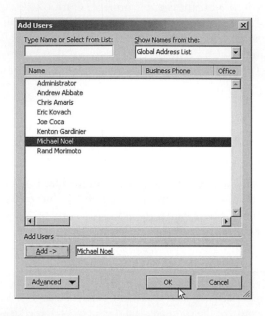

**FIGURE 25.11**    Sharing a Calendar with another user.

5. Click OK.

6. The end-user must now assign the permissions for other users of the Calendar. Outlook provides predefined roles for permissions that appear in the Permission Level box. Clicking the drop-down menu and choosing a predefined permission level shows what permissions are being granted, making it easy to choose the desired permissions. To create a unique set of permissions, choose an initial permissions level and then check the boxes and radio buttons to assign the unique permissions.

7. Click OK when completed. The user(s) specified will have those rights to the end-user's Calendar until the end-user specifically removes them by going through the same process mentioned, and then clicking on the user or group with permissions to the Calendar and choosing Remove.

## Sharing Other Personal Information

Outlook also enables a capability to share other users' personal information, such as the Inbox, contacts, and tasks. This is all done through the same method listed previously (except that the user must be in the Contacts or Tasks areas to access the proper hyperlink to share that component of Outlook). The exception is enabling mail sharing, which doesn't provide a hyperlink.

To enable mail sharing, follow these steps:

1. Right-click on the Inbox in the Folder view.

2. Choose Sharing.

3. Enter the users or groups and permissions levels, as described previously in the "Enabling Calendar Sharing" section.

## Delegating Rights to Send Email "On Behalf Of"

To enable a user to send email on someone's behalf, follow these steps:

1. Go to Tools, Options and select the Delegates tab.

2. Click Add.

3. Add the name of the user or group that needs the rights.

4. Click OK.

5. Choose the permission level for each component of Outlook.

6. Click OK when completed.

7. To send the delegates a summary message of their rights, click on the check box next to Automatically Send a Message to Delegate Summarizing These Permissions before clicking OK.

8. To enable the delegates to see private items, click on the box next to Delegate Can See My Private Items before clicking OK.

> **TIP**
>
> The Delegates tab found under the Tools, Options menu is also an easy option for the end-user to assign permissions. The end-user can permit others to view Outlook components, rather than requiring permission changes to be configured through the options individually. However, the permissions are less numerous and customizable than if done through the methods listed in the previous two sections.

## Sharing Information with Users Outside the Company

Throughout the different Outlook versions, collaborative functionality has constantly improved and enhanced with each version. Outlook 2003 provides some additional collaborative features not previously available, as well as some of the old tried-and-true features that have been around for many versions.

### Configuring Free/Busy Time to Be Viewed via the Internet

Exchange administrators and mailbox owners can publish free/busy information outside of the internal domain and company. If this option is desired, this information can be published by either using a company-published Web site designed for publishing this information or using through a service provided by Microsoft called the Microsoft Office Internet Free/Busy Service (both options require a user to have a Microsoft Passport account, which is used by the Microsoft Service). Via either method, any users outside of the company can view published free/busy information over the Internet from a shared location as well as use the same Web site to schedule meetings with internal mail recipients. This option is available for users accessing Exchange with the Outlook 2002 or later clients.

To configure free/busy time to be displayed on the Internet, follow these steps:

1. Go to Tools, Options, Calendar Options.

2. Click Free/Busy Options.

3. Choose the number of months of free/busy data to publish to the service, as shown in Figure 25.12.

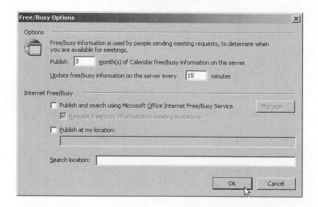

**FIGURE 25.12**   Providing three months of free/busy data publishing.

4. To also update how often Outlook updates the free/busy service with new information, under Options, type a number from 1 to 99 in the Update Free/Busy Information on the Server Every X Minutes check box.

To configure which service will publish the free/busy information, follow these steps:

1. To use a locally provided Web site, click Publish at My Location and enter the URL to the location. Go to step 10.

2. To use the Microsoft Office Free/Busy service, click the check box next to it and click the Manage button.

3. The user is directed to log in to the site using a Microsoft Passport username and password.

4. Agree to the terms of use by clicking on Yes, I Agree.

5. Click Continue.

6. Enter the email addresses of the users allowed to access the free/busy data.

7. Include a message to nonmembers that will be sent to them telling them that they have been authorized to view the free/busy information.

8. Click OK.

9. Close the Internet window after noting that the authorization process is complete.

10. Back in Outlook, click OK.

11. The user might be prompted to install some files to complete the installation of the added functionality.

12. Click Yes to install. The Outlook feature then is installed.

13. Click OK two more times.

### Viewing Free/Busy Time via the Internet

If permitted by the owner of the free/busy information, another end-user can view that information from the Web site. The user can send meeting requests, add the user to a group schedule, and see free/busy time. To do this, the end-user must access the free/busy information Web site, click on View Free/Busy Times on the Web, and enter the email address of the user whose free/busy time is to be viewed.

## Using iCalendar and vCalendar

iCalendar and vCalendar are RFC-compliant features of the Outlook 2003 Calendar that support communication between different types of Calendar clients. This allows a Calendar event created in one technology to import to a different Calendar technology.

vCalendar is the older version of the two Calendar features. It is widely supported by many different mail programs; when these options are being considered, it is best to use the vCalendar feature, which provides more compatibility. However, recurring appointments cannot be saved in the vCalendar format.

The iCalendar options are built on vCalendar technology. This option provides added journal entries and additional free/busy information. Also, because this option is built on the vCalendar technology, mail services set up to support iCalendar also support vCalendar. Using iCalendar also supports recurring appointments.

To send an iCalendar or vCalendar meeting request, first create the Calendar event. Then save it in the proper format and add it as an attachment to an email message; send it to the recipient, who can then import the iCalendar or vCalendar attachment.

To create an iCalendar entry, follow these steps:

1. Open or create the appointment that will become the iCalendar.

2. Choose File, Save As.

3. Click iCalendar Format, as shown in Figure 25.13, and then click on Save.

**FIGURE 25.13**    Saving an appointment as an iCalendar file.

4. Send the newly created .ics attachment in an email message to the recipient. The recipient will then import the attachment into his Calendar program.

To create a vCalendar entry, follow these steps:

1. Open or create the appointment that will become the vCalendar.

2. Choose File, Save As.

3. Click vCalendar Format (*.vcs) in the Save As box.

4. Send the newly created .vcs attachment in an email message to the recipient. The recipient will then import the attachment into his Calendar program.

Outlook 2003 can be also configured to always use the iCalendar format when meeting requests are sent directly over the Internet.

To enable the iCalendar functionality, follow these steps:

1. Go to the Calendar.

2. Go to Tools, Options, Calendar Options.

3. Click on Advanced Options.

4. Click the check box When Sending Meeting Requests over the Internet, Use iCalendar Format.

Now the end-user can send a meeting request as he would normally, but it will function across the Internet.

To turn off iCalendar, clear the check box mentioned in step 4.

### Sending Contact Information to Others

Another useful collaborative feature that isn't new to Outlook 2003 is Virtual Business Cards, or vCards. You can conveniently send the information of any Outlook contact to people either inside or outside the company. This vCard information can also be imported directly into your contact list program.

vCards can be emailed as attachments, included in auto signatures, saved to a file elsewhere, and imported and saved as contacts when received.

To email a vCard, follow these steps:

1. Open the contact that will become the vCard.

2. Go to Actions, Forward As vCard, as shown in Figure 25.14.

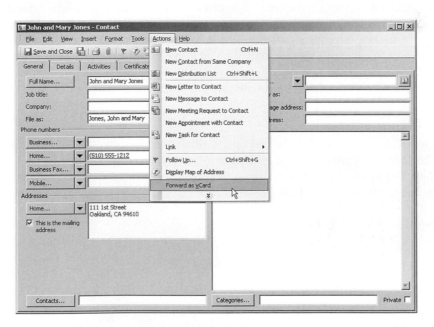

**FIGURE 25.14**   Forwarding a contact as a vCard.

3. Input information into the email and send the email.

When the user receives the card, he can open it, save, and close into his own contacts area.

To include a vCard in an auto signature, follow these steps:

1. Edit an existing auto signature or create a new one.

2. In the box below where the auto signature is entered, there is a vCard Options box. Choose an existing vCard.

3. If one doesn't exit, click on New vCard from Contact and choose the contact to create a vCard for.

4. Click Add.

5. Click OK.

## Using Public Folders to Share Information

Although using public folders to work collaboratively is not a concept new to Outlook 2003, it's worth mentioning its usefulness in collaborative business work environments. Public folders can be shared between different groups and users, across sites and servers. To support this configuration and provide acceptable performance, folders can be replicated across servers for fast receipt of information or, when needed, downloaded locally to client workstations for easy access while offline. These folders can all be repositories for email, documents of all types, group and contact lists, web pages and shared Calendars. They can be monitored so that posting is approved through a folder monitor before it is allowed. Public folders can also be mail-enabled allowing information to be sent directly to the folder through the GAL or SMTP address. These options make public folders a very powerful tool when establishing a collaborative work environment.

## Using Group Schedules

Group schedules are a new feature and only available to Outlook 2003 clients. Group schedules enable the user to create groups of users enabling a quick view of their Calendars. The Group Schedules feature also allows a user to send all the members of the group schedule an email or a meeting request using a single address.

### Configuring Group Schedules

Before anything can be done with a group schedule, one must be created by the end-user.

To create a new group schedule, follow these steps:

1. Select Action, View Group Schedules. The Group Schedules dialog box appears.

2. Click New.

3. Name the Group Schedule.

4. Click OK.

5. The Customized Group Schedules dialog box appears.

6. Click Add Others.

7. Type the name of the user(s) in the Type Name or Select from List box, and click To after the user has been selected (see Figure 25.15). Note that more than one user at a time can be selected and added to the To area.

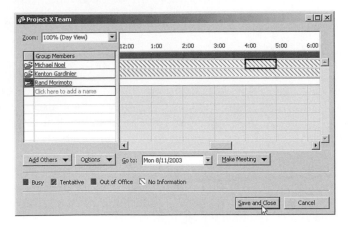

**FIGURE 25.15**    Adding usernames to the Group Schedules.

8. When all users are selected, click OK.

9. Click Save and Close.

After the Group Schedule has been created, to view it and work with it, follow these steps:

1. Click on the View Group Schedules button.

2. Select the group schedule to view.

3. Click Open.

### Sending Email or Meeting Requests to Group Schedules

After a group schedule is created, it is possible to send emails and meeting requests to the group from within the Group Schedule view.

To schedule a meeting, follow these steps:

1. Click on the Make Meeting button from within the Group Schedule view for the specific group.

2. Choose New Meeting to just send the meeting request to one member.

3. Choose New Meeting with All to send the meeting request to all members of the group schedule.

4. Fill out the meeting request as you would normally do.

To send an email, follow these steps:

1. Click on Make Meeting.

2. Choose New Mail Message to send to an individual member of the group.

3. Choose New Mail Message to All to send to the whole group.

4. Fill out the email message as you would normally do, and send the message.

## Using Synchronized Home Page Views

Using the Domain Group Policy or the Custom Installation Wizard, Outlook folders can be configured to view a Web page in the view pane when the end-user selects any of the root folders within Outlook (Inbox, Calendar, Notes, and so on). These web pages can exist as both intranet and Internet Web sites, providing end-users alternative options to share information in a collaborative workspace.

To configure shared Web home page views, do the following:

1. Open the Group Policy Object Editor (GPEdit.exe) using Start, Programs, Administrative Tools, Group Policy Object Editor.

2. Go to User Configuration, Administrative Tools. Right-click on Administrative Tools and select Add, Remote Templates.

3. Add the outlk11.adm template into Group Policy. Then click Close.

> **NOTE**
>
> outlk11.adm is installed in the \windows\inf directory when Office 2003 Resource Kit is installed on a system. outlk11.adm can be copied to the hard drive of the system being used to configure Group Policies, or the Office 2003 Resource Kit can be installed on the system.
>
> For more information on enabling and configuring this option, see Chapter 29.

4. Go to User Configuration, Administrative Tools, Microsoft Outlook 2003, Folder Home Pages for Outlook special folders, as shown in Figure 25.16.

5. Double-click on the Outlook home page to configure (for example, Inbox Folder home page, Calendar Folder home page, and so on).

6. Click Enabled.

7. Click Show Associated Web Page, and enter the URL of the web page.

8. Choose any other options and edit the default setting.

9. Click OK when completed.

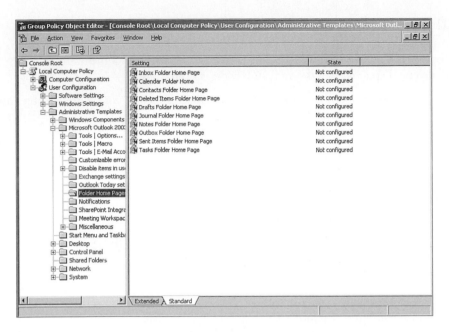

**FIGURE 25.16**   Configuring default folder locations for OWA.

## Using Outlook Cached Mode for Remote Connectivity

Outlook 2003 has another new feature with very familiar characteristics. To enhance the end-user experience for those who access Exchange information remotely, Cached Mode enables OST and OAB functionality with more seamless intertwined and easier-to-configure options. Using this option creates an experience to the end-user that should be faster and easier to manage than the PST options that were previously available.

The core idea behind Cached Mode is that remote and roving users maintain a full offline copy of their mailbox, which is stored locally (in an OST file) that automatically updates when online without user intervention. While using Cached Mode, the user can connect to Exchange, receive email, synchronize the mailbox information, and disconnect and reconnect to the network without exiting from Outlook—or experiencing any delays or the application hanging. The cached mailbox eliminates the constant need for a user to be connected to the Exchange server and the network while still providing the end-user the ability to work in the Outlook 2003 client.

The cached Exchange Mode is a very useful option when accessing Exchange over slow remote networks where network and server connectivity are known to be an issue (slow links as well as disconnections). It is a very useful option for users who frequently exchange portable PCs on and off the network during the day, preventing the user from being interrupted by network connectivity or slowness.

25

## The User Experience in Cached Mode

When the user is connected to the Exchange server, the word Connected appears in the lower-right corner of the Outlook window. The message "All folders are up-to-date" should also be displayed when synchronization is up to date.

When connectivity is lost, the message will say "Disconnected" and will give the date and time the offline folders were last updated.

When connectivity is first restored, the message will say "Trying to connect." As connectivity is re-established, the word "Connected" reappears; to the left are updates informing the user what is automatically occurring to get the mailbox up-to-date.

These messages could be

- Waiting to update the full items in Inbox

- Sending complete

- All folders are up-to-date

While the user is offline, some slowing when using Outlook might occur. However, the whole application will not hang as it would have previously.

## Deploying Cached Exchange Mode

Cached mode can be deployed by using a custom Outlook deployment and the Custom Installation Wizard or through enabling this option using domain Group Policy.

### Deploying Cached Mode Manually

When configuring a user's Outlook Profile manually, it's possible to configure Cached Mode at that time.

To configure Cached Mode manually, do the following:

1. Begin configuring a user profile in the standard manner.

2. When the Email Accounts page is reached, make sure the Use Cached Exchange Mode box is checked.

3. Finish configuring the Outlook profile.

### Deploying Cached Mode Using the Custom Installation Wizard

To deploy Cached Mode in Outlook 2003, one method is to use the Custom Installation Wizard to create a custom Outlook profile. The custom profile can be used to push out the same information or configuration to multiple users when Outlook is distributed to the client desktop.

> **NOTE**
>
> This section refers to the Custom Installation Wizard available with the Office 2003 Resource Kit.

To customize the Custom Installation Wizard, do the following:

1. While in the Custom Installation Wizard, go to the Outlook: Specify Exchange Settings page.

2. Click Configure an Exchange Server Connection.

3. Configure the following options:

   - To specify a new location for OST files (one method to change to Unicode OST files):

     1. Click on More Settings.

     2. Click Configure Cached Exchange Mode on the Outlook: Specify Exchange Settings page.

   - To configure a default behavior for downloading messages, do the following:

     1. Go to the Outlook: Specify Exchange Settings page.

     2. Click Configure New or Existing Profiles to Use a Local Copy of the Exchange Mailbox.

     3. Click the check box Configure an Exchange Local Mailbox.

     4. Click Use Local Copy of Mailbox.

     5. Choose the default download option desired for the default behavior: Download Only Headers, Download Headers Followed by the Full Item, or Download Full Items.

### Deploying Cached Mode Using Group Policy

Another method for configuring Cached Mode is to use Group Policy to push the new policy. If the Cached Mode Group Policy is assigned on a group-by-group basis (rather than to the whole domain at once), a phased approach to deployment will be achieved.

To access the Cached Mode Outlook configuration option (and any Outlook configuration options), the administrator must install the Outlook 2003 Group Policy template (outlk11.adm) first. The process for accessing the outlk11.adm in Group Policies is covered in the earlier section "Using Synchronized Home Page Views."

1. Open the Group Policy that has the Outlook administrative template installed. Go to User Configuration, Administrative Templates, Microsoft Outlook 2003, Tools, Email Accounts, Cached Exchange Mode.

2. Double-click on Disable Cached Exchange Mode on New Profiles.

3. Enable the policy.

4. Uncheck the Check to Disable Cached Exchange Mode on New Profiles check box, as shown in Figure 25.17.

**FIGURE 25.17** Enabling the Cached Exchange Mode by Group Policy.

5. Click OK.

6. Double-click the Cached Exchange Mode (File, Cached Exchange Mode) object.

7. Enable the policy.

8. In the drop-down list, select Cached Exchange Mode for New Profiles, and choose a download option (either Full Items, Headers Only, or Headers Followed By the Full Item).

9. Close the Group Policy.

### Deployment Considerations

Because enabling Cached Exchange Mode forces the end-users to synchronize a full copy of their mailbox to a local OST file as well as a full copy of the OAB, the demand on an Exchange server can be very substantial if a large number of users are initially configured to use Cached Mode at one time. The best choices for configuring Cached Mode initially are these:

- Continue to allow the users to use existing OST files. This prevents a full mailbox sync and only the changes are downloaded to the client. To do this, when deploying Outlook, clear the Replace Existing Accounts check box in the Outlook profiles.

Alternatively, do not specify a new Exchange server in the MAPI profile because this creates a new OST file.

- Deploy Cached Mode to groups of users rather than the whole enterprise. Combined with the next point in this list, the impact on the Exchange server will be the least and administrators can effectively enable this option centrally through the domain Group Policy.

- Initially deploy Outlook 2003 with Cached Mode disabled. When network bandwidth may be a concern, provide those users who will be enabling Cached Mode with an initial "seed" OST file. This is a capture of already populated OST that captures their mailbox, as well as a full OAB download on a CD and instructions on how to configure the OST and OAB. Then, when Cached Mode is enabled, the users will already have an OST file and the OAB relatively up to date, so downloading from the server is minimized.

## Using Cached Exchange Mode

Because Cached Mode somewhat changes the user experience, an administrator might consider some additional user training for those with Cached Mode enabled to train users on the differences. Some of these differences are mentioned next.

### The Send/Receive Button

It's important for Cached Mode users to know that it is unnecessary to click the Send/Receive messages button regularly when synchronizing with the new Cached Mode functionality. This now happens automatically.

### RPC over HTTP and the Cached Exchange Mode

It is recommended that users running RPC over HTTP also be users with Cached Exchange Mode enabled. This is because Cached Exchange Mode allows for "slow links and disconnections" to Exchange, which also might occur while the RPC over HTTP user is accessing Exchange information via the Internet.

### Slow-Link Connection Awareness

Cached Mode is enabled to address challenges when planning around links that are 128Kbps or slower. Using this option automatically implements the following email-synchronization behaviors:

- OAB is not downloaded (neither partial nor full download).

- Mail headers only are downloaded.

- The rest of the mail message and attachments are downloaded when the user clicks on the message or attachment to open it.

To change the slow link configuration, click on the On Slow Connection, Download Only Headers check box in Outlook 2003. This option can also be configured via Group Policy or custom Outlook installation files.

## Cached Exchange Mode and OSTs and OABs

Using Cached Mode will download a full copy of the user's mail to the OST file stored locally on the user's hard drive. However, administrators need to be aware of s ome considerations regarding OSTs and Cached Mode to plan and make their configuration choices for these Exchange clients, allowing optimal performance and efficient connectivity.

### Cached Mode OST Considerations

When configuring cached mode for users with large mailboxes, the new Outlook 2003 Unicode-formatted OST file should be enabled instead of using the older ANSI OST file method. This is because the Unicode OST files are capable of holding up to 20GB of data, whereas the old ANSI OST files have a limit of 2GB of data. Though large OSTs are not recommended in any environment, if the use of Unicode is enabled through Group Policy and Outlook identifies the file format on an OST and as ANSI, Outlook automatically creates a new Unicode OST and synchronizes it with Exchange. The policy can also be configured to prompt or not prompt the user before taking this action.

> **NOTE**
>
> This functionality will not automatically create new Unicode PST files. This option is only available when working with offline OST files.

To specify Unicode for new Outlook OST files through Group Policy, follow these steps:

1. Add the `outlk11.adm` template in Group Policy. The process for accessing `outlk11.adm` in Group Policy was covered in the previous section, "Using Synchronized Home Page Views."

2. Go to User Configuration, Administrative Templates, Microsoft Outlook 2003, Miscellaneous, PST Settings.

3. Click on Preferred PST Mode (Unicode/ANSI).

4. Enable the policy.

5. Choose the new default type for PST to be Enforce Unicode PST.

6. Click OK.

OST files can increase the size of the mailbox stated on the Exchange server by up to 50%–80%. This is because of the less efficient storage method used in OST files. For instance, Single Instance Storage functionality is lost when items are downloaded and synchronized. Exchange administrators may want to consider some of the following to decrease the size of mailboxes for users with Cached Mode enabled:

- Encouraging the use of autoarchiving of Exchange data for users with large mailboxes

- Not configuring synchronization of public folder Favorites unless absolutely necessary

It is imperative that any OST and OAB be configured to be stored on a local drive that has sufficient space to support the existing expected size and future growth expectation. If the client computer doesn't have enough space, errors will occur when Cached Mode attempts to download the mailbox locally. For example, it might be best to not configure the OST to reside on the system drive and instead to configure it on a data drive, if possible.

Caching Mode works best when the OST isn't close to its capacity. It is faster if only 5%–10% of the OST size is being used. Generally, it's best if the OST doesn't grow to be bigger than 1GB because the performance degrades.

### Cached Mode and Outlook Address Book (OAB) Implications

When using Cached Mode, it is possible to download a No Details Outlook address book, but users in Cached Mode should download the Full Details OAB because they can experience significant delays when they access the OAB and the full details are not locally accessible. When this occurs, the user's workstation must request the Exchange server to provide full data for the OAB, which can cause delays for the user experience during the download.

It's also a good idea for users running Cached Mode to download the Unicode OAB rather than the older ANSI OAB. This is because the Unicode OAB has more details held locally than the ANSI format, which decreases the number of server calls needed when a user accesses the OAB while online.

When Enabled, the OAB is synchronized every 24 hours, by default, down to the offline OAB. If there are no updates to the server OAB, there will be no updates to the offline OAB.

## Outlook Features That Decrease Cached Mode's Effectiveness

Cached Exchange Mode is easy to configure, but many Outlook 2003 features can decrease its effectiveness. The features discussed next can be considered the cause of Outlook 2003 sending calls to the Exchange server for information while in Cached Mode. For users using Cached Mode, these calls can greatly decrease the effectiveness and performance of the client and thus should be avoided if possible.

### Delegating Access and Accessing Shared Folders or Calendars

These two items both require access to the Exchange server to view other users' Outlook items. Cached Mode does not download another user's data to the local OST, so this nullifies the use of Cached Mode when the functionality is required.

### Outlook Add-ins

Outlook add-ins such as Activesync can result in Outlook not utilizing important items, such as the Download Headers Only functionality that allows Cached Mode to work so well. They also can cause excessive calls to the Exchange server or network. Avoid Outlook add-ins, if possible.

25

### Instant Messaging Integration

The use of Instant Messenger requires network connectivity. Thus, with Cached Mode, slow networks and bandwidth may be an issue when enabled with IM functionality.

### Digital Signatures

Verification of digital signatures requires Outlook to verify a valid signature for messages sent using digital encryption, requiring a server call as well.

### Noncached Public Folders

This, too, requires bandwidth and a call to the server. Consider synchronizing frequently used public folders to the OST (keeping an eye on the bandwidth needs and overall OST mailbox size as well).

### Customizing the User Object Properties

If the enterprise has created customized items on the General tab of the properties box of a user, this always requires a call to the server: When user properties are displayed, the General tab will always be displayed first. Therefore, if these are necessary, consider placing any customized fields in a different tab on the user properties pages, requiring a call to the server only when that tab is accessed, not every time the user properties are accessed.

## Summary

The Outlook client is a very versatile client and in today's business environment is used for much more than just for opening email messages, creating Calendar appointments, and sending messages. The Outlook 2003 client provides a whole lot more for organizations looking to expand the capabilities of the client and to provide group Calendar sharing, secure remote communications, and better information-management functionality when combined with Exchange.

Although hundreds of features were built into previous versions of the Outlook client, the new Outlook 2003 client has a variety of new ones regarding user productivity and group communications in an Exchange Server 2003 environment. Some of the new features include quick flags, the capability to propose new meeting times, the capability to associate items with a specific contact, and new message search capabilities.

Also new with Outlook 2003 are the tools that come with the Office 2003 Resource Kit. The new Resource Kit tools provide custom installation capabilities to automate the deployment of Outlook either through Group Policies or as integrated through other scripted installation tools.

Security is another major enhancement to Outlook 2003, with several new improvements for encrypted client-to-server communications using RPC over HTTP, the capability to add security to specific messages, and the capability to set security for an entire mailbox. Also, a powerful part of the secured client function in Outlook 2003 is the capability to set up junk mail filters to allow or deny incoming and outgoing messages between domains and specific users.

Finally, a new Cached Mode method of access enables a user to manage mail, Calendar appointments, and other content within Outlook, regardless of whether that user is connected to Exchange. Cached Mode access provides remote and roving users managed connectivity for unreliable remote access connections and improves the user experience when connection to an Exchange server is interrupted by either network failures or a temporary connection interruption.

All of the new capabilities of Outlook 2003, as well as the capability to leverage existing features in earlier versions of Outlook, provide an improved user experience within an Exchange Server 2003 environment.

## Best Practices

- Previous versions of the Outlook client are sufficient for most email users, but those who want to get the most out of Exchange Server 2003 should upgrade to Outlook 2003.

- Quick flags should be used to draw attention to messages that require follow-up or other attention.

- Key appointments can be flagged with colors to draw attention to appointments in user Calendars.

- Using the new search capabilities of Outlook 2003 can drastically improve the time it takes for a user to find messages or information within Outlook.

- The Custom Installation Wizard in the Office 2003 Resource Kit should be downloaded and used to help deploy Outlook configurations and manage Outlook settings either by script or through Group Policy.

- Instead of establishing a VPN before accessing an Exchange server from a remote Outlook 2003 client, the RPC over HTTP should be enabled to provide SSL-based 128-bit encrypted end-to-end communication from client to server.

- Calendars can be set up in group schedules to provide a side-by-side view of appointment Calendars for individuals or groups of users.

- Free/busy times can be configured to be viewable from the Internet, to provide nonconnected users access and views to appointment schedules.

- Outlook supports standard iCalendar, vCard, and vCalendar formats for the exchange of information across Exchange systems and cross-platforms.

- Cached Mode can be used to support users accessing Exchange across WAN links, saving bandwidth for other network needs such as business application access.

- Cached Mode for the Outlook client can improve performance for remote users across slow, unreliable, or failed client-to-server connections.

# CHAPTER 26

# Everything You Need to Know About the Outlook Web Access (OWA) Client

**IN THIS CHAPTER**

- Understanding Microsoft's Direction on OWA

- Using the Basics of OWA 2003

- What's New in the OWA Client (Since Exchange 2000 Server)

- Getting to Know the Look and Feel of OWA 2003

- Using OWA Mail Features

- Taking Advantage of Advanced OWA Features

- Customizing OWA Options

- Using the Calendar in OWA

- Gaining Functionality from the Meeting Invitation Functions

- Using Tasks in OWA

- Using Contacts in OWA

- Understanding OWA Security Features

- Tips for OWA Users with Slow Access

**M**any administrators and users found previous versions of the Outlook Web Access (OWA) client a less than appealing client substitute when they didn't have access to the full Microsoft Outlook client. With the release of OWA in Exchange Server 2003, many organizations are finding the Web client to have all the features needed to make OWA a great alternative when Outlook is not available as well as using OWA in some cases as a primary messaging client for certain types of users in an organization.

With this new version, Microsoft successfully has incorporated the most frequent customer requests for changes into OWA 2003. This chapter focuses on helping Exchange Server 2003 administrators and OWA users to become familiar with OWA and learn how to leverage the capabilities of Outlook Web Access in a business environment. The information in this chapter is useful for both new users and users familiar with OWA and, therefore, includes both basic instructions for how to use OWA and information on how to use the new and advanced features of the OWA client. Descriptions of the new features are discussed throughout, so to fully discover all the new features, read the chapter from start to finish.

# Understanding Microsoft's Direction on OWA

Outlook Web Access in Exchange Server 2003 provides a much more robust client interface, providing administrators more options when supporting clients accessing Exchange. In addition, OWA leverages newer technology, such as XML and the .NET Framework, to make it more powerful and useful in the day-to-day business communications needs of any organization. Arguably, OWA has changed the most of any aspect of Exchange Server 2003 from previous versions, allowing for a more complete useful client that can be accessed from a Web browser.

## Creating a Common Interface

The most obvious change in the 2003 OWA from its previous versions is its look and feel and its similarity to the full Outlook 2003. Although there are still differences between Outlook 2003 and OWA (including those inherent in using Web-based access and standard access), the look and feel along with key features are virtually exactly the same. Using the OWA client along with the latest Exchange service packs provide enhanced elements in areas such as spell checker, keyboard shortcuts, ability to configure rules, reading panes, and other improvements that help OWA feel familiar to end-users and, therefore, easier and friendlier to use, even for the least experienced end-user.

### The Outlook Client

Though OWA 2003 provides a very robust client access solution with many of the features of the full Outlook 2003 client, there are many features only available with Outlook 2003. For information on using the full client and all its features, see Chapter 25, "Getting the Most Out of the Microsoft Outlook Client."

## Making a Full-Feature Web Client

The biggest benefit of using OWA in this manner is that clients feel more comfortable using it as their only mail client, and that clients feel secure in the knowledge that they can do so without losing many features or functionality! With Exchange Server 2003 and the latest service packs, OWA is no longer regarded as only a remote access solution mail client, but can now be used day in and day out by users accessing mailbox information both in the office and from the Internet. In some cases, organizations might even decide not to deploy the full Outlook 2003 at all, and use OWA exclusively as the standard Exchange client for their users. However, it should be noted that limiting clients to OWA does limit features that Outlook 2003 provides and administrators should consider leveraging both solutions to provide users in the enterprise different solutions depending on the organizational needs of the business. Administrators should always plan to use both types of clients, and can certainly plan for more clients to use OWA, especially because it is a more robust solution, which certainly makes it an attractive alternative.

### Integrating XML in the Client Interface

Microsoft has also taken major steps to integrate XML into the OWA client interface; this is because the integration of XML into all Microsoft products that use the Web technology is a major push for Microsoft. This means that OWA can better integrate data, and a compatible code is used throughout Exchange and other Microsoft products that are served by Web-based technology, such as Outlook Mobile Access (OMA) devices and OWA. The result is that XML along with IIS 6 and its service packs means that OWA is more secure and better locked down than previous versions.

### Leveraging the .NET Framework

As with most Microsoft products today, OWA also uses the new .NET Framework and Internet-centric technology that enables applications more seamless integration with each other. The .NET technology sits on top of XML Web services and enables XML to be used by OWA. It uses the powerful .NET Framework to be more compatible with other technologies and provides access at a deeper level—to exchange data from a Web-based communications layer. The .NET Framework also enables users accessing OWA using Microsoft Internet Explorer 6 (SP1 or higher) to leverage Microsoft's Passport functionality with OWA along with MapPoint functionality available with contacts discussed later in this chapter. Using .NET Framework technology makes OWA a better Web interface and application all together.

# Using the Basics of OWA 2003

Older versions of OWA, just like previous versions of the Outlook client, was basically used for sending and receiving email. Basic email messaging has always been the focus for the Exchange client software programs and will continue to be, but now with OWA 2003, added features provide even more functionality and collaboration for even better business communications. Even with all this added functionality, there are cases when organizations don't want their employees to be bothered with all the features or are using older versions of Internet Explorer and even different browsers; for this, administrators can use the basic client. To accommodate all user needs, Microsoft created user modes built directly into Outlook Web Access 2003. These modes provide differing levels of feature availability and allow a user to choose which type of logon to use when accessing OWA. Some of the improvements and functionality changes in OWA 2003 are available only while using the Rich user mode, and not when using the Basic user mode.

### Understanding User Modes

OWA's logon, combined with the enhanced security feature called forms-based authentication, provides the end-user with two modes to choose from when logging on to Exchange via OWA. Depending on the application used to access OWA, for example, with Internet Explorer 5.01 or higher, users have the option to choose the Rich mode (or Premium Client Version) of OWA or the Basic user mode (or Basic Client Version). Users with Netscape or older versions of Internet Explorer or other Internet access methods must use the Basic mode for viewing OWA information.

## The Rich Mode

Using the Rich mode client definitely provides users with the full OWA experience. When using this mode, users can experience all available enhancements, views, and features available with OWA 2003 installed with the latest service packs, as shown in Figure 26.1.

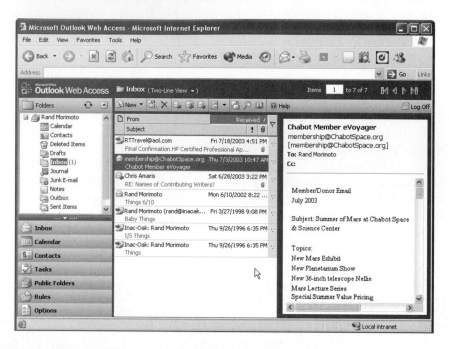

**FIGURE 26.1**    Rich mode Outlook Web Access.

One thing to keep in mind is that the Rich mode client is more bandwidth-intensive; to overcome this challenge for slow business networks, organizations can enable GZIP compression to increase performance up to 50% of that when OWA is used without compression. Administrators should review and test performance to determine if additional configurations are needed to maintain adequate performance when using the Rich mode client.

## The Basic Mode

With significantly fewer options and features available to the end-users accessing OWA, Basic mode, as shown in Figure 26.2, can still be used to access mail and calendaring information through the OWA forms-based interface. However, using Basic mode requires less bandwidth, while still providing any user with the ability to access OWA through any Internet application. Because of this, it provides a good alternative method for those with slow dial-up links to gain basic functionality without employing all the bells and whistles available to them via the Rich mode client.

**FIGURE 26.2**   Basic mode Outlook Web Access.

> **NOTE**
>
> This chapter is written from the viewpoint of a user who is accessing OWA via Rich mode. The experience for a user accessing OWA via Basic mode varies from the descriptions in this chapter.

Again, with forms-based authentication enabled on the configuration of a front-end or back-end Exchange server, the choice of whether to access OWA via Rich or Basic mode is presented at the user OWA logon screen. When users input their credentials, they also can choose the mode to use. By default, the Rich mode client is selected; the features presented when using OWA are dependent on this client selection before logon to OWA.

## What's New in the OWA Client (Since Exchange 2000 Server)

Many new features are available in OWA 2003. This section discusses old and new features. Table 26.1 details the new features and indicates which features are available in both Basic and Rich modes, and which are available only in Rich mode. However, the table does not include a full list of all OWA features.

TABLE 26.1   Features of OWA

| Feature | New Feature | Rich Mode *Only* | Basic and Rich Mode |
|---|---|---|---|
| **User Interface** | | | |
| New user interface | X | | X |
| Resize panes | | X | X |
| Public folders open in own window | X | X | |
| Last window size remembered | X | X | |
| Split screen view | X | X | |
| Logoff on toolbar | X | X | |
| Deferred View Update | X | X | |
| **General Functionality** | | | |
| Keyboard shortcuts | X | X | |
| Saved searches | X | X | |
| Items per page | X | | X |
| Search folders shown in folder tree | X | X | |
| GAL property sheets | More information in the sheets | X (But only in received items and draft items) | |
| Server-side rules | X | X | |
| Spell checker | X | X | |
| Context menus/right-click functionality | | X | X |
| Notifications of new email and reminder in Navigation pane | | X | X |
| **Mail Functionality** | | | |
| Send/receive email | | | X |
| Two-line view | X | X | |
| Preview pane | X | X | |
| New message notification | | X | |
| Quick flags | X | X | |
| Auto signature | X | | X |
| Mark message read/unread | X | X | |
| Message sensitivity Infobar | X | | X |
| Mail icons | X | | X |
| Find names from messages | X | X | |
| Customizable font in email editor | X | X | |
| Reply/forward in Infobar | X | | X |

**TABLE 26.1**   Continued

| Feature | New Feature | Rich Mode *Only* | Basic and Rich Mode |
| --- | --- | --- | --- |
| **Calendar Functionality** | | | |
| Reply to/forward meeting requests | X | | X |
| Preferred reminder time changes | X | X | |
| Launch invitation in own window | X | X | |
| Receive reminders | | | X |
| Set default reminder time | X | | |
| View Calendar from meeting request | X | X | |
| **Contact Functionality** | | | |
| Create contacts | | | X |
| Add recipients to contacts | X | X | |
| Send mail from Find Names | X | X | |
| **Tasks Functionality** | | | |
| Create tasks | X | | X (But no reminders) |
| Set default reminder time | X | | |
| **Security Upgrades** | | | |
| S/MIME support | X | X | |
| Clearing credentials at logoff | X | X | |
| **Internet Explorer 6 SP1 or Higher** | | | |
| Cookie authentication timeout | X | X | |
| Block external content— spam beacon blocking | X | | X |
| Timed logoff | X | | X |
| Attachment blocking (basic OK) | X | | X |

26

# Logging On

The logon interface might appear different from the older versions of OWA, depending on the configuration of the Exchange server. Users will experience different methods of authentication depending on if Exchange is installed with the default configuration or if forms-based authentication is enabled.

### Logon Screens

If the Exchange server is configured to use forms-based authentication, users are provided a customizable logon page with the options to choose the Basic or Rich mode OWA client. Using this feature requires the use of Internet Explorer 5.01 or higher, providing a user-friendly logon page, as shown in Figure 26.3.

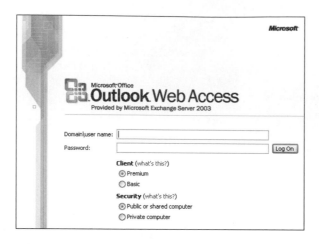

**FIGURE 26.3**    Prompt for Rich or Basic mode authentication.

If the Exchange server is configured for forms-based authentication but you are using an older version of Internet Explorer or another application, such as Netscape, you receive the authentication screen, but this type of access is limited and does not provide the choice of the Basic or Rich mode client.

One area not discussed in depth at this point is the default Outlook configuration. When a front-end or back-end Exchange server is installed and the server is not configured to use forms-based authentication, the user will receive a basic pop-up logon screen when the OWA Web page is accessed from a browser. After authentication or logon to Exchange is complete, the user receives access to the Rich or Basic mode clients. The client presented at logon is dependent on which Internet Explorer version or application is being used to access OWA.

> **TIP**
>
> When accessing an OWA server in the default OWA configuration, users accessing OWA with the latest Internet Explorer 6 SP1 browser are directed to the Rich mode OWA interface by default.

### Logon Credentials

Also depending on how the administrator has configured OWA, user authentication can be completed in different ways. The authentication configuration of OWA has users enter their domain name and then their username—for example, companyabc\Michele. The user may also use the fully qualified domain name, such as Michele@companyabc.com. And with the proper configuration, users also might be able to omit the domain name and enter just a username—for example, Michele. After successfully logging on, the user is presented with the default OWA screen.

### Security Options on Logon

Another important option to consider is the type of security embedded in the Forms-Based Authentication screen. When presented with the Basic/Rich Logon window, options are available regarding the type of security to use when logging on to Exchange. Users can choose whether they are on a public or shared computer or on a private computer. This option enables the client to address certain risks when accessing OWA.

If the Private Computer option is selected, the length of time before OWA automatically disconnects the session or logs off the user after inactivity is considerably longer than if the Public or Shared Computer option is selected.

By default, the Public or Shared Computer option is enabled when accessing the logon page. This option is defaulted and embedded into the Logon ASP page of OWA.

> **TIP**
>
> It is possible to change the default settings for the Private and Public or Shared computer setting. This is often a good option when supporting users with OWA on the internal network. This is done by modifying the logon.asp page. To do so, remove the rdoPublic information lines 685 and 691. Replace the entries in the rdotrusted lines with the following:
>
> ```
> INPUT id=""rdoTrusted"" checked name=""trusted""
> ```
>
> Always back up the logon.asp file before making any changes. Test all changes to ensure the desired results are applied when accessing the logon page of OWA.

## Getting to Know the Look and Feel of OWA 2003

As stated previously, the user interface (UI) of the new OWA client looks and feels almost exactly like the full Outlook 2003 client. It has the same basic pane structure, the same blue color scheme, the full folder tree, and the ability to change the widths of the columns, and it includes many similar elements and components found in Outlook 2003. With this familiar look and feel, even the most tentative user feels more comfortable using OWA. With this friendly UI, administrators can lessen the amount of training required for OWA client users. In addition to a similar look and feel, it also incorporates many of the same features that are included in Outlook 2003 when using the Rich version (and some in the Basic version) of OWA.

### Using Multiple Panes

By default, the OWA Rich client offers a very familiar pane when working within the UI. When users initially open OWA, they are presented with five basic panes, as shown in Figure 26.4. These panes were designed to help users cope with information overload by using better organization of data and better use of space.

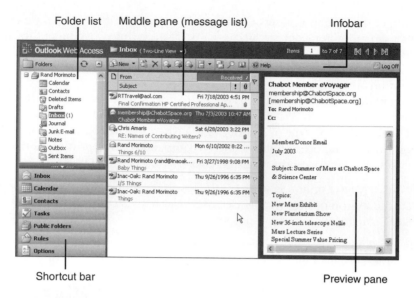

**FIGURE 26.4**   Outlook Web Access panes.

The Folder list is the upper-left pane, which, just like the Outlook client, lists all the folders available in the user's mailbox (Calendars, Journal, Inbox, Folders, Sync Issues, Sent Items, Junk Email, and even custom-created folders).

To help enhance navigation when working in OWA, below the Folder list is the Outlook or shortcut bar that lists shortcut icons to the Inbox, Calendar, Contacts, Tasks, Public Folders, Rules, and Options panes. Another helpful feature is the new mail notification pop-up. When new mail arrives, a vertical pop-up appears in the lower-left corner of OWA that notifies the user that she has new mail. The user can then click that button to refresh OWA and view the new message.

The middle pane lists the contents of whatever Exchange feature is selected in the Folder list or icon in the shortcut bar. For example, if Inbox is selected in the Folder list, the middle pane displays the existing and new messages in the Inbox. When using other options, such as the Calendar, there is one pane shown in the middle, not a split screen, as shown when the Inbox is highlighted.

The additional pane to the far-right is an optional pane called the reading pane. The reading pane is turned on by default and shown when viewing the Inbox. This pane shows the content or body of the message when highlighted in the center pane.

The toolbar across the top is called the Infobar. Like Outlook, it provides choices that are available while you view the information in the middle pane. The choices change depending on what a user is viewing when working within OWA. Different options are available when working with the Inbox, Calendar, and other options.

### Changing the Size of the Panes

To customize the OWA UI, a user can easily configure the width or height of the panes available. With OWA 2003, the adjustments of pane sizing can be saved when a user logs off. These sizing adjustments are remembered and restored when a user logs back on to OWA.

1.  To change the size of work area panes within OWA, move and hold the mouse pointer over the border between the panes, and wait for the double arrow or horizontal double arrow to appear.

2.  When the arrow appears, hold down the left mouse button and move the border right/left or up/down to resize the pane to the size you want.

3.  When the pane is in the proper place, release the left mouse button, and the pane will maintain the newly created size.

## Using Pull-Down Menus

To modify options within OWA, icons designate pull-down menus with an arrow next to them to allow users to choose different options. To view the choices available with these options, click the arrow to the right of the icon or the icon to see a menu similar to the one shown in Figure 26.5. To choose an option, move the mouse pointer down the list and view the choices as they are highlighted. To choose an option, highlight the option and click the desired choice.

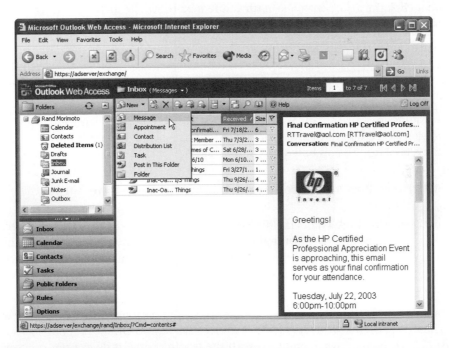

**FIGURE 26.5**    Pull-down menu in Outlook Web Access.

If there is no arrow next to the icon, the icon provides only a single choice, by clicking it.

## Moving Through the OWA Features

You can move through the different OWA features in a couple of ways. The first is by clicking the buttons that represent the feature you want to access. For example, the short-cut bar presents you with labeled icon buttons for options, such as the Contacts or the Inbox. By clicking once on the icon button, you can access the feature as it is opened in the center pane.

Another option is to select the desired options in the Folder list shown in the folder pane. Clicking the Inbox or any other folder in the list also allows the feature to be opened in the center pane.

## Moving Through Email Pages

When the Inbox folder is selected, email messages are displayed along with the reading pane. When working with the Inbox, you can now configure how many email messages are displayed on the screen at one time; an important thing to consider when configuring this option is, despite the number of messages configured to view, only a limited number of messages can fit in the middle pane, limiting the total number that can appear at one time.

As you well know, most users have many messages in a mailbox. To scroll through the pages of email messages when using OWA, click the arrows above the Infobar. Clicking the left- or right-arrow button moves you to the next page of email. To go to the end or beginning, click the arrow with the vertical line next to it. The arrow pointing left displays the beginning of the email pages; the arrow to the right displays the end.

You can also enter the page number of an email you want to view in the entry boxes that provide the ability to type in page numbers, for example, X to 1 of 45. However, this can be an inexact method to find an email because it's difficult to know exactly which page holds the email message you need, especially if you have many pages of emails.

Another way to organize emails is to use the Description bar, organizing emails by the From, Subject, Date Received, and more field options when the pane is moved over. Click the options to sort messages based on these criteria.

## Changing the Viewing Order and Using the Two-Line View

Users can change the viewing order of email messages in the Inbox or other email folders by using these selections. The default initial configuration is to display the most recent messages received by the users at the top of the email list. To change the view so the new messages go to the bottom of the list, click the word *Received* in the middle pane with a down-pointing arrow next to it. This rearranges the messages so the oldest received email is at the top.

Users can also choose to turn off the two-line view, eliminating the message preview pane. The two-line view enables the user to not only view an email title, but to also view the first line of the message. Combined with the reading pane, it gives users quicker access to view the core information of the message without having to open the message.

The two-line view is configured as on by default. To change the two-line view to a different view, click the drop-down menu next to the word Inbox above the Infobar and choose any of the other options. The choices are Messages, Unread Messages, By Sender, By Subject, By Conversation Topic, Unread By Conversation Topic, and Sent To:

- **Messages**—The Messages option removes the double-line view and shows the subject bars of the messages, ordered by date and time received.

- **Unread Messages**—The Unread Messages option shows only the messages that are unread. All other messages are hidden from view until another view is picked.

- **By Sender**—The By Sender option groups the messages by the sender's name. It creates an alphabetical list of those who have sent messages. Each sender has his own header with a plus sign next to the name. To show the messages sent by the senders, either double-click the sender name title bar or click the plus sign next to the name. The messages are then displayed, with the most recent at the top of the list.

- **By Subject**—The By Subject option displays the messages by the subject line of the messages and then displays all messages that share that heading (for example, replied-to emails) in a hierarchy below the initial subject heading message. This view can be useful when you're trying to find a particular message with a title and want to see all the corresponding/following messages. It lists all the empty subject headers and the reply messages first in a single group for each, however, which can be difficult to manage.

- **By Conversation Topic**—The By Conversation Topic groups messages by emails that have been replied to; this combines them as a type of discussion. This choice displays messages in the same type of hierarchy as the By Subject selection.

- **Unread by Conversation Topic**—The Unread by Conversation Topic option also groups messages by topic, but hides all messages except those that are unread.

- **Sent To**—The Sent To option groups the messages by recipient. This view shows groups as well as users to whom the messages were sent.

## Using the Reading Pane

As with previous versions of the Outlook Web Access client, the reading pane is an optional feature that can be toggled off and on. Turning on the reading pane opens a vertical pane on the far-right side of the OWA user interface, which shows the content of the message. The ability to scroll through the contents of the message in the reading pane enables you to view the whole message without having to physically open it. Even the location of the reading pane is customizable and can be located on the right vertical pane, or as a horizontal pane at the bottom of the page, or toggled off, removing the pane entirely.

To configure the reading pane, complete the following steps:

1. Click the reading pane icon. The drop-down menu provides choices as to where to put the reading pane (the default location is the right side of the OWA UI).

2. Choose Right to configure the vertical pane on the right side; choose Bottom to configure the horizontal pane.

3. Choose Off to turn the reading pane off. When the reading pane is removed, the middle pane expands to take up the space the reading pane used.

Attachments can now be accessed via the reading pane, using the methods discussed later in this chapter in the section "Using OWA Mail Features."

In addition, if the message has been viewed in the reading pane and another message in the message list is selected or OWA is refreshed, the previous message is no longer bold, changing the message status of the message to be marked as read, even if it hasn't been physically opened. When viewing messages in this manner, even though you have read the message, a read receipt does not go back to the requestor unless the message is actually opened.

> **TIP**
>
> To send a read receipt when viewing messages, you can click the Click Here icon in the far-right pane to send a read receipt without opening the message. If you open the message, use the Click Here button just below the toolbar at the top of the message to send a receipt.

## Creating New Folders

Folders and subfolders are also easily created and managed using OWA. You can easily create a type of additional folder that can be viewed and accessed in the Folder list:

1. To create a new folder, click anywhere in the Folder list (not the shortcut bar) in the left pane.

2. Right-click on any folder in the Folder list to see the menu shown in Figure 26.6.

3. Choose New Folder.

4. Name the folder.

5. Choose the location where it should be created by clicking the folder in which the new folder will reside.

6. Choose which type of folder to create:

    - Appointment Items creates a calendar container.

    - Contact Items creates a new contact list.

    - Journal Items creates a new journal folder.

    - Mail Items creates a new repository to hold email messages.

- Note Items creates a new Note folder.

- Task Items creates a new repository for task items.

7. Click OK when the folder is properly named and in the correct location.

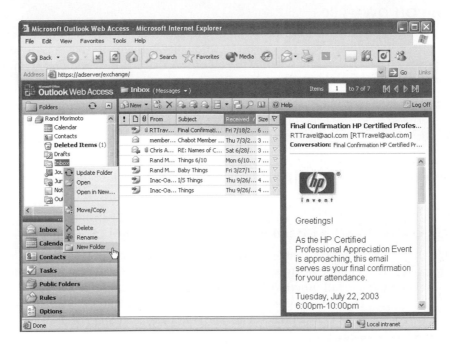

**FIGURE 26.6**    Adding a new folder to Outlook.

After being created, the new folder is immediately accessible for use and will appear in the location where it was placed in the Folder list.

## Displaying Public Folders in Their Own Windows

Access to public folders is also available through the Web interface, by clicking the Public Folders button on the shortcut bar; the public folders can be opened in their own, new Internet window. This gives users a great deal more space in which to work within OWA. When finished viewing and working with public folders, close the Public Folders window by clicking the X in the upper-right corner.

## Using OWA Help

As with all Microsoft applications, help is also available to users in OWA by clicking Help on the menu bar. The Help pages allow users access to information on features and steps for completing tasks. However, this Help feature does not enable searching or viewing by index as with its Windows cousin. OWA Help topics are segregated into groups according to the topic headings for simple access to any available topic. For example, if your

26

question deals with contacts, you can navigate to the contacts area, and all the topics dealing with contacts will be listed there. By clicking the plus sign (+), you can expand all the topics under the contact heading, enabling a view of all subheadings that become available. When you click a subheading, the Help information appears in the right pane.

## Logging Off OWA 2003

One feature also available with forms-based authentication is the Logoff button located on the right of the Infobar. With the logoff functionality being easily available at all times, it makes it much easier to securely log off of OWA and close a session than it was in previous versions of Outlook. Click the Logoff button to log off from OWA.

If the Exchange server is not configured to use forms-based authentication, users accessing OWA are forced to close the Internet browser window to finalize the OWA sessions and log off.

When logging off with forms-based authentication enabled, users are presented with the logon window after the logoff is complete, not forcing them to close the Internet browser window.

# Using OWA Mail Features

Although many features are available in OWA, the primary reason people use it is for the ability to access their email quickly and efficiently via the Internet. The new version of OWA makes using the email functionality portion of OWA easier and more robust than it has been previously. The following sections cover how to create and send email messages, including new features in OWA 2003 and advanced features available for dealing with sending and receiving email.

## Creating an Email

Many different methods exist for creating a new email message. The first is available regardless of what feature you are accessing and can be accomplished by clicking the drop-down arrow next to the New button on the Standard toolbar and choosing Message. The second is the simplest and is only available while you are in the Inbox or other mail folder in the Folder list. Click the envelope icon with the word New next to it. This pulls up a New Blank Message window, used to create email messages.

## Addressing an Email

Many methods also exist for addressing an OWA email message. When the message is open, the To, CC, and BCC boxes appear and are blank. These areas are used to enter recipient names to whom the message will be sent.

When sending a message, the primary recipients' names go into the To field of the message. Secondary recipients—those to whom the message is not primarily targeted—go in the CC (carbon copy) field. The BCC field stands for blind carbon copy, which means that the BCC recipient is invisible to all other recipients receiving the same message. In addition, when you use the Reply to All option, the recipient in the BCC box will not receive the reply.

To address an email, type a name (for example, `Kim Laur`) or an email address (for example, `Kim@companyabc.com`) into one of the three boxes. Note that multiple names can be entered into any of the fields; each name or address must be separated by a semicolon (;).

> **NOTE**
>
> When a name is entered and before it has been checked by Exchange and verified, it appears as a single line of text with no underline. After Exchange has checked the name—either against the Global Address List or contact list—or has confirmed that it is a legitimate formatted email address, the name becomes underlined, ensuring that Exchange regards the address as valid. Any subsequent unverified addresses go into the bottom box on the screen until they are checked, and then they are moved to the upper box.

Alternatively, use Find Names:

1. Click the To button to the left of the box area. This causes the Find Names dialog box to appear.

2. Enter the partial or full name of the recipient (for example, `Kim`).

3. Choose to find the names in the GAL or in the Contacts list, and then click OK. OWA lists all the *Kims* in the Global Address List (GAL) or the Contacts list, whichever was searched.

4. Click the recipient to highlight the name.

5. Click To, CC, or BCC.

6. Click Close.

The final method to add recipients to these fields can be done by using the Address Book. To add names via the Exchange Global Address List or any other available address book, see the section "Using the Address Book," later in this chapter.

### Removing a User from the To, CC, or BCC Fields in a Message

OWA 2003 makes it easier to remove a user from the address list of a message. To remove a user, simply right-click the recipient name or email address that needs to be removed, and then click Remove on the shortcut menu, or context menu. When removing names in the manner, it is important to know that there is no confirmation pop-up box; the name is immediately removed.

### Adding Attachments

Attachments are also supported when sending messages via OWA. Keep in mind that when sending attachments, uploads of the file or attachment is required and can be affected when doing so over slow links. In addition, when enabled at the server level, attachment size limits are also applied to OWA users when adding attachments. To add an attachment, the email being composed must be open:

1. Click the paper clip icon on the toolbar on top of the message, or click the Attachments button below the Subject line of the message. The Attachment dialog box opens.

2. Browse to the file to be attached and click it.

3. Click Attach, when completed, to attach the file to the email.

4. To add more attachments, click the Attachment icon again. Note that the same email size and attachment size limits apply in OWA as they do while in Outlook 2003, so be sure the attachments don't exceed those limits specified in Exchange.

5. Click Close when all attachments have been selected.

As shown in Figure 26.7, notice that all the attachments are listed below the Subject line, and the word Attachments is shown as an icon next to the attachment name.

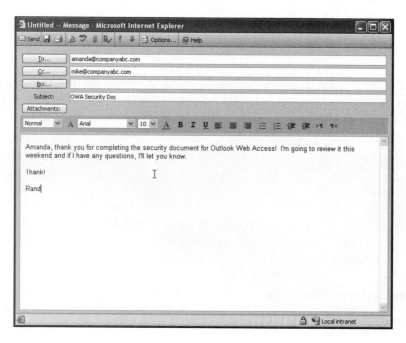

**FIGURE 26.7**    Attachments in Outlook Web Access.

## Sending an Email

After the information, attachments, and recipients have been entered in to the message, you can send the email by clicking the Send button with the envelope on it. At this time, if there are any issues with the names in the To, CC, or BCC boxes, OWA presents a dialog box highlighting the unresolvable address name. At this time, you can either delete this recipient from the list or choose a different user from a list by clicking Change To. If neither option is helpful, click Cancel and remove the address manually by using the method previously outlined for removing a user address from the To, CC, or BCC field list in the message.

After all changes are made to addresses, click OK and the message is immediately sent.

## Reading an Email

When an Inbox receives a new email message, a notification box appears in two places. A message window appears in the lower-right of the screen, and a message box appears in the shortcut bar. Both notify the user that a new message has arrived.

You can also force OWA to look for new email; to do this, click the Send/Receive Email button in the Infobar. This initiates a check with Exchange and updates OWA that a message has arrived.

To read an email, double-click the message in the message list. This opens the email message in its own window, enabling you to view the contents and access any attachments.

## Reading Attachments

If a message arrives with an attachment, it is indicated in the message list as a paper clip icon.

In the reading pane or in an opened email, an attachment can be identified to the left of the message list or listed below the Subject line and below the word "Attachment." To read the attachment, three options are available:

- The first option is to right-click on the underlined attachment name and choose Open. If allowed, the attachment opens in a new window.

- The second option is to right-click on the underlined attachment and choose Save Target As. This method downloads the attachment to the client accessing Exchange and allows the user to choose a target location locally to save the file. After the file has been saved, the user can browse to that location on the local client system and open the attachment there.

- The third option is to double-click on the underlined attachment, and if allowed, the attachment opens in a new window.

Some attachments that are at a high risk of containing viruses (such as executables) must be saved to a hard disk first, and cannot be opened directly from OWA. This is an intended security feature built in to OWA and keeps users from inadvertently opening a spamming virus that uses OWA/Outlook to send viruses to all entries in the user's Address Book. Forcing the file to be saved to disk provides another level of virus protection because generally, saving a file to a hard disk brings the machine's antivirus software into play, providing yet another assurance that the attachment isn't infected with a true virus.

26

When an attachment is considered high risk, OWA notifies the user that the attachment cannot be opened directly. The user then is forced to choose the Save Target As option.

## Replying or Forwarding an Email

Just as in the full Outlook 2003 client, OWA provides many options for emails to be replied to or forwarded. Three methods are available when choosing to reply or forward an email.

When a message is open, three buttons are available on the message dialog box toolbar. To reply to just the sender, click Reply to Sender and then click OK. To reply to all the recipients in the list, click Reply to All. Note that when the Reply to All option is used, it does not reply to any recipients listed in the BCC field. To forward the message to a different user not in the current recipient list, click Forward, and then enter the new recipient's address in the To field, using one of the addressing methods listed previously for addressing an email. When the message is properly addressed, click Send.

Another option is to right-click a message in the message list and choose Reply, Reply to All, or Forward from the shortcut menu, as shown in Figure 26.8.

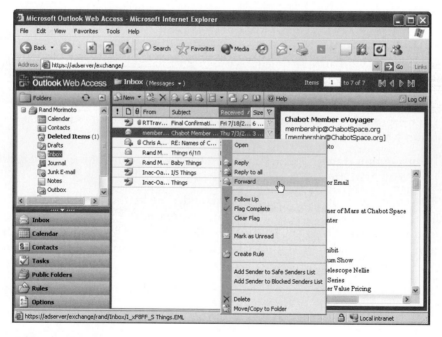

**FIGURE 26.8**    Reply, Reply to All, and Forward menu options.

The final method is to click a message once in the message list to highlight it and click one of the three envelope icons in the Infobar. Doing this allows a message to be replied to without actually opening the message. The left button is the Reply option, the middle is the Reply to All button, and the right button is the Forward button.

## Deleting Email

To delete a message while it's not open, simply highlight the email to be deleted and either press the Delete key or click the black X Delete button on the toolbar.

To delete more than one message at a time, press and hold the Ctrl key and click each message being selected, highlighting all the selected messages. After all are chosen, click the X button or press Delete.

To choose multiple messages in a row, press and hold the Shift key and click the top message; while still holding down the Shift key, click the bottom message of the group you want to select. When all are highlighted, delete the messages, using one of the two methods listed previously.

To delete an email while it's open, click the black X Delete button in the open email message.

## Configuring Message Options: Importance, Sensitivity, and Tracking Options

Certain options are available that can be applied to the current email message being created.

To access the options while the message is open, click the Options button in the toolbar of the message. The Message Options dialog box opens, as shown in Figure 26.9. Here, message sensitivity and tracking options for this particular message can be configured. Click Close when the options for the message are completed.

**FIGURE 26.9**   Message Options dialog box.

### Importance

Importance can be configured as Low, Medium, or High. By default, messages are marked as Medium. Configuring a message as Low Importance causes a down-pointing blue arrow icon to appear to the left of the message when the recipient receives the message.

Configuring an email message as High Importance attaches a red exclamation mark (!) icon to the message that appears in the message list when the user receives the message. These choices don't actually speed up the delivery of the message, but provide a visual clue as to the message importance.

26

### Sensitivity

Setting sensitivity options is a simple way for the sender to provide information about the message to any recipient receiving the message. Note that this option adds no security to the email message. When set, a visual clue appears at the top of the message (above the To and From boxes), suggesting the extra security assigned by the sender. The sensitivity setting also appears in the reading pane when the message is highlighted and is displayed in the Infobar when highlighted.

The choices for sensitivity settings are Normal, Personal, Private, and Confidential:

- **Normal**—Normal is the default setting for sensitivity: No message appears.

- **Personal**—The message reads: Please treat this as Personal.

- **Private**—The message reads: Please treat this as Private.

- **Confidential**—The message reads: Please treat this as Confidential.

Figure 26.10 is an example of a message that was marked Confidential and received.

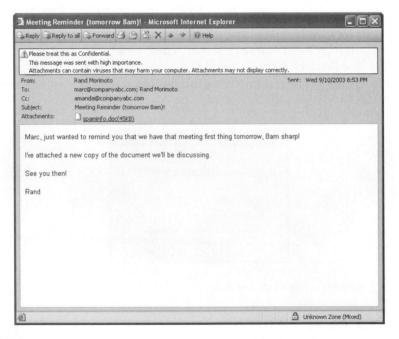

**FIGURE 26.10**    Treat-as-confidential notice on an email message.

### Tracking Options

Tracking options enable you to determine when the message has been delivered to a mailbox (which usually happens immediately) and request a read receipt be sent to the sender when the recipient(s) has read the message. If you enable these options, you receive a message when each recipient receives and/or opens the message.

However, the recipient also has the choice of whether to send a read receipt confirmation message. If the recipient chooses not to send the receipt, the sender does not receive a notification that the message was read.

In addition, if the recipient deletes an email configured with a read receipt without opening it, you receive a message stating that the message was deleted without being read.

### Changing the Look of the Text in an Email Message

The look of the text in an email can be easily changed and formatted. The choices for manipulating text include changing the font, font size, and font color; applying formatting, such as spacing, indentation and bullets, paragraph left/right, show paragraph markers, indent, and underline; and applying styles, such as headers and address.

To manipulate the text while the Create Message dialog box is open, highlight the text to be changed. Choose any of the options found on the Formatting toolbar below the Attachments area. There is no need to click an Apply or OK button—because these types of changes are immediately applied to the highlighted text.

## Taking Advantage of Advanced OWA Features

Many advanced features in OWA make finding users and user information and manipulating messages easier than in previous versions of OWA. Many of the features listed and discussed in this section are not available when using Basic mode.

To check whether the feature is available, see Table 26.1 in the beginning of this chapter.

### Moving Email Messages to Folders

You have the same visual folder view in OWA available as in Outlook 2003, meaning that all your folders and subfolders are available in OWA that are available in Outlook 2003. To move a message between folders, click the message once to highlight it and use the drag-and-drop functionality to move it into the desired folder. When moving messages and email items, there is no confirmation message displayed confirming that the message moved successfully, so to confirm the move was successfully completed, you must open the folder to verify the message is there.

### Using the Address Book

The Address Book has a much more robust search Address Book feature, which is new to OWA 2003. You can now use the Search feature to look for names and addresses listed in the Global Address List and any other address books configured in your mailbox. To access the Address Book, click the open Address Book icon located on the Infobar.

After clicking the icon, the Find Names dialog box opens. You can perform searches using any of the following criteria:

- Display name
- Last name
- First name
- Title
- Alias
- Company
- Department
- Office
- City

When you input information in any of the search fields available and click Find, as shown in Figure 26.11, OWA searches are performed against whatever list is configured in the Find Names pulldown option found at the top of the dialog box (for example, the Global Address List) and returns all the matches found only in that specific list.

**FIGURE 26.11**    Finding a name in Outlook Web Access.

To search a contact list or other custom list available in the GAL, click the Find Names In drop-down list arrow and choose the list from which to search. To see the properties of a user, click the desired user address and select the Properties button.

To create a new email message directly to a user found in the Address Book, click the New Message button at the bottom of the dialog box. When completed, click Close.

## Marking Messages Read/Unread

Additional organization of messages can be completed by marking a message read/unread (bold/not bold). To do so, right-click the message once to highlight it and choose Mark As Unread, or Mark As Read, as shown in Figure 26.12.

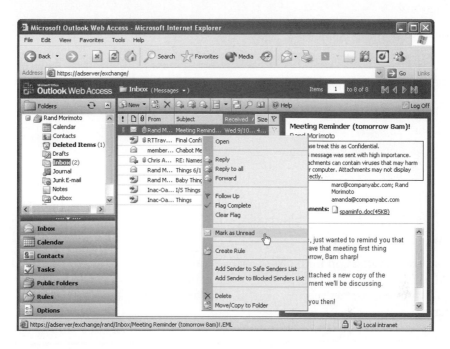

**FIGURE 26.12**   Marking a message as unread.

## Viewing User Property Sheets

To take advantage of the information provided through the Exchange Global Address List, OWA users can now view a great deal of information about address entries by viewing property sheets of names in the address list. Limited information is also available for senders from other organizations by viewing the properties of the addresses listed in the From field of any message received by a user.

To view property sheets of a user, sender, or any other type of recipient in a mail message, a username or address must be visually apparent. You can simply open an email message so the sender or recipients are displayed in the window or find the user in the Address Book. When viewing these Properties pages of an address in a mail message, this functionality is not available through the reading pane and can only be performed when the message is opened.

To view this information using the Address Book, click the name of the user and choose Properties. If the user is in an email message, double-click the username in the sender or recipients list.

The Properties page opens, which lists the following information about the user:

- Name (first and last)
- Initials
- Alias
- Display name
- Address
- Title
- Company
- Phone numbers
- Office

When viewing properties information, the data viewed is pulled directly from Active Directory if the user is viewable in the GAL. If the user is viewing a user object in the Contacts list, the data viewed is only information configured for that contact in the user's contacts list.

Note that user information in the Contacts list can be modified though OWA by clicking the Add to Contacts button while the properties sheet is open. Clicking Add to Contacts opens an Untitled Contact sheet, which enables the user to add/change any additional information.

After adding or modifying information, click Save and Close. When the contact closes, the Properties box must be closed by clicking Close. When completed, click Close again.

## Using the OWA 2003 Spell Checker

One of the most anticipated features of the new OWA 2003 is the Spell Check feature. And now, with Exchange Server 2003 and the latest service pack, this feature has been improved again.

This new functionality to OWA 2003 is very similar to the spell checker feature found in all Microsoft products, and should feel very familiar to users. Now, with the latest service pack, it includes some enhanced features making the spell checker more effective when using it with OWA:

1. To enable Spell Check while creating a message in a Create Message dialog box, click the Spell Check icon on the toolbar.

2. The first time Spell Check is used, a dialog box opens requesting a language selection. Choose the language by using the drop-down menu.

3. When completed, click the Check Document button.

4. Spell Check then checks the message. If it finds any errors, it highlights the error in the main text box, as shown in Figure 26.13. In the Suggestions box, it provides the recommended changes or suggestions of what OWA thinks the word should be.

**FIGURE 26.13**    Spell-checking a message.

5. Ignore the word and move to the next one, by clicking the Ignore button.

6. Manually change the word to a different spelling by entering the change in the Change To box. Then click the Change button.

7. Click a suggested word and click the Change button.

8. Spell Check will continue until it has checked the whole message. When completed, the Spelling dialog box closes.

> **TIP**
>
> Users can take advantage of specific options available regarding the functionality of the Spell Check feature (for example, configuring Spell Check to automatically occur before sending a message).

## Configuring Rules Using the Rules Editor

Another new powerful feature makes OWA an excellent option for users both as a remote access client and a day-to-day client. Now with the capability for users to configure server-based rules, end-users leveraging OWA as a client have a very powerful tool to assist with mail management. With full integration, users creating and leveraging rules through OWA will find and use the same rule in Outlook 2003, and vice versa.

To create a rule using the OWA UI, click the Rules icon button located on the shortcut bar. The rules pane then appears in the right pane of OWA. Any existing rules are listed in the rules pane.

When using rules, each rule is applied from the top down, in the order in which they reside in the list. Sometimes, the effectiveness of the rule depends on its place in the list; therefore, users can move the rules up and down in the list by clicking the Move Up or Move Down buttons to the right of the list of rules, changing the overall results when rules are applied. To create a rule, click the New button to open the Edit Rule dialog box, as shown in Figure 26.14. Many criteria are available to complete a rule.

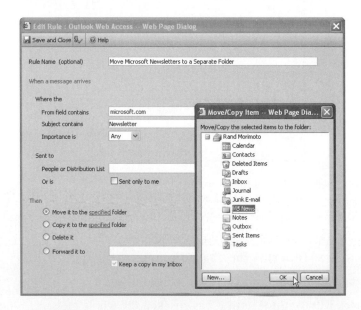

**FIGURE 26.14**    Edit Rule dialog box.

### Specifying Rule Criteria

The first section in the Edit Rule dialog box is used to specify the criteria used to put a rule into effect. When you configure one of the options in the When a Message Arrives section, the rule parses all incoming email messages to look for and identify if the message meets the rules criteria. If the criteria match the rule, the actions in the Then section are put into effect.

In the Where The area, specify a specific sender of the email message. If an email comes from that sender, the rule goes into effect.

In the Subject Contains area, specify any specific text to search for. However, the text must match exactly or the rule doesn't consider it a match. The Importance setting can also be configured as a criterion.

In the Sent To area, the rule searches names or lists in the recipients list. If the Sent Only to Me choice is selected, the rule looks for messages sent only to the user, not to a distribution list or an email sent to the user if there are other recipients in the email.

The Then section is the crux of the rule. It specifies what to do with the messages that are found via the criteria listed previously:

- To move a message to a specific folder, click the Move It to the Specified Folder radio button. When this is configured, specify a folder to which to move the message. Note that a folder can be created from the Folder Choice dialog box by clicking the New button and clicking OK after the folder is created.

- To copy the message to a specific folder, thereby leaving a copy in the Inbox and putting a copy elsewhere, click Keep a Copy in My Inbox.

- To configure the rule to delete the message, click the Delete It radio button.

- To forward the message to a specific user or a distribution group, click the Forward It To radio button and choose a user or group to receive the email.

- To keep a copy in the Inbox, make sure the Keep a Copy in My Inbox check box is checked.

As always, when completed, click Save and Close to complete the creation of the rule; the new rule is then added to the list of rules in the Rules pane.

## Displaying Context Menus

Message context menus are a new feature in OWA 2003. The context menus are available to perform a task or next step and can be accessed by right-clicking a message in the message list in the middle pane. The context list then provides the following choices:

- Open
- Reply
- Reply to All
- Forward
- Follow Up
- Flag Complete
- Clear Flag
- Mark As Unread
- Create Rule
- Delete
- Move/Copy to Folder

26

When you move the mouse over the desired choice and click once, the action is then taken. Each of these options is discussed in this chapter.

There also are folder context menu items available, which appear when the user right-clicks on a folder in the Folder list. The choices presented to the user are

- Update Folder
- Open
- Open in New Window
- Move/Copy
- Delete
- Rename
- New Folder

## Enabling Quick Flags for Easier Reminders

Continuing to improve on management tools, OWA supports Quick flags. Using this feature is an easy way to configure reminder notifications to follow up on emails, including specifying levels of importance for each of them, classifying each by one of six flag colors. The flags can also be cleared and marked Complete.

Quick flags can be configured on email messages in two methods. The first method is by accessing the context menu by right-clicking a message and choosing Follow Up. The other is to double-click the flag icon to the right of a message displayed in the middle-pane message list (under the word Received).

When a flag is configured on, right-clicking the flag gives you color options. Choose what color flag to apply to the specific message by highlighting a flag on the list and clicking it.

In a full mailbox, this feature can be very helpful to identify follow-up emails and emails you need to track. In addition, when you click the flag icon at the top of the message list, the messages are arranged by flag color making finding them even easier.

> **NOTE**
>
> The colors used for flags have no assigned significance within OWA or Outlook. Each user or organization can choose to designate certain colors for different levels of importance, priority, or even classification. The colored flags merely designate similarities or differences between messages, not specific priority.

When a flagged message no longer needs a flag, right-click the message and choose Clear Flag, which returns it to a grayed out flag, or Flag Complete, which is displayed as a check mark.

## Performing Searches with Outlook

Using saved searches are possible in OWA; however, it is the full Outlook 2003 client that makes this possible. By creating and saving frequently used searches in Outlook, a user is not required to reinput all the search criteria multiple times. These saved searches are then stored in the Folder list in a folder called Search Folder. Remember, the search folders and searches must be created in Outlook 2003 (not OWA) for a user in OWA to be able to use them.

To use already created searches, go to the Folder list, click Search Folder, and access the previously used searches to run them again.

Search functionality is available in OWA throughout the whole mailbox—and in every folder. The only limitation is that searches can't be saved in OWA. To use searches in OWA, follow these steps:

1. Click the highest folder in the folder hierarchy to search, and then click the Search icon in the Infobar. The Search dialog box opens, as shown in Figure 26.15.

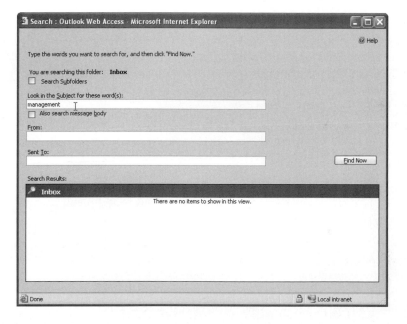

**FIGURE 26.15**    Search dialog box.

2. To search subfolders of the folder listed in the You Are Searching This Folder line, click Search Subfolders.

3. Input the search criteria in the Look in the Subject for These Words, if the text is in the subject line.

4. Click Also Search Message Body, if the search should also include the message body and not just the subject line.

5. To search for an email, narrow the search even further by choosing from whom the email was sent and/or to whom it was sent in the From and Sent To boxes.

6. After you input all the criteria, click Find Now. The results are then listed in the Search Results dialog box.

7. To open the results, double-click a result in the Search Results dialog box.

You cannot save a search in OWA, but you can delete a saved search. Click the X in the upper-right corner to delete a saved search.

## Using Keyboard Shortcuts to Save Time

A significant improvement, which makes many sophisticated typists happy, is that many of the familiar keyboard shortcuts used in Microsoft Office now also work while in OWA. Table 26.2 lists the keyboard shortcuts that can now be used in the OWA client.

**TABLE 26.2**  Keyboard Shortcuts Available in the OWA Client

| Shortcut | Option |
| --- | --- |
| **In Inbox View** | |
| Ctrl+N | Open a new message window |
| Ctrl+Q | Mark message as read |
| Ctrl+U | Mark message as unread |
| Ctrl+R | Reply to message |
| Ctrl+Shift+R | Reply to all selected messages |
| Ctrl+Shift+F | Forward the selected message |
| **In Message View** | |
| Ctrl+> | View the next message in the list |
| Ctrl+< | View the previous message in the list |
| **In Opened Message, While Creating a Message** | |
| Ctrl+S | Save the message |
| Ctrl+Enter or Alt+S | Send the message |
| [F7] | Activate Spell Check |
| Ctrl+K | Check names in the address boxes |
| Alt+T or Alt+C or Alt+B | Find names (look in Address Book) |
| **In Contacts View** | |
| Ctrl+Shift+L | Create a new contact distribution list |
| **In Public Folders View** | |
| Ctrl+N | Create a new posting in public folders |
| Ctrl+R | Reply to the posting |
| **In Task View** | |
| Ctrl+N | Create a new task |

## Understanding the Deferred View Update

To improve the speed of OWA, the new version includes a feature called Deferred View Update. This feature specifies how many changes to the window are enabled before the full OWA window refreshes. Changes can be things such as moving, copying, or deleting a message. In OWA 2003, the refresh is deferred until 20% of the window has changed. Until that threshold has been reached, the removed or moved items disappear but no additional or new items appear. The 20% is based not on the number of messages in the Inbox, but on the number of items set to display per page (which is configured in the Options area and discussed in the section "Configuring Items per Page," later in this chapter). If you don't refresh the entire screen with every change, the bandwidth and expense of OWA decreases.

# Customizing OWA Options

OWA enables you to customize and configure certain features universally for your OWA Inbox. When the options are saved, they apply until they are changed, whether you are in OWA or in Outlook 2003. To access the options area, click the Options button on the shortcut bar. A list of options becomes available for customization and configuration. To save the configuration changes, click Save and Close on the toolbar at the top of the Options page; otherwise, the options are discarded when the Options page is exited.

## Configuring the Out of Office Assistant

The Out of Office Assistant, shown in Figure 26.16, enables you to create a message that will automatically and instantly be sent to any senders who have sent a message to you while the Assistant is enabled. When a user enables the Out of Office Assistant, it remains on until you turn it off. Also, the enabling of and disabling of the Out of Office Assistant can be done in any of the Outlook clients, OWA, and Outlook:

- To enable the Out of Office Assistant, click I Am Currently Out of the Office. Then enter the text that will form the reply email back to the senders—for example, **Jane Doe will be out of the office until July 12, 2006.**

- To disable the Out of Office Assistant, click I Am Currently in the Office. OWA maintains the text from previous emails in the I Am Currently Out of the Office box until it is deleted manually or new text is entered.

- When you are finished, click Save and Close.

If a sender sends an email to a recipient with the Out of Office Assistant configured, the sender receives the Out of Office notification only once, even if he sends repeated messages or sends to a distribution list of which the out-of-office recipient is a member.

## Configuring Items Per Page

You can control how many items per page are shown. By default, OWA only displays 25 items, but this can be changed to show up to 100 objects per page, making visual

26

searching for messages much easier. To change this setting, click the Number of Items to Display Per Page drop-down list arrow and choose one of the provided numbers.

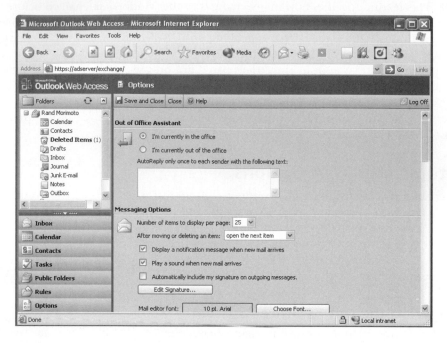

**FIGURE 26.16**    Out of Office Options page.

## Setting Default Signatures

Another option available in the OWA Messaging Options is the creation of an automatic signature. A signature is text composed in advance that appears at the bottom of new email messages. Signatures usually provide personal information about the sender—such as name, company, title, and phone number—enabling you to preconfigure the information so it doesn't have to be typed every time a message is created. You can also configure a signature to be automatically included in every message you send or to be added on a message-by-message basis:

1. To configure the signature, click the Edit Signature button under Messaging Options.

2. Enter the text that composes the signature.

3. After entering the text, choose to configure the font, font size, and color; to use bullets; or to use styles. Many other configuration choices are available as well.

4. When you are finished, click Save and Close.

When an initial signature is saved, its font size, choice of font, color, and choices such as bold, italic, and underline can be changed without opening the signature again. Click the Choose Font button under Messaging Options. Choose the options desired and then click OK.

If the Automatically Include My Signature on Outgoing Messages check box is checked, the signature appears on any messages created from scratch, forwarded, and replied to. If that option is not checked, you can add the signature on a message-by-message basis from within an open message you compose. To add the signature manually, click the Signature button (the icon with a piece of paper and hand with a pen) on the Standard toolbar within an open email message. It automatically inserts the signature after the button is clicked.

## Reading Pane Options

The reading pane options, shown in Figure 26.17, deal with the message list when Auto Preview is enabled. You must determine how long to wait with a message being previewed before it is marked as read. Choose from among the following options:

- **Mark Item Displayed in Reading Pane As Read**—After a specified amount of time that the message is viewed in the reading pane, the message becomes marked as read.

- **Mark Item As Read When the Selection Changes**—This option marks the message as read when the user clicks on a new message, no matter how long it was in the reading pane.

- **Do Not Automatically Mark Items As Read**—If configured, the messages are marked as read only when they are physically clicked on and opened.

## Spelling Options

The Spelling Options section provides configuration options for the Spell Check feature. If you check the Always Check Spelling Before Sending option, the spell checker automatically launches after Sent is clicked on a message but before it is sent.

A default language can also be configured in this location. OWA supports the following 10 language groups: English (Aus, UK, US, Canada), French, German (pre- and post-reform), Italian, Korean, and Spanish.

## Email Security

If S/MIME capabilities/compatibility is required, you must click the Download button to download and install the latest S/MIME version before OWA will be compatible with S/MIME functionality. See the section "Understanding OWA Security Features," later in this chapter for more detailed information about S/MIME support. To download S/MIME support, complete the following steps:

1. Click the Download button.

2. When presented with a security warning, click Yes to trust content from Microsoft. It will download some data and then present the security warning again. The download box disappears when the process has completed.

3. After the S/MIME capability is downloaded, several options appear. Choose which encryption options you want, or click the Reinstall button to reinstall the S/MIME support.

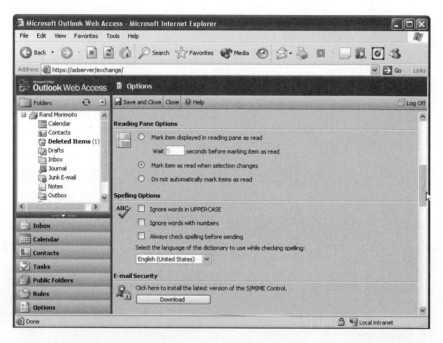

**FIGURE 26.17**    Reading Pane Options page.

## Privacy and Junk Email Prevention

OWA gives you many choices as to what to do with junk email, as shown in Figure 26.18, and provides default options, which are the minimum configuration suggested by Microsoft for spam control.

To filter junk email, click the check box next to Filter Junk Email. When configured, Exchange moves any mail it considers junk to your Junk Email Folder in the Folder list. When checked, you also must specify what is considered junk email by filling out the Manage Junk Email Lists dialog box. Specify Safe Senders, Safe Recipients, or Blocked Senders by adding their names or email addresses in the proper list.

The option to always trust email from contacts from your personal contact list is checked by default.

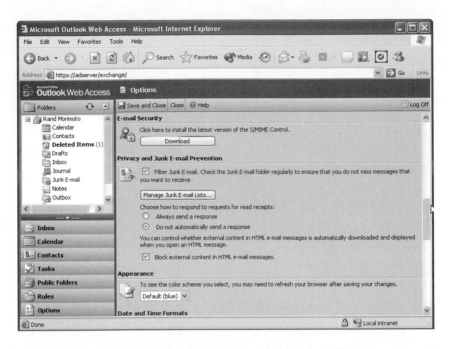

**FIGURE 26.18**    Privacy and Junk Email Options page.

> **NOTE**
>
> Users in the GAL will not be considered as coming from junk email addresses; therefore, there is no reason to manage addresses from the Global Address List unless you specifically want to flag messages from an individual or individuals.

The final option in the junk email area is whether to block external content, the implications of which are discussed in the section "Understanding Spam Beacon Blocking," later in this chapter.

## Color Scheme Appearance

The color scheme of OWA is configurable as well. The default is blue, but numerous choices are available. To choose a scheme, click the drop-down list arrow to the right of the 8-ball icon and choose the color scheme desired. Note that the color won't change until Save and Close is clicked.

## Configuring Date and Time Formats

The Date and Time Formats options enable you to configure the time zone, time style, long date style, and short date style:

- The short date style appears in areas such as the right side of the Inbox pane where it lists the time messages were received, in the appointment start/end times, or in the due date on a task.

- The long date style appears in areas such as in the Calendar at the top of a single day view.

Changing the time zone can be useful if you move to a different time zone and want OWA to reflect the new zone. To configure the time zone, click the drop-down list arrow and choose the proper time zone.

## Configuring Calendar Options

The Calendar options enable you to choose the day and times that describe a week in the Calendar. By default, the weeks begin on Sunday, the day start time is 8:00 a.m., and the end time is 5:00 p.m. This can be changed by clicking the drop-down menus to the right of the titles in the Calendar Options area in the Options menu.

The First Week of the Year choice specifies when the Calendar should consider the first week of the year.

## Configuring Reminder Options

Reminder options specify the default time of how soon before meetings, appointments, and tasks dates you are reminded. By default, all the configuration boxes are checked, and the default reminder time, which appears when you create a calendar or task item with a reminder, is 15 minutes. Configure any changes to reminders in this area by unchecking or checking the boxes or changing the reminder time by using the drop-down menu.

## Configuring Contact Options

Configuring Contact options enables you to determine where OWA checks first for resolution of addresses in the address boxes in emails. By default, OWA checks the GAL first. To configure OWA to check your contacts first before the GAL, click the Contacts radio button.

## Recovering Deleted Items

OWA also enables you to recover deleted Outlook items that have been purged from the Deleted Items folder. This option is dependent on the Deleted Items Retention setting configured on the Exchange server; thus, this option cannot be used to recover Outlook items older than the expired deleted item date.

> **TIP**
>
> When a deleted item has passed the Deleted Item Retention date, you will have to contact your administrator to retrieve the item or have the item restored from tape.

To recover a deleted item, complete the following steps:

1. Access the Outlook Options area and go to the Recover Deleted Items area.

2. Click View Items. The Recover Deleted Items dialog box opens, as shown in Figure 26.19, presenting a list of available files to be recovered.

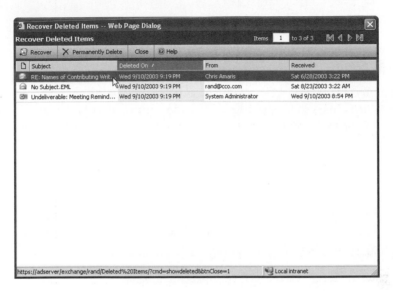

**FIGURE 26.19**    Recover Deleted Items dialog box.

3. Click the item(s) to recover.

4. Click Recover.

5. Click Close. After they're recovered, the item(s) will reappear in the location from which they were deleted.

6. Click Permanently Delete to purge the items completely. This makes them unavailable to be recovered through the Recover Deleted Items dialog box.

7. Click OK at the confirmation box.

8. Click Close to clear the dialog box from the screen.

## Changing the Active Directory Password

You can change your Active Directory password via OWA. This is extremely useful for mobile users who rarely come into the office. If you are on the road and your password expires, OWA enables you to access OWA and then forces you to change your password immediately. To change the password before being prompted, complete the following steps:

1. Access the Outlook options area and then click the Change Password button.

2. Enter the old password.

3. Enter the new password.

4. Confirm the new password.

5. Click OK.

# Using the Calendar in OWA

Outlook Web Access 2003 provides a fully functional calendar for managing personal meeting appointments, group appointments, and recurring events. The Calendar feature in Outlook Web Access includes the same functionality, including the new available features available with the full Outlook client. These options include appointment views, creation, and changes, and even changing meeting times as a meeting attendee.

## Using Views

You can view your calendar in many different ways, either by day, week, or month. To choose the view, click the icons in the Infobar that show Today, 1, 7, and 31:

- **Today view**—The Today view goes to today's date in the single day view.

- **Day view**—The Day view displays one day at a time. Users can move from day to day by clicking the day they want on the Calendar in the right pane.

- **Week view**—The Week view displays one week at a time in seven split panes in the middle pane. Brief descriptions of the day's appointments are shown in the seven panes.

- **Month view**—The Month view displays a one-month calendar, with brief titles for events in the Calendar.

## Creating an Appointment in Calendar

In OWA, all Calendar objects are initially called appointments, whether they are meeting requests with multiple invitees or appointments meant only for the individual user. To create a new appointment, complete the following steps:

1. Click the drop-down list arrow next to the New button on the toolbar and choose Appointment to see a screen similar to the one shown in Figure 26.20.

2. To maintain the appointment as an appointment and not a meeting request (meaning no one else is invited), use the default Appointments dialog box that opens. Enter the subject of the appointment in the Subject box.

3. Enter the location of the appointment in the Location box.

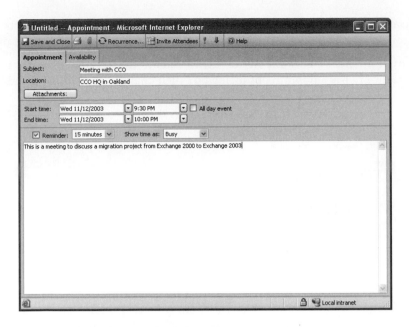

**FIGURE 26.20**    New Calendar Appointment page.

To specify a start time, there are two choices:

- To manually enter the time, type the time in the Start Time and End Time boxes.

- To use the OWA Calendar, click the drop-down menu boxes to the right of Start Time and End Time. From the calendar that is presented, click the date in the calendar to choose the date of the appointment.

To configure the time in a similar way, complete the following steps:

1. Click the drop-down menu to the right of Start Time and End Time and choose the start and end times.

2. It is optional to add text in the text area and to add attachments using the method discussed earlier in this chapter. If you want to do so, make these additions now.

3. To mark the appointment as important, click the ! icon located on the toolbar.

4. When you are finished, click Save and Close.

## Creating a Meeting Request in Calendar

When creating a new meeting, the same Appointment dialog box is used, but includes the ability to invite other users to the appointment:

- To create a new meeting request, click the drop-down list arrow next to the New button on the toolbar and choose Appointment. Input the subject of the meeting.

- To invite attendees, click the Invite Attendees button to display a page similar to Figure 26.21. The Appointment dialog box then changes appearance to add the Required, Optional, and Resources boxes.

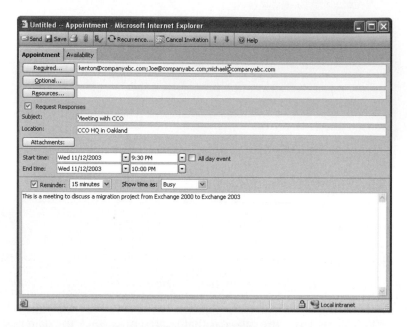

FIGURE 26.21    Calendar Appointment Invitation page.

### Inviting Attendees

Adding attendees to the meeting requires some extra steps. To add attendees, there are two choices:

- Enter the names directly into the Required or Optional boxes. If inviting multiple attendees, enter a semicolon (;) between the usernames.

- Click the Required or Optional buttons to use the Find Names OWA functionality. If using the Find Names functionality, locate the attendees using the methods listed earlier in this chapter and click the Required, Optional, or Resources buttons at the bottom of the Find Names dialog box to choose the box in which to put the invitees.

To use the attendee's calendars to view their availability, click the Availability tab. The Availability tab shows the schedules of the attendees by showing free time, busy time, or out-of-office time (not the details of what the attendees will be doing during those times, but whether they're available or not). If the attendees are busy at the specified time, you can choose a new time while viewing attendee availability.

To enter the new start and end times while viewing attendee availability, click the drop-down menus to the right of Start Time and End Time and Date and choose a new time. Another option is to click the actual calendar and move the start times and date by clicking and dragging the green and red vertical lines. The green line shows the start time, and the red line shows the end time.

Click the Appointment tab to complete the rest of the meeting request. Click Save and Close to exit the meeting request and send the request to all invited attendees.

### Setting Recurring Appointments/Meetings

If a meeting or appointment occurs with regularity, OWA enables the creation of multiple appointments with a single meeting request or appointment. To enable recurring appointments, while the Appointment dialog box is open, click the Recurrence button. The Recurrence Pattern dialog box opens, as shown in Figure 26.22.

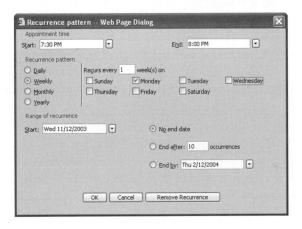

**FIGURE 26.22**    Recurrence Pattern dialog box.

To set the recurrence pattern, choose whether the meeting is Daily, Weekly, Monthly, or Yearly by clicking the radio button to the left of the appropriate choice.

Depending on which of those buttons is clicked, the items to the right change. The Weekly recurrence gives the options of what days the appointment occurs upon, as well as how often—for example, Every X Week(s). If Daily is chosen, the options display daily choices, such as Every X Days, or Every Week Day.

Range of recurrence enables the configuration of an end date for the recurrences. A specific end date can be specified, or the recurrence can be configured with No End Date or to End After X Occurrences, where X is the number of times the event will occur.

When you are finished, click OK. To exit the Recurrence Pattern dialog box without saving the recurrence configuration, click Remove Recurrence. The Appointment dialog box reappears. Complete the appointment or meeting request as needed and click Save and Close when you are finished.

# Gaining Functionality from the Meeting Invitation Functions

The meeting invitation function enables you to forward a meeting request to others, reply to the meeting request, set reminder times, launch an invitation, or receive task and calendar reminders.

## Forwarding and Replying to Meeting Requests

When forwarding or replying to a meeting request, users have the option of accepting, rejecting, or even requesting a different meeting time. To use these options, click the Forward To or Reply To context menus or the buttons on the Infobar. If the request is opened normally, the recipient will not be able to reply to or forward the meeting request without accepting or rejecting the request. By forwarding or replying to a request, you can create a discussion of the invitation or share its information with others without accepting or rejecting the original invitation.

## Setting Preferred Reminder Time Changes

When creating or setting reminders, the preferred reminder time is set to 15 minutes by default. This means that if you create a new Outlook item that uses a reminder time, 15 minutes prior to the reminder time, a notification will be displayed to remind the users of the upcoming item. This is a configurable option and can be changed in the Options section of OWA, as discussed previously in this chapter.

To change the reminder time provided by a meeting invitation, open the event and click in the drop-down menu that displays the reminder time. Choose the desired reminder time.

## Launching an Invitation in Its Own Window

To accept, request a change, or deny a meeting request, the request must be opened. To open it, double-click the invitation that arrives in the message Inbox pane.

The invitation then opens in its own separate window, enabling the invitees to accept the meeting, tentatively accept the meeting, or deny the request. This can be done by clicking the corresponding buttons on the toolbar in the meeting request box, and then clicking the Send button.

By accepting a meeting request, the meeting is automatically placed into your calendar with a dark blue heading on the left side of the meeting title. This can be seen in the Calendar view pane. Tentatively accepting the request also places the meeting in your calendar, but it appears in a light blue heading, indicating that the meeting is tentative. Denying the request doesn't alter your calendar at all.

All three choices result in an email being sent back to the original sender of the meeting request, stating the status that each attendee has placed for the meeting.

## Receiving Task and Calendar Reminders

When reminders occur in Tasks or your Calendar, a message similar to the one shown in Figure 26.23 appears in the shortcut bar and appears as a dialog box listing the reminders on your screen. You then can launch the task or appointment by clicking Open Item. You have three options:

- Dismiss all reminders at one time by clicking Dismiss All.

- Dismiss items individually by clicking once on the item and then clicking Dismiss.

- Snooze the reminder, and choose the amount of time to snooze by highlighting the reminder and clicking Snooze. In the time specified in the snooze time, the reminder will appear again.

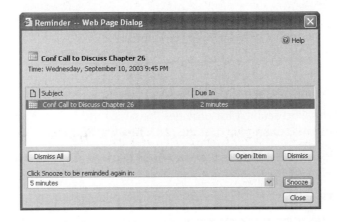

**FIGURE 26.23**    Calendar Reminder dialog box.

To view any reminders at any time, click the alarm icon button in the Infobar while in the Calendar view. The Reminder box appears after the button has been clicked.

# Using Tasks in OWA

The Tasks option in Outlook Web Access is similar to a to-do list. Tasks can be created, viewed, and organized.

## Creating Tasks

You can create tasks in OWA 2003 just as you do in Outlook 2003. Tasks are used to remind you of jobs that must be completed by a certain date or time. Tasks also enable you to set due dates and reminders and to follow the progress or percent of task that has been completed along with its status, enabling them to monitor areas such as works in progress. To make them even more effective, all criteria inside them can be easily changed when the task is saved, such as enabling frequent updates to the tasks' status and specifics about the tasks.

The Subject, Due Date, and Completion Status criteria can be sorted in the middle pane view while accessing tasks, making it easy to sort and view tasks.

To access tasks, click the Tasks button in the shortcut bar, or click New, Task in the Infobar. The New Task dialog box opens.

The methods used to input the subject, set the due dates and start dates, set a reminder, add attachments, complete text in the text box, and configure the task as recurring have been discussed earlier in the chapter and are applicable to configuring tasks.

When the task has been configured, click Save and Close to finish the task and save it to your Tasks list. The task will then appear on the list of tasks. The default order of the tasks is by due date, and tasks with no due date appear first.

### Task Views

Like other OWA functions, tasks provide you with multiple views that can make the organization and viewing of tasks easier:

- **Simple List**—The simple list provides a one-line list by subject and due date, and indicates whether the task is completed.

- **Detailed List**—The detailed list provides the same criteria as the simple list, but indicates percentage completed, status, attachments, and importance.

- **Active Tasks**—Active tasks include the same criteria as the detailed view, but don't show any tasks that are 100% completed.

- **Next 7 Days**—This view includes only the tasks that are due in the next seven days.

- **Overdue Tasks**—Overdue tasks are all the tasks that are overdue and aren't marked as completed.

- **Taskpad**—The Taskpad view shows only the subject and due date for all tasks, with the status of In Progress, Not Started, or Waiting on Someone Else.

## Using Contacts in OWA

Contacts enable you to create your own lists of users that might not be within the GAL. By entering them into the Contacts list, you can easily send emails and appointments to those contacts and create distribution lists made up of users in the GAL and those in your personal contact lists.

### Creating Contacts

Creating contacts is a simple three-step process:

1. Click New/Contact in the Infobar. The New Contact dialog box opens, as shown in Figure 26.24.

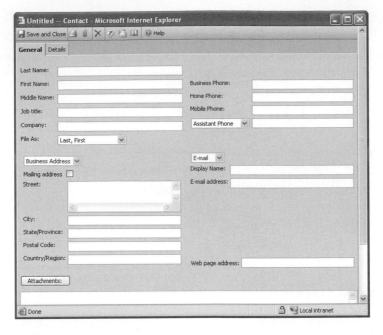

**FIGURE 26.24**   New Contact dialog box.

2. Enter all pertinent information about the contact. The Details tab enables even more details to be entered about the contact, such as nickname, manager, and even spouse name.

3. When completed, click Save and Close to save the contact in the contact list.

## Editing Contacts

To edit an already created contact, double-click the contact. Edit the contact sheet as needed, and then click Save and Close when completed.

## Mapping Addresses from Contacts

When you click the Mapping button icon, if you have access to the Internet, OWA contacts mappoint.msn.com and pulls up a map of the location stated in the Address portion of the Contacts sheet.

## Changing Contact Views

Just as the Inbox provides you with multiple views for email, Contacts provides six views for contacts:

- **Address Cards view**—Address Cards view is the standard, default view. The contacts look like Rolodex cards in the view, showing limited amounts of information about the contact.

- **Detailed Address Cards view**—Detailed Address Cards view shows a few more fields than the standard Address Cards view, but in the same format.

- **Phone List view**—Phone List view shows the contacts by name, company, and phone information in a single line per contact.

- **By Company view**—By Company view shows the contacts listed by company name headings. Contacts in the same company are listed below the company name heading.

- **By Location view**—By Location view shows the contacts in the same format as the By Company view, but by location (regions) rather than by company name.

- **By Follow-up Flag view**—Follow-up Flag view displays the contacts that require attention or need to be distinguished from other contacts.

## Deleting Contacts

To delete a contact, click the contact to highlight it and click the Delete button in the Infobar or press the Delete key.

## Finding Names

To find names in contacts, click the Address Book icon. When the familiar Find Names dialog box opens, click Contacts in the Look In box to search contacts instead of the GAL. This feature can be configured to always search Contacts rather than the GAL in the OWA options area in OWA.

## Sending Mail from Contacts

If a contact sheet is open, email can be sent directly to the contact if a correct email address is configured for the contact. To send an email directly, click the Send Email to Contact button on the toolbar.

OWA then opens a new email dialog box with the addressee information already completed, listing the contact as the intended recipient. Complete the email and send it.

## Creating New Distribution Lists

In the Contacts pane, you can also create custom distribution lists. These distribution lists are used to create a group mail address that can be represented as one single address for ease of sending messages to more than one user. All distribution lists are then saved in the Contacts list and differentiated from a standard contact with the group icon after it.

> **TIP**
>
> Contact distribution lists can include only recipients from the GAL, not from the user's contact list.

To create a new distribution list, enter the Contacts pane and do the following:

1. Click New, Distribution List. The New Distribution List box opens.

2. Enter the List Name (for example, **Local System Administrators**). To enter members of the list, complete the following:

   - Type the name of the users in the box under Add to Distribution List and click Add. The users must be entered one at a time. This method looks only in the GAL.

   - Click Find Names and find and enter names via the Find Name functionality discussed previously in this chapter.

3. When the names have been found, click the name and click the Distribution List button at the bottom of the Find Names dialog box. Then click Close to close the Find Names dialog box.

4. When the list is completed, click Save and Close.

## Understanding OWA Security Features

Outlook Web Access has several enhancements for security, including support for S/MIME attachments, spam beacon blocking, attachment blocking, cookie authentication, and clearing user credentials during the logoff process.

### S/MIME: Sending and Receiving Digitally Signed and Encrypted Messages

OWA 2003 now supports S/MIME functionality, giving you the ability to send and receive digitally signed messages using encryption. However, an ActiveX control must be loaded on each client. To download the ActiveX component manually, go to the OWA Options page. Configuration and loading of the S/MIME functionality was covered in the section "Email Security," earlier in the chapter.

### Understanding Spam Beacon Blocking

OWA 2003 provides additional security against spam. If configured, OWA does not enable spam beaconing technology to function in OWA; it blocks links to external content on the Internet from being accessed from the OWA interface. This greatly increases the anti-spam features of OWA by disabling the spammer's ability to hide beacons in unwanted spam messages. Those spam beacons automatically contact the spammers when the email messages are opened, letting the spammers know they have reached a live email address. By blocking this functionality, one more method of finding live addresses is eliminated from the spammer's arsenal.

## Understanding Attachment Blocking

OWA also provides built-in and configurable functionality to block Internet attachments, such as links to Web sites, music, and other Internet technologies available only outside the firewall (on the Internet).

OWA built on Exchange Server 2003 with the latest service packs contains a block list. Any attachments with an extension type in the block list are automatically blocked when sent to a user in Outlook or OWA. The latest service packs now also include blocking of XML MIME applications and test files.

When changing or modifying these options, only administrators can configure these options; this is not configured by users in OWA. When one of these types of files is blocked, users are sent a message notifying them that the attachment is blocked.

## Understanding Cookie Authentication Timeout and Timed Logoff

OWA 2003 uses cookies to hold the user authentication information. When a user logs off of OWA 2003, the cookie automatically expires, so a hacker can't use the cookie to gain authentication. In addition, the cookie is configured to automatically expire—after 20 minutes of inactivity in OWA if the user specified a private computer, or 10 minutes if the user specified a shared or public computer.

After timed logoff has occurred and a user tries to reaccess OWA, he has to re-enter user credentials.

The amount of time to wait before automatic logoff is configurable via the Registry by editing the Registry on the front-end Exchange server.

## Clearing User Credentials at Logoff

For users who access OWA 2003 via Internet Explorer 6.0 SP1 or higher and forms-based authentication, the user's logon credentials cache automatically clears when the user logs off from OWA 2003. It is no longer necessary to close the browser window to clear the cache. For users accessing OWA via other Internet browsers or via OWA servers that aren't configured to use forms-based authentication, users must still close the browser window to clear the cache and will be prompted to do so.

# Tips for OWA Users with Slow Access

Some users might need to access OWA through a slow dial-up connection. OWA provides them with many ways to enhance performance and speed to improve the overall OWA experience. Leveraging options built in to the Exchange operating systems and toggling off some OWA options can ensure that users accessing OWA experience a friendly, easy-to-use client.

When using forms-based authentication, making additional changes to the Exchange server can improve OWA performance. This option provides data compression on two levels when communicating with OWA and can improve the overall performance of OWA by up to 50%.

> **TIP**
>
> When enabling compression on the Exchange virtual server, test performance to validate that the change is addressing your performance concerns.

To enable compression on the Exchange virtual server, open the Exchange System Manager, expand the server name hosting OWA, and select the Protocols Folder/HTTP/Exchange Virtual Server. Open the properties page of the virtual server and select the level of compression based on the information provided in the following list.

- Low compression only compresses static components or pages seen in OWA.

- Using the high compression settings causes the server to compress both static and dynamic pages within OWA, allowing for a higher level of compression and performance.

There are options that can be configured from the server and through Group Policy to improve access speeds, but users can help speed up their access regardless of whether the server-side improvements are implemented. Major options are

- Choose Basic Mode When Logging into OWA

- Set Low Number of Messages to Be Displayed on the Page

- Turn Off the Reading Pane

- Turn on Two-Line Viewing

- Enable the Blocking of Internet Content

## Summary

Outlook Web Access in Exchange Server 2003 is more than just an alternative means of access when the user does not have the ability to connect with the full Outlook client. Because of significant enhancements added to Outlook Web Access 2003, along with forms-based authentication, many organizations are finding the security and features of the premium Outlook Web Access client robust enough to use OWA as a primary client for internal users as well. Because of continuing improvement available with service pack revision, features such as a spell checker, preview mode, filters, and Address Book lookup capabilities provide a robust set of features users leverage on a regular basis. When planning and deploying client access solutions, Outlook Web Access deserves much more consideration, so that it can also be used as a primary messaging client solution.

## Best Practices

The following are best practices from this chapter:

- Use the Basic mode OWA client when client bandwidth access is limited.

- Use the Rich mode (Premium) OWA client when full functionality is desired.

- Leverage compression on the Exchange server to improve performance by up to 50% when accessing OWA.

- Always back up or copy OWA files such as the original LOG.ASP page before making any changes.

- Change pane size to customize the OWA view and meet your needs.

- Use Ctrl or Shift when selecting emails for deletion; this speeds up the process of deleting several messages at the same time.

- Use Quick flags to create reminders or to bring attention to a message for Outlook users.

- Use keyboard shortcuts to simplify menu button tasks or functions.

- Customize task views to give a user the ability to see pertinent task information.

- Send mail to an email contact by selecting the contact and choosing to send the email to the contact.

- In contact distribution lists, include only recipients from the GAL, not from the user's contact list.

- Because S/MIME attachments are supported by OWA, use them to extend encryption and digitally signed messages for enhanced security.

# CHAPTER 27

# Outlook for Non-Windows Systems

**IN THIS CHAPTER**

- Understanding Non-Windows-Based Mail Client Options

- Outlook for Macintosh

- Outlook Express

- Configuring and Implementing Entourage 2004 for Mac

- Terminal Services Client for Mac

- Understanding Other Non-Windows Client Access Methods

In today's business networks, Exchange Server 2003 administrators are challenged with a variety of compatibility issues. One of the biggest challenges is the need to support today's complex mixed-Exchange client platforms often found when implementing or upgrading to Exchange Server 2003. With a diversity of different client needs to attach to Exchange data, administrators and IT managers are constantly challenged with the complexities of providing client access to corporate mail systems for a variety of different clients, including those running non-Windows-based client operating systems.

When administrators need to meet these specific requirements, many of the challenges involved with connecting non-Windows-based clients to Exchange Server 2003 mail information are overcome using the built-in functionality of Windows 2003 Server and Exchange Server 2003 technologies. Combining Microsoft technologies, administrators can provide support and establish compatibility to alternative messaging clients using remote technologies, Internet solutions, and Microsoft-developed alternative clients. This makes Exchange Server 2003 an effective all-in-one corporate mail solution to support non-Windows-based client operating systems, such as Apple's Mac platform and Unix-based platforms.

Using the information in this chapter, administrators will learn the options available for connecting these non-Windows-based client systems and the applications available to provide access to Exchange Server 2003 mailbox information.

This chapter discusses applications—such as Outlook Web Access and Entourage 2004—that provide connectivity for non-Windows-based clients to Exchange Server 2003 mail data. Each option is reviewed and discussed in detail to determine the different functions available with each solution and the compatibility when being used to connect to Exchange Server 2003 with the different alternative operating systems.

In addition to functionality and the conventional client/server connectivity methods, this chapter also provides systems administrators with the step-by-step instructions to configure access to Exchange Server 2003, using concepts such as Remote Desktop and Windows 2003 Terminal Services.

# Understanding Non-Windows-Based Mail Client Options

In most enterprise network environments today, the need to support non–Microsoft Windows client operating systems is almost guaranteed; administrators must plan and support alternative means of access to Exchange mail information.

To accomplish this goal, administrators can use several options available to provide Exchange data and calendaring information to a variety of alternative non-Windows-based client systems. Leveraging the built-in compatibility and functionality of Exchange Server 2003, access can be accomplished using any one or a combination of multiple familiar client options, depending on the operating system being used and the functionality needed by the individual client.

Using Exchange client options such as Entourage 2004, Outlook Web Access, and even Windows-based Remote Desktop (RDP), and others listed later in this chapter, administrators can identify the best solution available to provide Exchange Server 2003 server connectivity based on the operating system being used and functionality of each solution.

In addition, because these types of clients are usually the minority in most Exchange environments, administrators can also evaluate the functionality available with each of these client solutions and implement any specific one based on the requirements of the client accessing Exchange information.

## Supporting Mac Clients with Microsoft Solutions

When determining which Exchange client is best for supporting Mac users and desktops, the most important consideration is the required functionality of the client user and the limitations involved with each available option.

To support Mac desktops with Exchange Server 2003, Microsoft now provides the Entourage 2004, Outlook 2001, and Outlook Express clients designed specifically for the Macintosh desktop operating system.

Using any of these options, administrators can support internal network access and remote connectivity to Exchange Server 2003 using applications installed directly on the client desktop using protocols already enabled to support their Windows-based Outlook client cousins.

**Supporting Outlook Options**

For additional information on Entourage 2004, Outlook 2001, and support for Mac clients in an Exchange Server 2003 environment, Microsoft provides comprehensive information and instructions through the Mactopia support Web site at www.Microsoft.com/Mactopia.

Though most Windows users are familiar with the name Outlook and Outlook Express, Microsoft also provides another very powerful client option for connecting Macintosh clients to Exchange Server 2003. Using the Entourage 2004 client, Mac users can get a robust set of client options, such as mail and calendaring synchronization, junk email filtering, and contact management with the look and feel more familiar to Macintosh users. Not the Outlook client, this alternative to Outlook is available individually or as part of the Office 2004 Mac client suite or can be downloaded independently.

**TIP**

Using the free .PST Import tool available from Microsoft, upgrades from Outlook 2001 to Entourage 2004 can be a simple process. The Import tool can easily export and import data from Outlook to Entourage 2004 SP1 providing a simple upgrade path without data loss.

To download the Import tool, go to http://www.microsoft.com/mac/
downloads.aspx?pid=download&location=/mac/download/office2004/
pstimport.xml&secid=4&ssid=15&flgnosysreq=True.

To download or learn more about deploying the Entourage 2004 client for Macintosh, go to http://www.microsoft.com/mac/products/entourage2004/entourage2004.aspx.

## Providing Full Functionality with Virtual PC and Remote Desktop for Mac

What is probably the simplest and most popular option when supporting Mac clients in a predominantly Windows-based environment is using the Microsoft Virtual PC and Remote Desktop Client for Mac. Using these Mac client options provides any Mac user the full functionality of a Windows-based Outlook 2003 client on the Mac desktop. These are two options that can easily be implemented and allow Mac users full access to Windows client tools and functionality. Using this option, administrators can not only provide access to Microsoft Outlook, but they can also provide full functionality to Windows desktop applications and tools directly to the Mac client.

Using the Virtual PC for Mac, users can launch and work in a fully functional Virtual Windows-based PC loaded on the Mac desktop. Effective for Mac users with Windows experience, Virtual PC provides cross-platform functionality for users by allowing features such as access to Mac desktop peripherals, cut-and-paste features between VPC and the Mac OS, no configuration printing, and access to Windows network–based shares.

**NOTE**

Unlike the RDP client, Virtual PC runs the applications on the local Mac client. This means that any data, including saved files and offline folders, are stored on the local Mac desktop also.

27

> To get more information on Virtual PC, including updates, visit the Microsoft web page at `http://www.microsoft.com/mac/products/virtualpc/virtualpc.aspx?pid=virtualpc`.

Using the Remote Desktop Client or RDP, Mac users can access a Windows desktop functionality through sessions based on Terminal Services functionality, allowing full functionality in Windows through a remote connection. This function also gives Mac clients the ability to cut and paste information from the Remote Desktop Connection to the Mac operating system, full printing functionality to local connected Mac printers, as well as the ability to provide network access to shared Windows resources. The difference in these two options is the default storage of Exchange data and saved work; with the RDP client, when the RDP sessions are disconnected, all saved information remains on the network and not the attached client.

## Using the Internet for Exchange Connectivity

When access to Exchange information is all that is required, the most effective option available is leveraging the Outlook Web Access (OWA) functionality built in to the Exchange Server 2003 operating system. Because using this option is normally enabled for standard Windows-based remote access from the Internet, Mac users can also access OWA as they access a web page from both the internal network and the Internet.

By using Web-based access to provide Exchange Server 2003 client functionality, administrators can consider this solution for a variety of different non-Windows-based client systems with Internet browsing enabled. Though Outlook Web Access provides a limited set of Outlook functions, the Outlook 2003 version does provide all the basic needs, including spell checking, calendar appointments, rules wizard, and more. Even more important, this options requires no additional client software to be installed on any non-Windows-based client.

> **NOTE**
>
> Enabling Web Access to support non-Windows-based clients for both internal network access and access from the Internet requires additional configuration of the Exchange Server 2003 server and network firewall.
>
> For detailed information on how to design and enable Outlook Web services with Exchange Server 2003, see Chapter 10, "Configuring Outlook Web Access and Exchange Mobile Services."

## Comparing Client Functionality and Compatibility

With each option and method of access to Exchange Server 2003, different options and functionality are available. As mentioned in the review of each method of access, some methods enable full functionality and others are limited.

Review the operating system requirements in Table 27.1 to determine whether the Mac operating systems meet the required revision for the method of access being considered.

**TABLE 27.1**   Client Compatibility

| Outlook 2001 | Outlook Express | Remote Desktop | Entourage | OWA |
|---|---|---|---|---|
| OS 8.X | OS 8.1 | OS X 10.1 | OS X 10.1 | N/A |
| OS 9.X | OS 9.X | or | or | |
| OS X Classic | | Higher | Higher | |

| Entourage 2004 | Virtual PC | Outlook | Outlook Express | RDP |
|---|---|---|---|---|
| OS 10.2.8 | OS 10.2.8 | OS 8.X | OS 8.1 | OS X |
| or | or | OS 9.X | OS 9.1 | or |
| Higher | Higher | OS X Classic | | Higher |

> **NOTE**
>
> Entourage 2004 and Office 2004 provide full support for the Mac OS X v10.4 Tiger.
>
> The Mac Operating System OS X Classic is the additional software component that enables application compatibility for Mac OS 9 and earlier versions.

Determine the required functionality by using Table 27.2 to compare the features of each client access method. Review the functionality of each method and compare the result with the Mac OS with which you are working.

**TABLE 27.2**   Client Functionality

| Requirement | Outlook Express | Outlook Desktop | Remote | Entourage 2004 | OWA |
|---|---|---|---|---|---|
| Email | x | x | x | x | x |
| Calendaring | x | No | x | x | x |
| Contacts | x | x | x | x | x |
| Directory Search | x | x | x | x | Limited |
| Offline Access | x | x | x | x | No |
| PST Archive | x | No | x | x | No |
| PST Import/Export | x | No | x | x | No |
| Junk Mail Filtering | No | No | x | x | x |
| SLL Security | No | No | x | x | x |

# Outlook for Macintosh

With similar functionality to the Windows-based Outlook option for Exchange Server 2003, Outlook 2001 for Mac can easily provide many of the same functions as its Windows-based cousin.

Before installing, review the compatibility information in the next section for each client access method to ensure that the client operating system you're planning to deploy meets the minimum hardware and operating system requirements for installation.

## Outlook Options for Macintosh

With the Outlook 2001 client for Mac, Mac users can access and share information with Windows-based users with the same functionality as any Windows client. In addition to the standard email and calendaring functions of Outlook, Mac users can also access information through the Exchange Server 2003 public folders.

Functionality using the Outlook 2001 client for Mac includes

- **Email support**—With fully enabled email support for Exchange Server 2003, Outlook 2001 also includes message rules and the ability to enable message priority and message tracking.

- **Calendaring**—Mac users can use the calendaring feature of Outlook 2001 to create and send meeting requests and manage group calendaring functions.

- **Contacts**—Contact management is fully enabled and allows Mac users to access mail contacts and create a contact address list.

- **Public folders access**—Mac users can leverage Outlook 2001 to fully collaborate with Windows-based users through Exchange public folders.

- **Sharing panel**—Users can enable access to calendaring information to other Exchange users, send on-behalf permissions, and have the ability to allow other users to view private items.

- **Single sign-on**—Using Keychain from Apple, users can configure and enable this feature to provide single sign-on functionality when opening Outlook 2001.

- **Offline folders**—As with Windows Outlook, offline synchronization is fully enabled in Outlook 2001 for Mac, enabling users to synchronize email, calendars, contacts, and public folders.

- **Offline address book**—When Offline Synchronization is enabled, Mac users can also download the offline address book, enabling the email creation functionality when offline.

## Configuring Support for Mac Clients

Before installing the Mac Outlook client for Exchange Server 2003, administrators must configure support from the client to connect to the network. In addition, the Apple Mac hardware must be evaluated to ensure that it meets the minimum required hardware specifications to support the Outlook 2001 client.

To enable TCP/IP support on the Mac operating system, complete these steps:

1. From the Apple menu, select Control, TCP/IP properties.

2. In the TCP/IP dialog box, configure the TCP/IP properties, as shown in Figure 27.1.

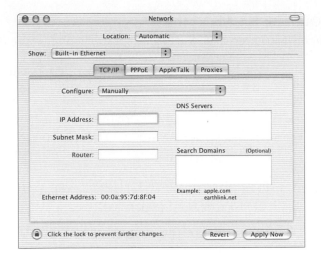

**FIGURE 27.1**    Mac client TCP/IP properties.

3. In this scenario, configure the TCP/IP properties using a Static setting. Select the Connect Via option and then select Ethernet.

4. From the Configure tab, select Manually.

5. Enter the TCP/IP properties and DNS address being used on your network.

6. Close the TCP/IP properties and reboot the Mac system.

---

**TIP**

To enhance and ensure optimal performance when using Outlook 2001 for Mac, turn on the Virtual Memory of the Mac client through the Memory Control Panel.

---

Before installing the Outlook 2001 client, ensure that the hardware being installed can meet the minimum requirement for supporting the Outlook client, as shown in Table 27.3.

**TABLE 27.3**    Outlook 2001 Hardware Requirements

| Processor | Memory | Hard Disk Space |
|-----------|--------|-----------------|
| Mac PowerPC | 32MB | 20MB available disk space |

---

**TIP**

If you are not sure which Mac platform and hardware you are using, use the Mac System Profiler tool available with the Mac operating system. To launch the Profiler tool, select the Apple menu and click the Apple System Profiler.

---

27

## Configuring Outlook for Macintosh

After all requirements have been met, you can install and configure the Outlook 2001 client for connectivity to Exchange Server 2003. To accomplish this, follow the steps in the next section and review the resources to troubleshoot any issues you might encounter.

### Installing Outlook 2001

To begin installing Outlook 2001, download or place the Outlook 2001 installation file in a folder on the Mac client. To begin the installation, follow these steps:

1. Select and click the installation file to expand it.

2. Start the setup of Outlook by clicking twice on the Outlook 2001.smi file.

3. From the desktop, click twice on the Outlook 2001 file.

4. In the Outlook 2001 window, select and move the Outlook 2001 file to a location on the Mac local disk.

---

**Downloading and Installing**

When downloading the installation file from Microsoft, problems might occur if Stuffit Expander is installed on the Mac client. Use Stuffit Expander 5.5 or later when installing from a download.

The Outlook 2001 client does not have an Uninstall feature, as with standard Windows installations. Remove the installation files from the download location when the installation is complete.

---

### Creating an Outlook Profile

After the installation of Outlook, you are prepared to configure the Outlook profile for the account that will be using the client. To create the first profile in a new installation of Outlook 2001, administrators can use the Run-First feature, which is launched the first time Outlook is opened.

To create the first profile in Outlook after the Run-First feature is launched, complete the following steps:

1. On the Create New Profile dialog box, enter the name for the new profile.

2. Enter the name of the account for which the profile is being created.

3. Enter the name of the Exchange Server 2003 server being used to house the client mailbox being configured.

4. Select the Yes option to enable the Is This Computer Always Connected to a Network option.

5. To test the configuration, select the Test Settings option to verify the Exchange server and account name.

6. After connectivity and the account information have been verified, select the Create Profile options to continue.

7. Test access to Exchange by launching Outlook 2001; enter the account name, password, and domain when prompted.

### Configuring the Profile to Use When Starting Outlook

Often, when Mac desktops are shared, administrators can create multiple profiles to enable access to Exchange for multiple Mac users by repeating the steps in the preceding section. To enable the prompt to choose which profile to use when starting Outlook, open the Control Panel and follow these steps:

1. From the Apple, Control Panel menu, select Outlook Settings.

2. To select the default profile, select the desired profile from the When Starting Outlook Use This Profile selection.

3. From the Outlook menu, select Edit, Preferences.

4. From the Preferences selection, click the General tab.

5. Click the Prompt for a Profile to Be Used under the setting When Starting Microsoft Outlook, and select OK to complete the task.

## Supporting Macintosh Clients

Administrators, in supporting Mac clients and Outlook for Mac, face some common issues when troubleshooting Mac clients, and tools are available to assist them. In addition, Microsoft provides links to support pages for Mac and Outlook for Mac.

One of the most common problems when dealing with Outlook connectivity is the TCP/IP configuration or functionality of the Mac client. Because there is no `ping` functionality with Mac, administrators can configure a static TCP/IP address on the client for testing connectivity.

By configuring a static TCP/IP address on the Mac client, administrators can perform a `ping` back to the client from a Windows server or workstation.

For more information on troubleshooting common issues with Outlook 2001, see the following links and references:

- For more information and Update downloads for Outlook 2001, go to
  `www.microsoft.com/mac/otherproducts/outlookformac/`
  `outlookformac.aspx?pid=outlookformac`.

- To troubleshoot common Outlook issues and find support, go to
  `http://support.microsoft.com/`
  `default.aspx?ID=FH;EN-US;outmac&SD=GN&LN=EN-US`.

27

# Outlook Express

Another option to support remote Macintosh users is the Outlook Express client; administrators can leverage the basic functionality of Outlook Express 5 for Mac to support clients requiring simple POP access to Exchange Server 2003. Using Outlook Express is an effective solution because remote users or mobile users can be supported using the limited functionality when emailing and working with address lists.

Although Outlook Express for Mac is not a full-function client like Outlook for Mac or Entourage 2004, Outlook Express still offers comprehensive support with the basic needs for mail and address books:

- **Email support**—Access to Exchange email using the Simple Mail Transport Protocol (SMTP) and Post Office Protocol (POP).

- **Address books**—Email addresses are stored in address books locally and within the Outlook Express client.

> **NOTE**
>
> Messages accessed through Outlook Express are downloaded to the local client and removed from the local server. All client messages using this option are downloaded and stored on the local Mac client only after a user accesses the Exchange server using any of the available methods.
>
> To avoid increasing Outlook Express file sizes over time, the Empty Deleted Item option is enabled by default when the client is installed.

- **Contact address list**—Outlook Express supports contacts and address lists, which can be used to select addresses when creating and sending messages and to store personal contact information.

- **LDAP support**—Lightweight Directory Access Protocol (LDAP) support enables an Outlook Express client's access to view information such as the Global Address List of an Exchange Server 2003 organization.

- **POP support**—POP is the primary method of supporting Express clients when accessing Exchange from the Internet. This option requires the POP protocol to be enabled on Exchange Server 2003 and might require additional configuration of the firewall to enable passthrough of the POP protocol.

- **Password support**—Usernames and passwords can be configured in advance, enabling users to open Outlook Express and access mail with a preconfigured account name and password.

## Compatibility with Non-Windows Systems

Before installing Outlook Express 5 for Mac, use the Mac System Profiler tool to determine whether the hardware being installed meets the minimum Microsoft requirements for installing the Mac client. See Table 27.4 for a list of Mac requirements.

**TABLE 27.4**    Outlook Express for Mac Hardware Requirements

| Processor | Memory | Hard Disk Space |
|-----------|--------|-----------------|
| Mac PowerPC | 7MB | 15MB available disk space |

## Installing and Enabling Support for Outlook Express 5

This section reviews the tasks required to configure the Mac client to support communication with Exchange Server 2003 from the internal network location and the Internet. After the network configuration has been completed, you will walk through the steps to install Outlook Express 5 onto the Mac operating system.

One common task when enabling support for Outlook Express 5 is to enable support for the client to use the TCP/IP protocol to communicate with and access Exchange mail. To enable support for TCP/IP, complete the following steps:

1. From the Apple menu, select the Control Panel and then TCP/IP properties.

2. In the TCP/IP dialog box, configure the TCP/IP properties.

3. Select the Connect Via option and then select Ethernet.

4. On the Configure tab, select the method by which the address will be assigned—in this case, Manual.

5. Enter the TCP/IP properties and DNS address being used on your network.

6. Close the TCP/IP properties and reboot the Mac system.

> **NOTE**
>
> Using TCP/IP enables client access from the internal network and from the Internet. This configuration is not the same as the protocol that will be used to access Exchange Server 2003 mail.

When installing Outlook Express for Mac, the installation file can be downloaded free from the Microsoft Web site at http://www.microsoft.com/mac/
downloads.aspx?pid=download&location=/mac/DOWNLOAD/OE/
oe5.xml&secid=40&ssid=6&flgnosysreq=True.

To begin installing Outlook Express 5, download the installation file to the Mac client and use the following steps:

1. Select and click the Download installation file to expand it.

2. In the Outlook Express 5 window, select and move the Outlook folder to a location on the Mac local disk.

27

## Configuring POP Access with Outlook Express 5 for Mac

The scenario in this section configures the Mac Outlook Express client to connect to Exchange Server 2003 through an Internet connection using the POP protocol. This enables Outlook Express to access the Exchange 2003 server and authenticate downloading messages.

> **NOTE**
>
> Before configuring client connectivity to Exchange Server 2003 using POP, additional configuration of the Exchange server to enable the protocol for the individual mail and server is required. In addition, if accessing with POP from the Internet, the network firewall should be configured to enable POP access and the domain name for the Exchange Server 2003 POP server populated to the Internet.
>
> For more information on DNS, see Chapter 7, "Domain Name System Impact on Exchange Server 2003."
>
> For information on configuring your firewall and security best practices when enabling support with POP, consult the firewall manufacturer's product information.

To configure Outlook Express to connect an Exchange Server 2003 server using POP, begin by opening Outlook Express and follow these steps:

1. From the Tools menu, select Accounts.

2. On the Internet Accounts tab, click the Mail tab and select New.

3. To create a new email account, enter the name for the account in the Display Name dialog box, enter the name for the account being created, and select Next.

4. On the email screen, select the I Already Have an Email Address That I'd Like to Use, and enter the email address for the user being configured. Select Next to continue.

5. At the Email Server Information page, type **POP** under the My Incoming Mail Server selection.

6. Enter the fully qualified mail server name as listed in the next example. Then click Next to continue.

   Example:

   Incoming Mail Server = `mail.companyabc.com`

   Outgoing Mail Server = `smtp.companyabc.com`

> **NOTE**
>
> The Incoming and Outgoing Mail Server names should be added and populated to the Internet for proper DNS name resolution.
>
> When configuring this option for Internet access, the outgoing mail server might need to be configured to point to the outgoing mail server of the Internet service provider (ISP) being used.

7. At the authentication screen, enter the logon name and password for the account accessing the Exchange Server 2003 POP server, as shown in the next example.

Example:

Account Name = **User@CompanyABC.com**

Password = \*\*\*\*\*\*\*\*\*\*\*

8. To enhance security and limit the ability for others to access the Exchange POP account, uncheck the Save Password option and click Next to continue.

> **Password and Best Practices**
>
> To enhance security, leave the password entry blank; this requires users to enter the password each time they access Exchange.
>
> In addition, when accessing Exchange through the POP protocol, it is best practice to use strong passwords to enhance security. Use the Active Directory Users and Computers management console to create a strong password for accounts using this method of access.

9. Complete the installation by entering the account name for the account being used and click Next to complete the installation.

10. Test accessing the Exchange Server 2003 POP services by selecting Send/Receive on the Outlook Express 5 toolbar.

## Migrating and Backing Up Personal Address Books

One of the most common tasks when managing Outlook Express clients is backing up the contacts from the Outlook Express 5 for Mac client. When performing this task, administrators can export contact information and create comma-separated files for import into other mail programs and Outlook clients.

To complete the export of contact information for backup and migration reasons, follow the example in the next section. In this scenario, you back up the Outlook Express 5 for Mac Contacts to a comma-delimited CSV file. After it is backed up, the contacts are then imported in the full version of Outlook 2001 for Mac.

### Backing Up Outlook Express Contacts

To begin, open the Outlook Express 5 for Mac client and complete the following steps to create a full backup of all the contact information.

1. From the File menu, select the Export Contact option.

2. In the Save dialog box, select the location where the export file will be saved by modifying the default Desktop location, as shown in Figure 27.2.

27

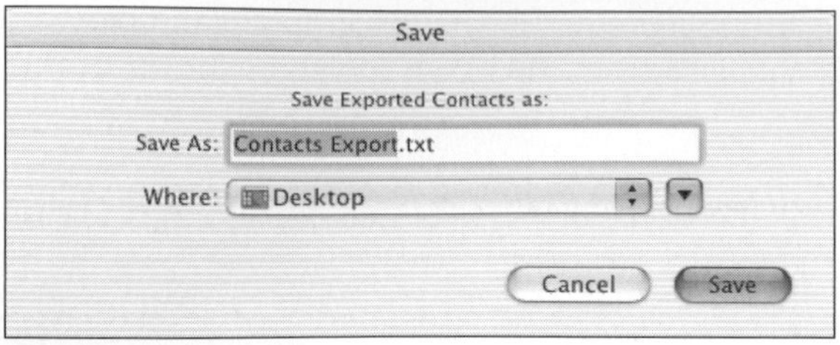

**FIGURE 27.2**    Exporting contacts.

3. In the Name dialog box, enter the name for the export file to create.

> **NOTE**
>
> By default, export files are created as tab-delimited files only and are placed on the desktop.
>
> To convert the export file to a CSV, use the steps in the next section, "Importing Contacts from Outlook Express 5 to Outlook 2001," to both convert the file and import contacts into other Outlook versions.

4. Click the Save button to create the export file and back up the Outlook Express contacts.

### Importing Contacts from Outlook Express 5 to Outlook 2001

To import files into Outlook 2001 for Mac from Outlook Express 5, administrators must first convert the export file to a CSV format using Microsoft Excel for Mac.

> **NOTE**
>
> To complete converting Outlook Express contact export files to CSVs, you must have Microsoft Office for Mac installed on the system being used.

To convert the export file to a CSV, launch the Excel for Mac application and follow these steps to create a CSV that will be used to import contacts into Outlook 2001 for Mac:

1. From the File menu, select Open.

2. Select the location and export file created in the previous steps and click Open.

3. When the Import Wizard begins, select Delimited in the original data type and select Next to continue.

4. Select the Tab option as the delimiter and click Next to continue.

5. On the Data Format tab, select General as the format and click Finish.

6. To save the new CSV file, on the File menu, select Save As. In the Save As dialog box, modify the file type to CSV Comma Delimited.

7. Enter the name for the new CSV file and select Save. This step creates a fully compatible CSV file for import into Outlook 2001.

---

**TIP**

To import the newly created CSV file into Outlook 2001 for Mac, select the Import option on the File menu and select the CSV file created in the previous steps. Selecting Open imports the CSV contacts into Outlook 2001.

---

# Configuring and Implementing Entourage 2004 for Mac

Understanding the need for a more comprehensive functional solution for Mac, Microsoft has released a powerful alternative client to the already available Outlook options. Available as a new release of a previous version, Microsoft now provides the Entourages 2004 client platform for the Mac operating system. This option is very effective for Mac users' both internal and external connectivity needs because it provides the same look and feel that Mac users are familiar with and many of the enhanced functions of the latest Windows-based Outlook client.

The most compatible platform with the Mac operating system, Entourage 2004 provides support for email, calendaring, contact management, junk email filtering, synchronization, and even support to handheld devices when combined with Exchange Server 2003. Exchange administrators can now leverage the Entourage client to provide Mac users a familiar look and feel while delivering full integration with added features and access to Exchange Server 2003 data.

27

## Features and Functionality

The Entourage 2004 client software combined with the Exchange Server 2003 platform and latest service packs can provide enhanced functionality of the Mac user in many areas not before available.

---

**CAUTION**

The Entourage 2004 client and Exchange Updates are available from Microsoft and have been fully certified for use on the Exchange Server 2003 platform. Test all components and functionality of Entourage in a lab environment before connecting any Entourage 2004 clients to the Exchange Server 2003 organization.

---

When combined with the Exchange Updates, Entourage 2004 provides extensive support and enhanced functionality in the following areas:

- **Message format support**—HTML and plaintext email format is fully supported, providing seamless integration with Windows-based Outlook clients.

- **Rules support**—As is with the Outlook for Windows client, Entourage 2004 support the creation of email rules at the client level.

- **Junk email filtering**—With today's unsolicited email issues, users can now filter junk mail by using three levels of filtering: Low, High, and Exclusive. This option also includes an exempt feature for all contacts stored that are associated with the Entourage client.

- **Outlook functions**—As with Outlook, Entourage 2004 provides full support for Exchange calendaring, scheduling appointments, contacts, and scheduled tasks.

- **Offline synchronization**—To support roaming users, Entourage can fully synchronize mailbox data between Exchange Server 2003 and the client.

- **Offline address book**—Entourage 2004 provides full synchronization of the Exchange Server 2003 offline address list.

- **LDAP support**—Using the Entourage client, Mac users can now access the Global Address List and Active Directory through LDAP lookups.

- **Palm support**—Sync and update information from the Entourage 2004 client to Palm handheld devices.

- **PST support**—Administrators can use the PST Import Tool to export and import Exchange data to Entourage 2004 from Outlook for Mac and the previous version of Entourage.

- **Integrated upgrade support**—With the 2004 version, administrators can complete an upgrade directly from Outlook, Outlook Express 5, and previous versions of Entourage, saving mail information, contacts, and identities using the built-in wizard available with the Office 2004 suite for Mac.

## Deploying Entourage 2004

Requirements for installing Entourage 2004 vary slightly from the requirements of Outlook and other Exchange solutions. Before installing and configuring Entourage 2004 clients, administrators must ensure that minimum hardware requirements at the Mac desktop are met and the Exchange Server 2003 prerequisites have been configured. In addition, the client must be updated and installed with the required updates and software to ensure proper functionality and connectivity when accessing Exchange mail data.

Before installing Entourage, ensure that the following requirements and configurations have been enabled on the Exchange server:

- Microsoft Exchange 2003 with the latest service pack

- IMAP/HTTP DAV/SMTP/LDAP

- Outlook Web Access

Though most of these settings are already enabled to support Windows-based client connectivity to Exchange Server, review and address any of the hardware and software requirements for installing Entourage by reviewing Table 27.5 and the software prerequisites for Exchange Server 2003.

Verify that the Mac client desktop hardware you are installing meets the minimum hardware requirements to install Entourage 2004, as listed in Table 27.5. If you do not know what hardware is installed on the Mac client, use the Mac System Profiler available on the Tools menu of the Mac desktop to display and evaluate the hardware installed on the Mac desktop.

**TABLE 27.5**    Entourage 2004 for Mac Hardware Requirements

| Processor | Memory | Hard Disk Space |
| --- | --- | --- |
| G3, Mac OS X–compatible | 128MB | 196MB available disk space |

After the Exchange server has been prepared and the hardware requirement for Entourage addressed, the next components to support Entourage are the updates and software requirements for the Mac client. Before the installation of Entourage 2004 can be completed, the following components must be installed or updated in the Mac client:

- **Office 2004 for Mac**—To install Entourage 2004, the Microsoft Office 2004 for Mac suite must be installed.

- **Install Updates**—Because upgrades can be completed after the installation of Office 2004 for Mac, administrators can install any available updates before running the upgrade wizard or configuring any identities.

- **Microsoft Exchange Update**—When connecting Entourage 2004 to Exchange Server 2003, be sure to install the Office 2004 Service Pack 1 update for Mac on the client computer. For download and additional information, go to `http://www.microsoft.com/mac/downloads.aspx?pid=download&location=/mac/download/office2004/update_11.1.1.xml&secid=4&ssid=14&flgnosysreq=True`.

> **TIP**
>
> To address Office 2004 updates, Microsoft provides an auto-update feature for the Office for Mac suite. Download and install the latest update version from Microsoft at `http://www.microsoft.com/mac/downloads.aspx?pid=download&location=/mac/download/office2004/mau.xml&secid=4&ssid=11&flgnosysreq=True`.
>
> To provide functionality for junk email filtering with the latest definition files, install the junk email filter update from Microsoft at `http://www.microsoft.com/mac/downloads.aspx?pid=download&location=/mac/download/office2004/junkfilter.xml&secid=4&ssid=13&flgnosysreq=True`.

After all updates have been completed and requirements met, the installation of Entourage 2004 can be completed and the Entourage client connected to Exchange. To configure the Entourage client for Exchange support, follow these steps:

27

**Enhancing Authentication with NTLM V2**

To further leverage the available features of Windows and Exchange, administrators can enable NTLM version 2 for authentication of Mac users when connecting with Entourage clients.

To encrypt a password using NTLM V2, select the properties of the Exchange mail account and select the Advance Features tab. Enable password encryption by selecting the Always Use Secure Passwords option.

Entourage 2004 does not support NTLM version 1.

**Important**

Entourage 2004 does not support NTLM version 1; ensure that the default domain policy is configured to support NTLM version 2 before connecting Entourage 2004 clients.

1. Launch the Entourage 2004 client, and select Tools, Accounts.

2. Select the Mail tab, select New from the New drop-down box, and enter the account type for connecting to Exchange Server 2003.

3. Enter the user information for the account connecting to Exchange with the client:

   - **Account Name**—Enter the name of the account created in Active Directory for the Mac user to connect to Exchange Server 2003.

   - **Password**—Provide the password for the Active Directory account or leave this entry blank to prompt the user to log on when connecting to Exchange.

   - **Domain Name**—Enter the name of the Active Directory domain where the account is a member.

# Terminal Services Client for Mac

The Terminal Services Client for Mac can be considered and planned in the same manner as its Windows counterpart. When the prerequisites are met, administrators can use the Terminal Services Client to provide full Windows and application functionality to Mac users requiring Exchange services and more.

Through Terminal Services technology, Mac users are able to fully access the Windows client and Outlook application with all the features and functionality of Windows-based users, including network shares and printers.

## Compatibility, Features, and Functionality

Because this Remote Desktop Connection for Mac uses Windows Terminal Services, the only compatibility concern to be considered is the actual connection manager. All applications, when being run, are executed remotely and do not require additional compatibility between Windows-based applications, such as Outlook and the Mac client.

The Remote Desktop Connection manager is compatible with the Mac OS X 10.1 version or later. If required on an earlier version of the Mac client, upgrade the Mac operating system to meet the operating system requirements. Also ensure that the Mac client hardware meets the minimum hardware requirements for installing the Remote Desktop Connection for Mac, as shown in Table 27.6.

**TABLE 27.6**    Remote Desktop Hardware Requirements

| Processor | Memory | Hard Disk Space |
| --- | --- | --- |
| Mac PowerPC | 128MB | 3MB for installation |
| | | 1.1MB after installation |

One of the biggest benefits to the Remote Desktop Connection client from Mac is its integration with Windows and Mac clients. Because of this compatibility, Mac users are able to leverage the functionality and features of Windows Outlook when accessing Exchange information and also leverage some of the following enhanced features when integrating Mac clients into a Windows Terminal Services environment:

- **Access to Windows**—The Remote Desktop Connection for Mac provides full access for Mac users into the Windows environment. This connection can be configured to the Windows desktop or restricted to an application such as Outlook.

- **Printing**—Through the Terminal Services connection, Mac users can access network printing and print information from applications to a networked Windows printer. To further enhance this feature, Mac users can print Windows information to the local Mac printer.

- **Access to data**—Through the Copy feature, Mac users are fully enabled to copy and paste data between the Mac client and the Windows Terminal Services session.

Before beginning any installation of the Remote Desktop Connection for Mac, Microsoft Windows Terminal Services and remote access must be enabled for supporting a remote connection with one or more of the following Microsoft Windows operating systems:

- **Windows XP**—Supported only through the Remote Desktop Connections feature of Windows XP, this method is limited to one concurrent connection.

- **Windows 2003**—Supported in all versions of Windows Server 2003, Terminal Services can be enabled to support remote access for multiple simultaneous connections.

- **Windows 2000**—Included in Windows 2000 Enterprise, Standard, and Datacenter Editions, the Terminal Service Application mode component must be enabled and will support multiple, simultaneous connections.

- **Windows NT 4.0 Terminal Server Edition**—This operating system enables support for multiple connections for both Windows sessions and application sessions.

27

**TIP**

When using Terminal Services for multiple client connections from Mac and Windows users, performance is dependent on the total amount of simultaneous connections and the total amount of available hardware resources installed in the server.

## Installing the Terminal Services Client

To install and configure the Remote Desktop Connection for Mac, you can begin with a simple scenario of creating a one-to-one connection. In this scenario, you configure a Windows XP desktop and a Mac client to provide remote desktop connectivity to Microsoft Outlook.

To begin, enable the remote desktop feature of the Windows XP client by following these steps:

1. From the Windows XP desktop, select Start, right-click on My Computer, and select Properties to open the Properties page.

2. Select the Remote tab and check the Allow Users to Connect Remotely to This Computer option, as shown in Figure 27.3.

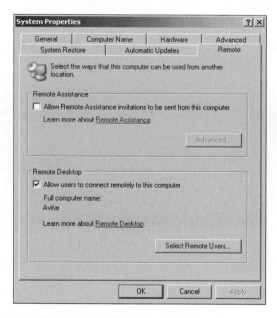

**FIGURE 27.3**    Remote desktop properties page.

3. Next, assign the account that may access the desktop remotely by clicking the Select the Remote Users button. Assign or create an account for the Mac users to authenticate with when accessing the Windows XP system remotely.

After the remote desktop configuration is complete and the client permissions to access Windows remotely have been configured, begin the installation of the Remote Desktop Connection for Mac by ensuring that the Mac client can communicate via TCP/IP on the network. Follow these steps to configure TCP/IP on the Mac client.

1. From the Apple menu, select Control, TCP/IP properties.

2. In the TCP/IP dialog box, configure the TCP/IP properties. In this scenario, configure the TCP/IP properties using a Static setting. Select the Connect Via option and select Ethernet.

3. From the Configure tab, select Manual.

4. Enter the TCP/IP properties for the client and Domain Name System address being used on your network.

5. Close the TCP/IP properties and reboot the Mac system.

To install the Remote Desktop Connection for Mac, download the installation file from Microsoft and place the file on the local Mac client where it will be installed.

To install the client, complete the following steps:

1. Expand the downloaded installation file by double-clicking the file.

2. Go to the Mac desktop and open the Remote Desktop Connection volume. Copy the Remote Desktop Connection folder into the local disk of the Mac client.

3. Remove the Remote Desktop Connection Volume and the original installation file by placing them in the Desktop Trash.

4. Launch the Remote Desktop Connection from the Remote Desktop Folder and enter the name of the system you are connecting to, as shown in Figure 27.4. Click Connect to establish the remote connection.

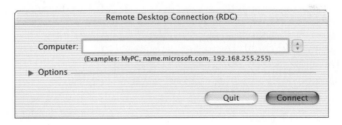

**FIGURE 27.4**    Remote Desktop Connection.

5. When prompted, enter the name and password of the account you configured to allow remote access to this desktop system.

# Understanding Other Non-Windows Client Access Methods

In addition to the Mac operating systems, Exchange Server 2003 can support a variety of clients by using virtual machines on the Mac client and leveraging support for Internet Message Access Protocol (IMAP), SMTP, and POP. Using these protocols, Exchange administrators can provide imitated email functionality and support a variety of clients throughout the Exchange environment for email and communication purposes.

## POP3 Access to Exchange

Most effective for users who are familiar with operating and working within Windows PC-based operating systems, the Virtual PC for Mac provides the same full functioning of a Windows PC client on the Mac OS desktop. Using this option can allow Mac users who are comfortable working in Windows full Microsoft Office and Outlook applications. Running within a virtual machine, a Windows domain client PC can allow the same features to a Mac desktop as any Windows domain client.

With a Virtual PC machine, the latest version of Outlook for Windows can be used on the Mac client desktop accessing Exchange Server 2003 data with full Windows-based support in areas such as offline files, multiple profiles, and Windows domain network resources. For more information regarding Virtual PC, go to the Mactopia web page at `http://www.microsoft.com/mac/products/virtualpc/virtualpc.aspx?pid=virtualpc`.

POP3 is one of the most popular methods of providing mail services on the Internet today. POP is highly reliable but has limited functionality. Users who access email using POP3 are limited to downloading all messages to the local client and can only send and receive messages when a connection is established with the POP server.

When enabled with Exchange Server 2003, the POP protocol can be leveraged to provide email support to additional non-Windows-based clients' platforms. Through the common method of sending mail, multiple client platforms can communicate over email regardless of the actual desktop operating system and client mail software being used.

The POP3 functionality of Exchange Server 2003 can support multiclient environments, including the Eudora Mail client, the Netscape Mail client, and other POP-compatible nonspecific client platforms. This protocol is best used when supporting single client systems that download mail and store mail information locally.

## IMAP Access to Exchange

IMAP is an additional method that can be used to support non-Windows-based client access to Exchange Server 2003 information. Designed to allow access to Information Stores located on a remote system, IMAP can also be used to support the Linux-based Netscape Mail clients.

Using the Netscape Mail client, Netscape users can access, collaborate, and store information on the Exchange Server 2003 server with the IMAP support built in to Netscape Communicator. With this functionality, networks can now incorporate additional operating systems, such as Linux with Netscape Mail, and still support email functionality between all network users.

Use the preferences option on the Netscape Mail client to configure and enable support for IMAP communication with Exchange Server 2003.

## Pocket PC Access

New to Exchange Server 2003, client mobile access is now fully integrated and supported when the Exchange Server 2003 server is installed.

Remote and mobile users can use the Outlook Pocket PC version to send, receive, and synchronize mail, calendaring, and task information, using the Windows Pocket PC 2003 platform over mobile information services built in to Exchange Server 2003.

For more information regarding the options and configuration to support Pocket PC access to Exchange Server 2003, see Chapter 24, "Configuring Client Systems for Mobility."

## HTML Access

Another new feature with Exchange Server 2003 is HTML access. With this feature, administrators can use Internet-ready cellular telephones to provide HTML access to Exchange information for mobile users regardless of where they might be.

By providing additional mobile services and client permissions through Active Directory, alternative access can be granted to email and Exchange using Internet-ready mobile phone devices over HTML access.

For more information regarding HTML access options and configurations, see Chapter 24.

## Outlook Web Access

One of the most effective methods of allowing access to Exchange information is OWA. Enhanced greatly in Exchange Server 2003, OWA can be used to provide HTML browser access to Exchange mailboxes from inside the network as well as the Internet.

Probably the biggest benefit to using the OWA solution to support non-Windows-based clients is that it is nondiscretionary as to which type of Internet browser can be used to access it. Effective in functionality, just like the full Outlook client, Linux-based users and others using non-Windows-based systems can access OWA for email and calendar management in the same fashion as any Windows-based users.

For more information regarding OWA and enabling support, see Chapter 26, "Everything You Need to Know About the Outlook Web Access (OWA) Client."

27

# Summary

In a Microsoft-centric environment, administrators of networks often focus solely on Windows-based connections to Exchange, spending little time on options for non-Windows-based users. When accessing Exchange Server 2003, there are many options for non-Windows users, including a whole suite of clients for the Macintosh—such as Entourage 2004, Outlook Express, Outlook for the Mac, and the Remote Desktop Connection. In addition, Outlook Express is available on other non-Windows platforms. To assist with alternative client platforms beyond the Mac OS, Exchange Server 2003 can be accessed using industry-standard protocols, such as POP3 and IMAP.

By choosing any one of a variety of client applications to access Exchange, an organization can leverage the capabilities of Exchange Server 2003 beyond just Windows-based users and provide seamless messaging communications throughout an entire enterprise. Depending on the client application selected, some options provide just email communications and others provide the full suite of Outlook and Exchange business productivity functions, such as calendaring, contacts, notes, to-do lists, journals, public folder access, offline files, junk email filtering, and more.

Using the information in this chapter, an organization should not be limited in its ability to extend Exchange Server 2003 to all users within the enterprise, and with the implementation of new client access capabilities, an organization can greatly improve its reach to all users in an organization well beyond Windows.

# Best Practices

The following are best practices from this chapter:

- When choosing a client configuration for Exchange, an organization should evaluate the different solutions available for non-Windows client connectivity.

- Outlook 2001 for the Macintosh will run on OS 9 as well as OS X; however, on OS X, the Outlook client runs in OS 9 emulation mode, so OS X users might consider using Entourage 2004, Outlook Web Access, or the Remote Desktop Connection client for access.

- To achieve the full Outlook functionality of Windows users, a non-Windows client might consider using a Terminal Services or the Virtual PC for Mac, which provides complete support to a full Windows client that is identical to the one Windows users access.

- Users who want calendar integration access tend not to want to use Outlook Express, which lacks calendar support, and should consider one of the other client applications when calendaring is required.

- For POP3 to work, the function should be enabled on the Exchange server and on the client Active Directory account. However, if POP3 will not be used, the service should be disabled on Exchange to minimize any security risk to unauthorized access to Exchange Server 2003.

- To improve security, leave the password entry on any client options configuration page blank so that the user will be prompted for a password every time logon is executed.

- Because different versions of client software for the Macintosh have different support requirements for various versions of the Mac OS, make sure to verify compatibility before installing any client software.

- To provide authentication to Entourage clients, NTLM v2 must be enabled on the default domain policy for access to Exchange Server 2003.

27

# PART IX

## Client Administration and Management

## IN THIS PART

**CHAPTER 28**   Deploying the Client for Exchange          829

**CHAPTER 29**   Group Policy Management for
                 Exchange Clients                          853

# Deploying the Client for Exchange

**IN THIS CHAPTER**

- Understanding Deployment Options
- Planning Considerations and Best Practices
- Preparing the Deployment
- Installing the Exchange Client
- Pushing Client Software with Windows 2003 Group Policies
- Deploying with Microsoft Systems Management Server
- Managing Post-Deployment Tasks

Whether you are implementing Exchange Server 2003 for the first time, or upgrading an organization from previous versions of Microsoft Exchange Server, client deployments are always a major component when planning and implementing Exchange messaging functionality to client desktop systems in the enterprise.

With many options available for deploying the Microsoft Exchange Outlook client, administrators can plan and leverage multiple options and technologies when configuring and pushing the Exchange Server 2003 Outlook client.

To assist in the planning and deploying of the Outlook client, this chapter provides information about the different options and the best practices when using them to deploy clients to the desktop, how to automate and configure the Exchange client profile, and how to work with automated configuration files—that is, Microsoft Outlook Profile (PRF) files. In addition, the basic tools are available for managing and administering the deployment of Exchange Server 2003 clients to the desktop.

## Understanding Deployment Options

To centralize Exchange management and deployments of the Outlook client, Microsoft has released standard tools and enhancements to technologies that can be found in the Office Resource Kit (ORK) and the Windows Server family operating system. Using these options enables Exchange administrators to leverage their features, and flexibility provides multiple options when deploying the Exchange 2003 Outlook client. Organizations can now use a variety of deployment methods and preconfiguration options to preconfigure and deploy, as well as support, Exchange Outlook clients and remote and mobile systems.

As organizations begin the planning process, administrators and architects can adopt different deployment methods and execute client installations based on the type of client and the specific need for each type of client desktop. This chapter explores these different options available to deploy the Exchange 2003 Outlook client software to desktops in the enterprise and the options and steps to configure the Outlook client including methods for generating Exchange client profiles during the deployment.

## Available Methods of Deployment

With multiple options available, client deployments can be performed on many levels not previously available to Exchange administrators when pushing and installing the Outlook desktop client software. With integration between Windows 2003 and Exchange Server 2003, along with new resource tools available to administrators, Outlook 2003 can be pushed to the desktop using any of the following methods:

- **Manual Installation**—Standard Installation enables administrators to incorporate wizards, profiles, generation tools, and configuration files into the client installation process. Using these methods, administrators can define baseline settings, standards, and manually test the installation when complete.

- **Windows 2003 Group Policy**—Leveraging Windows Group Policy Software deployment technologies and Microsoft Office 2003 Security Templates, Outlook clients and client updates can be pushed to desktop systems on the network. Using Group Policy, administrators can also centrally configure Outlook Security and User Options to enforce a baseline configuration to all client systems on the enterprise.

- **Imaging Technologies**—When upgrading to Outlook 2003 or deploying new installations, organizations can image the Outlook clients to the desktop or refresh the desktop images all together to support updates and the latest company standards.

- **Systems Management Server**—Using Microsoft Systems Management Server, you can centrally deploy and push the Outlook client and updates to large numbers of desktop systems in multiple locations throughout the enterprise. This option also enables tracking and reporting information to manage a full Exchange Outlook client deployment.

## Outlook Profile Generation

Most likely one of the biggest challenges Exchange administrators face when deploying Outlook 2003 and applying changes is configuring and modifying Outlook client Exchange sever profiles. To provide Exchange administrators a simple centralized means of automating this task, profile configurations and changes can be scripted using tools available from Microsoft and the Office 2003 Resource Kit (ORK).

Along with pushing clients using the methods described earlier, Outlook client profiles and Outlook Exchange Server settings can be configured using these technologies also.

Using the Office 2003 Custom Installation Wizard (CIW) to configure Outlook options and apply the initial profile configuration through PRF files is a very effective means of completing a deployment successfully. Also, administrators can use tools and functionality already in use like login scripts and Group Policy to modify and update an array of Outlook user property settings directly on the Outlook client.

> **Tool and Utilities**
>
> The Custom Installation Wizard and Microsoft Exchange Profile Update tool along with additional utilities can be found with the Office 2003 Resource Kit (ORK) or downloaded from Microsoft.
>
> Download the Office Resource Kit at `http://www.microsoft.com/office/orkarchive/2003ddl.htm`.

Another option for configuring Outlook profiles is the `NewProf.exe` utility. This executable file is used to automatically generate Outlook user profiles after the installation of the client software to the user desktop. Used in conjunction with a PRF file, this tool can also be used to specify user Outlook profile information and settings on a new Outlook client installation.

## Configuring Outlook Client Options

The most enhanced functionality available to administrators when installing the Exchange 2003 Outlook client is the ability to predefine and set configuration options and apply them dynamically after the installation of the Outlook client software has finished.

### Custom Installation Wizard

To deploy the Outlook client to desktops on the network with configuration options predefined, powerful tools such as the CIW are available from Microsoft. Working with Office configuration files OSPs and PRFs, the CIW can be leveraged to define Outlook client options and profile settings for large deployments, eliminating the need for administrators to visit desktops just to configure profile settings and Outlook options.

### Windows Server Group Policy

Another powerful configuration option is the centralized management option available through the Security Template for Outlook 2003 `Outlk11.adm`. With the Group Policy feature of Windows Server 2003, standard and advanced options can be configured and established after the client is deployed. The options are configured after all client settings are applied, regardless of which client desktop a users logs into.

> **NOTE**
>
> Using Group Policy is an effective way to apply settings and modify Outlook client profiles. This chapter will only cover Outlook client deployments. For additional information regarding the `Outlk11.adm` and applying settings, see Chapter 29, "Group Policy Management for Exchange Clients."

28

### Transforms

The final option for defining Outlook client settings and configuration options during a deployment is the Office Transforms. Transforms are configuration files used with the Windows Installer that contain information and modifications that will be applied to the Outlook client during installation.

This option is also created using the CIW and uses an MST file extension.

## Deploying Non–Windows-Based Options

With a variety of client systems to support, one other area administrators must consider is how to deploy the Microsoft Outlook client or provide Exchange access for non–Windows-based systems, such as Macintosh desktops. To understand more about these client options and the installation and configuration options available for the types of clients, see Chapter 27, "Outlook for Non-Windows Systems."

# Planning Considerations and Best Practices

Before deploying the Exchange 2003 Outlook client, organizations should consider all the details involved with the Outlook client deployment. Because most organizations support different types of clients and can have complicated messaging environments in multiple locations, client deployments should be reviewed and planned in detail to avoid any unforeseen issues that can affect a successful deployment.

Identifying and documenting the different client needs involved in each deployment and reviewing the overall network topology can allow planners and architects the ability to greatly enhance the performance of each deployment as well as assist with the transparent client installation on the desktop.

## Network Topology Bandwidth Consideration

In any situation, administrators must plan Outlook client deployments in a manner that avoids client network disruptions and bandwidth saturation during the deploying to local and remote locations.

Evaluating the network environment and determining the needs of the deployment, especially for remote location, can help ensure a transparent deployment of the Outlook client to enterprise workstations systems. In a single-site location network environment, planning the deployment can be accomplished by evaluating the bandwidth availability of the network to avoid network problems when pushing or deploying the Outlook with Group Policy. Because the installation can be pushed over the network during any time of the day, deployments should be planned and pushed in smaller groups to avoid running into pitfalls.

With multisite organizations, administrators must also plan and deploy the Outlook client locally and across Wide Area Network (WAN) links without causing network disruptions and communication issues between critical business systems. One larger factor in this scenario is WAN links. Because these types of connections are generally much slower than local network connections, it is difficult to complete multiple Outlook client deployments without possibly causing communication issues over the WAN links without taking advantage of the features and components designed to assist in these areas.

With shares called Administrative Distribution Points configured in each remote location, deployments can still be centrally managed while pushing client installation from a share located in the remote site. Using these Administrative Distribution Points can avoid bandwidth saturation over WAN links and enhance the overall time required to deploy the Outlook client in remote locations.

## Planning Best Practices

To assist in the planning process when deploying the Outlook client, study the following common considerations and best practices:

- Deploying the Outlook client with the Microsoft Office suite provides enhanced functionality, such as integration with Microsoft Word as the Outlook client email editor.

- Document all profile settings and configuration options for each Transform, PRF, and custom installation file.

- Testing deployment options and profile generations in a test environment before deployment to network desktops is always best practice.

- Always deploy Outlook to a smaller pilot group first.

- Perform deployments in small groups and phases for ease of management.

- Create and name configuration files based on the group or configuration options to which they will be applied. For example, create a file called Public.PRF to configure options for group workstations called Public Relations.

## Addressing Remote and Mobile Client Systems

Addressing remote and mobile Exchange Outlook client needs presents an entirely different challenge for administrators when planning the Outlook client deployment. With remote and mobile users accessing the business network environment using many different methods, administrators should consider the impact on the installation when clients access the network over low bandwidth links such as VPN or RAS dialup links.

Often, scheduling remote and mobile users to come into any business location where administrators can perform the installation manually or via a push can often be easier and cause less impact on the user than deploying over these types of slow network connections. If required to deploy Outlook for these types of clients, use the Installation State options page to install only the required components needed to support the Outlook client, reducing the overall size of the installation package. Leverage Administrative Installation Points located closest to the remote or mobile user's access point whenever possible to deploy the Outlook client.

## Managing the Outlook Deployment

It is difficult to manage the deployment of Outlook clients without additional software, such as Microsoft Systems Management Server (SMS). With Microsoft Systems Management Server, deployments are enhanced and can be tracked and managed down to the desktop level, enabling administrators to identify desktops needing the Outlook client, deploy Outlook, and even identify failed installations by using the reporting functionality built into SMS Server 2003.

When options such as SMS are not available, gathering this information can be difficult when determining how the deployment of the Outlook client is progressing. This is because all evidence of the Outlook client installation is not remotely present through the standard tools available in the ORK and Windows 2003 server group policy. To gather this information in a limited fashion, administrators must use other methods to determine whether a software installation was successful:

- Filter and look for MSI Installer events that are written into the Application Event logs on the server when using Windows Server Group Policy.

- On the local machine, view Add/Remove programs to see whether the Outlook update package is listed. This option can be accomplished remotely when the Remote Desktop feature of the Windows XP client desktop software is enabled.

# Preparing the Deployment

As the planning phase of the deployment comes to a close, administrators can focus on preparing the different areas of the Outlook client deployment.

For deploying the Outlook client successfully to desktop on the network, administrators can also use this time to prepare and test the different methods and configurations that will be used for the actual Outlook client deployment.

## Outlook Systems Requirements

Before pushing Outlook to desktop systems on the network, the desktop hardware must be evaluated to determine whether it meets the recommended Microsoft hardware and software requirements for installing the client.

> **TIP**
>
> With Microsoft Systems Management Server (SMS), inventories can be conducted on network desktop systems, creating a report to identify all hardware, software, and drive space availability needed to complete the install on each desktop.

Ensure that the desktop systems meet the installation requirements needed by reviewing Table 28.1.

**TABLE 28.1**    System Requirements

| Requirement | Outlook 2003 | Outlook 2002 |
| --- | --- | --- |
| Processor speed | P233MHz | P133MHz |
| Memory | 128MB | 136MB w/Windows XP |
|  |  | 72MB w/Windows 2000 |
| Hard disk space | 400MB | 135MB |

> **TIP**
>
> The installation of Outlook 2003 also requires Microsoft Internet Explorer 5.01 or higher.

## Planning Predefined Configuration Options

With a broad understanding of how the Outlook client can be deployed, another area to understand and plan for is which options can be configured when using the Custom Installation Wizard and Transform configuration files. Understanding the options available to administrators for configuring the Exchange Outlook client with PRF files, Transforms, and tools enables Exchange administrators to create a baseline plan of what options will be used prior to actually creating the individual configuration files.

Using the Custom Installation Wizard, you can configure the following features:

- **Outlook User Profile Settings**—Administrators can specify how users' profiles will be created. Using this option, administrators can set new profiles, modify existing profiles, and add additional user profiles.

- **Exchange Server Settings**—Settings defining Exchange Server names and specific options, such as Exchange 2003 connection options, can also be defined.

- **Installation States for Outlook and Features**—Using the installation options, you can define installation states to make features available, available at first use, or not available.

- **Mail Options**—Options such as PST and OST settings and synchronization options can be defined using the Custom Installation Wizard.

- **Settings and Options**—Many of the options available when configuring Outlook through the Tool, Options tab of the Outlook client can also be defined when creating custom installation files.

- **Installation Path**—Ensure that the installation directory path on the client desktop where the Outlook client will be installed contains enough free disk space to complete the installation.

28

## Creating Administrative Installation Points

If the deployment requires Administrative Installation Points, administrators can create them using the `Setup.exe` program of the Outlook or Office installation software.

Using the `Setup.exe` program with Outlook or Office 2003, you can create Administrative Installation Points by running the installation with the `/a` switch.

To create the Administrative Installation Point, complete these steps:

> **NOTE**
>
> In the following example, the Administrative Installation Point is created using the Microsoft Office 2003 installation media.

1.  Insert the Installation CD-ROM into the systems where the Installation Point will be created. Open a Run command dialog box by selecting Start, Run.

2.  At the Installation screen, enter the product key that came with the Office 2003 installation software and select Next to continue.

> **NOTE**
>
> Use the Install location option on this screen to change the installation path that Outlook will use when being deployed.

3.  Accept the End User License Agreement (EULA) and select Install; this begins the installation process.

4.  Select the Installation state for Outlook and Outlook options; select Next to continue.

## Automating Outlook Profile Settings

One positive change when dealing with Outlook client configurations is the ability for administrators and planners to use multiple options for configuring Outlook profiles when deploying and changing the client Exchange settings. When pushing a deployment, the most commonly used method is the use of PRF files. PRF files are used to generate the initial Outlook profile and apply Outlook settings as mentioned earlier in this chapter.

To configure profile settings using PRF files, you can use the Custom Installation Wizard to complete an all-in-one setup and configuration of the client. This means that the administrator can define the profile settings in the Outlook: Customizing Default Profile page. This section walks you through the standard configuration of the PRF file to generate a user's profile dynamically after the Outlook client installation has completed. In this scenario, you configure a single PRF file and create the Outlook profile for any user when the Outlook client is launched for the first time.

To create a new profile, open the CIW by selecting Start, Run, Microsoft Office, Microsoft Office Tools, Microsoft Office ORK, Custom Installation Wizard. Then follow these steps:

1. Select the default options until the Outlook: Customize Default Profile page appears. Select the New Profile option, enter `Outlook` for the profile name, and click Next.

---

**TIP**

To configure the PRF file to run when Outlook is launched for the first time, use the Add/Remove Registry Entries page of the Custom Installation Wizard.

To enable the run-once option, make the following Registry changes:

Delete the following key:

`HKEY_CURRENT_USER\Software\Microsoft\Office\10.0\Outlook\Setup\First-Run`

Expand the Registry tree to the following:

`HKEY_CURRENT_USER\Software\Microsoft\Office\10.0\Outlook\Setup`

Add the String Value and enter the path of the PRF file share created earlier.

---

2. To configure the PRF file to dynamically configure each user profile, enter the `%UserName%` syntax in the User Name field. Also, enter the name of your Exchange Server 2003, as shown in Figure 28.1.

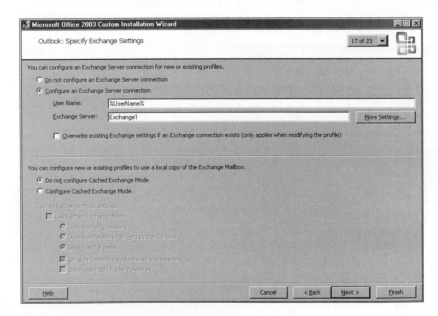

**FIGURE 28.1**   Exchange Server PRF file settings.

28

3. Because this PRF file is a default profile configuration file, select Next at the Add Accounts screen.

4. From the Remove Accounts and Export Settings screen, click the Export Profile settings. Enter the name **Outlook** for the name of the new PRF file and save the file to the desired location. Select Finish to complete the PRF file creation.

> **TIP**
>
> Microsoft PRF files can also be configured with additional Outlook profile settings, such as Personal folders and Outlook option settings. To understand more about configuring PRF files, go to www.microsoft.com/office/ork and search for .PRF.

## Creating Transforms and Profile Files

There are several different types of configuration files that can be used when pushing the Outlook client with predefined configuration settings to the desktop. In this section, you complete the steps needed to configure Outlook 2003 using the CIW to create Transforms and Profile files (PRF).

### Creating Transforms

Transform (MST) files are also created using the Office CIW available in the Office 2003 Resource Kit. Transforms can be used to create detailed custom settings when installing and configuring the Outlook client.

> **TIP**
>
> Use the Transform option when extensive settings are required for the Outlook deployment and when deploying Outlook as a component of a complete Office application suite installation. Transforms can be configured with custom settings and Outlook profile information making this option the most comprehensive of all initial configuration options when deploying.
>
> Be sure to document all settings expected to be used when creating configuration Transform files as part of the planning and testing process. Verify the successful application of settings and options in a lab before using transforms in a production deployment.

### Configuring Transforms

To create a Transform file, download and install the Office 2003 Resource Kit (ORK). Launch the Custom Installation Wizard by selecting Start, Run, Microsoft Office, Microsoft Office Tools, Microsoft Office ORK, Custom Installation Wizard. Then follow these steps:

1. From the Welcome to Microsoft Office Custom Installation Wizard Screen, select Next.

2. On the Open the MSI File page, enter the path and filename for the Outlook MSI Installation package, as shown in Figure 28.2. Use the Browse button to locate the

MSI installation package being used for this Microsoft Transform file. Click the Next button to continue.

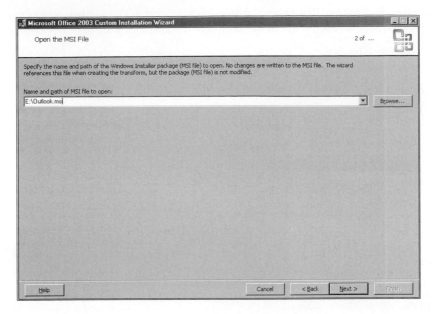

**FIGURE 28.2**    MSI selection page.

3. Because this scenario is creating a new Transform file, on the Open the MST File page, select the Create a New MST File option and select Next.

4. Select the location where the new MST file will be created and click Next.

5. Enter the location where the Outlook installation will be placed on the desktop when the client is deployed. Then enter the name of the organization that will be used for registration information.

6. If previous installations of Outlook and Microsoft Office exist on the desktop, select which installation version to remove.

> **NOTE**
>
> Using this option removes any selected version and component of Microsoft Office suite existing on the client desktop prior to installation of the new Outlook client or Office suite.

7. On the Set Feature Installation States page, select the Outlook components that will be installed. Click Microsoft Outlook for Windows and click the Run from My Computer option.

8. Use the Custom Default Application Settings page to define and add an Office Application Settings (OSP) file.

28

If upgrading, select the Migrate User's Settings check box to maintain the existing user-defined options after the upgrade.

9. Use the Change the Office User Settings page to define the setting and options to be applied to Outlook after the installation is finished.

10. Use the Options pages to modify the Outlook installation; continue through the configuration pages to create the Transform files.

11. Continue through the installation and configure the following:

    • Add/Remove additional custom installation files.

    • Add/Remove custom Registry Entries.

    • Modify Shortcuts and Outlook Icons.

    • If deploying across WAN links, select an additional installation point for the deployment.

    • Establish Outlook Security Settings.

    • Add additional programs to be installed with Outlook.

> **NOTE**
>
> For more information regarding options on each page and additional settings, use the help option on each page to review the Microsoft Custom Installation Wizard help file.

### Configuring Profiles with Transforms

Customizing the configuration of a profile during the installation can also be completed using transforms by configuring the Customize Default Profiles page. Using the options available, administrators can select the method in which to create the client profile with the Outlook Deployment tool.

For this Transform, select Apply PRF File and select the PRF file created in the previous section or select one of the following options, as shown in Figure 28.3:

• **Use Existing Profile**—Used when upgrading the Outlook client, this option maintains the existing setting.

> **NOTE**
>
> When Use Existing Profile is selected and no profile is found on the client desktop, this option prompts the user on the desktop to create the profile when Outlook is accessed for the first time.

- **Modify Profile**—Select this option to customize profile information and Exchange Outlook Options.

- **New Profile**—Use this option to create a single new profile and configure connection settings.

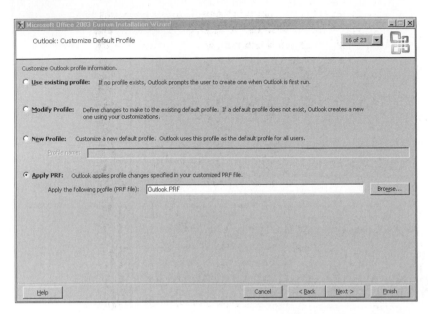

**FIGURE 28.3**    CIW profile options.

Additional options are available, such as Send and Receive Options and Mail settings; continue through the configuration screens by choosing the desired options for your organization's deployment. The creation of the PRF file can be completed at any time by selecting the Finish button on any setup screen.

After the Custom Installation Wizard has completed, document the command syntax for running the Outlook Setup.exe with the Transform just created, as in the example in Figure 28.4.

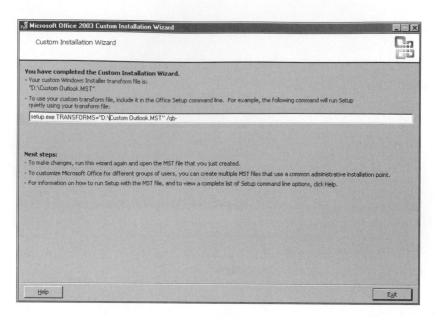

**FIGURE 28.4**    Completing the Custom Installation Wizard.

# Installing the Exchange Client

The options that require the most administrative attention—when manually installing the Outlook client—are also the options often configured when pushing Outlook using automated technologies. When considering these configuration and deployment options, administrators must determine which combination best fits the organization's needs by determining the overall manual effort required for the installation.

All the options can be used together, but they can also be incorporated into the deployment individually to enhance the options available when installing clients manually and configuring settings. In this section, you review the basic steps for installing the Outlook client to desktop systems using Transforms, PRF files, and the switches available when using these options.

## Using Transforms and PRF Files When Installing Outlook

When the options are not available to push the installation to client systems, administrators can still install the Outlook client and save valuable keystrokes and time by predefining Outlook information. Using these options with a manual installation scenario can greatly reduce the overall amount of time normally required to install the Outlook client manually. Administrators can now incorporate the manual installation process with preconfiguration files, such as PRFs and Transforms, and save time for each installation by eliminating the need to manually configure each installation after its completion.

When the required functionality is the client profile configuration setting and limited configuration options, the manual installation can easily be completed by using a simple

PRF file and a logon script to execute the tools such as the Exprofre.exe file. PRF files are simple to incorporate into the installation and require only the addition of a command-line switch with the Setup.exe installation program to deploy. Administrators can also avoid the need to configure the client profile by configuring the domain logon script to execute the Exprofre.exe file with the proper switches.

With more complex installation needs, administrators can create MST files to define these Outlook settings, security profiles, and user options. This option is most effective and enables administrators to continue with installations rather than manually configure each client setting individually.

## Installing the Outlook Clients with PRF Files

Using the steps in the last section to create a PRF file, administrators can then copy the file to the installation share for use when manually installing Outlook. This option prevents administrators from having to manually configure each client Outlook profile after the installation is complete.

To understand more about using PRF files when using the Windows installation program, complete these steps:

1. Create a folder share and place the Outlook.PRF file in the folder where it can be accessed from any location on the network.

> **TIP**
>
> When creating shares to support installs and PRF configuration file access, grant the account being used to install the client "Full Control" permissions to the PRF and installation share.

2. To open a command prompt and begin an installation in Outlook using PRF files, begin by selecting Start, Run, and enter **command**.

3. From the command prompt, type

   `d:\setup.exe /ImportPRF \\Outlook Files\Outlook.PRF`

   where d: represents the location of the Outlook installation files and *Outlook Files* is the name of the folder share created to host the PRF configuration files.

When errors occur or it appears that the Outlook profile has not been set correctly, the PRF file can be run by using the Open command and manually installing the configuration information.

## Manually Installing Outlook with Transforms

As stated earlier, using Transforms offer administrators the most functionality and flexibility when predefining Outlook settings and profile information. Using Transforms, administrators can leverage multiple options and even combine multiple Transforms when configuring Outlook clients. To understand the command lines and syntax used when

28

installing the Microsoft Outlook client with MST files, review the examples listed in the following sections.

### Applying Transforms with the Outlook `Setup.exe`

In these examples, you use the `OutlookSet1.MST` Transform filename to customize the Outlook Installation. To incorporate Transforms into the Outlook installation, use the following command:

```
Example: D:\setup.exe TRANSFORMS=OutlookSet1.mst
```

These Transforms can also be chained together when the application of settings residing in more than one Transform need to be applied during the installation of Outlook. When organizations create individual Transforms to specify different settings for individual groups or user types, the option to combine settings in multiple Transforms on a single installation is also still possible. For example, an organization creates a baseline Transform, defining settings that will be applied to all users and individual Transforms for specific groups. These files can be chained, making the Outlook settings easily manageable and simply modified and redeployed at any given time without affecting all users in the enterprise. Using a `Setup.ini` file with the proper syntax, you can link and apply Transforms in a very effective manner.

# Pushing Client Software with Windows 2003 Group Policies

Using Windows Server 2003 Group Policy management tools, administrators can easily and inexpensively deploy the Outlook client to desktops throughout the enterprise using Group Policy software installation functionality. Using Group Policy to deploy the Outlook client, administrators can centralize many of the duties and support tasks requiring administrative overhead and resources when working with other options.

Group Policies can provide extremely powerful administration and management control options when deploying the Outlook client to Organizational Units, Security Groups, and user accounts. Use the information provided in this section to set up and deploy the `Outlook.MSI` package.

For more detailed information regarding using Group Policy in the Exchange Server 2003 environment, see Chapter 29.

## Deploying Outlook with Group Policy Overview

Using Group Policy to deploy the Outlook client is one of the most effective and flexible options administrators can leverage. This option along with the new tool Exprofre.exe can almost be regarded as a hands-off installation without the use of management products such as SMS.

However, before using Group Policy and creating deployment packages, administrators should understand the basic functionality of Group Policy in Windows Server 2003 domains. Review the information and overview provided in the next sections before planning and setting up Windows Server 2003 Group Policy to support the Outlook client deployment.

### Administrative Options

Delegating the proper rights for administrators to manage and manipulate Group Policy when deploying Outlook clients is important. With the Delegation Wizard available in the Windows Group Policy snap-in, administrative rights can be assigned to Exchange administrators allowing control over the deployment without interfering with the day-to-day operations of the Windows systems. Using the Delegation Wizard to assign rights, administrators can grant permissions to individual accounts, groups, and Exchange Server administrators.

### Deployment Options

With Group Policy, the Outlook client can be deployed to the desktop using any of the following deployment methods:

- **Assigned to Computers**—This method of installation creates an Outlook installation package that is applied to workstations when a user logs on to the desktop. Using this option, all users have access to the Exchange client software after it's installed.

- **Assigned to Users**—When the installation package is assigned to users, application shortcuts are placed on the desktop of the user's profiles and in the Start menu of the individual user's profile. When these shortcuts are selected, the application installation is launched and completed.

- **Publishing the Installation**—When Outlook client software packages are published, the installation package is displayed in the Add/Remove Programs Group in the local desktop system control panel. Users can then initiate the installation by selecting the Install option.

> **TIP**
>
> When deploying any application with Windows Group Policy, it is best practice to deploy the Computer configuration application.

With each method, Exchange Server 2003 administrators use the MSI installation file format to push the Outlook client's software packages from a central location or from Administrative Installation Points to the workstation or users on the network.

> **CAUTION**
>
> When deploying Outlook software using Group Policy, *do not* assign the option Install to Users and Computers at the Same Time. Assigning both options can create conflicts when installing Outlook and possibly corrupt the installation of the Outlook client when applying the update.

28

## Best Practices for Deploying Outlook Clients

As with all aspects of Group Policy, the choices and configuration options of Outlook client deployment are numerous. Regardless of what method of Group Policy deployment is being used, some basic best practices apply to assist in avoiding unforeseen issues when deploying Outlook clients:

- Software packages must be in the format of an MSI package. Any other format type cannot be pushed using Group Policy.

- Always plan and configure Software Pushes at the highest levels possible in the domain tree. If the push is going out to more than one group or organizational unit, the software update should be configured to be pushed at the domain level. If the software update is being pushed to only a few groups or one organizational unit or multiple update packages are being pushed, configure the push at the group or organizational unit level.

- Deploy the Outlook client to the Computer Configuration rather than the User Configuration. Doing so keeps the installation from being applied more than once when a user logs on to a different desktop system.

- When pushing updates in multiple locations, use Administrative Installation Points and Windows Distributed File System (DFS). This enables software installations to be installed from packages located closest to the client being installed.

- Use Group Policy deployment options to push client software along with the PRF files to configure logon users' profiles at the time of the installation.

## Pushing Outlook Client

The steps in this scenario enable administrators to push the Exchange Server 2003 Outlook client package to workstations on the domain.

> **TIP**
>
> To enhance functionality when using Windows Server 2003 Group Policy, download and install the Microsoft Group Policy Management Console (GPMC) from Microsoft at
>
> http://www.microsoft.com/downloads/details.aspx?FamilyId=0A6D4C24-8CBD-4B35-9272-DD3CBFC81887&displaylang=en

Open the Group Policy Management Console by selecting Start, All Programs, Administrative Tools, Group Policy Management. To create Outlook client software Group Policy Objects, follow these steps:

1. Select the Default Domain Policy for your domain by expanding Forest/Domains/YourCompanyDomain/Group Policy Objects.

2. Select the Default Domain Policy, click Action, and then click Edit. This opens the Group Policy Editor to create the Software Push.

3. Select Computer Configuration and then Software Installation.

4. From the Action menu, select New/Package.

5. Navigate the Open dialog to the network share where the Outlook.MSI was placed and select the MSI package being applied. Select Open to continue.

---

**TIP**

If prompted that the Group Policy Editor cannot verify the network location, ensure that the share created to store the installation files has permission to allow users access to the share. Select Yes to continue when confirmed.

---

6. At the Deploy Software dialog, select Advance and click OK to continue. Windows Server 2003 will verify the installation package; wait for the verification to complete before continuing to the next step.

7. After the package is visible in the right pane of the software installation properties, highlight the install package and click Action/Properties.

8. On the Package properties page, select the Deployment tab. Review the configuration, click Assign, and ensure that the Install this Package at Logon option is selected, as shown in Figure 28.5. Select OK when complete.

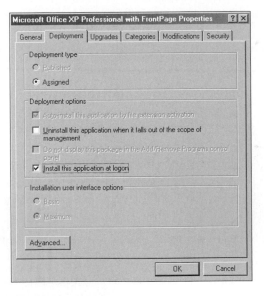

**FIGURE 28.5**   Outlook update properties.

When the new package is ready to deploy, test the update by logging on to a workstation and verifying that the package has installed correctly. If problems exist, redeploy the package by selecting the software update; click Action, All Tasks, Redeploy Application to force the deployment.

## Testing the Outlook Client Deployment

When using Group Policy, it can be difficult for administrators to determine whether a software package was pushed successfully or not without any additional management software such as Microsoft Systems Management Server. When reviewing installations and managing deployments, all evidence of a successful or failed client installation using Group Policy can only be seen using information at the client desktop. Using three areas to check and determine whether a software installation was successful, administrators must view the following manually:

- Look for MSI Installer events that are written into the Application Event Logs. This can be completed from the client desktop machine or by opening the computer management options and connecting the client desktop name.

- On the local machine, view Add/Remove programs to see whether the Outlook update package is listed. If the remote desktop options are enabled, administrators can remotely connect to the desktop and view this option.

# Deploying with Microsoft Systems Management Server

The most comprehensive option to deploy the Outlook client is Microsoft Systems Management Server (SMS). With the powerful software deployment functionality and management tools incorporated with SMS, this method becomes the best solution for deploying the Outlook client software to medium and large organizations.

## Planning and Preparing Outlook Deployments with SMS

To prepare the Outlook client installation for use with Microsoft Systems Management Server, administrators must plan and prepare the deployment in many of the same ways as when using other options.

This section reviews and outlines the following options and deployment preparation tasks involved with using Microsoft Systems Management Server (SMS):

- **Software Distribution**—Plan and create administrative installation points to support software pushes in remote locations and separate subnets. SMS site servers and remote distribution points can be used in remote locations to support software distribution without requiring pushes over WAN links.

- **Evaluate Client Needs**—Determine the specific client installation needs and document the deployment plan and order in which SMS will push the Outlook client.

- **Inventory Using and SMS Collections**—Leveraging the powerful functionality of SMS reporting, administrators can perform detailed inventories of the desktop client's hardware and software evaluating and determining Outlook requirements prior to deploying.

- **Create SMS Collections**—Use collections to create individual deployment groups based on the planned deployment scenario.

## Deploying with Systems Management Server 2003

When deploying the Outlook client with Microsoft Systems Management Server 2003, SMS leverages the Windows Installer to enhance the functionality of the deployment and add options and functionality to recover from failed installations.

When leveraging Windows Installer and SMS to push client software, the following options are available:

- **Pre-Defined Configuration Support**—Administrators can incorporate Transforms and PRF files with the distribution of the MSI package.

- **Per-system Pushes**—Users can establish a connection to the Web site without providing credentials.

- **Unattended Installation**—Using the /qb option with the installation syntax for the MSI package, administrators can force an unattended installation to the Outlook client.

- **Administrative Installation Points**—As with other options, remote location and alternate location can be defined to support client pushes over slower connections.

- **Advertised and Silent Installation**—Administrators can choose between the options of advertising the installation package in the SMS advance client or forcing for the installation without user intervention.

## Configuring the SMS Package for an Unattended Installation

Using the property pages of the Outlook MSI package being used with Systems Management Server to deploy clients, administrators can define the options to be used and characteristics of how the package will be installed.

In this scenario, you configure the basic installation package for an unattended installation with Microsoft Systems Management Server:

1. Select the Outlook MSI file and open the Programs property page. Modify the Installer package properties by adding the command-line switch **/qn**, as shown in Figure 28.6.

2. To complete configuring the unattended installation for the MSI package, click the Environment tab and uncheck the User Input Required option.

> **NOTE**
>
> To add a PRF file for use with the SMS package, add this command:
>
> `/ImportPRF \\Outlook Files\Outlook.PRF`
>
> after the /qn switch (where Outlook Files represents the share location where the packages can be found).

28

**FIGURE 28.6**    MSI general properties.

Now that the installation package has been prepared, Microsoft Systems Management Server can be configured to push Microsoft Outlook clients to the desktop.

# Managing Post-Deployment Tasks

Overall, without certain tools and management software such as Systems Management Server 2003, administrators are very limited in options for managing and validating Outlook client deployments. In this section, we will review methods and functionality already available in the Windows Enterprise that can be leveraged to help determine the overall success of a deployment and troubleshoot common deployment issues.

## Validating Successful Installations

When SMS is not available for managing and determining the success of the Outlook client deployments, administrators must take advantage of the standard tools and functionality available with Windows Server and Exchange Server 2003. Administrators can use several methods to review and validate successful and failed client installation as well as ensure that the client can authenticate after the Outlook client is installed and launched into the production environment.

Review the following options to determine methods and tricks that can assist in validating Outlook client functionality after the deployment is complete:

- Installations can be validated by reviewing the Application event logs of the client systems and identifying MSI Installer events that are written into the event logs.

- To avoid visiting every desktop to verify a successful installation, remotely connect to the event logs of the client systems through the Computer Management snap-in using the Connect to Another Computer option.

- On the local machine, view Add/Remove programs to see whether the Outlook update package is listed.

- Administrators can also leverage the remote desktop functionality of Windows XP to connect to client systems verifying all of the above options from a central location.

- Use the Logon page of the Exchange Mail Store to view and document Successful Client Logons as they access Exchange Server 2003 Mailboxes during the post deployment.

- Enable Diagnostic Logging on the Exchange Server 2003 properties page to monitor MSExchangeIS Mailbox activity when deploying clients.

## Summary

Overall, when planning a deployment of the Outlook client, organizations can leverage many different options depending on the type of client and the specific client needs identified during the discovery phase of the project. Whether you use manual installation or Windows Server 2003 Group Policy and Systems Management Server, extensive planning and testing of Outlook client Transforms and Outlook profiles should be performed prior and results documented well before deploying any clients to the production environment.

Regardless of the deployment method used, configuration settings and the procedures used to deploy should be documented and the production deployments of Outlook staged in groups for effective manageability.

## Best Practices

The following are best practices from this chapter:

- Use the Group Policy Management Console (GPMC) to plan and test policies prior to installation, as well as to debug policy problems after implementation.

- The Resultant Set of Policies (RSoP) should be used to analyze policy enforcement.

- Administrators should delegate rights to Exchange administrators to distribute, manage, and enforce group policies.

- Document all configuration settings being applied to Outlook Transform and PRF files.

- With Microsoft Systems Management Server (SMS), inventories using built-in reporting tools can be conducted on network desktop systems to identify hardware and software requirement needs on each.

28

- Review all prerequisites before installing Outlook. Ensure that all client systems meet the minimum requirement to avoid any installation failures.

- Always be aware of challenges with bandwidth availability prior to any deployment.

- To complete the installation of Outlook 2003 successfully, the desktop operating system also requires Microsoft Internet Explorer 5.01 or higher.

- To enhance functionality when using Windows Server 2003 Group Policy, download and install the Microsoft Group Policy Management Console (GPMC) from Microsoft.

- Use the Logon page of the Exchange Mail Store to view and document successful client logons and access to Exchange Server 2003 Mailboxes during the post deployment support and review.

- Enable Diagnostic Logging on the Exchange Server 2003 properties page to monitor MSExchangeIS Mailbox activity when deploying clients.

- Leverage built-in functionality, such as remote desktop and the Computer Management snap-in, to review the successes and failures of client installations.

CHAPTER **29**

# Group Policy Management for Exchange Clients

IN THIS CHAPTER

• Understanding Group Policy Management with Outlook

• Baseline Administration for Group Policy Deployment

• Outlook Client Group Policies

• Administering Outlook Through Group Policy

• Updates and Patch Management with Group Policies

To further enhance the features and options available when managing Microsoft Outlook clients with Exchange Server 2003 clients, Microsoft has developed new Windows features, tools, and add-on security templates. These new enhancements enable client configuration and options to be managed and pushed to client systems using these security templates along with Windows Group Policy.

Using Windows Group Policy management tools, administrators can easily and inexpensively centralize many of the duties and support tasks previously demanding time and resources when working with Exchange clients. With Windows Group Policy, additional Windows tools and resources available in the Office 2003 Resource Kit (ORK), Exchange client settings, and more can be configured centrally and applied to Exchange clients in the enterprise using Domain Group Policy functionality.

With Group Policy, administrators can provide powerful administration and management support to desktops and Exchange clients throughout the enterprise. This chapter provides insight to the resources, available options, and best practices, as well as the techniques used to minimize administrative overhead when supporting Exchange Server 2003 client systems.

Leveraging the information in this chapter, Exchange administrators will have a better understanding of how to integrate Group Policy and Exchange Server 2003 client support, the day-to-day tasks involved with managing Exchange Server 2003 users and client systems. In addition, the new tools enable administrators to have centralized management of Outlook and Outlook user preferences and to customize the look and feel of Outlook using only Windows Group Policy and policy security template files.

# Understanding Group Policy Management with Outlook

One of the most powerful tools administrators have—Group Policy available with Windows Server 2003—has become an even more comprehensive part of the network environment and the Exchange enterprise management strategy.

Group Policy functionality is used to deliver a standard set of security, controls, rules, and options to a user and workstation when authenticating to the domain. In addition, it can be used to configure everything from logon scripts and folder redirection to enabling desktop features and preventing users from installing software on network workstations. With Exchange Server 2003 and the Outlook client, Group Policy can be used to control the preferences and options available when configuring and customizing the Outlook client.

This section helps Exchange administrators understand Group Policy and its functionality and characteristics when they manage the enforcement of policies within an Exchange enterprise.

## Managing Group Policies

To manage Group Policy, administrators must understand that group policies apply only to Windows 2000 Professional, Windows XP, Windows Server 2000, and Windows Server 2003 server plaforms.

To access and manage Windows Group Policy, administrators can use the Group Policy snap-in available in the Administrative Tools program group of any Windows domain controller. In addition to the built-in tools available with Windows Server platforms, Microsoft has released another, more powerful option for managing Group Policy called the Group Policy Management Console (GPMC) for Windows Server 2003.

With the basic Group Policy Management snap-in, administrators are provided a standard management console through the built-in Administrative Tools of Windows Server. Through the standard method of accessing Group Policy, administrators are provided a single interface to access, manage, and configure policies with the standard options and functionality available in the built-in Windows tools.

The second option, the GPMC, is the new tool available from Microsoft for configuring and using Group Policy with Windows Server 2003. Using the GPMC, administrators are provided with a handy tool to manage group policies with all the standard options available with the Administrative Tools built-in Management snap-in. In addition, the GPMC provides enhanced functionality and options for planning and testing Group Policy implementations prior to deploying and enforcing them on the Windows domain.

> **GPMC in Windows 2000 Domains**
>
> To manage Group Policy using the GPMC tool in a Windows 2000 domain, the GPMC must be installed on a Windows XP desktop running Service Pack 1 or later with the Windows .NET component installed.

The `GPMC.msi` package can be downloaded from the `http://www.microsoft.com/Windows 2003/downloads/featurepacks` Web site. Search for `GPMC.msi` and download the add-on tool. After installing the GPMC, it can be found in the Administrative Tools program group or by selecting the Group Policy Management option.

> **CAUTION**
>
> Because Group Policy can cause tremendous impact on users, computers, and domain security, any Group Policy implementation should be tested using the Resultant Set of Policies (RSoP) tool included with the GPMC. When testing, use this tool in Planning mode and review all results before implementing any policy changes into a production domain. See the section titled "Working with Resultant Set of Policies (RSoP)" later in this chapter to learn more about testing Group Policy and using the Group Policy Management tool in Simulation mode.

## Understanding Policies and Preferences

When working with Group Policy, you have two methods for making changes on the local workstations: using preferences and using policies. With both preferences and policies, changes are applied and enforced using the local Registry of the machine on which they are being applied.

With preferences, changes to options such as wallpaper or screensavers and software settings are applied locally. With policies, changes to the Registry are applied that affect security and Registry keys, which are protected by access control lists (ACLs).

Although Group Policy overrides any preference settings at the desktop when working with applications such as Outlook and Office 2003, the policy does not overwrite the preference keys when preference options are set on the local desktop by the user or desktop administrator. This means that if a policy is configured and applied to systems or users, and then the policy is removed, the preferences that were set by the local user before the policy was applied will return.

This makes Group Policy a powerful tool when a network's administrator wants to control certain aspects of a client application such as Outlook options. Policy can also be used to disable end-users from changing the appearance, configuration, or functionality of the item to which the policy is applied.

## Group Policy Templates

One of the most important features for minimizing administrative overhead when working with Group Policy is leveraging security templates or the `.adm` file. Security templates are a powerful predefined set of security options and preferences available, from

29

Microsoft for applying Group Policy to a specific area or software component, available to users on the domain. Based on the type of users and environment needed, these templates can be a handy tool to create and enforce configuration settings already predefined in the template.

Though some templates are built in to the standard installation of Windows Server 2003, additional, more in-depth templates can be downloaded and imported into Group Policy Objects (GPOs), where they can then either be implemented as is, or modified to meet the specific needs to the areas and settings in which the template applies. However, when templates are used, they are a great starting point for network administrators to obtain a base-level security configuration standards settings policy on client workstations and software components.

Templates can also be used to configure settings such as account policies, event log settings, local policies, Registry permissions, file and folder permissions, and Exchange Server 2003 client settings.

## Defining the Order of Application

When applying Group Policy, each policy object is applied in a specific order. Computers and users whose accounts are lower in the AD tree may inherit policies applied at different levels within Active Directory. To help create a good, functional, structured policy model, Group Policy should be applied to objects in the Active Directory in the following order:

1. Local Security Policy

2. Site GPOs

3. Domain GPOs

4. OU GPOs

5. Nested OU GPOs

6. Security Group GPOs

If multiple GPOs are applied to a specific AD object—such as an organizational unit (OU) or group—they are applied in the reverse order from which they are listed. This means that the last GPO listed is applied first, and if conflicts exist with another applied GPO, settings in the higher listed GPO override those in the lower one that was applied first.

## Group Policy Refresh Intervals

When Group Policy is applied, the policy is refreshed and enforced at regularly scheduled intervals after a computer has been started and a user has logged on to the domain where that policy is applied. By default, Group Policy is refreshed every 90 minutes on workstation and member servers within the domain.

When you need to better control the refresh interval of a group policy, the refresh interval can be configured for each group policy by changing its time in the policy configuration. Using the GPMC, refresh intervals can be configured by going to the domain policy and selecting the following:

- Computer Configuration, Administrative Templates, System, Group Policy (to change the interval for computer policies and domain controllers)

- User Configuration, Administrative Templates, System, Group Policy (to change the interval for user policies)

Changes made to existing GPOs or new GPOs being created are enforced when the refresh cycle runs. However, with the following types or GPO settings, policies are enforced only at logon or when booting a workstation to the domain, depending on the GPO configuration settings:

- Software installation configured in the Computer Policies

- Software installation configured in the User Policies

> **NOTE**
>
> When working with application settings, refresh intervals can be configured and customized to fit the environment needs. You should leave the refresh interval as the default, however, unless requirements call them to be modified.

# Baseline Administration for Group Policy Deployment

Now that you have a base understanding of functionality and terminology of Group Policy, you can look at usage and how the configuration of Group Policy can vary greatly with each individual implementation.

Administrators can use this information to understand the more common methods of applying permissions to Group Policy for management purposes and the tools for testing Group Policy implementations prior to deployment in the production environment.

> **NOTE**
>
> In this section, some best practices for using Group Policy to manage Outlook client configurations are covered. For more information and details regarding Group Policy management, view the Help information for managing Group Policy with Windows Server 2003.

## Delegating GP Management Rights

It is important to delegate the proper rights for administrators to manage and manipulate Group Policy. For example, in larger organizations, a very small group of users normally has permission to edit a policy at the domain level. However, when specific requirements are needed to administer applications such as the Exchange client, permissions can be granted to accounts responsible for managing Exchange clients using the GPMC.

When creating specific permissions with the GPMC, administrators can delegate control for other administrators to manage the following areas within Group Policy:

- Create GPOs

- Create WMI filters

- Assign permissions on WMI filters

- Set permissions on an individual GPO to read and edit

- Assign permissions on individual locations to which the GPO is linked, called the scope of management (SOM)

To easily assign permissions to GPOs, administrators can use the Delegation Wizard in the GPMC, applied manually by selecting the Delegaton tab.

## Working with Resultant Set of Policies (RSoP)

The new GPMC provides administrators with a powerful tool for planning and testing Group Policy implementations prior to enforcing them on domain workstations and users. Using the RSoP tool in Planning mode, administrators can simulate the deployment of a specified group policy, evaluate the results of the test, make changes as needed, and then test the deployment again. After RSoP shows that the GPO is correct, the administrator can then back up the GPO configuration and import it into production.

To run RSoP in Simulation mode, right-click on Group Policy Modeling in the forest that will be simulated, and choose Group Policy Modeling Wizard. The wizard enables you to input slow links, loopback configurations, WMI filters, and other specific configuration choices to simulate the environment in which the policy will be deployed. Each model is presented in its own report as a subnode under the Group Policy Modeling node for review.

> **TIP**
>
> Because errors in Group Policy settings can impact users' domain security and client server connectivity, any Group Policy implementation should be tested using the RSoP tool in Planning mode before applying the policy on the production domain.

## Managing Group Policy Inheritance

To maximize the inheritance feature of Group Policy, keep the following in mind:

- Isolate the servers in their own OU: Create descriptive Server OUs and place all the non–domain controller servers in those OUs under a common Server OU. If software pushes are applied through Group Policy on the domain level or on a level above the Server OU and do not have the Enforcement option checked, the Server OU can be configured with Block Policy Inheritance checked to avoid the enforcement of the policy on the Server OU. As a result, the servers won't receive software pushes applied at levels above their OU.

• Use Block Policy Inheritance and Enforcement sparingly to make troubleshooting Group Policy less complex.

### Group Policy Backup, Restore, Copy, and Import

One new major improvement to Group Policy management offers the ability to back up (or export) the Group Policy data to a file. Using the backup functionality of the GPMC, any policy can be created and tested in a lab environment; after the results have been reviewed and issues resolved, the policy can then be exported to a file for deployment on the production domain.

When backing up Group Policy, you back up only data specific to that group policy itself. Other Active Directory objects that can be linked to GPOs, such as individual WMI filters and TCP/IP security policies, are not backed up because of complications with restores when working with these specific areas. When backup is completed, administrators can restore the Group Policy data in the same location, restoring proper functionality to misconfigured and accidentally deleted group policies.

The import functionality of the GPMC also enables administrators to take an exported Group Policy file and import the Group Policy data into a different location from its original one. This functionality is true even in scenarios in which no trust exists between domains.

Imports of Group Policy files can be completed using files from different domains, across forest domains, or within the same domain. This functionality is most powerful when you move a GPO from a test lab into production without having to manually re-create the policy setting tested in the lab environment.

Another helpful function of Group Policy Management is copying GPOs. If the administrator has configured a complex group policy and applied the setting to a specific OU in the domain, the group policy can be copied and duplicated for application to another OU. When using the copy function, a new group policy is created. This new policy can then be placed and applied to the new location.

## Outlook Client Group Policies

With a baseline understanding of how Group Policy functions in a Windows Server 2003 Active Directory domain environment, Microsoft Exchange Server 2003 administrators can look at how Group Policy, GPOs, and security templates can be leveraged to enhance the management of Outlook 2003 clients in the enterprise.

An all-in-one solution, Exchange administrators can also use the Group Policy function to create administrative installation points for pushing client software and updates to Windows desktops on the domain. Working with predefined Group Policy templates available from Microsoft, administrators can now manage areas and control access and options, ranging from restrictions and preventing configuration modifications to controlling the look and feel that affects the overall user experience and information delivered to clients when working with the Exchange Outlook 2003 client software.

29

In this section, you review the tools and options for managing the Exchange Outlook 2003 clients, specifically using Group Policy along with the predefined security templates or .adm files. You will explore the options available when deploying and working with the Outlook 2003 client, Microsoft Outlook Group Policy template, and the steps for configuring administration privileges for managing the Exchange client through Group Policy and the GPMC.

## Exchange Client Policy Options

To further enhance the management functionality when working with Exchange Outlook 2003 clients, the ORK now provides a predefined security template for managing Outlook 2003 on the domain using Group Policy functionality.

Called Outlk11.adm, this template enables administrators to centrally manage and configure many of the security functions and preferences normally required to be configured at each individual Outlook client. Using the Outlk11.adm security template, administrators can fully manage and configure the following areas defined by domain clients:

- **Outlook Preferences**—The Preferences options available with the security template can be enabled in the same manner as using the Options tab available on the Tools menu of the Outlook desktop client. When defining preferences, administrators can control the standard look and feel of each component available with Outlook. Options include areas for enforcing items such as spell check and email format, calendaring views, contacts options, and more.

- **Exchange Settings**—Configuration items, such as Outlook users profile configurations and auto archiving, can now be centrally configured.

- **Intranet and SharePoint Portal Server Settings**—In addition to the Outlook client settings, using the templates enables administrators to configure access to internal business information and SharePoint Portal server resources through Outlook client folders.

Though the Outlk11.adm template enables you to configure many important options and preferences with the Outlook 2003 Exchange client, not all areas are available using the template.

## Adding the Outlook Administrative Template

Because the additional administrative templates are not configured by default when Windows Server 2003 is installed, administrators must download or install the administrative Outlook Template Outlook11.adm manually. Available on the ORK, the Outlk11.adm is placed on the local drive of the systems on which the ORK is installed.

To begin setting up the Outlook security template Outlk11.adm, start by installing the GPMC on the domain controller on which the policy will be administered.

Next install the Microsoft ORK on a system on which the template can be accessed from a domain controller for import into the Domain Group Policy.

**TIP**

To download the GPMC from Microsoft, go to

http://www.microsoft.com/windowsserver2003/downloads/featurepacks/default.mspx

The Office 2003 Resource Kit (ORK) can be downloaded from the Microsoft Office Web site at

http://www.microsoft.com/office/orkarchive/2003ddl.htm

After the ORK is installed, the Outlk11.adm file is automatically extracted and placed in the C:\Windows\Inf directory (where C: represents the system root where the Windows installation resides) on the local system drive where the ORK was installed.

To import the Outlook security template Outlk11.adm into the Domain Group Policy using the Group Policy Management Tool, use the following steps:

**TIP**

When importing the Outlk11.adm security template, it is best practice to import the template to the Default Domain Group Policy. Review the event logs on additional domain controllers or use the Replmon tool available with Windows 2003 support tools to ensure the replication of the domain policy to all domain controllers occurs correctly.

1. From a domain controller in the domain where the policy will be applied, open the Group Policy snap-in by selecting Start, All Programs, Administrative Tools, Group Policy Management.

2. Select the location Default Domain Policy where Outlk11.adm will be imported to, as shown in Figure 29.1.

3. On the Action menu, select Edit; this opens the Group Policy Object Editor window.

4. In the Group Policy Object Editor window, select Administrative Templates under the User Configuration option and right-click to choose Add/Remove Templates, as shown in Figure 29.2.

5. From the Add/Remove Templates dialog box, click the Add button.

6. Navigate to the location where Outlk11.adm was placed, as noted in step 2. Select the template to import OUTLK11.ADM and click the Open button.

7. Ensure that the OUTLK11 template has been added to the Add/Remove Templates dialog box, and click Close to continue.

You should now see the Microsoft Outlook 2003 template under the Administrative Templates folder in the Group Policy Editor.

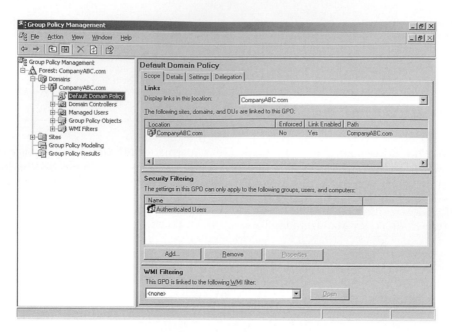

**FIGURE 29.1**    Group Policy Management Console.

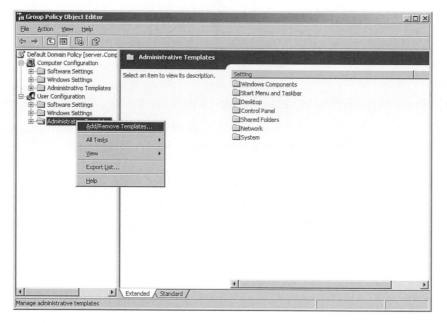

**FIGURE 29.2**    Group Policy Object Editor.

## Assigning Group Policy Delegates

Although Group Policy has traditionally been the management task of Windows domain administrators, with delegation, permissions can be assigned to additional resources and accounts such as Exchange administrators to manage Exchange 2003 Outlook clients. Using the Delegation Wizard of the GPMC, accounts can assign and delegate rights to add, modify, and delete Exchange Server 2003 related GPOs.

It is important to delegate the proper rights for administrators to manipulate the Microsoft Outlook 2003 Group Policy. Using the delegation option of the GPMC, administrators can assign a very small group of users permission to edit Outlook policies at the domain level. To enhance this functionality, it is also possible to allow diverse groups of administrators to configure group policies at lower levels of the Active Directory domain tree.

When assigning permissions, administrators can delegate the following rights:

- Create GPO

- Create WMI filters

- Assign permissions on WMI filters

- Set individual GPO permissions to read and edit

- Assign permissions on individual locations to which the GPO is linked (SOM)

Using the Group Policy Delegation Wizard makes it easy to give the appropriate security groups and account administrators the rights needed to manage Exchange connectivity and Outlook clients while maintaining Windows Server 2003 domain access in the most secure way possible.

### How to Delegate Rights over GPOs

To understand the steps using the Delegation Wizard required to assign rights over a GPO, let's look at the following scenario. Here, you will assign one Active Directory administrative account permission at the domain level. The rights for this exercise that will be assigned to the account will be the Edit Group Policy Objects Only permissions.

To begin, open the GPMC by selecting Start, All Programs, Administrative Tool, Group Policy Management. Then follow these steps:

1. On the GPMC, select Domain Folder, Your Domain, Group Policy Objects, Default Domain Policy.

2. Select the Delegation tab in the right pane of the Domain Group Policy Object.

3. To add an account, select the Add button, enter the name of the account to be added, and click the OK button.

4. Select the rights to be assigned to the account by selecting the permission Edit Settings in the drop-down box, as shown in Figure 29.3; select OK to continue.

29

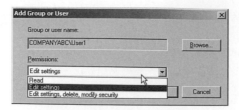

**FIGURE 29.3**    Add Group or User permissions.

The account has now been assigned rights to edit the domain-level GPO. Review the information and test settings to ensure that the permissions have been applied correctly.

## Managing Group Policy Configurations

Through Group Policy, Outlook configuration settings can be configured and applied differently depending on what level and what OU the GPO applies to the domain.

Applying GPOs to different OUs and groups, Exchange administrators can not only centrally manage one group of Exchange Server 2003 Outlook clients, but they can also configure and apply a completely different set of options and enforce them on a different group or OU in the domain. To complete an exercise using this method, follow these steps:

1. Open the GPMC and select the OU to which the GPO will be applied.

2. Select Action on the menu bar and select Link an Existing GPO.

3. From the Select GPO dialog box, choose the domain policy and click OK to link the domain policy to the desired OU.

> **TIP**
>
> This method can also be used when linking a specific GPO to any OU.
>
> When linking GPOs, access to the GPMC can be obtained through the Active Directory Users and Computers (ADUC) snap-in. Select the properties of the domain you are working with and select the Group Policy tab.

# Administering Outlook Through Group Policy

One option not available with previous Outlook versions is the ability to centrally manage Outlook options, preferences, and profiles when deploying clients to the enterprise. Using the Outlook Group Policy security template along with additional tools available with the latest service packs and updates, administrators can centrally manage Outlook configuration and settings through group policies that in previous versions required administrators to visit each Outlook client desktop.

**Configuring Profiles**

Though there are many options and configuration choices using the Outlk11.ADM security template, one option not available is setting or changing the profile information for Exchange 2003 Outlook clients.

To configure client profile information and settings using these new tools and GPO options, see Chapter 28, "Deploying the Client for Exchange."

## Defining Baseline Outlook Preferences

One option that Group Policy enables organizations to accomplish when managing Exchange Server 2003 Outlook clients is the ability to design, develop, and implement a baseline configuration for every Outlook 2003 client connecting to the domain and Exchange Server 2003. Often, this was not an option because of the exhaustive amount of administration involved, along with the inability to secure configurations from being modified by end-users without changing options at the client.

With the new options of standardizing configuration settings for all Outlook 2003 client systems, administrators must determine and plan which options can be used and configured to improve the productivity and functionality of the Exchange client for each domain user. Using the Group Policy Object settings to define simple Outlook preferences and configuration settings—such as Saving Sent Items, Spell Checking Messages Before Sending, and Auto Archive—can not only improve the functionality and performance of the Outlook client, but can also reduce administrative management and overhead when supporting Windows client workstations and Exchange Server 2003 users.

### Email Options

Some of the most useful email options available when configuring settings using Group Policy include

- **HTML/Microsoft Word Message Format**—The most enhanced of all Outlook Email Options is the Rich Text and HTML/Microsoft Word email format options. This option can be enabled to provide a robust email editor standard to all Exchange Server 2003 clients.

- **Junk Email Filtering**—Along with the latest service pack for Exchange 2003, enabling the Junk Email options allows the configuration of the Email Protection Level, filtering behavior, and deletion behavior of junk emails, and update behavior of the junk email list at the client level.

- **Cached Mode and PST Creation**—Disabling or enabling users' ability to use Cached mode is a powerful option for administrators to control internal network traffic. The OST and PST options can provide control over bandwidth utilization as well as local system disk space resources on domain client workstations.

- **Empty Deleted Items Folder**—Controlling the total amount of space each user mailbox can grow to helps control storage limits on the Exchange Server 2003

29

server; administrators can enable this option to control the total amount of deleted items that is retained by the client, based on date deleted or other options.

- **Auto Archiving**—One area often requiring administrative overhead, the Auto Archive option can now be toggled on or off via GPO settings. This option can also be used to specify the location both locally or on the network on which archived files will be stored.

- **Email Accounts**—Using this option, users can be prevented from adding additional account types such as POP Internet account. This option can be very effective when controlling the type of email and inbound virus scanned emails that are stored on domain client workstations.

### Calendaring Options

In addition to the email options available, robust Outlook calendaring options can also be defined to establish a base functionality for all domain Outlook 2003 users:

- **Free Busy Information**—The ability to publish or not publish user-free busy information to the Internet and local resources can now be controlled through GPOs. In addition to this, when enabled, the total amount, or duration, can be set—controlling and managing performance when enabled.

- **Reminders and Appointment Options**—The behavior of Calendar Reminders can also be enabled and disabled. In addition, options can also be set to determine how appointments are managed and displayed.

- **Working Hours and Workweek**—Administrators can control and define calendar views and workweek views for Outlook calendars. This option allows for work times to be adjusted depending on the business needs of your organization.

### Contact Options

One interesting setting is the option in the Outlook security template for Outlook contact management. For ease of management, administrators can now define how each contact will be filed, displayed, and even the language in which a contact is indexed for dealing with international Outlook client business needs. For example, the Display Name can be set as First [Middle], Last Name, and the File As option for the contact can be set as Last, First.

Many more options are available that extend beyond dealing with the Outlook client email settings. Additional options for dealing with Exchange Server 2003 settings also exist in the template, such as the ability to repair the `Mapi32.dll` and control client offline address book behavior when clients connect to Exchange Server 2003. Review all the administrative options available in the Outlook Security template and their descriptions to determine which settings and changes can best be applied to your organization using GPOs.

## Managing the Look and Feel of the Exchange Client

Another powerful function of the Outlook security template and Group Policy is the ability for administrators to control and define the look and feel of the Outlook client. Administrators can now configure and enforce options through these tools to deliver additional information to clients while also creating a specific look and feel within the Outlook 2003 interface.

Using Group Policy preferences, settings can also be defined to customize the look of the Exchange Server 2003 Outlook client. Options can be set to allow administrators to define folders within Outlook that can redirect users to information on intranet and Internet Web sites as well as SharePoint Portal Server workspaces, providing an enhanced user experience and access to business data within the Oulook 2003 client not previously available.

### Web Options Overview

Using the Outlook Today and Folder Home Pages from the Outlook Special Folders option, settings can be defined to integrate and redirect Outlook users to valuable Web and business data using technologies such as Microsoft SharePoint Portal and Internet Information Services:

- **Customize Outlook Today**—Administrators can use a Custom Outlook Today Properties setting to define a Web page that will be viewed when users access the Outlook Today folder. This option can be a great tool to direct Outlook users to an internal business intranet site.

- **Folder Home Page Settings**—Each default folder within Outlook can now be redirected to a predefined Web page or internal URL. For example, the default Contacts folder can be set to a URL of business contacts while users can still create subcontact folders for the additional contact information.

- **SharePoint Portal Server**—With Outlook 2003, policy preferences allow support for the integration of SharePoint Portal server with Outlook 2003 folders. When enabled, information in a SharePoint Portal server can be displayed in Outlook 2003; the update of this information is controlled through the GPO settings.

## Configuring and Applying Outlook Group Policy Settings

With all the information gathered in the previous sections, administrators can determine which options to implement and apply to the configuration of Outlook 2003 using the GPMC and Outlook 2003 security template. To better understand the effects of these settings before applying a group policy to the production domain, review the following mock installation scenario.

In this scenario, you will apply a standard set of preferences on the GPO to create an Exchange Server 2003 Outlook client baseline configuration. This GPO will be applied to one security group in the Users OU on the Active Directory domain. As described earlier, one additional setting will be applied to redirect the client's Outlook Today setting to a company Internet home page.

To begin, open the GPMC by selecting Start, All Programs, Administrative Tools, Group
Policy Management; then follow these steps:

1. Select the Default Domain Policy by selecting Forest, Domains,
   YourCompanydomain, Group Policy Objects.

2. Select the Default Domain Policy, click Action on the GPMC menu, and click Edit.
   This opens the Group Policy Editor.

3. Select Administrative Templates under the User Configuration and select the
   Microsoft Outlook 2003 folder.

From this point, you can begin to enable your options and apply preferences to the GPO.
After options are enabled, they appear in the GPMC to be tested through RSoP and
applied to the OU. In this scenario, you will also apply the Rich Text/Microsoft Word
email editor options and redirect the Outlook Today page to point to a Web page called
www.CompanyABC.com. To apply these settings, complete these steps:

1. Select the Microsoft Outlook 2003 folder and select Tools, Options, Mail Format,
   Message Format.

2. Double-click Message Format Editor in the right pane to open and configure the
   Message Format Policy settings.

3. As shown in Figure 29.4, select the Enabled Option and click Rich Text/Microsoft
   Word in the drop-down box. Select OK to continue.

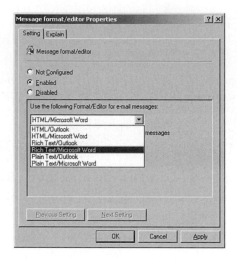

**FIGURE 29.4**    Message Format Editor properties.

4. Next select the Outlook Today folder by selecting Microsoft Outlook 2003, Outlook
   Today Settings.

5. Double-click URL for Custom Outlook Today Properties in the right pane.

6. To enable the redirection of the Outlook Today home page, click the Enable button and enter the URL to be displayed, as shown in Figure 29.5. Click OK when finished.

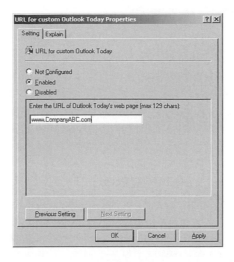

**FIGURE 29.5**    Custom Outlook Today properties.

7. Open the GPMC and confirm that the settings are ready to be applied. From the GPMC, select Default Domain Policy and ensure that the Outlook settings appear, as shown in Figure 29.6.

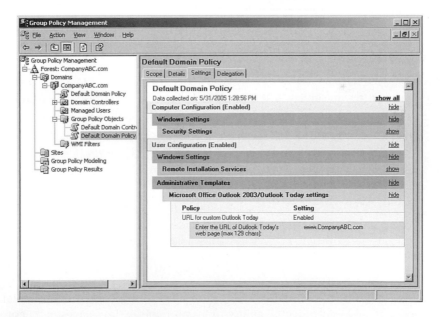

**FIGURE 29.6**    GPMC Outlook settings.

Now that the Group Policy options have been configured, you apply the settings to a group of users in the domain by following these steps:

8. To apply the settings to a group, click the Add button under Security Filtering in the right pane of the Default Domain Policy.

9. From the Select Users, Computers, or Groups search page, enter the name of a group in the Users OU that these Outlook 2003 settings will be applied to and click OK.

10. Check to see whether the group has been added to the Security Filtering pane.

After the configuration is complete and options saved, it is good practice to back up the configuration and ensure that all the settings are enabled on the GPO by selecting Action/GPO Status.

# Updates and Patch Management with Group Policies

One other advantage to using Group Policy is the centralized deployment options available to distribute the Exchange Outlook 2003 client updates and patches to domain workstations. Using any one of the following options, including a combination of each, Exchange administrators can use Group Policy to deploy updates using Microsoft MSI installation packages or Windows Updates security templates to push updates to the Microsoft Outlook 2003 client. Using GPO's installation of software updates can be deployed from the centralized administrative installation point to a predefined set of workstations or in the case of a wide area network (WAN), from any remote installation point or Windows Update site configured in the GPO settings.

## Deployment Options When Updating Exchange Clients

Using Group Policy, the Outlook 2003 client can be upgraded and patched using one of the following deployment methods:

- **Assigned to Computers**—This method of installation uses the Outlook Installation package on the workstation and is available when the workstation is restarted. Using this option, all users have access to the Exchange client software after it is installed.

- **Assigned to Users**—When the installation package is assigned to users, application shortcuts are placed on the desktop of the user's profile and on the Start menu. When these shortcuts are selected, the application installation will be completed.

> **TIP**
>
> When using the Assigned Application options for both users and computers only, when a package is uninstalled, Group Policy automatically reassigns the installation to the user or computer.

- **Publishing the Installation**—This option requires additional configuration at the desktop level to allow users the ability to install published packages on client systems. When a software package is published, the installation package is displayed in the Add/Remove Programs group in the local desktop system Control Panel. Users can then initiate the installation by selecting the update.

- **Using Windows Update Services**—This may be the most common method of deploying software updates to client desktop systems on any enterprise. Using Windows Server Update Services technology and Group Policy, security updates, patches, and critical updates can be deployed for Microsoft office platforms to the client workstion.

Each method enables Exchange Server 2003 administrators to deliver update packages to the Outlook 2003 client using a push or pull method. These updates can be configured for deployment from a central location or an administrative installation point somewhere on the network to allow for ease of download to the workstation anywhere in the enterprise.

---

**Windows Server Update Services**

For additional information and downloads for Windows Update services and the different update support options from Microsoft, go to www.microsoft.com/windowsserversystem/updateservices/default.mspx.

---

**CAUTION**

When deploying updates with GPOs, do not assign the option to install updates to users and computers at the same time. Assigning both options can create conflicts as to how updates are installed and possibly corrupt the installation to the Outlook 2003 client when applying the update.

---

## Deploying Client Updates

As with all aspects of Group Policy, the choices and configuration options of deployment updates are numerous. Regardless of which type of update package is being pushed, some basic best practices apply and can help make updates easier and less troublesome:

- When configuring clients to use update methods such as Windows Server Update Services, configure clients to use installation points that will allow clients to update systems from the local LAN rather than over WAN links.

- Software packages pushed with GPOs must be in the format of an MSI package. Any other format type than an MSI cannot be pushed using Group Policy. Using additional tools such as Marovision's Admin Studio can help administrators convert other update formats such as .exe files to customized MSI installation packages as well as custom configuration of predefined installation choices.

- When configuring software pushes using GPOs, configure the GPO at the highest levels possible in the domain tree. If the push is going out to more than one group or OU, the software update should be configured to be pushed at the domain level. If the software update is being pushed to only a few groups or one OU, or if multiple update packages are being pushed, configure the push at the group or OU level.

- Configure software pushes to the Computer Configuration rather than the User Configuration. This way, if users log on to multiple computer systems, updates are not applied more than once to the same system.

- When pushing updates to multiple locations, use technologies such as administrative distribution points and Distributed File System (DFS). This allows software updates to be installed from packages and sources close to the client being updated.

## Pushing Client Updates

With the options available and a good understanding of the best practices for deploying software using GPOs, the next step is to configure a GPO to push an update directly to the Outlook client. The steps in this scenario enable administrators to push a small update package to the Exchange Server 2003 Outlook client workstations on the domain.

Begin by downloading an update to use for this exercise ensuring an MSI format. Also, create a share on the network folder where the update will be placed and deployed. To begin, open the GPMC by selecting Start, All Programs, Administrative Tools, Group Policy Management. With the GPMC open, create an Outlook client software update GPO by following these steps:

1. Select the Default Domain Policy for your domain by selecting Forest, Domains, YourCompanyDomain, Group Policy Objects.

2. Select Default Domain Policy, click Action, and click Edit. This opens the Group Policy Editor to create the software push.

3. Select Computer Configuration and select Software Settings, Software Installation.

4. On the Action menu, select New, Package.

5. Navigate the Open dialog box to the network share where the MSI was placed and select the MSI package being applied. Select Open to continue.

> **TIP**
>
> If prompted that the Group Policy Editor cannot verify the network location, ensure that the share created earlier in these steps has permissions allowing user accounts in the domain access to the share. Select Yes to continue after confirming.

6. At the Deploy Software dialog box, select Advance and click OK to continue. Windows verifies the installation package; wait for the verification to complete before continuing to the next step.

7. When the package is visible in the right pane of the software installation properties, highlight the install package and click Action, Properties.

8. On the Package properties page, select the Deployment tab. Review the configuration, click Assign, and ensure that the Install This Package at Logon option is selected, as shown in Figure 29.7. Select OK when complete.

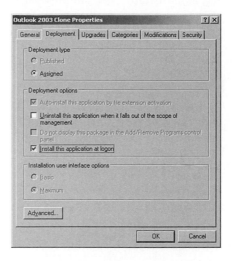

**FIGURE 29.7**    Outlook Update properties.

The new package is now ready to deploy; test the update by logging on to a workstation connected to the domain. Verify that the package has been installed. If problems exist, redeploy the package by selecting the software update in the GPMC and clicking Action, All Tasks, Redeploy Application to force the deployment.

### Determining the Success of a Push

Without additional management software such as Systems Management Server 2003, administrators cannot determine whether a software package was pushed successfully to a client system with a GPO. This is because all evidence of software pushes are only evident locally on the client machines on which the update logs are stored. To check and verify if an update has been installed successfully, you can check several areas:

- Look for MSI Installer events that are written into the application event logs.

- On the local machine, view Add/Remove programs to see whether the Outlook update package is listed.

- If using Windows Server Update Services, review the Windows Update Log located in the `Program Files\Windows Update` directory on the local machine.

## Summary

Group policies can be leveraged to help Exchange administrators manage client connections and configurations to Exchange Server 2003. Rather than accessing every user

29

profile, configuration, or Outlook property page, GPOs can be enabled that centralize the administration and management of any client authenticating to Exchange Server 2003 on a Windows 2003 domain. With new tools in Windows Server 2003 that provide better management of Group Policy, administrators can simplify their day-to-day tasks while expanding on the capabilities of client access to Exchange. From simple Outlook client preference changes to performing client software installation and patch management, Group Policy combined with additional technologies can be of significant help to Exchange Server 2003 administrators working in organizations of any size.

## Best Practices

The following are best practices from this chapter:

- Use the Group Policy Management Console (GPMC) to plan and test policies prior to any GPO deployment, as well as to debug policy problems after their implementation.

- Use the Resultant Set of Policies (RSoP) to verify and analyze policy enforcement.

- Domain administrators should delegate rights to distribute the management and enforcement of Outlook-related group policies to Exchange administrators.

- Limit the use of the Block Policy Inheritance option to minimize the administrative overhead of Group Policy management.

- Use the `Outlk11.adm` template file from the Office 2003 Resource Kit (ORK) to improve administrative capabilities of Outlook 2003.

- When importing the `Outlk11.adm` security template, import the template to the Default Domain Group Policy.

- Use Group Policy to manage the look and feel of the Outlook client.

- Use Windows Server Update Services as a global alternative to update clients accessing Exchange.

- Do not assign the option to install updates to users and computers at the same time. Assigning both options can create conflicts as to how updates are installed and corrupt the installation of the Outlook client when applying the update.

# PART X

# Fault Tolerance and Optimization Technologies

## IN THIS PART

**CHAPTER 30**  System-Level Fault Tolerance (Clustering/ Network Load Balancing)      877

**CHAPTER 31**  Backing Up the Exchange Server 2003 Environment      909

**CHAPTER 32**  Recovering from a Disaster      935

**CHAPTER 33**  Capacity Analysis and Performance Optimization      975

# System-Level Fault Tolerance (Clustering/Network Load Balancing)

**IN THIS CHAPTER**

- Clustering and Load Balancing with Exchange Server 2003

- Clusters and Load-Balancing Requirements

- Implementing Fault-Tolerant Exchange Systems

- Installing Exchange Server 2003 Clusters

- Managing Exchange Server 2003 Clusters

- Outlook Web Access Front-End Server and Load-Balancing Clusters

Today's business-critical business mail environments can leverage Microsoft Windows 2003 Cluster Service (MSCS) and Network Load Balancing (NLB) technologies to provide Exchange Server 2003 messaging systems with a high level of availability and performance. With these technologies, Exchange administrators can improve network reliability by providing high systems availability, Quality of Service (QOS), and immediate recovery from server hardware failures.

Using Windows clustering, load balancing, and the Automatic System Recovery (ASR) technologies available with Windows Server 2003, administrators can effectively provide enhanced reliability for Exchange Server 2003 environments in areas such as recovering from CPU hardware failures, memory problems, and entire Exchange Server 2003 failures.

In addition, Windows clustering services, combined with the Exchange Server 2003 Enterprise Edition, which is cluster aware, can now also be used as a tool to detect potential issues in the configuration and Exchange Server 2003 application. Using these new features available with Exchange Server 2003 Enterprise Edition and the latest Exchange service packs, administrators may be able to recover from potential issues before they occur by restarting the application or failing over the application to another node in the cluster.

In this chapter, administrators can review and understand the options available for designing and implementing system-level fault tolerance using Windows 2003 clusters and Windows 2003 NLB with Exchange Server 2003.

# Clustering and Load Balancing with Exchange Server 2003

First, understanding what Windows Server and Exchange Server platform versions are required to implement these technologies becomes the most important part of any fault-tolerant design. Though Network Load Balancing is supported in all four editions of the Windows 2003 server platforms, clustering technologies are only supported with the Microsoft Windows 2003 Enterprise Server and Datacenter Editions of Windows Server 2003. Fault-tolerant options such as clustering and load balancing provide Exchange mailbox clients with high availability and performance when accessing Exchange Server 2003 messaging systems and front-end Outlook Web Access.

Using the information in this section, administrators will understand the functionality and features of Windows 2003 clusters and NLB as they are implemented in Exchange Server 2003 environments. This section discusses the Exchange Server 2003 features that are available, and the best practices for determining which solution is best for Exchange Server 2003, and how to implement them.

## Clustering Terminology

Before implementing clustering technologies, it is important to understand that Windows Server 2003 clustering comes in different levels of availability or options. Determining which fault-tolerant option is best, the following list describes some of those options, how they work, and a few terms used to describe the way clustered Exchange Server 2003 operates:

- **Active/Active**—In Active/Active function clustering, all servers in the cluster are live and servicing clients at the same time. Active/Active clustering is limited to two clustered nodes and can only support 1,900 Exchange mailboxes.

- **Active/Passive**—In Active/Passive clustering, clustering is available when two or more nodes are available. Only one server in the cluster can service end-users at a time. Active/Passive clusters are also limited to a per-application basis while the other server(s) wait in a standby or offline mode until a failure occurs. If a failure occurs, the passive node then begins to service clients. In this configuration, one virtual server is configured and shared by both nodes.

- **Exchange virtual server**—An Exchange virtual server is really a cluster-configured resource group that contains all resources for Exchange to operate on the cluster. This includes a NetBIOS name of the virtual server, a TCP/IP address for the virtual server and all disk drives, and vital Exchange services required to operate in a clustered configuration. In an Active/Active two-node cluster, one Exchange virtual server is created per node while the NetBIOS name and TCP/IP address of the cluster form the virtual server. When failover occurs in this configuration, the entire Exchange virtual server fails over to the surviving node in the cluster dynamically.

- **Resource DLL or `Exres.dll`**—`Exres.dll` is the gateway responsible for communications between the cluster service and the Exchange services. This `.dll` is responsible for reporting failures in the cluster and bringing resources online and offline.

- **Heartbeat**—A single User Datagram Protocol (UDP) packet is sent every 500 milliseconds between nodes in the cluster across the internal private network that relays health information of the cluster nodes and on the health of the clustered application. If there is no response during a heartbeat, the cluster begins a failover.

- **Failover**—Failover is the process of one node in the cluster changing states from offline to online, resulting in the node taking over responsibility for the Exchange virtual server.

- **Failback**—Failback is the process of moving Exchange virtual server applications that failed over in the cluster back to the original online node.

- **Quorum resource**—This is the shared disk that holds the cluster server's configuration information. All servers must be able to contact the quorum resource to become part of an Exchange Server 2003 cluster.

- **Resource group**—A resource group is a collection of cluster resources, such as the Exchange NetBIOS name, TCP/IP address, and services of the Exchange cluster. A resource group also defines which items fail over to the surviving nodes during failover. This also includes cluster resource items, including cluster disk. A resource group is owned by only one node in the cluster at a time. The Exchange Server 2003 resource group is the first group created on the server and is responsible for all cluster resources.

- **Cluster resource**—Cluster resources are vital information of the Exchange virtual server and includes its network TCP/IP addresses, NetBIOS name, disks, and Exchange services—such as the System Attendant. These cluster resources are added to the cluster group when the virtual server is created to form Exchange virtual servers.

- **Dependency**—Dependencies are specified when creating the cluster resources. Similar to dependencies on Exchange services, a cluster resource that is specified as a dependency defines a mandatory relationship between resources. Before a cluster resource is brought online, whatever resource is defined as dependent must be brought online first. For instance, the virtual server NetBIOS name is dependent on the TCP/IP address; therefore, the TCP/IP address of the virtual server must be brought online before the NetBIOS name is brought online.

## Fault Tolerance Options

MSCS and NLB services support Exchange Server 2003 messaging by establishing high availability and Quality of Service (QOS) to messaging clients in the enterprise. By

30

supporting high availability with back-end Exchange Server 2003 mailbox servers and high performance to front-end Outlook Web Access systems, Exchange environments can be designed and implemented with more reliability than before. For these fault-tolerant technologies to be truly effective in a production environment, administrators must understand the characteristics of each option to choose which technology and configuration best fits their Exchange Server 2003 design and messaging application service needs.

### Microsoft Cluster Service (MSCS)

The Microsoft Windows 2003 Cluster Service (MSCS) technology provides high system-level fault tolerance by using failover technology. Unlike Windows versions that actually have built-in administration for clustering, Exchange Server 2003 does not. To implement clustering with Exchange Server 2003, the enterprise version must be used. This is because Exchange Server 2003 Enterprise Edition is "cluster aware." This means that no additional configuration is required from the Exchange System Manager to support clustering.

In Exchange Server 2003 environments, cluster services are best used to provide backup services such as access to Active Directory object mailbox information and public folder resources.

Because this is a high-availability option, when a problem is encountered with an Exchange Server 2003 cluster resource, the cluster service attempts to fix the problem before failing the virtual server over to the second node completely. The cluster node running the failing resource attempts to restart the resource on the same node first before taking the action to fail over. If the resource cannot be restarted, the cluster fails the resource, takes the cluster group offline, and moves it to another available node, where it can then be restarted and the virtual server can be brought back to an online state.

Several conditions can cause a cluster group to fail over. For example, a failover condition can occur when an active online node in the cluster loses power, loses network connectivity, or suffers a critical hardware failure. When a cluster resource cannot remain available on an active node, the resource's group is moved to an available node in the cluster, where it can then be restarted.

> **NOTE**
>
> In almost every case, client communications are affected by the failover process, causing a disruption in client/server communications. This only occurs if a client is attempting to access a message or information from the server during the time of failover; after the failover is complete, the resource then becomes fully available.

Cluster nodes also monitor the status of resources running on their local system; they also monitor and keep track of other nodes in the cluster through private network communication messages called heartbeats. The heartbeats are used similarly to pings except they also determine the status of a node and send updates of cluster configuration changes to the cluster quorum resource.

This is vital because the quorum resource contains the cluster configuration data necessary to restore or fail over the cluster back to a working state. So, each node in the cluster needs to have access to the quorum resource; otherwise, it will not be able to participate in the cluster. Windows Server 2003 provides two types of quorum resources, one for each cluster configuration model:

- **Majority-of-Node Cluster**—In this configuration, each node is responsible for contributing one local disk to the quorum disk set that is used as storage disks. This configuration limits the majority-of-node resource to one owner at a time. This configuration requires a minimum of two nodes to be available at all times.

- **Quorum-Device Cluster**—Using the quorum type resource requires the cluster storage resource to be connected with a Fiber Channel or small computer system interface (SCSI) bus. In this configuration, any physical disk can be configured as a quorum disk.

> **TIP**
>
> To avoid unwanted failover, power management should be disabled on each of the cluster nodes, both in the motherboard BIOS and in the Power applet in the operating system's Control Panel. Power settings that enable a monitor to shut off are okay, but the administrator must make sure that the disks are configured to never go into Standby mode.

### Network Load Balancing (NLB)

The second high-availability technology provided with the Windows Server 2003 Enterprise and Datacenter server platforms is Network Load Balancing (NLB). NLB clusters provide high network performance and availability by balancing client requests across several server systems. When the client load increases, Windows NLB clusters can easily be scaled out by adding more nodes to the NLB configuration to maintain an acceptable client response time to client requests.

Using NLB offers administrators the ability to leverage two dynamic features: First, to implement Windows NLB clusters, no proprietary hardware is required and NLB clusters can be implemented and configured through Windows management interfaces fairly easily and quickly.

NLB clusters are most effectively used to provide front-end support for Web applications, virus scanning, and Simple Mail Transfer Protocol (SMTP) gateways. Because they are a very effective solution when used for Web application functionality, NLB technology is a very effective solution for front-end access to Exchange Outlook Web Access and terminal servers maintaining Exchange client software.

NLB clusters can grow to 32 nodes, and if larger cluster farms are necessary, the Microsoft Application Center server can be considered as an option for server platform support, along with technologies such as Domain Name System round-robin to meet larger client access demands.

30

---

**NOTE**

When NLB clusters are configured in an Exchange Server 2003 environment, when changes in Windows or Exchange occurs, each additional server's configuration must also be updated independently. This makes the administrator responsible for ensuring that configuration and information changes are applied to each Exchange Server 2003 server, keeping all configurations consistent across each node.

---

For more detailed information on how to install and configure load balancing with Exchange Server 2003, refer to the section "Configuring Network Load Balancing with OWA," later in this chapter.

## Cluster Permissions with Exchange Server 2003 Environments

Unlike previous versions of Exchange Server in clustered environments, Exchange Server 2003 with the latest service pack does not require the cluster server account to be a Full Exchange Administrator at the Exchange organization or administrative group levels. With Exchange Server 2003, the account logon permissions are used to establish rights for the Cluster Administrator to manage Exchange Server 2003 cluster resource configurations. Using logon permission, the Cluster Administrator can create, delete, or modify Exchange virtual server configuration, depending on the level in which the permissions are applied and the mode (Mixed or Native) in which the clustered Exchange Server 2003 organization is in.

Keep in mind that, when working with Exchange 2003 Mixed and Native mode cluster environments and multidomain models, some common best practices can be applied to help administrators understand which permissions to apply to allow the ability to manage the Exchange cluster.

When clustering in Windows 2003 multidomain models and child domain configurations, Cluster Administrator accounts require a minimum of "Administrator Only" permissions at the Exchange organizational level. This permission can be applied using the Delegation Wizard in the Exchange System Manager and is required to configure and apply recipient policies as well as to configure the Exchange server responsible for providing the organization with the proper Recipient Update Services.

In addition, when the Exchange Server 2003 organization is in Native mode, if Exchange virtual servers are configured in routing groups and span multiple administrative groups, the Cluster Administrator must have Exchange Full Administrator permissions for this configuration to function correctly. This allows the account permissions to manage each administrative group and its Exchange virtual server members.

---

**TIP**

For more information on how to use the Exchange Server 2003 Delegation Wizard to apply permissions to the Exchange organization and administrative group levels, see Chapter 18, "Administering Exchange Server 2003."

---

## Management Options with Exchange Server 2003

As mentioned earlier in this chapter, when running Exchange Server 2003 in clustered and load-balanced environments, administrators must configure clusters and load-balancing technologies through Windows Server 2003 interfaces. Exchange Server 2003 does not provide any special or additional management options for administering load balancing and clustering Exchange and relies on the Windows Server 2003 clustering tools for administration and management.

---

**Managing Clustering with Exchange**

Because there are no options for managing clusters and load balancing with Exchange Server 2003, administrators can leverage the Windows Management Instrumentation (WMI) to monitor the state of the Exchange Server 2003 cluster resources.

---

Administrators can manage and configure clusters and load-balancing options through the Windows 2003 Cluster Administrator and Load Balance Manager snap-ins. For more information regarding cluster management and configuration options, see the section "Managing Exchange Server 2003 Clusters," later in this chapter.

# Clusters and Load-Balancing Requirements

When installing Exchange Server 2003 in a Windows Server 2003 clustered configuration, Exchange Server 2003 cluster-aware technologies complete checks to determine whether the hardware and software prerequisites for installation of Exchange Server 2003 in a Windows Server 2003 cluster are met. For a better understanding of the hardware and software requirements involved with installing Exchange Server 2003 in fault-tolerant environments, review the information provided in this section carefully to ensure that the basic prerequisites and requirements are met prior to attempting the installation of Exchange Server 2003 in a Windows cluster.

## Cluster Node Hardware Requirements

When installing a cluster with Windows Server 2003, the first step is determining the minimum server hardware requirements for a cluster server node. When reviewing this information, administrators must consider meeting the same hardware requirements for installing Exchange Server 2003 Enterprise Edition as are needed for installing Windows Server 2003 Enterprise Edition or Windows Server 2003, Datacenter Edition. Each server node to be incorporated in the cluster must meet the minimum hardware requirements for installing the Windows Server platform and must also be verified and tested in the cluster service Hardware Compatibility List (HCL). To verify that the proposed hardware meets these requirements, administrators can use the new Microsoft Windows Hardware Quality Labs site to access resources and test to verify hardware and gain access to additional resources related to clustering. To access the system testing resources for cluster services, go to http://www.microsoft.com/whdc/whql/system/SysSrv-Clstr.mspx.

As a best practice when implementing fault-tolerant servers, hardware, hardware configurations, and service packs on each server platform should always be identical. For

30

example, when installing PCI network cards, each card should be installed in the same slot on each server, maintain the same driver revision, and have the same settings in the server's configuration properties. This minimizes configuration errors and provides ease of troubleshooting when the server is implemented as a node in the cluster.

### Quorums with NAS and SANS

When implementing NAS and SANs in a cluster as a quorum resource type, check with the manufacturer to review the compatibility of their products with Exchange Server 2003, and to determine if the manufacturer has a recommendation in configuring quorum resources specific to their product.

For more information on using quorums with NAS and SAN devices, go to the Microsoft web page at `http://msdn.microsoft.com/library/default.asp?url=/library/enus/mscs/mscs/quorum_resource.asp`.

One of the greatest advantages of clustering Exchange Server 2003 is leveraging today's external high-availability, large disk space storage systems, such as NAS, SANs, and hybrid devices. When working with clustering, a single external disk storage cabinet, such as the devices mentioned previously, is required. This disk subsystem in a cluster is used to house the shared disks and quorum resources, whereas smaller servers provide processor resource performance to manage the Exchange application. It's best practice to configure these drives using a RAID level that provides fault tolerance to any data stored on these drives.

The following are requirements for *both nodes* in the cluster:

- A local server boot partition drive containing the Windows Server 2003 operating system. The OS should be installed on a disk controller that is *not* connected to the shared storage.

- Either a SCSI, Fiber Channel, or iSCSI technologies can be used to connect to the shared storage. In best practice, use iSCSI or GB Ethernet to test performance and ensure that adequate I/O-to-disk storage is available.

- Two network adapters per node in the cluster are required.

## Software Requirements

As mentioned previously, Microsoft Windows Server 2003 cluster services require either Windows Server 2003 Enterprise Edition or Windows Server 2003 Datacenter Edition. Always install and test the latest release of the Windows Server service pack, security updates, and critical updates. For additional information related to Windows Server service packs and updates, review the Windows Web site at `www.microsoft.com/Windows2003` and `www.windowsupdate.microsoft.com`.

## Networking Requirements

To support proper network communications, Windows Server 2003 clusters require five static TCP/IP addresses to be dedicated to the cluster. Two TCP/IP addresses are used to configure the network adapters on the private network. These two addresses control communication between the clustered Exchange Server nodes, and an additional two addresses are required for the network adapters on the public local area network (LAN). The additional TCP/IP address is the most important and should be planned because this address is used for the initial Windows 2003 cluster itself. There is also a requirement for an additional TCP/IP address, one per Exchange virtual server, which is the TCP/IP address that clients will use to access Exchange.

> **NOTE**
>
> An additional TCP/IP address is required per Exchange virtual server on the Windows 2003 cluster. Running Exchange Server in Active/Active mode requires two Exchange virtual servers. A two-node Active/Active Exchange Server 2003 cluster requires a total of seven static TCP/IP addresses. For more information about Exchange Server 2003 virtual servers, review the section "Installing Exchange Server 2003 Clusters," later in this chapter.

As is with servers on the network, the Windows 2003 cluster also requires a NetBIOS name to communicate on the domain. This is the same name that Exchange clients use to connect to the Exchange cluster and the cluster itself. In addition, each server node must also be configured as members of the same domain; however, they are not required to be a member of the same domain from which clients are connecting.

> **CAUTION**
>
> When clustering with Exchange Server 2003, each node must have two network adapters or network interface cards (NICs). When using clustered configurations like this, do not attempt to assign both the private and public TCP/IP addresses for the cluster nodes to the same network adapter. This configuration can cause the cluster to be inaccessible and even create instability in the cluster. This is because of disruption to the heartbeat communication between the clustered nodes, and is, therefore, unsupported by Microsoft technical support.

## Shared Storage and Disks Requirements

Review the following information to understand the disk storage requirements when working with clusters; here, you will find some best practices and requirements when working with clustered disk storage:

- All shared disks to be used in the cluster must be visible from both nodes. Check with the hardware vendor for known issues when using disk subsystem hardware in fault-tolerant environments. Always install the latest BIOS revisions and service packs before setting up any cluster. Getting both servers to recognize the shared storage is usually the most difficult part of the cluster configuration.

30

- Any logical disk in the shared disk storage system must be configured as a Windows 2003 basic disk. Do not configure a dynamic disk on the shared disk storage system for use with Windows clusters.

- All disk partitions used in the storage system must be formatted as NTFS.

- As a best practice, use hardware-based fault-tolerant RAID sets on physical drive configurations. This optimizes performance and disk redundancy.

- Separate the Exchange core application, transaction logs, and databases to separate disks. Use hardware RAID 1 or 0+1 for the Exchange Server transaction log drives and RAID 5 or 0+1 for database storage to optimize performance.

- When creating drive arrays on any shared storage device, be sure to create logical partitions in the RAID drive array utility so that Windows Server 2003 recognizes more than one hard drive. Five logical drives are usually optimum and can be extended to more drives depending on the total amount of Exchange mail stores in the organizational design. To begin planning your disk storage needs, provide one drive for the quorum resource and two drives for each Exchange virtual server. If possible, use additional separate drives for each mail store database and each database transaction log. Separating all databases and logs independently provides optimal performance and redundancy.

## Implementing Fault-Tolerant Exchange Systems

Before installing and configuring Exchange Server 2003 in a clustered or NLB Windows environment, administrators must first consider the design. When exploring which design is best, it is always best practice to implement an Exchange messaging environment that can support the demanding uptime needs and performance requirements of your business mail environment that Exchange Server 2003 will support. Begin by determining which cluster or NLB configuration is best for the specific area and function of Exchange. Ensure that the decision will provide adequate performance and redundancy while delivering reliable client/server communications to the entire Exchange client base. Leveraging Windows Server 2003 clustering technologies, implement Exchange messaging systems with fault tolerance based on the server function and QOS needs of your organization.

> **NOTE**
>
> When installing Exchange Server 2003 on a clustered Windows 2003 node, the cluster-aware version of Exchange is automatically installed. Also be sure to install the Exchange Server 2003 cluster-aware edition with the latest service packs and hot fixes as you would when installing any standalone Exchange Server 2003 server.

## Preparing to Install Exchange Server 2003 Clusters

Now that you have a good understanding of the functionality and options available when clustering with Exchange Server 2003 environments, administrators can begin implementing Windows Server 2003 in a cluster configuration and place Exchange Server 2003 virtual servers into the cluster configuration in multiple ways. Review these helpful hints before beginning the installation:

- **New installations**—Perform all Exchange Server 2003 preparation domain installation tasks as you would with a standalone installation. This includes ForestPrep and DomainPrep being performed prior to implementing Exchange Server 2003 on the clustered server nodes.

> **NOTE**
>
> For more information on preparing, planning, and deploying Exchange Server 2003, review Chapter 2, "Planning, Prototyping, Migrating, and Deploying Exchange Server 2003."

- **Post first Exchange server**—Clusters can be used to add functionality to an already prepped and functional Exchange Server 2003 environment. Implementing clustered and NLB nodes into existing Exchange Server 2003 organizations allows flexibility for the moving of services, users' mailboxes, and other Exchange resources without affecting the overall delivery of Exchange services.

- **Coexistence**—Leveraging compatibility provides administrators an excellent opportunity to allow coexistence with Exchange Server 2003 clusters and standalone servers. This configuration provides additional functionality and improved performance in areas such as Outlook Web Access (OWA) services and load-balanced mailboxes during large organizationwide demands and growth periods.

> **NOTE**
>
> If installing the new Exchange cluster in an existing Exchange 5.5 organization, an additional Exchange 2003 server is required to support the Microsoft Site Replication Service, or SRS. Exchange Server 2003 clusters cannot support SRS functionality.

This section introduces the features available within the cluster-aware version of Exchange Server 2003—what these features are and how it is installed in a Windows cluster. In addition, you will become familiar with the steps administrators are required to perform when implementing and configuring Windows Server 2003 clusters when supporting Exchange Server 2003 platforms.

## General Features Overview

Although there are obvious management tools and snap-ins installed with the Exchange Server 2003 cluster-aware installation, the cluster-aware version of Exchange Server 2003 does introduce new features and functionality not available with the Standard Edition of Exchange Server 2003.

Review the following list to learn more about the features and behavior of the Exchange Server 2003 Enterprise Edition cluster-aware functions:

- **Prerequisites checking**—During installation of the Exchange Server 2003 cluster-aware version, Exchange performs a prerequisite test to determine and validate that all requirements have been met in the cluster configuration before beginning the installation process.

- **Shared nothing architecture**—With Exchange Server 2003 Enterprise Edition, Windows Server 2003 server clustering behaves in a "Shared Nothing Architecture." This behavior means that, when nodes in the cluster are present, all can access the same shared data; however, no node in the cluster can access the shared data at the same time. For example, if node 1 of the cluster is accessed as a shared resource on a disk, node 2 cannot access the resource until node 1 is either manually placed in an offline state or the cluster is failed over.

- **Support for eight node clusters**—Clustering with Windows Server 2003 Enterprise Edition supports up to eight node clusters.

- **Kerberos authentication**—To provide enhanced security, Exchange Server 2003 clusters use Kerberos authentication; this feature is enabled by default.

- **Volume mount points**—New to Exchange Server 2003, support for volume mount points is now available for use in Windows Server 2003 clustered environments.

## Planning Exchange Server 2003 Clusters

When planning clustered Exchange Server 2003 designs, you have several areas to consider, such as the network environment, Exchange and Windows platform editions, third-party software and drivers, disk storage, and load-balancing configurations. All these areas can be vital to the success of a clustered Exchange implementation and must be considered and planned before installing onto the production network.

### Planning Network Resources

Exchange clusters, like any other Exchange installation, require TCP/IP addresses to communicate on the network. When planning and allocating cluster addresses, Exchange Server 2003 cluster systems require one TCP/IP address per virtual server. In addition, another five TCP/IP addresses are required to set up the Windows Server 2003 cluster environment. When addressing for a two-node Exchange cluster server in Active/Active mode, administrators are required to have two additional TCP/IP addresses to support the Exchange virtual servers. For example, to support a two-node cluster in an Active/Active mode configuration, plan for and allocate a total of seven static TCP/IP addresses.

### Planning a Heartbeat Configuration

To support the cluster heartbeat, it is best practice to connect the cluster network interfaces to a separate network. Isolating these TCP/IP addresses by connecting them to a separate switch creates a separate communication subnet. In this configuration, all cluster interfaces can be connected to the isolated subnet, providing clear heartbeat communications between nodes.

> **TIP**
>
> In the case of a two-node cluster, it is best practice not to use a cross cable to connect the two nodes. This ensures that the link state of the live node is not tied to the dead node of the cluster.

### Planning Cluster Disk Space

As important in a cluster as is with any standalone Exchange design, storage space is another important consideration when planning any Exchange cluster. Just like any standard installation of an Exchange environment, administrators must consider and allocate disk space to meet the immediate and future needs based on the expected growth of data and the existing mailbox and data population.

To plan database drives and drive size requirements, administrators must think through all aspects of the Exchange design. One method to help begin planning is to average the total amount of existing mail data and complete some additional calculations. To get a good understanding of the required disk space needs, begin by identifying the expected size limit per mailbox, multiply this number by the total number of expected mailboxes you plan Exchange to support. This will give you a good starting point. With the starting point size, factor in using deleted item retention, the company's growth rate, and the maximum number of mailboxes that will be supported on the cluster over its lifetime. To plan effectively, include an additional disk space in the final calculation to allow for maintenance, unforeseen growth, and buffer space.

> **NOTE**
>
> When planning drives to store Exchange Server logs, plan enough disk space to support the overall operation of Exchange Server 2003 and consider each log drive by storage group. In addition, plan to include additional drive space for managing and maintaining logs, should backups be missed and files not flushed.

To plan for Exchange Server 2003 disk storage and performance, use the following example. When evaluating performance needs, administrators must consider "Exchange being slow." This can be explained by disk queuing on a heavily used Exchange disk subsystem. If disks aren't sufficient to handle demands like the "Monday morning user load," performance will suffer as transactions are queued waiting for disks to respond. To ensure this is not the case when planning an Exchange cluster, I/O can be estimated by the peak number of users hitting the system multiplied by the modifier for the type of user. So, for example, for a server with 2,000 "heavy" users, you need to plan for a peak of 1,500 disk I/O per second. To explain, an Exchange database typically sees 70% read traffic and 30% write traffic. This is significant in determining the I/O potential of a disk configuration in RAID 5.

To determine the number of disks needed to support the 2,000 "heavy" users, the following calculation is used. With a 15,000RPM disk that can provide for 150 random I/Os per second (IOPS) and assuming (%Reads*IOPS per disk*(disks-1))+(%Writes*IOPS per disk*((disks-1)/4))= Total IOPS, to attain the 1,500 disk IOPS needed, 14 disks would be required for the databases.

> **NOTE**
>
> A RAID 0 configuration would not have the "((x-1/4)) penalty" for writes nor the "(x-1) penalty" for reads that RAID 5 has (due to the parity disk). It would be pure I/O so 1,500 I/O would be achieved by 10 disks.

Based on the "user profiles and corresponding usage patterns," you'd also expect each of the 2,000 users to have roughly 100MB of storage. This equates to 200GB of space. With 14 disks to get the I/O performance desired, smaller disks, such as 18GB drives, can reduce wasted space. If 36GB drives are used, they would allow for 100% growth.

15krpm disk = 150 random I/O per second

10krpm disk = 120 random I/O per second

7,200rpm disk = 100 random I/O per second

This concept can be taken a lot further if an organization can categorize their users into the various tiers of usage and configurations can be planned around those needs to maximize user experience.

### Software Requirements

Now you know clustering technology with the Exchange Server 2003 requires the Enterprise Edition platform. To install Exchange Server 2003 Enterprise Edition in the cluster, administrators must install the installation files on the same disk on each node in the cluster. For example, if administrators install the installation on node 1 in the C:\Exchsrvr directory, each node should also have the Exchange installation performed to C:\exchsrvr.

### Load Balancing Mailboxes and Exchange Data

Load balancing Exchange Server 2003 mailboxes and public folder information in multinode clusters is important. Considering the placement of resources on a cluster node can greatly improve the stability and performance of the Exchange Server 2003 cluster when in production. When evaluating the planning considerations of how to load balance Exchange Server 2003 resources, it's up to the administrator to properly allocate the total number of mailboxes per node in the cluster to maintain performance and stability.

In the most effective configuration of an Active/Passive configuration, the bottom line is ensuring that the surviving cluster node will be able to handle the total load should another server in the cluster be taken offline.

> **Leveraging an Active/Passive Cluster**
>
> Though Exchange can support both cluster configurations, Active/Passive configuration allows administrators more control when failing over a cluster. By manually failing over a cluster, Exchange administrators can choose which node to fail over to as well as verify the node is ready before bringing it online.

### Validating Design Decisions and Testing

As the information reviewed indicates, a properly installed front-end/back-end configuration can provide many benefits, including reducing the load on any surviving node in a cluster if there is a substantial number of Exchange Server 2003 clients accessing the node. As a best practice, be sure to prototype any cluster installations and configurations in a lab that is in a nonproduction environment. When testing, execute a detailed performance test to calculate the most effective hardware and software configurations based on the expected load each node is being designed to support should the cluster fail over.

When load testing to evaluate performance, perform tests on each node as it is online with other nodes at the same time. Validate functionality and performance and conduct the same set of tests on nodes as they are brought online after a failover condition.

## Installing Exchange Server 2003 Clusters

With all the information provided and a good solid plan in place, administrators can begin to install and configure Windows Server 2003 clusters to support Exchange Server 2003. The following section assists you in setting up Windows Server 2003 clusters and assumes that all hardware has been configured correctly and is compatible with clustering in the Windows Server 2003 Enterprise Edition.

On the cluster systems, install the Windows Server 2003 Enterprise Edition software and complete the following steps:

1. Configure the network TCP/IP address setting for both network adapters on the cluster node.

2. In the domain where the server resides, create an administrative account for the cluster service.

3. If additional disks have been created, format additional drives with NTFS and validate the disk configurations, ensuring that there are no dynamic disks configured. If dynamic disks were created, use the Disk Management configuration options in the Computer Management tool to change the disk back to the basic configuration setting, and format them using NTFS.

4. Review the server event logs and validate server functionality and domain membership.

30

## Setting Up Windows Server 2003 Clusters

When the installation of Windows 2003 Enterprise server is complete, it is time to set up and configure the Windows 2003 cluster. Unlike previous versions of Windows clustering services, the Windows Server 2003 clustering function is installed by default when the server operating system software is installed, requiring no additional steps to add the clustering functionality to the server installation.

With the server installed and configured, set up the cluster and nodes by performing the following steps:

1. Launch the Cluster Administrator by selecting Start, All Programs, Administrator Tools, Cluster Administrator.

2. Because this scenario is a new installation, when the Cluster Administrator snap-in is launched for the first time, you are prompted to select the type of connection. To create a new cluster, select Create New Cluster from the Connection tab, as shown in Figure 30.1.

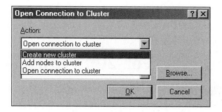

**FIGURE 30.1**    Choosing the connection type.

3. Selecting OK after choosing the connection type launches the New Server Cluster Wizard; at the Welcome screen, select Next.

4. From the Cluster Name and Domain screen, enter the name of the cluster and validate that the domain where the cluster is to be installed is selected.

5. Select the server where you are installing the cluster, and select Next to continue.

6. Run the analyzer to validate the configuration and environment where the cluster will be installed. Identify any warnings and view the logs to correct problems, should the analyzer identify any problems before continuing.

7. Enter the cluster TCP/IP address, and click Next.

8. Enter the Cluster Service account name and password created earlier and choose the correct domain. Click Next to continue.

> **NOTE**
>
> When the cluster service account was created, it was specified as a normal domain user. Adding this account as the Cluster Service in the snap-in automatically grants the account Local Administrator privileges on the cluster node and also delegates permissions to act as a part of the operating system and add computers to the domain.

9. On the Proposed Cluster Configuration screen, review the configuration and choose the correct quorum type by clicking the Quorum button.

   Review the information provided and select the proper quorum type for your installation:

   - To create a Majority Node Set (MNS) cluster, click the Quorum button on the Proposed Cluster Configuration screen, choose Majority Node Set, and click OK.

   - If a SAN is connected to the cluster node, the Cluster Administrator automatically chooses the smallest basic NTFS volume on the shared storage device. Make any changes to ensure the correct disk has been chosen and click OK.

   - If you're configuring a single node cluster with no shared storage, choose the local quorum resource and click OK.

10. Click Next to complete the cluster installation.

11. After the cluster is created, click Next and then click Finish to close the New Server Cluster Wizard and return to the Cluster Administrator screen.

## Adding Additional Nodes to a Cluster

With the cluster created and configured properly, it is time to add any additional nodes to the cluster that will be used to support Exchange Server 2003. After the cluster is configured, the first server is installed as a node in a cluster. Additional nodes can then be added to the cluster by completing the following steps:

1. Log on to the desired cluster node using the Cluster Administrator account.

2. Open the Cluster Administrator and choose Add Nodes to a Cluster. Enter the name of the cluster in the Cluster Name text box. Click OK to continue.

3. When the Add Nodes Wizard appears, click Next to continue.

4. Enter the server name of the new cluster node, and click Add. Repeat these steps to add any additional nodes to the Selected Computer text box. When complete, click Next to continue.

**NOTE**

When additional nodes are added, the cluster analyzer then analyzes the additional nodes for functionality and cluster requirements. Review the results of the test and make any changes to correct any potential issues, as shown in Figure 30.2.

To test the configuration again, click Re-analyze at any time.

30

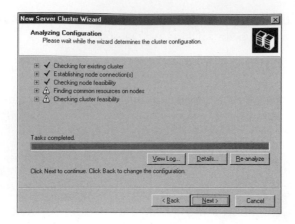

**FIGURE 30.2**    Node Wizard analyzer.

5. When all testing is completed, enter the Cluster Service account password, and click Next to continue.

6. Review the configuration on the Proposed Cluster Configuration screen, click Next, and then click Finish to complete the additional node installation.

## Installing the Cluster-Aware Version of Exchange Server 2003

When performing the installation of the Exchange Server 2003 platform, you will see that the Microsoft Exchange installation is cluster aware through the prompting of a dialog box during the installation.

One final step before you can install Exchange Server 2003 along with the latest service packs on any cluster node is to install the Microsoft Distributed Transaction Coordinator (MSDTC) on one Windows 2003 server node in the cluster. The MSDTC will later be used as part of the cluster configuration and will be used to support the Exchange Server 2003 cluster group. To install the MSDTC and configure the MSDTC cluster group, complete these steps:

1. Log on to the Windows 2003 server, click Start, Control Panel, and then click Add or Remove Programs.

2. Select the Add or Remove Windows Components option in the left pane.

3. From the Windows Component screen, choose the Application Server option and click Details.

4. Choose the Network DTC Access option, and install the component on the Windows 2003 server by selecting OK, Next, and then Finish.

5. After the MSDTC has been installed, reboot the server to stop and restart the MSDTC and other services on the Windows 2003 cluster node.

NOTE

With the MSDTC installed, it is now time to configure the MSDTC cluster group. Best practices when configuring the Exchange 2003 server in a cluster configuration dictates that the MSDTC be configured in its own cluster group. Doing so ensures that a failure of the MSDTC does not interfere with the operation of the Exchange cluster virtual server.

With the cluster administration and support applications having been installed, the cluster creation and configuration can begin. The steps are as follows:

1. After the server has rebooted, log on with the Cluster Administrator account, and launch the Cluster Administrator by selecting Start, All Programs, Administrative Tools, Cluster Administrator.

2. Select Groups, and then select Create a New Cluster group. In this example, call it "MSDTC Group."

3. Expand the groups. Right-click the MSDTC Group, point to New, and then click Resource Group.

4. Under New Resource, enter the name **MSDTC**. Under the Resource Type, select Distributed Transaction Coordinator, and under the group, select MSDTC Group. Click Next to continue.

5. At the Possible Owner dialog box, verify that all nodes appear and click Next.

6. On the Dependencies page, select the physical disk and network name already created for the MSDTC group. Click Finish to continue.

Now that the MSDTC installation and configuration is complete, it is time to install and understand how Exchange is installed on the first node of a cluster. When the program files for Exchange Server 2003 are installed into a clustered Windows 2003 server configuration, the Windows Installer detects the presence of the cluster environment and begins the installation of the Exchange Server 2003 cluster-aware version. Though its process is similar to a normal installation, the cluster-aware version requires administrators to confirm the installation of the cluster-aware version by accepting the Exchange dialog box prompt confirming the presence of the cluster. To install the cluster-aware version of Exchange Server 2003, use the following steps:

NOTE

In this scenario, the installation of Exchange Server 2003 and the configuration of the Exchange cluster is based on the post–first server environment. This scenario assumes that the Active Directory forest has already been prepared with ForestPrep and DomainPrep and the Exchange Server 2003 server is already in place servicing domain client systems.

1. Log on to Windows on the first node to be installed with the account that is a member of the Domain Admins and Exchange Admins security groups.

30

2. Install Exchange Server 2003, Enterprise Edition on the first node in the cluster from the Exchange Server 2003, Enterprise Edition installation CD-ROM.

3. Select to install Microsoft Messaging and Collaboration and Microsoft Exchange System Management Tools.

4. Install Exchange to a local drive in the clustered node, such as `C:\exchsrvr`.

> **NOTE**
>
> Use the same location and drive path for the core Exchange program files on each node in the cluster.

5. A dialog box should appear saying that setup has detected that the installation is on a cluster and will install a cluster-aware version. Select OK to continue.

> **TIP**
>
> If no dialog box prompts appear to confirm the installation of the cluster-aware version of Exchange Server 2003, check the configuration of the Windows 2003 cluster and ensure that the cluster is functioning correctly. Review the server Event Viewer and validate that each server in the cluster is aware of all nodes and all shared resources are available.

6. Install the Exchange server as you would any normal server. Place the new Exchange Server 2003 server into the proper administrative group and routing group and complete installation.

## Configuring Exchange Server 2003 in a Cluster

When the installation has completed, it is now time to configure Exchange Server 2003 in the cluster. To begin, launch the Cluster Administrator MMC snap–in and use the Application Wizard to create a new Exchange resource group and virtual server. Complete the following steps to set up the Exchange Server 2003 virtual server in the clustered environment:

1. From the Cluster Administrator, select the first node created earlier and select File, Configure Application to launch the Cluster Application Wizard.

2. On the Welcome screen, click Next.

3. On the Create New Virtual Server screen, select Create New Virtual Server, and click Next.

4. On the Resource Group screen, select Create New Resource, click Next, enter the name **ExchangeVS** and a description to be used for the new resource group, and then click Next.

5. Enter the TCP/IP address to be used for the virtual Exchange server, as shown in Figure 30.3.

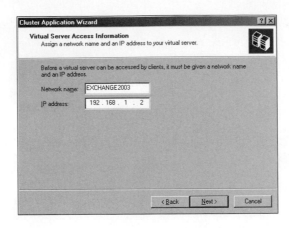

FIGURE 30.3    Virtual Server Access Information screen.

6. Use the Advance Properties screen to configure the properties and thresholds for the Exchange virtual server; click Next when you are finished.

7. On the Create Application Cluster Resource screen, click No and then click Next.

8. Open the Exchange Virtual Server Resource properties page, and configure all nodes as possible owners by clicking the Modify button under Possible Owners.

9. Next, create the Network Name resource for the Exchange virtual server resource and configure both nodes as possible owners. To do this, select the Exchange virtual server and select File, New, Resource.

10. Create the new network name resource and enter the network name to be used to access Exchange. When prompted, configure the dependencies, TCP/IP address, and DNS information for the Exchange resource.

11. Next, bring the IP address and network name resources online through Cluster Administrator by right-clicking the Exchange virtual server and selecting Bring Online, as shown in Figure 30.4.

12. Add disk resources to the Exchange virtual server resource group by dragging the disks to the Exchange virtual server resource group or by right-clicking the disk in cluster groups and selecting Change Group.

> **NOTE**
>
> Disk resources can belong to only one Exchange virtual server resource group. Configure both nodes as possible owners for each disk to be used for the Exchange cluster configuration.

13. Create the new Exchange 2003 System Attendant in the Exchange virtual server resource group by selecting File, New, Resource, and selecting Microsoft Exchange System Attendant under the resource type.

30

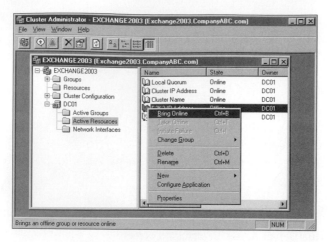

**FIGURE 30.4**    Bringing the cluster resources online.

14. Set the network name and disk resources as dependencies for the Exchange System Attendant, as you did earlier by completing the wizard steps.

15. Select the same administrative group and routing group for the Exchange Server 2003 virtual server. Use the same configuration information that was selected when the Exchange Server 2003 server was installed on the first node.

16. Enter the path to the data directory. Separate the paths for the logs and databases by placing them on separate shared disks, which were added to the Exchange virtual server resource group during the configuration.

17. The remaining services are added automatically to the Exchange virtual server resource group.

With an Active/Active cluster design, repeat these steps for each node in the cluster; when you are finished, configure the server cluster in an Active/Active configuration.

## Managing Exchange Server 2003 Clusters

After the Exchange Server 2003 clusters have been established and tested and are functional on the network, administrators can use the built-in Windows 2003 Cluster Administrator to manage and modify the overall configuration of the Exchange cluster.

In addition to the basic management tasks of Windows clusters, administrators must also understand the basics for backing up the Exchange Server 2003 cluster databases, along with the restore options and how to recover from failures. The following sections present the basic management options, best practices, and backup processes when working with Windows 2003 cluster administration.

## Configuration and Management Options

The Cluster Administrator tool that comes with Windows 2003 is the only management tool available for configuring and modifying an Exchange cluster. When working with Exchange Server 2003 and Windows clustering, administrators can also leverage Windows Management Instrumentation (WMI) to monitor the overall status of the Exchange Server 2003 cluster.

Another option for executing management commands with Windows clusters is using the Cluster.exe command-line utility. The Cluster.exe utility can be used to access a cluster and manage and modify cluster properties when the Cluster Administrator snap-in is not available.

## Backing Up and Restoring Exchange Server 2003 Clusters

To complete backups using Windows 2003 functionality, administrators can leverage ASR built in to Windows to back up and restore the Exchange Server 2003 cluster configurations on local cluster nodes or all nodes configured in the cluster.

Using an ASR, backup can be completed of the cluster node's disk signature or signatures and volume information, current system state—which includes Registry information—cluster quorum, Windows boot files, COM+ class registration databases, and system services. A backup of all local disks containing operating system files can also be completed, including the boot partitions and Exchange data.

Using the ASR utility, administrators can also leverage the new built-in functionality of Windows 2003 ASR cluster restoration to perform complete restores of the cluster and nodes in the cluster.

### Cluster Backups with Automated System Recovery

To perform an ASR backup, you need a blank floppy disk and a backup device—such as a tape device or disk storage system attached either locally to the server or a network share.

Keep in mind the tape drive or disk storage systems must be large enough to support the total amount of required disk space to back up the Exchange cluster service. Because ASR backs up all drives and data as well as applications, you should plan enough disk space to host backup in excess of 1GB above the total amount of space used by Exchange.

To create an ASR backup, perform the following steps:

1. Log on to the cluster node with an account that has the right to back up the system. (Any Local Administrator, Domain Administrator, or Cluster Service account has the necessary permissions to complete the operation.)

2. Select Start, All Programs, Accessories, System Tools, Backup.

3. If this is the first time you've run Backup, it opens in Wizard mode. Choose to run it in Advanced mode by clicking the Advanced Mode hyperlink. After you change to Advanced mode, the window should look similar to Figure 30.5.

30

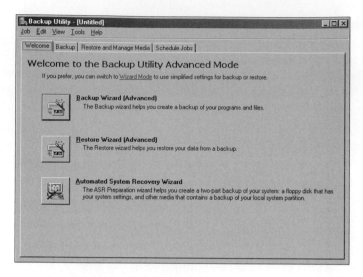

**FIGURE 30.5**    Windows Backup in Advanced mode.

4.  Click the Automated System Recovery Wizard button to start the Automated System Recovery Preparation Wizard.

5.  Click Next after reading the Automated System Recovery Preparation Wizard Welcome screen.

6.  Choose your backup media type and choose the correct media tape or file. If you're creating a new file, specify the complete path to the file; the backup creates the file automatically. Click Next to continue.

7.  If the file you specified resides on a network drive, click OK at the warning message to continue.

8.  Click Finish to complete the Automated System Recovery Preparation Wizard and to start the backup.

9.  After the tape or file backup portion completes, the ASR backup prompts you to insert a floppy disk that will contain the recovery information. Insert the disk and click OK to continue.

10. Remove the floppy disk as requested and label the disk with the appropriate ASR backup information. Click OK to continue.

11. When the ASR backup is complete, click Close on the Backup Progress window to return to the backup program or click Report to examine the backup report.

ASR backups should be performed periodically and immediately following any hardware changes to Exchange Server 2003 cluster nodes, including changes on a shared storage device or local disk configuration.

### Restoring Cluster Nodes After a Failure

Cluster nodes can also be restored after a cluster failure using a combination of restore methods. When one or all nodes in the cluster are nonoperational and the cluster node requires rebuilding, administrators can complete the following steps using the ASR to recover the lost Exchange Server 2003 cluster:

1. Shut down the failed cluster node.

2. On an available cluster node, log on using a Cluster Administrator account.

3. Select Start, Administrative Tools, Cluster Administrator.

4. If the Cluster Administrator does not connect to the cluster or connects to a different cluster, choose File, Open Connection.

5. From the Active drop-down box, choose Open Connection to Cluster. Then, in the Cluster or Server Name drop-down box, type a period (.) and click OK to connect.

6. Within each cluster group, make sure to disable failback to prevent these groups from failing over to a cluster node that is not completely restored. Close the Cluster Administrator.

7. Locate the ASR floppy created for the failed node or create the floppy from the files saved in the ASR backup media. For information on creating the ASR floppy from the ASR backup media, refer to Windows Server 2003 Help and Support tools.

8. Insert the operating system CD in the failed server and start the server.

9. If necessary, when prompted, press F6 to install any third-party storage device drivers. This includes any third-party disk or tape controllers that Windows Server 2003 does not recognize.

10. Press F2 when prompted to perform an Automated System Recovery.

11. When prompted, insert the ASR floppy disk and press Enter.

12. The operating system installation proceeds by restoring disk volume information and reformatting the volumes associated with the operating system. When this process is complete, restart the server as requested by pressing F3, and then click Enter in the next window.

13. After the system restarts, press a key if necessary to restart the CD installation.

14. If necessary, when prompted, press F6 to install any third-party storage device drivers. This includes any third-party disk or tape controllers that Windows Server 2003 does not recognize.

15. Press F2 when prompted to perform an Automated System Recovery.

16. When prompted, insert the ASR floppy disk and press Enter.

17. This time, the disks can be properly identified and are formatted, and the system files are copied to the respective disk volumes. When this process is complete, remove the ASR floppy when the ASR restore automatically reboots the server.

30

18. If necessary, specify the network location of the backup media using a Universal Naming Convention (UNC) path and enter authentication information if prompted. The ASR backup attempts to reconnect to the backup media automatically, but will be unable to if the backup media is on a network drive.

19. When the media is located, open the media and click Next. Finish recovering the remaining ASR data.

20. When the ASR restore is complete, if any local disk data was not restored with the ASR restore, restore missing information using the Windows NT Backup or a standard backup method being used in your organization.

## Failover and Failback

As discussed throughout this chapter, clusters that contain two or more Exchange nodes automatically have failover configured and enabled for each defined Exchange Server 2003 cluster group. When a node in a group becomes unavailable, the remaining server automatically becomes available and changes its state from Offline to Online. This server now inherits the role to service all Exchange Server 2003 clients accessing the cluster. By manually adding additional Exchange nodes to existing clusters, the administrator can add and modify the failover functionality to every node in the cluster as needed.

Unlike failover, the failback functionality of Exchange Server 2003 clusters is not configured by default. This functionality needs to be manually configured to allow a designated preferred server to always run a particular cluster group when it is available. Administrators can modify these settings to define the thresholds and expected characteristics when in a failover or failback mode.

### Cluster Group Failover Configuration

To create a failover and failback process, the cluster group failover configuration should be configured properly and tested to ensure proper functionality. Follow these steps to configure cluster group failover:

1. Select Start, Administrative Tools, Cluster Administrator.

2. When the Cluster Administrator opens, choose Open Connection to Cluster and type the name of the Exchange Server 2003 cluster to be configured.

3. Right-click the appropriate cluster group and select Properties.

4. Select the Failover tab and set the maximum number of failovers allowed during a predefined period of time. When the number of failovers is exceeded within the period interval, shown as a threshold of 10 in Figure 30.6, the cluster service changes the group to a failed state.

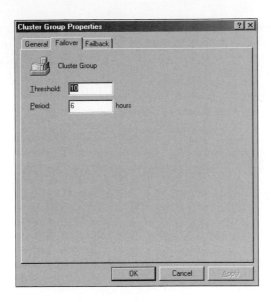

**FIGURE 30.6**    Failover Properties page.

5.  Click Next and then click Finish to complete the failover configuration.

6.  Close the Cluster Administrator page to complete the configuration.

# Outlook Web Access Front-End Server and Load-Balancing Clusters

One of the strongest options available to provide enhanced high performance and reliability when working with Exchange Server 2003 and OWA is Windows 2003 NLB. Windows Server 2003 NLB is also a built-in functionality and is a separate component than the Cluster Administrator. NLB works by establishing a different type of cluster containing two or more systems using a single TCP/IP address.

This functionality is often effective when load balancing front-end Exchange mail servers and Outlook Web Access with Exchange Server 2003. In this section, you explore NLB and Outlook Web Access, the steps to configure front-end Outlook Web Access servers using NLB options, the Network Load Balance MMC, and the best practices when working with OWA in a NLB configuration.

## Using Network Load Balancing

NLB is used to distribute network connections and clients between front-end servers to create fault tolerance to applications. Because of this functionality, using this feature is an exceptionally effective solution to provide high levels of availability and quality of service to users accessing Outlook Web Access services.

30

To simplify the decision even more with NLB, using this option requires no additional software and utilities other than the built-in functionality of Windows Server 2003 and the NICs configured in each server. After Exchange Outlook Web Access front-end servers have been configured, administrators can enable load-balancing functionality through the NLB Manager available in the Windows Server 2003 administrative tools.

When configuring NLB, servers are established in an NLB cluster. Other areas to consider when configuring NLB services are modes in which the NLB service will be configured and the configuration of NICs. Review the information in these sections for more information regarding these areas.

## NLB Modes and Port Configuration Overview

In the Unicast mode, clients and servers maintain a one-to-one relationship when communicating. In the Multicast mode, servers respond by broadcasting a single multicast address, which clients attach to when accessing information such as Web sites.

Another option when configuring NLB with Outlook Web Access is the ability to define the ports in which NLB cluster members will respond to client requests. This option is effective for the scenario because administrators can restrict and allow access to ports such as HTTP port 80 and Secure Sockets Layer (SSL) port 443.

## NLB Network Card Configurations

One of the first steps when configuring NLB cluster nodes is the configuration of the NICs in each server. A configuration of network cards can be completed using the NLB Manager and the TCP/IP properties of each node's network interface. One other option for configuring NICs is the command-line tool `nlb.exe`. This utility enables administrators to configure TCP/IP properties on NLB cluster nodes remotely and through the command line.

## Configuring Network Load Balancing with OWA

Using the NLB Manager is the simplest method in configuring Outlook Web Access servers into a load-balanced cluster configuration. When using the Network Load Balancing Manager, all information regarding the NLB cluster and load-balancing TCP/IP addresses is added dynamically to each cluster node when configured. Using the NLB Manager also simplifies the tasks of adding and removing nodes by enabling administrators to use the NetBIOS name or TCP/IP address to identify nodes.

> **TIP**
>
> To effectively manage NLB clusters on remote servers, install and configure two NICs on the local NLB Manager system.
>
> For more information regarding Network Load Balancing services with Windows Server 2003, go to `http://www.microsoft.com/windowsserver2003/default.mspx`.

In the following example, NLB services will be implemented to provide support with two separate Outlook Web Access servers. This scenario assumes that each Outlook Web Access server has already been installed and configured and is functioning.

To begin, configure the network cards for each Outlook Web Access system that you plan to configure in the NLB cluster:

1. Log on to the local console of a cluster node using an account with Local Administrator privileges.

2. Select Start, Control Panel, and select the properties of the Network Connections icon.

3. Open the properties of each network card to modify the properties by binding the appropriate cluster and dedicated IP addresses to each node's network card; use the advanced pages accessed through the General tab of the TCP/IP property page.

> **TIP**
>
> It is a good practice to rename each network card so you can easily identify it when configuring interfaces and troubleshooting problems.

After the TCP/IP properties of the network card for the two OWA servers have been configured and tested, configure the NLB cluster by accessing the NLB Manager in the Administrative Tools of the Windows 2003 server. To begin, open the NLB Manager and complete the following steps:

1. From the NLB Manager menu, select Cluster, New.

2. Enter the cluster IP address and subnet mask of the new cluster that will be used for both OWA servers' cluster members. Configure the following additional information, as shown in Figure 30.7:

    • Enter the fully qualified domain name for the cluster in the Full Internet name text box.

    • Enter the mode of operation (multicast because this is a Web-functional configuration).

    • Configure a remote control password if you will be using the command-line utility (nlb.exe) to remotely manage the NLB cluster.

    Click Next to continue.

3. Enter any additional TCP/IP addresses that will be load balanced and click Next to continue.

4. Configure the appropriate port rules for each IP address in the cluster. For OWA services being accessed from the Internet only, click the Edit tab and configure the port range to be 80, allowing HTTP traffic between cluster NLB servers.

30

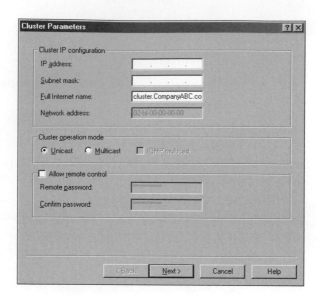

**FIGURE 30.7**    NLB Cluster Parameters page.

5. On the Connect page, type the name of the server you want to add to the cluster in the Host text box and click Connect. Review the server information and highlight the network interface to be used for the server; click Next to continue.

6. On the Host Parameters page, set the cluster node priority. Each node requires a unique host priority, and because this is the first node in the cluster, leave the default of 1; click the Finish option when complete.

Additional OWA servers can be added to the NLB cluster by repeating these steps at any time. Validate that the state of the clustered NLB system is listed in the NLB Manager as Started and close the Manager to complete the configuration of additional servers.

---

**TIP**

Use the NLB Manager when performing maintenance on any NLB cluster members. When maintenance is necessary, you can change the default state of a particular NLB cluster node by placing it in a Stopped or Suspended state. This enables administrators to perform maintenance, such as adding security updates and service packs, and keep the server from joining the cluster following a reboot.

For more information regarding load balancing and Exchange Server 2003, go to

`http://www.microsoft.com/technet/prodtechnol/windowsserver2003/library/DepKit/`
`2c1bfaca-5cb2-4790-a078-18bfdeb1f283.mspx`

---

## Summary

Administrators should review the information in this chapter carefully to understand the basic configuration options when working with Exchange Server 2003 and Microsoft clustering technologies. Information in this chapter provides insight to these technologies and how to configure the setup tasks and basic management options available with Exchange Server 2003 clustering environments and Network Load Balancing. Also, always exercise best practices when implementing any of the technologies and configurations listed in this chapter by testing and validating functionality in a nonproduction network environment. Use testing opportunities to ensure proper functionality and avoid unforeseen issues after these technologies are implemented into any production environment.

## Best Practices

The following are best practices from this chapter:

- Purchasing compatible server and network hardware is a good start to building fault-tolerant systems, but the proper configuration of this hardware is equally important.

- Create disk subsystem redundancy using hardware-based RAID technologies.

- Always plan for a sufficient amount of TCP/IP addresses in advance to support current and future cluster needs.

- Do not run both MSCS and NLB on the same computer; it is unsupported by Microsoft because of potential hardware-sharing conflicts between MSCS and NLB.

- Active/Passive mode is easiest to manage and maintain, and the licensing costs are generally lower.

- To avoid unwanted failover, power management should be disabled on each of the cluster nodes, both in the motherboard BIOS and in the power applet in the Control Panel of the operating system.

- Carefully choose whether to use a shared disk or a nonshared approach to clustering.

- Use the same type of card and driver when implementing multiple network cards in each node. This helps to ensure that one card can be dedicated to internal cluster communication and each functions properly.

- To reduce the chance of having a group fail back to a node during regular business hours after a failure, configure the failback schedule to allow failback only during nonpeak times.

- Thoroughly test failover and failback mechanisms after the configuration is complete and before adding mailboxes and public folders to a clustered Exchange Server 2003 server.

- Do not change the cluster service account password using the Active Directory Users and Computers tool or the Windows security box if logged on with the same account.

30

- Perform ASR backups periodically and immediately following any hardware changes to a cluster node, including changes on a shared storage device or local disk configuration.

- When possible, on internal network devices, create a port rule that allows only specific ports to the clustered IP address, and an additional rule blocking all other ports and ranges.

# CHAPTER **31**

# Backing Up the Exchange Server 2003 Environment

**IN THIS CHAPTER**

- Using Backup to Solve Department Challenges
- Maintaining Documentation on the Exchange Environment
- Developing a Backup Strategy
- Backing Up the Windows Server 2003 and Exchange Server 2003
- Volume Shadow Copy Services and Exchange Server 2003
- Using the Windows Backup Utility (Ntbackup.exe)
- Backing Up Specific Windows Services
- Managing Media in a Structured Backup Strategy

$A$ll network and messaging system administrators go to extensive lengths to ensure that the network and network data are backed up on a regular basis. And, in almost every organization, administrators go through some sort of process to either insert tapes into a tape backup system or use some kind of tape rotation to back up the network. Unfortunately, far too many organizations merely put tapes into their tape drives, without putting detailed thought into both the process and purpose of backing up network systems along with the validation and verification steps that make backups and restores truly successful.

Typically, the only time administrators worry about successful backups is during catastrophic network events that make backup restoral necessary. At that point, it is too late and far too common for administrators to find that a tape restoral was not successful due to improper backup planning, improper procedures, or lack of validation of tape media.

This chapter focuses on these areas, the planning process and technologies readily available, such as Volume Shadow Copy and backup programs, to create a successful backup and backup validation process that will significantly improve an organization's ability to successfully retrieve Exchange information and recover from a catastrophic network failure.

# Using Backup to Solve Department Challenges

Before creating a backup strategy or plan, administrators must understand what types of vulnerabilities and failures they must plan for and the mandatory recovery requirements for each of these failures. Because there are several different types of recovery situations, when planning a backup strategy, you must ensure that your organization has a process in place to respond to specific vulnerabilities with documented and tested recovery steps.

As an example, although a full tape backup of the entire Exchange database can enable an organization to restore the databases from a catastrophic failure, a full image of the database does not help the organization easily restore a single mailbox or messages within a mailbox. To restore a single mailbox or message from a full image of the entire Exchange databases, administrators are required to perform a full restore of the entire database, and then a manual extraction of the mailbox or message must be completed from the restored server. So if an organization has a need to restore a single message or a single mailbox, there are best-practice procedures to supplement a full image backup for the sole purpose of restoring individual items or mailboxes.

These other methods or procedures include using third-party disk and tape backup utilities that integrate with Windows server technology to do point-in-time snapshots of the Exchange database and brick level also known as mailbox-by-mailbox backups.

In addition to third-party and built-in backup tools, working with the Mailbox Recovery Center utility built in to Exchange Server 2003 is covered in detail in Chapter 32, "Recovering from a Disaster."

## Understanding What Should Be Ready for Restoral

To begin, learning what is necessary to complete a successful recovery gives administrators a list of all the elements that they might need to create good backups for recovery when a particular failure is encountered. When you know what needs to be backed up, you can then create the backup plan to address all the aspects of your business. So, it is recommended that administrators research each server function and service along with all applications to understand what is necessary for recovery so that their backup plan targets the correct information.

Along with these considerations, there are several reasons any organization should have a backup of its Exchange information. The reasons an Exchange administrator might need to restore Exchange include the following:

- In case of a server system failure

- In the event that the databases become corrupt, requiring restoration

- In a situation in which individual messages, folders, or mailboxes need to be restored

- For the purpose of restoring Exchange in a lab environment for testing and validation of Exchange changes prior to implementation on the production Exchange system

## Protecting Data in the Event of a System Failure

Server failures are the primary concern most organizations plan for, because a complete system failure creates the most impact and ultimate scenario in which data needs to be restored from backup tape. Server hardware failures include failed motherboards, processors, memory, network interface cards, disk controllers, power supplies, and, of course, hard disks. Each of these failures can be minimized through the implementation of RAID-configured hard disk drives, error-correcting memory, redundant power supplies, or redundant controller adapters. In a catastrophic system failure, however, it is likely that the entire data backup would have to be restored to a new system or repaired server.

Because data is read and written to hard drives on a constant basis, hard drives are frequently singled out as the most possible cause of a server hardware failure. To address this, Windows Server 2003 supports hot-swappable hard drives and RAID storage systems, allowing for the replacement of the drive without server downtime. However, this is only if the server chassis and disk controllers support such a change. Windows Server 2003 supports two types of disks: basic disks, which provide backward compatibility, and dynamic disks, which enable software-level disk arrays to be configured without a separate disk controller. Both basic and dynamic disks, when used as data disks, can be moved to other servers easily. This provides data or disk capacity elsewhere if a system hardware failure occurs and the data on these disks needs to be made available as soon as possible.

> **NOTE**
>
> If hardware-level RAID is configured, the controller card configuration should be backed up using a utility available through the vendor.
>
> With most array controllers today, dynamic reading of the disk configuration can be done as long as the disks are placed into a new system using the same disk order. If this is not supported, the controller can be moved to the new systems or the configuration might need to be re-created from scratch to complete a successful disk move to a new machine.
>
> This process should always be tested, verified, and documented in a lab environment before being considered as a valid recovery option.

To protect against a system failure, organizations need to have a full image backup that can then be restored in entirety to a new or repaired server system. This also requires completing and documenting these steps in advance to ensure that it can be completed and administrators understand the steps involved.

## Protecting Data in the Event of a Database Corruption

Data recovery also is needed in the event of a database corruption in Exchange. Unlike a catastrophic system failure, which can be restored from the last tape backup, data corruption creates a more challenging situation for information recovery. If data is corrupt on the server system, a restoral from the last backup might also contain corrupt information in its database, so a data restoral needs to predate the point of corruption. This typically requires the ability to restore the database from an older full backup tape and then recover incremental data since the clean database restoral.

**Providing the Ability to Restore a Message, Folder, or Mailbox**

In other situations, an organization might need to recover a single message, folder, or mailbox rather than a full database. With most full backups of an Exchange server, the restoral process requires a full restoral of all messages, folders, and mailboxes. If an administrator has to work with only a full image backup, typically a full restoral must be performed on a spare server and information extracted from the full restoral as necessary.

If message, folder, or mailbox recovery is required on a regular basis, the organization might elect to back up information in a format or process that provides an easier method of information recovery. This might involve the purchase and use of a third-party tape backup system, or a combination of various utilities available in Exchange Server 2003 to restore individual sets of information.

**Preparing a Backup for a Test Lab Restoral**

The last scenario in which a restoral is performed is the situation wherein an organization wants to re-create an Exchange server for the purpose of testing the server in a lab. In this situation, a full restoral is conducted in an isolated environment. Because Exchange Server 2003 requires Active Directory for the user address list and distribution list, a recovery of an Exchange server for this purpose requires the restoral of a global catalog server and potentially other support servers, such as front-end servers or bridgehead servers.

Instead of just restoring a single server into a production environment, the lab restoral for testing purposes requires the restoral of several dependency server systems. The process of restoral also requires certain servers to be restored in a logical sequence so that the right systems are in place, such as domain controllers, before member servers are restored. This sequence provides a more structured restoral that spans more than just the recovery of a system, but rather an entire system environment.

# Maintaining Documentation on the Exchange Environment

When performing system backups, many administrators merely back up servers and store tapes in-house or offsite, believing that the backup tape is the end goal of the backup process. Unfortunately, the backup tape is only part of the necessary process involved in creating a successful recovery process. As identified in the preceding section, many different scenarios require a data restoral, and in many cases, a full image restoral of an Exchange server is not the best solution to meet all situations.

A complete restoral of information presumes that the server the information being restored to is identical to the server that was backed up. If identical hard drive controller, network adapter, system board, and other server components do not exist, a full image restoral of a server will likely fail to recover from a server reboot—loaded drivers fail to enable. In these situations, the organization might choose to install the core Windows Server 2003 operating system on a new server with all the appropriate drivers for the new system, and then just restore the data.

To successfully restore just the Exchange data to a server, however, the server name, the domain the server is attached to, and the drive mappings must be identical to the server that was backed up. If the information is unknown, the ability for the organization to restore the information becomes a challenge.

This section covers the process of documenting key sets of information about each server, the server configuration, and the network information that can be used in the future as a server system requires recovery.

## Server Configuration Documentation

Server configuration documentation is essential for any environment regardless of size, number of servers, or disaster recovery budget. A server configuration document contains a server's name, network configuration information, hardware and driver information, disk and volume configuration, or information about the applications installed. This complete server configuration document contains all the necessary configuration information a qualified administrator would need if the server needed to be restored and the operating system could not be restored efficiently. A server configuration document also can be used as a reference when server information needs to be collected.

> **TIP**
>
> To assist with gathering information, administrators can use the WINMSD utility (standard utility installed as part of the base installation of Windows) to collect server data and configuration information to assist in producing server build documents. From the Run dialog box, enter **winmsd** and press Enter to view the Systems Information screen in Windows Server 2003.

## The Server Build Document

A server build document contains step-by-step instructions on how to build a particular type of server for an organization. The details of this document should be tailored to the skill of the person intended to rebuild the server. For example, if this document was created for disaster recovery purposes, it might be detailed enough that anyone with basic computer skills could rebuild the server. This type of information could also be used to help IT staff follow a particular server build process to ensure that when new servers are added to the network, they all meet company server standards.

## Hardware Inventory

Documenting the hardware inventory on an entire network might not be necessary. If the entire network does need to be inventoried, and if the organization is large, the Microsoft Systems Management Server can help automate the hardware inventory task. If the entire network does not need to be inventoried, hardware inventory can be collected for all the production and lab servers and networking hardware, including specifications such as serial numbers, amount of memory, disk space, processor speed, and, possibly, operating system platform and version.

## Network Configurations

Network configuration documentation is essential when network outages occur. Current, accurate network configuration documentation and network diagrams can help simplify and isolate network troubleshooting when a failure occurs.

### WAN Connection

WAN connectivity should be documented for enterprise networks that contain many sites to help IT staff understand the enterprise network topology. This document is very helpful when a server is restored and data should be synchronized enterprisewide after the restoral. Knowing the link performance between sites helps administrators understand how long an update made in Site A will take to reach Site B. This document should contain information about each WAN link, including circuit numbers, ISP contact names, ISP tech support phone numbers, and the network configuration on each end of the connection, and can be used to troubleshoot and isolate WAN connectivity issues.

### Router, Switch, and Firewall Configurations

Firewalls, routers, and sometimes switches can run proprietary operating systems with a configuration that is exclusive to the device. During a system recovery, certain gateway connections, configuration routing information, routing table data, and other information might need to be reset on the restored server. Information should be collected from these devices, including logon passwords and current configurations. When a configuration change is planned for any of these devices, the newly proposed configuration should be created using a text or graphical editor, but the change should be approved before it is made on the production device. A rollback plan should be created first to ensure that the device can be restored to the original state if the change does not deliver the desired results.

## Recovery Documentation

Recovery documentation, such as the server build document mentioned previously, can become reasonably complex and focused on a particular task. Recovery documentation aids an administrator in recovering from a failure for a particular server, server platform, specific service, or application. Recovery documentation is covered in Chapter 32.

## Updating Documentation

One of the most important, yet sometimes overlooked, areas concerning documentation is maintaining accuracy as changes are applied to server systems. Documentation is tedious, but outdated documentation can be worthless if changes have occurred to a server or software configuration since the document was created. For example, if a server configuration document was used to re-create a server from scratch but many changes were applied to the server after the document was created, the correct security patches might not be applied, applications might be configured incorrectly, or data restore attempts could be unsuccessful. Whenever a change will be made to a network device, printer, or server, documentation outlining the previous configuration, proposed changes, and rollback plan should be created before the change is approved and carried out on the

31

production device. After the change is carried out and the device is functioning as desired, the documentation associated with that device or server should be updated.

# Developing a Backup Strategy

Developing an effective backup strategy involves detailed planning around the logistics of backing up the necessary information or data via backup software, media type, and accurate documentation. To truly be effective, organizations should not limit a backup strategy by not considering the use of all available resources for recovery.

Along with planning and documentation, other aspects of a backup strategy include assigning specific tasks and responsibilities to individual IT staff members, considering the best person (depending on their strengths and areas of expertise) to be responsible for backing up a particular service or server and ensuring that documentation is accurate and current.

## Creating a Master Account List

Creating a master account list is a controversial subject because it contradicts what some security organizations call a best practice; however, many organizations follow this procedure. A master account list contains all the usernames and passwords with root privileges or top-level administrator privileges for network devices, servers, printers, and workstations.

Though this contradicts some best practices, organizations must plan for any, and even the worst, disaster scenarios. For example, a server restore might be required because of a disaster in a site that removed the server and the server administrator from accessibility. Without knowing the organizational-level password, site-level password, or server-level password on a system, an organization might be prevented from recovering server information. Even though this is considered, other areas such as employee changes can be a reason for having a master account list. To be effective, administrators should always plan for the worst, and hope for the best.

The master account list can be printed and stored in a sealed envelope in a safe at the office or in an electronically encrypted copy. This list should be used only when the assigned IT staff members are not available when recovering from a failure is necessary, and only one of the accounts on the list has the necessary access required. After the list is used, depending on who needed the temporary access, all the passwords on the list need to be changed for security purposes, and another sealed list created.

## Assigning Tasks and Designating Team Members

Each particular server or network device in the enterprise has specific requirements for backing up and creating documentation around hardware and the service it provides. To make sure that a critical system is being backed up properly, IT staff should designate a single individual to monitor that device and ensure the backup is completed and documentation is accurate and current at all times. Assigning a secondary staff member who has the same set of skills to act as a backup if the primary staff member is unavailable is a wise decision, to ensure that there is no point of failure among IT staff performing these tasks.

Assigning only primary and secondary resources to specific devices or services helps improve the overall security and reliability of the device and services provided to network users. By limiting who can back up and restore data—and even who can manage servers and devices—to just the primary and secondary qualified staff members, the organization can rest assured that only competent, trained individuals are working on systems they are assigned to manage. Even though the backup and restore responsibilities lie with the primary and secondary resources, the backup and recovery plans should still be documented and available to the remaining IT staff for additional training and final means of support if needed.

## Creating Regular Backup Procedures

Creating a regular backup procedure helps ensure that the entire enterprise is backed up consistently and properly on a regular basis. When a regular procedure is created, the assigned staff members soon become accustomed to the procedure as they are given a guide that walks through each required step. If there is no documented procedure, certain items might be overlooked and not be backed up, which can be a major problem if a failure occurs. For example, a regular backup procedure for an Exchange 2003 server might back up the Exchange databases on the local drives every night, and perform an Automated System Recovery (ASR) backup once per month and whenever a hardware change is made to a server. These differences might be overlooked if regular change control and documented procedures are not being followed.

> **TIP**
>
> It is best practice to add documentation updates into standard server change control processes. This ensures that any modifications to server configurations also get added into server build documents.

## Creating a Service-Level Agreement for Each Critical Service

A service-level agreement (SLA) defines the availability and performance of a particular server or application. This is usually linked to a failure. For example, a generic SLA could state that, for the Exchange server named EX01, if a failure occurs, it can be recovered and available on the network in four hours or less. These SLAs are commonly defined specifically within disaster recovery solutions; sometimes, the SLA is the *basis* for the disaster recovery solution. For example, if a company cannot be without its database for more than one hour, a disaster recovery solution must be created to meet that SLA.

Before an SLA can be defined, the IT staff member responsible for a device must understand what is necessary to recover that device from any type of failure. That person also must limit the SLA to only the failure types planned for in the approved disaster recovery solution. For example, suppose there is no plan for a site outage. The SLA might state that, if the device fails, it can be recovered using spare hardware and be back online in two hours or less. On the other hand, if a site failure occurs, there is no estimated recovery time because offsite backup media might need to be collected from an outside storage provider and hardware might need to be purchased or reallocated to rebuild the device. The more specific the SLA is, the better chance of covering every angle.

### Determining a Reasonable SLA

An SLA cannot be created until an IT staff member performs testing in a lab environment with backups and restores to verify that disaster recovery procedures are correct and that the data can be restored in a reasonable time frame according to your organization's SLA needs. When this method is not followed and an SLA is defined before the disaster recovery solution, the IT staff members need to see whether a standard recovery procedure will meet the SLA; otherwise, a creative, sometimes very expensive solution might be the only option to meet an SLA that is outside the abilities of existing solutions in your network.

## Selecting Devices to Back Up

Each device used on any network could have specific backup requirements. As mentioned earlier, each assigned IT staff member should also be responsible for researching and learning the backup and recovery requirements of each device to ensure that all backups will have everything that is necessary to recover from a device failure.

As a rule of thumb for network devices, the device configuration should be backed up whenever possible, using the device manufacturer's configuration software when possible or just by documenting the configuration for use as a reference should a device require reconfiguration.

> **TIP**
>
> It is also best practice to evaluate the hardware used in your environment to determine what areas might be the most likely points of failure. Having spare devices can reduce the overall downtime in case of a failure. When dealing with Exchange Server 2003 considerations, these spare hardware devices can be pieces such as hard drives to support a failed drive in a RAID configuration.

### Creating a Windows Server 2003 Boot Floppy

In previous versions of Windows, if RAID 1 volumes were created using the Windows operating system, instead of a hardware-based RAID solution, the administrator needed to create a specific boot disk allowing the operating system to boot to the second physical drive. This boot disk pointed to the remaining good disk to boot the server if the primary disk in the volume failed.

With Windows Server 2003, this dependency is removed because it adds additional lines in the server `boot.ini` file that point to the first and second disk's volumes, enabling the server to boot properly using the remaining disk in case of a failure. The only caveat to this is that the administrator needs to select the correct option when the `boot.ini` file displays the boot options on the screen when the server starts. The mirrored volume is referred to as a secondary plex in the following `boot.ini` file information:

```
[boot loader]
timeout=30
default=multi(0)disk(0)rdisk(0)partition(1)\WINDOWS
[operating systems]
multi(0)disk(0)rdisk(0)partition(1)\WINDOWS="C: Microsoft Windows Server _
 2003 Enterprise Server" /fastdetect
multi(0)disk(0)rdisk(1)partition(1)\WINDOWS="Boot Mirror C: - secondary plex"
```

The preceding example is taken directly from a boot.ini file of a Windows Server 2003 system using software-level RAID 1 arrays for the server operating system partition. The secondary subsystem is just a reference, but the disk controller and disk volume information point the boot loader to the correct remaining partition.

Note, sometimes a boot floppy is necessary though, especially if the boot and system volumes are different and the boot files are inaccessible. In a situation like this, a boot floppy can be priceless. To create a boot floppy, format a floppy disk. From the local server console, copy the boot.ini, NTLDR, and NTDETECT files to the floppy disk. When the BIOS cannot locate the boot loader files, this floppy can be used to boot the system and point the system to the correct volume containing the operating system files.

## Backing Up the Windows Server 2003 and Exchange Server 2003

The Windows Server 2003 operating system and the Exchange Server 2003 messaging system contain several features to enhance operating system stability, provide data and service redundancy, and deliver feature-rich client services.

And now, Windows Server 2003 provides additional services such as Volume Shadow Copy Service or VSS, which work to enhance backup capabilities when organizations use third-party backup products. Additional information around working with VSS is covered in the "Volume Shadow Copy Services and Exchange Server 2003" section later in this chapter.

Though other options have been mentioned, this section discusses ways to back up a Windows Server 2003 system, including key components of Exchange Server 2003 using the built-in backup utilities available with the Windows Server 2003 operating system. Also, additional Windows services are discussed, including built-in tools that aid in the backup and recovery process.

By preparing for a complete server failure and using the information in this section, an organization is more likely to successfully recover from a failed server, restoring it to its previous state.

### Backing Up Boot and System Volumes

A backup strategy for every Exchange Server 2003 system should always include the boot and system disk volumes of the server. For more Exchange Server installations, the boot and system volume are the same, but in some designs they can be located on completely separate volumes—as usually is the case with dual-boot computers. For the rest of this section and discussion, assume that they are both on the same partition. This volume contains all the files necessary to start the core operating system. It should be backed up before and after a change, such as the application of service packs, is made to the operating system and once every 24 hours, if possible.

When Exchange Server is installed on a Windows 2003 server, the installation, by default, will install on the system partition unless a different location is specified during installation. On average, the amount of information stored on the system volume, with applications, services, and all service packs installed, is typically less than 2GB.

> **NOTE**
>
> When system volumes are backed up, the system state should also be included in the backup at the same time to simplify recovery and restoration of the system to its original state if a server needs to be recovered from scratch.

## Backing Up Exchange Data Volumes

During the initial configuration, having the Exchange databases written to a completely separate data drive from the operating system is typically recommended; this improves overall system and user data access performance. When systems are built with this recommendation in mind, backing up just the system volume does not back up the Exchange databases. Backing up the Exchange databases that are stored on a separate drive set frequently requires the backup administrator to specifically define *both* the boot drive and the data drive in the backup selection. In far too many instances, organizations find out the hard way that they have been diligently backing up the Exchange server's C: drive, but have failed to back up the server's E: drive, which hosted the Exchange databases. Without a database backup, there is no data to be restored and recovered.

It is also important to note that the database volume usually has the most data needed for backup and recovery; this, of course, is dependent on the size of the mailbox information residing in the database. Always keep in mind, when planning, larger databases create longer backup intervals and might require more than one tape depending on the size of the Exchange databases and type of media used for the backup. For many organizations, a full backup of data volumes can be run only once per week, but to capture all new and modified data, incremental or differential backups can be run daily.

## Backing Up Windows Server 2003 Services

Many Windows Server 2003 services store configuration and status data in separate files or databases located in various locations on the system volume. If the service is native to Windows Server 2003, and a complete server backup on all drives and the system state is being performed, the critical data is almost certainly being backed up. A few services provide alternative backup and restore options. The procedures for backing up these services are outlined in the section titled "Backing Up Specific Windows Services," later in this chapter.

## Backing Up the System State

The system state of a Windows Server 2003 system contains, at a minimum, the System Registry, boot files, and the COM+ class registration database. Backing up the system state creates a point-in-time backup that can be used to restore a server to a previous working state. Having a copy of the system state is essential if a server restore is necessary.

How the server is configured determines what will be contained in the system state, other than the three items listed previously. On a domain controller, the system state also contains the Active Directory database and the SYSVOL share. On a cluster, it contains the cluster quorum data. When services such as Certificate Server and Internet Information Services, which contain their own service-specific data, are installed, these databases are not listed separately but are backed up with the system state.

Even though the system state contains many subcomponents, using the programs included with Windows Server 2003, the entire system state can be backed up only as a whole. When recovery is necessary, however, there are several different options. Recovering data using a system state backup is covered in Chapter 32.

The system state should be backed up every night to prepare for several server-related failures. A restore of a system state is very powerful and can return a system to a previous working state if a change needs to be rolled back or if the operating system needs to be restored from scratch after a complete server failure.

### Using the Active Directory Restore Mode Password

When a Windows Server 2003 system is promoted to a domain controller, one of the configurations is to create an Active Directory Restore mode password. This password is used only when booting into Active Directory Restore mode. Restore mode is used when the Active Directory database is in need of maintenance or needs to be restored from backup. Many administrators have found themselves without the ability to log on to Restore mode when necessary and have been forced to rebuild systems from scratch to restore the system state data. Many hours can be saved if this password is stored in a safe place, where it can be accessed by the correct administrators.

The Restore mode password is server-specific and created on each domain controller. If the password is forgotten, and the domain controller is still functional, it can be changed using the command-line tool `ntdsutil.exe`, as shown in Figure 31.1. The example in Figure 31.1 changes the password on the remote domain controller named `adserver.companyabc.com`.

# Volume Shadow Copy Services and Exchange Server 2003

Before discussing the backup process using Window NT backup, it is important for Exchange administrators to understand what Windows Server 2003 Volume Shadow Copy services are used for. With many third-party options available today, most Exchange Server 2003 organizations use these third-party backup products.

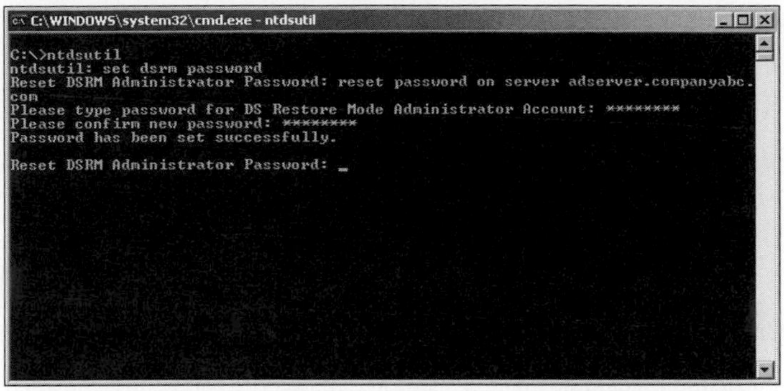

**FIGURE 31.1**    Changing the Active Directory Restore mode password (using `ntdsutil.exe`).

The Volume Shadow Copy service is a server service in Windows Server 2003 that is available as part of the operating system. Alone, VSS is a service, but when combined with backup applications, VSS become a vital part of every organization's backup strategy and recovery plan.

## What Role VSS Plays in Backup

Microsoft has created Volume Shadow Copy services to provide application platforms an infrastructure to enhance functionality when working with Microsoft services such as Exchange Server 2003. The key to Volume Shadow Copy is its ability to act as a go-between or coordinator for service providers (backup applications) and service writers (Exchange Server 2003 databases).

It is important to know that the VSS service does not function alone; VSS is designed to provide application developers a platform in which to build applications to create Exchange snapshots.

## Shadow Copies and Snapshots

The ability to enable third-party backup applications to create shadow copies or mirrors of the Exchange database allows administrators to design more dynamic backup strategies and reduce the overall cost of restoring servers. Using Show Copies (Mirror Copies) and Snapshots (Point-in-Time Mirror Copies), daily backups can be much smaller, and for vital messaging systems, snapshots can be taken several times a day.

## VSS Requirements and Prerequisites

When looking at third-party products as an option for backups with Volume Shadow Copy technology, you must evaluate the products to ensure that they are compatible with VSS. Compatibility is based on three specific areas.

First, backups of the Exchange Server 2003 database, logs, and checkpoint files must be completed by the application writer (Exchange Server 2003).

Second, the application must complete a full validation of the backup.

Last, when restoring data in Exchange, this must also be completed by the application writer (Exchange Server 2003).

VSS and third-party applications also require hardware compatibility. This is especially true when backing up to disk subsystems, such as network attached storage (NAS) and storage area network (SAN) solutions. To verify this information, review the application vendor support pages and verify that the application and hardware meet all requirements.

---

**TIP**

For more information regarding Volume Shadow Copy services and compatibility requirements, see the Microsoft article on the Microsoft Web site at support.microsoft.com/?kbid=822896.

---

# Using the Windows Backup Utility (Ntbackup.exe)

Windows Server 2003 includes several tools and services to back up and archive user data, but when it comes to backing up the entire operating system and disk volumes, Windows Server 2003 Backup is the program to use. Windows Server 2003 Backup is included on all the different versions of the Windows platform. Some Windows Server 2003 services provide alternative backup utilities, but they still can be backed up using Ntbackup.exe.

Windows Server 2003 Backup provides all the necessary functions to completely back up and restore a single file or the entire Windows Server 2003 system. Third-party, or even other Microsoft, applications installed on a Windows Server 2003 system should be researched to ensure that no special backup requirements or add-ons are necessary to back up the application data and configuration.

Windows Server 2003 Backup is capable of many types of backups; however, it is primarily used to back up the local server, but can also be used to back up remote server volumes. Although, in the case of backing up remote server volumes, open files are always skipped. Another limitation is that system state can be backed up only from the local server.

## Modes of Operation

The Windows Backup utility can run in two separate modes: Wizard and Advanced. Wizard mode provides a simple interface that enables a backup to be created in just a few simple steps:

1.  Choose to back up or restore files and settings.

2.  Choose to back up everything or specify what to back up.

3.  Choose what data to back up only if you do not choose the option to back up everything.

4.  Specify the backup media, tape, or file.

That is all it takes to use Wizard mode, but features such as creating a scheduled backup or choosing to use Volume Shadow Copy can be performed only using Advanced mode.

Advanced mode provides greater granularity when it comes to scheduling and controlling backup media security and other backup options. In the following sections concerning Windows Server 2003 Backup, you use Advanced mode.

## Using the Windows Backup Advanced Mode

Running the Windows Server 2003 Backup utility in Advanced mode enables administrators to configure all the available options for backups including using VSS. Scheduled backups can be created; specific wizards can be started; and advanced backup options can be configured, such as verifying backup, using volume shadow copies, backing up data in remote storage, and automatically backing up system-protected files.

To create a backup in Advanced mode, complete the following steps:

1. Click Start, All Programs, Accessories, System Tools, Backup.

2. If this is the first time you've run Backup, it opens in Wizard mode. Choose to run it in Advanced mode by clicking the Advanced Mode hyperlink.

3. Click the Backup Wizard (Advanced) button to start the Backup Wizard.

4. Click Next on the Backup Wizard Welcome screen to continue.

5. On the What to Back Up page, select Back Up Selected Files, Drives, or Network Data, and click Next to continue.

6. On the Items to Back Up page, expand Desktop, My Computer in the left pane, and choose each of the local drives and the system state, as shown in Figure 31.2. Then click Next to continue.

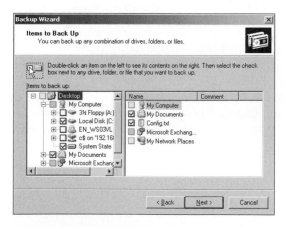

**FIGURE 31.2**    Selecting items to back up.

7. Choose your backup media type and choose the correct media tape or file. If you're creating a new file, specify the complete path to the file, and the backup creates the file automatically. Click Next to continue.

8. If the file you specified resides on a network drive, click OK at the warning message to continue.

9. If you chose tape for the backup, choose the media for the backup and choose to use a new tape.

10. Click the Advanced button on the Completing the Backup Wizard page to configure advanced options.

11. Choose the backup type and choose whether to back up migrated remote storage data. The default settings on this page will fit most backups, so click Next to continue.

12. Choose whether a verify operation will be run on the backup media and click Next. Disabling Volume Shadow Copy would be an option if a backup were just backing up local volumes, not the system state.

13. Choose the Media Overwrite option of appending or replacing the data on the media, and click Next.

14. On the When to Back Up page, choose to run the backup now or to create a schedule for the backup. If you chose Now, skip to step 18.

15. If a schedule will be created, enter a job name and click the Set Schedule button.

16. On the Schedule Job page, select the frequency of the backup, start time, and start date, as shown in Figure 31.3, and click OK when completed. You can set additional configurations using the Settings tab.

17. On the Set Account Information page, enter the user account name and password that should be used to run the scheduled backup and click OK when completed.

18. On the When to Back Up page, click Next to continue.

19. Click Finish to save the scheduled backup or immediately start the backup job.

20. When the backup is complete, review the backup log for detailed information, and click Close on the Backup Progress window when finished.

## Automated System Recovery

Automated System Recovery (ASR) is a backup option that is used to back up a system to recover from a complete server failure. An ASR backup contains disk volume information and a copy of all the data on the boot and system volumes, along with the current system state. ASR can be used to restore a system from scratch, and it will even re-create disk volumes and format them as previously recorded during the ASR backup. ASR does not back up the data stored on volumes that are solely used for data storage.

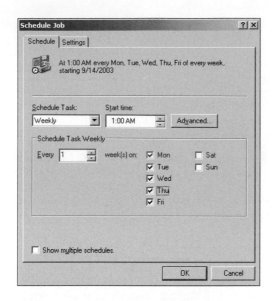

**FIGURE 31.3**   Creating a schedule for a backup.

To perform an ASR backup, you start with a blank floppy disk and a backup device; either a tape device or disk will suffice. One point to keep in mind is that an ASR backup will back up each local drive that contains the operating system and any applications installed. For instance, if the operating system is installed on drive C: and Microsoft Office is installed on drive D:, both of these drives will be completely backed up because the Registry has references to files on the D: drive. Although this can greatly simplify restore procedures, it requires additional storage and increases backup time for an ASR backup. Using a basic installation of Windows Server 2003 Enterprise Edition with only basic services installed, an ASR backup can average 1.3GB to less than 4GB or 5GB.

ASR backups should be created for a server before and after any hardware changes are performed or when a major configuration change occurs with the system. ASR backups contain disk information, including basic or dynamic configuration and volume set type. They save volume or partition data so that when an ASR restore is complete, only the data stored on storage volumes needs to be recovered.

### Creating an ASR Backup

An ASR backup can currently be created only from the local server console using the graphical user interface version of the Windows Server 2003 Backup utility.

To create an ASR backup, follow these steps:

1. Log on to the server using an account that has the right to back up the system. (Any Local Administrator or Domain Administrator has the necessary permissions to complete the operation.)

2. Click Start, All Programs, Accessories, System Tools, Backup.

3. If this is the first time you've run Backup, it opens in Wizard mode. Choose to run it in Advanced mode by clicking the Advanced Mode hyperlink.

4. Click the Automated System Recovery Wizard button to start the Automated System Recovery Preparation Wizard.

5. Click Next after reading the Automated System Recovery Preparation Wizard Welcome screen.

6. Choose your backup media type and choose the correct media tape or file. If you're creating a new file, specify the complete path to the file, and the backup creates the file automatically. Click Next to continue.

7. If you specified a file as the backup media and it resides on a network drive, click OK at the warning message to continue.

8. If you chose tape for the backup, choose the media for the backup and choose to use a new tape.

9. Click Finish to complete the Automated System Recovery Preparation Wizard and start the backup. As the ASR backup process begins, you will see the ntbackup utility processing the backup similar to what is shown in Figure 31.4.

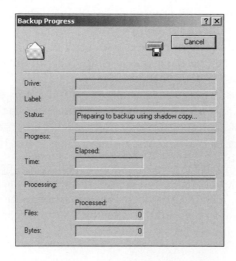

FIGURE 31.4   ASR backup in process.

10. After the tape or file backup portion completes, the ASR backup prompts you to insert a floppy disk to hold the recovery information. Insert the disk and click OK to continue.

11. Remove the floppy disk as requested and label the disk with the appropriate ASR backup information. Click OK to continue.

12. When the ASR backup is complete, click Close on the Backup Progress window to return to the backup program or click Report to examine the backup report.

> **NOTE**
>
> The information contained on the ASR floppy disk is also stored on the backup media. The ASR floppy contains only two files, `asr.sif` and `asrpnp.sif`, which can be restored from the backup media and copied to a floppy disk if the original ASR floppy cannot be located.

### Tips on Using ASR

One tip on using ASR is to ensure an ASR backup is completed after the server is built, updated with service packs, reconfigured, or security changes are applied. Also, an ASR backup should be performed when hardware configurations change and periodically otherwise. On domain controllers, this period should be less than 30 days to ensure that the domain can be up and running again if an Active Directory authoritative restore is necessary, but best practice is much sooner depending on the total amount of additions and changes occurring in Active Directory on a daily basis.

ASR backs up only the system and boot partitions. ASR does not back up the Exchange databases if they are installed on a separate drive. A normal tape backup of the drive(s) storing the Exchange databases or any other drive volume with critical data should be backed up separately. ASR backups, on average, are 1.3GB to 5GBs in size, so be sure to place the data in a location that can hold several copies of an ASR backup. To prevent ASR backups from getting too large, user data and file shares should be kept off the system and boot volumes.

## Backing Up Specific Windows Services

Most Windows Server 2003 services that contain a database or local files are backed up with the system state but also provide alternate backup and restore options. Because the system state restore is usually an all-or-nothing proposition, except when it comes to cluster nodes and domain controllers, restoring an entire system state might deliver undesired results if only a specific service database restore is required. This section outlines services that either have separate backup/restore utilities or require special attention to ensure a successful backup.

### Disk Configuration (Software RAID Sets)

Disk configuration is not a service but should be backed up to ensure that proper partition assignments can be restored. When dynamic disks are used to create complex volumes—such as mirrored, striped, spanned, or RAID 5 volumes—the disk configuration should be saved. This way, if the operating system is corrupt and needs to be rebuilt from scratch, the complex volumes need to have only their configuration restored, which could greatly reduce the recovery time. Only an ASR backup can back up disk and volume configuration.

### Certificate Services

Installing Certificate Services creates a certificate authority (CA) on the Windows Server 2003 system. The CA is used to manage and allocate certificates to users, servers, and workstations when files, folders, email, or network communication needs to be secured and encrypted. In many cases, the CA is a completely separate secured CA server; however, many organizations use their Exchange server as a CA server. This might be because of a limited number of servers with several different roles and services installed on a single server, or because the organization wants to use SSL and forms-based authentication for secured Outlook Web Access so they install Certificate Services on an Exchange server. Whatever the case, the CA needs to be backed up whether on the Exchange server or on any other server; if the CA server crashes and needs to be restored, it can be restored so users can continue to access the system after recovery.

---

**CAUTION**

For security purposes, it is highly recommended that the Certificate Services be enabled on a server other than the Exchange server. Definitely do not have the CA services on an Outlook Web Access server that is exposed to the Internet. The integrity of certificate-authenticated access depends on ensuring that certificates are issued only by a trusted authority. Any compromise to the CA server invalidates an organization's ability to secure its communications.

---

When the CA allocates a certificate to a machine or user, that information is recorded in the certificate database on the local drive of the CA. If this database is corrupted or deleted, all certificates allocated from this server become invalid or unusable. To avoid this problem, the certificates and Certificate Services database should be backed up frequently. Even if certificates are rarely allocated to new users or machines, backups should still be performed regularly.

Certificate Services can be backed up in three ways: backing up the CA server's system state, using the CA Microsoft Management Console (MMC) snap-in, or using the command-line utility `Certutil.exe`. Backing up Certificate Services by backing up the system state is the preferred method because it can be easily automated and scheduled. But using the graphic console or command-line utility adds the benefit of being able to restore Certificate Services to a previous state without restoring the entire server system state or taking down the entire server for the restore.

To create a backup of the certificate authority using the graphic console, follow these steps:

1. Log on to the certificate authority server using an account with Local Administrator rights.

2. Open Windows Explorer and create a folder named `CaBackup` on the C: drive.

3. Select Administrative Tools, Certificate Authority.

4. Expand the Certificate Authority server and select the correct CA.

5. Select Actions, All Tasks, Back Up CA.

6. Click Next on the Certification Authority Backup Wizard Welcome screen.

7. On the Items to Back Up page, check the Private Key and CA Certificate check box and the Certificate Database and Certificate Database Log check box, as shown in Figure 31.5.

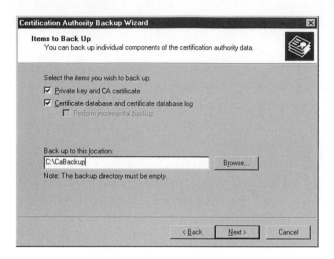

**FIGURE 31.5**   Selecting items for the certificate authority backup.

8. Specify the location to store the CA backup files. Use the folder created in the beginning of this process. Click Next to continue.

9. When the CA certificate and private key are backed up, this data file must be protected with a password. Enter a password for this file, confirm it, and click Next to continue.

> **NOTE**
>
> To restore the CA private key and CA certificate, you must use the password entered in step 9. Store this password in a safe place, possibly with the Master account list.

10. Click Finish to create the CA backup.

## Internet Information Services (IIS)

Internet Information Services (IIS) is Windows Server 2003's Web and FTP service that supports Web sites like OWA. It is included on every version of the Windows Server 2003 platform and is mandatory when installing Exchange Server 2003. IIS stores configuration information for Web and FTP site configurations and security, placing the information into the IIS metabase. The IIS metabase can be backed up by performing a system state backup of the server running IIS, but it can also be backed up using the IIS console. Best practice is that the IIS metabase should be backed up separately before and after any IIS configuration change is made. This ensures a successful rollback is available should issues occur and that the latest IIS configuration data is backed up after the change.

To back up the IIS metabase using the IIS console, use the following steps:

1. Log on to the IIS server using an account with Local Administrator access.

2. Click Start, All Programs, Administrative Tools, Internet Information Services (IIS).

3. If the local IIS server does not appear in the window, right-click Internet Information Services in the left pane, and select Connect.

4. Type in the fully qualified domain name for the IIS server, and click OK.

5. Right-click the IIS server in the left pane, and select All Tasks, Backup/Restore Configuration.

6. The Configuration Backup/Restore window lists all the automatic IIS backups that have been created. Click the Create Backup button.

7. Enter the backup name and, if necessary, check the Encrypt Backup Using Password check box, enter and confirm the password, and click OK when you're finished, as shown in Figure 31.6.

**FIGURE 31.6**    Creating an IIS configuration backup.

8. When the backup is complete, it is listed in the Configuration Backup/Restore window. Click Close to return to the IIS console.

Before a change is made to the IIS configuration, a backup should be manually created. When the change is completed, the administrator should either perform another backup or choose the option to save the configuration to disk. The administrator can save new IIS configuration changes to disk by right-clicking the IIS server, selecting All Tasks, and then choosing Save Configuration to Disk. This option works correctly only after a change has been made that has not yet been recorded in the IIS metabase.

## Managing Media in a Structured Backup Strategy

Windows Server 2003 Backup uses the Removable Storage service to allocate and deallocate media. The media can be managed using the Removable Storage console in the Computer Management Administrative Tools, as shown in Figure 31.7. The Removable Storage service allocates and deallocates media for these services by enabling each service to access media in media sets created for the respective program.

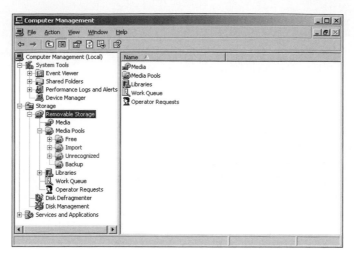

**FIGURE 31.7** Removable storage console.

## Media Pools

The Windows Server 2003 Removable Storage service organizes media so that policies and permissions can be applied and different functions can be performed. For example, the backup media pool is allocated for media created using Windows Server 2003 Backup. Only users granted the privilege to back up or restore the system, or administer the removable media service, will be granted access to this media pool.

### Free Pool

Media that can be used by any backup or archiving software that uses the Windows Server 2003 Removable Storage service is known as a free pool. Media in this pool are usually blank media or media marked as clean, and can be overwritten and reallocated.

### Remote Storage Pool

Use on a server only if the Remote Storage server has been installed. This pool stores media allocated for the Remote Storage service. If no tape is found, the device reallocates media from the free pool.

### Imported Pool

When media is inserted into a tape device and an inventory is run, if the media is not blank and not already allocated to the remote storage pool or backup media pool, this media is then stored in an imported media pool. If the media is known to have been created with Windows Server 2003 Backup, opening the backup program and performing a catalog should be sufficient to reallocate this media into the backup pool set.

### Backup Pool

This pool of media is clear and simple: It contains all the media allocated to the Windows Server 2003 Backup program.

### Custom Media Pools

Custom media pools can be created if special removable media options are required. Media pool options are very limited in Windows Server 2003, and there should be no compelling reason to create a custom media pool.

# Summary

Backing up an Exchange server is more than just putting in a tape every night and storing the tapes. Understanding what is occurring during a backup and the technologies used when working with backups are a bigger piece of the overall picture. Using this information to plan and test a backup strategy makes backups effective. If a data restoral becomes necessary, the administrator of the messaging system wants to ensure that the information on the tape has been properly backed up and verified so that the recovery goes as expected. The successful backup and restoral of key information is rarely successful by accident or by chance, and requires planning, extensive testing, and accurate documentation.

In addition, a backup of a system is not satisfied solely by a full image backup of a server. Although a full image backup provides an organization the ability to restore from a complete disaster, they are large and lengthy and also do not address the ability of the organization to restore portions of an Exchange environment, such as a specific message, folder, or mailbox. A full backup of an Exchange server also does not necessarily back up support functions of a fully operational Exchange environment, which include the directory in Active Directory, certificates for secured Exchange communications, or Web sites and services needed to complete the operational restoral of a server.

Because a successful restoral is so important to an organization after a system failure, take steps to ensure that a server restore will be successful.

# Best Practices

The following are best practices from this chapter:

- A successful backup and restoral plan includes backing up not only the Exchange server, but also any support servers, such as global catalog servers, certificate authority servers, or front-end Web servers.

- Always verify hardware and software compatibility before considering a solution for backing up your Exchange environment.

- Identify the different services and technologies, points of failure, and critical areas; prioritize in order of importance; and ensure all points of operation are backed up.

- Server configuration documentation is essential for any environment, regardless of size, number of servers, or disaster recovery budget. When restoring just the Exchange databases, other configuration information on Exchange, such as the server name, must be identical to the name of the server backed up; otherwise, the data will not successfully restore.

- Update documentation of an Exchange environment any time changes occur to ensure that core server and Exchange information is available should a component-level restoral be needed.

- When backing up system volumes, the system state should be backed up at the same time to simplify recovery if a server needs to be rebuilt from scratch.

- Perform an ASR backup after a server is built, updated, configured, and secured. Also, perform an ASR backup when hardware configurations change.

- Perform an ASR backup on domain controllers on a regular basis to ensure that if an Active Directory authoritative restore is necessary, you can get the domain up and running again.

- Consider using the remote storage management functions built in to Windows Server 2003 to better manage historical backup information and backup media.

# CHAPTER 32

# Recovering from a Disaster

W hen an Exchange server or environment isn't working properly, possibly due to database corruption, hardware failure, or just unknown reasons, there's an urgent need to get the Exchange system back up and running as quickly as possible. Several approaches can be used to recover depending on the type of disaster experienced.

Unfortunately, most organizations do not proactively create an environment with disaster-recovery processes in place. As a result, this chapter takes into account the information in Chapter 30, "System-Level Fault Tolerance (Clustering/Network Load Balancing)," and Chapter 31, "Backing Up the Exchange Server 2003 Environment," and also provides recommendations based on possible disaster scenarios.

## Identifying the Extent of the Problem

Before a successful recovery can be conducted, the type and extent of the problem must be determined. Otherwise, if the problem is not properly identified, additional issues may arise. For instance, considering there are different recovery strategies that exist for recovering a lost mail message than for recovering an entire mailbox, the strategy to recover may do the job but not in the time required. Moreover, the amount of data that must be recovered is equally important in determining how to recover from the failure. Using the right recovery process to solve the problem requires a pre-planned process to minimize the recovery time and the chance that a simple recovery will create bigger problems in the process. The most common scenarios are described next.

**IN THIS CHAPTER**

- Identifying the Extent of the Problem

- What to Do Before Performing Any Server-Recovery Process

- Preparing for a More Easily Recoverable Environment

- Recovering from a Site Failure

- Recovering from a Disk Failure

- Recovering from a Boot Failure

- Recovering from a Complete Server Failure

- Recovering Exchange Application and Exchange Data

- Recovering from Database Corruption

- Using the Recovery Storage Group in Exchange Server 2003

- Recovering Internet Information Services

- Recovering the Cluster Service

- Recovering Windows Server 2003 Domain Controllers

- Recovering Active Directory

> **Database Improvements Minimizes Corruption**
>
> Exchange Server 2003 Service Pack (SP) 1 and higher includes error correction (ECC) enhancements that help minimize the number of errors in the database. The ECC automatically identifies and fixes single-bit database page errors that commonly cause -1018 errors. Typically, these errors were caused by hardware issues and often required database repair or restoration.
>
> SP1 and higher also includes a performance improvement that significantly helps administrators during restoration. The enhancement allows log files to be replayed much faster than without the SP. A vast performance improvement will be noticed if hundreds or thousands of log files must be replayed.

## Mailbox Content Was Deleted, Use the Undelete Function of Exchange and Outlook

When information is deleted from a user's mailbox, whether it is an email message, a Calendar appointment, a contact, or a task, the information is not permanently deleted from the Exchange server. Deleted items go into the Deleted Items folder in the user's Outlook mailbox. The information is actually retained on the Exchange server for 30 days after deletion, even when it is supposedly permanently deleted from the Deleted Items folder.

> **NOTE**
>
> The Mail Retention feature needs to be enabled on the Exchange server for Outlook information to be retained on the Exchange server.

With a little training and documentation, end-users can recover their own deleted mail items with ease. To recover mailbox items that have been deleted within Outlook, do the following:

1. Highlight the Deleted Items folder.

2. From the Tools menu, choose Recover Deleted Items.

3. In the Recover Deleted Items From – Deleted Items window, select the items that you wish to restore.

4. Click the Recover Selected Items button.

## Data Is Lost, Must Restore from Backup

If data is lost and the undelete function will not recover the information, the information may need to be restored from a backup. Depending on how much information was lost, this might involve a full recovery of the Exchange server from tape or snapshot, or it might involve restoring just a single mailbox, folder, or message. Key to restoring information is determining what needs to be restored. If just a single message needs to be restored, there is no reason to recover the entire server in production. In many cases, when full tape backups have been conducted of an Exchange server, a full restore must be completed offline and then a specific mailbox, folder, or mail message must be extracted from the offline restored server to the production server. The restore process needs to take into account the restoration of the information desired without the restoration of the entire server, which might overwrite valid data.

The process of restoring all or partial data from tape is covered in the sections "Recovering from a Complete Server Failure" and "Recovering from Database Corruption," later in this chapter.

## Data Is Okay, Server Just Doesn't Come Up

The failure of a server does not necessarily mean that the data needs to be restored completely from tape. In fact, if the hard drives on a dead server are still operational, the hard drives should be moved to an operational server or, at the very least, the data should be transferred to a different server. By preserving the data on the drives, an organization can minimize the need to perform more complicated data reconstruction from a tape restore, which could result in the loss of data from the time of the last backup.

The process of recovering data from a drive and recovering a failed server is covered in the section "Performing a Restore of Only Exchange Database Files," later in this chapter.

## Data Is Corrupt—Some Mailboxes Are Accessible, Some Are Not

Data corruption typically occurs on Exchange servers because the time period since the last database maintenance is too long or maintenance has been neglected altogether. Without periodic maintenance, covered in Chapter 19, "Exchange Server 2003 Management and Maintenance Practices," the databases in Exchange are more susceptible to becoming corrupt. Exchange database corruption that is not repaired can make portions of mailboxes stored on an Exchange server inaccessible.

When a mailbox or multiple mailboxes are corrupt, the good data in the mailboxes can be extracted with minimal data loss. By isolating the corruption and extracting good data, an organization that might not need to recover the lost data can typically continue to operate with minimal downtime.

The process of extracting mail from an Exchange database is covered in the section "Recovering from Database Corruption," later in this chapter.

## Data Is Corrupt, No Mailboxes Are Accessible

Depending on the condition of an Exchange database, the information might be so corrupt that none of the mailboxes are accessible. Recovering data from a corrupt database that cannot be accessed is a two-step process. The first step is to conduct maintenance to attempt to get the database operational; the second step is to extract as much information from the database as possible.

The process of performing maintenance and extracting data from a corrupt database is covered in the section "Recovering from Database Corruption," later in this chapter.

## Exchange Server Is Okay, Something Else Is Preventing Exchange from Working

If you know that the Exchange server and databases are operational and something else is preventing Exchange from working, the process of recovery focuses on looking at things such as Active Directory, Internet Information Server (IIS), the Domain Name System (DNS), and the network infrastructure, as with site-to-site connectivity for replication.

The process of analyzing the operation of other services is covered in the sections "Recovering Windows Server 2003 Domain Controllers" and "Recovering Active Directory," later in this chapter.

# What to Do Before Performing Any Server-Recovery Process

If a full server recovery will be conducted, or if a number of different procedures will be taken to install service packs, patches, updates, or other server-recovery attempts as an attempt to recover the server, a full backup should be performed on the server.

It might seem unnecessary backing up a server that isn't working properly, but during the problem-solving and debugging process, it is quite common for a server to end up being in even worse shape after a few updates and fixes have been applied. The initial problem might have been that a single mailbox couldn't be accessed, and after some problem-solving efforts, the entire server might be inaccessible. A backup provides a rollback to the point of the initial problem state. When the backup is complete, verify that the backup is valid, ensuring that no open files are skipped during the backup process or that, if the files are skipped, they are backed up in other open file backup processes.

> **CAUTION**
>
> When performing any recovery of an Exchange server or resource, be careful what you delete, modify, or change. As a rule of thumb, *never* delete objects that are known throughout the directory; otherwise, you will not be able to restore the object due to the uniqueness of each object. As an example, if you plan to restore an entire server from tape, you do not want to first delete the server and then add the server back during the restoration process. The restoration process requires the existence of the old server in the directory. Deleting the server object and then adding the object again later gives the object a completely different globally unique identifier (GUID). Even though you restore the entire Exchange server from tape, the ID of the server and all of the objects in the server will be different, making it more difficult to recover the server. Other replicable objects that should not be deleted include public folders, public folder trees, groups, and distribution lists.

## Validating Backup Data and Procedures

Another very important task that should be done before doing any maintenance, service, or repairs on an Exchange server is to validate that a full backup exists on the server, test the condition of the backup, and then secure the backup so that it is safe. Far too many organizations proceed with risky recovery procedures, believing that they have a fallback position by restoring from tape, only to realize that the tape backup is corrupt or that a complete backup does not exist.

If the administrators of the network realize that there is no clean backup, the procedures taken to recover the system might be different than if a backup had existed. If a full backup exists and is verified to be in good condition, the organization has an opportunity to restore from tape if a full restore is necessary.

# Preparing for a More Easily Recoverable Environment

Steps can be taken to help an organization more easily prepare for a recoverable environment. This involves documenting server states and conditions, performing specific backup procedures, and setting up new features in Exchange Server 2003 that provide for a more simplified restoration process.

## Documenting the Exchange Environment

Key to the success of recovering an Exchange server or an entire Exchange environment is having documentation on the server configurations. Having specific server configuration information documented helps to identify which server is not operational, the routing of information between servers, and ultimately the impact that a server failure or server recovery will have on the rest of the Exchange environment.

> **NOTE**
>
> A utility called ExchDump can assist an administrator with baselining and improving the environment. Use ExchDump to export and document a server's configuration. The ExchDump utility can be downloaded from the Microsoft Exchange download page at http://www.microsoft.com/exchange/downloads/2003/default.mspx.

Some of the items that should be documented include these:

- Server name
- Version of Windows on servers (including Service Pack)
- Version of Exchange on servers (including Service Pack)
- Organization name in Exchange
- Site names
- Storage group names
- Database names
- Location of databases
- Size of databases
- Public folder tree name

- Replication process of public folders
- Security delegation and administrative rights
- Names and locations of Global Catalog servers

## Documenting the Backup Process

Important in simplifying a restore of an Exchange environment is to start with a clean backup to restore from. A clean backup is performed when the proper backup process is followed. Create a backup process that works, document the step-by-step procedures to back up the server, follow the procedures regularly, and then validate that the backups have been completed successfully.

Also, when configurations change, the backup process as well as system configurations should be documented and validated again, to make sure that the backups are being completed properly.

## Documenting the Recovery Process

An important aspect of recovery feasibility is knowing how to recover from a disaster. Just knowing what to back up and what scenarios to plan for is not enough. Restore processes should be created and tested to ensure that a restore can meet service level agreements (SLAs) and that the staff members understand all the necessary steps.

When a process is determined, it should be documented, and the documentation should be written to make sense to the desired audience. For example, if a failure occurs in a satellite office that has only marketing employees and one of them is forced to recover a server, the documentation needs to be written so that it can be understood by just about anyone. If the IT staff will be performing the restore, the documentation can be less detailed, but it assumes a certain level of knowledge and expertise with the server product. The first paragraph of any document related to backup and recovery should be a summary of what the document is used for and the level of skill necessary to perform the task and understand the document.

The recovery process involved in resolving an Exchange problem should also be focused not only on the goal of getting the entire Exchange server back up and operational, but also on considering smaller steps that might help minimize downtime. As an example, if an Exchange server has failed, instead of trying to restore 100GB of mail back to the server, which can take hours, if not days, to complete, an organization can choose to restore just the user inboxes, Calendars, and contacts. After a faster system recovery of core information on a server, the balance of the information can be restored over the next several hours.

## Including Test Restores in the Scheduled Maintenance

Part of a successful disaster-recovery plan involves periodically testing the restore procedures to verify accuracy and to test the backup media to ensure that data can actually be recovered. Most organizations or administrators assume that if the backup software reports "Successful," the backup is good and data can be recovered. If special backup consideration is not addressed, the successful backup might not contain everything necessary to restore a server if data loss or software corruption occurs.

Restores of file data, application data, and configurations should be performed as part of a regular maintenance schedule to ensure that the backup method is correct and that disaster-recovery procedures and documentation are current. Such tests also should verify that the backup media can be read from and used to restore data. Adding periodic test restores to regular maintenance intervals ensures that backups are successful and familiarizes the administrators with the procedures necessary to recover so that when a real disaster occurs, the recovery can be performed correctly and efficiently the first time.

# Recovering from a Site Failure

When a site becomes unavailable due to a physical access limitation or a disaster such as a fire or earthquake, steps must be taken to provide the recovery of the Exchange server in the site. Exchange does not have a single-step method of merging information from the failed site server into another server, so the process involves recovering the lost server in its entirety.

To prepare for the recovery of a failed site, an organization can create redundancy in a failover site. With redundancy built into a remote site, the recovery and restore process can be minimized if a recovery needs to performed.

## Creating Redundant and Failover Sites

Redundant sites are created for a couple of different reasons. First, a redundant site can have a secondary Internet connection and bridgehead routing server so that if the primary site is down, the secondary site can be the focus for inbound and outbound email communications. This redundancy can be built, configured, and set to automatically provide failover in case of a site failure. See Chapter 3, "Installing Exchange Server 2003," for details on creating Routing Group connectors and bridgehead servers.

The other reason for redundant site preparation is to provide a warm spare server site so that a company will be prepared to perform a restore of a site server in case of a site failure. The site recovery can simply be having server documentation available in another site or having a full image of server information stored in another site. The more preparatory work is conducted up front, the faster the organization will be able to recover from a system failure.

## Creating the Failover Site

When an organization decides to plan for site failures as part of a disaster-recovery solution, many areas need to be addressed and many options exist. For organizations looking for redundancy, network connectivity is a priority, along with spare servers that can accommodate the user load. The spare servers need to have enough disk space to accommodate a complete restore. As a best practice, to ensure a smooth transition, the following list of recommendations provides a starting point:

- Allocate the appropriate hardware devices, including servers with enough processing power and disk space to accommodate the restored machines' resources.

- Host the organization's DNS zones and records using primary DNS servers located at an Internet service provider (ISP) collocation facility, or have redundant DNS servers registered for the domain and located at both physical locations.

- Ensure that DNS record-changing procedures are documented and available at the remote site or at an offsite data storage location.

- For the Exchange servers, ensure that the host records in the DNS tables are set to low Time to Live (TTL) values so that DNS changes do not take extended periods to propagate across the Internet. The Microsoft Windows Server 2003 default TTL is 1 hour.

- Ensure that network connectivity is already established and stable between sites and between each site and the Internet.

- Create at least one copy of backup tape medium for each site. One copy should remain at one location, and a second copy should be stored with an offsite data storage company. An optional third copy could be stored at another site location and can be used to restore the file to spare hardware on a regular basis, to restore Windows if a site failover is necessary.

- Have a copy of all disaster-recovery documentation stored at multiple locations as well as at the offsite data storage company. This provides redundancy if a recovery becomes necessary.

Allocating hardware and making the site ready to act as a failover site are simple tasks in concept, but the actual failover and fail-back process can be troublesome. Keep in mind that the preceding list applies to failover sites, not mirrored or redundant sites configured to provide load balancing.

## Failing Over Between Sites

Before failing over between sites can be successful, administrators need to be aware of what services need to fail over and in which order of precedence. For example, before an Exchange server can be restored, Active Directory domain controllers, Global Catalog servers, and DNS servers must be available.

To keep such a cutover at a high level, the following tasks need to be executed in a timely manner:

1. Update Internet DNS records pointing to the Exchange server(s).

2. Restore any necessary Windows Server 2003 domain controllers, Global Catalog servers, and internal DNS servers.

3. Restore the Exchange server(s).

4. Test client connectivity, troubleshoot, and provide remote and local client support as needed.

## Failing Back After Site Recovery

When the initial site is back online and available to handle client requests and provide access to data and networking services and applications, it is time to consider failing back the services. This can be a controversial subject because fail-back procedures are usually more difficult than the initial failover procedure. Most organizations plan on the failover and have a tested failover plan that might include database log shipping to the disaster-recovery site. However, they do not plan how they can get the current data back to the restored servers in the main or preferred site.

Questions to consider for failing back are as follows:

- Will downtime be necessary to restore databases between the sites?

- When is the appropriate time to fail back?

- Is the failover site less functional than the preferred site? In other words, are only mission-critical services provided in the failover site, or is it a complete copy of the preferred site?

The answers really lie in the complexity of the failed-over environment. If the cutover is simple, there is no reason to wait to fail back.

## Providing Alternative Methods of Client Connectivity

When failover sites are too expensive and are not an option, that does not mean that an organization cannot plan for site failures. Other lower-cost options are available but depend on how and where the employees do their work. For example, many times users who need to access email can do so without physically being at the site location. Email can be accessed remotely from other terminals or workstations.

The following are some ways to deal with these issues without renting or buying a separate failover site:

- Consider renting racks or cages at a local ISP to collocate servers that can be accessed during a site failure.

- Have users dial in from home to a terminal server hosted at an ISP to access Exchange.

- Set up remote user access using Terminal Services or Outlook Web Access at a redundant site so that users can access their email, Calendar, and contacts from any location.

- Rent temporary office space, printers, networking equipment, and user workstations with common standard software packages such as Microsoft Office and Internet Explorer. You can plan for and execute this option in about one day. If this is an option, be sure to find a computer rental agency first and get pricing before a failure occurs and you have no choice but to pay the rental rates.

# Recovering from a Disk Failure

Organizations create disaster-recovery plans and procedures to protect against a variety of system failures, but disk failures tend to be the most common in networking environments. The technology used to create processor chips and memory chips has improved drastically over the past couple decades, minimizing the failure of system boards. And while the quality of hard drives has also drastically improved over the years, because hard drives are constantly spinning, they have the most moving parts in a computer system and tend to be the items of most failure.

Key to a disk fault-tolerant solution is creating hardware fault tolerance on key server drives that can be recovered in case of failure. Information is stored on system, boot, and data volumes that have varying levels of recovery needs. Many options exist such as SAN or various RAID levels to minimize the impact of drive failures.

## Hardware-Based RAID Array Failure

Common uses of hardware-based disk arrays for Windows servers include RAID 1 (mirroring) for the operating system and RAID 5 (striped sets with parity) for separate data volumes. Some deployments use a single RAID 5 array for the OS, and data volumes for RAID 0+1 (mirrored striped sets) have been used in more recent deployments.

RAID controllers provide a firmware-based array-management interface, which can be accessed during system startup. This interface enables administrators to configure RAID controller options and manage disk arrays. This interface should be used to repair or reconfigure disk arrays if a problem or disk failure occurs.

Many controllers offer Windows-based applications that can be used to manage and create arrays. Of course, this requires the operating system to be started to access the Windows-based RAID controller application. Follow the manufacturer's procedures on replacing a failed disk within hardware-based RAID arrays.

> **NOTE**
>
> Many RAID controllers allow an array to be configured with a *hot spare disk*. This disk automatically joins the array when a single disk failure occurs. If several arrays are created on a single RAID controller card, hot spare disks can be defined as global and can be used to replace a failed disk on any array. As a best practice, hot spare disks should be defined for arrays.

## System Volume

If a system disk failure is encountered, the system can be left in a completely failed state. To prevent this problem from occurring, the administrator should always try to create the system disk on a fault-tolerant disk array such as RAID 1 or RAID 5. If the system disk was mirrored (RAID 1) in a hardware-based array, the operating system will operate and boot normally because the disk and partition referenced in the boot.ini file will remain the same and will be accessible. If the RAID 1 array was created within the operating system using Disk Manager or `diskpart.exe`, the mirrored disk can be accessed upon bootup by choosing the second option in the `boot.ini` file during startup. If a disk failure occurs on a software-based RAID 1 array during regular operation, no system disruption should be encountered.

## Boot Volume

If Windows Server 2003 has been installed on the second or third partitions of a disk drive, a separate boot and system partition will be created. Most manufacturers require that for a system to boot up from a volume other than the primary partition, the partition must be marked active before functioning. To satisfy this requirement without having to change the active partition, Windows Server 2003 always tries to load the boot files on the first or active partition during installation, regardless of which partition or disk the system files will be loaded on. When this drive or volume fails, if the system volume is still intact, a boot disk can be used to boot into the OS and make the necessary modification after changing the drive.

## Data Volume

A data volume is by far the simplest of all types of disks to recover. If an entire disk fails, simply replacing the disk, assigning the previously configured drive letter, and restoring the entire drive from backup will restore the data and permissions.

A few issues to watch out for include these:

- Setting the correct permissions on the root of the drive

- Ensuring that file shares still work as desired

- Validating that data in the drive does not require a special restore procedure

# Recovering from a Boot Failure

Occasionally, a Windows Server 2003 system can suffer a service or application startup problem that could leave a server incapable of completing a normal bootup sequence. Because the operating system cannot be accessed in this case, the system remains unavailable until this problem can be resolved.

Windows Server 2003 includes a few alternative bootup options to help administrators restore a server to a working state. Several advanced bootup options can be accessed by pressing the F8 key when the boot loader screen is displayed (see Figure 32.1). If the Recovery Console was previously installed, it is listed as an option in the boot loader screen. The advanced boot options include these:

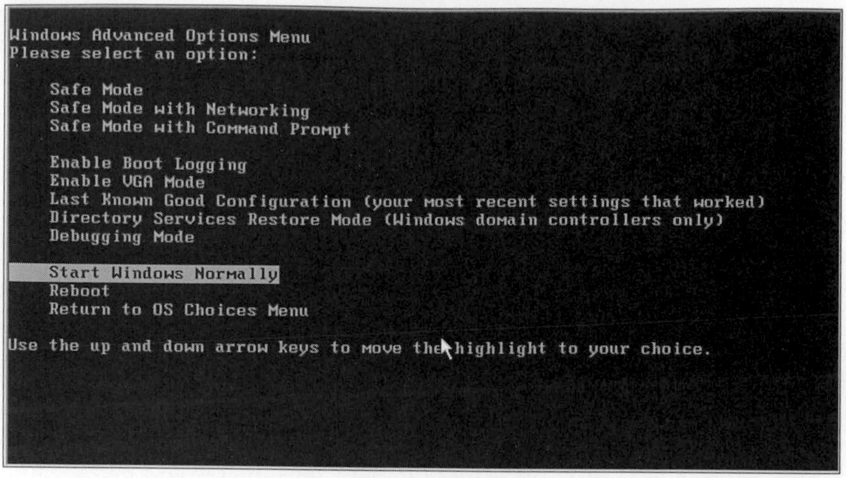

**FIGURE 32.1**    The advanced boot options of Windows 2003.

- **Safe Mode**—This mode starts the operating system with only the most basic services and hardware drivers, and disables networking. This allows administrators to access the operating system in a less functional state to make configuration changes to service startup options, some application configurations, and the system Registry.

- **Safe Mode with Networking**—This option is the same as Safe Mode, but networking drivers are enabled during operation. This mode also starts many more operating system services upon startup.

- **Safe Mode with Command Prompt**—This option is similar to the Safe Mode option; however, the Windows Explorer shell is not started by default.

- **Enable Boot Logging**—This option boots the system normally, but all the services and drivers loaded at startup are recorded in a file named `ntbtlog.txt`, located in the `%systemroot%` directory. The default location for this file is `C:\Windows\ntbtlog.txt`. To simplify reading this file, the administrator must delete the existing file before a bootup sequence is logged so that only the information from the last bootup is logged.

- **Enable VGA Mode**—This mode loads the current display driver, but it displays the desktop at the lowest resolution. This mode is handy if a server is plugged into a different monitor that cannot support the current resolution.

- **Last Known Good Configuration**—This mode starts the operating system using Registry and driver information saved during the last successful logon.

- **Directory Services Restore Mode**—This mode is only for domain controllers and allows for maintenance and restoration of the Active Directory database or the SYSVOL folder.

- **Debugging Mode**—This mode sends operating system debugging information to other servers through a serial connection. This requires a server on the receiving end with a logging server that is prepared to accept this data. Most likely, standard administrators will never use this mode.

- **Start Windows Normally**—As the name states, this mode loads the operating system as it would normally run.

- **Reboot**—This option reboots the server.

- **Return to OS Choices Menu**—This option returns the screen to the boot loader page so that the correct operating system can be chosen and started.

## The Recovery Console

The Recovery Console provides an option for administrators to boot up a system using alternate configuration files to perform troubleshooting tasks. Using the Recovery Console, the bootup sequence can be changed, alternate boot options can be specified, volumes can be created or extended, and service startup options can be changed. The Recovery Console has only a limited number of commands that can be used, making it a simple console to learn. If Normal or Safe Mode bootup options are not working, the administrator can use the Recovery Console to make system changes or read the information stored in the boot logging file using the `type` command. The boot logging file is located at `C:\Windows\ntbtlog.txt` by default and exists only if someone tried to start the operating system using any of the Safe Mode options or the boot logging option.

# Recovering from a Complete Server Failure

Because hardware occasionally fails and, in the real world, operating systems do have problems, a server-recovery plan is essential, even though it might never be used. The last thing any administrator wants is for a server failure to occur and to end up on the phone with Microsoft technical support asking for the server to be restored from backup when no plan is in place. To keep from being caught unprepared, the administrator should have a recovery plan for every possible failure associated with Windows Server 2003 systems.

## Restoring Versus Rebuilding

When a complete system failure occurs, whether it is due to a site outage, a hardware component failure, or a software corruption problem, the method of recovery depends on the administrator's major goal. The goal is to get the server up and running, of course, but behind the scenes, many more questions should be answered before the restore is started:

- How long will it take to restore the server from a full backup?

- If the server failed due to software corruption, will restoring the server from backup also restore the corruption that actually caused the failure?

- Will reloading the operating system and Exchange manually followed by restoring the system state be faster than doing a full restore?

Loading the Windows Server 2003 operating system and Exchange Server 2003 software can be a relatively quick process. This ensures that all the correct files and drivers are loaded correctly and all that needs to follow is a system state restore to recover the server configuration and restore the data. One of the problems that can occur is that, upon installation, some applications generate Registry keys based on the system's computer name, which can change if a system state restore is performed.

Exchange Server 2003 has a `setup /disasterrecovery` installation option and does not need the server's system state restore—just the original computer name and domain membership, as long as computer and user certificates are not being used.

The key to choosing whether to rebuild or restore from backup is understanding the dependencies of the applications and services to the operating system, and having confidence in the server's stability at the time of the previous backups. The worst situation is attempting a restore from backup that takes several hours, only to find that the problem has been restored as well.

## Manually Recovering a Server

When a complete server system failure is encountered and the state of the operating system or an application is in question, the operating system can be recovered manually. Locating the system's original configuration settings is the first step. This information is normally stored in a server build document or wherever server configuration information is kept.

Because each system is different, as a general guideline for restoring a system manually, perform the following steps:

1. Install a new operating system on the original system hardware and disk volume, or one as close to the original configuration as possible. Be sure to install the same operating system version—for example, Windows Server 2003 Enterprise or Standard Server.

2. During installation, name the system using the name of the original server, but do not join a domain.

3. Do not install additional services during installation, and proceed by performing a basic installation.

4. When the operating system completes installation, install any additional hardware drivers as necessary and update the operating system to the service pack and security patches that the failed server was expected to have installed. To reduce compatibility problems, install the service packs and updates as outlined in the server build document to ensure that any installed applications will function as desired. During a restore is not the time to roll out additional system changes. The goal is to get the system back online, not to upgrade it.

5. Using the Disk Management console, create and format disk volumes and assign the correct drive letters as recorded in the server build document.

6. If the server was originally part of a domain, join the domain using the original server name. Because many Windows Server 2003 services use the server name or require the service to be authorized in a domain, perform this step before installing any additional services or applications.

7. Install any additional Windows Server 2003 services as defined in the server build document.

8. Install Exchange Server 2003 using the same version of Exchange (Standard or Enterprise) that was originally installed. Apply any Exchange Service Packs and updates that were expected to be on the original server as well. When installing Exchange, use the `setup /disasterrecovery` installation process that will install Exchange but will not add new databases.

9. Restore Exchange data to the new server.

10. Test functionality, add this system to the backup schedule, and start a full backup.

> **NOTE**
>
> If certificates were issued to the previous server, the new server must enroll with the Certificate Authority (CA) for a new certificate before encrypted communication can occur.

## Restoring a Server Using a System State Restore

The restoration of an Exchange Server 2003 system into an existing Active Directory domain does not require the installation of the system state because the procedures covered in the previous section will recover the server and database for the server replacement. However, if the failure of Exchange also included the loss of the Active Directory Global Catalog and there is no other Global Catalog in the organization, a system state restore of the Global Catalog needs to be performed before Exchange can be restored.

Exchange Server 2003 requires a valid Active Directory to be in place. This process might be required if the Exchange server was the only server in the network and, thus, the loss of the Exchange server also meant the loss of the only Global Catalog server. This also might be the case if there was a site failure and all servers, including the Exchange Server and Active Directory Global Catalog server, were lost.

To recover the system state, follow these steps:

1. Shut down the original server or build a new server hardware system.

2. Install a new copy of Windows 2003 on the system hardware and disk volume, or one as close to the original configuration as possible. Be sure to install the same operating system version—for example, Windows Server 2003 Enterprise or Standard Server.

3. During installation, name the system using the name of the original server, but do not join a domain.

> **NOTE**
>
> If the machine is joined to the original domain during the clean installation, a new security identifier (SID) will be generated for the machine account. A system state restore after this restores an invalid computer SID, and many services and applications will fail.

4. Do not install additional services during installation, and proceed by performing a basic installation.

5. When the operating system completes installation, install any additional hardware drivers as necessary and update the operating system to the latest service pack and security patches. To reduce compatibility problems, install the service packs and updates as outlined in the server build document, to ensure that any installed applications will function as desired.

6. Using the Disk Management console, create and format disk volumes and assign the correct drive letters as recorded in the server build document.

7. After the installation, restore any necessary drivers or updates to match the original configuration. This information should be gathered from a server configuration document (server build document). Then reboot as necessary.

After all the updates have been installed, restore the previously backed-up system state data; afterward, restore any additional application or user data.

### System State Restore

This section outlines how to restore the system state to a member or standalone Windows Server 2003 system. To restore the system state, perform the following steps:

1. Click Start, All Programs, Accessories, System Tools, Backup.

2. If this is the first time you've run Backup, it opens in Wizard mode. Choose to run it in Advanced mode by clicking the Advanced Mode hyperlink.

3. Click the Restore Wizard (Advanced) button to start the Restore Wizard.

4. Click Next on the Restore Wizard welcome screen to continue.

5. On the What to Restore page, select the appropriate cataloged backup medium, expand the catalog selection, and check system state. Click Next to continue.

6. If the correct tape or file backup medium does not appear in this window, cancel the restore process. Then, from the Restore Wizard, locate and catalog the appropriate medium and return to the restore process from step 1.

7. On the Completing the Restore Wizard page, click Finish to start the restore. The restore will look something similar to Figure 32.2.

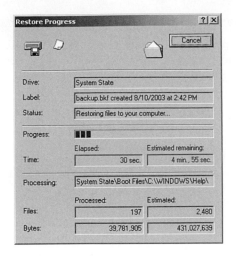

**FIGURE 32.2**   Performing a system state restore on an Exchange server.

8. When the restore is complete, review the backup log for detailed information and click Close on the Restore Progress window when finished.

9. Reboot the system as prompted.

10. When the system restarts, log in using an account with Local and/or Domain Administrator rights, as necessary.

11. After the system state is restored, Exchange Server 2003 can be installed.

## Restoring a System Using an Automated System Recovery Restore

When a system has failed and all other recovery options have been exhausted, an Automated System Recovery (ASR) restore can be performed, provided that an ASR backup has been previously performed. The ASR restore will restore all disk and volume configurations, including redefining volumes and formatting them. This means that the data stored on all volumes needs to be restored after the ASR restore is complete. This restore brings a failed system back to complete server operation, except for certain applications that require special configurations after the restore. For example, the Remote Storage service data needs to be restored separately.

> **NOTE**
>
> An ASR restore re-creates all disk volumes, but if a new or alternate system is being used, each disk must be of equal or greater size to the disks on the original server. Otherwise, the ASR restore will fail.

To perform an ASR restore, follow these steps:

1. Locate the ASR floppy created for the failed node, or create the floppy from the files saved in the ASR backup medium. For information on creating the ASR floppy from the ASR backup medium, refer to Help and Support from any Windows Server 2003 Help and Support tool.

2. Insert the Windows Server 2003 operating system medium in the CD-ROM drive of the server you are restoring to, and start the installation from this CD.

3. When prompted, press F6 to install any third-party storage device drivers, if necessary. This includes any third-party disks or tape controllers that Windows Server 2003 will not natively recognize.

4. Press F2 when prompted to perform an Automated System Recovery.

5. Insert the ASR floppy disk into the floppy drive and press Enter when prompted. If the system does not have a local floppy drive, one must temporarily be added; otherwise, an ASR restore cannot be performed.

6. The operating system installation proceeds by restoring disk volume information and reformatting the volumes associated with the operating system. When this process is complete, the operating system will restart after a short countdown, the graphic-based OS installation will begin, and the ASR backup will attempt to reconnect to the backup medium automatically. If the backup medium is on a network drive, the ASR backup reconnection will fail. If it fails, specify the network location of the backup medium using a UNC path, and enter authentication information, if prompted.

7. When the medium is located, open the medium and click Next and then Finish to begin recovering the remaining ASR data.

8. When the ASR restore is complete, if any local disk data was not restored with the ASR restore, restore all local disks.

9. Click Start, All Programs, Accessories, System Tools, Backup.

10. If this is the first time you've run Backup, it opens in Wizard mode. Choose to run it in Advanced mode by clicking the Advanced Mode hyperlink.

11. Click the Restore Wizard (Advanced) button to start the Restore Wizard.

12. Click Next on the Restore Wizard welcome screen to continue.

13. On the What to Restore page, select the appropriate cataloged backup medium, expand the catalog selection, and check the desired data on each local drive. Click Next to continue.

14. On the Completing the Restore Wizard page, click Finish to start the restore. Because you want to restore only what ASR did not, you do not need to make any advanced restore configuration changes.

15. When the restore is complete, reboot the server, if prompted.

16. After the reboot is complete, log on to the restored server and check server configuration and functionality.

17. If everything is working properly, perform a full backup and log off the server.

## Restoring the Boot Loader File

When a Windows Server 2003 system is recovered using an ASR restore, the boot.ini file might not be restored. This file contains the options for booting into different operating systems on multiboot systems and booting into the Recovery Console if it was previously installed. To restore this file, simply restore it from backup to an alternate folder or drive. Delete the boot.ini file from the C:\ root folder and move the restored file from the alternate location to C:\ or whichever drive the boot.ini file previously was located on.

# Recovering Exchange Application and Exchange Data

To recover an Exchange server, there are several different ways of rebuilding the core Exchange server and restoring the Exchange data. The restoration of Exchange databases must be done to a server with the exact same server name as the original server where the databases were backed up from.

After the Active Directory and base Windows server(s) have been installed, the first process is installing or restoring the Exchange application software; the second process is installing the data files for Exchange.

## Recovering Using Ntbackup.exe

When program and data files are corrupt or missing, or a previously backed-up copy is needed, the information can be restored using Ntbackup.exe if a previous backup was performed using this utility. The following process should be followed:

1. Log on to the server using an account that has at least the privileges to restore files and folders. Backup Operators and Local Administrator groups have this right, by default.

2. Click Start, All Programs, Accessories, System Tools, Backup.

3. If this is the first time you've run Backup, it opens in Wizard mode. Click on Next to continue with a restore.

4. Select Restore Files and Settings, and then click Next.

5. On the What to Restore page, select the appropriate cataloged backup medium, expand the catalog selection, and select to restore all applicable volumes (C:, D:, E:, and so on) and the system state. Then click Next.

6. If the correct tape or file backup medium does not appear in this window, cancel the restore process. Then, from the Restore Wizard, locate and catalog the appropriate medium and return to the restore process from step 4.

7. On the Completing the Restore Wizard page, click Finish to start the restore.

8. When the restore is complete, review the backup log for detailed information, and click Close on the Restore Progress window when finished.

9. Reboot the server. The system should come up as a complete replacement of the original server system.

> **NOTE**
>
> Third-party backup products for Exchange Server 2003 offer various backup and restore options that go beyond Ntbackup's functionality including individual mailbox or message restores as well as integration with Volume Shadow Copy Services (VSS).

## Performing a Restore of Only Exchange Database Files

If Exchange server program files have been corrupt or the restore of the full backup information from tape might restore corruption and server instability, an administrator can choose to install Exchange Server 2003 from scratch and restore just the database files. This process involves installing the Exchange program files from CD-ROM and then restoring a copy of the Exchange databases.

To install Exchange and restore the Exchange database files, do the following:

1. Log on to the server using an account that has administrative privileges to install application software as well as restore data from tape.

2. Ensure that the server has the exact same server name as it had before. Also make sure that the version of Windows is the same version.

3. Install Exchange Server 2003 using the setup /disasterrecovery command. When prompted, confirm the Disaster Recovery method of installation, as shown in Figure 32.3.

4. After Exchange Server 2003 has been installed, restore data files to the Exchange server.

### Restoring Exchange Data Files from Tape

If the Exchange data files are stored on tape, restore just the Exchange database files by doing the following:

1. Click Start, All Programs, Accessories, System Tools, Backup.

2. If this is the first time you've run Backup, it opens in Wizard mode. Choose to run it in Advanced mode by clicking the Advanced Mode hyperlink.

3. Click the Restore Wizard (Advanced) button to start the Restore Wizard.

4. Click Next on the Restore Wizard welcome screen to continue.

5.  On the What to Restore page, select the appropriate cataloged backup medium, expand the catalog selection, and select the *.edb and *.stm files for restoration.

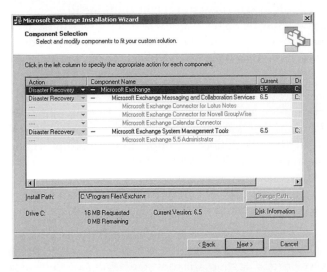

**FIGURE 32.3**    Selecting the Disaster Recovery method of installation.

The Exchange database files have the extension .edb while streaming message databases files have the .stm extension. The files are typically stored in `\Program Files\Exchsrvr\mdbdata`. However, in Exchange Server 2003, administrators can name Exchange database files and specify folder locations differently than the default settings. Also, the Enterprise edition of Exchange Server 2003 allows for up to five databases for each storage group, with up to four storage groups on a server. So, an Exchange server could potentially have 20 different directories each with a *.edb and *.stm file for the databases stored.

6.  If the correct tape or file backup medium does not appear in this window, cancel the restore process. Then, from the Restore Wizard, locate and catalog the appropriate medium and return to the restore process from step 4.

7.  On the Completing the Restore Wizard page, click Finish to start the restore.

8.  When the restore is complete, review the backup log for detailed information, and click Close on the Restore Progress window when finished. Reboot the Exchange server to restart all services. (Alternately, after a restore of data, the individual databases can just be mounted to get the Exchange server back and operational.)

# Recovering from Database Corruption

If an Exchange database is corrupt, it is not extremely effective to restore the corrupt database to a production server. The server might continue to operate, but database corruption never goes away on its own, and you eventually will have to repair the database. In fact, when minor database corruption is not repaired, the corruption can get to the point that entire sections of the Exchange database become inaccessible.

A couple methods can be used to repair a corrupt Exchange database, or at least restore the database and extract good information from the database. Key to the successful recovery of as much information as possible is using the right tool. In many cases, administrators jump right into using the ESEUTIL /p repair command; instead of repairing the Exchange database to 100% condition, the utility finds a corrupt section of the database and deletes all information from that portion of the database on. So, although the Exchange system becomes 100% clean, the utility deleted 20%–30% of the data that was in the database to get the database to a clean state. The ESEUTIL /P command is the task of last resort: Other tools work around corrupt database areas and allow the administrator to recover as much of the data as possible.

Going all the way back to the start of the chapter in the "What to Do Before Performing Any Server-Recovery Process" section, this is where having a complete backup of the databases in Exchange is really important. If a process to repair or recover information causes more harm to the database than good, there is still a backup copy to restore and start again.

## Flat File Copying the Exchange Databases

One of the best techniques Exchange experts use when working to recover corruption in a database is to make a flat file copy of the Exchange databases. A flat file copy is merely an exact copy of the Exchange databases copied to another portion of the server hard drive or to another server. To do a manual copy of the databases, do the following:

1. Unmount the Exchange database stores by going into the Exchange System Manager. Traverse the tree past Administrative Groups, Servers, Storage Group. Right-click on the mailbox store and select Dismount Store.

2. Dismount the store for all mailbox stores you will be working on.

3. Copy (using Windows Explorer, or XCOPY) the *.edb and *.stm files to a safe location (usually the filenames are priv1.edb and priv1.stm and are stored in \Program Files\Exchsrvr\mdbdata\ for the default—however, as additional databases are created, the directory names and filenames can differ).

> **NOTE**
>
> If the databases need to be manually restored, a simple XCOPY (or Windows Explorer copy) of the databases back to the original subdirectories will bring the data back to the condition the databases were in at the time the databases were copied off the system. Inside the directories (\Program Files\Exchsrvr\mdbdata or the like) are other files, such as tmp.edb, *.log, files.

These files are support files to the Exchange databases. These files could be copied off the system and then copied back if a restore is desired. The support files beyond the basic `priv1.edb`, `priv1.stm`, `pub1.edb`, and `pub1.stm` files typically need to be copied as a group. After maintenance is run on the main *.edb and *.stm files, the support files are typically unuseable because they are no longer associated with the master database files.

# 32

## Moving Mailboxes to Another Server in the Site

One way of extracting mail from a corrupt database is to move the mailbox or mailboxes to a different server in the site. Instead of trying to run utilities to fix the corruption in the database, which can take several hours (or even days, depending on the size of the database and the amount of corruption that needs to be fixed), an administrator can set up another server in the Exchange site and move the mailboxes to a new server.

Moving mailboxes grabs all of the mail, Calendar, contacts, and other mailbox information from one server and moves the information to a new server. As the information is written to the new server, the information is automatically defragmented and corruption is not migrated. Additionally, mailboxes can be moved from one server to another without ever having to bring down the production server. A mailbox user must be logged out of Outlook and must not be accessing Exchange before the mailbox can be moved. However, if mailboxes are moved when individuals are out of the office or at lunch, or on weekends, the mailboxes can be moved without users ever knowing that their information was moved from one system to another.

The two caveats to moving mailboxes are these: Corrupt mailboxes will not move, and user Outlook profiles will be changed. For Outlook profiles, because a user's Outlook profiles point to a specific server, when a mailbox is moved from one server to another, the user's profile also needs to point to the new server. Fortunately, with Exchange and Outlook, when a user's mailbox is moved, Outlook tries to access the mailbox on the original server, and the server notifies Outlook that the mailbox has been moved to a new Exchange server. The user's Outlook profile automatically changes to associate the profile to the new server where the user's mailbox resides. So, as long as the old server remains operational and the user attempts to access email from the old server, the profiles will be automatically changed the next time the user tries to access email. Typically within 1–2 weeks after moving mailboxes from one server to another, the user profiles are all automatically changed.

As for corrupt mailboxes, unfortunately, Exchange typically does not move a corrupt mailbox. So, if a user's mailbox has been corrupted, the mailbox will remain on the old server. Moving the data from the corrupt mailbox will need to be handled in a manner specified in the following section, "Extracting Mail from a Corrupt Mailbox." However, if 80%–90% of the user mailboxes can be moved to a new server, the administrators are trying to recover only a handful of mailboxes instead of all mailboxes on a server. This could mean far less downtime for all users who had mail on the server and could limit the exposure of data loss to a limited number of users.

To move mailboxes between servers in a site, do the following:

1. Open the Exchange System Manager.

2. Select the Administrative Group where the mailboxes to be moved reside.

3. Highlight the mailboxes to be moved.

4. From the Action menu, select the Exchange Tasks option and click the Next button on the welcome screen.

5. At the Available Tasks page, select Move Mailbox and click the Next button to continue.

6. Click the Mailbox Store option and choose the destination store where the mailboxes will be moved. Select Next when complete.

7. Configure the options for addressing corruption, and set the desired limits for this move. Select the Next button to begin the mailbox move.

8. Review the results of the mailbox move, and click Finish to complete the move.

## Extracting Mail from a Corrupt Mailbox

When mailboxes cannot be moved between servers, either due to mailbox corruption or because the organization does not have a spare server to move mailboxes between, one option is to use the exmerge.exe utility to export mailboxes to a file. The ExMerge utility is freely downloadable from the Microsoft downloads page at www.microsoft.com/downloads (search for "ExMerge" or "Mailbox Merge Wizard").

ExMerge allows an administrator to select specific mailboxes and export the data from the mailbox into a PST file. The PST file can then be imported (using the ExMerge utility) into another server. Unlike the Move Mailbox tool, which is an all-or-nothing migration tool, ExMerge extracts information on an item-by-item basis. When corruption is found in a user's mailbox, the corrupted item is skipped and the balance of the user's information is extracted.

The ExMerge utility can be used to extract all mailboxes from a server and import the information back into a new server. However, because ExMerge extracts and imports information item by item, it could take more than an hour to extract 1GB of mail and another hour to import that 1GB of mail back into a new server. So, if the Move Mailbox tool can migrate the information directly from one server to another over the wire, the migration process of good mailboxes goes much faster. However, for corrupt mailboxes, the ExMerge method does skip corrupt portions of mailboxes and minimizes the loss of information.

To use the ExMerge utility, do the following:

1. Download the ExMerge utility from Microsoft.

2. Extract the exmerge.exe file (this explodes out four to five ExMerge utility files).

3. Copy the files into the \Program Files\Exchsrvr\Bin directory on the Exchange server.

4. Launch the exmerge.exe program and click Next through the welcome screen.

5. Choose Export or Import (Two-Step Procedure) and click Next.

> **NOTE**
>
> The ExMerge utility has an Export and Import (One-Step Procedure) option that exports the information from one server and imports the information into another server. Exchange experts do not commonly use this because they want to isolate the export and import functions to have better control over the results. If during the export or import processes an error occurs when performing both the export and import processes, it's harder to determine whether the problem was an export problem or an import problem. It's also harder to know where the problem faulted and where to pick up to complete the data-migration process. Using the two-step procedure ensures that a clean export can be successfully completed before an import is begun. Any problem in the export or import process also can more easily be identified.

6. Select Step 1 to extract data from an Exchange server, and click on Next.

7. Enter the name of the server where the information is being extracted; then click Next.

8. Select the storage group from which the mailboxes will be extracted; then select Next.

9. Choose the mailboxes that are to be extracted (hold down the Ctrl key to select individual mailboxes, or click on the Select All button to select all mailboxes to be extracted). Click on Next to continue.

> **NOTE**
>
> The ExMerge utility extracts information from the source server, but it leaves a copy of the information in the server. This allows information to be extracted without impacting the pre-existing state of information in the source server.

10. Select the default locale or language set used for the mailbox (for example, English US). Then click Next to continue.

11. Select the drive and subdirectory where the mailbox(es) should be extracted to; then click Next.

> **NOTE**
>
> Even if the data will ultimately reside on another server, if the server being extracted has ample disk space, it is faster to have the mailboxes extracted from the server to a local hard drive than to try to write the exported data across a LAN or WAN connection to another server. Remember, you might be extracting gigabytes of information, and it's a lot faster to extract the information to a local hard drive than over even a 100Mb Ethernet connection.

12. Choose to change the filenames during the extract process and to save the settings of the configuration information, or just leave them as the default and select Next to continue. A summary screen displays the results of the extraction, as shown in Figure 32.4.

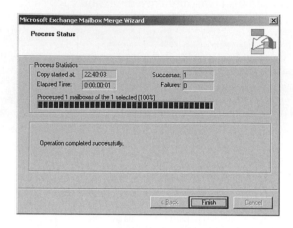

**FIGURE 32.4**    Extracting information from an Exchange database.

To import the ExMerge information to another server, the process is very similar. Do the following:

1. Launch the `exmerge.exe` program and click Next through the welcome screen.

2. Choose the Export or Import (Two-Step Procedure) option, and click Next.

3. Select Step 2 to import data into an Exchange server, and click on Next.

4. Enter the name of the server where the information will be imported, and then click Next.

5. Select the storage group into which the mailboxes will be imported; then select Next.

6. Choose the mailboxes that are to have data imported (hold down the Ctrl key to select individual mailboxes, or click on the Select All button to select all mailboxes to be extracted). Click on Next to continue.

7. Select the default locale or language set used for the mailbox (such as English US). Then click Next to continue.

8. Select the drive and subdirectory where the mailbox(es) should be imported from; then click Next.

**NOTE**

If the data currently resides on another server and there is a lot of information to import (more than 1GB), you might consider copying the files onto the hard drive of the server where the data will be imported from. This can drastically improve the import time because the file read is done on a message-by-message basis, and an XCOPY or Windows Explorer transfer of files is compressed.

9. Choose to change the filenames during the extraction process and to save the settings of the configuration information, or just leave them as default and select Next to continue. After completing, a summary screen displays the results of the import.

## Running the ISINTEG and ESEUTIL Utilities

When a database is determined to be corrupt, usually an administrator is directed to run the built-in utilities on Exchange to run maintenance on the databases. The utilities are the ISINTEG ("eye-ess-in-tehg") and ESEUTIL ("ee-ess-ee-u-tihl"). However, depending on the condition of the database, a very corrupt database can take several hours to run, only to result in the loss of data. Some administrators are incorrectly told to never run the utilities because they will always result in loss of data. It's typically just a lack of knowledge of how the utilities work that leads to misunderstanding the potential results of the databases.

As noted in the previous two sections, there might be better options for recovering information from a corrupt database. Instead of trying to fix a known corrupt database, simply migrating the information off a server or extracting information from corrupt databases is frequently a better fix. However, if the determination is to run the utilities, a few things should be noted:

1. The ISINTEG utility is a high-level utility that checks the consistency of the database, validating the branches of the database that handle data, data directory tables, attachment objects, and the like. Fixing the database table makes way for a more intensive data integrity check of the database.

2. The ESEUTIL utility is a low-level utility that checks the data within the database. ESEUTIL does not differentiate between a corrupt section of the database and how that section impacts mailboxes or messages. So, when a complete repair is performed using ESEUTIL, entire mailboxes can be deleted or all attachments for the entire database can be eliminated to fix the corruption. This is why running ESEUTIL to repair a database is a function of last resort.

3. To run ISINTEG on a database takes around 1 hour for every 10GB being scanned for a moderately corrupt database. The repairs are done relatively quickly, and the database is ready for more extensive scanning.

4. Running ESEUTIL on a database takes anywhere from 1 hour for every 10GB to up to 1 hour per 1GB, depending on the level of repair being performed. It is not unreasonable to see a relatively corrupt 30GB database take more than 24 hours to complete the repair.

5. ISINTEG and ESEUTIL can be performed only offline, meaning that the Exchange server is offline during the process. Users cannot access their mailboxes during the ISINTEG and ESEUTIL processes. Thus, if it takes 20–40 hours of downtime to complete the repair of a database, the Move Mailbox method that can be run without bringing servers offline is frequently a more palatable solution.

6. However, if run on a regular basis, the ISINTEG and ESEUTIL utilities can clean up an Exchange database before serious corruption occurs. Administrators who get scared off performing maintenance because of the potential threat of losing data could actually minimize their chance of data corruption if the utilities are run regularly. See Chapter 19 for recommended maintenance practices.

The common parameters used for the ISINTEG and ESEUTIL utilities are as follows. For regular maintenance such as checking the database structure's integrity and performing defragmentation of the database, the following commands should be run:

```
isinteg –s SERVERNAME –test allfoldertests
```

```
eseutil /d priv1.edb
```

When run against an Exchange Server 2003 system, the ISINTEG utility produces a summary similar to the one in Figure 32.5.

**FIGURE 32.5**    Results from an ISINTEG utility run.

> **NOTE**
>
> The ISINTEG and ESEUTIL utilities typically reside in the \Program Files\Exchsrvr\Bin directory of the Exchange server. The databases that are typically specified in ESEUTIL are the priv1.edb and pub1.edb. However, if an organization has multiple database and storage groups, several databases might need to be checked separately for integrity.

When a database needs to be repaired, eseutil /p priv1.edb can be run. Beware: The /p repair command is a brute-force repair and deletes sections of the database to make the integrity of the database clean. A message provides an additional warning about ESEUTIL, as shown in Figure 32.6. When running the /p command in ESEUTIL, entire sections of the database might be deleted to repair and recover the state of the database.

> **NOTE**
>
> Prior to a disaster, if the ISINTEG or ESEUTIL utilities have not been run against an Exchange database for a long period of time, restore the database from tape to an Exchange server in a lab environment to run tests. These tests can tell you how much corruption may be present as well as give an indication of how long it may take to repair the database.

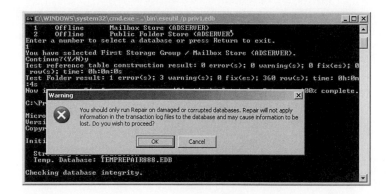

**FIGURE 32.6**   ESEUTIL warning when a database repair (/p) is run.

## Using the Recovery Storage Group in Exchange Server 2003

When an administrator wants to recover a mail message, a Calendar appointment, a contact, a folder, or entire user mailboxes, Exchange Server 2003 has a Recovery Storage Group function and wizard that provides a recovery mechanism. In the past, if an administrator wanted to recover a mailbox or information, the administrator would have to build a brand-new Exchange server with the exact same server name in the lab and then restore a database to the lab server. After the restore, the administrator could run the ExMerge utility to export the desired mailbox or information, and then transfer the information to the production server and ExMerge the information back into the production server.

The recovery storage group in Exchange Server 2003 facilitates the restore of any database, including an Exchange 2000 SP3 or higher database from any server within an Administrative Group. So, an Exchange database can be restored to the recovery storage group, and then information can be extracted without ever having to bring up another server or shut down the production server.

## Recovering Data with a Recovery Storage Group

A recovery storage group is created on any Exchange Server 2003 system in an Administrative Group where the original database resides. To create a recovery storage group, do the following:

1.  Launch the Exchange System Manager utility.

2.  Traverse the tree past the Administrative Group and past the servers. Right-click on the name of the server that will host the recovery storage group and select New, Recovery Storage Group, as shown in Figure 32.7.

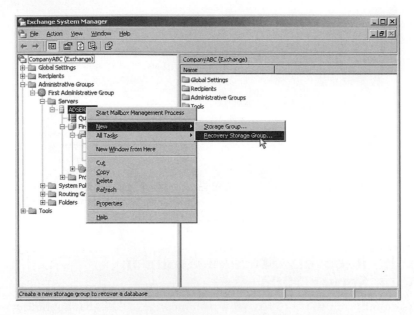

**FIGURE 32.7**  Adding a recovery storage group to Exchange Server 2003.

---

**NOTE**

The server that will host the recovery storage group must have enough disk space to allow for the full restore of the database that will be hosted on the system.

---

3.  Specify the name of the recovery storage group as well as the location of the database and logs, or just select the defaults and click OK to continue. A recovery storage group container is added to the server.

4.  Right-click on the recovery storage group container and select Add Database to Recover. Select the mailbox store you want to recover, and click OK.

5.  Launch your tape software and restore the database you want to recover to a temporary subdirectory.

6. When the restore is complete, right-click on the mailbox store in the recovery storage group and select Mount Store.

7. Optionally, you can use the ExMerge utility covered in the section "Extracting Mail from a Corrupt Mailbox," earlier in this chapter or use the Recovery Storage Group (RSG) Wizard as described in the following steps.

> **NOTE**
>
> The RSG Wizard is available with Exchange SP1 and higher. Use ExMerge to obtain mailbox rules and permissions or to filter items.

8. In the left pane, expand the mailbox store and then click the Mailboxes folder.

9. In the right pane, right click the mailbox to restore and then click Exchange Tasks. This action will display the Exchange Task Wizard window.

10. Click Next at the Welcome screen and then select Recover Mailbox Data. Click Next when done.

11. Verify the destination and then click Next.

12. The next screen gives you the option to either merge or copy the data as shown in Figure 32.8. Copying the data will place the recovered items into a separate folder whereas the merge feature merges the items into the mailbox. Select either option and click Next.

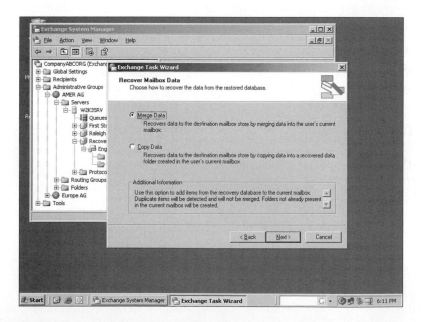

**FIGURE 32.8**    Choosing between merging and copying recovered items using the RSG Wizard.

13. Either run the recovery process now or schedule it and then click Next. If it was scheduled to run immediately, the process will kick off after clicking Next.

14. Click Finish when done.

# Recovering Internet Information Services

When Internet Information Services (IIS) data is erased or the service is not functioning as desired, restoring the configuration might be necessary. To restore the IIS metabase data, perform the following steps:

1. Log on to the desired IIS server using an account with Local Administrator privileges.

2. Click Start, Programs, Administrative Tools, Internet Information Services (IIS) to start the IIS Manager.

3. Select the Web server in the left pane.

4. Select Action, All Tasks, Backup/Restore Configuration.

5. On the Configuration Backup/Restore page appears a listing of automatic backups that IIS has already performed. Select the desired backup and click the Restore button to perform a manual restore.

6. A pop-up window opens stating that all Internet services will be stopped to restore the data and restarted afterward. Click Yes to begin the restore.

7. When the restore is complete, a confirmation pop-up window is displayed. Click OK to close this window.

8. Click Close on the Configuration Backup/Restore page.

9. Back in the IIS Manager window, verify that the restore was successful, close the window, and log off the server when you're finished.

Backups are stored in `%systemroot%\system32\Inetsrv\MetaBack`, by default.

### Recovering IIS Data and Logs

IIS Web and FTP folders are stored in the `C:\InetPub\` directory. The default location for the IIS logs is `C:\Windows\system32\LogFiles`. To recover the IIS Web site, FTP site, or IIS logs, restore the files using either shadow copy data or a backup/restore tool such as Ntbackup.exe.

# Recovering the Cluster Service

Cluster nodes require that special backup and restore procedures be followed to ensure a successful recovery if a cluster failure is encountered. For detailed information on backing up and restoring a cluster node, refer to Chapter 30, or use the Windows Server 2003 Help and Support tool.

# Recovering Windows Server 2003 Domain Controllers

When a Windows Server 2003 domain controller fails, the administrator needs to either recover this server or understand how to completely and properly remove this domain controller from the domain. The following are some questions to consider:

- Did this domain controller host any of the domain or forest Flexible Single Master Operations (FSMO) roles?

- Was this domain controller a Global Catalog (GC) server and, if so, was it the only GC in a single Active Directory site?

- If the server failed due to Active Directory corruption, has the corruption been replicated to other domain controllers?

- Is this server a replication hub or bridgehead server for Active Directory site replication?

Using the preceding list of questions, the administrator can decide how best to deal with the failure. For example, if the failed domain controller hosted the PDC emulator FSMO role, the server could be restored or the FSMO role could be manually seized by a separate domain controller. If the domain controller was the bridgehead server for Active Directory site replication, recovering this server might make the most sense so that the desired primary replication topology remains intact. The administrator should recover a failed domain controller as any other server would be recovered, restore the OS from an ASR restore or build a clean server, restore the system state, and perform subsequent restores of local drive data as necessary.

# Recovering Active Directory

When undesired changes are made in Active Directory or the Active Directory database is corrupted on a domain controller, recovering the Active Directory database might be necessary. Restoring Active Directory can seem like a difficult task, unless frequent backups are performed and the administrator understands all the restore options.

## The Active Directory Database

The Active Directory database contains all the information stored in Active Directory. The Global Catalog information is also stored in this database. The actual filename is `ntds.dit` and, by default, is located in `C:\Windows\NTDS\`. When a domain controller is restored from server failure, the Active Directory database is restored with the system state. If no special steps are taken when the server comes back online, it will ask any other domain controllers for a copy of the latest version of the Active Directory database. This situation is called a *nonauthoritative restore* of Active Directory.

When a change in Active Directory needs to be rolled back or the entire database needs to be rolled back across the enterprise or domain, an authoritative restore of the Active Directory database is necessary.

### Active Directory Nonauthoritative Restore

When a domain controller is rebuilt from a backup after a complete system failure, simply recovering this server using a restore of the local drives and system state is enough to get this machine back into the production network. When the machine is back online and establishes connectivity to other domain controllers, any Active Directory and SYSVOL updates will be replicated to the restored server.

Nonauthoritative restores are also necessary when a single domain controller's copy of the Active Directory database is corrupt and is keeping the server from booting up properly. To restore a reliable copy of the Active Directory database, the entire system state needs to be restored; if additional services reside on the domain controller, restoring the previous configuration data for each of these services might be undesirable. In a situation like this, the best option is to try to recover the Active Directory database using database maintenance and recovery utilities such as Esentutl.exe and Ntdsutil.exe. These utilities can be used to check the database consistency, defragment, and repair and troubleshoot the Active Directory database. For information on Active Directory maintenance practices with these utilities, refer to Windows Server 2003 Help and Support.

To restore the Active Directory database to a single domain controller to recover from database corruption, perform the following steps:

1. Power up the domain controller and press the F8 key when the boot loader is displayed on the screen.

2. When the advanced boot options are displayed, scroll down, select Directory Services Restore Mode, and then press Enter to boot the server. This mode boots the Active Directory database in an offline state. When you choose this boot option, you can maintain and restore the Active Directory database.

3. When the server boots up, log on using the username Administrator and the Restore Mode password specified when the server was promoted to a domain controller. To change the Restore Mode password on a domain controller running in Normal Mode, use the Ntdsutil.exe utility; this process is covered in Chapter 31.

4. Click Start, Run.

5. Type **Ntbackup.exe** and click OK.

6. When the Backup or Restore window opens, click the Advanced Mode hyperlink.

7. Select the Restore and Manage Media tab.

8. Select the appropriate backup medium, expand it, and check the system state. If the correct medium is not available, the file must be located or the tape must be loaded in the tape drive and cataloged before it can be used to restore the system state.

9. Choose to restore the data to the original location, and click the Start Restore button in the lower-right corner of the backup window.

10. A pop-up window indicates that restoring the system state to the original location will overwrite the current system state. Click OK to continue.

11. A confirm restore window opens in which you can choose advanced restore options. Click OK to initiate the restore of the system state.

12. When the restore is complete, a system restart is necessary to update the services and files restored during this operation. Because only a nonauthoritative restore of the Active Directory database is necessary, click Yes to restart the server.

13. After the server reboots, log in as a domain administrator.

14. Check the server event log and Active Directory information to ensure that the database has been restored successfully. Then log off the server.

### Active Directory Authoritative Restore

When a change made to Active Directory is causing problems, or when an object is modified or deleted and needs to be recovered to the entire enterprise, an Active Directory Authoritative Restore is necessary.

To perform an authoritative restore of the Active Directory database, follow these steps:

1. Power up the domain controller and press the F8 key when the boot loader is displayed on the screen.

2. When the advanced boot options are displayed, scroll down, select Directory Services Restore Mode, and press Enter to boot the server. This mode boots the Active Directory database in an offline state. When you choose this boot option, you can maintain and restore the Active Directory database.

3. When the server boots up, log in using the username Administrator and the Restore Mode password specified when the server was promoted to a domain controller. To change the Restore Mode password on a domain controller running in Normal Mode, use the Ntdsutil.exe utility; this process is covered in Chapter 31.

4. Click Start, Run.

5. Type **Ntbackup.exe** and click OK.

6. When the Backup or Restore window opens, click the Advanced Mode hyperlink.

7. Select the Restore and Manage Media tab.

8. Select the appropriate backup medium, expand it, and check the system state. If the correct medium is not available, the file must be located, or the tape must be loaded in the tape drive and cataloged before it can be used to restore the system state.

9. Choose to restore the data to the original location, and click the Start Restore button in the lower-right corner of the backup window.

10. A pop-up window indicates that restoring the system state to the original location will overwrite the current system state. Click OK to continue.

11. A confirm restore window opens in which you can choose advanced restore options. Click OK to initiate the restore of the system state.

12. When the restore is complete, a system restart is necessary to update the services and files restored during this operation. Because only a nonauthoritative restore of the Active Directory database is necessary, click No.

13. Close the backup window and click Start, Run.

14. Type `cmd.exe` and click OK to open a command prompt.

15. At the command prompt, type `ntdsutil.exe` and press Enter.

16. Type `Authoritative restore` and press Enter.

17. Type `Restore Database` and press Enter to restore the entire database. The respective Active Directory partitions, such as the schema partition and the domain-naming context partition, are replicated to all other appropriate domain controllers in the domain and/or forest.

18. An authoritative restore confirmation dialog box appears; click Yes to start the authoritative restore.

19. The command prompt window displays whether the authoritative restore was successful. Close the command-prompt and reboot the server.

20. Boot up the server in Normal mode, log in, and open the correct Active Directory tools to verify whether the restore was successful. Also, check on other domain controllers to ensure that the restore is being replicated to them.

21. When you're done, perform a full backup of the domain controller or at least the system state; then log off the server when the backup is complete.

### Partial Active Directory Authoritative Restore

Most Active Directory authoritative restores are performed to recover from a modification or deletion of an Active Directory object. For example, a user account might have been deleted instead of disabled, or an Organizational Unit's security might have been changed and the administrator is locked out. Recovering only a specific object, such as a user account or an Organizational Unit or a container, requires the distinguished name (DN) of that object. To find the distinguished name, the administrator can use the Ntdsutil utility; however, if an LDIF dump of Active Directory exists, this file is more helpful. If no LDIF file exists and the DN of the object to be recovered is unknown, the recovery of the single object or container is not possible.

To simplify the steps to partial recovery, you will recover a single user account using the logon john that was previously contained in the Users container in the Companyabc.com domain. To restore the user account, follow these steps:

1. Power up the domain controller and press the F8 key when the boot loader is displayed on the screen.

2. When the advanced boot options are displayed, scroll down, select Directory Services Restore Mode, and press Enter to boot the server. This mode boots the

Active Directory database in an offline state. When you choose this boot option, you can maintain and restore the Active Directory database.

3.  When the server boots up, log in using the username Administrator and the Restore Mode password specified when the server was promoted to a domain controller. To change the Restore Mode password on a domain controller running in Normal Mode, use the Ntdsutil.exe utility; this process is covered in Chapter 31.

4.  Click Start, Run.

5.  Type **Ntbackup.exe** and click OK.

6.  When the Backup or Restore window opens, click the Advanced Mode hyperlink.

7.  Select the Restore and Manage Media tab.

8.  Select the appropriate backup medium, expand it, and check the system state. If the correct medium is not available, the file must be located, or the tape must be loaded in the tape drive and cataloged before it can be used to restore the system state.

9.  Choose to restore the data to the original location, and click the Start Restore button in the lower-right corner of the backup window.

10. A pop-up window indicates that restoring the system state to the original location will overwrite the current system state. Click OK to continue.

11. A confirm restore window opens in which you can choose advanced restore options. Click OK to initiate the restore of the system state.

12. When the restore is complete, a system restart is necessary to update the services and files restored during this operation. Because only a nonauthoritative restore of the Active Directory database is necessary, click No.

13. Close the backup window and click Start, Run.

14. Type **cmd.exe** and click OK to open a command prompt.

15. At the command prompt, type **ntdsutil.exe** and press Enter.

16. Type **Authoritative restore** and press Enter.

17. Type **Restore Object "cn=John,cn=Users,dc=companyabc,dc=com"** and press Enter.

18. The success or failure status of the restore appears in the command prompt. Now type **quit** and press Enter. Repeat this step until you reach the C: prompt.

19. Close the command-prompt windows and reboot the server.

20. Log on to the server with a Domain Administrator account, and verify that the account has been restored. Then log off the server.

### Global Catalog

No special restore considerations exist for restoring a Global Catalog server other than those outlined for restoring Active Directory in the previous sections. The Global Catalog data is re-created based on the contents of the Active Directory database.

### Restoring the SYSVOL Folder

The SYSVOL folder contains the system policies, Group Policies, computer startup/ shutdown scripts, and user logon/logoff scripts. If a previous version of a script or Group Policy Object is needed, the SYSVOL folder must be restored. As a best practice and to keep the process simple, the SYSVOL folder should be restored to an alternate location where specific files can be restored. When the restored files are placed in the SYSVOL folder, the File Replication Service recognizes the file as new or a changed version and replicates it to the remaining domain controllers. If the entire SYSVOL folder needs to be pushed out to the remaining domain controllers and the Active Directory database is intact, a primary restore of the SYSVOL is necessary.

To perform a primary restore of the SYSVOL folder, follow these steps:

1. Power up the domain controller and press the F8 key when the boot loader is displayed on the screen.

2. When the advanced boot options are displayed, scroll down, select Directory Services Restore Mode, and press Enter to boot the server. This mode boots the Active Directory database in an offline state. When you choose this boot option, you can maintain and restore the Active Directory database.

3. When the server boots up, log in using the username Administrator and the Restore Mode password specified when the server was promoted to a domain controller. To change the Restore Mode password on a domain controller running in Normal Mode, use the Ntdsutil.exe utility; this process is covered in Chapter 31.

4. Click Start, Run.

5. Type **Ntbackup.exe** and click OK.

6. When the Backup or Restore window opens, click the Advanced Mode hyperlink.

7. Select the Restore and Manage Media tab.

8. Select the appropriate backup medium, expand it, and check the system state. If the correct medium is not available, the file must be located, or the tape must be loaded in the tape drive and cataloged before it can be used to restore the system state.

9. Choose to restore the data to the original location, and click the Start Restore button in the lower-right corner of the backup window.

10. A pop-up window indicates that restoring the system state to the original location will overwrite the current system state. Click OK to continue.

11. A confirm restore window opens in which you can choose advanced restore options. Click the Advanced button to view the advanced restore options.

12. Check the box labeled When Restoring Replicated Data Sets, Mark the Restored Data as the Primary Data for All Replicas.

13. Click OK to return to the Confirm Restore page, and click OK to start the restore.

14. When the restore is complete, a system restart is necessary to update the services and files restored during this operation. Because only a nonauthoritative restore of the Active Directory database is necessary, click Yes to restart the server.

15. After the server reboots, log in using an account with Domain Administrator access.

16. Check the server event log and the SYSVOL folder to ensure that the data has been restored successfully. Log off the server when you're finished.

## Summary

Recovering from a disaster in Exchange Server 2003 involves a variety of different options. Exchange Server 2003 provides several ways to recover from a variety of different disasters—not simply recovering an entire server in case of a major disaster, but also recovering information that was lost due to data corruption or simply because a user deleted a message or a folder. Disaster recovery takes several different forms and levels based on the recovery needs of the organization.

An important factor in any recovery is to have proper documentation on the configuration of the Exchange environment. Be sure to have documented server names, server configurations, and messaging routing information so that when a recovery process needs to be conducted, the administrators know the impact that a change in one site might have on other sites and locations.

When performing recovery of information in Exchange, the process needs to involve the isolation of the problem, whether the problem is specific to Exchange or is related to Active Directory or other network services. Because the Global Catalog in Active Directory is the core directory for Exchange, knowing how to recover the Active Directory Global Catalog is an important task for an Exchange administrator to understand.

And if the recovery process involves recovery due to database corruption, instead of jumping in and running Exchange utilities to repair the Exchange database, other alternatives can be used, such as migrating mailboxes off of production servers onto new servers within a site. The tools involve not only the Mailbox Move function, but also the ExMerge utility.

Finally, with tools such as the recovery storage group, the administrators of an Exchange environment can restore an Exchange database to a server without having to rebuild an entire server in the lab. Just restoring the data to a temporary server allows the administrator to extract the necessary information needed to recover information.

With all the tools available for recovery, an administrator of an Exchange Server 2003 environment has far more options available for recovery of a single message, folder, mailbox, or entire server than ever. By using the right tool for the right task, the administrator can provide a much better response to resolving Exchange server–related problems.

## Best Practices

- Consider multiple alternatives beyond restoring an entire server or running the built-in Exchange utilities when analyzing recovery methods.

- Having good documentation on the Exchange environment makes for an easier time in recovering from system failures.

- Use the `setup /disasterrecovery` command to greatly simplify the recovery process in Exchange.

- Perform an offline copy of the database using XCOPY before performing any maintenance.

- Move mailboxes from an old server with corrupt databases to a new server in the same site to minimize downtime.

- Extract mail from an old server using the ExMerge utility to a new server to extract good data and leave corrupt portions of information on the old system.

- Running the `ISINTEG` and `ESEUTIL` utilities on a regular basis for maintenance helps maintain the integrity of Exchange databases.

- Use a recovery storage group whenever possible to simplify the recovery of information from backup.

- Test Active Directory recovery in a lab.

# CHAPTER 33

# Capacity Analysis and Performance Optimization

**IN THIS CHAPTER**

- Examining Exchange Server 2003 Performance Improvements
- Analyzing Capacity
- Monitoring Exchange Server 2003
- Analyzing and Monitoring Core Elements
- Properly Sizing Exchange Server 2003
- Optimizing Exchange Through Ongoing Maintenance
- Monitoring Exchange with Microsoft Operations Manager

Technology enhancements in Exchange Server 2003, in comparison to its predecessor, Exchange Server 2000, afford new optimization in performance. These enhancements can improve the messaging environment's reliability, availability, and scalability. In order to be able to make use of these features, however, you must carefully plan the deployment of Exchange Server 2003. This involves proper capacity planning and analysis of areas wherein a well-planned configuration can make an enormous difference in performance.

Capacity analysis and performance optimization processes and procedures are, most often, low-priority tasks. This is frequently because productivity is regularly measured by what can be achieved now and not always what can be properly planned or designed. The benefits of capacity analysis and performance monitoring can be obtained in the short term, but they are more important when established over longer periods of time. As a result, the main focus of most IT departments shifts to the more immediate and more tangible day-to-day processes and IT needs.

The results of capacity analysis and performance optimization save organizations of all sizes time, effort, and expenditures. This chapter is designed to provide best practices for properly and proactively performing capacity analysis and performance optimization so that IT personnel can work more effectively and efficiently, organizations can capture savings, and the Exchange Server 2003 infrastructure can optimally operate.

# Examining Exchange Server 2003 Performance Improvements

Before delving into ways to tweak Exchange Server 2003 performance, it is important to have an understanding of the performance improvements that have been made since its predecessor, Exchange 2000. Although some of these performance improvements are more noticeable than others, Exchange Server 2003 has proven its ability to scale into the enterprise and beyond.

## Communication Improvements

Exchange Server 2003 includes major improvements in the way it handles client/server communications. These improvements entail changes made to communication links between sites, servers, and users. Implemented changes translate into a fundamentally different approach toward how Exchange Server 2003 handles routing of messages from site to site as well as to and from the client computer.

### Improvements in Link State Connections

In order to determine the best possible route to send a message between servers, Exchange uses link state routing technology. The best route is chosen based on the status and the cost of the connections. While routing messages between servers and sites, no alternate paths might be available to Exchange Server 2003 servers, or the existing connectors might be intermittently available. By determining whether there are alternate and available connections, Exchange Server 2003 significantly reduces the amount of traffic between servers.

Another performance improvement with Exchange Server 2003 analyzing links between servers is how it efficiently propagates link status information to other servers in and between sites. If no alternate paths are detected for a message to take, the available route is marked as always in service. Exchange will never change this state back to an out-of-service state unless an alternate path becomes available. As a result, propagation of link state information in and between sites is reduced, and consequently overall network traffic is optimized.

### Global Catalog Placement and Caching

The Active Directory (AD) global catalog is intimately tied to the operation of Exchange Server 2003. Exchange uses the global catalog server for queries and is critical for services such as logon, group membership, global address list (GAL), and more.

For many organizations, following the golden rule of using a global catalog server in the same site and domain as a mailbox server serves the purpose of improving performance for the types of services described earlier. In addition, with the combination of Windows Server 2003 and Exchange Server 2003 Service Pack (SP) 1 or later, Exchange provides the ability to cache group and distribution list membership. This speeds up membership lookup prior to sending messages. For more information on planning and designing Exchange Server 2003, refer to chapters in Part II, "Exchange Server 2003."

### Synchronization and Replication Enhancements

Synchronization and replication enhancements available in Exchange Server 2003 can be analyzed from various viewpoints. Generally speaking, these enhancements include changes made to the Outlook client, Outlook Web Access client, and public folders.

## Client-Side Performance Enhancements

Among the new performance-enhancing features of Exchange Server 2003 and Outlook 2003 is the ability to collect client-side data by recording RPC errors that occur on the client. This information is then reported in the Event Viewer.

### Outlook 2003 Client Synchronization

Significant reduction of Remote Procedure Calls (RPCs) to the Exchange Server from the Outlook 2003 client has resulted in noticeable improvements in client performance even in low-bandwidth conditions. This improvement was primarily made available through the employment of the following features:

- **Cached Exchange Mode**—Cached Exchange Mode refers to the Outlook 2003 client keeping a local copy of the user's mailbox on the client computer. This is similar to an Offline Folder (OST) file in earlier versions of Exchange. There are some differences, however: This mode requires less configuration (as shown in Figure 33.1), uses the Offline Address Book (OAB) by default, and copies the entire mailbox rather than relying on the user to specify which folders to synchronize with Exchange Server 2003. Although this reduces the number of data requests sent to the server, this mode also determines whether or not the connection with Exchange is slow (128KB or less) and then adapts accordingly. For instance, if the user connects via the corporate LAN, the full message, including attachments, is copied to the local cached copy. If the user later connects using a 56KB modem, only headers are copied unless the user opens the message. This is done automatically and is transparent to the user.

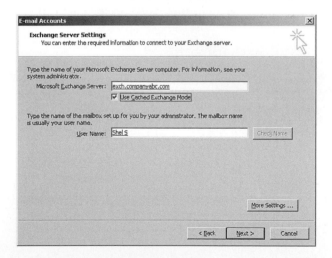

**FIGURE 33.1**   Cached Exchange Mode option.

- **Outlook Synchronization**—Synchronization communication between the Outlook client and Exchange Server 2003 uses data compression to reduce traffic overhead. Changes that are made through the Outlook client are also sent to Exchange Server 2003 incrementally, thereby providing additional network traffic optimization.

## Outlook Web Access (OWA) Performance Enhancements

An abundance of new features are available in OWA, and the biggest one by far is the interface. However, the following primary features contribute to performance enhancements:

- **Compression Support**—OWA compression uses GZip to keep bandwidth requirements low and improves response times even over dial-up or other low-bandwidth connections. Configuring OWA to use high compression (that is, compression of static and dynamic pages) can reduce bandwidth requirements as much as 50%. It is important to note that clients must use Internet Explorer (IE) 6 (or Netscape 6) or higher in order to take advantage of OWA compression.

- **Logon Options**—Outlook Web Access is now available in two configurations: Premium and Basic Experience. These two configurations are presented to users at the time of login and depending on available bandwidth, the user can choose which version of OWA to load, thus improving performance.

## Improved Public Folder Store Replication

Public folder store replication has greatly improved in respect to the way Exchange Server 2003 handles the receipt of updates from various other servers. In Exchange 2000 Server, a server holding the largest number of needed updates would always be chosen regardless of its transport cost. When determining update status during the replication process, Exchange Server 2003 takes the following three main elements into account on a priority basis and calculates the replication algorithm based on the data gathered from these questions:

- Which server has the lowest transport cost?

- For servers with equal transport costs, which server is the newest version of Exchange?

- For servers with equal transport costs and versions, which server owns the greater number of updates?

This architecture enables reduction of replication traffic over slower links because lower-cost servers (servers in the same site) always take precedence over higher-cost servers (those located in remote sites).

> **NOTE**
>
> Exchange Server 2003 Service Pack 2 (SP2) minimizes public folder replication storms by giving administrators the ability to temporarily stop public folder content replication before performing any administration or reconfiguration. Administrators can stop and then later resume replication by right-clicking within the public folder hierarchy. In addition, administrators can right-click the top-level folder structure and select Synchronize Hierchary to synchronize just the folder structure (that is, not the contents).

## Performance Scalability Improvements

Some of the Exchange Server 2003 enhancements to performance and scalability are

- **Improved Distribution List Member Caching**—The processing resources required to look up the membership of Distribution Lists has been greatly reduced by redesigning the cache rule in a way that lookups and insertions can be achieved by 60% fewer Distribution List–related queries made against the Active Directory. Therefore, a small AD performance optimization has been achieved by changes made to the cache rule.

- **Enhanced Internet Mail Delivery**—Exchange Server 2003 relies heavily on Windows Server 2003 DNS for message delivery, and the algorithms used relating to load-balanced DNS-based Internet delivery have been enhanced. In circumstances where the external DNS Server is not available or the network is experiencing latency, Exchange Server 2003 has greater tolerance, which results in a greater reliability of message delivery.

# Analyzing Capacity

Capacity analysis for an Exchange Server 2003 environment requires a well-established understanding of the business and messaging needs of the organization and a well-documented outline of the organization's expectations of its messaging environment. Business constantly undergoes change, and so do capacity requirements and measurements of an organization.

The first step in capacity analysis is to grasp an understanding of these changes and define performance expectations. This can be done by establishing policies and service-level agreements. It is in these policies and service-level agreements that an administrator can outline acceptable performance thresholds and more accurately gauge the capacity needs of Exchange Server 2003. These thresholds can also be used to accurately establish performance baselines from which to analyze the requirements against available resources.

To help develop the policies and service-level agreements, use questionnaires, interviews, business objectives, and the like along with performance measurements.

## Establishing Baselines

The importance of establishing meaningful baselines of the messaging environment cannot be underscored enough. Baselines are particularly important in the sense that they are the measurable tools that can be used to balance what is required of Exchange Server 2003 with what resources are needed to fulfill those requirements. Achieving this balance can be made simpler if an administrator consults performance metrics, such as industry-standard benchmarks.

> **NOTE**
>
> Use ExchDump to assist with baselining the environment. ExchDump exports a server's configuration, which can be useful to determine whether or not the build follows company standards. This is particularly important with Exchange clusters since each node in the cluster should be a replica of the other.

In order to establish an accurate baseline of Exchange Server 2003, there are a number of tools that can help an administrator in this process. These tools are discussed in detail in the following sections. Some of these capacity analysis tools are built in to Windows Server 2003, and others are built in to Exchange Server 2003. Many third-party tools and utilities are also available for the careful measurement of Exchange Server 2003 capacity requirements and performance analysis.

### Using the Exchange Best Practices Analyzer Tool

The Exchange Best Practices Analyzer (ExBPA) is a utility provided by Microsoft that analyzes an Exchange server's configuration and informs administrators on possible configuration changes that can be made to improve performance or mitigate problems. More specifically, ExBPA can be used to perform a health check, a health and performance check, a connectivity test, and baseline test. This tool can be downloaded at `http://www.microsoft.com/downloads` by searching on ExBPA. After downloading ExBPA.msi, double-click the file and follow the installation steps. Once installed, ExBPA can be executed from the Start, All Programs, Microsoft Exchange menu by selecting Best Practices Analyzer Tool.

To begin the analysis to determine what configuration parameters you may want to consider modifying, do the following:

1. Open ExBPA and then click Connect to the Active Directory Server. ExBPA will try and locate the nearest global catalog server but you can also specify a specific server.

2. Label the test and then select the scope of the scan.

3. Select the type of scan (for example, Health Check) and then click Start Scanning. By default, ExBPA will set to scan all Exchange servers it can locate within the scope that you have set. Optionally, you can define the network speed to optimize scanning time as well as schedule the scan.

4. Once the scanning is complete, click View a Report of This Best Practice Scan to display the generated report. As Figure 33.2 shows, there are many different reports viewing options and you can drill down to see the issue and any recommendations that may be provided.

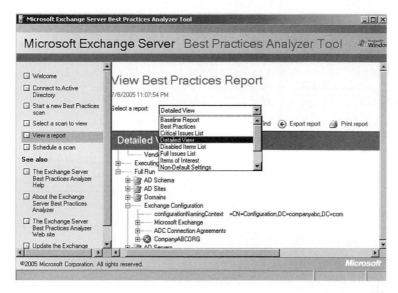

**FIGURE 33.2**   Viewing ExBPA reports.

# Monitoring Exchange Server 2003

A variety of built-in Microsoft tools is available to help an administrator establish the baseline of the Exchange Server 2003 environment. Among these, the Performance Monitor Microsoft Management Console (MMC) snap-in is one of the most common tools used to measure the capacity requirements of Exchange Server 2003.

## Using the Performance Monitor Console

The Performance snap-in enables an in-depth analysis of every measurable aspect of the Exchange server. The information that is gathered using the Performance snap-in can be presented in a variety of forms—including reports, real-time charts, or logs—which add to the versatility of this tool. The resulting output formats enable an administrator to present a baseline analysis in real-time or through historical data. The Performance snap-in, shown in Figure 33.3, can be launched from the Start, Administrative Tools menu.

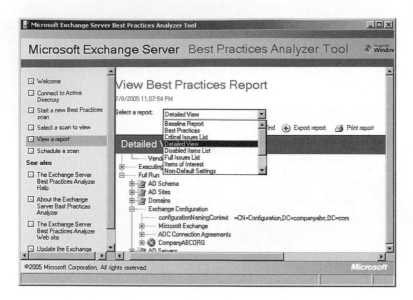

**FIGURE 33.3**    The Performance snap-in.

## Using Network Monitor

The Network Monitor, as illustrated in Figure 33.4, is a reliable capacity-analysis tool used specifically to monitor network traffic. There are two flavors of the Network Monitor: one that is built in to Windows Server 2003 and one that is provided in System Management Server (SMS). The one included with Windows Server 2003 is a more downscaled version. It is capable of monitoring network traffic to and from the local server on which it runs. The SMS version monitors network traffic coming to or from any computer on the network and enables you to monitor network traffic from a centralized machine. This facilitates gathering capacity analysis data, but it is also important to note that it could present possible security risks because of its ability to promiscuously monitor traffic throughout the network.

## Using Task Manager

Task Manager displays real-time performance metrics, so an administrator can quickly get an overall idea of how Exchange Server 2003 is performing at any given time. Its biggest downfall, however, is that it does not store any historical data, so it not a suitable tool for capacity analysis purposes.

## Simulating Stress with Jetstress

Jetstress is a tool written by the Microsoft Exchange product group to help IT personnel with capacity and performance analysis of the disk subsystem on an Exchange system prior to deploying in a production environment.

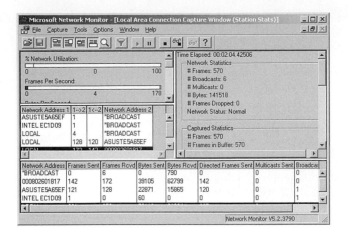

**FIGURE 33.4**   The Network Monitor interface.

An administrator can put the Exchange server's disk subsystem to the test using simulated I/O workloads mimicking an Exchange environment. Jetstress is broken into two tests (Jetstress Disk Performance Test or the Jetstress Disk Subsystem Stress Test), which can be used to test Exchange storage or the entire disk subsystem. The tests run for 2 and 24 hours, respectively, and Microsoft recommends running both tests to adequately determine the Exchange Server 2003 disk subsystem configuration, performance, and reliability.

> **NOTE**
>
> Jetstress is a free utility that can be downloaded from Microsoft's Web site:
>
> http://www.microsoft.com/exchange/downloads/2003/default.mspx
>
> It is recommended that you read the Jetstress documentation before installing and using this tool.

## Analyzing and Monitoring Core Elements

The capacity analysis and performance optimization process can be intimidating because there can be an enormous amount of data to work with. In fact it can easily become unwieldy if not done properly. The process is not just about monitoring and reading counters; it is also an art.

As you monitor and catalog performance information, keep in mind that more information does not necessarily yield better optimization. Tailor the number and types of counters that are being monitored based on the server's role and functionality within the network environment. It's also important to monitor the four common contributors to bottlenecks: memory, processor, disk, and network subsystems. When monitoring

Exchange Server 2003, it is equally important to understand the various Exchange roles to keep the number of counters being monitored to a minimum.

## Memory Subsystem Optimizations

As with earlier versions of Windows, Windows Server 2003 tends to use the amount of memory that you throw at it. However, it outperforms its predecessors in terms of how efficiently memory is managed. Nevertheless, fine-tuning system memory can go a long way toward making sure that Exchange has adequate amounts of memory.

Memory management is performed by Windows Server 2003 and is directly related to how well applications such as Exchange Server 2003 perform. Exchange Server 2003 also has greatly enhanced memory management and the way it uses virtual memory. This reduces memory fragmentation and enables more users to be supported on a single server or cluster of servers.

> **TIP**
>
> Use the /3GB /USERVA=3030 parameters in boot.ini for any Exchange Server 2003 server with 1GB of memory or more installed. This enables Exchange Server 2003 to manage memory more efficiently and support a greater number of users.

With the Performance Monitor Console, there are a number of important memory-related counters that can help in establishing an accurate representation of the system's memory requirements. The primary memory counters that provide information about hard pages (pages that are causing the information to be swapped between the memory and the hard disk) are

- **Memory—Pages/sec**—The values of this counter should range from 5–20. Values consistently higher than 10 are indicative of potential performance problems, whereas values consistently higher than 20 might cause noticeable and significant performance hits.

- **Memory—Page Faults/sec**—This counter, together with the Memory—Cache Faults/sec and Memory—Transition Faults/sec counters, can provide valuable information about page faults that are not committed to disk. They were not committed to disk because the memory manager allocated those pages to a standby list, also known as transition faults. Most systems today can handle a large number of page faults, but it is important to correlate these numbers with the Pages/sec counter as well to determine whether Exchange is configured with enough memory.

Figure 33.5 shows some of the various memory-related and process-related counters.

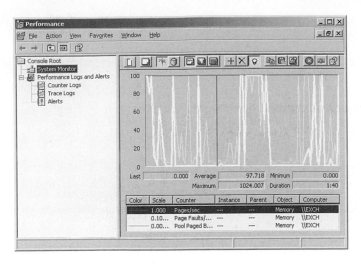

**FIGURE 33.5**    Memory-related counters in Windows Server 2003.

## Improving Virtual Memory Usage

Calculating the correct amount of virtual memory is one of the more challenging parts of planning a server's memory requirements. While trying to anticipate growing usage demands, it is critical that the server has an adequate amount of virtual memory for all applications and the operating system. This is no different for Exchange Server 2003.

Virtual memory refers to the amount of disk space that is used by Windows Server 2003 and applications as physical memory gets low or when applications need to swap data out of physical memory. Windows Server 2003 uses 1.5 times the amount of RAM as the minimum paging file size by default, which for many systems is adequate. However, it is important to monitor memory counters to determine whether this amount is truly sufficient for that particular server's resource requirements. Another important consideration is the maximum size setting for the paging file. As a best practice, this setting should be at least 50% more than the minimum value to enable paging file growth, should the system require it. If the minimum and maximum settings are configured with the same value, there is a greater risk that the system could experience severe performance problems or even crash.

The most indicative sign of low virtual memory is the presence of 9582 warning events logged by the Microsoft Exchange Information Store service that can severely impact and degrade the Exchange Server's message-processing abilities. These warning events are indicative of virtual memory going below 32MB. If unnoticed or left unattended, these warning messages might cause services to stop or the entire system to crash.

---

**TIP**

Use the Performance snap-in to set an alert for Event ID 9582. This helps proactively address any virtual memory problems and possibly prevent unnecessary downtime.

---

To get an accurate portrayal of how Exchange Server 2003 is using virtual memory, monitor the following counters within the `MSExchangeIS` object:

- **VM Largest Block Size**—This counter should consistently be above 32MB.

- **VM Total 16MB Free Blocks**—This counter should remain over three 16MB blocks.

- **VM Total Free Blocks**—This value is specific to your messaging environment.

- **VM Total Large Free Block Bytes**—This counter should stay above 50MB.

Other important counters to watch closely are

- **Memory—Available Bytes**—This counter can be used to establish whether the system has adequate amounts of RAM. The recommended absolute minimum value is 4MB.

- **Paging File—% Usage**—% Usage is used to validate the amount of the paging file used in a predetermined interval. High usage values might be indicative of requiring more physical memory or needing a larger paging file.

## Monitoring Processor Usage

Analyzing the processor usage can reveal invaluable information about system performance and provide reliable results that can be used for baselining purposes. There are three major Exchange-related processor counters that are used for capacity analysis of an Exchange Server 2003:

- **% Privileged Time**—This counter indicates the percentage of non-idle processor time spent in privileged mode. The recommended ideal for this value is under 55%.

- **% Processor Time**—This counter specifies the processor use of each processor or the total processor use. If these values are consistently higher than 50%–60%, consider upgrade options or segmenting workloads.

## Monitoring the Disk Subsystem

Exchange Server 2003 relies heavily on the disk subsystem and it is therefore a critical component to properly design and monitor. Although the disk object monitoring counters are by default enabled in Windows Server 2003, it is recommended that these counters be disabled until such time that an administrator is ready to monitor them. The resource requirements can influence overall system performance. The syntax to disable and reenable these counters is as follows:

*diskperf -n* (to disable)
*diskperf -y* [\\computer_Name] (to reenable)

Nevertheless, it is important to gather disk subsystem performance statistics over time.

The primary Exchange-related performance counters for the disk subsystem are located within the Physical and Logical Disk objects. Critical counters to monitor include, but are not limited to, the following:

- **Physical Disk—% Disk Time**—This counter analyzes the percentage of elapsed time that the selected disk spends on servicing read or write requests. Ideally this value should remain below 50%.

- **Logical Disk—% Disk Time**—This counter displays the percentage of elapsed time that the selected disk spends fulfilling read or write requests. It is recommended that this value be 60%–70% or lower.

- **Current Disk Queue Length (Both Physical and Logical Disk Objects)**—This counter has different performance indicators depending on the monitored disk drive (Database or Transaction Log volume). On disk drives storing the Exchange Database, this value should be below the number of spindled drives divided by 2. On disk drives storing transaction log data, this value should be below 1.

### Monitoring the Network Subsystem

The network subsystem is one of the more challenging elements to monitor because there are a number of factors that make up a network. In an Exchange messaging environment, site topologies, replication architecture, network topologies, synchronization methods, the number of systems, and more are among the many contributing factors.

In order to satisfactorily analyze the network, all facets must be considered. This will most likely require using third-party network monitoring tools in conjunction with built-in tools such as the Performance snap-in and Network Monitor.

## Properly Sizing Exchange Server 2003

Before delving into recommended configurations for Exchange Server 2003, it is essential to not only understand the fundamentals of this messaging system but also the dependencies and interactions those components have with the underlying operating system (that is, Windows Server 2003). Being a client-server messaging application, maximizing Exchange Server 2003 involves fine-tuning all of its core and extended components. Optimization of each of these components affects the overall performance of Exchange.

The core components of Exchange Server (for example, the information stores, connectors, transaction logs, and more) have a direct bearing on gauging resource requirements. The number of users in a messaging environment and the various Exchange functions are equally influential.

### Optimizing the Disk Subsystem Configuration

There are many factors—such as the type of file system to use, physical disk configuration, database size, and log file placement—that need to be considered when you are trying to optimize the disk subsystem configuration.

## Choosing the File System

Among the file systems supported by Windows Server 2003 (that is, FAT and NTFS), it is recommended to use only NTFS on all servers—especially those in production environments. NTFS provides the best security, scalability, and performance features. For instance, NTFS supports file and directory-level security, large file sizes (files of up to 16TB), large disk sizes (disk volumes of up to 16TB), fault tolerance, disk compression, error detection, and encryption.

## Choosing the Physical Disk Configuration

Windows Server 2003, like its predecessors, supports RAID (Redundant Array of Inexpensive Disks). The levels of RAID supported by the operating system are

- RAID 0 (Striping)

- RAID 1 (Mirroring)

- RAID 5 (Striping with Parity)

There are various other levels of RAID that can be supported through the use of hardware-based RAID controllers.

The deployment of the correct RAID level is of utmost importance because each RAID level has a direct effect on the performance of the server. From the viewpoint of pure performance, RAID level 0 by far gives the best performance. However, fault tolerance and the reliability of system access are other factors that contribute to overall performance. The skillful administrator strikes a balance between performance and fault tolerance without sacrificing one for the other. The following sections provide recommended disk configurations for Exchange Server 2003.

> **NOTE**
>
> As mentioned earlier, there are various levels of RAID, but for the context of Exchange Server 2003 there are two recommended basic levels to use: RAID 1 and RAID 5. Other forms of RAID, such as RAID 0+1 or 1+0, are also optimal solutions for Exchange Server 2003. These more advanced levels of RAID are supported only when using a hardware RAID controller. As a result, only RAID 1 and 5 are discussed in this chapter.

## Disk Mirroring (RAID 1)

In this type of configuration, data is mirrored from one disk to the other participating disk in the mirror set. Data is simultaneously written to the two required disks, which means read operations are significantly faster than systems with no RAID configuration or with a greater degree of fault tolerance. Write performance is slower, though, because data is being written twice—once to each disk in the mirror set.

Besides adequate performance, RAID 1 also provides a good degree of fault tolerance. For instance, if one drive fails, the RAID controller can automatically detect the failure and run solely on the remaining disk with minimal interruption.

The biggest drawback to RAID 1 is the amount of storage capacity that is lost. RAID 1 uses 50% of the total drive capacity for the two drives.

---
**TIP**

RAID 1 is particularly well suited for the boot drive and for volumes containing Exchange Server 2003 log files.

---

### Disk Striping with Parity (RAID 5)

In a RAID 5 configuration, data and parity information is striped across all participating disks in the array. RAID 5 requires a minimum of three disks. Even if one of the drives fails within the array, the Exchange Server 2003 server can still remain operational.

After the drive fails, Windows Server 2003 continues to operate because of the data contained on the other drives. The parity information gives details of the data that is missing due to the failure. Either Windows Server 2003 or the hardware RAID controller also begins the rebuilding process from the parity information to a spare or new drive.

RAID 5 is most commonly used for the data drive because it is a great compromise among performance, storage capacity, and redundancy. The overall space used to store the striped parity information is equal to the capacity of one drive. For example, a RAID 5 volume with three 200GB disks can store up to 400GB of data.

### Hardware Versus Software RAID

Hardware RAID (configured at the disk controller level) is recommended over software RAID (configurable from within Windows Server 2003) because of faster performance, greater support of different RAID levels, and capability of recovering from hardware failures more easily.

## Database Sizing and Optimization

As mentioned throughout this book, Exchange Server 2003 is available in two versions: Standard and Enterprise. The Standard Edition supports one storage group with one private and one public information store. The maximum information store (database) size is 75GB with Exchange Server 2003 Standard Edition at Service Pack 2 or higher. The Enterprise Edition provides support for up to four storage groups with a combined total of 20 useable databases per server with practically unlimited database size.

The flexibility with the Enterprise Edition is beneficial not just in terms of growth but also performance and manageability. More specifically, the advantages for segmenting can include the following:

- Administrators are able to segment the user population on a single Exchange server.

- Multiple mailboxes can more evenly distribute the size of the messaging data and help prevent one database from becoming too large and possibly unwieldy for a given system.

- Multiple databases present greater opportunities for faster enumeration of database indexing.

- Multiple databases can be segmented onto different RAID volumes and RAID controller channels.

- Transaction logs can be segmented from other log files using separate RAID volumes.

- Failures such as database corruption affect a smaller percentage of the user population.

- Offline maintenance routines require less scheduled downtime, and fewer users are affected.

> **TIP**
>
> If using the Enterprise Edition, the recommended best practice is to keep database sizes in the 10–20GB range. An administrator can use this guideline to gauge or plan for the number of users each database should optimally contain. This best practice is also useful in determining the appropriate number of Exchange Server 2003 servers that are required to support the number of users in the organization.

Determining the number of storage groups and databases for Exchange Server 2003 should also be based on workload characterization. Users can be grouped based on the how they interact with the messaging system (for example, in terms of frequency, storage requirements, and more). Users placing higher demands on Exchange Server 2003 can be placed into a separate storage group and separate databases so that the greater number of read/write operations do not occur in the same database and are more evenly distributed.

## Optimizing Exchange Logs

Similar to the previous versions of Exchange, transaction log files should be stored on separate RAID volumes. This enables significant improvements in disk input/output (I/O) operations. Transaction logs are created on a per-storage group level rather than per-database. Therefore, when you have multiple storage groups, multiple log files are created that enable simultaneous read and write operations. If the transaction logs are then placed on separate RAID volumes, there can be significant improvements to performance.

> **TIP**
>
> Because transaction logs are as important to Exchange Server 2003 as the data contained in the databases, the most suitable RAID configuration to use for transaction log files is RAID 1. This provides suitable performance without sacrificing fault tolerance.

## Sizing Memory Requirements

The recommended starting point for the amount of memory an Exchange Server 2003 server is installed with is 512MB. The specific memory requirements naturally vary based on server roles, server responsibilities, and the number of users to support. In addition, some organizations define certain guidelines that must be followed for base memory configurations. A more accurate representation of how much memory is required can be achieved by baselining memory performance information gathered from the Performance snap-in or third-party tools during a prototype or lab testing phase.

Another important factor to take into consideration is when the organization adds functionality to Exchange Server 2003 or consolidates users onto fewer servers. This obviously increases resource requirements, especially in terms of adding more physical memory. In these scenarios, it is recommended to use the base amount of memory (for example, 512MB) and then add the appropriate amount of memory based on vendor specifications. It is also important to consult with the vendor to determine what the memory requirements may be on a per-user basis. This way the organization can plan ahead and configure the proper amount of memory prior to needing to scale to support a larger number of users in the future.

## Sizing Based on Server Roles

Server roles can have a considerable bearing on both the performance and capacity of Exchange Server 2003. Based on the various roles of the Exchange servers, the strategic placement of Exchange services and functionality can greatly improve performance of the overall messaging system while reducing the need for using additional resources. By the same token, a misplaced Exchange service or functional component can noticeably add to network traffic and degrade the overall performance of the messaging system.

Servers are generally divided into two sets of roles: front-end and back-end servers. Within these two sets of roles are several key roles that an Exchange Server 2003 server can serve, including, but not limited to, OWA, public folder, mailbox store, or bridgehead server.

Front-end servers are the first point of contact for client messaging requests. The servers proxy these requests to the back-end servers for processing. The front-end/back-end topology is recommended for organizations that use OWA, POP, or IMAP for employees accessing the messaging system over the Internet.

Another key difference between a front-end and back-end server is storage requirements. Back-end servers usually host mailbox or public folder stores, and front-ends have minimal requirements. Back-end servers, therefore, usually have much higher and greater storage requirements, as well as processing power and memory requirements.

### Front-End Server Sizing

There are various factors that affect the performance of a front-end server, including the following:

- The number and type of protocols supported
- The number of users supported

- The authentication methods supported

- Encryption requirements

Tables 33.1 through 33.3 show the recommended resource requirements of various dedicated front-end servers. It is important to note that these guidelines are minimum recommendations, and actual requirements may vary depending upon the organization.

**TABLE 33.1**   Recommended Minimum POP3 Front-End Server Configurations

| Resource | Description |
| --- | --- |
| RAM | 512MB. |
| Processor | Pentium III 800MHz or higher processor. |
| Hard disk | RAID 1 for Windows Server 2003 and Exchange Server 2003 (assuming no mail is stored on the front-end server and logging is not enabled). |
| Network | 100Mbps or higher NIC(s). |
| Other considerations | If connections to this server are over *SSL,* consider using a NIC that offloads SSL processing. |

**TABLE 33.2**   Recommended Minimum OWA or IMAP4 Front-End Server Configurations

| Resource | Description |
| --- | --- |
| RAM | 512MB plus 512KB of RAM per active, concurrent client connection. |
| Processor | Dual Pentium III 800MHz or higher processors. |
| Hard disk | RAID 1 for Windows Server 2003 and Exchange Server 2003 (assuming no mail is stored on the front-end server and logging is not enabled). |
| Network | 100Mbps or higher NIC(s). |
| Other considerations | If connections to this server are over *SSL,* consider using a NIC that offloads SSL processing. |

**TABLE 33.3**   Recommended Minimum SMTP Front-End Server Configurations

| Resource | Description |
| --- | --- |
| RAM | Recommended 512MB to manage large queues. |
| Processor | Dual Pentium III 800MHz or higher processors. |
| Hard disk | RAID 1 can be used for Windows Server 2003 and Exchange Server 2003. If large amounts of disk space are required for SMTP queues, a separate RAID 0+1 volume can be used. |
| Network | 100Mbps or higher NIC(s). |
| Other considerations | Encrypting the SMTP traffic using *TLS* (Transport Layer Security) does not necessarily require significantly more memory or processing power. |

**TIP**

Similar front-end servers can be combined for additional availability and performance requirements using Microsoft's Network Load Balancing (NLB).

### Back-End Server Sizing

As mentioned earlier, back-end servers generally host mailbox and public folder stores. They can also provide various other functions, including features that are typically thought of as front-end functions.

The myriad of functional options and other considerations (for example, the number of users to support, mailbox store size(s), incoming and outgoing message size restrictions, security requirements, and more) can make back-end server sizing a daunting task at best. As a best practice, it is recommended that an Exchange Server 2003 server be configured with a minimum of 512MB of memory and dual processors. Physical memory has been, and continues to be, an inexpensive component and is one of the easiest ways to upgrade a server. As such you might even consider using 1GB as a minimum standard for back-end servers. For the disk subsystem, it is recommended to implement three hardware-based RAID volumes: a RAID 1 volume for Windows Server 2003 and Exchange Server 2003 system-related files, a RAID 5 volume for the mailbox and public folder stores, and another RAID 1 volume for transaction logs. The number of volumes for the transaction logs may vary depending on the number of storage groups configured on the server.

> **TIP**
>
> Another best practice is to thoroughly test server configurations in a lab environment prior to deploying in production.

## Optimizing Exchange Through Ongoing Maintenance

Through typical usage, Exchange databases become fragmented. This fragmentation gradually slows server performance and can also lead to corruption over extended periods of time. In order to ensure that an Exchange server continues to service requests in an optimized manner and the chances of corruption are minimized, it is important to perform regular maintenance on Exchange.

Although Exchange Server 2003 performs online maintenance tasks on a nightly basis, this accounts for roughly only 60%–70% of the maintenance tasks that are recommended. Offline maintenance, on the other hand, achieves the true optimization of the information stores, as well as prevents and fixes corruption. Offline optimization routines help keep the messaging server operating like a well-oiled engine and ensure that Exchange provides the highest serviceability and reliability.

> **CAUTION**
>
> It is of utmost importance to perform a full backup of Exchange Server 2003 prior to and immediately after running offline maintenance. After the backup has completed, it is equally important to verify the backups.

Because offline maintenance procedures require at least one database or that the entire server is offline, it is also important to schedule maintenance during the off-peak hours and notify the end-users in advance.

> **NOTE**
>
> If Exchange Server 2003 Enterprise Edition is being used, you can perform maintenance on a single database and not affect other data that is stored within other databases. In addition, the entire server does not have to be offline.

The utilities to use for offline maintenance are ESEUTIL (ESEUTIL.EXE) and the Integrity Checker (ISINTEG.EXE). These utilities perform a number of functions, including, but not limited to, checking database and table integrity, identifying and correcting corruption, and defragmenting databases. For further information on the recommended best practices on maintaining Exchange Server 2003 and step-by-step instructions for offline maintenance, refer to Chapter 19, "Exchange Server 2003 Management and Maintenance Practices."

# Monitoring Exchange with Microsoft Operations Manager

Microsoft Operations Manager (MOM) is an application that can be used to actively monitor Exchange Server 2003. Employing MOM in an Exchange messaging environment offers administrators the following benefits:

- MOM has the capability of detecting even the smallest of problems that, if gone unnoticed, can lead to more complicated issues. Early detection of problems enables an administrator to troubleshoot the problem areas well in advance.

- MOM can monitor all Exchange-related system health indicators.

- The Exchange Server 2003 Management Pack leverages all the new features of Exchange Server 2003.

- The Exchange Server 2003 Management Pack also includes the Microsoft Knowledge Base, which can be used for fast and reliable resolution of issues.

- MOM can centrally manage a large number of Exchange Server 2003 servers over widely dispersed deployments.

- MOM can actively monitor server availability by verifying that services are running, databases are mounted, messages are flowing, and users are able to log on.

- MOM can actively monitor server health by monitoring free disk space thresholds, mail queues, security, performance thresholds, and more.

- MOM provides detailed reports on database sizes, traffic analysis, and more.

- Alerts can be sent based on customized thresholds and events.

In short, MOM is an excellent tool that administrators can use to proactively monitor the Exchange environment from a centralized location.

Figure 33.6 shows the various Mail Queue performance counters.

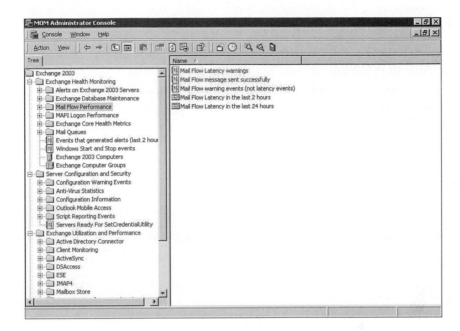

**FIGURE 33.6**   MOM Mail Queue performance counters.

## Summary

Despite all the performance, reliability, scalability, and availability enhancements of Exchange Server 2003, capacity analysis and performance optimization are still a necessity. The techniques and processes described in this chapter not only help you determine how to size a server or tweak it to operate optimally, they also reflect a methodology for continually monitoring a changing environment. By keeping one step ahead of the system, an organization can use resources more efficiently and effectively and in return save time, effort, and costs associated with supporting Exchange Server 2003.

## Best Practices

The following are best practices from this chapter:

- Begin capacity analysis and performance optimization sooner rather than later.

- Create performance baselines in which to gauge the changing requirements and performance levels of Exchange Server 2003.

- Establish SLAs and other policies that reflect the business expectations of the messaging environment.

- Monitor only those counters that are pertinent to the server's configuration.

- Always monitor the four common contributors to bottlenecks: memory, disk subsystem, processor, and network.

- Run performance and stress tests in a lab environment prior to implementing in a production environment.

- Establish regular maintenance routines, including those for offline maintenance tasks.

- Set an alert for Event ID 9582 to proactively address any memory or virtual memory problems.

- Use the `/3GB /USERVA=3030` parameters in `boot.ini` for any Exchange Server 2003 server with 1GB of memory or more installed.

- Keep Exchange Server 2003 database sizes in the 10–20GB range whenever possible.

- Use separate, hardware-based RAID 1 volumes for system files and transaction logs.

# PART XI

## Cross-Platform Migrations to Exchange 2003

## IN THIS PART

**CHAPTER 34**   Migrating from Novell GroupWise to
Exchange 2003                                        999

**CHAPTER 35**   Migrating from Lotus Notes to
Exchange Server 2003                              1057

CHAPTER **34**

# Migrating from Novell GroupWise to Exchange 2003

**IN THIS CHAPTER**

- Similarities and Differences Between GroupWise and Exchange Server 2003
- Exchange Migration and the Impact of Active Directory
- Evaluating the Existing Environment
- Understanding the Tools Available to Migrate from NDS/eDirectory to Active Directory
- Automating the Migration Using Services for NetWare 5.03
- Planning Your Migration from GroupWise
- Conducting Preinstallation Checks on Exchange Server 2003
- Performing a Core Installation of Exchange Server 2003
- Detailing the Exchange Server 2003 Installation
- Performing Postinstallation Configurations
- Installing and Configuring a Gateway Between GroupWise and Exchange
- Installing and Configuring Calendar Connector in a GroupWise Environment
- Using the Exchange Migration Wizard to Migrate User Data
- Details on the Effects of the GroupWise Migration Tools

Many organizations are choosing to migrate from GroupWise to Microsoft Exchange because Novell has changed their operating system platform from NetWare to SuSE Linux, forcing organizations to perform a relatively substantial migration. Other organizations have found that GroupWise has limited support for integration with business applications and tools, such as application integration with Enterprise Resource Planning (ERP) systems, customer relationship management (CRM) systems, and mobile devices.

The migration process from Novell GroupWise to Microsoft Exchange is greatly simplified by several tools provided by Microsoft to help organizations make the transition to the new messaging system. Microsoft has a free migration tool called Services for Netware (SfN) that migrates Novell Directory Services (NDS) and eDirectory for user accounts, groups, and security to Active Directory. In addition, Microsoft also provides GroupWise-to-Exchange migration tools to help an organization migrate mailboxes, calendars, and address books from GroupWise to Exchange.

Whether an organization is looking to perform a quick migration from GroupWise to Exchange, or an extended migration that will involve the coexistence of GroupWise and Exchange in an environment, the tools exist to assist with the migration process. This chapter highlights the tools, tips, tricks, and best practices used by hundreds of organizations in their successful migration from GroupWise to Exchange.

# Similarities and Differences Between GroupWise and Exchange Server 2003

In general feature comparisons, Novell GroupWise and Exchange are very similar. They are both enterprise email and calendar systems that provide contact management, task management, and collaboration. However, beyond the basic functionality of email, there are differences between the two systems.

## Comparing Messaging and Collaboration Capabilities

Some of the similarities and differences between GroupWise and Exchange relative to messaging and collaboration capabilities include

- **Microsoft Exchange as a reliable email server**—Email is a critical application for most companies today and when it doesn't work, it can seriously affect business. Exchange supports online backup and restore, allowing end-users to keep working while their email is backed up. Transaction logging guarantees that no messages are ever lost. On the other hand, GroupWise utilizes a legacy-file–based architecture for its data store, which does not provide up-to-the-minute data recovery. For a complete backup or restore of GroupWise 4.x or 5.x to be successful, all end-users must be logged off the system. Although Novell added online backup capability for GroupWise 6, write-ahead transaction logging is still not provided. This feature is promised as a future major release. Finally, GroupWise users in Direct Access mode connect to the GroupWise post office through a mapped network drive. If users inadvertently modify or delete files on this drive, the entire mail system could be seriously affected. With Exchange, messaging components are stored in a transactional database and users don't have access to the messaging system files.

- **Third-party tools**—Companies using GroupWise are required to look to third-party providers if they want features such as rich workflow tools, online meetings, or audio- or videoconferencing. This functionality is included in a default installation of Exchange Server 2003.

- **Familiar Outlook client**—The Microsoft Outlook client is installed with the Microsoft Office suite of products. Microsoft Office and Outlook are familiar applications for users. The GroupWise client, on the other hand, requires end-user training to users because the client software is not commonly used by home users or businesses. The GroupWise client software provides little or no support for online meetings or SendTo Office Routing Recipients and SendTo GroupWise Folder. There is no application integration with Office documents and properties, which are simply treated as attachments. Users cannot use the File Save As function to save to a GroupWise shared folder.

- **User experience across client access technologies**—User experience is enhanced in Exchange Server 2003 through the use of a consistent user interface (UI) across the client access technologies, including Outlook, Outlook Web Access, Outlook Mobile Access, and Pocket Outlook, which improves user productivity and reduces the need for IT support.

- **Built-in mobile device support**—Outlook Mobile Access and Exchange Server ActiveSync are mobile features built in to Exchange Server 2003. Outlook Mobile Access and Exchange Server ActiveSync also help provide security for corporate email on a range of mobile devices, including browser-based mobile phones and Microsoft Windows Powered Mobile Devices. Currently, GroupWise requires third-party mobile server products to provide synchronization between GroupWise and Exchange.

- **Single password**—Users can log on with a single password in both the Windows Active Directory network logon and the Exchange messaging system. This is possible using Novell Single Sign On, but GroupWise does not actually use NDS authentication. There is a separate password for GroupWise and NDS, and these passwords are not synchronized.

### Comparing Administrative Tools

There are also similarities and differences in the administrative tools between Novell GroupWise and Exchange:

- **Multiple organization directory hosting**—Both GroupWise and Exchange Server 2003 support multiple-organization, directory hosting; however, in Groupwise there needs to be multiple domains and multiple Simple Mail Transfer Protocol (SMTP) mail connectors.

- **Wizards**—Both GroupWise and Exchange messaging systems have setup and configuration wizards. Both messaging systems support Windows Installer Support, which is used for Deploying Desktop Messaging and Collaboration Software.

- **Network security**—NetWare 5.x and later versions provide a set of network services that are similar to Active Directory. These include support for Secure Sockets Layer (SSL), X.509 digital certificates, and security policies. If interoperability between security implementations is desired, companies should focus on the use of SSL and Public Key Infrastructure (PKI) to ensure a good level of interoperability. Both platforms support many similar security policies, including account lockout, access control, and password policies.

## Exchange Migration and the Impact of Active Directory

Exchange is usually implemented as the messaging system in an environment that uses Windows Active Directory as the primary network logon, file system, and network operating system. However, Exchange can also be implemented in an environment that uses Novell NDS or eDirectory as the primary network operating system and file and print environment. Exchange requires Active Directory to operate, so even if an organization uses NDS or eDirectory for their network logon authentication system, Active Directory still needs to be installed and operating for Exchange to operate.

## Implementing Exchange in a Native Active Directory Environment

For an organization looking to migrate from Novell GroupWise to Exchange, the organization needs to determine whether it will also migrate from Novell NDS or eDirectory to Active Directory, or whether it will have a dual Active Directory and NDS/eDirectory environment.

Many organizations that have Novell NDS or eDirectory also have a Windows network infrastructure for application servers, such as Microsoft SQL Server or Citrix, or Windows-based ERP or CRM applications. The Windows-based network infrastructure may be running on Windows NT 4.0 domains that will need to be migrated to Active Directory (see Chapter 14, "Migrating from NT4 to Windows Server 2003"), or the organization might already have Active Directory in place.

Later in this chapter in the section "Understanding the Tools Available to Migrate from NDS/eDirectory to Active Directory," the procedures for migrating from Novell NDS and eDirectory to Active Directory are highlighted. Although an organization does not need to completely remove NDS or eDirectory from their network before beginning a migration from GroupWise to Exchange, the Active Directory infrastructure needs to be established for user authentication and directory lookup of the Active Directory for Microsoft Exchange Server 2003 to run properly.

## Running Exchange in an NDS/eDirectory Environment

Although some organizations may choose to fully migrate from Novell NDS or eDirectory to Microsoft Active Directory as a strategic business decision to consolidate their directories and operating systems, some organizations may choose to run both NDS/eDirectory and Active Directory.

Having a dual-directory strategy is fully supported with Exchange. Although in many cases having a dual directory is redundant, the organization can run both directories in their environment. Key to having a dual-directory strategy is ensuring that the directories are synchronized. With synchronized directories, a user who logs on to Novell NDS or eDirectory will have his user account and password pass to Exchange, allowing the user to access his Exchange mailbox without having to log on a second time. This single sign-on capability requires the directories to be synchronized, and Microsoft provides a free tool called the Microsoft Directory Synchronization Services, or MSDSS, that is covered later in this book in the section titled "Microsoft Directory Synchronization Services."

# Evaluating the Existing Environment

It is critical to fully understand the current environment before designing the environment to which you plan to upgrade. It is important to allow time in the planning process to collect information about the existing environment and evaluate that information to determine the appropriate next steps in the planning process.

This discovery process can also shed light on constraints to the implementation process that weren't considered previously, such as time restrictions that would affect the window of opportunity for change. These restrictions can include seasonal businesses as well as company budgeting cycles or even vacation schedules.

Ultimately, although the amount of time spent in the discovery and evaluation process will vary greatly from organization to organization, the goals are the same: to really understand the technology infrastructure in place and the risks involved in the project, and to limit the surprises that might occur during the build and deploy phases.

In preparation for development of the functional specifications document, the following information discovery tasks should be performed:

- **Diagram the existing network, including hardware and software**—Diagram the network and all its components. Identify which servers are file and print servers, Web servers, mail servers, and database servers. Document servers thoroughly, including NetWare versions, transport protocols, NDS partitioning, and directory versions (Bindery or NDS).

- **Identify all types of information stored on the network, including its owners, users, locations, and security**—Identify all types of information stored on the NetWare network (not just NDS or Bindery information), where it is stored, who is responsible for which information, which subsets of users have access to which data, and what the associated security requirements are.

- **Identify all Novell-dependent software**—Before the migration begins, decide whether you will replace all Bindery-, NDS-, or NLM-dependent software (such as NDS-compliant Domain Name System [DNS], Dynamic Host Configuration Protocol [DHCP], ZENworks, and so on) with Active Directory–compatible software (leading to a direct migration), or whether you want to continue to use some or all of the Bindery- or NDS-integrated services or applications (leading to a phased migration). Be sure to include the email system in this list.

- **Determine the systems to be migrated**—Determine which systems will be migrated or decommissioned. Determine the affected users, groups, objects, folders, files, databases, and email systems.

- **Review WAN/LAN links and their available bandwidth**—This will help you decide how you can effectively design the Active Directory topology in respect to the current Novell environment on the existing network.

- **Plan for future hardware, software, and network bandwidth needs**—Research what additional functionality your organization plans to implement in the future. Factor these features into your migration planning (for example, when you plan namespace design, wide area network (WAN) links, application software needs, and so on).

- **Analyze the current and future namespace design**—Familiarize yourself with the current Novell namespace design and with Active Directory namespace design principles.

- **Review user environment components involved in the migration**—Primarily, you should review logon scripts and group/system policies.

34

- **Perform a directory health check**—This is the process of going through the Novell NDS or eDirectory, to determine if the directory is working properly. In addition, if there is already an Active Directory infrastructure in place, it should be verified to ensure that it is working properly. The health check ensures that the objects scheduled for migration are appropriate and that they can be migrated to the new environment.

You can perform an eDirectory health check in a number of different ways. Step-by-step procedures for verifying the Novell DS versions, time synchronization using DSREPAIR, and making sure that all of the servers are in sync, using DSTRACE to verify that the servers have replicated properly, can be found in the Novell white paper TID #10012858 found on `http://support.novell.com/search/kb_index.jsp`.

## Understanding the Tools Available to Migrate from NDS/eDirectory to Active Directory

If you don't already have an Active Directory environment in your network, you can plan the directory migration portion of your project more effectively if you know which tools are available to assist with the directory migration process. Although a number of tools are available to assist with the migration, this chapter focuses on the Microsoft Services for NetWare 5.03 (SfN) tool that is free from Microsoft.

### Services for NetWare

Services for NetWare 5.03 (SfN) and Windows Server 2003 provide protocols and services that enable migration, synchronization, and limited interoperability with Novell NetWare networks. These protocols and services enable network managers and technical staff to integrate computers running Windows Server 2003 into a NetWare network to facilitate migration and/or coexistence. To enhance interoperability with NetWare networks, Services for NetWare 5.03 includes MSDSS and the File Migration Utility (FMU).

### Microsoft Directory Synchronization Services

Microsoft Directory Synchronization Services (MSDSS) is a tool used for two-way synchronization of directory information stored in the Active Directory and NDS or eDirectory. MSDSS also synchronizes directory information stored in Active Directory with all versions of NetWare 3.x bindery services on a one-way basis.

MSDSS is the cornerstone of any NDS/eDirectory/Bindery–to–Active Directory migration strategy. MSDSS also plays a critical role in long-term coexistence strategies by allowing NetWare customers to deploy Active Directory services without having to replace existing directories or bear the cost of managing two separate directories. As a result, customers have the flexibility to consolidate network management when multiple directories are required, manage accounts from either directory, and use directory-enabled applications, devices, and services based on Active Directory.

## File Migration Utility

The File Migration Utility (FMU) is an add-on utility included in Services for NetWare 5.03 that provides a central management console to automatically manage the migration of files from NetWare file and print servers to Windows 2003 servers. Although the migration of file and print services are not directly part of a GroupWise-to-Exchange migration, many times users store their email archives in files on a network, or the migration to Exchange is preceded by a migration of the organization from NDS, eDirectory, and Novell NetWare file and print services to Windows Active Directory.

The FMU helps customers migrate their NetWare files to a Windows 2003 server by

- Accelerating the migration process through automation

- Preserving file security information

- Simplifying migration management

The FMU reduces the time and cost of migration by copying multiple NetWare files and their associated permissions to one or more Windows 2003 servers automatically.

The FMU preserves the permissions and access control lists (ACLs) associated with each file it copies. Through granular mapping support and integration with MSDSS, files and the rights they have inherited or been assigned in NetWare are calculated and maintained in the Windows 2003–based network, preserving security and minimizing the time-consuming process of reassigning file rights and permissions.

The FMU migrates files simply, as well as quickly and securely, by providing a central point of administration for migration management. As such, administrators can monitor which files have been migrated and which haven't in a detailed status report. Incremental migration support also allows customers to perform a gradual migration. Finally, both the TCP/IP and IPX/SPX protocols are supported to allow the migration of NetWare files and their permissions.

Table 34.1 provides a summary of the NetWare-based elements that can be migrated automatically from the major versions of NetWare to the Windows Server 2003 server using the previously described tools and services.

**TABLE 34.1**    Summary of Migration Services

| NetWare Element | NetWare Versions | Microsoft Migration Tool Available? | Tool Name |
| --- | --- | --- | --- |
| Files | NetWare 3.x | Yes | FMU |
| | NetWare 4.x | Yes | FMU |
| | NetWare 5.x | Yes | FMU |
| Directories | NetWare 3.x | Yes | MSDSS |
| | NetWare 4.x | Yes | MSDSS |
| | NetWare 5.x | Yes | MSDSS |
| | NDS 8 | Yes | MSDSS |

34

In addition to the tools outlined, Services for NetWare 5.03 provides troubleshooting support that enables you to troubleshoot connectivity problems, logon scripts, and password synchronization. Services for NetWare 5.03 also provides utilities for monitoring network traffic.

# Automating the Migration Using Services for NetWare 5.03

Services for NetWare 5.03 can be used in the prototype test phase and can be initiated using the following key steps:

- Identifying the sample data that will be migrated. This can consist of a server or a single NetWare volume.

- Creating test users and necessary accounts.

- Migrating groups from NDS/eDirectory to Active Directory.

- Choosing to migrate specific sets of file data from NetWare file servers to Active Directory file servers.

- Applying security to the migrated data.

- Migrating client functionality, such as logon scripts, drive mappings, printer mapping, and so on.

> **NOTE**
>
> Although this book focuses on the full server edition of Microsoft Exchange, if you deploy SfN on Small Business Server (SBS 2003), you need to stop Exchange services before installing SfN or it will fail.

## Setting Up Directory Synchronization

After deploying Microsoft Services for NetWare 5.03, MSDSS can be used to set up directory replication between Active Directory and NDS/Bindery as well as prepare for file migration.

MSDSS requires the use of Novell's Client for Windows. If you performed a clean installation of the Windows Server 2003 operating system, you must download and install Novell's Client for Windows before you install Services for NetWare 5.03 MSDSS. In addition, the user account that runs the install process must have Schema Admin rights to the forest as the MSDSS install process will extend the Active Directory schema.

The general installation steps for MSDSS are as follows:

1. Install the latest version of Novell's Client for Windows.

2. Download (from `http://www.microsoft.com/windowsserver2003/sfn/default.mspx`) the latest version of Services for NetWare software.

3. Launch the Services for NetWare installer to install the software on your Windows server system. (You need to have Schema Admin rights to the Active Directory forest to install the product.)

4. Restart the computer after installation.

5. To manage MSDSS after you have installed it, open Administrative Tools, and then click Directory Synchronization.

The next step is to create sessions for each Novell organizational unit that is to be migrated or synchronized. In addition to selecting the appropriate OUs in each directory for the session, you must select the migration of the session.

After the sessions are defined according to the design criteria, a schedule can be set to regularly update the appropriate directories. An initial manual synchronization can be performed as well. It is highly recommended that all objects are set up to be synchronized between NetWare and Active Directory from the moment of the Pilot setup, through the implementation, and all the way to the end of the project, as this ensures that all changes that are made to both directories are reflected in both places.

To set up an MSDSS synchronization session, perform the following tasks on the server on which MSDSS is installed:

1. Click Start, point to All Programs, point to Administrative Tools, and then click Directory Synchronization.

2. In the console tree, right-click MSDSS, and then click New Session to start the New Session Wizard.

3. On the Synchronization and Migration Tasks page, under Select NDS or Bindery, choose whether objects will be copied from NDS or Bindery.

4. Under Select a Task, click Migration (from NDS or Bindery to Active Directory), as shown in Figure 34.1, and then click Next.

   If files will be migrated with directory objects, you need to click to select the Migrate Files check box. This creates the file migration log that is required by the FMU.

5. On the Active Directory Container and Domain Controller page, under Active Directory Container, type the path to the container in which you want to copy items, or click Browse to locate the Active Directory container.

   Use the syntax in the following example to type the path:

   LDAP://OU=Sales,DC=Server1,DC=Companyabc,DC=com

   All subcontainers in the selected containers will be copied.

6. Under Domain Controller, accept the default domain controller in which you want to store the migration log, or click Find to locate a different domain controller to store the log, and then click Next.

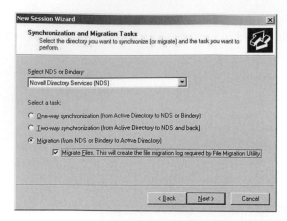

**FIGURE 34.1**    Migrating objects from NDS/eDirectory to Active Directory.

7.  On the NDS Container and Password or Bindery Container and Password page, type the appropriate NDS or Bindery syntax as indicated here, or click Browse to locate the container or server:

    NDS://Tree1/O=Companyabc/OU=Sales

    NWCOMPAT://Server

8.  Under User Name, type the name of the administrative account. In the Password box, type the password for that account, and then click Next.

    You must type the NDS administrative account by using the full NDS context, such as "Admin.companyabc". Do not include the NDS tree name.

9.  On the Initial Reverse Synchronization page, click Password Options, and then click one of the following password schemes:

    - Set Passwords to Blank

    - Set Passwords to the User Name

    - Set Passwords to a Random Value

    - Set All Passwords to the Following Value

10. If you do not select a scheme, the default Set Passwords to the User Name scheme is applied. After you have selected a password scheme, click OK, click Next, and then click Finish.

## Migrating Data with the File Migration Utility (FMU)

Although not specific to a GroupWise-to-Exchange migration, SfN can not only migrate users and groups using the MSDSS tool, but it can also migrate files using the FMU. The users and groups that are created in Active Directory using MSDSS are then used for the application of security to the data that is migrated with the FMU.

As part of the pilot process, a sample set of data can be migrated from NetWare to the new Windows Server 2003 file servers as a test of the FMU capabilites. This sample set of data can consist of the data from a single NetWare server or a single volume of NetWare data from the server. The data should then be migrated using the FMU, which preserves the file security structure from the NetWare side and re-creates it using the users and groups that were synchronized with the MSDSS utility.

To set up an FMU session to migrate the data, perform the following high-level steps on the server on which FMU is installed:

1. Start the File Migration Utility (Start, All Programs, Administrative Tools, File Migration Utility).

2. Click Next at the welcome screen.

3. Browse for the migration log that was created by using MSDSS with the Migration option selected.

4. Click the Load Data button.

5. Click Next.

6. Verify the Security Accounts and click Next.

7. Select the source volume and target location, as shown in Figure 34.2; then click Next.

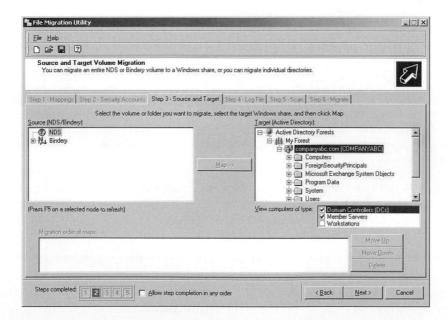

**FIGURE 34.2**   Selecting source and target locations for migration.

8. Enable logging by checking the Enable Logs check box.

9. Click the Scan button to check whether the target source and roots are valid. After verification, click Next.

10. Click the Migrate button on the last screen. The logs are displayed as the file data and permissions are migrated.

## Planning Your Migration from GroupWise

Before migrating from Novell GroupWise to Exchange, a planning process should be conducted to develop the plan, create a project plan, and outline the steps that will be taken to successfully migrate the organization to Exchange Server 2003. When developing a migration strategy, you must make a number of decisions:

- **Plan a phased or direct migration**—Plan an immediate, one-time migration, or a phased migration over time (synchronizing Active Directory and your NDS directory during the transitional period). Phased and direct migrations are covered in detail in the following section.

- **Identify containers and servers to migrate or synchronize**—Identify the containers that you want to migrate or synchronize and the Active Directory and NDS or Bindery servers between which you want to establish relationships.

- **Identify and obtain administrator accounts with sufficient permissions to successfully complete the migration**—If you will use synchronization, ensure that you have the required accounts with permissions to extend the Active Directory schema (even though the Services for NetWare 5.03 tool, MSDSS, does this automatically, you must have schema-extending administrative authority). If you will use two-way synchronization, ensure that you have the necessary permissions to extend the NDS schema.

> **NOTE**
>
> When you set up a two-way synchronization session with MSDSS, you must have full administrator privileges to the entire NDS container in which you are creating the session. Ensure that these privileges are maintained for the life of the session—if these privileges are changed, objects might be deleted from one or both of the directories.

- **Choose the migration administrators**—Decide who you will add as a member of the MSDSS Admins group that is created automatically when you install MSDSS. Choose the users to whom you will delegate specific MSDSS administrative tasks.

- **Determine the need for migration tools**—Determine whether the migration should be performed manually or whether you should employ migration tools and services. For details on selecting migration tools, see the "Details on the Effects of the GroupWise Migration Tools" section of this chapter.

## Choosing a Phased Migration from GroupWise

If you want to maintain an environment that contains both Active Directory and Bindery/NDS directory services, you can perform a phased migration and run the two systems in parallel. If you choose to run the two systems in parallel, you will be able to perform additional migration tasks (other than synchronizing the two directory services), such as replacing applications that are dependent on Novell services with Active Directory–compatible applications.

A phased migration reduces the risk of data loss because you can migrate in managed stages and you can reverse the process if necessary. However, maintaining two separate directory services can, over time, add additional administrative costs to the migration.

In a phased migration, you use MSDSS to copy all Bindery or NDS user accounts, groups, and distribution lists, and (for NDS only) organizational units and organizations to Active Directory. At the same time, these objects are maintained in NDS or Bindery. While you gradually move resources to the Windows Server 2003–based environment, the MSDSS-provided directory synchronization enables users to continue to access those resources that remain on NetWare servers. As the changeover continues, users begin to access resources on Windows Server 2003–based servers with their new accounts and associated migrated permissions.

If you plan to perform the migration over several months or longer, two-way synchronization is recommended. This allows you to make changes in both Active Directory and NDS environments, such as adding user accounts and modifying group membership and have those changes reflected in the other respective directory. Two-way synchronization should be used if the long-term goal is to interoperate using the two directory services. In this scenario, you can replace existing NetWare technologies with the latest comparable Microsoft technologies over a period of time.

After you have moved all resources to Windows Server 2003, converted all Novell services and applications to Active Directory–based counterparts, and moved object security permissions and objects that MSDSS does not migrate (such as computer accounts, printer objects, and application objects), synchronization between the two directory services might no longer be necessary. This allows you to delete the synchronization sessions and decommission remaining NetWare servers.

If you choose a phased migration, you should

- **List migration priorities**—List the departments or other groupings, the software, and the hardware that you must migrate immediately, and which resources can be migrated over time. List the order in which you want to accomplish each stage.

- **Choose one-way or two-way synchronization**—Decide whether one-way synchronization (using Active Directory to manage objects in both directories) or two-way synchronization (using either Active Directory or NDS to manage shared data) is appropriate to the situation. Take network traffic into account. Decide the timetable for replacing any of the Bindery- or NDS-dependent software with Active Directory–enabled counterparts.

### Synchronizing NDS/eDirectory with Active Directory

The administration of multiple directory services often leads to time-consuming and redundant management. Establishing a periodic synchronization, using MSDSS, of both directories will help you reduce the time you spend on directory management.

When you introduce Windows Server 2003 and Active Directory into an existing Novell network, you can facilitate directory management and improve data availability by establishing directory interoperability. Central to interoperability is the ability to synchronize the information stored in Active Directory with the Novell directory information within your organization. MSDSS, included with Services for NetWare 5.03, makes Active Directory synchronization with NDS and NetWare 3.x binderies possible.

By default, MSDSS synchronization duplicates the Bindery or NDS structure in Active Directory. Also like migration, synchronization maps Novell user, group, and distribution list objects to Active Directory user, group, and distribution list objects, and (for NDS only) it maps Novell OUs and organizations to Active Directory OUs. In addition, MSDSS synchronization optionally provides custom object mapping (for NDS only) that enables you to map objects in dissimilar directory structures to each other.

Synchronization and Active Directory setup are easy to do through the MSDSS management interface. MSDSS provides two options for managing synchronization as part of a migration strategy.

**Using One-Way Synchronization**    One-way synchronization enables you to manage objects in both directories from Active Directory. Reasons to select one-way synchronization include

- The desire to centralize directory administration from Active Directory

- The consideration that the network is predominantly Windows-based (with some NDS-based computers), or the network is currently NDS-based, but you plan to reduce the number of directories over time

- The interest to administer and update NDS user account passwords to support a single set of logon credentials that enable users to log on to both a Windows-based and a Novell-based network

- The intent to prepare to migrate an NDS-based directory environment to Active Directory

**Using Two-Way Synchronization**    Two-way synchronization enables the administrator to manage shared data, such as user account information, from either directory. Reasons to select two-way synchronization include

- The expectation of having both Active Directory and NDS administered by two sets of network administrators

- The anticipation that the network environment will contain NDS as the primary directory and the organization has no plans to consolidate the number of directory platforms

- The plan to maintain and actively administer both directory environments for an extended period of time

### Preparing the Project Team for the Migration

After the project team determines what the new Exchange Server 2003 environment will look like, they are ready to determine how to migrate their existing GroupWise environment to the new Exchange Server 2003 environment.

The first step in planning a migration from GroupWise should be to explain to both end-users and administrators how their worlds will change after the new messaging environment is deployed. Most administrators and end-users will not fear the change if they are properly informed and educated about the changes. In addition, if the migrations are planned correctly, it should be seamless and transparent to end-users, which lessens the impact on end-users. However, rather than overconfidently telling the users and the executives of the organization that the migration will be simple and seamless, it is safer to describe a much more complex scenario, giving the users a vision of the benefits they'll receive after the migration is completed, and if the migration happens with minimal interruption, the users and executives will be pleasantly surprised.

The next important step in planning a migration involves system readiness. All systems involved directly or indirectly in the migration process, such as Windows Server 2003, Active Directory, and Exchange Server 2003, must be ready. After all systems are operational, project teams should attempt to reduce the amount of data to be migrated. They must also ensure they grant the appropriate permissions for the service account that will be used to migrate the GroupWise data. Sufficient access rights are necessary to extract data from mailboxes. For example, you must grant the migration account Novell GroupWise proxy rights for all mailboxes. Next, a decision needs to be made on whether to carry out a direct migration or a phased migration. A company's assessment of its existing environment should help it identify the most logical and effective migration approach: direct or phased.

### Identifying the Tools Needed for the Phased Migration

An organization that chooses a phased migration also needs to identify the tools needed to maintain coexistence between their legacy messaging system, GroupWise, and their new messaging system, Exchange Server 2003. Through coexistence, users who are still part of the legacy messaging system will be able to communicate with users who have already migrated to Exchange Server 2003.

Exchange Server 2003 and Exchange Server 2003 Service Pack 1 have readily available tools that support interoperability, such as

- **Connector for Novell GroupWise**—Connector for Novell GroupWise is a gateway component that allows both messaging systems to coexist for either a short period of time or a long period of time. Users of the separate messaging systems interact as if they belong to the same messaging system.

34

- **Calendar Connector**—Together with Connector for Novell GroupWise, the Calendar Connector provides users access to free/busy calendar information that is almost real time. It is important to realize that Calendar Connector always looks for the Schedule+Free Busy folder on the local Exchange 2003 server. Therefore, Exchange Server 2003 should have a local replica of the public folder.

For communication between GroupWise and Exchange Server 2003, an additional component is required. The GroupWise API Gateway version 4.1 with Novell GroupWise Patch 2 for API must be deployed when connecting GroupWise to Exchange. It is important to consider the security ramifications of deploying the API Gateway directory because it is able to perform management functions similar to a Novell NetWare Administrator. After the project team installs and configures Novell GroupWise API Gateway and Connector for GroupWise, they can think about synchronization. Synchronization allows users to work on both systems without losing data or having versioning problems. For instance, the GroupWise system address book and the Exchange Global Address List can be synchronized to provide a unified address list for both GroupWise and Exchange clients.

> **NOTE**
>
> The GroupWise-to-Exchange synchronization tool only synchronizes the address lists between the two environments in which the Exchange Global Address List is synchronized with the GroupWise system address book. No other data is synchronized via the directory synchronization tool.

During the interoperability stage of the migration, it is very important to maintain accurate directory information on both messaging systems. Connector for Novell GroupWise supports the synchronization of directory information. Directory synchronization consists of two sequential processes: synchronizing mail-enabled users from Active Directory to GroupWise and synchronizing recipients from Novell GroupWise to Active Directory. When using the Connector for Novell GroupWise to synchronize directories, the project team should consider the following:

- **Attributes to be synchronized**—If all of the attributes for each user are not required to be synchronized to the Exchange Server 2003 messaging system, the administrator can exclude attributes from the directory synchronization process. For example, the project team might choose to synchronize the directory information for all mailbox-enabled user accounts, but not to synchronize contacts or mail-enabled groups.

- **Organizational units in Active Directory**—Based on the organizational units that are selected, the project team can specify which recipient objects are synchronized with the legacy messaging system. The project team can also specify a target organizational unit for all recipient objects that point to legacy mailboxes.

- **Types of recipient objects to be created**—An administrator can create disabled Windows user accounts, enabled Windows user accounts, or contacts in Active Directory.

- **Replicate groups or distribution lists**—When the project team configures the connector to replicate distribution lists from GroupWise, a mail-enabled contact item is created in Active Directory for that distribution list. When the Exchange Server 2003 end-users send email to that contact, the message is sent to the email address that is specified on the contact, and the message is delivered to the other messaging system where the list is expanded and the email is distributed to all of the recipients on the list.

When synchronizing users from GroupWise to Active Directory, an organizational unit for all contacts representing GroupWise users should be created in Active Directory. After configuring directory synchronization, the project team may want to install and configure the Exchange Calendar Connector to allow calendar lookups to be performed between Exchange and a GroupWise environment. Calendar synchronization consists of two sequential processes: synchronization from GroupWise to Exchange Server 2003 and synchronization from Exchange Server 2003 to GroupWise. After the Calendar Connector is installed, users on Exchange Server 2003 and GroupWise can access each other's free/busy information. The most appropriate thing to do is install Calendar Connector on the server running Connector for Novell GroupWise.

> **NOTE**
>
> The process that occurs when an Exchange Server 2003 end-user queries the free/busy information for a user on GroupWise is different than the process used when the user querying the calendar information for an Exchange Server 2003 end-user is on GroupWise.

When establishing interoperability, companies using Connector for Novell GroupWise should consider installing the connector on a dedicated Exchange bridgehead server. A specific bridgehead server can run exactly one connector instance. One connector can service one direct GroupWise domain and an entire Exchange Server 2003 environment. A GroupWise Message Transfer Agent (GWMTA) is required in the GroupWise domain to route messages within the GroupWise environment to post offices, other domains, or external foreign domains. After interoperability is established, users can be migrated to Exchange.

## Choosing the Direct Migration Approach

The direct migration path is suitable for small- to medium-sized organizations that have not deployed NDS-dependent applications. Migration in these cases can normally be accomplished in a short amount of time with minimal time and effort spent in designing, testing, and implementing multiplatform directory and application sharing across both the Novell and Microsoft environments.

A direct migration is also feasible if the organization is deploying a large number of new desktops or has an older Bindery or NDS network and needs to move the entire organization to a more current operating system. For example, environments that only provide limited services, such as account information and file and print services, are relatively simple migration projects.

The direct migration is exactly what it sounds like. The migration of the existing directory and all file and print data is performed as part of a single process. Immediately following, the printers are migrated and then the workstations are migrated. After the core infrastructure has been migrated, the organization can migrate applications such as GroupWise to Microsoft Exchange because user authentication, file, and print have been previously migrated to Windows.

This process can only be performed if there are no requirements to maintain legacy Novell systems and the environment, and the organization is small enough or there are enough resources to migrate all of the workstations in the environment in a short period of time. In addition, all applications must be fully tested before migration to verify that there is no longer a requirement for a Novell server.

If there is no need to maintain GroupWise and the messaging system is small and not complex, an immediate, one-time migration can be planned by the project team. For example, the company can schedule downtime and migrate the GroupWise data over a weekend or in the evening.

> **NOTE**
>
> The Exchange connector is the conduit by which all mailbox data will be moved from GroupWise to Exchange, so the connector is required to migrate mail from GroupWise in either a direct or phased migration scenario. If the connector is omitted, there is no way to transfer mailbox data from GroupWise into Exchange.

After the interoperability and migration strategy is developed, it is time to deploy the new Exchange Server 2003 environment. The next step is to connect Exchange Server 2003 to GroupWise using a connector tool. After coexistence is established, it is recommended that a client technology such as Outlook 2003 be deployed followed by the task of migrating user data. The Exchange Migration Wizard requires access to the mailbox of each user it is migrating; however, only users can grant access to their accounts. Users need to grant full proxy access using the Novell GroupWise client. After the migration is completed, the project team needs to decommission GroupWise.

This process should be fully tested in the test environment to identify any issues and verify that there are no application requirements for Novell servers. After Novell servers are retired, the client will no longer be able to communicate with a server until it has been migrated to the Windows environment.

# Conducting Preinstallation Checks on Exchange Server 2003

When it comes to the actual installation of Exchange Server 2003, you can run setup manually or you can create an unattend file so that the install can be automated for a branch office with no technical staff at the site. There are also different configurations of Exchange, such as Mailbox Server, Public Folder Server, Front-End Server, Back-End Server, and Bridgehead Server. This section covers the preinstallation tasks prior to installing the first Exchange server in the environment.

## Verifying Core Services Installation

When installing Exchange Server 2003 on a Windows 2003 server, you must make sure that Internet Information Services (IIS), Network News Transfer Protocol (NNTP), and SMTP are installed and running. This can be done by checking the Services applet within Administrative Tools from the Start menu. The setup program looks for IIS, NNTP, and SMTP services before it begins the install and fails if they are not present. In addition, ASP.net and .NET framework need to be installed on the server. None of these services are enabled by default. You have to enable these services manually prior to running the Exchange 2003 setup program.

## Preparing the Forest

The ForestPrep process extends the Active Directory schema to include the Exchange Server 2003 classes and attributes required for the application to run. To run the ForestPrep process, you must have the following permissions by belonging to these groups: enterprise admins, schema admins, domain admins, and local administrator on the Exchange server. During the ForestPrep process, you assign an account that has full Exchange administrator rights to the organization object in Exchange Server 2003.

> **NOTE**
>
> Those familiar with the installation of Exchange 2000 Server will notice that you no longer have to enter an organization name for Exchange during the ForestPrep process with Exchange Server 2003. This is now entered only at the point of installation.

## Preparing the Domain

The DomainPrep process creates groups and permissions within the Active Directory forest so that Exchange Server 2003 can modify user attributes. To run the DomainPrep setup parameter, you must be a member of the domain admins and local administrator groups.

The groups that are created during this process are Exchange domain servers and Exchange enterprise servers. The Exchange domain servers group is a domain global security group and the Exchange enterprise servers group is a domain local security group.

## Reviewing All Log Files

Each of the utilities that you execute has some output in its respective log files. Review the log file after running each utility to ensure no errors are encountered.

# Performing a Core Installation of Exchange Server 2003

When installing Exchange Server 2003 for the first time in an environment, the easiest way to conduct the installation is to insert the Exchange 2003 CD and follow the step-by-step installation instructions. This section of the chapter focuses on the step-by-step installation of a basic Exchange Server 2003 installation.

> **NOTE**
>
> For those who have installed previous versions of Exchange, the setup program now has a new switch that can be used during installation. Running setup with a /ChooseDC {dcname}, followed by the name of a domain controller, tells the setup program to look for a specific DC to write schema changes to or check for permissions and groups.

## Implementing Active Directory

Before you install Exchange Server 2003 on your network, you need to make sure that Active Directory is properly deployed. The Active Directory infrastructure and DNS need to be healthy and without replication errors prior to installing your first Exchange 2003 server. It is so important to perform health checks and verification steps in your environment prior to installation that the Exchange development team has designed the installation program to include these steps. Exdeploy walks you through all the preinstallation health checks before running the setup program for Exchange Server 2003.

## Extending the Active Directory Schema

The first step to the actual implementation of Exchange Server 2003 is to extend the Active Directory schema. The schema comprises the rules that apply to the directory and controls what type of information can be stored in the directory. It also describes how that information is stored in the directory—such as string, string length, integer, and so on. Exchange Server 2003 almost doubles the amount of attributes in the Active Directory schema.

Extending the schema is the easiest part of the installation, but it is also the place where many organizations make mistakes. To extend the Active Directory schema, use the /forestprep switch on setup.exe for Exchange Server 2003 or follow the steps outlined in the deployment tool. The following list contains a few tips to note before extending the Active Directory schema:

- The schema must be extended on the server that holds the Schema Master Flexible Single Master Operations (FSMO) role. By default, the first server installed in the forest contains the Schema Master; however, this role could have been moved to another server. To locate which server contains the Schema Master FSMO role, use the Active Directory Schema Microsoft Management Console (MMC) snap-in, right-click the Active Directory Schema icon under the console root, and select Operations Master.

> **TIP**
>
> To use the Active Directory Schema MMC snap-in, the `adminpak.msi` file must be installed on the server. Use the run command and execute `adminpak.msi` to install the adminpak. After the adminpak is installed, open the MMC from the run prompt by executing MMC; then use the Add/Remove snap-in option from the Console menu to add the Active Directory Schema MMC snap-in.

- The account used to extend the schema must be a member of the schema admins group and domain admins or enterprise admins groups. The schema admins and enterprise admins groups are available only in the first domain in the forest. If the messaging group does not control the forest root domain, this process must be delegated to the group that does.

- A schema change forces a full replication of domain databases and global catalog information in Active Directory. Many administrators are scared of full replications and have heard stories of bandwidth-saturated WAN links due to schema extensions. However, when a full replication occurs, the directory information is compressed before it is sent across the network. The actual amount of data sent across the wire will be approximately 15%–20% of the actual Active Directory database size.

> **NOTE**
>
> For Windows NT 4.0 organizations still in the Active Directory planning stages, to get an approximate size of the Active Directory database size, you multiply the Windows NT 4.0 SAM database by a factor of 3. This is a good ballpark estimate to use for the database size that will be seen immediately after migration. To calculate the size after implementing Exchange Server 2003 and other new directory information, use the AdSizer tool from Microsoft, available at `http://www.microsoft.com/downloads/`.

## Preparing the Windows 2003 Domain

The second step in preparing to install Exchange Server 2003 is to prepare the Windows Server 2003 domain that will host the Exchange servers or mailbox-enabled users. To prepare the Windows Server 2003 domain, use the `/domainprep` switch on `setup.exe` for Exchange Server 2003 or follow the steps outlined in the deployment tool.

The account used to prepare the Windows Server 2003 domain must be a member of the domain admins group in the domain where the /domainprep command is being run. Running DomainPrep performs the following operations on the domain:

- Creates the global security group Exchange Domain Servers
- Creates the domain local security group Enterprise Exchange Servers

- Adds the Exchange Domain Servers group to the Enterprise Exchange Servers group

- Grants appropriate rights to the domain controller used for the Recipient Update Service

For domains that will host mailbox-enabled users and not host Exchange servers, administrators have the choice of running DomainPrep or manually creating a Recipient Update Service for the domain in Exchange System Manager. If the domain will never host Exchange servers, the Recipient Update Service should be manually created. If the domain will eventually host Exchange servers, DomainPrep should be used.

## Step-by-Step Installation of Exchange Server 2003

To install the first Exchange server in an organization using the interactive installation process of Exchange Server 2003:

1. Insert the Exchange Server 2003 CD (Standard or Enterprise).

2. Autorun should launch a splash screen with options for Resources and Deployment Tools. (If autorun does not work, select Start, Run. Then type **CDDrive:\setup.exe** and click OK.)

3. Click Exchange Deployment Tools.

4. At the Deployment Tools welcome screen, click Deploy the First Exchange 2003 Server.

5. Click New Exchange 2003 installation.

6. Verify that your server has met all the operating system and Active Directory requirements. (Click the reference link in the right column.)

7. Check that your server is running NNTP, SMTP, and World Wide Web Services. If you're running Windows 2003, you also need ASP.NET. (Check the reference link to the right of the window for details.)

8. Install the Windows 2003 Support Tools to use the preinstallation utilities (located on the Windows 2003 CD under \support\tools\).

9. Run DCDiag and view the log file output. Click the reference link to the right for details. The syntax is

   ```
   DCDiag /f: log file /s:domain controller
   ```

10. Run NetDiag and view the log file output in netdiag.log.

11. Click Run Forestprep Now.

12. Click Next.

13. Read the license agreement,  and then click I Agree if you agree with the licensing. Click Next.

14. Click Next to accept the default administrator account.

15. Click Finish when the ForestPrep is done.

The next step is to run the DomainPrep on the domain that will hold the Exchange servers and user accounts. To prepare the domain:

1. Click Run Domainprep Now.

2. Click Next.

3. After reading the license agreement, click I Agree, and then click Next.

4. Click Next again.

5. Click Finish.

After the domain has been prepared, it's time to install the Exchange messaging system:

1. Run Setup Now.

2. Click Next.

3. Select I Agree after agreeing with the licensing requirements, and then click Next.

   In the Component Selection window, the default will be Typical for Microsoft Exchange, Install for Microsoft Exchange Messaging and Collaboration Services, and Install for Microsoft Exchange System Management Tools. The configuration screen should look similar to Figure 34.3.

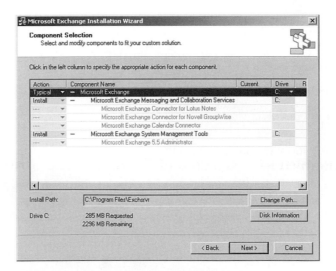

**FIGURE 34.3** Component Selection screen for installation.

4. Click Next.

5. Select Create New Exchange Organization, and click Next.

6. Type the Exchange organization name, and click Next.

7. Select I Agree That I Have Read and Will Be Bound by the License Agreements for this product.

8. Click Next.

9. If you already created the admin group and routing group structure, you are prompted to select where to install this server. Choose an administrative group and click Next. Then choose a routing group, and click Next.

10. Review the Installation Summary and click Next.

11. If you are installing in a Mixed mode domain, you receive a security warning. Click OK to the security group warning.

12. Click Finish.

13. Click OK if prompted to reboot.

# Detailing the Exchange Server 2003 Installation

After the first Exchange Server 2003 server has been installed, the Exchange environment will likely need to be customized to meet the needs and requirements of the organization. The custom options include

- Creating administrative groups

- Creating routing groups

- Creating storage groups

- Creating additional mailbox databases

- Creating a public folder store

## Creating Administrative Group and Routing Group Structure

By default, the Exchange installation program creates an administrative group and routing group called first administrative group and first routing group. If your company wants to create an administrative group structure prior to installing Exchange, it can do so by installing the Exchange System Manager and creating the group structure.

### Setting Administrative Views

To begin managing and administering the administrative groups and routing groups in Exchange Server 2003, administrative views need to be configured. To enable administrative views:

1. Start the Exchange System Manager.

2. Right-click and select Properties on the Exchange organization.

3. On the properties page, select Display Routing Groups and Display Administrative Groups, as shown in Figure 34.4.

4. Click OK.

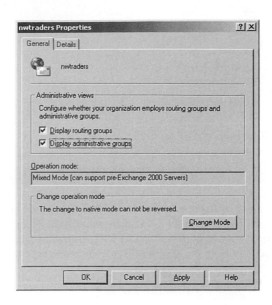

**FIGURE 34.4**    Enabling administrative views.

### Creating Administrative Groups

For a clean installation of Exchange, the organization is set up in a single administrative group. The Exchange administrator can create additional administrative groups to delegate the administration of the organization to other administrators. To create an additional administrative group:

1. Start Exchange System Manager.

2. Right-click Administrative Groups and select New, Administrative Group, as shown in Figure 34.5.

3. Type the name of the group, and click OK.

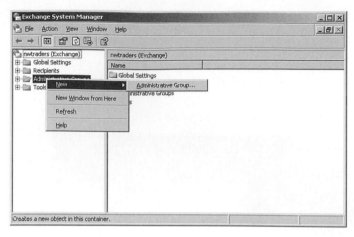

**FIGURE 34.5**    Adding an administrative group.

## Creating Routing Groups

The default installation of administrative groups is to create a single administrative boundary; routing groups also create a single boundary for mail delivery. Routing groups are created to control message flow. A routing group connector then connects routing groups. A new routing group is usually created when there is a transition in bandwidth, such as from a local area network (LAN) to a WAN. Servers separated by a WAN link or highly saturated or unstable LAN link are usually contained in separate routing groups.

In every routing group, one server is identified as the routing group master (RGM). This server is responsible for propagating link state information to other servers in the routing group. The RGM is responsible for tracking which servers are up or down in their own routing group and propagating that information to the RGM servers in other routing groups on the network. Only two states are tracked for the message link, which are up or down.

Routing groups also affect a client's connection to a public folder. When a client attempts to access a public folder, the client uses the copy of the folder on its home server if it exists. If the folder cannot be located on the home server, the client uses a copy in its home server's routing group. If a copy is not available in the local routing group, clients attempt to locate the folder in a remote routing group. The arbitrary cost assigned to the routing group connector by the administrator determines which routing group is selected first.

If the organization has only a single location, a complicated routing structure is unnecessary. However, routing groups can provide the Exchange administrator(s) the ability to throttle the routing of messages between servers and sites. This can be done if an organization has a very low bandwidth between sites and wants to prevent large attachments from saturating the limited bandwidth between locations. Standard messages could be sent throughout the day; however, messages with large attachments can be delayed until the evening when bandwidth is more readily available.

To create an additional routing group:

1. Start Exchange System Manager.

2. Expand the administrative groups/administrative group name.

3. Right-click Routing Groups, and then select New Routing Group, as shown in Figure 34.6.

4. Type the routing group name, and click OK.

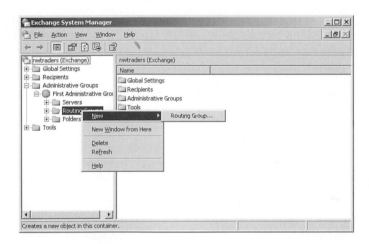

**FIGURE 34.6**    Adding a routing group.

> **NOTE**
>
> You can also rename any new administrative group you create and any of the routing group names after the first server is installed in your organization. To do so, right-click, click Properties, and then click Rename.

## Creating Storage Groups

Storage groups are collections of Exchange databases that the Exchange server manages with a separate process. Each storage group shares a set of transaction logs. Log files are not purged until the entire storage group has been backed up. All databases in the storage group are also subject to the Circular Logging setting on the storage group. Exchange Server 2003, Standard Edition supports a single storage group on a server, and a total of four storage groups are supported on each Exchange Server 2003, Enterprise Edition server.

> **NOTE**
>
> Circular logging is a process that can be enabled to save disk space by overwriting transaction logs. Enabling circular logging is dangerous because, in the event the database fails and has to be restored from tape, a replay of the information in the logs might not contain all the messages since the last backup. For data integrity and recovery reasons, Exchange administrators should never enable circular logging on the storage group. Instead, they should allocate sufficient disk space for the transaction logs and verify that a successful backup of the storage group is being performed each night. Running a full backup and then flagging the tape backup software to purge the log files is the best practice of ensuring that the database has been properly backed up and logs have been cleared.

As an administrator, you should create additional storage groups when

- You can use separate physical transaction log drives to increase performance. Putting an additional storage group on the same physical transaction log drive might actually reduce performance because of transaction log management and should be considered only if the first storage group is full.

- You need to back up multiple databases simultaneously. Databases are backed up at the storage group level. Using multiple storage groups allows simultaneous backups of each storage group.

- The first storage group already has the maximum number of databases supported. When another database is required on a server where the first storage group has the maximum number of supported databases, an additional storage group has to be created.

To create a new storage group, right-click the Exchange server in Exchange System Manager and select New, Storage Group. A set of options, as shown in Figure 34.7, is shown:

- **Name**—The name of the storage group appears in Exchange System Manager and Active Directory Users and Computers when managing users.

- **Transaction Log Location**—Put transaction logs on a different drive than the databases that will be part of this storage group; if the hard drive that the database is on crashes and you have to restore the database from tape, the logs are not affected by the database drive hardware failure. This method can improve data integrity and recoverability.

- **System Path Location**—The system path is the location of temporary files, such as the checkpoint file and reserve logs.

- **Log File Prefix**—The log file prefix is assigned to each log file and is automatically assigned by the server.

- **Zero Out Deleted Database Pages**—This option clears deleted data from the drive, and although that process creates additional overhead, it also increases security.

- **Enable Circular Logging**—Never enable this setting. Make sure the backup jobs are completingsuccessfully to prevent filling the transaction log drive.

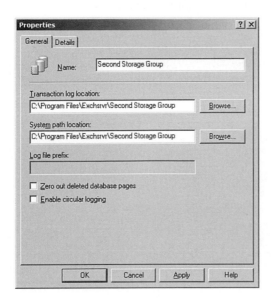

**34**

**FIGURE 34.7**    Options for creating a new storage group.

## Managing Databases

Exchange Server 2003 Enterprise Edition allows five databases per storage group. The number of databases can be any combination of public and private stores. Exchange Server 2003 stores data in two types of databases:

- **EDB**—Stores rich text messages and Internet message headers.

- **STM**—Stores all Multipurpose Internet Mail Extensions (MIME) content. Stores audio, voice, and video as a stream of MIME data without conversion. This reduces the amount of space for storage and reduces the overhead on the server by not converting the data. Message bodies from the Internet messages are also stored in the STM database; the message header is converted to rich text format and stored in the EDB database.

A feature in Exchange Server 2003 mailbox and public store databases is full-text indexing. In earlier versions of Exchange, every folder and message was searched when users initiated a search. In Exchange Server 2003, the administrator can configure an index that is updated and rebuilt periodically. This enables fast searches for Outlook 2003, Outlook XP, and Outlook 2000 users. The following attachment types are also included in the index: .doc, .xls, .ppt, .html, .htm, .asp, .txt, and .eml (embedded MIME messages). Binary attachments are not included in the index. To initiate a full-text index, right-click the Mail or Public store and select Create Full Text Index.

## Creating Additional Mailbox Stores

New mailbox stores should be created when the size of the existing mailbox store is growing too large to manage. To create a new mailbox store, right-click the storage group and select New, Mailbox Store. When creating a new mailbox store, the options to configure appear as tabs, as shown in Figure 34.8:

**FIGURE 34.8**    Options for creating a new database.

- **General**—Defines the database name, the offline address book to use, message archiving, whether digitally signed messages are allowed, and plain text display.

- **Database**—Sets the location for the EDB and STM databases. These should be stored on a hardware RAID 5 or 0+1 drive. Also controls the online database maintenance schedule.

- **Limits**—Configures the message storage limit at which users are warned that sending and receiving are prohibited. Also sets the deleted items and mailbox policy.

- **Full-Text Indexing**—Configures how often the full-text index is updated and rebuilt.

- **Details**—Notes any information about the configuration that is manually keyed in to this page by an administrator or Exchange Server manager.

- **Policies**—Defines the system mailbox store policies that apply to the mailbox store.

Three entries are listed below the mailbox store that can provide the administrator information regarding the status of the store:

- **Logons**—Last logon time, last access time, client type used to log on, and the Windows 2000 or Windows 2003 account that was used

- **Mailboxes**—Number of items in the mailbox, mailbox size, and last log on and log off time

- **Full-Text Indexing**—Index information, such as location, size, state, number of documents, and the last build time

## Creating a Public Folder Store

Unlike the mailbox store, new public stores should be created only when there is a need for a new public folder tree, because each public folder store needs to be associated with a public folder tree. Public folder trees can be created under the folders container in each storage group. Only one public store from each Exchange server can be associated with a public folder tree. To create a new public store, right-click the storage group and select New, Public Store. The majority of the tabs are identical to those of the mailbox store. The following are tabs that contain unique public folder store settings:

- **Replication**—Sets the replication schedule, interval, and size limit for public folder replication messages

- **Limits**—Includes an age limit setting for the number of days for folder content to be valid

The entries listed below the public folder store provide the administrator information regarding the status of the store:

- **Logons**—Last logon time, last access time, client type used to log on, and the Windows 2000 or Windows 2003 account that was used

- **Public Folder Instances**—Information about folders that are being replicated to other servers

- **Public Folders**—Folder size, number of items, creation date, and last access time

- **Replication Status**—Replication status of each folder in the public folder store—for example, In Sync indicates that the folder is up to date

- **Full-Text Indexing**—Index information, such as location, size, state, number of documents, and the last build time

# Performing Postinstallation Configurations

After Exchange Server 2003 has been installed and customized, you should take a few cleanup and implementation steps. These steps help to clean up and remove services, connectors, and logging functions enabled as part of the installation process. The cleanup task involves the following:

- Disabling unnecessary services

- Removing Information Stores that won't be used

- Setting up routing group connections

- Enabling logging and message tracking

- Deleting mailbox and public folder stores

## Disabling Services

Although Exchange Server 2003 does a much better job by not automatically installing dozens of different utilities and services the way previous versions of Exchange did, it still installs some default services that might not be used by the organization. For security and administration purposes, if a service is not used, it should be disabled. To disable services that are commonly unused—such as Internet Message Access Protocol (IMAP), Post Office Protocol 3 (POP3), NNTP, or SMTP—do the following:

1. Select Start, All Programs, Administrative Tools, Services.

2. Scroll down to the IMAP4 Service.

3. Double-click on the service.

4. Under the Startup Type section, choose Disabled.

5. Under the Service Status section, click Stop.

6. Repeat steps 1–5 for POP3, NNTP, and SMTP, as applicable.

> **NOTE**
>
> If IMAP, POP3, and NNTP are used on a server, such as a front-end system hosting remote mail users, those services should not be disabled. It's common on back-end servers on which IMAP or POP3 is not used that the service could be disabled; it's also common for organizations that use Exchange just for email and do not need NNTP on any of their servers. For servers or systems that are not routing mail, such as those set up solely as Exchange System Manager administration servers, the SMTP service should be disabled.

## Removing Information Stores

By default, an Information Store that holds Exchange databases is created on each Exchange server installed in the organization. However, dedicated front-end servers that are just the Web front-end systems do not require Information Stores or databases. In those cases, the Information Stores should be deleted. To delete the Information Stores that are unneeded on front-end servers:

1. Select Start, All Programs, Microsoft Exchange, System Manager.

2. Navigate to Administrative Groups, Administrative Group Name, Servers, Server Name, Storage Groups.

3. Right-click on the mailbox store and choose Delete.

4. Click Yes.

5. Click OK and delete the database files manually.

---

**CAUTION**

Before deleting any database or Information Store, unless you are positive the database or Information Store is completely empty and unused, you might want to do a full backup of the database, store, and system—in case a user's mailbox was inadvertently hosted on the system. Sometimes during an early implementation of Exchange, an organization might start with just one or two servers in a pilot test environment. If a mailbox was stored on one of the test servers, it might eventually become the front-end server for the organization. Backing up a system is safer than making assumptions and regretting the decision later. Using the NTBackup utility covered in Chapter 31, "Backing Up the Exchange Server 2003 Environment," is a quick way to back up a system.

---

## Setting Up Routing Group Connectors

Routing group connectors should be used in situations in which there is greater than 64Kbps of available bandwidth between the routing groups. If there is not sufficient bandwidth, SMTP or X.400 connectors should be used to connect the routing groups. Routing group and routing group connector designs should follow the organization's physical connectivity links. Four basic routing group connector strategies can be implemented based on the organization's physical network links:

- **Full mesh**—In a full mesh, all routing groups connect to all other routing groups. Unless there are only a few routing groups, the administrative overhead for implementation becomes unbearable. This design can also be a waste of administrative resources if there isn't the WAN link redundancy to support the design.

- **Partial mesh**—A partial mesh tries to create the benefits of a full mesh without the added administrative overhead. If the WAN design is a partial mesh, build the routing groups to follow the partial mesh.

- **Hub-and-spoke**—In a hub-and-spoke design, one routing group becomes the center of the universe and all other routing groups connect to it. In larger networks, there can be multiple hubs in the enterprise, and the hubs are joined together in a full or partial mesh. This design is simple to implement and maintain but creates a single point of failure at the hub. This design is an option for locations that do not have any WAN link redundancy.

- **Linear**—In a linear design, routing groups connect to only one other routing group in a straight line. Linear designs are not recommended.

To create a new routing group:

1. Navigate to Administrative Groups, Admin Groups, Routing Groups, HO, as shown in Figure 34.9.

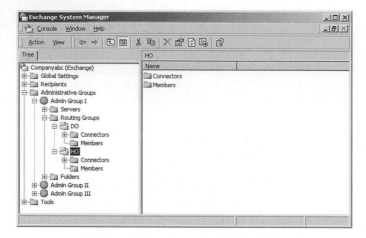

**FIGURE 34.9**    Traversing the Exchange System Manager for routing groups.

2. Right-click Connectors and choose New Routing Group Connector.

3. Type a name for the connector, as shown in Figure 34.10.

4. Click These Servers Can Send Mail over This Connector, and click Add to choose a server or check Any Local Server Can Send Mail over This Connector.

The General tab of the routing group connector defines a few significant items that administrators should understand when configuring the connector:

- **Connects This Routing Group With**—Specifies the destination routing group for the RGC.

- **Cost**—Identifies the arbitrary cost assigned by the administrator, which can be used to control which connector is used first if multiple connectors exist.

- **Server**—Allows any server, or specifies specific servers allowed, to transfer mail to the destination routing group. By specifying specific servers, a bridgehead server is nominated. By specifying multiple servers, backup bridgehead servers are identified. The order of the servers in the list specifies which server is used first.

- **Do Not Allow Public Folder Referrals**—Disables the user's ability to access public folder content that is homed in the routing group connected to that server.

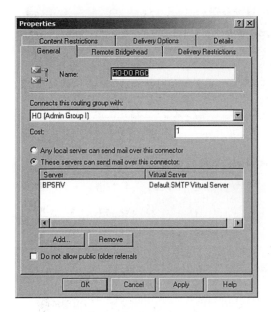

**FIGURE 34.10**    Routing group configuration screen.

5. Click the Remote Bridgehead tab, and click Add to choose a server. After entering the bridgehead server selection, you see a screen similar to Figure 34.11.

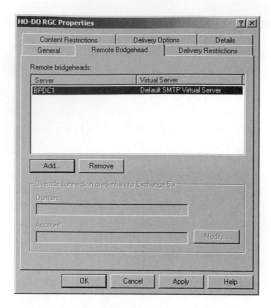

**FIGURE 34.11**    Bridgehead server configuration.

6. Click OK.

7. Select Yes to create a routing group connector in the remote routing group.


## Enabling Logging and Message Tracking

Logging and message tracking are common functions enabled by Exchange administrators early on in an Exchange implementation to help the administrator validate that messages are flowing through the environment. By enabling the logging and message tracking function, the administrator can then run a report to find out which route a message took to get from one server to another, and how long it took for the message to be transmitted.

Many administrators never use the logging and message tracking function and simply assume that messages are getting from point A to point B successfully. In many environments, although messages reach their destination, they are routed from one site to another and once around the globe before being received by a mail user in the same site facility. Misconfigured routing group connectors, DNS errors, or other networking problems are often the cause. So it's usually helpful to monitor messages to ensure that they are being routed and processed as expected.

To enable logging and message tracking:

1. Open Exchange System Manager.

2. Navigate to Administrative Groups, Admin Groups, Servers, Server Name.

3. Right-click the server object and choose Properties.

4. Select Enable Subject Logging and Display and Enable Message Tracking.

5. Type a number for days to keep the message tracking log files, as shown in Figure 34.12.

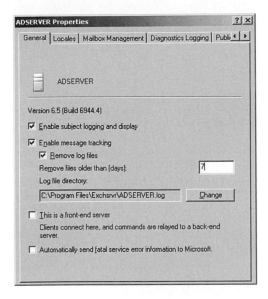

**FIGURE 34.12**   Configuring logging for message tracking.

## Installing and Configuring a Gateway Between GroupWise and Exchange

After you configure your new Microsoft Exchange environment, you can establish a connection between GroupWise and Exchange for email flow using the Connector for Novell GroupWise. The connector is installed on an Exchange Server 2003 server. This includes installing the connector, which you can do as part of the server setup or afterward, when you start the Exchange setup program on a server on which Exchange Server 2003 is already installed. For the purposes of these instructions, it is assumed that you are performing the connector installation during the initial server setup.

### Prerequisites for Migrating to Exchange Server 2003

Before implementing the Exchange Server 2003 server that will host the gateway between GroupWise and Exchange, the organization needs to keep in mind some basic system requirements. Those requirements are

- You already have an existing Microsoft Windows® network, including an Exchange organization, and the Active Directory® directory service is deployed.

- You have Exchange Administrator permissions to install an Exchange Server 2003 server in the Exchange organization.

- You have network connectivity to the server running Novell GroupWise.

- You can resolve the NDS name of the server running Novell NetWare.

- In Exchange System Manager, you have selected the Display Routing Groups and Display Administrative Groups options on the properties page for the organization object.

Organizations must ensure the server running Novell NetWare and Novell GroupWise has the following software installed:

- Novell NetWare 3.x or later

- Novell NetWare Administrator

- Novell GroupWise 4.1 or later

From an Exchange migration perspective, Microsoft offers connectors for coexistence and migration support between GroupWise and Exchange. The level of coexistence is dependent on the Exchange version a company is running. Currently, the migration and connectivity tools between GroupWise and Microsoft Exchange support Novell GroupWise versions 4.1x, 5.0, 5.1, 5.2x, 5.5x, 6.x, and 6.5x.

## Migration Considerations for All GroupWise Environments

Although the Migration Wizard permits the migration of mail, calendar items, and contact information to Exchange Server 2003 from any of the GroupWise product versions listed previously, you should review a number of items in the planning of any GroupWise-to-Exchange migration.

One key consideration when planning a migration from GroupWise is the level of support that can be expected for legacy versions of GroupWise products. Currently, all versions of GroupWise prior to version 6.x are no longer supported by Novell. Novell has a policy of continuing to provide best-effort paid support for these products, but it frequently proves to be a challenge obtaining patches and updates for these unsupported versions. As a result, companies must assess the health of their GroupWise environment and identify and address all issues prior to doing a migration.

Another issue to be aware of when considering a migration of any GroupWise environment is the limitations end-users of GroupWise 4.1 API Gateway impose. The GroupWise 4.1 API Gateway is used by the Connector for Novell GroupWise to transfer mail, appointments, and directory information between GroupWise and Exchange during the migration period. Unfortunately, the API Gateway is no longer supported by Novell, and no replacement solution currently exists.

There are a number of other limitations that frequently come up during a GroupWise migration that cannot be directly addressed by any migration tool:

- Proxy access granted to other GroupWise users cannot be migrated to Exchange. Users who rely on proxy access to other GroupWise users' mailboxes will need to be migrated together and existing GroupWise mailbox proxy rights must be re-created in each user's mailbox. The GroupWise GWCHECK tool can be used to report on proxy access for an entire post office. This information can be used to reassign the appropriate mailbox permission settings as users are migrated to Exchange.

- Shared folders that currently exist in GroupWise will not be accessible to Exchange users. While each user who is migrated receives her own copy of all GroupWise folders in her mailbox (shared or otherwise), the shared folder permissions are not migrated. The GWCHECK tool can be used to report on shared folder permissions and these permissions reapplied as users are migrated to Exchange.

- No migration path of any type exists for GroupWise document libraries. Customers with access to a product such as Adobe Acrobat have sometimes elected to generate PDFs or other electronic versions of the documents stored in the GroupWise document management library.

## Installing an Exchange Server 2003 Server with the Connector for GroupWise

After the initial migration requirements have been met and the GroupWise API Gateway has been configured, the next step is to install the Connector for GroupWise on an Exchange Server 2003 system. Follow these steps to install the Connector for GroupWise:

1. Insert the Exchange Server 2003 CD into the CD-ROM drive of a computer running Windows Server 2003.

2. At a command prompt, type **cd e:\setup\i386**, where *e* is the drive letter for the CD-ROM drive.

3. Type **setup.exe** and press Enter.

4. On the Microsoft Exchange Installation Wizard Welcome page, click Next.

5. On the License Agreement page, if you agree with the terms of the license agreement, click I Agree, and then click Next.

6. On the Product Identification page, enter your CD key and then click Next.

7. On the Component Selection page, in the Action drop-down list next to Exchange Server 2003, click Change.

8. In the Microsoft Connector for Novell GroupWise and Microsoft Exchange Calendar Connector drop-down list, click Install, as shown in Figure 34.13, and then click Next.

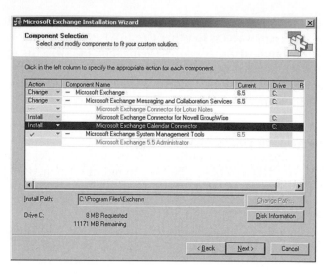

**FIGURE 34.13**    Installing Connector for Novell GroupWise.

9. If you are installing your first Exchange Server 2003 server, an Installation Type page appears. Ensure that Create a New Exchange Organization is selected, and click Next.

10. If you are creating a new Exchange organization, on the Organization Name page, enter an organization name, and click Next.

11. On the Licensing Agreement page, if you agree, click I Agree That I Have Read and Will Be Bound by the License Agreements for This Product, and then click Next.

12. On the Component Summary page, ensure that Connector for Novell GroupWise is selected, and then click Next.

13. If a Microsoft Exchange Installation Wizard message box appears informing you that your domain has been identified as an insecure domain for mail-enabled groups with hidden distribution list membership, click OK.

14. After setup completes successfully, click Finish.

> **NOTE**
>
> If Exchange Server 2003 Service Pack 1 is installed on the system, you need to reinstall Service Pack 1 after the connector is installed.

## Enabling and Customizing Novell GroupWise Proxy Addresses

After the Connector for GroupWise component has been installed, the administrator needs to enable and customize the Novell GroupWise proxy addresses to properly set the default naming scheme that will be used for recipients and to ensure messages are directed to the correct server system. The process for enabling and customizing Novell GroupWise proxy addresses is as follows:

1. Start Exchange System Manager: On the Start menu, point to All Programs, point to Microsoft Exchange, and then click System Manager.

2. Expand Recipients, and then click Recipient Policies.

3. In the details pane, right-click Default Policy, and then click Properties. You can also create a new recipient policy.

4. On the policy's E-Mail Addresses (Policy) tab, select the GWISE check box (this enables the address), ensure that the GWISE address entry is selected, and then click Edit.

5. In the Address box, modify the address format. For example, you can set the address format to first name and last name, or first initial and last name, or something similar.

6. After you configure the address formula, click OK.

7. In the Default Policy Properties dialog box, click OK.

8. A message box appears asking whether you want to update all corresponding recipient email addresses to match the new addresses. To run the Recipient Update Service immediately, click Yes. To update the addresses the next time the Recipient Update Service runs, click No. Non-Exchange addresses are always updated, even if you made manual changes to specific addresses.

9. Wait for the Recipient Update Service to populate the Exchange address lists. The time required to populate the lists varies depending on the update interval set on the service.

## Configuring the Connector for Novell GroupWise

With the Connector for Novell GroupWise installed and the default proxy address established for the GWISE namespace, you need to perform a few configuration steps for the connector to work properly. The configuration steps are as follows:

1. In Exchange System Manager, expand Administrative Groups, expand Routing Groups, and expand the First Routing Group. Expand the Connectors container, right-click Connector for Novell GroupWise, and then click Properties.

2. On the General tab, shown in Figure 34.14, in the API Gateway Path box, type the full path to your Novell GroupWise API Gateway directory in Universal Naming Convention (UNC), including the server name. For example: `\\NWSERVER01\SYS\Mail\GWDom\WPGate\API41`.

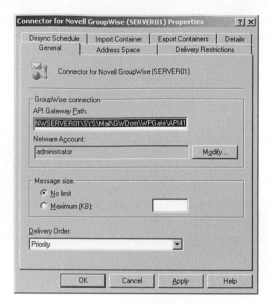

**FIGURE 34.14**    Connector for Novell GroupWise General tab settings.

3. Under Netware Account, click Modify. Type the account name in the NetWare Account box (for example, Exchange). Under Password and Confirm Password, enter the password that was defined in NetWare Administrator.

4. Under Message Size, specify a maximum size for messages that are allowed to pass this Connector for Novell GroupWise instance, or accept the default setting of No Limit.

5. In the Delivery Order list, choose the order in which messages are to be delivered from Exchange Server 2003 to Novell GroupWise. The order you specify controls the sequence in which Exchange messages are placed in the MTS-OUT queue by the Exchange message transfer agent (MTA), and hence the sequence in which messages are delivered to the API Gateway. The options are

   - **Priority**—High-priority messages, such as urgent messages, are delivered to the outbound queue first. This is the default setting.

   - **FIFO**—Messages are delivered to the outbound queue on a first in, first out (FIFO) basis.

   - **Size**—Smaller messages are delivered to the outbound queue before larger messages.

6. On the Address Space tab, click Add to add the address space for Novell GroupWise.

7. On the Add Address Space tab, click GWISE, and then click OK.

8. On the Novell GroupWise Address Space Properties tab, in the Address box, type *
   to allow all users to connect to Novell GroupWise using Connector for Novell
   GroupWise, and then click OK.

9. Click OK to close the Connector for Novell GroupWise Properties dialog box and
   apply the settings.

## Starting the Connector for Novell GroupWise

After being configured, the Windows service that manages the Connector for Novell
GroupWise needs to be started. You can do this by completing the following steps:

1. Start the Services tool: Click Start, point to All Programs, point to Administrative
   Tools, and then click Services.

2. Right-click Microsoft Exchange Connector for Novell GroupWise, and then click
   Start.

3. Verify that Connector for Novell GroupWise starts successfully, and then close the
   Services tool.

## Configuring Directory Synchronization

After the configuration of the Connector for Novell GroupWise is completed, the Novell
GroupWise and Exchange Server 2003 directories can be synchronized, either manually or
on a schedule that you establish. Prior to configuring automatic directory synchronization, at least one manual synchronization should be completed to verify that directory
entries are correctly synchronized to both systems.

### Requirements for Configuring Directory Synchronization

To establish directory synchronization between Novell GroupWise and Exchange, a
number of prerequisite steps must be completed to allow directory information to be
synchronized across the Connector for Novell GroupWise. Review your environment to
confirm that the following requirements are met:

- You have Exchange Administrator permissions.

- You have network connectivity to the Novell NetWare server running Novell
  GroupWise.

- You can resolve the NDS name of the Novell NetWare server running Novell
  GroupWise from the Exchange server running the Connector for Novell GroupWise.

- You have installed and configured the Novell GroupWise client software.

- You have installed and configured Connector for Novell GroupWise.

To configure directory synchronization with Novell GroupWise, perform the following steps:

1. In Exchange System Manager, right-click Connector for Novell GroupWise, and then click Properties.

2. On the Import Container tab, shown in Figure 34.15, to specify the Active Directory container (or organizational unit) to which Novell GroupWise users are imported, click Modify. It is recommended that you create a special organizational unit for all of your Novell GroupWise users and select that organizational unit here.

3. On the Choose a Container tab, browse to the container to which you want to import Novell GroupWise users. Click the container and then click OK.

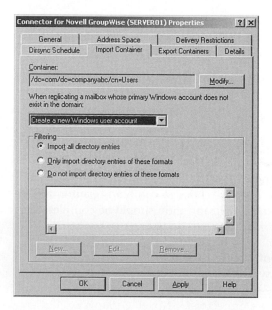

**FIGURE 34.15**    Configuring inbound directory synchronization.

> **NOTE**
>
> You might receive an error message that reads, "The machine account must be granted permission to create and modify recipients in the selected import container. Continue?" If you receive this error message, click Yes. This is necessary for directory synchronization from Novell GroupWise to Exchange Server 2003 to work. When you click Yes, you add the computer account with the permissions required to manipulate objects in the selected container.

4. When replicating a mailbox whose primary Windows account does not exist in the domain list, choose one of the following options for Active Directory to use when new users are imported:

- Create a Disabled Windows User Account
- Create a New Windows User Account
- Create a Windows Contact

This setting applies only to new users. If you change this setting later, it does not affect Novell GroupWise users who are already replicated to Active Directory. If you are not sure which option to choose, click Create a Disabled Windows User Account or Create a Windows Contact. Click Create a New Windows User Account only if Novell GroupWise users are logging on to the Windows domain.

5. Under Filtering, choose one of the following options to determine which GroupWise directory entries to replicate to Active Directory:

- Import All Directory Entries
- Only Import Directory Entries of These Formats
- Do Not Import Directory Entries of These Formats

The default setting, Import All Directory Entries, imports all GroupWise directory objects with a visibility set to System in GroupWise without applying any filters. The remaining two options allow you to define a filter when you click the New button to display the Import Filter dialog box. In the Import Filter dialog box, you can use wildcard characters—asterisk (*) and question mark (?)—to create your filter, where an asterisk denotes any number of characters of any value, and a question mark denotes one character of any value.

6. On the Export Containers tab, to specify which groups or organizational units to export from Active Directory to the Novell GroupWise directory, click Add.

7. On the Choose a Container tab, click the organizational unit that you want to export to the Novell GroupWise directory, and then click OK.

> **NOTE**
>
> You might receive an error message that reads, "The machine account must be granted permission to read the deleted recipients in the selected domain. Continue?" If you receive this error message, click Yes. This is necessary for directory synchronization from Novell GroupWise to Exchange Server 2003 to work. When you click Yes, you add the computer account with the permissions required to manipulate objects in the selected container.

8. Repeat the preceding two steps for each organizational unit that you want to export. Nested organizational units are not selected for export if you select the parent organizational unit. You must select each organizational unit individually.

9. On the Dirsync Schedule tab, in the Exchange-GroupWise directory update schedule list, select the schedule for directory synchronization. Connector for Novell GroupWise performs the directory synchronization.

> **TIP**
>
> Do not schedule synchronization during peak traffic hours because it can slow message through-put. If your directory information changes infrequently, schedule synchronization for once per day. If your directory information changes frequently, schedule synchronization for two or more times per day.

10. Click Customize to schedule synchronization for a period other than those provided by default in the Exchange-GroupWise directory update schedule list.

11. Click OK to close each dialog box.

## Manually Testing Directory Synchronization

To confirm that directory synchronization is working properly, perform the following test to verify that the process is working:

1. In Exchange System Manager, right-click Connector for Novell GroupWise, and then click Properties.

2. On the Dirsync Schedule tab, under Exchange to GroupWise Directory Synchronization, click Immediate Full Reload. In the Exchange System Manager message box informing you that a process has been started to synchronize the directories, click OK. This process synchronizes directory objects from Active Directory to the Novell GroupWise directory.

3. Under GroupWise to Exchange Directory Synchronization, click Immediate Full Reload. Again, a message box appears informing you that directory synchronization has begun. This process synchronizes directory objects from the Novell GroupWise directory to Active Directory. Click OK.

# Installing and Configuring Calendar Connector in a GroupWise Environment

The Connector for Novell GroupWise can only synchronize address book entries between GroupWise and Exchange messaging systems. To allow the exchange of calendar information and free/busy data between GroupWise and Exchange users, the Calendar Connector needs to be installed on the Exchange server and configured to connect to the GroupWise environment. The following procedure identifies the steps to configure the Microsoft Exchange Calendar Connector. The Calendar Connector needs to be installed on a server running Exchange. The most straightforward option is to install the Calendar Connector on the same server running the Connector for Novell GroupWise.

## Prerequisites for the Calendar Connector for GroupWise

Similar to the Connector for GroupWise, there are prerequisites for the system and system access to ensure the Calendar Connector will work properly. The server on which the Calendar Connector is installed must meet the following requirements:

- The server is running Exchange Server 2003.

- The server running Exchange Server 2003 has a local replica of the SCHEDULE+ FREE BUSY public folder.

- The server is part of the same routing group as the server running Connector for Novell GroupWise.

- You have Exchange Administrator permissions, and you are a member of the Administrators group on the computer on which you install Calendar Connector.

- You have network connectivity to the Novell NetWare server running the Novell GroupWise API Gateway.

## Installing the Calendar Connector

To install the Calendar Connector for GroupWise, you should complete following steps:

1. Insert the Exchange Server 2003 CD into the CD-ROM drive of the server running Exchange Server 2003.

2. At a command prompt, type **cd e:\setup\i386**, where *e* is the drive letter for the CD-ROM drive.

3. Type **setup.exe**, and then press Enter.

4. On the Microsoft Exchange 2003 Installation Wizard Welcome page, click Next.

5. On the Component Selection page, in the Action list next to Microsoft Exchange, click Change.

6. In the Action list next to Microsoft Exchange Messaging and Collaboration Services, click Change.

7. In the Microsoft Exchange Calendar Connector list, click Install, and then click Next.

8. On the Installation Summary page, verify your installation choices, and then click Next.

9. After the installation is complete, click Finish.

## Adding a Local Replica for the Schedule+ Free/Busy Public Folder

One of the prerequisites for configuring the Calendar Connector is that a local replica of the Schedule+ Free/Busy public folder needs to reside on the Exchange server where the Calendar Connector is installed. To add a local replica on the server, do the following:

1. In Exchange System Manager, expand Administrative Groups, expand the administrative group that contains the server running Exchange with Calendar Connector (for example, First Administrative Group), and then expand Folders.

2. Expand Public Folders. If you do not see the SCHEDULE+ FREE BUSY public folder, right-click Public Folders, and then click View System Folders.

3. Expand Public Folders, expand SCHEDULE+ FREE BUSY, right-click the public folder that refers to your administrative group that contains the Exchange server running Calendar Connector (for example, EX:/o=Companyabc /ou=First Administrative Group), and then click Properties.

4. On the Replication tab, click Add.

5. On the Select a Public Store page, select the server running Exchange Server 2003 with Calendar Connector, and then click OK.

6. In the Public folder replication interval list, click Always Run. This causes replication to occur whenever there is a change in free/busy information. Click OK.

## Configuring the Calendar Connector

After the Calendar Connector is installed and a replica of the Schedule+ Free/Busy information has been added to the Exchange server, the Calendar Connector can be configured. Perform the following steps to complete the configuration:

1. In Exchange System Manager, expand Administrative Groups, and then expand the administrative group that contains the server running Exchange with Calendar Connector (for example, First Administrative Group).

2. Expand Routing Groups and then expand the routing group in which you installed Calendar Connector (for example, First Routing Group).

3. Expand Connectors, right-click Calendar Connector, and then click Properties.

4. On the General tab, shown in Figure 34.16, next to the Connector Used to Import Users into Active Directory box, click Modify.

5. In the Select Exchange Notes or Groupwise Connector dialog box, select the Connector for Novell GroupWise instance that is used to connect to the Novell GroupWise API Gateway, and then click OK.

6. In the Number of Days of Free/Busy Information to Request from Foreign Calendars box, enter the number of days that users are able to see free/busy information for users on the foreign messaging server. Free/busy information beyond the number of days specified is not retrieved by Calendar Connector and appears as free, even if meetings are scheduled during this time. Remember that the maximum value for GroupWise is 389 days.

7. In the Maximum Age in Minutes of Foreign Free/Busy data in Exchange That Can Be Used Without Querying the Foreign Calendar box, enter the age limit for free/busy information in minutes. If the free/busy information is beyond the specified number of minutes and a user requests the information, Calendar Connector queries the non-Exchange messaging system for updated data. If the free/busy information is within the specified number of minutes, Calendar Connector uses the current free/busy information.

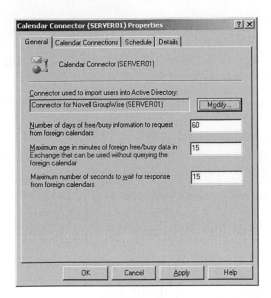

**FIGURE 34.16** Setting the General tab Calendar Connector options.

8. In the Maximum Number of Seconds to Wait for Response from Foreign Calendars box, enter the number of seconds that you want Calendar Connector to wait for a response after it requests an individual user's free/busy information. Set this to a low number because each recipient on a meeting request is handled in turn, and a long response interval can cause the mail client to stop responding as it proceeds down the list of recipients.

9. On the Calendar Connections tab, click New.

10. In the Calendar Type dialog box, click Novell GroupWise, and then click OK.

11. In the GroupWise Calendar Connection dialog box, in the GroupWise API Gateway box, type the domain and gateway name of the Connector for Novell GroupWise that interfaces with the API Gateway. Do not include the certifier information. For example, if your Novell GroupWise domain name is COMPANYABC_DOM, and the API gateway name is Exchange Gateway, type **COMPANYABC_DOM.Exchange Gateway**, and then click OK.

12. On the Schedule tab, click Always. This causes Calendar Connector to create a free/busy record for Novell GroupWise recipients in the Exchange public folder. This happens every 15 minutes for new recipients. Alternatively, click Selected Times to Specify a Custom Time for the Connector to Create New Records in the Server's Public Folder. Click OK.

## Starting Calendar Connector Service

After the Calendar Connector has been installed and configured on the Exchange server, the Calendar Connector service needs to be started. Do the following to start the Calendar Connector service:

1. Open the Services Microsoft Management Console (MMC) snap-in: Click Start, point to All Programs, point to Administrative Tools, and then click Services.

2. In the details pane, right-click Microsoft Exchange Calendar Connector, and then click Start.

3. The default startup type for Calendar Connector is Manual. You should change the startup type to Automatic. To do this, right-click Microsoft Exchange Calendar Connector, and then click Properties. In the Startup type list, click Automatic, and then click OK. The next time the server starts, the Calendar Connector service starts automatically.

## Reviewing the Results of the Lab Environment

Based on the results of the migration lab testing, it is important to review and adjust your migration plans as appropriate based on the results of the test lab. It is expected that problems will arise in the test lab. Repeat the test migration process to refine the migration process until you are comfortable with the results. This process leads into the next phase of the migration, the stabilizing phase, where the process is finalized.

# Using the Exchange Migration Wizard to Migrate User Data

With the new Microsoft Exchange environment created, user accounts migrated to Microsoft Exchange environment, and the Connector for Novell GroupWise exchanging information between Novell GroupWise and Exchange, existing mailbox information can be migrated to the new Exchange environment.

The Exchange Migration Wizard is a free tool from Microsoft that is installed by default as part of Exchange Server 2003. This utility can migrate mailbox data from a variety of messaging platforms, including Microsoft Mail, Microsoft Exchange v5.5, Lotus cc:Mail, Lotus Notes, Novell GroupWise, LDAP via ADSI, and IMAP4. This chapter focuses on the use of the Exchange Migration Wizard to migrate mailbox data from Novell GroupWise to Exchange Server 2003.

## Setting Up a Migration Server for Novell GroupWise and Exchange Server 2003

For the purposes of this chapter, the server that runs the Exchange Migration Wizard is referred to as a migration server. The migration server must have both the Novell GroupWise client and the Novell NetWare client installed to allow access to the

GroupWise mailboxes that will be migrated. The following versions of the Novell GroupWise and Novell NetWare clients are recommended for use on the migration server:

- **GroupWise Client version 5.2.5 or higher**—This recommendation pertains only to the migration server. GroupWise users can use the latest GroupWise client.

- **Novell Client version 4.8 or higher**—This recommendation pertains only to the migration server. Novell users can use the latest NDS client.

> **TIP**
>
> If possible, multiple migration servers should be deployed to allow multiple GroupWise mailboxes to be migrated simultaneously. Because the migration process is a single-threaded operation that only migrates one mailbox at a time, having multiple migration servers available greatly reduces the time required to complete the migration to Exchange. The migration servers can be workstation-class machines or older servers that have been decommissioned, with a minimum recommendation of 128MB of RAM for each migration server.

**34**

## Preparing the Users' Novell GroupWise Mailboxes

For the Migration Wizard to access users' GroupWise mailboxes, the GroupWise account that is being used to perform the migration must be granted proxy access to the GroupWise users' mailboxes. This can be accomplished by having the GroupWise user who is being migrated grant full proxy access to the account being used to perform the migration.

To ensure that any corruption or other GroupWise database issues are corrected prior to the migration, it is recommended that the Novell GWCHECK utility be used to scan the mailbox databases of the GroupWise accounts that are being migrated. GWCHECK is a free tool that is available from the Novell support Web site at http://support.novell.com/filefinder/; search for the keyword GWCHECK. Be sure to download the most current version of GWCHECK for the version of GroupWise that is running in your environment. If issues are encountered when running GWCHECK, the utility can be run multiple times to correct any issues that are encountered. If GroupWise database issues are encountered that GWCHECK is unable to correct, it may be possible to correct the issue by moving the affected user's mailbox to a different GroupWise post office. This process copies the user's entire mailbox to the new post office location and writes a fresh copy of the mailbox data into the new post office database, ensuring that the data can be read in its entirety by the GroupWise post office agents. After the mailbox move is completed, the user's mailbox can be migrated directly to Exchange from the new post office location, or moved back to the original post office if necessary.

In addition to running the GWCheck tool, you might want to perform the following Novell GroupWise tasks:

- Delete users who no longer exist from Novell GroupWise.

- Run the Novell VREPAIR tool, available from Novell, to repair any problems on traditional Novell NetWare volumes.

- Run the Novell Timesync tool, available from Novell, at the server console to ensure that the time on all servers across the network is consistent.

- Clean all mail queues of old mail.

## Deploying Outlook 2003 Client Software to Pilot User Workstations

To access their new Exchange mailboxes, Outlook 2003 client software must be deployed to all client workstations. In an automated deployment scenario, Outlook 2003 can be automatically installed using the Custom Installation Wizard.

1. Configure directory synchronization between GroupWise and Exchange. Directory synchronization must be configured between GroupWise and Exchange using the Connector for Novell GroupWise and the GroupWise API Gateway.

2. Migrate data from Novell GroupWise to Exchange Server 2003. The next step in performing migration from Novell GroupWise to Exchange Server 2003 is to migrate the users and mailboxes from Novell GroupWise to the Exchange 2003 server. You do this by running the Exchange Migration Wizard on an Exchange 2003 server with Novell NetWare client and Novell GroupWise client installed (for example, the server that you configured to run Connector for Novell GroupWise). The Exchange Migration Wizard uses the Novell GroupWise client API to access GroupWise mailboxes.

> **NOTE**
>
> It is important that the Connector for Novell GroupWise service be stopped during migration to prevent directory synchronization from occurring during the migration process. Because it is possible that migration of mailbox data from GroupWise to Exchange will not complete successfully, stopping the Connector for Novell GroupWise service ensures that no directory synchronization is performed until it is determined that the migration process completed successfully. After the migration process finishes without errors, the Connector for Novell GroupWise should be restarted and a manual synchronization performed to synchronize the GroupWise and Exchange directories with the updated information.

## Running the Exchange Migration Wizard Process

With the GroupWise and Exchange environments configured, mailbox accounts created, and configurations finalized, it is now time to migrate mailbox data. This is performed by doing the following:

1. Launch the Microsoft Exchange Migration Wizard. To do so, click Start, point to All Programs, point to Microsoft Exchange, point to Deployment, and then click Migration Wizard.

2. Click Next at the welcome screen.

3. At the second screen, select Migrate from GroupWise.

4. Read the window and click Next if you have completed the prerequisites. If you have not read the prerequisites, please go back and review them now.

5. Choose the recommended option of a one-step migration, as shown in Figure 34.17, and select a location for the migrated files.

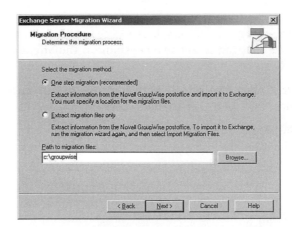

**FIGURE 34.17**    Choosing a one-step migration.

6. At the next screen, choose your Exchange server and Information Store that contains your mailbox objects. If you are using an Exchange cluster, choose the name of the Exchange virtual server. You have already mailbox-enabled the accounts within Active Directory; be sure to choose the correct Information Store.

7. If you have not mailbox-enabled the accounts, go back and review the prerequisites section.

8. Configure the tool to connect to GroupWise.

9. Choose which objects you are planning to migrate.

10. Select the accounts you want to migrate to Exchange. You may select individual mailboxes or click Select All for all mailboxes.

11. Select the container within Active Directory in which new accounts will be created if necessary. It is recommended to create all accounts in Active Directory, and create mailboxes for these users, in advance of starting the wizard.

12. Select your choice of password creation for newly created accounts. It is highly recommended you force users to change their password on their first logon.

13. The Exchange Migration Wizard displays a screen with the results from matching the accounts specified for migration. This screen denotes whether an existing account was found and its location or if a new account will be created in the location specified on the last screen.

14. Check this screen carefully. The tool does not always properly find accounts and you might need to manually link accounts. This is possible by clicking the account name and then selecting Find Existing Account. You can then find the account within Active Directory.

15. Select Next to begin the migration process.

It is often sufficient to accept the defaults in the Exchange Migration Wizard. If you have specific needs, you can change the following options on the Migration Information Wizard page:

- **Information to Create Mailboxes**—When selected, a new mailbox is created for users migrated from Novell GroupWise to Exchange.

- **Personal E-Mail Messages**—When selected, the user's email stored on Novell GroupWise is migrated to Exchange. You can select either All to migrate all of the user's mail or Dated From to specify a date range of messages to migrate.

- **Calendar Items**—When selected, the user's appointments, notes, and tasks are migrated to Exchange. You can select either All to migrate all of the user's information or Dated From to specify a date range of schedule information to migrate.

> **NOTE**
>
> Any meeting requests in users' Inboxes that have not been accepted are migrated as text messages. Users must manually add these meetings to their calendars. Before you complete the migration, ensure that users accept any outstanding meeting requests.

The Exchange Migration Wizard creates a mailbox-enabled Active Directory account for each user being migrated. All new user accounts are placed in the target organizational unit that you select on the Container for New Windows Accounts page. If accounts already exist in Active Directory, for example because you created disabled Windows accounts for all Novell GroupWise users through directory synchronization beforehand, you must verify that the accounts are matched correctly. You can associate the correct account using the Find Existing Account option on the Windows Account Creation and Association page. You can also choose to create a new account using the Create New Account option. For new accounts, the Exchange Migration Wizard can generate a random strong password, which is stored in the `Accounts.Password` file in the `\Program Files\Exchsrvr\Bin` directory on the Exchange Server 2003 server.

## Confirming Migration Operations

This section highlights information on how to validate that the Exchange Migration Wizard is working properly. Check the Windows application event log for any errors or information about the migration. You should see something similar to the following:

```
The 'Import ' of mail from 'File   - C:\MigratedFiles\GW.001\GW.PKL' completed with
the following results:

Start Time:        12:51:00
Elapsed Time:      00:07:43

Accounts:               1
Public folders:         0
E-Mail Messages:                 351
PABs:                   0
Warnings:               0
Errors:                 0
```

The key is to note no errors took place during the migration.

In addition, you can test the migration by opening Outlook with the account you created for the migration. Do the following:

1. Click File, Open, Other User's Folder.

2. Type the name of a user you have migrated, and select Inbox to open. You should see the migrated mail in the user's Inbox.

Ensure all Outlook clients are set to connect to their mailbox via a MAPI Exchange connection. This might require changing user account profiles from POP3 or IMAP to Exchange (MAPI). A Microsoft Office transform is available and deployable via a logon script or Group Policy Object (GPO) for mass conversion of client settings.

# Details on the Effects of the GroupWise Migration Tools

This section explains some of the effects of the GroupWise Migration Tool. These effects identify how folders, content, and other user data is migrated or not migrated as part of the conversion process.

## Migration of Local Archives

The Exchange Migration Wizard migrates data stored on the Novell GroupWise server, but does not migrate data stored in local archives by Novell GroupWise clients. Novell GroupWise clients include the option to automatically archive messages to local message archive databases. For the Exchange Migration Wizard to migrate archived GroupWise mailbox data, the messages in the archive must be unarchived back to the user's GroupWise mailbox, where it can then be migrated to Exchange.

> **NOTE**
>
> After the migration is complete, your users can create local personal folder (.pst) files to store the email data that they previously stored in GroupWise local archives on the client computer.

## Migration of Personal Address Books

The Exchange Migration Wizard is unable to migrate personal address books from Novell GroupWise to Exchange Server 2003. However, it is possible to export personal address books from GroupWise into .nab files, which are text-based files that can be converted into comma-separated value (.csv) files using a macro in Microsoft Excel, for example. The primary task is to reorder the fields to match the layout required by Outlook. Outlook provides the functionality to import Contact objects from a .csv file.

To determine the order of fields in a .csv file for Outlook, create a sample contact object in Outlook and then export this contact into a .csv file using the Import and Export command on the File menu in Outlook 2003. Choose Export to a File and then select Comma Separated Values (Windows). Select the Contacts folder where you created the sample contact, and complete the export procedure. Open the resulting .csv file in Excel. You should find the list of fields in the first row.

> **NOTE**
>
> Users can re-create personal contacts as well as personal distribution lists in a Contacts folder in Outlook.

## Migration of Personal Dictionaries

Personal dictionaries cannot be migrated from Novell GroupWise to Exchange Server 2003 and Outlook. The Novell GroupWise spelling checker dictionary is stored in separate, identifiable files. However, these files are encrypted and encoded and cannot be migrated to Outlook. Users must add their words to the spelling checker dictionaries in Outlook and Microsoft Office manually.

## Migration of Client Rules and Proxy Access

The Exchange Migration Wizard cannot migrate client rules from Novell GroupWise clients to Outlook 2000. Users must re-create their rules in Outlook. Users can access the Rules and Alerts command from the Tools menu in Outlook 2003 to re-create their rules.

Users must also migrate proxy access permissions to the mailboxes manually. In Outlook, proxy access is referred to as delegate access. In Outlook 2003, from the Tools menu, click Options, and then in the Options dialog box, switch to the Delegates tab, where you can click the Add button to configure delegate access. Because Outlook and Exchange Server 2003 handle delegate access differently than Novell GroupWise does, it is recommended that you train your users to set up delegates and send messages on behalf of another user in Outlook before you perform the migration.

> **NOTE**
>
> Exchange users can grant delegate access only to accounts in the Exchange Server 2003 organization. Exchange users cannot grant delegate access to Novell GroupWise users.

### Migration of Shared Folders

Novell GroupWise users can share their mailbox folders with other users, and the Exchange Migration Wizard can migrate the shared folders to Exchange Server 2003, but shared folder permissions cannot be migrated. To share folders after the migration, users must re-create these permissions on the appropriate folders in Outlook. To grant another user access to a folder in Outlook 2003, right-click the folder, select Properties, and then switch to the Permissions tab.

> **NOTE**
>
> Exchange users can share their folders only with other Exchange users. They cannot give access to their folders to Novell GroupWise users.

### Migration of External Entities

The Novell GroupWise directory is separate from NDS, and Novell GroupWise allows objects to exist in the GroupWise directory without having an NDS linked object. This kind of object is called an external entity. In Exchange, external entities are handled as normal mailbox-enabled accounts and are migrated using the Exchange Migration Wizard.

## Summary

Organizations choosing to migrate from Novell GroupWise to Exchange are helped by several tools from Microsoft. The tools include SfN that migrates user accounts, groups, and other directory information to establish the Active Directory that is a requirement for Exchange to operate.

Some organizations that already have Windows NT 4.0 in their environment may choose to migrate NT 4.0 to Active Directory as part of their conversion process. After Active Directory is installed, the organization may choose to use the SfN tool MSDSS to keep the NDS or eDirectory and Active Directory in sync.

With an established Active Directory in place, the organization can install Exchange Server 2003 and then begin the process of connecting GroupWise to Exchange, move mailboxes, and route mail between the two messaging systems until all users have been migrated to Exchange.

After all users have been migrated to Exchange, the GroupWise messaging system can be removed.

## Best Practices

The following are best practices from this chapter:

- Review Chapter 1 to understand the common reasons organizations plan and deploy the Exchange Server 2003 messaging system.

- Leverage the planning and design details in Chapters 4 and 5 of this book to prepare the business for an appropriate Exchange Server 2003 messaging system design and configuration.

- Install Exchange Server 2003 to establish the foundation for the new Exchange messaging environment.

- Use the Microsoft SfN tool to migrate user accounts from NDS or eDirectory to Active Directory, and continue to use the MSDSS tool in SfN to keep the directories synchronized.

- Install the Connector for GroupWise on an Exchange Server 2003 server that will be used to route messages between the two environments.

- Install the Calendar Connector on the same server as the Connector for GroupWise to minimize the number of servers needed to interconnect the two environments.

- Perform database integrity checks on existing GroupWise mailbox databases prior to migration to reduce the possibility of corrupted mailbox data causing errors in the migration process.

- If possible, plan to deploy multiple migration servers to decrease the time required to migrate mailbox data from GroupWise to Exchange.

# Migrating from Lotus Notes to Exchange Server 2003

**IN THIS CHAPTER**

- Similarities and Differences Between Lotus Notes and Exchange Server 2003

- Exchange Migration and the Impact of Active Directory

- Evaluating the Existing Environment

- Planning Your Migration from Lotus Notes

- Conducting Preinstallation Checks on Exchange Server 2003

- Performing a Core Installation of Exchange Server 2003

- Detailing the Exchange Server 2003 Installation

- Performing Postinstallation Configurations

- Installing and Configuring a Gateway Between Lotus Notes and Exchange

- Installing and Configuring Calendar Connector in a Lotus Notes Environment

- Using the Exchange Migration Wizard to Migrate User Data

- Details on the Effects of the Lotus Notes Migration Tools

Many organizations are choosing to migrate off of Lotus Notes to Microsoft Exchange because IBM/Lotus has changed their messaging platform for Notes, forcing organizations to perform a relatively substantial migration. Other organizations have found that Lotus Notes has limited support for integration with business applications and tools such as application integration with Enterprise Resource Planning (ERP) systems, customer relationship management (CRM) systems, or mobile devices.

The migration process from Lotus Notes to Microsoft Exchange is greatly simplified by several tools provided by Microsoft to help organizations make the transition to the new messaging system. Microsoft has a free migration tool called Exchange 2003 Migration Wizard that migrates mailboxes and calendar accounts from Lotus Notes to Exchange. In addition, there is the Connector for Lotus Notes that comes with Exchange Server 2003 that synchronizes Active Directory with Lotus Notes, exchanges email messages between the two environments, and provides free/busy calendar views between Lotus Notes and Exchange messaging systems.

Whether an organization is looking to perform a quick migration from Lotus Notes to Exchange or an extended migration that'll involve the coexistence of Lotus Notes and Exchange in an environment, the tools exist to assist with the migration process. This chapter highlights the tools, tips, tricks, and best practices used by hundreds of organizations in their successful migration from Lotus Notes to Exchange.

# Similarities and Differences Between Lotus Notes and Exchange Server 2003

In very simple comparisons, Lotus Notes and Microsoft Exchange are very similar. They are both enterprise email and calendar systems that provide contact management, task management, and collaboration. However, beyond the basic functionality of email, there are differences between the two systems.

## Comparing Messaging and Collaboration Capabilities

Some of the similarities and differences between Lotus Notes and Exchange relative to messaging and collaboration capabilities include

- **Microsoft Exchange as a reliable email server**—Email is a critical application for most companies today and when it doesn't work, it can seriously affect business. Microsoft Exchange supports online backup and restore allowing end-users to keep working while their email is backed up. Transaction logging guarantees that no messages are ever lost.

- **Third-party tools**—Companies using Lotus Notes are required to look to third-party providers if they want features such as online meetings or audio- or videoconferencing. This functionality is included in a default installation of Exchange Server 2003 installations.

- **Familiar Outlook client**—The Microsoft Outlook client is installed with the Microsoft Office suite of products. Microsoft Office and Outlook are familiar applications for users. The Lotus Notes client, on the other hand, requires end-user training to users because the client software is not commonly used by home users or businesses. The Lotus Notes client software provides little or no support for online meetings or SendTo Office Routing Recipients and SendTo Lotus Notes Folder. There is no application integration with Office documents and properties, which are simply treated as attachments. Users cannot use the File Save As function to save to a Lotus Notes shared folder.

- **User experience across client access technologies**—User experience is enhanced in Exchange Server 2003 through the use of a consistent user interface (UI) across the client access technologies, including Outlook, Outlook Web Access, Outlook Mobile Access, and Pocket Outlook, which improves user productivity and reduces the need for IT support.

- **Built-in mobile device support**—Outlook Mobile Access and Exchange Server ActiveSync are mobile features built in to Exchange Server 2003. Outlook Mobile Access and Exchange Server ActiveSync also help provide security for corporate email on a range of mobile devices, including browser-based mobile phones and Microsoft Windows Powered Mobile Devices. Currently, Lotus Notes requires third-party mobile server products to provide synchronization between Lotus Notes and Exchange.

- **Single password**—Users can log on with a single password in both the Windows Active Directory network logon and the Exchange messaging system. This is possible using a third-party Single Sign-on solution, but Lotus Notes does not actually use network logon authentication like Active Directory. There is a separate password for Lotus Notes and the network directory, and these passwords are not natively synchronized.

## Comparing Administrative Tools

There are also similarities and differences in the administrative tools between Lotus Notes and Microsoft Exchange:

- **Multiple organization directory hosting**—Both Lotus Notes and Exchange Server 2003 support multiple-organization, directory hosting; however, in Lotus Notes there needs to be multiple domains and multiple Simple Mail Transfer Protocol (SMTP) mail connectors.

- **Wizards**—Both Lotus Notes and Microsoft Exchange messaging systems have setup and configuration tools. Both messaging systems support Windows Installer Support, which is used for Deploying Desktop Messaging and Collaboration Software.

- **Network security**—Lotus Notes does not directly tie into network security. The security in Notes is separate from the security of the operating system. If interoperability between security implementations for Lotus Notes is desired, organizations need to focus on the use of Secure Sockets Layer (SSL) and Public Key Infrastructure (PKI) to ensure a good level of interoperability. Both platforms support many similar security policies, including account lockout, access control, and password policies.

# Exchange Migration and the Impact of Active Directory

Exchange is usually implemented as the messaging system in an environment that uses Windows Active Directory as the primary network logon, file system, and network operating system. Because Lotus Notes does not come with its own network operating system, organizations using Lotus Notes frequently have Windows NT4 Domains or Windows Active Directory for their file, print, and networking infrastructure. When an organization migrates from Lotus Notes to Exchange, the core network operating system (if running Windows Active Directory) might not need to be modified.

## Implementing Exchange in a Native Active Directory Environment

For an organization looking to migrate from Lotus Notes to Exchange, if the organization already has Active Directory in place, the only decision that needs to be made is whether the current Active Directory forest, domain, organizational unit, site, group, or user structure needs to be modified.

If the organization has a Windows-based network infrastructure based on Windows NT4 domains, the organization needs to migrate their NT4 structure to Active Directory, or build a brand-new Active Directory environment to support Exchange Server 2003 (see Chapter 14, "Migrating from NT4 to Windows Server 2003").

### Migrating to Exchange in an Environment That Has No Windows Network

Although some organizations may already have Active Directory in place, or others may be in the process of migrating their Windows NT4 environment to Active Directory, some organizations running Lotus Notes may not have any Windows in their environment. Lotus Notes runs on top of Unix systems as well as AS/400 minicomputers and IBM mainframe systems.

In the cases in which an organization has no existing Windows NT4 or Active Directory infrastructure, a Windows Active Directory needs to be implemented to support the directory system needed to run Exchange Server 2003. See the Sams Publishing book *Windows 2003 Unleashed, 2nd Edition* (ISBN# 0-672-32667-1) for detailed information on planning, designing, and implementing a Microsoft Windows 2003 Active Directory environment from scratch.

# Evaluating the Existing Environment

It is critical to fully understand the current environment before designing the environment to which you plan to upgrade. It is important to allow time in the planning process to collect information about the existing environment and evaluate that information to determine the appropriate next steps in the planning process.

This discovery process can also shed light on constraints to the implementation process that weren't considered previously, such as time restrictions that would affect the window of opportunity for change. These restrictions can include seasonal businesses as well as company budgeting cycles or even vacation schedules.

Ultimately, although the amount of time spent in the discovery and evaluation process will vary greatly from organization to organization, the goals are the same: to really understand the technology infrastructure in place and the risks involved in the project, and to limit the surprises that might occur during the build and deploy phases.

In preparation for development of the functional specifications document, the following information discovery tasks should be performed:

- **Diagram the existing network, including hardware and software**—Diagram the network and all its components. Identify which servers are file and print servers, Web servers, mail servers, and database servers. Document servers thoroughly, including network operating system versions, transport protocols, and data replication methods.

- **Identify all types of information stored on the network, including its owners, users, locations, and security**—Identify all types of information stored on the existing network (such as mailboxes, shared folder information, Web mail server systems, and so on), where information is stored, who is responsible for which information, which subsets of users have access to which data, and what the associated security requirements are.

- **Identify all Lotus Notes–dependent applications**—Before the migration begins, the organization needs to decide whether they will be migrating just Lotus Notes email and calendaring to Exchange, or whether the organization will be migrating Lotus Notes applications as well. Typically, organizations running Lotus Notes have created an extensive suite of business applications on Lotus Notes for purchase requests, client relationship management information, help desk support systems, and the like. If the Lotus Notes applications will be migrated as part of the migration project, the conversion process needs to be addressed. It is out of the scope of this chapter to address the migration of Lotus Notes applications to Microsoft SQL, Microsoft Access, or other Microsoft application systems. For more information on migrating Lotus Notes applications to Microsoft platforms, start with reviewing the "Exchange Server Application Analyzer 2003 for Lotus Notes" found on `http://www.microsoft.com/exchange/downloads/2003/default.mspx`.

- **Determine the systems to be migrated**—Determine which systems will be migrated or decommissioned. Determine the affected users, groups, objects, folders, files, databases, and email systems.

- **Review WAN/LAN links and their available bandwidth**—This will help you decide how you can effectively design the Active Directory topology in respect to the current environment supporting the Lotus Notes messaging environment.

- **Plan for future hardware, software, and network bandwidth needs**—Research what additional functionality your organization plans to implement in the future. Factor these features into your migration planning (for example, when you plan namespace design, wide area network [WAN] links, application software needs, and so on).

- **Review user environment components involved in the migration**—Primarily, you should review logon scripts and group/system policies.

- **Perform a directory health check**—This is the process of going through the Lotus Notes directory as well as the existing network security Lotus Notes is running on, to determine if the directory is working properly. In addition, if there is already an Active Directory infrastructure in place, it should be verified to ensure that it is working properly. The health check ensures that the objects scheduled for migration are appropriate and that they can be migrated to the new environment.

## Planning Your Migration from Lotus Notes

Before migrating from Lotus Notes to Exchange, a planning process should be conducted to develop the plan, create a project plan, and outline the steps that will be taken to

35

successfully migrate the organization to Exchange Server 2003. When developing a migration strategy, you should make a number of decisions:

- **Plan a phased or direct migration**—Plan an immediate, one-time migration, or a phased migration over time (synchronizing Active Directory and your Lotus Notes directory during the transitional period). Phased and direct migrations are covered in detail in the following section.

- **Identify containers and servers to migrate or synchronize**—Identify the data that you want to migrate or synchronize and the Active Directory and Lotus Notes servers between which you want to establish relationships.

- **Identify and obtain administrator accounts with sufficient permissions to successfully complete the migration**—If you will use synchronization, ensure that you have the required accounts with permissions to extend the Active Directory schema, read and write Active Directory container information, and access to the Lotus Notes directory.

> **NOTE**
>
> When you set up a two-way synchronization session with Lotus Notes, you must have full administrator privileges to the entire Lotus Notes organization in which you are creating the session. You must also have administrative permissions on each user's individual Lotus Notes mailbox (.nsf file) as they are not enabled by default. Ensure that these privileges are maintained for the life of the session. If these privileges are changed, objects will not be updated properly between Active Directory and Lotus Notes.

- **Determine the need for migration tools**—Determine whether the migration should be performed manually or whether you should employ migration tools and services. For details on selecting migration tools, see the "Details on the Effects of the Lotus Notes Migration Tools" section of this chapter.

## Choosing a Phased Migration from Lotus Notes

If you want to maintain an environment that contains both Exchange Active Directory and Lotus Notes directory services, you can perform a phased migration and run the two systems in parallel. If you choose to run the two systems in parallel, you will be able to perform additional migration tasks (other than synchronizing the two directory services), such as replacing applications that are dependent on Lotus Notes services with Active Directory–compatible applications.

A phased migration reduces the risk of data loss because you can migrate in managed stages and you can reverse the process if necessary. However, maintaining two separate directory services can, over time, add additional administrative costs to the migration.

In a phased migration, you use the Microsoft Exchange Connector for Lotus Notes to copy all Lotus Notes user accounts, groups, and distribution lists to Active Directory. At the same time, these objects are maintained in Lotus Notes. While you gradually move resources to the Windows Server 2003–based environment, the Connector for Lotus Notes directory synchronization enables users to continue to access Lotus Notes resources. As the changeover continues, users begin to access resources on Windows Server 2003–based servers with their new accounts and associated migrated permissions.

If you plan to perform the migration over several months or longer, two-way synchronization is recommended. This allows you to make changes in both Active Directory and the Lotus Notes environment, such as adding user accounts and modifying group membership and have those changes reflected in the other respective directory. Two-way synchronization should be used if the long-term goal is to interoperate using the two directory services.

After you have moved all resources to Windows Server 2003, you can choose to convert all Lotus Notes applications to Active Directory–based counterparts. After mail, calendaring, and applications are migrated off Lotus Notes, the organization can then delete the synchronization sessions and decommission remaining Lotus Notes servers.

If you choose a phased migration, you should

- **List migration priorities**—List the departments or other groupings, the Lotus Notes applications, and the hardware that you must migrate immediately, and which resources can be migrated over time. List the order in which you want to accomplish each stage.

- **Choose one-way or two-way synchronization**—Decide whether one-way synchronization (using Active Directory to manage objects in both directories) or two-way synchronization (using either Active Directory or Lotus Notes to manage shared data) is appropriate to the situation. Take network traffic into account. Decide the timetable for replacing any of the Lotus Notes–dependent applications with Active Directory–enabled counterparts.

### Synchronizing Lotus Notes with Active Directory
The administration of multiple directory services often leads to time-consuming and redundant management. Establishing a periodic synchronization, using the Connector for Lotus Notes, of both directories will help you reduce the time you spend on directory management.

When you introduce Windows Server 2003 and Active Directory into an existing Lotus Notes environment, you can facilitate directory management and improve data availability by establishing directory interoperability. Central to interoperability is the ability to synchronize the information stored in Active Directory with the Lotus Notes directory information within your organization.

By default, Lotus Notes synchronization duplicates the Notes directory structure in Active Directory. Also like migration, synchronization maps Lotus Notes user, group, and distribution list objects to Active Directory user, group, and distribution list objects.

**Using One-Way Synchronization**   One-way synchronization enables you to manage objects in both directories from Active Directory. Reasons to select one-way synchronization include

- The desire to centralize directory administration from Active Directory

- The consideration that the network is predominantly Windows-based (with some independent Lotus Notes accounts)

- The interest to administer and update Lotus Notes user accounts from Active Directory

- The intent to prepare to migrate the entire Lotus Notes directory environment to Active Directory

**Using Two-Way Synchronization**    Two-way synchronization enables the administrator to manage shared data, such as user account information, from either directory. Reasons to select two-way synchronization include

- The expectation of having both Active Directory and Lotus Notes administered by two sets of network administrators

- The anticipation that the network environment will contain both Active Directory and Lotus Notes with no plans to eliminate Lotus Notes in the near term

### Preparing the Project Team for the Migration

After the project team determines what the new Exchange Server 2003 environment will look like, they are ready to determine how to migrate their existing Lotus Notes environment to the new Exchange Server 2003 environment.

The first step in planning a migration from Lotus Notes should be to explain to both end-users and administrators how their worlds will change after the new messaging environment is deployed. Most administrators and end-users will not fear the change if they are properly informed and educated about the changes. In addition, if the migrations are planned correctly, it should be seamless and transparent to end-users, which lessens the impact on end-users.

However, rather than overconfidently telling the users and the executives of the organization that the migration will be simple and seamless, it is safer to describe a much more complex scenario, giving the users a vision of the benefits they'll receive after the migration is completed, and if the migration happens with minimal interruption, the users and executives will be pleasantly surprised.

The next important step in planning a migration involves system readiness. All systems involved directly or indirectly in the migration process such as Windows Server 2003, Active Directory, and Exchange Server 2003 must be ready. After all systems are operational, project teams should attempt to reduce the amount of data to be migrated. They must also ensure they grant the appropriate permissions for the service account that will be used to migrate the Lotus Notes data. Sufficient access rights are necessary to extract data from mailboxes. For example, you must grant the migration account Lotus Notes proxy rights for all mailboxes. Next, a decision needs to be made on whether to carry out a direct migration or a phased migration. A company's assessment of its existing environment should help it identify the most logical and effective migration approach: direct or phased.

### Identifying the Tools Needed for the Phased Migration

An organization that chooses a phased migration also needs to identify the tools needed to maintain coexistence between their legacy messaging system, Lotus Notes, and their new messaging system, Exchange Server 2003. Through coexistence, users who are still part of the legacy messaging system will be able to communicate with users who have already migrated to Exchange Server 2003.

Exchange Server 2003 Service Pack 1 provides basic tools that support interoperability from Lotus Notes to Exchange. Some tools considerations for an organization include

- **Connector for Lotus Notes**—Connector for Lotus Notes is a gateway component that allows both messaging systems to coexist for either a short period of time or a long period of time. Users of the separate messaging systems interact as if they belong to the same messaging system.

- **Calendar Connector**—Together with Connector for Lotus Notes, the Calendar Connector provides users access to free/busy calendar information that is almost real time. It is important to realize that Calendar Connector always looks for the Schedule+Free Busy folder on the local Exchange 2003 server. Therefore, Exchange Server 2003 should have a local replica of the public folder.

- **Microsoft Exchange Migration Wizard**—Part of the Exchange System Manager installation is the installation of the Microsoft Exchange Migration Wizard that migrates mailbox data from Lotus Notes to Microsoft Exchange.

- **Third-party tools**—Although Microsoft provides a free migration wizard and connector between Lotus Notes and Exchange, there are limitations to the Microsoft tools (such as the inability to migrate archives, phone messages, proxy rights, and signatures). An organization might need to evaluate third-party tools as part of a complete migration strategy from Lotus Notes to Exchange Server 2003.

During the interoperability stage of the migration, it is very important to maintain accurate directory information on both messaging systems. Connector for Lotus Notes supports the synchronization of directory information. Directory synchronization consists of two sequential processes: synchronizing users from Active Directory to Lotus Notes and synchronizing user accounts from Lotus Notes to Active Directory.

After configuring directory synchronization, the project team might want to install and configure Calendar Connector in a Lotus Notes environment. Calendar synchronization consists of two sequential processes: synchronization from Lotus Notes to Exchange Server 2003 and synchronization from Exchange Server 2003 to Lotus Notes. After the Calendar Connector is installed, users on Exchange Server 2003 and Lotus Notes can access each other's free/busy information. The most appropriate thing to do is install Calendar Connector on the server running Connector for Lotus Notes.

> **NOTE**
>
> The process that occurs when an Exchange Server 2003 end-user queries the free/busy informa-
> tion for a user on Lotus Notes is different than the process used when the user querying the
> calendar information for an Exchange Server 2003 end-user is on Lotus Notes.

When establishing interoperability, companies using Connector for Lotus Notes should consider installing the connector on a dedicated Exchange bridgehead server. A specific bridgehead server can run exactly one connector instance. One connector can service one or more direct Lotus Notes connections and an entire Exchange Server 2003 environment.

## Choosing the Direct Migration Approach

The direct migration path is suitable for small- to medium-sized organizations that have none or limited Lotus Notes applications. Migration in these cases can normally be accomplished in a short amount of time with minimal time and effort spent in designing, testing, and implementing multiplatform directory sharing across both the Lotus Notes and Microsoft environments.

A direct migration is also feasible if the organization is deploying a large number of new desktops or has an older Lotus Notes messaging system and needs to move the entire organization to a more current messaging system. For example, environments that only provide limited services such as just email messaging are relatively simple migration projects.

The direct migration is exactly what it sounds like. The migration of the Lotus Notes directory and all user accounts and mailboxes is performed as part of a single process. Immediately following, the users are exclusively on Exchange for messaging and calendaring.

This process can only be performed if there are no requirements to maintain legacy Lotus Notes applications and the organization is small enough or there are enough resources to migrate all of the Lotus Notes mailboxes in the environment in a short period of time.

If there is no need to maintain Lotus Notes and the messaging system is small and not complex, an immediate, one-time migration can be planned by the project team. For example, the company can schedule downtime and migrate the Lotus Notes data over a weekend or in the evening. With direct migration, the project team will save time in preparing their environments because they are not required to install or configure an Exchange connector.

After the interoperability and migration strategy is developed, it is time to deploy the new Exchange Server 2003 environment. The next step is to begin the migration of mailboxes from Lotus Notes to Microsoft Exchange. The Exchange Migration Wizard requires access to the mailbox of each user it is migrating. After the migration is completed, the project team needs to decommission Lotus Notes.

This process should be fully tested in the test environment to identify any issues and verify that there are no application requirements for the Lotus Notes servers. After the

Lotus Notes servers are retired, the client will no longer be able to communicate with the Notes environment.

# Conducting Preinstallation Checks on Exchange Server 2003

When it comes to the actual installation of Exchange Server 2003, you can run setup manually or you can create an unattend file so that the install can be automated for a branch office with no technical staff at the site. There are also different configurations of Exchange, such as Mailbox Server, Public Folder Server, Front-End Server, Back-End Server, and Bridgehead Server. This section covers the preinstallation tasks prior to installing the first Exchange server in the environment.

## Verifying Core Services Installation

When installing Exchange Server 2003 on a Windows 2003 server, you must make sure that Internet Information Services (IIS), Network News Transfer Protocol (NNTP), and SMTP are installed and running. This can be done by checking the Services applet within Administrative Tools from the Start menu. The setup program looks for IIS, NNTP, and SMTP services before it begins the install and fails if they are not present. In addition, ASP.net and .NET framework need to be installed on the server. None of these services are enabled by default. You have to enable these services manually prior to running the Exchange Server 2003 setup program.

## Preparing the Forest

The ForestPrep process extends the Active Directory schema to include the Exchange Server 2003 classes and attributes required for the application to run. To run the ForestPrep process, you must have the following permissions by belonging to these groups: enterprise admins, schema admins, domain admins, and local administrator on the Exchange server. During the ForestPrep process, you assign an account that has full Exchange administrator rights to the organization object in Exchange Server 2003.

> **NOTE**
>
> Those familiar with the installation of Exchange 2000 Server will notice that you no longer have to enter an organization name for Exchange during the ForestPrep process with Exchange Server 2003. This is now entered only at the point of installation.

## Preparing the Domain

The DomainPrep process creates groups and permission within the Active Directory forest so that Exchange Server 2003 can modify user attributes. To run the DomainPrep setup parameter, you must be a member of the domain admins and local administrator groups.

The groups that are created during this process are Exchange domain servers and Exchange enterprise servers. The Exchange domain servers group is a domain global security group and the Exchange enterprise servers group is a domain local security group.

### Reviewing All Log Files

Each of the utilities that you execute has some output in its respective log files. Review the log file after running each utility to ensure no errors are encountered.

# Performing a Core Installation of Exchange Server 2003

When installing Exchange Server 2003 for the first time in an environment, the easiest way to conduct the installation is to insert the Exchange Server 2003 CD and follow the step-by-step installation instructions. This section of the chapter focuses on the step-by-step installation of a basic Exchange Server 2003 installation.

> **NOTE**
>
> For those who have installed previous versions of Exchange, the setup program now has a new switch that can be used during installation. Running setup with a /ChooseDC {dcname}, followed by the name of a domain controller, tells the setup program to look for a specific domain controller (DC) to write schema changes to or check for permissions and groups.

### Implementing Active Directory

Before you install Exchange Server 2003 on your network, you need to make sure that Active Directory is properly deployed. The Active Directory infrastructure and Domain Name Service (DNS) need to be healthy and without replication errors prior to installing your first Exchange 2003 server. It is so important to perform health checks and verification steps in your environment prior to installation that the Exchange development team has designed the installation program to include these steps. Exdeploy walks you through all the preinstallation health checks before running the setup program for Exchange Server 2003.

### Extending the Active Directory Schema

The first step to the actual implementation of Exchange Server 2003 is to extend the Active Directory schema. The schema comprises the rules that apply to the directory and controls what type of information can be stored in the directory. It also describes how that information is stored in the directory—such as string, string length, integer, and so on. Exchange Server 2003 almost doubles the amount of attributes in the Active Directory schema.

Extending the schema is the easiest part of the installation, but it is also the place where many organizations make mistakes. To extend the Active Directory schema, use the /forestprep switch on setup.exe for Exchange Server 2003 or follow the steps outlined in the deployment tool. The following list provides a few tips to note before extending the Active Directory schema:

- The schema must be extended on the server that holds the Schema Master flexible single master operations (FSMO) role. By default, the first server installed in the forest contains the Schema Master; however, this role could have been moved to another server. To locate which server contains the Schema Master FSMO role, use the Active Directory Schema Microsoft Management Console (MMC) snap-in, right-click the Active Directory Schema icon under the console root, and select Operations Master.

---

**TIP**

To use the Active Directory Schema MMC snap-in, the `adminpak.msi` file must be installed on the server. Use the run command and execute `adminpak.msi` to install the adminpak. After the adminpak is installed, open the MMC from the run prompt by executing MMC; then use the Add/Remove snap-in option from the Console menu to add the Active Directory Schema MMC snap-in.

---

- The account used to extend the schema must be a member of the schema admins group and domain admins or enterprise admins groups. The schema admins and enterprise admins groups are available only in the first domain in the forest. If the messaging group does not control the forest root domain, this process must be delegated to the group that does.

- A schema change forces a full replication of domain databases and global catalog information in Active Directory. Many administrators are scared of full replications and have heard stories of bandwidth-saturated WAN links due to schema extensions. However, when a full replication occurs, the directory information is compressed before it is sent across the network. The actual amount of data sent across the wire will be approximately 15%–20% of the actual Active Directory database size.

---

**NOTE**

For Windows NT 4.0 organizations still in the Active Directory planning stages, to get an approximate size of the Active Directory database size, you multiply the Windows NT 4.0 SAM database by a factor of 3. This is a good ballpark estimate to use for the database size that will be seen immediately after migration. To calculate the size after implementing Exchange Server 2003 and other new directory information, use the AdSizer tool from Microsoft, available at `http://www.microsoft.com/downloads/`.

---

## Preparing the Windows 2003 Domain

The second step in preparing to install Exchange Server 2003 is to prepare the Windows Server 2003 domain that will host the Exchange servers or mailbox-enabled users. To prepare the Windows Server 2003 domain, use the `/domainprep` switch on `setup.exe` for Exchange Server 2003 or follow the steps outlined in the deployment tool.

The account used to prepare the Windows Server 2003 domain must be a member of the domain admins group in the domain where the /domainprep command is being run. Running DomainPrep performs the following operations on the domain:

35

- Creates the global security group Exchange Domain Servers

- Creates the domain local security group Enterprise Exchange Servers

- Adds the Exchange Domain Servers group to the Enterprise Exchange Servers group

- Grants appropriate rights to the domain controller used for the Recipient Update Service

For domains that will host mailbox-enabled users and not host Exchange servers, administrators have the choice of running DomainPrep or manually creating a Recipient Update Service for the domain in Exchange System Manager. If the domain will never host Exchange servers, the Recipient Update Service should be manually created. If the domain will eventually host Exchange servers, DomainPrep should be used.

## Step-by-Step Installation of Exchange Server 2003

To install the first Exchange server in an organization using the interactive installation process of Exchange Server 2003:

1. Insert the Exchange 2003 CD (Standard or Enterprise).

2. Autorun should launch a splash screen with options for Resources and Deployment Tools. (If autorun does not work, select Start, Run. Then type `CDDrive:\setup.exe` and click OK.)

3. Click Exchange Deployment Tools.

4. At the Deployment Tools welcome screen, click Deploy the First Exchange 2003 Server.

5. Click New Exchange 2003 Installation.

6. Verify that your server has met all the operating system and Active Directory requirements. (Click the reference link in the right column.)

7. Check that your server is running NNTP, SMTP, and World Wide Web Services. If you're running Windows 2003, you also need ASP.NET. (Check the reference link to the right of the window for details.)

8. Install the Windows 2003 Support Tools to use the preinstallation utilities (located on the Windows 2003 CD under `\support\tools\`).

9. Run DCDiag and view the log file output. Click the reference link to the right for details. The syntax is

   `DCDiag /f: log file /s:domain controller`

10. Run NetDiag and view the log file output in `netdiag.log`.

11. Click Run Forestprep Now.

12. Click Next.

13. Read the license agreement, and then click I Agree if you agree with the licensing. Click Next.

14. Click Next to accept the default administrator account.

15. Click Finish when ForestPrep is done.

The next step is to run DomainPrep on the domain that will hold the Exchange servers and user accounts. To prepare the domain:

1. Click Run Domainprep Now.

2. Click Next.

3. After reading the license agreement, click I Agree, and then click Next.

4. Click Next again.

5. Click Finish.

After the domain has been prepared, it's time to install the Exchange messaging system:

1. Run Setup Now.

2. Click Next.

3. Select I Agree after agreeing with the licensing requirements, and then click Next.

   In the Component Selection window, the default is Typical for Microsoft Exchange, Install for Microsoft Exchange Messaging and Collaboration Services, and Install for Microsoft Exchange System Management Tools. The configuration screen should look similar to Figure 35.1.

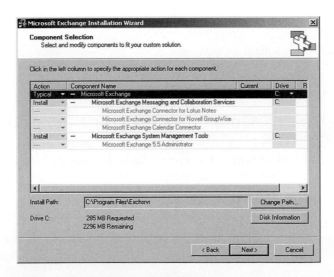

**FIGURE 35.1**  Component Selection screen for installation.

35

4. Click Next.

5. Select Create New Exchange Organization, and click Next.

6. Type the Exchange organization name, and click Next.

7. Select I Agree That I Have Read and Will Be Bound by the License Agreements for This Product.

8. Click Next.

9. If you already created the admin group and routing group structure, you are prompted to select where to install this server. Choose an administrative group and click Next. Then choose a routing group and click Next.

10. Review the Installation Summary and click Next.

11. If you are installing in a Mixed mode domain, you receive a security warning. Click OK to the security group warning.

12. Click Finish.

13. Click OK if prompted to reboot.

# Detailing the Exchange Server 2003 Installation

After the first Exchange Server 2003 server has been installed, the Exchange environment will likely need to be customized to meet the needs and requirements of the organization. The custom options include

- Creating administrative groups

- Creating routing groups

- Creating storage groups

- Creating additional mailbox databases

- Creating a public folder store

## Creating the Administrative Group and Routing Group Structure

By default, the Exchange installation program creates an administrative group and routing group called first administrative group and first routing group. If your company wants to create an administrative group structure prior to installing Exchange, it can do so by installing the Exchange System Manager and creating the group structure.

### Setting Administrative Views

To begin managing and administering the administrative groups and routing groups in Exchange Server 2003, administrative views need to be configured. To enable administrative views:

1. Start the Exchange System Manager.

2. Right-click and select Properties on the Exchange organization.

3. On the Properties page, select Display Routing Groups and Display Administrative Groups, as shown in Figure 35.2.

4. Click OK.

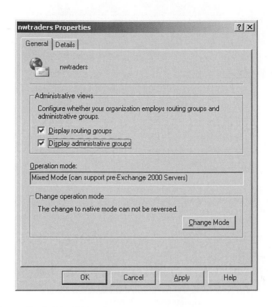

**FIGURE 35.2**   Enabling administrative views.

### Creating Administrative Groups

For a clean installation of Exchange, the organization is set up in a single administrative group. The Exchange administrator can create additional administrative groups to delegate the administration of the organization to other administrators. To create an additional administrative group:

1. Start Exchange System Manager.

2. Right-click Administrative Groups and select New Administrative Group, as shown in Figure 35.3.

3. Type the name of the group, and click OK.

> **NOTE**
>
> For many organizations that have multiple sites or multiple administrators, the common practice is to share administrative duties; all administrators in the organization can add, delete, or modify users in all sites. This is frequently used as a backup administration function when one administrator is not available—any other administrator in the organization can provide assistance. When

administration tasks are shared, the organization may choose to have a single administrative group.

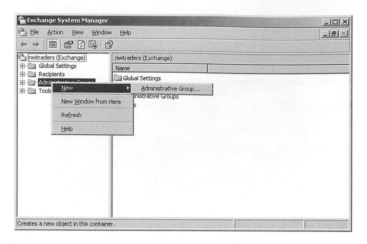

**FIGURE 35.3**    Adding an administrative group.

## Creating Routing Groups

The default installation of administrative groups is to create a single administrative boundary; routing groups also create a single boundary for mail delivery. Routing groups are created to control message flow. A routing group connector then connects routing groups. A new routing group is usually created when there is a transition in bandwidth, such as from a local area network (LAN) to a WAN. Servers separated by a WAN link or highly saturated or unstable LAN link are usually contained in separate routing groups.

In every routing group, one server is identified as the routing group master (RGM). This server is responsible for propagating link state information to other servers in the routing group. The RGM is responsible for tracking which servers are up or down in their own routing group and propagating that information to the RGM servers in other routing groups on the network. Only two states are tracked for the message link, which are up or down.

Routing groups also affect a client's connection to a public folder. When a client attempts to access a public folder, the client uses the copy of the folder on its home server if it exists. If the folder cannot be located on the home server, the client uses a copy in its home server's routing group. If a copy is not available in the local routing group, clients attempt to locate the folder in a remote routing group. The arbitrary cost assigned to the routing group connector by the administrator determines which routing group is selected first.

If the organization has only a single location, a complicated routing structure is unnecessary. However, routing groups can provide the Exchange administrator(s) the ability to throttle the routing of messages between servers and sites. This can be done if an organization has a very low bandwidth between sites and wants to prevent large attach-ments from saturating the limited bandwidth between locations. Standard messages could be sent throughout the day; however, messages with large attachments can be delayed until the evening when bandwidth is more readily available.

To create an additional routing group:

1. Start Exchange System Manager.

2. Expand the administrative groups/administrative group name.

3. Right-click Routing Groups, and then select New Routing Group, as shown in Figure 35.4.

4. Type the routing group name, and click OK.

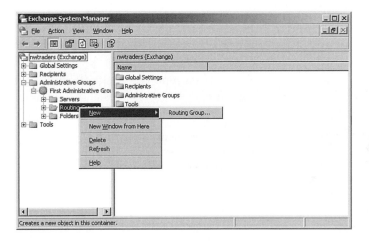

**FIGURE 35.4** Adding a routing group.

> **NOTE**
>
> You can also rename any new administrative group you create and any of the routing group names after the first server is installed in your organization. To do so, right-click, click Properties, and then click Rename.

## Creating Storage Groups

Storage groups are collections of Exchange databases that the Exchange server manages with a separate process. Each storage group shares a set of transaction logs. Log files are not purged until the entire storage group has been backed up. All databases in the storage group are also subject to the Circular Logging setting on the storage group. Exchange Server 2003, Standard Edition supports a single storage group on a server, and a total of four storage groups are supported on each Exchange Server 2003, Enterprise Edition server.

35

> **NOTE**
>
> Circular logging is a process that can be enabled to save disk space by overwriting transaction logs. Enabling circular logging is dangerous because, in the event the database fails and has to be restored from tape, a replay of the information in the logs might not contain all the messages since the last backup. For data integrity and recovery reasons, Exchange administrators should never enable circular logging on the storage group. Instead, they should allocate sufficient disk space for the transaction logs and verify that a successful backup of the storage group is being performed each night. Running a full backup and then flagging the tape backup software to purge the log files is the best practice of ensuring that the database has been properly backed up and logs have been cleared.

As an administrator, you should create additional storage groups when

- You can use separate physical transaction log drives to increase performance. Putting an additional storage group on the same physical transaction log drive might actually reduce performance because of transaction log management and should be considered only if the first storage group is full.

- You need to back up multiple databases simultaneously. Databases are backed up at the storage group level. Using multiple storage groups allows simultaneous backups of each storage group.

- The first storage group already has the maximum number of databases supported. When another database is required on a server where the first storage group has the maximum number of supported databases, an additional storage group has to be created.

To create a new storage group, right-click the Exchange server in Exchange System Manager and select New, Storage Group. A set of options, as shown in Figure 35.5, is shown:

- **Name**—The name of the storage group appears in Exchange System Manager and Active Directory Users and Computers when managing users.

- **Transaction log location**—Put transaction logs on a different drive than the databases that will be part of this storage group; if the hard drive that the database is on crashes and you have to restore the database from tape, the logs are not affected by the database drive hardware failure. This method can improve data integrity and recoverability.

- **System path location**—The system path is the location of temporary files, such as the checkpoint file and reserve logs.

- **Log file prefix**—The log file prefix is assigned to each log file and is automatically assigned by the server.

- **Zero out deleted database pages**—This option clears deleted data from the drive, and although that process creates additional overhead, it also increases security.

- **Enable circular logging**—Never enable this setting. Make sure the backup jobs are completing successfully to prevent filling the transaction log drive.

**FIGURE 35.5**  Options for creating a new storage group.

## Managing Databases

Exchange Server 2003, Enterprise Edition allows five databases per storage group. The number of databases can be any combination of public and private stores. Exchange Server 2003 stores data in two types of databases:

- **EDB**—Stores rich text messages and Internet message headers.

- **STM**—Stores all Multipurpose Internet Mail Extensions (MIME) content. Stores audio, voice, and video as a stream of MIME data without conversion. This reduces the amount of space for storage and reduces the overhead on the server by not converting the data. Message bodies from the Internet messages are also stored in the STM database; the message header is converted to rich text format and stored in the EDB database.

A feature in Exchange Server 2003 mailbox and public store databases is full-text indexing. In earlier versions of Exchange, every folder and message was searched when users initiated a search. In Exchange Server 2003, the administrator can configure an index that is updated and rebuilt periodically. This enables fast searches for Outlook 2003, Outlook XP, and Outlook 2000 users. The following attachment types are also included in the index: .doc, .xls, .ppt, .html, .htm, .asp, .txt, and .eml (embedded MIME messages). Binary attachments are not included in the index. To initiate a full-text index, right-click the Mail or Public store and select Create Full Text Index.

## Creating Additional Mailbox Stores

New mailbox stores should be created when the size of the existing mailbox store is growing too large to manage. To create a new mailbox store, right-click the storage group and select New, Mailbox Store. When creating a new mailbox store, the options to configure appear as tabs, as shown in Figure 35.6:

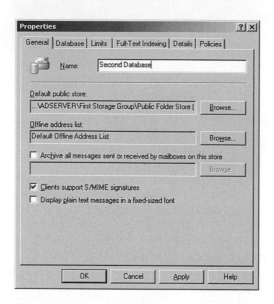

**FIGURE 35.6**    Options for creating a new database.

- **General**—Defines the database name, the offline address book to use, message archiving, whether digitally signed messages are allowed, and plain text display.

- **Database**—Sets the location for the EDB and STM databases. These should be stored on a hardware RAID 5 or 0+1 drive. Also controls the online database maintenance schedule.

- **Limits**—Configures the message storage limit at which users are warned that sending and receiving are prohibited. Also sets the deleted items and mailbox policy.

- **Full-Text Indexing**—Configures how often the full-text index is updated and rebuilt.

- **Details**—Notes any information about the configuration that is manually keyed in to this page by an administrator or Exchange Server manager.

- **Policies**—Defines the system mailbox store policies that apply to the mailbox store.

Three entries are listed below the mailbox store that can provide the administrator information regarding the status of the store:

- **Logons**—Last logon time, last access time, client type used to log on, and the Windows 2000 or Windows 2003 account that was used

- **Mailboxes**—Number of items in the mailbox, mailbox size, and last logon and logoff time

- **Full-Text Indexing**—Index information, such as location, size, state, number of documents, and the last build time

### Creating a Public Folder Store

Unlike the mailbox store, new public stores should be created only when there is a need for a new public folder tree because each public folder store needs to be associated with a public folder tree. Public folder trees can be created under the folders container in each storage group. Only one public store from each Exchange server can be associated with a public folder tree. To create a new public store, right-click the storage group and select New, Public Store. The majority of the tabs are identical to those of the mailbox store. The following are tabs that contain unique public folder store settings:

- **Replication**—Sets the replication schedule, interval, and size limit for public folder replication messages

- **Limits**—Includes an age limit setting for the number of days for folder content to be valid

The entries listed below the public folder store provide the administrator information regarding the status of the store:

- **Logons**—Last logon time, last access time, client type used to log on, and the Windows 2000 or Windows 2003 account that was used

- **Public Folder Instances**—Information about folders that are being replicated to other servers

- **Public Folders**—Folder size, number of items, creation date, and last access time

- **Replication status**—Replication status of each folder in the public folder store—for example, In Sync indicates that the folder is up to date

- **Full-Text Indexing**—Index information, such as location, size, state, number of documents, and the last build time

# Performing Postinstallation Configurations

After Exchange Server 2003 has been installed and customized, you should take a few cleanup and implementation steps. These steps help to clean up and remove services, connectors, and logging functions enabled as part of the installation process. The cleanup task involves the following:

35

- Disabling unnecessary services
- Removing Information Stores that won't be used
- Setting up routing group connections
- Enabling logging and message tracking
- Deleting mailbox and public folder stores

## Disabling Services

Although Exchange Server 2003 does a much better job by not automatically installing dozens of different utilities and services the way previous versions of Exchange did, it still installs some default services that might not be used by the organization. For security and administration purposes, if a service is not used, it should be disabled. To disable services that are commonly unused—such as Internet Message Access Protocol (IMAP), Post Office Protocol 3 (POP3), NNTP, or SMTP—do the following:

1. Select Start, All Programs, Administrative Tools, Services.

2. Scroll down to the IMAP4 Service.

3. Double-click on the service.

4. Under the Startup Type section, choose Disabled.

5. Under the Service Status section, click Stop.

6. Repeat steps 1–5 for POP3, NNTP, and SMTP, as applicable.

> **NOTE**
>
> If IMAP, POP3, and NNTP are used on a server, such as a front-end system hosting remote mail users, those services should not be disabled. It's common on back-end servers where IMAP or POP3 is not used that the service could be disabled; it's also common for organizations that use Exchange just for email and do not need NNTP on any of their servers. For servers or systems that are not routing mail, such as those set up solely as Exchange System Manager administration servers, the SMTP service should be disabled.

## Removing Information Stores

By default, an Information Store that holds Exchange databases is created on each Exchange server installed in the organization. However, dedicated front-end servers that are just the Web front-end systems do not require Information Stores or databases. In those cases, the Information Stores should be deleted. To delete the Information Stores that are unneeded on front-end servers:

1. Select Start, All Programs, Microsoft Exchange, System Manager.

2. Navigate to Administrative Groups, Administrative Group Name, Servers, Server Name, Storage Groups.

3. Right-click on the mailbox store and choose Delete.

4. Click Yes.

5. Click OK and delete the database files manually.

---

**CAUTION**

Before deleting any database or Information Store, unless you are positive the database or Information Store is completely empty and unused, you might want to do a full backup of the database, store, and system—in case a user's mailbox was inadvertently hosted on the system. Sometimes during an early implementation of Exchange, an organization might start with just one or two servers in a pilot test environment. If a mailbox was stored on one of the test servers, it might eventually become the front-end server for the organization. Backing up a system is safer than making assumptions and regretting the decision later. Using the NTBackup utility covered in Chapter 31, "Backing Up the Exchange Server 2003 Environment," is a quick way to back up a system.

---

35

## Setting Up Routing Group Connectors

Routing group connectors should be used in situations in which there is greater than 64Kbps of available bandwidth between the routing groups. If there is not sufficient bandwidth, SMTP or X.400 connectors should be used to connect the routing groups. Routing group and routing group connector designs should follow the organization's physical connectivity links. Four basic routing group connector strategies can be implemented based on the organization's physical network links:

- **Full mesh**—In a full mesh, all routing groups connect to all other routing groups. Unless there are only a few routing groups, the administrative overhead for implementation becomes unbearable. This design can also be a waste of administrative resources if there isn't the WAN link redundancy to support the design.

- **Partial mesh**—A partial mesh tries to create the benefits of a full mesh without the added administrative overhead. If the WAN design is a partial mesh, build the routing groups to follow the partial mesh.

- **Hub and spoke**—In a hub-and-spoke design, one routing group becomes the center of the universe and all other routing groups connect to it. In larger networks, there can be multiple hubs in the enterprise, and the hubs are joined together in a full or partial mesh. This design is simple to implement and maintain but creates a single point of failure at the hub. This design is an option for locations that do not have any WAN link redundancy.

- **Linear**—In a linear design, routing groups connect to only one other routing group in a straight line. Linear designs are not recommended.

To create a new routing group:

1. Navigate to Administrative Groups, Admin Groups, Routing Groups, HO, as shown in Figure 35.7.

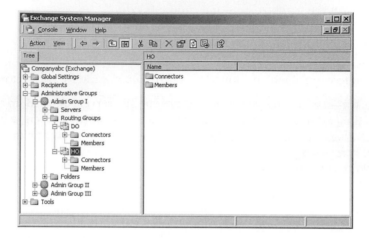

**FIGURE 35.7**    Traversing the Exchange System Manager for routing groups.

2. Right-click Connectors and choose New Routing Group Connector.

3. Type a name for the connector, as shown in Figure 35.8.

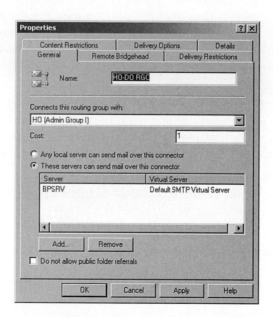

**FIGURE 35.8**    Routing group configuration screen.

4. Click These Servers Can Send Mail over This Connector, and click Add to choose a server or check Any Local Server Can Send Mail over This Connector.

The General tab of the routing group connector defines a few significant items that administrators should understand when configuring the connector:

- **Connects This Routing Group With**—Specifies the destination routing group for the RGC.

- **Cost**—Identifies the arbitrary cost assigned by the administrator, which can be used to control which connector is used first if multiple connectors exist.

- **Server**—Allows any server, or specifies specific servers allowed, to transfer mail to the destination routing group. By specifying specific servers, a bridgehead server is nominated. By specifying multiple servers, backup bridgehead servers are identified. The order of the servers in the list specifies which server is used first.

- **Do Not Allow Public Folder Referrals**—Disables the user's ability to access public folder content that is homed in the routing group connected to that server.

5. Click the Remote Bridgehead tab, and click Add to choose a server. After entering the bridgehead server selection, you see a screen similar to Figure 35.9.

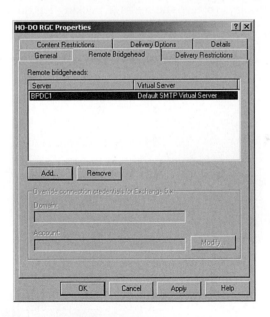

**FIGURE 35.9**   Bridgehead server configuration.

6. Click OK.

7. Select Yes to create a routing group connector in the remote routing group.

## Enabling Logging and Message Tracking

Logging and message tracking are common functions enabled by Exchange administrators early on in an Exchange implementation to help the administrator validate that messages are flowing through the environment. By enabling the logging and message tracking function, the administrator can then run a report to find out which route a message took to get from one server to another, and how long it took for the message to be transmitted.

Many administrators never use the logging and message tracking function and simply assume that messages are getting from point A to point B successfully. In many environments, although messages reach their destination, they are routed from one site to another and once around the globe before being received by a mail user in the same site facility. Misconfigured routing group connectors, DNS errors, or other networking problems are often the cause. So it's usually helpful to monitor messages to ensure that they are being routed and processed as expected.

To enable logging and message tracking:

1.  Open Exchange System Manager.

2.  Navigate to Administrative Groups, Admin Groups, Servers, Server Name.

3.  Right-click the server object and choose Properties.

4.  Select Enable Subject Logging and Display and Enable Message Tracking.

5.  Type a number for days to keep the message tracking log files, as shown in Figure 35.10.

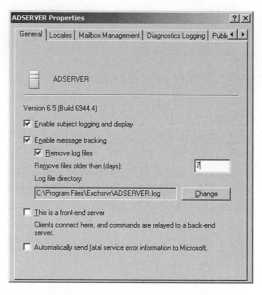

**FIGURE 35.10**    Configuring logging for message tracking.

# Installing and Configuring a Gateway Between Lotus Notes and Exchange

After you configure your new Microsoft Exchange environment, you can establish a connection between Lotus Notes and Exchange for email flow using the Connector for Lotus Notes. The connector is installed on an Exchange Server 2003 server. This includes installing the connector, which you can do as part of the server setup or afterward, when you start the Exchange setup program on a server on which Exchange Server 2003 is already installed. For the purposes of these instructions, it is assumed that you are performing the connector installation during the initial server setup.

## Prerequisites for Migrating to Exchange Server 2003

Before implementing the Exchange Server 2003 server that will host the gateway between Lotus Notes and Exchange, the organization needs to keep in mind some basic system requirements. Those requirements are

- You already have an existing Microsoft Windows® network, including an Exchange organization, and the Active Directory® directory service is deployed.

- You have Exchange administrator permissions to install an Exchange Server 2003 server in the Exchange organization.

- You have network connectivity to the server running Lotus Notes.

- You can resolve the name of the server running Lotus Notes.

- In Exchange System Manager, you have selected the Display Routing Groups and Display Administrative Groups options on the Properties page for the organization object.

From an Exchange migration perspective, Microsoft offers a few connectors for coexistence and migration support between Lotus Notes and Exchange. The level of coexistence is dependent on the Exchange version a company is running. Currently, the migration and connectivity tools between Lotus Notes and Exchange support Lotus Notes version 4.6 or higher.

## Migration Considerations for All Lotus Notes Environments

Although the Migration Wizard permits the migration of mail, calendar items, and contact information to Exchange Server 2003 from any v4.6 or higher of Lotus Domino or Notes, you should review a number of items in the planning of any Lotus Notes-to-Exchange migration.

Some of the limitations that frequently come up during a Lotus Notes migration that cannot be directly addressed by any migration tool:

- Proxy access granted to other Lotus Notes users cannot be migrated to Exchange. Users who rely on proxy access to other Lotus Notes users' mailboxes will need to be migrated together and existing Lotus Notes mailbox proxy rights must be re-created in each user's mailbox.

- Shared folders that currently exist in Lotus Notes will not be accessible to Exchange users. Although each user who is migrated receives his own copy of all Lotus Notes folders in his mailbox (shared or otherwise), the shared folder permissions are not migrated.

- No migration path of any type currently exists for Lotus Notes application libraries. Organizations with access to a product such as Adobe Acrobat have sometimes elected to generate PDFs or other electronic versions of the documents stored in the Lotus Notes document management library.

## Installing an Exchange Server 2003 Server with the Connector for Lotus Notes

After the prerequisites have been identified, and the migration criteria have been reviewed, the next step is to install the Connector for Lotus Notes on an Exchange Server 2003 system. Follow these steps to install the Connector for Lotus Notes:

1. Insert the Exchange Server 2003 CD into the CD-ROM drive of a computer running Windows Server 2003.

2. At a command prompt, type **cd e:\setup\i386**, where *e* is the drive letter for the CD-ROM drive.

3. Type **setup.exe** and press Enter.

4. On the Microsoft Exchange Installation Wizard Welcome page, click Next.

5. On the License Agreement page, if you agree with the terms of the license agreement, click I Agree, and then click Next.

6. On the Product Identification page, enter your CD key and then click Next.

7. On the Component Selection page, in the Action drop-down list next to Exchange Server 2003, click Change.

8. In the Microsoft Connector for Lotus Notes and Microsoft Exchange Calendar Connector drop-down list, click Install, as shown in Figure 35.11, and then click Next.

9. If you are installing your first Exchange Server 2003 server, an Installation Type page appears. Ensure that Create a New Exchange Organization is selected, and click Next.

10. If you are creating a new Exchange organization, on the Organization Name page, enter an organization name, and click Next.

11. On the Licensing Agreement page, if you agree, click I Agree That I Have Read and Will Be Bound by the License Agreements for This Product, and then click Next.

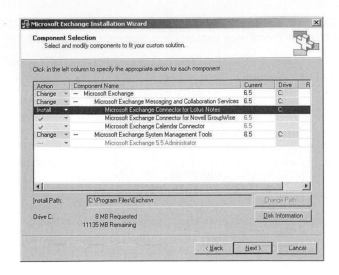

**FIGURE 35.11**    Installing Connector for Lotus Notes.

12. On the Component Summary page, ensure that Connector for Lotus Notes is selected, and then click Next.

13. If a Microsoft Exchange Installation Wizard message box appears informing you that your domain has been identified as an insecure domain for mail-enabled groups with hidden distribution list membership, click OK.

14. After setup completes successfully, click Finish.

> **NOTE**
>
> With Exchange Server 2003 Service Pack 1 installed on the system, you will need to reinstall Service Pack 1 after the connector is installed to update the binary files updated in Exchange Server 2003 Service Pack 1.

## Enabling and Customizing Lotus Notes Proxy Addresses

After the core Connector for Lotus Notes has been installed, the administrator will need to enable and customize the Lotus Notes proxy addresses to properly set the default naming scheme that'll be used for recipients and to ensure messages are directed to the right server system. The process for enabling and customizing Lotus Notes proxy addresses is as follows:

1. Start Exchange System Manager: On the Start menu, point to All Programs, point to Microsoft Exchange, and then click System Manager.

2. Expand Recipients, and then click Recipient Policies.

3. In the details pane, right-click Default Policy, and then click Properties. If you do not have a Default Policy, you can create a new recipient policy.

4. On the policy's E-Mail Addresses (Policy) tab, select the NOTES check box (this enables the address), ensure that the NOTES address entry is selected, and then click Edit.

5. In the Address box, modify the address format. For example, you can set the address format to first name and last name, or first initial and last name, or something similar.

6. After you configure the address formula, click OK.

7. In the Default Policy Properties dialog box, click OK.

8. A message box appears asking whether you want to update all corresponding recipient email addresses to match the new addresses. To run the Recipient Update Service immediately, click Yes. To update the addresses the next time the Recipient Update Service runs, click No. Non-Exchange addresses are always updated, even if you made manual changes to specific addresses.

9. Wait for the Recipient Update Service to populate the Exchange address lists. The time required to populate the lists varies depending on the update interval set on the service.

## Configuring the Connector for Lotus Notes

With the Connector for Lotus Notes installed and the default proxy address generator set, you need to set a few configuration steps for the connector to work properly. The configuration steps are as follows:

1. In Exchange System Manager, expand Administrative Groups, expand Routing Groups, and expand the First Routing Group. Expand the Connectors container, right-click Connector for Lotus Notes, and then click Properties.

2. On the General tab, shown in Figure 35.12, in the Notes Server box, type the full name of your Lotus Notes servers.

3. Under the Notes INI file location, click Modify. Type the location of the NOTES.INI file (for example, `c:\windows\notes.ini`). Under Password and Confirm Password, enter the password used for the user ID for this notes.ini configuration.

4. On the Address Space tab, click Add to add the address space for Lotus Notes.

5. On the Add Address Space tab, click NOTES, and then click OK.

6. On the Lotus Notes Address Space Properties tab, in the Address box, type * to allow all users to connect to Lotus Notes using Connector for Lotus Notes, and then click OK.

7. Click OK to close the Connector for Lotus Notes Properties dialog box and apply the settings.

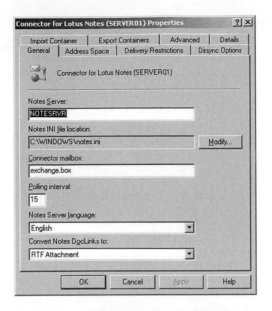

**FIGURE 35.12**    Connector for Lotus Notes General tab settings.

## Starting the Connector for Lotus Notes

After being configured, the Windows service that manages the Connector for Lotus Notes needs to be started. You can do this by completing the following steps:

1. Start the Services tool: Click Start, point to All Programs, point to Administrative Tools, and then click Services.

2. Right-click Microsoft Exchange Connector for Lotus Notes, and then click Start.

3. Verify that Connector for Lotus Notes starts successfully, and then close the Services tool.

## Configuring Directory Synchronization

After you configure the Connector for Lotus Notes, you can synchronize directories between Lotus Notes and Exchange Server 2003 (Active Directory). It is recommended that you test the directory synchronization process manually to ensure that everything works as expected.

### Requirements for Configuring Directory Synchronization

To be able to configure the directory synchronization between Lotus Notes and Exchange, certain permissions, connectivity, client software, and configurations need to be properly set up. Ensure that your environment meets the following requirements:

• You have Exchange administrator permissions.

• You have network connectivity to the server running Lotus Notes.

- You can resolve the name of the server running Lotus Notes.

- You have installed and configured the Lotus Notes client software.

- You have installed and configured Connector for Lotus Notes.

To configure directory synchronization with Lotus Notes, perform the following steps:

1. In Exchange System Manager, right-click Connector for Lotus Notes, and then click Properties.

2. On the Import Container tab, shown in Figure 35.13, to specify the Active Directory container (or organizational unit) to which Lotus Notes users are imported, click Modify. It is recommended that you create a special organizational unit for all of your Lotus Notes users and select that organizational unit here.

3. On the Choose a Container tab, browse to the container to which you want to import Lotus Notes users. Click the container, and then click OK.

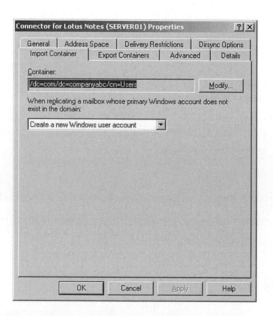

**FIGURE 35.13**    Configuring inbound directory synchronization.

> **NOTE**
>
> You might receive an error message that reads, "The machine account must be granted permission to create and modify recipients in the selected import container. Continue?" If you receive this error message, click Yes. This is necessary for directory synchronization from Lotus Notes to Exchange Server 2003 to work. When you click Yes, you add the computer account with the permissions required to manipulate objects in the selected container.

4.  In the When Replicating a Mailbox Whose Primary Windows Account Does Not Exist in the Domain list, choose one of the following options for Active Directory to use when new users are imported:

    • Create a Disabled Windows User Account

    • Create a New Windows User Account

    • Create a Windows Contact

This setting applies only to new users. If you change this setting later, it does not affect Lotus Notes users who are already replicated to Active Directory. If you are not sure which option to choose, click Create a Disabled Windows User Account or Create a Windows Contact. Click Create a New Windows User Account only if Lotus Notes users are logging on to the Windows domain.

5.  On the Export Containers tab, to specify which groups or organizational units to export from Active Directory to the Lotus Notes directory, click Add.

6.  On the Choose a Container tab, click the organizational unit that you want to export to the Lotus Notes directory, and then click OK.

> **NOTE**
>
> You might receive an error message that reads, "The machine account must be granted permission to read the deleted recipients in the selected domain. Continue?" If you receive this error message, click Yes. This is necessary for directory synchronization from Lotus Notes to Exchange Server 2003 to work. When you click Yes, you add the computer account with the permissions required to manipulate objects in the selected container.

7.  Repeat the preceding two steps for each organizational unit that you want to export. Nested organizational units are not selected for export if you select the parent organizational unit. You must select each organizational unit individually.

8.  On the Dirsync Schedule tab, in the Exchange-Notes directory update schedule list, select the schedule for directory synchronization. Connector for Lotus Notes performs the directory synchronization.

> **TIP**
>
> Do not schedule synchronization during peak traffic hours because it can slow message throughput. If your directory information changes infrequently, schedule synchronization for once per day. If your directory information changes frequently, schedule synchronization for two or more times per day.

9.  Click Customize to schedule synchronization for a period other than those provided by default in the Exchange–Lotus Notes directory update schedule list.

10. Click on Address Book Settings and Add the Source Name and Address Book file-name of the `names.nsf` file for Lotus Notes that has an updated directory for Notes. Click OK.

11. Click OK to close each dialog box.

## Manually Testing Directory Synchronization

To make sure that directory synchronization is working properly, a test can be performed to validate the process is working. To test directory synchronization, do the following:

1. In Exchange System Manager, right-click Connector for Lotus Notes, and then click Properties.

2. On the Dirsync Schedule tab, under Exchange to Lotus Notes directory synchronization, click Immediate Full Reload. In the Exchange System Manager message box informing you that a process has been started to synchronize the directories, click OK. This process synchronizes directory objects from Active Directory to the Lotus Notes directory.

3. Under Lotus Notes to Exchange directory synchronization, click Immediate Full Reload. Again, a message box appears informing you that directory synchronization has begun. This process synchronizes directory objects from the Lotus Notes directory to Active Directory. Click OK.

# Installing and Configuring Calendar Connector in a Lotus Notes Environment

The Connector for Lotus Notes only exchanges messaging objects between the Lotus Notes and Exchange environments. For calendar objects to be exchanged between the two environments, the Calendar Connector needs to be installed and configured so users on Lotus Notes and Exchange can see each others' free or busy schedule information.

The following procedure identifies the steps to configure the Microsoft Exchange Calendar Connector. The Calendar Connector needs to be installed on a server running Exchange. The most straightforward option is to install the Calendar Connector on the same server running the Connector for Lotus Notes.

## Prerequisites for the Calendar Connector for Lotus Notes

Similar to the Connector for Lotus Notes, there are prerequisites for the system and system access to ensure the Calendar Connector will work properly. The server on which the Calendar Connector is installed must meet the following requirements:

- The server is running Exchange Server 2003.

- The server running Exchange Server 2003 has a local replica of the SCHEDULE+ FREE BUSY public folder.

- The server is part of the same routing group as the server running Connector for Lotus Notes.

- You have Exchange administrator permissions, and you are a member of the Administrators group on the computer on which you install Calendar Connector.

- You have network connectivity to the server running Lotus Notes.

## Installing the Calendar Connector

To install the Calendar Connector for Lotus Notes, you should complete the following steps:

1. Insert the Exchange Server 2003 CD into the CD-ROM drive of the server running Exchange Server 2003.

2. At a command prompt, type **cd e:\setup\i386**, where *e* is the drive letter for the CD-ROM drive.

3. Type **setup.exe**, and then press Enter.

4. On the Microsoft Exchange 2003 Installation Wizard Welcome page, click Next.

5. On the Component Selection page, in the Action list next to Microsoft Exchange, click Change.

6. In the Action list next to Microsoft Exchange Messaging and Collaboration Services, click Change.

7. In the Microsoft Exchange Calendar Connector list, click Install, and then click Next.

8. On the Installation Summary page, verify your installation choices, and then click Next.

9. After the installation is complete, click Finish.

## Adding a Local Replica for the Schedule+ Free/Busy Public Folder

As noted in one of the prerequisites, a local replica of the Schedule+ Free/Busy public folder needs to be on the Exchange server where the Calendar Connector is installed. To add a local replica on the server, do the following:

1. In Exchange System Manager, expand Administrative Groups, expand the administrative group that contains the server running Exchange with Calendar Connector (for example, First Administrative Group), and then expand Folders.

2. Expand Public Folders. If you do not see the SCHEDULE+ FREE BUSY public folder, right-click Public Folders, and then click View System Folders.

3. Expand Public Folders, expand SCHEDULE+ FREE BUSY, right-click the public folder that refers to your administrative group that contains the Exchange server running

Calendar Connector (for example, EX:/o=Companyabc /ou=First Administrative Group), and then click Properties.

4. On the Replication tab, click Add.

5. On the Select a Public Store page, select the server running Exchange 2003 with Calendar Connector, and then click OK.

6. In the Public Folder Replication Interval list, click Always Run. This causes replication to occur whenever there is a change in free/busy information. Click OK.

## Configuring the Calendar Connector

After the Calendar Connector is installed on the system and a replica of the Schedule+ Free/Busy information has been added to the system, the Calendar Connector can be configured. The configuration steps are as follows:

1. In Exchange System Manager, expand Administrative Groups, and then expand the administrative group that contains the server running Exchange with Calendar Connector (for example, First Administrative Group).

2. Expand Routing Groups, and then expand the routing group in which you installed Calendar Connector (for example, First Routing Group).

3. Expand Connectors, right-click Calendar Connector, and then click Properties.

4. On the General tab next to the Connector used to import users into Active Directory box, click Modify.

5. In the Select Exchange Notes or GroupWise Connector dialog box, select the Connector for Lotus Notes instance that is used to connect to the Lotus Notes server, and then click OK.

6. In the Number of days of free/busy information to request from foreign calendars box, enter the number of days that users are able to see free/busy information for users on the foreign messaging server. Free/busy information beyond the number of days specified is not retrieved by Calendar Connector and appears as free, even if meetings are scheduled during this time.

7. In the Maximum Age in Minutes of Foreign Free/Busy Data in Exchange That Can Be Used Without Querying the Foreign Calendar box, enter the age limit for free/busy information in minutes. If the free/busy information is beyond the specified number of minutes and a user requests the information, Calendar Connector queries the non-Exchange messaging system for updated data. If the free/busy information is within the specified number of minutes, Calendar Connector uses the current free/busy information.

8. In the Maximum Number of Seconds to Wait for Response from Foreign Calendars box, enter the number of seconds that you want Calendar Connector to wait for a response after it requests an individual user's free/busy information. Set this to a low number because each recipient on a meeting request is handled in turn, and a long

response interval can cause the mail client to stop responding as it proceeds down the list of recipients.

9. On the Calendar Connections tab, click New.

10. In the Calendar Type dialog box, click Lotus Notes, and then click OK.

11. In the Notes Calendar Connection dialog box, shown in Figure 35.14, for the NT Server Hosting the Notes Server box, type the domain and server name of the Lotus Notes server that interfaces with the connector system. For Notes.INI file location and password, click Modify and enter the notes.ini filename along with the associated password for the ID account associated with the notes.ini file. Click OK.

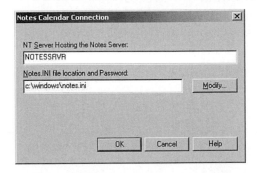

**FIGURE 35.14**    Notes Calendar Connection dialog box options.

12. On the Schedule tab, click Always. This causes Calendar Connector to create a free/busy record for Lotus Notes recipients in the Exchange public folder. This happens every 15 minutes for new recipients. Alternatively, click Selected Times to specify a custom time for the connector to create new records in the server's public folder. Click OK.

## Starting Calendar Connector Service

After the Calendar Connector has been installed and configured on the Exchange Server system, the Calendar Connector service has to be started. Do the following to start the Calendar Connector service:

1. Open the Services Microsoft Management Console (MMC) snap-in: Click Start, point to All Programs, point to Administrative Tools, and then click Services.

2. In the details pane, right-click Microsoft Exchange Calendar Connector, and then click Start.

3. The default startup type for Calendar Connector is manual. You should change the startup type to Automatic. To do this, right-click Microsoft Exchange Calendar Connector, and then click Properties. In the Startup Type list, click Automatic, and then click OK. The next time the server starts, the Calendar Connector service starts automatically.

## Reviewing the Results of the Lab Environment

Based on the results of the migration lab testing, it is important to review and adjust your migration plans as appropriate based on the results of the test lab. It is expected that problems will arise in the test lab. Repeat the test migration process to hone the process until you are comfortable with the results. This process leads into the next phase of the migration, the Stabilizing phase, in which the process is perfected.

# Using the Exchange Migration Wizard to Migrate User Data

With the new Exchange environment created, user accounts migrated to the Exchange environment, and the connector gateway exchanging information between Lotus Notes/Domino and Exchange, existing mailbox information can be migrated to the new Exchange environment.

Microsoft provides a free tool that is installed as part of the default installation of Exchange called the Exchange Migration Wizard. The Exchange Migration Wizard migrates mailbox data from Microsoft Mail, Microsoft Exchange v5.5, Lotus cc:Mail, Novell GroupWise, Lotus Notes, LDAP via ADSI, and IMAP4. This chapter focuses on using the Exchange Migration Wizard to migrate mailbox data from Lotus Notes/Domino to Exchange.

## Prerequisites for the Exchange Migration Wizard

The Exchange Migration Wizard can be installed on a Windows XP desktop or Windows Server 2003 system. Although the tool is automatically installed when Exchange Server 2003 is installed on a server, the tool can also be installed on a workstation or non-Exchange Server system by just installing the Exchange Server 2003 administration tools on a system.

The Exchange Server 2003 administration tools can be installed on a system using the following steps:

1. Insert the Exchange Server 2003 CD into a system.

2. Click Setup and choose Exchange Deployment Tools from the Exchange 2003 setup screen.

3. Choose Install Exchange System Management Tools Only.

4. Select Run Setup Now and install the tools on the system.

5. Click Finish when done.

---

**NOTE**

Service Pack 1 for Exchange Server 2003 has an updated version of the Exchange Migration Wizard. Run the Exchange setup from the Exchange Server 2003 Service Pack 1 files for the latest version of the installation files.

---

Another prerequisite is to ensure your Lotus Domino server is running release 4.6 or higher. Release 4.6 and 5.x of Domino are inherently supported, whereas release 6.x is supported with a patch available from the Microsoft Web site.

Select the system you will use for migration. It cannot be either a Lotus Domino/Notes server or an Exchange server. It must be a standalone system that can access the Active Directory root for the forest in which your Exchange organization resides, the Exchange server, and the Lotus Domino server. Ensure DNS is properly configured to allow this system to connect to your Active Directory, Exchange, and Domino servers.

> **CAUTION**
>
> Ensure your Lotus Domino server is not configured as an SMTP Internet mail gateway. If it *is* configured as the SMTP Internet mail gateway, see `http://go.microsoft.com/fwlink/ ?LinkID=3052&kbid=255160` for resolution.

## Preparing Your Lotus Domino Environment

For the Exchange Migration Wizard to work, the Lotus Domino environment needs to be prepared with the necessary user accounts and information access rights. To prepare the Lotus Domino environment, do the following:

1. Create a Lotus Notes user ID with administrative privileges. On a server with Lotus Domino Administrator installed, start the tool and log on as a current Domino Administrator.

2. Click People and then click Register.

3. Select the Certifier ID (often found in "Notes installation directory\Data").

4. Enter the password for the Certifier ID.

5. A warning may appear. This warning explains the Certifier ID has no recovery information. You may click Yes to continue.

6. A Register Person – New Entry dialog box opens; choose Advanced Options and enter the first and last name of your user.

7. Set the password to something easy to remember but hard to guess.

8. Click the ID Info box and select the In File check box.

9. Click Set ID File and choose a path for the new ID file. Choose a location you'll remember as you will use this file later during the migration.

10. Select Groups and add the Lotus Domino Administrators group.

11. Select Mail and select None for Mail System.

12. Click Add Person, Register.

13. After the user is registered, click Done.

## Creating a Mail File for the Lotus Notes Account

After the Lotus Notes account has been created, create a mail file for the account. To do so, perform the following steps:

1. Add the Lotus Notes account as a Domino administrator with full access for all the mailboxes (.nsf files) you want to migrate.

2. Click File, Open Server.

3. Select your Domino server and click OK.

4. Click the Files tab and expand Tools, then Folder, and then click New Link.

5. The Create New Link screen appears; add a unique name for the link.

6. For "link to a," select Folder.

7. In the Path and Filename to the Folder field, type the path to the Lotus Domino mail database.

8. For Who Should Be Able to Access This Account, add the account you created for migration purposes.

9. Press F9 to refresh. You should now see a folder for the link you created.

10. Click the link for your new folder and you should see a list of mailboxes in the right frame.

11. Press Ctrl+A to select All Users.

12. In the right frame, right-click the list of selected users.

13. Select Access Control, Manage.

14. Click Add in the Multi ACL Management window.

15. Select Browse for the Add ACL Entry window.

16. In the Names window, select the user you created for migration purposes, click Add, and then click OK.

17. Select Person from the User Type list.

18. Select Reader from the Access list, and click OK.

19. Force directory synchronization.

## Preparing Your Microsoft Exchange 2003 Server

After the Lotus Domino account and mailbox configurations have been completed, prepare the Exchange Server 2003 server for the migration process. Perform the following steps:

1. Open Active Directory Users and Computers from the Microsoft Exchange menu.

2. Create an account for the migration. This account does not need a mailbox.

3. Give the account a password that is easy to remember, but hard to guess.

4. Place this account in the Enterprise Admins Group.

5. If you have not already done so, create accounts for all the users you plan to migrate. A Lightweight Directory Access Protocol (LDAP) connector is often used to import user objects from another environment.

6. Select all the accounts for users you plan to migrate.

7. Right-click the selected group and choose Exchange Tasks.

8. Click Next at the welcome screen.

9. Select Create Mailbox.

10. If you selected multiple users, the alias is assigned automatically; otherwise, it defaults to the user's logon name.

11. Choose the server on which the mailbox will reside.

12. Choose the storage group in which to store the mailbox. Make note of this storage group because you will need it later.

13. If there are no errors, click Finish.

With the Lotus Notes and Exchange servers configured and mailboxes identified, final configuration steps will complete the Exchange server mailbox process. The configuration steps include

1. Double-click the first account planned for migration to bring up the Properties screen.

2. Select the E-mail Addresses tab. Make sure the SMTP address matches what you want the external email address to be. If it does not match what you want, either add a new SMTP address or edit the current SMTP address.

3. Select the Exchange Advanced tab.

4. Select Mailbox Rights, click Add, and then add the user you created earlier.

5. Select the Take Ownership and Full Access options, and click OK. Click OK again to save your settings.

6. Repeat this process for every user you want to migrate.

## Running the Exchange Migration Wizard Process

With the Lotus Notes and Exchange servers configured, mailbox accounts created, and configurations finalized, it is now time to migrate mailbox data. You can perform this by doing the following:

1. Launch the Microsoft Exchange Migration Wizard. To do so, click Start, point to All Programs, point to Microsoft Exchange, point to Deployment, and then click Migration Wizard.

2. Click Next at the welcome screen.

3. At the second screen, select Migrate from Lotus Notes.

4. Read the window and click Next if you have completed the prerequisites. If you have not read the prerequisites, please go back and review them now.

5. Choose the recommended option of a one-step migration and select a location for the migrated files.

6. At the next screen, choose your Exchange server and Information Store that contains your mailbox objects. If you are using an Exchange cluster, choose the name of the Exchange virtual server. You have already mailbox-enabled the accounts within Active Directory; be sure to choose the correct Information Store.

7. If you have not mailbox-enabled the accounts, go back and review the prerequisites section.

8. Configure the tool to connect to Notes.

9. Select your Notes.ini file from the Notes installation directory.

10. On the Access Information Page, as shown in Figure 35.15, select the Notes user ID with administrative privileges that you created earlier.

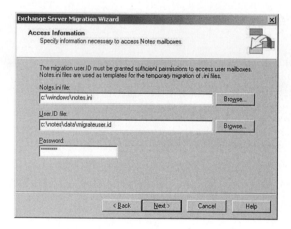

**FIGURE 35.15**    Configuring the Access Information settings for migration.

11. Enter the password for the Notes user ID.

12. Select the hierarchical name of your Notes server.

13. Choose which objects you are planning to migrate.

14. Select the accounts you want to migrate to Exchange. You can select individual mailboxes or click Select All for all mailboxes.

15. Select the container within Active Directory in which new accounts will be created if necessary. It is recommended to create all accounts in Active Directory, and create mailboxes for these users, in advance of starting the Exchange Migration Wizard.

16. Select your choice of password creation for newly created accounts. It is highly recommended you force users to change their password on their first logon.

17. The Exchange Migration Wizard displays a screen with the results from matching the accounts specified for migration. This screen denotes whether an existing account was found and its location or if a new account will be created in the location specified on the last screen.

18. Check this screen carefully. The tool does not always properly find accounts and you might need to manually link accounts. This is possible by clicking the account name and then selecting Find Existing Account. You can then find the account within Active Directory.

19. Click Next to begin the migration process.

## Confirming Migration Operations

This section highlights information on how to validate that the Exchange Migration Wizard is working properly. Check the Windows application event log for any errors or information about the migration. You should see something similar to the following:

```
The 'Import ' of mail from 'File  - C:\MigratedFiles\Notes.001\Notes.PKL' completed
with the following results:

Start Time:       12:51:00
Elapsed Time:     00:07:43

Accounts:              1
Public folders:        0
E-Mail Messages:                   351
PABs:                  0
Warnings:              0
Errors:                0
```

The key is to note no errors took place during the migration.

In addition, you can test the migration by opening Outlook with the account you created for the migration. Do the following:

1. Choose File, Open, Other User's Folder.

2. Type the name of a user you have migrated, and select Inbox to open. You should see the migrated mail in the user's Inbox.

35

Ensure all Outlook clients are set to connect to their mailbox via a MAPI Exchange connection. This might require changing user account profiles from POP3 or IMAP to Exchange (MAPI). A Microsoft Office transform is available and deployable via logon script or Group Policy Object (GPO) for mass conversion of client settings.

Instruct users to import their calendar data. All users will have an item in their Inbox with an SC2 attachment and instructions on how to import this data to Exchange.

## Problems and Errors That May Occur During the Migration Process

The following are problems that may occur during the migration process, and the event errors that will indicate the problem.

- Event ID 181 and/or 10052

  - Event ID: 181
    Source:MSExchangeMigDS
    Type: Error
    Description: Could not bind to the Microsoft Exchange Directory server *Server_name*.
    The Microsoft Exchange Server computer does not respond.
    Event ID: 10052
    Source:MSExchangeMig
    Type: Error
    Description: Invalid server specified or you do not have the permission required to complete the operation.

  - Resolution

    - Run Nltest.exe /sc_reset:<domain_name> to ensure a reliable connection with the domain.

    - Run ping <FQDN for exchange server name>.

    - See http://support.microsoft.com/default.aspx?scid=kb;en-us;275341.

- Event ID 12019

  - Event ID: 12019
    Source: MSExchangeMig
    Type: Error
    Description: Invalid user ID file.

  - Resolution

    - The specified user ID may not exist or is incorrect.

      - Correct the user ID (*.id file).

    - See http://support.microsoft.com/default.aspx?scid=kb;en-us;274130.

- The Exchange Migration Wizard fails for large mailboxes.

    - Not all mail is imported from a Notes mailbox to Exchange, yet the Exchange Migration Wizard did not throw an error.

    - Resolution

        - For very large mailboxes, use the Microsoft Importer for Lotus Notes Mail Tool. It is available at `http://www.microsoft.com/exchange/downloads/2000/NotesImporter.asp`.

- The Exchange Migration Wizard does not import folders with leading or trailing whitespace.

    - This issue only exists when migrating from Lotus Notes 5.x.

    - Resolution

        - Using the Lotus Notes client removes the leading or trailing whitespace.

- The Exchange Migration Wizard does not migrate items only in All Documents mail view.

    - The All Documents view is a complete catalog of all of the documents (messages) in the Notes mail database, which can contain items that are not in any visible folder.

    - Resolution

        - Move the documents to a folder, such as the Inbox folder.

- The Exchange Migration Wizard does not import calendar items with no end date.

    - In this situation, the Microsoft Exchange Migration Wizard crashes.

    - Lotus Notes uses the value -1 to designate a recurring meeting that does not have an ending date. This value is equivalent to hexadecimal FFFF. In this scenario, the Exchange Migration Wizard interprets the recurring meeting as having an ending date of hexadecimal FFFF for the day, hexadecimal FFFF for the month, and hexadecimal FFFF for the year.

    - Resolution

        - Set an end date for calendar items using the Notes client.

        - Or, re-create these items after the migration is complete.

        - Contact Microsoft support to obtain the hotfix for Exchange Server 2003.

            - `http://support.microsoft.com/default.aspx?scid=fh;[LN];CNTACTMS`

- Event ID 283

    - Event ID: 283

35

Source: MSExchangeMIGDS

Description: Could not remove object <UserID> because the directory service reported the following error: Changes cannot be written to this directory object. Try connecting to a Microsoft Exchange Server computer in the same site as this object.

- Resolution

  - The account used has inadequate privileges to perform the migration.

  - Use an account with the appropriate level of permissions.

  - See http://support.microsoft.com/kb/162833/EN-US/.

- The Exchange Migration Wizard may "freeze" or stop responding when it encounters a corrupt mailbox in Lotus Notes.

  - When the Exchange Server 2003 Migration Wizard encounters a corrupt calendar item in a Lotus Notes mailbox, it freezes and crashes.

  - Resolution

    - Contact Microsoft support to obtain the hotfix for Exchange Server 2003.

      - http://support.microsoft.com/
        default.aspx?scid=fh;[LN];CNTACTMS

- Notes mailboxes may not be properly migrated to Exchange Server 2003.

  - The Lotus Notes mailbox may contain messages that have two or more Lotus Notes domains in the header.

  - See http://support.microsoft.com/default.aspx?scid=kb;en-us;887577.

  - Resolution

    - Contact Microsoft support to obtain the hotfix for Exchange Server 2003.

      - http://support.microsoft.com/
        default.aspx?scid=fh;[LN];CNTACTMS

- Calendar items are not imported to Exchange Server 2003.

  - The Migration Wizard places a mail message in the user's Inbox with an SC2 attachment and instructions on how to import the data to Exchange.

    - Often, even after importing this file, the location field is left blank.

- Event ID 8084

  - Event Type: Error
    Event Source: MSExchangeMig
    Event ID: 8084
    Computer: *ComputerName*

Description: MAPI Section *FilePath\FileName*.PRI
Line: *LineNumber* Failed to set a property on a message.
Error code: 0x80070057

- Lotus Notes .pkl file is not imported to Exchange Server 2003 by the Exchange Migration Wizard.

- Resolution

  - Contact Microsoft support to obtain the hotfix for Exchange Server 2003.

    - `http://support.microsoft.com/`
      `default.aspx?scid=fh;[LN];CNTACTMS`

  - Hotfix requires Exchange Server 2003 SP1.

- After migration is complete, you cannot access any mailboxes in the same Information Store as the migrated mailboxes.

  - On rare occasions, the Exchange Migration Wizard may halt the Microsoft Exchange Information Store service.

  - Resolution

    - Restart the Microsoft Exchange Information Store service.

- The Exchange Migration Wizard finished but with errors.

  - This is most likely due to corrupt objects or attachments in Notes.

    - Check the application log in Event Viewer for the specific errors.

    - Corrupt objects or attachments that were not migrated are not indicative of a failed migration and should be noted and can otherwise be ignored.

# Details on the Effects of the Lotus Notes Migration Tools

This section explains some of the effects of the Lotus Notes Migration tool. These effects identify how folders, content, and other user data is migrated or not migrated as part of the conversion process.

## Migration of Local Archives

The Exchange Migration Wizard migrates data stored on the Lotus Notes server, but not data in local archives on Lotus Notes clients. Lotus Notes clients include automatic archive functionality to store messaging data locally. To migrate local archives, users must convert their local archives back to standard email data and transfer it back into the Lotus Notes mailboxes.

Lotus Notes users can store large amounts of email data in their local archives, which means putting these items back into their Lotus Notes mailboxes greatly increases the amount of data that must be migrated. You must ensure that your Lotus Notes system and the Exchange Server 2003 server have sufficient disk space to store the data. If you are concerned that migrating local archives impedes your migration process, you might want to consider migrating local archives for executives and employees with specific permission only.

> **NOTE**
>
> After migration is complete, your users can create local personal folder (.pst) files to store the email data that they previously stored in Lotus Notes local archives on the client computer.

## Migration of Personal Address Books

The Exchange Migration Wizard is unable to migrate personal address books from Lotus Notes to Exchange Server 2003. However, it is possible to export personal address books from Lotus Notes into text-based files that can be converted into comma-separated value (.csv) files using a macro in Microsoft Excel, for example. The primary task is to reorder the fields to match the layout required by Outlook. Outlook provides the functionality to import Contact objects from a .csv file.

To determine the order of fields in a .csv file for Outlook, create a sample contact object in Outlook and then export this contact into a .csv file using the Import and Export command on the File menu in Outlook 2003. Choose Export to a File and then select Comma Separated Values (Windows). Select the Contacts folder where you created the sample contact, and complete the export procedure. Open the resulting .csv file in Excel. You should find the list of fields in the first row.

> **NOTE**
>
> Users can re-create personal contacts as well as personal distribution lists in a Contacts folder in Outlook.

## Migration of Personal Dictionaries

Personal dictionaries cannot be migrated from Lotus Notes to Exchange Server 2003 and Outlook. The Lotus Notes spelling checker dictionary is stored in separate, identifiable files. However, these files are encrypted and encoded and cannot be migrated to Outlook. Users must add their words to the spelling checker dictionaries in Outlook and Microsoft Office manually.

## Migration of Client Rules and Proxy Access

The Exchange Migration Wizard cannot migrate client rules from Lotus Notes clients to Microsoft Outlook. Users must re-create their rules in Outlook. Users can access the Rules and Alerts command from the Tools menu in Outlook 2003 to re-create their rules.

Users must also migrate proxy access permissions to the mailboxes manually. In Outlook, proxy access is referred to as delegate access. In Outlook 2003, from the Tools menu, click

Options, and then in the Options dialog box, switch to the Delegates tab, where you can click the Add button to configure delegate access. Because Outlook and Exchange Server 2003 handle delegate access differently than Lotus Notes does, it is recommended that you train your users to set up delegates and send messages on behalf of another user in Outlook before you perform the migration.

> **NOTE**
>
> Exchange users can grant delegate access only to accounts in the Exchange Server 2003 organization. Exchange users cannot grant delegate access to Lotus Notes users.

## Migration of Shared Folders

Lotus Notes users can share their mailbox folders with other users, and the Exchange Migration Wizard can migrate the shared folders to Exchange Server 2003, but shared folder permissions cannot be migrated. To share folders after the migration, users must re-create these permissions on the appropriate folders in Outlook. To grant another user access to a folder in Outlook 2003, right-click the folder, select Properties, and then switch to the Permissions tab.

> **NOTE**
>
> Exchange users can share their folders only with other Exchange users. They cannot give access to their folders to Lotus Notes users.

# Summary

Organizations choosing to migrate from Lotus Notes to Microsoft Exchange are helped by several tools from Microsoft. The tools include the Microsoft Exchange Migration Wizard, Connector for Lotus Notes, and Calendar Connector.

Some organizations that already have Windows NT4 in their environment may choose to migrate NT4 to Active Directory as part of their conversion process. After Active Directory is installed, the organization may choose to use the Connector for Lotus Notes to keep the Lotus Notes directory and Active Directory in sync.

With an established Active Directory already in place, the organization can install Microsoft Exchange Server 2003 and then begin the process of connecting Lotus Notes to Exchange, move mailboxes, and route mail between the two messaging systems until all users have been migrated to Exchange.

After all users have been migrated to Exchange, the Lotus Notes messaging system can be removed.

# Best Practices

The following are best practices from this chapter:

- Review Chapter 1 to understand the common reasons organizations plan and deploy the Exchange Server 2003 messaging system.

- Leverage the planning and design details in Chapters 4 and 5 of this book to prepare the business for an appropriate Exchange Server 2003 messaging system design and configuration.

- Install Exchange Server 2003 to establish the foundation for the new Exchange messaging environment.

- Use the Connector for Lotus Notes to migrate user accounts from Lotus Notes to Active Directory, and continue to use the connector to keep the directories synchronized.

- Install the Connector for Lotus Notes on an Exchange Server 2003 server that will be used to route messages between the two environments.

- Install the Calendar Connector on the same server as the Connector for Lotus Notes to minimize the number of servers needed to interconnect the two environments.

# Index

## NUMBERS

**8-node clustering, 18**

## A

**acceleration**
  ISA Server 2004, 234
    creating OWA publishing rules, 243-247
    customizing OWA FBA, 252
    EMS, 237-239, 252-258
    IMAP/POP3, 261-266
    logging, 277-279
    MAPI, 258-260
    monitoring, 279-283
    moving OWA certificates, 240-243
    OWA, 239-240
    redirecting OWA traffic, 247-251
    role of, 234-237
    SMTP, 266-276
**access, 629**
  administrative rights, 537-538
  Cached Mode Outlook configuration option, 741
  Calendars Additional calendars, 729
  clients, 125-127
    front-end server design, 155
    integrating, 154-155
    large businesses, 157
    mid-sized businesses, 156
    small businesses, 156
  extended permissions, 536
  GPMC, 864
  IMAP security, 261-266
  Internet (Outlook 2003), 344-346
  logon, 370
  mailboxes, 937
  mobile devices, 647-648, 673-674

applying Pocket PC, 693-695
connecting Pocket PC, 679-683,
    688-693
mobile phone connections, 699-700
smartphones, 695-698
synchronizing Pocket PC, 674-678,
    683-688
mobile Web access, 643-644
new features, 114
non-Windows clients, 822
    HTML, 823
    IMAP, 822
    OWA, 823
    pocket PCs, 823
    POP, 822
offline, 114
OMA, 114, 701
    comparing to ActiveSync, 658
    configuring, 254-257
Outlook
    configuring, 715
    connecting with VPN, 641-643
OWA, 9-10, 114, 126, 287-288, 642
    configuring architecture, 289-294
    enabling SSL, 294-299
    infrastructure, 288
    optimizing slow access, 798-799
    servers, 756
POP (Outlook Express), 812-813
POP3, 822
proxy servers, 1054, 1106-1107
remote access, 644
SMTP virtual servers, 410
transport-level security layers, 391-392
Windows 2003 support tools, 71

**accounts**
    email, 715
    Lotus Notes, 1098
    master account lists, 915
    migrating, 438-448
    provisioning, 166
    users, 872
**ACT (Windows Application Compatibility
toolkit), 527-528**
**Active Directory, 8-9, 116-118**
    core installations
        extending schemas, 1068-1069
        implementing, 1068

design, 136-137
    configuring DNS, 139
    domains, 137
    forests, 137
    large businesses, 142
    mid-sized businesses, 140
    replication, 138
domain controllers, 138, 214
    authentication, 214-215
    placement, 215
domain structures, 120
DSAccess, 222-223
DSProxy, 224
eDirectory
    NDS tools, 1004-1006
    synchronizing, 1012
forest migration, 458-460
functionality, 225-229
Global Catalog, 215
    demoting, 219
    deploying domain controllers, 220
    domain controllers, 216
    optimizing promotion, 219
    placement of, 219
    server relationships, 216
    structures, 216
    universal group caching, 221-222
    verifying, 218
implementing, 70, 1018
infrastructure components, 120-122
integration
    replication, 192
    zones, 189
Lotus Notes, 1063
managing, 588-589
migrating, 1001-1002, 1059-1060
MMS, 123
modes
    group models, 71-73
    selecting, 71
NDS, 1012
objects, 540-541
populating, 478-480
recovering, 967-973
Restore mode password, 920
schemas, 73-74, 458, 492-493,
    1018-1019
SMTP Categorizer, 224

structure, 212
  domains, 212
  forests, 212
  replication, 213
  trees, 212
  Windows NT 4.0, 427-429
**Active Directory Application Mode (ADAM), 165**
**Active Directory Connector (ADC), 460-466**
**Active Directory Migration Tool (ADMT), 433-448**
**Active Directory Replication Monitor, 71**
**Active Directory Schema MMC snap-in, 74, 1069**
**Active Directory Users and Computers (ADUC), 401, 864**
**active prototypes (mobile devices), 651-652**
**Active/Active clustering, 878**
**Active/Passive clustering, 878**
**ActiveSync.** *See also* **synchronization**
  configuring, 254-257
  functionality, 650-651
  installing, 486
  leveraging, 29
  mobile services, 668-670
  OMA, 658
  OWA, 315-321
  PDA connections, 643-646
**ADAM (Active Directory and Active Directory Application), 165**
**adapters, clustering networks, 885**
**ADC (Active Directory Connector)**
  deleting, 479
  installing, 460-466
**ADClean, 481**
**add-ins (Outlook), 745**
**adding**
  Administrative Outlook Template, 860-861
  attachments to email, 765-766
    deleting, 769
    forwarding, 768
    reading, 767-768
    replying, 768
  codes, 893
  email addresses, 553

  Exchange 2003 Server, 12-13
  folders (Outlook), 762
  front-end servers, 664
  groups, 85
  IP addresses to OWA servers, 323
  layers to security, 391-392
  memberships to Group Distribution, 555
  replicas, 1093
  SRSs, 469-470
**address books**
  migrating, 1054, 1106
  OWA, 771
**addresses**
  contacts, 552
    adding, 553
    types, 553
  email, 764-765
    configuring, 542
    defining recipient policies, 565
    editing recipient policies, 567
    implementing recipient policies, 566-567
    naming recipient policies, 565
    recipient policies, 564
    sharing, 388
  Exchange 5.5, 453
  Global Catalogs, 70-71
  IP, 323
  OAB, 600, 977
  OAL, 600
  personal address books, 813-814
  proxy
    customizing GroupWise, 1038-1039
    Lotus Notes, 1087-1088
  validating, 765
**administration, 21, 581**
  Active Directory, 588-589
  Administrative Outlook Template, 860-861
  backups, 590, 910-912
    database corruption, 911-912
    devices, 917
    documentation, 912-915
    media, 930-932
    Ntbackup.exe, 922-927
    servers, 918-920
    services, 927-930

strategies, 915-917
system failures, 911
client options, 845
contacts, 551
   adding addresses, 553
   address types, 552
   creating, 551-552
   forwarding mail, 552
creating, 1072-1073
Delegation Wizard, 533-534
   auditing tasks, 539
   extended permissions, 536
   implementing roles, 538
   rights, 537-538
   role-based, 534-535
deleting, 97
directories, 22-23
Distribution Groups, 557
documentation, 616-617
dynamic distribution lists, 21
eseutil utility, 591-592
ESM, 587-588
Exchange 5.5, 452
isinteg utility, 590-591
knowledge, 607
LDAP, 175-178
Mailbox Manager tool, 574-578
mailboxes, 540
   customizing, 541-543
   enabling Active Directory objects,
      540-541
   implementing limitations, 541
   modifying status, 545
   moving, 547-551
   speed of, 21
   user protocols, 544
   wireless services, 543
maintenance, 602
message tracking, 592
migration, 23
MOM, 24
ntdsutil utility, 590
Outlook, 715, 834
Queue Viewer, 592
Recipient Update Services, 568-571
recipients, 563-564
   defining, 565
   editing, 567
   implementing, 566-567
   naming, 565

remote, 586-587
Remote Desktop for Administration,
   625-631
roles/responsibilities, 582-583
server roles, 368-369
tools, 15, 115
Administrative Groups, 82, 123, 558
   creating, 560, 1022-1025
   databases recovery, 21
   delegating, 560-561
   design, 149
   email policies, 365
   mailboxes, 550
   models, 559
   modes, 559
   selecting number of, 123
   tools
      GroupWise, 1001
      Lotus Notes, 1059
   views, 1022
Administrative Installation Points
   (Outlook), 836
Administrative Outlook Template, 860-
   861
Administrator role, 535
ADMT (Active Directory Migration Tool),
   433-448
AdSizer tool, 74
ADUC (Active Directory Users and
   Computers), 401, 864
agents
   account provisioning, 166
   MA role of, 167-168
aging indexes, 594
alerts
   Event ID 9582, 985
   ISA Server 2004, 280
allocation
   hardware, 525
   memory, 30
   NOS, 525-526
analysis
   capacity, 979-980
   core elements, 983
   database free space, 601
   MBSA, 374
   processor usage, 986
   resource utilization, 600
Anti-Virus API (AVAPI), 131, 383

**antispam, 387**
design, 150
filters, 722
tools, 349-350
**antivirus applications, 132**
design, 150
DNS, 201-203
Exchange 2003 Servers, 382-383
**application-layer filtering, 236-237**
**applications**
antispam, 387
antivirus, 132, 382-383
compatibility, 519-524
components
large businesses, 146
mid-sized businesses, 146
selecting, 142-144
small businesses, 145
disaster recovery, 953-955
gateways, 201
Group Policy, 845
ISA Server 2004, 234
creating OWA publishing rules, 243-247
customizing OWA FBA, 252
EMS, 237-239, 252-258
IMAP/POP3, 261-266
MAPI, 258-260
OWA, 239-243
redirecting OWA traffic, 247-251
role of, 234-237
lab-testing, 525-528
multiple forests, 119
noncompatible, 522. *See also* compatibility
Ntbackup.exe, 953
prioritizing, 518-519
requirements, 884
researching, 517-519
testing, 510-513
**applying**
Active Directory Schema MMC snap-in, 74, 1069
Group Policy settings, 867-869
internal CAs, 300-303
MSDSS, 170-175
multiple forests, 119
Pocket PC 2002, 693-695

Pocket PC 2003, 693-695
PRF files, 718-719
Routing Groups, 563
RPC over HTTP(S), 127, 326-329
Schema Master, 1068
undelete functions, 936
**appointments**
calendars, 788-789
Outlook, 711
Recovery Storage Group, 963-964
**approval for statement of work, 46**
**architecture**
Active Directory, 212
authentication, 214-215
domain controllers, 214
domains, 212
DSAccess, 222-223
DSProxy, 224
forests, 212
functionality, 225-229
Global Catalog, 215-220
placement, 215
replication, 213
SMTP Categorizer, 224
trees, 212
universal group caching, 221-222
OWA, 289-294
**archives**
local, 1053
migrating, 1105-1106
**as-built documentation, 615**
**ASR (Automated System Recovery), 899, 924-927, 951-953**
**assessment, risk, 362-363**
**Assigned Application options, 870**
**assigning**
IP addresses, 254
permissions, 731
**assumptions/risks, 45**
**attachments**
blocking, 27, 348
email
adding, 765-766
deleting, 769
forwarding, 768
reading, 767-768
replying, 768

Outlook 2003, 348
OWA, 354
S/MIME encryption, 27
**attacks, 391-392**
**attributes, MIIS, 165**
**auditing, 583**
logging, 584-585
protocols, 584
tracking messages, 585
policies, 371
security events, 370
tasks, 539
**authentication**
Active Directory, 214-215
cookies, 798
cross-forest Kerberos, 25
domain controllers, 490
FBA, 309
customizing, 252
OWA, 415
Internet (Outlook 2003), 347
smartcards, 399
SMTP, 408
**authoritative restores, Active Directory, 969**
**authority over DNS zones, 189**
**Automated System Recovery (ASR), 899, 924-927, 951-953**
**Automatic Signature, 783**
**automation**
Outlook
configuring profiles, 830-831
profiles, 836-841
SfN, 1006-1010
SSL redirection, 416
updates, 131, 644, 817
**AVAPI (Anti-Virus API), 131, 383**
**Average Response Time, 660**
**avoiding VM fragmentation, 128**


# B

**back-end servers**
architecture, 289-294
IPSec, 25
locking down, 416-417
sizing, 993

**backups, 95, 910-912, 993**
ASR, 924-927
clustering, 899-902
controller card configurations, 911
databases, 663, 911-912, 1081
devices, 917
documentation, 619, 912-915, 940
domain controllers, 429
eseutil utility, 592
Group Policy, 859
information stores, 601
mailboxes, 547
managing, 590
media, 930-932
MSDSS, 174-175
Ntbackup.exe, 922-927
online, 19, 598
personal address books, 813-814
pools, 931
procedures, 938
restoring from, 936
servers, 918-920
services, 927-930
single member server migrations, 425
strategies, 915-917
system failures, 911
Volume Shadow Copy services, 921
**balancing loads, 203-204**
**bandwidth topologies, 832-833**
**baselines**
establishing, 980
Group Policy, 857-859
Outlook, 865
records, 607
**basic mode, OWA user mode, 752**
**BCC (blind carbon copy), 764**
**beaconing**
spam, 725, 797
Web, 350
**benefits of documentation, 606-607**
**best practices**
databases, 592-596
deployment, 832-833
Outlook, 846
scheduling, 597-601
storage groups, 96-97
**binary emulation, 678.** *See also* **emulation**
**blacklists, 386.** *See also* **spam**

**blind carbon copy (BCC), 764**

**Blocked Senders list, 724**

**blocking**
attachments, 27, 354
lists, 26, 352-355
read receipts, 353

**booting**
disaster recovery, 945-947
loader files, 953
volumes
backups, 918
troubleshooting, 945

**breaches, cost of security, 234**

**bridgehead server configuration, 93, 98, 583**

**bridges, 198**

**browser-based devices, 647-648**

**budgets, 45**
compatibility testing, 515
hardware, 525
Migration document, 59
NOS, 525-526

**burn-in, enabling servers, 500**

**business unit messaging goals, 41**


# C

**CA (Certificate Authority)**
backups, 927-929
PKI, 392-396

**CAs (connection agreements)**
configuring, 461-469
enterprise root, 394
third-party, 296-299

**Cached Exchange Mode, 977**

**Cached Mode, 739-746**

**caches**
distribution lists, 30, 979
GC, 17, 121
Universal Group Caching, 122, 221-222

**calculations**
free space, 596
virtual memory, 985-986

**Calendar, 8**
customizing, 786
formatting, 711
Group Policy, 866
managing, 647
meetings, 711-712
multiple, 729
OWA, 788-791
Pocket PC 2002/2003, 694-695
Recovery Storage Group, 963-964
sharing, 729-731
versions, 733-735

**Calendar Connector**
GroupWise, 1014
configuring, 1046-1047
installing, 1044-1045
starting, 1048
Lotus Notes
configuring, 1092-1095
starting, 1095

**Calendars Additional calendars, opening, 729**

**Cals (client access licenses), 632**

**canonical name (CNAME), 195**

**capacity**
analysis, 979
baselines, 980
Jetstress, 982

**carbon copy (CC), 764**

**cards, networks, 904**

**Categorizer, 224-225**

**CC (carbon copy), 764**

**CD (connected directory), 165**

**centralized administrative models, 559**

**Certificate Authority (CA)**
backups, 927-929
PKI, 392-396

**Certificate Manager window, 401**

**Certificate Practice Statement (CPS), 394**

**Certificate Revocation List (CRL), 402**

**Certificate Services, 928**

**certificates, 396**
Active Directory Users and Computers snap-in, 401
enrollment, 400-402
OWA, 240-243
S/MIME, 402-403

templates, 397-399
User, 397
**change control, 621**
**Change Password button (OWA), 313**
**charts, Gantt Chart, 54**
**checking versions, 807**
**checklists**
administration, 617
maintenance, 617
migration documentation, 613
**Checkpoint-Meta IP, 188**
**CHTML (Compact HTML), 658**
**circular logging, 1076**
**CIW (Custom Installation Wizard), 831**
Cached Mode, 741
Outlook, 715-719
predefined configuration options, 835
**cleaning mailboxes, 548, 576**
**clearing credentials, 798**
**clients**
access, 125-127, 632
front-end server design, 155
IMAP, 126
integrating, 154-155
large businesses, 157
MAPI compression, 125
mid-sized businesses, 156
OMA, 126
OWA, 126
POP3, 126
RPC over HTTP, 127
security, 337
small businesses, 156
SMTP, 127
administrative, 845
clustering, 878-883
permissions, 882
requirements, 883-886
configuring, 806-809
managing, 715
predefined options, 835
proposing meetings, 711-712
public folders, 736
remote connections, 739-746
requirements, 834-835
RPC over HTTP, 725-728
searching, 712-713
security, 719-725

shared Web home page views, 738
testing, 848
connection failures, 943
deploying, 829
configuring Outlook profiles, 830-831
customizing, 831-832
managing Outlook, 834
methods, 830
planning, 832-833
desktop migration procedures, 613
DNS, 186-187
need for, 187
SMTP, 199
troubleshooting, 205
Entourage 2004 client and Exchange Updates, 815
Group Policy, 831, 859-864
GroupWise, 1000
installing, 842-843, 850-851
Lotus Notes, 1058
Macintosh
Entourage X, 815-818
Terminal Services Client, 818-821
mobile communications, 10
multiple client, 820
non-Windows access methods, 822
HTML, 823
IMAP, 822
OWA, 823
pocket PCs, 823
POP, 822
Outlook
best practices, 846
Calendar, 733-735
collaboration, 729-733
comparing versions, 708
Group Schedules, 736-738
highlighting, 710-711
installing, 715-719
interfaces, 709
linking, 713-714
Macintosh, 806
Outlook Express, 810-814
OWA, 9-10, 749-751
calendar, 788-791
Contacts option, 794-797
customizing email features, 771-781
email features, 764-771

interfaces, 750-751
leveraging .NET framework, 751
login interfaces, 755-756
meeting invitations, 792-793
navigating, 757-764
new features, 753-756
optimizing slow access, 798-799
options, 781-787
redirecting, 305-306
security, 797-798
Task option, 793-794
user modes, 753
post-deployment tasks, 850-851
rules, 1106-1107
security
hardening Windows, 337
lockdown guidelines, 343
new features, 343-344
optimizing, 338
patches/updates, 342-343
templates, 340-341
virus protection, 343
servers, 976-977
synchronization, 977
Terminal Services, 633
transforms, 832
transport-level security, 415-416
updating, 871-873
VPN, 641-643
Windows-based mail, 802
Macintosh support, 802-803
OWA functionality, 804-805
wireless technologies, 10
Cluster Resources, 879
clustering, 130, 878-883
8-node, 18
configuring, 896-898
design, 145
fault tolerance
installing, 887-896
optimizing, 886
managing, 898-902
network adapters, 885
NLB, 904
NLB Manager, 906
nodes, 893
OWA, 903-906
permissions, 882

planning, 888-890
recovering, 966
requirements, 883-886
software requirements, 890
support, 144
CNAME (canonical name), 195
coexistence, 117
collaboration, 48
GroupWise, 1000-1001
Lotus Notes, 1058-1059
Outlook, 729-733
Calendar, 733-735
Group Schedules, 736-738
public folders, 736
shared Web home page views, 738
colors
Outlook, 711
OWA, 785
combined migration approach, 488
command-line utilities, 587. See also tools
commands, Outlook Mobile Access, 647
communication, optimizing, 362, 976-977
community, 362
Compact HTML (CHTML), 658
compacting Exchange 5.5 organizations, 456
comparing
Exchange Server 2003
and GroupWise, 1000-1001
and Lotus Notes, 1058-1059
PDAs/tablet PCs, 654
versions of Outlook, 708
compatibility
between DNS platforms, 188
clients, 804-805
hardware, 424
Outlook Express, 810-814
states of, 520
Terminal Services Client, 818-821
testing, 510-516
documenting, 516-517, 528
lab-testing applications, 525-528
prototype phase, 529
researching applications, 517-519
training, 516
verifying, 519-524
complete server failures, 947-949

**components**
  Active Directory, 120-122
  ADMT, 434-449
  applications
    large businesses, 146
    mid-sized businesses, 146
    selecting, 142-144
    small businesses, 145
  design, 113
    coexistence, 117
    functionality, 113-116
    scaling, 117
    third-party functionality, 118
  DNS, 185-189
    need for, 187
    queries, 191-192
    replication, 192
    resource records, 192-197
    servers, 187-188
    zones, 189-191
  Entourage X, 815-816
  hardware
    large businesses, 146
    mid-sized businesses, 146
    selecting, 142-144
    small businesses, 145
  ISA SMTP Screener
    enabling, 269
    installing, 268
  mobility, 658
  SFU (Interix), 180-181
**compression**
  enabling, 799
  MAPI, 125
  OWA, 978
**computer accounts, 445.** *See also*
  **accounts**
**computers.** *See* **desktops**
**configuration**
  Active Directory, 118, 136
    DNS, 139
    domain controllers, 138
    domain structures, 120
    domains, 137
    forests, 137
    infrastructure components, 120-122
    large businesses, 142
    mid-sized businesses, 140

  MMS, 123
    replication, 138
  ActiveSync, 254-257
  Administrative Groups, 560-561,
    1022-1025, 1072-1073
  administrative views, 1022
  ADMT, 434-449
  bridgehead servers, 93
  Calendar Connector, 1092-1095
    GroupWise, 1044-1047
    starting, 1095
  clustering, 896-898
    managing, 898-902
    OWA, 903-906
  compatibility
    documenting, 516-517, 528
    lab-testing applications, 525-528
    prototype phase, 529
    researching applications, 517-519
    testing, 510-516
    training, 516
    verifying, 519-524
  components, 113
    coexistence, 117
    functionality, 113-116
    scaling, 117
    third-party functionality, 118
  connection agreements, 461-469
  contacts, 551-552
    adding addresses, 553
    address types, 552
    forwarding mail, 552
  databases, 96-97
  Date & Time Formats, 785
  directory synchronization, 1006-1008,
    1065, 1089
  disks
    backups, 927
    subsystems, 986-988
  Distribution Groups, 553-556
    mail-enabled, 558
    managing, 557
    scope, 554
  DNS
    namespaces, 121
    servers, 204-208
    troubleshooting, 205
  documents, 491
  domain trusts, 430-432
  email, 542, 769

environment documentation, 614
  as-built, 615
  server build procedure, 614
  topology diagrams, 615
Exchange 5.5 limitations, 452-454
extended permissions, 536
FMU, 1009
folders, 762
forward outbound messages, 275-276
free/busy time, 732-733
front-end servers, 662
Global Catalogs, 70-71
Group Policy, 867-869
Group Schedules, 736-738
GroupWise connectors, 1039-1041
hardware, 525
IIS, 486
IMAP
  publishing rules, 264-266
  SSL, 265
IPSec, 405-407
items per page, 781
Lotus Notes
  connectors, 1088
  gateways, 1085-1092
mailboxes, 1098
  cleanup tasks, 576
  customizing, 541-543
  limitations, 541
  stores, 1028, 1078-1079
message delivery limitations, 407-408
migration options, 1101
MIIS, 168
mobile devices, 673-674
  applying Pocket PC, 693-695
  connecting Pocket PC 2002, 679-
    683, 688-693
  mobile phone connections, 699-700
  smartphones, 695-698
  synchronizing Pocket PC 2002,
    674-678, 683-688
mobile services, 666-670
mobility, 648, 658-659
  active prototypes, 651-652
  adding front-end servers, 664
  creating front-end servers, 662-663
  defining device use, 648-649
  firewalls, 664
  functionality, 650-651

installing, 662
optimizing front-end servers,
  659-660
pilot testing, 651-652
scalability, 652
selecting, 650
testing, 661
MSDSS, 1007
multiple mailboxes, 715
network documentation, 914
NOS, 525-526
OMA, 254-257
optimizing, 127
  AVAPI, 131
  avoiding VM fragmentation, 128
  backup/restore, 131
  clustering, 130
  disk options, 128
  MOM, 131
  multiple databases, 129-130
  operating systems, 127-128
Out of Office Assistant, 781
Outlook
  Administrative Installation Points,
    836
  automating profiles, 836-841
  Group Policy, 864
  Macintosh, 806-809
  predefined options, 835
  profiles, 715, 808, 830-831
  secure messaging, 357-358
Outlook Express, 810-814
OWA, 288
  ActiveSync, 315-321
  applying internal CAs, 300-303
  customizing, 306-308
  deploying multiple, 322-326
  enabling FBA, 309-310
  forcing, 303
  formatting SSL, 294-297
  front-end/back-end architecture,
    289-294
  installing third-party CAs, 297-299
  modifying passwords, 313
  secure messaging, 358
  summarizing, 310-312
physical disk, 988
placement, 123

administrative groups, 123
client access points, 125-127
environment sizing, 125
public folders, 125
routing group topology, 124
POP3, 261-264
postinstallation, 1030, 1079
  deleting Information Stores, 1030,
    1080-1081
  disabling services, 1030, 1080
  enabling logging/message tracking,
    1084
  formatting routing groups,
    1081-1083
  tracking, 1034
PRF files, 837-838
profiles, 809
public folder stores, 1029, 1079
quick flags, 778
reading pane (OWA), 761
Registry keys, 718
rights, 537-538
role-based administration, 534-535
routing groups, 561-563, 1022-1025,
  1074
  connectors, 91-93, 1031-1033
  installing, 562-563
  modes, 562
  moving, 563
RPC over HTTP, 725-728
RPC over HTTP(S), 327-328
  creating virtual directories, 330
  Outlook 2003, 331-333
Rules Editor, 775-777
SCW, 19-20, 374-376
security, 361
servers
  documenting, 913
  Global Catalog, 216
  secure messaging environments,
    364-366
  services, 98-106
signatures, 783
SMS packages, 849-850
SMTP, 407-411
SRSs, 469-470
storage groups, 96-97, 1025-1027,
  1076-1077
transforms, 838-841
wizards, 15
X.400, 412-413

confirming migration, 1052
connected directory (CD), 165
connection agreements (CAs)
  configuring, 461-469
  enterprise root, 394
  third-party, 296-299
connections
  ADC, 460-466
  bandwidth topologies, 832-833
  client site failures, 943
  environment documentation, 614
    as-built, 615
    server build procedure, 614
    topology diagrams, 615
  FE servers, 583
  GroupWise, 1035
    Calendar Connector, 1046-1048
    configuring connectors, 1039-1041
    customizing, 1038-1039
    environments, 1036
    installing Calendar Connector,
      1044-1045
    installing Exchange servers, 1037
    migrating prerequisites, 1035
    starting connectors, 1041
    synchronizing directories,
      1041-1044
    testing directories, 1044
  link state, 976
  mobile phones, 699-700
  multiple clients, 820
  new features, 114
  PDA
    ActiveSync, 643-645
    customizing synchronization, 645
    optimizing synchronization, 646
    securing, 646
  Pocket PC 2002, 679-683
  Pocket PC 2003, 688-693
  remote, 739-746
  RPC over HTTP, 725-728
  SSL, 416
  VPN, 641-643
  WAN, 914
  wireless, 29, 643-644
Connectivity verifiers (ISA Server 2004),
  283
connector namespace (CS), 165

**connectors**
ADC, 460-466
Calendar Connector
configuring, 1092-1095
starting, 1095
deleting, 479
GroupWise, 1035
Calendar Connector, 1046-1048
configuring connectors, 1039-1041
customizing, 1038-1039
environments, 1036
installing Calendar Connector, 1044-1045
installing Exchange servers, 1037
migrating prerequisites, 1035
starting connectors, 1041
synchronizing directories, 1041-1044
testing directories, 1044
Lotus Notes
configuring, 1088
installing from, 1086-1087
migration, 1065
starting, 1089
migrating, 475-477
moving, 503
PROFS/SNADS, 456
routing groups, 91-93, 412, 561-562
configuring, 1031-1033, 1081-1083
installing, 562-563
Internet Mail Wizard, 413-414
modes, 562
moving, 563
X.400, 412-413
SMTP, 104-105
**contacts**
address types, 553
customizing, 786
Group Policy, 866
linking, 713-714
managing, 551, 647, 715
adding addresses, 553
address types, 552
creating, 551-552
forwarding mail, 552
Outlook Express
importing, 814
migrating, 813

Pocket PC 2002/2003, 694-695
Recovery Storage Group, 963-964
**Contacts option (OWA), 794-797**
**context menus, viewing, 777**
**controller card configuration, backing up, 911**
**controls**
authentication, 408
outbound security, 413
**conversion, Native Mode, 478-480**
**cookies, 798**
**copying**
flat files, 956
Group Policy, 859
Volume Shadow Copy services, 921
**core elements, analyzing, 983**
**core installations, 1018, 1068**
Active Directory, 1018-1019, 1068-1069
customizing, 1022-1029
domains, 1019-1020
interactive process of, 1020-1022
preparing domains, 1069-1070
step-by-step instructions, 1070-1072
**core services**
installing, 1067
verifying, 77, 1017
**core technologies, solidifying, 31-32**
**corporate email policies, creating, 364-365**
**costs**
of migrations, 11
of security breaches, 234
**CPS (Certificate Practice Statement), 394**
**credentials**
clearing, 798
OWA client login, 756
**criteria for email rules, 776**
**CRL (Certificate Revocation List), 402**
**CRM (customer relationship management), 999**
**cross-forest Kerberos authentication, 25**
**cryptography, 720**
**CS (connector namespace), 165**
**CSV files, importing, 815**

**Custom Installation Wizard (CIW), 831**
Cached Mode, 741
Outlook, 715-719
predefined configuration options, 835
**custom media pools, 932**
**customer relationship management (CRM), 999**
**customization**
alerts, 280
boot failures, 945-947
calendars, 786
certificates templates, 398-399
clients
administration, 845
deployment, 831-832
installing, 842-843
clustering, 880-883, 898-902
OWA, 903-906
permissions, 882
requirements, 883-886
contacts, 552, 786
disaster recovery, 49
disk options, 128
email, 769-781
FBA, 252
Group Policy, 855
GroupWise, 1038-1039
installations, 1022-1029
ISA Server 2004, 278
mailboxes, 541-543
migration, 424
combined approach, 488
deploying prototype labs, 489-491
in-place upgrade method, 486-497
move mailbox upgrade method, 487-488, 497-506
optimizing deployment, 485
options, 1101
planning, 484-485
restoring prototype labs, 491
validating documents, 491
Outlook
colors, 711
interfaces, 867
Macintosh, 806
properties, 746
OWA
new features, 753-756
options, 781-787

proxy addresses (Lotus Notes), 1087-1088
Reading Panes, 783
recovery, 150
redundancy, 145
reminders, 786
RUS, 504
servers, 366-369
SMTP, 276-277
Spell Check feature, 783
SSL, 306-308
synchronization, 645
Windows, 338
hardening, 337
lockdown guidelines, 343
patches/updates, 342-343
security templates, 340-341
virus protection, 343
Windows-based mail clients, 802
Macintosh support, 802-803
OWA functionality, 804-805

# D

**daily maintenance, 598.** *See also* **maintenance**
**data loss, restoring from backups, 936**
**data volumes, troubleshooting, 945**
**databases**
Active Directory, 967-973
backing up, 115, 1081
configuring, 96-97
corruption, 956-963
deleting, 91, 663, 1081
design, 149
Enterprise Edition, 990
ESE, 454
files, 954-955
free space analysis, 601
Global Catalog, 215
demoting, 219
deploying domain controllers, 220
domain controllers, 216
optimizing promotion, 219
placement, 219
server relationships, 216
structures, 216

universal group caching, 221-222
verifying, 218
integrity, 591
mailboxes, 500
maintenance
best practices, 592-596
post-maintenance procedures, 602
scheduling best practices, 597-601
managing, 87, 1027-1028, 1077
multiple, 129-130
public folders, 125
recovery, 21
sizing, 116, 148, 599
STM, 596
testing, 591-592
Date & Time Formats, configuring, 785
decentralized administrative models, 560
decision matrices, creating, 524
decommissioning versions, 65
dedicated public folder servers, 102
default installations, 362
default public folders, 486
default signatures, configuring, 783
defaults, 16
Deferred View Update, OWA, 781
defining
baselines (Outlook), 865
Group Policy, 856
mobile device use, 648-649
recipient policies, 565
Delegates tab, 731
delegation
administration, 97
Administrative Groups, 560-561
GP management rights, 857-858
Group Policy, 863-864
Delegation Wizard, 533-534
auditing tasks, 539
extended permissions, 536
rights, 537-538
role-based administration, 534-535, 538
Deleted Item Retention dates, 786
deleting
ADC, 479
administration, 97
contacts, 796
databases, 91, 663, 1081

Directory Replication Connectors, 479
email, 769, 786-787
information stores, 90-91, 663, 1030, 1080-1081
public folder stores, 95
recovery, 938
servers, 479
SRSs, 480
undelete function, 936
delivery messages, limiting, 407-408
demotion, optimizing Global Catalog, 219
departmental messaging goals, 41
dependencies, clustering, 879
Deploy Software dialog box, 872
deployment, 362
ADMT, 434
applications (Group Policy), 845
Cached Mode, 740-746
clients, 829
configuring Outlook profiles, 830-831
customizing, 831-832
managing Outlook, 834
methods, 830
planning, 832-833
post-deployment tasks, 850-851
pushing updates, 872-873
updating, 871
domain controllers, 220
Entourage X, 816-818
Exchange Deployment Tools, 454
MAPI filtering, 260
migration
combined approach, 488
in-place upgrade method, 486-497
move mailbox upgrade method, 487-488, 497-506
optimizing, 485
prototype labs, 489-491
validating documents, 491
MIIS (Novell eDirectory), 169-170
multiple OWA servers, 322-326
Outlook, 838
Administrative Installation Points, 836
automating profiles, 836-841
best practices, 846
Group Policy, 844-845
testing, 848

placement, 123
  administrative groups, 123
  client access points, 125-127
  environment sizing, 125
  public folders, 125
  routing group topology, 124
Recipient Update Services, 569-571
SMS, 848-850
Terminal Services Client, 820-821
tools, 114, 485
**design.** *See also* **configuration**
Active Directory, 118, 136-137
  configuring DNS, 139
  domains, 120, 137-138
  forests, 137
  infrastructure components, 120-122
  large businesses, 142
  mid-sized businesses, 140
  MMS, 123
  placement of domain controllers,
    215
  replication, 138
compatibility
  documenting, 516-517, 528
  lab-testing applications, 525-528
  prototype phase, 529
  researching applications, 517-519
  testing, 510-516
  training, 516
  verifying, 519-524
components, 113
  coexistence, 117
  functionality, 113-116
  scaling, 117
  third-party functionality, 118
DNS, 121
documentation, 608-609
  outlining migration, 610-612
  planning migration, 610
  testing, 611-612
  validating migration, 491
examples, 157
Exchange 5.5, 452-454
front-end servers, 155
infrastructure, 147
  administration groups, 149
  antispam, 150
  antivirus, 150
  databases, 149
  large businesses, 153

  mid-sized businesses, 151
  monitoring, 151
  public folders, 149
  recovery, 150
  routing groups, 149
  small businesses, 151
  storage groups, 149
  versions, 148
large businesses, 136, 159-160
mid-sized businesses, 136, 158-159
mobility, 648, 658-659
  active prototypes, 651-652
  adding front-end servers, 664
  configuring firewalls, 664
  creating front-end servers, 662-663
  defining device use, 648-649
  functionality of, 650-651
  installing, 662
  optimizing front-end servers,
    659-660
  pilot testing, 651-652
  scalability, 652
  selecting, 650
  testing, 661
MOM, 131
OWA, 288
  ActiveSync, 315-321
  applying internal CAs, 300-303
  configuring architecture, 294
  customizing, 306-308
  deploying multiple, 322-326
  enabling FBA, 309-310
  forcing, 303
  formatting SSL, 294-297
  front-end/back-end architecture,
    289-294
  installing third-party CAs, 297-299
  modifying passwords, 313
  summarizing, 310-312
placement, 123
  administrative groups, 123
  client access points, 125-127
  environment sizing, 125
  public folders, 125
  routing group topology, 124
public folders, 102
security, 361
small businesses, 135-136, 157-158
validating, 891
**Design documents, upgrading, 48-53**
**designating IT members for backups, 915**

**desktops**
Active Directory, 588-589
migration, 613
remote, 587
**devices**
backups, 917
mobile, 673-674
active pilot testing, 651-652
active prototypes, 651-652
applying Pocket PC, 693-695
connecting Pocket PC, 679-683,
688-693
defining use, 648-649
executive use, 653
functionality, 650-651
GroupWise, 1001
mobile phone connections, 699-700
replacing laptops with, 653-654
scalability, 652
selecting, 650
smartphones, 695-698
synchronizing Pocket PC, 674-678,
683-688
spare, 917
**diagram topologies, 615**
**dialog boxes**
Deploy Software, 872
Edit Rules, 776
Exchange System Manager Proxy
Address, 566
Find Names, 765
New Contact, 794
Search, 779
Virtual Directory Access Permissions,
307
Virtual Directory Alias, 307
**dictionaries, migrating, 1054, 1106**
**digital signatures**
Outlook, 720-721, 746
S/MIME, 356-359, 402-403
**direct migration approaches, 1015-1016**
**directories**
Active Directory, 8-9. *See also* Active
Directory
authentication, 214-215
domains, 212-214

DSAccess, 222-223
DSProxy, 224
forests, 212
functionality, 225-229
Global Catalog, 215-220
implementing, 70
migrating, 1059
non-Windows environments, 1060
placement, 215
replication, 213
SMTP Categorizer, 224
structure, 212
synchronizing Lotus Notes, 1063
trees, 212
universal group caching, 221-222
configuring, 1006-1008, 1089-1092
eDirectory/NDS migration tools,
1004-1006
forests, 22-23
GroupWise
hosting, 1001
synchronizing, 1014, 1041-1044
testing synchronizing, 1044
hosts (Lotus Notes), 1059
lookup, 32
MIIS, 164-166
account provisioning, 166
group management, 168
installing, 168
role of MAs, 167-168
Novell eDirectory, 169
applying MSDSS, 170-175
deploying MIIS, 169-170
synchronizing, 1065
testing, 1092
virtual, 330
**Directory Replication Connector**
deleting, 479
viewing, 469
**disabling**
front-end servers, 293
services, 90, 1030, 1080
**disaster recovery**
Active Directory, 967-973
applications, 953-955
boot failures, 945-947
clusters, 966
database corruption, 956-963

disk failures, 944-945
documentation, 617-619, 939-941
    benefits of, 606-607
    planning, 606
domain controllers, 967
identifying, 935
    applying undelete functions, 936
    mailbox access, 937
IIS, 966
options, 49
planning, 938
Recovery Storage Group, 963-964
sever failures, 947-953
site failures, 941-943
testing, 61

**disclaimers, email, 365-366**

**disconnections, 571.** *See also* **connections**

**discovery, planning phase of upgrades, 46-48**

**disks**
clustering, 885. *See also* clustering
configuration backups, 927
mirroring, 988
options, 128
subsystems, 986-988
troubleshooting, 944-945

**dismounting public folder stores, 95**

**Distribution Groups, 225-226, 553-554**
creating, 555-556
expanding, 408
mail-enabled, 558
managing, 557
scope, 554

**distribution lists**
caching, 30
creating, 796
restricting, 25
security, 387

**DNS (Domain Name Service), 31, 185-187**
components, 189
    queries, 191-192
    replication, 192
    resource records, 192-197
    zones, 189-191
configuring, 139
design, 121
migrating, 199
namespaces, 121

need for, 187
requirements, 199-204
security, 201-203
servers
    configuring, 204-208
    types of, 187-188
SMTP, 197-199
troubleshooting, 205

**dnscmd utility, 209**

**DNSLINT, 208**

**documentation, 598, 605**
administration, 616-617
backups, 912-915
benefits of, 606-607
compatibility testing, 516-517, 528-529
databases, 601
design, 608-609
    outlining migration, 610-612
    planning migration, 610
    testing, 611-612
disaster recovery, 617-619, 939-941
environments, 614
    as-built, 615
    server build procedure, 614
    topology diagrams, 615
maintenance, 616-617
migration, 612
    checklists, 613
    desktop configuration procedures, 613
    mail procedures, 613
    servers, 612
    validating, 491
network configuration, 914
Outlook
    linking, 713-714
    managing, 715
performance, 619-620
planning, 606
recovery, 914
security, 621-622
servers, 913
training, 622
troubleshooting, 608
updating, 914-916
upgrades, 36
    migration, 53-62
    pilot phase, 62-64

planning phase, 46-53
prototype phase, 60-62
statement of work, 42

**domain controllers**
Active Directory, 214
authentication, 214-215
design, 138
Global Catalog, 216
placement, 215
authentication, 490
backing up, 429
deploying, 220
GC caching, 17
recovering, 967
Windows NT 4.0, 427

**Domain Local scope, 554**

**DomainPrep, 494-495, 1017-1020, 1067**

**domains**
Active Directory, 120, 137, 212
controllers. *See* domain controllers
DNS. *See* DNS
functionality, 449
installing, 74-75, 430
local groups, 226
migrating, 432-435, 458-460
policies, 435
preparing, 77
RUS, 504
trusts, 430-432
Windows 2003, 1069-1070
Windows NT 4.0, 429-432

**downloading**
Outlook Mobile Access, 647-648
Pocket PC 2002 emulation, 675
Pocket PC 2003 emulation, 685

**drag-and-drop capabilities, 15**

**DSAccess, 222-223**

**DSProxy, 224**

**dual-authentication, 253.** *See also*
authentication

**dynamic distribution lists, 21**


# E

**E2k3SecOps11.exe, 376**

**EAS (Exchange ActiveSync), 126, 154**

**.edb file extensions, 955**

**eDirectory, 999**
Active Directory, 1012
MIIS, 169-170
MSDSS, 170-175
running in, 1002
tools, 1004-1006

**Edit Rule dialog box, 776**

**editing**
contacts, 795
email, 774-775
recipient policies, 567
Spell Check, 783

**email, 8**
Active Directory, 8-9
addresses
adding, 553
defining recipient policies, 565
editing recipient policies, 567
implementing recipient policies,
566-567
naming recipient policies, 565
recipient policies, 564
sharing, 388
addressing, 764-765
attachments
adding, 765-766
reading, 767-768
Blocked Senders list, 724
configuring, 542
contacts, 694-695
corporate policies, 364-365
deleting, 769, 786-787
disclaimers, 365-366
flow, 107
folders
adding, 762
moving messages to, 771
forwarding, 768
Group Policy, 865
Group Schedules, 737
GroupWise, 1000
inboxes, 693
internal routing, 205
Internet Mail Wizard, 413-414
junk, 817
limitations, 541-543
linking, 713-714

Lotus Notes, 1058
mailboxes, 470-474
managing, 647, 715
migration, 613
"On Behalf Of", 731
options, 769
outbound routing, 205
Outlook 2003
    attachments, blocking, 348
    authenticating, 347
    encrypting, 346-347
    Internet access, 344-346
OWA, 764-771
    creating, 764
    customizing, 771-781
    modifying viewing order, 760-761
    navigating, 760
passwords, 787-788
policies, 365
privacy, 784
reading, 767, 773
recovering, 958-960
Recovery Storage Group, 963-964
replying, 768
routing, 198-201
Safe Recipients list, 724
Safe Senders list, 723
searching, 779
security, 201-203, 720-721, 783
sending, 766
spam, 349
    IRM, 353-354
    junk mail, filtering, 351-353
    read receipts, blocking, 353
    tools, 349-350
    Web beaconing, 350
text
    modifying, 771
    Spell Check feature, 774-775
tracking, 770
viewing, 711
**eMbedded Visual C++ 4.0, 686**
**eMbedded Visual Tools 3.0, installing, 675-677**
**EMS (Exchange Mobile Services)**
ISA Server 2004, 252-258
threats, 237-239

**emulation**
Pocket PC 2002, 675-678
Pocket PC 2003
    downloading, 685
    installing, 685-688
smartphones, 696-698
Web-enabled, 700
**enabling**
Active Directory objects, 540-541
compression, 799
FBA on OWA servers, 309-310
ISA SMTP Screener component, 269
logging, 93-94, 1084
message tracking, 586
notifications, 669
POP
    enabling, 262
    SSL, 263
    support
proxy addresses (Lotus Notes), 1087-1088
quick flags, 778
relaying, 411
Remote Administration (HTML), 627-631
Remote Desktop for Administration, 626
services, 77
SSL, 99-100, 294-299
tracking, 1034
**encryption**
Internet (Outlook 2003), 346-347
Outlook, 720-721
S/MIME, 27, 356-359, 402-403
SSL, 238
**end-user training documentation, 622**
**enhancements.** *See* **new features; optimization**
**enrollment**
CAs, 949
certificates, 400-402
**Enterprise Edition**
databases, 990
Exchange 2003 Server, 14
**enterprise management, 854**
baselines, 857-859
clients, 859-864
customizing, 855
levels of, 856

Outlook, 864-870
refreshing, 856
templates, 855
updating, 870-873
**Enterprise Resource Planning, (ERP), 999**
**enterprise root CAs, 393-394**
**Enterprise Server 2003, 116**
**enterprise subordinate CA, 393**
**entities, migrating, 1055**
**Entourage 2004 client and Exchange Updates, 815**
**Entourage X (Macintosh), 815**
deploying, 816-818
functionality, 815-816
**environments**
auditing, 583
logging, 584-585
protocols, 584
tracking messages, 585
documentation, 614, 939
as-built, 615
server build procedure, 614
topology diagrams, 615
documenting, 939-941
evaluating, 1002-1004, 1060-1061
GroupWise, 1036
Lotus Domino, 1097
sizing, 125
**equipment, upgrade prototype phase, 60**
**ERP (Enterprise Resource Planning), 999**
**ESE (Extensible Storage Environment), 454**
**ESEUTIL, 961-963**
**eseutil utility, 591-592**
**ESM (Exchange System Manager), 587-588**
installing, 107-108
remote management, 635-636
SMTP, 407-411
SSL, 325-326
**evaluating environments, 1002-1004, 1060-1061**
**Event ID 9582, alerts for, 985**
**Event Viewer**
DNS, 205-206
logs, 598

**events**
disaster recovery
Active Directory, 967-973
applications, 953-955
boot failures, 945-947
clusters, 966
database corruption, 956-963
disk failures, 944-945
documenting, 939-941
domain controllers, 967
identifying, 935-937
IIS, 966
planning, 938
Recovery Storage Group, 963-964
server failures, 947-953
site failures, 941-943
validating procedures, 938
security, 370
**ExBPA (Exchange Best Practices Analyzer), 411**
**Exchange 5.5**
Exchange Server 2003, 466-470
migrating, 452-454
Active Directory forests/domains, 458-460
ADC, 460-466
Exchange Deployment Tools, 454
optimizing, 457-458
preparing, 454-457
name resolution requirements, 199
**Exchange ActiveSync (EAS), 126, 154**
**Exchange Administration Delegation Wizard, 369**
**Exchange Administrator role, 368**
**Exchange Best Practices Analyzer (ExBPA) tool, 411**
**Exchange Deployment Tools, 454**
**Exchange Features tab, 545**
**Exchange Full Administrator role, 368, 535**
**Exchange Migration Wizard, 1048**
GroupWise, 1048-1053
user data, 1096-1105
**Exchange Mobile Service (EMS), 252-258**
**Exchange Server 2003, 52**
adding, 12
backups, 918-920
capacity analysis, 979-980

connectors, 475-477
deleting, 479
GroupWise, 1000-1001
installing, 69, 466-470
    extending Active Directory schema, 73-74
    finalizing, 82-89
    groups models, 71-73
    interactive, 78-80
    planning, 69-71
    postinstallation, 89-98
    preinstallation checks, 76-77
    preparing, 74-76
    scripted, 80-82
    selecting modes, 71
    testing, 106-108
Lotus Notes
    administrative tool differences, 1059
    collaboration/messaging, 1058-1059
    comparing, 1058
    configuring gateways, 1085-1092
    formatting connectors, 1088
    starting connectors, 1089
mailboxes, 470-474
migration, 483
    combined approach, 488
    deploying prototype labs, 489-491
    from Exchange 5.5, 12-13
    from Exchange 2000, 12
    finalizing, 478-480
    in-place upgrade method, 423, 486-497
    from Lotus Notes, 13
    move mailbox upgrade method, 487-488, 497-506
    from Novell GroupWise, 13
    objectives, 422
    optimizing deployment, 485
    options, 424
    phases, 422-423
    planning, 484-485
    restoring prototype labs, 491
    single member servers, 424-427
    strategies, 423
    validating documents, 491
MOM, 994-995
monitoring, 981-983
    analyzing processor usage, 986
    calculating virtual memory, 985-986

    configuring disk subsystems, 986-988
    optimizing memory subsystems, 984
name resolution requirements, 199
new features, 15
    8-node clustering, 18
    configuration/management wizards, 15
    drag-and-drop capabilities, 15
    functionality, 17
    GC caching, 17
    performance, 17
    reliability, 20-21
    remote installation, 17-18
    security, 16
    VSS, 19
optimizing, 976-978
    communicating with clients, 976-977
    ongoing maintenance, 993-994
    reporting RPC errors, 977
    scalability, 979
    sizing, 987-993
preinstallation checks, 1016
    configuring domains, 1017
    preparing forests, 1017
    reviewing log files, 1017
    verifying core services, 1017
public folder migration, 475
remote management, 635-636
replicating public folders, 978
retiring, 505-506
security enhancements, 343
service migration, 475-477
transport-level security, 392
versions, 13
    Enterprise Edition, 14
    Standard Edition, 14
**Exchange Server 2003 Delegation Wizard, 882**
**Exchange Server 2003 Service Pack 2 (SP2), 979**
**Exchange System Manager (ESM)**
    installing, 107-108
    remote management, 635-636
    SMTP, 407-411
    SSL, 325-326
**Exchange System Manager Proxy Address dialog box, 566**

Exchange Task Wizard, 540, 544
Exchange View Only Administrator role, 368
Exchange View Only role, 535
Exchange-specific functionality, 119
ExchDAV procedures, 320
ExchDump utility, 939
executing
    ntdsutil, 590
    OM seizing, 490
Executive Summary, design documents, 51
executive use, mobility, 653
existing applications, lab-testing, 525-528
existing environments, discovery phase of, 46
existing NT4 domains, migrating, 429-432
ExMerge, 21, 473-474, 958-959
expanding Distribution Groups, 408
expiration messages, 594
exploits, HTTP, 237
exporting
    OWA certificates, 240-243
    passwords, 436
Exres.dll, clustering, 879
extended permissions, 536
extending Active Directory schemas, 73-74, 1018-1019, 1068-1069
Extensible Storage Environment (ESE), 454
external DNS servers, Internet, 205
external entities, migrating, 1055
extracting email from corrupt mailboxes, 958-960

**F**

failback
    clustering, 879
    troubleshooting, 902
failover
    clustering, 879
    documentation, 619
    MSCS, 880

site failures, 941-943
troubleshooting, 902
fault tolerance
    clustering, 878-883
        permissions, 882
        requirements, 883-886
    configuring, 896-898
    disk failures, 944-945
    managing, 898-902
    optimizing, 886-896
    options, 879-883
    OWA, 903-906
FBA (forms-based authentication), 309
    customizing, 252
    enabling, 309-310
    OWA, 415
FE (front-end) servers, 582
    adding, 664
    clustering, 903-906
    configuring, 662
    creating separate, 662-663
    design, 155
    functionality, 132
    IPSec, 25
    locking down, 416-417
    optimizing number of, 659-660
    RPC over HTTP(S), 328
    sizing, 991
    SSL, 99-100
    transport-level security, 415-416
File Migration Utility (FMU), 1005-1010
file systems, selecting, 988
files
    boot loader, 953
    CSV, 815
    databases, 954-955
    flat file copying, 956
    locking down, 373
    logs, 78, 1017, 1068
    mail, 1098
    online backup of, 19
    OST, 977
    .pfx (security), 241
    PRF
        applying, 718-719
        configuring, 837-838
        creating, 716
        installing Outlook, 842-843

setup.exe, 81
STM, 596
transforms
    configuring, 838-841
    creating, 838
    installing Outlook, 842-843
unattended installations, 81
**filtering**
    application-layer, 236-237
    block/safe lists, 352-353
Blocked Senders list, 724
    IMF, 384
    IPSec, 405
    ISA Server 2004, 278
    junk email, 351-353, 722, 817
    MAPI, 260
    rules, 259
    Safe Recipients list, 724
    Safe Senders list, 723
    SMTP, 276-277
    spam, 725
**finalizing Exchange 2003 installations,
    82-89**
**finalizing migration, 478-480**
**financial benefit of documentation, 607**
**Find Names dialog box, 765**
**firewalls**
    documenting, 914
    front-end/back-end servers, 291
    mobile access, 664
    role of, 235
    Windows, 339
**flags**
    email, 778
    Outlook, 710-711
**flat file copying, 956**
**Flexible Single Master Operations
    (FSMO), 1018, 1068**
**floppy disks, creating, 917**
**flow, testing mail, 107**
**FMU (File Migration Utility), 1005-1010**
**folders.** *See also* **files**
    email
        modifying viewing order, 760-761
        moving messages to, 771
    OWA, 762

public, 486
    adding replicas, 1093
    connection agreements, 464
    creating trees, 101-102
    dedicated servers, 102
    deleting, 95
    design, 102, 125, 149
    managing, 100-101
    message expiration, 594
    migrating, 475
    Outlook, 746
    replicating, 103, 502
    servers, 582
    sharing, 736
    stores, 89, 1079
    verifying replication, 599
    viewing, 763
Recovery Storage Group, 963-964
restoring, 912
sharing, 1055, 1107
system, 103
SYSVOL, 972-973
**fonts, modifying, 771**
**forcing SSL encryption (for OWA traffic),
    303**
**foreign mail connectors, migrating, 477**
**ForestPrep process, 492-493, 1017, 1067**
**forests**
    Active Directory, 212
        design, 137
        domain structures, 120
        migrating, 458-460
    cross-forest Kerberos authentication,
        25
    directories, 22-23
    installing, 430
    MMS, 123
    multiple, 119
    preparing, 77
**formatting**
    Active Directory, 118
        domain structures, 120
        infrastructure components, 120-122
        MMS, 123
    Administrative Groups, 560,
        1022-1025, 1072-1073
    Administrative Installation Points, 836
    calendars, 711
    components, 113

coexistence, 117
functionality, 113-116
scaling, 117
third-party functionality, 118
contacts, 551-552, 794
adding addresses, 553
address types, 552
forwarding mail, 552
corporate email policies, 364-365
Distribution Groups, 553-556
mail-enabled, 558
managing, 557
scope, 554
distribution lists, 796
email, 764
folders, 762
Group Schedules, 736-738
IMAP publishing rules, 264-266
mail files, 1098
mailbox stores, 87-88, 106, 540, 1028, 1078-1079
Migration documents, 58-59
Outlook profiles, 808
OWA publishing rules, 243-247
POP3 publishing rules, 261-264
PRF files, 716
public folders
stores, 89, 1029, 1079
trees, 101-102
reading pane (OWA), 761
Routing Groups, 561-562, 1022-1025, 1074
installing, 562-563
modes, 562
moving, 563
shares, 843
storage groups, 85-87, 1025-1027, 1075-1077
transforms, 838
unattended installation files, 81
**forms-based authentication (FBA), 309**
customizing, 252
enabling, 309-310
OWA, 415
**forward lookup zones, 189**
**forward outbound messages, 275-276**
**forwarding email, 552, 768**
**fragmentation, avoiding, 128**
**free disk space, checking, 598**
**free media pools, 931**

**free space, calculating, 596**
**free/busy time, configuring, 732-733**
**front-end architecture, 289-294**
**front-end (FE) servers, 582**
adding, 664
clustering, 903-906
configuring, 662
creating separate, 662-663
design, 155
functionality, 132
IPSec, 25
locking down, 416-417
optimizing number of, 659-660
RPC over HTTP(S), 328
sizing, 991
SSL, 99-100
transport-level security, 415-416
**FSMO (Flexible Single Master Operations), 1018, 1068**
**functional roles, 380-381**
**functional specifications documents, 1003**
**functionality, 113-116, 588**
Active Directory, 225-229
dnscmd, 209
domains, 449
email, 764-771
Entourage X, 815-816
front-end server, 132
IPSec, 404
Macintosh, 803
mobile devices, 650-651
mobility, 658
multiple forests, 119
optimizing, 17
Outlook (Macintosh), 806
OWA, 753-756, 804-805
Search In, 712
Terminal Services Client, 818-821
third-party, 118
wireless services, 543
**functions, undelete, 936**

# G

**GAL (Global Address List), 403, 765**
**Gantt Chart, 54**

**gateways**
   applications, 201
   GroupWise, 1035
      configuring connectors, 1039-1041
      customizing, 1038-1039
      environments, 1036
      installing Exchange servers, 1037
      migrating prerequisites, 1035
      starting connectors, 1041
      synchronizing directories,
         1041-1044
      testing directories, 1044
   Lotus Notes, 1085-1092
   mail, 198
   scanning, 383
**GC (Global Catalog)**
   Active Directory, 215
      demoting, 219
      domain controllers, 216, 220
      optimizing promotion, 219
      placement, 219
      server relationships, 216
      structure, 216
      universal group caching, 221-222
      verifying, 218
   caching, 17, 121
   placement, 70-71, 138
   restoring, 972
**geographic distribution of resources, 47**
**Global Address List (GAL), 403, 765**
**Global Catalog**
   Active Directory, 215
      demoting, 219
      domain controllers, 216, 220
      optimizing promotion, 219
      placement, 219
      server relationships, 216
      structure, 216
      universal group caching, 221-222
      verifying, 218
   caching, 17, 121
   placement, 70-71, 138
   restoring, 972
**Global Distribution Groups, 554**
**global groups, 226**
**goals, 43**

**GPMC (Group Policy Management
   Console), 854-855**
   accessing, 864
   downloading, 861
   installing, 846
**GPOs (Group Policy Objects), linking, 864**
**granular permissions improvements, 485**
**Group Policy**
   applications, 845
   baselines, 857-859
   Cached Mode, 741
   clients, 831, 859-864
   configuring, 867-869
   customizing, 855
   levels of, 856
   management, 854
   Outlook, 720, 864-870
   pushing, 844-847
   refreshing, 856
   templates, 855
   updating, 870-873
**Group Policy Management Console
   (GPMC), 854-855**
   accessing, 864
   downloading, 861
   installing, 846
**Group Policy Objects (GPOs), linking, 864**
**Group Schedules, 736-738**
**groups**
   Active Directory functionality, 225-229
   administration design, 149
   Administrative, 82, 123, 558
      creating, 560, 1022-1025, 1072-
         1073
      delegating, 560-561
      models, 559
      modes, 559
      moving mailboxes, 550
      selecting number of, 123
   Distribution Groups, 225-226, 553-554
      creating, 555-556
      mail-enabled, 558
      managing, 557
      scope, 554
   domain local, 226
   global, 226
   machine local, 226
   mail-enabled, 226
   membership, 73

migrating, 438-447
MIIS, 168
models, 71-73
permissions, 72
Recovery Storage Group, 963-964
Routing Groups, 561-562
    configuring, 563
    connectors, 91-93, 1031-1033
    creating, 1022-1025, 1074
    design, 149
    installing, 562-563
    Internet Mail Wizard, 413-414
    modes, 562
    moving, 563
    security, 412
    X.400, 412-413
scope, 226
security, 225, 372-373
storage, 129-130
    configuring, 96-97
    creating, 85-87, 1025-1027,
      1075-1076
    design, 149
    managing databases, 1077
universal, 221-222, 227
viewing, 72
Windows, 225
GroupWise, 999
    administrative tools, 1001
    Calendar Connector
        configuring, 1046-1047
        installing, 1044-1045
        starting, 1048
    collaboration, 1000-1001
    connecting, 1035
        configuring connectors, 1039-1041
        customizing, 1038-1039
        environments, 1036
        installing Exchange servers, 1037
        migrating prerequisites, 1035
        starting connectors, 1041
        synchronizing directories,
          1041-1044
        testing directories, 1044
    directories, 1014
    Exchange Migration Wizard,
      1048-1053
    Exchange Server 2003, 1000-1001
    mailboxes, 1049

messaging, 1000-1001
migrating
    planning, 1010-1015
    selecting direct approach of,
      1015-1016
GroupWise Migration Tool, 1053
    external entities, 1055
    local archives, 1053
    personal address books, 1054
    personal dictionaries, 1054
    proxy access, 1054
    shared folders, 1055
guidelines for security, 374


H

hardening, 337
    IIS, 378-380
    ISS, 378-379
    Windows Server 2003, 370-374
hardware
    components
        large businesses, 146
        mid-sized businesses, 146
        selecting, 142-144
        small businesses, 145
    configuring, 525
    Entourage X, 817
    inventories, 913
    Macintosh. See Macintosh
    new hardware migration, 423
    requirements, 115
        clustering, 883-884
        Outlook, 834-835
    Terminal Services Client, 818
Hardware RAID, 989
hardware-based RAID array failures, 944
heartbeats
    clustering, 879-880
    planning configurations, 888
Help, OWA, 763. See also troubleshooting
high-level messaging goals, 40
highlighting Outlook items, 710-711
home pages, sharing views, 738

**hosts**
directories
GroupWise, 1001
Lotus Notes, 1059
records, 193
**hot spare disks, 944**
**hotfixes**
MBSA, 374
servers, 377
**HTML (Hypertext Markup Language)**
access, 823
Remote Desktop for Administration,
627-631
**HTTP (Hypertext Transfer Protocol)**
exploits, 237
OWA traffic, 247-251
RPC over, 127, 725-728, 743
**HTTP Proxy, connecting, 642**
**HTTP(S)**
OWA traffic, 247-251
servers, 258
**Hypertext Markup Language.** *See* **HTML**
**Hypertext Transfer Protocol.** *See* **HTTP**

# I

**iCalendar, 733-735**
**identities (MIIS), 164-166**
account provisioning, 166
group management, 168
installing, 168
role of MAs, 167-168
**IIS (Internet Information Services)**
backups, 929-930
configuring, 486
hardening, 378-379
metabase, 583
recovering, 966
security, 486
servers, 378-380
**IMAP (Internet Message Access Protocol),
822**
clients, 126
security, 261-266
**IMF (Intelligent Message Filter), 384**

**implementation**
Active Directory, 70, 1018
core installations, 1068
extending schemas, 1018-1019
DNS, 185-187
components, 189-192
configuring servers, 204-208
need for, 187
requirements, 199-204
resource records, 192-197
servers, 187-188
SMTP, 197-199
troubleshooting, 205
Exchange in a native Active Directory,
1059
extended permissions, 536
LDAP, 177-178
mailboxes
customizing, 541-543
limitations, 541
maintenance, 131
antivirus applications, 132
front-end server functionality, 132
patching operating systems, 131
scheduling, 132
Mixed Mode, 71
MSDSS, 173
native Active Directory environments,
1002
preinstallation checks, 1067
DomainPrep process, 1067
ForestPrep process, 1067
reviewing log files, 1068
verifying core services installation,
1067
recipient policies, 566-567
rights, 537-538
role-based administration, 534-535
roles, 538
security, 131
antivirus applications, 132
front-end server functionality, 132
patching operating systems, 131
scheduling maintenance, 132
servers
extending Active Directory schema,
73-74
finalizing installation, 82-89
group models, 71-73

interactive installation, 78-80
planning installations, 69-71
postinstallation, 89-98
preinstallation checks, 76-77
preparing, 74-76
scripted installation, 80-82
selecting modes, 71
testing installation, 106-108
**importance, configuring email options, 769**
**imported media pools, 931**
**importing**
contacts, 814
CSV files, 815
Group Policy, 859
Outlk11.adm security template, 861
OWA certificates, 240-243
**in-place upgrade method, 486-497**
of migration, 423
Windows NT 4.0, 427-429
**inbound recipients, filtering, 26**
**inboxes**
Pocket PC 2002/2003, 693
viewing, 760-761
**indexes, aging, 594**
**Information Rights Management (IRM), 353-354**
**information store backups, validating, 601**
**information stores, deleting, 90-91, 663, 1030, 1080-1081**
**infrastructure**
Active Directory components, 120-122
antispam, 150
antivirus, 150
coexistence, 117
databases, 149
design, 147
administration groups, 149
public folders, 149
routing groups, 149
versions, 148
environment documentation, 614
as-built, 615
server build procedure, 614
topology diagrams, 615
large businesses, 153
mid-sized businesses, 151

monitoring, 151
OWA, 288
PKI smartcards, 399
recovery, 150
small businesses, 151
**inheritance, Group Policy management, 858**
**initiation phase (upgrades), 37**
budgets, 46
business unit messaging goals, 40-42
departmental unit messaging goals, 40-42
goals, 38-39
goals, summarizing, 43
high-level messaging goals, 40
resource requirements, 44-45
risks/assumptions, 45
statement of work, 42, 46
timelines/milestones, 44
**installation**
ActiveSync, 486
ADC, 460-466
ADMT, 434-449
bridgehead servers, 98
CA, 395-396
Calendar Connector, 1044-1045, 1092-1095
clients, 842-843
configuring Outlook profiles, 830-831
customizing, 831-832
deployment methods, 830
managing Outlook, 834
planning, 832-833
validating, 850-851
clustering, 887-896
connectors for GroupWise, 1037
core installations, 1018, 1068
customizing, 1022-1029
extending Active Directory, 1018-1019, 1068-1069
implementing Active Directory, 1018, 1068
interactive process of, 1020-1022
preparing domains, 1019-1020, 1069-1070
step-by-step instructions, 1070-1072

default, 362
domains, 430
eMbedded Visual C++ 4.0, 686
eMbedded Visual Tools 3.0, 675-677
Entourage X, 816-818
ESM, 588
Exchange Server 2003, 466-470,
    1086-1087
Exchange System Manager, 107-108
forests, 430
GPMC, 846
internal CAs, 300
ISA SMTP Screener component, 268
Lotus Notes
    connectors, 1088
    gateways, 1085-1092
MIIS, 665-666
mobility, 662
    adding front-end servers, 664
    configuring firewalls, 664
    creating front-end servers, 662-663
MSDSS, 172-173
multiple servers, 368-369
OMA, 486
Outlook, 715-719, 808
    Administrative Installation Points,
        836
    automating profiles, 836-841
    Macintosh, 807
    predefined options, 835
    requirements, 834-835
Outlook Express, 811-814
Pocket PC 2002 emulation, 675-677
Pocket PC 2003 emulation, 685-688
postinstallation configuration, 1079
    configuring routing groups, 1031-
        1033, 1081-1083
    deleting Information Stores, 1030,
        1080-1081
    disabling services, 1030, 1080
    enabling logging/message tracking,
        1084
    tracking, 1034
preinstallation checks, 1016, 1067
    DomainPrep process, 1067
    ForestPrep process, 1067
    preparing domains, 1017
    preparing forests, 1017
    reviewing log files, 1017, 1068
    verifying core services, 1017, 1067

remote, 17-18
Remote Administration (HTML),
    627-631
Routing Groups, 562-563
RPC over HTTP, 725-728
RPC over HTTP(S), 326
servers, 69
    extending Active Directory schema,
        73-74
    finalizing, 82-89
    groups models, 71-73
    interactive, 78-80
    planning, 69-71
    postinstallation, 89-98
    preinstallation checks, 76-77
    preparing, 74-76
    scripted, 80-82
    selecting modes, 71
    testing, 106-108
SMTP (ISA Server 2004), 268
Terminal Services Client, 820-821
third-party CAs, 297-299
unattended, 849-850
updates, 871
versions, 148
**Instant Messenger, integrating, 746**
**integration, 163**
    client access, 154-155
        front-end server design, 155
        large businesses, 157
        mid-sized businesses, 156
        small businesses, 156
    Instant Messenger, 746
    LDAP, 175-178
    MIIS, 164-166
        account provisioning, 166
        group management, 168
        installing, 168
        MAs, 167-168
    Novell eDirectory, 169
        applying MSDSS, 170-175
        deploying MIIS, 169-170
    SFU, 178-181
    XML, 751
    zones, 189
**integrity, testing, 590-591**
**Intelligent Message Filter (IMF), 384**
**intelligent setup, migrating, 486**
**interactive core installation, 1020-1022**

interactive Exchange 2003 installation, 78-80
interactive installation, 1070-1072
interfaces
  browser-based devices, 647-648
  Cached Mode, 740
  highlighting, 710-711
  MAPI, 258-260
  MMC, 586
  NSPI, 219
  Outlook, 709, 867
  OWA, 9-10, 750
    integrating XML, 751
    login, 755-756
    navigating, 757-764
    optimizing, 978
internal CAs, applying, 300-303
internal DNS servers, outbound mail routing, 205
internal email routing, 205
internal Ethernets 679, 689
Internet
  connectivity, 804
  external DNS servers, 205
  free/busy time, 732-733
  Outlook 2003
    accessing, 344-346
    authenticating users, 347
    blocking attachments, 348
    encrypting, 346-347
  security
    ISA 2004 enhancements, 16-18
    SCW, 19-20
Internet Mail Service, migrating, 476
Internet Mail Wizard, 413-414
Internet Message Access Protocol (IMAP), 822
  clients, 126
  security, 261-266
Internet Protocol. See IP (Internet Protocol) addresses
Internet Security and Acceleration Server. See ISA (Internet Security and Acceleration Server) 2004
Internet Security and Acceleration Server 2004. See ISA (Internet Security and Acceleration Server) 2004

Interrix, SFU, 180-181
intervals, Group Policy, 856
inventories
  hardware, 913
  messaging applications, 518
invitations to meetings, 711-712
IP (Internet Protocol) addresses
  adding to OWA servers, 323
  assigning, 254
IP Security (IPSec), 16, 25
ipconfig utility, 206
IPSec (IP Security), 16, 25
IRM (Information Rights Management), 353-354
ISA (Internet Security and Acceleration Server) 2004
  EMS, 252-258
  IMAP/POP3, 261-266
  logging, 277-279
  MAPI, 258-260
  monitoring, 279-283
  OWA, 239-240
    creating publishing rules, 243-247
    customizing FBA, 252
    exporting/importing certificates, 240-243
    redirecting traffic, 247-251
  role of, 234-237
  security enhancements, 16-18
  SMTP, 266-276
  threats, 237-239
ISA SMTP Screener component, 268-269
ISINTEG, 961-963
isinteg utility, 590-591
items per page, configuring, 781
iterative queries, 192

# J – K – L

Jetstress, 982
junk email
  prevention, 784
  filtering, 351-353, 722, 817
junk senders, lists of, 725

Kerberos authentication, 25
keyboard shortcuts, OWA, 780
keys, configuring, 718
knowledge management, 607
knowledge sharing, 607

lab-testing applications, 525-528
labels, security, 722
laptops, replacing, 653-654
large businesses
    Active Directory, 142
    client access, 157
    components, 146
    design, 136, 159-160
    infrastructure, 153
Last Response Time, 660
layers
    application-layer filtering, 236-237
    security, 370-372
    SSL, 238
    transport-level security, 391-392
LDAP (Lightweight Directory Access Protocol), 464
leapfrogging migrations, 472
legacy Exchange 2000 Server, retiring, 505-506
levels
    Active Directory, 227
    service packs, 457
leveraging (ActiveSync), 29
licenses, Terminal Services, 632-633
Lightweight Directory Access Protocol (LDAP), 464
limitations
    of Exchange 5.5, 452-454
    mailboxes, 541-543
    message delivery, 407-408
    message size, 486
link state connections, optimizing, 976
linking
    GPOs, 864
    Outlook, 713-714
lists
    block/safe, 352-355
    Blocked Senders, 724
    contacts
        adding addresses, 553
        address types, 552

        creating, 551-552
        forwarding mail, 552
    junk senders, 725
    master account list, 915
    Safe Senders, 723
load balancing, 203-204
    clustering, 883-886
    front-end servers, 294
    NLB, 881
    OWA, 903-906
local archives, 1053, 1105-1106
local scans, MBSA, 374
locking down
    files, 373
    servers, 416-417
    SMTP, 407-411
    Terminal Services, 633
logging
    audits, 584-585
    circular, 1076
    enabling, 93-94, 1084
    Event Viewer, 598
    IIS, 966
    ISA traffic, 277-279
    off OWA, 764
    optimizing, 990
    protocols, 584
    reviewing, 78, 1017, 1068
    tracking, 1034
    transactions, 990
login, OWA client interfaces, 755-756
logon
    access, 370
    OWA, 978
    screens, 756
lookups
    directories, 32
    nslookup, 207-208
    reverse zones, 189
Lotus Domino environment, preparing, 1097
Lotus Notes
    accounts, 1098
    Active Directory, 1063
    Calendar Connector
        configuring, 1092-1095
        starting, 1095

connectors
    configuring, 1088
    installing from, 1086-1087
    starting, 1089
environments, 1060-1061
Exchange Server 2003, 13
    administrative tool differences, 1059
    collaboration/messaging, 1058-1059
    comparing, 1058
gateways, 1085-1092
migrating, 1085-1086
    planning from, 1061-1066
    selecting paths, 1066
proxy addresses, 1087-1088

**Lotus Notes Migration tool, 1105-1107**

**Lucent Vital QIP, 188**

# M

**MAs (management agents), role of, 167-168**

**Mac System Profiler tool, 807**

**machine local groups, 226**

**Macintosh**
client support, 802-803
compatibility, 804-805
Entourage X, 815
    deploying, 816-818
    functionality, 815-816
Outlook, 805
    configuring, 806-809
    options, 806
Outlook Express, 810-814
Terminal Services Client, 818-821

**mail.** *See also* **email**
addresses
    defining recipient policies, 565
    editing recipient policies, 567
    implementing recipient policies, 566-567
    naming recipient policies, 565
    recipient policies, 564
bridges, 198
exchange records, 193
files, 1098
flow, 107

gateways, 198
migration, 613
mixed environment routing, 201
outbound routing, 205
recovering, 958-960
relays, SMTP, 105-106
security, 201-203
viewing, 711

**mail-enabled**
Distribution Groups, 558
groups, 226

**Mailbox Manager tool, 574-578**

**Mailbox Move tool, 548-549**

**Mailbox Move Wizard, 547**

**Mailbox Recovery Center tool, 571-574**

**mailboxes**
access, 937
backing up, 547
cleaning, 548, 576
clustering, 878-883
    permissions, 882
    requirements, 883-886
creating, 106, 540
email, 958-960
GroupWise, 1049
Mailbox Recovery Center, 20
maintenance, 597
managing, 95-96, 540
    customizing, 541-543
    enabling Active Directory objects, 540-541
    implementing limitations, 541
migrating, 470-474, 665. *See also* migration
moving, 470-472, 500, 547-551, 957
multiple mailboxes, 715
recipient policies, 566-567
Recipient Update Services, 568-571
recovering, 19, 573-574
Recovery Storage Group, 963-964
restoring, 912
scanning, 383
security, 721
speed of, 21
status, 545
stores
    creating, 87-88, 1028, 1078-1079
    servers, 582

user protocols, 544
VSS, 19
wireless services, 543
**maintenance.** *See also* **troubleshooting**
best practices, 592-601
documentation, 616-617
    benefits of, 606-607
    design, 608-609
    outlining migration, 610-612
    planning, 606
    planning migration, 610
    testing, 611-612
implementing, 131
    antivirus applications, 132
    front-end server functionality, 132
    patching operating systems, 131
    scheduling, 132
mailboxes, 597
managing, 602
NLB Manager, 906
post-maintenance procedures, 602
scheduling, 940-941
servers, 993-994
tasks, 599
tombstones, 594
tools
    Active Directory, 588-589
    backup, 590
    eseutil utility, 591-592
    ESM, 587-588
    isinteg utility, 590-591
    message tracking, 592
    ntdsutil utility, 590
    Queue Viewer, 592
**management, 21, 581**
Active Directory, 588-589
Administrative Outlook Template,
    860-861
backups, 590, 910-912
    database corruption, 911-912
    devices, 917
    documentation, 912-915
    media, 930-932
    Ntbackup.exe, 922-927
    servers, 918-920
    services, 927-930
    strategies, 915-917
    system failures, 911

client options, 845
contacts, 551
    adding addresses, 553
    address types, 552
    creating, 551-552
    forwarding mail, 552
creating, 1072-1073
Delegation Wizard, 533-534
    auditing tasks, 539
    extended permissions, 536
    implementing roles, 538
    rights, 537-538
    role-based, 534-535
deleting, 97
directories, 22-23
Distribution Groups, 557
documentation, 616-617
dynamic distribution lists, 21
eseutil utility, 591-592
ESM, 587-588
Exchange 5.5, 452
isinteg utility, 590-591
knowledge, 607
LDAP, 175-178
Mailbox Manager tool, 574-578
mailboxes, 540
    customizing, 541-543
    enabling Active Directory objects,
        540-541
    implementing limitations, 541
    modifying status, 545
    moving, 547-551
    speed of, 21
    user protocols, 544
    wireless services, 543
maintenance, 602
message tracking, 592
migration, 23
MOM, 24
ntdsutil utility, 590
Outlook, 715, 834
Queue Viewer, 592
Recipient Update Services, 568-571
recipients, 563-564
    defining, 565
    editing, 567
    implementing, 566-567
    naming, 565
remote, 586-587

Remote Desktop for Administration, 625-631

roles/responsibilities, 582-583

server roles, 368-369

tools, 15, 115

**management agents (MAs), role of, 167-168**

**management-level reporting, 620**

**manual installation, Outlook, 843**

**manual modification, avoiding, 593**

**manual recovery, servers, 948.** *See also* **disaster recovery**

**MAPI (Messaging Application Programming Interface)**

compression, 125

security, 258-260

**mapping names (SFU), 181**

**marking email messages read/unread, 773**

**master account lists, 915**

**master-slave replication, 192**

**matching mailboxes, 573-574**

**MBSA (Microsoft Baseline Security Analyzer), 374**

**media backups, 930-932**

**Media option, domain controllers, 220**

**meetings**

Group Schedules, 737

invitations (OWA), 792-793

proposing, 711-712

**memberships**

Group Distribution, 555

groups

modifying, 73

viewing, 72

recipient policies, 565

**memory**

/3GB /USERVA=3030 parameters, 984

alerts (Event ID 9582), 985

allocating, 30

servers, 143

sizing, 991

subsystems, 984

virtual, 985-986

VM, 128

**menus**

context, 777

pull-down, 759

**merging (ExMerge), 473-474**

**messages.** *See also* **email**

applications, 518

communication restriction, 26

delivery limitations, 407-408

expiration, 594

flow, 26

folders

adding, 762

moving to, 771

forward outbound, 275-276

Global Catalog, 70-71

GroupWise, 1000-1001

limitations, 541-543

Lotus Notes, 1058-1059

notification, 30-31

options, 769

Outlook 2003, 357-358

OWA, 358, 764-771

creating, 764

customizing, 771-781

modifying viewing order, 760-761

navigating, 760

queues, 598

reading, 773

Recovery Storage Group, 963-964

restoring, 912

scanning, 385

searching, 779

security, 238, 358, 364-366

sizing, 486

text

modifying, 771

Spell Check feature, 774-775

tracking, 93-94, 585, 592, 1034, 1084

X.400, 412-413

**Messaging Application Programming Interface (MAPI), 258-260**

**metabases, IIS, 929**

**metadirectories (MIIS), 165**

**metaverse namespace (MV), 165**

**methods, client deployment, 830**

**Microsoft Directory Synchronization Services (MSDSS), 170-175, 1004-1008**

**Microsoft Exchange Migration Wizard, 1065**

**Microsoft Identity Integration Services (MIIS), 164-166**

**Microsoft Management Console (MMC),** 586

**Microsoft Operations Manager (MOM),** 24, 131, 602, 994-995

**Microsoft Server 2003**
fault tolerance, 886
configuring, 896-898
installing, 887-896
managing, 898-902
OWA, 903-906

**Microsoft Systems Management Server (SMS),** 848-850

**Microsoft Trustworthy Computing Initiative,** 361-362

**Microsoft Windows 2003 Cluster Service (MSCS),** 880

**mid-sized businesses**
Active Directory, 140
client access, 156
components, 146
design, 136, 158-159
infrastructure, 151

**migration,** 7, 421, 451, 483
Active Directory, 1001-1002, 1059
eDirectory/NDS tools, 1004-1006
non-Windows environments, 1060
ADC, 460-466
ADMT, 433-449
client rules, 1106-1107
compatibility
documenting, 516-517, 528
prototype phase, 529
researching applications, 517-519
testing, 510-516
training, 516
verifying, 519-524
confirming, 1052
connectors, 475-477
cost of, 11
DNS, 199
documentation, 612
checklists, 613
desktop configuration procedures, 613
mail procedures, 613
servers, 612
documents, 53-59
domains, 429-435
Exchange 5.5, 452-454

Active Directory forests/domains, 458-460
Exchange Deployment Tools, 454
optimizing, 457-458
preparing, 454-457
Exchange Server 2003
adding, 12
from Exchange 5.5, 12-13
from Exchange 2000, 12
installing, 466-470
from Lotus Notes, 13
from Novell GroupWise, 13
finalizing, 478-480
GroupWise
planning, 1010-1015
prerequisites, 1035
selecting direct approach of, 1015-1016
GroupWise Migration Tool, 1053
external entities, 1055
local archives, 1053
personal address books, 1054
personal dictionaries, 1054
proxy access, 1054
shared folders, 1055
in-place upgrades, 423-429
leapfrogging, 472
local archives, 1105-1106
Lotus Notes, 1085-1086
planning from, 1061-1066
selecting paths, 1066
Lotus Notes Migration tool, 1105-1107
mailboxes, 470-474, 665
Microsoft Exchange Migration Wizard, 1065
MIIS, 665-666
objectives, 422
options, 424
personal address books, 813-814, 1106
personal dictionaries, 1106
PFMigrate tool, 503
phase objectives, 422-423
planning, 484-485, 610
combined approach, 488
deploying prototype labs, 489-491
in-place upgrade method, 486-497
move mailbox upgrade method, 487-488, 497-506
optimizing deployment, 485
outlining, 610-612

restoring prototype labs, 491
validating documents, 491
post-migration cleanup, 480
prerequisites, 484-485, 1085
production migration/upgrade, 64-65
project teams, 1013
proxy server access, 1106-1107
public folders, 475
services, 475-477, 1005
SfN, 999, 1006-1010
shared folders, 1107
simulating, 489
single member servers, 424
backing up, 425
standalone server upgrades, 426-427
testing hardware, 424
verifying applications, 425
SRS, 469-470
strategies, 423
testing, 1096
tools, 23
troubleshooting, 1102-1104
upgrades, 62
user data, 1096-1105
Windows 2003 Server, 32
**Migration document**
background, 58
budget estimates, 60
executive summary, 56
Gantt Charts, 59
goals/objectives, 57
risks/assumptions, 58
roles/responsibilities, 58
timeline/milestones, 58
training, 59
validation (final), 62
**MIIS (Microsoft Identity Integration Services) 2003, 164-166**
account provisioning, 166
group management, 168
installing, 168
migrating from, 665-666
Novell eDirectory, 169-170
role of MAs, 167-168
scripts, 123
**milestones, 44**
**mirroring disks, 988**
**misconfiguration, MBSA, 374**

**mixed environment mail routing, 201**
**mixed Exchange environments, 636**
**mixed modes**
Administrative Groups, 559
implementation, 71
Routing Groups, 562
selecting, 71
**MMC (Microsoft Management Console), 586**
**MMS (Microsoft Metadirectory Services), 123**
**mobile communications, 10**
Active Directory, 8-9
optimizing, 27
applying over HTTPS, 28
connecting wireless technologies, 29
leveraging ActiveSync, 29
OWA, 28
synchronization, 10
**mobile devices, 673-674**
GroupWise, 1001
mobile phones, 699-700
Pocket PC 2002
applying, 693-695
connecting, 679-683
synchronizing, 674-678, 683
Pocket PC 2003
applying, 693-695
connecting, 688-693
synchronizing, 684-688
smartphones, 695-698
support (Lotus Notes), 1058
**mobile phones**
connecting, 699-700
Pocket PC 2002, 682
Pocket PC 2003, 690
smartphones, 695-698
**mobile services, configuring, 666-670**
**mobile users, scheduling, 833**
**mobile Web access, 643-644**
**mobility, 657**
automatic updates, 644
browser-based devices, 647-648
components, 658
design, 648
active prototypes, 651-652
defining device use, 648-649

functionality of, 650-651
pilot testing, 651-652
scalability, 652
selecting, 650
executive use, 653
functionality, 658
installing, 662
adding front-end servers, 664
configuring firewalls, 664
creating front-end servers, 662-663
laptops, 653-654
OMA, 701
Outlook
browser-based devices, 647-648
connecting with VPN, 641-643
PDA connections, 645
comparing to tablet PCs, 654
customizing synchronization, 645
optimizing synchronization, 646
securing, 646
planning, 658-659
optimizing front-end servers, 659-660
testing, 661
Terminal Services, 633

**models**
Administrative groups, 559
groups, 71-73

**modes**
Administrative groups, 559
backup, 922-924
Cached Mode (Outlook), 739-746
mixed. *See* mixed modes
NLB, 904
Restore (Active Directory), 920
Routing Groups, 562
users (OWA clients), 753

**modification.** *See also* **customization**
contacts, 795
domain policies, 435
email
addresses, 553
viewing order (OWA), 760-761
group memberships, 73
OWA settings, 757
passwords
email, 787-788
OWA, 313
reading pane (OWA), 761
recipient policies, 567

replication, 213. *See also* replication
RPC over HTTP(S), 329
RUS, 504
status, 545
text (email), 771

**MOM (Microsoft Operations Manager), 24, 131, 602, 994-995**

**monitoring**
clustering, 880
design, 151
ISA traffic, 279-283
MOM, 131, 994-995
performance documentation, 620
Performance Monitor, 207
servers, 981-983
analyzing processor usage, 986
calculating virtual memory, 985-986
configuring disk subsystems, 986-988
optimizing memory subsystems, 984
subsystems, 987

**monthly maintenance, 600.** *See also* **maintenance**

**Move Mailbox tool, 549**

**move mailbox upgrade method, 487-488, 497-506**

**moving**
connectors, 503
email to folders, 771
ExMerge, 473-474
mailboxes, 470-474, 547-551, 957
between administrative groups, 550
maintenance, 597
Move Mailbox tool, 548-549
objects, 547
public folders, 475
Routing Groups, 563

**MSCS (Microsoft Windows 2003 Cluster Service), 880**

**MSDSS (Microsoft Directory Synchronization Services), 170-175, 1004-1008**

**MSI package file, 849-850**

**multihomed DNS servers, 196**

**multiorganization Exchange 5.5 migration, 458**

**multiple back-end mailbox servers, 155**

**multiple calendars, viewing, 729-731**

multiple client connections, 820

multiple databases, 129-130

multiple forests, 119-123

multiple front-end servers, 659-660

multiple mailboxes
  configuring, 715
  moving, 549

multiple OWA servers, deploying, 322-326

multiple panes, OWA, 757-760

multiple servers, installing, 368-369

multiple-organization directory hosting (Lotus Notes), 1059

multisite Exchange 5.5 migration, 458

MV (metaverse namespace), 165

# N

Name Service Provider Interface (NSPI), 219

naming
  DNS, 185-187
    components, 189-192
    configuring servers, 204-208
    namespaces, 121
    need for, 187
    requirements, 199-204
    resource records, 192-197
    servers, 187-188
    SMTP, 197-199
    troubleshooting, 205
  email addresses, 764-765
  recipient policies, 565
  resolution requirements, 199
  records, 193
  searching, 796
  servers, 148
  SFU, 181

NAT-T (NAT Traversal), 404-405

native Active Directories, 1022, 1059

native mode
  Administrative Groups, 559
  converting, 478-480
  Routing Groups, 562
  selecting, 71

navigating OWA clients, 757-764

NDS (Novell Directory Services), 999
  Active Directory, 1012
  running in, 1002
  tools, 1004-1006

.NET, leveraging OWA clients, 751

NetWare
  eDirectory, 172
  FMU (File Migration Utility), 1005-1010
  migration tools, 1004-1006
  SfN (Services for NetWare), 999, 1004-1010

Network Load Balancing (NLB), 203-204, 881, 903-906

Network Monitor, 982

Network Operating System (NOS), 525-526

networks
  adapters, 885
  cards, 904
  coexistence, 117
  configuring, 914
  load balancing, 294
  Pocket PC 2002
    applying, 693-695
    connecting, 679-683
  Pocket PC 2003
    applying, 693-695
    connecting, 688-693
  renaming, 905
  requirements, 885
  security
    GroupWise, 1001
    Lotus Notes, 1059
  subsystems, 987
  topologies (bandwidth), 832-833

New Contact dialog box, 794

new features, 15
  8-node clustering, 18
  access, 114
  client-level security, 343-344
  configuration/management wizards, 15
  connections, 114
  drag-and-drop capabilities, 15
  functionality, 17
  GC caching, 17
  mobile communications, 27-28

applying over HTTPS, 28
connecting wireless technologies, 29
leveraging ActiveSync, 29
OWA clients, 753-756
performance, 17, 29
    allocating memory, 30
    caching, 30
    controlling message notification, 30-31
reliability, 20-21
remote installation, 17-18
security, 16, 25
    controlling message flow, 26
    cross-forest Kerberos authentication, 25
    filtering, 26
    IPSec, 25
    restricting distribution lists, 25
VSS, 19

**new hardware migration, 423**
**NLB (Network Load Balancing)**, 203-204, **881, 903-906**
**No Service Account, 469-470**
**nodes**
8-node clustering, 18
clustering, 880
    adding, 893
    troubleshooting, 901
**non-Windows**
client access methods, 822
    HTML, 823
    IMAP, 822
    OWA, 823
    pocket PCs, 823
    POP, 822
deployment options, 832
environment integration, 163
    account provisioning (MIIS), 166
    applying MSDSS, 170-175
    deploying MII, 169-170
    group management (MIIS), 168
    installing, 168
    LDAP, 175-178
    MIIS, 164-166
    Novell eDirectory, 169
    role of MAs (MIIS), 167-168
    SFU, 178-181
systems, 644, 810. *See also* Macintosh

**nonauthoritative restores, 968**
**noncompatible applications, 522**
**NOS (Network Operating System), 525-526**
**notifications**
enabling, 669
messages, 30-31
**Novell Directory Services (NDS), 999**
Active Directory, 1012
running in, 1002
tools, 1004-1006
**Novell eDirectory, 999**
Active Directory, 1012
MIIS, 169-170
MSDSS, 170-175
running in, 1002
tools, 1004-1006
**Novell GroupWise.** *See* **GroupWise**
**nslookup, troubleshooting, 207-208**
**NSPI (Name Service Provider Interface), 219**
**NT4 (Windows NT version 4), 199**
**Ntbackup.exe, 922-927, 953**
**ntdsutil utility, 490, 590**

# O

**OAB (Offline Address Book), 600, 744-745, 977**
**OAL (Offline Address List), 600**
**objects**
Active Directory, 540-541
mailboxes, 540
MMS, 123
moving, 547
**Office 2003 Resource Kit (ORK), 830, 853, 861**
**offline access, 114**
**Offline Address Book (OAB), 600, 744-745, 977**
**Offline Address List (OAL), 600**
**offline database maintenance, 594**
**Offline Folder (OST), 744-745, 977**
**offline maintenance, 601**
**OM (Operations Master), seizing, 490**

**OMA (Outlook Mobile Access), 114, 154, 486, 701**
ActiveSync, 658
clients, 126
configuring, 254-257
functionality, 650-651
mobile services, 670
**"On Behalf Of", sending email, 731**
**one way synchronization, 463**
**ongoing maintenance, servers, 993-994**
**online backups, 19, 598**
**online database maintenance, 593**
**opening**
Calendars Additional calendars, 729
multiple panes (OWA), 757-760
**Openwave mobile phone simulator, 652**
**operating systems**
NOS, 525-526
optimizing, 127-128
patching, 131
requirements, 115-117
servers, 144
upgrading, 496-497
Windows
hardening, 337
lockdown guidelines, 343
optimizing Windows Server 2003, 338
optimizing Windows XP Professional, 338
patches/updates, 342-343
security templates, 340-341
virus protection, 343
**Operations Master (OP), seizing, 490**
**optimization, 127**
AVAPI, 131
backup/restore, 131
capacity analysis, 979-980
clustering, 130
disk options, 128
documentation, 619-620
Exchange 5.5 migration, 457-458
fault tolerance, 886
configuring, 896-898
installing, 887-896
managing, 898-902
OWA, 903-906

Global Catalog, 219
link state connections, 976
logs, 990
mailbox speed, 21
memory
calculating virtual memory, 985-986
subsystems, 984
migration
combined approach, 488
deploying, 485-491
in-place upgrade method, 486-497
move mailbox upgrade method, 487-488, 497-506
restoring prototype labs, 491
validating documents, 491
mobile communications, 27
applying over HTTPS, 28
connecting wireless technologies, 29
leveraging ActiveSync, 29
OWA, 28
MOM, 131
monitoring, 981-983
multiple databases, 129-130
new features, 15
8-node clustering, 18
configuration/management wizards, 15
drag-and-drop capabilities, 15
functionality, 17
GC caching, 17
performance, 17
reliability, 20-21
remote installation, 17-18
security, 16
VSS, 19
number of front-end servers, 659-660
operating systems, 127-128
Outlook 2001, 807
OWA
Deferred View Update, 781
new features, 753-756
slow access, 798-799
performance, 29
allocating memory, 30
caching, 30
controlling message notification, 30-31

replication, 977
security, 25
   controlling message flow, 26
   cross-forest Kerberos authentication, 25
   filtering, 26
   IPSec, 25
   restricting distribution lists, 25
servers, 143, 976
   communicating with clients, 976-977
   new features, 366-369
   ongoing maintenance, 993-994
   OWA, 978
   replicating public folders, 978
   reporting RPC errors, 977
   scalability, 979
   sizing, 987-993
synchronization, 646, 977
VM, 128
Windows Server 2003, 338
Windows XP Professional, 338

**options.** *See also* **customization**
boot failures, 945-947
certificate templates, 398-399
clients
   administrative, 845
   installing, 842-843
clustering, 880-883, 898-902
   OWA, 903-906
   permissions, 882
   requirements, 883-886
contacts, 552
deployment of clients, 831-832
disks, 128
email, 769
fault tolerance, 879-883
Group Policy, 855
Mailbox Move tool, 549
mailboxes, 541-543
media, 220
migration, 424
   combined approach, 488
   configuring, 1101
   deploying prototype labs, 489-491
   in-place upgrade method, 486-497
   move mailbox upgrade method, 487-488, 497-506
   optimizing deployment, 485
   planning, 484-485

   restoring prototype labs, 491
   validating documents, 491
Outlook
   colors, 711
   interfaces, 867
   Macintosh, 806
   predefined, 835
   properties, 746
OWA
   calendar, 788-791
   Contacts, 794-797
   customizing, 781-787
   meeting invitations, 792-793
   optimizing slow access, 798-799
   publishing rules, 247
   security, 797-798
   Task, 793-794
Reading Pane, 783
recovery, 150
redundancy, 145
RUS, 504
Spell Check, 783
viewing, 542
Windows
   hardening, 337
   lockdown guidelines, 343
   patches/updates, 342-343
   security templates, 340-341
   virus protection, 343
   Windows Server 2003, 338
   Windows XP Professional, 338
Windows-based mail clients, 802-805
**order of application, Group Policy, 856**
**organization names, 148**
**organization roles, managing, 534-535**
**organizational email policies, creating, 364-365**
**organizational policy documents, 617**
**OrgPrepCheck tool, 460**
**ORK (Office 2003 Resource Kit), 830, 853, 861**
**OST (Offline Folder), 744-745, 977**
**Out of Office Assistant, configuring, 781**
**outbound mail routing, internal DNS servers, 205**
**outbound messages, ISA, 275-276**
**outbound security controls, 413**
**outlining migration, 610-612**

**Outlk11.adm security templates, importing, 861**
**Outlook**
  add-ins, 745
  Administrative Installation Points, 836
  baselines, 865
  Calendar, 711-712
  clients
    best practices, 846
    testing, 848
  collaboration, 729-733
    Calendar, 733-735
    Group Schedules, 736-738
    public folders, 736
    shared Web home page views, 738
  deployment, 838
  email, 764. *See also* email
  folders, 762
  Group Policy, 864-870
    baselines, 857-859
    clients, 859-864
    customizing, 855
    levels of, 856
    managing, 854
    refreshing, 856
    templates, 855
    updating, 870-873
  GroupWise, 1000
  highlighting, 710-711
  installing, 715-719, 808
  interfaces, 709
  junk mail filters, 722
  linking, 713-714
  Lotus Notes, 1058
  Macintosh, 805
    configuring, 806-809
    options, 806
    support, 802-803
  managing, 715
  mobile access, 647-648
  predefined options, 835
  PRF files, 837-838
  profiles
    automating, 836-841
    configuring, 715, 830-831
    creating, 808
  remote connections, 739-746
  requirements, 834-835

  RPC over HTTP, 725-728
  RPC over HTTP(S), 331-333
  searching, 712-713, 779
  security, 719-725
  SMS, 848-850
  synchronizing, 978
  Transforms, 844
  versions, 708
  VPNs, 641-643
**Outlook 2001, optimizing, 807**
**Outlook 2003, 8**
  security, 344
    attachments, blocking, 348
    authenticating users, 347
    encrypting, 346-347
    Internet access, 344-346
    secure messaging, 357-358
  spam, 349
    IRM, 353-354
    junk mail, filtering, 351-353
    read receipts, blocking, 353
    tools, 349-350
    Web beaconing, 350
**Outlook Express, configuring, 810-814**
**Outlook Mobile Access.** *See* **OMA**
**Outlook Web Access.** *See* **OWA**
**overriding ESM, 325-326**
**OWA (Outlook Web Access), 114, 154, 287-288, 642**
  access, 823
  ActiveSync, 315-321
  attachments, 27
  clients, 126, 749-751
    calendar, 788-791
    Contacts option, 794-797
    email features, 764-781
    interfaces, 750-751
    leveraging .NET framework, 751
    login interfaces, 755-756
    meeting invitations, 792-793
    navigating, 757-764
    new features, 753-756
    optimizing slow access, 798-799
    options, 781-787
    security, 797-798
    Tasks option, 793-794
    user modes, 753

colors, 785
Deferred View Update, 781
FBA, 253, 309-310, 415
front-end/back-end architecture,
    289-294
Help, 763
infrastructure, 288
interfaces, 9-10
ISA Server 2004, 239-240
    creating publishing rules, 243-247
    customizing FBA, 252
    exporting/importing certificates,
        240-243
    redirecting OWA traffic, 247-251
logging off, 764
mail flow, 107
mobile communications, 28
multiple, 322-326
optimizing, 978
passwords, 313
saved searches, 713
secure messaging, 358
security, 354
    attachments, blocking, 354
    block/safe lists, 355
SSL
    applying internal CAs, 300-303
    customizing, 306-308
    enabling, 294-297
    forcing, 303
    installing third-party CAs, 297-299
summarizing, 310-312
threats, 237-239
Web sites
    redirecting clients, 305-306
    security, 304

**P**

**packages, configuring, 849-850**
**packets (IPSec), 403-404**
    configuring, 405-407
    NAT-T, 404-405
**panes.** *See also* **interfaces**
    OWA, 759
    reading
        options, 783
        OWA, 761

**parameters, /3GB /USERVA=3030
    parameters, 984**
**partial authoritative restores, 970**
**Password Migration DLL, 436-437**
**passwords**
    Active Directory Restore mode, 920
    email, 787-788
    exporting, 436
    GroupWise, 1001
    Lotus Notes, 1059
    OWA, 313
    SFU, 181
    Telnet, 587
**patches**
    Group Policy, 870-873
    security, 342-343
    servers, 377
**patching**
    compatibility, 522-524
    operating systems, 131
**paths, selecting migration, 1066**
**PDAs (personal digital assistants)**
    connections
        ActiveSync, 643-645
        customizing ActiveSync, 645
        optimizing ActiveSync, 646
        securing, 646
    table PCs, 654
    Terminal Services, 633
**performance, 127.** *See also* **optimization**
    AVAPI, 131
    backup/restore, 131
    capacity analysis, 979-980
    clustering, 130-883
        permissions, 882
        requirements, 883-886
    disk options, 128
    documentation, 619-620
    MOM, 131
    monitoring, 981-983
        analyzing processor usage, 986
        calculating virtual memory, 985-986
        configuring disk subsystems,
            986-988
        optimizing memory subsystems,
            984
    multiple databases, 129-130
    operating systems, 127-128

optimizing, 17, 29
  allocating memory, 30
  caching, 30
  controlling message notification,
    30-31
  servers, 976
    communicating with clients,
      976-977
    ongoing maintenance, 993-994
    OWA, 978
    replicating public folders, 978
    reporting RPC errors, 977
    scalability, 979
    sizing, 987-993
  VM, 128
**Performance Monitor, 207, 981**
**permissions**
  assigning, 731
  clustering, 882
  extended permissions, 536
  GP, 857-858
  granular, 485
  Group Policy, 863-864
  groups, 72
  registry, 438
  source domains, 435
  user accounts, 872
**personal address books, migrating,
  813-814, 1054, 1106**
**personal dictionaries, migrating, 1054,
  1106**
**personal digital assistants.** *See* **PDAs**
**pfmigrate tool, 475, 503**
**.pfx files, security, 241**
**PGP (Pretty Good Privacy), 403**
**phased migration**
  from GroupWise, 1011-1015
  from Lotus Notes, 1062-1066
  tools, 1065
**phases**
  of migration, 422-423
  upgrades, 36
    documentation, 36
    initiation, 37-40
    pilot, 62-64
    planning, 46-55, 58-59
    prototype, 60-62

**phones (mobile)**
  connecting, 699-700
  Pocket PC 2002, 682
  Pocket PC 2003, 690
  smartphones, 695-698
**physical disk configuration, 988**
**physical security, 370**
**pilot phase**
  groups, 63-64
  success of, 64
**pilot testing**
  migration, 500
  mobile devices, 651-652
**PKI (Public Key Infrastructure), 392**
  CA, 392-396
  certificates, 396
    enrollment, 400-402
    templates, 397-399
  planning, 394-395
  private/public keys, 396
  smartcards, 399
**placeholder domain structures, 120**
**placement, 123**
  Active Directory, 215
  administrative groups, 123
  client access points, 125-127
  environment sizing, 125
  GC, 138
  GC/DC, 121
  Global Catalog, 219
  public folders, 125
  routing group topology, 124
  servers, 142
**planning**
  backups, 910-912
    database corruption, 911-912
    devices, 917
    documentation, 912-915
    media, 930-932
    Ntbackup.exe, 922-927
    servers, 918-920
    services, 927-930
    strategies, 915-917
    system failures, 911
  clustering, 888-890
  deployment
    clients, 832-833
    Outlook, 848-850

disaster recovery, 618-619, 938
Distribution Groups, 553-554
    creating, 555-556
    mail-enabled, 558
    managing, 557
    scope, 554
documentation, 606
Exchange 5.5 migration, 454-457
installations, 69-71
migration, 484-485, 610
    combined approach, 488
    deploying prototype labs, 489-491
    from GroupWise, 1010-1015
    in-place upgrade method, 486-497
    from Lotus Notes, 1061-1066
    move mailbox upgrade method,
        487-488, 497-506
    optimizing deployment, 485
    outlining, 610-612
    restoring prototype labs, 491
    selecting direct approach of,
        1015-1016
    validating documents, 491
mobility, 657-659
    components, 658
    functionality, 658
    optimizing front-end servers,
        659-660
    testing, 661
Outlook, 835
PKI, 394-395
Remote Desktop for Administration,
    626
Terminal Services, 631
upgrade phase, 46-48
**planning phase (upgrades)**
Design documents, 49-53
    collaboration sessions, 48
    creating, 48
migration documents, 53-59
prototype, 60-62
**platforms, DNS compatibility between,
188**
**pocket devices, Terminal Services, 633**
**Pocket PC 2002**
connecting, 679-683
synchronizing, 674-678, 683

**Pocket PC 2003**
applying, 693-695
connecting, 688-693
synchronizing, 684-688
**policies**
audits, 371
corporate email, 364-365
domains, 435
email, 365
Group Policy. *See also* Group Policy
    clients, 831
    pushing, 844-847
IPSec, 405-407
recipients, 563-564
    defining, 565
    editing, 567
    implementing, 566-567
    naming, 565
security documentation, 621-622
system, 95-96
SYSVOL folder, 972-973
**political limitations, multiple forests, 119**
**pools, media, 931.** *See also* **media**
**POP (Post Office Protocol), 812-813, 822**
**POP3 (Post Office Protocol version 3)**
access, 822
clients, 126
security, 261-266
**populating Active Directory, 478-480**
**ports.** *See also* **connections**
firewalls, 664
searching, 464, 904
servers, 416
**Post Office Protocol (POP), 812-813, 822**
**Post Office Protocol version 3.** *See* **POP3**
**post-deployment client tasks, 850-851**
**post-maintenance procedures, 602**
**post-migration cleanup, 480**
**postinstallation, 1079-1083**
configuring, 1030
    deleting Information Stores, 1030
    disabling services, 1030
    routing group connectors, 1031-
        1033
    tracking, 1034
deleting Information Stores, 1080-1081
disabling services, 1080

enabling logging/message tracking, 1084

Exchange 2003 installations, 89-98

**predefined configuration options, Outlook, 835**

**preferences.** *See also* **customization**

boot failures, 945-947

certificate templates, 398-399

clustering, 880-883, 898-902

OWA, 903-906

permissions, 882

requirements, 883-886

Group Policy, 855

mailboxes, 541-543

migration, 424

Outlook

colors, 711

interfaces, 867

Macintosh, 806

properties, 746

Windows-based mail clients, 802

Macintosh support, 802-803

OWA functionality, 804-805

**preinstallation checks, 1016, 1067**

core services, 1017, 1067

DomainPrep process, 1067

domains, 1017

Exchange 2003 installations, 76-77

ForestPrep process, 1067

forests, 1017

log files, 1017

reviewing log files, 1068

**preparing**

deployment (Outlook), 848-850

domains, 77, 1017

for core installations, 1019-1020

for installation, 74-75

forests, 77, 1017

Lotus Domino environments, 1097

project teams for migration, 1013, 1064

Windows 2003 domains, 1069-1070

**prerequisites**

Exchange Migration Wizard, 1096-1097

migration, 484-485, 1035, 1085

Volume Shadow Copy services, 921

**Pretty Good Privacy (PGP), 403**

**prevention of spam beaconing, 725**

**PRF files**

applying, 718-719

configuring, 837-838

creating, 716

Outlook, 842-843

**primary domain controllers, upgrading, 427**

**primary zones, DNS, 190-191**

**primary-secondary replication, 192**

**prioritizing**

applications, 518-519

maintenance, 597-601

**privacy**

email, 784

PGP, 403

statements, 388

**Private (OWA) setting, modifying, 757**

**private keys, 396**

**procedures**

for backups, 916

security, 621. *See also* documentation

**processes**

DomainPrep, 1017-1020, 1067

ForestPrep, 1017, 1067

interactive core installation, 1020-1022

interactive installation (Exchange Server 2003), 1070-1072

**processor usage, analyzing, 986**

**production migration/upgrade, 64-65**

**profiles**

configuring, 809

Group Policy, 865

Outlook

automating, 836-841

configuring, 715, 830-831

creating, 808

RPC over HTTP(S), 331-333

**PROFS/SNADS connectors, 456**

**project schedules, 54**

**project teams, preparing for, 1013, 1064**

**promotion, optimizing Global Catalog, 219**

**properties**

ActiveSync, 668-670

OMA, 670

Outlook, 746
sheets, 774
**proposing meetings, 711-712**
**protocols**
    IPSec, 403-404
        configuring, 405-407
        NAT-T, 404-405
    logging, 584
    mailboxes, 544
    RDP, 626
    SMTP, 407-411
    transport-level security, 414
    WEP, 633
**prototyping**
    compatibility testing, 529
    Exchange 2003 installations, 76
    labs (Exchange Server 2003)
        deploying, 489-491
        restoring, 491
    upgrades, 60-62
**provisioning accounts, 166**
**proxy servers**
    access, 1106-1107
    DNS, 201-203
    GroupWise, 1038-1039
    HTTP, 642
    Lotus Notes, 1087-1088
    migrating, 1054
**Public (OWA) setting, modifying, 757**
**public folders, 486**
    connection agreements, 464
    dedicated servers, 102
    design, 102, 125, 149
    managing, 100-101
    message expiration, 594
    migrating, 475
    Outlook, 746
    replicating, 103, 502, 599
    Schedule+ Free/Busy, 1093
    servers, 582
    sharing, 736
    stores
        creating, 89, 1029, 1079
        deleting, 95
        replicating, 978
    trees, 101-102
    viewing, 763

**Public Key Infrastructure (PKI), 392**
    CA, 392-396
    certificates, 396
        enrollment, 400-402
        templates, 397-399
    planning, 394-395
    private/public keys, 396
    smartcards, 399
**public keys, 396**
**publishing rules**
    IMAP, 264-266
    OWA, 243-247
    POP3, 261-264
**pull-down menus (OWA), 759**
**pushing clients, updating, 872-873**

# Q – R

**quarterly maintenance, 601**
**queries**
    Distribution Groups, 556
    DNS, 191-192
**Queue Viewer, 592**
**queues, 598**
**Quick flags, 710, 778**
**quorum resources, clustering, 879**

**RAID (Redundant Array of Inexpensive Disks), 944, 989**
**RAM (random access memory), 145**
**read receipts, blocking, 353**
**readiness of applications, 425**
**reading**
    email, 767
        attachments, 767-768
        marking read/unread, 773
    panes (OWA), 761, 783
**rebuilding, comparing to restoring, 947**
**Recipient Connection Agreements, 464**
**Recipient Update Service (RUS), 470, 504, 568-571**
**recipients.** *See also* **contacts**
    email, 764-765
    policies, 563-564
        defining, 565
        editing, 567

implementing, 566-567
naming, 565
Safe Recipients list, 724

**records**
baselining, 607
CNAME, 195
hosts, 193
mail exchange, 193
name server, 193
service, 195

**recovery**
ASR, 899, 916, 951-953
backups, 910-912
database corruption, 911-912
devices, 917
documentation, 912-915
media, 930-932
Ntbackup.exe, 922-927
servers, 918-920
services, 927-930
strategies, 915-917
system failures, 911
databases, 21
deleted items, 786-787, 938
disaster recovery options, 49
documentation, 619, 914
email, 958-960
Mailbox Recovery Center Tool, 571-574
mailboxes, 19, 573-574
Mailbox Recovery Center, 20
VSS, 19
options, 150
single member server migrations, 425
storage group, 20

**Recovery Console, boot failures, 947**
**Recovery Storage Group, 963-964**
**recursive queries, 191-192**
**redirecting**
automatic SSL, 416
clients, 305-306
OWA traffic, 247-251

**redundancy, 453-454**
Exchange 5.5, 453
options, 145
servers, 143

**Redundant Array of Inexpensive Disks (RAID), 944, 989**

**redundant site preparation, 941**
**refreshing Group Policy, 856**
**registries**
permissions, 438
RPC over HTTP(S), 329

**Registry, configuring keys, 718**
**relationships, 216**
**relaying**
enabling, 411
SMTP, 105-106, 387, 410-411, 583

**reliability, 20-21, 127, 1058**
AVAPI, 131
backup/restore, 131
clustering, 130
disk options, 128
MOM, 131
multiple databases, 129-130
operating systems, 127-128
scaling, 18

**reminders**
customizing, 786
enabling quick flags, 778

**remote access.** *See also* **access**
Active Directory, 8-9
mobile devices, 644
OWA, 642
PDA connections
ActiveSync, 643-645
customizing synchronization, 645
optimizing synchronization, 646
securing, 646

**Remote Administration (HTML) tool, 627-631**
**remote connections (Outlook), 739-746**
**Remote Desktop for Administration, 625-631**
**Remote Desktop Protocol (RDP), 626**
**remote desktops, 587**
**remote installation, 17-18**
**remote management, 586-587, 635-636**
**Remote Procedure Calls.** *See* **RPC**
**remote scans, 374**
**remote users, scheduling, 833**
**Removable Storage, 930-932**
**renaming networks, 905**
**replacing backup domain controllers, 429**

**replicas, adding, 1093**

**replication**

Active Directory, 138, 213

ActiveSync, 29

deleting, 479

directories, 22-23

Directory Replication Connector, 469

Distribution Groups, 557

DNS, 192

MMS, 123

optimizing, 977

public folders, 103, 149, 502, 599

Site Replication Service, 466

SRS, 469-470

**ReplMon (Active Directory Replication Monitor), 71**

**replying to email, attachments, 768**

**reports**

Mailbox Manager, 575-576

performance, 620

RPC errors, 977

spammers, 386

**requests, Group Schedules, 737**

**requirements**

Active Directory, 116

clustering, 883-886

DNS, 199-204

Exchange versions, 116

hardware, 115, 883-884

load balancing, 883-886

memory, 991

migration, 484-485

operating systems, 115-117

Outlook, 834-835

software clustering, 890

Volume Shadow Copy services, 921

**Research in Motion (RIM), 658**

**researching applications, 517-519**

**resolution, Exchange 5.5 name requirements, 199**

**resource groups, clustering, 879**

**Resource Mailbox Wizard, 461**

**resource records, DNS, 192-197**

**resources, 44**

compatibility testing, 515-516

geographic distribution of, 47

utilization analysis, 600

**responsibilities, servers, 582-583**

**Restore Wizard, 950**

**restoring, 115, 131**

Active Directory domain controllers, 491

backups, 590, 910-912, 936

database corruption, 911-912

devices, 917

documentation, 912-915

media, 930-932

Ntbackup.exe, 922-927

servers, 918-920

services, 927-930

strategies, 915-917

system failures, 911

boot loader files, 953

clustering, 899-902

databases, 954-955

Exchange Server 2003, 491

Global Catalog, 972

Group Policy, 859

MSDSS, 174-175

servers, 937

system state, 950

testing, 940-941

**restrictions**

access

login, 370

SMTP virtual servers, 410

distribution lists, 25

mailboxes, 541-543

of message communications, 26

**Resultant Set of Policies (RSoP), 855-858**

**retirement of legacy Exchange 2000 Servers, 505-506**

**return on investment (ROI), 607**

**reverse lookup zones, 189**

**reviewing**

log files, 78, 1017, 1068

message queues, 598

migration lab results, 1096

**revisions**

contacts, 795

email, 774-775

Spell Check, 783

**rich mode, OWA client user mode, 752**

**rights**

delegating, 537-538

Group Policy, 857-858, 863-864

**RIM (Research in Motion), 658**

**risk**
    assessing, 362-363
    assumptions, 45
**ROI (return on investment), 607**
**role-based administration, 534-535**
**roles**
    Delegation Wizard, 538
    DSAccess, 223
    Exchange Full Administrator, 535
    Exchange Server 2003, 368-369
    Exchange View Only, 535
    FSMO, 1018
    of MAs, 167-168
    OP, 490
    scope of, 537
    servers, 582-583
        functional roles, 380-381
        sizing, 991-992
    SMTP Categorizer, 224
**routers, documenting, 914**
**routing**
    email, 198
    Exchange 5.5, 452
    groups. *See* Routing Groups
    internal email, 205
    mixed environments, 201
    outbound, 205
**Routing Groups, 82, 124, 200, 561-562**
    adding, 85
    configuring, 561-563
    connectors, 91-93, 412-414, 1031-
        1033, 1081
    creating, 1022, 1024-1025, 1074
    design, 149
    installing, 562-563
    modes, 562
    moving, 563
    security, 412
**RPC (Remote Procedure Calls), 977**
    error reporting, 977
    ISA Server 2004, 258
    MAPI, 259
**RPC over HTTP, 725-728**
    Cached Mode, 743
    clients, 127

**RPC over HTTP(S), 154**
    applying, 326-329
    Outlook 2003, 331-333
    virtual directories, 330
**RSG Wizard, 965**
**RSoP (Resultant Set of Policies), 855-858**
**rules**
    clients, 1106-1107
    filtering (MAPI RPC), 259
**Rules Editor, configuring, 775-777**
**RUS (Recipient Update Service), 470, 504,
    568-571**


**S**

**S/MIME (Secure/Multipurpose Internet
    Mail Extensions), 356-359, 402-403**
    attachments, 27
    functionality, 797
    Outlook, 720-721
**safe lists, 26, 352-355**
**Safe Recipients list, 724**
**Safe Senders list, 723**
**saving.** *See also* **backups**
    mailboxes, 547
    searches, 712
**scalability, 117, 453**
    8-node clustering, 18
    Exchange 5.5, 452
    front-end servers, 664
    mobile devices, 652
    servers, 979
    SMTP, 203-204
**scans**
    antivirus applications, 383
    MBSA, 374
    messages, 385
**Schedule+ Free/Busy public folders, 1093**
**scheduling**
    Group Schedules, 736-738
    Mailbox Manager, 577
    maintenance, 132, 597-601, 940-941
    remote users, 833
**Schema Master, 1018, 1068**

**schemas**
Active Directory
extending, 73-74, 1018-1019, 1068-1069
upgrading, 492-493
Active Directory Schema MMC snap-in, 74
**SCL (Spam Confidence Level), 26**
**scope**
applications, 511
Distribution Groups, 554
groups, 226
of management (SOM), 858
of roles, 537
**of work, 43scripted Exchange 2003 installations, 80-82**
**scripts**
Interix, 180
MIIS 2003, 123
SYSVOL folder, 972-973
WSH, 587
**SCW (Security Configuration Wizard), 19-20, 374-376**
**Search Based on Exchange Mailboxes Only option, 481**
**Search dialog box, 779**
**Search In functionality, 712**
**searching**
Address Book (OWA), 771
email, 779
LDAP ports, 464
names, 796
Outlook, 712-713
recipient policies, 565
saving searches, 712
**secondary zones, 190-191**
**secure messaging**
Outlook 2003, 357-358
OWA, 358
**Secure Sockets Layer.** *See* **SSL**
**Secure/Multipurpose Internet Mail Extensions.** *See* **S/MIME**
**security, 16**
Active Directory authentication, 214-215
breaches, 234
Certificate Services, 928

clients, 337, 343
hardening Windows, 337
lockdown guidelines, 343
new features, 343-344
patches/updates, 342-343
templates, 340-341
virus protection, 343
Windows Server 2003, 338
Windows XP Professional, 338
distribution lists, 387
documentation, 621-622
email, 783-788
events, 370
firewalls, 235
front-end servers, 290-291
Group Policy (Outlook), 864-870
groups, 225, 372-373
IIS, 486
implementing, 131
antivirus applications, 132
front-end server functionality, 132
patching operating systems, 131
scheduling maintenance, 132
IPSec, 403-404
configuring, 405-407
NAT-T, 404-405
ISA Server 2004, 16-18, 234
creating OWA publishing rules, 243-247
customizing OWA FBA, 252
EMS, 237-239, 252-258
IMAP/POP3, 261-266
logging, 277-279
MAPI, 258-260
monitoring, 279-283
OWA, 239-243
redirecting OWA traffic, 247-251
role of, 234-237
SMTP, 266-276
junk mail filters, 722
labels, 722
layers, 370-372
mobile, 646
multiple forests, 119
networks
GroupWise, 1001
Lotus Notes, 1059

optimizing, 25
    controlling message flow, 26
    creating cross-forest Kerberos
        authentication, 25
    filtering, 26
    integrating IPSec, 25
    restricting distribution lists, 25
Outlook, 344, 708, 719-725
    attachments, 348
    authenticating users, 347
    encrypting, 346-347
    Internet access, 344-346
OWA, 354, 797-798
    attachments, blocking, 354
    block/safe lists, 355
    client interfaces, 757
    redirecting clients, 305-306
    Web sites, 304
passwords, 181
.pfx files, 241
routing groups, 412
RPC over HTTP, 725-728
SCW, 19-20
servers
    antivirus applications, 382-383
    assessing risk, 362-363
    configuring secure messaging,
        364-366
    functional roles, 380-381
    hardening, 370-374
    IIS, 378-380
    Microsoft Trustworthy Computing
        Initiative, 361-362
    new features, 366-369
    patches/updates, 377
    spam, 384-388
    standardizing, 382
    templates, 376
services, 373
SMTP, 105-106, 201-203
spam beaconing, 725
standards, 374
templates, 340, 376
    customizing, 341
    importing, 861
Terminal Services, 631-632
transport-level, 391
    automatic SSL redirection, 416
    CA, 392-394

certificates, 396-399
clients, 415
enrollment of certificates, 400-402
installing CA, 395-396
Internet Mail Wizard, 413-414
layers, 391-392
locking down, 407-417
PKI, 392
planning PKI, 394-395
private/public keys, 396
protocols, 414
routing group connectors, 412
smartcards (PKI), 399
X.400, 412-413
virus protection (client-based), 343
Windows Firewall, 339
Security Configuration and Analysis tool,
340-341
Security Configuration Wizard (SCW),
19-20, 374-376
security identifier (SID), 432, 950
seizing OM, 490
selecting
    components
        applications, 142-144
        hardware, 142-144
        large businesses, 146
        mid-sized businesses, 146
        small businesses, 145
    direct migration approaches,
        1015-1016
    DNS namespaces, 121
    file systems, 988
    group models, 71-73
    migration paths, 1066
    mixed/native modes, 71
    mobile devices, 650
    objects, 547
    phased migration from Lotus Notes,
        1062-1066
    tools for phased migrations, 1065
Send/Receive messages, cached Mode,
743
Sender ID, 27, 385-386
sending
    email, 766
        adding attachments, 765-766
        configuring options, 769

deleting, 769
forwarding, 768
Group Schedules, 737
modifying text, 771
"On Behalf Of", 731
reading attachments, 767-768
replying, 768
Safe Senders list, 723
secure messages, 358
text via Telnet, 587
**sensitivity, configuring email options, 770**
**separate front-end servers, creating, 662-663**
**Server 2003 environments, supporting, 65**
**servers**
antivirus applications, 382-383
ASR, 951-953
auditing, 584-585
back-end, 993
backups, 918-920
media, 930-932
Ntbackup.exe, 922-927
services, 927-930
bridgehead, 583
configuring, 93
installing, 98
capacity analysis, 979-980
clients, 844-847
clustering, 878-883
permissions, 882
requirements, 883-886
configuring, 913
connectors, 475-477
deleting, 479
disaster recovery, 947-953
DNS, 186-187
configuring, 204-208
multihomed, 196
need for, 187
troubleshooting, 205
types of, 187-188
documentation, 614, 913
fault tolerance, 886
configuring, 896-898
installing, 887-896
managing, 898-902
OWA, 903-906

floppy disks, 917
front-end, 582
adding, 664
automatic SSL redirection, 416
configuring, 662
creating separate, 662-663
optimizing number of, 659-660
sizing, 991
transport-level security, 415
functionality, 132
Global Catalog
configuring, 216
demoting, 219
deploying domain controllers, 220
optimizing promotion, 219
placement, 70-71, 219
verifying, 218
Group Policy
baselines, 857-859
clients, 859-864
customizing, 855
levels of, 856
managing, 854
Outlook, 864-870
refreshing, 856
templates, 855
updating, 870-873
hardening, 370-374
HTTPS, 258
installing, 69, 466-470
extending Active Directory schema, 73-74
finalizing, 82-89
groups models, 71-73
interactive, 78-80
planning, 69-71
postinstallation, 89-98
preinstallation checks, 76-77
preparing, 74-76
scripted, 80-82
selecting modes, 71
testing, 106-108
inventory lists, 518
ISA Server 2004, 234
creating OWA publishing rules, 243-247
customizing OWA FBA, 252
EMS, 252-258
exporting/importing certificates, 240-243

IMAP/POP3, 261-266
logging, 277-279
MAPI, 258-260
monitoring, 279-283
OWA, 239-240
redirecting OWA traffic, 247-251
role of, 234-237
SMTP, 266-276
threats, 237-239
location of, 455
locking down, 416-417
mailboxes, 582
migrating, 470-474
moving, 548-551
management, 581
Active Directory, 588-589
backup, 590
eseutil utility, 591-592
ESM, 587-588
isinteg utility, 590-591
message tracking, 592
ntdsutil utility, 590
Queue Viewer, 592
remote, 586-587
roles/responsibilities, 582-583
memory, 143
migration, 483
combined approach, 488
deploying prototype labs, 489-491
documenting, 612
finalizing, 478-480
in-place upgrade method, 486-497
in-place upgrades, 423
move mailbox upgrade method,
487-488, 497-506
objectives, 422
optimizing deployment, 485
options, 424
phases, 422-423
planning, 484-485
restoring prototype labs, 491
single member servers, 424-427
strategies, 423
validating documents, 491
MIIS, 665-666
monitoring, 981-983
analyzing processor usage, 986
calculating virtual memory, 985-986

configuring disk subsystems,
986-988
optimizing memory subsystems,
984
naming, 148
operating systems, 144
optimizing, 143, 976
communicating with clients,
976-977
ongoing maintenance, 993-994
OWA, 978
replicating public folders, 978
reporting RPC errors, 977
scalability, 979
sizing, 987-993
OWA
applying internal CAs, 300-303
configuring ActiveSync, 315-321
customizing, 306-308
deploying multiple, 322-326
enabling FBA, 309-310
forcing, 303
front-end/back-end architecture,
289-294
installing third-party CAs, 297-299
modifying passwords, 313
SSL, 294-297
summarizing, 310-312
placement, 123, 142
administrative groups, 123
client access points, 125-127
environment sizing, 125
public folders, 125
routing group topology, 124
primary-secondary replication, 192
proxy, 1106-1107
public folders, 475, 582
redundancy, 143
relationships, 216
remote management, 635-636
restoring, 937
RPC over HTTP, 725-728
RPC over HTTP(S)
applying, 326-329
configuring Outlook 2003, 331-333
creating virtual directories, 330

security
    assessing risk, 362-363
    configuring secure messaging,
      364-366
    functional roles, 380-381
    IIS, 378-380
    Microsoft Trustworthy Computing
      Initiative, 361-362
    new features, 366-369
    patches/updates, 377
    templates, 376
services
    configuring, 98-106
    migrating, 475-477
SMS, 834, 848-850
SMTP relay, 583
spam, 384-388
standardizing, 382
Terminal Services, 632-633
testing, 993
transport-level security, 392
upgrading
    Active Directory forests/domains,
      458-460
    Exchange Deployment Tools, 454
    migrating Exchange 5.5, 452-458
virtual servers, 104-105, 288
virtual SMTP, 200, 408-411
VPN, 641-643
Windows Server 2003, 338
Windows XP Professional, 338
**service (SRV) records, 195**
**service packs, 14**
    servers, 377
    upgrading, 457
**service patches, compatibility, 522-524**
**service-level agreement (SLA), 41,
916-917**
**services**
    backups, 919, 927-930
    core, 77, 1017, 1067
    disabling, 90, 1030, 1080
    enabling, 77
    migrating, 448-449, 475-477, 1005
    mobile, 666-670
    security, 373
    servers, 98-106
    SRS, 469-470
    SSL, 99-100

Terminal Services, 625, 631-633
    locking down, 633
    pocket devices, 633
    Remote Desktop for Administration,
      625-631
Volume Shadow Copy, 921
**Services for NetWare (SfN), 999,
1004-1010**
**Services for Unix (SFU), 178-181**
**sessions**
    HTML, 627-631
    Remote Desktop for Administration,
      625-626
**setup.exe, 81**
**SfN (Services for NetWare), 999,
1004-1010**
**SFU (Services for Unix), 178-181**
**Shared (OWA) setting, modifying, 757**
**shared folders, migrating, 1055**
**shares, creating, 843**
**sharing**
    Calendars, 729-731
    email addresses, 388
    folders, 1107
    knowledge, 607
    Outlook, 731-733
    public folders, 736
    Web home page views, 738
**SID (security identifier), 432, 950**
**signatures**
    configuring, 783
    Outlook, 720-721
    S/MIME, 356-359, 402-403
**Simple Mail Transport Protocol. *See* SMTP**
**simulating migration, 489**
**single member server migration, 424**
    applications, 425
    backing up, 425
    hardware, 424
    standalone server upgrades, 426-427
**single site Exchange 5.5 migration, 457**
**Site Connectors, migrating, 477**
**site failures, disaster recovery, 941-943**
**Site Replication Service (SRS), 466-470,
480**
**sizing**
    back-end servers, 993
    databases, 116, 148, 599, 990

environments, 125
Exchange Server 2003, 987-993
front-end servers, 991
interfaces, 759
memory, 991
messages, 486
**SLA (service level agreement), 41, 916-917**
**slow access, optimizing OWA, 798-799**
**slow-link connection awareness, 743**
**small businesses**
client access, 156
components, 145
design, 135-136, 157-158
infrastructure, 151
**smartcards, PKI, 399**
**SMS (Systems Management Server), 834, 848-850**
**SMTP (Simple Mail Transfer Protocol)**
authentication, 408
Categorizer, 224
clients, 127
connectors, 104-105
DNS, 197-199
locking down, 407-411
mail relays, 105-106
relay servers, 583
relays, 387
scalability, 203-204
security, 201-203, 266-276
**snap-ins, Active Directory Schema MMC, 74**
**snapshots, Volume Shadow Copy services, 921**
**SOA (Start of Authority), 193**
**software.** *See* applications
**Software Update Services (SUS), 377**
**solidifying core technologies, 31-32**
**SOM (scope of management), 858**
**source domains.** *See also* domains
Password Migration DLL, 436-437
permissions, 435
registry permissions, 438
two-way domains, 435
**SP2 (Exchange Server 2003 Service Pack 2), 979**
**space, planning clusters, 889-890**

**spam, 349**
antispam filters, 722
beaconing, 725
beacons, 797
IRM, 353-354
junk mail, filtering, 351-353
read receipts, 353
reporting, 386
servers, 384-388
tools, 349-350
Web beaconing, 350
**Spam Confidence Level (SCL), 26**
**spare devices, 917**
**specifications documents, development of, 1003**
**specifying email rule criteria, 776**
**Spell Check, 774-775**
**Spelling Options, 783**
**spoofing, 409**
**SQL 2000, 168**
**SRS (Site Replication Service), 469-470, 480**
**SRV (service) records, 195**
**SSL (Secure Sockets Layer), 238, 626**
automatic redirection, 416
enabling, 99-100
ESM, 325-326
IMAP, 265
OWA
applying internal CAs, 300-303
assigning certificates, 325
customizing, 306-308
enabling, 294-297
forcing, 303
installing third-party CAs, 297-299
publishing rules, 244
POP, 263
**stability, 453-454**
**standalone root CA, 394**
**standalone servers, upgrading, 426-427**
**standalone subordinate CAs, 394**
**Standard Edition, Exchange 2003 Servers, 14**
**Standard version, 116**
**standards**
Exchange 2003 Servers, 382
recipient policies, 565

security, 374
X.400, 412-413
**Start of Authority (SOA), 193**
**starting**
    Calendar Connector, 1095
    connectors, 1089
    GroupWise, 1041, 1048
    Pocket PC 2002, 677-678
    Pocket PC 2003, 688
    Smartphone 2003 Emulator, 698
**state**
    backups, 920
    restoring, 949-950
**statement of work**
    approvals, 46
    budgets, 46
    creating, 42
    goals, 43
    resource requirements, 44-45
    risks/assumptions, 45
    scope of work, 42
    Scope section, 43
    timelines/milestones, 44
**status, modifying, 545**
**step-by-step procedure documents, 616**
**STM (streaming database file), 596**
**storage.** *See also* **backups**
    Active Directory, 212
        authentication, 214-215
        domain controllers, 214
        domains, 212
        DSAccess, 222-223
        DSProxy, 224
        forests, 212
        functionality, 225-229
        Global Catalog, 215-220
        placement, 215
        replication, 213
        SMTP Categorizer, 224
        trees, 212
        universal group caching, 221-222
    groups. *See* storage groups
    limitations, 541
    Recovery Storage Group, 963-964
    requirements, clustering, 885. *See also*
      clustering
**storage group recovery, 20**

**storage groups, 20, 129-130, 548-551**
    configuring, 96-97
    creating, 85-87, 1025-1027, 1075-1076
    databases, 1077
    design, 149
**stores**
    backups, 601
    Information Stores, 90-91, 1030,
      1080-1081
    mail, 548
    mailboxes
        creating, 87-88, 1028, 1078-1079
        servers, 582
    public folders, 89, 125
        creating, 1029, 1079
        deleting, 95
        replicating, 978
**strategies**
    backups, 915-917
    migration, 423, 1010-1013
    selecting direct approach of, 1015-
      1016
    tools for phased migrations, 1013-1015
    migration, 451
**streaming database file (STM), 596**
**stub zones, creating, 191**
**subsystems**
    memory, 984
    monitoring, 987
**summarizing OWA settings, 310-312**
**support**
    clustering, 144
    digital signatures, 402
    mobile devices, 673-674
        applying Pocket PC, 693-695
        connecting Pocket PC, 679-683,
          688-693
        mobile phone connections, 699-700
        smartphones, 695-698
        synchronizing Pocket PC, 674-678,
          683-688
    RAM, 145
    SenderID, 27
**SUS (Software Update Services), 377**
**switches, documenting, 914**
**synchronization**
    ActiveSync, 254-257, 1012
    clients, 977
    directories

configuring, 1006-1008, 1065, 1089-1092
GroupWise, 1014, 1041-1044
testing, 1044, 1092
Lotus Notes with Active Directory, 1063
MIIS, 164-166
   account provisioning, 166
   group management, 168
   installing, 168
   role of MAs, 167-168
mobile communications, 10
mobile devices, 645
   customizing, 645
   optimizing, 646
   securing, 646
mobility
   adding front-end servers, 664
   components, 658
   configuring firewalls, 664
   creating front-end servers, 662-663
   functionality, 658
   installing, 662
   optimizing front-end servers, 659-660
   planning, 657-659
   testing, 661
optimizing, 977
Outlook, 641-643, 978
Pocket PC 2002, 674-678, 683
Pocket PC 2003, 684-688
SFU, 181
smartphones, 698
system failover documentation, 619
system failure backups, 911
system folders, 103
system policies, 95-96
system state
   backups, 920
   restoring, 949-950
system volumes
   backups, 918
   troubleshooting, 944
Systems Management Server (SMS), 834
SYSVOL folder, restoring, 972-973

**T**

tablet PCs, comparing to PDAs, 654
tacks, managing, 647
tape, restoring databases, 954
target domains. *See also* domains
   policies, 435
   two-way domains, 435
target OU structures, creating, 435
Task Manager, 982
Task option (OWA), 793-794
tasks
   auditing, 539
   Mailbox Manager tool, 577
   maintenance, 599
technical documentation, 622
technical reporting, 620
technical training documentation, 622
Telnet, 587
templates
   Administrative Outlook Template, 860-861
   as-built documentation, 615
   certificates, 397-399
   Group Policy, 855
   security, 340-341, 376, 861
   security templates, 341
   servers, 376
temporary prototype domain controllers, 489
Terminal Services, 625, 631-633
   locking down, 633
   multiple client connections, 820
   pocket devices, 633
   Remote Desktop for Administration, 625-631
Terminal Services Client, 818-821
testing
   applications, 425, 510, 513
   compatibility, 510-516
      documenting, 516-517, 528
      lab-testing applications, 525-528
      prototype phase, 529
      researching applications, 517-519
      training, 516
      verifying, 519-524

databases, 591-592
design, 891
directory synchronization, 1044, 1092
disaster recovery, 61
documentation, 611-612
environments, 1060-1061
free disk space, 598
Group Policy implementations, 855, 858
hardware, 424
installation, 106-108
integrity, 590-591
migration, 500, 1096
mobility, 661
Outlook, 848
pilot, 651-652
restores, 940-941
servers, 993
UPS, 600

**text**
email, 771
Telnet, 587

**third-party applications, 512**

**third-party CAs, 296-299**

**third-party DNS, 188**

**third-party functionality, 118**

**third-party tools**
Exchange VSS recovery, 19
GroupWise, 1000
Lotus Notes, 1058

**threats, transport-level security, 391-392**

**time frames, compatibility testing, 514**

**timelines, 44**

**timing migration, 11**

**TLS (Transport Layer Security), 407**

**tombstones, 594**

**tools**
ACT, 527-528
ADC, 460-466
ADClean, 481
administration, 115
comparing Exchange Server 2003/Lotus Notes, 1059
GroupWise, 1001
ADMT, 433-449
AdSizer, 74
collaboration
Calendar, 733-735
Group Schedules, 736-738

Outlook, 729-733
public folders, 736
shared Web home page views, 738
command-line, 587
deployment, 114, 485
dnscmd, 209
DNSLINT, 208
DomainPrep, 494-495
drag-and-drop capabilities, 15
eDirectory, 1004-1006
ESEUTIL, 961-963
eseutil utility, 592
Exchange Deployment Tools, 454
Exchange Migration Wizard, 1048-1053
ExchDump, 939
ExMerge, 21, 473-474, 958-959
ExPBA, 411
FMU, 1005-1010
ForestPrep, 492-493
GroupWise Migration Tool, 1053
external entities, 1055
local archives, 1053
personal address books, 1054
personal dictionaries, 1054
proxy access, 1054
shared folders, 1055
ipconfig, 206
ISINTEG, 961-963
Lotus Notes Migration, 1105-1107
Mac System Profiler, 807
Mailbox Manager, 574-578
Mailbox Move, 548-549
Mailbox Recovery Center, 20, 571-574
maintenance
Active Directory, 588-589
backup, 590
best practices, 592-596
eseutil utility, 591-592
ESM, 587-588
isinteg utility, 590-591
managing, 602
message tracking, 592
ntdsutil utility, 590
post-maintenance procedures, 602
Queue Viewer, 592
scheduling best practices, 597-601
management, 115
MBSA, 374
migration, 23, 610-612

MOM, 24, 994-995
Move Mailbox, 549
MSDSS, 1004-1008
NDS, 1004-1006
nslookup, 207-208
Ntbackup.exe, 922-927, 953
ntdsutil, 490, 590
OrgPrepCheck, 460
Performance Monitor, 207
pfmigrate, 475, 503
phased migrations, 1013-1015, 1065
remote management, 586
RSoP, 855
SCW, 374-376
Security Configuration and Analysis, 340-341
SfN, 999
spam, 349-350
third-party
    GroupWise, 1000
    Lotus Notes, 1058
Windows 2003 support, 71
WINMSD, 913

**topologies**
Active Directory, 138
bandwidth, 832-833
diagrams, 615
routing groups, 124

**tracking**
application compatibility, 520
email, 713-714, 770
logging, 1034
messages, 93-94, 585, 592, 1034, 1084

**traffic**
encrypting, 238
IPSec, 403-404
    configuring, 405-407
    NAT-T, 404-405
ISA
    logging, 277-279
    monitoring, 279-283
OWA, 247-251
SMTP, 266-276

**training**
compatibility testing, 516
documentation, 622

**transactions, logs, 990**

**transfers, DNS zones, 192**

**Transform option, 838**

**transforms**
clients, 832
configuring, 838-841
creating, 838
Outlook, 842-844

**transport-level security, 391, 407**
clients, 415-416
IPSec, 403-404
    configuring, 405-407
    NAT-T, 404-405
layers, 391-392
PKI, 392
    CA, 392-394
    certificates, 396-399
    enrollment of certificates, 400-402
    installing CA, 395-396
    planning, 394-395
    private/public, 396
    smartcards, 399
protocols, 414
routing group connectors, 412
    Internet Mail Wizard, 413-414
    X.400, 412-413
S/MIME, 403
servers, 416-417
SMTP, 407-411

**trees**
Active Directory, 212
public folders, 101-102

**troubleshooting**
ADMT, 433-449
applications, 425
ASR, 951-953
backups, 910-912
    database corruption, 911-912
    devices, 917
    documentation, 912-915
    media, 930-932
    Ntbackup.exe, 922-927
    servers, 918-920
    services, 927-930
    strategies, 915-917
    system failures, 911
Cached mode, 745
Categorizer, 225

clustering, 878-883, 901
    permissions, 882
    requirements, 883-886
compatibility, 510-516
    documenting, 516-517, 528
    lab-testing applications, 525-528
    prototype phase, 529
    researching applications, 517-519
    training, 516
    verifying, 519-524
disaster recovery
    Active Directory, 967-973
    applications, 953-955
    boot failures, 945-947
    clusters, 966
    database corruption, 956-963
    disk failures, 944-945
    documentation, 617-619, 939-941
    domain controllers, 967
    identifying, 935-937
    IIS, 966
    planning, 938
    Recovery Storage Group, 963-964
    server failures, 947-953
    site failures, 941-943
    validating procedures, 938
dnscmd, 209
DNSLINT, 208
documentation, 608
    benefits of, 606-607
    design, 608-609
    outlining migration, 610-612
    planning, 606, 610
    testing, 611-612
Event Viewer, 205
Exchange Deployment Tools, 454
failback/failover, 902
hardware, 424
hot spare disks, 944
ipconfig utility, 206
mail stores, 548
Mailbox Manager, 574-578
Mailbox Recovery Center, 20, 571-574
maintenance
    best practices, 592-596
    scheduling best practices, 597-601
migration, 500, 1102-1104
mobility, 661
MSDSS, 174-175

NLB Manager, 906
nslookup, 207-208
Ntbackup.exe, 953
ongoing maintenance, 993-994
Outlook deployment, 848
OWA, 763
Performance Monitor, 207
post-maintenance procedures, 602
post-migration cleanup, 480
servers
    antivirus applications, 382-383
    spam, 384, 387-388
spam, 349-350
    filtering junk mail, 351
    IRM, 353-354
    junk mail, filtering, 352-353
    read receipts, blocking, 353
    Web beaconing, 350
tools
    Active Directory, 588-589
    backup, 590
    eseutil utility, 591-592
    ESM, 587-588
    isinteg utility, 590-591
    message tracking, 592
    ntdsutil utility, 590
    Queue Viewer, 592
transport-level security layers, 391-392
visibility, 72
VM, 128
volumes, 944
Windows Server 2003, 370-374
**trusts**
    domains, 430-432
    two-way, 435
**two-way synchronization, 463**
**two-way trusts, 435**
**types**
    of addresses, 552
    of contacts, 553
    of groups, 225
    of servers, 187-188

## U

UI (user interface), 757-764. *See also* interfaces
unattended installations, 81, 849-850
undelete function, 936
Universal Group Caching, 122, 221-222
universal groups, 227
Universal scope, 554
Unix
  BIND DNS, 188
  SFU, 178-181
unread, marking email messages, 773
unsupported connectors, 477
updating, 16, 36
  autoupdates, 817
  clients, 871-873
  compatibility, 522-524
  Deferred View Update, 781
  disaster recovery options, 49
  DNS, 199
  documentation, 36, 914-916
  Entourage 2004 client and Exchange Updates, 815
  Group Policy, 870-873
  initiation phase, 37
    budgets, 46
    business unit messaging goals, 40-42
    departmental messaging goals, 40-42
    goals, 38-39, 43
    high-level messaging goals, 40
    resource requirements, 44-45
    risks/assumptions, 45
    statement of work, 42, 46
    timelines/milestones, 44
  installing, 871
  mobile devices, 644
  pilot phase
    groups, 63-64
    plans, 62
    server implementation, 63
    success, 64
  planning phase
    Design documents, 48-53
    discovery, 46-48
    migration documents, 53-55, 59

production migration/upgrade, 64-65
prototype phase, 60-62
Recipient Update Services, 568-571
roles, 45
RUS, 504
scope of project, 37
security, 342-343
servers, 377
versions, 594
Windows 2003 Server Automatic Updates, 131
Windows Update, 342
upgrading
  compatibility, 522-524
    documenting, 516-517, 528
    prototype phase, 529
    researching applications, 517-519
    testing, 510-516
    training, 516
    verifying, 519-524
  decision matrices, 524
  Exchange 5.5, 452-454
    Active Directory forests/domains, 458-460
    Exchange Deployment Tools, 454
    optimizing migration, 457-458
    preparing migration, 454-457
  in-place upgrades, 423
  migration
    combined approach, 488
    in-place upgrade method, 486-497
    move mailbox upgrade method, 487-488, 497-506
  operating systems, 496-497
  planning phase, 58
  schemas, 492-493
  server prerequisites, 484-485
  service packs, 457
  standalone servers, 426-427
  Windows NT 4.0
    domains, 429-432
    in-place upgrades, 427-429
UPS (Uninterruptible Power Supply), testing, 600
User certificates, 397
user data, migrating, 1096-1105
user interface (UI), 757-764. *See also* interfaces

**user protocols, mailboxes, 544**

**users**

accounts, 872

Active Directory, 8-9, 588-589

authenticating, 347

end-user training documentation, 622

MIIS, 164-166

account provisioning, 166

group management, 168

installing, 168

role of MAs, 167-168

modes, 753

property sheets, 774

Telnet, 587

**utilities.** *See* **tools**

**utilization, resource analysis, 600**


# V

**validation**

addresses, 765

backup procedures, 938

client installation, 850-851

design, 891

document migration, 491

information store backups, 601

Migration document, 62

OrgPrepCheck tool, 460

plans, 62

**vCalendar, 733-735**

**verification**

Active Directory, 218

application readiness, 425

compatibility, 519-524

core services, 77, 1017, 1067

hardware compatibility, 424

ISA Server 2004 connections, 283

maintenance tasks, 599

online backups, 598

OrgPrepCheck tool, 460

public folder replication, 599

**versions, 116**

Calendar, 733-735

decommissioning, 65

Exchange Server 2003, 13

Enterprise Edition, 14

Standard Edition, 14

installing, 148

LDAP, 177-178

Mac System Profiler tool, 807

Outlook, 708

updating, 594

**viewing**

contacts, 694-695

context menus, 777

Directory Replication Connector, 469

email, 711, 760-761

Event Viewer, 598

free/busy time, 732-733

groups, 72

inboxes, 693

mobile services, 666

multiple calendars, 729

options, 542

public folders, 763

Queue Viewer, 592

reading pane (OWA), 761

user property sheets, 774

Windows NT Accounts, 456

**views**

administrative, 1022

calendars, 788

contacts, 795

Deferred View Update, 781

Outlook, 867

tasks, 794

web pages, 738

**virtual directories, 330**

**Virtual Directory Access Permissions dialog box, 307**

**Virtual Directory Alias dialog box, 307**

**virtual private network (VPN0, 641-643**

**virtual servers, 104-105, 288**

clustering, 878

OWA

assigning SSL certificates, 325

creating additional, 323-324

summarizing settings, 310-312

RPC over HTTP(S), 330

SMTP, 200, 408-411

**Virus Scanning Application Programming Interface (VSAPI), 150**

**viruses, 343**

**visibility, 72**

**VM (virtual memory), 128**

**Volume Shadow Copy Service (VSS), 19**

**volumes**
backups, 918-919
troubleshooting, 944
**VPN (virtual private network), 641-643**
**VSAPI (Virus Scanning Application Programming Interface), 150**
**VSS (Volume Shadow Copy Service), 19**

# W

**WAN (wide area network), 914**
**Web**
beaconing, 350
mobile access, 643-644
OWA, 9-10, 642
**web pages, sharing views, 738**
**Web sites, 304-306**
**Web view (Outlook), 867**
**weekly maintenance.** *See* **maintenance**
**WEP (Wired Equivalent Protocol), 633**
**wide area network (WAN), 914**
**Windows**
Certificate Manager, 401
groups, 225
hardening, 337
impact on Exchange, 70
implementing Exchange, 1060
non-Windows environment
integration, 163, 644
account provisioning (MIIS), 166
applying MSDSS, 170-175
deploying MIIS, 169-170
group management (MIIS), 168
installing MIIS, 168
LDAP, 175-178
MIIS, 164-166
Novell eDirectory, 169
role of MAs (MIIS), 167-168
SFU, 178-181
security
lockdown guidelines, 343
patches/updates, 342-343
templates, 340-341
virus protection, 343
**Windows 2000 Server, 496-497**

**Windows 2003 Server, 1069-1070**
antivirus applications, 382-383
Automatic Updates, 131
backups, 590, 918-920
Ntbackup.exe, 922-927
services, 927-930
existing NT4 domains, 429-432
floppy disks, 917
Group Policy, 844-847
baselines, 857-859
clients, 859-864
customizing, 855
levels of, 856
managing, 854
Outlook, 864-870
refreshing, 856
templates, 855
updating, 870-873
migration, 32
optimizing, 338
security, 337-338
functional roles, 380-381
IIS, 378-380
patches/updates, 377
standardizing, 382
templates, 376
support tools, 71
Terminal Services, 625, 631-633
locking down, 633
pocket devices, 633
Remote Desktop for Administration, 625-631
troubleshooting, 370-374
upgrading from Windows 2000, 496-497
**Windows Application Compatibility toolkit (ACT), 527-528**
**Windows Backup Wizard, 922-924**
**Windows Firewall, 339**
**Windows NT 4.0**
domain migration, 429-432
in-place upgrades, 427-429
viewing, 456
**Windows Script Host (WSH), 587**
**Windows Server Update Services (WSUS), 342**

**Windows Update, 342, 377**

**Windows XP Professional**
optimizing, 338
security improvements, 338

**Windows-based mail clients, 802**
Macintosh support, 802-803
OWA functionality, 804-805

**WINMSD utility, 913**

**WINS (Windows Internet Naming Service), 199**

**Wired Equivalent Protocol (WEP), 633**

**wireless connections, 643-644**

**wireless network adapters, 679, 689**

**wireless services, mailboxes, 543**

**wireless technologies, 10**
connecting, 29
security, 16

**wizards**
configuration, 15
Connection Agreement, 462-469
Custom Installation, 831
Cached Mode, 741
Outlook, 715-719
predefined configuration options, 835
Delegation, 533-534
auditing tasks, 539
extended permissions, 536
implementing roles, 538
rights, 537-538
role-based administration, 534-535
Exchange Administration Delegation, 369
Exchange Migration, 1048
GroupWise, 1048-1053
migrating user data, 1096-1105
Exchange Server 2003 Delegation, 882
Exchange Tasks, 540
GroupWise, 1001
Internet Mail, 413-414
Lotus Notes, 1059
Mailbox Move, 547
Mailbox Resource, 461
management, 15
Microsoft Exchange Migration, 1065
Restore, 950

RSG, 965
SCW, 19-20, 374-376
Windows Backup, 922-924

**WSH (Windows Script Host), 587**

**WSUS (Windows Server Update Services), 342**


# X – Y – Z

**X.400 Connectors, 117, 412-413**

**zones**
DNS, 189-192
reverse lookup, 189
secondary, 191
stub, 191